R. Gupta's®

POPULAR MASTER GUIDE

DSSB

Delhi Subordinate Services Selection Board

TGT Computer Science

Recruitment Exam

by

RPH Editorial Board

2027
EDITION

RAMESH PUBLISHING HOUSE, NEW DELHI

Published by
O.P. Gupta *for* Ramesh Publishing House

Admin. Office
12-H, New Daryaganj Road, Opp. Officers' Mess,
New Delhi-110002 ✆ 23275224, 23245124

E-mail: info@rameshpublishinghouse.com
For Online Shopping: www.rameshpublishinghouse.com

Showroom
• Balaji Market, Nai Sarak, Delhi-110006 ✆ 23282525 📱 9354373464
• 4457, Nai Sarak, Delhi-110006

Book Code: R-1697

ISBN: 978-93-5012-482-6

Price: ₹ 940

Printed at: Deepak Offset, Delhi

CONTENTS

SECTION–A

SECTION–B

Previous Years' Paper

Delhi Subordinate Services Selection Board (DSSSB)

TGT—COMPUTER SCIENCE, EXAM-2025

(Exam held on 12-09-2025)

SECTION-A

GENERAL INTELLIGENCE AND REASONING ABILITY

1. Which of the given letter-number clusters will replace the question mark (?) in the following series to make it logically complete?

DWP 6, HAT 15, LEX 24, PIB 33, TMF 42, ?

1. XQI 51
2. XQJ 51
3. XAJ 51
4. YQJ 51

2. Reena ranked 7th from the top and 28th from the bottom in her class. How many students are there in the class?

1. 34
2. 36
3. 33
4. 35

3. Select the triad which follows the same pattern as that followed by the triads given below.

EACH - HEAC - CHEA

HACK - KHAC - CKHA

1. SACK - ASKC - SKAC
2. PACK - PKAC - PCKA
3. LACE - ELAC - CELA
4. OAKS - AKSO - KSOA

4. What should come in place of the question mark (?) in the given series?

231 224 214 207 197 190 ?

1. 170
2. 183
3. 173
4. 180

5. Read the given statements and conclusions carefully. Assuming that the information given in the statements is true, even if it appears to be at variance with commonly known facts, decide which of the given conclusions logically follow(s) from the statements.

Statements:

All stones are rocks.

All rocks are pebbles.

Some stones are hills.

Conclusions:

(I) All rocks are hills.

(II) All pebbles are hills.

1. Only conclusion (I) follows.
2. Neither conclusion (I) nor (II) follows.
3. Only conclusion (II) follows.
4. Both conclusions (I) and (II) follow.

6. 206 is related to 135 following a certain logic. Following the same logic, 178 is related to 107. To which of the given options is 194 related, following the same logic?

(NOTE: Operations should be performed on the whole numbers, without breaking down the numbers into their constituent digits. E.g. 13 – Operations on 13 such as adding to/subtracting from/multiplying with 13 can be performed. Breaking down 13 into 1 and 3 and then performing mathematical operations on 1 and 3 is not allowed.)

1. 123
2. 133
3. 127
4. 117

7. Mr. E starts from Point A and drives 12 km towards the North. He then takes a right turn, drives 6 km, turns right and drives 9 km. He then takes a left turn, drives 12 km, turns right and drives 6 km. He then takes a right turn and drives 21 km. He takes a final right turn, drives 3 km and stops at Point P. How far (shortest distance) and towards which direction should he drive in order to reach Point A again? (All turns are 90 degrees turns only unless specified)

1. 4 km to the north
2. 6 km to the south
3. 5 km to the west
4. 3 km to the east

1. 2	**2.** 1	**3.** 3	**4.** 4	**5.** 2	**6.** 1	**7.** 4

8. Below are given two sets of numbers. In each set of numbers, a certain mathematical operation on the first number results in the second number. Similarly, certain mathematical operation on the second number results in the third number and so on.

Which of the given options follows the same set of operations as in question?

(NOTE – A two/three-digit number cannot be broken into individual digits for operations e.g. if 37 is followed by 10, the operation cannot be 3+7 as a two-digit number cannot be broken into individual digits)

3 – 27 – 37 – 32 ; 8 – 72 – 82 – 77

1. 12 – 108 – 118 – 113
2. 11 – 121 – 132 – 162
3. 6 – 54 – 84 – 42
4. 4 – 36 – 52 – 62

9. In this question, a statement is given, followed by two assumptions numbered I and II. You have to assume everything in the statement to be true and decide which of the assumptions is implicit in the statement.

Statement:

Roads of City B are congested due to high vehicle movement.

Assumptions:

I. Metro rail of City B also gets delayed due to congestion.

II. Influx of people to City B is higher than that to other cities of the country.

1. Both assumptions I and II are implicit.
2. Neither assumption I nor II is implicit.
3. Only assumption I is implicit.
4. Only assumption II is implicit.

10. Based on the English alphabetical order, three of the following four letter-clusters are alike in a certain way and thus form a group. Which letter-cluster DOES NOT belong to that group?

(Note: The odd one out is not based on the number of consonants/vowels or their position in the letter-cluster.)

1. RVY 2. MQT
3. CGJ 4. INR

11. In a certain code language, 'TYRE' is coded as '5127' and 'TREK' is coded as '7253'.

What is the code for 'K' in the given code language?

1. 2 2. 3
3. 5 4. 7

12. Based on the English alphabetical order, three of the following four letter-clusters are alike in a certain way and thus form a group. Which letter-cluster DOES NOT belong to that group?

(Note: The odd one out is not based on the number of consonants/vowels or their position in the letter-cluster.)

1. AWDG 2. KGNQ
3. SOWY 4. VRYB

13. Six students are sitting around a circular table, facing the centre. Himani is an immediate neighbour of both Evan and Charu. Gauri is sitting to the immediate right of Evan. Firoz is sitting second to the left of Himani. Danish is an immediate neighbour of both Firoz and Gauri. How many people sit between Danish and Himani when counted from the right of Himani?

1. One 2. Two
3. Four 4. Three

14. What will come in the place of the question mark (?) in the following equation, if '+' and '–' are interchanged and '×' and '÷' are interchanged?

34 – 20 ÷ 8 × 2 + 16 = ?

1. 96 2. 98
3. 95 4. 93

15. This question is based on the following words.

(Left) REAL, FAIR, LIKE, PITY (Right)

In each of the words, each vowel is changed to the letter immediately following it in the English alphabetical order and each consonant is changed to the letter immediately preceding it in the English alphabetical order. In how many letter-clusters thus formed, will no vowel appear?

1. Two 2. One
3. Three 4. Four

16. If 'A' stands for '÷', 'B' stands for '×', 'C' stands for '+' and 'D' stands for '–', then what will come in place of the question mark (?) in the following equation?

9 D 35 C 48 B 30 A 12 = ?

1. 95 2. 94
3. 96 4. 92

17. Which of the following letter-number clusters will replace the question mark (?) in the given series to make it logically complete?

QIM 1 PLK 3 ? NRG 27 MUE 81

1. MOI 6 2. OIN 7
3. OOI 9 4. NOM 5

8. 1	9. 2	10. 4	11. 2	12. 3	13. 2	14. 2	15. 1	16. 2	17. 3

18. Seven boxes, P, Q, R, S, T, Y and Z, are kept one over the other but not necessarily in the same order. T is kept second from the top. Only three boxes are kept between P and T. Y is kept at one of the positions below P. Only Q is kept between T and R. S is kept at one of the positions above T. How many boxes are kept between R and Y?

1. One
2. Three
3. Four
4. Two

19. This question is based on the following four words.

(Left) RAT ANT FAN TON (Right)

In each of the given words, each vowel is changed to the letter immediately following it in the English alphabetical order and each consonant is changed to the letter immediately preceding it in the English alphabetical order. In how many letter-clusters thus formed will no vowel appear?

1. One
2. Three
3. Four
4. Two

20. D is the sister of E. F is the mother of G. H is the daughter of G. E is the mother of H. How is D related to F ?

1. Son's wife's mother
2. Sister
3. Mother
4. Son's wife's sister

GENERAL AWARENESS

21. Which animal is renowned for its ability to regenerate lost body parts?

1. Eagle
2. Zebrafish
3. Dog
4. Snail

22. According to Article 165, which of the following qualifications is required for a person to be appointed as the Advocate General of a State?

1. Qualified to be appointed a Judge of the Supreme Court
2. Qualified to be appointed a Magistrate
3. Qualified to be appointed a Judge of a High Court
4. Qualified to be appointed a Judge of a District Court

23. The prestigious National School Games 2024, known for showcasing young athletic talent (Under 17) from across the country, were hosted in which state?

1. Punjab
2. Maharashtra
3. Gujarat
4. Uttar Pradesh

24. As per the Provision of ______ of the Indian Constitution, the Lok Sabha is the lower house of the Parliament.

1. Article 56
2. Article 79
3. Article 64
4. Article 87

25. Kabini and Bhavani are tributaries of the ______ river.

1. Indus
2. Kaveri
3. Narmada
4. Godavari

26. Which of the following is a rabi crop?

1. Cotton
2. Maize
3. Tur
4. Rapeseed

27. Which country banned the entry of the UN Secretary-General António Guterres in October 2024 for 'failing' to condemn Iran's attack?

1. Israel
2. Thailand
3. Turkmenistan
4. Oman

28. Who designed the impressive Albert Hall building in Jaipur, India, in the Indo-Saracenic style?

1. Charles Correa
2. Samuel Swinton Jacob
3. Edwin Lutyens
4. Le Corbusier

29. Which of the following Fundamental Duties of the Indian Constitution was inserted through the 86th Constitutional Amendment Act of 2002?

1. To develop the scientific temper, humanism and the spirit of inquiry and reform
2. To provide opportunities for education to his child or as the case may be, ward between the age of six and fourteen years
3. To safeguard public property and to abjure violence
4. To value and preserve the rich heritage of our composite culture

30. Narasimham Committee-1998 is related to ______.

1. agricultural reform
2. police reform
3. banking sector reform
4. educational reform

18. 4	19. 2	20. 4	21. 2	22. 3	23. 4	24. 2	25. 2	26. 4	27. 1	28. 2	29. 2	30. 3

31. Which of the following statements regarding quantum science and technology are correct?
   1. The United Nations has designated 2025 as the International Year of Quantum Science and Technology, marking the centenary of quantum mechanics.
   2. The National Quantum Mission, launched in 2023, focusses on scaling up scientific and industrial research and development in quantum technology.
   3. Quantum Computing Applications Lab (QCAL) aims to accelerate research in quantum computing and facilitate new scientific discoveries.

1. 1 and 2 only 2. 1, 2 and 3
3. 1 and 3 only 4. 2 and 3 only

32. Who among the following was one of the founders of the 'Hindustan Republican Association' in 1924?
1. Surya Sen 2. Bir Tikendrajit Singh
3. Ram Prasad Bismil 4. Lala Lajpat Rai

33. The unit of force is different from the unit of ________.
1. weight
2. pressure × area
3. mass × acceleration
4. rate of change of angular momentum

34. In which year did Babasaheb Ambedkar organise a non-violent struggle for entry into the Kala Ram Temple in Nasik?
1. 1930 2. 1934
3. 1925 4. 1921

35. Which of the following equations correctly represents the calculation of speed?
1. Speed = Distance/Time
2. Speed = Energy/Time
3. Speed = Force × Time
4. Speed = Mass × Acceleration

36. In which type of forests are Sal, Shisham and Hurra trees found in India?
1. Littoral and swamp forests
2. Tropical deciduous forests
3. Tropical thorn forests
4. Tropical evergreen forests

37. Which of the following stages are involved in beer-production?
1. Fermentation and brewing only
2. Brewing and pasteurisation only
3. Malting, brewing and fermentation
4. Fermentation and finishing only

38. Which of the following books was NOT written by Jhumpa Lahiri?
1. Whereabouts
2. The Lowland
3. The Ministry of Utmost Happiness
4. Unaccustomed Earth

39. In February 2025, Rekha Gupta took oath as the Chief Minister of ________.
1. Rajasthan 2. Delhi
3. Madhya Pradesh 4. Andhra Pradesh

40. During which of the following years was gender budgeting introduced in India?
1. 2005-2006 2. 1965-1966
3. 1986-1987 4. 1972-1973

ARITHMETICAL AND NUMERICAL ABILITY

41. The area of a square plot is 38809 m^2. The length of each side of the plot (in m) is:
1. 173 2. 203 3. 197 4. 217

42. A shopkeeper lists the price of a fan at 50% above its cost price and offers a 30% discount on its list price. If he earns a profit of ₹ 159, then what is the list price (in ₹) of the fan?
1. 4,657 2. 4,951
3. 4,741 4. 4,770

43. A garrison of 1210 men has provisions for 15 days. How long (in days) will the provisions last if the garrison is increased to 1815 men?
1. 10 2. 11 3. 9 4. 12

44. There are 7597 students in a school and the ratio of boys to girls is 50 : 21. Find the number of boys in the school.
1. 5350 2. 5367 3. 5333 4. 5359

45. A person borrows ₹ 87,900 at 10% compound interest per year, compounded annually. At the end of every year, he pays ₹ 9,900 as part payment. How much does he still owe after two such instalments?
1. ₹ 85,569 2. ₹ 85,439
3. ₹ 85,556 4. ₹ 85,382

46. The value of 2.5555... + 1.2727... − 1.8888... is:
1. $\frac{64}{33}$ 2. $\frac{61}{39}$ 3. $\frac{62}{39}$ 4. $\frac{60}{35}$

31. 2	32. 3	33. 4	34. 1	35. 1	36. 2	37. 3	38. 3
39. 2	40. 1	41. 3	42. 4	43. 1	44. 1	45. 1	46. 1

47. Pinki is twice as competent a worker as Sabina. Sabina can complete a task in 48 days. If Pinki and Sabina work together, the time it will take to finish the work is:

1. 18 days 2. 18.6 days
3. 17.9 days 4. 16 days

48. Amit purchased 10 kg of rice at the rate of ₹ 38 per kg and 32 kg of rice at ₹ 46 per kg. He sold the whole mixture at the rate of ₹ 43 per kg. Find his loss (in ₹).

1. 54 2. 41 3. 51 4. 46

49. The average price of three items of furniture is ₹ 17,295. If their prices are in the ratio 3 : 5 : 7, the price of the costliest item (in ₹) is:

1. 8,071 2. 10,377
3. 5,765 4. 24,213

50. Three men complete a work in 27 hours. In how many hours will 9 men complete the same work?

1. 30 2. 81 3. 3 4. 9

51. If curved surface area of a cylinder is 880 cm. If the circumference of its base is 88 cm, find its volume. (Use $\pi = 22/7$)

1. 6120 cm^3 2. 6180 cm^3
3. 6140 cm^3 4. 6160 cm^3

52. The average marks of 16 students in a class is 53. If the marks of each student are doubled, find the new average.

1. 106 2. 32 3. 53 4. 16

53. The speed of a stream is 3 km/hr. A person can row 26 km downstream in the same time as he can row 14 km upstream. Find the speed of the boat in still water (in km/hr).

1. 9 2. 8 3. 7 4. 10

54. Sapna invested ₹ 21,300 on simple interest, partly at 7% per annum and partly at 13% per annum. If she earns equal interests from the two investments after 5 years, then find the sum (in ₹) invested at 7% per annum.

1. 13,843 2. 13,845
3. 13,846 4. 13,847

55. Simplify: $(96 \div 4) \times \left\{\frac{18}{6} + \frac{34}{3} \times (9-6)\right\}$

1. 888 2. 896
3. 895 4. 901

56. Convert 4.6833333... into a fraction.

1. $\frac{185}{77}$ 2. $\frac{247}{55}$
3. $\frac{209}{65}$ 4. $\frac{281}{60}$

57. Water flows out through a circular pipe whose internal diameter is 2 cm, at the rate of 2 metres per second into a cylindrical tank with base radius of 50 cm. By how much will the level of water rise in the tank in 20 minutes?

1. 94 cm 2. 91 cm
3. 96 cm 4. 93 cm

58. The price of fuel decreases by 30%, 20% and 10% in three successive months, but increases by 65% in the fourth month. What is the percentage increase/ decrease in the price of fuel in the fourth month as compared to its original price?

1. Decreases by 19.82%
2. Increases by 21.97%
3. Increases by 20.21%
4. Decreases by 16.84%

59. Amit's income in 2019 was ₹ 24,100. He gets an increment of 30% every year. What was his income (in ₹) in 2021?

1. 38,560 2. 40,729
3. 31,330 4. 24,100

60. Simplify: $\sqrt[6]{729} + \sqrt[4]{6561} + \sqrt[3]{6859} + \sqrt{8649}$

1. 107 2. 152
3. 58 4. 124

TEST OF ENGLISH LANGUAGE AND COMPREHENSION

61. Select the option that can be used as a one-word substitute for the given group of words.

A thing no longer in use

1. Obsolete 2. New
3. Waste 4. Held

62. Sentences of a paragraph are given below. While the first and the last sentences (S1 and S6) are in the correct order, the sentences in between are jumbled up. Arrange the sentences in the correct order to form a meaningful and coherent paragraph.

47. 4	**48.** 4	**49.** 4	**50.** 4	**51.** 4	**52.** 1	**53.** 4	**54.** 2
55. 1	**56.** 4	**57.** 3	**58.** 4	**59.** 2	**60.** 4	**61.** 1	

S1. Yes, a mirage can be photographed.
P. That is hallucination.
Q. Anything reflected by the lens of the human eye will naturally be picked up by photographic lens.
R. Sometimes, however, a person imagines he is seeing something but actually he is not.
S. The image, of course, will be hazy and simmering because of refraction of light.
S6. That kind of mirage obviously cannot be photographed.

1. QRPS
2. QSRP
3. SPRQ
4. PSQR

63. Select the most appropriate meaning of the given proverb.

Don't count your chickens before they hatch

1. Planning for the future guarantees results
2. Avoid making assumptions about future
3. Focus on small goals before aiming higher
4. Prepare in advance for better results

64. Select the correct spelling of the incorrectly spelt word in the given sentence.

He gave a detailed recomendation for the new policy.

1. recomendation
2. recomendition
3. reccommendation
4. recommendation

65. Select the most appropriate article to fill in the blank. If no article is needed, select 'No article required'.

The number and proportion of people aged 60 years and older in ______ population is increasing.

1. an
2. a
3. the
4. No article required

66. Select the most appropriate ANTONYM of the underlined word in the given sentence.

My friend Sita has impeccable manners.

1. Immaculate
2. Imperfect
3. Unblemished
4. Seamless

67. Select the most appropriate one-word substitute for the group of words given in the brackets to fill in the blank.

Sita has a high knowledge of music, which she has acquired from her grandmother who was a renowned musician. So, her father calls her a/an _______ (a person with a good knowledge of music).

1. amateur
2. maestro
3. incompetent
4. beginner

68. Select the most appropriate option to fill in the blank.

Despite his extensive knowledge, he has no real insight ______ how human emotions work under extreme stress.

1. on 2. into 3. with 4. over

69. Select the most appropriate option to fill in the blanks.

______ sudden change in weather caused ______ unexpected delay in the flight.

1. A; an 2. An; a 3. A; a 4. An; an

70. Select the most appropriate synonym of the given word.

Draconian

A. Lenient
B. Clement
C. Benignant
D. Vicious

1. D 2. A 3. B 4. C

71. Select the most appropriate option to fill in the blank.

He worked ______ for his success.

1. hardly
2. harder
3. hardest
4. hard

72. Identify the INCORRECTLY spelt word in the given sentence and select the option that rectifies it.

Many metals that react to the vaccuum which electron-beam requires for the generation of intense heat cannot be welded properly.

1. intence
2. vacuum
3. electron-beem
4. wellded

73. Select the most appropriate meaning of the given proverb.

Don't put all your eggs in one basket

1. Diversify your risks to avoid complete loss
2. Save your resources for future use
3. Simplicity leads to better decisions
4. Avoid multitasking to achieve better results

74. Select the most appropriate option to fill in the blank.

Each of the players ______ awarded a trophy.

1. have 2. was 3. are 4. were

75. Sentences of a paragraph are given below in jumbled order. Arrange the sentences in the correct order to form a meaningful and coherent paragraph.

A. It is known for its elaborate, traditional dancing.
B. Bali is the capital of Indonesia.
C. The dancing is inspired by its Hindi beliefs.
D. To watch this dancing is a breathtaking experience.

1. DCBA
2. BADC
3. ABCD
4. BACD

62. 2	**63.** 2	**64.** 4	**65.** 3	**66.** 2	**67.** 2	**68.** 2	**69.** 1	**70.** 1	**71.** 4	**72.** 2	**73.** 1	**74.** 2	**75.** 4

Directions (Qs. No. 76-80): *Read the given passage and answer the questions that follow.*

In the age of algorithmic decision-making, predictive governance has emerged as a dominant paradigm for public administration. Governments are increasingly deploying data-driven models to pre-empt criminal activity, optimise urban planning, and forecast economic volatility. While ostensibly rational, this model introduces a paradox: the more predictive power a system accumulates, the more it flattens human agency into statistical probabilities. The future becomes not an open horizon but a quantifiable extension of past behaviours. This technobureaucratic reliance risks marginalising outliers — those whose experiences fall outside normative data sets — and institutionalising bias under the guise of objectivity. Moreover, the ethical oversight of such systems lags far behind their deployment, creating a governance vacuum wherein accountability is outsourced to opaque algorithms. In prioritising efficiency and foresight, predictive governance often bypasses deliberative democracy, weakening participatory channels in favour of streamlined outcomes.

Citizens are recast as data points, their individual complexities reduced to patterns in a machine-readable format. This mechanistic interpretation of society may inadvertently erode trust in institutions that no longer appear responsive but merely anticipatory. Therefore, the question is not only whether predictive systems function but also for whom they function — and who is excluded by their logic. A governance structure that projects authority through prediction must be tempered by transparent frameworks, ethical scrutiny, and above all, a reaffirmation of the human condition as more than a predictable variable.

76. What best summarises the passage?

1. Algorithms have no place in governance due to their inherent inaccuracies.
2. While predictive governance improves foresight, it risks diminishing human agency and democratic processes.
3. Predictive governance enhances citizen engagement through efficient data systems.
4. Predictive models have revolutionised public administration with minimal drawbacks.

77. What is the central theme of the passage?

1. The ethical and democratic implications of data-driven governance
2. The future of AI in economics
3. The superiority of algorithmic decision-making in policy
4. The technical limitations of predictive models

78. What best describes the structure of the passage?

1. Concept Introduction → Benefits → Risks → Philosophical Reflection
2. Anecdote → Research Findings → Political Critique
3. Case Study → Rebuttal → Policy Proposal
4. Problem → Historical Context → Solution

79. Which real-world issue best parallels the concerns raised in the passage?

1. The automation of social welfare decisions via predictive analytics
2. The privatisation of education in developing countries
3. International trade agreements excluding local voices
4. Judicial delays in underfunded rural courts

80. Select the most appropriate ANTONYM of the word 'marginalising' as used in the given segment.

This techno-bureaucratic reliance risks marginalising outliers — those whose experiences fall outside normative data sets

1. Ignoring
2. Integrating
3. Suppressing
4. Isolating

हिन्दी भाषा और अवतरण

81. निम्नलिखित वाक्य के रेखांकित पद में वर्तनी संबंधी अशुद्धि है। दिए गए विकल्पों में से सही वर्तनी वाला शब्द चुनिए–

उसने <u>हस्ताक्छर</u> किए

1. हस्ताक्षर
2. हाश्ताक्षर
3. हस्तक्षर
4. हश्ताक्षर

82. निम्नलिखित वाक्यांश के लिए एक शब्द का चयन कीजिए:

जो अपने निश्चित स्थान से डिग गया हो

1. च्युत
2. देय
3. चिरकुट
4. दुर्बोध

76. 2	**77.** 1	**78.** 1	**79.** 1	**80.** 2	**81.** 1	**82.** 1

83. 'अनिष्ट' शब्द के उपयुक्त पर्यायवाची का चयन करें:

1. अपरिहार्य 2. अनिर्णीत
3. अधीर 4. अमंगल

84. निम्नलिखित वाक्य के रिक्त स्थान में उचित क्रिया की पूर्ति कीजिए–

'वह नरेन्द्र से कपड़े ________।'

1. धुलवाता है। 2. पहचानता है।
3. पाया है। 4. गाता है।

85. निम्नलिखित लोकोक्ति के उपयुक्त अर्थ का चयन करें

बाप न मारे मेंढकी बेटा तीरंदाज

1. अच्छे दिनों में सब दोस्त बनते हैं
2. बड़े से छोटा बढ़ गया
3. चुप्पा बहुत चालक होता है
4. छोटों की आपस में मित्रता

86. दिए गए वाक्यों में से तीन का संबंध एक ही संदर्भ से जुड़ा हुआ है, जबकि एक वाक्य अतिरिक्त है। इनमें से अतिरिक्त वाक्य का चयन करें।

1. आधुनिक हिंदी साहित्य में कई लेखक सामाजिक मुद्दों को अपने लेखन में स्थान दे रहे हैं।
2. क्रिकेट विश्व कप में भारत ने कई बार शानदार प्रदर्शन किया है।
3. मुंशी प्रेमचंद को हिंदी उपन्यास लेखन का पितामह माना जाता है।
4. हिंदी साहित्य में अनेक विधाएँ पाई जाती हैं, जैसे कविता, कहानी और नाटक।

87. उपयुक्त 'विशेषण' का प्रयोग कर वाक्य को पूर्ण कीजिए।

नितांशी के फ्राक का रंग ________ है।

1. गीला 2. दुबला
3. ऊपरी 4. नीला

88. 'उदयाचल' का विलोम शब्द निम्नलिखित में से कौन-सा होगा?

1. सीमांचल 2. अस्ताचल
3. अरुणाचल 4. पूर्वांचल

89. निम्नलिखित वाक्य के रिक्त स्थान में उचित कारक का प्रयोग कीजिए–

'मोहन .... तीन भाई हैं।'

1. को 2. ने
3. के द्वारा 4. के

90. 'परीक्षा ________ दिन नजदीक आ गए हैं। वाक्य के रिक्त स्थान के लिए उपयुक्त कारक चिह्न है–

1. के 2. के लिए
3. का 4. में

91. दिए गए वाक्य के किस भाग में त्रुटि है?

'इन्दरियों को वश में रखना चाहिए।'

1. इन्दरियों 2. वश
3. को 4. रखना

92. निम्नलिखित में से अतिरिक्त उचित वाक्य का चयन करें–

'विश्व के विशाल भू-भाग में ________'

1. सैकड़ों-हजारों मील का सफर तय कर मिलती हैं।
2. किनारा मिलना बहुत ही मुश्किल बात है।
3. बोली जाने वाली हिन्दी एक वेगवती नदी की भाँति है।
4. जिसमें अनेक नदियाँ अपने उदगम से।

93. उपयुक्त 'क्रियाविशेषण' का प्रयोग कर वाक्य को पूर्ण कीजिए।

'वह ________ सड़क पार करता है।'

1. देश-विदेश 2. यथाक्रम
3. घर-बाहर 4. धीरे-धीरे

94. 'जिसकी गिनती प्रमुख व्यक्तियों में हो' वाक्यांश के लिए सार्थक शब्द होगा–

1. अग्रणी 2. प्रमुखता
3. मुख्यत: 4. अगड़ी

95. 'गिरगिट की तरह रंग बदलना' मुहावरे का एक उचित अर्थ कौन-सा **नहीं** है?

1. एक बात पर स्थिर न रहना।
2. व्यर्थ समय खोना।
3. एक रंग-ढंग न रखना।
4. काम निकल जाने पर वायदा पूरा न करना।

निर्देश (प्र. सं. 96-100): *दिए गए गद्यांश को पढ़कर नीचे लिखे प्रश्नों के उत्तर दीजिए।*

जनसंख्या घनत्व बढ़ने से महानगरों में तरह-तरह के प्रदूषण बढ़ रहे हैं। सबसे भीषण वायु प्रदूषण है। बड़े शहरों में लोग स्वस्थ हवा में साँस नहीं ले सकते। लोगों को सड़क पर चलते समय वाहनों का काला धुआँ पीना पड़ रहा है। भीड़ अधिक होने के कारण जगह-जगह कूड़े के ढेर लगे हैं। कल-कारखानों का धुआँ पर्यावरण को जहरीला बनाता है, इसलिए मनुष्य भी स्वच्छ हवा के लिए तरसता है। बड़े शहरों में जल प्रदूषण एक बड़ी समस्या बन गया है। कारखानों का पानी प्रदूषित होने से भू-जल भी लाल और काला हो गया है। ध्वनि प्रदूषण की वर्तमान स्थिति यह है कि महानगरों के निवासियों के लिए बहरापन और तनाव आम समस्या हो गई है और शांत स्थानों की जगह शोर ने ले ली है। इस

83. 4	**84.** 1	**85.** 2	**86.** 2	**87.** 4	**88.** 2	**89.** 4	**90.** 1	**91.** 1	**92.** 3	**93.** 4	**94.** 1	**95.** 2

संबंध में वैज्ञानिक साधनों की तरह आम लोग भी समान रूप से दोषी हैं। हमें प्रदूषण के कारणों और इससे बचने के तरीकों को समझना होगा। लोगों की सचेत करें और उपायों को व्यापक रूप से प्रचारित करें। सरकार और जनता का संयुक्त सहयोग ही प्रदूषण मुक्त वातावरण को निर्माण हो सकता है।

96. उपर्युक्त गद्यांश का शीर्षक है–
1. वैज्ञानिक साधनों का दुरुपयोग
2. जनसंख्या घनत्व के दुष्प्रभाव
3. प्रदूषण के कारण, दुष्प्रभाव, बचाव
4. पर्यावरण संरक्षण के उपाय

97. उपर्युक्त गद्यांश में किस प्रकार के पर्यावरण प्रदूषण का उल्लेख नहीं किया गया है–
1. वायु प्रदूषण 2. भूमि प्रदूषण
3. ध्वनि प्रदूषण 4. जल प्रदूषण

98. निम्नलिखित में से कौन-सा एक कारण प्रदूषण का नहीं है–
1. पर्यावरण संरक्षण अधिनियम
2. जनसंख्या घनत्व
3. वैज्ञानिक साधन
4. औद्योगीकरण

99. 'घनत्व' शब्द का अर्थ है–
1. घनात
2. घनापन
3. घनागम
4. घनाक्षरी

100. निम्नलिखित में से कौन-सा शब्द 'कल' का अनेकार्थी शब्द नहीं है–
1. चैन 2. मशीन
3. कक्ष 4. सुंदर

SECTION-B

POST SPECIFIC SUBJECT-RELATED QUESTIONS

101. How does the receiver handle out-of-order frames in Selective Repeat?
1. Buffers them until all missing frames arrive
2. Discards them immediately
3. Sends a cumulative acknowledgment
4. Requests retransmission of all frames

102. Which SQL statement is used to update data in a table?
1. SET
2. MODIFY
3. CHANGE
4. UPDATE

103. Which of the following is NOT a benefit of distributed systems?
1. Scalability
2. Fault tolerance
3. High communication latency
4. Resource sharing

104. Which of the following statements is false about universal logic gates?
1. All basic logic gates cannot be implemented using universal logic gates.
2. All basic logic gates can be implemented through universal logic gates.
3. NAND gate is known as universal logic gate.
4. NOR gate is known as universal logic gate.

105. Select the correct SQL statement which will correctly insert a new row into the Customer table with only the CustomerID, Name, and Product columns specified, assuming the table allows NULLs for other columns.
1. INSERT INTO Customer VALUES (101, 'Alice', 'Pen');
2. INSERT Customer SET CustomerID=101, Name='Alice', Product='Pen';
3. INSERT INTO Customer (CustomerID, Name, Product) VALUES (101, 'Alice', 'Pen');
4. INSERT INTO Customer (101, 'Alice', 'Pen');

106. In public key cryptography, which key is used for decrypting a message encrypted with the public key?
1. Another public key
2. A symmetric key
3. The recipient's private key
4. The sender's private key

107. What does the XNOR gate output when A=1 and B=0?
1. B 2. 0
3. A 4. 1

108. What is the overall design of a database called?
1. Database Table 2. Database Schema
3. Database Instance 4. Database Model

96. 3	97. 2	98. 1	99. 2	100. 3	101. 1	102. 4	103. 3	104. 1	105. 3	106. 3	107. 2	108. 2

109. Which technology is commonly used in Wi-Fi to enhance signal range and reliability?

1. CDMA (Code Division Multiple Access)
2. WEP (Wired Equivalent Privacy)
3. TDMA (Time Division Multiple Access)
4. MIMO (Multiple Input Multiple Output)

110. What is typically returned by the getpid system call in Unix-based operating systems?

1. Process ID of the parent process
2. The process ID of the kernel
3. Process ID of the current process
4. Process ID of the first process

111. _________ is NOT allowed in a SQL:1999 view definition.

1. Use of nested queries
2. Use of aggregate formulas
3. Use of ORDER BY clause
4. Use of subqueries

112. What does the TCP service model guarantee about the order of data delivery?

1. Data may arrive out of order and is handled by the application layer.
2. Data is not guaranteed to arrive in any specific order.
3. Data is delivered as fast as possible.
4. Data is delivered in the order it is transmitted.

113. In an acyclic graph directory structure, what is a common method used to implement shared directories or files?

1. File duplication
2. Directory pointers
3. Symbolic (soft) links
4. Hard links

114. If a process arrives at time 5, what is the latest possible time for it to start execution if there are no other processes in the system?

1. Time 5 2. Time 4
3. Time 0 4. Time 6

115. Which of the following describes the use of digital certificates in authentication?

1. They store user passwords.
2. They verify the identity of entities using public key infrastructure (PKI).
3. They encrypt data transmissions.
4. They compress large files for secure transfer.

116. How does the Best Fit algorithm impact system performance?

1. It always improves system performance.
2. It improves system performance by reducing memory wastage.
3. It may reduce system performance due to increased search time for free blocks.
4. It improves system performance by reducing external fragmentation.

117. Which of the following SQL expressions evaluates to TRUE, according to SQL-99?

1. NULL IS NULL returns FALSE
2. NULL >= NULL returns UNKNOWN
3. NULL <= NULL returns UNKNOWN
4. NULL IS NULL returns TRUE

118. In which scheduling algorithm does the disk head move in one direction, satisfying all requests until it reaches the end, and then reverses direction?

1. FCFS 2. SSTF
3. SCAN 4. LOOK

119. What happens if a RST (reset) packet is received during the connection management process?

1. The sender continues retransmissions.
2. The receiver sends another SYN packet.
3. The connection remains active.
4. The connection is immediately terminated.

120. What is the ARP reply's scope in terms of message type?

1. Unicast 2. Multicast
3. Broadcast 4. Anycast

121. What will be the output of the following code?

```
#include <stdio.h>
int main() {
int a = 10, b = 20;
int max = (a > b) ? a : b;
printf("%d", max);
return 0;
}
```

1. 10 2. 30
3. compile time error 4. 20

122. What is the objective of encapsulation in object-oriented programming?

1. To enable one class to inherit from another class
2. To allow objects to take multiple forms
3. To create multiple instances of a class
4. To combine data and methods that operate on that data within a single unit

109. 4 **110.** 3 **111.** 3 **112.** 4 **113.** 3 **114.** 1 **115.** 2 **116.** 3 **117.** 4 **118.** 3 **119.** 4 **120.** 1 **121.** 4 **122.** 4

123. class Parent {

```
class Parent {
protected void protectedMethod() {
System.out.println("Protected method in Parent");
}
}
class Child extends Parent {
public void childMethod() {
protectedMethod();
}
}
public class Test {
public static void main(String[] args) {
Child child = new Child();
child.childMethod();
}
}
```

What will happen when the code is executed?

1. The code will compile and print 'Protected method in Parent'.
2. Runtime Error: Cannot access protectedMethod from the Child class.
3. Compilation Error: The protectedMethod is not visible in the Child class.
4. Compilation Error: childMethod is not visible due to access restrictions.

124. Which of the following is true about nested switch statements in C?

1. A switch statement cannot contain another switch.
2. Inner switch cases should not contain break statement
3. A switch statement can contain another switch statement inside any of its cases.
4. Both inner and outer switch statements must have a default case.

125. What does the super keyword in Java do?

1. Used to define static variables
2. Refers to high performing objects
3. Refers to the parent class
4. Refers to the current object

126. Which of the following techniques can be used to modify the actual variable passed to a function?

1. Standard C has no options for modifying actual variables passed to a function.
2. Pass a copy of the actual parameter to function.
3. Pass the address of the actual parameters to function.
4. Use a local variable instead of passing any parameters.

127. What will be the output of the following code snippet?

```
#include<stdio.h>
int main() {
int a = 5, b = 3, c = 0;
if (a > b > c) {
printf("True\n");
} else {
printf("False\n");
}
return 0;
}
```

1. FALSE
2. undefined behavior
3. TRUE
4. compile time error

128. What does the first dimension and the second dimension represents in a two-dimensional character array?

1. The first dimension stores the length of each name, and the second stores the number of names.
2. The first dimension represents the maximum length of the names, and the second dimension represents the number of names.
3. The first dimension represents the number of names in the array, and the second dimension represents the maximum length of each name.
4. The first dimension holds the total number of characters, and the second dimension stores the number of names.

129. What is the output of the following code?

```
#include <stdio.h>
int main() {
int i = 5;
do {
printf("%d ", i);
i--;
} while (i > 5);
return 0;
}
```

1. 5 4 3 2 1
2. Infinite loop
3. No output printed
4. 5

130. What will be the output of the following code?

```
#include <stdio.h>
int main() {
int x = -1, y = 0, z = 1;
int result = (x > 0) ? x : (y == 0) ? z : y;
printf("%d", result);
return 0;
}
```

1. compile time error
2. 1
3. −1
4. 0

123. 1	124. 3	125. 3	126. 3	127. 3	128. 3	129. 4	130. 2

131. How many times will the innermost loop execute in the below code?

```
#include <stdio.h>
int main() {
for(int i=0; i<3; i++)
{
for(int j=0; j<2; j++)
{
printf("%d ",i);
}
}
return 0;
}
```

1. 2 times
2. 5 times
3. 3 times
4. 6 times

132. What happens when the following code executes?

```
#include <stdio.h>
int main() {
char buffer[50];
int n = sprintf(buffer, "Hello, World!");
printf("%d %s", n, buffer);
return 0;
}
```

1. Prints '13 Hello, World!'
2. Prints '12 Hello, World!'
3. Prints '13 Hello'
4. Prints '12 Hello'

133. What will be the output of the following program?

```
class CustomException extends Exception {
public CustomException(String message) {
super(message);
}
}
public class TestCustomException {
public static void main(String[] args) {
try {
validateAge(15);
} catch (CustomException e) {
System.out.println("Caught Exception:" +
e.getMessage());
} finally {
System.out.println("Execution finished.");
}
}
public static void validateAge(int age) throws
CustomException {
if (age < 18) {
throw new CustomException("Age must be 18 or
above.");
}
System.out.println("Age is valid.");
}
}
```

1. Compilation error because custom exceptions cannot extend Exception.
2. Age is valid.
Execution finished.
3. Caught Exception: Age must be 18 or above.
Execution finished.
4. Caught Exception: null
Execution finished.

134. What does the below code snippet represent?
myObject.doActivity();

1. Sending a message to the doActivity class
2. Calling a method named doActivity on the object myObject
3. Creating an object myObject
4. Sending a message to the child class of myObject

135. Which of the following statements is false about simplification of Boolean functions using Karnaugh Map technique?

1. In Karnaugh Map, you group adjacent squares in the form of power of two and try to cover as many minterms or maxterms as you can in one group.
2. In Karnaugh Map, the rows and columns are represented in binary code sequence.
3. Karnaugh Map technique is used to simplify Sum of Product (SOP) form of Boolean functions.
4. Karnaugh Map technique is used to simplify Product of Sum (POS) form of Boolean functions.

136.
```
public class ExceptionTest {
public static void main(String[] args) {
try {
System.out.println("Result: " + calculate(10, 0));
} catch (ArithmeticException e) {
System.out.println("ArithmeticException caught: "
+ e.getMessage());
} catch (Exception e) {
System.out.println("General exception caught: " +
e.getMessage());
} finally {
System.out.println("In finally block.");
}
}
public static int calculate(int a, int b) throws
Exception {
try {
return a / b;
} catch (ArithmeticException e) {
throw new Exception("Division by zero not allowed");
} finally {
```

131. 4	**132.** 1	**133.** 3	**134.** 2	**135.** 2

```
System.out.println("Inner finally block executed.");
}
}
}
```

What will be the output of the program?

1. Inner finally block executed. General exception caught: Division by zero not allowed
   In finally block.
2. Inner finally block executed. General exception caught: / by zero In finally block.
3. Inner finally block executed.
   Result: 0
   In finally block.
4. Inner finally block executed.
   ArithmeticException caught: / by zero
   In finally block

137. Given the following code snippet, what is the value of the variable *c*?

int *a*, *b*, *c*;
a = *b* = *c* = 15;
c = *c* + 10;

1. 10 2. 25
3. 15 4. Undefined

138. Which arithmetic operator has the highest precedence in C?

1. + 2. − 3. % 4. =

139. Which of the following causes an infinite loop?

1. for (int i = 0; i < 10; i++) { }
2. for (int i = 10; i >5; i--) { }
3. do { } while (0);
4. while (1) { }

140. What is the 2's complement of the binary number 1100?

1. 1001 2. 1111
3. 11 4. 0100

141. Which tool is used to adjust the brightness and contrast of an image in Adobe Photoshop?

1. Paint bucket tool 2. Healing brush tool
3. Adjustments panel 4. Selection tool

142. Which of the following DHTML methods is used to change the style of an HTML element using CSS dynamically?

1. document.getElementById("element").setCSS()
2. element.style.backgroundColor = "red"
3. document.createElement("style")
4. window.addEventListener("resize")

143. In singly linked list, each node of the list consists of __________.

1. data value and address of next node
2. data value and address of previous node
3. NULL and address of the previous node
4. NULL and address of the next node

144. Which of the following PHP functions is used to sort an array in ascending order without affecting the keys?

1. asort() 2. array_sort()
3. sort() 4. ksort()

145. Which of the following is NOT a correct way of declaring and initializing array in C?

1. char arr[6];
   arr = "consultancy";
2. char arr[6] ={ };
3. char arr[6] ={2};
4. char arr[ ] = "consultancy";

146. Which of the following statements is correct about the divide and conquer approach of binary search technique?

1. The best-case time complexity of binary search is O(log*n*).
2. The worst-case time complexity of binary search is O(log*n*).
3. The recurrence relation of binary search is written as T(*n*) = 2T(*n*/2) + O(1), where *n* is the number of elements in the array.
4. The average-case time complexity of binary search is O(*n*).

147. What will be the output of the given C program?

```
#include <stdio.h>
int main()
{
{
int x = 10, y = 20;
{
{
int y = 40;
x++;
y++;
}
printf("x = %d, y = %d\n", x, y);
}
}
return 0;
}
```

1. x = 10, y = 20 2. x = 11, y = 41
3. x = 10, y = 41 4. x = 11, y = 20

136. 1	**137.** 2	**138.** 3	**139.** 4	**140.** 4	**141.** 3	**142.** 2	**143.** 1	**144.** 1	**145.** 1	**146.** 2	**147.** 4

148. Which of the following formats is commonly used for exporting images for the web?

1. BMP
2. TIFF
3. PNG
4. PSD

149. Which sorting technique is best for sorting a linked list with *n* elements?

1. Selection sort
2. Insertion sort
3. Merge sort
4. Bubble sort

150. Which of the following asymptotic notation gives asymptotically tight upper bound as well as asymptotically tight lower bound?

1. Omega (Ω)
2. Theta (θ)
3. Big Oh (O)
4. Small Omega (ω)

151. What is the main function of the 'cutting' tool in image editing?

1. To change the image resolution
2. to apply color effects
3. To resize the image
4. To remove parts of the image

152. What is the output of the following JavaScript code?

```
let x = 10;
if (x > 5) {
console.log("Greater");
} else {
console.log("Smaller");
}
```

1. "undefined"
2. Error
3. "Smaller"
4. "Greater"

153. Which of the following statements is INCORRECT about the storage classes in C?

1. In Register storage class, the storage of a variable is CPU register.
2. The scope of variable in automatic storage class is local to the block in which the variable is defined.
3. In static storage class, the default initial value of the variable is zero.
4. In Register storage class, the default initial value of the variable is zero.

154. What will be the output of the C program given below?

```
#include <stdio.h>
int* func()
{
static int arr[5] = { 1, 2, 3, 4, 5 };
return arr;
}
int main()
{
int* ptr = func();
printf("Array Elements: ");
for (int i = 0; i < 5; i++) {
printf("%d ", *ptr);
}
return 0;
}
```

1. 1 1 1 1 1
2. 1 1 3 4 1
3. 1 2 3 4 5
4. 2 3 4 5 0

155. Which of the following DHTML methods is used to control the browser window size, such as resizing it dynamically via JavaScript?

1. document.resizeWindow()
2. window.changeSize()
3. window.resizeTo()
4. window.setSize()

156. Which of the following options is correct about the functions in C language?

1. Actual parameters are always variables.
2. Actual parameters are declared in the function definition.
3. Actual parameters are used to define the function signature and to specify the type and number of arguments that a function can accept.
4. Actual parameters are the values that are passed to a function when it is called.

157. What is the primary function of a web browser?

1. To send and receive emails
2. To display and navigate web pages
3. To create websites
4. To store large amounts of data

158. Which advantage of AJAX helps in reducing bandwidth consumption?

1. AJAX sends and retrieves only small amounts of data from the server.
2. AJAX uses less JavaScript.
3. AJAX increases data transfer.
4. AJAX only loads images on the page.

159. What will be the output of the given C program?

```
#include <stdio.h>
int main() {
int a = 4;
int b = 3;
int result;
```

148. 3	149. 3	150. 2	151. 4	152. 4	153. 4	154. 1	155. 3	156. 4	157. 2	158. 1

```
result = a ^ b;
printf("%d", result);
return 0;
}
```

1. 3 2. 0
3. 4 4. 7

160. Which of the following cases DOES NOT exist when one computes the time complexity of an algorithm?

1. Average case 2. Worst case
3. Test Case 4. Best Case

161. The total Purchases of ABC Ltd., during the FY 2024-25 was ₹ 1,90,000. If the gross profit of ABC Ltd. was 20% on sales and closing stock was more than the opening stock by ₹ 30,000 the gross profit earned by ABC Ltd., during the year 2024-25 was:

1. ₹ 35,000.00 2. ₹ 25,000.00
3. ₹ 40,000.00 4. ₹ 52,000.00

162. Calculate the time complexity of deleting an element from the beginning of a dynamic array.

1. O(log n) 2. O(log)
3. O(1) 4. O(n)

163. Which logical operation does the ALU perform that results in a 1 output only when both inputs are different?

1. NOR 2. XOR
3. OR 4. AND

164. What will be the output of the following C program?

```
#include <stdio.h>
int main()
{
int a[5];
for (int i = 0; i < 5; i++)
{
a[i] = i * i - 2 * i + 1;
}
for (int i = 0; i < 5; i++)
{
printf("%d ", a[i]);
}
return 0;
}
```

1. 1 2 3 4 9 2. 1 0 2 4 9
3. 1 1 2 4 9 4. 1 0 1 4 9

165. What is the main purpose of virtual memory?

1. To provide cache storage
2. To extend the physical memory using secondary storage
3. To increase CPU speed
4. To store BIOS settings

166. Which of the following is true about the for loop in C?

1. A for loop must always have all three components: initialization, condition, and increment/decrement.
2. The increment/decrement part of the for loop is mandatory.
3. The condition in a for loop is optional, and it can result in an infinite loop if omitted.
4. A for loop cannot be nested inside another for loop.

167. Which of the following is a disadvantage of singly linked list?

1. Linked lists have a variable size.
2. Insertion operation at the beginning of the linked list is performed in O (1) time.
3. Deletion operation at the beginning of the linked list is performed in O(1) time.
4. Accessing an element in a singly linked list requires traversal from the head, making it slower than arrays.

168. Which of the following options is the differential equation corresponding to $y = ae^{2x} + be^{-x}$ where a and b are arbitrary?

1. $y'' - 2y' + y = 0$
2. $y'' - y' - 2y = 0$
3. $y'' + 2y' - y = 0$
4. $y'' + 2y' + y = 0$

169. The characteristic equation of matrix A = $\begin{bmatrix} 1 & 4 \\ 3 & 5 \end{bmatrix}$ is _____.

1. $\lambda^2 - 6\lambda + 7 = 0$
2. $\lambda^2 + 6\lambda - 7 = 0$
3. $\lambda^2 - 6\lambda - 7 = 0$
4. $\lambda^2 + 6\lambda + 7 = 0$

170. Which of the following is NOT a tertiary business activity?

1. Manufacturing 2. Warehousing
3. Transportation 4. Insurance

171. Which of the following options is the particular solution of the differential equation $y'' - 6y' + 9y = 2e^{3t}$?

1. $\frac{e^{3t}}{2}$ 2. $\frac{e^{3t}}{9}$
3. t^2e^{3t} 4. e^{3t}

159. 4	160. 3	161. 3	162. 4	163. 2	164. 4	165. 2	166. 3	167. 4	168. 2	169. 3	170. 1	171. 3

172. Which of the following will terminate the loop immediately in C?

1. When the loop condition is not given
2. When the loop variable reaches a certain value
3. When a continue statement is encounted
4. When a break satement is encountered

173. Two identical cells of *emf* = 1.5 V and internal resistance = 0.5 Ω are connected in series. If 1 A is the allowed current through the cell, the effective terminal potential difference of the cells is ______.

1. 0.75 V 2. 1 V
3. 2 V 4. 0.5 V

174. If $A = \begin{bmatrix} 1 & 0 & 0 \\ 0 & -1 & 0 \\ 1 & 0 & 1 \end{bmatrix}$ then the matrix for A^6 is ______

1. $\begin{bmatrix} 1 & 0 & 0 \\ 0 & -1 & 0 \\ 6 & 0 & 1 \end{bmatrix}$ 2. $\begin{bmatrix} 1 & 0 & 0 \\ 0 & -1 & 0 \\ 1 & 0 & 1 \end{bmatrix}$

3. $\begin{bmatrix} 1 & 0 & 0 \\ 0 & 1 & 0 \\ 6 & 0 & 1 \end{bmatrix}$ 4. $\begin{bmatrix} 6 & 0 & 0 \\ 0 & 6 & 0 \\ 6 & 0 & 6 \end{bmatrix}$

175. On 15 December 2024, a fire occurred in the godown of M Ltd., and the entire stock was destroyed. The value of the stock salvaged was ₹ 3,00,000. The following transactions took place between 1 October 2024 and 15 December 2024. Study the table and answer the question that follows.

Purchases

Sales

Wages

Opening Stock

Gross Profit

The value of stock lost by fire was ______.

1. ₹ 6,75,000 2. ₹ 2,55,000
3. ₹ 5,92,000 4. ₹ 6,30,000

176. MC Publications has received rent amounting to ₹ 2,50,000 during the financial year ending 31st March 2024. Out of this ₹ 50,000 represents rent relating to next financial year. The rent account to be credited to the profit and loss account for the year ended 31st March 2024 is ______ and the rent received in advance will be shown as a/an ______.

1. ₹ 2,00,000; Asset 2. ₹ 3,00,000; Asset
3. ₹ 1,50,000; Liability 4. ₹ 2,00,000; Liability

177. The particular solution of the differential equaion $(D^4 - 18D^2 + 81)y^2$

1. $\dfrac{72x^2e^{3x}}{104}$ 2. x^2e^{3x}
3. $2x^2e^{3x}$ 4. $12x^2e^{3x}$

178. Which cycle is primarily managed by the Control Unit?

1. Arithmetic cycle
2. Instruction cycle (Fetch-Decode-Execute cycle)
3. Memory refresh cycle
4. I/O cycle

179. The magnetic moment of a bar magnet is ______ the magnetic moment of an equivalent solenoid if the solenoid's magnetic field is ______ that of the bar magnet.

1. more than ; same as
2. equal to ; same as
3. less than ; same as
4. equal to ; different from

180. Which of the following is a key design goal of an Instruction Set Architecture?

1. Minimizing the transistor count
2. Maximizing the instruction decode time
3. Ensuring only complex instructions are supported
4. Balancing simplicity and performance for ease of programming and efficiency

181. Which of the following statement is correct for a business organisation?

1. Centralisation leads to autonomy
2. Responsibility leads to decentralisation
3. Authority leads to decentralisation
4. Delegation leads to decentralisation

182. Eighty eight residents of a city, who were interviewed in a city are classified as male or female and also as drinkers or non-drinkers of tea. For testing association between sex and drinking of tea, the test statistic follows:

1. Chi Square distribution with 2 degrees of freedom
2. Normal distribution
3. Chi square distribution with 1 degree of freedom
4. *t* distribution with 1 degree of freedom

183. Suppose a six faced die is thrown. Then the probability that the number appearing on the top is even is equal to:

1. $\frac{1}{2}$ 2. $\frac{1}{4}$
3. $\frac{1}{9}$ 4. $\frac{1}{6}$

172. 4	173. 3	174. 3	175. 4	176. 4	177. 2	178. 2	179. 2	180. 4	181. 4	182. 3	183. 1

184. Select an appropriate ROM type from the options, where data can be erased or destroyed using ultraviolet light.

1. PROM 2. EPROM
3. EEPROM 4. Flash ROM

185. How can you add an emoji to an email?

1. Use the delete key
2. Reply to the email
3. Click the emoji icon in the toolbar
4. Change the font style

186. What does the term 'bootstrapping' refer to in the context of starting a business?

1. Obtaining bank loans for initial capital
2. Self-funding the business using personal resources
3. Raising funds through venture capitalists
4. Crowdfunding through online platforms

187. Which of the following is an example of open-source application software?

1. Microsoft Excel 2. CorelDRAW
3. GIMP 4. Adobe Illustrator

188. Select the INCORRECT option among the phases of the CPU Instruction Cycle.

1. Execute 2. Fetch
3. Encode 4. Store

189. Which of the following smileys express happiness in text communication?

1. :-(2. : (
3. :-) 4. :

190. WhatsApp was founded by ________.

1. Jan Koum and Brian Acton
2. Mark Zuckerberg and Sheryl Sandberg
3. Larry Page and Sergey Brin
4. Allan Musk and Bill Steve

191. Which law legally mandates the inclusion of children with disabilities into mainstream schools in India?

1. RTI Act, 2009
2. National Curriculum Framework, 2005
3. RPwD Act, 2016
4. NEP, 2020

192. Aesthetic education primarily develops ________.

1. logical reasoning 2. sensory responsiveness
3. speed in recall 4. factual knowledge

193. ______ is a methodical approach. It suggests a logical and well-organised sequence of actions. It follows more steps.

1. Teaching technique
2. Teaching method
3. Teaching strategy
4. Teaching approach

194. Piaget's formal operational stage begins at approximately ________

1. 7 years 2. 8 years
3. 14 years 4. 11 years

195. Which of the following is NOT one of the five steps in Herbartian lesson planning?

1. Application 2. Association
3. Evaluation 4. Presentation

196. Gender inequality refers to which of the following?

1. Uniform distribution of resources
2. Differences in hairstyles
3. Biological differences only
4. Social and economic disparities between genders

197. Diagnostic assessment mainly helps in which of the following?

1. Identifying misconceptions
2. Grading performance
3. Standardising content
4. Promoting learners

198. You are designing a curriculum for vocational education. To ensure learners can transfer skills to actual work settings, which principle should you emphasise most?

1. Principle of economy
2. Principle of recency
3. Principle of activity and practicality
4. Principle of articulation

199. What is the core principle of the multilingual approach in early education?

1. Welcoming the child's language and using it to build understanding
2. Teaching only in the national language
3. Prioritising grammar over communication
4. Replacing mother tongue with the target language quickly

200. A 'subject' in school differs from a 'discipline' because it is ________.

1. a philosophical field
2. more deeply systematic
3. a classroom-taught branch of a discipline
4. an external research domain

184. 2	**185.** 3	**186.** 2	**187.** 3	**188.** 3	**189.** 3	**190.** 1	**191.** 3	**192.** 2
193. 2	**194.** 4	**195.** 3	**196.** 4	**197.** 1	**198.** 3	**199.** 1	**200.** 3	

EXPLANATORY ANSWERS

1. The first letters follow D → H → L → P → T → X, increasing by four alphabetical positions. The second letters follow W → A → E → I → M → Q, while the third letters follow P → T → X → B → F → J, both also increasing by four positions cyclically. The numbers increase by 9 each time: 6, 15, 24, 33, 42, 51; therefore, the missing cluster is XQJ 51.

2. Total number of students = Rank from top + Rank from bottom – 1

$= 7 + 28 - 1 = 34$

Reena herself is counted in both rankings, so one is subtracted to avoid counting her twice. Therefore, there are 34 students in the class.

3. In the given pattern, the fourth letter is moved to the beginning to form the second cluster: EACH → HEAC and HACK → KHAC. To form the third cluster, the third and fourth letters are placed before the first and second letters: EACH → CHEA and HACK → CKHA. Applying the same operations, LACE becomes ELAC and then CELA; therefore, option 3 follows the required pattern.

4. $231 - 7 = 224$

$224 - 10 = 214,\ 214 - 7 = 207$

$207 - 10 = 197,\ 197 - 7 = 190$

$190 - 10 = 180$

The series alternately subtracts 7 and 10. Therefore, the number that should replace the question mark is 180, which is option 4, not 183.

5. From the statements, all stones are rocks and all rocks are pebbles, so every stone is necessarily a pebble. Some stones are hills, which proves only that some rocks and some pebbles are hills; it does not establish that all rocks or all pebbles are hills. Therefore, neither "All rocks are hills" nor "All pebbles are hills" logically follows.

6. $206 - 71 = 135$

$178 - 71 = 107$

$194 - 71 = 123$

The same operation, subtraction of 71 from the whole number, is used in each pair. Therefore, 194 is related to 123.

7. A = (0, 0)

$(0, 0) \xrightarrow{\text{12 km North}} (0, 12) \xrightarrow{\text{6 km East}} (6, 12)$

$(6, 12) \xrightarrow{\text{9 km South}} (6, 3) \xrightarrow{\text{12 km East}} (18, 3)$

$(18, 3) \xrightarrow{\text{6 km South}} (18, -3) \xrightarrow{\text{21 km West}} (-3, -3) \xrightarrow{\text{3 km North}} (-3, 0)$

Point P is 3 km west of Point A. Hence, Mr. E must drive 3 km to the east to reach Point A again.

8. $3 \times 9 = 27,\ 27 + 10 = 37,\ 37 - 5 = 32$

$8 \times 9 = 72,\ 72 + 10 = 82,\ 82 - 5 = 77$

Applying the same operations:

$12 \times 9 = 108,\ 108 + 10 = 118,\ 118 - 5 = 113$

Therefore, 12 – 108 – 118 – 113 follows the same sequence of operations.

9. The statement only establishes that the roads of City B are congested because a large number of vehicles move on them. Metro trains do not travel on ordinary roads, so their delay due to road congestion cannot be assumed. The statement also gives no comparison between the influx of people into City B and that into other cities; therefore, neither assumption is implicit.

10. In RVY, the alphabetical gaps are R → V = +4 and V → Y = +3. The same pattern occurs in MQT and CGJ, where the respective gaps are also +4 and +3. In INR, however, I → N = +5 and N → R = +4; therefore, INR does not belong to the group.

11. The letters common to TYRE and TREK are T, R and E, while their common code digits are 5, 2 and 7. The only letter occurring in TREK but not in TYRE is K, and the only digit occurring in 7253 but not in 5127 is 3. Therefore, the code assigned to K is 3.

12. In AWDG, the letter movements are A → W = –4, W → D = +7 and D → G = +3, considering the alphabet cyclically. The same pattern of –4, +7 and +3 is followed by KGNQ and VRYB. In SOWY, however, the movements are S → O = –4, O → W = +8 and W → Y = +2; therefore, SOWY does not belong to the group.

13. Fixing Himani at one position, Evan and Charu occupy the two immediately adjacent positions. Gauri sits immediately to the right of Evan, Firoz sits second to the left of Himani, and Danish must occupy the common neighbouring position of Firoz and Gauri. The clockwise arrangement is Himani–Charu–Firoz–Danish–Gauri–Evan; when counted from the right of Himani, Evan and Gauri sit between Himani and Danish. Therefore, two people sit between Danish and Himani.

14. $34 - 20 \div 8 \times 2 + 16$

After interchanging the signs: $34 + 20 \times 8 \div 2 - 16$

$= 34 + 160 \div 2 - 16 = 34 + 80 - 16 = 98$

Therefore, the value replacing the question mark is 98.

15. REAL changes to QFBK, in which no vowel appears, while FAIR changes to EBJQ, which contains the vowel E. LIKE changes to KJJF, in which no vowel appears, whereas PITY changes to OJSX, which contains the vowel O. Thus, exactly two of the resulting letter-clusters contain no vowel.

16. 9 D 35 C 48 B 30 A 12

Replacing the symbols: $9 - 35 + 48 \times 30 \div 12$

$= 9 - 35 + 1440 \div 12 = 9 - 35 + 120 = 94$

Therefore, the required value is 94.

17. The first letters follow Q, P, O, N, M, decreasing by one position each time. The second letters follow I, L, O, R, U, increasing by three positions, while the third letters follow M, K, I, G, E, decreasing by two positions. The numbers follow 1, 3, 9, 27, 81, with every number multiplied by 3; therefore, the missing term is OOI 9.

18. T is second from the top, and P must be sixth because exactly three boxes lie between T and P. Y is below P, so Y occupies the seventh position; Q is the only box between T and R, placing Q third and R fourth. S occupies the first position, and the complete order from top is S, T, Q, R, Z, P, Y; hence, Z and P are the two boxes between R and Y.

19. RAT changes to QBS and ANT changes to BMS; neither resulting cluster contains a vowel. FAN changes to EBM, which contains the vowel E, while TON changes to SPM, which contains no vowel. Therefore, three resulting letter-clusters contain no vowel.

20. F is the mother of G, and H is the daughter of G. E is also the mother of H, so E is the wife of G and consequently the son's wife of F. D is the sister of E; therefore, D is related to F as her son's wife's sister.

21. Zebrafish are renowned for their remarkable regenerative abilities and can repair several damaged or lost body parts. They can regenerate portions of their fins, heart, spinal cord, retina and certain other tissues through controlled cellular growth. This exceptional capacity has made zebrafish an important model organism for studying tissue regeneration and possible applications in human medicine.

22. Article 165 of the Indian Constitution provides that the Governor of each State shall appoint a person qualified to be appointed a Judge of a High Court as the Advocate General of the State. Such qualification generally requires Indian citizenship and at least ten years of judicial office or advocacy in a High Court. The Advocate General is the highest law officer of the State and advises the State Government on legal matters.

23. The Under-17 athletics competition of the 68th National School Games 2024–25 was entrusted to Uttar Pradesh and was organised under the aegis of the School Games Federation of India. The competition brought together school-level athletes from different States and units of the country. Therefore, among the given options, the host State was Uttar Pradesh.

24. Article 79 of the Indian Constitution provides for the constitution of Parliament, consisting of the President and two Houses known respectively as the Council of States and the House of the People. The House of the People is commonly called the Lok Sabha and functions as the lower House of Parliament. The Council of States, known as the Rajya Sabha, is the upper House.

25. Kabini and Bhavani are important tributaries of the Kaveri River, which flows through the southern part of India. The Kabini originates in the Western Ghats region of Kerala and joins the Kaveri in Karnataka, while the Bhavani originates in the Nilgiri Hills and joins it in Tamil Nadu. These tributaries contribute substantially to the Kaveri river system and support irrigation and water supply.

26. Rapeseed is a major rabi oilseed crop that is generally sown during the winter season and harvested during the spring season. It grows well under cool and comparatively dry climatic conditions and is cultivated extensively along with mustard. Cotton, maize and tur are principally classified as kharif crops, although cultivation seasons may vary in some regions.

27. On 2 October 2024, Israel declared United Nations Secretary-General António Guterres persona non grata and prohibited him from entering the country. Israel's foreign minister alleged that Guterres had failed to condemn Iran's missile attack on Israel unequivocally. Therefore, the country referred to in the question is Israel.

28. The Albert Hall Museum building in Jaipur was designed by British architect Sir Samuel Swinton Jacob in the Indo-Saracenic architectural style. This style combines Indian architectural features, including domes, arches, chhatris and ornamental stonework, with European design elements. The building was named after Albert Edward, the Prince of Wales, and is one of Jaipur's most prominent architectural landmarks.

29. The 86th Constitutional Amendment Act, 2002 inserted clause (*k*) in Article 51A concerning the Fundamental Duties. It makes it the duty of every parent or guardian to provide opportunities for education to a child or ward between six and fourteen years of age. The same amendment also inserted Article 21A, making free and compulsory education for children of this age group a Fundamental Right.

30. The Narasimham Committee of 1998, formally known as the Committee on Banking Sector Reforms, examined measures required to strengthen India's banking system. It recommended greater capital adequacy, reduction of non-performing assets, stronger banking supervision, improved risk management and structural consolidation of banks. Its recommendations formed an important part of the second phase of banking-sector reforms in India.

31. Statement 1 is correct because the United Nations designated 2025 as the International Year of Quantum Science and Technology, coinciding with one hundred years since the foundational development of modern quantum mechanics. Statement 2 is correct because India's National Quantum Mission was approved in April 2023 to nurture and scale up scientific and industrial research and development in quantum technologies. Statement 3 is also correct because the Quantum Computing Applications Lab seeks to accelerate quantum-computing research and enable discoveries by supporting the development and testing of practical applications. Therefore, all three statements are correct.

32. Ram Prasad Bismil was among the principal founders of the Hindustan Republican Association, established in 1924 as a revolutionary organisation against British rule. Sachindra Nath Sanyal, Jogesh Chandra Chatterjee and other revolutionaries were also associated with its formation. The organisation aimed to establish a federal republic in India through an organised revolutionary struggle and later became closely associated with the Kakori train action of 1925.

33.

$$\text{Force} = \text{mass} \times \text{acceleration}$$

$$[\text{Force}] = MLT^{-2}$$

$$\text{Pressure} \times \text{area} = \frac{\text{Force}}{\text{Area}} \times \text{area} = \text{Force}$$

$$\frac{d(\text{angular momentum})}{dt} = \text{torque} = \text{force} \times \text{distance}$$

Thus, weight, pressure multiplied by area and mass multiplied by acceleration have the unit of force, whereas the rate of change of angular momentum has the unit of torque.

34. Babasaheb B. R. Ambedkar launched the non-violent Kala Ram Temple Entry Satyagraha at Nashik in 1930. The movement challenged caste-based restrictions that prevented members of the oppressed communities from entering the temple and exercising equal religious rights. Thousands of people participated in this organised struggle, which became an important event in Ambedkar's campaign for social equality, dignity and the abolition of untouchability.

35.

$$\text{Speed} = \frac{\text{Distance travelled}}{\text{Time taken}}$$

Speed measures the distance travelled by an object per unit of time and is a scalar quantity because it has magnitude but no specified direction. Its SI unit is:

$$\frac{\text{Metre}}{\text{Second}} = \text{m/s}$$

Therefore, the equation Speed = $\frac{\text{Distance}}{\text{Time}}$ correctly represents the calculation of speed.

36. Sal, shisham and hurra are characteristic trees found in India's tropical deciduous forests, also called monsoon forests. These forests occur in regions receiving seasonal rainfall and shed their leaves during the dry season to conserve water. Sal is especially common in the moist deciduous forests of central and eastern India, while shisham occurs extensively in deciduous and riverine tracts of northern India.

37. Beer production begins with malting, in which cereal grains—usually barley—are germinated and dried to develop enzymes required for converting starch into fermentable sugars. During brewing, the malt is mashed with water, and the resulting liquid is boiled, generally with hops, to produce wort. Yeast is then added during fermentation to convert sugars into alcohol and carbon dioxide; subsequent maturation and finishing prepare the beer for packaging.

38. *The Ministry of Utmost Happiness* was written by Arundhati Roy and published as her second novel after *The God of Small Things*. Jhumpa Lahiri wrote *Whereabouts*, originally composed in Italian and later translated into English by the author herself. She also wrote *The Lowland* and the short-story collection *Unaccustomed Earth;* therefore, *The Ministry of Utmost Happiness* was not written by her.

39. Rekha Gupta took oath as the Chief Minister of Delhi on 20 February 2025 at Ramlila Maidan. She became the ninth Chief Minister of the National Capital Territory of Delhi after being elected from the Shalimar Bagh Assembly constituency. The oath of office and secrecy was administered following her selection as leader of the newly elected Bharatiya Janata Party legislature group.

40. Gender budgeting was formally introduced in India through the Union Budget for the financial year 2005–2006. A separate Gender Budget Statement was included to analyse allocations and expenditure relating to women and girls across different ministries and government programmes. Gender budgeting is not a separate budget for women; it is a policy tool for assessing whether public expenditure and revenue measures promote gender equality and adequately address gender-specific needs.

41.
$$\text{Area of square} = (\text{side})^2$$
$$\text{Side} = \sqrt{38809} = \sqrt{197\times197} = 197 \text{ m}$$
Therefore, the length of each side of the square plot is 197 m.

42. Let the cost price be ₹ x.
$$\text{List price} = x+\frac{50}{100}x = 1.5x$$
$$\text{Selling price} = 70\% \text{ of } 1.5x = 1.05x$$
$$\text{Profit} = 1.05x - x = 0.05x$$
$$0.05x = 159 \Rightarrow x = \frac{159}{0.05} = 3180$$
$$\text{List price} = 1.5 \times 3180 = ₹\ 4770$$
Therefore, the list price of the fan is ₹ 4,770.

43.
$$\text{Men} \times \text{Days} = \text{Constant}$$
$$1210 \times 15 = 1815 \times d$$
$$d = \frac{1210\times15}{1815} = \frac{2\times15}{3} = 10$$
Therefore, the provisions will last for 10 days.

44.
$$\text{Boys : Girls} = 50:21$$
$$\text{Total ratio} = 50 + 21 = 71$$
$$\text{Value of one part} = \frac{7597}{71} = 107$$
$$\text{Number of boys} = 50 \times 107 = 5350$$
Therefore, the number of boys in the school is 5350.

45. Amount due at the end of the first year:
$$87900 + \frac{10}{100} \times 87900 = 87900 + 8790 = 96690$$
After the first instalment: $96690 - 9900 = 86790$
Amount due at the end of the second year:
$$86790 + \frac{10}{100} \times 86790 = 86790 + 8679 = 95469$$
After the second instalment:
$$95469 - 9900 = ₹\ 85569$$
Therefore, he still owes ₹ 85,569.

46.
$$2.5555... = 2+\frac{5}{9}=\frac{23}{9}$$
$$1.2727... = 1+\frac{27}{99}=1+\frac{3}{11}=\frac{14}{11}$$
$$1.8888... = 1+\frac{8}{9}=\frac{17}{9}$$
$$\frac{23}{9}+\frac{14}{11}-\frac{17}{9} = \frac{6}{9}+\frac{14}{11}=\frac{2}{3}+\frac{14}{11}=\frac{22+42}{33}=\frac{64}{33}$$

47. Sabina's one-day work: $\frac{1}{48}$

Pinki is twice as competent as Sabina:

Pinki's one-day work = $2\times\frac{1}{48}=\frac{1}{24}$

Their combined one-day work:
$$\frac{1}{48}+\frac{1}{24}=\frac{1+2}{48}=\frac{3}{48}=\frac{1}{16}$$
Therefore, Pinki and Sabina together will complete the work in 16 days.

48. Cost price of 10 kg rice: $10 \times 38 = ₹\ 380$
Cost price of 32 kg rice: $32 \times 46 = ₹\ 1472$
$$\text{Total cost price} = 380 + 1472 = ₹\ 1852$$
$$\text{Total quantity} = 10 + 32 = 42 \text{ kg}$$
$$\text{Selling price} = 42 \times 43 = ₹\ 1806$$
$$\text{Loss} = 1852 - 1806 = ₹\ 46$$
Therefore, Amit incurred a loss of ₹ 46.

49. Total price of three items = $17295 \times 3 = ₹\ 51885$
$$\text{Sum of ratio terms} = 3 + 5 + 7 = 15$$
$$\text{Value of one part} = \frac{51885}{15} = ₹\ 3459$$
$$\text{Price of costliest item} = 7 \times 3459 = ₹\ 24213$$
Therefore, the price of the costliest item is ₹ 24,213.

50.
$$\text{Men} \times \text{Hours} = \text{Constant}$$
$$3 \times 27 = 9 \times h$$
$$h = \frac{3\times27}{9} = 9 \text{ hours}$$
Therefore, 9 men will complete the same work in 9 hours.

51. Curved surface area = Circumference of base × height
$$880 = 88 \times h \Rightarrow h = 10 \text{ cm}$$

$$2\pi r = 88 \Rightarrow 2 \times \frac{22}{7} \times r = 88$$

$$\Rightarrow r = 14 \text{ cm}$$

$$\text{Volume} = \pi r^2 h = \frac{22}{7} \times 14^2 \times 10 = 6160 \text{ cm}^3$$

Therefore, the volume of the cylinder is 6160 cm^3.

52. Original average = 53

When every observation is multiplied by the same number, its average is also multiplied by that number.

New average = 53 × 2 = 106

Therefore, after doubling the marks of every student, the new average marks will be 106.

53. Let the speed of the boat in still water be x km/hr.

Downstream speed = $x + 3$, Upstream speed = $x - 3$

$$\frac{26}{x+3} = \frac{14}{x-3}$$

$$26(x-3) = 14(x+3)$$

$$26x - 78 = 14x + 42$$

$$12x = 120 \Rightarrow x = 10 \text{ km/hr}$$

Therefore, the speed of the boat in still water is 10 km/hr.

54. Let the sum invested at 7% per annum be ₹ x.

Sum invested at 13% = 21300 – x

Since the interests earned after five years are equal:

$$\frac{x \times 7 \times 5}{100} = \frac{(21300 - x) \times 13 \times 5}{100}$$

$$7x = 13(21300 - x)$$

$$7x = 276900 - 13x$$

$$20x = 276900 \Rightarrow x = 13845$$

Therefore, the sum invested at 7% per annum is ₹ 13,845.

55. $(96 \div 4) \times \left\{\frac{18}{6} + \frac{34}{3} \times (9-6)\right\} = 24 \times \left\{3 + \frac{34}{3} \times 3\right\}$

$= 24 \times (3 + 34) = 24 \times 37 = 888$

Therefore, the simplified value of the given expression is 888.

56. $x = 4.6833333...$

$x = 4.68 + 0.0033333...$

$$= \frac{468}{100} + \frac{1}{300} = \frac{1404 + 1}{300} = \frac{1405}{300} = \frac{281}{60}$$

Therefore, 4.6833333... expressed as a fraction is $\frac{281}{60}$.

57. Radius of pipe = $\frac{2}{2}$ = 1 cm

Speed of water = 2 m/s = 200 cm/s

Time = 20 × 60 = 1200 seconds

Length of water column = 200 × 1200 = 240000 cm

Volume of water = $\pi(1)^2 \times 240000 = 240000\pi$ cm^3

Let the rise in the tank be h cm:

$$\pi(50)^2 h = 240000\pi$$

$$2500h = 240000 \Rightarrow h = 96 \text{ cm}$$

Therefore, the water level will rise by 96 cm.

58. Decreases by 16.84%:

Let the original price of fuel be ₹ 100.

$$100 \times \frac{70}{100} = 70\ ; \qquad 70 \times \frac{80}{100} = 56$$

$$56 \times \frac{90}{100} = 50.4\ ; \qquad 50.4 \times \frac{165}{100} = 83.16$$

Percentage decrease = 100 – 83.16 = 16.84%

Therefore, the price after the fourth month is 16.84% lower than the original price.

59. Income in 2019: ₹ 24100

Income in 2020: $24100 \times \frac{130}{100}$ = ₹ 31330

Income in 2021: $31330 \times \frac{130}{100}$ = ₹ 40729

Therefore, Amit's income in 2021 was ₹ 40,729.

60. $\sqrt[6]{729} + \sqrt[4]{6561} + \sqrt[3]{6859} + \sqrt{8649}$

$= \sqrt[6]{3^6} + \sqrt[4]{9^4} + \sqrt[3]{19^3} + \sqrt{93^2} = 3 + 9 + 19 + 93 = 124$

Therefore, the simplified value of the expression is 124.

61. The word "obsolete" refers to something that is no longer used because it has become old-fashioned, outdated or has been replaced by something newer. It can describe an object, method, technology or practice that is no longer in active use. Therefore, "a thing no longer in use" can be substituted by the word obsolete.

62. Sentence Q logically follows S1 because it explains why a real mirage can be captured by a photographic lens. Sentence S then describes how the photographed image will appear hazy and shimmering because of the refraction of light. Sentence R introduces a contrasting situation in which a person merely imagines seeing something, and sentence P identifies this experience as a hallucination, which connects directly with S6. Hence, the correct sequence is Q–S–R–P.

63. The proverb "Don't count your chickens before they hatch" advises a person not to assume that an expected result has already been achieved. Future events may not happen exactly as anticipated, and plans based on uncertain outcomes may lead to disappointment. Therefore, the proverb means that one should avoid making assumptions about the future.

64. The correctly spelt word is "recommendation," which is formed from the verb "recommend" and the suffix "-ation." It contains a double "m" in "recommend" but only one "c" at the beginning. Therefore, the incorrect spelling "recomendation" in the sentence should be replaced with recommendation.

65. The phrase refers to the population as a whole within which the number and proportion of people aged sixty years and above are increasing. The definite article "the" is used because "population" denotes a specific collective population under discussion. Therefore, the grammatically correct expression is "in the population."

66. The word "impeccable" means faultless, flawless or without any defect, especially when describing behaviour or manners. "Imperfect" means having faults, weaknesses or defects and is therefore opposite in meaning to "impeccable." The other options—immaculate, unblemished and seamless—are similar in meaning to impeccable rather than its antonyms.

67. A "maestro" is a person who possesses exceptional knowledge, skill or mastery in music, particularly as a performer, conductor or composer. Sita has extensive musical knowledge acquired from her renowned musician grandmother, so the term suitably describes her musical expertise. The other options refer to inexperienced or unskilled persons; therefore, maestro is the most appropriate substitute.

68. The noun "insight" is conventionally followed by the preposition "into" when it means a deep and accurate understanding of a subject or process. Thus, "insight into how human emotions work" is the grammatically and idiomatically correct construction. Therefore, the sentence should read, "he has no real insight into how human emotions work under extreme stress."

69. The word "sudden" begins with the consonant sound /s/, so it takes the indefinite article "a." The word "unexpected" begins with a vowel sound, so it takes the indefinite article "an." Therefore, the correct sentence is: "A sudden change in weather caused an unexpected delay in the flight."

70. "Draconian" means extremely harsh, severe, cruel or oppressive, especially when describing laws, rules or punishments. Among the given words, "vicious" most closely conveys the sense of cruelty and severity associated with "draconian." Lenient, clement and benignant express mildness, mercy or kindness and are therefore opposite rather than similar in meaning.

71. The word "hard" functions as an adverb meaning diligently or with great effort and correctly modifies the verb "worked." "Hardly" means scarcely or almost not, which would change the intended meaning of the sentence. "Harder" and "hardest" are comparative and superlative forms and require an explicit comparison; therefore, the correct sentence is "He worked hard for his success."

72. The word "vaccuum" in the sentence is incorrectly spelt and must be written as "vacuum." The correct spelling contains one "c" followed by two consecutive "u" letters: v-a-c-u-u-m. The other alternatives—"intence," "electron-beem" and "wellded"—are themselves incorrect spellings of "intense," "electron-beam" and "welded"; therefore, vacuum is the required correction.

73. The proverb "Don't put all your eggs in one basket" advises against committing all one's resources, money or effort to a single plan or opportunity. If that single option fails, everything may be lost at once. Dividing resources among several alternatives reduces dependence on one outcome; therefore, the proverb means diversify your risks to avoid complete loss.

74. The subject of the sentence is "each," which is a singular distributive pronoun even though it is followed by the plural noun "players." A singular subject requires a singular verb, and the passive construction in the past tense is "was awarded." Therefore, the grammatically correct sentence is "Each of the players was awarded a trophy."

75. Sentence B introduces Bali as the subject of the paragraph, while sentence A follows it through the pronoun "It" and introduces Bali's elaborate traditional dancing. Sentence C then explains that the dancing is inspired by its Hindu beliefs, providing further information about the dance already mentioned. Sentence D concludes by describing the experience of watching this dancing as breathtaking; therefore, the correct sequence is B–A–C–D.

76. The passage acknowledges that predictive governance can anticipate criminal activity, assist urban planning and forecast economic changes. However, its principal concern is that algorithmic systems reduce complex human beings to statistical patterns and may institutionalise bias. It further argues that opaque decision-making weakens accountability, participation and deliberative democracy; therefore, option 2 best summarises the passage.

77. The passage primarily examines how predictive algorithms affect human agency, fairness, transparency, accountability and citizen participation. It warns that supposedly objective data systems may exclude outliers and reproduce existing biases while bypassing democratic deliberation. Its focus is not merely on technical performance but on the ethical question of who benefits and who is excluded; therefore, option 1 expresses the central theme.

78. The passage first introduces predictive governance as an emerging model of public administration and briefly identifies its practical uses. It then moves to the risks of statistical reduction, exclusion, bias, opacity and weakening democratic participation. Finally, it reflects on human dignity and argues that governance must recognise people as more than predictable variables; therefore, the structure is Concept Introduction → Benefits → Risks → Philosophical Reflection.

79. Automated welfare systems use data and algorithms to determine eligibility, assess risk or distribute public benefits. Such systems closely reflect the passage's concerns because they may reduce citizens to data profiles, exclude unusual cases and make consequential decisions through opaque models. They can also shift accountability away from human officials and disadvantage vulnerable individuals; therefore, option 1 is the closest real-world parallel.

80. In the passage, "marginalising" means pushing certain people or groups to the edge, excluding them or making their experiences less significant. "Integrating" means bringing people into the main group or system and ensuring their inclusion and participation. "Ignoring," "suppressing" and "isolating" are similar to exclusion rather than opposite to it; therefore, the most appropriate antonym is integrating.

81. 'हस्ताक्षर' शब्द की शुद्ध वर्तनी में 'हस्त' और 'अक्षर' का संयोग होता है। इसका अर्थ किसी व्यक्ति द्वारा अपने नाम को विशिष्ट रूप में लिखना है, जिसका प्रयोग सहमति या प्रमाण के लिए किया जाता है। अतः वाक्य का शुद्ध रूप होगा—'उसने हस्ताक्षर किए।'

82. 'च्युत' का अर्थ अपने निश्चित स्थान, पद, अवस्था अथवा मार्ग से हट गया या गिर गया होता है। यह शब्द संस्कृत की 'च्यु' धातु से बना है, जिसका भाव स्थान से विचलित होना है। इसलिए 'जो अपने निश्चित स्थान से डिग गया हो' वाक्यांश के लिए उपयुक्त एक शब्द च्युत है।

83. 'अनिष्ट' का अर्थ अहित, अशुभ, बुरा परिणाम अथवा अमंगल होता है। 'अमंगल' भी किसी अप्रिय, अशुभ या हानिकारक घटना का बोध कराता है, इसलिए यह 'अनिष्ट' का उपयुक्त पर्यायवाची है। 'अपरिहार्य', 'अनिर्णीत' और 'अधीर' के अर्थ इससे भिन्न हैं।

84. वाक्य में नरेन्द्र से कपड़े साफ करवाने का भाव व्यक्त किया गया है, इसलिए यहाँ प्रेरणार्थक क्रिया की आवश्यकता है। 'धुलवाता है' का अर्थ है कि कर्ता स्वयं कपड़े नहीं धोता, बल्कि नरेन्द्र से धुलवाने का कार्य कराता है। अतः पूर्ण वाक्य होगा—'वह नरेन्द्र से कपड़े धुलवाता है।'

85. 'बाप न मारे मेंढकी बेटा तीरंदाज' लोकोक्ति का प्रयोग तब किया जाता है जब पुत्र या छोटा व्यक्ति अपने पिता अथवा बड़े से भी अधिक योग्यता या वीरता का दिखावा करता है। इसमें वास्तविक उपलब्धि की अपेक्षा बढ़-चढ़कर किए गए दावे पर व्यंग्य किया जाता है। अतः इसका उपयुक्त अर्थ बड़े से छोटा बढ़ गया है।

86. वाक्य 1, 3 और 4 आधुनिक हिंदी साहित्य, हिंदी साहित्यकार तथा साहित्य की विधाओं से संबंधित हैं। ये तीनों वाक्य एक ही साहित्यिक संदर्भ के अंतर्गत आते हैं। क्रिकेट विश्व कप से संबंधित वाक्य का हिंदी साहित्य से कोई संबंध नहीं है, इसलिए वही अतिरिक्त वाक्य है।

87. 'रंग' की विशेषता बताने के लिए रंगवाचक विशेषण का प्रयोग किया जाता है। 'नीला' शब्द फ्रॉक के रंग की विशेषता स्पष्ट करता है, जबकि 'गीला', 'दुबला' और 'ऊपरी' रंग के उपयुक्त विशेषण नहीं हैं। अतः शुद्ध वाक्य होगा—'निताशी के फ्रॉक का रंग नीला है।'

88. 'उदयाचल' का अर्थ वह पर्वत या दिशा है जहाँ सूर्य का उदय माना जाता है। इसके विपरीत 'अस्ताचल' उस स्थान या दिशा को कहते हैं जहाँ सूर्य अस्त होता हुआ प्रतीत होता है। इसलिए 'उदयाचल' का उचित विलोम शब्द अस्ताचल है।

89. यहाँ मोहन और उसके तीन भाइयों के बीच संबंध अथवा अधिकार का भाव प्रकट किया गया है। संबंध कारक का चिह्न 'का, के, की' होता है और 'भाई' बहुवचन होने के कारण 'के' का प्रयोग उचित है। अतः शुद्ध वाक्य होगा—'मोहन के तीन भाई हैं।'

90. रिक्त स्थान में परीक्षा और दिन के बीच संबंध स्थापित करने के लिए संबंध कारक 'के' का प्रयोग होगा। 'दिन' बहुवचन में प्रयुक्त है, इसलिए 'का' के स्थान पर 'के' व्याकरणसम्मत है। अतः शुद्ध वाक्य होगा—'परीक्षा के दिन नजदीक आ गए हैं।'

91. 'इन्दरियों' शब्द की वर्तनी अशुद्ध है; इसका शुद्ध रूप 'इन्द्रियों' होता है। 'इन्द्रिय' के बहुवचन रूप 'इन्द्रियाँ' में परसर्ग 'को' जुड़ने पर 'इन्द्रियों' बनता है। अतः शुद्ध वाक्य होगा—'इन्द्रियों को वश में रखना चाहिए।'

92. दिए गए आरम्भिक अंश 'विश्व के विशाल भू-भाग में' के साथ विकल्प 3 व्याकरण और अर्थ दोनों की दृष्टि से उचित संबंध बनाता है। इससे यह भाव व्यक्त होता है कि विस्तृत भू-भाग में प्रयुक्त हिन्दी निरन्तर प्रवाहित और परिवर्तनशील भाषा है। पूर्ण वाक्य होगा—'विश्व के विशाल भू-भाग में बोली जाने वाली हिन्दी एक वेगवती नदी की भाँति है।'

93. 'धीरे-धीरे' रीतिवाचक क्रियाविशेषण है, क्योंकि यह सड़क पार करने की क्रिया के ढंग अथवा रीति को प्रकट करता है। 'देश-विदेश', 'यथाक्रम' और 'घर-बाहर' इस वाक्य में क्रिया की उपयुक्त विशेषता व्यक्त नहीं करते। अतः पूर्ण वाक्य होगा—'वह धीरे-धीरे सड़क पार करता है।'

94. 'अग्रणी' उस व्यक्ति को कहते हैं जो किसी क्षेत्र, समूह अथवा कार्य में आगे हो और जिसकी गणना प्रमुख व्यक्तियों में की जाती हो। यह शब्द नेतृत्व करने वाले या विशिष्ट स्थान रखने वाले व्यक्ति का बोध कराता है। अतः 'जिसकी गिनती प्रमुख व्यक्तियों में हो' वाक्यांश के लिए सार्थक शब्द अग्रणी है।

95. 'गिरगिट की तरह रंग बदलना' मुहावरे का अर्थ परिस्थितियों या स्वार्थ के अनुसार बार-बार अपना व्यवहार, विचार अथवा पक्ष बदलना होता है। एक बात पर स्थिर न रहना और अलग-अलग रंग-ढंग अपनाना इसके अर्थ से संबंधित हैं। 'व्यर्थ समय खोना' इस मुहावरे का अर्थ नहीं है।

96. गद्यांश में जनसंख्या घनत्व, वाहनों, कूड़े, कारखानों और वैज्ञानिक साधनों को प्रदूषण के कारणों के रूप में प्रस्तुत किया गया है। इसमें वायु, जल और ध्वनि प्रदूषण से होने वाली स्वास्थ्य तथा पर्यावरण संबंधी समस्याएँ भी बताई गई हैं। अंत में जागरूकता, प्रचार तथा सरकार और जनता के संयुक्त सहयोग को बचाव का उपाय बताया गया है, इसलिए यही सर्वाधिक उपयुक्त शीर्षक है।

97. गद्यांश में वाहनों और कारखानों के धुएँ के माध्यम से वायु प्रदूषण का स्पष्ट उल्लेख किया गया है। प्रदूषित औद्योगिक जल से जल प्रदूषण तथा अत्यधिक शोर से ध्वनि प्रदूषण की समस्या भी बताई गई है। भूमि प्रदूषण का स्वतंत्र और स्पष्ट रूप से उल्लेख नहीं किया गया है।

98. जनसंख्या घनत्व, वैज्ञानिक साधनों का अनुचित प्रयोग और औद्योगीकरण प्रदूषण को बढ़ाने वाले कारण हो सकते हैं। इसके विपरीत पर्यावरण संरक्षण अधिनियम का उद्देश्य पर्यावरण की रक्षा करना तथा प्रदूषण को नियंत्रित करना है। इसलिए पर्यावरण संरक्षण अधिनियम प्रदूषण का कारण नहीं है।

99. 'घनत्व' का सामान्य अर्थ किसी स्थान या क्षेत्र में वस्तुओं अथवा व्यक्तियों की सघनता या घनापन होता है। 'जनसंख्या घनत्व' से आशय किसी निश्चित क्षेत्रफल में रहने वाले लोगों की संख्या से है। अतः दिए गए विकल्पों में 'घनत्व' का सही अर्थ घनापन है।

100. 'कल' एक अनेकार्थी शब्द है, जिसके अर्थ बीता अथवा आने वाला दिन, मशीन, चैन या सुख तथा मधुर या सुंदर भी हो सकते हैं। 'कक्ष' का अर्थ कमरा, श्रेणी अथवा किसी भवन का भाग होता है और यह 'कल' का अर्थ नहीं है। इसलिए कक्ष 'कल' का अनेकार्थी शब्द नहीं है।

101. In the Selective Repeat ARQ protocol, the receiver accepts frames that arrive correctly even when they are out of order. Such frames are stored temporarily in the receiver's buffer while the missing or damaged frames are retransmitted individually. After all preceding missing frames arrive, the receiver rearranges the buffered frames in the correct sequence and passes them to the upper layer.

102. The SQL UPDATE statement is used to modify existing data stored in one or more rows of a table. It is generally used with the SET clause to specify new values and the WHERE clause to identify the rows that must be changed. For example, UPDATE Student SET Marks = 80 WHERE Roll No = 5; updates the marks of the specified student.

103. Scalability, fault tolerance and resource sharing are important benefits of distributed systems because multiple interconnected computers can cooperate and share workloads and resources. High communication latency is not a benefit; it is a disadvantage that may occur because data and messages must travel across a network. Such delays can reduce system performance, especially when frequent communication between distributed nodes is required.

104. This statement is false because universal gates can be used to construct all basic and complex logic gates. Both NAND and NOR are called universal logic gates since NOT, AND and OR operations can be implemented using only NAND gates or only NOR gates. Therefore, the statement that all basic logic gates cannot be implemented using universal logic gates is incorrect.

105. This statement correctly specifies the table name, the three columns receiving values and the corresponding values in the same order. Since the remaining columns allow NULL values, they may be omitted from the INSERT statement. The syntax INSERT INTO table_name (column_list) VALUES (value_list); is the standard SQL form for inserting values into selected columns.

106. In public-key cryptography, the sender encrypts a confidential message using the recipient's public key. The encrypted message can then be decrypted only with the corresponding private key held securely by the recipient. This relationship ensures confidentiality because possession of the public key does not allow an unauthorised person to recover the original message.

107. An XNOR gate produces an output of 1 when its two inputs are identical and an output of 0 when they are different. Here, the inputs are A = 1 and B = 0, so they are unequal. Therefore:

$$A \odot B = 1 \odot 0 = 0$$

Hence, the output of the XNOR gate is 0.

108. A database schema is the overall logical design or structure of a database. It defines tables, attributes, data types, keys, relationships, constraints and other structural components without referring to the particular data stored at a specific moment. A database instance represents the actual data present at a given time, whereas the schema describes the permanent organisational framework.

109. MIMO technology uses multiple transmitting and receiving antennas to send and receive several data signals simultaneously. It improves Wi-Fi coverage, signal reliability, data speed and resistance to interference by using techniques such as spatial diversity and spatial multiplexing. CDMA and TDMA are access methods, while WEP is an outdated wireless security mechanism rather than a range-enhancement technology.

110. In Unix-based operating systems, the getpid() system call returns the unique process identifier assigned to the process that invokes it. This Process ID enables the operating system and applications to identify and manage the running process. The parent process ID is obtained using getppid(), not getpid().

111. In SQL:1999, a view represents a virtual table derived from a query, but the rows of a relational table or view have no inherent ordering. Therefore, an ORDER BY clause is not permitted as part of a standard view definition because ordering is applied when retrieving data from the view. Nested queries, subqueries and aggregate expressions may be used in view definitions, subject to the applicable SQL rules.

112. TCP provides a reliable, connection-oriented byte-stream service and assigns sequence numbers to transmitted data. If segments arrive out of order, TCP temporarily stores and rearranges them before delivering the data to the receiving application. Thus, the application receives the data in the same logical order in which it was transmitted.

113. An acyclic graph directory structure permits a file or directory to be shared through more than one directory path while preventing cycles. A common method is to place a symbolic link in another directory, with the link containing the pathname of the shared object. This avoids creating a separate physical copy of the file and allows several users or directories to access the same object.

114. A process cannot begin execution before its arrival time because it does not yet exist in the ready queue. If the process arrives at time 5 and there are no other processes competing for the CPU, the processor is immediately available to execute it. Therefore, its earliest as well as latest possible starting time under the stated condition is time 5.

115. A digital certificate electronically binds the identity of a person, organisation, server or other entity to its public key. It is issued and digitally signed by a trusted Certificate Authority within a Public Key Infrastructure. During authentication, the certificate's signature, validity and identity details are checked to establish that the public key belongs to the claimed entity.

116. The Best Fit memory-allocation algorithm searches for the smallest available block that is large enough to satisfy a request. Although this can reduce the amount of unused space left within the selected block, finding the closest-sized block may require examining many or all free blocks. Consequently, its longer search time can reduce allocation speed and overall system performance.

117. In SQL, ordinary comparison operators such as =, > = and < = do not determine equality or order when an operand is NULL; such comparisons produce the logical value UNKNOWN. The special predicate IS NULL is specifically designed to test whether a value is null. Therefore, the expression NULL IS NULL evaluates to TRUE.

118. In the SCAN disk-scheduling algorithm, the disk arm moves continuously in one direction and services all pending requests encountered along its path. It continues until it reaches the physical end of the disk and then reverses its direction to service requests on the return journey. This movement resembles an elevator travelling up and down, so SCAN is also known as the elevator algorithm.

119. A TCP segment carrying the RST flag indicates that the connection must be reset because it is invalid, refused or cannot continue normally. When a valid reset is received during connection establishment or management, the current connection attempt or established connection is aborted immediately. The endpoint does not continue normal retransmissions or preserve the connection as active.

120. An ARP request is normally broadcast on the local network because the sender does not yet know the hardware address associated with the target IP address. The device possessing that IP address responds directly to the requesting device using its known MAC address. Therefore, an ARP reply is ordinarily transmitted as a unicast message.

121. The conditional operator first checks the condition $a > b$. Here, 10 > 20 is false, so the expression selects the value after the colon, which is b. Therefore, max receives the value 20 and the program prints 20.

122. Encapsulation binds data members and the methods that manipulate them together inside a class. It also controls direct access to the internal data through access modifiers such as private, protected and public. Thus, encapsulation promotes data hiding, security and controlled interaction with an object.

123. A protected member of a parent class is directly accessible inside its child class through inheritance. Therefore, childMethod() can call protectedMethod() without any access violation. When the program runs, it prints Protected method in Parent.

124. C permits a switch statement to be nested inside another switch statement. The inner switch may be written within any case of the outer switch and operates independently. The break statements and default cases are optional, although break is normally used to prevent fall-through.

125. In Java, the super keyword refers to the immediate parent class of the current object. It can be used to access parent-class variables and methods that are hidden or overridden in the child class. It is also used through super() to invoke the constructor of the parent class.

126. C uses pass-by-value, so passing an ordinary variable gives the function only a copy of its value. To modify the original variable, its memory address must be passed through a pointer. The function can then dereference that pointer and change the value stored in the actual variable.

127. $a > b > c$

$5 > 3 = 1$

$1 > 0 = 1$ (true)

In C, relational operators are evaluated from left to right, so the expression is interpreted as $(a > b) > c$, not as a mathematical chained comparison. Therefore, the program prints True.

128. In a declaration such as char names[10][20], the first dimension specifies that ten character strings or names can be stored. The second dimension reserves twenty character positions for each name, including space for the null terminator. Thus, rows represent the number of names and columns represent the maximum storage for each name.

129. A do-while loop executes its body at least once before testing the condition. The program first prints 5 and then decreases i from 5 to 4. The condition 4 > 5 is false, so the loop terminates immediately and the only output is 5.

130. The outer conditional expression first checks x > 0, and −1 > 0 is false. It therefore evaluates the nested expression (y == 0) ? z : y. Since y = 0, the condition is true and z = 1 is assigned to result; hence, the program prints 1.

131. The outer loop executes for i = 0, 1, 2, so it runs three times. For each iteration of the outer loop, the inner loop executes for j = 0, 1, which means two executions. Therefore, the total number of executions of the innermost loop is:

$3 \times 2 = 6$ times

132. The sprintf() function writes the string "Hello, World!" into the character array buffer and returns the number of characters written, excluding the terminating null character. The string contains 13 characters: five in "Hello", one comma, one space, five in "World" and one exclamation mark. Hence, n = 13, and the program prints 13 Hello, World!

133. The method validateAge(15) checks whether the supplied age is below 18. Since 15 < 18, it throws a CustomException carrying the message "Age must be 18 or above.", which is caught by the corresponding catch block. The finally block executes afterwards, so the conceptual output matches option 3; because the code contains no space after the colon, the exact first line is Caught Exception:Age must be 18 or above.

134. In the expression myObject.doActivity();, myObject is an object reference and doActivity() is a method invoked through that object. The dot operator is used to access an object's members, including its methods. Therefore, the statement represents a call to the method named doActivity on the object myObject.

135. The rows and columns of a Karnaugh Map are arranged in Gray-code order rather than ordinary binary numerical order. In Gray code, two consecutive cells differ in only one binary variable, which makes adjacent grouping possible. The other statements are correct because K-maps group 1,2,4,8,... adjacent cells and can simplify both SOP and POS forms.

136. The expression a / b attempts 10/0, initially causing an ArithmeticException. The inner catch block catches it and throws a new general Exception with the message "Division by zero not allowed", while the inner finally block executes before control leaves calculate(). The new exception is caught by catch (Exception e), not by catch (ArithmeticException e), and the outer finally block then executes.

137. a = b = c = 15

Thus, the initial value of c is 15.

c = c + 10 = 15 + 10 = 25

Therefore, the final value stored in the variable c is 25.

138. Among the given operators, the modulus operator % belongs to the multiplicative group and has higher precedence than the additive operators + and −. The assignment operator = has much lower precedence than arithmetic operators. Therefore, % has the highest precedence among the listed operators.

139. In C, any non-zero value is treated as true, so the condition 1 in while (1) always remains true. Since the loop body contains no break, return or condition-changing statement, the loop never terminates. The other loops either have finite control conditions or, in the case of do { } while (0);, execute only once.

140. Given binary number = 1100

First, invert every bit: 1100 → 0011

Then add 1: 0011 + 1 = 0100

Therefore, the 4-bit 2's complement of 1100 is 0100.

141. The Adjustments panel in Adobe Photoshop contains the Brightness/Contrast adjustment used to modify an image's brightness and tonal contrast. It may also be applied as an adjustment layer, allowing non-destructive editing without permanently changing the original pixels. The Paint Bucket fills areas with colour, the Healing Brush repairs imperfections, and the Selection Tool selects portions of an image.

142. In JavaScript, the style property of an HTML element is used to modify its CSS dynamically. This statement directly changes the selected element's background colour to red. setCSS() is not a standard DOM method, while the other options do not directly modify the existing CSS style of the element in the required manner.

143. Each node of a singly linked list consists of a data field and a link field. The data field stores the actual value, while the link field stores the address of the next node in the list. The link field of the final node contains NULL, indicating the end of the linked list.

144. The PHP function asort() arranges array values in ascending order while preserving the association between each value and its original key. The sort() function also sorts values in ascending order, but it reindexes numeric keys. The ksort() function sorts an array according to its keys rather than its values.

145. In C, an entire character array cannot be assigned a string using the assignment operator after the array has been declared. Moreover, the string "consultancy" requires twelve character positions including the null terminator, while the declared array has only six positions. A character array should be initialised at declaration with adequate size or populated using an appropriate string-copying function. Strictly under standard C, option 2 using an empty initializer is also invalid, but option 1 is the clearly intended answer.

146. Binary search reduces the search interval to approximately half after each comparison. Therefore, the maximum number of comparisons increases in proportion to $\log_2 n$, giving a worst-case complexity of $O(\log n)$. Its best-case complexity is O(1), and its correct recurrence relation is $T(n) = T(n/2) + O(1)$.

147. The outer block declares x = 10 and y = 20. The inner block declares another variable y = 40, which temporarily hides the outer variable y; inside that block, x++ changes the outer x to 11 and y++ changes only the inner y to 41. After the inner block ends, its local y is destroyed, so the program prints x = 11, y = 20.

148. PNG is a commonly used image format for the web because it supports lossless compression and transparency. It is especially suitable for logos, icons, screenshots and graphics with sharp edges. BMP and TIFF files are generally much larger, while PSD is Photoshop's editable working format rather than a standard web-display format.

149. Merge sort is highly suitable for linked lists because the list can be divided and merged efficiently by changing links rather than moving elements. It does not require random access and has a time complexity of $O(n \log n)$. Selection sort, insertion sort and bubble sort generally have a worst-case time complexity of $O(n^2)$.

150. Theta notation represents an asymptotically tight bound on a function. If $f(n) = \theta(g(n))$, then $g(n)$ provides both an asymptotic upper bound and an asymptotic lower bound for $f(n)$. Big Oh gives an upper bound, Omega gives a lower bound, whereas Theta expresses both simultaneously.

151. The cutting or cropping tool is mainly used to remove unwanted portions from the edges or selected areas of an image. It helps improve composition by retaining only the required part of the picture. It does not primarily change resolution, apply colour effects or proportionally resize the entire image.

152. The variable x is assigned the value 10, and the condition x > 5 is evaluated. Since 10 > 5 is true, the statement inside the if block executes. Therefore, the JavaScript console displays "Greater", while the else block is skipped.

153. A register variable declared locally without explicit initialisation has an indeterminate or garbage value, not a default value of zero. Register variables are intended to be stored in CPU registers when possible, and their scope is generally limited to the block in which they are declared. Static variables, in contrast, are automatically initialised to zero when no explicit value is supplied.

154. The function returns a pointer to the first element of the static array, so ptr initially points to the value 1. Inside the loop, the expression *ptr is printed, but the pointer is never incremented. Therefore, the same first element is accessed during all five iterations, producing:

1 1 1 1 1

155. The JavaScript method window.resize To (width, height) is used to resize a browser window to specified dimensions. It accepts the desired width and height in pixels and attempts to adjust the outer window accordingly. The other listed methods are not standard JavaScript window-resizing methods.

156. Actual parameters, also called arguments, are the values, variables or expressions supplied in a function call. Formal parameters are the variables declared in the function definition that receive those values. Thus, actual parameters appear at the point of calling the function and need not always be variables.

157. A web browser retrieves web resources from servers and presents them to the user in a readable and interactive form. It interprets technologies such as HTML, CSS and JavaScript and allows navigation through hyperlinks and web addresses. Sending emails, creating websites and storing large amounts of data are not its primary functions.

158. AJAX allows a web page to exchange data with a server asynchronously without reloading the entire page. Only the required portion of data is transmitted and the relevant part of the page is updated. This partial communication reduces unnecessary data transfer and therefore helps lower bandwidth consumption.

159. The operator ^ in C performs a bitwise XOR operation.

$$4 = (100)_2,\ 3 = (011)_2$$

$$100 \oplus 011 = 111$$

$$(111)_2 = 7$$

Therefore, the program prints 7.

160. The commonly analysed cases in algorithmic time complexity are the best case, average case and worst case. These describe the minimum, expected and maximum amounts of computational work required for inputs of a particular size. A test case is merely a specific input used to examine or verify a program and is not a standard complexity case.

161. Cost of goods sold = Opening stock + Purchases – Closing stock

Since closing stock exceeds opening stock by ₹ 30,000:

Cost of goods sold = 190000 – 30000 = ₹ 160000

Gross profit is 20% of sales; therefore, cost of goods sold is 80% of sales:

$$\text{Sales} = \frac{160000 \times 100}{80} = ₹\ 200000$$

$$\text{Gross profit} = 200000 - 160000 = ₹\ 40000$$

Therefore, the gross profit earned was ₹ 40,000.00.

162. In a dynamic array, deleting the first element creates an empty position at the beginning. Every remaining element must be shifted one position towards the beginning to maintain contiguous storage. For an array containing n elements, up to $n - 1$ elements are shifted; therefore, the time complexity is $O(n)$.

163. The XOR operation produces an output of 1 only when its two input bits are different. Thus, $0 \oplus 1 = 1$ and $1 \oplus 0 = 1$, while equal inputs produce 0. Therefore, the logical operation performed by the ALU under the stated condition is XOR.

164. $a[i] = i^2 - 2i + 1 = (i - 1)^2$

$i = 0: a[0] = 0 - 0 + 1 = 1$

$i = 1: a[1] = 1 - 2 + 1 = 0$

$i = 2: a[2] = 4 - 4 + 1 = 1$

$i = 3: a[3] = 9 - 6 + 1 = 4$

$i = 4: a[4] = 16 - 8 + 1 = 9$

Therefore, the output is 1 0 1 4 9.

165. Virtual memory allows an operating system to use a portion of secondary storage, such as a hard disk or SSD, as an extension of main memory. It enables programs larger than the available physical RAM to execute by transferring pages between RAM and secondary storage. Therefore, its main purpose is to extend the effective memory available to processes.

166. In C, the initialisation, condition and update expressions of a for loop are all syntactically optional. When the condition is omitted, it is treated as always true, as in for(;;), so the loop continues indefinitely unless interrupted by break, return or another control statement. A for loop may also be nested inside another loop.

167. A singly linked list does not support direct or random access to its elements. To reach a particular element, traversal must begin at the head and proceed node by node, giving an access time of O(n) in the worst case. Arrays provide indexed access in O(1), making element retrieval faster.

168. $y = ae^{2x} + be^{-x}$

The corresponding auxiliary roots are:

$$m = 2, -1$$

Therefore, the auxiliary equation is:

$$(m - 2)(m + 1) = 0$$
$$m^2 - m - 2 = 0$$

Hence, the required differential equation is:

$$\boxed{y'' - y' - 2y = 0}$$

169. $$A = \begin{bmatrix} 1 & 4 \\ 3 & 5 \end{bmatrix}; \quad |A - \lambda I| = \begin{vmatrix} 1-\lambda & 4 \\ 3 & 5-\lambda \end{vmatrix} = 0$$

$$(1 - \lambda)(5 - \lambda) - (4 \times 3) = 0$$
$$5 - 6\lambda + \lambda^2 - 12 = 0$$
$$\lambda^2 - 6\lambda - 7 = 0$$

Therefore, the characteristic equation of the matrix is $\lambda^2 - 6\lambda - 7 = 0$.

170. Tertiary business activities provide services that support production and distribution, including warehousing, transportation and insurance. Manufacturing involves converting raw materials into finished or semi-finished goods and belongs to the secondary sector. Therefore, manufacturing is not a tertiary business activity.

171. $$(D^2 - 6D + 9)y = 2e^{3t}$$
$$(D - 3)^2 y = 2e^{3t}$$

Since 3 is a repeated root of multiplicity 2,

$$\text{P.I.} = \frac{2t^2e^{3t}}{2!} = t^2e^{3t}$$

Therefore, the particular solution is t^2e^{3t}.

172. The break statement immediately terminates the nearest enclosing loop in C, irrespective of whether the loop condition is still true. Control then passes to the first statement following that loop. A continue statement does not terminate the loop; it skips only the remaining statements of the current iteration and begins the next iteration.

173. Total emf = 1.5 + 1.5 = 3V

Total internal resistance = 0.5 + 0.5 = 1 Ω

Terminal potential difference = E – Ir = 3 – (1 × 1) = 2V

Therefore, the effective terminal potential difference of the two cells is 2 V.

174. $$A = \begin{bmatrix} 1 & 0 & 0 \\ 0 & -1 & 0 \\ 1 & 0 & 1 \end{bmatrix}$$

The (3, 1) element increases by 1 with every successive power, while the middle diagonal element becomes $(-1)^n$. Thus,

$$A^n = \begin{bmatrix} 1 & 0 & 0 \\ 0 & (-1)^n & 0 \\ n & 0 & 1 \end{bmatrix}; \quad A^6 = \begin{bmatrix} 1 & 0 & 0 \\ 0 & 1 & 0 \\ 6 & 0 & 1 \end{bmatrix}$$

Therefore, the required matrix is option 3.

175. A Memorandum Trading Account is prepared to estimate the stock available immediately before the fire.

Stock available for sale = Opening stock + Purchases + Wages

Cost of goods sold = Sales – Gross profit

Estimated stock on date of fire = Stock available for sale – Cost of goods sold = ₹ 9,30,000

Stock lost by fire = Estimated stock – Salvaged stock = ₹ 9,30,000 – ₹ 3,00,000 = ₹ 6,30,000.

176. Total rent received = ₹ 2,50,000

Rent relating to next financial year = ₹ 50,000

Rent income for current year = 2,50,000 – 50,000 = ₹ 2,00,000

The amount of ₹ 50,000 received for the next year is unearned income and creates an obligation to provide the benefit in the future. Therefore, ₹ 2,00,000 is credited to the Profit and Loss Account, while rent received in advance is shown as a liability.

177. The printed differential equation contains a typographical omission; the intended equation is evidently

$$(D^4 - 18D^2 + 81)y = 72e^{3x}$$
$$(D^2 - 9)^2 y = (D - 3)^2(D + 3)^2 y = 72e^{3x}$$

Since 3 is a repeated root of multiplicity 2,

$$\text{P.I.} = \frac{72x^2e^{3x}}{2!(3+3)^2} = \frac{72x^2e^{3x}}{2 \times 36} = x^2e^{3x}$$

Therefore, the particular solution is x^2e^{3x}.

178. The Control Unit directs and coordinates the sequence in which the processor fetches an instruction from memory, decodes it and executes it. It generates the control signals required to move data among registers, memory and the Arithmetic Logic Unit. Therefore, the principal cycle managed by the Control Unit is the Fetch-Decode-Execute instruction cycle.

179. The magnetic field of a bar magnet can be represented by that of an equivalent current-carrying solenoid. For the solenoid to be magnetically equivalent to the bar magnet, both must produce the same external magnetic field pattern and possess the same magnetic moment. Therefore, the magnetic moment of the bar magnet is equal to that of the equivalent solenoid when their magnetic fields are the same as each other.

180. An Instruction Set Architecture defines the instructions, registers, data types, addressing modes and programmer-visible behaviour of a processor. A major design objective is to keep the instruction set sufficiently simple for efficient implementation while providing enough capability for high performance and convenient programming. Minimising transistor count or supporting only complex instructions is not the primary goal of ISA design.

181. Delegation means assigning authority and responsibility by a superior to subordinate employees for performing specific tasks. When delegation takes place systematically at different organisational levels, decision-making authority becomes dispersed rather than remaining concentrated at the top. Therefore, extensive and systematic delegation leads to decentralisation in a business organisation.

182. The residents are classified according to two attributes—sex with two categories and tea-drinking status with two categories—forming a 2 × 2 contingency table. For testing the association between these attributes, the chi-square test of independence is used.

Degrees of freedom = $(r - 1)(c - 1) = (2 - 1)(2 - 1) = 1$

Therefore, the test statistic follows a chi-square distribution with 1 degree of freedom.

183. Total possible outcomes = {1, 2, 3, 4, 5, 6}

Favourable even outcomes = {2, 4, 6}

$$P(\text{even number}) = \frac{3}{6} = \frac{1}{2}$$

Therefore, the probability of obtaining an even number is $\frac{1}{2}$.

184. EPROM stands for Erasable Programmable Read-Only Memory. The information stored in an EPROM chip can be erased by exposing the chip to ultraviolet light through a transparent quartz window provided on it. After erasure, the memory can be programmed again, unlike PROM, which can generally be programmed only once.

185. Most email applications provide an emoji or smiley icon in the message-composition toolbar. Clicking this icon opens a collection of emojis from which the desired symbol can be selected and inserted into the email. The delete key, reply command and font-style options do not directly add an emoji.

186. Bootstrapping refers to starting and developing a business with the founder's own savings, personal income or revenue generated by the business itself. It involves operating with limited external financial assistance and controlling expenditure carefully. Bank loans, venture capital and crowdfunding are external financing methods and therefore do not represent bootstrapping in its usual sense.

187. GIMP, or GNU Image Manipulation Program, is open-source application software used for image editing, graphic design and digital artwork. Its source code is publicly available and may be studied, modified and distributed under its licence conditions. Microsoft Excel, CorelDRAW and Adobe Illustrator are proprietary commercial applications.

188. The principal stages of the CPU instruction cycle include fetching the instruction from memory, decoding it, executing it and storing or writing back the result when required. "Encode" is not a standard phase of the instruction cycle because instructions are decoded by the Control Unit rather than encoded during execution. Therefore, Encode is the incorrect option.

189. The symbol :-) represents a smiling face when viewed sideways and is commonly used to express happiness, friendliness or amusement in text communication. The symbols :-(and :(indicate sadness or disappointment, while :| generally represents neutrality or an expressionless mood. Therefore, :-) is the smiley that expresses happiness.

190. WhatsApp was founded by Jan Koum and Brian Acton, both of whom had previously worked at Yahoo. They developed the application as a mobile messaging service that allowed users to exchange messages through an internet connection. The other pairs listed are associated with organisations such as Facebook and Google or do not represent the founders of WhatsApp.

191. The Rights of Persons with Disabilities Act, 2016 legally requires government-funded or recognised educational institutions to provide inclusive education to children with disabilities. Such institutions must admit them without discrimination, ensure accessibility, provide reasonable accommodation and offer necessary individualised support. The National Curriculum Framework and NEP are policy documents rather than the principal statutory mandate among the given options.

192. Aesthetic education develops a learner's sensitivity towards beauty, harmony, form, colour, sound and artistic expression. It refines perception and enables learners to respond thoughtfully and emotionally to art, music, literature and nature. Therefore, its primary focus is the development of sensory responsiveness, rather than factual recall or purely logical reasoning.

193. A teaching method is a systematic and methodical way of presenting subject matter to learners. It follows a logical, organised sequence of several steps to achieve predetermined instructional objectives. A technique is a specific classroom action, while a strategy is a broader plan; therefore, the description most appropriately refers to a teaching method.

194. According to Piaget, the formal operational stage generally begins at approximately eleven years of age and continues into adulthood. During this stage, learners develop the ability to think abstractly, reason hypothetically and solve problems systematically. They can consider possibilities beyond immediate concrete experiences and use deductive reasoning.

195. The five traditional Herbartian steps are Preparation, Presentation, Association or Comparison, Generalisation and Application. These steps proceed from connecting prior knowledge to presenting new material and applying the developed general principle. Evaluation is important in modern lesson planning, but it is not one of the original five Herbartian steps.

196. Gender inequality refers to unequal rights, opportunities, treatment, responsibilities and access to resources based on gender. It may be reflected in education, employment, income, political participation, healthcare and decision-making power. It is a socially produced disparity and cannot be reduced merely to biological differences or personal appearance.

197. Diagnostic assessment is conducted to discover specific learning difficulties, misconceptions, knowledge gaps and weaknesses before or during instruction. Its results help the teacher identify the causes of poor performance and design suitable remedial teaching. It is not primarily intended for grading, promotion or standardising the curriculum.

198. Vocational education should provide learners with opportunities to perform authentic tasks, operate tools and practise procedures resembling actual workplace conditions. The principle of activity and practicality connects theoretical knowledge with hands-on experience and promotes the transfer of learning to real occupational settings. Therefore, it is the most important principle for developing usable vocational competence.

199. A multilingual approach recognises the child's home language as a valuable resource for learning rather than treating it as an obstacle. Teachers use familiar languages to explain concepts, support participation and gradually connect learners with additional languages. This approach strengthens comprehension, confidence, identity and meaningful communication in the early years.

200. A discipline is a broad and systematically organised field of knowledge involving specialised concepts, methods of inquiry and research traditions. A school subject is a selected, reorganised and age-appropriate part of that discipline designed for classroom teaching. Thus, a subject is a classroom-taught branch of a discipline, shaped according to educational aims and learners' needs.

Previous Years' Paper

Delhi Subordinate Services Selection Board (DSSSB)

TGT—COMPUTER SCIENCE, EXAM-2024

(Exam held on 07-02-2024)

SECTION-A

GENERAL INTELLIGENCE AND REASONING ABILITY

1. A statement is followed by two arguments in the given question. Choose the correct option after deciding which of the arguments is a 'strong' argument and which is a 'weak' argument.

Statement: Should we repeat our clothes?

Argument:

I. Yes. It helps in developing a sustainable environment.

II. No. New clothes means new beginnings.

1. Only argument II is strong
2. Both I and II are strong arguments
3. Neither I nor II argument is strong
4. Only argument I is strong

2. In a certain code language, 'LOMQG' is written as '16', 'WTQMC' is written as '19'. What is the code for 'LSOMI' in that code language?

1. 18 2. 16
3. 17 4. 20

3. A series is given with one term missing. Select the correct alternative from the given ones that will complete the series.

NRCH, IYNJ, FJUE, AQFB, ?

1. XBMW 2. QRST
3. XTQR 4. XMNO

4. In the following, select the odd letter/letters from the given alternatives.

1. MKH 2. MPR
3. WUR 4. KIF

5. In a certain code language, 'STOPWARS' is written as 'POTSSRAW', 'LOGIPERT' is written as 'IGOLTREP'. What is the code for 'LAPTOPST' in that code language?

1. TATPOTSP 2. TATPPOTS
3. TAPTSOPS 4. TPALTSPO

6. A statement is followed by a set of conclusions in the given question. Identify which conclusion follows logically from the following statement.

Statement: Raveena goes to the gym daily, as her father has advised her to exercise.

Conclusion:

I. Raveena's father cares for her daughter health.

II. Raveena is suffering from some chronic disease.

1. Both I and II follow 2. Only I follow
3. Neither I nor II follow 4. Only II follow

7. If '÷' means '×', '–' means '+', '×' means '÷' and '+' means '–', then 38 × 57 ÷ 9 – 18 + 12 = ?

1. 10 2. 12 3. 6 4. 7

8. Select that missing pair (Third number : Fourth number) which is related in the same way as the first number is related to the second number and fifth number is related to sixth number. (NOTE: Operations should be performed on the whole numbers, without breaking down the numbers into its constituent digits. E.g.13 – Operations on 13 such as adding /subtracting /multiplying etc. to 13 can be performed. Breaking down 13 into 1 and 3 and then performing mathematical operations on 1 and 3 is not allowed)

442 : 633 :: ? :: 186 : 377

1. 313 : 504 2. 518 : 719
3. 111 : 292 4. 277 : 467

9. P, Q, R, S, T, U and V are seven friends sitting in a single row facing North. S is to the immediate right of R. T and P are neighbours of U. Q is to the immediate left of R and on second place from left most end. P is at the right most end. Who is sitting on the immediate left of P?

1. U 2. R 3. T 4. S

1. 4	**2.** 3	**3.** 1	**4.** 2	**5.** 4	**6.** 2	**7.** 2	**8.** 1	**9.** 1

10. In the following question below are given some statements followed by some conclusions based on those statements. Taking the given statements to be true even if they seem to be at variance from commonly known facts. Read all the conclusions and then decide which of the given conclusion logically follows the given statements.

Statements: I. Some C are D.
II. Some D are E.
III. No E is G.

Conclusions: I. Some E are C.
II. No D is G.
III. Some G are C.

1. Neither conclusion follows
2. Only conclusion II follows
3. Only conclusion I follows
4. Only conclusion III follows

11. Mona is 13th from the right end in a row of 40 girls. What is his position from the left end?

1. 29 2. 27 3. 28 4. 26

12. In the following question, select the missing number from the given series.

200, 197, 206, 179, 260, ?

1. –83 2. –80 3. –100 4. 17

13. In the following, select the odd letter/letters from the given alternatives.

1. WXUZ 2. EFCG
3. NOLQ 4. IJGL

14. In the following question, select the related letters from the given alternatives.

NQT : ORU :: ADH : ?

1. ACZ 2. UVZ
3. BEI 4. SPQ

15. If A + B means 'A' is the husband of 'B', A – B means 'A' is the wife of 'B', A × B means 'A' is the mother of 'B', A ÷ B means 'A' is the son of 'B'. If J ÷ P + K × M – R, then How is P related to R?

1. Husband 2. Wife's brother
3. Father 4. Wife's father

16. By Interchanging the given two numbers which of the following equation will be not correct?

7 and 9

1. 9 – 7 + 3 = 1
2. 9 × 4 – 7 × 3 = 4
3. 9 × 1 – 7 × 2 = –11
4. 7 × 2 + 9 – 4 = 21

17. Select the option that is related to the fifth number cluster in the same way as the second number cluster is related to the first number cluster and fourth number cluster is related to third number cluster.

6 : 180 :: 8 : 448 :: 10 : ?

1. 900 2. 990
3. 800 4. 999

18. In the given question, a statement is followed by two courses of action. Based on the information given in the statement, you have to assume everything in the statement to be true. Identify which course(s) of action logically follows.

Statement: A bridge collapsed in town Y due to poor construction.

Course of Action:

I. Search-and-rescue operations should be conducted immediately.
II. People should leave town Y and move to town X.

1. Only I follows
2. Only II follows
3. Neither I nor II follows
4. Both I and II follow

19. A statement is followed by a set of conclusions in the given question. Identify which conclusion follows logically from the following statement.

Statement: For the past three years the ABC Corporation has been planning to expand its operations in order to reach out to the world market.

Conclusions:

I. The ABC corporation is not competitive.
II. The ABC corporation wants to capture the global market.

1. Neither I nor II follows
2. Only I follows
3. Both I and II follow
4. Only II follows

20. How many workers are uneducated?

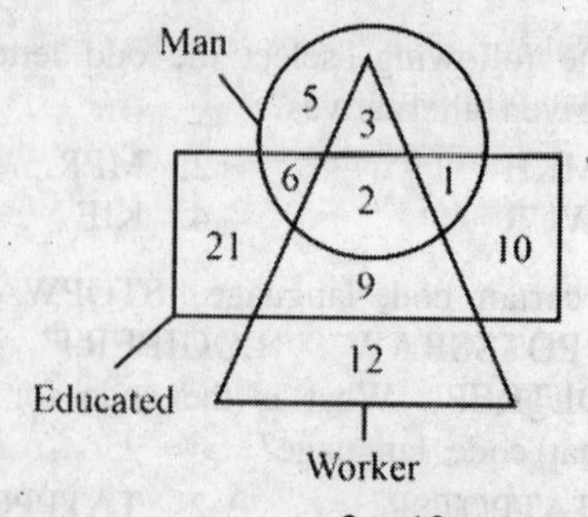

1. 17 2. 12
3. 8 4. 10

10. 1 **11.** 3 **12.** 4 **13.** 2 **14.** 3 **15.** 4 **16.** 2 **17.** 1 **18.** 1 **19.** 4 **20.** 2

GENERAL AWARENESS

21. Which Indian badminton player secured a bronze medal in the men's singles at the BWF World Badminton Championships 2023?

1. Srikanth Kidambi
2. HS Prannoy
3. Lakshya Sen
4. B. Sai Praneeth

22. ISRO signed MoU with which of the following companies in January 2023 to support space-tech startups in India?

1. Cognizant 2. Microsoft
3. Oracle 4. Capgemini

23. Which of the following articles of the Indian Constitution mentions that the official language of the Union shall be Hindi in the Devanagari script?

1. Article 343 2. Article 280
3. Article 324 4. Article 226

24. Narmada originates from which of the following places?

1. Amarkantak plateau
2. Mahabaleshwar
3. Brahmagiri hills
4. Chotanagpur Plateau

25. In which year did the Battle of Seringapatam, a war between Mysore and the British, take place?

1. 1799 2. 1764
3. 1767 4. 1805

26. Article 315 of the Indian Constitution is related to which of the following?

1. Finance Commission
2. Public Service Commissions for the Union and for the States
3. Administrative tribunals
4. Election Commission

27. Nalwari Fair is a cattle fair celebrated in which of the following states?

1. Tamil Nadu 2. Himachal Pradesh
3. Assam 4. Gujarat

28. Which of the following articles of the Indian Constitution provides protection of life and personal liberty?

1. Article 29 2. Article 25
3. Article 21 4. Article 19

29. Who among the following composed the famous Tamil epic Silappadikaram?

1. Kovalan 2. Thiruvalluvar
3. Sattanar 4. Ilango

30. What was the repo rate of RBI announced in December 2023?

1. 3.5 per cent 2. 8.5 per cent
3. 6.5 per cent 4. 2.5 per cent

31. In which of the following years was the Indian National Congress established?

1. 1906 2. 1893
3. 1885 4. 1875

32. Which is the most populous state in India according to 2011 census?

1. Madhya Pradesh 2. West Bengal
3. Bihar 4. Uttar Pradesh

33. Which of the following ministries had signed a MoU with the International Society of Krishna Consciousness (ISKCON) in New Delhi on 23 November 2023 to spread the message of Nasha Mukt Bharat Abhiyan among youth, women, students etc.?

1. Ministry of Home Affairs
2. Ministry of Social Justice and Empowerment
3. Ministry of Health and Family Welfare
4. Ministry of Food Processing Industries

34. What is the name of the artificial intelligence project that Jio is working on with IIT Bombay, announced by Akash Ambani in December 2023?

1. Bharat GPT 2. Chat GPT
3. Chat Bot 4. India GPT

35. Which of the following is NOT a rich source of Vitamin A?

1. Carrot 2. Mango
3. Amla 4. Papaya

36. Who among the following started the Young Bengal Movement in Calcutta?

1. Dadabhai Naoroji 2. W.C. Bonnerji
3. Henry Derozio 4. A.O. Hume

37. Which of the following acids is found in orange?

1. Citric acid 2. Oxalic acid
3. Methanoic acid 4. Lactic acid

21. 2 **22.** 2 **23.** 1 **24.** 1 **25.** 1 **26.** 2 **27.** 2 **28.** 3 **29.** 4
30. 3 **31.** 3 **32.** 4 **33.** 2 **34.** 1 **35.** 3 **36.** 3 **37.** 1

38. Which of the following Articles of the Indian Constitution empowers the Vice President to act as President or discharge his functions during casual vacancies in the office or during the absence of the President?

1. Article 72
2. Article 61
3. Article 65
4. Article 52

39. Which of these hills is NOT included in Purvanchal or Eastern hills?

1. Manipur hills
2. Shevroy hills
3. Patkai hills
4. Naga hills

40. In which of the following years was ICICI formed at the initiative of World Bank, the Government of India and representative of Indian Industry?

1. 1982
2. 1975
3. 1955
4. 1966

ARITHMETICAL AND NUMERICAL ABILITY

41. The ratio of Amit's and Ankit's present age is 10 : 13. Amit is 18 years younger than Ankit. What will be the ratio of Amit's age to Ankit's age after 12 years?

1. 4 : 5
2. 3 : 5
3. 4 : 9
4. 4 : 7

42. If E1 is 8 times more than E2, then E2 is what percentage less than E1?

1. 96.96 per cent
2. 88.88 per cent
3. 80.88 per cent
4. 84.88 per cent

43. The line chart given below shows the production of 6 companies in 2 years P and Q.

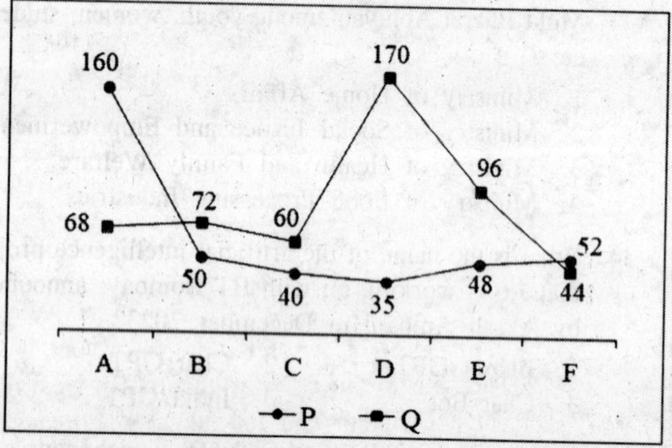

J1 = The total production of all companies in year P.
J2 = The total production of all companies in year Q.
What is the value of (J2 – J1)?

1. 125
2. 110
3. 150
4. 85

44. The average age of 40 students is 21 years. It was observed that while calculating the average age, the age of a student was taken as 20 years instead of 30 years. What will be the correct average age?

1. 21.25 years
2. 21.22 years
3. 12.12 years
4. 23.84 years

45. Three numbers P, Q and R are in the ratio of 6 : 5 : 3 respectively. If R is 32 less than the sum of P and Q, then what is the value of Q?

1. 24
2. 48
3. 20
4. 32

46. What is the compound interest on (compounding annually) ₹ 14400 at the rate of 10 per cent for 3 years?

1. ₹ 4214.8
2. ₹ 4712.6
3. ₹ 4812.6
4. ₹ 4766.4

47. Each of the length, breadth and height of a cuboid is decreased by 12 per cent. What is the percentage decrease in the total surface area of the cuboid?

1. 20.24 per cent
2. 24.78 per cent
3. 18.92 per cent
4. 22.56 per cent

48. For what value of M, 859M is divisible by 9?

1. 5
2. 3
3. 7
4. 2

49. Cost price of an article is ₹ 230. If the profit percentage is 12 per cent, then what is the value of profit?

1. ₹ 27.6
2. ₹ 30
3. ₹ 32.8
4. ₹ 35

50. After giving a discount of 25 per cent a cycle is sold for ₹ 7200. What is the marked price of the cycle?

1. ₹ 9500
2. ₹ 10000
3. ₹ 9000
4. ₹ 9600

51. Simple interest and compound interest (compounding annually) on a principal at a certain rate of interest for 2 years is ₹ 28800 and ₹ 36000 respectively. What is the principal?

1. ₹ 30000
2. ₹ 28800
3. ₹ 29750
4. ₹ 28850

38. 3	**39.** 2	**40.** 3	**41.** 1	**42.** 2	**43.** 1	**44.** 1
45. 3	**46.** 4	**47.** 4	**48.** 1	**49.** 1	**50.** 4	**51.** 2

52. A train of length 210 metres is running at a speed of 54 km/hr. In how much time it will completely cross a platform of 390 metres?

1. 50 seconds 2. 60 seconds
3. 40 seconds 4. 30 seconds

53. What is the value of 33 ÷ 11 + 75 ÷ 5 × 2 – 6 ÷ 12 × 30?

1. 15 2. 18
3. 9 4. 42

54. The population of a town is 30000. If every year the population increases by 20 per cent, then what will be the population of the town after 3 years?

1. 51840 2. 51720
3. 50820 4. 48000

55. What is the Highest Common Factor of 12, 36 and 240?

1. 12 2. 30
3. 18 4. 480

56. The breadth of a rectangular hall is 5/8 of its length. If the area of the floor is 160 metre^2, then what is the difference between the length and breadth of the hall?

1. 8 metre 2. 6 metre
3. 10 metre 4. 4 metre

57. X and Y together can complete a work in 60 days. Y and Z together can complete the same work in 90 days. If X, Y and Z all work together, then the same work gets completed in 45 days. How many days will X and Z together take to complete the same work?

1. 120 days 2. 90 days
3. 60 days 4. 150 days

58. The pie chart given below shows the number of employees in 6 different companies. The total number of employees in all these 6 companies 18000. The number of employees in a particular company is shown in terms of degree with respect to the total number of employee in all these 6 companies.

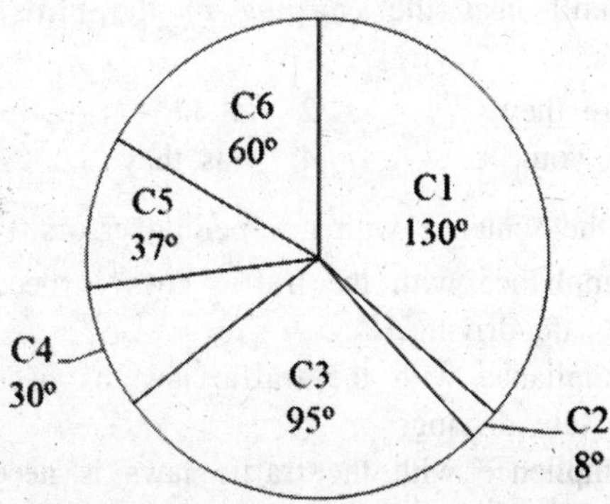

Which of the following statement is correct?

I. The difference between average number of employee in company C1 and C2 and the average number of employee in company C3 and C5 are 150.
II. The number of employee in company C6 is 50 per cent of the number of employee in company C4.
III. The ratio of number of employee in company C2 to the number of employee in C6 are 2 : 15.

1. I, II and III 2. I and II
3. II and III 4. I and III

59. A truck left 8 hours early than the scheduled time and in order to reach its destination 600 km away on time, it had to decrease its usual speed by 20 km/hr. What is the usual speed of the truck?

1. 30 km/hr 2. 50 km/hr
3. 40 km/hr 4. 60 km/hr

60. The simple interest on a sum for 11 years is ₹ 42000. The rate of interest for the first 4 years is 3 per cent per annum and for the next 7 years is 9 per cent per annum. What is the sum?

1. ₹ 70000 2. ₹ 56000
3. ₹ 60000 4. ₹ 58000

ENGLISH LANGUAGE AND COMPREHENSION

61. Choose the most appropriate synonym of the given word.

Obstinate

1. Headstrong 2. Devilish
3. Joyful 4. Agreeable

62. Choose the most appropriate antonym of the given word.

Quarantine

1. Quarrel 2. Assimilate
3. Mourn 4. Circumstance

52. 3	**53.** 2	**54.** 1	**55.** 1	**56.** 2	**57.** 3
58. 4	**59.** 2	**60.** 2	**61.** 1	**62.** 2	

63. Choose the most appropriate option for the given blank.

You can't hear the chirping of the birds from outside, ... ?

1. were they
2. is she
3. can you
4. was they

64. Select the sentence with no spelling errors.

1. Compliance with the traffic laws is neccesary for safe driving.
2. Compliance with the traffic laws is necessary for safe driving.
3. Complience with the traffic laws is necessary for safe driving.
4. Compliance with the traffic laws is necessary for safe driving.

65. Choose the most appropriate antonym of the underlined word in the given sentence.

We should always be <u>friendly</u> to others and help them in need.

1. Hostile
2. Igneous
3. Scorching
4. Mammoth

66. Rearrange the parts of the sentence in correct order.

Developing basic

P. is the only way to face an
Q. infrastructure and the production sector
R. responsibility to help states in this respect
S. economic crisis and the Centre has the

1. QPSR
2. RSPQ
3. SRPQ
4. PRSQ

67. Choose the most appropriate idiom for the given situation.

The team stopped working since they had been working for 6 hours continuously.

1. Down to the wire
2. Cracked someone up
3. Flip the bird
4. Call it a day

68. Select the sentence with no spelling errors.

1. I'd like to rich a consensus on the isue before we take a formal vote.
2. I'd like to reach a consensus on the essue before we take a formal vote.
3. I'd like to reach a conssensus on the issue before we take a formal vote.
4. I'd like to reach a consensus on the issue before we take a formal vote.

69. The question below consists of a set of labelled sentences. Out of the four options given, select the most logical order of the sentences to form a coherent paragraph.

P. As the Plains was settled and grassland converted for crops and grazing, fires were seen as a threat and extinguished.
Q. Historically, fires set by lightning burned naturally at regular intervals across the Great Plains.
R. Native Americans, who saw the benefits, periodically burned the prairie to improve grazing conditions for buffalo.
S. In the last 50 years, as woody plants began increasing and transforming the grassland into a shrub ecosystem, fire has returned to the Plains in the form of controlled burns.

1. SRQP
2. PSQR
3. RSQP
4. QRPS

70. A sentence has been given with a blank to be filled with an appropriate option. Choose the correct alternative.

He took another bite and chewed ....

1. slow
2. slower
3. slowly
4. slowest

71. A sentence has been given with a blank to be filled with an appropriate option. Choose the correct alternative.

Nina felt her eyes brim .... tears and blinked hard.

1. with
2. by
3. of
4. off

72. A sentence has been given with a blank to be filled with an appropriate option. Choose the correct alternative.

The sea provides humanity with a bounty of nutrient-rich food, which we have benefited .... thousands of years.

1. for since
2. for
3. of from
4. from of

73. A sentence has been given with a blank to be filled with an appropriate option. Choose the correct alternative.

Melitopol residents .... the streets following the alleged kidnapping of mayor.

1. took on
2. took to
3. taken off
4. taken at

63. 3 **64.** 4 **65.** 1 **66.** 1 **67.** 4 **68.** 4 **69.** 4 **70.** 3 **71.** 1 **72.** 2 **73.** 2

74. Choose the most appropriate option for the given blank.

She was wearing a ball gown in the party, ...?

1. wasn't them
2. wasn't she
3. weren't they
4. isn't she

75. Choose the most appropriate idiom for the given situation.

She prepared herself for hard work as her exams were near.

1. Drag one's feet
2. Roll up one's sleeves
3. Back to square one
4. Hit the books

Directions (Qs. No. 76-80): *Read the following passage and answer the questions given below.*

The two main reasons of this chronic and unmanageable problem is rapidly ever increasing population and defective education system. Such a huge population, India finds it difficult to make any significant success in the areas of employment, alleviation of poverty and backwardness. Every sixth person in the world is an Indian. In other words, we are adding an Australia to our population every year or to Japan every ten years. There are about 31 new babies every minute or 45,000 new people daily. Thus, every year there are about 16 million more people to feed, cloth, educate and give employment. This prevailing trend of population growth is quite disturbing.

Unemployment rate in India is showing an increasing trend since 2011 when it was 3.5 per cent. The same rose to 3.6 per cent in 2012 and climbed to 3.7 per cent last year.

76. Through this passage, the author's main idea is to bring to your notice the ....

1. population growth of Japan and Australia
2. low population growth and its benefits
3. rate of poverty in India and its cause
4. population explosion in India and the resulting problems

77. According to the passage, which of these problems cannot be successfully tackled due to a large population?

I. Unemployment
II. Poverty
III. Backwardness

1. Only I
2. Only III
3. Only II and III
4. I, II and III

78. Through the given statement 'we are adding an Australia to our population every year', the author implies that ....

1. our population growth is equivalent to that of Australia
2. population composition of India and Australia, is similar.
3. the number of people added to Australia's population is equal to India's entire population
4. the number of people added to India's population every year is equal to Australia's entire population

79. Choose the word that has the most nearly the same meaning as the word given.

Alleviation

1. Eradicate
2. Indigenous
3. Intensify
4. Impressive

80. Which of the following words is opposite in meaning to the word 'extinct' as used in the passage?

1. prevailing
2. lost
3. obsolete
4. defunct

हिन्दी भाषा और अवतरण

81. (*i*) कहानियाँ, जिसमें बेहतर सीख, संस्कार व जीवन में अच्छी चीज

(*ii*) बच्चों के कोमल मन में बातों को गहराई तक पहुँचाने का

(*iii*) की ओर बढ़ने की प्रेरणा मौजूद होती है

(*iv*) तरीका कहानियों से बेहतर और क्या हो सकता है। खासकर, पंचतंत्र की

प्रस्तुत खंडित वाक्य में वाक्य संरचना का सही क्रम क्या होगा?

1. (*i*), (*ii*), (*iv*), (*iii*)
2. (*iv*), (*iii*), (*i*), (*ii*)
3. (*ii*), (*iv*), (*i*), (*iii*)
4. (*iii*), (*iv*), (*i*), (*ii*)

82. निम्नलिखित प्रश्न में, दिए गए चार विकल्पों में से, उस विकल्प का चयन करें जो दिए गए मुहावरे के अर्थ को सर्वश्रेष्ठ रूप से व्यक्त करता है।

टुकुर-टुकुर देखना

1. बहुत लज्जित होना
2. बुरा-भला होना
3. खूब परिश्रम करना
4. टकटकी लगाकर देखना

83. दिए गए वाक्य में उचित विशेषण का चयन करके रिक्त स्थान की पूर्ति करें।

महाराज जी के चर्चे तो .... लोकों में फैले हुए हैं।

1. तीनों
2. स्वभाव
3. प्रत्येक
4. जिसको

74. 2	**75.** 2	**76.** 4	**77.** 4	**78.** 4	**79.** 1	**80.** 1	**81.** 3	**82.** 4	**83.** 1

84. निम्नलिखित प्रश्न में, दिए गए चार विकल्पों में से, उस विकल्प का चयन करें जो दिए गए मुहावरे के अर्थ को सर्वश्रेष्ठ रूप से व्यक्त करता है।

तौल-तौल कर मुँह से शब्द निकालना

1. क्रोध दबाना
2. बातें बदलना
3. बहुत सोच-विचार कर बोलना
4. नुकसान पहुँचाना

85. निम्नलिखित शब्द का संधि विच्छेद करें।

प्रमाण

1. पर + मान
2. प्रा + माण
3. प्र + मान
4. परम + अण

86. निम्नलिखित प्रश्न में, दिए गए चार विकल्पों में से, उस विकल्प का चयन करें जो दी गई लोकोक्ति के अर्थ को सर्वश्रेष्ठ रूप से व्यक्त करता है।

अपना हाथ जगन्नाथ

1. दोहरा फायदा होना
2. पूरी तरह अनियंत्रित होना
3. स्वयं द्वारा किया गया कार्य अच्छा होता है
4. दोनों ओर संकट होना

87. *(i)* आश्विन के महीने का तीसरा पहर था। हर तरफ रामलीला का उत्साह था

(ii) अचानक एक व्यक्ति वहाँ मेरे बारे में पूछते हुए व मेरा नाम लेते हुए वहाँ आया

(iii) मैं भी अपने एक दोस्त के घर था, वहां ताश की बाजी चल रही थी

(iv) और मेरे बगल की कुर्सी पर आकर बैठ गया। मैं उसे नहीं जानता था

प्रस्तुत खंडित वाक्य में वाक्य संरचना का सही क्रम क्या होगा?

1. *(iv)*, *(i)*, *(ii)*, *(iii)*
2. *(ii)*, *(i)*, *(iii)*, *(iv)*
3. *(i)*, *(iii)*, *(ii)*, *(iv)*
4. *(iii)*, *(iv)*, *(i)*, *(ii)*

88. दिए गए वाक्य में उचित संज्ञा का चयन करके रिक्त स्थान की पूर्ति करें।

माही ने आते ही .... से सबका दिल जीत लिया।

1. लकड़ी
2. प्रार्थना
3. प्लास्टिक
4. प्यार

89. नीचे दिए गए शब्द का पर्यायवाची शब्द ज्ञात करें।

गणेश

1. नीरद
2. चक्रपाणि
3. कौशलेन्द्र
4. लम्बोदर

90. निम्नलिखित शब्द के अनेकार्थी शब्द का चयन करें।

गुण

1. लाल
2. धतूरा
3. इच्छा
4. विशेषता

91. निम्नलिखित शब्द का विलोम शब्द ज्ञात करें।

मोक्ष

1. खगोल
2. शाश्वत
3. बंधन
4. सभ्य

92. दिए गए वाक्य में उचित कारक का चयन करके रिक्त स्थान की पूर्ति करें।

मिठाई .... डब्बे में से एक मिठाई निकालकर ले आओ।

1. का
2. में
3. के
4. पर

93. निम्नलिखित शब्द का संधि विच्छेद करें।

इत्यादि

1. इत + आदि
2. इट + आदि
3. इदः + आदि
4. इति + आदि

94. दिए गए वाक्य में उचित क्रिया का चयन करके रिक्त स्थान की पूर्ति करें।

ठंड के मारे मेरे दांत भी .... लगे।

1. लंगड़ाने
2. कटकटाने
3. सठियाने
4. कांपने

95. नीचे दिए गए शब्द का पर्यायवाची शब्द ज्ञात करें।

रमा

1. निशा
2. फूल
3. कटक
4. श्री

निर्देश (प्र.सं. 96 से 100 तक) : *निम्नलिखित गद्यांश के आधार पर पाँच प्रश्न दिए गए हैं। गद्यांश को ध्यानपूर्वक पढ़ें तथा प्रत्येक प्रश्न के चार विकल्पों में से सही विकल्प चुनें।*

एक शोध के अनुसार, जलवायु परिवर्तन के कारण गर्म तापमान यूरोपीय आल्पस में पहाड़ी बकरियों की जीवन शैली को बदल रहा है। अल्पाइन आइबेक्स (कैपरा आइबेक्स) एक पहाड़ी बकरी की प्रजाति है जो गर्म दिनों से बचने के लिए अपनी दैनिक आदतों को रात की आदतों में बदलने के लिए मजबूर हैं। जीवनशैली में यह बदलाव उन्हें भेड़ियों जैसे शिकारियों के प्रति संवेदनशील बना रहा है, जिससे उनकी आवाजाही में बाधा आ रही है और अंततः उनकी जनसंख्या में गिरावट आ सकती है।

84. 3 **85.** 3 **86.** 3 **87.** 3 **88.** 4 **89.** 4 **90.** 4 **91.** 3 **92.** 3 **93.** 4 **94.** 2 **95.** 4

इटली में सासारी विश्वविद्यालय और फेरारा विश्वविद्यालय के शोधकर्ताओं ने 14 वर्षों की अवधि में 47 आइबेक्स का अध्ययन किया। अध्ययन, जिसका शीर्षक है–''सीकिंग टेम्पोरल रिफ्यूजिया टू हीट स्ट्रेस : परभक्षी जोखिम के बावजूद रात्रिकालीन गतिविधि में वृद्धि'', रॉयल सोसाइटी जर्नल में प्रकाशित हुई थी। मोशन सेंसर और ग्लोबल पोजिशनिंग सिस्टम ट्रैकर्स का उपयोग करके बकरियों को 2006 और 2019 के बीच ट्रैक किया गया था।

शोधकर्ताओं ने नोट किया कि चंद्रमा की रोशनी के कारण गर्म दिनों और चमकदार रातों के दौरान आइबेक्स की रात्रि गतिविधियां बढ़ गईं। ''मनुष्यों की व्यापक उपस्थिति या भूदृश्य संरचना के कारण अनुकूल क्षेत्रों में प्रवास में बाधा उत्पन्न हो सकती है। ऐसे मामलों में, जानवर अस्थायी आयाम में अपने पारिस्थितिक स्थान, यानी उनकी दैनिक गतिविधि लय को संशोधित करके अपनी वर्तमान वितरण सीमा और इष्टतम थर्मल आला को बनाए रख सकते हैं'', उन्होंने लिखा। जानवर शाम के ठंडे घंटों के कारण ऊर्जा संतुलन और कुशल गर्मी अपव्यय प्राप्त करने के लिए ऐसा करते हैं। व्यवहार पैटर्न में बदलाव इस बात का प्राथमिक प्रमाण है कि जानवर गर्मी के तनाव से बच रहे हैं और रात की गतिविधियों को अपना रहे हैं और इस प्रक्रिया में, शिकार के जोखिम बढ़ रहे हैं।

जलवायु परिवर्तन के अलावा, मानव गतिविधियाँ, शहरी विकास, कृषि, शिकार और अन्य जैसे अन्य दबाव भी स्तनपायी प्रजातियों की रात्रिचर गतिविधि में वैश्विक वृद्धि को बढ़ा रहे हैं।

96. गद्यांश के आधार पर उचित केन्द्रीय विषय का चयन करें।
1. शोध और उनमें प्रकाशित तथ्य की जांच जरूरी है
2. अल्पाइन आइबेक्स की बदलती गतिविधियाँ और घटती जनसंख्या का जोखिम
3. परिवर्तन मानव जीवन की महत्वपूर्ण शैली है
4. अल्पाइन आइबेक्स की विविध प्रजातियाँ

97. गद्यांश के आधार पर उस विकल्प का चयन करें जिसमें दिया गया तथ्य नहीं है।
1. अल्पाइन आइबेक्स (कैपरा आइबेक्स) एक पहाड़ी बकरी की प्रजाति है।
2. व्यवहार पैटर्न में बदलाव से शिकार के जोखिम कम हो रहे हैं।
3. जीवनशैली में बदलाव के कारण अल्पाइन आइबेक्स की जनसंख्या में गिरावट आ सकती है।
4. गर्म दिनों से बचने के लिए अल्पाइन आइबेक्स अपनी दैनिक आदतों को रात की आदतों में बदलने के लिए मजबूर है।

98. गद्यांश में दिए गए निम्नलिखित शब्द का उचित विलोम शब्द चुनें।

परिवर्तन

1. प्रवर
2. बहुज्ञ
3. प्रस्थान
4. स्थिरता

99. गद्यांश को ध्यान में रखते हुए 'जीवनशैली' शब्द का उपयुक्त अर्थ ज्ञात करें।
1. किसी व्यक्ति, समूह या संस्कृति के घूमने का विशिष्ट तरीका
2. किसी व्यक्ति, समूह या संस्कृति के जीवन का विशिष्ट तरीका
3. किसी व्यक्ति, समूह या संस्कृति के बदलाव का विशिष्ट तरीका
4. किसी व्यक्ति, समूह या संस्कृति के ठहरने का विशिष्ट तरीका

100. गद्यांश में दिए गए निम्नलिखित शब्द का उचित पर्यायवाची शब्द चुनें।

प्रमाण

1. मिथ्या
2. कृत्रिम
3. काल्पनिक
4. साक्ष्य

SECTION-B

POST SPECIFIC SUBJECT-RELATED QUESTIONS

101. Match the AI Ethics with its correct description.

AI Ethics	Description
I. Data privacy	1. It is a standard metric that measures how many users in a database share a particular attribute.
II. K-anonymity	2. It is a trade-off between the amount of data collected and the performance of a product or service.
III. L-diversity	3. It extends the idea by merging several sensitive attributes together.

1. I-1, II-3, III-2
2. I-2, II-3, III-1
3. I-1, II-2, III-3
4. I-2, II-1, III-3

102. What is the advantage of exploratory Data Analysis in Big Data and Analytics?
1. Less realistic statements of accuracy
2. Flexible ways to generate hypotheses
3. Usually does not provide definitive answers
4. More realistic statements of accuracy

96. 2 **97.** 2 **98.** 4 **99.** 2 **100.** 4 **101.** 4 **102.** 2

103. In computer networking, a Repeater is a device that operates only in the .... layer.

1. Physical
2. Network
3. Data link
4. Session

104. Which of the following data function in SQL returns the current database system timestamp as a 'date time' value without the database time zone offset?

1. GET TIME
2. GET DATE
3. CAST DATE
4. CAST TIME

105. Which of the following type of function used with strings in the Python language returns the character with the highest ASCII value?

1. len ( )
2. hvalue ( )
3. max ( )
4. long ( )

106. Which of the following command is used in the communication system call of an operating system?

1. Request device, release device
2. Attach or detach remote devices
3. Allocate and free memory
4. Read, write, reposition

107. A .... index is an ordered file whose records are of fixed length with two fields primary key and a pointer to a disk block.

1. Secondary
2. Multilevel
3. Primary
4. Clustering

108. In AI biases many AI models are ....

I. deepfakes
II. Black boxes
III. K-anonymity

1. Only II
2. Only I
3. I, II and III
4. Only I and III

109. Select the correct output for the following python code?

```
a = 20
b = 35
if a > = b:
    print ("yes")
else:
    print ("No")
```

1. Syntax
2. No
3. Yes
4. Error

110. In cyber security, what remedy does the law provide?

1. Apology
2. Imprisonment
3. Technologies
4. Computer networks

111. Which of the following is an input device which can detect the presence or absence of a pencil or pen mark on a paper?

1. Optical Mark Reader (OMR)
2. Light pen
3. Digitizer
4. Optical Character Recognizer (OCR)

112. Which of the following type conversion function in the Python language, is used to convert a character into an integer?

1. tuple ( )
2. dict ( )
3. set ( )
4. ord ( )

113. Using K-map, simplify the Boolean function: $F(x, y, z) = S\ (0, 2, 4, 5, 6)$

Which of the following is simplified function?

1. $F = z + x'y'$
2. $F = z' + xy'$
3. $F = z + x'y$
4. $F = z' + xy$

114. In Python language, which of the following is correct for 'strip ( )' function?

1. In returns the string by removing trailing and leading white spaces
2. It returns a list from the string depending upon the delimiter that we specify
3. It returns the power of values passed
4. It returns the string with the first character in upper case and lowering the case for rest of the string

115. Which of the following statement is correct for DATEDIFF function in SQL?

I. This function reports difference between the arguments 'startdate' and 'enddate'.
II. In this, 'datepart' argument/value can be specified in a variable.

1. Only I
2. Neither I nor II
3. Both I and II
4. Only II

116. In the data link layer, ... is based on automatic repeat request, which is the retransmission of data.

1. Framing
2. Physical addressing
3. Error control
4. Flow control

117. In Python language, which of the following method of lists is used to add an element to the end of the list?

1. index ( )
2. sort ( )
3. pop ( )
4. append ( )

103. 1	**104.** 2	**105.** 3	**106.** 2	**107.** 3	**108.** 1	**109.** 2	**110.** 2
111. 1	**112.** 4	**113.** 2	**114.** 1	**115.** 1	**116.** 3	**117.** 4	

118. Which of the following part of the CPU has the necessary electronic circuitry toper form binary addition and shift operations in computer system?

1. Arithmetic Logic Unit (ALU)
2. Memory Buses
3. Registers
4. Control Unit

119. Match the categories of AI with its correct description.

Categories of AI	Description
I. Artificial Narrow Intelligence	1. Level of general and strong AI that is smarter than humans if that's possible.
II. Artificial General Intelligence	2. Such system seems to act intelligently but they don't have any awareness of what they are doing.
III. Super Intelligence	3. Acting like a smart human and thinking like one with a conscious.

1. I-2, II-3, III-1
2. I-2, II-1, III-3
3. I-1, II-2, III-3
4. I-1, II-3, III-2

120. Choose the correct output for the following Python code.

tuple_var_mix = ("Example", 1, "Tuple")
print (tuple_var_mix)

1. {Example, 1, Tuple}
2. (Example, 1, tuple)
3. ('Example', 1, 'Tuple')
4. [Example, 1, 'Tuple']

121. In which of the following condition of Deadlock Prevention, at least one resource must be non-sharable?

1. Circular wait
2. Hold and wait
3. Mutual Exclusion
4. No preemption

122. Which of the following notation of ERD (Entity – Relationship Diagram) shows the 'Weak Entity'?

1. 
2. 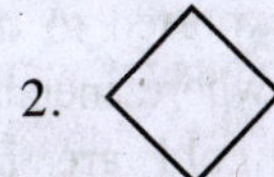
3. 
4. 

123. Which of the following statement is correct for a 'Volume Control block' in File-System Implementation?

1. It is used to organize the files
2. It has a unique identifier number to allow association with a directory entry
3. It contains the number of block in the partition
4. It can contain information needed by the system to boot an operating system from that volume

124. In Python language, which of the following mode for opening the file, opens the file for both reading and writing and file pointer will be placed at the start of the file?

1. ab
2. rb
3. r^+
4. a^+

125. Which of the following is characteristic of a RISC (Reduced Instruction Set Computer) processor?

1. Microprogrammed control
2. Instruction that manipulate operands in memory
3. Fixed-length, easily decoded instruction format
4. A large number (typically from 100 to 250) of instructions

126. Which among the following given below is correct in context of privacy issues in social media and online platforms?

1. The sharing on social media especially by children must be monitored at all times.
2. The addiction of social media does not hamper the academic performance of a student.
3. Rumours and fake news cannot put the administration at risk.
4. Mishandling of social media cannot create tension in the law and order.

127. In which of the following type of addressing mode, the instruction specifies a register in the CPU whose contents give the address of the operand in memory?

1. Register indirect mode
2. Indirect address mode
3. Implied mode
4. Immediate mode

128. In HTML body tag, which of the following attribute indicates the colour of the hyperlinks after the mouse is clicked on it?

1. VLINK
2. ALINK
3. LINK
4. HLINK

118. 1	**119.** 1	**120.** 3	**121.** 3	**122.** 3	**123.** 3
124. 3	**125.** 3	**126.** 1	**127.** 1	**128.** 1	

129. Which of the following statement(s) is/are correct regarding Assembly language?

I. An assembler converts (or assembles) the symbolic program of an Assembly language into its equivalent machine program.

II. A program written in an assembly language is machine dependent.

1. Both I and II
2. Only II
3. Only I
4. Neither I nor II

130. Which of the following Instruction format use an implied accumulator (AC) register for all data manipulation?

1. One-address instructions
2. Three-address instructions
3. Zero-address instructions
4. Two-address instructions

131. In context of the Digital Personal Data Protection Act, 2023, which of the given following is correct?

1. "Child" means an individual who has not completed the age of eighteen years
2. "Digital personal data" means personal data in physical form
3. "Chairperson" does not mean the chairperson of the board
4. "Data" means representation of facts only

132. Which of the following File operation need not involve any actual I/O (Input/Output) and is also known as 'File Seek'?

1. Deleting a file
2. Repositioning within a file
3. Reading a file
4. Truncating a file

133. In CPU, which of the following type of register is required by the control unit and contains the instruction currently being executed?

1. Instruction register
2. Accumulator
3. Program register
4. Memory data register

134. The values in a dictionary can be .... but the keys in the dictionary should be .... in Python programming languages.

1. repeated, repeated
2. repeated, unique
3. unique, repeated
4. unique, unique

135. Which of the following part of operating system allocates the CPU to next scheduled process in the system?

1. File manager
2. Dispatcher
3. Scheduler
4. Input/output handler

136. Which of the following printer is type of impact printer?

1. Ink-Jet
2. Laser
3. Dot matrix
4. Thermal

137. Which of the following statement is correct regarding point-to-point connection in the data communication?

I. It provides a dedicated link between two devices.

II. It is a time shared connection.

1. Only II
2. Both I and II
3. Neither I nor II
4. Only I

138. In Direct Memory Access (DMA) ...., a block sequence consisting of a number of memory words is transferred in a continuous burst.

1. Bus granting
2. Burst transfer
3. Cycle stealing
4. Controller count

139. Which of the following normal form of normalization in relational model, disallows relations within relations or relations as attribute values within tuples?

1. Fourth
2. First
3. Second
4. Third

140. Which of the following is NOT an attribute that included by the HR tag which puts a horizontal line on the page?

1. SHADE
2. SIZE
3. ALIGN
4. WIDTH

141. .... enables the creator owner to earn recognition or financial benefit by using their creation or invention.

1. Patent
2. Copyright
3. Intellectual property right
4. Data protection

142. Over half of the e-waste generated in the developed world are exported to developing countries, mainly to ...., where metals like copper, iron, silicon, nickel and gold are recovered during recycling process.

1. Afghanistan
2. Kazakistan
3. UAE
4. India

129. 1	**130.** 1	**131.** 1	**132.** 2	**133.** 1	**134.** 2	**135.** 2
136. 3	**137.** 4	**138.** 2	**139.** 2	**140.** 1	**141.** 3	**142.** 4

143. .... is a two-dimensional labelled data structure with columns of potentially different type, in data handling with pandas.

1. Series 2. Missing data
3. Iteration 4. Data frames

144. A semaphore is an integer variable that, apart from initialization, is accessed only through which of the following standard atomic operation?

1. release ( ) 2. lock ( )
3. acquire ( ) 4. signal ( )

145. From the challenges given below, which of the challenge does IoT adoption include?

1. Deepfake 2. Black box
3. Security 4. Cloud storage

146. Which of the following tag of HTML language is a container for the tags that contain information about the page?

1. <title> 2. <html>
3. <head> 4. <body>

147. Irreparable computer and other electronic goods are known as .... in tech world.

1. Man made waste 2. Natural waste
3. Waste 4. Electronic waste

148. Which of the following is a one-dimensional labelled array capable of holding any data type (integers, strings, floating point numbers, python objects, etc) in data handling with pandas?

1. Series 2. Missing data
3. Data frames 4. Iteration

149. The E-waste (management) rules 2016 of India, recognizes two broad categories: IT and tele-communication equipment and consumer electrical and electronics including which of the following material?

I. Fluorescent
II. Mercury

1. Only I 2. Only II
3. Both I and II 4. Neither I nor II

150. Which of the following form is correct to show a 'comments' in the HTML language?

1. < – – This is a comment – – >
2. < – – This is a comment – –! >
3. < !– – This is a comment – –! >
4. < !– – This is a comment – – >

151. If you encounter an import Error, what does it mean?

I. Python could find pandas in list of available libraries
II. Pandas couldn't find python in list of available libraries
III. Python couldn't find Pandas in list of available libraries

1. Only III 2. I, II and III
3. Only I 4. Only I and III

152. Data frame in Pandas has a method which takes a column name (for a regular index) or a list of column names to create a new, re-indexed data frame, which of the following is correct method?

1. dFb 2. data.index ( )
3. set_index ( ) 4. dFmi

153. Which of the following is correct for Identifiers name used in Python language?

1. An identifier can have underscore (_) symbol
2. We must use keywords as identifier
3. There is restriction the length of an identifier
4. An identifier must start with a digit

154. Which of the following rule is needed to be followed while declaring the XML (Extensible Markup Language) elements name?

1. Name must start with a number
2. Name can contain spaces
3. Name must not start with the letter xml
4. Name cannot contain letter, numbers and other characters

155. In digital realm, which refers to the legal rights to protect invention or creation in intellectual property, are given to whom?

1. Employee
2. Seller
3. Creator/invertor
4. Buyers

156. Which of the following symbol is used to add comments in the Python language?

1. * 2. #
3. ! 4. //

157. Which operation is provided in Pandas, when multiple tables can be concatenated both column wise and row wise as database?

1. SUM 2. MERGE
3. GROUP BY 4. SELECT

143. 4	**144.** 4	**145.** 3	**146.** 3	**147.** 4	**148.** 1	**149.** 3	**150.** 4
151. 1	**152.** 3	**153.** 1	**154.** 3	**155.** 3	**156.** 2	**157.** 2	

158. IPR (Intellectual Property Right) is given for how much time, in digital realm?

1. Certain period of time
2. Unlimited period of time
3. Uncertain period of time
4. Depending on case to case basis

159. In E-waste management, from which factors, there comes the exposure variability in electronic waste?

1. Type of E-waste
2. Quantity of the Pollutants in air
3. Management processes of the air pollution
4. Medical waste

160. Which of the following HTML tag is used to puts a line break in the text?

1. <B> 2. <BL>
3. <L> 4.

161. Which of the following maths function in SQL returns the smallest integer greater than, or equal to, the specified numeric expression?

1. ROUND 2. CEILING
3. ABS 4. FLOOR

162. Which of the following page replacement algorithms(s) does not suffer from Belady's anomaly in Operating System?

I. Least-Recently Used (LRU) page replacement.
II. First-In, First-Out (FIFO) page replacement.

1. Only I 2. Neither I nor II
3. Only II 4. Both I and II

163. String is a collection of one or more character which consists of .... in programming language.

I. Letters
II. Numbers
III. Symbols

1. I, II and III 2. Only I
3. Only I and III 4. Only II

164. Which of the following symbol is used with SELECT command of SQL, to retrieve all the attribute values of the selected tuples?

1. # 2. %
3. * 4. :

165. Which of the following is commonly used in UNICODE encoding schemes and number system in computer science?

1. UTF-17 2. UTF-61
3. UTF-8 4. UTF-35

166. Extensions like .txt, .py, .CSV, etc in python language are example of ....

1. text files 2. text editor
3. UNI CODE 4. ASCII

167. Which of the following logic gate is shown in the given Graphic Symbol? (where, A and B = inputs, x = output)

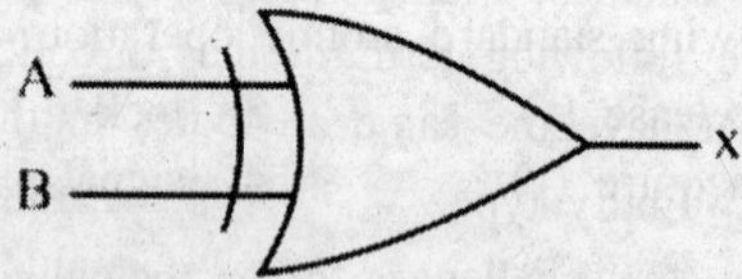

1. OR gate
2. NAND gate
3. NOR gate
4. Exclusive – OR (XOR) gate

168. Which of the following phase of the compiler, gathers type information and saves it in either the syntax tree or the symbol table, for subsequent use during intermediate code generation?

1. Semantic Analyzer 2. Code Analyzer
3. Syntax Analyzer 4. Lexical Analyzer

169. Number with decimal points is called .... in programming language.

1. Fractional point numbers
2. Complex numbers
3. Imaginary Numbers
4. Integer

170. Which of the following operation includes all tuples that are in R-set but not in S-set?

1. R – S 2. R Ç S
3. R È S 4. R × S

171. Which of the following is NOT an aggregate function in SQL?

1. CROSS PRODUCT
2. MAXIMUM
3. COUNT
4. SUM

172. .... has been developed to incorporate all the character of every written language of the world. It provides a unique number for every character, irrespective of device[server, desktop, mob], OS [linux, win] or software application.

1. UNICODE 2. Binary Code
3. ISCII 4. ASCII

158. 1	**159.** 1	**160.** 4	**161.** 2	**162.** 1	**163.** 1	**164.** 3	**165.** 3
166. 1	**167.** 4	**168.** 1	**169.** 1	**170.** 1	**171.** 1	**172.** 1	

173. ASCII (American Standard Code for Information Interchange) can only handle .... or at most .... languages and that shows its limitation to handle all world languages.

1. 2, 5
2. 1, 2
3. 1, 5
4. 3, 4

174. In Database Management System (DBMS), which of the following term defines a collection of entities that have the same attributes in the database?

1. Entity type
2. Value set
3. Entity set
4. Value type

175. Which symbol is used to add the comment in the code or program to make it more readable and understandable in Python programming language?

1. #
2. *
3. –
4. :

176. Which of the following statement(s) is/are correct for context switching in Operating System?

I. When a context switch occurs, the kernel saves the context of the old process in its PCB (Process Control Block).

II. Context-Switch time is pure overhead, because the system does no useful workwhile switching.

1. Neither I nor II
2. Only I
3. Only II
4. Both I and II

177. Which of the following statement(s) is/are correct regarding AND logic gate?

I. The AND gate produces the output value 1 if input A and input B are both equal to 1.

II. The algebraic operation symbol of the AND function is the same as the multiplication symbol of ordinary arithmetic.

1. Neither I ncr II
2. Only I
3. Both I and II
4. Only II

178. Which of the following term of ER model (Entity – Relationship) is corresponding to the foreign key (or relationship relation) in the relational model of database?

1. Composite attribute
2. Entity type
3. 1 : 1 (one to one) or 1 : N (one to many) relationship type
4. M : N (many to many) relationship type

179. In relational databases, which of the following integrity constraint is specified between two relations and is used to maintain the consistency among tuples in the two relations?

1. Entity integrity constraint
2. Semantic integrity constraint
3. Functional integrity constraint
4. Referential integrity constraint

180. Match the following Process states of Operating System with their definitions.

State	Definition
I New	1. The process is waiting to be assigned to a processor
II. Running	2. Instructions are being executed
III. Ready	3. The process is being created

1. I-3, II-1, III-2
2. I-1, II-3, III-2
3. I-1, II-2, III-3
4. I-3, II-2, III-1

181. Which of the following operator is used as concatenation operator in SQL?

1. + +
2. " "
3. # #
4. | |

182. Which of the following statement is correct regarding unguided media (wireless)?

I. Unguided media transport electromagnetic waves without using a physical conductor.

II. Unguided signals can travel from the source to destination in ground propagation way.

1. Only II
2. Both I and II
3. Only I
4. Neither I nor II

183. Which of the following is correct formula for calculating wavelength (λ) of a signal in the data communication?

1. λ = propagation speed + frequency
2. λ = propagation speed × period
3. λ = propagation speed + period
4. λ = propagation speed × frequency

184. In periodic analog signals, which of the following is NOT a parameter to describe a sine wave in data communication?

1. Wavelength
2. Phase
3. Frequency
4. Peak amplitude

185. Which of the following operator of SQL is used in WHERE clause for match a character pattern in database?

1. LIKE
2. IN
3. IS NULL
4. OR

173. 2 **174.** 3 **175.** 1 **176.** 4 **177.** 3 **178.** 3 **179.** 4
180. 4 **181.** 4 **182.** 2 **183.** 2 **184.** 1 **185.** 1

186. In SQL, which of the following is correct command for schema evolution, if the RESTRICT option is chosen than the schema is dropped only if schema has no element in it?

1. DELETE 2. UPDATE
3. ALTER 4. DROP

187. .... files are spreadsheet files in a text format of data when cell contents are separated by a character for example a comma or semi-colon.

1. Comma-Separated-Values
2. Semi-colon Separated Values
3. Column and Row Headers
4. CVS

188. Unicode in the programming language can be represented using which of the bit format standards in computer science?

1. 8-bit 2. 17-bit
3. 65-bit 4. 9-bit

189. Which of the following type of guided transmission media are categorized by their Radio Government (RG) ratings in computer networking?

1. Fiber-Optic Cable 2. Coaxial Cable
3. Metallic Cable 4. Twisted-Pair Cable

190. Which of the following system call include 'wait for time' operation command in Operating System?

1. Process Control 2. Device Management
3. File Management 4. Communications

191. Which of the following stage is used for child cognition development at the age from 2 years to 7 years?

1. Sensori-motor 2. Pre-operational
3. Formal operational 4. Concrete operational

192. The Government of India adopted the National Policy for Empowerment of Women in ....

1. 2001 2. 2005
3. 2000 4. 2003

193. In which of the following approach Pedagogy indicate learning by doing based on engagement of students through different activities?

I. Teacher centered approach
II. Student centered approach

1. Both I and II 2. Only I
3. Neither I nor II 4. Only II

194. Which of the following approach of Assessment for Learning is the assessment of classmates on the response and performance of the learner?

1. Teacher-led assessment
2. Learner self-assessment
3. Computer-based assessment
4. Peer assessment

195. Which of the following language was included through the 71st constitutional amendment (1992) in 8th schedule of the Indian Constitution?

1. Bengali 2. Nepali
3. Boro 4. Gujarati

196. Art education is the area of learning that is based upon which of the following?

I. The visual, tangible art
II. The performing arts

1. Only I 2. Both I and II
3. Neither I nor II 4. Only II

197. In which of the following approach to learning and teaching, both the teacher and the students perform activities strictly confined to the prescribed contents/textbooks in the subject being taught?

1. Learner centered 2. Teacher-centered
3. Subject-centered 4. Discipline centered

198. Piaget divided which of the following domain of development into four stages: The Sensorimotor Stage, The Pre-Operational Stage, Concrete Operational Stage and The Formal Operational Stage?

1. Moral development
2. Physical and motor development
3. Cognitive development
4. Socio-emotional development

199. Match the following Classification of Cognitive Disability (Mental Retardation) with their range of intelligence quotient (IQ).

Severity Levels	Range of IQ
I. Profound Mentally Retarded	1. 20-34
II. Mild Mentally Retarded	2. Below 20
III. Severe Mentally Retarded	3. 50-75

1. I-2, II-3, III-1 2. I-1, II-3, III-2
3. I-3, II-2, III-1 4. I-2, II-1, III-3

200. In the types of Learning resources, the term .... denotes a partially three-dimensional, full-size replica or scale model of a landscape typically showing historical events, nature scenes or city scapes, for purposes of education or entertainment.

1. cartoons 2. Globes
3. realia 4. diorama

186. 4	**187.** 1	**188.** 1	**189.** 2	**190.** 1	**191.** 2	**192.** 1	**193.** 4
194. 4	**195.** 2	**196.** 2	**197.** 3	**198.** 3	**199.** 1	**200.** 4	

EXPLANATORY ANSWERS

1. Repeating our clothes is a practical and socially relevant idea because it directly connects to reducing waste and promoting sustainability.

Argument I gives a logical, objective reason (supporting a sustainable environment), so it is a strong argument.

Argument II is based on a subjective feeling ("new beginnings") and does not address whether repeating clothes is good or bad in a rational way, so it is a weak argument.

2. Convert letters into their alphabetical positions and add them, then divide by 4.

For LOMQG:

L(12) + O(15) + M(13) + Q(17) + G(7) = 64, and 64 ÷ 4 = 16.

For WTQMC:

W(23) + T(20) + Q(17) + M(13) + C(3) = 76, and 76 ÷ 4 = 19.

For LSOMI:

L(12) + S(19) + O(15) + M(13) + I(9) = 68, and 68 ÷ 4 = 17.

3. Compare each letter position-wise across the series and observe the shifting pattern in alphabetical positions.

The first letters go

N(14) → I(9) (–5),
I(9) → F(6) (–3),
F(6) → A(1) (–5),

so the next shift continues with (–3):

A(1) – 3 = X(24).

The second letters go

R(18) → Y(25) (+7),
Y(25) → J(10) (–15),
J(10) → Q(17) (+7),

so the next shift is (–15):

Q(17) – 15 = B(2).

Continuing the same position-wise pattern for the remaining letters gives M and W, so the missing term is XBMW.

4. In MKH, WUR, and KIF, the letter positions decrease by 2 and then by 3 (e.g., M(13) → K(11) is –2, K(11) → H(8) is –3).

MKH follows –2, –3;

WUR follows –2, –3;

KIF follows –2, –3.

But MPR increases by +3 and then +2 (M(13) → P(16) is +3, P(16) → R(18) is +2), so it does not follow the common pattern and is the odd one out.

5. The rule is: first reverse the word, then interchange the first half and the second half.

STOPWARS → reverse = SRAWPOTS,
split as SRAW | POTS,
interchange → POTS + SRAW = POTSSRAW.
LOGIPERT → reverse = TREPIGOL,
split as TREP | IGOL,
interchange → IGOL + TREP = IGOLTREP.
LAPTOPST → reverse = TSPOTPAL,
split as TSPO | TPAL,
interchange → TPAL + TSPO = TPALTSPO.

6. From the statement, Raveena's father advises her to exercise and she goes to the gym daily due to that advice. Advising regular exercise logically indicates concern for maintaining or improving health. Nothing in the statement suggests that Raveena has any chronic disease; she may simply be exercising for general fitness.

Hence, only Conclusion I follows.

7. Replace the symbols as given: '×' means '÷', '÷' means '×', '–' means '+', and '+' means '–'.

So, 38 × 57 ÷ 9 – 18 + 12 becomes

38 ÷ 57 × 9 + 18 – 12.

Now 38 ÷ 57 × 9 = (38/57) × 9 = 6.

Then 6 + 18 – 12 = 12.

8. In the given relation, 442 becomes 633 by adding 191 (442 + 191 = 633).

Similarly, 186 becomes 377 by adding 191 (186 + 191 = 377).

So the missing pair must also follow "add 191".

Among the options, 313 + 191 = 504, which matches exactly.

9. Q is second from the left and is immediately left of R, so Q is in position 2 and R in position 3.

S is immediately right of R, so S is in position 4.

P is at the rightmost end, so P is in position 7.

Since U has neighbours T and P, U must be in position 6 (adjacent to P), and T in position 5.

Therefore, the person immediately left of P (position 6) is U.

10. From "Some C are D" and "Some D are E," the overlapping parts of D may be different, so "Some E are C" is not guaranteed.

"No E is G" only restricts E, not all D, so "No D is G" does not follow.

Also, nothing given forces any relation between C and G, so "Some G are C" does not follow.

Hence, none of the conclusions follows.

11. Total girls = 40. Mona is 13th from the right.

Position from the left = 40 – 13 + 1 = 28,

So, Mona is 28th from the left end.

12. Differences are

197 – 200 = –3,
206 – 197 = +9,

179 – 206 = –27,

260 – 179 = +81.

Each difference is multiplied by –3 (–3, +9, –27, +81), so next difference = +81 × (–3) = –243.

Hence next term = 260 – 243 = 17.

13. In WXUZ, NOLQ, and IJGL, the pattern is 1st → 2nd is +1, 2nd → 3rd is –3, and 3rd → 4th is +5 (e.g., W → X +1, X → U –3, U → Z +5). In EFCG, E → F is +1 and F → C is –3, but C → G is +4 (not +5), so it is the odd one.

14. NQT becomes ORU by shifting each letter one step forward (N → O, Q → R, T → U). Applying the same to ADH gives A → B, D → E, H → I, so the related letters are BEI.

15. J ÷ P means J is the son of P. P + K means P is the husband of K (so K is P's wife). K × M means K is the mother of M, so P (husband of K) is the father of M. M – R means M is the wife of R, so R is M's husband. Therefore, P is the father of R's wife, i.e., P is R's wife's father.

16. 9 × 4 – 7 × 3 = 4:

Interchanging 7 and 9 makes the equation become

7 × 4 – 9 × 3 = 4.

Now, 7 × 4 = 28

and 9 × 3 = 27,

so LHS = 28 – 27 = 1.

Since 1 ≠ 4, this equation becomes not correct after the interchange.

17. Observe the pattern:

$6 \to 6^3 - 6^2 = 216 - 36 = 180$

and $8 \to 8^3 - 8^2 = 512 - 64 = 448$.

So the rule is

$$n^3 - n^2 = n^2(n - 1).$$

For 10, $10^3 - 10^2 = 1000 - 100 = 900$.

18. A bridge collapse can trap or injure people, so immediate search-and-rescue is a direct and necessary response.

Course I is practical, urgent, and logically connected to the situation.

Course II is extreme and not supported because one collapse does not logically require everyone to leave the entire town.

19. The statement says ABC Corporation has been planning expansion for three years to reach the world market. That directly supports that the corporation wants to capture or enter the global market.

Nothing in the statement proves the corporation is not competitive, so Conclusion I does not follow.

20. The triangle represents Workers, the rectangle represents Educated, and the circle represents Man.

We need the number of workers who are uneducated, i.e., the parts of the triangle that do not lie inside the rectangle. From the diagram, the region marked 12 lies entirely inside the triangle and completely outside the rectangle, meaning these are workers who are not educated. All other numbers within the triangle are either partially or fully inside the rectangle (educated), so they are excluded.

Hence, the required number is 12.

21. In the BWF World Badminton Championships 2023, HS Prannoy reached the semi-finals in the men's singles category.

In badminton world championships, both losing semi-finalists are awarded bronze medals.

Prannoy's consistent performance and his advancement to the semi-finals ensured that he secured the bronze medal for India in the tournament.

22. In January 2023, ISRO signed a Memorandum of Understanding with Microsoft to support space-tech startups in India. This collaboration aimed to provide startups with access to cloud computing, artificial intelligence, and other advanced technological tools, helping them scale and innovate within the space sector.

23. Article 343 of the Indian Constitution clearly states that the official language of the Union shall be Hindi in the Devanagari script. It also mentions that the form of numerals to be used for official purposes shall be the international form of Indian numerals, establishing the linguistic framework for official communication.

24. The Narmada River originates from the Amarkantak Plateau in Madhya Pradesh. It flows westward across central India and drains into the Arabian Sea. The river is one of the major west-flowing rivers of India and holds geographical as well as cultural significance.

25. The Battle of Seringapatam took place in the year 1799 during the Fourth Anglo-Mysore War. This battle resulted in the defeat and death of Tipu Sultan and marked the end of the Mysore Kingdom's resistance against British expansion in southern India.

26. Article 315 of the Indian Constitution provides for the establishment of Public Service Commissions for the Union and for each State. These commissions are responsible for conducting examinations and advising on recruitment, promotions, and disciplinary matters in civil services, ensuring merit-based selection.

27. Nalwari Fair is a famous traditional cattle fair celebrated in Bilaspur district of Himachal Pradesh. It is an important cultural and economic event where livestock trading takes place along with various cultural activities, attracting people from nearby regions.

28. Article 21 of the Indian Constitution guarantees the protection of life and personal liberty. It states that no person shall be deprived of his life or personal liberty

except according to procedure established by law, and it has been widely interpreted by courts to include various rights necessary for a dignified life.

29. The Tamil epic Silappadikaram was composed by Ilango Adigal, a Jain monk and prince. It is one of the five great epics of Tamil literature and narrates the story of Kannagi and Kovalan, highlighting themes of justice and morality.

30. The Reserve Bank of India maintained the repo rate at 6.5 per cent in its monetary policy announcements during 2023, including December. The repo rate is the rate at which RBI lends money to commercial banks and is a key tool for controlling inflation and liquidity.

31. The Indian National Congress was established in the year 1885. It was founded by A.O. Hume, along with Indian leaders like Dadabhai Naoroji and Dinshaw Wacha. The first session was held in Bombay under the presidency of W.C. Bonnerjee, marking the beginning of organized political activity in India.

32. According to the Census of India 2011, Uttar Pradesh is the most populous state in the country. It has a population of over 19.9 crore, making it not only the most populous state in India but also one of the most populous sub-national entities in the world.

33. The Ministry of Social Justice and Empowerment signed a Memorandum of Understanding with ISKCON on 23 November 2023. This collaboration aimed to spread awareness about the Nasha Mukt Bharat Abhiyan, focusing on reducing substance abuse among youth, women, and students.

34. In December 2023, Akash Ambani announced that Reliance Jio was working with IIT Bombay on an artificial intelligence project named Bharat GPT. The aim of this initiative is to develop AI models tailored for Indian languages and needs, promoting digital inclusion.

35. Vitamin A is abundantly found in foods like carrots, mangoes, and papaya, which are rich in beta-carotene. Amla, on the other hand, is primarily known for its high Vitamin C content and is not considered a rich source of Vitamin A.

36. The Young Bengal Movement was started by Henry Louis Vivian Derozio in Calcutta during the early 19th century. He was a teacher at Hindu College and inspired his students to question orthodox traditions, promote rational thinking, and embrace modern ideas. The movement played a key role in social and intellectual reform in Bengal.

37. Oranges are rich in citric acid, which gives them their characteristic sour taste. Citric acid is commonly found in citrus fruits like oranges, lemons, and limes. It also acts as a natural preservative and antioxidant.

38. Article 65 of the Indian Constitution provides that the Vice President shall act as President or discharge the functions of the President during any vacancy in the office or when the President is unable to perform duties. This ensures continuity in the executive funcions of the country.

39. The Purvanchal or Eastern Hills include ranges such as the Patkai Hills, Naga Hills, and Manipur Hills, which lie in the northeastern part of India. The Shevroy Hills, however, are located in Tamil Nadu in southern India and are part of the Eastern Ghats, so they are not included in the Purvanchal Hills.

40. ICICI (Industrial Credit and Investment Corporation of India) was established in 1955 at the initiative of the World Bank, the Government of India, and representatives of Indian industry. It was created to provide medium and long-term project financing to Indian businesses.

41. Let present ages be $10x$ and $13x$

Given difference $= 13x - 10x = 3x = 18$

$\Rightarrow \quad x = 6.$

Amit $= 10x = 60$ years,

Ankit $= 13x = 78$ years.

After 12 years:

Amit $= 60 + 12 = 72,$

Ankit $= 78 + 12 = 90.$

Required ratio $= 72 : 90 =$ (divide by 18) $= 4 : 5.$

42. Let, E2 $= 1$ unit.

Then, E1 $= 8 \times 1 = 8$ units.

Difference $= 8 - 1 = 7.$

Percentage less $= \frac{7}{8} \times 100 = 87.5\%.$

Given options do not include 87.5%, hence the closest matching option is 88.88 per cent.

43. Carefully reading the graph again is essential.

The circular markers represent year P and the square markers represent year Q.

For year P (circle points):

A = 160, B = 50, C = 40, D = 35, E = 48, F = 52

So, J1 $= 160 + 50 + 40 + 35 + 48 + 52$

$= 385$

For year Q (square points):

A = 68, B = 72, C = 60, D = 170, E = 96, F = 44

So, J2 $= 68 + 72 + 60 + 170 + 96 + 44$

$= 510$

Now, J2 − J1 $= 510 - 385 = 125$

Hence, the correct value is 125.

44. Given average $= 21$ for 40 students

$\Rightarrow$ Total $= 21 \times 40 = 840.$

One age was taken as 20 instead of 30,

so actual total should be $840 + (30 - 20) = 850.$

Correct average $= 850 \div 40 = 21.25$ years.

45. Let, $P : Q : R = 6x : 5x : 3x$

Given R is 32 less than the sum of P and Q, so

$3x = (6x + 5x) - 32$

$3x = 11x - 32$

$8x = 32 \Rightarrow x = 4$

Thus, $Q = 5x = 5 \times 4 = 20.$

46. Given, Principal = 14400,

Rate = 10% per annum,

Time = 3 years

$$\text{Amount} = 14400 \times \left(1+\frac{10}{100}\right)^3$$

$$= 14400 \times \left(\frac{11}{10}\right)^3$$

$$= 14400 \times \frac{11 \times 11 \times 11}{10 \times 10 \times 10}$$

$$= 14400 \times \frac{1331}{1000} = 19166.4$$

Compound Interest = Amount − Principal

= 19166.4 − 14400 = ₹ 4766.4.

47. Each dimension decreases by 12%, so new factor = 0.88

Surface area depends on product of two dimensions

New factor = 0.88 × 0.88 = 0.7744

Decrease = (1 − 0.7744) × 100 = 22.56%.

48. Sum of digits of 859M = 8 + 5 + 9 + M = 22 + M

For divisibility by 9, sum must be divisible by 9

Nearest multiple of 9 = 27.

22 + M = 27 → M = 5.

49. Profit = 12% of 230

$$= \frac{12}{100} \times 230 = 27.6.$$

50. Selling price = 75% of marked price

$$7200 = \frac{75}{100} \times MP$$

$$MP = 7200 \times \frac{100}{75} = 9600.$$

51. Let Principal = P and Rate = r% per annum

Simple Interest for 2 years

$$= \frac{P \times r \times 2}{100} = 28800$$

So, $$\frac{P \times r}{100} = 14400 \quad \text{...(1)}$$

Compound Interest for 2 years

$$= P\left[\left(1+\frac{r}{100}\right)^2 - 1\right] = 36000$$

Add Principal to both sides:

$$\text{Amount} = P\left(1+\frac{r}{100}\right)^2$$

$$= P + 36000 \quad \text{...(2)}$$

Also, for 2 years:

$$CI - SI = P \times \left(\frac{r}{100}\right)^2$$

$$36000 - 28800 = P \times \left(\frac{r}{100}\right)^2$$

$$7200 = P \times \left(\frac{r}{100}\right)^2 \quad \text{...(3)}$$

Divide (3) by (1):

$$\frac{r}{100} = \frac{7200}{14400} = \frac{1}{2}$$

Substitute in (1):

$$P \times \frac{1}{2} = 14400$$

P = 28800.

52. Total distance = 210 + 390 = 600 metres

Speed = 54 km/hr

$$= \frac{54 \times 1000}{3600} = 15 \text{ m/s}$$

$$\text{Time} = \frac{\text{Distance}}{\text{Speed}}$$

$$= \frac{600}{15} = 40 \text{ seconds.}$$

53. 33 ÷ 11 + 75 ÷ 5 × 2 − 6 ÷ 12 × 30

$$= 3 + 15 \times 2 - \frac{6}{12} \times 30$$

$$= 3 + 30 - \frac{1}{2} \times 30$$

= 3 + 30 − 15 = 18.

54. Population = 30000

After 1 year = 30000 × 1.2 = 36000

After 2 years = 36000 × 1.2 = 43200

After 3 years = 43200 × 1.2 = 51840.

55. 12 = 2 × 2 × 3

36 = 2 × 2 × 3 × 3

240 = 2 × 2 × 2 × 2 × 3 × 5

Common factors = 2 × 2 × 3 = 12.

56. Let, length = L and breadth = $\frac{5L}{8}$

$$\text{Area} = L \times \frac{5L}{8} = 160$$

$$\frac{5L^2}{8} = 160$$

$$L^2 = 160 \times \frac{8}{5} = 256$$

L = 16 m

$$\text{Breadth} = \frac{5}{8} \times 16 = 10 \text{ m}$$

Difference = 16 − 10 = 6 m

57. $X + Y = \frac{1}{60}$

$Y + Z = \frac{1}{90}$

$X + Y + Z = \frac{1}{45}$

$Z = \frac{1}{45} - \frac{1}{60} = \frac{4-3}{180} = \frac{1}{180}$

$Y = \frac{1}{90} + \frac{1}{180} = \frac{2-1}{180} = \frac{1}{180}$

$X = \frac{1}{60} - \frac{1}{180} = \frac{3-1}{180} = \frac{2}{180} = \frac{1}{90}$

$X + Z = \frac{1}{90} + \frac{1}{180} = \frac{2+1}{180} = \frac{3}{180} = \frac{1}{60}$

Time = 60 days.

58. Total employees = 18000,

Total degrees = 360°,

So, $1° = \frac{18000}{360} = 50$ employees

Employees in each company:

C1 = 130 × 50 = 6500

C2 = 8 × 50 = 400

C3 = 95 × 50 = 4750

C4 = 30 × 50 = 1500

C5 = 37 × 50 = 1850

C6 = 60 × 50 = 3000

Statement I:

Average of C1 and C2 = $\frac{6500+400}{2} = 3450$

Average of C3 and C5 = $\frac{4750+1850}{2} = 3300$

Difference = 3450 – 3300 = 150 → Correct

Statement II: C6 = 3000, C4 = 1500

3000 is double of 1500, i.e., 200%, not 50% → Incorrect

Statement III:

C2 : C6 = 400 : 3000 = 2 : 15 → Correct.

59. Let usual speed = v km/hr

Usual time = $\frac{600}{v}$

New speed = $v - 20$

New time = $\frac{600}{v-20}$

Given difference = 8 hours

$\frac{600}{v-20} = \frac{600}{v+8}$

$600v = 600(v - 20) + 8v(v - 20)$

$600v = 600v - 12000 + 8v^2 - 160v$

$0 = 8v^2 - 160v - 12000$

Divide by 8:

$v^2 - 20v - 1500 = 0$

$(v - 50)(v + 30) = 0$

$v = 50$ km/hr.

60. Let principal = P

Interest for 4 years at 3% = $\frac{P \times 3 \times 4}{100} = \frac{12P}{100}$

Interest for 7 years at 9% = $\frac{P \times 9 \times 7}{100} = \frac{63P}{100}$

Total SI = $\frac{12P + 63P}{100} = \frac{75P}{100}$

$\frac{75P}{100} = 42000$

$P = 42000 \times \frac{100}{75}$

P = 56000.

61. The word "obstinate" means stubborn or refusing to change one's opinion. "Headstrong" also means determined to do what one wants despite advice, so it is the closest synonym.

62. "Quarantine" means isolation to prevent spread. Its opposite would be mixing or integrating, which is conveyed by "assimilate," meaning to absorb or integrate.

63. The main clause is negative ("You can't hear..."), so the tag must be positive. With auxiliary "can," the correct tag is "can you."

64. Compliance with the traffic laws is necessary for safe driving : The sentence has all words spelled correctly. In option 1, "necessary" is misspelled as "neccesary." In option 2, "traffic" is misspelled as "trafic." In option 3, "Compliance" is misspelled as "Complience." Hence, option 4 is the only sentence without any spelling errors.

65. "Friendly" means kind and pleasant, while "hostile" means unfriendly or antagonistic, making it the correct antonym.

66. The sentence begins with "Developing basic infrastructure and the production sector," followed by "is the only way to face an economic crisis," and ends with "and the Centre has the responsibility to help states in this respect," forming a meaningful sentence.

67. This idiom means to stop working for the day, which fits the situation where the team stopped after working for hours.

68. I'd like to reach a consensus on the issue before we take a formal vote.: All words are correctly spelled here, unlike other options which contain errors like "rich," "isue," or "conssensus."

69. The paragraph starts with natural fires (Q), then actions of Native Americans (R), followed by change due to settlement (P), and finally modern controlled burns (S), forming a logical chronological sequence.

70. The verb "chewed" requires an adverb to describe how the action is done, so "slowly" is grammatically correct.

71. The correct phrase is "brim with tears," which means the eyes are filled with tears. The preposition "with" correctly completes the expression.

72. The sentence requires a preposition indicating duration of time. The phrase "for thousands of years" correctly expresses a continuous period during which humanity has benefited from the sea. "For" is used with a span of time, whereas "since" is used with a specific starting point. Hence, "for" is the most appropriate choice among the given options.

73. "Took to the streets" is an idiomatic expression meaning to protest or gather publicly. Hence, "took to" is the correct phrasal verb.

74. The main clause is in past tense ("was wearing"), so the tag question should also be in past tense. Since the subject is "she," the correct tag is "wasn't she."

75. The idiom "roll up one's sleeves" means to prepare oneself for hard work or to get ready to tackle a difficult task. In the given situation, the emphasis is on preparing oneself mentally for effort due to upcoming exams, not just the act of studying. Therefore, this idiom fits more accurately than others.

76. The passage mainly discusses the rapid increase in population and its negative effects like unemployment and poverty, highlighting population explosion.

77. The passage clearly states that due to the huge population, India struggles with employment, poverty alleviation, and backwardness. Hence, all three problems are included.

78. The number of people added to India's population every year is equal to Australia's entire population: The statement implies that the increase in India's population annually is as large as the total population of Australia.

79. "Alleviation" means reducing or lessening a problem. Among the options, "eradicate" (to remove or reduce completely) is the closest in meaning.

80. "Extinct" means no longer existing. The opposite is something that still exists or is widespread, which is "prevailing."

81. वाक्य को अर्थपूर्ण बनाने के लिए पहले विचार आता है कि बच्चों के कोमल मन में बातों को गहराई तक पहुँचाने का तरीका क्या हो सकता है (*ii*), फिर कहा जाता है कि कहानियों से बेहतर और क्या हो सकता है (*iv*)। इसके बाद कहानियों का विवरण आता है (*i*) और अंत में पंचतंत्र की ओर बढ़ने की प्रेरणा का उल्लेख किया जाता है (*iii*), जिससे वाक्य का क्रम सही बनता है।

82. 'टुकुर-टुकुर देखना' का अर्थ होता है बिना पलक झपकाए लगातार देखना, अर्थात किसी चीज को ध्यान से या आश्चर्य से घूरते रहना।

83. 'तीनों लोकों में फैले हुए हैं' एक प्रचलित वाक्यांश है, जो स्वर्ग, पृथ्वी और पाताल तीनों लोकों को दर्शाता है, इसलिए 'तीनों' उपयुक्त विशेषण है।

84. 'तौल-तौल कर मुँह से शब्द निकालना' का अर्थ है बहुत सोच-समझकर, सावधानी से बोलना ताकि कोई गलती न हो।

85. 'प्रमाण' शब्द का संधि-विच्छेद 'प्र + मान' होता है, जहाँ 'प्र' उपसर्ग है और 'मान' मूल शब्द है।

86. 'अपना हाथ जगन्नाथ' लोकोक्ति का अर्थ है कि अपना काम स्वयं करना ही सर्वोत्तम होता है, दूसरों पर निर्भर नहीं रहना चाहिए।

87. पहले समय और वातावरण का वर्णन (*i*), फिर व्यक्ति का स्थान (*iii*), फिर घटना (*ii*), और अंत में उसका परिणाम (*iv*) आता है, जिससे वाक्य क्रम सही बनता है।

88. वाक्य में भावनात्मक संज्ञा की आवश्यकता है, 'प्यार से सबका दिल जीत लिया' एक स्वाभाविक और अर्थपूर्ण वाक्य है।

89. 'गणेश' के अनेक पर्याय हैं जैसे गजानन, विनायक, लम्बोदर आदि। यहाँ 'लम्बोदर' सही पर्यायवाची है।

90. 'गुण' शब्द के कई अर्थ होते हैं जैसे विशेषता, गुणधर्म, सद्‌गुण आदि। 'विशेषता' इसका उपयुक्त अनेकार्थी अर्थ है।

91. 'मोक्ष' का अर्थ मुक्ति या छुटकारा होता है, जबकि इसका विलोम 'बंधन' है, जिसका अर्थ बंध जाना या जकड़न है।

92. वाक्य में स्थान सूचक कारक की आवश्यकता है। 'मिठाई के डब्बे में से' सही प्रयोग है, जिससे स्थान और स्रोत दोनों का संकेत मिलता है।

93. 'इत्यादि' शब्द का संधि-विच्छेद 'इति + आदि' होता है, जिसका अर्थ है 'आदि आदि' अर्थात अन्य भी।

94. ठंड के कारण दाँत बजने लगते हैं, जिसे 'दाँत कटकटाना' कहा जाता है। इसलिए यह उपयुक्त क्रिया है।

95. 'रमा' देवी लक्ष्मी का एक नाम है और 'श्री' भी लक्ष्मी का पर्यायवाची है, इसलिए यह सही उत्तर है।

96. गद्यांश का मुख्य विषय जलवायु परिवर्तन के कारण अल्पाइन आइबेक्स की जीवनशैली में बदलाव और उससे जुड़े खतरों को दर्शाना है।

97. गद्यांश में बताया गया है कि बदलाव से शिकार का जोखिम बढ़ रहा है, इसलिए यह कथन गद्यांश के विपरीत है और सही विकल्प है।

98. 'परिवर्तन' का अर्थ बदलाव है, जिसका विलोम 'स्थिरता' होता है, अर्थात बिना परिवर्तन के स्थिति।

99. किसी व्यक्ति, समूह या संस्कृति के जीवन का विशिष्ट तरीका : 'जीवनशैली' का अर्थ जीवन जीने का तरीका होता है, इसलिए यह विकल्प उपयुक्त है।

100. 'प्रमाण' का अर्थ सबूत या evidence होता है, जिसका पर्यायवाची 'साक्ष्य' है।

101. Data privacy is commonly discussed through the privacy–utility trade-off, meaning that collecting more data can improve performance but increases privacy risk, which matches statement 2.

K-anonymity is about ensuring each record is indistinguishable from at least k–1 others based on identifying attributes, so it aligns with the idea of "how many users share a particular attribute," matching statement 1.

L-diversity extends k-anonymity by requiring that sensitive information within each anonymized group is not all the same, i.e., there is diversity in sensitive attributes/values, which corresponds best to statement 3.

102. Exploratory Data Analysis (EDA) is used to discover patterns, relationships, trends, and anomalies without fixing a rigid model first. Because of this open-ended approach, it supports forming multiple plausible hypotheses from the data. In big data contexts, where structure and quality can vary, EDA helps decide what is worth testing further. This flexibility is the key advantage compared to purely confirmatory analysis.

103. A repeater works by regenerating or amplifying signals to overcome attenuation and extend the transmission distance. It does not interpret frames, addresses, or routing information; it simply deals with the raw bit/signal level. That function belongs to the Physical layer of the OSI model.

Hence, a repeater operates only at the Physical layer.

104. The intent of this question is the SQL function that returns the current system date and time as a datetime value without any time zone offset. "GET DATE" corresponds to the commonly used function that provides the current database system timestamp in date-time form. It returns a date-time value rather than a time-zone-aware timestamp. Therefore, among the given choices, option 2 is the correct match.

105. In Python, max() applied to a string returns the character with the greatest value under the character ordering used by Python. For standard ASCII letters and symbols, this corresponds to the highest ASCII code among the characters present.

For example, between 'A' and 'z', the one with the larger code point is returned by max().

Hence, max() is the function that gives the character with the highest ASCII value in a string.

106. Communication system calls in an operating system are used to establish, manage, and terminate communication between processes or systems, especially over networks. These calls include operations such as connecting to remote devices, sending/receiving data, and disconnecting from communication channels. "Attach or detach remote devices" correctly represents such communication-oriented operations, unlike memory allocation or device request functions which belong to other categories.

107. A primary index is an ordered file in which records are arranged based on the primary key, and the index entries are of fixed length. Each entry contains the primary key value and a pointer to the corresponding disk block where the record is stored. This type of index helps in efficient searching because the data file itself is sorted on the primary key.

Hence, the description exactly matches the primary index.

108. In the context of AI bias, many AI models are considered "black boxes" because their internal decision-making process is not easily interpretable. Deepfakes are synthetic media generated using AI but are not a type of bias. K-anonymity is a privacy-preserving technique, not related to bias in models. Therefore, only statement II correctly relates to AI model characteristics in the context of bias discussion.

109. The given Python code checks the condition a >= b. Here, a = 20 and b = 35.

Since 20 is not greater than or equal to 35, the condition evaluates to false.

Therefore, the else block is executed, which prints "No".

The syntax >= is valid in Python, so there is no syntax error.

110. Cyber security laws provide legal remedies against cyber crimes such as hacking, data theft, identity fraud, etc. These remedies include punishments like fines and imprisonment depending on the severity of the offense. Legal frameworks such as IT laws aim to deter cyber crimes through penal provisions. Hence, imprisonment is the appropriate remedy provided by law.

111. Optical Mark Reader is a specialized input device used to detect marks made by pencil or pen on predefined positions of paper, such as in answer sheets or surveys. It works by sensing the presence or absence of marks in specific areas and converting them into digital data. Light pen and digitizer are used for pointing and drawing, while OCR is used for reading printed text, not marks.

112. In Python, the ord() function is used to convert a character into its corresponding integer value based on the Unicode (ASCII for standard characters).

For example, ord('A') returns 65. Other functions like tuple(), dict(), and set() are used for data structure conversions and do not convert characters into integers.

113. The given function is $F(x, y, z) = \Sigma(0, 2, 4, 5, 6)$.

Writing minterms in binary:

$0 \to 000$, $2 \to 010$, $4 \to 100$, $5 \to 101$, $6 \to 110$.

In the K-map, groupings are formed:

Group of four covering minterms 0, 2, 4, 6 gives z' (since $z = 0$).

Pair of minterms 4 and 5 gives $x\ y'$.

Combining these terms gives the simplified expression $F = z' + xy'$.

114. In Python, the strip() function removes whitespace (or specified characters) from both the beginning and end of a string. It does not split strings or perform exponentiation. Functions like split() or title() correspond to the other options, but strip() specifically trims leading and trailing spaces.

115. The DATEDIFF function in SQL is used to find the difference between two dates, typically expressed in terms of a specified unit such as days, months, or years, so statement I is correct.

However, the datepart argument (like DAY, MONTH, YEAR) must be specified explicitly and cannot generally be passed as a variable in standard SQL syntax, making statement II incorrect.

116. In the data link layer, error control ensures reliable transmission of data across a physical link. It detects errors and uses techniques like Automatic Repeat reQuest (ARQ), where erroneous or lost frames are retransmitted. ARQ mechanisms such as Stop-and-Wait, Go-Back-N, and Selective Repeat are used to maintain data integrity. Therefore, retransmission based on error detection is a part of error control.

117. In Python, the append() method is used to add a single element at the end of a list. It modifies the original list by inserting the element as the last item.

For example, if L = [1, 2], then L.append(3) results in [1, 2, 3]. Other methods like index() search elements, sort() arranges elements, and pop() removes elements.

118. The ALU is the component of the CPU responsible for performing arithmetic operations such as addition, subtraction, and logical operations like AND, OR, and shift operations.

It contains the necessary electronic circuitry to carry out binary arithmetic and bit manipulation. Registers store data, the control unit manages execution, and memory buses transfer data, but actual computation is done by the ALU.

119. Artificial Narrow Intelligence refers to systems designed for specific tasks; they may appear intelligent but lack real understanding, matching description 2.

Artificial General Intelligence aims to perform any intellectual task that a human can do, including reasoning and awareness, aligning with description 3.

Super Intelligence represents a level beyond human intelligence, capable of outperforming humans in all aspects, matching description 1.

120. In Python, a tuple is defined using parentheses and elements are separated by commas. When printed, string elements inside a tuple are displayed with quotes.

The given tuple contains a string, an integer, and another string, so the output will be shown with quotes around string elements.

Hence, the correct output is ('Example', 1, 'Tuple').

121. Deadlock prevention involves breaking at least one of the necessary conditions for deadlock. Mutual exclusion is the condition where at least one resource cannot be shared and must be held by only one process at a time. If resources were shareable, multiple processes could use them simultaneously, and deadlock would not occur. Therefore, the condition stating that at least one resource must be non-sharable is mutual exclusion.

122. In an Entity-Relationship Diagram (ERD), a weak entity is represented by a double rectangle. A weak entity does not have a primary key of its own and depends on a strong entity for identification.

Option 1 shows a single rectangle (strong entity), option 2 shows a diamond (relationship), and option 4 shows a double diamond (identifying relationship).

Therefore, the correct notation for a weak entity is the double rectangle shown in option 3.

124. In Python, the file mode *r+* is used to open a file for both reading and writing. The file pointer is positioned at the beginning of the file. It does not truncate the file and allows modification of existing content.

Other modes like *a+* open the file for reading and writing but place the pointer at the end, while *rb* and *ab* are used for binary modes.

125. RISC processors are designed with a simplified instruction set to achieve high performance. They use fixed-length instructions, which makes decoding simpler and faster. They emphasize register-based operations and reduce complexity by avoiding memory-to-memory operations. This contrasts with CISC architectures, which have variable-length instructions and more complex operations.

126. Privacy issues in social media are serious, especially for children who may unknowingly share sensitive personal information. Continuous monitoring helps prevent misuse, cyberbullying, and exposure to harmful content.

The other statements are incorrect because social media addiction can affect academics, fake news can destabilize administration, and misuse of social media can disturb law and order.

127. In register indirect addressing mode, the instruction specifies a register, and the contents of that register give the memory address of the operand. This means the register holds the address rather than the actual data. Indirect mode generally refers to memory-based addressing, while immediate and implied modes do not use such addressing.

128. In HTML (older versions before HTML5), the <body> tag had attributes to define link colors. LINK specifies the color of unvisited links, ALINK specifies the color of a link while it is being clicked (active state), and VLINK specifies the color of a link after it has been clicked and visited. Since the question asks for the color of hyperlinks after the mouse is clicked on them (visited state), the correct attribute is VLINK.

129. An assembler is a program that translates assembly language into machine code, so statement I is correct. Assembly language is closely tied to the hardware architecture, making it machine dependent, so statement II is also correct.

Hence, both statements are correct.

130. In one-address instruction format, the accumulator (AC) is implied as one of the operands, and operations are performed using it.

For example, instructions like ADD X assume AC = AC + X.

Thus, the accumulator is implicitly used for data manipulation, making one-address instructions the correct answer.

131. Under the Digital Personal Data Protection Act, 2023, a "child" is defined as an individual who has not completed eighteen years of age. "Digital personal data" refers to data in digital form, not physical form. "Chairperson" specifically refers to the chairperson of the Data Protection Board. "Data" includes representation of information, not only facts. Therefore, option 1 is correct.

132. Repositioning, also known as file seek, changes the file pointer to a different location without actually reading or writing data. It only updates the pointer position in the file, so no actual input/output operation is required.

Other operations like reading, deleting, or truncating involve actual disk I/O.

133. The instruction register (IR) holds the instruction that is currently being executed by the CPU. The control unit fetches the instruction from memory and stores it in the IR, then decodes and executes it. The accumulator stores intermediate results, the program counter holds the next instruction address, and the memory data register holds data being transferred.

134. In Python dictionaries, values can be repeated because multiple keys can map to the same value. However, keys must be unique to ensure proper identification and retrieval of values. If duplicate keys are used, the last assigned value overwrites the previous one.

135. The scheduler selects which process should run next, but the dispatcher is responsible for actually allocating the CPU to that process. It performs context switching, switching from the current process to the selected process, and starts its execution.

Hence, the dispatcher is the component that gives control of the CPU to the chosen process.

136. Impact printers work by physically striking an ink ribbon against paper to print characters. A dot matrix printer uses pins to strike the ribbon and form characters as a pattern of dots. Inkjet and laser printers are non-impact printers that use spray or laser technology, and thermal printers use heat, so they are not impact printers.

137. A point-to-point connection provides a direct and dedicated communication link between exactly two devices. It is not shared with other devices, so it is not a time-shared connection. Time-sharing occurs in multipoint connections where multiple devices share the same link.

Hence, only statement I is correct.

138. In Direct Memory Access (DMA), burst transfer mode allows a block of data (multiple memory words) to be transferred continuously without interruption. During this transfer, the CPU is temporarily halted while the DMA controller takes control of the bus. Cycle stealing transfers one word at a time, not a continuous block.

139. First Normal Form (1NF) requires that all attributes in a relation must have atomic (indivisible) values. It does not allow nested relations or repeating groups within tuples. Therefore, relations cannot contain other relations as attribute values, ensuring a flat table structure.

140. In HTML, the <HR> tag supports attributes such as SIZE (thickness), WIDTH (length), and ALIGN (alignment). The attribute "SHADE" is not a standard attribute for the <HR> tag.

Hence, it is the correct answer.

141. Intellectual Property Rights (IPR) provide legal protection to creators and inventors for their creations, inventions, designs, and artistic works. It ensures that the owner can gain recognition and financial benefits from their work. Patents and copyrights are specific types of IPR, but the general concept covering all such protections is intellectual property rights.

142. A significant portion of e-waste from developed countries is exported to developing nations like India, where informal recycling sectors recover valuable metals such as copper, iron, silicon, nickel, and gold.

Due to lower labor costs and less strict environmental regulations, such activities are commonly carried out in countries like India.

143. In pandas, a DataFrame is a two-dimensional, labeled data structure with rows and columns. Each column can contain data of different types, making it suitable for handling structured data. A Series is one-dimensional, while missing data and iteration are concepts, not data structures.

144. A semaphore is an integer variable used for process synchronization and is accessed only through atomic operations such as wait() and signal(). The signal() operation increments the semaphore value and can wake up a waiting process.

Other options like lock() or acquire() are not standard semaphore operations.

145. One of the major challenges in IoT adoption is security. IoT devices are often connected to networks and may be vulnerable to cyber-attacks, data breaches, and unauthorized access. Ensuring secure communication, authentication, and data protection is critical. Deepfake and black box relate to AI, while cloud storage is a supporting technology, not a challenge.

146. The <head> tag in HTML acts as a container for metadata and information about the webpage. It includes elements such as <title>, <meta>, <link>, and <style>, which define the page's title, character encoding, styles, and other settings.

The <body> contains visible content, while <html> is the root element.

Therefore, <head> is the correct container for page-related information.

147. Irreparable or discarded electronic devices such as computers, mobiles, and other electronic goods are termed electronic waste or e-waste.

These include obsolete or damaged electronic items that are no longer usable. E-waste contains hazardous materials and requires proper disposal and recycling methods.

148. In pandas, a Series is a one-dimensional labeled array capable of holding data of any type such as integers, floats, strings, or Python objects. Each element in a Series has an associated index label. DataFrames are two-dimensional, while missing data and iteration are concepts, not data structures.

149. The E-waste (Management) Rules, 2016 of India classify e-waste into categories including IT and telecommunication equipment and consumer electrical and electronics.

These categories include items containing hazardous substances such as fluorescent materials (like in lamps) and mercury (used in various electronic components).

Hence, both statements are correct.

150. In HTML, comments are written using the syntax <!-- comment -->. It begins with <!-- and ends with -->. These comments are ignored by the browser and are used to explain code.

Among the options, only option 4 correctly represents this structure.

151. An ImportError in Python occurs when the interpreter is unable to locate the specified module or library in the available paths. Statement III correctly states that Python could not find the pandas library in the list of available libraries. Statement I is incorrect because it says Python could find pandas, which would not produce an error. Statement II is incorrect because pandas does not search for Python libraries.

152. In pandas, the set_index() method is used to set one or more existing columns as the index of a DataFrame. It can take a single column name or a list of column names and returns a new DataFrame with the updated index. Other options are not valid methods for re-indexing in pandas.

153. In Python, identifiers are names used for variables, functions, classes, etc. They can contain letters, digits, and underscores, but they cannot start with a digit and cannot be reserved keywords. There is no strict maximum length restriction, so using underscore is allowed and correct.

154. In XML, element names must follow certain rules: they cannot start with numbers or punctuation, cannot contain spaces, and must not start with the string "xml" (in any case variation). They must begin with a letter or underscore and can include letters, digits, hyphens, and periods.

Therefore, option 3 is correct.

155. Intellectual Property Rights are legal rights granted to the creator or inventor of an original work or invention. These rights allow them to control the use of their creation and benefit financially or gain recognition. Employees, sellers, or buyers do not automatically receive these rights unless transferred legally.

156. In Python, the # symbol is used to write single-line comments. Any text written after # on the same line is ignored by the Python interpreter. This is useful for explaining code or temporarily disabling parts of it. Symbols like *, !, or // are not used for comments in Python.

157. In pandas, the merge() function is used to combine multiple DataFrames based on common columns or indices, similar to database joins. It allows combining data both column-wise and row-wise depending on the join type. Operations like SUM, GROUP BY, and SELECT are related to aggregation or querying, not merging tables.

158. Intellectual Property Rights are granted for a limited or fixed period depending on the type of intellectual property. For example, patents and copyrights have defined durations after which the rights expire and the work enters the public domain.

Therefore, IPR is not permanent but valid for a certain period.

159. Exposure variability in e-waste management depends largely on the type of e-waste being processed. Different electronic items contain different hazardous materials such as lead, mercury, or cadmium, leading to varying levels of exposure. Thus, the type of e-waste is a key factor affecting exposure variability.

160. In HTML, the <BR> tag is used to insert a line break in the text. It does not require a closing tag and is used to move the text to the next line.

Other options like <B> are used for bold text, while <BL> and <L> are not valid HTML tags.

161. The CEILING function in SQL returns the smallest integer that is greater than or equal to a given numeric expression. For example, CEILING(4.3) gives 5.

FLOOR gives the largest integer less than or equal to the number, ROUND rounds to nearest value, and ABS returns absolute value.

162. Belady's anomaly refers to the situation where increasing the number of page frames leads to more page faults. This anomaly occurs in FIFO page replacement but not in stack algorithms like LRU.

LRU always shows non-increasing page faults with more frames, so it does not suffer from Belady's anomaly, while FIFO does.

163. A string in programming is a sequence of characters which can include letters (alphabets), numbers (digits), and symbols (special characters).

Therefore, all three components—letters, numbers, and symbols—can be part of a string.

164. In SQL, the * symbol is used with the SELECT command to retrieve all columns (attributes) of a table.

For example, SELECT * FROM table_name; returns all the attribute values of selected tuples.

Other symbols like #, %, and : are not used for this purpose.

165. UTF-8 is a widely used Unicode encoding scheme in computer science. It encodes characters using one to four bytes and is compatible with ASCII.

It is commonly used for text representation across systems and the internet. Other options like UTF-17, UTF-61, and UTF-35 are not standard encoding schemes.

166. Extensions such as .txt, .py, .csv represent types of files that store data in text format. Python files (.py) and CSV files are also text-based, meaning they store human-readable characters.
These are not editors or encoding systems but types of text files.

167. The given logic symbol is similar to an OR gate but with an additional curved line at the input side. This extra curved line is the distinguishing feature of the XOR (Exclusive-OR) gate. An OR gate has only a single curved input line, while XOR has two. Also, there is no inversion bubble at the output, so it is not NOR or NAND.
Therefore, the symbol represents an Exclusive-OR (XOR) gate, which gives output 1 only when the inputs are different.

168. In a compiler, the semantic analysis phase checks for type correctness and gathers type-related information. It ensures variables are declared, types are compatible, and operations are valid. This information is stored in the symbol table or syntax tree for later stages like intermediate code generation. Lexical analysis only tokenizes input, and syntax analysis checks grammar structure.

169. Numbers that include a decimal point are referred to as fractional or floating-point numbers in programming. They represent real values such as 3.14 or 2.5. Integers do not have decimal points, while complex and imaginary numbers involve additional components beyond simple decimals.

170. The set difference operation R-S returns all tuples that are present in relation R but not in relation S. It removes any tuples that appear in both sets, leaving only the distinct elements of R. Intersection gives common tuples, union combines all tuples, and Cartesian product pairs every tuple of R with S.

171. Aggregate functions in SQL operate on a set of values and return a single value, such as COUNT, SUM, MAX, etc. CROSS PRODUCT is not an aggregate function; it is a relational operation (Cartesian product) that combines rows from two tables.
Therefore, it is not an aggregate function.

172. Unicode is a universal character encoding standard designed to represent characters from all writing systems of the world. It assigns a unique code point to each character, independent of platform, program, or language. This ensures consistent representation of text across different systems and devices.

173. ASCII is a limited character encoding scheme that primarily supports English characters. It can handle only one language (English) or at most a very few variations (like extended ASCII handling limited characters). Hence, it cannot represent most world languages, which shows its limitation.

174. In DBMS, an entity set is a collection of similar entities that share the same attributes. For example, a set of all students in a database forms an entity set. An entity type defines the structure, while an entity set is the actual collection of entities of that type.

175. In Python, the # symbol is used to add comments. Comments are ignored by the interpreter and are used to explain the code for better readability and understanding. Other symbols like *, –, and : are not used for commenting.

176. During a context switch, the operating system kernel saves the state (context) of the currently running process into its Process Control Block (PCB) so that it can resume execution later. This includes registers, program counter, etc. Also, context switching consumes CPU time without performing any useful computation for user processes, so it is considered pure overhead. Hence, both statements are correct.

177. The AND gate produces an output of 1 only when both inputs are 1, which matches statement I. In Boolean algebra, the AND operation is represented using multiplication (•), which is similar to the multiplication symbol in arithmetic, confirming statement II. Therefore, both statements are correct.

178. In the relational model, foreign keys are used to represent relationships between tables. For a one-to-many relationship, the primary key of the "one" side is stored as a foreign key in the "many" side table. For a one-to-one relationship, a foreign key can be placed in either of the related tables. Many-to-many relationships require a separate relation and cannot be represented using a single foreign key directly.

179. Referential integrity ensures that a foreign key in one relation correctly refers to a primary key in another relation. It maintains consistency between related tables by preventing invalid references. This constraint ensures that relationships between tuples in different tables remain valid.

180. In operating systems, the "New" state refers to a process that is being created, so I-3 is correct. The "Running" state means the CPU is executing instructions, so II-2 is correct. The "Ready" state indicates the process is waiting to be assigned to the CPU, so III-1 is correct.

181. In SQL, the concatenation operator is represented by || (two vertical bars). It is used to combine two strings into one.

For example, 'Hello' || 'World' results in HelloWorld. Other symbols like ++, quotes, or ## are not used for string concatenation in standard SQL.

182. Unguided media refers to wireless communication where electromagnetic waves travel without a physical medium, so statement I is correct.

These waves can propagate through space in different ways, including ground propagation, sky propagation, and line-of-sight transmission. Therefore, statement II is also correct, making both statements correct.

183. λ = propagation speed × period:

The wavelength (λ) of a signal is calculated as the product of propagation speed (v) and the time period (T) of the signal. Since period is the inverse of frequency, this formula is correct.

Other options involving addition or multiplication with frequency directly in that form are incorrect.

184. A sine wave in data communication is primarily described using parameters such as amplitude, frequency, and phase. Wavelength is derived from these parameters and is not considered a fundamental parameter for describing a sine wave in signal analysis. Hence, wavelength is not a basic descriptive parameter.

185. The LIKE operator in SQL is used in the WHERE clause to search for a specified pattern in a column. It uses wildcard characters such as % (for multiple characters) and _ (for a single character).

Other operators like IN, IS NULL, and OR serve different purposes and are not used for pattern matching.

186. In SQL, schema evolution operations include commands like CREATE, ALTER, and DROP. The DROP command is used to remove a schema. When the RESTRICT option is used with DROP, the schema will be dropped only if it contains no objects such as tables or views. If elements exist, the operation is prevented.

Therefore, DROP is the correct command.

187. CSV (Comma-Separated Values) files store tabular data in plain text format, where each value is separated by a delimiter such as a comma or sometimes a semicolon. These files are widely used for data exchange and can be opened in spreadsheet software. Hence, Comma-Separated-Values is the correct option.

188. Unicode can be represented using various encoding formats, and UTF-8 is the most commonly used format. UTF-8 uses an 8-bit (byte) unit for encoding characters and is backward compatible with ASCII. It can represent all Unicode characters using one to four bytes.

Hence, 8-bit format is correct.

189. Coaxial cables are categorized using RG (Radio Guide or Radio Grade) ratings such as RG-58, RG-59, etc. These ratings define characteristics like impedance and shielding. Fiber-optic and twisted-pair cables are not classified using RG ratings. Therefore, coaxial cable is correct.

190. System calls related to process control include operations like create process, terminate process, and wait operations. The "wait for time" or delay operation is associated with controlling process execution and scheduling. Therefore, it falls under process control system calls.

191. According to Jean Piaget's theory of cognitive development, the pre-operational stage occurs between 2 to 7 years of age. In this stage, children begin to use symbols, language, and imagination, but their thinking is still intuitive and not yet logical. The sensori-motor stage is from birth to 2 years, concrete operational is 7 to 11 years, and formal operational begins from around 11 years onward.

192. The Government of India adopted the National Policy for Empowerment of Women in the year 2001. This policy aimed at advancing, developing, and empowering women in all spheres of life by creating an environment for equal opportunities and participation in social, economic, and political activities.

193. Learning by doing, where students actively engage in activities, is a key feature of the student-centered approach. In this approach, learners participate actively in constructing knowledge through experience and interaction. The teacher-centered approach focuses more on lectures and passive learning, so it does not align with this concept.

194. Peer assessment refers to the evaluation of a student's work by fellow students. In this method, classmates assess each other's responses and performance, providing feedback. It helps develop critical thinking, responsibility, and collaborative learning among students.

195. The 71st Constitutional Amendment Act, 1992 added three languages—Konkani, Manipuri, and Nepali—to the Eighth Schedule of the Indian Constitution. Therefore, among the given options, Nepali is the correct answer.

196. Art education includes both visual/tangible arts such as painting, sculpture, and drawing, as well as performing arts like music, dance, and drama. It focuses on creativity, expression, and appreciation of artistic forms. Therefore, both visual arts and performing arts are included in art education.

197. In the subject-centered approach, teaching and learning are strictly based on the prescribed syllabus or textbooks. Both teacher and students follow the content without deviation, focusing mainly on subject matter rather than learner needs or experiences. Hence, activities remain confined to the textbook content.

198. Jean Piaget proposed four stages of cognitive development—Sensorimotor, Pre-operational, Concrete operational, and Formal operational. These stages describe how children's thinking and reasoning abilities develop over time. Thus, these stages belong to cognitive development.

199. In the classification of intellectual disability based on IQ levels, profound mental retardation corresponds to IQ below 20, mild mental retardation corresponds to IQ range 50–75, and severe mental retardation corresponds to IQ range 20–34.

Therefore, the correct matching is I-2, II-3, III-1.

200. A diorama is a three-dimensional model that represents a scene, such as historical events, natural environments, or cityscapes. It is used as an educational tool to provide a realistic and visual understanding of concepts. Unlike globes or realia, a diorama specifically depicts scenes in a structured display.

Previous Paper (Solved)

DSSSB—TRAINED GRADUATE TEACHER (TGT) COMPUTER SCIENCE EXAM, 2023*

SECTION-A

GENERAL INTELLIGENCE AND REASONING ABILITY

1. Four number-pairs have been given, out of which three are alike in some manner and one is different. Select the one that is different.

A. 67-469 B. 69-483
C. 81-567 D. 87-609

2. Read the given statements and conclusions carefully. Assuming that the information given in the statements is true, even if it appears to be at variance with commonly known facts, decide which of the given conclusions logically follow(s) from the statements.

Statements:

(*a*) All troupes are flowers.
(*b*) All flowers are jungles.
(*c*) All jungles are gangs.

Conclusions:

I. Some gangs are jungles.
II. Some jungles are flowers.
III. All troupes are jungles.

A. Only conclusions II and III follow.
B. Only conclusions I and II follow.
C. All the conclusions I, II and III follow.
D. Only conclusion III follows.

3. If

A + B means A is the brother of B,
A – B means A is the sister of B, and
A × B means A is the father of B,

then how is P related to S in the expression 'P × Q – R + S'?

A. P is the father of S B. P is the son of S
C. P is the brother of S D. P is the uncle of S

4. Select the figure from among the given options that can replace the question mark (?) in the following series.

A. C.

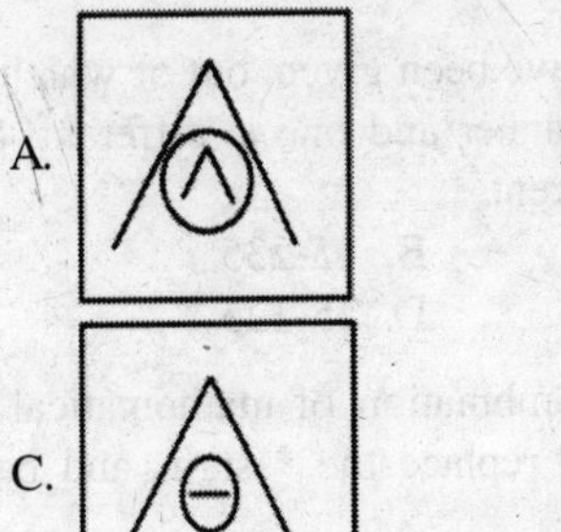

B. D.

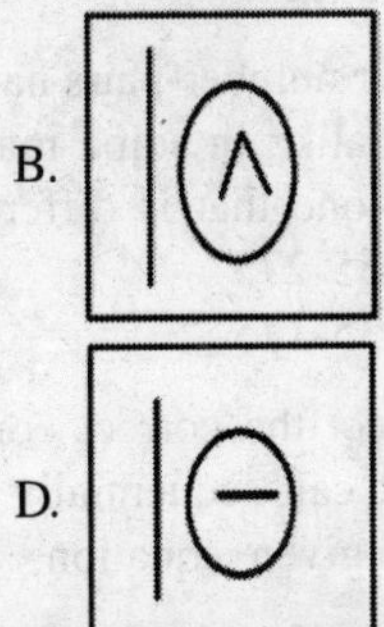

5. Read the given statement and conclusions carefully. Assuming that the information given in the statement is true, even if it appears to be at variance with commonly known facts, decide which of the given conclusions logically follow(s) from the statement.

Statement:

Health is the best wealth of an individual.

Conclusions:

I. People do not think too much about health while making efforts to earn.
II. Wealth is of no use without health.

A. Only conclusion I follows.
B. Either conclusion I or II follows.
C. Only conclusion II follows.
D. Both I and II follow.

6. Which two signs should be interchanged to make the following equation correct?

105 ÷ 21 + 67 – 64 × 16 = 287

A. ÷ and × B. × and +
C. + and – D. × and –

7. ABCDEFGHIJKLMNOPQRSTUVWXYZ

If the 1st, 3rd, 5th, 8th, 12th, 15th and 18th letters of the English alphabet (given above) are chosen to form a meaningful word (name of a disease), which letter will come in the middle of all? Each letter must be used and only once.

A. A B. E
C. C D. L

* Exam held on 25/06/2023.

8. Four letter-cluster pairs have been given, out of which three are alike in some manner and one is different. Select the one that is different.
A. INSPIRING : KMUOKQKMI
B. CABALETTA : ABZBJFRUY
C. FACULTIES : HZETNSKDU
D. ABANDONED : CACMFNPDF

9. Ramesh secured the 15th position from the top and is just 3 positions behind of his best friend Arvind in a class of 50 students. What will be the rank of Arvind from the bottom?
A. 36th B. 40th
C. 39th D. 38th

10. Four number-pairs have been given, out of which three are alike in some manner and one is different. Select the one that is different.
A. 55-275 B. 45-235
C. 35-175 D. 25-125

11. Select the correct combination of mathematical signs that can sequentially replace the * signs and balance the given equation.

37 * 42 * 21 * 37 * 67 * 44

A. ×, +, ÷, –, = B. –, ÷, +, ×, =
C. ÷, +, ×, –, = D. +, ÷, ×, –, =

12. A question is given followed by two statements labelled I and II. Identify which of the statements is/are sufficient to answer the question.

Question: Who is the shortest of all?

Statements:

I. Sachin is taller than Mohan and shorter than Vipin.
II. Devika is shorter than Gangan.

A. Both the statements I and II are insufficient to answer the question.
B. Either statement I alone or statement II alone is sufficient to answer the question.
C. Statement II alone is sufficient to answer the question, while statement I alone is not sufficient to answer the question.
D. Statement I alone is sufficient to answer the question, while statement II alone is not sufficient to answer the question.

13. Read the given statement and courses of action carefully. Assuming that the information given in the statement is true, even if it appears to be at variance with commonly known facts, decide which of the given courses of action logically follow(s) from the statement.

Statement: In the last few years, the condition of roads in the state has continuously deteriorated.

Courses of Action:

I. State Government should take strict action against all the employees of Road Development Authority.
II. State Government should instruct Road Development Authorities to take regular inspection and necessary action to maintain roads.

A. Only II follows. B. Only I follows.
C. Both I and II follow. D. Either I or II follows.

14. How many even numbers are immediately followed by an odd number but not immediately preceded by an even number in the following series?

3 4 3 2 5 6 7 4 3 4 5 6 7 8 9 6 5 4
3 2 2 4 5 6 7 8 9 9 7 6 0 7 6 5 4 3

A. 13 B. 14
C. 12 D. 11

15. What approximate value should come in place of the question mark (?) in the following equation?

56.43 ÷ 27.89 – 67.78 + 98.19 × 13.67 = ?

A. 1235 B. 1238
C. 1123 D. 1306

16. Select the option that contains figure X as its part.

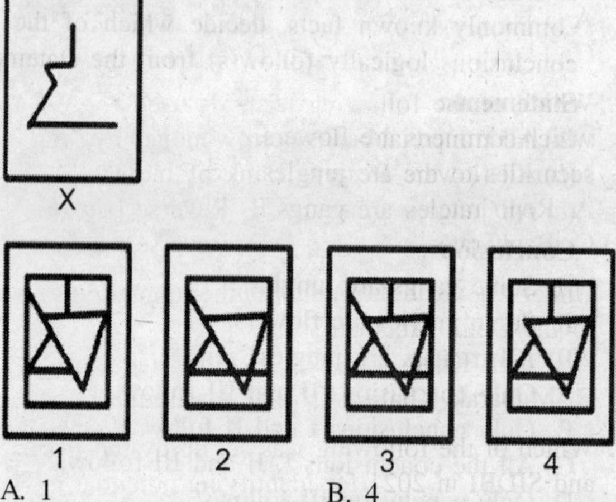

A. 1 B. 4
C. 3 D. 2

17. In the early morning after sunrise, the football coach of Argentina is discussing the strategies for the next match with Messi on the ground such that the coach's shadow falls exactly in front of Messi. In which direction is Messi facing?
A. South B. North
C. East D. West

18. There are six persons. P, Q, R, S, T and U. T is older than no one. S is older than P. Q is younger than P. U is older than T but younger than Q. S is older than R. Who is the third youngest among all?
A. Q B. P
C. R D. U

19. Select the option with the second term related to the first term in the same way as the second term is related to the first term in the given pair.

MATTER : BNUUSF

A. HOTELS : PIFTUM B. HOTELS : PIFUTM
C. HOTELS : PIFUMT D. HOTELS : PFIUTM

20. Select the correct mirror image of the given figure when the mirror is placed at the right side.

A.  B. 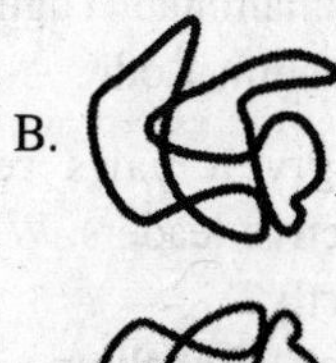

C.  D. 

GENERAL AWARENESS

21. Which ministry has launched the Digital India Awards?
A. Ministry of Electronics and Information Technology
B. Ministry of Education
C. Ministry of Information and Broadcasting
D. Ministry of Commerce and Industry

22. How many scientists were awarded the Shanti Swarup Bhatnagar Award, 2021 for Science and Technology?
A. 14 B. 8
C. 11 D. 5

23. Which of the following terms is used for the rate at which commercial banks borrow money by selling their securities to the Reserve Bank of India?
A. Repo rate B. Reverse bank rate
C. Bank rate D. Reverse repo rate

24. Under whose rule were the southern kingdoms annexed to the Delhi Sultanate?
A. Ulugh Khan B. Shershah Suri
C. Mubarak Khalji D. Nasiruddin Khan

25. Which of the following was set up by the Exim Bank and SIDBI in 2021 for identifying potential mid-sized and small companies as India's new champions in exports?
A. Prabasi Tarakki fund
B. National Investment fund
C. Ubharte Sitaare fund
D. Stand Up India scheme

26. As of 2022, which of the following states has the highest number of assembly constituencies?
A. Maharashtra B. Gujarat
C. Uttar Pradesh D. Tamil Nadu

27. What is the minimum age requirement, as prescribed by the Constitution, to become a member of a Panchayat?
A. 18 years B. 28 years
C. 36 years D. 21 years

28. Which of the following is a vector borne disease?
A. Diabetes B. Breast Cancer
C. Covid-19 D. Malaria

29. Who among the following won the Golden Boot award during the 2022 FIFA World Cup awards?
A. Lionel Messi B. Kylian Mbappe
C. Enzo Fernandez D. Emiliano Martinez

30. The final match of Ranji Trophy, 2022 was played between which two teams?
A. Rajasthan and Maharashtra
B. Haryana and Punjab
C. Mumbai and Madhya Pradesh
D. Delhi and Himachal Pradesh

31. With reference to the constitutional provisions regarding Rajya Sabha, which of the following statements is correct?
A. The Attorney General of India is the ex-officio chairman of the Rajya Sabha.
B. The Prime Minister of India is the ex-officio chairman of the Rajya Sabha.
C. The Vice-President of India is the ex-officio chairman of the Rajya Sabha.
D. The President of India is the ex-officio chairman of the Rajya Sabha.

32. Which of the following man-made objects was the first one to cross the heliosphere of our solar system?
A. Sputnik-1 B. New Horizons
C. Messenger-1 D. Voyager-1

33. Which of the following aims to create a competent civil service, rooted in Indian ethos, with a shared understanding of India's priorities, working in harmonisation for effective and efficient public service delivery?
A. Mission Karmayogi
B. Rashtriya Gokul Mission
C. Atmanirbhar Bharat Abhiyan
D. Samarth Scheme

34. Who among the following is NOT amongst the Trinity of Carnatic music?
A. Tyagaraja B. Syama Sastri
C. Tenali Raman D. Muthuswami Dikshitar

35. Who among the following planned to launch a military expedition to bring the Khurasan region under Delhi Sultanate's submission?

A. Muhammad Tughluq B. Ghiyasuddin Khan
C. Ibrahim Lodi D. Alauddin Khalji

36. The given pairs represent movements with the respective leaders. Which of these pairs is/are matched correctly?

I. Koya Rebellion — Tomma Dora
II. Pabna Peasant Uprising — Bhagirath Manjhi
III. Kharwar Uprising — Shambhunath Pal

A. Only II B. II and III
C. I and III D. Only I

37. The temples at Khajuraho, a UNESCO World Heritage Site, were built during the reign of which of the following dynasties?

A. Maurya B. Chandela
C. Pallava D. Kakatiya

38. Terms such as 'Pada Bheda', 'Chalis' and 'Bhramaris' are associated with the techniques of which of the following dance forms?

A. Odissi B. Kathakali
C. Ghoomar D. Manipuri

39. Which of the following Indian monuments is NOT a UNESCO World Heritage Site?

A. Red Fort B. Char Minar
C. Taj Mahal D. Humayun's Tomb

40. In terms of power generation from renewable sources, which of the following sectors has the highest installed capacity in India as per the Annual Report, 2021-22 of the Ministry of New and Renewable Energy, Government of India?

A. Small hydro B. Wind
C. Bio-energy D. Solar

ARITHMETICAL AND NUMERICAL ABILITY

41. The ratio of spirit and water in solution A is 3 : 4, and the ratio of spirit and water in solution B is 5 : 9. Later, 5 L of A is mixed with 6 L of B. In 462 mL of the resulting solution, how much water (in mL) should be added so that the ratio of spirit and water in it becomes 1 : 2?

A. 87 B. 182
C. 78 D. 178

42. When 3336, 4188 and 5679 are divided by a 2-digit number p, the remainder in each case is q. What is the value of $(p - q)$?

A. 13 B. 3
C. 1 D. 11

43. A is 60% more than B. C is 55% more than the difference between A and B. If A is decreased by 40% and C is increased by $33\frac{1}{3}\%$, then C is what percentage more than A (correct to one decimal place)?

A. 22.6% B. 29.2%
C. 28.5% D. 25.4%

44. Study the following graph and answer the question.

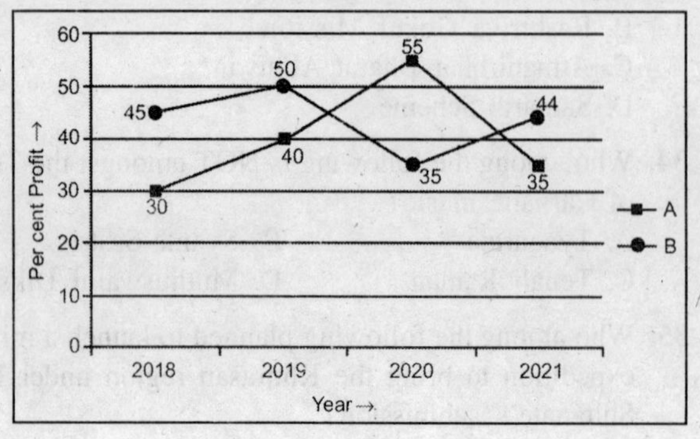

$$\text{Per cent profit} = \frac{\text{Income} - \text{Expenditure}}{\text{Expenditure}} \times 100$$

Profit = Income – Expenditure

In 2018, if the expenditure of the company B is ₹ 300 crores and the income of company A is 390 crores, then by what percentage was the profit of company B more than that of A in that year?

A. 40% B. 55%
C. 50% D. 42%

45. The volume of a right circular cylinder of height 32 cm and base diameter 36 cm is equal to the volume of a right circular cone of height 24 cm. What is the curved surface area (in cm²) of the cone?

A. $432\sqrt{13}\pi$ B. $288\sqrt{13}\pi$
C. $240\sqrt{15}\pi$ D. $360\sqrt{15}\pi$

46. The value of

$$\left(5\frac{1}{9} - 7\frac{7}{8} \div 9\frac{9}{20}\right) \div 1.\overline{2} - \left(5\frac{1}{4} \div \frac{3}{7} \text{ of } \frac{1}{4} \times \frac{2}{7}\right) \times \frac{3}{14} + \frac{3}{4}$$

is:

A. $2\frac{1}{2}$ B. $1\frac{1}{4}$
C. $2\frac{1}{3}$ D. $1\frac{1}{3}$

47. P varies directly as Q and inversely as R. When Q = 2.7 and R = 1.6, then P = 4.5. What is the value of R when P = 6 and Q = 15?

A. 5 B. $\frac{20}{3}$
C. 10 D. $\frac{5}{2}$

48. When Savita sells 46 articles for ₹ 2,070, she suffers a loss of 10%. To earn a profit 20%, she should sell 46 articles for:

A. ₹ 2,852 B. ₹ 2,668
C. ₹ 2,760 D. ₹ 2,990

49. An article is sold for ₹ 1,683 after giving three successive discounts of x%, 10% and 12% on its marked price of ₹ 2,500. If a single discount of $3x$% is given on the same marked price, then the selling price (in ₹) of the article will be:

A. 1,450 B. 1,300
C. 1,375 D. 1,150

50. What is the area (in cm^2) of a circle that circumscribes a triangle with sides 28 cm, 45 cm and 53 cm?

A. 702.25 π B. 729 π
C. 784 π D. 506.25 π

51. Study the following table and answer the question:

Production and Export of cement by companies A and B from 2017 to 2020 (in million tonnes)

Year	Company			
	A		B	
	Production	Export	Production	Export
2017	250	170	320	190
2018	340	275	360	280
2019	370	220	425	320
2020	450	245	470	275

The total export of cement by both the companies in 2017 and 2019 is what percentage less than the total production of cement by the two companies in 2018 and 2020 (correct to one decimal place)?

A. 45.5% B. 44.4%
C. 43.2% D. 43.8%

52. A man covers a distance of 180 km at a speed of 45 km/h, the next 150 km at a speed of 50 km/h and the next 120 km at a speed of x km/h. If his average speed for the whole journey is $47\frac{7}{19}$ km/h, then what is the value of x?

A. 48 B. 52
C. 42 D. 40

53. The height of a cylinder inscribed in a sphere is 1.2 times the radius of the sphere. The radius of the sphere is 10 cm, and the volume of the cylinder is x% of the volume of the sphere. The value of x is:

A. 58.2 B. 56.4
C. 60.4 D. 57.6

54. A loan of ₹ 13,500 is to be paid back in two equal annual instalments. If the rate of interest is 16% p.a. compounded annually, then what is the total interest paid in this instalment scheme?

A. ₹ 3,300
B. ₹ 3,320
C. ₹ 3,360
D. ₹ 3,350

55. A and B started a business by investing their capitals in the ratio $\frac{5}{8}:\frac{3}{5}$. After 6 months, A reduced his capital by 20% and B increased his capital by 50%. After 1 year, the share of A in the total profit was ₹ 15 lakhs. The total profit (in ₹ lakhs) was:

A. 35 B. 27
C. 40 D. 30

56. The speed of a boat going upstream is 40% of its speed going downstream. It takes a total time of $4\frac{2}{3}$ hours in going 15 km upstream and the same distance downstream. What is the speed (in km/h) of the boat in still water?

A. $8\frac{3}{8}$ B. $7\frac{7}{8}$
C. $7\frac{1}{2}$ D. $8\frac{1}{2}$

57. Pipes A and B can fill a tank in 18 hours and 27 hours, respectively. Pipe C is an outlet pipe. When all the three pipes are opened for 15 hours, then $\frac{5}{36}$ part of the tank is filled. How much time (in hours) will C alone take to empty one-third of the tank?

A. 4 B. 3
C. 6 D. 5

58. In a test consisting of 150 questions, a candidate correctly answers 60% of the first 90 questions. What percentage of the remaining questions does he need to answer correctly so that he has 64% of all the questions answered correctly in the test?

A. 68% B. 72%
C. 70% D. 66%

59. If $x = \sqrt{19+4\sqrt{15}} - \sqrt{19-4\sqrt{15}}$, then what is the value of x?

A. $2\sqrt{5}$ B. 4
C. 2 D. $8\sqrt{15}$

60. A certain sum invested at 10% p.a. simple interest amounts to ₹ 9,417 in 4 years 4 months. What will be the amount of the same sum at $12\frac{1}{2}$% p.a. in $2\frac{2}{5}$ years at simple interest?

A. ₹ 8,641
B. ₹ 8,531
C. ₹ 8,541
D. ₹ 8,631

ENGLISH LANGUAGE AND COMPREHENSION

61. Select the most appropriate ANTONYM of the given word.

Predictable

A. Foreseeable B. Improbable
C. Certain D. Expected

62. Select the most appropriate meaning of the given idiom.

Miss the boat

A. Miss a chance
B. Narrow escape
C. Forget something important
D. Miss travelling by boat

63. Sentences of a paragraph are given below in jumbled order. Arrange the sentences in the correct order to form a meaningful and coherent paragraph.

(*a*) Two IAF MiG fighters from the Adampur base crashed following a mid-air collision.
(*b*) As a result, a fire broke out in four houses, and four boys playing in a field were wounded when the debris fell on them.
(*c*) The other fighter plane crashed in the fields of Chansu Jattan.
(*d*) According to reports, one plane crashed near Pensara.

A. (*a*), (*b*), (*c*), (*d*) B. (*d*), (*c*), (*b*), (*a*)
C. (*a*), (*c*), (*b*), (*d*) D. (*a*), (*d*), (*c*), (*b*)

64. Parts of the following sentence have been given as options. Select the option that contains an error.

It is so refreshing to walk through the beach early in the morning.

A. refreshing to walk B. early in the morning
C. through the beach D. It is so

65. Select the option that can be used as a one-word substitute for the given phrase.

A collection of weapons and military equipment

A. Arsenal B. Archive
C. Apiary D. Asylum

66. Select the most appropriate option to fill in the blanks.

My injured _____ will ______ soon.

A. heel; heel B. heal; heel
C. heel; heal D. heal; heal

67. Sentences of a paragraph are given below in jumbled order. Arrange the sentences in the correct order to form a meaningful and coherent paragraph.

(*a*) We can request the public library to send us all the books that they will be replacing this year.
(*b*) However, I think, I have solution to this problem.
(*c*) That means, no books till the next academic session.
(*d*) Yesterday I was told that we had exhausted our library funds for this year.

A. (*c*), (*b*), (*a*), (*d*) B. (*d*), (*b*), (*c*), (*a*)
C. (*a*), (*b*), (*c*), (*d*) D. (*d*), (*c*), (*b*), (*a*)

68. Select the most appropriate option that can substitute the underlined word in the given sentence. If there is no need to substitute it, select 'No substitution required'.

Post covid, international air travel is <u>hopping</u> back to normalcy.

A. limping
B. No substitution required
C. faltering
D. lumbering

69. Select the most appropriate meaning of the given idiom.

Short fuse

A. Dangerous situation B. Control anger quickly
C. A tricky problem D. Get angry quickly

70. Select the correctly spelt word.

A. Competance B. Cammand
C. Complexety D. Crucial

71. Select the most appropriate option that can substitute the underlined phrase in the given sentence. If there is no need to substitute it, select 'No substitution required'.

The Mysore palace is <u>gearing up</u> for the winter festival.

A. setting up B. No substitution required
C. fortifying D. dressing up

72. Select the most appropriate option to fill in the blank.

There is a ______ train from Mysore to Chennai.

A. speedy B. brisk
C. quick D. fast

73. Select the option that can be used as a one-word substitute for the given phrase.

The study of evolution of mankind

A. Geology B. Archaeology
C. Anthropology D. Cartography

74. Parts of the following sentence have been given as options. Select the option that contains an error.

Whether I do not agree with her views, I respect her for her honesty.

A. for her honesty B. with her views
C. I respect her D. Whether I do not agree

75. Select the INCORRECTLY spelt word.

A. Associate B. Attendance
C. Accept D. Alott

Directions (Qs. No. 76-80): *Read the given passage and answer the questions that follow.*

"Any bicycle repair shop around? Can anyone share the location please?" That was a desperate appeal from a woman in our residents' association's WhatsApp group. Her child's bicycle needed urgent mending.

"There is one around 2 km away." Soon came the first response. "No. The shop shut long ago, even before COVID," someone else chipped in. Where have the bicycle repairers gone? The wayside mechanics who would do a gamut of works on your bicycles for a paltry sum have almost gone extinct. These days, only children use bicycles, and you know a mechanic needs regular customers to survive. There is a time in almost everyone's life when they become proud owners of their first bicycle. And there comes a stage when we abandon the prized possession and graduate ourselves to a motorised vehicle. Unused and unattended, the bicycles rust and disintegrate and finally end up at scrap dealers.

City roads in Kerala have now become totally unfriendly for bicycles. A cyclist is an odd man out on the chaotic road, an unwelcome disruptor among the automobiles arrogantly jostling for space. There are people out there who love to bicycle to their workplaces but dare not, dreading the reckless traffic on the way.

Is speed synonymous with progress? The transition from bullock carts to bullet trains denotes mankind's journey toward development. However, passion for speed and more speed could trigger a gasping race to nowhere. To find time to relish the fruits of development, the curve has to slow down and plateau somewhere.

A bicycle is silent like a butterfly, easy like a true friend to possess and maintain. A bicycle symbolises fine balancing, not just on its narrow wheels but a balanced living. This simple carbon-free mode of transport helps the rider to be healthy and heal the habitat. People who cycle to work tend to be less stressed out at workplaces. Motorcyclists whiz past, hiding their heads and thoughts in full-face helmets. Car owners roll up their glasses and cocoon their mind and body from the outside world. A cyclist pedals under the open sky, opens up to friends and fellows on the way and forgets one's own worries. It seems egalitarianism is part and parcel of the cycling culture.

76. Who is referred to as an 'unwelcome disrupter'?

A. Scrap dealer
B. Motorcyclist
C. Cyclist
D. Car owner

77. Which of these advantages of a bicycle does the writer NOT mention in the passage?

A. It is an eco-friendly means of transport.
B. It symbolises balance in life.
C. It easily navigates in traffic jams.
D. It acts as stress buster.

78. Select the synonym of 'unfriendly' as used in the passage.

A. Inhospitable
B. Estranged
C. Aloof
D. Lonely

79. What is the purpose of the conversation at the beginning of the passage?

A. No particular purpose
B. An interesting way of introducing the topic of disappearing cycle mechanics.
C. To express anger against the disappearing cycle mechanics.
D. To bring to everyone's notice the chaotic state of roads in Kerala.

80. What does the writer mean when he says, "It seems egalitarianism is part and parcel of cycling culture"?

A. Cycling culture isolates the poor.
B. Cycling culture encourages the polarisation of the community.
C. Cycling promotes an elitist culture.
D. Cycling symbolises the removal of inequalities among people.

HINDI LANGUAGE AND COMPREHENSION

81. 'तीन बेर खाती थीं ते वे तीन बेर खाती हैं।'

उक्त पंक्तियाँ, निम्न में से किस अलंकार का उदाहरण हैं?

A. यमक
B. अनुप्रास
C. उत्प्रेक्षा
D. श्लेष

82. 'बायीं ओर को घूमा हुआ'– इस वाक्यांश के लिए उपयुक्त शब्द का चयन करें।

A. वसितव्य
B. वामोरू
C. वायव्य
D. वामावर्त

83. 'ठोकर लगी पहाड़ की, तोड़े घर की सील'– उक्त लोकोक्ति का कोई खंड अशुद्ध है। शुद्ध भाग का चयन करें।

A. ठोकर लगी कंकड़ की
B. तोड़े घर की खटिया
C. तोड़े घर की सिल
D. ठोकर लगी पत्थर की

84. निम्नलिखित में से शुद्ध वाक्य का चयन करें।

A. सेठ माणिकचंद के घर रोज लड़ाई-झगड़ा हुआ करता था।
B. जागुआ कहकर पुकारते जग्गू को लोग थे।
C. लड़का जैसा सुन्दर है, सुशील भी और वैसा बुद्धिमान है।
D. निकट का गुणी व्यक्ति कम सम्मान पर दूर का ज्यादा पाता है।

85. 'मात्रुपदेश' शब्द के शुद्ध संधि-विच्छेद का चयन कीजिये।

A. मातृ + उपदेश

B. मातृ + ओपदेश

C. मात्र + उपदेश

D. मात्रु + उपदेश

86. 'मेरे घर में एक _______ है।' निम्न में से विदेशज शब्द चुनकर वाक्य को पूर्ण करें।

A. घोंसला B. लोटा

C. झरोखा D. नौकर

87. उपयुक्त 'करण कारक' चुनकर निम्न वाक्य को पूर्ण करें।

'_______ सुनी बात हमेशा सत्य होती है।'

A. मेरी B. कानों

C. कान D. आपकी

88. निम्नलिखित में से उस वाक्य का चयन करें जिसका पदक्रम शुद्ध हो?

A. व्यापक और संकीर्ण अर्थों में इसकी परिभाषा निश्चित करने की चेष्टा की गयी है।

B. इन शब्दशक्तियों पर आधार के काव्य की रचना होती है।

C. इन आचार्यों ने रस को प्रधानता न देकर अलंकार में काव्य में प्रधानता दी है।

D. अलंकृत करे किसी वस्तु को वह जो अलंकार है।

89. 'पीपर पात सरिस मन डोला'

उपर्युक्त पंक्ति में मुख्यतः कौन-सा अलंकार है?

A. उत्प्रेक्षा B. रूपक

C. उपमा D. अतिशयोक्ति

90. दिए गए शब्दों में से 'गरल' के विलोमार्थी शब्द की पहचान करें।

A. औरस B. विरल

C. सुधा D. कालकूट

91. 'अधक _______ और सतत लगन से कोई भी व्यवसाय चरमसीमा प्राप्त कर सकता है।'

स्व विवकानुसार उचित शब्द चुनकर, उपरोक्त वाक्य में रिक्त स्थान की पूर्ति करें।

A. ज्ञान B. परिश्रम

C. व्यवहार D. जानकारी

92. जीभ पर लक्ष्मी बसना– अशुद्ध मुहावरे के रेखांकित शब्द को सही शब्द से बदलें।

A. कौस्तुभी B. इंदुमती

C. सरस्वती D. पार्वती

93. 'जीवन तो क्षणभंगुर होता है।'

उचित पर्यायवाची शब्द चुनकर रेखांकित शब्द को प्रतिस्थापित करें।

A. यक्ष B. नश्वर

C. स्वत्व D. कृश

94. 'इस सोसाइटी में _______ रहते हैं।'

उस शब्द का चयन करके वाक्य पूर्ण करें जो 'समाहार द्वंद्व' का उदाहरण हो।

A. सेठ-साहूकार

B. हृष्ट-पुष्ट

C. परिवार

D. स्त्री-पुरुष

95. 'वर्द्धिक-रेखांकित शब्द का उपयुक्त तद्भव रूप चुनकर निम्न वाक्य को पूर्ण करें।

'इस _______ के पैसे दे दो।'

A. दुकानदार B. बनिया

C. बढ़ई D. भाई

निर्देश (प्र.सं. 96-100): *दिए गए गद्यांश को ध्यान से पढ़ें और प्रश्न के उत्तर दें।*

डॉ. रामकुमार वर्मा ने ऐतिहासिक एवं समस्या मूलक एकांकियों की रचना की है। उनके एकांकियों का मूल स्वर आदर्शवादी है। प्रेम, सेवा, उदारता, त्याग और बलिदान की भावनाओं से ओतप्रोत इन ऐतिहासिक एकांकियों में भारत के अतीत गौरव को प्रस्तुत करते हुए राष्ट्रीयता की भावना जगाने का प्रयास किया गया है। समस्यामूलक एकांकियों में वर्मा जी ने शिक्षित मध्यमवर्गीय दंपत्तियों की अनेक समस्याओं प्रेम, सहवास, संदेह, दंभ आदि को कथानक का विषय बनाया है, किंतु उनकी परिणति आदर्श में हुई है क्योंकि उनके एकांकियों की नायिकाएं अंततः अपने पति के सम्मान की रक्षा करती हुई दिखाई पड़ती हैं, यथा 'रेशमी टाई', 'ललिता' और 'एक्ट्रेस' एकांकी की नायिका प्रभाव कुमारी। अतिशय आदर्शवाद के कारण वर्मा जी के एकांकी यथार्थ से दूर हो गए जान पड़ते हैं, किंतु एकांकी शिल्प की दृष्टि से वे हिंदी के युग प्रवर्तक एकांकी माने जा सकते हैं। आरंभ, कुतूहल, संकलन त्रय, चरम सीमा आदि तत्व उनके एकांकियों में बड़ी सूक्ष्मता से विद्यमान हैं। रंगमंचीयता एवं अभिनेयता के गुणों से भी उनके एकांकी संपन्न हैं तथा उनमें सरसता के साथ-साथ शिल्प की पौढ़ता भी विद्यमान है। वस्तुतः एकांकी को चरम पर पहुँचाने का श्रेय डॉ. राजकुमार वर्मा को ही दिया जाता है।

96. उपर्युक्त गद्यांश के लिए उचित शीर्षक का चयन करें।

A. डॉ. रामकुमार वर्मा के एकांकी

B. एकांकी शिल्प और डॉ. रामकुमार वर्मा

C. एकांकियों की विषय-वस्तु

D. एकांकी कला और शिल्प

97. 'प्रौढ़ता' के विपरीतार्थक शब्द का चयन कीजिये।

A. अप्रौढ़ता B. बौड़मपन

C. निजता D. परिपक्वता

98. उपर्युक्त अवतरण किस शैली में लिखा गया है?

A. वर्णनात्मक B. आत्मपरक

C. विवरणात्मक D. आलोचनात्मक

99. निम्नलिखित में से किस वाक्य में 'परिणति' शब्द का उचित प्रयोग किया गया है?

A. दूल्हा-दूल्हन का परिणति संस्कार संपन्न हो गया।
B. आपके व्यवहार की परिणति है कि इतने लोग आपको पसंद करते हैं।
C. आपकी उम्र में परिणति हो जानी चाहिए।
D. उसने नौकरी पाने की अच्छी परिणति खो दी।

100. निम्नलिखित में से कौन-सा शब्द 'सम्मान' का पर्यायवाची नहीं है?

A. सरंजाम B. प्रतिष्ठा
C. आदर D. आवभगत

SECTION-B

POST SPECIFIC SUBJECT

101. Too many packets present in (a part of) the network causes packet delay and loss that degrades performance. This situation is referred to as ______.

A. throttling B. chocking
C. congestion D. collapse

102. With reference to CSS, which of the following allows to change property values smoothly over a given duration?

A. Masking B. Transitions
C. Web Fonts D. Text Effects

103. Which of the following identifies, controls, audits and reports modifications that invariably occur while software is being developed and after it has been released to a customer?

A. Software Process Model
B. Software Quality Assurance
C. Software Cost Estimation
D. Software Configuration Management

104. Which of the following is an illusion of an extremely large main memory?

A. Cache memory B. Virtual memory
C. Hard Disk D. Associative memory

105. Which of the following is a relational operator in the C programming language?

A. && B. !
C. != D. ||

106. Which of the following statements is/are true with reference to java servlets?

(*i*) A Servlet is a Java program that runs without a web server.
(*ii*) It receives the requests and responds to them using related protocols (usually HTTP).

A. Only (*i*) B. Both (*i*) and (*ii*)
C. Neither (*i*) nor (*ii*) D. Only (*ii*)

107. Which of the following refers to focusing on determining, organising, directing, facilitating and monitoring knowledge-related practices and activities required to achieve the desired business strategies and objectives with reference to knowledge management in organisations?

A. Business point of view
B. Education point view
C. Hands-on operational point of view
D. Management point of view

108. Which of the following refers to a system test that forces a software to fail in a variety of ways and verifies that recovery is properly performed?

A. Recovery testing B. Stress testing
C. Security testing D. Performance testing

109. By default, the BASH shell of the Linux environment has a ______ prompt.

A. # B. &
C. $ D. %

110. Which of the following is NV RAM memory that retains its data even when turned off?

A. Cache memory B. Flash memory
C. Register memory D. Main memory

111. Which of the following is NOT a method of solving quadratic equations?

A. By completing the square
B. By using the quadratic formula
C. By factorisation
D. By using convergence

112. The technology of .Net is developed by ______ and was launched in ______.

A. Microsoft; 2002 B. Oracle; 2002
C. Microsoft; 2010 D. Google; 2002

113. Which of the following is a software application that helps developers to build attractive website layouts and apps with ease?

A. Database design tools
B. Front-end development tools
C. Logic programming tools
D. Back-end development tools

114. A cube is a square prism. If all the sides of a cube are x, then volume = ______ and surface area = ______.

A. x^3; $6x^2$ B. x^2; $6x^3$
C. $6x^3$; x^2 D. $6x^2$; x^3

115. Which of the following is a valid syntax for the XML element in a DTD?
A. <!ELEMENT element-name category>
B. <!ATTLIST element-name attribute-name attribute-type attribute-value>
C. <#ELEMENT element-name category>
D. <!ENTITY entity-name "entity-value">

116. Which of the following statements is FALSE?
A. Microkernel is smaller in size.
B. It is not easy to extend a Monolithic kernel.
C. In Monolithic kernel, both user services and kernel services are kept in a separate address space.
D. To design a Microkernel, more codes are required.

117. Which of the following process models are the oldest software engineering paradigms and suggest a linear process flow that is often inconsistent with modern realities?
A. Incremental Process Models
B. Sequential Process Models
C. Evolutionary Process Models
D. Concurrent Process Models

118. What is the output of the following java program?

```
public class Solution{
  public static void main(String[] args){
    int[] p ={121, 201, 017};
    for(int j = 0; j < p.length; j++){
      System.out.print(p[j] + " ");
    }
  }
}
```

A. 121 201 17 B. 121 201 15
C. Compilation error D. Runtime error

119. The demand is said to be ______ when a very insignificant change in price leads to an infinite change in quantity demanded.
A. perfectly inelastic B. relatively elastic
C. relatively inelastic D. perfectly elastic

120. Which of the following displays uses an electron beam that operates like a pencil to create a line image on the CRT screen?
A. Rotate Scan B. Roster Scan
C. Random Scan D. Raster Scan

121. Consider the following data set: 6, 20, 25, 63, 92, 101. What is the range of the data set?
A. 63 B. 6
C. 95 D. 101

122. Which of the following is a graphical representation of an algorithm?
A. Flowchart B. Source code
C. Program D. Pseudo code

123. In connectionless services offered by the network layer, packets are injected into the network individually and routed independently of each other. In this context, the packets are frequently called ______, and the network is called a ______ network.
A. datagrams; virtual-circuit
B. datagrams; datagram
C. virtual circuits; datagram
D. virtual circuits; virtual-circuit

124. Which of the following can be used for the frontend or user interface while developing a web application?
A. JavaScript B. PHP
C. Django D. SQL

125. Any process in the transport layer wishing to remotely retrieve mail from a host can connect to the destination host's port ______ to contact its IMAP daemon.
A. 443 B. 80
C. 143 D. 20

126. Which of the following refers to expertise and skills acquired by a person through experience or education, the theoretical or practical understanding of a subject?
A. Synthesis B. Reference
C. Knowledge D. Problem solving

127. Which of the following software quality factors refers to the degree to which the software makes optimal use of system resources as indicated by the sub-attributes time behaviour and resource behaviour?
A. Maintainability B. Usability
C. Portability D. Efficiency

128. Which of the following is a type of Discrete Probability Distribution?
A. Log-Normal Distribution
B. Exponential Distribution
C. Normal Distribution
D. Poisson Distribution

129. Which of the following is a router in a foreign network to which the mobile node is currently connected with reference to mobile communication?
A. Foreign agent B. Home agent
C. Foreign agent COA D. Co-located COA

130. Which of the following are two arguments that 'chmod' takes to change different permission configurations of files in KDE Linux shell?
A. Permission changes and network names
B. Permission changes and user names
C. Permission changes and system names
D. Permission changes and file names

131. Which of the following symbols of a flow chart represents the processing phase?
A. [diamond] B. [parallelogram]
C. [oval] D. [rectangle]

132. Which of the following curves is particularly a kind of spline generated from a set of control points by forming a set of polynomial functions with reference to computer graphics?
A. Explicit B. Parametric
C. Implicit D. Bezier

133. Which of the following refers to messages sent from transport entity to transport entity in the transport layer of the ISO/OSI network model?
A. Packet B. Block
C. Frame D. Segment

134. Which of the following is defined as that branch of economic analysis that studies the economic behaviour of the individual unit and may be a person, a particular household or a particular firm?
A. International Economics
B. Macro Economics
C. Environmental Economics
D. Micro Economics

135. In Cohen Sutherland Line clipping algorithm, if a line ______ the clipping window, then the line is required to clip as it is considered partially visible.
A. falls inside B. falls outside
C. intersects D. falls on

136. What is the output of following C program?

```
#include<stdio.h>
int  main()
{
  int  x  =  8,  *y,  z;
  y =  &x;
  printf("%d\n",  x  *  *  y  *  x  + *y);
  return  0;
}
```

A. 8 B. Runtime error
C. 520 D. Compilation error

137. Which of the following options describes the desirable property of a good operating system?
A. Low throughput and low turnaround time
B. High throughput and high turnaround time
C. Low throughput and high turnaround time
D. High throughput and low turnaround time

138. Which step of the knowledge management process involves adding value by discovering relationships, abstracting and sharing?
A. Knowledge refining
B. Knowledge gathering or acquisition
C. Knowledge organisation
D. Knowledge sharing

139. Which of the following ciphers reorders the letters but does NOT disguise them?
A. Quantum B. One time pad
C. Transposition D. Substitution

140. Which of the following is an action or occurrence such as a mouse click, a key press, mouse movements or any system-generated notification in ASP.NET?
A. Directive B. Validator
C. Control D. Event

141. Which characteristic of business refers to 'various components of a business system are highly interacting and interdependent'?
A. Interdependence B. Complexity
C. Creativity D. Goal-orientation

142. Suppose we are given values of $y = f(x)$ for a set of values of x, the process of finding the value of y corresponding to any value of $x = x_i$ between x_0 and x_n is called ______.
A. bias B. variance
C. hypothesis D. interpolation

143. Which of the following is NOT a front-end design tool?
A. Angular JS B. PHP
C. Chrome Dev Tools D. jQuery

144. Which of the following is the proper sequence of the accounting cycle?
A. Recording of Transaction → Journal → Ledger → Trial Balance → Adjusted Trial Balance → Adjustment Entries → Closing Entries → Financial Statement
B. Recording of Transaction → Journal → Ledger → Trial Balance → Adjustment Entries → Adjusted Trial Balance → Closing Entries → Financial Statement
C. Recording of Transaction → Journal → Ledger → Trial Balance → Adjustment Entries → Closing Entries → Adjusted Trial Balance → Financial Statement
D. Recording of Transaction → Journal → Ledger → Trial Balance → Adjustment Entries → Adjusted Trial Balance → Financial Statement → Closing Entries

145. Which of the following operators has the highest precedence in the C programming language?
A. ^ B. !=
C. * D. ( )

146. Interpretability, Format, Coherence and Compatibility refer to which quality of information with reference to Management Information System?
A. Contextual B. Representational
C. Intrinsic D. Accessibility

147. The 'DEFAULT constraint' of SQL will ______.
A. ensure that a column cannot have a NULL value
B. ensure that all the values in a column satisfy certain conditions

C. ensure that all values in a column are different
D. provide a default value for a column when none is specified

148. Which of the following refers to the art of recoding, classifying and summarising in a significant manner, and in terms of money, transactions and events that are in part at least of a financial character, and interpreting the results thereof?
A. Financial Accounting
B. Cost Accounting
C. Management Accounting
D. Book Keeping

149. Which of the following types of XML parsers is an object that contains all the information of an XML document and is composed like a tree structure?
A. DOS B. SAX
C. DOM D. SAY

150. Activities like packing goods, loading goods and shipping goods belong to which step of the e-commerce primary process?
A. Contract conclusion B. Delivery/fulfilment
C. Billing/invoice D. Service/support

151. Which of the following algebraic functions represents NAND gate?
A. $(xy)'$ B. $(x + y)'$
C. $x + y$ D. $x*y$

152. Which of the following front-end tools is one of the most widely used CSS extension languages across the world?
A. Visual Studio Code B. Git
C. TypeScript D. Sass

153. Which of the following methods is used for the function $y = f(x)$, with the given discrete set of points (x_i, y_i), $i = 0, 1, 2, 3, ..., n$ where x_i 's are NOT equispaced?
A. Newton's backward interpolation formula
B. Newton's divided difference formula
C. Newton's forward interpolation formula
D. Gauss's forward difference formula

154. In which of the following radio channel sharing methods several users share the same frequency channel of higher bandwidth by dividing it into different time slots?
A. Time Division Multiple Access
B. Network Division Multiple Access
C. Frequency Division Multiple Access
D. Packet Division Multiple Access

155. Which of the following with reference to digital electronics is a device that stores (and sometimes displays) the number of times a particular event or process has occurred, often in relationship to a clock signal?
A. Latch B. Flip-Flop
C. Counter D. Register

156. The operations of a ______ require that the first element that is inserted is the first one to be removed?
A. union B. graph
C. stack D. queue

157. Which of the following belongs to the fixed and wireless configuration category of mobile devices?
A. Wi-Fi router B. Desktop computer
C. Wi-Fi Dongle D. Laptop

158. The ______ economic system is characterised by free markets and the absence of government intervention in the economy.
A. private B. capitalist
C. public D. socialist

159. Which of the following is designed in such a way that all the stations are connected through a single cable known as a backbone cable in the computer network?
A. Bus topology B. Mesh topology
C. Star topology D. Ring topology

160. The algorithm that manages routing tables and makes routing decisions in the network layer of the ISO/OSI model is called:
A. network algorithm
B. routing algorithm
C. table algorithm
D. IP algorithm

161. With reference to Management Information System, which of the following categories refers to information that is concerned with long-term policy decisions that define the objectives of a business and check how well these objectives are met?
A. Tactical information
B. Strategic information
C. Operational information
D. Planning information

162. The semiconductor memory Dynamic RAM (DRAM) stores each bit of information in a/an ______.
A. diode B. electrical capacitor
C. flip-flop D. resistor

163. C++ provides inline functions to facilitate a reduced function call overhead mainly for ______.
A. non-member functions
B. library functions
C. small functions
D. large functions

164. AB is a tangent to a circle at B. O is the centre of the circle. If the circle radius is 40 mm and AB = 150 mm, calculate the length of AO.
A. 57.30 mm B. 962 mm
C. 155.2 mm D. 235.6 mm

165. Which of the following effects is the phenomenon of emission of electrons from the surfaces of certain substances, mainly metals, when light of a shorter wavelength is incident upon them?
A. Photo-light B. Photo-mechanic
C. Photo-electric D. Photo-magnetic

166. Which characteristic of an algorithm refers to 'each instruction is clear and unambiguous'?
A. Definiteness B. Finiteness
C. Effectiveness D. Indefiniteness

167. Which of the following is a java primitive data type?
A. Array B. String
C. Classes D. Byte

168. What will be the output of the Linux shell command *rm doc*'?
A. Erase all files beginning with the pattern 'doc'
B. Erase all files ending with the pattern 'doc'
C. List filenames ending with the pattern 'doc'
D. List filenames beginning with the pattern 'doc'

169. Which of the following is a Microsoft ActiveX control that will soil through a data file, extrapolate the necessary information and produce that information in specified areas on the web page?
A. Dialog Bars B. Tabular Data Control
C. Control Bars D. Dialog Boxes

170. Which of the following is known as an association among several entities?
A. Instance B. Key
C. Relationship D. Participation

171. Which of the following controls in VB.NET is used to select one option from a number of choices?
A. Label B. Button
C. ListBox D. RadioButton

172. The Insert key in a keyboard of a computer system is used to toggle between ______ and ______ modes during data entry.
A. backspace; overwrite B. delete; overwrite
C. insert; overwrite D. delete; replace

173. Which of the following is NOT a component of Management Information System?
A. People B. Software
C. Education procedures D. Data

174. Which of the following is a symbolic name given to a memory location in any programming language?
A. Variable B. Constant
C. Literal D. Attribute

175. Which of the following helps to make predictions from data?
A. Prescriptive statistics B. Inferential statistics
C. Sample statistics D. Descriptive statistics

176. What is the amount of rotation between two straight lines?
A. Revolution B. Degree
C. Transversal D. Angle

177. Which of the following is FALSE with reference to constructor in C#.NET?
A. It can have a return type.
B. All classes have constructors by default.
C. Constructor name must match the class name.
D. The constructor is called when the object is created.

178. Which of the following is NOT a storage class in the C programming language?
A. Register B. Extern
C. Auto D. Intern

179. Which of the following is FALSE with reference to peer-to-peer network?
A. This network has a dedicated server.
B. It is useful for small environments, usually up to 10 computers.
C. Special permissions are assigned to each computer for sharing the resources.
D. All the computers are linked together with equal privilege and responsibilities for processing data.

180. Which of the following is true with reference to Queue Data Structure in the C programming language?
(*i*) Insertion can take place from the front end.
(*ii*) Deletion can take place from the rear end.
A. Neither (*i*) nor (*ii*) B. Both (*i*) and (*ii*)
C. Only (*i*) D. Only (*ii*)

181. What is the binary equivalent of the decimal number 10.25?
A. 1010.01 B. 1011.01
C. 1101.01 D. 1111.01

182. Match the system with the respective unit to represent heat.

(System)	*(Unit)*
(*a*) CGS	(*i*) BTU
(*b*) FPS	(*ii*) Joule
(*c*) SI	(*iii*) Calorie

	(*a*)	(*b*)	(*c*)
A.	(*iii*)	(*i*)	(*ii*)
B.	(*ii*)	(*i*)	(*iii*)
C.	(*i*)	(*ii*)	(*iii*)
D.	(*ii*)	(*iii*)	(*i*)

183. What is the key length for the Triple DES cryptography algorithm?
A. 46 bits B. 32 bits
C. 168 bits D. 56 bits

184. Which of the following refers to the kind of problems that require the identification of the best solution to a search problem from a given set of solutions?

A. Training B. Optimisation
C. Counting D. Decision

185. Which of the following internet protocols provides a way for applications to send encapsulated IP datagrams without having to establish a connection?
A. Telnet
B. User Datagram Protocol
C. Transmission Control Protocol
D. rlogin

186. With reference to stakeholders of e-commerce, business organisations abbreviated by 'B' may include ______.
A. government B. consumers
C. customers D. producers

187. Which of the following is the fundamental state of business activity and involves the sale and purchase of goods and services?
A. Enterprise B. Trade
C. Supply D. Industry

188. Which of the following refers to a planned system of collecting, storing and disseminating data in the form of information needed to carry out the functions of management?
A. Computer Networks
B. Software Engineering
C. Management Information System
D. Database Management System

189. 'As the stock of a commodity increases with the consumer, its marginal utility to the consumer decreases'. To which of the following laws does the given statement refer to?
A. Law of Diminishing Marginal Utility
B. Law of Supply
C. Law of Elasticity
D. Law of Demand

190. In a Client/server network, the central controller is known as a ______, while all other computers in the network are called ______.
A. peer; servers B. client; servers
C. server; clients D. server; peers

191. Considering the benefits to children with disability, which of the following provisions of Sarva Shiksha Abhiyan is correct?
I. Stipend for girls with disabilities
II. Braille textbooks
A. Only II B. Only I
C. Neither I nor II D. Both I and II

192. Reinforcement strengthens the occurrence of the emitted behaviour in the students. Which of the following is the correct example of positive reinforcement?
A. Teacher assigning high grades.
B. Teacher finding loopholes in work.
C. Teacher detaining the student after class hours.
D. Teacher giving threat of failure.

193. Which of the following does not come under lower form of writing?
A. Dictation
B. Picture composition
C. Paragraph writing
D. Independent writing

194. Which of the following is NOT correct in regard of Piagetian perspective of play?
A. Play is not possible for child without toys
B. The play is something which transcends both culture and time
C. Play have biological foundation
D. The play is something related to nature

195. Which activity children's do to expand their vocabulary?
I. Fast mapping
II. Sorting
A. Only I B. Only II
C. Both I and II D. Neither I nor II

196. In which method of learning by work, student themselves decide objective and prepare plan for an activity?
A. Project method B. Excursion method
C. Observation method D. Demonstration method

197. The 'Kesari' newspaper was published in which language?
A. Marathi B. Odiya
C. Bengali D. Hindi

198. According to the Indian Penal Code, an offence is not punishable for a child below ______ of age.
A. 10 years B. 5 years
C. 7 years D. 12 years

199. Parent and family involvement decreases student's ______.
I. Achievement
II. Success
A. Only I B. Both I and II
C. Neither I nor II D. Only II

200. Read the following characteristics of one of the piaget's stages of cognitive development given as (*a*), (*b*) and (*c*).
Select the correct stage from the options.
(*a*) Complete generality of thought.
(*b*) Development of strong idealism.
(*c*) Propositional thinking.
A. Concrete operations stage
B. Preoperational stage
C. Formal operations stage
D. Sensorimotor

ANSWERS

1. (A): 67 – 469 is not divisible by 3
69 – 483 is divisible by 3
81 – 567 is divisible by 3
87 – 609 is divisible by 3
Hence, 67 – 469 is different.

2. (C)

3. (A): P × Q – R + S

$P \xrightarrow{\text{Father}} Q \xrightarrow{\text{Sister}} R \xrightarrow{\text{Brother}} S$

Clearly, P is the father of S.

4. (C) **5. (A)**

6. (B): Given, 105 ÷ 21 + 67 – 64 × 16 = 287
105 ÷ 21 × 67 – 64 + 16
= 5 × 67 – 64 + 16
= 335 + 16 – 64
= 351 – 64 = 287

Hence, making equation correct, we should interchanged the signs × and +.

7. (D): ACEHLOR
The word is C H O [L] E R A
Hence, the middle letter of the word is L.

8. (B):

I	N	S	P	I	R	I	N	G
+2↓	–1↓	+2↓	–1↓	+2↓	–1↓	+2↓	–1↓	+2↓
K	M	U	O	K	Q	K	M	I

F	A	C	U	L	T	I	E	S
+2↓	–1↓	+2↓	–1↓	+2↓	–1↓	+2↓	–1↓	+2↓
H	Z	E	T	N	S	K	D	U

C	A	B	A	L	E	T	T	A
–2↓	+1↓	–2↓	+1↓	–2↓	+1↓	–2↓	+1↓	–2↓
A	B	Z	B	J	F	R	U	Y

A	B	A	N	D	O	N	E	D
+2↓	–1↓	+2↓	–1↓	+2↓	–1↓	+2↓	–1↓	+2↓
C	A	C	M	F	N	P	D	F

Hence, CABALETTA : ABZBJFRUY is different.

9. (C):

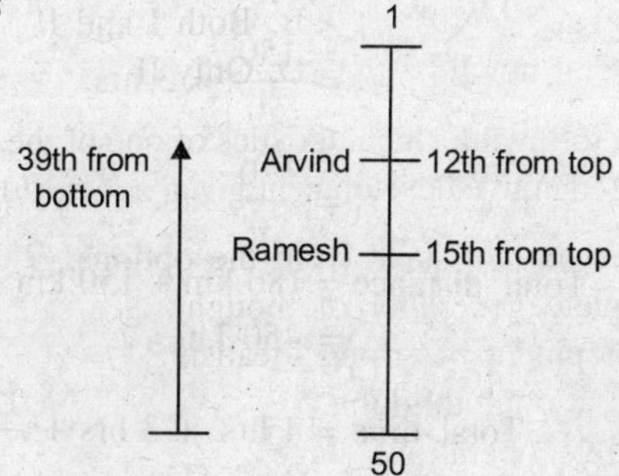

Hence, the rank of Arvind from the bottom
= 50 – 11 = 39th.

10. (B): A. 55 – 275 (× 5) B. 45 – 235 (× 5 + 10)
C. 35 – 175 (× 5) D. 25 – 125 (× 5)

Hence, 45 – 235 is different.

11. (D): 37 * 42 * 21 * 37 * 67 * 44
37 + 42 ÷ 21 × 37 – 67 = 44
⇒ 37 + 2 × 37 – 67
= 37 + 74 – 67
= 111 – 67 = 44

Hence, +, ÷, ×, –, = signs can replace the signs * then balance the given equation.

12. (A) **13. (A)** **14. (A)**

15. (D): 56 ÷ 28 – 68 + 98 × 14 = ?
= 2 – 68 + 1372
= 1374 – 68 = 1306

Hence, 1306 will come at the place of question mark.

16. (C)	**17. (C)**	**18. (A)**
19. (B)	**20. (B)**	**21. (A)**
22. (C)	**23. (A)**	**24. (C)**
25. (C)	**26. (C)**	**27. (D)**
28. (D)	**29. (B)**	**30. (C)**
31. (C)	**32. (D)**	**33. (A)**
34. (C)	**35. (A)**	**36. (D)**
37. (B)	**38. (A)**	**39. (B)**
40. (D)	**41. (C)**	**42. (C)**

43. (B): Let, B = 100
A = 160
A – B = 160 – 100 = 60

$C = 60 + \frac{55}{100} \times 60 = 93$

Now, $A = 160 - \frac{40}{100} \times 160$
= 160 – 64 = 96

$C = 93 + \frac{100}{300} \times 93$
= 93 + 31 = 124

Difference = 124 – 96 = 28

Required% $= \frac{28}{96} \times 100 = \frac{175}{6}\% = 29.166$
= 29.2
[correct to one decimal place]

44. (C): Export of company B in 2018 = ₹ 300

Profit % of company B in 2018 = 45%

Let income = ₹ x

$$\therefore \quad 45 = \frac{x-300}{300}\times 100$$

$$\Rightarrow \quad x - 300 = 135$$

$$\Rightarrow \quad x = 300 + 135 = ₹\ 435$$

Profit of B = 435 – 300 = 135

Income of company A = ₹ 390

Profit % of company A = ₹ 30%

$$30 = \left(\frac{390-y}{y}\right)\times 100$$

$$\Rightarrow \quad 30y = 39000 - 100y$$

$$\Rightarrow \quad 130y = 39000$$

$$\therefore \quad y = \frac{39000}{130} = 300$$

$\therefore$ Profit of A = 390 – 300 = ₹ 90

Difference = 135 – 90 = 45

$$\text{Required\%} = \frac{45}{90}\times 100 = 50\%.$$

45. (A): Volume of Cylinder = Volume of Cone

$$\Rightarrow \pi \times 18 \times 18 \times 32 = \frac{1}{3}\pi \times r^2 \times 24$$

$$\Rightarrow \quad 24r^2 = 18 \times 18 \times 32 \times 3$$

$$\Rightarrow \quad r^2 = \frac{18\times 18\times 32\times 3}{24}$$

$$\Rightarrow \quad r^2 = 18 \times 18 \times 4$$

$$\Rightarrow \quad r = 18 \times 2 = 36 \text{ cm}$$

Slant height of cone $= \sqrt{r^2+h^2}$

$= \sqrt{36^2+24^2}$

$= \sqrt{1872} = 12\sqrt{13}$ cm

Curved surface area of cone = πrl

$= \pi \times 36 \times 12\sqrt{13}$

$= 432\sqrt{13}\pi \text{ cm}^2$.

46. (B):

$$\left(\frac{46}{9}-\frac{63}{8}\div\frac{189}{20}\right)\div\frac{12-1}{9}-\left(\frac{21}{4}\div\frac{3}{28}\times\frac{2}{7}\right)\times\frac{3}{14}+\frac{3}{4}$$

$$=\left(\frac{46}{9}-\frac{63}{8}\times\frac{20}{189}\right)\div\frac{11}{9}-(14)\times\frac{3}{14}+\frac{3}{4}$$

$$=\left(\frac{46}{9}-\frac{5}{6}\right)\div\frac{11}{9}-3+\frac{3}{4}$$

$$=\left(\frac{92-15}{18}\right)\div\frac{11}{9}-3+\frac{3}{4} = \frac{77}{18}\times\frac{9}{11}-3+\frac{3}{4}$$

$$=\frac{7}{2}-3+\frac{3}{4} = \frac{14-12+3}{4} = \frac{5}{4} = 1\frac{1}{4}.$$

47. (B)

48. (C): S.P. = ₹ 2070

Loss = 10%

$$\text{C.P.} = \frac{100}{90}\times 2070 = ₹\ 2300$$

Now, C.P. = ₹ 2300

Profit % = 20%

$$\therefore \quad \text{S.P.} = \frac{120}{100}\times 2300 = ₹\ 2760$$

Hence, Savita should sell 46 articles = ₹ 2760.

49. (C)

50. (A): Sides of triangles are 28 cm, 45 cm and 53 cm

$(53)^2 = 2809$

$(28)^2 + (45)^2 = 784 + 2025 = 2809$

$\therefore$ It is right triangle whose longest side = 53 cm

Hence, radius of the circle $= \frac{53}{2}$ cm

Area of the circle = πr^2

$$= \pi\times\left(\frac{53}{2}\right)^2 = \pi\times\frac{2809}{4}$$

$$= \pi \times 702.25 = 702.25\ \pi \text{ cm}^2.$$

51. (B): Total export of cement by both the companies in 2017 and 2019

= 170 + 190 + 220 + 320 = 900

Total production of cement by the two companies in 2018 and 2020

= 340 + 360 + 450 + 470 = 1620

Difference = 1620 – 900 = 720

$$\text{Required \%} = \frac{720}{1620}\times 100 = \frac{7200}{162}$$

= 44.444 = 44.4%

(correct to one decimal place)

52. (A):

$$t_1 = \frac{180}{45} = 4 \text{ hrs.}$$

$$t_2 = \frac{150}{50} = 3 \text{ hrs.}$$

$$t_3 = \frac{120}{x} \text{ hrs.}$$

Total distance = 180 km + 150 km + 120 km

= 450 km

$$\text{Total time} = 4 \text{ hrs.} + 3 \text{ hrs} + \frac{120}{x} \text{ hrs.}$$

$$= \left(\frac{7x+120}{x}\right) \text{ hrs.}$$

$$\text{Average speed} = \frac{\text{Total distance}}{\text{Total time}}$$

$$\Rightarrow \frac{900}{19} = \frac{450 \times x}{7x+120}$$

$$\Rightarrow \frac{2}{19} = \frac{x}{7x+120}$$

$$\Rightarrow 19x = 14x + 240$$

$$\Rightarrow 5x = 240$$

$$\Rightarrow x = \frac{240}{5} = 48$$

Hence, the value of x = 48 km/hr.

53. (D)

54. (B): Loan = ₹ 1350

Let each instalment = ₹ x

Present value of two instalments

$$= \frac{100 \times x}{16}\left[1-\left(1+\frac{16}{100}\right)^{-2}\right]$$

$$= \frac{25x}{4}\left[1-\left(\frac{25}{29}\right)^2\right]$$

$$= \frac{25x}{4}\left[\frac{841-625}{841}\right]$$

$$= \frac{25x}{4} \times \frac{216}{841} = \frac{25x \times 54}{841}$$

But, $\frac{25x \times 54}{841} = 13500$

$$\Rightarrow x = \frac{841 \times 13500}{25 \times 54} = 8410$$

Total given amount = 8410 × 2 = ₹ 16820

Hence, total interest charged

= 16820 − 13500 = ₹ 3320.

55. (A) **56. (B)**

57. (A): (A + B − C)'s 15 hrs. work = $\frac{5}{36}$ part

(A + B − C)'s 1 hr. work = $\frac{5}{36 \times 15} = \frac{1}{108}$ part

(A + B)'s 1 hr. work = $\frac{1}{18} + \frac{1}{27} = \frac{5}{54}$ part

C's 1 hr. work = $\frac{5}{54} - \frac{1}{108} = \frac{10-1}{108}$

$= \frac{9}{108} = \frac{1}{12}$ part

Pipe C alone can empty $\frac{1}{12}$ part in 1 hr.

Pipe C alone can empty $\frac{1}{3}$ part in = $\frac{1}{\left(\frac{1}{12}\right)} \times \frac{1}{3}$ hrs.

$= 12 \times \frac{1}{3}$ hrs. = 4 hrs.

58. (C): 64% of 150 = $\frac{64}{100} \times 150$ = 96 marks

$\frac{60}{100} \times 90$ = 54 marks

96 − 54 = 42 marks

150 − 90 = 60 questions

Required % = $\frac{42}{60} \times 100$ = 70%.

59. (B): ∵ $x = \sqrt{19+4\sqrt{15}} - \sqrt{19-4\sqrt{15}}$

Squaring both sides

$$(x)^2 = \left(\sqrt{19+4\sqrt{15}} - \sqrt{19-4\sqrt{15}}\right)^2$$

$$\Rightarrow x^2 = 19+4\sqrt{15}+19-4\sqrt{15} - 2\left(\sqrt{19+4\sqrt{15}}\right)\left(\sqrt{19-4\sqrt{15}}\right)$$

$$\Rightarrow x^2 = 38 - 2\sqrt{(19)^2 - \left(4\sqrt{15}\right)^2}$$

$$\Rightarrow x^2 = 38 - 2\sqrt{361-240}$$

$$\Rightarrow x^2 = 38 - 2 \times 11$$

$$\Rightarrow x^2 = 16$$

$$\Rightarrow x = 4$$

Hence, the value of x = 4

60. (C): Let P = ₹ 100, r = 10%, $t = 4\frac{4}{12} = 4\frac{1}{3} = \frac{13}{3}$ years

$$\text{S.I.} = \frac{100 \times 10 \times 13}{100 \times 3} = \frac{130}{3}$$

$$\text{Amount} = 100 + \frac{130}{3} = \frac{430}{3}$$

When amount is ₹ $\frac{430}{3}$, then P = ₹ 100

When amount is ₹ 9417, then P = $\frac{100 \times 3 \times 9417}{430}$ = ₹ 6570

Now, P = ₹ 6570

$$r = 12\frac{1}{2}\% = \frac{25}{2}\%$$

$$t = 2\frac{2}{5} \text{ years} = \frac{12}{5} \text{ years}$$

∴ S.I. = $\frac{6570 \times 25 \times 12}{100 \times 2 \times 5}$ = ₹ 1971

∴ Amount = P + SI

= 6570 + 1971 = ₹ 8541.

61. (B) **62. (A)** **63. (D)**
64. (C) **65. (A)** **66. (C)**
67. (D) **68. (A)** **69. (D)**
70. (D) **71. (B)** **72. (D)**
73. (C) **74. (D)** **75. (D)**
76. (C) **77. (C)** **78. (A)**
79. (B) **80. (D)** **81. (A)**
82. (D) **83. (C)** **84. (A)**
85. (A) **86. (D)** **87. (B)**
88. (A) **89. (C)** **90. (C)**
91. (B) **92. (C)** **93. (B)**
94. (A) **95. (C)** **96. (A)**
97. (A) **98. (D)** **99. (B)**
100. (A)

101. (C): Congestion in a computer network occurs when there is an excessive amount of data traffic or packets being transmitted through a specific portion of the network infrastructure, such as a router or a network link. When this congestion happens, it can lead to several issues that degrade network performance.

With too many packets trying to pass through a network element at the same time, some packets may have to wait in a queue before they can be transmitted. This waiting time is known as packet delay. High levels of congestion can result in significant delays, which can be particularly problematic for real-time applications like video conferencing or online gaming.

102. (B): In CSS, transitions are a powerful way to add smooth and gradual changes to property values of elements over a specified duration. This allows for more visually appealing and interactive user experiences on websites and web applications. You can apply transitions to specific CSS properties, such as color, size, opacity, and more. When a property's value changes, the transition effect smoothly interpolates between the old and new values over a specified duration.

103. (D): The process that identifies, controls, audits, and reports modifications that invariably occur while software is being developed and after it has been released to a customer is known as Software Configuration Management.

Software Configuration Management (SCM) is a discipline within software engineering that focuses on managing and controlling changes to software artifacts, such as source code, documentation, and configuration settings, to ensure the integrity and consistency of the software throughout its lifecycle. SCM helps teams keep track of different versions of the software, manage concurrent development efforts, and ensure that the correct version of the software is delivered to customers. It plays a critical role in maintaining software quality and reliability.

104. (B): An illusion of an extremely large main memory is typically provided by Virtual memory.

Virtual memory is a memory management technique that uses a combination of physical RAM (main memory) and disk storage to create the illusion of a much larger and contiguous memory space than is physically available. It allows programs to access more memory than is physically installed in the computer by using a portion of the hard disk as an extension of RAM. This makes it appear as if there is a large amount of memory available to the software, even if the physical RAM is limited.

105. (C): A relational operator in the C programming language is represented by the symbol != . This operator is used to test if two values are not equal.

Here's what each of the options represents:

A. && is a logical AND operator.

B. ! is a logical NOT operator.

C. != is the "not equal to" relational operator.

D. || is a logical OR operator.

Relational operators are used to compare values and return a Boolean result (true or false) based on the comparison. != checks if two values are not equal, and if they are not equal, it returns true; otherwise, it returns false.

106. (D): (*i*) A Servlet is a Java program that runs without a web server: This statement is not true. Servlets are Java programs designed to run within a web server or servlet container. They are part of the Java EE (Enterprise Edition) or Jakarta EE platform, and their main purpose is to handle HTTP requests and generate responses in the context of web applications. Servlets rely on the web server or servlet container to provide the infrastructure and environment for their execution. Without a web server or servlet container, servlets cannot function properly.

(*ii*) It receives the requests and responds to them using related protocols (usually HTTP): This statement is true. Servlets are specifically designed to receive HTTP requests from clients (such as web browsers) and respond to those requests. They can also handle other related protocols, but HTTP is the most common one. Servlets can process incoming data, perform actions, and generate dynamic web content as responses, making them an integral part of web applications.

In summary, Java Servlets are Java programs that run within a web server or servlet container, and their primary role is to handle HTTP requests and generate responses for web applications. They cannot run independently without the support of a web server or servlet container. Statement (*ii*) correctly describes the role and function of Java Servlets.

107. **(D):** The approach that focuses on determining, organizing, directing, facilitating, and monitoring knowledge-related practices and activities required to achieve the desired business strategies and objectives with reference to knowledge management in organizations is referred to as the Management point of view.

Knowledge management is a discipline that involves the systematic management of an organization's knowledge resources to create value, improve efficiency, and support the achievement of business goals. The management perspective ensures that knowledge-related practices are aligned with the organization's strategic objectives and that knowledge assets are effectively utilized to drive success.

108. **(A): Recovery testing:** Recovery testing is a critical part of quality assurance and software testing. It focuses on assessing how well a system or software application can recover from unexpected failures, errors, or faults. The goal is to ensure that when the software encounters unexpected issues, it can gracefully recover without data loss or critical system failures. This testing helps identify vulnerabilities and weaknesses in the recovery mechanisms of the software and allows for necessary improvements to be made.

109. **(C):** By default, the BASH shell in the Linux environment has a $ prompt.

The $ symbol is the default command prompt in the BASH shell, indicating that the shell is ready to accept commands from the user. When you open a terminal or command prompt in a Linux system you typically see a prompt.

110. **(B): Flash memory:** Flash memory is a type of non-volatile memory that is commonly used for long-term storage in devices like USB flash drives, solid-state drives (SSDs), memory cards, and more. It can retain data even when the power is turned off, making it suitable for storing programs, files, and other data that needs to be preserved when the device is not in use.

111. **(D):** The method that is NOT typically used for solving quadratic equations is: By using convergence completing the square, using the quadratic formula, and factorization are the common methods for solving quadratic equations. Convergence, on the other hand, is a concept related to iterative algorithms in mathematics and is not a standard method for solving quadratic equations.

112. **(A):** .Net is a software framework developed by Microsoft. It was officially launched in the year 2002. The .Net framework provides a comprehensive and consistent programming model for building a wide variety of applications, from desktop and web applications to mobile and cloud-based applications.

113. **(B):** The software application that helps developers to build attractive website layouts and apps with ease is: **Front-end development tools**

Front-end development tools are specifically designed to assist developers in creating the user interface and user experience of websites and applications. These tools often include features for designing layouts, working with HTML, CSS, and JavaScript, and optimizing the visual aspects of the application. Examples of front-end development tools include web design software, integrated development environments (IDEs) with web development features, and user interface design tools.

114. **(A):** A cube is indeed a type of square prism where all sides are of equal length. If all the sides of a cube are x, then:

Volume of the cube is calculated as the side length cubed, so it's x^3.

Surface area of the cube is calculated as 6 times the side length squared, so it's $6x^2$.

So, the correct answer is:

x^3; $6x^2$.

115. **(A):** The valid syntax for declaring an XML element in a Document Type Definition (DTD) is:

<!ELEMENT element-name category>

In this syntax:

<!ELEMENT is used to declare an element.

element-name is the name of the XML element you're defining.

category represents the content model for the element, which specifies what kind of content can appear within the element (e.g., EMPTY, ANY, a specific set of child elements).

116. **(C):** The statement that is FALSE is: In Monolithic kernel, both user services and kernel services are kept in a separate address space.

In Monolithic kernel architecture, user services and kernel services share the same address space. This is one of the characteristics of Monolithic kernels. In contrast, Microkernels often separate user services and kernel services into different address spaces for better modularity and isolation.

117. **(B):** Sequential or Waterfall process models are among the oldest and most traditional software development paradigms. They follow a linear and sequential approach where each phase of software development (such as requirements analysis, design, implementation, testing, and maintenance) is completed one after the other in a predetermined order. This approach assumes that each phase must be completed before moving on to the next, which can be inflexible and less adaptive to changing requirements or unexpected issues.

Modern software development often favors more iterative and flexible approaches, such as Agile methodologies, which emphasize collaboration, continuous feedback, and adaptability throughout the development process.

118. (B)

119. (D): The demand is said to be perfectly elastic when a very insignificant change in price leads to an infinite change in the quantity demanded. In this case, consumers are extremely sensitive to price changes, and they will only buy a particular quantity at a specific price. Consumers are so sensitive to changes in price that even the slightest increase in price (no matter how small) will cause them to completely stop buying the product. Conversely, a decrease in price (no matter how small) will cause them to buy an infinite quantity of the product.

120. (C): The display that uses an electron beam operating like a pencil to create a line image on the CRT (Cathode-Ray Tube) screen is called Random Scan.

In a Random Scan display, also known as a Vector Display, the electron beam is directed to specific points on the screen to draw lines and shapes, similar to how a pencil is used to draw on paper. This approach is particularly useful for applications that require precisc line drawing, such as computer-aided design (CAD) systems.

121. (C): The range of a data set is the difference between the maximum and minimum values in the set.

In the given data set: 6, 20, 25, 63, 92, 101,

The minimum value is 6, and the maximum value is 101.

So, the range is:

Maximum value (101) – Minimum value (6)

$= 101 - 6 = 95.$

Therefore, the range of the data set is 95.

122. (A): A graphical representation of an algorithm is typically done using a Flowchart.

Flowcharts are visual diagrams that use standardized symbols to represent the steps and logic of an algorithm or process. They are commonly used in software engineering and other fields to visually represent the flow of control and decision-making in a program or system. Flowcharts are a useful tool for planning, designing, and documenting algorithms and processes.

123. (B): In connectionless services offered by the network layer, packets are injected into the network individually and routed independently of each other. In this context:

The packets are frequently called datagrams.

The network is called a datagram network.

In networking, a datagram is a self-contained, independent packet of data that contains both the actual data being transmitted and the addressing information required to route it to its destination. Datagrams are used in connectionless communication, where each packet is treated separately and does not rely on a pre-established connection. Each datagram can take a different route through the network to reach its destination. Datagram packets can be of varying sizes, and they are often associated with the Internet Protocol (IP), where IP datagrams carry data across the internet.

124. (A): JavaScript is a scripting language commonly used for frontend web development. It allows developers to add interactivity, manipulate the DOM (Document Object Model), and create dynamic user interfaces within web applications. JavaScript is an essential technology for building interactive and responsive web pages.

The other options:

PHP is a server-side scripting language primarily used for backend web development and server-side processing.

Django is a high-level Python web framework used for building the backend or server-side logic of web applications.

SQL is a query language used for managing and retrieving data from databases and is not directly related to frontend development.

125. (C): IMAP (Internet Message Access Protocol) is a widely used email retrieval protocol that allows email clients to access and manage email messages stored on a mail server. When an email client wants to connect to a mail server to retrieve email messages using IMAP, it needs to establish a connection to the appropriate port on the server where the IMAP daemon (server software) is listening.

In the case of IMAP, the default port used for incoming IMAP connections is port 143. This means that when an email client (such as Outlook, Thunderbird, or a mobile mail app) wants to retrieve emails from a mail server via IMAP, it will initiate a connection to the mail server's IP address on **port 143**. The server's IMAP daemon will be listening on this port to receive incoming IMAP requests.

126. (C): Knowledge refers to the information, facts, expertise, skills, and understanding that a person has acquired over time through various means, including education, experience, and learning. It encompasses both theoretical and practical understanding of a subject or domain.

127. (D): The software quality factor that refers to the degree to which the software makes optimal use of system resources, as indicated by the sub-attributes time behavior and resource behavior, is: **Efficiency**

Efficiency in software quality assesses how well the software utilizes system resources such as CPU time, memory, and network bandwidth while performing its functions. It focuses on ensuring that the software operates smoothly and without unnecessary resource consumption. The sub-attributes, time behavior (response time, processing speed) and resource behavior (memory usage, CPU utilization), are used to evaluate efficiency.

128. (D): The type of Discrete Probability Distribution among the options provided is: **Poisson Distribution**

The Poisson Distribution is a discrete probability distribution that describes the number of events occurring in a fixed interval of time or space, given a known average rate of occurrence. It is commonly used to model rare events, such as the number of customer arrivals at a store in a minute, the number of phone calls at a call center in an hour, or the number of accidents at a particular intersection in a day. The Poisson Distribution is characterized by a single parameter, which is the average rate of occurrence.

129. (A): In mobile communication, the router in a foreign network to which the mobile node is currently connected is referred to as: **Foreign agent**

The foreign agent is a key component in mobile IP networks. It assists in the mobility of a mobile node (such as a Smartphone or laptop) by helping it maintain its connection as it moves from its home network to foreign networks. When a mobile node roams into a foreign network, it registers with the foreign agent, which then forwards packets between the mobile node and its home network. This allows the mobile node to maintain connectivity even when it's not in its home network.

130. (D): The 'chmod' command is used to change the permissions (read, write, execute) of files and directories in a Linux-based operating system, including KDE Linux. It allows you to control who can access and modify files and what actions they can perform.

Options: The 'chmod' command can include various options to specify how the permissions are modified. Common options include:

R: Recursively change permissions for files and directories within a directory.

V: Verbosely display the changes made.

C: Report only when a change is made.

F: Suppress error messages.

And others, depending on the specific Linux distribution.

Permissions: This part of the command specifies the changes you want to make to the permissions of the file(s). The permissions are usually expressed using symbolic notation or octal (numeric) notation:

Symbolic notation: Uses letters (u for user, g for group, o for others) and symbols (+ for adding permission, – for removing permission, = for setting permission).

Octal notation: Uses a three-digit number (e.g., 755) to represent permissions for user, group, and others, with each digit indicating read (4), write (2), and execute (1) permissions.

File(s): This is the name or names of the files or directories for which you want to change permissions. You can specify multiple files or use wildcard characters (*).

131. (D)

132. (D): A Bezier curve is a type of spline curve that is widely used in computer graphics and animation. It is defined by a set of control points, and the curve itself is generated by blending or interpolating between these control points using polynomial functions. Bezier curves are commonly used for creating smooth and aesthetically pleasing curves in various applications, including vector graphics, 3D modeling, and animation software.

133. (D): In the ISO/OSI network model, messages sent from a transport entity to another transport entity in the transport layer are typically referred to as: **Segment**

A packet typically refers to a unit of data in the network layer (Layer 3).

A block is a more generic term that can refer to a group of data, but it doesn't have a specific layer association.

A frame usually refers to a unit of data in the data link layer (Layer 2).

A segment specifically pertains to the transport layer (Layer 4), where data is divided into segments for transmission, and each segment may include additional transport layer information such as sequence numbers and checksums to ensure reliable delivery.

134. (D): . The branch of economic analysis that studies the economic behavior of individual units, which can be a person, a particular household, or a particular firm, is called: **Microeconomics**

Microeconomics focuses on examining the economic decisions, choices, and interactions of individual economic agents, such as consumers, businesses, and small groups, within a specific market or industry.

It deals with topics like supply and demand, pricing, market structures, consumer behavior, and firm behavior at the micro level. In contrast, macroeconomics deals with the overall behavior and performance of an entire economy.

135. (C): In the Cohen-Sutherland Line Clipping Algorithm: If a line intersects the clipping window, then the line is required to clip because it is considered partially visible.

The algorithm checks whether a line segment intersects the boundary of the clipping window or has at least one endpoint inside the window. If either condition is met, the line is considered partially visible and needs to be clipped.

136. (C): int $x = 8$: This declares an integer variable x and initializes it with the value 8.

int *y: This declares an integer pointer variable y.

y = &x;: This assigns the address of variable x to pointer y. Now, y points to x.

printf("%d\n", x * * y * x + *y);: This line calculates the expression x * *y * x + *y and prints it using printf. Let's break down the calculation:

*y is the value pointed to by y, which is the value of x, so *y is 8.

x is 8.

Now, the expression becomes: 8 * 8 * 8 + 8, which simplifies to 512 + 8.

So, the correct output of the program is 520.

137. (D): . The desirable property of a good operating system is: High throughput and low turnaround time

Throughput: Throughput refers to the rate at which a system or program can process or complete a task. In the context of an operating system, high throughput means that the OS can efficiently handle a large number of tasks or processes in a given time period. This is desirable because it indicates the system's efficiency in executing tasks.

Turnaround Time: Turnaround time is the time it takes for a task or process to be completed from the moment it is submitted or started. Low turnaround time is desirable because it means that tasks are processed quickly and users do not have to wait for extended periods to see the results.

A good operating system aims to achieve a balance between high throughput (efficient resource utilization) and low turnaround time (quick task completion), providing users with a responsive and efficient computing environment.

138. (A): Knowledge refining, also known as knowledge refinement, is a process in knowledge management that involves improving the quality and relevance of existing knowledge. This can include activities such as:

Discovering Relationships: Identifying connections and associations between different pieces of knowledge to enhance understanding.

Abstracting: Summarizing or distilling complex knowledge into simpler and more actionable forms.

Sharing: Making refined knowledge available to others in a way that is understandable and accessible.

If "knowledge refining" is the terminology used in your context to describe these activities. Different organizations and sources may use slightly different terminology for the steps in the knowledge management process, which can lead to variations in how these processes are labeled.

139. (C): Transposition: In a transposition cipher, the letters of the plaintext message are rearranged or shuffled to form the ciphertext. However, the actual letters themselves are not substituted or disguised; their positions within the message are changed. This is different from a substitution cipher, where letters are replaced with other letters or symbols to create the ciphertext. Transposition ciphers are a form of encryption that relies on the rearrangement of characters rather than substitution.

140. (D): The term that describes an action or occurrence such as a mouse click, a key press, mouse movements, or any system-generated notification in ASP.NET is: **Event**

In ASP.NET, an event is a specific action or occurrence that triggers code execution in response. For example, a button click event or a page load event can be used to execute code when a user interacts with a web application. Events are a fundamental part of the ASP.NET framework and are used to create dynamic and interactive web applications.

141. (A): The characteristic of business that refers to "various components of a business system being highly interacting and interdependent" is: **Interdependence**

In the context of business, interdependence means that different parts or components of a business organization rely on each other and have a significant impact on each other's operations and success. This interconnectedness is a fundamental aspect of how businesses function, as changes or actions in one area of the business can have ripple effects throughout the entire organization.

142. (D): Interpolation: Interpolation is a mathematical technique used to estimate the value of a function at a point within the range of known data points. It involves constructing a curve or function that passes through the given data points and allows for the estimation of values at intermediate points.

Interpolation is commonly used in various fields, including mathematics, statistics, engineering, and computer science, to approximate values between known data points.

143. (B): PHP: PHP is a server-side scripting language primarily used for backend web development. It is used to handle server-side logic, process data, and generate dynamic web content. While PHP can be used in conjunction with front-end technologies to create full-stack web applications, it is not a front-end design tool itself.

The other options:

AngularJS and jQuery are JavaScript libraries/ frameworks commonly used for front-end development.

Chrome Dev Tools is a browser-based developer toolset that helps developers inspect and debug web pages, which is often used during front-end development.

144. (B): Recording of Transaction → Journal → Ledger → Trial Balance → Adjustment Entries → Adjusted Trial Balance → Closing Entries → Financial Statement

Recording of Transaction: This is the initial step in the accounting cycle. Whenever a financial transaction occurs within a business or organization, it needs to be recorded. This recording process captures the details of the transaction, such as the date, accounts involved, and amounts.

Journal: Transactions recorded in the first step are then entered into a journal. The journal is a chronological record of all financial transactions. Each entry in the journal includes information about the specific transaction, including the accounts affected and whether it's a debit or credit.

Ledger: The ledger is where the details from the journal are transferred to individual accounts. Each account in the ledger represents a specific type of asset, liability, revenue, or expense. Entries in the ledger help organize financial information by account.

Trial Balance: After all transactions are recorded and posted to the ledger, a trial balance is prepared. The trial balance lists all the accounts and their respective debit and credit balances. Its purpose is to verify that the total debits and total credits are equal, which is a fundamental principle of double-entry accounting.

Adjustment Entries: Adjustment entries are made to correct the accounts for certain transactions or events that have occurred but were not captured in the initial recording. Common adjustments include recognizing accrued expenses, prepaid income, and depreciation.

Adjusted Trial Balance: Following the adjustment entries, a new trial balance is created. This adjusted trial balance includes the impact of the adjustment entries. Its purpose is to ensure that the financial records are up to date and accurate.

Closing Entries: Closing entries are made to close temporary accounts, such as revenue and expense accounts, at the end of the accounting period. The goal is to prepare these accounts for the next accounting period and determine net income or loss.

Financial Statement: Finally, the financial statements are prepared based on the information in the adjusted trial balance. The key financial statements include the income statement (which shows revenue and expenses), the balance sheet (which presents assets, liabilities, and equity), and the cash flow statement (which details cash inflows and outflows).

This sequence of steps ensures that a company's financial records are accurate and that its financial statements provide an accurate representation of its financial position and performance for a specific period, such as a fiscal quarter or year.

145. (D): ( ) - Parentheses: Parentheses are used to group expressions and force a specific order of evaluation. Any expression within parentheses is evaluated first, and this takes precedence over all other operators. This allows you to control the order of operations in complex expressions and ensure that certain calculations are performed before others.

146. (B): Interpretability, Format, Coherence, and Compatibility are qualities of information that refer to the "Representational" quality of information within a Management Information System (MIS).

Interpretability: This refers to how easily the information can be understood by the users of the MIS. Information should be presented in a way that users can easily comprehend and make decisions based on it.

Format: Format refers to the structure and presentation of information. It's about how data and information are organized, formatted, and displayed within the MIS. A well-organized format makes it easier for users to access and use the information effectively.

Coherence: Coherence relates to the logical consistency and clarity of the information. It ensures that the information provided in the MIS is free from contradictions or conflicting data, making it more reliable and trustworthy.

Compatibility: Compatibility refers to the ability of the information to work seamlessly with other systems or tools within the organization. Information should be compatible with other data sources and technologies to ensure efficient data exchange and analysis.

These qualities collectively contribute to the representational quality of information in an MIS, ensuring that the data and information presented are meaningful, reliable, and usable for decision-making and analysis.

147. (D): The 'DEFAULT constraint' in SQL is used to provide a default value for a column when no value is specified during the insertion of a new row.

This means that if a user does not explicitly provide a value for a column, the default value specified in the constraint will be used. It does not enforce that a column cannot have a NULL value or that all values in a column are different. It also does not ensure that values satisfy certain conditions unless those conditions are related to the default value itself.

148. (A): The activity described, involving the recoding, classifying, summarizing, and interpreting of financial transactions and events, is typically associated with "Financial Accounting". Financial accounting is primarily concerned with preparing financial statements such as income statements, balance sheets, and cash flow statements that provide a summary of an organization's financial performance and position. It is essential for external stakeholders, such as investors and regulatory authorities, to assess the financial health and performance of a business.

149. (C): The type of XML parser that creates an object representing the entire XML document as a tree structure is the DOM (Document Object Model) parser. DOM is a standard interface for representing and interacting with structured documents, including XML documents. It treats an XML document as a tree-like structure in memory, where each element, attribute, and piece of content is represented as a node in the tree. When you use a DOM parser to process an XML document, it reads the entire document and constructs an in-memory representation of it as a tree of objects. Each XML element becomes a node in the tree, with attributes and content represented as properties of those nodes.

150. (B): Activities like packing goods, loading goods, and shipping goods belong to the "Delivery/fulfilment" step of the e-commerce primary process.

In the e-commerce process, once a customer places an order and the contract is concluded (step A), the next phase involves preparing the ordered items for shipment, loading them for transport, and finally shipping them to the customer's location. This phase is often referred to as the "Delivery/fulfilment" step, as it involves fulfilling the customer's order by ensuring that the products are delivered to them in a timely and satisfactory manner.

151. (A)

152. (D): One of the most widely used CSS extension languages across the world is Sass (Syntactically Awesome Stylesheets). It is a popular tool that extends the capabilities of CSS by adding features like variables, nesting, mixins, and more, making it easier and more efficient to write and maintain stylesheets.

153. (B): When you have a set of discrete points (x_i, y_i), where the x_i values are not equispaced, one of the commonly used methods for interpolating the function $y = f(x)$ is Newton's Divided Difference Formula. This formula allows you to calculate the coefficients of a polynomial that can interpolate the given set of points. It works well with non-equispaced data points.

154. (A): In the context of radio channel sharing methods, the method where several users share the same frequency channel of higher bandwidth by dividing it into different time slots is known as Time Division Multiple Access (TDMA).

In TDMA, each user is allocated a specific time slot during which they can transmit or receive data on the shared frequency channel. This allows multiple users to share the same channel without interfering with each other's transmissions.

155. (C): The device that stores (and sometimes displays) the number of times a particular event or process has occurred, often in relationship to a clock signal, is called a Counter.

Counters are digital circuits or devices that count the number of clock pulses or events and represent the count in binary or other numerical formats. They are commonly used in various applications, including frequency measurement, timers, and digital displays.

156. (D): The operations of a queue require that the first element that is inserted is the first one to be removed. This behavior is often referred to as "First-In-First-Out" or FIFO.

A queue is a fundamental data structure in computer science and is used to store and manage a collection of elements. In a queue, the order in which elements are inserted is important. The first element inserted is the first one to be removed. This behavior is often referred to as "First-In-First-Out" or FIFO. Imagine a queue like a line of people waiting for a bus. The person who arrives first (is inserted into the line first) is the one who gets on the bus first (is removed from the line first). Queues are used in a variety of applications in computer science and software engineering. For example, they are commonly used in task scheduling, process management, print spooling, and network data packet management.

157. (A): The device that belongs to the fixed and wireless configuration category of mobile devices is a Wi-Fi router.

A Wi-Fi router is a device that provides wireless connectivity to devices like laptops, smartphones, and tablets while also being fixed in one location, typically at a home or office. It allows multiple devices to connect to the internet or a local network wirelessly through Wi-Fi.

158. (B): The economic system characterized by free markets and the absence of government intervention in the economy is often referred to as a "capitalist" economic system.

A capitalist economic system, also known as capitalism, is an economic system where the means of production, distribution, and exchange are primarily owned and controlled by private individuals and businesses, rather than the government or state. In this system, individuals and companies are free to make economic decisions based on their own self-interest.

159. (A): The network topology designed in such a way that all the stations are connected through a single cable known as a backbone cable is called Bus topology. Bus topology is a type of network topology in which all devices or stations are connected to a single central cable, known as the "backbone" or "bus." This central cable serves as the communication medium through which data is transmitted. All devices share this single communication line.

160. (B): The algorithm that manages routing tables and makes routing decisions in the network layer of the ISO/OSI model is called a "routing algorithm". The routing algorithm is the core component of the network layer responsible for calculating the best path or route for data packets based on the information in the routing tables. The routing algorithm considers various factors, such as the network topology, link costs, and the current state of network links, to make routing decisions.

161. (B): With reference to Management Information Systems (MIS), the category of information that is concerned with long-term policy decisions that define the objectives of a business and check how well these objectives are met is "Strategic information".

Strategic information is essential for top-level management to make decisions that shape the overall direction and goals of the organization. It helps in planning for the future and assessing the organization's performance in achieving its strategic objectives.

162. (B): Dynamic RAM (DRAM) stores each bit of information in an electrical capacitor.

In DRAM, each memory cell consists of a capacitor that can either be charged or discharged to represent the binary values 0 and 1. The charge in the capacitor needs to be refreshed periodically to prevent data loss, which is why it's called "dynamic" RAM.

163. (C): C++ provides inline functions to facilitate a reduced function call overhead mainly for small functions.

Inline functions are a feature in C++ that allows the compiler to insert the code of a function directly into the calling code, rather than performing a standard function call. This can lead to a reduction in overhead for small functions because it avoids the cost associated with function call setup and teardown.

164. (C)

165. (C): The phenomenon of emission of electrons from the surfaces of certain substances, mainly metals, when light of a shorter wavelength is incident upon them is known as "Photo-electric" effect.

This effect was one of the key pieces of evidence in the development of quantum theory in physics. It demonstrated that light exhibits both wave-like and particle-like properties, and it played a significant role in the understanding of the behavior of electrons and photons.

166. (A): The characteristic of an algorithm that refers to "each instruction is clear and unambiguous" is called "Definiteness."

This means that each step or instruction in an algorithm must be well-defined, leaving no room for ambiguity or multiple interpretations. It ensures that the algorithm can be precisely followed to achieve the desired outcome.

167. (D): The Java primitive data type is Byte.

In Java, primitive data types are the basic building blocks for data manipulation. They are not objects and are treated more efficiently by the Java Virtual Machine (JVM) compared to objects created from classes. "byte" is one of the primitive data types in Java, used to store 8-bit integer values.

168. (A): The Linux shell command rm doc* will erase all files beginning with the pattern 'doc'.

The asterisk (*) is a wildcard character in Linux that matches zero or more characters. In this context, it matches files with names starting with "doc." Be cautious when using the rm command with wildcards, as it will delete files without asking for confirmation.

169. (B): The Microsoft ActiveX control that is used to scroll through a data file, extrapolate the necessary information, and display that information in specified areas on a web page is called the "Tabular Data Control". The Tabular Data Control (TDC) is an ActiveX control developed by Microsoft for web applications. It is designed to facilitate the display and interaction with tabular data, such as database records, in web pages. It's important to note that ActiveX controls like TDC were primarily used in older web technologies, such as Internet Explorer, and may not be commonly employed in modern web development. Modern web development tends to rely more on HTML5, CSS, JavaScript, and web frameworks to achieve similar functionality while ensuring cross-browser compatibility and security.

170. (C): The term that is known as an association among several entities is "Relationship".

In the context of databases or data modeling, a relationship defines how entities or tables are connected or associated with each other, often indicating how data in one entity relates to data in another entity. Relationships can be one-to-one, one-to-many, or many-to-many, depending on the specific data modeling needs.

171. (D): The control in VB.NET that is used to select one option from a number of choices is the "RadioButton" control.

Radio buttons are typically used in groups where only one option can be selected at a time, and selecting one option deselects any previously selected option in the same group. They are often used in user interfaces for making exclusive choices or selecting options from a list of mutually exclusive items.

172. (C): The Insert key on a keyboard of a computer system is used to toggle between "insert" and "overwrite" modes during data entry.

Insert mode: When the Insert key is activated (usually by pressing it), it allows you to insert new characters into existing text without overwriting the characters that come after the insertion point.

Overwrite mode: When the Insert key is deactivated (pressed again), it switches to overwrite mode, where typing new characters replaces the existing characters at the insertion point.

173. (C): Education procedures. In some contexts, the term "education procedures" may be considered a component or aspect of a Management Information System (MIS) as it pertains to training and educating personnel in how to use the system effectively. However, it's not traditionally listed as one of the core components of an MIS, which typically include people, software, data, hardware, and procedures. Thank you for pointing out the clarification.

174. (A): The symbolic name given to a memory location in any programming language is called a "Variable."

Variables are used to store and manage data in a program, and they can represent various types of information, including numbers, text, and more. They are essential for working with data and performing computations in programming.

175. (B): The statistical method that helps to make predictions from data is Inferential statistics.

Inferential statistics involves using data from a sample to make inferences or predictions about a larger population. It includes techniques like hypothesis testing, regression analysis, and confidence intervals, which allow you to draw conclusions about characteristics of a population based on observed data from a sample.

176. (D): The amount of rotation between two straight lines is typically measured in "Angle."

An angle represents the amount of rotation or deviation between two lines or line segments. It is typically measured in degrees, radians, or other angular units, and it quantifies how much one line has been turned or tilted with respect to another line. Angle measurement is a fundamental concept in geometry and trigonometry.

177. (A): The statement that is FALSE with reference to constructors in C#.NET is: It can have a return type.

In C#.NET, constructors do not have a return type. They have the same name as the class and are used to initialize the object of the class. Constructors are responsible for setting up the initial state of an object and cannot return a value, not even void. They are automatically called when an object of the class is created.

178. (D): The storage class that is NOT a storage class in the C programming language is "Intern." "Intern", it is not a recognized or standard storage class in the C programming language. The storage classes mentioned earlier are the primary ones used in C to define the characteristics of variables. "Intern" is not part of the standard C language, and you wouldn't typically encounter it in C programming. If you come across "Intern" in a specific context, it might be a custom or non-standard term used in a particular programming environment or framework.

179. (A): The statement that is FALSE with reference to a peer-to-peer network is: This network has a dedicated server.

In a peer-to-peer network, there is typically no dedicated server. Instead, all computers (peers) on the network have equal status and can act as both clients and servers. Each computer can share its resources (such as files or printers) with others on the network, and all computers have similar privileges and responsibilities for processing data.

180. (A)

181. (A): To convert the decimal number 10.25 to binary, we can handle the integer and fractional parts separately.

Integer Part (10):

Convert the integer part (10) to binary:

10 in decimal is 1010 in binary.

Fractional Part (0.25):

Convert the fractional part (0.25) to binary:

Multiply the fractional part by 2.

0.25 * 2 = 0.5 (First binary digit after the decimal point)

Continue this process with the new fractional part:
0.5 * 2 = 1.0 (Second binary digit after the decimal point)
Note: Since we reached 1.0, we don't need to continue further.
Combine the binary digits obtained:
0.25 in decimal is 0.01 in binary.
Now, combine the integer and fractional parts to get the binary representation of 10.25:
10.25 in binary is 1010.01.
So, the correct answer is 1010.01.

182. **(A)**

183. **(C):** The key length for the Triple DES (Data Encryption Standard) cryptography algorithm is 168 bits.

Triple DES uses three 56-bit keys for a total key length of 168 bits. It applies the Data Encryption Standard algorithm three times to enhance security, making it more resistant to brute-force attacks compared to the original DES with its 56-bit key.

184. **(B):** The kind of problems that require the identification of the best solution to a search problem from a given set of solutions is referred to as "Optimization" problems.

Optimization problems involve finding the most favorable or optimal solution from a set of possible solutions while satisfying certain constraints or criteria. These problems are commonly encountered in various fields, including mathematics, computer science, engineering, economics, and operations research, among others.

185. **(B):** The internet protocol that provides a way for applications to send encapsulated IP datagrams without having to establish a connection is "User Datagram Protocol (UDP)."

UDP is a connectionless protocol in the Internet Protocol (IP) suite. Unlike Transmission Control Protocol (TCP), which establishes a connection and ensures reliable data delivery, UDP allows applications to send datagrams without a prior connection setup. It is often used for real-time communication and applications where a slight loss of data is acceptable, such as streaming media and online gaming.

186. **(D):** With reference to stakeholders of e-commerce, business organizations abbreviated by 'B' may include: **Producers**

Business organizations or producers are among the key stakeholders in e-commerce. They create and supply products or services that are offered through e-commerce platforms. Other stakeholders may include government (A), consumers (B), and customers (C), but business organizations or producers are specifically identified by the letter 'B' in your list.

187. **(B):** The fundamental state of business activity that involves the sale and purchase of goods and services is "Trade."

Trade is at the core of business activity, where products or services are exchanged between buyers and sellers. It encompasses various aspects of commerce, including buying, selling, distribution, and the flow of goods and services in the marketplace. Trade is a fundamental driver of economic activity in both domestic and international contexts.

188. **(C):** The term that refers to a planned system of collecting, storing, and disseminating data in the form of information needed to carry out the functions of management is Management Information System (MIS).

A Management Information System (MIS) is a computerized system that provides managers with the tools and information they need to effectively organize, analyze, and make decisions based on data relevant to their organization's operations. MIS helps in collecting, storing, processing, and delivering information to support management's decision-making process. It plays a crucial role in facilitating efficient management and decision-making within an organization.

189. **(A):** The given statement, "As the stock of a commodity increases with the consumer, its marginal utility to the consumer decreases," refers to the "Law of Diminishing Marginal Utility."

The Law of Diminishing Marginal Utility is a fundamental concept in economics that states that as a consumer consumes more units of a good or service, the additional satisfaction or marginal utility derived from each successive unit tends to decrease. This law helps explain consumer behavior and the downward-sloping demand curve in microeconomics.

190. **(C):** In a client/server network, the central controller is known as a "server," while all other computers in the network are called "clients."

In a client/server architecture, servers typically provide resources or services to clients, which request and use these resources or services. Servers are central controllers that manage and distribute resources, while clients are the devices or software applications that request and utilize these resources.

191. **(D):** In the context of the Sarva Shiksha Abhiyan (SSA) in India, both provisions mentioned are correct: Both I and II

I. Stipend for girls with disabilities: SSA includes provisions to provide financial incentives and support to encourage the enrollment and retention of children with disabilities, including girls.

Stipends or scholarships are often provided to support their education.

II. Braille textbooks: SSA recognizes the need for accessible education materials for children with visual impairments. As part of this effort, Braille textbooks are provided to students with visual disabilities to ensure they have access to educational content.

So, both of these provisions are part of the efforts to benefit children with disabilities under the Sarva Shiksha Abhiyan.

192. (A): Teacher assigning high grades: Positive reinforcement involves the presentation of a desirable stimulus or reward after a behavior to increase the likelihood of that behavior occurring again. In this case, when the teacher assigns high grades (a desirable stimulus) to a student, it is intended to reinforce and strengthen the student's behavior (such as good academic performance) to encourage them to continue performing well in their studies.

193. (C): "Paragraph writing" does not come under the lower form of writing. "Paragraph writing" is typically considered a foundational skill in writing and is often taught at an earlier stage of writing development. It involves structuring and organizing ideas within a single paragraph.

In the context of educational progression, "independent writing" generally represents a higher level of writing proficiency where students are expected to compose original and extended pieces of writing without direct guidance or prompts.

194. (A): The statement that is NOT correct in regard to the Piagetian perspective of play is: Play is not possible for a child without toys.

Jean Piaget's perspective on play emphasizes that play is a crucial part of a child's cognitive development and that it is not dependent solely on the presence of toys. According to Piaget, play involves the child's exploration of the environment and interactions with objects and people. While toys can be tools for play, play can also occur through imaginative and symbolic activities that do not necessarily require physical toys.

195. (A): The activity that children engage in to expand their vocabulary is: Only I - Fast mapping

Fast mapping is a cognitive process through which children quickly learn and expand their vocabulary by making connections between new words and their meanings. It allows children to rapidly acquire and store new words in their mental lexicon based on limited exposure. Sorting (II) is not typically associated with vocabulary expansion; it may involve categorization and organization of objects or concepts but does not directly relate to learning new words.

196. (A): . The method of learning by work in which students themselves decide the objectives and prepare a plan for an activity is: **Project method**

In the project method of learning, students take an active role in defining the project's goals and planning how to achieve them. They often work on a specific project or task that requires them to apply their knowledge and skills to solve real-world problems or explore a particular topic in depth. This method promotes hands-on learning, critical thinking, and independent decision-making among students.

197. (A): The "Kesari" newspaper was published in the Marathi language.

The Kesari, founded by Lokmanya Bal Gangadhar Tilak in 1881, was a prominent Marathi-language newspaper in India. It played a significant role in the Indian independence movement and was known for its contributions to the socio-political discourse of the time.

198. (C): According to the Indian Penal Code (IPC), an offence is not punishable for a child below 7 years of age.

Under Section 82 of the IPC, it is stated that nothing is an offense that is done by a child who is under seven years of age. This means that children below the age of seven are considered legally incapable of committing an offense and are not subject to punishment under the IPC.

199. (C)

200. (C): The characteristics described as (*a*) Complete generality of thought, (*b*) Development of strong idealism, and (*c*) Propositional thinking are typically associated with Piaget's "Formal Operations Stage" of cognitive development.

So, the correct answer is: **Formal Operations Stage**

During the formal operations stage, individuals develop abstract and propositional thinking abilities, which involve reasoning about hypothetical situations, considering multiple possibilities, and engaging in more systematic and logical thought processes. Idealism and generality of thought also become prominent during this stage.

Previous Paper (Solved)

DSSSB—TRAINED GRADUATE TEACHER (TGT) COMPUTER SCIENCE EXAM, 2023*

SECTION-A

GENERAL INTELLIGENCE AND REASONING ABILITY

1. Select the correct mirror image of the given figure when the mirror is held at the right side.

A.  B. 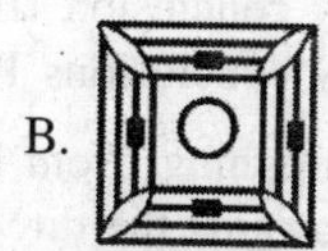

C. D. 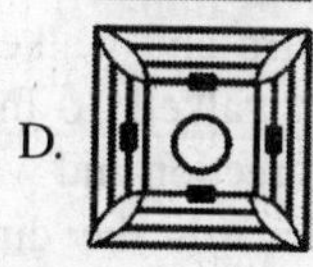

2. Study the following (English alphabetical) series and answer the question that follows.

A B C D E F G H I J K L M

N O P Q R S T U V W X Y Z

If the 2nd, 5th, 12th, 13th, 15th, 16th and 18th letters from the series are chosen to form a meaningful word, which letter will come in the middle of that word? Each letter must be used and only once.

A. E B. B
C. L D. O

3. In a row of 50 students, Rahul is 15th to the left of Ravi, who is 20th from the right end. What will be the position of Rahul from the left end?

A. 16th
B. 14th
C. 17th
D. 15th

4. Six friends, A, B, C, D, E and F, are sitting around a round table facing toward the centre and equidistant from each other. A is sitting second to the left of C. D is sitting opposite to B. F is sitting to the immediate right of B. Who is sitting second to the right of E?

A. A B. F
C. D D. B

5. Three different positions of the same dice are shown. Which pattern will be on the face opposite to the one having 'O'?

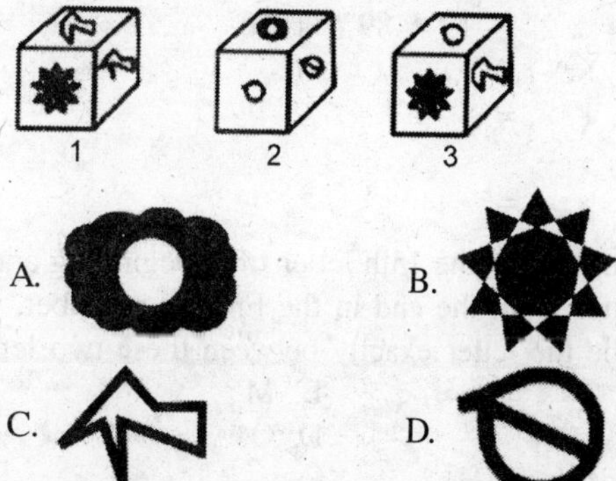

6. There are six persons, P, Q, R, S, T and U. T is older than P and R. U is younger than Q. T is younger than S. R is older than Q but younger than P. Who is the second youngest of all?

A. U B. P
C. R D. Q

7. In a family, there are 3 fathers, 3 mothers, 3 daughters, 3 sons, 2 nieces, 2 nephews, 1 son-in-law and 1 daughter-in-law. How many minimum members are there in the family?

A. 10 B. 12
C. 11 D. 13

8. Four letter-cluster pairs have been given, out of which three are alike in some manner and one is different. Select the one that is different.

A. SX–UZ
B. AF–CI
C. HM–JO
D. EJ–GL

9. Four number-pairs have been given, out of which three are alike in some manner and one is different. Select the one that is different.

A. 19–47.5 B. 17–47.5
C. 29–78.3 D. 23–57.5

* Exam held on 24/06/2023.

10. Select the number from among the given options that can replace the question mark (?) in the following series.

6, 7, 15, 24, 88, ?, 329

A. 114 B. 116
C. 115 D. 113

11. Which two signs should be interchanged to make the following equation correct?

$100 \div 20 + 67 - 64 \times 16 = 2063$

A. ÷ and + B. + and –
C. ÷ and × D. × and –

12. Select the correct combination of mathematical signs that can sequentially replace the * signs and balance the given equation.

45 * 44 * 22 * 17 * 89 * 1556

A. ÷, +, ×, –, =
B. –, ÷, +, ×, =
C. ×, +, ÷, –, =
D. +, ÷, ×, –, =

13. If a man reaches the 15th letter from beginning and the 14th letter from the end in the English alphabet, what would be the letter exactly between these two letters?

A. N B. M
C. L D. O

14. A question is given, followed by two statement labelled I and II. Identify which of the statements is/are sufficient/necessary to answer the question.

Question: How is Mahesh related to Bipin?

Statements:

I. Mahesh is the son of Devika.
II. Devika is the only daughter of Bipin's father.

A. Statement II alone is sufficient to answer the question, while statement I alone is not sufficient to answer the question
B. Both statement I and II are necessary to answer the question
C. Statement I alone is sufficient to answer the question, while statement II alone is not sufficient to answer the question
D. Either statement I alone or statement II alone is sufficient to answer the question

15. Select the letter-cluster from among the given options that can replace the question mark (?) in the following series.

HXK, MUC, ?, WOP, BLK

A. SRV B. RRU
C. RRV D. RSV

16. What approximate value should come in place of the question mark (?) in the following equation?

$45.67 \div 22.89 - 56.69 + 23.89 \times 13.37 = ?$

A. 345 B. 216
C. 378 D. 257

17. Read the given statements and conclusions carefully. Assuming that the information given in the statements is true, even if it appears to be at variance with commonly known facts, decide which of the given conclusions logically follow(s) from the statements.

Statements:

(*a*) All ducks are cats.
(*b*) All cats are lions.
(*c*) Some lions are jungles.

Conclusions:

I. No lions are cats.
II. No cat is a duck.
III. All ducks are lions.

A. Only conclusions II and III follow
B. All the conclusions I, II and III follow
C. Only conclusion III follows
D. Only conclusions I and II follow

18. In the morning, from Point A, a man started walking 10 m towards the direction of the Sun, and then took a right turn and walked 10 m. Again, he took a right turn and walked 10 m, and then took another turn in the left direction and walked 10 m. After this, he walked 20 m towards the direction of the Sun, and finally walked 20 m towards the north direction. In what direction and at what distance is he now from his initial point?

A. 20 m, west
B. 10 m, east
C. 10 m, west
D. 20 m, east

19. Select the alternative figure in which given figure (X) is embedded.

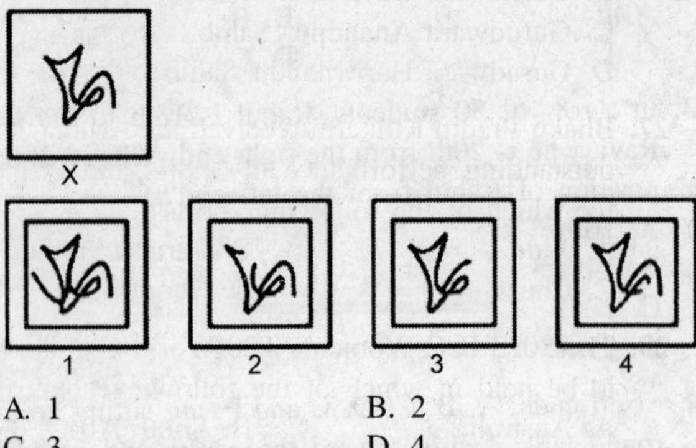

A. 1 B. 2
C. 3 D. 4

20. Four letter-cluster pairs have been given, out of which three are alike in some manner and one is different. Select the one that is different.

A. VXZ – ACF
B. FHJ – KMO
C. CEG – HJL
D. KMO – PRT

GENERAL AWARENESS

21. Hydrogen peroxide is decomposed by the enzymes _______.
A. catalase B. isomerases
C. lyases D. oxidoreductases

22. Which of the following political parties recorded its victory in the Municipal Corporation of Delhi (MCD) elections in 2022 by winning 134 seats?
A. Indian National Congress (INC)
B. Nationalist Congress Party (NCP)
C. Bharatiya Janata Party (BJP)
D. Aam Aadmi Party (AAP)

23. Alfred High School, from which Mahatma Gandhi completed his schooling, is located in which of the following cities of Gujarat?
A. Porbandar B. Ahmedabad
C. Bhavnagar D. Rajkot

24. The first Lodi ruler Bahlol Lodi ruled between _______.
A. 1452 AD and 1499 AD
B. 1454 AD and 1501 AD
C. 1453 AD and 1500 AD
D. 1451 AD and 1489 AD

25. In October 2022, the Department of Telecommunications (DoT) initially announced that 5G services would be launched in how many cities?
A. 14 B. 15
C. 12 D. 13

26. In which of the following Gurdwara did Guru Gobind Singh establish the Khalsa Panth in 1699?
A. Gurudwara Takht Sri Patna Sahib
B. Gurudwara Baba Atal Sahib
C. Gurudwara Anandpur Sahib
D. Gurudwara Hari Mandir Sahib

27. Bhakti Pradip Kulkarni received the Arjuna Award for outstanding performance in Sports and Games 2022 for which of the following sports?
A. Judo B. Para swimming
C. Chess D. Shooting

28. The 2023 ICC Women's T20 World Cup is scheduled to be held in which of the following countries?
A. Australia B. South Africa
C. India D. New Zealand

29. Malus' law is related to which of the following subjects?
A. Surface tension B. Light
C. Gravity D. Inertia

30. Sukhna Lake is located in which of the following union territories?
A. Jammu and Kashmir B. Chandigarh
C. Ladakh D. Lakshadweep

31. The Deposit Insurance Corporation commenced functioning in which of the following years?
A. 1963 B. 1965
C. 1964 D. 1962

32. Sultan Garhi, built in 1231 for Prince Nasiruddin, said to be the first Islamic mausoleum in India, is located in which of the following cities of India?
A. Panipat B. Lucknow
C. Delhi D. Agra

33. As per RBI guidelines for licensing of small finance banks in the private sector, the minimum initial share of the promoter in the paid up equity capital will be at least _______.
A. 60 per cent B. 45 per cent
C. 50 per cent D. 40 per cent

34. Which of the following national parks is known for the Lesser Panda or Red Panda?
A. Bandipur National Park
B. Jim Corbett National Park
C. Nagarhole National Park
D. Singalila National Park

35. What is the number of deaths of women as a result of complications from pregnancy or childbirth during a given year per 100,000 live births during that year?
A. Maturation Mortality Rate (MMR)
B. Maternal Mortality Rate (MMR)
C. Motherly Mortality Rate (MMR)
D. Mother Mortality Rate (MMR)

36. The report of which of the following committee was challenged in the Supreme Court in 2021? The committee was constituted to examine the social, economic and educational condition of the Muslim community.
A. Shah Committee
B. Mahajan Committee
C. Khusro Committee
D. Sachar Committee

37. Which of the following pair is not correctly matched?
A. Battle of Khanwa – Year 1527
B. Battle of Chausa – Year 1539
C. Battle of Chanderi – Year 1544
D. Battle of Kannauj – Year 1540

38. Gardi dance is a popular folk dance of which of the following parts of India?
A. Northeast India B. Western India
C. Northern India D. Southern India

39. According to the Sample Registration System Statistical Report 2020 released by the Registrar General of India on September 22, 2022, what was the infant mortality rate of India in the year 2020?
A. 30 B. 24
C. 28 D. 26

40. In which city was the Indian Mobile Congress-2022 organized?
A. Mysore
B. Bengaluru
C. New Delhi
D. Mumbai

ARITHMETICAL AND NUMERICAL ABILITY

41. Study the given graph and answer the following question.

Rice production by States A, B and C during 2018 to 2020 (in lakh tonnes)

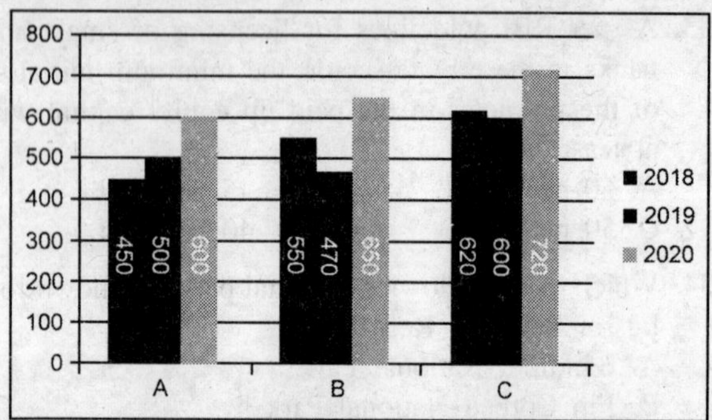

The average production (per year) of rice by A, B, and C in 2018 is what per cent less than the production of rice by state C in 2020?
A. $33\frac{1}{3}\%$ B. 25%
C. 18% D. 20%

42. An article is sold at ₹ 351.91 on its marked price ₹ 450 after giving two successive discounts of x and 15%. If a single discount of $2x\%$ is given on its marked price, what will be its selling price?
A. ₹ 387.50
B. ₹ 378
C. ₹ 360
D. ₹ 382.50

43. Solution A contains spirit and water in the ratio 6 : 7 and solution B contains water and spirit in the ratio 9 : 4. 3L of A is mixed with 5L of B. What is the amount (in mL) of spirit in 780 mL of the resulting solution?
A. 304 B. 266
C. 270 D. 285

44. The time taken by a boat to go 21 km downstream is equal to the time taken by it to go 9 km upstream. To go 12 km downstream and the same distance upstream, it takes a total of $5\frac{5}{7}$ hours. How much time (in hours) will the boat take to go 28 km downstream?
A. 4 B. $3\frac{1}{9}$
C. $3\frac{1}{2}$ D. 5

45. The curved surface area of a right circular cone is 444 π cm^3 and the diameter of its base is 24 cm. What is the volume of the cone (in cm^3)?
A. 840 π B. 1400 π
C. 1120 π D. 1680 π

46. Study the given pie chart and answer the following question.

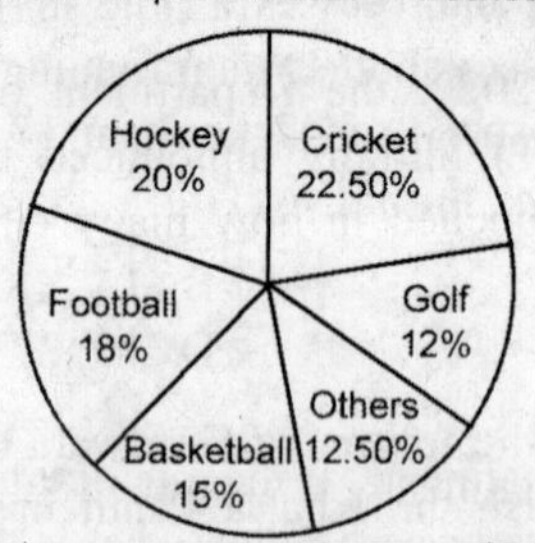

If the total amount spent on Basketball and Hockey is ₹ x more than the total amount spent on Football and Golf, then the value of x lies between:
A. 3,800 and 4,200 B. 3,600 and 3,800
C. 4,200 and 4,400 D. 4,400 and 4,600

47. The price of tea increased by 40% and then decreased by 20%. If a person now reduces his consumption of tea by $6\frac{1}{4}\%$, then what is the percentage change in his expenditure?
A. Increase, 15% B. Decrease, 15%
C. Decrease, 5% D. Increase, 5%

48. The area of a rectangular field is 1008 m^2. Its shorter side is $\frac{1}{8}$ of the sum of its longer side and one of its diagonals. What is the cost of fencing the field at ₹ 24 per m?
A. ₹ 3,744 B. ₹ 3,840
C. ₹ 3,792 D. ₹ 3,696

49. The value of $\dfrac{\frac{1}{2}\times\frac{3}{4}\div\frac{2}{5}\text{ of }1\frac{1}{4}}{5\frac{1}{2}\div3\frac{2}{3}\text{ of }\frac{1}{2}-3\frac{1}{2}+7\frac{1}{2}\div\frac{2}{5}\text{ of }3\frac{3}{4}}$ is:

A. $\frac{1}{2}$ B. $\frac{5}{4}$
C. $\frac{3}{2}$ D. $\frac{1}{6}$

50. Let x be the least number which when divided by 11, 21, 24 and 28, leaves a remainder of 10 in each case. If x is divisible by 37, what will be the sum of the digits of x?

A. 17 B. 15
C. 16 D. 13

51. Pipes A and B can fill a tank in 20 hours and 30 hours, respectively. Pipe C is an emptying pipe. When all the three pipes are opened together, $\frac{2}{9}$th part of the tank is filled in 8 hours. Pipe C alone can empty $\frac{1}{3}$rd part of the tank in:

A. 4 hours B. 3 hours
C. 5 hours D. 6 hours

52. A 240-m-long train passes a pole in 18 seconds and completely passes another train running in the opposite direction at a speed of 42 km/h in 17 seconds. What is the length of the other train?

A. 200 m B. 195 m
C. 170 m D. 185 m

53. A loan of ₹ 10,200 is to be paid back in two equal half-yearly instalments. If the rate of interest is 8% p.a., compounded half-yearly, then what is the total interest charged in this scheme?

A. ₹ 616 B. ₹ 636
C. ₹ 620 D. ₹ 600

54. x varies directly as y and inversely as z. When $y = 1.5$ and $z = 2$, then $x = 5$. If $z = 2.5$ and $y = 9$, then what is the value of x?

A. 15 B. 12
C. 20 D. 24

55. Two numbers, A and B are in the ratio of 10 : 13. If 90 is subtracted from each of them, the resulting numbers are in the ratio of 7 : 10. If 57 is added to A and 16 is subtracted from B, then the ratio of the resulting numbers will be:

A. 20 : 21 B. 19 : 20
C. 22 : 23 D. 21 : 22

56. P and Q started a business by investing their capitals in the ratio of 1 : 2 and the period of P's investment is three times that of Q. If P received a profit of ₹ 22,800, then what is the total profit?

A. ₹ 38,000 B. ₹ 36,000
C. ₹ 36,900 D. ₹ 42,000

57. The volume of a right circular cylinder is 554.4 cm^3 and its height is 10 cm. What is the perimeter of the base of the cylinder? (Use $\pi = 22/7$)

A. 22 cm B. 44 cm
C. 26.4 cm D. 17.6 cm

58. The simple interest on a certain sum for 10 years at 9.5% p.a. is ₹ 2,832 less than the amount of the same sum for $3\frac{1}{2}$ years at 7% p.a, simple interst. The sum (in ₹) is:

A. 9,600 B. 9,500
C. 9,800 D. 9,200

59. By selling an article at $\frac{23}{40}$ of its selling price, a shopkeeper loses 8%. If it is sold at 90% of its original selling price, then the profit percentage is:

A. 44% B. 35%
C. 38% D. 40%

60. A man travels the first 2 hours at a speed of 45 km/h, the next $3\frac{1}{2}$ hours at a speed of 60 km/h and the next $4\frac{1}{2}$ hours at a speed of 70 km/h. What is his average speed (in km/h) for the entire journey?

A. 63 B. 62
C. 60.5 D. 61.5

ENGLISH LANGUAGE AND COMPREHENSION

61. Select the ***most appropriate*** meaning of the underlined proverb.

By arresting all the group leaders, they nipped the rebellion in the bud.

A. To halt something at an early stage
B. To fight back
C. To punish the opponents
D. To create a commotion

62. Select the ***most appropriate*** option to fill in the blank with the correct collocation.

The jeep crashed and ______ flames.

A. burst into B. burst onto
C. burst in D. bursts out

63. Select the ***most appropriate*** option to fill in the blanks.

There can be several _____ of indoor air pollution. Tobacco smoke is one of the _____ important air pollutants in closed places. 'Passive smoking' or environmental tobacco smoke (ETS) pollution can lead to all the harmful _____ of tobacco smoking seen in the smokers in their non-smoking companions. The children of smoking parents are among the worst _____ persons.

A. sources, much, effects, affected
B. sources, many, effects, affected
C. sources, most, effects, affected
D. sources, most, affects, effected

64. Select the ***most appropriate*** option to fill in the blanks.

Travellers to space go beyond the orbit of the earth and _______ the orbit of the moon. On the other _____, the suborbital tourist will travel in a rocket _____ the International Space Station only. Space travel is not possible for everyone, ______ suborbital tourism is a possible alternative.

A. reach, hands, into, and
B. reach, hand, upto, but
C. reached, hand, upto, because
D. reach, hand, onto, since

65. Select the ***most appropriate*** option to fill in the blanks.

Call it a blessing or a _____ of Mother Nature, we have to breathe in _____ 10,000 litres of air in a day to remain alive. By making it essential for life, God has wished that we try to _____ the air we breathe clean. Everyone can see the food that is not clean and perhaps refrain from eating it, _____ one cannot stop breathing even if one can feel the air to be polluted.

A. curse, over, keep, but
B. curse, over, keeping, yet
C. curse, between, keep, because
D. cursing, over, keep, since

66. Sentences of a paragraph are given below in jumbled order. Arrange the sentences in the correct order to form a meaningful and coherent paragraph.

1. I carried a small load on my back as others knowing that it will help in getting to a new nation that is about to be my nation and build a new life.
2. In the dead of the night, I walked with my family, away from my home, my street, my town, and what was till yesterday - my country.
3. Even if they get on that train to Amritsar and arrive there in one piece, they would just be a wisp of what they once were.
4. There were other families with us, snaking their way to Lahore railway station in fear, pain and certainty that their lives are not theirs anymore.

A. 2, 4, 3, 1　　B. 1, 2, 3, 4
C. 4, 1, 3, 2　　D. 3, 4, 1, 2

67. Select the ***most appropriate*** option to fill in the blanks.

Spam is the flooding of the internet with _____ copies of the same message, in an attempt to force the ______ on people who would not otherwise _____ to receive it. Spam is basically ______ junk mail or junk newsgroup postings. It is sometimes confused with any unsolicited email.

A. more, massage, choose, electronics
B. much, message, chose, electronic
C. many, message, choose, electronic
D. many, massage, chosen, electronic

68. Select the ***most appropriate*** meaning of the given idiom.

Up a creek without a paddle

A. To be in an unlucky/bad situation
B. To work hard to achieve success
C. To wish for something good to happen
D. To take revenge

69. Select the option that can be used as a one-word substitute for the given group of words.

Statistical study of the human population

A. Lexicography　　B. Demography
C. Silvology　　D. Econometrics

70. Select the option that contains no spelling error.

A. While turmeric is completely safe as a food ingredient and safe for most people as a suplement, there can be side affects.
B. While turmeric is completely safe as a food ingredient and safe for most people as a supplement, there can be side effects.
C. While turrmeric is completely safe as a food ingredeint and safe for most people as a supplement, there can be side affects.
D. While turmerric is completely safe as a food ingredient and safe for most people as a suppliment, there can be side effects.

71. Select the ***most appropriate*** option to fill in the blanks.

I thanked my friend who _____ me a 99 _____ worth imported _____ for my birthday.

A. cent, scent, sent　　B. sent, cent, scent
C. scent, sent, cent　　D. sent, scent, cent

72. Sentences of a paragraph are given below in jumbled order. Arrange the sentences in the correct order to form a meaningful and coherent paragraph.

1. She was at the university working on her PhD thesis.
2. It was approaching 2 a.m. when Lexi made the discovery that would fracture the world.
3. The research involved creating controlled, miniature black holes in a Vacuity Machine and then testing its potential for hyper-space travel which was mostly hypothetical research.

4. She skulled the rest of her black coffee and sat the paper cup down on the smooth, white table.

A. 1, 2, 3, 4 B. 3, 2, 4, 1
C. 2, 4, 1, 3 D. 2, 4, 3, 1

73. Select the ***most appropriate*** option that can substitute the underlined segment in the given sentence. If there is no need to substitute it, select 'No substitution required'.

No sooner did we arrived at the railway station than we got into an argument with the auto driver.

A. No sooner had we arrive
B. No substitution required
C. No sooner did we arrives
D. No sooner did we arrive

74. Select the ***most appropriate*** option that can substitute the underlined segment in the given sentence. If there is no need to substitute it, select 'No substitution required'.

When plastic waste was burnt, a complex weave of toxic chemicals is released.

A. is burnt B. No substitution required
C. were burnt D. are burnt

75. Select the one-word substitute for the underlined group of words that can fill in the blank.

A _____ is an industrial facility which manufactures coins that can be used as currency.

A. mint B. bank
C. kiln D. treasury

Directions (Qs. No. 76-80): *Read the given passage and answer the questions that follow.*

Good health is the soundness of body, mind and soul. It is that condition in which the body and mind duly discharge their functions. Good health helps everyone to be creative and work for the welfare of the society. He has to be, therefore, free from diseases: or, if he suffers from a disease he needs treatments not only for that particular disease but for the whole body, mind and soul. In other words, a doctor has to have a sound approach to the patients.

In these days of specialisation, doctors cure a patient only for his immediate disease, treating it in isolation. Such an approach goes against the old aphorism that 'prevention is better than cure'. Dr. Hedge provides insight into the overall causes of simple and serious disease and describes the methods of preventing them without having to take medicine but exercising, self-control on food consumption, smoking and intake of alcoholic drinks. He also advocates regular yoga exercise and meditation to keep fit, but at the same time warns against over indulgence.

Hedge stresses the importance of laughter because laughter induces secretion of good catecholamine, which is a hormone produced by adrenal glands; they can be both beneficial and harmful. They are harmful when a person is angry, but beneficial if he laughs. For a healthy living, "Laughter proves to be great boon," Hedge says.

In these days of hectic life, full of stress, strain and emotions, everyone needs to lead a relaxed life. The best form of relaxation, according to Hedge, is sound sleep. "Restful sleep at night will recharge our batteries for the following day's fruitful endeavour," he says. There is no use of lying on the bed and tossing without sleep. Under those circumstances it is better to read or engage oneself in some light mental activities which are useful. But never seek refuge in alcoholic drinks or pills for inducing sleep, as these are not refreshing for an individual. For a normal human being, eight hours of sleep a day is sufficient to keep him free from stress. More than nine to ten hours of sleep a day would produce increased muscle protein loss in the body and might even shorten one's life.

76. Identify the tone of the passage.

A. Humanistic
B. Ethical
C. Cynical
D. Emotional

77. From the given options identify the ***most appropriate*** synonym of the underlined word as used in the passage.

Good health helps everyone to be creative and work for the welfare of the society.

A. Imitative B. Fertile
C. Innovative D. Enervated

78. Identify the most suitable title for the given passage.

A. The Importance of Laughter
B. Yoga Exercise and Meditation
C. Good Health for All
D. Good sleep of 15 hours

79. Which of the following sentences is NOT true in the context of the given passage?

A. A restful sleep at night will recharge our batteries for the following day's cataclysmic endeavour.
B. In these days of specialisation, doctors cure a patient only for his immediate disease, treating it in quarantine.
C. Good health is that condition in which the body and mind duly discharge their functions.
D. Dr. Hedge advocates regular yoga exercise and meditation to keep fit, but at the same time cautions against overindulgence.

80. From the given options identify the ***most appropriate*** ANTONYM of the underlined word as used in the passage.

In these days of hectic life, full of stress, strain and emotions, everyone needs to lead a relaxed life.

A. Frenzied B. Postponed
C. Leisurely D. Delayed

HINDI LANGUAGE AND COMPREHENSION

81. 'जो विधि के विरुद्ध है'– इस वाक्यांश के लिए एक शब्द का चयन करें।

A. अविधिक B. वैधानिक

C. अवैध D. अक्षम

82. उचित तद्भव शब्द का चयन करके निम्न वाक्य पूर्ण करें।

'______ आजकल हर जगह उपलब्ध है।

A. नारिकेल B. गेहूँ

C. गोधूम D. खेत

83. 'सदाचार' शब्द के शुद्ध संधि-विच्छेद का चयन कीजिये।

A. सत् + आचार B. सद् + आचार

C. सद् + अचार D. सत् + अचार

84. 'उन्नति के लिए मानसिक और आर्थिक ______ की आवश्यकता होती है।

स्व विवेकानुसार उचित शब्द चुनकर, उपरोक्त वाक्य में रिक्त स्थान की पूर्ति करें।

A. सक्षमता B. सकारात्मकता

C. आत्मनिर्भरता D. विविधता

85. निम्नलिखित में से कौन-सा शब्द 'थकान' का पर्याय नहीं है?

A. आश्विन B. श्रान्ति

C. क्लान्ति D. परिश्रान्ति

86. 'सोहत ओढ़े पीत-पट स्याम सलोने गात।
मनो नील मनि शैल पर आतप परयो प्रभात।।'

उक्त पंक्तियाँ, निम्न में से किस अलंकार का उदाहरण हैं?

A. अतिशयोक्ति B. उत्प्रेक्षा

C. उपमा D. रूपक

87. ''केकी-रव की नूपुर ध्वनि सुन,
जगती जगती की मूक प्यास।''

इन पंक्तियों में कौन-सा अलंकार है?

A. यमक B. श्लेष

C. वीप्सा D. वक्रोक्ति

88. 'देवता ______ कर जाना'– मुहावरे के रिक्त स्थान को सही शब्द से भरें।

A. देख B. भाग

C. कूच D. आ

89. 'मीनकेतु' शब्द के उचित विग्रह की पहचान करें।

A. मीन की आँख है जिनकी वे कामदेव

B. मील वाला केतु

C. मछली की ध्वजा वाले कामदेव

D. मीन की केतु है जिनकी अर्थात कामदेव

90. 'एक दिन का आवना, दूजे दिन अनखावना'– उक्त लोकोक्ति का प्रथम खंड अशुद्ध है। शुद्ध खंड का चयन करें।

A. चार दिन का पाहुना B. एक दिन का पाहुना

C. एक दिन का खावना D. अच्छे दिन का आवना

91. निम्नलिखित में से शुद्ध वाक्य का चयन करें।

A. एक ऐसा जीवन है राजपथ जिससे होकर सभी को चलना पड़ता है।

B. एक ऐसा राजपथ जिससे होकर चलना पड़ता है सभी को जीवन है।

C. एक ऐसा जीवन राजपथ है जिससे होकर चलना पड़ता है सभी को।

D. जीवन एक ऐसा राजपथ है जिससे होकर सभी को चलना पड़ता है।

92. दिए गए शब्दों में से शुद्ध विलोमार्थी-युग्म की पहचान करें।

A. व्याप्त – संकुचित B. शम्बर – पार्वती

C. शानदार – शर्मनाक D. शुभ्र – श्वेत

93. 'अन्वेषण' शब्द के शुद्ध संधि-विच्छेद का चयन कीजिये।

A. अना + एषण B. अनु + वेषण

C. अन्ते + षण D. अनु + एषण

94. 'कानून की अनभिज्ञता से बहुत हानि होती है इसलिए उसकी ______ आवश्यक है।'

उपयुक्त शब्द चुनकर, उपरोक्त वाक्य में रिक्त स्थान की पूर्ति करें।

A. अल्पज्ञता B. अज्ञानता

C. विज्ञता D. अज्ञता

95. निम्न वाक्य में रेखांकित शब्द में क्रिया का कौन-सा रूप है?

'कृष्ण बाँसुरी <u>बजाकर</u> गोपियों को नचाते है।'

A. पूर्वकालिक क्रिया B. संयुक्त क्रिया

C. नामबोधक क्रिया D. क्रियार्थक संज्ञा

निर्देश (प्र.सं. 96-100): *दिए गए गद्यांश को ध्यान से पढ़ें और प्रश्न के उत्तर दें।*

मनुष्य उत्सव प्रिय होते हैं। उत्सव का एकमात्र उद्देश्य आनंद प्राप्ति है। यह तो सभी जानते है कि मनुष्य अपनी आवश्यकता की पूर्ति के लिए आजीवन प्रयत्न करता रहता है। आवश्यकता की पूर्ति होने पर सभी को सुख होता है पर उस सुख और उत्सव के इस आनंद में बड़ा अंतर है। आवश्यकता अभाव सूचित करती है। उससे यह प्रकट होता है कि हमें किसी बात की कमी है। मनुष्य-जीवन ही ऐसा है कि वह किसी भी अवस्था में यह अनुभव नहीं कर सकता कि अब उसके लिए कोई आवश्यकता नहीं रह गई है। एक के बाद दूसरी वस्तु की चिंता उसे सताती ही रहती है। इसलिए किसी एक आवश्यकता की पूर्ति से उसे जो सुख होता है, वह अत्यंत क्षणिक होता है; क्योंकि तुरंत ही दूसरी आवश्यकता

उपस्थित हो जाती है। उत्सव में हम किसी बात की आवश्यकता का अनुभव नहीं करते। यह आनंद जीवन का आनंद है, काम का नहीं। उस दिन हम अपनी सारी आवश्यकताओं को भूल कर केवल मनुष्यत्व का ख्याल करते हैं। उस दिन हम अपनी स्वार्थ-चिंता छोड़ देते हैं, कर्तव्य-भार की उपेक्षा कर देते हैं तथा गौरव और सम्मान को भूल जाते हैं। उस दिन हममें उच्छृंखलता आ जाती है, स्वच्छंदता आ जाती है। उस रोज हमारी दिनचर्या बिल्कुल नष्ट हो जाती है। व्यर्थ घूम कर, व्यर्थ काम कर, व्यर्थ खा-पीकर हम लोग अपने मन में अनुभव करते हैं कि हम सच्चा आनंद पा रहे हैं।

96. गद्यांश में प्रयुक्त शब्द 'सम्मान' के विलोम-युग्म का चयन कीजिये।

A. निरादर
B. बेइज्जती
C. आदर
D. अपमान

97. निम्नलिखित में से किस वाक्य में 'क्षणिक' शब्द का उचित प्रयोग किया गया है?

A. यह विपत्ति तो क्षणिक है, चली जायेगी।
B. मेरे घर बहुत से क्षणिक अतिथि आये हैं।
C. आज हमारे समाज में क्षणिक उत्सव है।
D. अपनी क्षणिक भूख के लिए तुमने सारी रोटियाँ खा ली।

98. गद्यांश में जीवन का कौन-सा गहन तथ्य छुपा हुआ है?

A. उत्सव में हम किसी बात की आवश्यकता का अनुभव नहीं करते जिससे सब अभाव खत्म हो जाते हैं।
B. मनुष्य अपनी आवश्यकता की पूर्ति के लिए आजीवन प्रयत्न करता रहता है, किन्तु सुख की प्राप्ति नहीं कर पाता। आवश्यकताओं की पूर्ति और आनंद का एकमात्र साधन उत्सव हैं।
C. मनुष्य-जीवन ऐसा है कि वह किसी भी अवस्था में यह अनुभव नहीं कर सकता कि अब उसके लिए कोई आवश्यकता नहीं रह गई है इसलिए आवश्यकता की पूर्ति होने पर उसे सुख होता है।
D. उत्सव में किसी अभाव का अनुभव न होने से विशुद्ध आनंद की प्राप्ति होती है और हम सही अर्थों में चिन्ता-मुक्त और स्वच्छंद होकर, कुछ समय के लिए, जीवन का रसास्वादन कर पाते हैं, किन्तु यह आनंद वास्तविक और स्थायी होता है मन को नयी शक्ति देता है।

99. निम्नलिखित में से कौन-सा शब्द 'केवल' का पर्यायवाची नहीं है?

A. निरा
B. एकमात्र
C. सिर्फ
D. भी

100. उपर्युक्त गद्यांश के लिए उचित शीर्षक का चयन करें।

A. उत्सव का महत्व
B. कार्य-भार और उत्सव
C. स्वछंद उत्सव
D. निरुद्देश्य उत्सव

SECTION-B

POST SPECIFIC SUBJECT

101. Haptic technology is used to provide ______ feedback to a user.

A. olfactory
B. innovative
C. visual
D. tactile

102. What is the number of terms in the given expression?

$$\left(x^2 + \frac{2}{x}\right)^{11}$$

A. 24
B. 12
C. 11
D. 22

103. An unhappy employee because of ______ processes in a business can negatively affect the corporate image of the business and make the business less successful.

A. easy communication
B. instant communication
C. poor communication
D. frequent communication

104. The given diagram expresses ______.

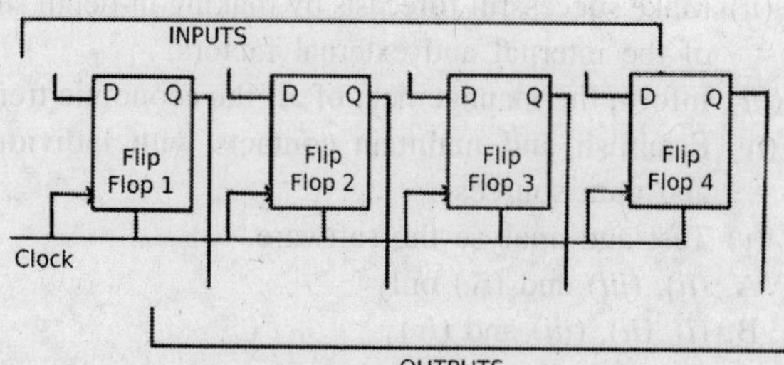

A. Serial-In Serial-Out Shift Register
B. Parallel-In Parallel-Out Shift Register
C. Serial-In Parallel-Out Shift Register
D. Parallel-In Serial-Out Shift Register

105. Which of the following is a storage allocation scheme in which secondary memory can be addressed as though it were part of the main memory?

A. CPU register memory
B. Virtual memory
C. Secondary memory
D. CPU buffer memory

106. Which of the following are the advantages of using the NEFT system?

Advantages:
(*i*) The transaction has legal backing.
(*ii*) Round the clock availability on all days of the year.
(*iii*) Near-real-time funds transfer to the beneficiary account and settlement in a secure manner.
(*iv*) Positive confirmation to the remitter by SMS/ e-mail on credit to the beneficiary account.

A. (*i*), (*ii*), (*iii*) and (*iv*)
B. (*ii*), (*iii*) and (*iv*) only
C. (*i*) and (*ii*) only
D. (*i*), (*ii*) and (*iii*) only

107. Which of the following database management systems is developed by Microsoft?

A. SQL Server B. MySQL
C. PostgreSQL D. Oracle

108. The process of organising the contents of each file into contiguous regions and creating larger areas of free space on the hard disk is called ______ and ______ is the process of making computer files take up less space on your computer by reducing the size of the file.

A. compression; formatting
B. defragmentation; compression
C. debugging; assembly
D. defragmentation; mirroring

109. Which of the following are responsibilities of a Business Economist?

Responsibilities:
(*i*) Make a reasonable profit on capital employed.
(*ii*) Make successful forecasts by making in-depth study of the internal and external factors.
(*iii*) Inform the management of all the economic trends.
(*iv*) Establish and maintain contacts with individuals and data sources.
(*v*) Test and analyse the software.

A. (*ii*), (*iii*) and (*iv*) only
B. (*i*), (*ii*), (*iii*) and (*iv*)
C. (*i*), (*ii*) and (*v*) only
D. (*i*), (*iii*) and (*v*) only

110. Which of the following is/are key knowledge management process(es)?

Processes:
(*i*) Knowledge gathering
(*ii*) Knowledge storage and organisation
(*iii*) Knowledge distribution
(*iv*) Knowledge use

A. (*i*), (*ii*) and (*iv*) only B. (*iii*) only
C. (*ii*), (*iii*) and (*iv*) only D. (*i*), (*ii*), (*iii*) and (*iv*)

111. Which of the following is a barrier to e-commerce relevant to micro-environmental issues (external to the organisation)?

A. Business models
B. Culture
C. Internet infrastructure
D. Lack of experts

112. Which of the given options best describes the truthfulness of the following statements?

(*i*) Assembly languages are machine dependent.
(*ii*) A compiler is a program which produces a machine level program from the specifications of a high-level language.
(*iii*) An interpreter translates and executes each program statement, one at a time.
(*iv*) 'BASIC' language is an interactive programming language.

	(*i*)	(*ii*)	(*iii*)	(*iv*)
A.	True	True	True	True
B.	True	True	False	True
C.	False	True	True	True
D.	True	False	True	True

113. Which of the following is NOT a front-end technology?

A. HTML B. JavaScript
C. PL/SQL D. CSS

114. A/An ______ is a user-defined datatype which has data members and member functions.

A. package
B. class
C. method
D. object

115. Match the column JavaScript-Events with the column Descriptions.

(JavaScript-Events)	***(Descriptions)***
(*a*) onchange	(*i*) The browser has finished loading the page.
(*b*) onmouseover	(*ii*) An HTML element has been changed.
(*c*) onkeydown	(*iii*) The user moves the mouse over an HTML element.
(*d*) onload	(*iv*) The user pushes a keyboard key.

	(*a*)	(*b*)	(*c*)	(*d*)
A.	(*iii*)	(*ii*)	(*iv*)	(*i*)
B.	(*ii*)	(*iv*)	(*iii*)	(*i*)
C.	(*ii*)	(*iii*)	(*iv*)	(*i*)
D.	(*iv*)	(*iii*)	(*i*)	(*ii*)

116. A ______ is the subset of a process and is also known as the lightweight process.

A. Process B. Library
C. Program D. Thread

117. Which of the following statements is/are INCORRECT about the Z-buffer algorithm in computer graphics?

Statements:

(*i*) It is an image space method to detect visible surface.

(*ii*) In this method, a depth buffer is used to store the depth values of each position and a refresh (frame) buffer is used to store the intensity values or colour values for each position.

(*iii*) In this method, object edges can be anti aliased.

(*iv*) This method can only find one visible surface at each pixel position.

A. (*iii*) only B. (*i*), (*ii*), (*iii*) and (*iv*)
C. (*ii*), (*iii*) and (*iv*) only D. (*i*), (*ii*) and (*iv*) only

118. Which of the given options best describes the truthfulness of the following statements?

(*i*) VB.NET is an object-oriented programming language implemented in the .NET Framework.

(*ii*) VB.NET is subset of Visual basic 6.0.

(*iii*) .NET is a free, cross-platform, open-source developer platform for building many different types of applications.

	(*i*)	(*ii*)	(*iii*)
A.	False	True	True
B.	True	True	True
C.	False	False	True
D.	True	False	True

119. Match the column Functions with the column descriptions.

(Functions)	*(Descriptions)*
(*a*) Multiprocessing	(*i*) Two or more users can work with programs and share peripheral devices, such as printers, at the same time.
(*b*) Multithreading	(*ii*) The computer can have two or more central processing units (CPUs) that programs share.
(*c*) Multiuser	(*iii*) A program can be broken into smaller parts that can be loaded as needed by the operating system.

	(*a*)	(*b*)	(*c*)
A.	(*ii*)	(*i*)	(*iii*)
B.	(*i*)	(*iii*)	(*ii*)
C.	(*ii*)	(*iii*)	(*i*)
D.	(*iii*)	(*ii*)	(*i*)

120. Mobile Agents are also called ______ agents. They are of two types: Mobile Agents with pre-defined path and Mobile Agents with undefined path.

A. connector
B. transportable
C. linker
D. migrator

121. The main purpose of a/an ______ is to record, process validate and store transition that take place in various function areas of a business for future retrieval of use.

A. transaction processing sytem
B. knowledge management system
C. executive support system
D. decision support system

122. Which of the following Linux commands is/are used to search content from files?

Commands:

(*i*) grep (*ii*) egrep
(*iii*) fgrep (*iv*) find
(*v*) tail (*vi*) tr

A. (*ii*), (*iii*) and (*iv*) only B. (*i*), (*ii*) and (*iii*) only
C. (*v*) and (*vi*) only D. (*iv*) only

123. If A = {1, 2, 3, 4}, B = {2, 4, 5} and C = {2, 5} then (A – B) × (B – C) = ?

A. {1, 4} B. {1, 3}
C. {1, 3, 4, 5} D. {1, 3, 4}

124. Which of the following are the objectives of financial accounting?

(*i*) Proper recording of transactions

(*ii*) Ascertainment of the financial position

(*iii*) Reporting financial information

(*iv*) Defalcation prevention

(*v*) Digital marketing

A. (*i*), (*ii*), (*iii*) and (*iv*) only
B. (*ii*) and (*iii*) only
C. (*i*), (*iii*) and (*iv*) only
D. (*i*) and (*ii*) only

125. What is the output of the following 'C' language statements?

```
#include <stdio.h>
int main () {
int a = 10, b = 20, *p1 = & a, *p2 = &b;
printf("Before : **p1 = %d **p2 = %d", *p1,
*p2);
*p1 = *p1 + *p2;
*p2 = *p1 - *p2;
*p1 = *p1 - *p2;
printf("\nAfter : **p1 = %d **p2=%d", *p1,
*p2);
return 0;
}
```

A. Before : **p1 = 10 **p2 = 20
After : **p1 = 20 **p2 = 10
B. Before : *p1 = 10 *p2 = 20
After : *p1 = 20 *p2 = 20
C. Before : p1 = 10 p2 = 20
After : p1 = 20 p2 = 10
D. Before : **p1 = 20 **p2 = 10
After : **p1 = 10 **p2 = 20

126. Select the option that best describes the truthfulness of the following statements.

(*i*) RAM is a volatile memory having a limited storage capacity.

(*ii*) Secondary memory is storage other than the RAM and ROM.

	(*i*)	(*ii*)
A.	True	False
B.	False	False
C.	False	True
D.	True	True

127. Which of the following is NOT an input/output redirection symbol that Linux shell assigns?

A. < B. >
C. >> D. !

128. Consider the following disk request sequence for a disk with 100 tracks:

60, 45, 21, 67

Head pointer starting at 60 and moving in the left direction. Find the number of head movements in cylinders using FCFS scheduling.

A. 85 B. 90
C. 80 D. 193

129. Which of the given options best describes the truthfulness of the following statements?

(*i*) In the probability theory, an outcome is the result of random experiment.

(*ii*) The purpose of statistical inference is to estimate the uncertainty or sample to sample variation.

(*iii*) A sampling error is the difference between the true population values (called parameters) and the measured sample values (called statistics).

	(*i*)	(*ii*)	(*iii*)
A.	True	True	True
B.	False	False	True
C.	True	False	True
D.	False	True	True

130. Which of the following languages is a non .NET language?

A. Pascal B. C#
C. F# D. J#

131. In Managed Ad-hoc Network (MANET), under which attack, malicious node injects fault routing information to the network, in order to locate packets into a loop?

A. Snooping attack B. Worm Hole attack
C. DNS attack D. Byzantine attack

132. Which of the following is/are associated with turbulent flow?

(*i*) Flow of liquid is orderly.

(*ii*) Flow of liquid is zigzag and random.

A. Only (*ii*) B. Neither (*i*) nor (*ii*)
C. Only (*i*) D. Both (*i*) and (*ii*)

133. Match the column 'Moduli of elasticity' with the column 'Descriptions'.

(Moduli of elasticity)	***(Descriptions)***
(*a*) Young's modulus	(*i*) It is the ratio of the shearing stress applied to the body to the shearing strain produced
(*b*) Bulk (or) Volume modulus	(*ii*) It is defined as the ratio of linear stress to linear strain
(*c*) Shearing (or) Rigidity modulus	(*iii*) It is defined as the ratio of bulk stress to bulk strain.

	(*a*)	(*b*)	(*c*)
A.	(*iii*)	(*ii*)	(*i*)
B.	(*ii*)	(*iii*)	(*i*)
C.	(*ii*)	(*i*)	(*iii*)
D.	(*i*)	(*iii*)	(*ii*)

134. Which of the following firewalls examine traffic and filter on application-specific commands such as http:post or http:get?

A. Packet filters
B. Stateful multilayer inspection firewalls
C. Application gateways
D. Circuit level gateways

135. Which of the following software is used by a wide range of industries for project planning, resource allocation and scheduling?

A. Firewall software
B. Project management software
C. CRM software
D. Word process

136. Which of the given options best describes the truthfulness of the following statements?

(*i*) When a Java program is compiled, it generates Byte code.

(*ii*) SOAP and RESTFUL are java web services.

(*iii*) PATH Environment variable identifies the location of Java compiler.

(*iv*) The || logical operator returns true if both statement are true.

	(*i*)	(*ii*)	(*iii*)	(*iv*)
A.	True	False	True	False
B.	True	False	True	True
C.	False	True	True	False
D.	True	True	True	False

137. Which of the given options best describes the truthfulness of the following statements?

(*i*) Class is one of the HTML global attributes which specifies one or more class names for an element (refer to a class in a style sheet).

(*ii*) HTML is a markup language used for server-side processing.

(*iii*) CSS describes how HTML elements are to be displayed on screen paper, or in other media.

	(i)	(ii)	(iii)
A.	False	True	True
B.	True	True	True
C.	False	True	False
D.	True	False	True

138. A ______ counter is a cascaded arrangement of flip-flops where the output of one flip-flop drives the clock input of the following flip-flop.

A. ring B. synchronous
C. ripple D. cascaded

139. Which of the following is/are type(s) of business communication?

Types:
(i) Internal Business Communication
(ii) Lateral Business Communication
(iii) External Business Communication
(iv) Protected Business Communication

A. (i) only B. (i) and (ii) only
C. (ii), (iii) and (iv) only D. (i), (ii) and (iii) only

140. Which of the given options best describes the truthfulness of the following statements?

(i) XML schemas define datatype for elements and attributes, while DTD doesn't support datatypes.
(ii) DTD are the declarations that define a document type for SGML.
(iii) In XML, Tag names can begin with a numeric value.

	(i)	(ii)	(iii)
A.	True	True	False
B.	False	False	False
C.	True	False	False
D.	False	True	False

141. Which of the following is NOT a valid Software Life Cycle Model?

A. Iterative B. Prototype
C. JAD D. Circular

142. Which of the following protocols assign(s) dynamic IP?

(i) POP (ii) DHCP
(iii) BOOTP (iv) SNMP
(v) ICMP

A. (ii) and (iii) only
B. (ii), (iii), (iv) and (v) only
C. (i), (ii) and (iii) only
D. (i), (ii), (iii) and (v) only

143. Which of the given options best describes the truthfulness of the following statements?

(i) Service Set Identification (SSID) is human readable text string with a maximum length of 2000 bytes.
(ii) Service Set Identification (SSID) acts as a single shared identifier between the access points and clients.

	(i)	(ii)
A.	False	False
B.	True	False
C.	False	True
D.	True	True

144. Which of the following languages are object-oriented programming languages?

Languages:
(i) LISP (ii) Java
(iii) C++ (iv) Simula
(v) SQL (vi) C

A. (ii), (iii) and (iv) only
B. (i), (ii), (iii) and (iv) only
C. (i), (ii), (iii), (iv), (v) and (vi)
D. (i) and (ii) only

145. What is the full form of WPF with respect to ASP.NET?

A. Windows Presentation File
B. Windows Presentation Framework
C. Windows Presentation Foundation
D. Windows Programming Force

146. What is the expected output of the following Python code?

```
print("\nDictionary Iteration")
d = dict()
d['lmn'] = 123
d['abc'] = 345
for i in d:
    print("%s%d" %(i, d[i]))
```

A. Dictionary Iteration'
123 lmn
345 abc

B. Dictionary Iteration'
123 lmn
abc 345

C. Dictionary Iteration
lmn 123
abc 345

D. Dictionary Iteration'
lmn 345
abc 123

147. Which of the given options best describes the truthfulness of the following statements?

(i) Clipping process determines each element into the visible and invisible portion. The visible portion is selected. An invisible portion is discarded.
(ii) Clipping can be applied through hardware as well as software.
(iii) Point clipping, area clipping and text clipping are the types of clipping.

	(i)	(ii)	(iii)
A.	True	False	True
B.	True	True	True
C.	False	Flase	False
D.	True	True	False

148. Which of the following is NOT a key driver of e-business?

A. Supplementary workforce
B. Requirements of customers and suppliers
C. Commercial benefits
D. Skilled and committed workforce

149. Solid modeling is based on _____, _____ and _____ geometric representation of physical object.
A. incomplete; valid; unambiguous
B. complete; valid; undefined
C. complete; valid; unambiguous
D. complete; valid; varying

150. _____ is a discipline which deals with the application of economic theory to business management.
A. Business economics
B. Information processing
C. Decision Support System
D. Management Information System

151. Which of the following are management information system resources?

Resources:
(*i*) Hardware (*ii*) Software
(*iii*) People (*iv*) Data
A. (*ii*), (*iii*) and (*iv*) only
B. (*iii*) and (*iv*) only
C. (*i*) and (*ii*) only
D. (*i*), (*ii*), (*iii*) and (*iv*)

152. Which of the given options best describes the truthfulness of the following statements?
(*i*) Just-In-Time compiler (JIT) is a part of Common Language Runtime (CLR).
(*ii*) NET Framework is part of the .NET platform, a collection of technologies for building apps for Linux, macOS, Windows, iOS, Android.
(*iii*) ASP.NET applications are compiled codes, written using the extensible and reusable components or objects present in .NET framework.

	(*i*)	(*ii*)	(*iii*)
A.	False	Flase	True
B.	True	True	True
C.	False	True	True
D.	True	False	True

153. What is the expected output of the following Java code?

```
public class operators {
  public static void main(String[] args)
  {
    int a = 5;
    int b = 7;
    System.out.println("a&b = " + (a & b));
    }
}
```

A. a&b = 5 B. a&b = 2
C. a&b = 7 D. a&b = 35

154. Which of the following security services protects against repudiation?
A. Nonrepudiation B. Access control
C. Authentication D. Data integrity

155. What is the degree of the following function?
F(A, B, C, D) = A′ B′ C′ D′
A. 8 B. 5
C. 4 D. 0

156. Which of the following correctly defines coplanar force?
A. A single force which produces the same effect as that produced by two or more force acting on the body.
B. Two or more than two forces acting at a point.
C. When the lines of the action of all forces lie in one plane.
D. A single force, which acting along with other forces, keeps the body in equilibrium.

157. Which of the following are the dimensions of communication?

Dimensions:
(*i*) Downward
(*ii*) Upward
(*iii*) Horizontal/Lateral
(*iv*) Diagonal
(*v*) Grapevine
(*vi*) Circular
A. (*i*), (*iv*) and (*vi*) only B. (*i*) and (*ii*) only
C. (*ii*), (*iii*) and (*v*) only D. (*i*), (*ii*), (*iii*), (*iv*) and (*v*)

158. Match the column List-I with the column List-II:
(*a*) Front-End Framework (*i*) React JS
(*b*) Front-End Asset (*ii*) Tailwind CSS
(*c*) Front-End Boilerplate (*iii*) Font Awesome
(*d*) JavaScript Library: (*iv*) Reset CSS

	(*a*)	(*b*)	(*c*)	(*d*)
A.	(*ii*)	(*iii*)	(*iv*)	(*i*)
B.	(*iii*)	(*i*)	(*iv*)	(*ii*)
C.	(*i*)	(*ii*)	(*iv*)	(*iii*)
D.	(*ii*)	(*i*)	(*iv*)	(*iii*)

159. Which of the given options best describes the truthfulness of the following statements?
(*i*) Physical quantities which have magnitude only are called scalar quantities.
(*ii*) Physical qunatities which have both magnitude and direction are called vector quantities.
(*iii*) Two equal and opposite parallel forces acting at different points in a body constitute a couple.

	(*i*)	(*ii*)	(*iii*)
A.	True	True	False
B.	True	False	True
C.	True	True	True
D.	False	True	True

160. A/An _____ is a rectangular array of numbers arranged in rows and columns enclosed by brackets.
A. matrix B. record
C. object D. field name

161. Match the column Well-known ports used by TCP with the column Protocol.

(Well-known ports used by TCP)	*(Protocol)*
(*a*) 7	(*i*) Daytime
(*b*) 9	(*ii*) Echo
(*c*) 11	(*iii*) Discard
(*d*) 13	(*iv*) SYSTAT

	(*a*)	(*b*)	(*c*)	(*d*)
A.	(*ii*)	(*iii*)	(*iv*)	(*i*)
B.	(*iii*)	(*i*)	(*iv*)	(*ii*)
C.	(*ii*)	(*i*)	(*iv*)	(*iii*)
D.	(*i*)	(*ii*)	(*iv*)	(*iii*)

162. Which of the following languages is referred to as a database language?

A. Python B. SQL
C. HTML D. VJ++

163. Find the rank of the given matrix.

$$\begin{bmatrix} 1 & 5 & 6 \\ 2 & 3 & 4 \\ -1 & 2 & 2 \end{bmatrix}$$

A. 2 B. 6
C. 4 D. 9

164. Which of the following are managerial functions?

Functions:
(*i*) Planning (*ii*) Organising
(*iii*) Staffing (*iv*) Directing
(*v*) Controlling (*vi*) Coding
(*vii*) Testing

A. (*i*), (*ii*), (*iii*) and (*iv*) only
B. (*v*) and (*vii*) only
C. (*ii*), (*iii*) and (*iv*) only
D. (*i*), (*ii*), (*iii*), (*iv*) and (*v*) only

165. Which of the following projects deals with developing a well understood application program, the size of the development team is reasonably small, and the team members are experienced in developing similar types of projects?

A. Embedded
B. Semidetached
C. Flexible
D. Organic

166. Which of the following devices works at the network layer of the ISO-OSI reference model?

A. Router B. Repeater
C. Hub D. Amplifier

167. ______ is a method of constructing new data points within a range of discrete set of known data points.

A. Limit B. Integration
C. Interpolation D. Isolation

168. Which of the following are limitations of mobile computing?

Limitations:
(*i*) Device mobility
(*ii*) Power consumption
(*iii*) Human interface with device
(*iv*) Range and Bandwidth
(*v*) Transmission interferences
(*vi*) Wireless connectivity

A. (*ii*), (*iii*), (*iv*) and (*v*) only
B. (*i*), (*ii*) and (*v*) only
C. (*i*), (*iii*) and (*vi*) only
D. (*i*), (*ii*) and (*iv*) only

169. Which of the following statements is/are true for the Waterfall Model?

Statements:
(*i*) This model does not work smoothly if there are some issues left at the previous step.
(*ii*) It projects the process of development in a cyclic manner, repeating every step after every cycle of software development life cycle process.
(*iii*) This model considers risk, which often goes unnoticed by most other models.
(*iv*) This model provides means of testing of software at each stage in a reverse manner.

A. (*i*), (*iii*) and (*iv*) only B. (*ii*) and (*iii*) only
C. (*i*) only D. (*i*) and (*ii*) only

170. Which of the given options best describes the truthfulness of the following statements?

(*i*) The clock signal is required for sequential circuits.
(*ii*) In the sequential circuit, memory elements play an important role and are required.

	(*i*)	(*ii*)
A.	True	False
B.	False	True
C.	False	False
D.	True	True

171. Which of the following commands is used to comment out multiple lines in an XML file?

A. <-- This XML file contains a list of custom information -->
B. /* This XML file contains a list of custom information */
C. <!-- This is a multi-line XML comment -->
D. // This is a multi-line XML comment //

172. Which of the following is an accounting application software?

A. OpenOffice B. MS-Word
C. Tally D. MS-Access

173. The term ______ in ASP.NET means that data that is collected from a source is bound to the controls that provide the read and write connection to the data.

A. control variable B. data controlling
C. data binding D. binding hierarchy

174. Which of the following commands is/are used to create files in Linux?

Commands:
(*i*) touch (*ii*) cat
(*iii*) head (*iv*) finger

A. (*i*) and (*ii*) only B. (*i*) only
C. (*i*), (*ii*) and (*iii*) only D. (*ii*), (*iii*) and (*iv*) only

175. Which of the following input devices is used to detect orientation and angular velocity?

A. Light pen B. Gyroscope
C. Proximity sensor D. Magnetometer

176. What is/are the purpose(s) of JavaScript events?

(*i*) Provide a dynamic interface to a webpage.
(*ii*) Provide a static interface to a webpage.

A. Only (*ii*) B. Neither (*i*) nor (*ii*)
C. Both (*i*) and (*ii*) D. Only (*i*)

177. Which of the following is/are feature(s) of inheritance in OOPs?

Features:
(*i*) Sub Class
(*ii*) Super Class
(*iii*) Reusability
(*iv*) Operator Overloading

A. (*iii*) only B. (*i*), (*ii*) and (*iii*) only
C. (*ii*) and (*iii*) only D. (*i*) and (*ii*) only

178. Which of the given, options best describes the truthfulness of the following statements?

(*i*) A compiler translates the entire source code line by line.
(*ii*) Computer architecture refers to those attributes of a system visible to a programmer.
(*iii*) The Reduced Instruction Set Architecture (RISC) computer organisation reduces the cycles per instruction at the cost of the number of instructions per program to increase the CPU performance.
(*iv*) All the arithmetic and logical processing is performed by the Arithmetic Logic Unit under the supervision of a control unit.

	(*i*)	(*ii*)	(*iii*)	(*iv*)
A.	True	False	True	True
B.	True	True	True	True
C.	False	False	True	False
D.	False	True	True	True

179. A stack is a liner data structure in which insertion and deletion of elements are done at only one end, which is known as the top of the stack. Stack is called a last-in, first-out (LIFO) structure because the last element which is added to the stack is the first element which is deleted from the stack.

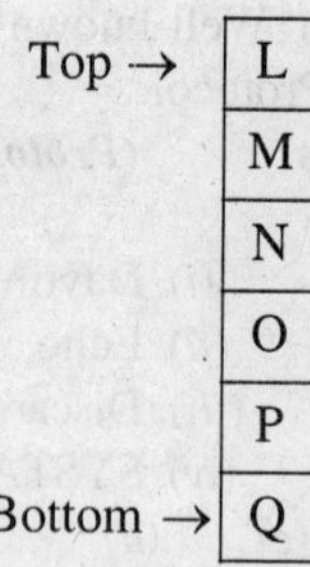

Read the above paragraph and answer the following.

Which of the following items will be at the top in the stack after removing three items?

A. N B. O
C. P D. L

180. Which of the given options best describes the truthfulness of the following statements?

(*i*) The 'communications', 'Schedules' and 'Task lists' are key functionality aspects of project management software to guide you in your decision.
(*ii*) A data warehouse is a relational database that is designed for query and analysis rather than transaction processing.
(*iii*) Software integration option is one of the criteria for selecting project management software.

	(*i*)	(*ii*)	(*iii*)
A.	False	True	True
B.	True	False	True
C.	True	True	False
D.	True	True	True

181. Match the column Mobility with the column Descriptions.

(Mobility)	***(Descriptions)***
(*a*) Macro-mobility	(*i*) This is mobility within an MANET, caused by device mobility constantly changing the network topology.
(*b*) Micro-mobility	(*ii*) This is mobility through a global network.
(*c*) Ad hoc mobility	(*iii*) This is mobility of a device in one single administrative domain of the global network.

	(*a*)	(*b*)	(*c*)
A.	(*i*)	(*iii*)	(*ii*)
B.	(*iii*)	(*ii*)	(*i*)
C.	(*ii*)	(*iii*)	(*i*)
D.	(*i*)	(*ii*)	(*iii*)

182. Which of the given options best describes the truthfulness of the following statements?

(*i*) In connectionless services of transport layer protocol, the packets are sent from one party to another with no need for connection establishment or connection release.

(*ii*) In connection-oriented service of transport layer protocol, a connection is first established between the sender and the receiver.

(*iii*) The User Datagram Protocol (UDP) is called a connectionless, unreliable transport protocol.

	(*i*)	(*ii*)	(*iii*)
A.	True	False	True
B.	False	True	True
C.	True	True	True
D.	False	False	False

183. Match the column Types of knowledge with the column Descriptions.

(Types of knowledge)	***(Descriptions)***
(*a*) Tacit knowledge	(*i*) This type of knowledge is captured within various document types such as manuals, reports, and guides, allowing organisations to easily share knowledge across teams.
(*b*) Implicit knowledge	(*ii*) This type of knowledge is typically acquired through experience, and it is intuitively understood.
(*c*) Explicit knowledge	(*iii*) This type is also referred to as 'know-how' knowledge'

	(*a*)	(*b*)	(*c*)
A.	(*i*)	(*iii*)	(*ii*)
B.	(*i*)	(*ii*)	(*iii*)
C.	(*iii*)	(*ii*)	(*i*)
D.	(*ii*)	(*iii*)	(*i*)

184. Which of the given options best describes the truthfulness of the following statements?

(*i*) Interpolation is a statistical method by which related known values are used to estimate an unknown value of set of values.

(*ii*) In the Inverse Distance Weighted (IDW) interpolation method, estimation of cell values is done by averaging values of sample data points in the neighbourhood of each processing cell.

	(*i*)	(*ii*)
A.	True	False
B.	False	True
C.	True	True
D.	False	False

185. ______ is a study of economics based on facts, is verifiable, and you can prove or disprove it.

A. Positive economics B. Basic economics
C. Regular economics D. Negative economics

186. Which of the following is NOT a system call category?

A. Device Manipulation
B. File Manipulation
C. Data Compilation
D. Process Control

187. Which of the given option best describes the truthfulness of the following statements?

(*i*) A tuple is a sequence of immutable Python objects, in the given tuple course = "*l*", "*m*", "*n*", "*o*" has four elements.

(*ii*) To explicitly remove an entire tuple, use the drop statement.

	(*i*)	(*ii*)
A.	True	True
B.	False	True
C.	True	False
D.	False	False

188. Which of the following is/are Interpolation Methods in Computer Graphics?

(*i*) Inverse Distance Weighted
(*ii*) Kriging
(*iii*) Natural Neighbour
(*iv*) Spline
(*v*) Topo to raster
(*vi*) Compiler

A. (*i*), (*ii*), (*iii*), (*iv*), (*v*) and (*vi*)
B. (*i*), (*ii*) and (*iv*) only
C. (*i*) only
D. (*i*), (*ii*), (*iii*), (*iv*) and (*v*) only

189. Which of the following does the actual display in a computer?

A. VRAM B. GPU
C. CRT D. DPU

190. When a plane is perpendicular to a reference plane, its projection on that plane is a/an ______.

A. apparent line B. straight line
C. curve D. point

191. Which of the following is an element of effective learning activity?

I. Automatic participation
II. Challengingness

A. Only I B. Both I and II
C. Only II D. Neither I nor II

192. 'Problem related to languages' is one of the hurdles to school-family-community partnerships. Which of the following actions can be taken with respect to this hurdle?

I. Set aside a room in the school in which to provide child care during events.
II. Have printed materials translated into home languages.
III. Help parents set up car pools.

A. I and II B. Only II
C. II and III D. I, II and III

193. The initial Juvenile Justice Act, 1986, defined a boy child below ______ of age and a girl child as below ______ of age, a juvenile.

A. 14 years, 16 years B. 16 years, 18 years
C. 12 years, 15 years D. 20 years, 14 years

194. What is regional art?

I. It is the work of a community of unschooled artists keeping alive the traditions specific to its particular culture.

II. It reflects the traditional art forms of diverse community groups.

A. Only II B. Only I
C. Neither I nor II D. Both I and II

195. Sarva Shiksha Abhiyan was launched in ______ year.

A. 2012 B. 2001
C. 2005 D. 2007

196. The objective type items are normally used in most of the tests. Which of the following is the correct example of closed-ended items?

A. Which numbers when added give 7?
B. Write down as many words adding 'ed' like played, created, etc.
C. Who controls the teachers and students in a school?
D. In how many ways can you draw a triangle?

197. The Rishi valley approach in pedagogy was designed to make the students:

I. Capable of acquiring mastery in learning competencies through both group and individual learning

II. Understand the importance of physical environment in the classroom

A. Only II B. Only I
C. Neither I nor II D. Both I and II

198. Which of the following comes under socio-emotional development of play?

A. By play children learn or develop the ability to keep their mind on task at hand
B. Playing improves brain cognition
C. Playing helps to develop memory, and the ability to analyse
D. Play provides opportunity for children to demonstrate their abilities and skills

199. Which of the following statements is correct regarding formative assessment?

I. It is conducted at regular intervals on informal basis.
II. It involves self-assessment and peer appraisal.
III. It is diagnostic and remedial.

A. II and III B. I, II and III
C. Only III D. Only I

200. The ways in which the government has tried to implement the equality that is guaranteed in the constitution is ______.

I. through laws
II. through government programmes

A. Only I B. Both I and II
C. Neither I nor II D. Only II

ANSWERS

1. (A)

2. (B): BELMOPR

The word is P R O [B] L E M

Hence, the middle letter of the word is B.

3. (A):

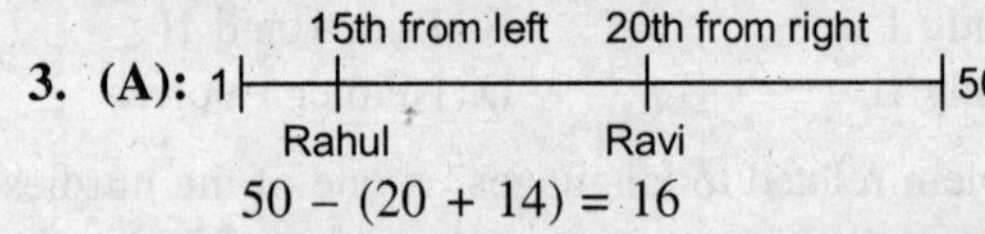

50 − (20 + 14) = 16

Hence, position of Rahul from left = 16th.

4. (B):

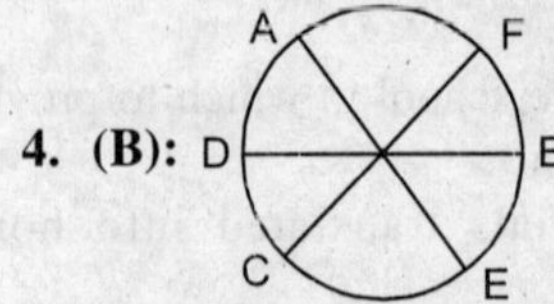

Hence, F is sitting second to the right of E.

5. (C) **6. (D)** **7. (A)**

8. (B): A. SX — UZ (+2, +2)

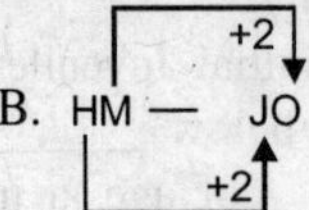

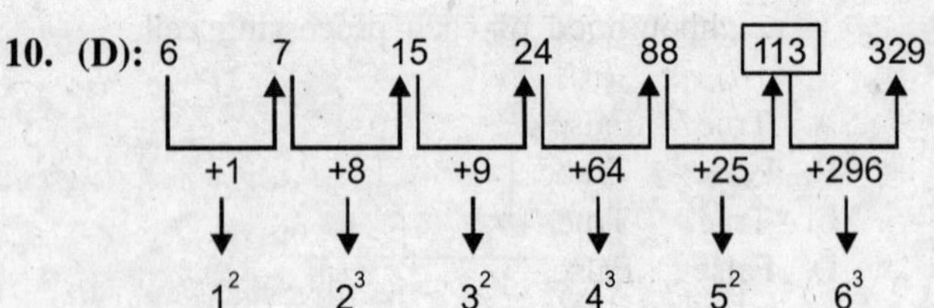

Clearly AF − CI is different.

9. (C)

10. (D): 6 7 15 24 88 [113] 329

+1 +8 +9 +64 +25 +296

1^2 2^3 3^2 4^3 5^2 6^3

Hence, 113 will come at the place of question mark.

11. (C): 100 ÷ 20 + 67 − 64 × 16 = 2063

100 × 20 + 67 − 64 ÷ 16

= 2000 + 67 − 4

= 2067 − 4

= 2063

Hence, ÷ and × sign should be interchanged to make the equation correct.

12. (B): $45 - 44 \div 22 + 17 \times 89 = 1556$

$45 - 2 + 1513 = 43 + 1513 = 1556$

Hence, –, ÷, +, ×, = signs should come at the place of * signs to balance the equation.

13. (A) **14. (B)** **15. (C)**

16. (D): $46 \div 23 - 57 + 24 \times 13$

$= 2 - 57 + 312$

$= 314 - 57 = 257$

Hence, 257 will come at the place of question mark.

17. (C)

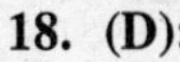

18. (D):

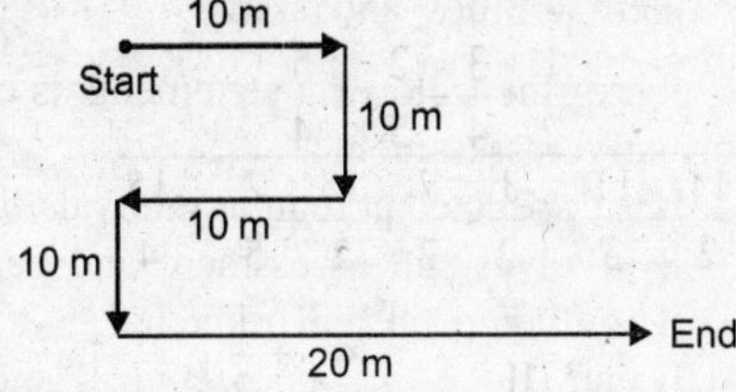

Now, he is 20 m in East direction for the initial point.

19. (A)

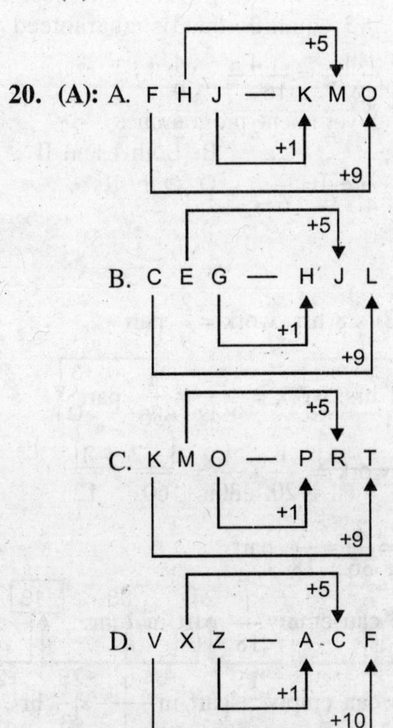

Hence, VXZ – ACF is different.

21. (A) **22. (D)** **23. (D)**

24. (D) **25. (D)** **26. (C)**

27. (C) **28. (B)** **29. (B)**

30. (B) **31. (D)** **32. (C)**

33. (D) **34. (D)** **35. (B)**

36. (D) **37. (C)** **38. (D)**

39. (C) **40. (C)**

41. (B): In 2018, total production of A, B, C

$= 450 + 550 + 620 = 1620$

$$\text{Average} = \frac{1620}{3} = 540$$

In 2020, production of rice by state C = 720

Difference = $720 - 540 = 180$

$$\text{Required \%} = \frac{180}{720} \times 100 = 25\%.$$

42. (B):

$$\text{1st Discount} = 450 \times \frac{x}{100} = \frac{9x}{2}$$

$$\text{S.P.} = 450 - \frac{9x}{2} = \frac{900 - 9x}{2}$$

$$\text{2nd Discount} = \left(\frac{900 - 9x}{2}\right) \times \frac{15}{100} = \frac{2700 - 27x}{40}$$

$$\text{S.P.} = \frac{900 - 9x}{2} - \frac{2700 - 27x}{40} = 351.90$$

$$\frac{18000 - 180x - 2700 + 27x}{40} = 351.90$$

$$15300 - 153x = 351.90 \times 40$$

$$15300 - 14076 = 153x$$

$$1224 = 153x \Rightarrow x = 8\%$$

Again when single discount = $2x$

Then, $$\text{Discount} = \frac{16}{100} \times 450 = 72$$

S.P. = 450 – 72 = ₹ 378

Hence, required S.P. = ₹ 378.

43. (D)

44. (A): $$\frac{21}{x + y} = \frac{9}{x - y}$$

$$\Rightarrow \quad 21u = 9v \quad \left[\frac{1}{x + y} = u \text{ and } \frac{1}{x - y} = v\right]$$

$$7u = 3v$$

$$u = \frac{3v}{7}$$

$$\frac{12}{x + y} + \frac{12}{x - y} = \frac{40}{7}$$

$$\Rightarrow \quad 12u + 12v = \frac{40}{7}$$

$$\Rightarrow \quad 12 \times \frac{3v}{7} + 12v = \frac{40}{7}$$

$$\Rightarrow \quad \frac{36v + 84v}{7} = \frac{40}{7}$$

$$\Rightarrow \quad v = \frac{1}{3}$$

$$\therefore \quad u = \frac{3}{7} \times \frac{1}{3} = \frac{1}{7}$$

$$\frac{1}{x+y} = \frac{1}{7} \Rightarrow x + y = 7 \quad ...(i)$$

$$\frac{1}{x-y} = \frac{1}{3} \Rightarrow x - y = 3 \quad ...(ii)$$

From (*i*) and (*ii*) $x = 5$ and $y = 2$

Required time $= \frac{28}{x+y} = \frac{28}{7} = 4$ hrs.

45. (D): Curved surface area of cone $= \pi rl$

$\Rightarrow \quad \pi \times 12 \times l = 444\pi$

$\Rightarrow \quad l = \frac{444}{12} = 37$ cm

$h^2 = l^2 - r^2 = (37)^2 - (12)^2$

$= 1369 - 144 = 1225$

$\therefore \quad h = \sqrt{1225} = 35$ cm

Volume of cone $= \frac{1}{3}\pi r^2 h$

$= \frac{1}{3} \times \pi \times 12 \times 12 \times 35$

$= \pi \times 12 \times 140 = 1680\pi$ cm^3.

46. (A): 22.50% of $x = 18000$

$\Rightarrow \quad x =$ ₹ 80000

$\because \quad$ 35% of x = X + 30% of x

$\frac{35}{100} \times 80000 = \text{X} + \frac{30}{100} \times 80000$

$\Rightarrow \quad 28000 = \text{X} + 24000$

$\Rightarrow \quad \text{X} = 28000 - 24000$

$= 4000$

Hence, the value of X lies between 3800 and 4200.

47. (D)

48. (C):

D, C, A, B, x, y

Area of rectangle $= xy$

According to the question

$xy = 1008$ m^2

Diagonal $\text{AC}^2 = x^2 + y^2$

$\text{AC} = \sqrt{x^2 + y^2}$

$\Rightarrow \quad y = \frac{1}{8}\left(x + \sqrt{x^2 + y^2}\right)$

$\Rightarrow \quad 8y = x + \sqrt{x^2 + y^2}$

$\Rightarrow \quad 8y - x = \sqrt{x^2 + y^2}$

Squaring both sides

$64y^2 + x^2 - 16xy = x^2 + y^2$

$\Rightarrow \quad 63y^2 = 16xy = 16 \times 1008$

$\Rightarrow \quad y^2 = \frac{16 \times 1008}{63} = 256$

$\Rightarrow \quad y = 16$

$x = \frac{1008}{y} = \frac{1008}{16} = 63$

Perimeter of rectangle $= 2(x + y)$

$2(x + y) = 2(63 + 16) = 2(79) = 158$ m

$\therefore \quad$ Cost of fencing = 158 × 24 = ₹ 3792.

49. (D): $\dfrac{\frac{1}{2} \times \frac{3}{4} \div \frac{2}{5} \text{ of } \frac{5}{4}}{\frac{11}{2} \div \frac{11}{3} \text{ of } \frac{1}{2} - \frac{7}{2} + \frac{15}{2} \div \frac{2}{5} \text{ of } \frac{15}{4}}$

$= \dfrac{\frac{1}{2} \times \frac{3}{4} \div \frac{1}{2}}{\frac{11}{2} \div \frac{11}{6} - \frac{7}{2} + \frac{15}{2} \div \frac{3}{2}} = \dfrac{\frac{1}{2} \times \frac{3}{2}}{3 - \frac{7}{2} + 5}$

$= \dfrac{\frac{3}{4}}{8 - \frac{7}{2}} = \dfrac{\frac{3}{4}}{\frac{16-7}{2}} = \dfrac{\frac{3}{4}}{\frac{9}{2}}$

$= \frac{3}{4} \times \frac{2}{9} = \frac{1}{6}$.

50. (C)

51. (D): (A + B − C)'s 8 hrs. work $= \frac{2}{9}$ part

(A + B − C)'s 1 hrs. work $= \frac{2}{9 \times 8} = \frac{1}{36}$ part

(A + B)'s 1 hr. work $= \frac{1}{20} + \frac{1}{30} = \frac{3+2}{60} = \frac{1}{12}$

C's 1 hr. work $= \frac{2}{36} = \frac{1}{18}$ part

$\because$ Pipe C alone can empty $\frac{1}{18}$ part in 1 hr.

$\therefore$ Pipe C alone can empty $\frac{1}{3}$ part in $\frac{1}{\left(\frac{1}{18}\right)} \times \frac{1}{3}$ hrs.

$= 18 \times \frac{1}{3}$ hrs. = 6 hrs.

52. (D): Speed of the train $= \frac{240}{18} = \frac{40}{3}$ m/s

Speed of the other train $= 42 \times \frac{5}{18}$ m/s $= \frac{35}{3}$ m/s

Relative speed $= \left(\frac{40}{3} + \frac{35}{3}\right)$ m/s = 25 m/s

Let length of the other train = x m

$$\frac{x+240}{25} = 17$$

$\Rightarrow$ $x + 240 = 425$

$\Rightarrow$ $x = 425 - 240 = 185$ m

Hence, length of other train = 185 m.

53. (A): Loan = ₹ 10200

Let each instalment = ₹ x

Present value of two instalments

$$= \frac{100 \times x}{4}\left[1-\left(1+\frac{4}{100}\right)^{-2}\right]$$

$$= 25x\left[1-\left(\frac{26}{25}\right)^{-2}\right]$$

$$= 25x\left[1-\left(\frac{25}{26}\right)^{2}\right]$$

$$= 25x\left[\frac{26^2-25^2}{26^2}\right]$$

$$= \frac{25x \times 51 \times 1}{676}$$

But $\frac{25x \times 51}{676} = 10200$

$\Rightarrow$ $x = \frac{676 \times 10200}{25 \times 51} = 5408$

Total given amount = 5408 × 2 = ₹ 10816

Hence, total interest charged = 10816 − 10200 = ₹ 616.

54. (D)

55. (D): Let A = $10x$ and B = $13x$

$$\frac{10x-90}{13x-90} = \frac{7}{10}$$

$\Rightarrow$ $100x - 900 = 91x - 630$

$\Rightarrow$ $9x = 270$

$\Rightarrow$ $x = 30$

A = 300 and B = 390

Now, A = 300 + 57 = 357

B = 390 − 16 = 374

$$\text{Required ratio} = \frac{357}{374} = \frac{21}{22}.$$

56. (A): Let P invest ₹ 1000, Q invest ₹ 2000

P invest in 12 months, Q invest in 4 months

P : Q = 12000 : 8000 = 12 : 8 = 3 : 2

According to the question,

Let total profit = ₹ x

$$\frac{3}{5} \text{ of } x = 22800$$

$\Rightarrow$ $3x = 22800 \times 5$

$\Rightarrow$ $x = \frac{22800 \times 5}{3}$

$= 7600 \times 5 = 38000$

Hence, total profit = ₹ 38000.

57. (C): Volume of cylinder = $\pi r^2 h$

$\Rightarrow$ $\pi r^2 h = 554.4$

$\Rightarrow$ $\frac{22}{7} \times r^2 \times 10 = \frac{5544}{10}$

$\Rightarrow$ $r^2 = \frac{5544 \times 7}{22 \times 10 \times 10} = \frac{1764}{100}$

$\Rightarrow$ $r = \frac{42}{10} = 4.2$ cm

C = $2\pi r$

$= 2 \times \frac{22}{7} \times 4.2$

$= 44 \times 0.6 = 26.4$ cm

Hence, the perimeter of the base of the cylinder = 26.4 cm.

58. (A): Let P = ₹ 100

$$\text{S.I.} = \frac{100 \times 9.5 \times 10}{100} = ₹\ 95$$

Again, $\text{S.I.} = \frac{100 \times 7 \times 7}{2 \times 100} = ₹\ \frac{49}{2}$

$$A = 100 + \frac{49}{2} = ₹\ \frac{249}{2}$$

$$\text{Difference} = \frac{249}{2} - 95 = \frac{249-190}{2} = \frac{59}{2}$$

When difference is ₹ $\frac{59}{2}$, then P = ₹ 100

When difference is ₹ 2832, then P = $\frac{100 \times 2 \times 2832}{59}$

$= 200 \times 48 = ₹\ 9600$

Hence, required sum = ₹ 9600.

59. (A)

60. (D): Distance = 45 × 2 = 90 km

Again distance = $60 \times \frac{7}{2} = 210$ km

Again distance = $70 \times \frac{9}{2} = 315$ km

Total distance = (90 + 210 + 315) km = 615 km

Total time = 2 hrs. + $\frac{7}{2}$ hrs. + $\frac{9}{2}$ hrs. = 10 hrs.

$$\text{Average speed} = \frac{\text{Total distance}}{\text{Total time}}$$

$$= \frac{615}{10} = 61.5 \text{ km/hr.}$$

Hence, average speed for the entire journey = 61.5 km/hr.

61. (A)	**62. (A)**	**63. (C)**
64. (B)	**65. (A)**	**66. (A)**
67. (C)	**68. (A)**	**69. (B)**
70. (B)	**71. (B)**	**72. (C)**
73. (D)	**74. (A)**	**75. (A)**
76. (A)	**77. (C)**	**78. (C)**
79. (A)	**80. (C)**	**81. (C)**
82. (B)	**83. (A)**	**84. (A)**
85. (A)	**86. (B)**	**87. (A)**
88. (C)	**89. (D)**	**90. (B)**
91. (D)	**92. (C)**	**93. (D)**
94. (C)	**95. (A)**	**96. (D)**
97. (A)	**98. (D)**	**99. (D)**

100. (A)

101. (D): Haptic technology is used to provide tactile feedback to a user. Haptic technology is a technology that simulates the sense of touch, allowing users to feel physical sensations through electronic devices. It provides tactile feedback, which means it uses various mechanisms to create the sensation of touch or pressure on the user's skin or other parts of the body. This feedback can be in the form of vibrations, force, or other tactile sensations.

102. (B)

103. (C): An unhappy employee because of poor communication processes in a business can negatively affect the corporate image of the business and make the business less successful. Poor communication processes can create a toxic work environment, resulting in unhappy employees who are less engaged and less productive. This, in turn, can negatively impact a company's reputation, customer satisfaction, and overall success in the long run. Effective communication is essential for fostering a positive work culture and ensuring a company's continued growth and success.

104. (B)

105. (B): Virtual memory is a memory management technique that allows a computer's operating system to use secondary storage, typically a hard drive or solid-state drive (SSD), as an extension of the main physical memory (RAM). This approach enables the computer to address more memory than is physically installed, effectively providing the illusion to both the operating system and applications that there is more RAM available than there actually is. Virtual memory is a storage allocation scheme that expands a computer's addressable memory space by using secondary storage as an extension of the main memory. It plays a crucial role in modern computing environments, allowing for efficient multitasking and the execution of larger applications while maintaining system stability.

106. (A): The NEFT (National Electronic Funds Transfer) system is a popular electronic payment system used for transferring funds from one bank account to another in India. The advantages listed in the question highlight the benefits of using this system:

(*i*) **The transaction has legal backing:** This means that NEFT transactions are regulated and governed by legal frameworks and guidelines, providing a secure and legitimate means for transferring funds. It ensures that the transactions are recognized and protected under the law.

(*ii*) **Round the clock availability on all days of the year:** NEFT offers the convenience of 24/7 availability, including weekends and holidays. This means you can initiate NEFT transactions at any time, making it a flexible option for fund transfers that aren't restricted to banking hours or working days.

(*iii*) **Near-real-time funds transfer to the beneficiary account and settlement in a secure manner:** NEFT transactions are processed relatively quickly, and the funds are transferred to the beneficiary account in near-real-time. While it may not be instantaneous like some other payment systems, it offers a timely and secure way to transfer money.

(*iv*) **Positive confirmation to the remitter by SMS/ email on credit to the beneficiary account:** NEFT provides a confirmation mechanism that informs the person initiating the transaction (remitter) when the funds have been successfully credited to the beneficiary's account. This confirmation is usually sent through SMS or email, providing peace of mind to the sender that the transaction was completed.

NEFT is a reliable and widely used electronic funds transfer system in India, offering several advantages including legal backing, round-the-clock availability, near-real-time fund transfers, and confirmations to both the sender and receiver. These features make NEFT a convenient and secure method for transferring money between bank accounts.

107. (A): Microsoft SQL Server, commonly referred to as SQL Server, is a relational database management system (RDBMS) developed and marketed by Microsoft.

It is a robust and feature-rich database platform designed for managing and storing data in a structured manner. SQL Server is developed and maintained by Microsoft Corporation, one of the world's largest technology companies. Microsoft has been continuously improving and enhancing SQL Server since its initial release.

108. (B): The process of organizing the contents of each file into contiguous regions and creating larger areas of free space on the hard disk is called defragmentation, and compression is the process of making computer files take up less space on your computer by reducing the size of the file.

Defragmentation: Over time, as you use your computer, files and data on your hard drive can become fragmented. This means that parts of the same file or data are scattered in different physical locations on the hard drive. Fragmentation can slow down the performance of your computer because it takes longer to access fragmented files.

Defragmentation is the process of reorganizing these scattered file fragments and storing them in contiguous (continuous) regions on the hard drive. This reduces the seek time when accessing files and can improve overall system performance. Regular defragmentation helps maintain the efficiency and speed of your computer's file access. Many operating systems, including Windows, offer built-in defragmentation tools or utilities to automate this process.

Compression: Compression is the process of reducing the size of a file or data to save storage space. It works by encoding data in a more efficient way, removing redundancy, and using algorithms to represent the data in a smaller form.

When you compress a file, it is transformed into a smaller version while retaining the essential data. This smaller version is often referred to as a compressed file or archive. When you want to use the file again, you need to decompress it to restore it to its original size and format. Compression is used to save disk space and reduce storage requirements. It's especially valuable for tasks like archiving files, sending files over the internet, and storing large datasets efficiently. Common compression formats include ZIP, GZIP, and JPEG (used for image compression).

109. (B): *(i)* **Make a reasonable profit on capital employed:** Business Economists are often responsible for analyzing financial data and economic conditions to ensure that a business is making a reasonable profit on the capital (money) it has invested in its operations. This involves assessing the return on investment (ROI) and profitability of various business activities.

(ii) **Make successful forecasts by making an in-depth study of the internal and external factors:** Business Economists are tasked with forecasting economic trends and conditions that can impact a company's performance. They conduct in-depth studies of both internal factors (company-specific data) and external factors (macroeconomic and industry trends) to make accurate predictions about the future.

(iii) **Inform the management of all the economic trends:** Business Economists play a crucial role in keeping management informed about relevant economic trends and conditions. They provide regular updates and reports on factors like inflation, interest rates, consumer behavior, and market dynamics. This information helps management make informed decisions and adapt strategies accordingly.

(iv) **Establish and maintain contacts with individuals and data sources:** To gather the necessary data and insights for their economic analysis and forecasting, Business Economists often establish and maintain contacts with various individuals and data sources. These contacts can include government agencies, industry experts, financial institutions, and other relevant stakeholders. Building a network of reliable sources is essential for accurate economic analysis.

110. (D): The key knowledge management processes typically include:

(i) **Knowledge gathering:** This process involves collecting relevant knowledge and information from various sources, such as employees, documents, databases, and external resources. It's the initial step in building a knowledge repository.

(ii) **Knowledge storage and organization:** After gathering knowledge, it needs to be stored and organized in a structured manner. This includes creating databases, categorizing information, and ensuring easy retrieval.

(iii) **Knowledge distribution:** Knowledge is valuable when shared. This process involves disseminating knowledge to those who need it within the organization. It can take the form of training sessions, documentation, intranet portals, and more.

(iv) **Knowledge use:** The ultimate goal of knowledge management is to apply knowledge to solve problems, make informed decisions, and improve processes. This process involves employees utilizing the stored knowledge effectively in their work.

111. (C): Internet infrastructure: Internet infrastructure refers to the availability and quality of internet connectivity, including factors like broadband access, network reliability, and bandwidth. In some regions, limited or unreliable internet infrastructure can be a significant barrier to the successful implementation of e-commerce because it can affect website accessibility, page load times, and the overall user experience. Inadequate internet infrastructure is an external micro-environmental factor that can impact e-commerce operations.

112. (A): Here's the assessment of the truthfulness of each statement:

(*i*) **Assembly languages are machine dependent:** This statement is generally true. Assembly languages are closely tied to the architecture and instruction set of a specific computer or processor. Code written in assembly language is specific to a particular machine or family of machines.

(*ii*) **A compiler is a program that produces a machine-level program from the specifications of a high-level language:** This statement is generally true. A compiler is a program that translates high-level programming code (e.g., written in languages like C++, Java, or Python) into machine-level code or an intermediate representation that can be executed by a computer's processor.

(*iii*) **An interpreter translates and executes each program statement, one at a time:** This statement is generally true. An interpreter is a program that reads and executes high-level code line by line or statement by statement. It translates each statement into machine-level code and immediately executes it.

(*iv*) **'BASIC' language is an interactive programming language:** This statement is generally true. BASIC (Beginner's All-purpose Symbolic Instruction Code) is often used as an interactive programming language, especially for beginners. It allows users to write and execute code interactively, making it suitable for learning and quick prototyping.

113. (C): PL/SQL (Procedural Language/Structured Query Language): PL/SQL is not a front-end technology; it is a server-side programming language used for database operations and stored procedures in database management systems like Oracle Database. It is primarily used for back-end development and database-related tasks, not for front-end web development.

114. (B): In object-oriented programming (OOP), a class is a blueprint or a template for creating objects (instances). It defines a user-defined datatype that encapsulates both data members (attributes or properties) and member functions (methods or operations). These are variables or fields within the class that store data or attributes associated with the objects created from that class. For example, in a class representing a "Person," data members could include attributes like "name," "age," and "address." These data members define the properties of objects created from the class.

115. (C)

116. (D): A thread is the subset of a process and is also known as a lightweight process.

Threads are smaller units of execution within a process. Unlike processes, which have their own separate memory and resources, threads within the same process share memory and resources. This sharing makes threads more lightweight and efficient in terms of resource consumption compared to separate processes.

Threads allow a program to perform multiple tasks concurrently, making them useful for tasks like parallel processing, multi-threaded applications, and improving the responsiveness of software in various computing scenarios.

117. (A)

118. (D): (*i*) VB.NET is an object-oriented programming language implemented in the .NET Framework.

This statement is true. VB.NET (Visual Basic .NET) is indeed an object-oriented programming language that is part of the .NET Framework. It allows developers to build object-oriented applications for the Windows platform.

(*ii*) VB.NET is a subset of Visual Basic 6.0.

This statement is false. VB.NET is not a subset of Visual Basic 6.0. VB.NET is a successor to Visual Basic 6.0 and is a part of the .NET Framework, while Visual Basic 6.0 is an earlier version of the language that is not part of the .NET Framework.

(*iii*) .NET is a free, cross-platform, open-source developer platform for building many different types of applications.

This statement is true. .NET is a free, cross-platform, and open-source developer platform developed by Microsoft. It allows developers to build a wide range of applications, including web applications, desktop applications, mobile apps, and more.

119. (C)

120. (B): Transportable agents are mobile software components that can move from one location to another in a networked environment to perform tasks or gather information. Mobile agents are a type of software program or code that have the ability to move autonomously from one computer or system to another within a networked environment. They are designed to perform specific tasks, gather information, or carry out operations on behalf of a user or a system administrator. Mobile agents can "travel" from one host to another over a network, executing tasks at different locations. Mobile agents are often referred to as "transportable" because their mobility allows them to be transported from one host to another. They "transport" their code, data, and mission as they move around the network. This term emphasizes the agent's ability to move and execute tasks in different locations.

121. **(A):** The main purpose of a transaction processing system is to record, process, validate, and store transactions that take place in various functional areas of a business for future retrieval and use.

Transaction processing systems are designed to handle routine, day-to-day transactions such as sales, purchases, payments, and inventory updates. They play a crucial role in ensuring the accuracy and integrity of a business's operational data and provide a foundation for generating reports and making informed decisions.

122. **(B):** The Linux commands used to search content from files are:

(*i*) **grep:** This command is used to search for text patterns or regular expressions within files.

(*ii*) **egrep:** This is an extended version of grep that supports more complex regular expressions.

(*iii*) **fgrep:** This is a faster version of grep that searches for fixed strings in files, not regular expressions.

123. **(D)**

124. **(A):** (*i*) **Proper recording of transactions:** This objective emphasizes the accurate and systematic recording of all financial transactions that occur within a business or organization. It involves documenting each financial event, such as sales, purchases, expenses, and investments, in a consistent and organized manner. Proper recording ensures that financial data is reliable and can be used for decision-making, analysis, and compliance with accounting standards.

(*ii*) **Ascertainment of the financial position:** This objective is about determining and presenting an organization's financial position at a specific point in time. It involves assessing the company's assets (what it owns), liabilities (what it owes), and equity (the residual interest of the owners) to provide a clear snapshot of its financial health. The balance sheet is a key financial statement used to ascertain the financial position.

(*iii*) **Reporting financial information:** Financial accounting aims to communicate financial information to various stakeholders, including shareholders, investors, creditors, management, and regulatory authorities. This objective involves preparing and presenting financial statements like the income statement, balance sheet, and cash flow statement. These reports provide a comprehensive view of a company's financial performance and help stakeholders make informed decisions.

(*iv*) **Defalcation prevention:** Defalcation prevention is related to safeguarding company assets and preventing fraudulent activities such as embezzlement or misappropriation of funds. While it's not a primary objective of financial accounting, it does involve implementing internal controls, audit procedures, and risk management measures to reduce the risk of financial misconduct.

These objectives collectively ensure that financial accounting serves as a critical tool for businesses and organizations to maintain accurate records, assess their financial health, communicate financial information transparently, and mitigate the risk of financial fraud or mismanagement.

125. **(A)**

126. **(D):** (*i*) RAM is a volatile memory having a limited storage capacity.

This statement is partially true. RAM (Random Access Memory) is indeed volatile, meaning it loses its data when the computer is powered off or restarted. However, the statement about limited storage capacity is not entirely accurate. RAM comes in various capacities, and its storage capacity can vary from a few gigabytes to many gigabytes in modern computers. It is typically larger in capacity compared to cache memory but smaller than secondary storage like hard drives or SSDs.

(*ii*) Secondary memory is storage other than the RAM and ROM.

This statement is true. Secondary memory refers to storage devices that are separate from RAM (primary memory) and ROM (Read-Only Memory). Secondary memory includes devices like hard disk drives (HDDs), solid-state drives (SSDs), optical drives, USB drives, and more. These devices provide non-volatile storage for data and programs.

127. (D): In the Linux shell, the following symbols are commonly used for input/output redirection:

A. <: Used for input redirection, where a command takes input from a file.

B. >: Used for output redirection, where the output of a command is saved to a file, overwriting the file if it exists.

C. >>: Used for output redirection, where the output of a command is appended to a file, creating the file if it doesn't exist.

D. !: Not used for input/output redirection. Instead, the exclamation mark (!) is often used in shell commands for history expansion and other purposes, but it is not an input/output redirection symbol.

128. (A): To find the number of head movements using the FCFS (First-Come-First-Serve) scheduling algorithm, we need to calculate the total distance the disk arm (head) moves as it services the given disk request sequence. In this case, the head starts at track 60 and moves in the left direction.

Disk Request Sequence: 60, 45, 21, 67

Here's how the head moves to service the requests:

Move from track 60 to track 45 : 60 – 45 = 15 cylinders

Move from track 45 to track 21 : 45 – 21 = 24 cylinders

Move from track 21 to track 67 : 67 – 21 = 46 cylinders

Now, calculate the total number of head movements:

Total head movements = 15 + 24 + 46 = 85 cylinders

129. (A): (*i*) In probability theory, an outcome is the result of a random experiment.

This statement is true. In probability theory, an outcome refers to a specific result or event that can occur as a result of a random experiment. Outcomes are the possible results that are considered in probability calculations.

(*ii*) The purpose of statistical inference is to estimate the uncertainty or sample-to-sample variation.

This statement is true. Statistical inference involves making predictions or inferences about a population based on data collected from a sample. One of the primary purposes of statistical inference is to estimate the uncertainty or variation from sample to sample in order to draw conclusions about the entire population.

(*iii*) A sampling error is the difference between the true population values (called parameters) and the measured sample values (called statistics).

This statement is true. A sampling error refers to the discrepancy or difference between the true values (parameters) of a population and the values obtained from a sample (statistics). It quantifies the level of uncertainty introduced by using a sample to estimate population characteristics.

130. (A): Pascal is a programming language that predates the .NET framework and is not inherently part of the .NET ecosystem. It is not considered a .NET language. In contrast, C#, F#, and J# are all .NET languages, as they are designed to work with the .NET framework and are part of the Microsoft .NET ecosystem.

131. (D): The attack in which a malicious node injects false routing information into a Managed Ad-hoc Network (MANET) with the intention of causing packets to loop is typically referred to as a Byzantine attack.

In a Byzantine attack, the malicious node behaves arbitrarily and can send misleading or contradictory routing information to other nodes in the network. This can disrupt the routing process and lead to problems such as loops in the network, making it challenging to establish efficient communication paths.

132. (A): Turbulent flow is characterized by chaotic and random fluid motion, and it is associated with high levels of fluid disorder and irregularity.

(*i*) Flow of liquid is orderly. This statement is not associated with turbulent flow. Turbulent flow is precisely the opposite, where the flow of liquid is highly disordered and irregular.

(*ii*) Flow of liquid is zigzag and random. This statement is associated with turbulent flow. Turbulent flow is known for its zigzagging and random motion of fluid particles.

133. (B)

134. (C): The type of firewall that examines traffic and filters on application-specific commands such as HTTP POST or HTTP GET is: Application gateways

Application gateways, also known as application layer or proxy firewalls, operate at the application layer of the OSI model. They have the capability to understand and filter traffic based on specific application protocols, such as HTTP, FTP, or SMTP. This allows them to inspect and control application-specific commands and actions, making them effective at filtering and securing application-level traffic.

135. (B): The software used by a wide range of industries for project planning, resource allocation, and scheduling is: **Project management software**

Project management software is specifically designed to help plan, manage, and execute projects efficiently.

It allows users to create project schedules, allocate resources, set milestones, track progress, and collaborate with team members. It is a valuable tool for industries ranging from construction and engineering to information technology, marketing, and many others for effective project management.

136. (D): (*i*) When a Java program is compiled, it generates Byte code.

This statement is true. When you compile a Java program, it is translated into bytecode, which is a platform-independent intermediate code that can be executed on a Java Virtual Machine (JVM).

(*ii*) SOAP and RESTFUL are Java web services.

This statement is true in the sense that Java can be used to implement web services using both SOAP and RESTFUL architectures. However, they are not exclusive to Java, as they can be implemented in other programming languages as well.

(*iii*) PATH Environment variable identifies the location of Java compiler.

This statement is true. The PATH environment variable can be configured to include the directory containing the Java compiler (javac), allowing you to run the compiler from any location in the command prompt or terminal.

(*iv*) The || logical operator returns true if both statements are true.

I made an error in my previous response. This statement is false. The || logical operator in Java returns true if at least one of the statements is true, not necessarily both. It performs a logical OR operation.

137. (D): (*i*) Class is one of the HTML global attributes which specifies one or more class names for an element (refer to a class in a style sheet).

This statement is true. In HTML, the class attribute is used to specify one or more class names for an HTML element. These class names can then be referenced in a CSS stylesheet to apply styling rules to the element.

(*ii*) HTML is a markup language used for server-side processing.

This statement is false. HTML (Hypertext Markup Language) is primarily used for defining the structure and content of web pages. It is a client-side language that web browsers use to render and display web pages. Server-side processing is typically done using server-side scripting languages like PHP, Python, or JavaScript (Node.js).

(*iii*) CSS describes how HTML elements are to be displayed on screen, paper, or in other media.

This statement is true. CSS (Cascading Style Sheets) is used to describe how HTML elements should be presented and styled in various media, including screen displays, print, and other devices. It allows web developers to control the layout, colors, fonts, and other visual aspects of web pages.

138. (C): A ripple counter is a cascaded arrangement of flip-flops where the output of one flip-flop drives the clock input of the following flip-flop. Ripple counters are relatively simple but may have issues with timing and propagation delays due to the ripple effect of clock transitions from one flip-flop to the next.

139. (D): Business communication can be categorized into various types based on the nature and direction of the communication.

(*i*) **Internal Business Communication:** This type of communication takes place within the organization and involves communication among employees, departments, or teams. It includes messages, emails, meetings, and reports that are intended for internal use.

(*ii*) **Lateral Business Communication:** Lateral communication refers to communication that occurs horizontally or at the same hierarchical level within an organization. It typically involves communication between colleagues or peers within the same department or team.

(*iii*) **External Business Communication:** External communication involves interactions and exchanges of information between the organization and external entities such as customers, suppliers, partners, regulatory authorities, and the general public. It includes marketing communication, customer support, public relations, and more.

(*iv*) **Protected Business Communication:** "Protected" is not a recognized type of business communication. Business communication can have various purposes and content, but "protected" is not a standard category.

140. (A): (*i*) XML schemas define datatypes for elements and attributes, while DTD doesn't support datatypes.

This statement is true. XML schemas (XSD) allow you to define datatypes for elements and attributes, specifying the expected data format, such as string, integer, date, etc.

DTD (Document Type Definition) does not provide built-in support for specifying datatypes.

(*ii*) DTDs are the declarations that define a document type for SGML.

This statement is true. DTDs are used to define the structure and rules for valid documents in SGML (Standard Generalized Markup Language) and are also applicable to XML. DTDs declare the elements, attributes, and their relationships within a document type.

(*iii*) In XML, tag names can begin with a numeric value.

This statement is false. In XML, tag names must adhere to specific naming rules. They cannot start with a numeric value. A valid XML tag name should start with a letter or underscore, followed by letters, digits, hyphens, underscores, or periods.

141. (D): Circular is NOT a valid Software Life Cycle Model. The other options-Iterative, Prototype, and JAD (Joint Application Development)-are recognized software development life cycle models.

The Circular model is not a commonly known or accepted software development life cycle model in the same way as the others. Instead, it may refer to a general concept of iterative or recurring development processes.

142. (A): (*i*) **POP (Post Office Protocol):** POP is used for email retrieval and does not assign dynamic IP addresses.

(*ii*) **DHCP (Dynamic Host Configuration Protocol):** DHCP is specifically designed to assign dynamic IP addresses to devices on a network.

(*iii*) **BOOTP (Bootstrap Protocol):** While BOOTP is primarily used for network booting and can assign IP addresses, it is often considered a precursor to DHCP and is not as commonly used for dynamic IP address assignment today.

(*iv*) **SNMP (Simple Network Management Protocol):** SNMP is used for network management and does not assign dynamic IP addresses.

(*v*) **ICMP (Internet Control Message Protocol):** ICMP is not used for IP address assignment, whether static or dynamic. It is a network protocol primarily used for diagnostic and control purposes, including error reporting and network troubleshooting.

143. (C): (*i*) Service Set Identification (SSID) is a human-readable text string with a maximum length of 2000 bytes.

This statement is false. An SSID is indeed a human-readable text string, but it typically has a maximum length of 32 characters, not 2000 bytes. The specific length may vary depending on the network configuration.

(*ii*) Service Set Identification (SSID) acts as a single shared identifier between the access points and clients.

This statement is true. The SSID is used as the network identifier that allows wireless clients (devices) to connect to a specific wireless network. It acts as a shared identifier that all clients and access points in the same network use to communicate with each other.

144. (B): Object-oriented programming (OOP) languages are designed to support the principles of object-oriented programming, which includes concepts like classes, objects, encapsulation, inheritance, and polymorphism. Let's evaluate the provided languages:

(*i*) **LISP:** LISP is not typically considered an object-oriented programming language. It is primarily associated with functional programming.

(*ii*) **Java:** Java is a well-known object-oriented programming language.

(*iii*) **C++:** C++ is a widely used object-oriented programming language that extends the C programming language with OOP features.

(*iv*) **Simula:** Simula is considered one of the earliest object-oriented programming languages and played a significant role in the development of OOP concepts.

(*v*) **SQL:** SQL (Structured Query Language) is a domain-specific language used for managing relational databases. While it is not primarily an OOP language, some database systems have added support for object-oriented extensions.

(*vi*) **C:** C is not an object-oriented programming language. It is a procedural programming language.

Based on this evaluation, the object-oriented programming languages among the provided options are: (*i*), (*ii*), (*iii*) and (*iv*) only

These languages (Java, C++, and Simula) are known for their object-oriented capabilities.

145. (C): WPF (Windows Presentation Foundation) is a graphical subsystem for rendering user interfaces in Windows-based applications. It is part of the .NET framework and provides a framework for creating rich and interactive user interfaces for Windows applications. While ASP.NET is primarily used for web-based applications, WPF is used for building Windows desktop applications with advanced graphical interfaces.

146. (C): The provided Python code contains some formatting issues that would prevent it from running successfully. The correct code with proper formatting is as follows:

```
print("\nDictionary Iteration")
d = dict()
d['lmn'] = 123
d['abc'] = 345
for i in d:
print("%s %d" % (i, d[i]))
```

With this corrected code, the expected output is:

Dictionary Iteration lmn 123 abc 345

So, the correct answer is: Dictionary Iteration lmn 123 abc 345.

147. (B): (*i*) Clipping process determines each element into the visible and invisible portion. The visible portion is selected. An invisible portion is discarded.

This statement is true. Clipping is a process in computer graphics where it determines which parts of an object or image are visible (inside the viewing area) and which parts are invisible (outside the viewing area). The visible portion is retained, and the invisible portion is discarded.

(*ii*) Clipping can be applied through hardware as well as software.

This statement is true. Clipping can be implemented both in hardware (graphics hardware) and in software (using algorithms and programming techniques).

(*iii*) Point clipping, area clipping, and text clipping are the types of clipping.

This statement is true. Point clipping, area clipping, and text clipping are indeed considered types or categories of clipping in computer graphics.

148. (A): The other options—Requirements of customers and suppliers, Commercial benefits, and Skilled and committed workforce—are key drivers of e-business. E-business often aims to meet the requirements of customers and suppliers, generate commercial benefits such as increased sales and cost savings, and rely on a skilled and committed workforce to implement and manage digital strategies effectively.

149. (C): Solid modeling is based on complete, valid, and unambiguous geometric representation of physical objects.

Complete: Solid models aim to represent the entire volume and shape of an object accurately. In other words, they provide a comprehensive and detailed representation of the object, including its interior and exterior surfaces.

Valid: The geometric information in a solid model must conform to the rules and constraints of Euclidean geometry. This means that the relationships between points, lines, curves, and surfaces must be mathematically accurate and consistent.

Unambiguous: Solid models should be free from ambiguity or uncertainty. It should be clear and well-defined how different parts of the model relate to each other. This clarity ensures that the model can be used for various purposes, including analysis, manufacturing, and visualization, without misinterpretation.

By adhering to these principles, solid modeling allows engineers, architects, and designers to create digital representations of physical objects that are highly accurate, reliable, and suitable for a wide range of applications, from prototyping and simulation to manufacturing and architectural design.

150. (A): The discipline that deals with the application of economic theory to business management is: **Business economics**

Business economics, also known as managerial economics, is a field of study that applies economic principles and concepts to practical business decision-making. It involves the use of economic theories, tools, and methodologies to analyze and solve various business-related problems.

Business economics is a valuable tool for managers, entrepreneurs, and decision-makers in various industries. It helps them make rational and data-driven choices that contribute to the success and sustainability of their organizations.

151. (D): Management Information System (MIS) resources typically include the following:

(*i*) **Hardware:** This refers to the physical components of the information system, such as computers, servers, storage devices, networking equipment, and peripheral devices.

(*ii*) **Software:** This includes the software applications and programs used to process, store, and manage data and information within the MIS. It encompasses operating systems, database management systems, application software, and more.

(*iii*) **People:** People resources are essential for the effective operation of an MIS. This includes the individuals who design, develop, operate, and manage the system, such as IT professionals, analysts, and end-users.

(*iv*) **Data:** Data is a fundamental resource for an MIS. It includes the raw facts and information that are collected, processed, and stored within the system. Data is essential for generating meaningful information and reports.

152. (B): (*i*) Just-In-Time compiler (JIT) is a part of Common Language Runtime (CLR).

This statement is true. The Just-In-Time (JIT) compiler is indeed a component of the Common Language Runtime (CLR) in the .NET framework. It compiles Intermediate Language (IL) code into native machine code at runtime.

(*ii*) .NET Framework is part of the .NET platform, a collection of technologies for building apps for Linux, macOS, Windows, iOS, Android.

This statement is true. .NET Framework is a component of the .NET platform, which includes technologies for building cross-platform applications, including those for Linux, macOS, Windows, iOS, and Android.

(*iii*) ASP.NET applications are compiled codes, written using the extensible and reusable components or objects present in .NET framework.

This statement is true. ASP.NET applications are typically compiled, and they make use of the extensible and reusable components and objects provided by the .NET framework.

153. (A)

154. (A): Nonrepudiation is a security service that ensures that a party cannot deny the authenticity or validity of a transaction or communication. It provides proof that a transaction occurred and that the parties involved cannot later deny their participation in it. This helps in legal and dispute resolution scenarios where the parties involved need to be held accountable for their actions.

155. (C): The degree of a Boolean function is determined by the number of literals in its most complex term. In the given function:

$$F(A, B, C, D) = A' B' C' D'$$

Each term consists of four literals (A′, B′, C′, and D′), so the degree of this function is 4.

So, the correct answer is: 4.

156. (C): Coplanar forces are a set of forces whose vectors all lie within the same two-dimensional plane. This means that if you were to represent each force as an arrow (vector), all these arrows would be contained within a single flat surface. In a three-dimensional space, a plane is like a flat sheet of paper, and coplanar forces are forces that can be drawn or represented on that sheet without any of them "popping out" of it.

157. (D): The dimensions of communication in an organizational context typically include the following:

(*i*) **Downward:** This dimension involves communication flowing from higher levels of management or authority to lower levels. It includes instructions, directives, goals, and feedback.

(*ii*) **Upward:** Upward communication is the reverse of downward communication. It involves communication from lower levels of the organization to higher levels. This can include feedback, reports, suggestions, and concerns from employees to managers or executives.

(*iii*) **Horizontal/Lateral:** Horizontal or lateral communication occurs between individuals or groups at the same hierarchical level within the organization. It facilitates coordination, collaboration, and information sharing among peers.

(*iv*) **Diagonal:** Diagonal communication involves communication that cuts across different levels and departments of the organization. It often occurs when individuals from different parts of the organization need to work together or share information.

(*v*) **Grapevine:** The grapevine represents informal communication channels within an organization. It includes rumors, gossip, and informal discussions among employees. While not an official channel, the grapevine can have a significant impact on organizational culture and communication.

(*vi*) **Circular:** Circular communication involves communication that moves in a circular or cyclical pattern. It often occurs in team-based or project-based settings where information or decisions need to be shared among team members in a circular manner.

So, the correct answer is: (*i*), (*ii*), (*iii*), (*iv*), and (*v*)

These dimensions encompass various ways in which communication occurs within an organization, both formally and informally.

158. (A)

159. (C): (*i*) Physical quantities which have magnitude only are called scalar quantities.

This statement is true. Scalar quantities are physical quantities that have magnitude (size) but no direction. Examples include mass, speed, and temperature.

(*ii*) Physical quantities which have both magnitude and direction are called vector quantities.

This statement is true. Vector quantities are physical quantities that have both magnitude (size) and direction. Examples include velocity, force, and displacement.

(*iii*) Two equal and opposite parallel forces acting at different points in a body constitute a couple.

This statement is true. A couple is a pair of forces of equal magnitude and opposite direction that act along parallel lines but at different points. Couples are often used to describe rotational effects.

160. **(A):** A matrix is a mathematical and data structure concept used to represent and manipulate collections of numbers, symbols, or other mathematical entities arranged in a rectangular grid or array. Matrices are commonly used in various fields, including mathematics, computer science, engineering, physics, and statistics. Matrices are versatile and are used for various purposes, such as solving systems of linear equations, representing transformations in linear algebra, storing and manipulating data in computer programming, and conducting statistical analyses. They play a fundamental role in many mathematical and computational operations, making them an essential concept in various domains.

161. **(A)**

162. **(B):** SQL (Structured Query Language) is specifically designed for managing and querying relational databases. It is used for tasks such as creating, modifying, and querying database structures and data. SQL allows users to interact with databases to retrieve, update, insert, and delete data, making it a fundamental language for working with databases.

163. **(A)**

164. **(D): Planning:** Planning is the foundation of effective management. It involves setting organizational goals, defining strategies to achieve those goals, and developing detailed plans and actions. This function requires managers to anticipate future needs, allocate resources, and create a roadmap for the organization. Planning ensures that everyone in the organization knows what needs to be accomplished and how it will be achieved.

Organizing: Organizing is the process of arranging resources, both human and material, in a structured way to achieve organizational objectives. It involves creating an organizational structure, defining roles and responsibilities, and establishing lines of authority and communication. Organizing ensures that tasks are distributed efficiently, and people are coordinated in their efforts.

Staffing: Staffing involves acquiring, training, and developing the workforce necessary to accomplish organizational goals. It includes recruiting and selecting employees, providing training and development opportunities, and ensuring that the organization has the right people in the right positions. Effective staffing ensures that the organization has the skills and talents needed to succeed.

Directing: Directing is the function of guiding and leading employees to achieve their assigned tasks and contribute to the overall success of the organization. It includes motivating employees, providing clear instructions, and supervising their work. Directing ensures that individuals and teams are aligned with the organization's goals and are working effectively.

Controlling: Controlling is the process of monitoring and measuring performance against established standards and taking corrective actions as needed. It involves comparing actual results with planned outcomes and making adjustments to ensure that the organization stays on track. Controlling helps in identifying and addressing issues and deviations from the plan.

Managers at various levels within an organization are responsible for carrying out these functions to ensure effective and efficient operations. These functions are essential for achieving the organization's goals and adapting to changes in the business environment. Each function plays a crucial role in the management process, and successful managers often excel in all of them. Coding and testing are not considered managerial functions; they are technical activities associated with software development and quality assurance.

165. **(D):** In the context of software project management, projects are often categorized into different types based on their characteristics, and these categories are known as project types.

Organic projects involve well-understood applications, small teams, and experienced team members. These projects are typically relatively straightforward, and the development process is well-established. There's a low level of risk associated with organic projects.

166. **(A):** Routers operate at the network layer (Layer 3) of the OSI model. They are responsible for forwarding data packets between different networks, making decisions based on network addresses, and determining the best path for data to travel from the source to the destination. Routers are essential for connecting and routing data between multiple networks in a complex network infrastructure.

167. **(C):** Interpolation is a mathematical technique used to estimate values between two or more known data points. It is commonly used in various fields, including mathematics, science, engineering, and computer graphics, to approximate values that fall within the range of existing data points. There are various interpolation methods, such as linear interpolation, polynomial interpolation, and spline interpolation, each suited to different types of data and applications.

168. **(A):** *(ii)* **Power consumption:** Mobile devices are often powered by batteries, and power consumption is a critical limitation. High power consumption can result in shorter battery life, requiring frequent recharging.

(iii) **Human interface with the device:** Interacting with a mobile device's small screen and input methods can be challenging, especially for complex tasks or users with limited dexterity.

(iv) **Range and Bandwidth:** Mobile devices may have limitations in terms of the range over which they can connect to wireless networks and the available bandwidth, which can affect data transfer speeds.

(v) **Transmission interferences:** Mobile devices can experience interference from other electronic devices or physical obstacles, affecting the quality of wireless communication.

169. **(C):** This model does not work smoothly if there are some issues left at the previous step.

True. The Waterfall Model is a linear and sequential approach where each phase depends on the deliverables of the previous phase. If issues or errors are left unresolved in earlier phases, they can carry over and cause problems in subsequent phases.

170. **(D):** *(i)* The clock signal is required for sequential circuits.

True. In sequential circuits, a clock signal is essential to synchronize the operation of memory elements and control the timing of state transitions.

(ii) In the sequential circuit, memory elements play an important role and are required.

True. Sequential circuits rely on memory elements (such as flip-flops or latches) to store and retain information about the circuit's current state. These memory elements are crucial for sequential circuits to maintain and update their state over time.

171. **(C):** <!-- This is a multi-line XML comment -->

In XML (eXtensible Markup Language), comments are used to add explanatory notes or remarks within an XML document. Comments are not processed by XML parsers, and they do not affect the functionality of the document. Instead, they serve as a way for developers to include human-readable information or annotations for documentation or debugging purposes.

Comments in XML are a helpful tool for improving the readability and maintainability of your XML documents. However, it's essential to note that comments should not contain critical information or data required for processing the document, as they are intended for human consumption and not machine interpretation.

172. **(C):** Tally is an accounting application software widely used for various accounting and financial management tasks. It is designed to help businesses and individuals manage their accounts, financial transactions, and related activities efficiently. Tally provides features for bookkeeping, financial reporting, inventory management, taxation compliance, and more, making it a popular choice in the field of accounting and finance.

173. **(C):** In ASP.NET, data binding refers to the process of connecting data from a data source to controls (such as text boxes, labels, grids, etc.) that display or manipulate the data. Data binding allows you to associate data with the controls, making it easier to display and manipulate data in web applications. This connection between the data source and controls is often referred to as data binding.

174. **(A):** In Linux, the commands for creating files are:

(i) touch: Used to create empty files or update the access and modification timestamps of existing files.

(ii) cat: Used to concatenate and display the contents of files, but it can also be used to create and write to files by redirecting input from the keyboard or another source.

(iii) head and *(iv)* finger are not typically used to create files. head is used to display the beginning lines of a file, and finger is used to display information about user accounts.

175. **(B):** A gyroscope is an input device used to detect orientation and angular velocity. It measures the rate of rotation or angular displacement around one or more axes. Gyroscopes are commonly used in various applications, including mobile devices (such as smartphones and tablets) for features like screen rotation, gaming controllers, drones, and navigation systems. They are essential for determining the orientation and movement of objects in three-dimensional space.

176. **(D):** The purpose of JavaScript events is to provide a dynamic interface to a webpage. JavaScript events allow you to define how a webpage or web application responds to user interactions and other events, such as mouse clicks, keyboard input, form submissions, and more. You can use JavaScript to create interactive and responsive web pages by adding event listeners to HTML elements and defining actions or behaviors to be triggered when events occur.

JavaScript events do not provide a static interface; their primary role is to add interactivity and make web pages more dynamic by responding to user actions and events.

177. (B): Inheritance is a fundamental concept in object-oriented programming (OOP) that allows one class (the subclass or derived class) to inherit the properties and behaviors of another class (the superclass or base class). The features of inheritance are as follows:

(*i*) **Sub Class:** This refers to the class that inherits properties and behaviors from another class. It is also called the derived class.

(*ii*) **Super Class:** This refers to the class from which properties and behaviors are inherited. It is also called the base class or parent class.

(*iii*) **Reusability:** Inheritance allows for the reuse of code. The properties and behaviors defined in the superclass can be reused in the subclass, promoting code reusability and reducing redundancy.

(*iv*) **Operator Overloading:** Operator overloading is not a direct feature of inheritance. It is a separate concept in OOP that allows the definition of custom behavior for operators in a class. It is not inherently tied to inheritance.

178. (D): (*i*) A compiler translates the entire source code line by line. - **False.** A compiler translates the entire source code as a whole, not line by line.

(*ii*) Computer architecture refers to those attributes of a system visible to a programmer. - **True.** Computer architecture encompasses the attributes of a computer system that are visible to a programmer, such as the instruction set and memory hierarchy.

(*iii*) The Reduced Instruction Set Architecture (RISC) computer organization reduces the cycles per instruction at the cost of the number of instructions per program to increase CPU performance. - **True.** RISC architecture aims to reduce the number of cycles per instruction to improve CPU performance, which may result in more instructions per program.

(*iv*) All the arithmetic and logical processing is performed by the Arithmetic Logic Unit under the supervision of a control unit. - **True.** In a computer's central processing unit (CPU), the Arithmetic Logic Unit (ALU) is responsible for performing arithmetic and logical operations, and it operates under the control of the control unit.

179. (B)

180. (D): (*i*) The 'communications,' 'Schedules,' and 'Task lists' are key functionality aspects of project management software to guide you in your decision. - **True.** Project management software typically includes features for managing communications, schedules, and task lists, which are crucial for effective project management.

(*ii*) A data warehouse is a relational database that is designed for query and analysis rather than transaction processing. - **True.** A data warehouse is a specialized database designed for storing and retrieving data for analytical and reporting purposes, rather than transaction processing.

(*iii*) Software integration option is one of the criteria for selecting project management software. - **True.** Integration capabilities with other software and systems can be an important criterion when selecting project management software, as it affects how well it can work with your existing tools.

181. (C)

182. (C): (*i*) In connectionless services of the transport layer protocol, the packets are sent from one party to another with no need for connection establishment or connection release. - **True.** In connectionless services, such as UDP (User Datagram Protocol), packets are sent independently without establishing a connection.

(*ii*) In connection-oriented service of the transport layer protocol, a connection is first established between the sender and the receiver. - **True.** Connection-oriented services, such as TCP (Transmission Control Protocol), involve a three-way handshake to establish a connection before data transfer.

(*iii*) The User Datagram Protocol (UDP) is called a connectionless, unreliable transport protocol. - **True.** UDP is a connectionless protocol, and it is considered unreliable because it does not guarantee the delivery of packets.

183. (D)

184. (C): (*i*) Interpolation is a statistical method by which related known values are used to estimate an unknown value of a set of values. - **True.** Interpolation is a method used to estimate values within a range based on known values at data points within that range.

(*ii*) In the Inverse Distance Weighted (IDW) interpolation method, estimation of cell values is done by averaging values of sample data points in the neighborhood of each processing cell. - **True.** In the IDW interpolation method, values are estimated based on a weighted average of neighboring sample data points, where the weights are inversely proportional to the distance from the processing cell.

185. **(A):** Positive economics is an approach to economics that focuses on objective analysis and the examination of empirical data to understand and explain economic phenomena. Positive economics relies on empirical analysis, which means it looks at real-world data and observations. It aims to provide a description and explanation of economic events and behaviors based on concrete evidence. Positive economics is a branch of economics that seeks to understand economic phenomena through the collection and analysis of empirical data. It provides a foundation for making informed decisions and policies based on factual evidence rather than personal opinions or value judgments.

186. **(C):** System calls primarily fall into the following categories:

Process Control: System calls related to the creation, termination, scheduling, and management of processes (e.g., fork, exec, exit, wait).

File Manipulation: System calls that allow processes to read, write, create, delete, and manipulate files and directories (e.g., open, read, write, close).

Device Manipulation: System calls that deal with input and output devices, including reading from or writing to devices (e.g., read, write, ioctl).

Information Maintenance: System calls that provide information about the system and allow processes to retrieve information such as time, date, and system parameters (e.g., time, getpid, getuid).

Communication: System calls used for inter-process communication, including mechanisms like message passing and shared memory (e.g., pipe, socket).

"Data Compilation" is not a standard category of system calls in this context. System calls are typically classified into the categories mentioned above based on their primary functions and purposes.

187. **(C):** (*i*) A tuple is indeed a sequence of immutable Python objects, and the tuple course = "*l*", "*m*", "*n*", "*o*" contains four elements. So, statement (*i*) is **true.**

(*ii*) In Python, you don't use the "drop" statement to remove an entire tuple. Instead, you can use the "del" statement to delete the tuple itself. So, statement (*ii*) is **false.**

188. **(D):** Interpolation methods in computer graphics are techniques used to estimate values between known data points. These methods are particularly useful when you have a set of discrete data points and need to infer values at positions that lie between these points. Here's an explanation of some common interpolation methods:

Inverse Distance Weighted: This method estimates values by considering the influence of nearby data points on the interpolated value. Data points closer to the target point have a stronger influence, while those farther away have a weaker influence. It's often used in spatial analysis and geostatistics.

Kriging: Kriging is a geostatistical interpolation technique that takes into account the spatial correlation between data points. It provides not only an interpolated value but also an estimation of the uncertainty associated with that value.

Natural Neighbour: This method uses the natural neighbors of a point to interpolate values. It calculates weights for each neighbor based on proximity and assigns a weighted average value to the target point. It's particularly useful for irregularly spaced data points.

Spline: Splines are a type of curve-fitting technique. They involve fitting a piecewise continuous function to the data points, ensuring that the resulting curve is smooth and continuous. There are various types of splines, such as cubic splines and B-splines, each with its own characteristics.

Topo to Raster: This method is often used in geographic information systems (GIS). It converts topographic data, which includes elevation information at discrete points, into a raster or grid format. Interpolated values are assigned to each cell in the grid, creating a continuous representation of the terrain.

These interpolation methods are essential tools in computer graphics, GIS, geostatistics, and other fields where you need to estimate values between known data points to create smooth and visually pleasing representations of data. The choice of which method to use depends on factors like the nature of the data, the desired level of smoothness, and the application's specific requirements.

189. **(C):** The CRT (Cathode Ray Tube) is a type of display technology that was commonly used in older monitors and television sets. It's the component responsible for displaying images and text on the screen by using electron beams to excite phosphors on the screen's surface.

While VRAM (Video Random Access Memory) and GPU (Graphics Processing Unit) are important for handling and processing graphics data, they don't directly produce the visual display on the screen. The GPU processes graphics data and sends it to the display device, which in the case of CRT monitors, is the CRT itself.

DPU is not a standard term related to computer displays.

190. (B): When a plane is perpendicular to a reference plane, its projection on that plane is a straight line. When a plane is parallel to a reference plane, its projection on that plane shows its true shape and size. This is because all points on the perpendicular plane project onto the reference plane as a single line. Imagine shining a light on the perpendicular plane, and its shadow on the reference plane will be a straight line.

191. (B): Automatic Participation: Automatic participation refers to the active involvement of learners in the learning process. It means that learners are engaged and participating willingly in the learning activity without external pressure. This involvement can include asking questions, sharing thoughts and ideas, discussing topics, and actively seeking to understand the subject matter. Automatic participation is a positive sign of engagement and interest in the learning process. It often leads to a deeper understanding of the material.

Challengingness: Challengingness in a learning activity refers to the level of difficulty or complexity presented to the learners. An effective learning activity should strike a balance between being too easy (which can lead to boredom) and too difficult (which can lead to frustration). Challengingness encourages learners to think critically, problem-solve, and stretch their capabilities. When a learning activity is appropriately challenging, it can motivate learners to stay engaged and persevere through the material.

Effective learning activities should promote active participation from learners and offer an appropriate level of challenge. When learners are actively engaged and find the material appropriately challenging, they are more likely to have a meaningful and effective learning experience.

192. (B): "Only II," suggests having printed materials translated into home languages as a way to address the hurdle related to languages in school-family-community partnerships.

While translating materials is an important step to improve communication and engagement between schools and families with diverse language backgrounds, it's worth noting that a comprehensive approach, can be more effective. This approach includes not only translating materials but also providing childcare during events (option I) and assisting parents in setting up car pools (option III). These additional measures can further enhance the partnership between the school and families by addressing various aspects of the language-related hurdle.

193. (B): The Juvenile Justice Act, initially enacted in 1986, was aimed at addressing the issues related to children and adolescents who were in conflict with the law. It defined a juvenile as follows:

A boy child below 16 years of age.

A girl child below 18 years of age.

In essence, anyone falling below these age limits was considered a juvenile under the law. The purpose of this legislation was to ensure that children and adolescents who committed offenses were treated differently from adults within the criminal justice system. The idea was to provide them with a more rehabilitative and protective approach, acknowledging that young individuals might lack the maturity and understanding of their actions that adults possess.

194. (D): I. It is the work of a community of unschooled artists keeping alive the traditions specific to its particular culture. This statement highlights that regional art often involves artists who are not formally trained but have deep-rooted cultural traditions and artistic practices. They create art that is closely tied to their culture and heritage.

II. It reflects the traditional art forms of diverse community groups. Regional art reflects the traditional artistic expressions of various community groups within a specific region. These traditional art forms can include painting, sculpture, music, dance, crafts, and other cultural expressions that have been passed down through generations.

195. (B): Sarva Shiksha Abhiyan (SSA) is a flagship program of the Government of India launched in 2001 with the aim of achieving universalization of elementary education in a time-bound manner. The primary objective of SSA is to provide free and compulsory quality education to all children in the age group of 6 to 14 years. The program aims to ensure that every child has access to elementary education, regardless of their background or location. Sarva Shiksha Abhiyan has made significant strides in improving access to elementary education in India, especially in rural and underserved areas. It has contributed to increasing literacy rates and reducing educational disparities among various sections of society. The program has been instrumental in achieving the goal of universal elementary education and continues to evolve to meet the changing needs of India's education system.

196. (C): "Who controls the teachers and students in a school?" is a closed-ended question because it can be answered with a specific response, such as "school administration" or "principal," from a predetermined list of options.

Closed-ended questions are valuable when you want to gather structured data efficiently and analyze responses quantitatively. They are particularly useful in situations where you want to compare responses across a large number of respondents or when you need to measure specific variables or opinions. Closed-ended items, also known as closed-ended questions or objective-type items, are a type of question format commonly used in tests, surveys, and questionnaires. These questions are designed to elicit specific, predetermined responses from respondents.

197. (B): The Rishi Valley approach in pedagogy is designed to make students capable of acquiring mastery in learning competencies through both group and individual learning. It does not specifically focus on understanding the importance of the physical environment in the classroom.

198. (D): "Play provides opportunity for children to demonstrate their abilities and skills," is indeed related to socio-emotional development as well. It highlights how play can help children build self-confidence, express themselves, and showcase their abilities and skills to others, which are important aspects of socio-emotional development.

199. (B): **I. It is conducted at regular intervals on an informal basis:** Formative assessment is not a one-time event but a continuous process. Teachers use various methods, such as quizzes, discussions, observations, or homework, to gauge students' understanding of the material regularly. These assessments are often informal in nature and can occur daily or weekly.

II. It involves self-assessment and peer appraisal: Formative assessment doesn't only involve teachers assessing students. Students are encouraged to assess their understanding of the material as well. This can include reflecting on their own learning progress, identifying areas where they need improvement, and even peer evaluations, where students provide feedback to their classmates. Self-assessment and peer appraisal help students become more self-aware and take responsibility for their learning.

III. It is diagnostic and remedial: Formative assessments are designed to diagnose or identify areas where students are struggling or need further support. When a teacher identifies areas of weakness in a student's understanding, they can take remedial actions. These actions might include re-teaching certain concepts, providing additional resources, or adjusting the teaching approach to better address students' needs.

200. (B): The government has implemented the guaranteed equality in the constitution through both laws and government programs. Laws, such as anti-discrimination laws, are enacted to ensure equal treatment and protection of the rights of all citizens. Government programs and policies are also put in place to address issues related to equality, such as affirmative action programs aimed at promoting equal opportunities for disadvantaged groups. Together, these mechanisms help to uphold and promote the principle of equality as enshrined in the constitution.

Previous Paper (Solved)

DSSSB—TRAINED GRADUATE TEACHER (TGT) COMPUTER SCIENCE EXAM, 2021*

SECTION-A

GENERAL AWARENESS

1. Rice needs ______ temperature and ______ humidity.
A. high; high B. low; low
C. low; high D. high; low

2. Which article of Indian constitution is related to uniform civil code for citizens?
A. 44 B. 49
C. 46 D. 52

3. During a recession when GDP falls, disposable income ______.
A. falls less sharply B. increases less sharply
C. becomes zero D. becomes constant

4. Where are the headquarters of IAEA situated?
A. Vienna B. Copenhagen
C. Geneva D. Oslo

5. Which of the following is correct about insolation?
I. It influences distribution of temperature.
II. It increases from the equator towards the poles.
A. Both I and II B. Neither I nor II
C. Only II D. Only I

6. The size of pupil is controlled by the ______.
A. cornea B. iris
C. retina D. lens

7. ______ fight against germs that may enter our body.
A. Platelets B. White blood cells
C. Red blood cells D. Hemoglobin

8. Which of the following statement is correct?
I. Lord Dalhousie introduced doctrine of lapse.
II. Company took over Awadh in 1856.
A. Both I and II B. Only II
C. Only I D. Neither I nor II

9. 51st amendment of Indian constitution happened in which year?
A. 1973 B. 1984
C. 1989 D. 1969

10. Who won the Golden Boot award at 2019 FIFA U20 World Cup?
A. Lee Kangin B. Erling Haaland
C. Sekou Koita D. Andriy Lunin

11. Which country hosted the 2018 Asian games?
A. Malaysia B. Thailand
C. Qatar D. Indonesia

12. ______ compiled the Puranas and the Mahabharata.
A. Vyas B. Banabhatta
C. Tulsidas D. Kalidas

13. Which of the following pair of act - year is correct?
I. Child marriage restraint act - 1929
II. Window remarriage act - 1858
A. Both I and II B. Only II
C. Neither I nor II D. Only I

14. Which of the following is NOT a member of ASEAN?
A. Fiji B. Cambodia
C. Singapore D. Vietnam

15. ______ is located in Telangana.
A. Kangra Fort
B. Bibi-ka-Maqbara
C. Shershah Suri's Tomb
D. Khazana Building Museum

16. India launched supply chain resilience initiative in April, 2021 with ______.
A. Russia and Japan
B. Brazil and South Africa
C. Australia and Japan
D. Australia and Brazil

17. Which of the following pair of river - tributary is correct?
I. Krishna - Bhavani
II. Kaveri - Bhima
A. Only II B. Both I and II
C. Only I D. Neither I nor II

18. Which method of separation is used for seperating heavier and lighter components by bowing air?
A. Hand picking B. Sieving
C. Winnowing D. Threshing

19. Which of the following pair of type - instrument is correct?
I. Tata - Flute
II. Sushir - Table

* Exam for **TGT Computer Science** held on 07/08/2021.

A. Only I B. Only II
C. Neither I nor II D. Both I and II

20. Which of the following statement(s) is/are correct about Direct Taxes?

I. Direct taxes consist of taxes on incomes of individuals.

II. Income tax is one of the direct taxes.

A. Both I and II B. Neither I nor II
C. Only II D. Only I

GENERAL ABILITY

21. Five boxes B1, B2, B3, B4 and B5 are placed one above the other in racks. The lowermost rack is numbered as one and just above the lowermost is numbered as two and so on. Each box is coloured with different colour such as L1, L2, L3, L4 and L5 (not necessarily in the same order). Two boxes are placed between L2 coloured box and L5 coloured box. Box B1 is not placed immediately above box B3. Box B4 is placed in the top most rack. L1 coloured box is placed immediate above L5 coloured box. Box B3 is coloured with L4. L5 coloured box is placed above L4 coloured box. Box B2 is coloured with L1. Which of the following boxes are placed immediately above and immediately below B5 box respectively?

A. B4 and B1 B. B3 and B2
C. B2 and B3 D. B1 and B3

22. A series is given with one term missing. Select the correct alternative from the given ones that will complete the series.

SJ20, WF42, AB86, ?, IT370

A. EX174 B. FX172
C. EX172 D. FX174

23. In the following question below are given some statements followed by some conclusions based on those statements. Taking the given statements to be true even if they seem to be at variance from commonly known facts. Read all the conclusions and then decide which of the given conclusion logically follows the given statements.

Statements:

I. All A are S.
II. No D is A.

Conclusions:

I. Some S are A.
II. All S are D.
III. No A is D.

A. Both conclusions I and III follow
B. Both conclusions I and II follow
C. Only conclusion III follows
D. All conclusion follow

24. In the following question, select the number which can be placed at the sign of question mark (?) from the given alternatives.

19, 4, 14, 7, 10, 11, 7, ?

A. 24 B. 32
C. 40 D. 16

25. In the following question, a group of letters is given. The letters of each group are related with the letters of the same group by some Logic/Rule/Relation. From the given alternatives, select a group of letters which follows the same Logic/Rule/Relation.

(GROB, EKUC, FQNA)

A. (CGND, GJJY, BFMD)
B. (RFID, GECV, YYHC)
C. (LAPT, WLDH, KZOS)
D. (NEFT, WBHJ, MDEA)

26. A series is given with one term missing. Select the correct alternative from the given ones that will complete the series.

LXMG, TPUY, ?, JZKI, RRSA

A. BHCR B. BHDQ
C. BHCQ D. BHDR

27. In a certain code language, 'LACKEY' is written as '121311525', 'LUSTER' is written as '1221192051 8'. What is the code for 'KIPPER' in that code language?

A. 1191616518 B. 1191622522
C. 1191640532 D. 1191617520

28. Pairs of adjacent sides of a big cube are coloured with red, yellow and brown colour. Now this big cube is divided into 64 small equal cubes. How many small cubes will have 3 faces painted with different colours?

A. 8 B. 0
C. 2 D. 6

29. In the following question, select the related letters from the given alternatives.

KOM : LPN :: TIP : ?

A. UHQ B. VJQ
C. VHQ D. UJQ

30. Pointing towards a woman in a photograph, Vipin said, "She is the daughter of my son's wife". How is the woman related to Vipin?

A. Grand daughter B. Daughter in law
C. Daughter D. Niece

31. In the following question, select the related letters from the given alternatives.

AMD : FOC :: TRV : ?

A. YTV B. YTU
C. XTV D. XTU

32. If 'A' means '+', 'B' means '–', 'C' means '×' and 'D' means '÷', then which of the following equation is correct?

A. 8 A 15 D 5 C 11 B 7 = 35
B. 9 A 16 D 64 C 32 B 3 = 14
C. 26 D 14 C 7 A 9 B 3 = 20
D. 6 C 21 D 7 A 9 B 15 = 10

33. In the following question, four letter pairs are given. The letters on left side of (–) is related to the letters on the right side of (–) with some Logic/Rule/Relation. Three are similar on basis of same Logic/Rule/Relation. Select the odd one out from the given alternatives.

A. NO – MN B. LX – WK
C. TA – ZS D. CR – QB

34. Seven boys A, B, C, P, Q, R and S are sitting around a circular table facing towards the centre (not necessarily in the same order). S is second to the left of C. P is second to the left of S. Q is not the immediate neighbour of P or S. B is fourth to the right of A.

Which of thc following statement is correct?

A. B is second to the right of Q.
B. B is the immediate neighbour of S and C.
C. A is not the immediate neighbour of P or Q.
D. P is third to the left of C.

35. In the following question, select the missing number from the given series.

8, 31, 123, ?, 1963

A. 491 B. 461
C. 481 D. 471

36. In evening, Prema and Radhika were facing each other. Radhika's shadow was to the left of Prema. In which direction was Prema facing?

A. North B. East
C. West D. South

37. In the following question below are given some statements followed by some conclusions based on those statements. Taking the given statements to be true even if they seem to be at variance from commonly known facts. Read all the conclusions and then decide which of the given conclusion logically follows the given statements.

Statements:

I. Some land are hard.
II. No stone is land.

Conclusions:

I. Some hard are land.
II. Some stone are hard.

A. Both conclusions I and II follow
B. Neither conclusion follows
C. Only conclusion I follows
D. Only conclusion II follows

38. Ramesh is facing towards south direction. He rotates by 140 degrees in clockwise direction. He again rotates by 362 degrees in anti-clockwise direction. In which direction is he facing now?

A. North-east B. East
C. West D. North-west

39. In the certain code language, 'I think I can' is written as '6 8 6 4', 'We can think about' is written as '5 4 8 9'. What is the code for 'think, can' in that code language?

A. 6 9 B. 6 4
C. 8 5 D. 8 4

40. A series is given with one term missing. Select the correct alternative from the given ones that will complete the series.

GRZ, KWV, OBR, SGN, ?

A. XMJ B. XLJ
C. WMJ D. WLJ

ARITHMETIC ABILITY

41. Income of A is 20 per cent more than the income of B and income of B is 30 per cent more than the income of C. The income of C is (approximately) how much percentage less than the income of A?

A. 36 B. 30
C. 40 D. 32

42. Length of the largest side of an isosceles right angle triangle is 30 cm. What will be the area of this triangle?

A. 225 cm^2 B. 450 cm^2
C. 550 cm^2 D. 350 cm^2

43. If $(x + y) : (y + z) : (z + x) = 2 : 3 : 4$ and $(x + y + z) = 27$, then what is the value of z?

A. 17 B. 12
C. 15 D. 10

44. Which of the following statement is correct?

I. A boat travels 84 km downstream and 42 km upstream. If speed of boat and speed of stream are 6 km/hr and 2 km/hr respectively, then total time taken is 20 hours.

II. Length of a platform is 1200 meters. If a 600 meter long train can cross it in 30 seconds, then speed of train is 54 km/hr.

A. Only II B. Neither I nor II
C. Only I D. Both I and II

45. Diameter of wheel of a cycle is 17.5 cm. A cyclist takes 165 minutes to travel a distance with speed of 90 km/hr. How many revolutions will the wheel make during journey?

A. 425000 B. 525000
C. 450000 D. 500000

46. Marked price of an article is ₹ 4000. Selling price of the article is ₹ 2600. What is the discount percentage?

A. 20 B. 30
C. 35 D. 25

47. The downstream speed of a boat is 20 km/hr and the speed of stream is 4 km/hr. What will be the total time taken by the boat to cover 160 km downstream and 96 km upstream?

A. 10 hours B. 16 hours
C. 12 hours D. 14 hours

48. An article is sold for ₹ 864 at a loss of 28 per cent. If it is sold at 20 per cent profit, then what will be the selling price?

A. ₹ 1240 B. ₹ 1380
C. ₹ 1440 D. ₹ 1560

49. Total surface area of a solid hemisphere is 4158 cm^2. It is melted to form cylinder whose height is 1 cm and radius of base 7 cm. How many cylinders will be formed?

A. 136 B. 156
C. 96 D. 126

50. The line chart given below shows the marked price and selling price of six articles A, B, C, D, E and F.

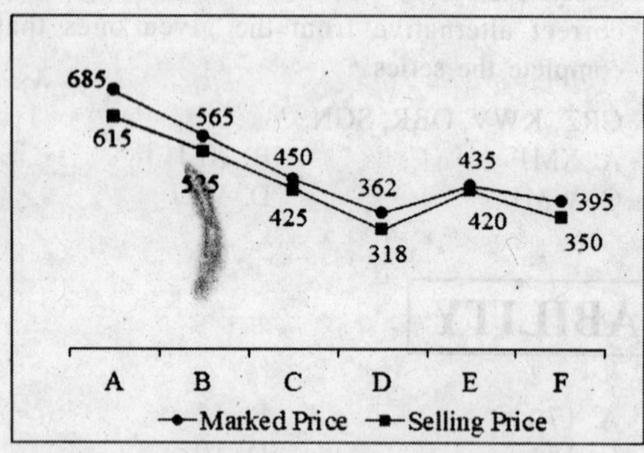

discount = (Marked price – Selling price)

$$\text{discount\%} = \frac{\text{Marked price} - \text{Selling price}}{\text{Marked price}} \times 100$$

J1 = Value of sum of discount on articles C and D

J2 = Value of difference of discount on articles D and E

What is the value of J1 – J2?

A. 29 B. 69
C. 20 D. 40

51. If (9835 × 88A) is divisible by 15, then what is the value of A?

A. 2 B. 6
C. 3 D. 7

52. What is the value of 24 per cent of 35 per cent of 6500?

A. 576 B. 648
C. 546 D. 612

53. The line chart given below shows the birth rate (per thousand persons) and death rate (per thousand persons) of countries P, Q, R and S in the year 2018.

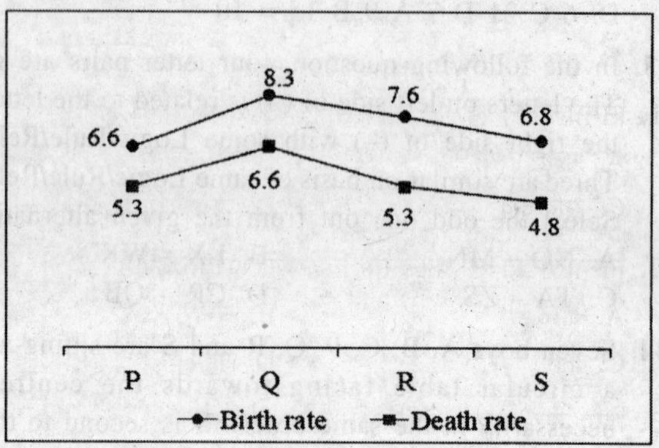

Which of the following statement(s) is/are correct?

I. Birth rate of country Q is 9.2 per cent more than country R.

II. Birth rate of country R is 11.76 per cent more than the birth rate of country S.

III. Birth rate of country Q is 32 per cent more than the birth rate of country S.

A. Both I and II B. Both I and III
C. Only I D. Only II

54. Which of the following fraction is highest?

A. $\frac{7}{8}$ B. $\frac{13}{16}$
C. $\frac{31}{40}$ D. $\frac{63}{80}$

55. The sum of two numbers is 66 and their difference is 22. What is the ratio of the two numbers?

A. 6 : 5 B. 17 : 5
C. 2 : 1 D. 5 : 1

56. The decimal notation of one-hundredth is:

A. 0.1 B. 0.25
C. 0.01 D. 2.5

57. A sum of ₹ 1200 becomes ₹ 1560 at a rate of simple interest in 3 years. In how many years will the sum of ₹ 800 amounts to ₹ 1120 at the same rate of simple interest?

A. 5 years B. 4 years
C. 3 years D. 6 years

58. Highest common factor of three distinct numbers is 7 and their least common multiple is 42. If all numbers are less than the least common multiple, then what is the product of these three numbers?

A. 686 B. 6174
C. 4116 D. 2058

59. P, Q and R alone can do a work in 12, 18 and 24 days respectively. They worked for 5 days, 4 days and 6 days respectively. They received ₹ 32000. What is the share of Q?

A. 6000 B. 8000
C. 12000 D. 15000

60. What is the value of 153 ÷ 17 × 8?
A. 81 B. 72
C. 63 D. 99

GENERAL HINDI

61. निम्नलिखित में से कौन-सा शब्द युग्म सही नहीं है?
A. भलाई-बुराई B. काम-बाम
C. सुख-दुख D. पाया-खोया

62. निम्नलिखित में कौन-सा विशेषण गुणवाचक है?
A. आठ B. सुन्दर
C. कोई D. यह

63. दिए गए वाक्य में क्रिया ज्ञात कीजिए।
बच्चे रो रहे हैं।
A. सामान्य B. अकर्मक
C. सकर्मक D. संयुक्त

64. कौन-सा शब्द कवि शब्द का स्त्रीलिंग है?
A. कविकी B. कवियत्री
C. कवयित्री D. कवयित्रि

65. निम्नलिखित वाक्यों में से मिश्र वाक्य ज्ञात कीजिए।
A. जो व्यक्ति बूढ़ा है उसे दवा पिला दो।
B. बूढ़े व्यक्ति को दवा पिला दो।
C. व्यक्ति बूढ़ा है इसलिए उसे दवा पिला दो।
D. व्यक्ति बूढ़ा है, अतः उसे दवा पिला दो।

66. निम्नलिख्ति वाक्यों में से शुद्ध वाक्य का चयन कीजिए।
A. कई रेलवे के अनेक कर्मचारियों की गिरफ्तारी हुई।
B. अनेक रेलवे के कर्मचारियों की गिरफ्तारी हुई।
C. रेलवे के कई कर्मचारियों की गिरफ्तारी हुई।
D. कई रेलवे के कर्मचारियों की गिरफ्तारी हुई।

67. निम्नलिखित में से कौन-सा शब्द 'अ' प्रत्यय से नहीं बना है?
A. वासुदेव B. ममत्व
C. राघव D. लाघव

68. 'को' और 'के लिए' किस कारक के चिन्ह हैं?
A. संबोधन B. संप्रदान
C. अपादान D. करण

69. दिए गए शब्द युग्म का सही शब्द युग्म ज्ञात कीजिए।
हय : हेय
A. घोड़ा : नीचा B. नीचा : कारण
C. कारण : नीचा D. नीचा : घोड़ा

70. निम्नलिखित प्रश्न में, दिए गए चार विकल्पों में से, उस विकल्प का चयन करें जो दिए गए मुहावरे के अर्थ को सर्वश्रेष्ठ रूप से व्यक्त करता है।
घड़ों पानी पड़ना
A. बात को और बढ़ाना B. संकट में पड़ना
C. अत्यन्त लज्जित होना D. ईर्ष्या से जलना

71. निम्नलिखित प्रश्न में, दिए गए चार विकल्पों में से, उस विकल्प का चयन करें जो दिए गए मुहावरे के अर्थ को सर्वश्रेष्ठ रूप से व्यक्त करता है।
अधर में लटकना
A. दुःख होना B. बाधक होना
C. घबराना D. दुविधा में पड़ा रह जाना

72. दिए गए वाक्य में उपयुक्त विराम चिह्न का चयन कीजिए।
अहिंसा मनुष्यता है हिंसा पशुत्व
A. – B. :-
C. : D. ॰

73. दिए गए वाक्य में उपयुक्त विराम चिह्न का चयन कीजिए।
अरे वर्षा होने लगी
A. :- B. ( )
C. ! D. ...

74. दिए गए वाक्यांश के लिए उचित शब्द का चयन कीजिए।
जो प्रतिदिन होता है।
A. अर्धवार्षिक B. दैनिक
C. साप्ताहिक D. वार्षिक

75. दिए गए शब्द युग्म का सही शब्द युग्म ज्ञात कीजिए।
शांति : श्रांति
A. स्थिरता : थकावट B. शक्तिशाली : सार
C. स्थिरता : विश्रांति D. श्याम : थकावट

निर्देश (प्र.सं. 76-80): *दिए गए गद्यांश को ध्यानपूर्वक पढ़ें और दिए गए प्रश्न के उत्तर दें।*

हर वर्ष 26 जनवरी को हमारे देश में गणतंत्र दिवस के रूप में मनाया जाता है। हम सभी देशवासियों को भारत का नागरिक होने का गर्व

है। 26 जनवरी, 1950 को हमारा देश एक प्रजातान्त्रिक गणतंत्र देश बना था। इस दिन हमारे देश में संविधान लागू हुआ था। हमारी मातृभूमि भारत लंबे समय तक ब्रिटिश शासन की गुलाम रही तथा ब्रिटिश शासन द्वारा बनाये गये कानूनों का भारतीय लोगों को पालन करना पड़ता था व कानूनों को मानने के लिये मजबूर थे, भारतीय स्वतंत्रता सेनानियों द्वारा लंबे संघर्ष के बाद भारतीय स्वतंत्रता सेनानियों ने अंततः 15 अगस्त, 1947 को भारत को आजादी दिलाई। लगभग 2 साल 11 महीने 18 दिन बाद 26 जनवरी, 1950 को हमारी संसद द्वारा भारतीय संविधान पारित किया गया। भारत ने अपना संविधान लागू किया और खुद को संप्रभु, लोकतांत्रिक, गणराज्य के रूप में घोषित किया। भारत में आजादी के बाद 'विविधता में एकता' के अस्तित्व को दिखाने के लिए देश के अलग-अलग राज्य खूबसूरत झांकियों के जरिए अपनी संस्कृति, परंपरा और प्रगति को दिखाते हैं। अतः यह और भी आवश्यक हो जाता है कि इस विशेष दिन को हम उचित सम्मान दें और इसे साथ मिलकर मनायें, जिससे हमारे देश की एकता और अखंडता जिसके लिए कई वीरों ने अपने प्राणों की आहुति दी है, इसी प्रकार से बनी रहे। गणतंत्र दिवस का यह राष्ट्रीय पर्व हमारे लिए बहुत ही महत्वपूर्ण है क्योंकि हमारे देश का संविधान तथा इसका गणतांत्रिक स्वरूप ही हमारे देश को कश्मीर से कन्याकुमारी तक जोड़ने का कार्य करता है।

76. गणतांत्रिक स्वरूप हमारे देश को कहां से कहां तक जोड़ने का कार्य करता है?

A. कन्याकुमारी से दिल्ली B. कश्मीर से कन्याकुमारी
C. कश्मीर से लद्दाख D. कन्याकुमारी से लेह

77. दिए गए गद्यांश का उपयुक्त शीर्षक क्या होगा?

A. भारत का नागरिक B. स्वतंत्रता दिवस
C. जोड़ने का कार्य D. गणतंत्र दिवस

78. हमारे देश के कई वीरों ने अपने प्राणों की आहुति क्यों दी थी?

A. संस्कृति और परम्परा
B. लोकतांत्रिक और कानूनों
C. एकता और अखंडता हेतु
D. विविधता में एकता

79. हमारा देश कब आजाद हुआ था?

A. 15 अगस्त, 1950 B. 26 जनवरी, 1947
C. 15 अगस्त, 1947 D. 26 जनवरी, 1950

80. हमारी मातृ भूमि भारत लंबे समय तक किस शासन का गुलाम रही?

A. संसदात्मक शासन प्रणाली B. ब्रिटिश शासन
C. एकात्मक शासन D. संघात्मक शासन

GENERAL ENGLISH

81. In the following question, out of the given four alternatives, select the alternative which best expresses the meaning of the Idiom/Phrase.

To raise a dust

A. To treat someone indifferently
B. To bring lots of energy in an event
C. To spend extravagantly
D. To cause commotion

82. A sentence has been given with a blank to be filled with an appropriate word/words. Choose the correct alternative.

They ______ it difficult to read that book.

A. founded B. founds
C. found D. find

83. Rearrange the parts of the sentence in correct order.

The common goals of the Stop TB Partnership
P: efforts aimed at preventing and
Q: developing a cure for the disease
R: of tuberculosis and supporting
S: include raising global awareness

A. SRPQ B. PRQS
C. SPQR D. SRQP

84. In the given question, four words are given out of which one word is correctly spelt. Choose the correctly spelt word.

A. Trensmission B. Tranmission
C. Transmission D. Transmession

85. A sentence has been given with a blank to be filled with an appropriate word. Choose the correct alternative.

Mental stress can make a person ____ in many ways.

A. inspirit B. lunatic
C. rally D. hail

86. In the following question, out of the given four alternatives, select the alternative which best expresses the meaning of the Idiom/Phrase.

Bolt from the blue

A. A sudden and entirely unforeseen event
B. A catastrophic happening
C. An apparition
D. A violent thunderstorm

87. Choose the word that can substitute the given sentence.

An act of remembering or telling about past experiences

A. Indictment B. Blockade
C. Vengeance D. Reminiscence

88. Select the most appropriate option to substitute the underlined segment in the given sentence. If no substitution is required, select No improvement.

The meeting had evoked curiosity in regards to the recent panchayat.

A. No Improvement B. with regards to
C. in view of D. in regarding to

89. Select the most appropriate option to substitute the underlined segment in the given sentence. If no substitution is required, select No improvement.

Although, he comes to the event but he was as usual late.

A. No Improvement B. comes to
C. came to D. will come to

90. Choose the word that means the same as the given word.

Warning

A. Caution B. Victim
C. Accuse D. Attention

91. Rearrange the parts of the sentence in the correct order.

P: spite of sometimes anaemic comic book sales
Q: has appeared on all manner of merchandise and
R: has remained a presence in the pop culture consciousness in
S: appealing to a vast demographic, Wonder Woman

A. RQPS B. SQRP
C. RPSQ D. PSQR

92. Find the part of the given sentence that has an error in it. If there is no error, choose 'No error'.

My son is the most /bravest of all /other men in the city. / No error

A. My son is the most B. other men in the city
C. bravest of all D. No error

93. Find the part of the given sentence that has an error in it. If there is no error, choose 'No error'.

India's forest and tree cover has/increased by nearly 4,000 sq km/for the last assessment report in 2017./ No error

A. No error
B. for the last assessment report in 2017.
C. India's forest and tree cover has
D. increased by nearly 4,000 sq km

94. In the given question, four words are given out of which one word is incorrectly spelt. Choose the incorrectly spelt word.

A. Gathering B. Comisson
C. Brightness D. Assumption

95. Choose the word that is opposite in meaning to the given word.

Altercate

A. Concurrent B. Contend
C. Coexist D. Nitpick

Directions (Qs. No. 96-100): *Read the following information carefully and answer the given questions.*

Assessing women's access to equal opportunity and resources against the access that men have would be a scientific way of evaluating a nation's commitment to the advancement of its citizens. But going by the World Economic Forum's Global Gender Gap Index 2020, released last week, questions can easily be raised about whether this government is doing the right thing by the country's women. India has dropped four points from 2018, to take the 112th rank on the Index. The Index measures the extent of gender-based gaps on four key parameters - economic participation and opportunity, educational attainment, health and survival, and political empowerment. Notably, it measures gender-based gaps in access to resources and opportunities in countries, rather than the actual levels of the available resources and opportunities. Despite a small score improvement, India has lost four positions as some countries ranked lower than India have shown better improvement. The country has reportedly closed two-thirds of its overall gender gap, with a score of 66.8 per cent, but the report notes with concern that the condition of women in large fringes of Indian society is 'precarious'. Of significant concern is the economic gender gap, with a score of 35.4 per cent, at the 149th place, among 153 countries, and down seven places since the previous edition, indicating only a third of the gap has been bridged. The participation of women in the labour force is also among the lowest in the world, and the female estimated earned income is only one-fifth of male income. An alarming statistic is India's position (150th rank) on the very bottom of the Health and Survival subindex, determined largely by the skewed sex ratio at birth, violence, forced marriage and discrimination in access to health. It is on the educational attainment (112th rank) and political empowerment (18th rank) fronts that the relatively good news is buried.

96. Which of the following is not one of the key parameters to measure the extent of gender based gap?

A. Educational attainment
B. Economic participation
C. Political empowerment
D. Labour force

97. In what context, the word 'precarious' is used in the passage?

A. Women conditions in larger part of India is balanced.
B. The condition of women in less important parts of India is dangerous.
C. The condition of women in India is at a risk.
D. The role of women in India is in jeopardy.

98. What can be the suitable title for the given passage?

A. Economic Gender Gap
B. Mind the gap: On Gender gap
C. Prevailing Inequality in India
D. India's Rank

99. Identify the nearby antonym of the word 'Alarming'?

A. Dread B. Ghastly
C. Unwary D. Exonerate

100. Which of the following statements is/are not correct as per the given passage?

I. The participation of women in the labour force is lowest in the whole world.

II. In India, female income is only one-fifth of female income.

A. Only I
B. Neither I nor II
C. Only II
D. Both I and II

SECTION-B

COMPUTER SCIENCE

POST SPECIFIC SUBJECT

101. What is the full form of 'The EDVAC', the first generation computer?

A. The electronic discrete variable automatic computer
B. The electronic discrete variable automatic calculator
C. The electronic digital variable automatic computer
D. The electronic digital variable automatic calculator

102. What is the output of the code written in C?

```
void main()
{
int k, val=1;
k= ++val*++val;
printf("%d",k);
}
```

A. 4
B. 1
C. 9
D. 16

103. Which one is the reserved word in C language?

A. Integer
B. Volatile
C. Constant
D. Automatic

104. The height of a tree is the length of the longest path from root to leaf. What is the maximum and minimum number of nodes in a binary tree of height 'n'?

A. $2^{n+1} - 1$, $n + 1$
B. $2^{n-1} - 1$
C. 2^{n-1}, $n - 1$
D. 2^n, $n + 1$

105. 2 Dimensional array (Matrices) with relatively high proportion of zero entries are called ______ while with low proportion of zero entries are called ______.

A. Regular Matrix; Non-Regular Matrix
B. Square Matrix; Dense Matrix
C. Transpose Matrix; Inverse Matrix
D. Sparse Matrix; Dense Matrix

106. How many interchanges will happen when the sequence of letters of "SORTED" is sorted using bubble sort?

A. 6
B. 36
C. 18
D. 11

107. Perverse Software is also known as ______.

A. application software
B. utility software
C. malicious software
D. diagnostic software

108. Which of the following is the feature(s) of High level programming languages?

I. Portability

II. Easy debugging

A. Only II
B. Both I and II
C. Only I
D. Neither I nor II

109. Which of the following are the key feature(s) of cloud computing?

I. Scalability

II. Self service

III. Pay-per-use

A. I and II
B. I, II and III
C. I and III
D. II and III

110. Which of the following is a non-positional number system?

A. Decimal
B. Octal
C. Binary
D. Roman

111. What is the function of Ctrl + T in MS Word?

A. Justify paragraph alignment
B. Hanging indent
C. Redo the last action
D. Undo last action

112. ______ mode allows transmission in both directions simultaneously.

A. Duplex
B. Half simplex
C. Half duplex
D. Simplex

113. Which of the following statement(s) is/are true about control unit?

I. It manages and coordinate the entire computer system.

II. It does not perform any actual processing on data.

A. Only I
B. Only II
C. Both I and II
D. Neither I nor II

114. Which of the following is a shortcut key to justify paragraph alignment in MS-Word?

A. Ctrl + S
B. Ctrl + Y
C. Ctrl + I
D. Ctrl + J

115. What will be the quotient when $(100001)_2$ is divided by $(110)_2$?

A. $(001)_2$
B. $(110)_2$
C. $(100)_2$
D. $(101)_2$

116. How many bits are required to represent $(1000)_{10}$ in BCD code?

A. 10 bits
B. 16 bits
C. 32 bits
D. 4 bits

117. Which of the following is/are the open-source software(s)?
I. PHP
II. Apache
A. Only II B. Only I
C. Both I and II D. Neither I nor II

118. Which of the following is/are true about little oh(o) asymptotic notation?
I. $f(x) = o(g(x))$ iff $f(x) = O(g(x))$
II. $f(x) = o(g(x))$ iff $f(x) \neq W(g(x))$
A. Only II B. Both I and II
C. Only I D. Neither I nor II

119. Which generation of computer used transistor?
A. Fourth B. Second
C. Third D. First

120. Which of the following statement(s) is/are true about binary search algorithm?
I. It is implemented on sorted array.
II. One must have direct access to the middle element in any sub-list.
III. It is implemented on sorted linked list.
A. I, II and III B. I and III
C. II and III D. I and II

121. Which of the following pair is correct?
I. RTL - Saturated bipolar logic family
II. ECL - Non-Saturated bipolar logic family
A. Only II B. Neither I nor II
C. Both I and II D. Only I

122. How many NOR gates are used to get AND gate from them?
A. 4 B. 3
C. 1 D. 2

123. ______ describes the process of deciding about putting data to different sites in distributed database system.
A. Data allocation B. Data mining
C. Data sharing D. Data storing

124. Which of the following is a Comparison operator in Structured Query Language?
A. + B. >=
C. / D. *

125. Which of the following is an alternative to the log-based recovery schemes in database recovery system?
A. Demand paging B. Prepaging
C. Shadow paging D. Defragmentation

126. ______ is a unique identifier created by database management system to identify the relative starting time of a transaction.
A. Shadow paging B. Spoofing
C. Deadlock D. Timestamp

127. In a JK flip flop, if J = K, then resulting flip flop is ______.
A. D B. SR
C. Clocked SR D. T

128. Which of the following is NOT a variant of time stamp-based method of concurrency control in database management system?
A. Multilevel time stamp ordering
B. Multi version time stamp ordering
C. Partial time stamp ordering
D. Total time stamp ordering

129. What is the meaning of this arithmetic micro-operation?
A. Content of R1 plus the 2's complement of R2 transferred to R3
B. Content of R1 plus R2 after increments transferred to R3
C. Content of R1 plus the 1's complement of R2 transferred to R3
D. Content of R1 plus R2 transferred to R3

130. ______ is a technique of breaking up database into logical units, which may be assigned for storage at the various sites in distributed database system.
A. Data fragmentation B. Data mining
C. Data normalization D. Data binding

131. Both the inputs of NAND gate are connected to A. What will be the output?
A. 1 B. A
C. 0 D. $\bar{A}$

132. Which of the following statement(s) is/are true about wire framing of website?
I. Showing which content will appear on which page.
II. Showing navigator between pages.
A. Only I B. Neither I nor II
C. Both I and II D. Only II

133. In a multiplexer, the number of input lines is 'n' and the number of select lines is 'm'. Which of the following is correct?
A. $2^m = n$ B. $2m = n$
C. $2^n = m$ D. $2n = m$

134. How many bits are required to distinguish between a direct and an indirect address?
A. 1 B. 3
C. 2 D. 4

135. Which logical gate is used to represent product of sum expression?
A. EX-OR gate B. AND gate
C. NOR gate D. OR gate

136. In D flip-flop, if D = 1, then the output of the D flip-flop is ______, but if D = 0, then the output of D flip-flop goes to ______ state.
A. 0; 0 B. 1; 0
C. 1; 1 D. 0; 1

137. Which of the following is an advantage of use of multiplexers?

I. Logic design is simplified.

II. Minimizes IC package count.

III. Simplification of logic expression is not required.

A. I, II and III B. II and III

C. I and II D. I and III

138. By how many different ways micro-operation encountered in digital computers are classified?

A. Three B. Two

C. Four D. One

139. 2 resistors of 4 ohm each are connected in series. What is their equivalent resistance?

A. 2 ohm B. 8 ohm

C. 4 ohm D. 16 ohm

140. Simplify the following Boolean Expression?

A. A – B B. B

C. A + B D. AB

141. What is the other name of Linear Sequential model in software engineering?

A. Spiral model B. Prototype model

C. Waterfall model D. RAD model

142. In ______ model, software is developed in a series of incremental releases.

I. Spiral

II. Sequential

A. Only I B. Neither I nor II

C. Only II D. Both I and II

143. Which of the following is/are correct about java programming?

I. All functions in java must be members of some class.

II. Member functions are called methods in java.

A. Neither I nor II B. Only II

C. Both I and II D. Only I

144. What is the full form of WDMA protocol?

A. Wide Division Multiple Access Protocol

B. Wavelength Digital Multiple Access Protocol

C. Wavelength Division Multiple Access Protocol

D. Wide Digital Multiple Access Protocol

145. What is the other name of White-box testing?

A. Glass-box testing

B. Open-box testing

C. Red-box testing

D. Close-box testing

146. Which of the following is/are correct regarding accounting process?

I. A provision is a charge against profit.

II. Reserve is an appropriation of profit.

A. Both I and II B. Neither I nor II

C. Only I D. Only II

147. A 500 kbyte memory is managed using variable memory partitions and are allowed for compaction. It is currently using 2 partitions of sizes 100 kbytes and 130 kbytes respectively. The smallest allocation request in kbytes that could be denied is for ______.

A. 270 B. 250

C. 271 D. 170

148. Which principles are used in digitization of multimedia content?

I. Sampling

II. Quantization

A. Only II B. Only I

C. Neither I nor II D. Both I and II

149. What is the full form of MTTF in software reliability?

A. Median time to failure

B. Minimum time to failure

C. Mean time to failure

D. Maximum time to failure

150. A computer system has 7 tape drives. There are '*n*' processes competing for them. Each process may need 2 tape drives. What is the maximum value of '*n*' for which the system is guaranteed to be deadlock free?

A. 1 B. 4

C. 3 D. 2

151. Which of the following is not an example of unguided transmission media?

A. Radio transmission

B. Light transmission

C. Coaxial cable

D. Microwave transmission

152. ______ is used to reduce the size of multimedia files.

A. Data handling B. Data coupling

C. Data compression D. Data dependency

153. ______ model is a "high speed" adaption of the linear sequential model in software engineering.

A. Prototype model

B. Rapid Application development model

C. Waterfall model

D. Spiral model

154. ______ is used to transfer the data directly to main memory without using CPU.

A. Memory Address Register

B. Device driver

C. Input/Output interface

D. DMA controller

155. Which of the following statement(s) is/are true regarding PERT chart in software project management?

I. PERT charts consists of a network of boxes and arrows.

II. In PERT chart, the boxes represent activities and the arrow represents task dependencies.

A. Neither I nor II B. Only I

C. Only II D. Both I and II

156. Which of the following is not a project estimation technique in software engineering?
A. Heuristic techniques B. Prototyping techniques
C. Empirical techniques D. Analytical techniques

157. ARQ (Automatic Repeat Request) is:
A. asking question and getting the reply
B. protocol in which the sends for positive acknowledgement before advancing to the next data item
C. protocol allows both manual IP address assign infant and automatic assignment
D. protocol allows a newly booted workstation to broadcast its Ethernet address

158. The time required to wait until Read/Write head comes under a desired sector is known as ______.
A. Rotational delay B. Seek time
C. Wait time D. Execution time

159. What is COHESION in software design?
A. Cohesion is a measure of complexity of module of a software
B. Cohesion is a measure of efficiency of a module of a software
C. Cohesion is a measure of functional weakness of a module of a software
D. Cohesion is a measure of functional strength of a module of a software

160. What is the output of the following java code?

```
int m = 1000;
int k = 3000;
while (+ + m < - - k);
System.out.println(m);
```

A. 2000 B. Error
C. 1000 D. 4000

161. Which of the following statement(s) is/are correct regarding m-commerce?
I. Mobile security is one of the prominent impediments of m-commerce.
II. M-commerce reduces overall transaction cost through streamlined business processes.
III. Mobile coupons and mobile ticket delivery are m-commerce services.
A. I and II B. I, II and III
C. II and III D. Only III

162. Which of the following is NOT the correct characteristic of Security Socket Layer (SSL)?
A. It requires a server certificate.
B. It operates between the network and transport layer.
C. It uses a dedicated TCP/IP socket.
D. It operates at TCP/IP transport layer.

163. Which of the following is a component of Management Information System (MIS)?
A. Inquiry processing
B. Data entry
C. External database
D. Knowledge engine

164. If an image has a width of 4 inch and an aspect ratio of 3 : 2, then what is its height?
A. 16/3 inch B. 8/3 inch
C. 4/3 inch D. 2/3 inch

165. Which of the following statement(s) is/are correct regarding On-Line Transaction Processing (OLTP)?
I. Responses to the user inquiry are immediate.
II. The associated cost is economical with efficient utilization of resources.
III. The database is always up-to-date.
A. Only II B. I and III
C. I and II D. Only III

166. Extension of bootstrap protocol is known as ______.
A. Dynamic Host Configuration Protocol
B. Direct Source Routing Protocol
C. Dynamic Source Routing Protocol
D. Direct Host Configuration Protocol

167. ______ gives the location of a resource on the internet.
A. Domain name B. TCP/IP
C. URL D. IP address

168. Rearrange steps involved in two dimensional viewing transformation.
I. Map normalized viewport to device co-ordinates.
II. Convert world co-ordinate to viewing co-ordinates.
III. Construct world - co-ordinate scene using modelling coordinate transformation.
IV. Map viewing co-ordinates to normalized viewing co-ordinates using window-viewport specification.
A. II → III → IV → I
B. III → II → I → IV
C. I → II → IV → III
D. III → II → IV → I

169. Which component of CRT regulate the intensity of electron beam?
A. Focusing Anode B. Control Grid
C. Heating Filament D. Accelerating Anode

170. ______ lets users to show their location with websites they trust.
A. OLTrust B. Geolocation
C. Geotrust D. Loctrust

171. ______ is a set of rules that governs how two computer system interact.
A. Syntax B. Rules
C. Protocol D. Grammar

172. Consider a max heap, represented by the array 400, 300, 200, 100, 150, 160, 170, 80, 40.

What will be the new heap after insertion of 350?
A. 400, 350, 200, 100, 150, 160, 170, 80, 40, 300
B. 400, 300, 200, 100, 150, 160, 170, 80, 40, 350

C. 400, 350, 200, 100, 300, 160, 170, 80, 40, 150
D. 400, 300, 200, 100, 350, 160, 170, 80, 40, 150

173. Which of the following is stable sort?
A. Quick sort B. Heap sort
C. Merge sort D. Selection sort

174. ______ is a symbol used to represent special files in Linux OS.
A. d B. e
C. s D. c

175. ______ is a CPU independent machine language style instruction set into which .NET Framework program are compiled.
A. Machine language B. Intermediate language
C. Assembly language D. High level language

176. What is the full form of GSM in mobile computing?
A. Global Services for mobile computing
B. Global Scientific mobile computing
C. Global Signalling for mobile computing
D. Global Systems for mobile communication

177. Post-order Binary tree traversal is ______.
A. Right, Left, Node B. Left, Right, Node
C. Left, Node, Right D. Node, Left, Right

178. What will be the balancing factor of node 14 in an AVL tree when a node 13 is deleted from it?
A. BF(14) = 1 B. B(14) = 2
C. BF(14) = –2 D. BF(14) = –1

179. Rearrange steps involved in top-down design programming?
I. Analyze the problem
II. Revise and resequence
III. Write the main module
IV. Connect the modules in proper order
V. Write the remaining modules
A. III → I → V → IV → II
B. V → III → I → IV → II
C. II → IV → V → III → I
D. I → III → V → IV → II

180. Which of the following is not the collision resolution technique of hashing?
A. Quadratic probing B. Double hashing
C. Chaining D. Folding

181. Which of the following statement(s) is/are true about Algorithm?
I. It is step by step solution of problem
II. It is difficult to debug
III. It is not dependent on the programming language
A. I, II and III B. I and II
C. I and III D. II and III

182. If the probability of winning a match is 0.7, then what is the value of variance?
A. 0.3 B. 0.21
C. 0.7 D. 0.31

183. When contacting a large number of people for some information, which of the following methods of data collection is considered to be convenient?
A. Official Records
B. Questionnaires
C. Personal Observation
D. Interview

184. If loop does not terminate at all and keeps on executing endlessly, then it is known as ______.
A. for loop B. infinite loop
C. finite loop D. white loop

185. A question in mathematics is given to three students P, Q and R whose chances of solving are 1/3, 1/4, 1/5 respectively. What is the probability that the problem will be solved?
A. 0.6 B. 0.7
C. 0.8 D. 0.4

186. The two-dimensional perspective of knowledge management includes which of the following element(s)?
I. Strategy
II. Content
A. Neither I nor II B. Both I and II
C. Only I D. Only II

187. ______ URL is used to send electronic mail.
A. EURL B. Email UR
C. Mailto D. Eto

188. If $f(1) = 4$ and $f(5) = 6$, then what is the value of $f(3)$ using Lagrange's interpolation?
A. 4 B. 6.5
C. 5 D. 3

189. Efficiency of an algorithm is measured in terms of ______.
A. Response time and completion time
B. Data and space
C. Memory and processor speed
D. Time and space

190. 20 per cent of the pens produced in a factory are of red colour and 4 per cent are red and defective. If one pen is picked up at random, then what is the probability of its being defective if it is red?
A. 0.6 B. 0.4
C. 0.8 D. 0.2

191. Which of the following statement(s) is/are correct?
I. Discrimination disregards individual need, merit and potential.
II. Providing separate toilets for boys and girls does not tantamount to discrimination.
A. Only I B. Only II
C. Neither I nor II D. Both I and II

192. Which of the following is/are the component(s) of Lesson Plan?

I. What to teach
II. Who to teach
III. How to teach
A. I, II and III
B. I and II
C. Only III
D. II and III

193. As per National Curriculum Framework (2005), which of the following statement(s) is/are NOT correct about subject-centered approach?
I. Text book is the only source and main source for the teacher.
II. Insistence on the students to memorise the facts by repeated reading.
A. Only I
B. Both I and II
C. Only II
D. Neither I nor II

194. Which of the following statement(s) is/are correct?
I. Multilinguality is an integral part of the Indian linguistic heritage.
II. The culture and attitude towards language has a prominent role to play in a country being monolingual or multilingual.
A. Both I and II
B. Neither I nor II
C. Only I
D. Only II

195. While working with clay, which of the following precaution(s) needs to be taken?
I. Using too much water will make the clay weak and later cracks will develop in the slabs.
II. Children should maintain cleanliness and hygiene while working with clay.
A. Only II
B. Only I
C. Both I and II
D. Neither I nor II

196. In contrast to other approaches to assessment of learning, assessment as learning is entirely ______ controlled.
I. Student
II. Teacher
A. Neither I nor II
B. Only I
C. Only II
D. Both I and II

197. Which of the following are those teaching learning materials that are prepared by teachers and students in most of the schools?
I. Graphs
II. Number and alphabet cards
III. Flash cards on different themes
A. I and IV
B. I and II
C. I, II and III
D. II and III

198. The basics of all performing arts is ______.
I. Exploring
II. Expressing
III. Listening
A. II and III
B. I, II and III
C. Only II
D. I and III

199. When we gather new experiences while assessing our own performance or performance of others, then the processes of learning and assessment lose the line of demarcation between them. In such instances assessment becomes a ______ process.
A. speaking
B. reading
C. teaching
D. learning

200. Which article of Indian Constitution empowered the state to make special provisions for the welfare of the women and children?
A. Article 15(3)
B. Article 11(2)
C. Article 2
D. Article 45

ANSWERS

1	2	3	4	5	6	7	8	9	10
A	A	A	A	D	B	B	A	B	B
11	**12**	**13**	**14**	**15**	**16**	**17**	**18**	**19**	**20**
D	A	D	A	D	C	D	C	C	A
21	**22**	**23**	**24**	**25**	**26**	**27**	**28**	**29**	**30**
C	A	A	D	C	C	A	C	D	A
31	**32**	**33**	**34**	**35**	**36**	**37**	**38**	**39**	**40**
C	B	A	B	A	D	C	D	D	D
41	**42**	**43**	**44**	**45**	**46**	**47**	**48**	**49**	**50**
A	A	C	B	C	C	B	C	D	D
51	**52**	**53**	**54**	**55**	**56**	**57**	**58**	**59**	**60**
A	C	A	A	C	C	B	D	B	B
61	**62**	**63**	**64**	**65**	**66**	**67**	**68**	**69**	**70**
B	B	B	C	A	C	B	B	A	C

71 D	**72** C	**73** C	**74** B	**75** A	**76** B	**77** D	**78** C	**79** C	**80** B
81 D	**82** C	**83** A	**84** C	**85** B	**86** A	**87** D	**88** C	**89** C	**90** A
91 B	**92** B	**93** B	**94** B	**95** C	**96** D	**97** C	**98** B	**99** C	**100** C
101 A	**102** C	**103** B	**104** A	**105** D	**106** D	**107** C	**108** B	**109** B	**110** D
111 B	**112** A	**113** C	**114** D	**115** D	**116** B	**117** C	**118** B	**119** B	**120** D
121 C	**122** B	**123** A	**124** B	**125** C	**126** D	**127** D	**128** A	**129** A	**130** A
131 D	**132** C	**133** A	**134** A	**135** C	**136** B	**137** A	**138** C	**139** B	**140** B
141 C	**142** A	**143** C	**144** C	**145** A	**146** A	**147** C	**148** D	**149** C	**150** C
151 C	**152** C	**153** B	**154** D	**155** D	**156** B	**157** B	**158** A	**159** D	**160** A
161 B	**162** B	**163** C	**164** B	**165** B	**166** A	**167** C	**168** D	**169** B	**170** B
171 C	**172** C	**173** C	**174** D	**175** B	**176** D	**177** B	**178** C	**179** D	**180** B
181 C	**182** B	**183** B	**184** B	**185** A	**186** B	**187** C	**188** C	**189** D	**190** D
191 D	**192** A	**193** D	**194** A	**195** C	**196** B	**197** C	**198** B	**199** D	**200** A

EXPLANATORY ANSWERS

21. We have, arranging order of boxes are:

B4 → L2
B1 → L3
B2 → L1
B5 → L5
B3 → L4

Hence, box B2 immediately above B5 and box B3 is immediately box B3.

22.

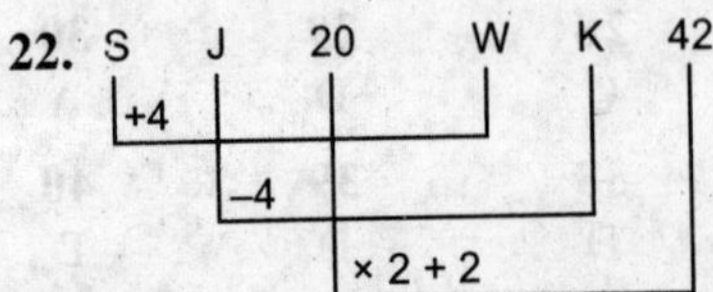

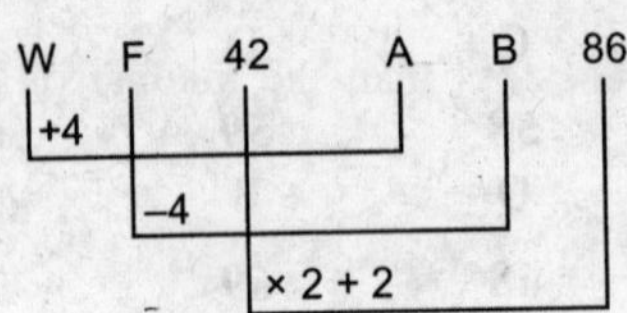

Similarly,

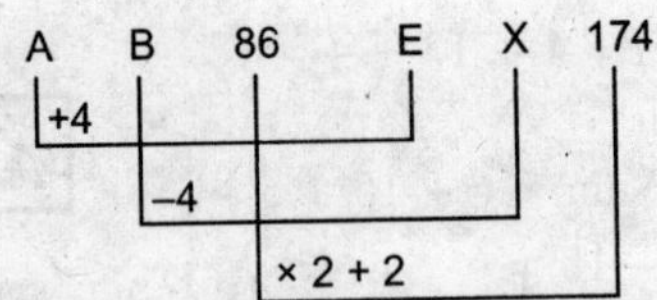

Hence, the milling term in the series = EX174.

24. We have,

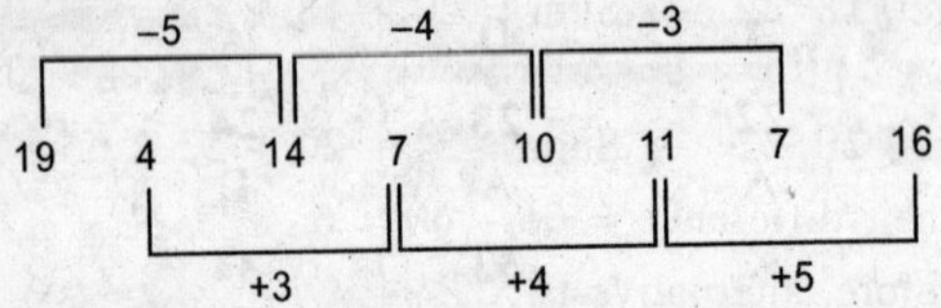

Hence, correct answer is D.

26.

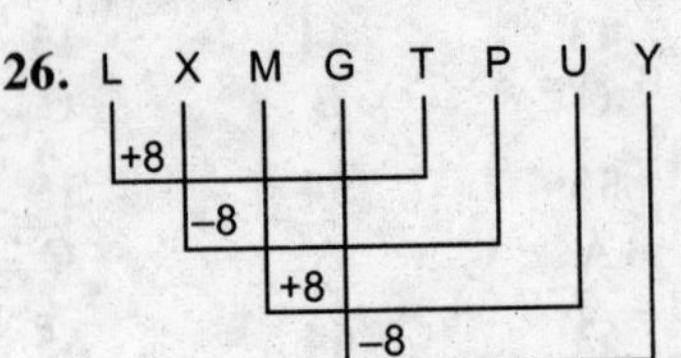

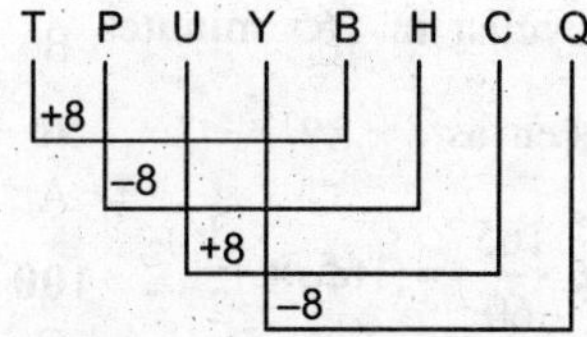

Similarly,

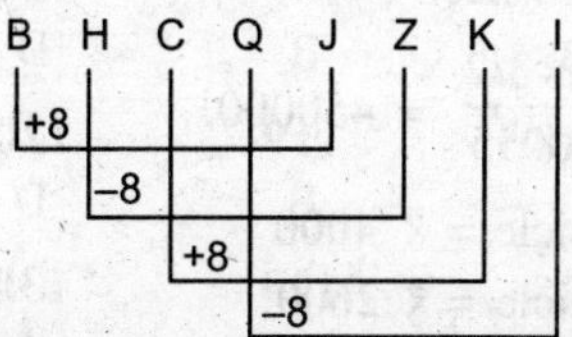

The letter of the word are coded by moving 8 steps forward and 8 steps backward alternately.

Hence, the missing term = BHCQ.

27. Given, L A C K E Y , L U S T E R

12 1 3 11 5 25 12 21 19 20 5 18

Similarly,

K I P P E R

11 9 16 16 5 18

30.

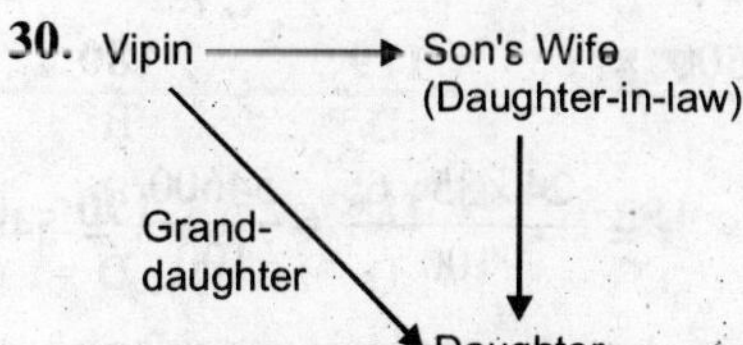

As, Son's wife → Daughter-in-law

Daughter of Son's wife is grand daughter

Hence, women is grand daughter of Vipin.

31. Given,

A M D

1 13 4 Sum = 1 + 13 + 4 = 18

and F O C

6 15 3 → Sum = 6 + 15 + 3 = 24

∴ Difference = 24 – 18 = 6

Similarly,

T R V

20 18 22 → Sum = 20 + 18 + 22 = 60

and X T V

24 20 22 → Sum = 24 + 20 + 22 = 66

∴ Their difference = 66 – 60 = 6

Therefore, alternative is XTV.

32. Given options:

A. 8 A 15 D 5 C 11 B 7 = 35

$= 8 + 15 \div 5 \times 11 - 7$

$= 8 + 3 \times 11 - 7$

$= 8 + 33 - 7 = 41 - 7 = 34 \neq 35$

B. 9 A 16 D 64 C 32 B 3 = 14

$= 9 + 16 \div 64 \times 32 - 3$

$= 9 + \dfrac{16}{64} \times 32 - 3$

$= 9 + 8 - 3 = 17 - 3 = 14.$

C. 26 D 14 C 7 A 9 B 3 = 20

$= 26 \div 14 \times 7 + 9 - 3$

$= \dfrac{26}{14} \times 7 + 9 - 3$

$= 13 + 9 - 3 = 22 - 3 = 19 \neq 20$

D. 6 C 21 D 7 A 9 B 15 = 10

$= 6 \times 21 \div 7 + 9 - 15$

$= 6 \times \dfrac{21}{7} + 9 - 15$

$= 6 \times 3 + 9 - 15$

$= 18 + 9 - 15 = 27 - 15 = 12 \neq 10.$

Hence, correct answer is B.

33. For NO – MN

The given letters NO of N is the left side is related to the letters MN of letter N on the right side are same.

i.e.,

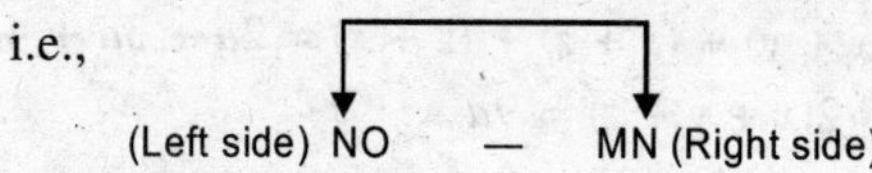

Hence, correct answer is A.

34. We have,

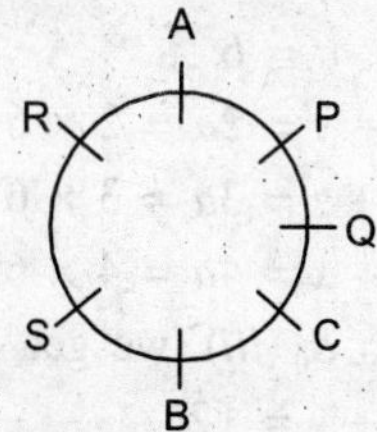

Hence, B is immediate neighbour of S and C.

41. Let income of B = 100

According to question

∴ Income of A = 120

Income of C, $C \times \dfrac{130}{100} = 100$

$\therefore \quad C = \dfrac{100 \times 100}{130} = \dfrac{1000}{13}$

Now, $A - C = 120 - \dfrac{1000}{13}$

$= \dfrac{1560 - 1000}{13} = \dfrac{560}{13}$

∴ Required percentage less than the income of A

$= \dfrac{\frac{560}{13}}{120} \times 100 = \dfrac{560}{13 \times 12} \times 10 = \dfrac{5600}{156} \simeq 36\%$

42. Let length of other two sides of an isosceles triangle be x

Given, largest side AC = 30 cm

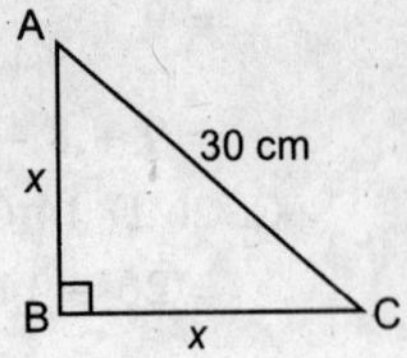

From Pythagorous theorem,

$$AC^2 = AB^2 + BC^2$$

$$\Rightarrow \quad 30^2 = x^2 + x^2$$

$$\Rightarrow \quad 2x^2 = 900$$

$$\Rightarrow \quad x^2 = \frac{900}{2} = 450$$

$$\therefore \quad x = 15\sqrt{2} \text{ cm}$$

Now, area of isosceles rt-angled triangle,

$$A = \frac{1}{2} \times AB \times BC$$

$$= \frac{1}{2} \times 15\sqrt{2} \times 15\sqrt{2}$$

$$= \frac{450}{2} = 225 \text{ cm}^2.$$

43. Given, $(x + y) : (y + z) : (z + x) = 2 : 3 : 4$

and $\quad x + y + z = 27 \quad$ ...(*i*)

Let the value of $(x + y)$, $(y + z)$ and $(z + x)$ be $2a$, $3a$ and $4a$

Then, $(x + y) + (y + z) + (z + x) = 2a + 3a + 4a$

$$\Rightarrow \quad 2(x + y + z) = 9a$$

$$\Rightarrow \quad 2 \times 27 = 9a$$

$$\Rightarrow \quad 9a = 54$$

$$\therefore \quad a = 6$$

$$x + y = 2a = 2 \times 6 = 12 \quad \text{...(ii)}$$

$$y + z = 3a = 3 \times 6 = 18 \quad \text{...(iii)}$$

$$z + x = 4a = 4 \times 6 = 24 \quad \text{...(iv)}$$

From equation (*ii*) & (*iii*), we get

$$\begin{array}{r} x + y = 12 \\ \underset{-}{y} + \underset{-}{z} = \underset{-}{18} \\ \hline x - z = -6 \end{array} \quad \text{...(v)}$$

From equation (*iv*) & (*v*), we get

$$\begin{array}{r} z + x = 24 \\ \underset{-}{x} \underset{+}{-} z = \underset{+}{-6} \\ \hline 2z = 30 \end{array}$$

$$\therefore \quad z = \frac{30}{2} = 15$$

Hence, $z = 15$.

45. Perimeter of wheel = $\pi D = \frac{22}{7} \times 17.5$

$= 55$ cm $= 0.00055$ km

Distance covered by cyclist in 165 minutes or $\frac{165}{60}$ hrs can be given as

$$= 90 \times \frac{165}{60} = 165 \times \frac{3}{2}$$

$\therefore$ Revolution can be given as total distance covered by cycle/perimeter of wheel

$$= \frac{165 \times 3/2}{0.00055} = 450000.$$

46. Given, MP of an article = ₹ 4000

SP of an article = ₹ 2600

$\therefore$ Total discount = MP − SP

= 4000 − 2600 = ₹ 1400

$$\therefore \quad \text{Discount\%} = \frac{\text{Discount} \times 100}{\text{MP}}$$

$$= \frac{1400 \times 100}{4000} = \frac{140}{4} = 35\%.$$

52. Let value be x

According to question,

$$\frac{24}{100} \times \frac{35}{100} \times 6500 = x$$

$$\therefore \quad x = \frac{24 \times 35 \times 65}{100} = \frac{54600}{100} = 546$$

55. Let numbers be x and y, then ratio is $x : y$.

According to question,

$$x + y = 66 \quad \text{...(i)}$$

$$x - y = 22 \quad \text{...(ii)}$$

From eqution (*i*) & (*ii*), we get

$$x = 44 \text{ and } y = 22$$

$$\therefore \text{ Their ratio} = \frac{x}{y} = \frac{44}{22} = 2$$

$$= x : y = 2 : 1.$$

59. Ratio of P : Q : R = $\frac{5}{12} : \frac{4}{18} : \frac{6}{24} = \frac{5}{12} : \frac{2}{9} : \frac{1}{4}$

$$= 15 : 8 : 9$$

$$\therefore \quad \text{Sum} = 15 + 8 + 9 = 32$$

$$\therefore \quad \text{Share of Q} = 32000 \times \frac{8}{32} = ₹\ 8000$$

60. Given, $153 \div 17 \times 8 = \frac{153}{17} \times 8$

$$= 9 \times 8 = 72.$$

Previous Paper (Solved)

DSSSB—TRAINED GRADUATE TEACHER (TGT) COMPUTER SCIENCE EXAM 2017*

SECTION-A

GENERAL AWARENESS

1. Certain events of the eastern coast of South America can affect the Indian Monsoon. What is the event called which can increase the Monsoon intensity in India?

A. Trade oscillation B. Humboldt current
C. El Nino D. La Nina

2. During the war of Independence in 1857, the British beseiged the fortified city of Delhi. In September 1857, they blew up one of the city gates and entered Delhi. Which gate was it?

A. Lahori Gate B. Kashmere Gate
C. Turkman Gate D. Delhi Gate

3. Which fuel is used in a 'Fast Breeder Reactor'?

A. Uranium – 235 B. Plutonium
C. Thorium D. Radium

4. Which sector contributes the most to savings in the Indian economy?

A. Households B. Corporates
C. State Governments D. Central Government

5. Which agency is mainly responsible for formulating fiscal policy in India?

A. NITI Aayog B. RBI
C. Ministry of Finance D. Parliament

6. Which among the following, was a famous inmate of the Cellular Jail in Port Blair, Andamans?

A. Lokmanya Tilak
B. Mahatma Gandhi
C. Damodar Savarkar
D. Subhash Chandra Bose

7. What is the function of MUDRA bank which was recently set up by Government of India?

A. To print currency
B. To allow deposits of untaxed income
C. To provide insurance cover to the poor
D. To provide refinance to Micro enterprises

8. Sharing of which river's waters are a bone of contention between India and Bangladesh?

A. Kosi B. Brahmaputra
C. Teesta D. Baghmati

9. Which Constitutional Writ is issued by the Supreme Court or High Court directing a public authority to perform some specific action?

A. Habeas Corpus B. Mandamus
C. Certiorari D. Quo Warranto

10. Which among the following is a famous Indian sculptor?

A. Jamini Roy B. Satish Gujral
C. Khushwant Singh D. All of the above

11. 'To be or not to be, thats the question', is a very famous line from one of Shakespeare's plays. Which play is it?

A. Hamlet B. McBeth
C. Julius Ceaser D. Antony and Cleopatra

12. In plants, glucose is stored as reserve energy in form of starch. In which form is glucose stored as reserve energy in humans?

A. Glycogen B. Sucrose
C. Starch D. Cellulose

13. Which of the following acids, can dissolve glass?

A. Nitric acid B. Fuming sulfuric acid
C. Hydrochloric acid D. Hydrofluoric acid

14. Mirza Ghalib was a famous poet of 19th century who lived in Delhi. Where is Ghalib's house (Haveli) in Delhi?

A. Gali Samosan B. Ballimaran
C. Churiwalan D. Gali Kasimjan

15. Who among the following is credited with introducing paper currency?

A. Akbar B. Sher Shah Suri
C. Mohd. Bin Tughlaq D. Ala-uddin Khilji

16. Bismillah Khan was a proponent of which?

A. Sarod B. Shehnai
C. Santoor D. Sarangi

* Exam held on 21/05/2017.

17. Which movie won the best picture honour at Oscar 2017?
A. Moonlight B. La La Land
C. Hacksaw Ridge D. Fences

18. Who was recently elected as the President of France?
A. Marine Le Pen B. Jacques Chirac
C. Emmanuel Macron D. Francois Hollande

19. Which is not a Kharif crop?
A. Jowar B. Maize
C. Groundnut D. Wheat

20. Principle of electromagnetic induction is not used in which of the following appliances?
A. Electric fan
B. Generator
C. Electric oven
D. Choke coil of tubelight

GENERAL INTELLIGENCE AND REASONING ABILITY

Directions (Q. Nos. 21 and 22): *Given below is a statement and two conclusions. Analyse whether the conclusions logically follow from the statement and answer as follows.*
A. If only conclusion I follows
B. If only conclusion II follows
C. If both I and II follow
D. If neither I, nor II follows

21. **Statement:** With respect to its nuclear weapons, India follows a No First Use (NFU) Policy meaning thereby that it shall not be the first to use nuclear weapons in a conflict situation.

Conclusions:
I. Both China and Pakistan have a first use policy for nuclear weapons.
II. Indian nuclear weapons are mainly for deterrence.

22. **Statement:** $L = C, P < C, G \geq P$.

Conclusions:
I. $L > G$
II. $L > P$

Directions (Q. Nos. 23 and 24): *Select the answer figure which will continue the pattern given in the question figure.*

23.

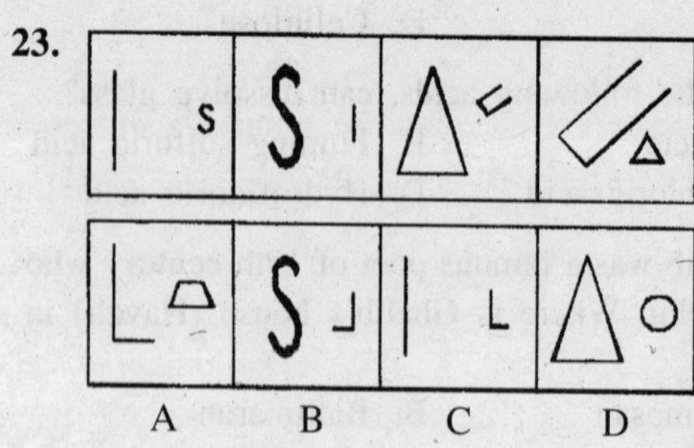

A B C D

24.

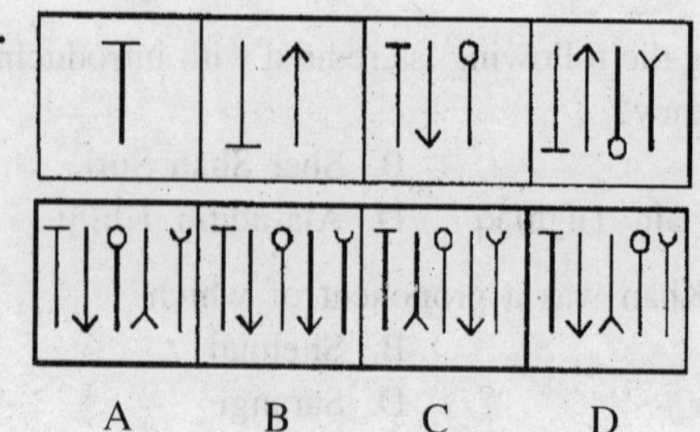

A B C D

Directions (Q. Nos. 25 and 26): *Find the missing term in the series.*

25. 22, 21, 23, 22, 24, 23, ?
A. 26 B. 24
C. 25 D. 23

26. B_2CD, ____ , BCD_4, B_5CD, BC_6D.
A. BCD_3 B. B_2C_2D
C. BC_3D D. BCD_7

27. How many dots will be present on the face which is opposite to the face having three dots, when the figure is folded to form a cube?

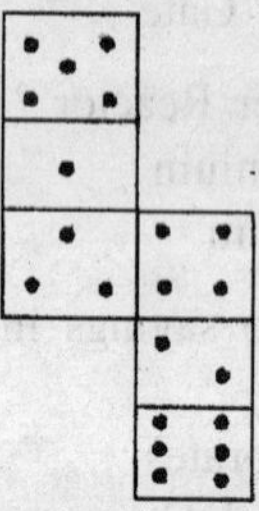

A. 6 B. 4
C. 1 D. 5

28. Which cube will be formed if the sheet shown below is folded?

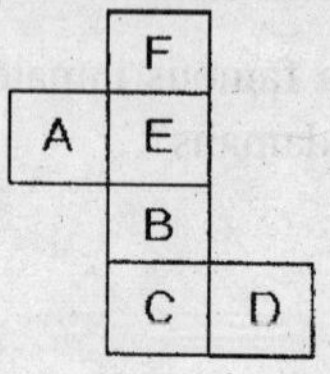

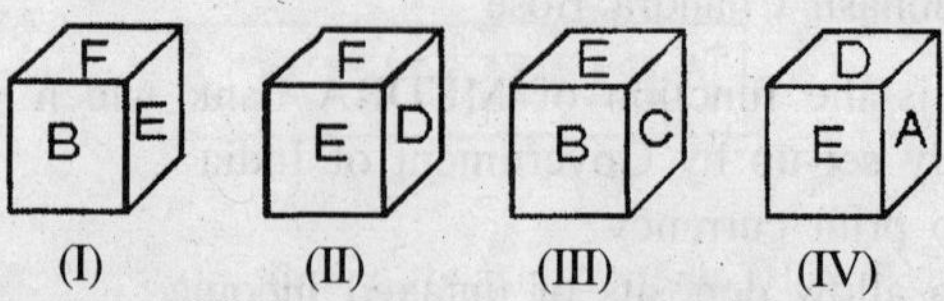

(I) (II) (III) (IV)

A. only I B. only II
C. I and III D. I, II, III and IV

29. Snake is to Cobra as Flower is to:
A. Petal B. Rose
C. Smell D. Plant

30. Pride is to Lion as School is to:

A. Teacher　　B. Student
C. Fish　　D. Books

31. Select a suitable figure to complete the pattern.

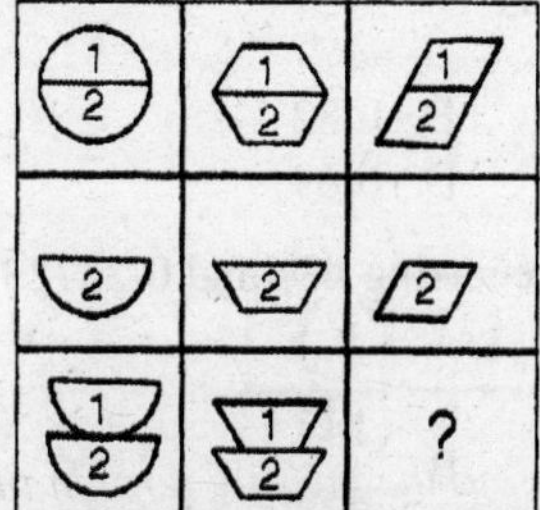

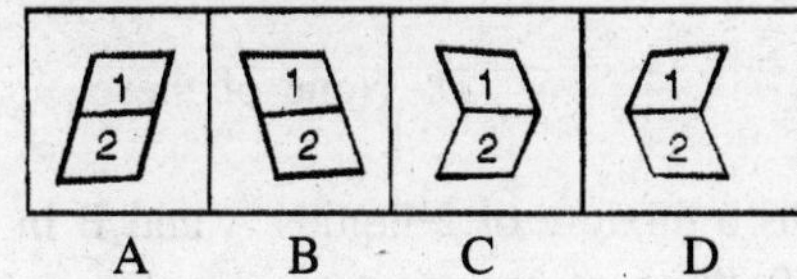

32. In a certain code 'TREAD' is written as '7%#94' and 'PREY' is written as '$%#8'. How is 'ARTERY' written in the code?

A. 9#7%#8　　B. 9#%7#8
C. 9%7#%8　　D. 9%#7%8

33. Find the missing letter.

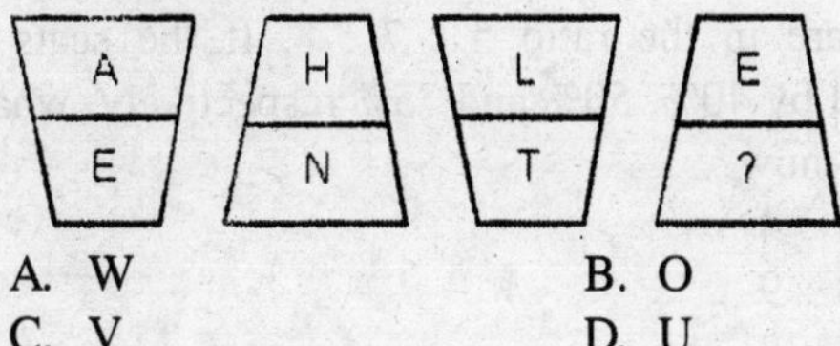

A. W　　B. O
C. V　　D. U

34. Which diagram best describes the relation between Doctors, Artists, Men?

A. 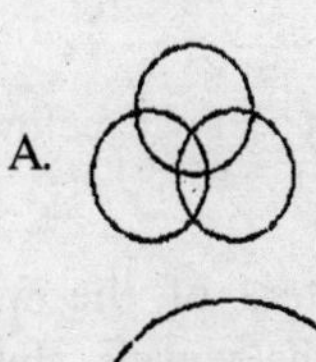

B. 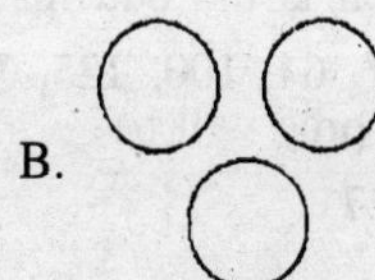

C. 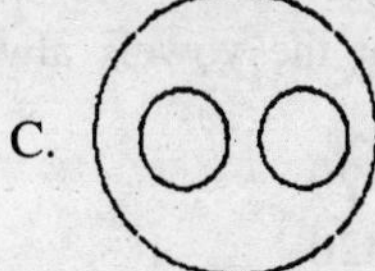

D. 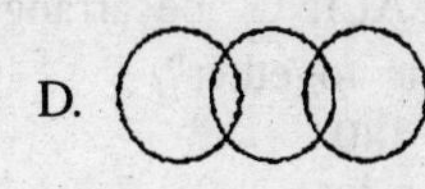

35. If 6% of the population of Rampur is postgraduate and 19% are plain graduates, then which diagram best represents the proportion of graduates as shaded portion

A. 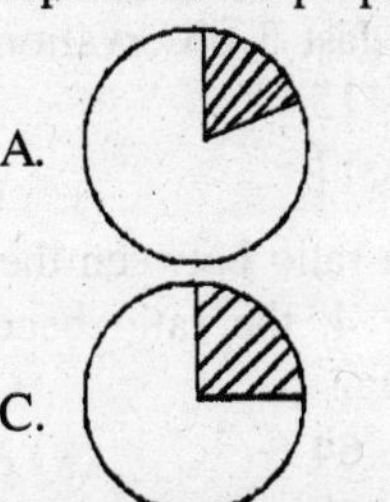

B. 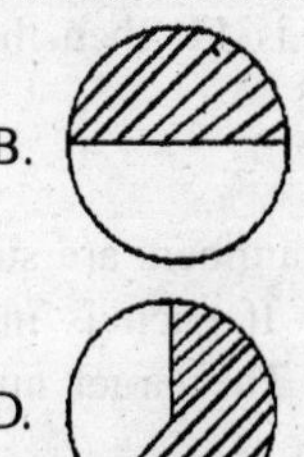

C.

D.

Directions (Q. Nos. 36 to 38): *Read the following information carefully to answer the questions.*

There are six books kept in a shelf and are labelled as L, M, N, O, P and Q. M, P, N and Q have brown covers while others have black covers. L, M and O are new volumes while others are old. L, M and N are computer books while the rest are law books.

36. Which 2 volumes are old law books with brown covers?

A. P and N　　B. P and O
C. P and Q　　D. Q and L

37. Which new law book has a black cover?

A. L　　B. O
C. Q　　D. P

38. Which new computer book has a brown cover?

A. P　　B. N
C. L　　D. M

39. How many pentagons?

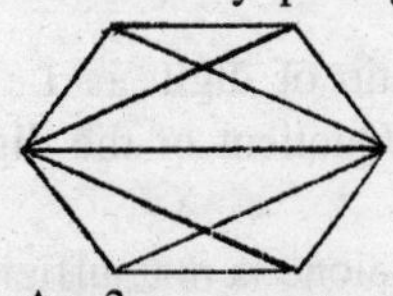

A. 3　　B. 4
C. 5　　D. 6

40. Reaching the place of meeting 20 minutes before 8:50 A.M., Rajesh found himself 30 minutes earlier than the person who came 40 minutes late. When was the scheduled time of meeting?

A. 8:10 A.M.　　B. 8:20 A.M.
C. 8:35 A.M.　　D. 8:45 A.M.

ARITHMETICAL & NUMERICAL ABILITY

41. If $3^{\frac{x}{7}} \times 2^{\frac{y}{5}} = 10$, then values of x and y would be:

A. 5, 7　　B. 4, 4
C. 3, 4　　D. 4, 3

42. If $\left(x+\frac{1}{x}\right) = 3$ then $\left(x^2+\frac{1}{x^2}\right)$ is:

A. 11　　B. $\frac{83}{9}$
C. 7　　D. $\frac{13}{4}$

43. If $\sqrt{5} = 2.236$, then the value of $\frac{1}{\sqrt{5}}$ is:

A. 0.367 B. 0.447
C. 0.745 D. 0.926

44. If the mean of 5 observations x, $x + 2$, $x + 4$, $x + 6$ and $x + 8$ is 11, then the mean of last 3 observations is:
A. 13 B. 15
C. 17 D. 11

45. Two numbers are such that the ratio between them is 4 : 7. If each is increased by 4, the ratio becomes 3 : 5. The larger number is:
A. 36 B. 64
C. 56 D. 48

46. 10% of 20 plus 20% of 10 equals:
A. 10% of 20
B. 20% of 10
C. 1% of 200
D. 2% of 200

47. Depreciation applicable to an equipment is 20%. Value of the equipment 3 years from now will be:
A. 47.6% B. 51.2%
C. 40% D. 60%

48. The speed of a boat in still water is 15 km/hr and the rate of current is 3 km/hr. Distance travelled downstream in 12 minutes is:
A. 1.2 km B. 5.4 km
C. 4.8 km D. 3.6 km

Directions (Q. Nos. 49 and 50): *A question is given followed by two statements I and II. You have to decide if one or both statements are sufficient to answer the question.*

49. What is the number?
I. Sum of the digits is 12. Ratio of digits is 1 : 3.
II. Product of the digits is 27. Quotient of the digits is 3.
A. I alone is sufficient while II alone is not sufficient
B. II alone is sufficient while I alone is not sufficient
C. Either I or II alone is sufficient
D. Neither I nor II are sufficient

50. What is the two-digit number whose first digit is '*p*' and second is '*q*'? The number is greater than 9
I. The number is a multiple of 53.
II. Sum of the digits of the number is 8.
A. I alone is sufficient while II is not sufficient
B. II alone is sufficient while I is not sufficient
C. Both I and II are necessary to answer
D. Neither I nor II are sufficient

51. If an error of 2% is made in measures the side of a square, what will be the percentage error in area?
A. 2% B. 4%
C. 2.2% D. 4.04%

52. A man walks diagonally across a square lawn. What % of distance approximately was saved by not walking along the edges?
A. 25 B. 30
C. 35 D. 40

53. The value of

$$\frac{(0.83)^3-(0.1)^3}{(0.83)^2+0.083+(0.1)^2} \text{ is}$$

A. 0.76 B. 0.82
C. 0.73 D. 0.69

54. The rational number for recurring decimal 0.237237 ... is:
A. $\frac{234}{997}$ B. $\frac{147}{459}$
C. $\frac{237}{999}$ D. None of these

55. A can contains a mixture of 2 liquids A and B in the ratio 7 : 5. 9 litres of the mixture are drawn and replaced by B. Now the ratio is 7 : 9. What was the volume of liquid A contained by the mixture originally?
A. 10 B. 20
C. 21 D. 25

56. Sets for English, Maths and Computer Science in a college are in the ratio 5 : 7 : 8. If the seats are increased by 40%, 50% and 75% respectively, what is the ratio now?
A. 2 : 3 : 4
B. 6 : 8 : 9
C. 6 : 7 : 8
D. None of these

57. Which is the odd man out?
8, 27, 64, 100, 125, 343
A. 100 B. 125
C. 27 D. 64

58. In how many ways can the letters of the word 'HEALING' be arranged so that the vowels always come together?
A. 480 B. 720
C. 960 D. 320

59. If $\left(\frac{a}{b}\right)^{x-1}=\left(\frac{b}{a}\right)^{x-3}$ then x = ?
A. $\frac{7}{2}$ B. $\frac{5}{2}$
C. 2 D. –1

60. The greatest number of 4 digits which is divisible by 15, 25, 40 and 75 is:
A. 9200 B. 9800
C. 9000 D. 9600

भाषा परीक्षण : हिन्दी

निर्देश (प्र.सं. 61-65): *रिक्त स्थान भरें।*

61. मौसम विभाग ने तूफान आने की .... दी है।
A. भविष्यवाणी B. चेतावनी
C. घोषणा D. कोई भी नहीं

62. प्रेमचंद की कहानियों में हमें ग्रामीण जीवन की .... देखने को मिलती है।
A. मेला B. परछाई
C. झांकी D. सतरंगी

63. सीमा पर सैनिकों का जीवन बहुत .... होता है।
A. मधुर B. शौर्य
C. स्वस्थ D. कठोर

64. समझदार को .... ही काफी होता है।
A. धमकी B. ईशारा
C. कहना D. आदेश

65. बेटे की सफलता का समाचार सुनकर पिता का हृदय .... हो उठा।
A. कमजोर B. हर्ष
C. प्रफुल्लित D. खुशी

निर्देश (प्र.सं. 66-68): *पर्यायवाची शब्द चुनें।*

66. पादप
A. खाद B. पौधा
C. पशु D. कोई भी नहीं

67. गिरी
A. वृक्ष B. शिव
C. पर्वत D. समुद्र

68. शिखा
A. कंकड B. चट्टान
C. पहाड़ी D. पहाड़

निर्देश (प्र.सं. 69-71): *विलोम शब्द चुनें।*

69. गोपनीय
A. पारदर्शी B. राज
C. शासकीय D. कोई भी नहीं

70. शिथिल
A. मृत B. बलवान
C. चंचल D. जीव

71. एकरस
A. समरस B. विविध
C. कला D. कोई भी नहीं

निर्देश (प्र.सं. 72-75): *इन प्रश्नों में एक वाक्य को तीन भागों में विभक्त किया गया है। जिसमें से एक भाग में त्रुटि हो सकती है। यदि है तो उस भाग का चयन करें, अन्यथा (D) का चयन करें।*

72. A. घोड़ा गाड़ी B. सड़क ऊपर
C. दौड़ रही थी D. कोई त्रुटि नहीं

73. A. किसी भी काम में B. समय का पाबंदी
C. अनिवार्य है D. कोई त्रुटि नहीं

74. A. उस स्थान में B. एक बहुत बड़ी
C. झील है D. कोई त्रुटि नहीं

75. A. समय पर सोना और जागना B. स्वास्थ्य के लिए
C. बहुत जरूर है D. कोई त्रुटि नहीं

76. "लाल पीला होना" का अर्थ है
A. शर्म महसूस करना B. बहुत क्रोधित होना
C. आलस करना D. कोई भी नहीं

77. "चार दिन की चांदनी" का मतलब
A. कम पुरानी दोस्ती B. उज्जवल रात
C. क्षणिक सुख D. खतरा टल जाना

78. बाघ का स्त्रीलिंग
A. बाघनी B. बाघिन
C. बाघी D. कोई भी नहीं

79. जिसमें बड़े जंगली जानवर रहते हैं
A. मैदान B. घोसला
C. कंदरा D. दलदल

80. पूजा का विशेषण
A. पूजा B. पूजन
C. पूज्य D. कोई भी नहीं

LANGUAGE : ENGLISH

Directions (Q. Nos. 81 and 82): *Replace the sentence/group of word with a word of similar meaning.*

81. One who reacts at the slightest stimulus
A. Angry B. Emotional
C. Excitable D. Placid

82. The colour green
A. Azure B. Verdant
C. Auburn D. Sanguine

Directions (Q. Nos. 83 to 85): *Select the word which has the most similar in meaning to the given word.*

83. AUDACIOUS
A. Cowardly B. Excited
C. Brave D. Soldier

84. OBDURATE
A. Bold B. Stabborn
C. Fighter D. Obnoxious

85. REMORSE
A. Remark B. Scold
C. Condemn D. Regret

Directions (Q. Nos. 86 to 88): *Select the word which is most opposite in meaning to the given word.*

86. ABUNDANT
A. Rich B. Pennyless
C. Scarce D. Infertile

87. DISMAL
A. Appoint B. Dark
C. Dismiss D. Cheerful

88. ONEROUS
A. Trivial B. Punishing
C. Painful D. Major

Directions (Q. Nos. 89 and 90): *Select the option which gives the nearest meaning of the idiom/phrase.*

89. To let the chips fall where they may
A. To start a war
B. To let something happen regardless of consequences
C. To teach someone a lesson
D. None of the above

90. By the skin of your teeth
A. just avoid failing
B. to catch a criminal
C. bring to justice
D. none of the above

Directions (Q. Nos. 91 to 93): *Fill in the blanks with appropriate choices.*

91. The servant .... the master by .... thieves to the house while the family was away.
A. helped, helping B. condemned, allowing
C. robbed, assisting D. betrayed, admitting

92. The movie .... for more than six months.
A. played B. ran
C. attended D. was on

93. The exam is going to start in an hour. You need to .... if you want to reach on time.
A. show the door B. stand on your toes
C. shake a leg D. cast a long shadow

Directions (Q. Nos. 94 to 96): *A sentence is divided into three parts out of which one part may have error(s). If so, select that part. If there is no error, select (D).*

94. A. The headquarters of B. the Indian army are
C. locating in New Delhi D. No error

95. A. The ship went round B. the lighthouse and
C. into the lagoon D. No error

96. A. Who are you going B. to invite for
C. inaugurating the show D. No error

97. Select the incorrect spelling
A. EXHBITION B. MENDICANT
C. BRISTLE D. BEAUTIFY

98. Select the correct spelling
A. PULVARISE B. DIEGNOSTIC
C. SYSTEMETIC D. PRONUNCIATION

99. Adjective of Glory is
A. Glorify B. Glory
C. Glorification D. Glorious

100. Verb form of simple is
A. Simple B. Simplification
C. Simplify D. Simpleton

SECTION-B

POST SPECIFIC SUBJECT

COMPUTER AWARENESS

101. In a relational database a referential integrity constraint can be specified with the help of
A. Primary key B. Foreign key
C. Secondary key D. None of the above

102. Which layer of TCP/IP is responsible for getting data to its destination?
A. Link layer B. Application layer
C. Network layer D. Transport layer

103. The .... standard promises to provide enough characters to cover all the world's language.
A. ASCII B. EBDIC
C. Unicode D. EASCII

104. Which of the following is a private IP Address?
A. 12.0.0.1
B. 172.168.2.3
C. 168.202.32.4
D. 192.168.12.12

105. Which of the following is responsible for converting higher level protocol addresses (IP Addresses) to Physical network addresses?
A. IP
B. ICMP
C. ARP
D. BOOTP

106. Socket and Winsock are examples of this type of software
A. API
B. VCRs
C. DSL
D. IPX

107. In Java, which exception is thrown when divide by zero executes
A. Array Index Out of Bound
B. Arithmetic Exception
C. Illegal State Exception
D. Null Pointer Exception

108. Which of the following protocols can automate IP configuration (IP Address, Subnet mask, DNS, default gateway)?
A. SMTP
B. DHCP
C. SNMP
D. ARP

109. In IPv4, every IP address is formed using
A. 64 bits
B. 32 bits
C. 128 bits
D. 12 bits

110. 127.0.0.1 is an example of
A. Class A address
B. Class C address
C. Local loop back address
D. Global IP address

111. In an SQL Query involving NOT, OR and AND without parenthesis, what is the order of evaluation?
A. NOT followed by AND followed by OR
B. NOT followed by OR followed by AND
C. AND followed by OR followed by NOT
D. OR followed by AND followed by NOT

112. Where is the default session data stored in ASP.NET?
A. Session object
B. State server
C. SQL server
D. In process

113. Which of the following is not a valid formula in MS Excel?
A. = AVG(A1 : A6)
B. = AVERAGE(A1 : A6)
C. = MEDIAN(A1 : A6)
D. = MEDIAN(2, 4, 4, 5)

114. In ASP.NET, which namespace provides forms authentication?
A. System.Web.Ui.Forms.Security
B. System.Web.Configuration
C. System.Web.Security
D. System.Web.Services

115. Octal equivalent of $(111101000)_2$ is
A. 456
B. 556
C. 750
D. 550

116. Default subnet mask for a class
A. 255.255.255.0
B. 255.0.0.0
C. 255.255.0.0
D. All of the above

117. RAID configuration of disks are used to provide
A. Fault tolerance
B. High speed
C. High data density
D. None of these

118. .... contains the swap space.
A. RAM
B. Disk
C. ROM
D. On-chip cache

119. .... is a protocol used in sending and receiving email.
A. BGP
B. HTTP
C. RTP
D. SMTP

120. The length of IPv6 is
A. 64 bits
B. 32 bits
C. 128 bits
D. 12 bits

121. Which of the following is not an advantage of multiprocessing system?
A. increased throughput
B. shorter response time
C. decreased operating system overhead
D. ability to assign priorities to jobs

122. Multiprogramming was made possible by
A. I/O units that operate independently of the CPU
B. Operating system
C. Both A and B
D. Neither A nor B

123. A DMA controller is connected to the
A. Processor bus
B. System bus
C. SPI bus
D. None of the above

124. Which of the following statements declares a one-dimensional array named item that consists of five elements?
A. charitem[0 to 4) =" ";
B. charitem={1, 2, 3, 4}
C. charitem=' ';
D. charitem[5] =" ";

125. A logical schema in a database
A. is the entire database
B. is the standard way of organizing information into accessible parts
C. describes how data actually stored on disk
D. all of the above

126. In SQL, which of the following is not a data manipulation language command?

A. DELETE B. SELFCT
C. UPDATE D. CREATE

127. In SQL, which command is used to make permanent changes made by statements issue since the beginning of a transaction?
A. COMMIT B. PACK
C. SAVE D. DONE

128. In Linux, which option of rm command is used to remove a directory with all its subdirectories?
A. –b B. –o
C. –p D. –r

129. Which command will create a new, empty file in Linux?
A. touch B. make
C. mv D. cpy

130. To access the services of operating system, interface is provided by
A. RPC B. System call
C. DLL D. API

131. Frames from one LAN can be transmitted to another LAN via
A. Repeater B. Bridge
C. Modem D. Router

132. An attribute of table cannot hold multiple values is the property of
A. First Normal Form (1NF)
B. Second Normal Form (2NF)
C. Third Normal Form (3NF)
D. None of these

133. Register storage class can be specified to global variables
A. true B. false
C. depends on compiler D. depends on program

134. Which among the following is NOT a logical or relational operator in C?
A. ! = B. ||
C. = D. = =

135. The disadvantage of using parallel mode of communication is
A. It is costly B. It is slower
C. No security D. All of these

136. Which option of the kill command sends the given signal name to the specified process?
A. –l B. –n
C. –s D. –a

137. In a linux/unix system, process information in the current shell can be obtained by using
A. bg B. processor – status
C. ps D. fg

138. The command syntax to display the file 'sample.txt' one page at a time is
A. man sample.txt>more
B. cat sample.txt<more
C. cat sample.txt|more
D. none of the above

139. The permission –rwxr.–r– represented in octal expression will be
A. 777 B. 666
C. 744 D. 711

140. At the end of kernel bootstrap, which process is started?
A. /etc/init B. /etc/sched
C. /etc/swap D. /etc/kernel

141. Which of the following is not a type of constructor in C++ ?
A. Copy constructor
B. Friend constructor
C. Default constructor
D. Parameterized constructor

142. Which of the following is not the member of class?
A. Static function B. Friend function
C. Const. function D. Virtual function

143. In ASP.NET, what is Global. asax used for
A. To implement application and session level events
B. To store configuration information
C. To store styling information
D. None of the above

144. Which of the following tag is used to mark a beginning of paragraph?
A. <par> B.
C. <P> D. <tr>

145. Correct HTML tag for the largest heading is
A. <head> B. <h6>
C. <heading> D. <h1>

146. What does the following statement declare?
int(*f)(int*);
A. Integer pointer f
B. A function pointer f which takes integer argument
C. A pointer to a function that takes integer pointer as an argument
D. A function that takes integer pointer as an argument

147. What is the output of the following code snippet?
```
int a = 3; int b = 5;
int*p = &b;
int**q = &p;
*q = &a;
printf("%d",*p);
```
A. Segmentation fault B. 0XF3000H
C. 5 D. 3

148. In ASP.NET, difference between Response. Write() and Response. Output. Write() is

A. Response.Output.Write() allows Cached output
B. Response.Output.Write() allows Formatted output
C. Response.Output.Write() allows Buffered output
D. Response.Output.Write() allows Streamed output

149. In Linux, which command is used to record a user login session in a file (by recording terminal session)?
A. screen B. script
C. sed D. r view

150. Under virtual storage
A. a signal program is processed by two or more CPUs
B. two or more programs are used concurrently in primary storage
C. only the active pages of a program are stored in primary storage
D. interprogram interference may occur

151. A situation where two or more concurrent processes access shared data and they try to change it concurrently is
A. critical section B. intolerance
C. race condition D. synchronization

152. A situation where a group of processes are permanently blocked waiting for a particular event that will not occur
A. race condition B. intolerance
C. critical section D. None of these

153. Removing of suspended process from memory to disk and their subsequent return is called
A. Swapping B. Segmentation
C. I/O operation D. Replacement

154. .... is a scheme where only a portion of the job's address space is actually loaded into physical memory.
A. Swapping B. Virtual memory
C. Kernel Swap D. SPOOL

155. A relation may have nor than one key. In this case, each of these keys is called a
A. Primary key B. Secondary key
C. Foreign key D. Candidate key

156. The information stored in the catalog of a database is called
A. Distributed data B. Raw data
C. Encapsulated data D. Meta data

157. Which SQL operator tests if any of the sub-query value meets the condition?
A. LIKE operator B. SOME operator
C. OR operator D. IN operator

158. To add two cells (A1 and A2) together you use the following formula
A. A1plusA2 B. =A1+A2
C. =Add(A1+A2) D. =together(A1:A2)

159. How many primitive data types are there in Java?
A. 6 B. 7
C. 8 D. 9

160. Routing algorithm used in MANETs is
A. Routing information protocol
B. Distance vector protocol
C. Shortest path first
D. Ad-hoc on-demand distance vector protocol

161. In RDBMS, B+trees are preferred to binary trees since
A. Disk capacities are higher than memory capacities
B. Memory access is faster than disk access
C. Disks are more reliable than memory
D. None of the above

162. What does the VLOOKUP function do?
A. Looks up text that contain 'V'
B. Checks whether text is the same in one cell as in the next
C. Finds related records
D. All of the above

163. Which of the following is an absolute cell reference?
A. !B!1 B. B1
C. #b#1 D. B1

164. Which of the following formulas will Excel not be able to calculate?
A. = SUM(Sales) – A3
B. = SUM(A1 : A5)*.5
C. = SUM(A1 : A5)/(10 – 10)
D. = SUM(A1 : A5) – 10

165. Addition of 1101_2 and 1000_2 is
A. 10110_2 B. 1000_2
C. 10101_2 D. None of these

166. Which of the following is an example of nonvolatile memory?
A. ROM B. VLSI
C. LSI D. RAM

167. What is the minimum number of stacks of size n required to implement a queue of size n?
A. One B. Two
C. Three D. Four

168. A sorting algorithm is called stable if
A. It takes O(n log n) time
B. It maintains relative order of occurrence of non-distinct elements
C. It uses divide and conquer paradigm
D. It takes linear time

169. .... is a line drawing algorithm based only on integer calculation.
A. Digital Differential Analyzer (DDA) line drawing algorithm
B. Bresenham's line drawing algorithm

C. Caman's line drawing algorithm
D. All of the above

170. Hexa-decimal equivalent of $(101010011011)_2$ is
A. A9B B. B9A
C. 129B D. A29

171. .... contains the information about a file that is needed by the system programs that access the file records.
A. A file header B. A file descriptor
C. Bootstrap D. Both A and B

172. In C language, conditional operator is also called as
A. logical operator B. unary operator
C. ternary operator D. binary operator

173. In C language. % Id is used as the format of .... data type.
A. int B. long int
C. double int D. long distant

174. Stacks data structures are also called as .... list.
A. FIFO B. LIFO
C. DEQUEUE D. None of these

175. In SQL, to DROP a constraint from a table we use the
A. ALTER statement with a DROP clause
B. DROP statement with CHANGE clause
C. MODIFY statement with CHANGE clause
D. CHANGE statement with MODIFY clause

176. Trigger code is written in
A. SQL B. PL/SQL
C. JAVA D. Machine language

177. By default the return type of any user defined function in 'C' is
A. void B. float
C. integer D. None of these

178. Object Oriented Programming uses .... approach.
A. Top-down B. Bottom-up
C. Hybrid approach D. Mixed approach

179. The insulation of data from direct access by the program is called as
A. Encapsulation B. Data hiding
C. Inheritance D. Polymorphism

180. The property or the ability to take more than one form is called as
A. Encapsulation B. Polymorphism
C. Inheritance D. Data transform

181. Choose the statement that are syntactically incorrect in C language.
A. for(; ;);
B. /*this is/*a valid */comment */
C. return 5;
D. return(6+3);

182. Increasing the RAM of a computer typically improves performance because
A. Virtual memory increase
B. Larger RAMs are faster
C. Fewer page faults occur
D. Fewer segmentation fault occurs

183. In computer communication network the term baud rate means
A. The number of bits transmitted per unit time
B. The number of bytes lost per unit time
C. The rate at which signal change
D. None of the above

184. Error detection at the data link level is achieved by
A. Bit stuffing
B. Cyclic redundancy code
C. Hamming code
D. Equalization

185. Which of the following decides if a function declared in line indeed is going to treated inline in the executable code?
A. Compiler B. Operating system
C. Linker D. Loader

186. Consider the statement.
int val[2] [4] = {1, 2, 3, 4, 5, 6, 7, 8};
4 will be the value of
A. val[1] [4] B. val[1] [1]
C. val[0] [4] D. None of these

187. PID of the Kernel process is
A. Undefined B. 0
C. 1 D. 3

188. Which of the sorting algorithm has the worst case time complexity of n log n?
A. Heap sort B. Quick sort
C. Insertion sort D. Selection sort

189. Sparse matrices have
A. Many zero entries than non-zero entries
B. Many non-zero entries than zero-entries
C. Higher dimension
D. None of the above

190. The maximum degree of any vertex in a simple graph with n vertices is
A. n B. n − 1
C. n + 1 D. 2n − 1

191. Random scan monitors are also referred as
A. Stroke writing display
B. Calligraphic display
C. Vector display
D. All of these

192. The refresh rate below which picture flickers is
A. 25 B. 35
C. 40 D. 45

193. The time a magnetic disk takes to position a head on the selected track is
A. Latency
B. Access time
C. Seek time
D. Turn around time

194. Which one of the following is not used to generate dynamic web pages?
A. PHP
B. ASP.NET
C. JSP
D. None of these

195. The group of digits stored at each address in memory is generally referred as
A. memory bit
B. memory byte
C. memory word
D. memory block

196. Defects are less costly if detected in which of the following phases?
A. Requirements gathering
B. Coding
C. Design
D. Implementation

197. In .... testing only the functionality of the software module is tested.
A. White box testing
B. Black box testing
C. Gray box testing
D. None of the above

198. Pareto principle advocates
A. 20 – 80 rule
B. 80 – 20 rule
C. 40 – 60 rule
D. 60 – 40 rule

199. Page fault occurs when
A. The page is corrupted by the application software
B. The page is in main memory
C. The page is not available in main memory
D. One tries to divide by zero

200. Semaphores are used to solve the problem of
A. race condition
B. process synchronization
C. cache replacement
D. None of the above

ANSWERS

1	2	3	4	5	6	7	8	9	10
D	B	C	A	C	C	D	C	B	B
11	**12**	**13**	**14**	**15**	**16**	**17**	**18**	**19**	**20**
A	A	D	C	C	B	A	C	D	C
21	**22**	**23**	**24**	**25**	**26**	**27**	**28**	**29**	**30**
B	B	A	A	C	C	D	B	B	C
31	**32**	**33**	**34**	**35**	**36**	**37**	**38**	**39**	**40**
C	C	B	A	C	C	B	D	D	B
41	**42**	**43**	**44**	**45**	**46**	**47**	**48**	**49**	**50**
B	C	B	A	C	D	B	D	C	A
51	**52**	**53**	**54**	**55**	**56**	**57**	**58**	**59**	**60**
D	B	C	C	C	A	A	B	C	D
61	**62**	**63**	**64**	**65**	**66**	**67**	**68**	**69**	**70**
B	C	D	B	C	B	C	B	A	C
71	**72**	**73**	**74**	**75**	**76**	**77**	**78**	**79**	**80**
B	D	B	A	C	B	C	B	C	C
81	**82**	**83**	**84**	**85**	**86**	**87**	**88**	**89**	**90**
C	A	C	B	D	C	D	A	B	A
91	**92**	**93**	**94**	**95**	**96**	**97**	**98**	**99**	**100**
D	B	C	C	A	A	A	D	D	C
101	**102**	**103**	**104**	**105**	**106**	**107**	**108**	**109**	**110**
B	C	C	D	C	A	B	B	B	C
111	**112**	**113**	**114**	**115**	**116**	**117**	**118**	**119**	**120**
A	D	A	C	C	A	A	B	D	C
121	**122**	**123**	**124**	**125**	**126**	**127**	**128**	**129**	**130**
C	C	B	D	B	D	A	D	A	B
131	**132**	**133**	**134**	**135**	**136**	**137**	**138**	**139**	**140**
B	A	B	C	A	C	C	C	C	A

141	142	143	144	145	146	147	148	149	150
B	C	A	C	D	C	D	B	B	C
151	**152**	**153**	**154**	**155**	**156**	**157**	**158**	**159**	**160**
C	D	A	B	D	D	B	B	C	D
161	**162**	**163**	**164**	**165**	**166**	**167**	**168**	**169**	**170**
B	C	B	A	C	A	B	B	B	A
171	**172**	**173**	**174**	**175**	**176**	**177**	**178**	**179**	**180**
D	C	B	B	A	D	C	B	B	B
181	**182**	**183**	**184**	**185**	**186**	**187**	**188**	**189**	**190**
B	C	A	B	A	D	B	A	A	B
191	**192**	**193**	**194**	**195**	**196**	**197**	**198**	**199**	**200**
D	A	C	D	C	A	B	B	C	B

EXPLANATORY ANSWERS

22. ∵ $L = C$

and $C > P$

∴ $L > P$

Again $L = C$

$C > P$

$P \leq G$

or $G \geq P$

Therefore, it is not clear that $L > P$.

25.

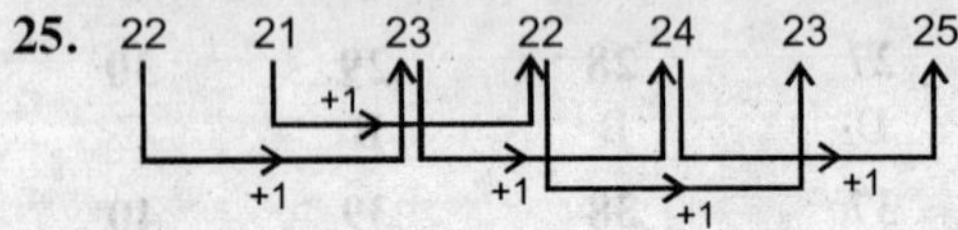

26. $B_2CD \rightarrow BC_3D \rightarrow BCD_4 \rightarrow B_5CD \rightarrow BC_6D$

29. Since, Cobra comes under snake category.

Similarly, Rose comes under flower category.

32. Here,

T	R	E	A	D
↓	↓	↓	↓	↓
7	%	#	9	4

and

P	R	E	Y
↓	↓	↓	↓
$	%	#	8

Similarly,

A	R	T	E	R	Y
↓	↓	↓	↓	↓	↓
9	%	7	#	%	8

33. Here,

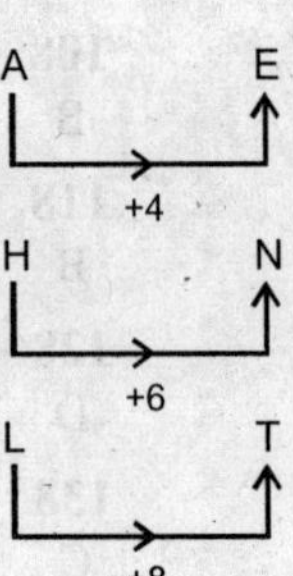

Therefore,

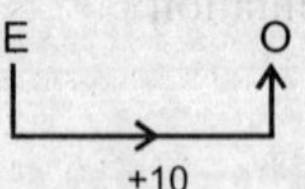

36-38.

M, P, N & Q = Brown cover

and L & O = Black cover

Again L, M & O = New volumes

N, P & Q = Old volumes

and L, M & N = Computer Book

O, P & Q = Law Book

40. Rajesh reached the place 20 minutes before 8.50 AM *i.e.*, at 8.30 AM.

Clearly, the man who was 40 minutes late would reach the place at 9.00 AM.

So, the scheduled time of the meeting was 40 minutes before 9.00 AM, *i.e.*, 8.20 AM.

41. ∵ $3\frac{x}{7} \times 2\frac{y}{5} = 10$

Put $x = 4$, $y = 4$

$$3\frac{4}{7} \times 2\frac{4}{5} = \frac{25}{7} \times \frac{14}{5}$$

$$= 5 \times 2 = 10$$

Hence, the value of x and $y = (4, 4)$

42. ∵ $x + \frac{1}{x} = 3$

Squaring both sides

$$\left(x + \frac{1}{x}\right)^2 = (3)^2$$

$\Rightarrow \quad x^2 + \frac{1}{x^2} + 2(x)\left(\frac{1}{x}\right) = 9$

$\Rightarrow \quad x^2 + \frac{1}{x^2} = 9 - 2 = 7.$

43. $\because \quad \sqrt{5} = 2.236$

$\therefore \quad \frac{1}{\sqrt{5}} = \frac{1}{\sqrt{5}} \times \frac{\sqrt{5}}{\sqrt{5}} = \frac{\sqrt{5}}{5}$

$= \frac{2.236}{5}$

$= 0.447$

Hence, the value of $\frac{1}{\sqrt{5}} = 0.447$.

44. $\frac{x+x+2+x+4+x+6+x+8}{5} = 11$

$\Rightarrow \quad 5x + 20 = 55$

$\Rightarrow \quad 5x = 35$

$\Rightarrow \quad x = 7$

Sum of last three observations

$= x + 4 + x + 6 + x + 8$

$= 3x + 18$

$= 3 \times 7 + 18$

$= 21 + 18 = 39$

$\therefore$ Mean of last three observations

$= \frac{39}{3} = 13.$

45. Let numbers are $4x$ and $7x$

According to the question,

$\frac{4x+4}{7x+4} = \frac{3}{5}$

$\Rightarrow \quad 21x + 12 = 20x + 20$

$\Rightarrow \quad x = 8$

Numbers are 32 and 56

Hence, the larger number = 56.

46. $\frac{10}{100} \times 20 + \frac{20}{100} \times 10 = 2 + 2 = 4$

A. $\frac{10}{100} \times 20 = 2$

B. $\frac{20}{100} \times 10 = 2$

C. $\frac{1}{100} \times 200 = 2$

D. $\frac{2}{100} \times 200 = 2 \times 2 = 4$

Option (D) is correct.

Hence, 10% of 20 + 20% of 10 = 2% of 200.

47. $\frac{20}{100} \times 100 = 20$

$100 - 20 = 80$

$\frac{20}{100} \times 80 = 16$

$80 - 16 = 64$

$\frac{20}{100} \times 64 = \frac{64}{5} = 12.8$

$64 - 12.8 = 51.2$

Hence, value of the equipment 3 years from now will be 51.2%.

48. Speed of boat in down stream

$= 15 + 3 = 18$ km/hr

time = 12 minutes

$= \frac{12}{60} = \frac{1}{5}$ hrs.

Distance travelled by the boat in down stream

= Speed × time

$= 18 \times \frac{1}{5}$ km = 3.6 km.

49. I. $x + y = 12$ ...(*i*)

and $\frac{x}{y} = \frac{1}{3}$

$\Rightarrow \quad 3x = y$

From (*i*) $x + 3x = 12$

$\Rightarrow \quad 4x = 12 \Rightarrow x = 3$

and $y = 9$

$\therefore$ Number = 39

II. $x \times y = 27 = 3 \times 9$

$\because$ Quotient $= 3 = \frac{9}{3}$

$\therefore$ Digits are 3 and 9

Number = 39

Hence, option (C) is correct.

51.

x

x x

x

Let side of square = x

Area of square = x^2

New length of square = $x + \frac{2x}{100} = \frac{102x}{100}$

Area of new square = $\left(\frac{102x}{100}\right)^2$

$= \frac{10404x^2}{10000}$

$= 1.0404x^2$

Area increased = $1.0404x^2 - x^2$

$= x^2(1.0404 - 1)$

$= 0.0404x^2$

Percentage area increased = $\frac{0.0404x^2}{x^2} \times 100$

$= \frac{404}{10000} \times 100$

$= \frac{404}{100}\% = 4.04\%$

Hence, the percentage error in area = 4.04%.

52. 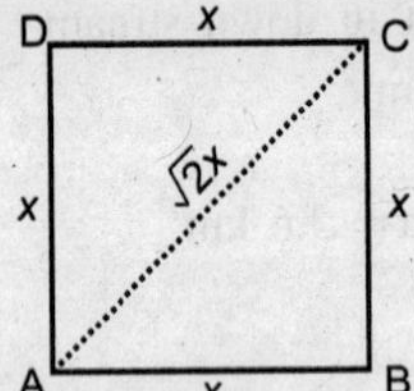

ABCD is a square whose each side = x

Man walks diagonally

$\therefore$ AC = $\sqrt{2}x$

If he can go along the side

AC = $x + x = 2x$

Distance saved = $2x - \sqrt{2}x$

$= x(2 - \sqrt{2})$

$= x(2 - 1.414)$

$= 0.586x$

% distance saved = $\frac{0.586x}{2x} \times 100$

$= 50 \times \frac{586}{1000}$

$= \frac{29300}{1000} = \frac{293}{10}$

$= 29.3\% \cong 30\%$.

53. $\frac{(0.83)^3 - (0.1)^3}{(0.83)^2 + 0.083 + (0.1)^2}$

Let 0.83 = a

and 0.1 = b

$\therefore$ Given expression can be written as

$\frac{a^3 - b^3}{a^2 + ab + b^2} = \frac{(a-b)(a^2 + ab + b^2)}{(a^2 + ab + b^2)}$

$= a - b = 0.83 - 0.1$

$= 0.73.$

54. 0.237237 ....

$= 0.\overline{237} = \frac{237}{999}$.

55. % of liquid B initially present

$= \frac{5}{12} \times 100 = \frac{125}{3}\%$

% of liquid B finally present

$= \frac{9}{16} \times 100 = \frac{225}{4}\%$

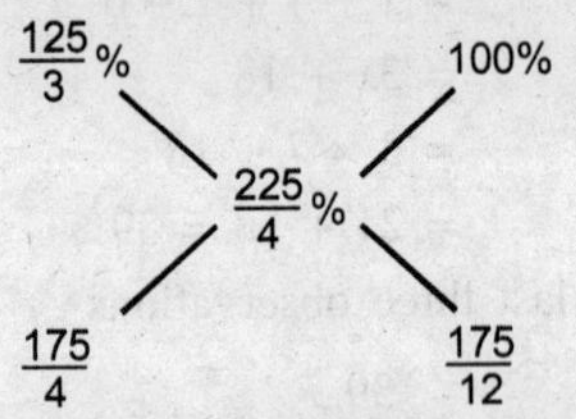

Ratio $\frac{\frac{175}{4}}{\frac{175}{12}} = \frac{175}{4} \times \frac{12}{175} = 3 : 1$

$\therefore$ Total quantity of liquid initially present

= 27 + 9 = 36 litres

Quantity of liquid A = $\frac{7}{12} \times 36$

= 21 litres.

56. Let no. of seats are $5x$, $7x$ and $8x$

$5x$ of $\frac{140}{100} = 7x$

$7x$ of $\frac{150}{100} = \frac{21x}{2}$

$8x$ of $\frac{175}{100} = 14x$

Required ratio $= 7x : \frac{21x}{2} : 14x$

$= 14 : 21 : 28$
$= 2 : 3 : 4.$

57.

8	27	64	100	125	343
↓	↓	↓	↓	↓	↓
2^3	3^3	4^3	10^2	5^3	7^3

Hence, 100 is the odd man out.

58. There are 3 vowels in the word HEALING namely E, A and I. Since these 3 vowels have to occur together, we treat them as one letter. This reduces the no. of letters to be arranged to 5 and accordingly the no. of places to be filled also gets reduces to 5.

No. of permutations $= 5! = 5 \times 4 \times 3 \times 2 \times 1$
$= 120$

Now, the 3 vowels can be arranged among them selves in $3! = 3 \times 2 \times 1 = 6$

∴ Total no. of words in which vowels occur together
$= 120 \times 6 = 720.$

59. $\because \left(\frac{a}{b}\right)^{x-1} = \left(\frac{b}{a}\right)^{x-3}$

$\Rightarrow \left(\frac{a}{b}\right)^{x-1} = \left(\frac{a}{b}\right)^{-x+3}$

$\Rightarrow x - 1 = -x + 3$

$\Rightarrow 2x = 4$

$\Rightarrow x = 2$

60. The greatest no. of 4 digits = 9999

L.C.M. of 15, 25, 40 and 75 = 600

```
600)9999(16
    600
    ----
    3999
    3600
    ----
     399
```

$9999 - 399 = 9600$

Hence, the greatest number of 4 digits which is divisible by 15, 25, 40 and 75 = 9600.

ARITHMETIC & NUMERICAL ABILITY

1 SIMPLIFICATION

BODMAS-RULE

This rule is very important for the arithmetical simplification. When vinculum, bracket, of, division, multiplication, addition, subtraction all or two or more than two operations are present in any question, then we can find out the result (answer) with the help of BODMAS-Rule. Details of BODMAS-Rule is given below :

Order	Abbreviated Letter Used in rule	Meaning	Notation
1.	V	Vinculum or Bar	——
2.	B	Brackets	[ ], { }, ( )
3.	O	Of	of
4.	D	Division	÷
5.	M	Multiplication	×
6.	A	Addition	+
7.	S	Subtraction	–

Note :

(*i*) Order of the letter which is used in BODMAS Rule is always fixed.

(*ii*) Absence of any operation or more than one operations does not changes the order of BODMAS.

(*iii*) 'of' means multiplication.

BRACKETS

When all brackets are present in a question, in that condition **ViCiCuSq-Rule** is applied. This ViCiCuSq-Rule stands for brackets and represents the order of calculation of brackets. Details are given below :

Order	Abbreviated Letter Used in rule	Meaning	Notation
1.	Vi	Vinculum	——
2.	Ci	Circular Bracket	( )
3.	Cu	Curly Bracket	{ }
4.	Sq	Square Bracket	[ ]

Note : This order of brackets (ViCiCuSq) is also fixed and not variable.

SOLVED EXAMPLES

Example 1: $\frac{3}{5}$ of $\frac{5}{7}$ of 357 = ?

A. 51 B. 153
C. 255 D. 159

Solution: $357 \times \frac{5}{7} \times \frac{3}{5} = 153$

Example 2: 125% of 860 + 75% of 480 = ?

A. 1415 B. 1385
C. 1435 D. 1365

Solution: $\frac{860 \times 125}{100} + \frac{480 \times 75}{100}$

= 1075 + 360

= 1435

Example 3: 1121.21 + 121.021 + 21.0021 = ?

A. 1263.2331
B. 1263.2121
C. 1163.2121
D. 1163.2331

Solution: 1121.21 + 121.021 + 21.0021
= 1263.2331

Example 4: $\left(\sqrt{5}-\sqrt{6}\right)^2 + \left(\sqrt{3}+\sqrt{10}\right)^2 = (?)^3 - 40$

A. 8 B. 4
C. 3 D. 6

Solution: Let ? = x

$\therefore \left(\sqrt{5}-\sqrt{6}\right)^2 + \left(\sqrt{3}+\sqrt{10}\right)^2 = (x)^3 - 40$

$\Rightarrow 5+6-2\sqrt{30}+3+10+2\sqrt{30} = x^3 - 40$

$\Rightarrow 24 = x^3 - 40$

$\Rightarrow x^3 = 40 + 24$

$= 64 = 4^3$

$\Rightarrow x = 4$

MULTIPLE CHOICE QUESTIONS

1. 68% of $\sqrt{2916} \times 25 = ? + 189$

A. 728 B. 718
C. 729 D. 739

2. $\sqrt{5^2 \times 41 \times 5 - 17^2 - 75} = ?$

A. 69 B. 61
C. 71 D. 79

3. 8.88 × 88.8 × 88 = ?

A. 68301.142 B. 79391.642
C. 65365.824 D. None of these

4. $\frac{9 \div 2 \times 27 \div 9}{18 \div 7.5 \times 5 \div 4} = ?$

A. 4.5 B. 5.7
C. 2.5 D. 6.8

5. $\sqrt{\sqrt{2500} + \sqrt{961}} = (?)^2$

A. 81 B. 3
C. 6561 D. 9

6. $64^{12} \div 4^{15} = 64^{?}$

A. 9 B. 3
C. 12 D. 7

7. $\sqrt{97344} = ?$

A. 302 B. 322
C. 292 D. None of these

8. 14% of 255 + ?% of 405 = 124.8

A. 22 B. 24
C. 18 D. 15

9. 19.25 × 16.4 × ? = 3472.7

A. 15 B. 17
C. 12 D. None of these

10. 83.04 – 66.46 – 11.71 = ?

A. 5.63 B. 2.92
C. 3.87 D. None of these

11. $\sqrt{529} \div 46 \times 7.4 + (8)^3 - 251 = ?$

A. 265.1 B. 246.1
C. 256.4 D. None of these

12. $(16 \times 4)^3 \div (4)^5 \times (2 \times 8)^2 = (4)^?$

A. 5 B. 6
C. 3 D. 8

13. 534.58 – 386.89 + 221.45 – 195.42 = ?

A. 162.65 B. 109.65
C. 173.72 D. None of these

14. $\sqrt{5625} \times \frac{3}{5} + (85)^2 = ?$

A. 7270 B. 7280
C. 7260 D. 7250

15. $(7)^3 \times (3)^3 \div (6)^2 = ?$

A. 12348 B. 85.75
C. 1543.5 D. 257.25

16. $\frac{17^{6.87}}{17^{4.23}} = 17^{(?)}$

A. 1.62 B. 2.64
C. 11.1 D. 29.06

17. $\sqrt{2401} \times \sqrt{3249} = ?$

A. 2793 B. 2842
C. 2679 D. 2891

18. (5967 – 2437 – 1910) ÷ ? = 27

A. 60 B. 50
C. 65 D. 45

19. $\sqrt[3]{12167} \times \sqrt{?} = 621$

A. 841 B. 27
C. 625 D. None of these

20. 4.5% of 800 ÷ 0.5% of 640 = ?

A. 11.75 B. 12
C. 112.05 D. 11.25

21. 383 ÷ 25 × 2.5 + 12 = ?

A. 50.30 B. 222.14
C. 68.30 D. 124.24

22. 5083 + 25% of ? + 289 = 6385.5

A. 4044 B. 4054
C. 4154 D. 4104

23. $0.2 \times 10^{-2} = ?$

A. 2 B. 0.02
C. 0.002 D. 0.0002

24. 15 – 10 + 5 × 2 ÷ 5 = ?

A. 70 B. 4
C. 5 D. None of these

25. 37% of 150 – 0.05% of 1000 = ?

A. 50 B. 55
C. 55.5 D. 55.55

26. $(15)^{98} \times (15)^{-95} = ?$

A. 3375 B. 225
C. 45 D. 75

27. $\sqrt[3]{?} = (36 \times 24) \div 9$

A. 884736 B. 804036
C. 854734 D. 814736

28. (43% of 2750) – (38% of 2990) = ?

A. 49.3 B. 44.7
C. 43.6 D. 46.3

29. $40 \times 2 \div 10 + 5 - 4 = ?$

A. 5
B. 8
C. 11
D. 9

30. $28 \times 104 \div (18 + 6) + 3 = ?$

A. $124\frac{1}{3}$
B. $104\frac{1}{3}$
C. $125\frac{1}{3}$
D. 128

ANSWERS

1	2	3	4	5	6	7	8	9	10
C	A	D	A	B	D	D	A	D	D
11	**12**	**13**	**14**	**15**	**16**	**17**	**18**	**19**	**20**
D	D	D	A	D	B	A	A	D	D
21	**22**	**23**	**24**	**25**	**26**	**27**	**28**	**29**	**30**
A	B	C	D	B	A	A	D	D	A

SOME SELECTED EXPLANATORY ANSWERS

1. $\sqrt{2916} \times 68\% \times 25 = ? + 189$

$\Rightarrow 54 \times \frac{68}{100} \times 25 = ? + 189$

$\Rightarrow 918 = ? + 189$

$\Rightarrow ? = 918 - 189 = 729$

2. $? = \sqrt{25 \times 41 \times 5 - 17^2 - 75}$

$= \sqrt{5125 - 289 - 75} = \sqrt{4761} = 69$

3. $8.88 \times 88.8 \times 88 = 69391.872$

4. $\frac{9 \div 2 \times 27 \div 9}{18 \div 7.5 \times 5 \div 4} = \frac{\frac{9}{2} \times \frac{27}{9}}{\frac{18}{7.5} \times \frac{5}{4}} = \frac{\frac{27}{2}}{3} = 4.5$

5. $\sqrt{\sqrt{2500 + 961}}$

$= \sqrt{\sqrt{50 + 31}} = \sqrt{9} = \sqrt{(3)^2} = 3.$

6. Let $(64)^x = 64^{12} \div 4^{15}$

$\Rightarrow \quad 4^{3x} = 4^{36-15} = 4^{21}$

$\therefore \quad 3x = 21 \quad \therefore x = 7$

7. $\sqrt{97344} = 312$

8. $\because$ 14% of 255 + ?% of 405 = 124.8

$\Rightarrow \quad 35.7 + 405 \times ? = 124.8$

$\Rightarrow \quad \frac{405 \times ?}{100} = 124.8 - 35.7 = 89.1$

$\therefore \quad ? = \frac{98.1 \times 100}{405} = \frac{891 \times 10}{405}$

$= \frac{891 \times 2}{81} = \frac{1782}{81} = 22.$

9. $\because \ 19.25 \times 16.4 \times ? = 3472.7$

$\therefore \quad ? = \frac{3472.7}{19.25 \times 16.4} = 11$

10. $83.04 - 66.46 - 11.71 = 4.87$

11. $\sqrt{529} \div 46 \times 7.4 + (8)^3 - 251$

$= \frac{23}{46} \times 7.4 + 512 - 251$

$= 3.7 + 512 - 251 = 264.7$

12. $(4)^? = (16 \times 4)^3 \div (4)^5 \times (2 \times 8)^2$

$(4)^? = \frac{(4)^9}{(4)^5} \times (4)^4 = (4)^{9+4-5}$

$\therefore \quad ? = 8.$

13. $534.58 - 386.89 + 221.45 - 195.42 = 172.72$

14. $\sqrt{5625} \times \frac{3}{5} + (85)^2 = 75 \times \frac{3}{5} + 7225 = 7270$

15. $343 \times 27 \div 36 = 257.25$

16. $17^{(?)} = \frac{17^{6.87}}{17^{4.23}} = 17^{6.87-4.23} = 17^{2.64}$

$\therefore \ ? = 2.64.$

17. $\sqrt{2401} \times \sqrt{3249} = 49 \times 57 = 2793.$

18. $(5967 - 2437 - 1910) \div ? = 27$

$\therefore \quad \frac{1620}{?} = 27$

$\therefore \quad ? = \frac{1620}{27} = 60$

19. $\because \ \sqrt[3]{12167} \times \sqrt{?} = 621$

$\Rightarrow \quad 23 \times \sqrt{?} = 621$

$\Rightarrow \quad \sqrt{?} = \frac{621}{23} = 27$

$\therefore \quad ? = (27)^2 = 729$

20. $\frac{4.5}{100}$ of $800 \div \frac{0.5}{100}$ of 640

$= 36 \div 3.2 = 11.25$

21. $383 \div 25 \times 2.5 + 12$

$= \frac{383}{25} \times 2.5 + 12 = 50.30.$

22. $\because 5083 + \frac{25}{100}$ of $? + 289 = 6385.5$

$\Rightarrow 0.25 \times ? = 6385.5 - 5083 - 289$

$\therefore \quad ? = \frac{1013.5}{0.25} = 4054.$

23. $0.2 \times 10^{-2} = 0.2 \times \frac{1}{100} = 0.002$

24. $15 - 10 + 5 \times 2 \div 5$

$= 15 - 10 + \frac{5 \times 2}{5} = 15 - 10 + 2 = 7$

25. 37% of 150 – 0.05% of 1000

$= \frac{37}{100}$ of $150 - \frac{0.05}{100}$ of 1000

$= \frac{111}{2} - 0.5 = 55.5 - 0.5 = 55.$

26. $(15)^{98} \times (15)^{-95} = (15)^3 = 3375$

27. $(36 \times 24) \div 9 = \sqrt[3]{?}$

$\Rightarrow 4 \times 24 = \sqrt[3]{?}$

$\therefore ? = 96^3 = 884736$

28. (43% of 2750) – (38% of 2990)

$= 0.43 \times 2750 - 0.38 \times 2990 = 46.3$

29. $\because 40 \times 2 \div 10 + 5 - 4$

$= 40 \times \frac{2}{10} + 5 - 4$

$= 8 + 5 - 4 = 9$

30. $\because 28 \times 104 \div (18 + 6) + 3$

$= 28 \times 104 \div 24 + 3$

$= 28 \times \frac{104}{24} + 3 = 28 \times \frac{13}{3} + 3$

$= \frac{364}{3} + 3 = \frac{373}{3} = 124\frac{1}{3}$

❑❑❑

2 L.C.M. & H.C.F.

LCM

Multiple : A number is said to be multiple of other when it is exactly divisible by the other.

Common multiple : A common multiple of two or more numbers is a number which is exactly divisible by each of them. For example, for 2 and 3, common multiples are 6, 12, 18, 24 and so on.

Explanation:

Consider the two numbers 2 and 3

Multiple of 2 are 2, 4, 6, 8, 10, 12, ...

Multiple of 3 are 3, 6, 9, 12, 15, ...

∴ Common multiples are 6, 12, 18, ...

Least Common Multiple (L.C.M.) : L.C.M. of two or more given numbers is the least number which is exactly divisible by each of them. For example,

6 is a common multiple of 2 and 3

12 is also common multiple of 2 and 3

18 is also common multiple of 2 and 3

But 6 is the least common multiple (L.C.M.) of 2 and 3.

Methods to find out L.C.M.

L.C.M. of two or more given numbers is determined by following two methods:

1. By prime factorization method
2. By division method

1. By prime factorization method : Resolve the given numbers into their prime factors and then find the product of the highest power of all the factors that occur in the given numbers. This product will be the L.C.M.

Example 1 : Find the L.C.M. of 40, 50, 60 and 80.

Sol :

$$40 = 2 \times 2 \times 2 \times 5 = 2^3 \times 5$$
$$50 = 2 \times 5 \times 5 = 2 \times 5^2$$
$$60 = 2 \times 2 \times 3 \times 5 = 2^2 \times 3 \times 5$$
$$80 = 2 \times 2 \times 2 \times 2 \times 5 = 2^4 \times 5$$

Here, the prime factors that occur in the given numbers are 2, 3 and 5 and their highest powers are respectively 2^4, 5^2 and 3.

Hence, the required L.C.M. $= 2^4 \times 3 \times 5^2 = 1200$.

2. By division method : This is the quicker method to find the prime factors and hence L.C.M.

For determining L.C.M. of the numbers 40, 50, 60 and 80, following process of division is adopted:

2	40, 50, 60, 80
2	20, 25, 30, 40
2	10, 25, 15, 20
5	5, 25, 15, 10
	1, 5, 3, 2

Now required L.C.M. $= 2 \times 2 \times 2 \times 5 \times 5 \times 3 \times 2 = 1200$

L.C.M. of decimal : First of all, we find out the L.C.M. of numbers without decimal and then, we see the number in which decimal is given in the minimum digit from right to left. We put the decimal in our result which is equal to that number of digits.

Example : Find the L.C.M. of 0.6, 9.6 and 0.36.

Sol : The given numbers are equivalent to 0.60, 9.60 and 0.36.

Now, we find out the L.C.M. of 60, 960 and 36, which is equal to 2880.

Hence, the required L.C.M. = 2880.

L.C.M. of fraction : The L.C.M. of two or more fractions is the least fraction or integer which is exactly divisible by each of them.

If $\frac{a}{b}, \frac{c}{d}, \frac{e}{f}$ be the proper fractions, then their L.C.M. is given by

$$\frac{\text{L.C.M. of numerators } a, c, e}{\text{H.C.F. of denominators } b, d, f}$$

An example : Find the L.C.M. of $\frac{1}{2}, \frac{3}{5}, \frac{4}{7}$ and $\frac{5}{12}$

Sol : $$\text{L.C.M.} = \frac{\text{L.C.M. of } 1, 3, 4, 5}{\text{H.C.F. of } 2, 5, 7, 12} = \frac{60}{1} = 60$$

HCF

Factor : One number is said to be a factor of other when it divides the other exactly. Hence, 5 and 7 are factors of 35.

Common factor : A common factor of two or more numbers is a number that divides each of them exactly. Hence, 5 is a common factor of 15, 25, 35 and 55.

Highest Common Factor (H.C.F.) : H.C.F. of two or more numbers is the largest number by which each given number is divisible without leaving any remainder.

An example : It is required to find the H.C.F. of 6 and 8.

Factors of 6 are 1, 2, 3, 6 and

Factors of 8 are 1, 2, 4, 8.

The common factors are 1, 2, but highest of these is 2. Hence, 2 is the H.C.F.

Note : *The terms Highest Common Divisor (H.C.D.) and Greatest Common Measure (G.C.M.) are often used in the sense of Highest Common Factor (H.C.F.)*

We can find H.C.F. by two methods:

1. By prime factorization method :

An example : Find the H.C.F. of 144, 336 and 2016.

Sol : $144 = 2 \times 2 \times 2 \times 2 \times 3 \times 3 = 2^4 \times 3^2$

$336 = 2 \times 2 \times 2 \times 2 \times 3 \times 7 = 2^4 \times 3 \times 7$

$2016 = 2 \times 2 \times 2 \times 2 \times 2 \times 7 \times 3 \times 3 = 2^5 \times 7 \times 3^2$

$\therefore$ H.C.F. of given numbers $= 2^4 \times 3 = 48$.

2. By division method : Divide the greater number by the smaller number, divide the divisor by the remainder, divide the remainder by the next remainder, and so on until no remainder is left. The last divisor is the required H.C.F.

An example : Find the H.C.F. of 48, 168 and 324.

Sol :

```
48 ) 168 ( 3
     144
     24 ) 48 ( 2
          48
          ××
```

Thus, the H.C.F. of 48 and 168 is 24.

Now, we find out the H.C.F. of 24 and 324

```
24 ) 324 (13
     24
     84
     72
     12 ) 24 (2
          24
          ××
```

$\therefore$ Required H.C.F. = 12.

H.C.F. of Decimals : First of all find the H.C.F. of the given numbers ignoring decimals and then put decimal at maximum digits from right to left.

An example : Find the H.C.F. of 0.0012, 1.6 and 2.8.

Sol : First we find the H.C.F. of 12, 16 and 28, which comes to 4.

So, H.C.F. of 0.0012, 1.6 and 2.8 will be 0.0004.

H.C.F. of Fractions : If $\frac{a}{b}, \frac{c}{d}, \frac{e}{f}, \ldots$ be the proper fraction, their H.C.F. is equal to $\frac{\text{H.C.F. of numerators}}{\text{L.C.M. of denominators}}$

An example : Find the H.C.F. of $\frac{54}{9}, 3\frac{9}{17}$ and $\frac{36}{51}$

Sol : Here, $\frac{54}{9} = \frac{6}{1}$; $3\frac{9}{17} = \frac{60}{17}$ and $\frac{36}{51} = \frac{12}{17}$

Hence, the fractions are $\frac{6}{1}, \frac{60}{17}$ and $\frac{12}{17}$

$\therefore$ H.C.F. $= \frac{\text{H.C.F. of } 6, 60, 12}{\text{L.C.M. of } 1, 17, 17} = \frac{6}{17}$.

Relationship Between Two Numbers and Their L.C.M. and H.C.F.

Product of the H.C.F. and the L.C.M. of two numbers is equal to the product of the given numbers.

i.e., 1st number × 2nd number = H.C.F. × L.C.M.

MULTIPLE CHOICE QUESTIONS

1. The largest three-digit number, when divided by 6, 9 and 12 leaves 1 as remainder in each case, will be
A. 887 B. 987
C. 973 D. 730

2. Two numbers are in the ratio of 8 : 15. If their H.C.F. is 4, the numbers are
A. 32 and 60 B. 16 and 30
C. 80 and 150 D. 64 and 120

3. The largest number that will divide 226 and 272 leaving 1 and 2 as remainders respectively, is
A. 36 B. 45
C. 55 D. 59

4. Which of the following is the greatest common divisor of 1170 and 102?
A. 8 B. 4
C. 6 D. 3

5. A number, when 3 is added to it, becomes divisible by 36, 45 and 50. The smallest such number is
A. 987 B. 798
C. 986 D. 897

6. The least perfect square number which is completely divisible by 10, 20, 30 and 40 is
A. 4800 B. 3600
C. 4400 D. 2500

7. The product of two numbers is 2160 and their H.C.F. is 12. How many such pairs of numbers can be possibly formed?
A. 3 B. 1
C. 2 D. None of these

8. The greatest number that will divide 366, 513 and 324 leaving the same remainder in each case is
A. 21 B. 18
C. 27 D. 42

9. The sum of two numbers is 216 and their H.C.F. is 27. These numbers are
A. 60 and 90 B. 81 and 135
C. 64 and 128 D. 30 and 84

10. The L.C.M. of two numbers is 45 times their H.C.F. If the sum of the L.C.M. and the H.C.F. of these two numbers is 1150 and one of the numbers is 125, then the other number is
A. 256 B. 225
C. 250 D. 255

11. The H.C.F. and the L.C.M. of two numbers are 50 and 250 respectively. On dividing one of these numbers by 2, 50 is obtained as quotient. The numbers are
A. 100, 125 B. 80, 100
C. 125, 100 D. 200, 250

12. The largest three-digit number, which when successively divided by 6, 9 and 12, leaves 3 as remainder in each case, is
A. 575 B. 795
C. 975 D. 525

13. The greatest number that will divide 33, 64 and 80 leaving 3, 4 and 5 as remainders respectively, is
A. 10 B. 20
C. 15 D. 22

14. The H.C.F. of three numbers is 12. If the three numbers are in the ratio of 1 : 2 : 3, then the numbers are
A. 14, 28, 42 B. 12, 24, 36
C. 15, 30, 45 D. 24, 48, 72

15. The greatest four-digit number completely divisible by 2, 3, 4 and 5 is
A. 9960 B. 9690
C. 8990 D. 9980

16. Three bells ring respectively at an interval of 15 seconds, 20 seconds and 24 seconds. If they ring continuously for 12 minutes then how many times, during this period, will they ring together?
A. 2 times B. 6 times
C. 5 times D. 3 times

17. The smallest number, on being successively divided by 5, 6, 8, 9 and 12 leaves 1 as remainder in each case and is completely divisible by 13, will be
A. 4603 B. 6305
C. 4503 D. 3601

18. If in the process of finding H.C.F. of two numbers by continued division method, 49 is the last divisor and quotients obtained (from the beginning) are 17, 3 and 2 respectively, then the numbers are
A. 432 and 4929 B. 343 and 5829
C. 388 and 5880 D. 472 and 5930

19. A, B and C start running together in a particular direction from a particular point on a 12 kms long circular path. If the speeds of A, B and C are 3 kms/h, 7 kms/h and 13 kms/h respectively, then after how many hours will they meet together again?
A. 8 B. 6
C. 12 D. 10

20. Which of the following has most numbers of divisors?
A. 182 B. 176
C. 101 D. 99

ANSWERS

1	2	3	4	5	6	7	8	9	10
C	A	B	C	D	B	C	A	B	B
11	**12**	**13**	**14**	**15**	**16**	**17**	**18**	**19**	**20**
A	C	C	B	A	B	D	B	C	B

SOME SELECTED EXPLANATORY ANSWERS

1. L.C.M. of 6, 9 and 12

3	6, 9, 12
2	2, 3, 4
	1, 3, 2

$\therefore$ LCM $= 3 \times 2 \times 3 \times 2 = 36.$

$\because$ Largest 3-digit number = 999

36) 999 (27
72
279
252
×27

$\therefore$ Largest 3-digit number which is exactly divisible by 6, 9 and 12

$= 999 - 27 = 972$

$\therefore$ The required number $= 972 + 1 = 973$

2. Let the numbers be $8x$ and $15x$

$8x = 2 \times 2 \times 2 \times x$

$15x = 3 \times 5 \times x$

$\therefore$ LCM of $8x$ and $15x = 2 \times 2 \times 2 \times x \times 3 \times 5$

$= 120x$

Now, 1st number × 2nd number = HCF × LCM

$\Rightarrow \quad 8x \times 15x = 4 \times 120x$

$\Rightarrow \quad 120x^2 = 4 \times 120x$

$\Rightarrow \quad x = 4$

$\therefore$ Numbers are $8 \times 4 = 32$ and $15 \times 4 = 60$

3. $226 - 1 = 225$ and $272 - 2 = 270$

Now, HCF of 225 and 270

```
225 ) 270 ( 1
      225
      ----
       45 ) 225 ( 5
            225
            ---
             ×
```

$\therefore$ The required number is 45.

4. $1170 = 2 \times 5 \times 3 \times 3 \times 13$

$102 = 2 \times 3 \times 17$

$\therefore$ Greatest common divisor $= 2 \times 3 = 6$

5. It is clear from the given conditions of the problem that the smallest number will be 3 less than the LCM of 36, 45 and 50.

$\therefore$ LCM of 36, 45 and 50

3	36, 45, 50
2	12, 15, 50
3	6, 15, 25
5	2, 5, 25
	2, 1, 5

$\therefore$ LCM $= 3 \times 2 \times 3 \times 5 \times 2 \times 5 = 900$

$\therefore$ Required number $= 900 - 3 = 897$.

6. LCM of 10, 20, 30 and 40

2	10, 20, 30, 40
5	5, 10, 15, 20
2	1, 2, 3, 4
	1, 1, 3, 2

$\therefore$ LCM $= 2 \times 2 \times 5 \times 3 \times 2$

But the number is a perfect square number

$\therefore$ Required number

$= 2 \times 2 \times 5 \times 5 \times 3 \times 3 \times 2 \times 2 = 3600.$

7. Product of two numbers = their HCF × their LCM

$2160 = 12 \times \text{LCM}$

$\therefore \quad \text{LCM} = \dfrac{2160}{12} = 180$

Therefore such pairs of numbers in which product of numbers is 2160 and HCF is 12 will be only 2.

i.e., 12×180 and 36×60.

8. Difference between 366 and 513

$= 513 - 366 = 147$

and difference between 513 and 324

$= 513 - 324 = 189$

$\therefore$ HCF of 147 and 189

```
147 ) 189 ( 1
      147
      ---
     × 42 ) 147 ( 3
            126
            ---
          × 21 ) 42 ( 2
                 42
                 --
                  ×
```

$\therefore$ The required largest number is 21.

9. Let the numbers be x and y.

$\therefore x + y = 216 = 27 \times 8$

Since HCF of these two numbers is 27, hence, common factor of these two numbers is 27.

Therefore these numbers will be of the form of 27×1, 27×2, 27×3, ... etc.

According to the condition of the problem sum of these numbers is 216.

$\therefore$ The numbers will be $27 \times 3 = 81$

and $\quad 27 \times 5 = 135$

10. LCM of the two numbers $= 45 \times$ HCF

and $\quad$ LCM + HCF = 1150

$\Rightarrow \quad 45 \times \text{HCF} + \text{HCF} = 1150$

$\Rightarrow \quad \text{HCF}(45 + 1) = 1150$

$\Rightarrow \quad \text{HCF} = \dfrac{1150}{46} = 25$

$\therefore \quad \text{LCM} = 45 \times 25 = 1125$

$\because$ 1st number × 2nd number = LCM × HCF

$\therefore$ 125 × 2nd number $= 1125 \times 25$

$\therefore \quad \text{2nd number} = \dfrac{1125 \times 25}{125} = 225.$

11. According to the condition of the problem, 50 is obtained on dividing one of the numbers by 2

$\therefore$ One of the numbers $= 50 \times 2 = 100$

Now, 1st number × 2nd number = LCM × HCF

$\therefore \quad 100 \times \text{2nd number} = 250 \times 50$

$\therefore \quad \text{2nd number} = \dfrac{250 \times 50}{100} = 125$

Hence, numbers are 100 and 125.

12. LCM of 6, 9 and 12 = 36 and largest 3-digit number = 999

$\therefore$ HCF of 36 and 999

```
36 ) 999 ( 27
     72
     ---
     279
     252
     ---
      27
```

$\therefore$ Largest three-digit number completely divisible by 6, 9 and 12

$= 999 - 27 = 972$

Since 3 is left as remainder in each case,

$\therefore$ Required largest number of 3-digit

$= 972 + 3 = 975.$

13. $33 - 3 = 30$, $64 - 4 = 60$ and $80 - 5 = 75$

Now, HCF of 30, 60 and 75:

$30 = 2 \times \underline{3 \times 5}$

$60 = 2 \times 2 \times \underline{3 \times 5}$

$75 = \underline{3 \times 5} \times 5$

$\because \quad$ Common factor $= 3 \times 5 = 15$

$\therefore$ Required largest number = 15.

14. Let the numbers be x, $2x$ and $3x$ respectively.
Here, HCF of the three numbers is 12, therefore 12 is the largest common factor of these three numbers. Thus, it is clear that $x = 12$
∴ These numbers are 12, 24 and 36 respectively.

15. LCM of 2, 3, 4 and 5 = 60
Largest 4-digit number = 9999

Now, 60) 9999 (166
60
399
360
×399
360
39

∴ Largest 4-digit number completely divisible by 2, 3, 4 and 5
= 9999 − 39 = 9960
∴ Required number = 9960

16. LCM of 15, 20 and 24

5	15,	20,	24
4	3,	4,	24
3	3,	1,	6
	1,	1,	2

LCM = 5 × 4 × 3 × 2 = 120
∵ 12 minutes = 12 × 60 = 720 seconds
∴ Number of times the bells will ring together during 12 minutes

$$= \frac{720}{120} = 6 \text{ times.}$$

17. LCM of 5, 6, 8, 9 and 12 = 360. Hence, the smallest number which when divided by 5, 6, 8, 9 and 12 leaves 1 as remainder in each case will be 360 + 1 = 361. But 361 is not completely divisible by 13. Hence, on considering 360 × 2 + 1, 360 × 3 + 1,... , 360 × n + 1, we conclude that 360 × 10 + 1 = 3601 is the required number.

18. This question is based on finding HCF by continued division method. Now according to the condition of the problem,
Last divisor = 49
and Last quotient = 2
∴ dividend = 49 × 2 = 98
Now, divisor = 98 and quotient = 3
and remainder = 49
∴ dividend = 98 × 3 + 49 = 343
Now, divisor = 343
quotient = 17
and remainder = 98
∴ Dividend = 343 × 17 + 98 = 5829
Therefore, these numbers are 343 and 5829.

19. A, B and C will take 4 hours, $\frac{12}{7}$ hours and $\frac{12}{13}$ hours respectively in completing one round on the circular path.

$$\therefore \text{ LCM of } \frac{4}{1}, \frac{12}{7} \text{ and } \frac{12}{13}$$

$$= \frac{\text{LCM of 4,12 and 12}}{\text{HCF of 1,7 and 13}}$$

∵ LCM of 4, 12 and 12= 12 and HCF of 1, 7 and 13 = 1

$$\therefore \quad \text{Required LCM} = \frac{12}{1} = 12$$

Hence, they will meet together again after 12 hrs.

20.

Numbers		***Their divisors***
182	→	1, 2, 7, 13, 14, 26, 91 and 182
176	→	1, 2, 4, 8, 16, 22, 44, 88 and 176
101	→	1 and 101
99	→	1, 3, 9, 11, 33 and 99

Therefore, 176 has the most number of divisors.

❑❑❑

3 RATIO & PROPORTION

Some Important Facts:

1. If a and b are two quantities, then
   (*a*) Duplicate ratio of $a : b = a^2 : b^2$
   (*b*) Sub-duplicate ratio of $a : b = \sqrt{a} : \sqrt{b}$
   (*c*) Triplicate ratio of $a : b = a^3 : b^3$
   (*d*) Sub-triplicate ratio $a : b = \sqrt[3]{a} : \sqrt[3]{b}$
   (*e*) Inverse or reciprocal ratio of $a : b = \frac{1}{a} : \frac{1}{b}$
2. If $a : b = c : d$, then
   (*a*) Third proportional (c) to 'a' and 'b' $= \frac{b^2}{a}$
   (*b*) Fourth proportional (d) $= \frac{bc}{a}$
   (*c*) Mean proportional between a and $b = \sqrt{ab}$
   (*d*) If $\frac{a}{b} = \frac{c}{d}$ then $\frac{a+b}{a-b} = \frac{c+d}{c-d}$
   (Componendo and dividendo)
3. (*a*) Comparision of ratios $(a : b) > (c : d) \Leftrightarrow \frac{a}{b} > \frac{c}{d}$
   (*b*) Compounded ratio of $(a : b)$, $(c : d)$, $(e : f) = \frac{ace}{bdf}$
4. If A : B = $x : y$ and B : C = $p : q$, then
   (*a*) $A : C = \frac{x \times p}{y \times q}$
   (*b*) A : B : C = $px : py : qy$
5. In what *ratio* the two kinds of tea must be mixed together one at ₹ x per kg and another at ₹ y per kg, so that the mixture may cost ₹ z per kg?
   $$\text{Ratio} = \frac{z-y}{x-z}$$
6. A grey hound persues a hare as takes J_1 leaps for every J_2 leaps of the hare. If K_1 leaps of the hound are equal to K_2 leaps of the hare, then the Ratio of speeds of the hound and hare is
   $$\frac{J_2 \times K_1}{J_1 \times K_2}$$
7. The incomes of two persons are in the ratio of $a : b$ and their expenditure are in the ratio of $x : y$. If the saving of each person is ₹ s, then income of each is ₹ $\frac{as(y-x)}{ay-bx}$ and ₹ $\frac{bs(y-x)}{ay-bx}$ respectively.
8. In a mixture of z litre, the ratio of milk and water is $x : y$. If another p litres of water is added to the mixture, the ratio of milk and water in the resulting mixture $= \frac{xz}{yz + p(x+y)}$.
9. There are four members a, b, c and d, then formula for
   (*a*) What should be added to each of these numbers so that the remaining numbers may be proportional $= \frac{ad - bc}{(b+c)-(a+d)}$.
   (*b*) What should be subtracted from each of these numbers so that the remaining numbers may be proportional $= \frac{ad-bc}{(a+d)-(b+c)}$.
10. In a mixture the ratio of milk and water is $a : b$. If in this mixture another K litre of water is added, then the ratio of milk and water in the resulting mixture becomes $a : m$. Then the quantity of milk in the original mixture $= \frac{ak}{m-b}$ and quantity of water $= \frac{bk}{m-b}$.

SOLVED EXAMPLES

Example 1: The ratio between the three angles of a quadrilateral is 6 : 7 : 8 respectively. The value of the fourth angle of the quadrilateral is 108°. What is the difference between the largest and the smallest angles of the quadrilateral?

Solution: $6x + 7x + 8x = 360° - 108°$

$\Rightarrow 21x = 252°$

$\Rightarrow x = 12°$

$\therefore$ Required difference $= 108° - 6 \times 12°$
$= 108° - 72° = 36°$.

Example 2: Three-fifth of a number is equal to 70% of another number. What is the ratio between the first number and the second number respectively?

Solution: Let the numbers are x and y respectively.

$\therefore \quad x \times \frac{3}{5} = y \times \frac{70}{100}$

$\Rightarrow \quad x \times \frac{3}{5} = y \times \frac{7}{10}$

$\Rightarrow \quad \frac{x}{y} = \frac{7}{10} \times \frac{5}{3} = 7 : 6.$

Example 3: The respective ratio between the speeds of a car, a train and a bus is 5 : 9 : 4. The average speed of the car, the bus and the train is 72 km/hr together. What is the average speed of the car and the train together?

Solution: Let the speed of car, train and bus be $5x$, $9x$ and $4x$ km/hr respectively.

$\because \quad 5x + 9x + 4x = 72 \times 3$

$\therefore \quad x = 12$

$\therefore$ Average speed of car and train

$= \frac{5x + 9x}{2} = \frac{14 \times 12}{2} = 84$ km/hr

Example 4: The ratio between the present ages of Meena and Priya is 3 : 4 respectively. Ten years ago the ratio between their ages was 4 : 7 respectively. What will be Meena's age after 5 years?

Solution: Let the present age of Meena be $3x$ years

$\therefore$ The present age of Priya = $4x$ years

$\frac{3x - 10}{4x - 10} = \frac{4}{7}$

$21x - 70 = 16x - 40$

$x = \frac{70 - 40}{5} = 6$

$\therefore$ Meena's age after 5 years $= 3 \times 6 + 5$

$= 23$ years.

MULTIPLE CHOICE QUESTIONS

1. An amount of rupees 4500 is to be distributed among Shrinath, Ramnath and Raghunath in the ratio of 3 : 7 : 5 respectively. If ₹ 500 is added to each of the share, the new ratio will become ......?

A. 7 : 10 : 13 B. 9 : 16 : 13
C. 2 : 4 : 3 D. 4 : 5 : 2

2. The total number of students studying in a school is 10396. The ratio of the total number of girls to the total number of boys studying in the school is 52 : 61 respectively. What is the total number of girls studying in the school?

A. 4874 B. 4784
C. 5216 D. 5612

3. In a box the numbers of one rupee, half rupee and quarter rupee are in the ratio 3 : 4 : 5 and the total value of the coins is ₹ 100. Find the number of each kind of coins respectively—

A. 48, 64, 80 B. 48, 60, 70
C. 55, 78, 90 D. 44, 68, 80

4. The ratio of the ages of two persons is 4 : 7 and the age of one of them is more than the other by 30 years. What is the sum of their ages in years?

A. 100 B. 110
C. 120 D. 130

5. The ratio of the amounts of A and B is 4 : 3 and the sum of their amount is ₹ 700. What amount in rupees should A give B to make the ratio 1 : 1?

A. 100 B. 200
C. 150 D. 50

6. The ratio of the volumes of water and glycerine in 240 c.c. glycerine mixed with water is 1 : 3. What additional volume of water should be mixed with it so that the ratio of the volumes of water and glycerine becomes 2 : 3?

A. 70 c.c. B. 80 c.c.
C. 60 c.c. D. 50 c.c.

7. If 15% of A is the same as 20% of B, then A : B is :

A. 9 : 11 B. 4 : 3
C. 3 : 4 D. 6 : 7

8. The fourth proportional to 1, 3 and the third proportional to 1 and 3 is :

A. 9 B. 81
C. 3 D. 27

9. The ratio of third proportional to 12 and 30 and the mean proportional to 9 and 25 is :

A. 5 : 1 B. 2 : 1
C. 9 : 14 D. 7 : 15

10. If $a + b : b + c : c + a = 6 : 7 : 8$ and $a + b + c = 14$ then the value of c is :

A. 14 B. 7
C. 8 D. 6

11. ₹ 120 are divided among P, Q, R such that P's share is ₹ 20 more than Q's and ₹ 20 less than R's share. What is Q's share?

A. ₹ 20 B. ₹ 15
C. ₹ 25 D. ₹ 10

12. If four numbers are in the ratio 5 : 7 : 11 : 13 be such that the sum of their cubes is 3996, find the average of four numbers.

A. 13 B. 11
C. 12 D. 9

13. If 2A = 3B = 4C, then A : B : C is :
A. 2 : 3 : 4 B. 4 : 3 : 2
C. 6 : 4 : 3 D. 3 : 4 : 6

14. If $\frac{1}{5} : \frac{1}{x} = \frac{1}{x} : \frac{1}{1.25}$, then the value of x is :
A. 1.25 B. 1.5
C. 2.5 D. 2.25

15. A fraction bears the same ratio to $\frac{1}{27}$ as $\frac{3}{7}$ does to $\frac{5}{9}$. The fraction is :
A. $\frac{7}{45}$ B. $\frac{1}{35}$
C. $\frac{45}{7}$ D. $\frac{5}{21}$

16. The fourth proportional to 0.2, 0.12 and 0.3 is:
A. 0.13 B. 0.15
C. 0.18 D. 0.8

17. A bag contains 25 paise, 10 paise and 5 paise coins in the ratio 1 : 2 : 3. If their total value is ₹ 30, the number of 5 paise coins is :
A. 50 B. 100
C. 150 D. 200

18. In a class, the number of boys is more than the number of girls by 12% of the total strength. The ratio of boys to girls is :
A. 11 : 14 B. 14 : 11
C. 25 : 28 D. 28 : 25

19. A right cylinder and a right circular cone have the same radius and the same volume. The ratio of the height of the cylinder to that of the cone is :
A. 3 : 5 B. 2 : 5
C. 3 : 1 D. 1 : 3

20. The speeds of three cars are in the ratio 3 : 4 : 5. The ratio between times taken by them to travel the same distance is :
A. 3 : 4 : 5 B. 5 : 4 : 3
C. 12 : 15 : 20 D. 20 : 15 : 12

21. A and B are two alloys of gold and copper prepared by mixing metals in proportions 7 : 2 and 7 : 11 respectively. If equal quantities of the alloys are melted to form a third alloy C, the proportion of gold and copper in C will be :
A. 5 : 9 B. 5 : 7
C. 7 : 5 D. 9 : 5

22. If $a : b = c : d$, then $\frac{ma + nc}{mb + nd}$ is equal to :
A. $m : n$ B. $na : mb$
C. $a : b$ D. $md : nc$

23. Vijay got thrice as many marks in Maths as in English. The proportion of his marks in Maths and History is 4 : 3. If his total marks in Maths, English and History are 250, what are his marks in English?
A. 120 B. 90
C. 40 D. 80

24. A mixture contains milk and water in the ratio 5 : 1. On adding 5 litres of water, the ratio of milk and water becomes 5 : 2. The quantity of milk in the mixture is:
A. 16 litres B. 25 litres
C. 32.5 litres D. 22.75 litres

25. Two equal glasses are respectively $\frac{1}{3}$ and $\frac{1}{4}$ full of milk. They are then filled up with water and the contents mixed in a tumbler. The ratio of milk and water in the tumbler is:
A. 7 : 5 B. 7 : 17
C. 3 : 7 D. 11 : 23

26. The ratio between two numbers is 3 : 4 and their L.C.M. is 180. The first number is :
A. 15 B. 20
C. 45 D. 60

27. A man has some hens and cows. If the number of heads be 48 and number of feet equals 140, the number of hens will be :
A. 22 B. 23
C. 24 D. 26

28. The ratio between the ages of Kamal and Savita is 6 : 5 and the sum of their ages is 44 years. The ratio of their ages after 8 years will be :
A. 5 : 6 B. 7 : 8
C. 8 : 7 D. 14 : 13

29. One year ago the ratio between Laxmi's and Gopi's salary was 3 : 4. The ratios of their individual salaries between last year's and this year's salaries are 4 : 5 and 2 : 3 respectively. At present the total of their salary is ₹ 4160. The salary of Laxmi now, is :
A. ₹ 1040 B. ₹ 1600
C. ₹ 2560 D. ₹ 3120

30. If 15% of x = 20% of y, then $x : y$ is :
A. 3 : 4 B. 4 : 3
C. 17 : 16 D. 16 : 17

ANSWERS

1	2	3	4	5	6	7	8	9	10
E	B	A	B	D	C	B	D	A	D
11	**12**	**13**	**14**	**15**	**16**	**17**	**18**	**19**	**20**
A	D	C	C	B	C	C	B	D	D
21	**22**	**23**	**24**	**25**	**26**	**27**	**28**	**29**	**30**
C	C	C	B	B	C	D	C	B	B

SOME SELECTED EXPLANATORY ANSWERS

2. From question,
The total number of students in the school = 10396 and ratio of number of girls : boys = 52 : 61
∴ The total number of girls in that school
$= \frac{10396 \times 52}{(52+61)} = \frac{10396 \times 52}{113}$
$= 92 \times 52 = 4784.$

3. $3x + 4x \times \frac{1}{2} + 5x \times \frac{1}{4} = 100$
$12x + 8x + 5x = 400$
$x = 16$
Number of 1 rupee = 48
Number of 1/2 rupee = 64
Number of quarter rupee = 5 × 16 = 80

4. ∵ $7x - 4x = 30,$
$x = 10$
∴ Sum of their ages = (4 + 7) × 10
= 11 × 10
= 110 years

5. ∵ $4x + 3x = 700$
⇒ $x = 100$
400 300
(A) (B)
∵ $\frac{400-x}{300+x} = \frac{1}{1}$
⇒ $400 - x = 300 + x$
∴ $x = 50$

6. Quantity of water in 240 cc glycerine and water
$= \frac{1}{4} \times 240 \text{ cc} = 60 \text{ cc}$
Quantity of glycerine = (240 – 60) cc
= 180 cc
∵ $\frac{60+x}{180} = \frac{2}{3}$
⇒ $x = 60$ cc.

8. First we find the third proportional to 1 and 3.
Let the third proportional to 1 and 3 is
⇒ $1 : 3 :: 3 : x$
⇒ $x = 3 \times 3$
⇒ $x = 9$
The fourth proportional to 1, 3 and the third proportional to 1 and 3
= The fourth proportional to 1, 3 and 9. Let the fourth proportional to 1, 3 and 9 is y, then $1 : 3 :: 9 : y$
⇒ $1 \times y = 3 \times 9$
⇒ $y = 27$
∴ Required answer is 27.

9. Let the third proportional to 12 and 30 be y, then $12 : 30 :: 30 : y$
⇒ $12y = 30 \times 30$
$y = \frac{30 \times 30}{12} = 75$
Mean proportional to 9 and 25
$= \sqrt{9 \times 25} = 3 \times 5 = 15$
∴ The required ratio is 75 : 15 = 5 : 1

10. Given
$$\left.\begin{aligned} a+b &= 6x \\ b+c = 7x \text{ and } c+a &= 8x \end{aligned}\right\} \quad ...(1)$$
and $a + b + c = 14$
adding equations in (1), we get
$2(a + b + c) = 21x$
using (2), we get
$2 \times 14 = 21x$
⇒ $x = \frac{2 \times 14}{21}$
$= \frac{2 \times 2}{3} = \frac{4}{3}$
$a + b = 6x = 6 \times \frac{4}{3} = 8.$
Using $a + b + c = 14$ and $a + b = 8$
We get $c = 6$.

11. Given P's share = Q's share + ₹ 20
P's share = R's share – ₹ 20
let Q's share be y.
then P's share = $y + 20$
$y + 20$ = R's share – ₹ 20
⇒ R's share = $y + 40$
P's share + Q's share + R's share = 120
$y + 20 + y + y + 40 = 120$
$3y + 60 = 120$
$3y = 120 - 60 = 60$
$y = 20$
∴ Q's share = y = ₹ 20.

12. Let the four numbers be $5x$, $7x$, $11x$ and $13x$.
Given $(5x)^3 + (7x)^3 + (11x)^3 + (13x)^3 = 3996.$
$125x^3 + 343x^3 + 1331x^3 + 2197x^3 = 3996$
⇒ $3996x^3 = 3996$
⇒ $x^3 = 1$ ⇒ $x = 1$
∴ The four numbers are 5, 7, 11 and 13. Average of these four numbers
$= \frac{5+7+11+13}{4} = \frac{36}{4} = 9.$

13. Let 2A = 3B = 4C = x.

Then, A = $\frac{x}{2}$, B = $\frac{x}{3}$ and C = $\frac{x}{4}$.

$\therefore$ A : B : C = $\frac{x}{2} : \frac{x}{3} : \frac{x}{4}$ = 6 : 4 : 3.

Hence, A : B : C = 6 : 4 : 3.

14. $\frac{1}{x}\times\frac{1}{x} = \frac{1}{5}\times\frac{1}{1.25}$

or, $\frac{1}{x^2} = \frac{4}{25}$

or, $x^2 = \frac{25}{4}$

$\therefore$ $x = \frac{5}{2} = 2.5.$

15. $x : \frac{1}{27} = \frac{3}{7} : \frac{5}{9} \Rightarrow \frac{5}{9}x = \frac{1}{27}\times\frac{3}{7}.$

$\therefore \frac{5}{9}x = \frac{1}{63}$ or $x = \left(\frac{1}{63}\times\frac{9}{5}\right) = \frac{1}{35}.$

16. Let 0.2 : 0.12 :: 0.3 : x.
Then, $0.2x = 0.12 \times 0.3$ or

$$x = \frac{0.12\times0.3}{0.2} = 0.18.$$

17. Ratio of their values = $\frac{1}{4} : \frac{2}{10} : \frac{3}{20}$

= 5 : 4 : 3.

$\therefore$ Value of 5-paise coins = ₹ $\left(30\times\frac{3}{12}\right)$

= ₹ 7.50.

$\therefore$ Number of 5-paise coins = $\frac{750}{5}$ = 150.

19. Let the heights of the cylinder and cone be h and H respectively. Then, $\pi r^2 h = \frac{1}{3}\pi r^2$ H or $\frac{h}{H} = \frac{1}{3}.$

So, their heights are in the ratio 1 : 3.

20. Ratio of time taken = $\frac{1}{3} : \frac{1}{4} : \frac{1}{5}$ = 20 : 15 : 12.

21. Gold in C = $\left(\frac{7}{9}+\frac{7}{18}\right) = \frac{21}{18} = \frac{7}{6}.$

Copper in C = $\left(\frac{2}{9}+\frac{11}{18}\right) = \frac{15}{18} = \frac{5}{6}.$

$\therefore$ Gold : Copper = $\frac{7}{6} : \frac{5}{6}$ = 7 : 5.

22. Let $\frac{a}{b} = \frac{c}{d} = k$. Then, $a = bk$ and $c = dk$.

$\therefore \frac{ma+nc}{mb+nd} = \frac{mbk+ndk}{mb+nd} = k\left(\frac{mb+nd}{mb+nd}\right)$

$= k = \frac{a}{b}.$

23. M = 3E and $\frac{M}{H} = \frac{4}{3}.$

$\therefore$ H = $\frac{3}{4}$M = $\frac{3}{4}\times 3$E = $\frac{9}{4}$E.

Now, M + E + H = 250

$\Rightarrow$ 3E + E + $\frac{9}{4}$E = 250

$\therefore$ 25E = 1000 or E = 40.

24. Let quantity of milk and water be $5x$ and x litres.

Then, $\frac{5x}{x+5} = \frac{5}{2}$ or, $10x = 5x + 25$

or, $x = 5.$

$\therefore$ Quantity of milk = $5x$ = 25 litres.

26. Let the numbers be $3x$ and $4x$.
Then, their L.C.M. = $12x$.
$\therefore$ $12x = 180$ or $x = 15$.
Hence, the first number = 45.

27. Let the number of hens = x and number of cows = y.
Then, $x + y = 48$ and $2x + 4y = 140$.
Solving these equations, we get, $2y = 44$
or $y = 22$.
So, $x = (48 - 22) = 26$.
$\therefore$ Number of hens = 26.

28. Let their ages be $6x$ and $5x$ years.
$\therefore$ $6x + 5x = 44$ or, $x = 4$.
So, their present ages are 24 years and 20 years.
Ratio of their ages after 8 years = 32 : 28
= 8 : 7.

29. Let the salaries of Laxmi and Gopi one year before be x_1, y_1 respectively and now x_2, y_2 respectively. Then,

$\frac{x_1}{y_1} = \frac{3}{4}, \frac{x_1}{x_2} = \frac{4}{5}, \frac{y_1}{y_2} = \frac{2}{3}$ and $x_2 + y_2 = 4160$.

Solving these equations, we get $x_2 = 1600$.

30. 15% of x = 20% of y

$\Rightarrow \frac{15x}{100} = \frac{20y}{100}$

$\Rightarrow \frac{x}{y} = \left(\frac{20}{100}\times\frac{100}{15}\right) = \frac{4}{3}$

$\Rightarrow x : y = 4 : 3.$

□□□

4 AGE AND AVERAGE

IMPORTANT FACTS

1. The present age of the father is x times the age of his son. T years hence, the father's age become y times the age of his son. Then the present ages of the father and his son are:

   Present age of the son = $\frac{(y-1)T}{x-y}$ years and age of the father = $\frac{(y-1)T \times x}{x-y}$ years.

2. T years ago, the father's age was x times that of his son and at present the father's age is y times the age of his son. Then their present ages are:

   Son's age = $\frac{T(x-1)}{x-y}$ years;

   Father's age = $\frac{T(x-1)}{x-y} \times y$ years.

3. Average Speed = $\frac{\text{Total travelled distance}}{\text{Total taken time}}$

4. If equal distances are travelled at the rate X and Y, then Average Speed = $\frac{2XY}{X+Y}$

5. When a person leaves a group and another person joins the group in the place of person left, then

   I. In the case of increasing of average age, Age of the newcomer = Age of person left + no. of persons in the group X increase in average age.

   II. In the case of decreasing of average age, Age of the newcomer = Age of person left – no. of persons in the group X decrease in average age.

6. When a person joins a group without replacing any previous person from that group, then

   I. In the case of increasing of average age, Age of the newcomer = Previous of the age + no. of all persons (including newcomer) × increaser in average age.

   II. In the case of decreasing of average age, Age of the newcomer = Previous average age – no. of all persons (including new comer) × decrease in average age.

7. When a person leaves the group but nobody joins this group, then

   I. In the case of increasing of average age, Age of man left = Previous Average of the age – no. of present persons × decrease in the average age.

   II. In the case of decreasing of average age, Age of man left = Previous Average age + no. of present persons × increase in average age.

8. Average related to Natural Numbers

   I. Average of consecutive natural numbers till n $= \frac{(n+1)}{2}$

   II. Average of squares of numbers till n $= \frac{(n+1)(2n+1)}{6}$

   III. Average of cubes of consecutive natural numbers till $n = \frac{n(n+1)^2}{4}$

9. Average related to Even Numbers

   I. Average of n = consecutive even numbers $= n + 1$

   II. Average of consecutive even number till n $= (n/2 + 1)$

   III. Average of squares of n consecutive even numbers = $\frac{2(n+1)(2n+1)}{3}$

   IV. Average of squares of consecutive even numbers till $n = \frac{(n+1)(2n+1)}{3}$

10. Average related to Odd Numbers

    I. Average of n consecutive odd numbers = n

    II. Average of consecutive odd numbers till n $= \frac{n(n+1)}{3}$

    III. Average of squares of consecutive odd numbers till $n = \frac{n(n+1)}{3}$

SOLVED EXAMPLES

Example 1: Ankur's present age is 12 years more than Raman's age 5 years ago. Presently Raman is 24 years older than Raju's present age who is 12 years younger than Amit. If Amit's present age is 42 years, what is Ankur's age 3 years ago?

Solution: Amit's present age = 42 years

Raju's present age = 42 – 12 = 30 years

Raman's present age = 30 + 24 = 54 years

Ankur's present age = 54 – 5 + 12 = 61 years

∴ Ankur's age 3 years ago = 58 years

Example 2: Present ages of Leela and Shivani are in the ratio of 4 : 5 respectively. Three years hence this ratio becomes 5 : 6. What is the difference between their present ages?

Solution: Let Leela's and Shivani's present ages be $4x$ and $5x$ years respectively.

After 3 years,

$$\frac{4x+3}{5x+3} = \frac{5}{6}$$

⇒ $25x + 15 = 24x + 18$

⇒ $25x - 24x = 18 - 15 = 3$

∴ $x = 3$ = Required difference

Example 3: Radha's present age is three years less than twice her age 12 years ago. Also the respective ratio between Raj's present age and Radha's present age is 4 : 9. What will be Raj's age after 5 years?

Solution: Let the present age of Radha be x years. As per question,

∵ $x = (x - 12) \times 2 - 3$

⇒ $x = 2x - 27$

∴ $x = 27$

∵ Present age of Raj

$$= \frac{4}{9} \times 27 = 12 \text{ years}$$

∴ Raj's age after 5 years = 12 + 5 = 17 years

Example 4: If $12a + 12b = 45$, what is the average of a and b?

Solution: ∵ $12a + 12b = 45$

⇒ $12(a + b) = 45$

∴ $$\frac{a+b}{2} = \frac{45}{12\times 2} = 1.875.$$

Example 5: The sum of five numbers is 555. The average of first two numbers is 75 and the third number is 115. What is the average of last two numbers?

Solution: Average of last two numbers

$$= \frac{555 - 2\times 75 - 115}{2}$$

$$= \frac{555 - 150 - 115}{2} = \frac{290}{2} = 145.$$

MULTIPLE CHOICE QUESTIONS

1. The sum of 8 consecutive odd numbers is 656. Also average of four consecutive even number is 87. What is the sum of the smallest odd number and second largest even number?

A. 165 B. 175

C. 163 D. Cannot be determined

2. The ages of Meena, Tina and Seema are in the ratio of 6 : 4 : 7 respectively. If the sum of their ages is 34 years, what is Seema's age?

A. 12 years B. 10 years

C. 18 years D. None of these

3. The average of 4 positive integers is 52.5. The highest integer is 76 and the lowest integer is 34. The difference between the remaining two integers is 4. Which of the following integers is higher of the remaining two integers?

A. 52 B. 54

C. 48 D. Cannot be determined

4. The present age of Deepa is 3 times the present age of his son. Five years hence the ratio of their ages will be 34 : 13 respectively. What is the present age of Deepa?

A. 63 years B. 68 years

C. 58 years D. 60 years

5. The average of 5 consecutive even numbers A, B, C, D and E is 66. What is the product of B and E?

A. 4352 B. 4340

C. 4620 D. None of these

6. The present age of father is 34 years more than that of his son. Twelve years ago father's age was 18 times the age of his son. What is the present age of the son in years?

A. 16 B. 14

C. 12 D. 18

7. A father is older than his first son by 30 years, the first son is older than the second son by 10 years. If the sum of their ages by 95 years, find the age of father–

A. 65 years B. 55 years

C. 45 years D. 50 years

8. In 10 years, Alok will be twice as old as Babul was 10 years ago. If Alok is now 9 years older than Babul, the present age of Babul is :

A. 19 years B. 29 years

C. 39 years D. 49 years

9. The difference between the ages of two persons is 10 years. 15 years ago, the elder one was twice as old as the younger one. The present age of the elder person is :

A. 25 years B. 35 years
C. 45 years D. 55 years

10. Ratio of Anshu's age to Jolly's age is equal to 4 : 3. Anshu will be 26 years old after 6 years. How old is Jolly now?

A. 12 years B. 15 years
C. $19\frac{1}{2}$ years D. 21 years

11. The ratio between the ages of Asha and Bhushan at present is 2 : 3. Five years hence the ratio of their ages will be 3 : 4. What is the present age of Asha?

A. 10 years B. 15 years
C. 25 years D. data inadequate

12. Three years ago the average age of A and B was 18 years. With C joining them, the average becomes 22 years. How old is C now?

A. 24 years B. 27 years
C. 28 years D. 30 years

13. Ten years ago A was half of B in age. If the ratio of their present ages is 3 : 4, what will be the total of their present ages?

A. 8 years B. 20 years
C. 35 years D. 45 years.

14. Out of three numbers, the first is twice the second and is half of the third. If the average of the three numbers is 56, the three numbers in order are :

A. 48, 96, 24 B. 48, 24, 96
C. 96, 24, 48 D. 96, 48, 24

15. The average of 50 numbers is 38. If two numbers, namely 45 and 55 are discarded, the average of the remaining numbers is :

A. 36.5 B. 37.0
C. 37.5 D. 37.52

16. The average temperature of the first three days is 27° C and that of the next three is 29° C. If the average of the whole week is 28.5° C, the temperature of the last day of the week is:

A. 10.5°C B. 21°C
C. 31.5°C D. 42°C

17. The average of an adult class is 40 years. 12 new students with an average age of 32 years join the class, thereby decreasing the average by 4 years. The original strength of the class was :

A. 10 B. 11
C. 12 D. 15

18. The average weight of 8 persons is increased by 2.5 kg when one of them whose weight is 56 kg is replaced by a new man. The weight of the new man is :

A. 66 kg B. 75 kg
C. 76 kg D. 86 kg

19. In a TV factory, an average of 60 TVs are produced per day for the first 25 days of the month. A few workers fell ill for the next five days, reducing the daily average for the month to 58 sets per day. The average production per day for the last 5 days is :

A. 45 B. 48
C. 52 D. 58

20. The average expenditure of a man for the first five months is ₹ 120 and for the next seven months it is ₹ 130. If he saves ₹ 290 in that years, his monthly average income is :

A. ₹ 140 B. ₹ 150
C. ₹ 160 D. ₹ 170

21. The average age of 24 students in a class is 10. If the teacher's age is included, the average increases by one. The age of the teacher is :

A. 25 years B. 30 years
C. 35 years D. 40 years

22. A batsman has a certain average runs for 11 innings. In the 12th inning he made a score of 90 runs and thereby decreased his average by 5. His average after 12th inning is :

A. 127 B. 145
C. 150 D. 217

23. The average weight of three men A, B and C is 84 kg. Another man D joins the group and the average now becomes 80 kg. If another man E, whose weight is 3 kg more than that of D, replaces A, then the average weight of B, C, D and E becomes 79 kg. The weight of A is :

A. 70 kg B. 72 kg
C. 75 kg D. 80 kg

24. A man whose bowling average is 12.4 takes 5 wickets for 26 runs and thereby decreases his average by 0.4. The number of wickets, taken by him, before his last match, is :

A. 85 B. 78
C. 72 D. 64

25. The present ages of three persons are in proportions 4 : 7 : 9. Eight years ago, the sum of their ages was 56. Find their present ages (in years).

A. 8, 20, 28 B. 16, 28, 36
C. 20, 35, 45 D. Cannot be determined

26. A is two years older than B who is twice as old as C. If the total of the ages of A, B and C be 27, then how old is B?

A. 7 B. 8
C. 9 D. 10

27. A person's present age is two-fifth of the age of his mother. After 8 years, he will be one-half of the age of his mother. How old is the mother at present?

A. 32 years B. 36 years
C. 40 years D. 48 years

28. Quasab is as much younger than Rahim as he is older than Tanveer. If the sum of the ages of Rahim and Tanveer is 50 years, what is definitely the difference between Rahim's and Quasab's age?

A. 1 year B. 2 years
C. 25 years D. Can not be determined

29. A father said to his son, "I was as old as you are at present at the time of your birth." If the father's age is 38 years now, the son's age five years back was :

A. 14 years B. 19 years
C. 33 years D. 38 years

30. Asha's father was 38 years of age when she was born while her mother was 36 years old when her brother four years younger to her was born. What is the difference between the ages of her parents?

A. 2 years B. 4 years
C. 6 years D. 8 years

ANSWERS

1	2	3	4	5	6	7	8	9	10
C	D	A	A	D	B	B	C	B	B
11	**12**	**13**	**14**	**15**	**16**	**17**	**18**	**19**	**20**
A	A	C	B	C	C	C	C	B	B
21	**22**	**23**	**24**	**25**	**26**	**27**	**28**	**29**	**30**
C	B	C	A	B	D	C	D	A	C

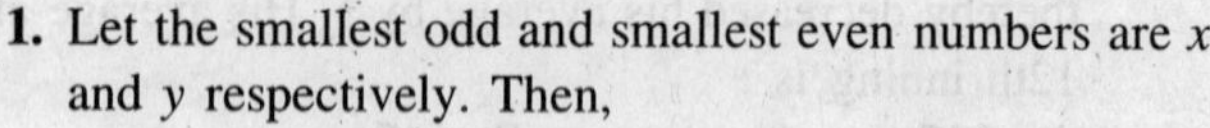

SOME SELECTED EXPLANATORY ANSWERS

1. Let the smallest odd and smallest even numbers are x and y respectively. Then,

$\because\ x + (x + 2) + (x + 4) + (x + 6) + (x + 8) + (x + 10) + (x + 12) + (x + 14) = 656$

$\Rightarrow\ 8x + 56 = 656$

$$x = \frac{656 - 56}{8} = 75$$

$\because\ y + (y + 2) + (y + 4) + (y + 6) = 4 \times 87$

$\Rightarrow\ 4y + 12 = 348$

$$y = \frac{348 - 12}{4} = 84$$

$\therefore$ Reqd. sum of the smallest odd number and second largest even number

$= x + (y + 4) = 75 + (84 + 4) = 163$

2. Seema's age $= \dfrac{7 \times 34}{(6 + 4 + 7)} = 14$ years.

3. Let the 4 positive integers, kept in descending order be a, b, c and d respectively. Then from question,

$\because\ a + b + c + d = 4 \times 52.5 = 210$

$\Rightarrow\ 76 + (b + c) + 34 = 210$

$\Rightarrow\ (b + c) = 100$ ...(*i*)

Again from question,

$b - c = 4$ ...(*ii*)

Solving (*i*) and (*ii*), we get

$b = 52$

and $c = 48$

Hence, higher integer $= b = 52$

4. Let the present age of Deepa's son $= x$ years.

Then from question,

Deepa's present age $= 3x$ years

$$\therefore\ \frac{3x + 5}{x + 5} = \frac{34}{13}$$

$\Rightarrow\ 39x + 65 = 34x + 170$

$\Rightarrow\ 5x = 105$

$\therefore\ x = 21$

Deepa's present age $= 3x = 3 \times 21 = 63$ years

5. From question,

$A + B + C + D + E = 66 \times 5 = 330$

Let the 1st even number A be n, then

$\because\ n + (n + 2) + (n + 4) + (n + 6) + (n + 8) = 330$

$\Rightarrow\ 5n + 20 = 330$

$\Rightarrow\ 5n = 310$

$\therefore\ n = 62$

Thus the required product

$= B \times E = (n + 2) \times (n + 8)$

$= 64 \times 70 = 4480$

7. Age of 1st son $= x$

Father's age $= x + 30$

Age of 2nd son $= x - 10$

$\because\ x + (x + 30) + (x - 10) = 95$

$\Rightarrow\ 3x + 20 = 95$

$\Rightarrow\ 3x = 75$

$x = 25$

$\therefore$ Father's age $= (25 + 30)$ years $= 55$ years

8. Let the present ages of Babul and Alok be x years and $(x + 9)$ years respectively.
Then, $(x + 9 + 10) = 2(x - 10)$ or $x = 39$.

9. Let the present age of the elder person be x years. Then, the present age of the other person $= (x - 10)$ years
$(x - 15) = 2(x - 10 - 15)$ or $x = 35$
$\therefore$ The present age of the elder person is 35 years.

10. Let Anshu's age $= 4x$ and Jolly's age $= 3x$ years.
$\therefore$ $4x + 6 = 26 \Rightarrow x = 5$
$\therefore$ Jolly's age $= 3x = 15$ years.

11. Let the ages of Asha and Bhushan be $2x$ and $3x$ years.
$$\frac{2x+5}{3x+5} = \frac{3}{4}$$
$\Rightarrow$ $4(2x + 5) = 3(3x + 5)$
$\Rightarrow$ $x = 5$.
$\therefore$ Asha's present age $= 2x = 10$ years.

12. Sum of ages of A and B, 3 years ago $= (18 \times 2) = 36$ years.
Sum of ages of A, B and C $= (22 \times 3) = 66$ years.
Sum of ages of A and B $= (36 + 6)$ years $= 42$ years.
$\therefore$ C's age $= (66 - 42)$ years $= 24$ years.

14. Let second number $= x$. Then, first one $= 2x$ and third number $= 4x$.
$$\therefore \frac{x+2x+4x}{3} = 56 \Rightarrow 7x = 168 \text{ or } x = 24.$$
So, the numbers are 48, 24, 96.

15. Total of 50 numbers $= (50 \times 38) = 1900$.
Total of 48 numbers $= [1900 - (45 + 55)] = 1800$.
$$\therefore \text{Required average} = \frac{1800}{48} = \frac{225}{6} = 37.5.$$

16. $3 \times 27 + 3 \times 29 + x = 7 \times 28.5$
$\therefore$ $x = 31.5$

17. Let original strength $= x$. Then,
$40x + 12 \times 32 = (x + 12) \times 36$
or $40x + 384 = 36x + 432$ or $4x = 48$
or $x = 12$.

18. Total increase $= (8 \times 2.5)$ kg $= 20$ kg.
Weight of new man $= (56 + 20)$ kg $= 76$ kg.

19. Production during these 5 days $= (30 \times 58 - 25 \times 60) = 240$.
$$\therefore \text{Average for 5 days} = \frac{240}{5} = 48.$$

20. Total income $=$ ₹ $120 \times 5 + 130 \times 7 + 290)$ $=$ ₹ 1800.
Average monthly income $=$ ₹ $\left(\frac{1800}{12}\right)$ $=$ ₹ 150.

21. Age of the teacher $= (25 \times 11 - 24 \times 10)$ years $= 35$ years.

22. $11x + 90 = (x - 5) \times 12$ or $x = 150$.
$\therefore$ Average after 12th inning $= (150 - 5) = 145$.

23. $A + B + C = 3 \times 84 = 252$, $A + B + C + D = (4 \times 80) = 320$.
$\therefore$ $D = (320 - 252) = 68$ and so $E = (68 + 3) = 71$.
Now, $B + C + D + E = (4 \times 79) = 316$
So, $A = (320 - 245) = 75$ kg.

24. Let the number of wickets taken before the last match $= x$.
$$\text{Then, } \frac{12.4x+26}{x+5} = 12 \Rightarrow x = 85.$$

25. Let their present ages be $4x$, $7x$ and $9x$ years respectively.
Then, $(4x - 8) + (7x - 8) + (9x - 8) = 56$
$\Rightarrow 20x = 80 \Rightarrow x = 4$.
$\therefore$ Their present ages are 16 years, 28 years and 36 years respectively.

26. Let C's age be x years.
Then, B's age $= 2x$ years.
A's age $= (2x + 2)$ years.
$\therefore$ $(2x + 2) + 2x + x = 27 \Rightarrow 5x = 25 \Rightarrow x = 5$.
Hence, B's age $= 2x = 10$ years.

27. Let the mother's present age be x years. Then, the person's present age $= \left(\frac{2}{5}x\right)$ years.
$$\therefore \left(\frac{2}{5}x+8\right) = \frac{1}{2}(x+8)$$
$\Rightarrow 2(2x + 40) = 5(x + 8) \Rightarrow x = 40$.

28. Rahim $-$ Quasab $=$ Rahim $-$ Tanveer
$\Rightarrow$ Quasab $=$ Tanveer
Also, Rahim $+$ Tanveer $= 50$
$\Rightarrow$ Rahim $+$ Quasab $= 50$.
So, (Rahim $-$ Quasab) cannot be determined.

29. Let the son's present age be x years.
Then, $(38 - x) = x$
$\Rightarrow$ $2x = 38$
$\Rightarrow$ $x = 19$.
$\therefore$ Son's age 5 years back $= (19 - 5)$ years $= 14$ years.

30. Mother's age when Asha's brother was born $= 36$ years.
Father's age when Asha's brother was born $= (38 + 4)$ years $= 42$ years.
$\therefore$ Required difference $= (42 - 36)$ years $= 6$ years.

❑❑❑

5 PERCENTAGE

IMPORTANT FACTS

To solve quickly the problems related to percentage, remember following rules:

Rule 1:

(*a*) Of the given two numbers if the first is $x\%$ more than the second, then the second will be $\left(\frac{100 \times x}{100 + x}\right)\%$ less than the first.

(*b*) Of the given two numbers if the first is $x\%$ less than the second, then the second will be $\left(\frac{100 \times x}{100 - x}\right)\%$ more than the first.

(*c*) If two numbers are respectively $x\%$ and $y\%$ more than a third number, then the first number will be $\left(\frac{100 + x}{100 + y} \times 100\right)\%$ of the second.

(*d*) If two numbers are respectively $x\%$ and $y\%$ less than a third number, then the first number will be $\left(\frac{100 - x}{100 - y} \times 100\right)\%$ of the second.

Rule 2 :

(*a*) If a number or quantity is increased by $x\%$ then in order to restore its original value it must be decreased by $\left[\frac{100 \times x}{100 + x}\right]\%$.

(*b*) If a number or quantity is decreased by $x\%$ then in order to restore its original value it must be increased by $\left[\frac{100 \times x}{100 - x}\right]\%$.

Rule 3 :

(*a*) If a number is successively increased by $x\%$ and $y\%$ then a single equivalent increase in that number will be $\left(x + y + \frac{xy}{100}\right)\%$.

(*b*) If two successive discounts of $x\%$ and $y\%$ are allowed on a particular amount, then a single discount that is equivalent to the two successive discounts will be $\left(x + y - \frac{xy}{100}\right)\%$.

(*c*) If a number is successively increased by $x\%$, $y\%$ and $z\%$, then a single equivalent increase in that number will be $\left[(x + y + z) + \left(\frac{xy + yz + zx}{100}\right) + \frac{(xyz)}{10000}\right]\%$.

(*d*) If three successive discounts of $x\%$, $y\%$ and $z\%$ are allowed on an amount, then a single discount that is equivalent to the three successive discounts will be $\left[x + y + z - \frac{(xy + yz + zx)}{100} + \frac{xyz}{10000}\right]\%$.

Rule 4 :

(*a*) If a number is increased by $x\%$ and thereafter reduced by $x\%$, then the number will be reduced by $\left(\frac{x^2}{100}\right)$ per cent.

(*b*) If a number is reduced by $x\%$ and thereafter increased by $x\%$ then the number will be reduced by $\left(\frac{x^2}{100}\right)$ per cent.

(*c*) If due to an increase of $x\%$ in the selling price of certain commodity the sell/consumption of the commodity decreases by $y\%$, then gross receipts on account of sale of that commodity will be increased or decreased by $\left(x - y - \frac{xy}{100}\right)\%$, where $x > y$ and will be decreased by $\left(y - x + \frac{xy}{100}\right)\%$, where $y > x$.

SOLVED EXAMPLES

Example 1: If the numerator of a fraction is increased by 200% and the denominator is increased by 400%. The resultant fraction is $1\frac{1}{20}$. What was the original fraction?

Solution: Let original fraction = $\frac{x}{y}$; then

$$\frac{x+2x}{y+4y} = \frac{21}{20}$$

$$\frac{3x}{5y} = \frac{21}{20}$$

$$\frac{x}{y} = \frac{21\times5}{20\times3} = \frac{7}{4} = 1\frac{3}{4}$$

Example 2: In a class of 65 students and 4 teachers, each student got sweets that are 20% of the total number of students and each teacher got sweets that are 40% of the total number of students. How many sweets were there?

Solution: The share of each student = $\frac{20}{100}\times65$ = 13 sweets

The share of each teacher = $\frac{40}{100}\times65$ = 26 sweets

Total number of sweets = 65 × 13 + 4 × 26 = 845 + 104 = 949.

Example 3: Bovina spent ₹ 44,668/- on her air tickets, ₹ 56,732/- on buying gifts for the family members and the remaining 22% of the total amount had as cash with her. What was the total amount?

Solution: Let total amount = ₹ x ; then

$$\frac{78}{100}\times x = 44668 + 56732$$

$$\Rightarrow x = \frac{101400\times100}{78} = ₹\ 1{,}30{,}000.$$

Example 4: Rubina decided to donate 16% of her monthly salary to an NGO. On the day of donation she changed her mind and donated ₹ 6,567/- which was 75% of what she had decided earlier. How much is Rubina's monthly salary?

Solution: Let her monthly salary be ₹ x ; then

$$\frac{16}{100}\times\frac{75}{100}\times x = 6567$$

$$\Rightarrow \frac{3}{25}x = 6567$$

$$\Rightarrow x = \frac{6567\times25}{3} = ₹\ 54725$$

Thus, her monthly salary = ₹ 54725.

MULTIPLE CHOICE QUESTIONS

1. Mr. Rajesh spent 20% of his monthly income on grocery and household expenses. Out of the remaining he spent 25% on children's education 20% on transport and 15% on entertainment. He is left with an amount of ₹ 14,400 after incurring above expenses. What was his monthly income?

A. ₹ 45,000
B. ₹ 24,000
C. ₹ 36,000
D. ₹ 32,000

2. Number of students in a school in June every year increases by 10% from the previous year. If the school had 2,400 students in 2009, how many students did it have in June 2011?

A. 2,840 B. 2,880
C. 2,904 D. 2,920

3. On a test consisting of 150 questions, Reema answered 40% of the first 75 questions correctly. What per cent of the other 75 questions does she need to answer correctly for her grade on the entire exam to be 60%?

A. 80 B. 70
C. 40 D. 50

4. If the numerator of a fraction is increased by 200% and the denominator is increased by 300%. The resultant fraction is $\frac{9}{17}$. What was the original fraction?

A. $\frac{11}{17}$ B. $\frac{9}{11}$
C. $\frac{13}{17}$ D. None of these

5. One-sixth of a number is 53. What will 57% of that number be?

A. 181.26 B. 136.74
C. 197.16 D. 149.46

6. Mrs. Sudha Jain invests 14% of her monthly salary, *i.e.* ₹ 7,014 in Insurance Policies. Later she invests 21% of her monthly salary on Family Mediclaim Policies; also she invests another 6.5% of her salary on Mutual Funds. What is the total annual amount invested by Mrs. Sudha Jain?

A. ₹ 25,050 B. ₹ 50,100
C. ₹ 2,42,550 D. ₹ 2,49,498

7. A sum of ₹ 817 is divided among A, B and C such that 'A' receives 25% more than 'B' and 'B' receives 25% less than 'C'. What is the 'A's share in the amount?

A. ₹ 228 B. ₹ 247
C. ₹ 285 D. ₹ 304

8. Ms. Sujan invests 7% *i.e.* ₹ 2170 of her monthly salary in mutual funds. Later she invests 18% of her monthly salary in recurring deposits also, she invests 6% of her salary on NSC's. What is the total annual amount invested by Ms. Sujan?

A. ₹ 1,25,320 B. ₹ 1,13,520
C. ₹ 1,35,120 D. ₹ 1,15,320

9. What is the 30% of 40% of $\frac{2}{5}$th of 2500?

A. 500 B. 400
C. 360 D. 120

10. A sum of ₹ 731 is divided among A, B and C, such that 'A' receives 25% more than 'B' and 'B' receives 25% less than 'C'. What is C's share in the amount?

A. ₹ 172 B. ₹ 200
C. ₹ 262 D. None of these

11. Thirty five per cent of 740 is 34 more than a number. What is two-fifth of the number?

A. 45 B. 90
C. 180 D. 120

12. Ramu scored 456 marks in an exam and Shama got 54 per cent marks in the same exam which is 24 marks less than Ramu. If the minimum passing marks in the exam is 34 per cent, then how much more marks did Ramu score than the minimum passing marks?

A. 184 B. 196
C. 190 D. 180

13. Shreyas bought an article and sold for 125% of its cost price. What was the cost price of the article, if Shreyas sold it for ₹ 30,750?

A. ₹ 24,600 B. ₹ 25,640
C. ₹ 24,250 D. ₹ 23,200

14. When 20% of a number is added to another number the number increases by 50%. What is the respective ratio between the first and the second number?

A. 3 : 2
B. 2 : 3
C. 5 : 2
D. Cannot be determined

15. If a number is added to seven-ninth of thirty five per cent of 900, the value so obtained is 325. What is the number?

A. 60 B. 120
C. 90 D. None of these

16. The difference between 60% of a number and 20% of the same number is 316. What is 35% of that number?

A. 270.5 B. 285.5
C. 276.5 D. 275

17. In an examination it is required to get 36% of the aggregate marks to pass. A student gets 174 marks and is declared failed by 96 marks. What is the maximum aggregate marks a student can get?

A. 750
B. 650
C. 600
D. Cannot be determined

18. There is a rebate of 15%, if electric bills are paid in time. A man got a rebate of ₹ 54 by paying the bill in time. What was his electric bill in rupees?

A. 300 B. 350
C. 360 D. 380

19. A number is increased by 20% then again by 20%. By what per cent the original number is changed?

A. 40% B. 50%
C. 44% D. 36%

20. In an examination 62% of the examinees got plucked in Mathematics, 52% passed in English and 22% failed in both the subjects. If 108 is the number of examinees who passed in both the subjects then find out the total number of candidates—

A. 1200 B. 900
C. 800 D. 1000

21. Ramesh gets 10% more than Mohan. How much per cent will Mohan get less than Ramesh?

A. 10% B. 9%
C. $9\frac{1}{11}$% D. 11%

22. By what quantity the use of coal is to be reduced to keep one's family budget same when the price of coal is increased by 25%?

A. 25% B. 20%
C. 30% D. 15%

23. The percentage equivalent to the fraction 3/4 is :

A. 75% B. 25%
C. 60% D. 80%

24. If each side of a square be increased by 10%, what is the percentage increase of the area?

A. 21% B. 10%
C. 20% D. 100%

25. Suppose 35% of the males are married. Find the percentage of unmarried females in the total population, if $\frac{5}{7}$ part of the population in a village are males.

A. 21%
B. 25%
C. $3\frac{4}{7}$%
D. 28%

ANSWERS

1	2	3	4	5	6	7	8	9	10
A	C	A	D	A	D	C	D	D	D
11	12	13	14	15	16	17	18	19	20
B	A	A	C	D	C	A	C	C	B
21	22	23	24	25					
C	B	A	A	C					

SOME SELECTED EXPLANATORY ANSWERS

1. Let Rajesh's monthly income be ₹ 100.

∴ Expenditure on grocery and household expenses = ₹ 20.

Expenditure on education etc.

$= \frac{80 \times 60}{100} =$ ₹ 48

Saving = 100 − 20 − 48 = ₹ 32

Now,

when saving ₹ 32 then income = ₹ 100

when saving ₹ 14400 then income

$= \frac{100}{32} \times 14400 =$ ₹ 45000

2. Required number of students

$= 2400\left(1+\frac{10}{100}\right)^2 \quad \left[P = P_0\left(1+\frac{R}{100}\right)^T\right]$

$= 2400 \times \frac{11}{10} \times \frac{11}{10} = 2904.$

3. Required % $= \frac{150 \times \frac{60}{100} - 75 \times \frac{40}{100}}{75} \times 100\%$

$= \frac{90-30}{75} \times 100\% = 80\%$

4. Let the fraction be $\frac{x}{y}$

$\therefore \quad \frac{x+2x}{y+3y} = \frac{9}{17}$

$\Rightarrow \quad \frac{3x}{4y} = \frac{9}{17}$

$\therefore \quad \frac{x}{y} = \frac{9}{17} \times \frac{4}{3} = \frac{12}{17}$

5. Let the number be x

$\because \quad \frac{x}{6} = 53$

$\Rightarrow \quad x = 53 \times 6$

$\therefore \quad x \times \frac{57}{100} = \frac{53 \times 6 \times 57}{100} = 181.26$

6. Let the monthly salary be ₹ x

$\because \quad x \times \frac{14}{100} = 7014$

$\Rightarrow \quad x = \frac{7014 \times 100}{14} =$ ₹ 50100

∴ Total amount of annual investment

$= \frac{(14+21+6.5)}{100} \times 50100 \times 12 =$ ₹ 249498

8. Monthly salary of Ms. Sujan $= \frac{2170 \times 100}{7}$

= ₹ 31,000.

∴ Total money invested by her in a year

$= 31000 \times \frac{(7+18+6)}{100} \times 12$

= ₹ 9610 × 12

= ₹ 115320

9. $2500 \times \frac{30}{100} \times \frac{40}{100} \times \frac{2}{5} = 120.$

10. Let the share of C be ₹ x

∴ Share of B $= \frac{75x}{100} =$ ₹ $0.75x$

and share of A $= 0.75x \times \frac{125}{100} =$ ₹ $0.9375x$

$\because 0.9375x + 0.75x + x = 731$

$\therefore \quad x = \frac{731}{2.6875} =$ ₹ 272

11. Number $= 740 \times \frac{35}{100} - 34 = 225$

$\therefore \quad \frac{2}{5}$ of the number $= 225 \times \frac{2}{5} = 90.$

12. Let the maximum marks of the eximination be x. Then, from question—

$\because \quad 54\%$ of $x = 456 - 24 = 432$

$x = \frac{432 \times 100}{54} = 800$

$\Rightarrow$ Minimum passing marks = $\frac{34}{100}\times 800$

= 272

$\therefore$ Required difference = 456 – 272 = 184.

13. C.P. of the article = $\frac{30750\times 100}{125}$ = ₹ 24600.

14. Let the two numbers be x and y respectively. Then,

$\because \quad \frac{20x}{100}+y = y+\frac{50y}{100}$

$\Rightarrow \quad \frac{x}{5}+y = y+\frac{y}{2}$

$\Rightarrow \quad \frac{x}{5} = \frac{y}{2}$

$\Rightarrow \quad \frac{x}{y} = \frac{5}{2}$

$\therefore \quad x : y = 5 : 2$

15. Let the number be x.

$\because \quad 900\times\frac{35}{100}\times\frac{7}{9}+x = 325$

$\therefore \quad x = 325 - 245 = 80$

16. Let the number be 'n', then from question,

$\because$ (60% – 20%) of n = 316

$\Rightarrow$ 40% of n = 316

$\Rightarrow$ 35% of n = $\frac{316}{40}\times 35$

= 276.5

17. Let the maximum marks of the exam. paper = n.

Then from question,

$n\times\frac{36}{100} = 174 + 96$

$\Rightarrow \quad n = \frac{270\times 100}{36}$

$\therefore \quad n = 750$

18. 15% = ₹ 54

100% = ₹ $\frac{54}{15}\times 100$

= ₹ 360

19. Let the first number be 100.

After 20% increase, the number becomes = 120

After again 20% increase, the number becomes

$= 120\times\frac{120}{100} = 144$

$\therefore$ Original number is changed by (144 – 100)% = 44%

20. Failed in Mathematics = 62%

Failed in English = (100 – 52)% = 48%

Failed in both = 22%

Failed only in Maths = (62 – 22)% = 40%

Failed only in English = (48 – 22)% = 26%

$\therefore$ Total failed = (40 + 26 + 22)%

= 88%

$\therefore$ Passed in both = (100 – 88)% = 12%

12% = 108

100% = $\frac{108}{12}\times 100$ = 900

21. Ramesh gets = 110,

Mohan = 100

Required percentage = $\frac{10}{110}\times 100 = 9\frac{1}{11}\%$.

22. Required percentage = $\frac{25}{(100+25)}\times 100$

$= \frac{25}{125}\times 100 = 20\%$.

23. Required percentage = $\frac{3}{4}\times 100\% = 75\%$.

24. Percentage increase in area

$= \frac{(110)^2-(100)^2}{(100)^2}\times 100\%$

$= \frac{210\times 10}{100\times 100}\times 100\% = 21\%$.

❑❑❑

6 PROFIT & LOSS

GENERAL FORMULAE

1. $\text{Gain \%} = \left(\frac{\text{Gain}}{\text{C.P.}} \times 100\right)$
2. $\text{Loss \%} = \left(\frac{\text{Loss}}{\text{C.P.}} \times 100\right)$
3. $\text{S.P.} = \left(\frac{100 + \text{Gain \%}}{100}\right) \times \text{C.P.}$
4. $\text{S.P.} = \left(\frac{100 - \text{Loss \%}}{100}\right) \times \text{C.P.}$
5. $\text{C.P.} = \left(\frac{100}{100 + \text{Gain \%}}\right) \times \text{S.P.}$
6. $\text{C.P.} = \left(\frac{100}{100 - \text{Loss \%}}\right) \times \text{S.P.}$

Formulae For Short Cut Solution

Type 1 :

Conditional Tricks

If cost price of X goods = Selling price of Y goods then,

I. $\text{Gain \%} = \frac{X - Y}{Y} \times 100$ (In case of $X > Y$)

II. $\text{Loss \%} = \frac{Y - X}{Y} \times 100$ (in case of $X < Y$)

Type 2 :

I. If X_1 and X_2 both are the rate of gain or both are the rate of loss, then, $\text{C.P.} = \left(\frac{100}{X_1 - X_2}\right) \times$ amount of difference between S.Ps.

II. If in X_1 and X_2 one is the rate of gain and another is the rate of loss, then $\text{C.P.} = \left(\frac{100}{X_1 + X_2}\right) \times$ amount of difference between S.P.s.

Type 3 :

Miscellaneous Tricks

I. When a man buys two things on equal price and in those things one is sold on the profit of X % and another is sold on the loss of X %, then there is no loss or gain percent.

II. When a man sells two things at the same price each and in this process his loss on first thing is X % and gain on second thing is X % then in such type of questions, there is always a loss.

$$\text{Loss \%} = X\text{ \% of } X = \frac{X^2}{100} = \left(\frac{X}{10}\right)^2$$

III. Dishonest dealer and less weight

$$\text{Gain} = \frac{\text{Error}}{\text{True value} - \text{Error}} \times 100$$

Where, error = 100 gm – used weight of goods

IV. If A sells a thing to B at a gain of R_1 %, B sells it to C at a gain of R_2 % and C sells it to D at a gain of R_3 % Then, cost price of D = Cost Price of A $(1 + R_1/100)(1 + R_2/100)(1 + R_3/100)$

V. If A sells a thing, to B at a loss of R %, B sells it to C at a loss of R % and C sells it to D at a loss of R % then, Cost price of D = Cost price of A $(1 - R_1/100)(1 - R_2/100)(1 - R_3/100)$

SOLVED EXAMPLES

Example 1: Suman purchased an item of ₹ 72,000 and sold it at a loss of 27 percent. With that amount she purchased another item and sold it at a gain of 30 percent. What is her overall profit/loss?

Solution: First S.P. = $\frac{72000 \times 73}{100}$ = ₹ 52560

Second S.P. = $\frac{52560 \times 130}{100}$ = ₹ 68328

Loss = 72000 – 68328 = ₹ 3672.

Example 2: Mr. Babulal purchased 100 pieces of an article at the rate of ₹ 480 per piece. He then listed the price so as to gain a profit of 25%. While selling the articles he offered a discount of 5%. What is the percentage of profit earned in the deal?

Solution: Profit per cent = $\left(x+y+\frac{xy}{100}\right)\%$

Here, $x = 25\%$, $y = -5\%$

$= \left(25-5-\frac{25\times5}{100}\right)\% = 18.75\%.$

Example 3: The profit earned after selling an article for ₹ 625 is the same as loss incurred after selling the article for ₹ 435. What is the cost price of the article?

Solution: C.P. of the article = $\frac{625+435}{2}$ = ₹ 530.

Example 4: A man sold an item for ₹ 6,750 at a loss of 25%. What will be the selling price of same item if he sells it at a profit of 15%?

Solution: C.P. of the item = $\frac{6750\times100}{75}$ = ₹ 9000

∴ Required S.P. of the item = $\frac{9000\times115}{100}$ = ₹ 10350.

Example 5: A man sold a wristwatch for ₹ 2,400 at a loss of twenty-five per cent. At what rate should he have sold the wristwatch to earn a profit of twenty five per cent?

Solution: C.P. of the wristwatch = $\frac{100\times2400}{100-25}$ = ₹ 3200

∴ Required S.P. of the wristwatch

= $\frac{125\times3200}{100}$ = ₹ 4000.

MULTIPLE CHOICE QUESTIONS

1. What profit / loss per cent did Raveena earn if she purchased an item of ₹ 5,600 and sold it at three-fourth of its cost price?
   A. Loss of 20 per cent B. Gain of 25 per cent
   C. Neither gain nor loss D. Loss of 15 per cent
2. By what per cent must the cost price be raised in fixing the sale price in order that there may be a profit of 20% after allowing a commission of 10%?
   A. 30% B. $33\frac{1}{3}\%$
   C. 25% D. 40%
3. A sold a watch to B at a loss of 10%. B sold it to C at a gain of 10%. If A had sold at the same price which C paid for it, what would have been his gain or loss per cent?
   A. 1% loss B. 10% gain
   C. 12% gain D. 11% loss
4. A shopkeeper purchased two cycles at ₹ 1600 and sold the first at 10% profit and second one at 20% profit. If he could sell the first cycle at a profit of 20% and the second one at a profit of 10% then he could get ₹ 5 more. What will be the cost price of each in rupees?
   A. 925, 675 B. 1000, 600
   C. 825, 775 D. 900, 700
5. A person makes a profit of 25%, by selling an article for ₹ 35.50. By how much should he increase his selling price so as to make a profit of 40%?
   A. ₹ 4.60 B. ₹ 4.26
   C. ₹ 4 D. ₹ 3.90
6. A man bought a pen and sold it at a loss of 20%. If he had bought it for 30% less and sold it for ₹ 60 more, he would have made a profit of 50%. Find the C.P. of the article.
   A. ₹ 200 B. ₹ 140
   C. ₹ 240 D. ₹ 210
7. The cost price of 15 article is equal to S.P. of 10 articles. The gain percent is:
   A. 50% B. 25%
   C. $16\frac{2}{3}\%$ D. 100%
8. Raghav bought a radio with 20% discount on the labelled price. Had he bought it with 25% discount, he would have saved ₹ 500. At what price did he buy the radio?
   A. ₹ 1000 B. ₹ 500
   C. ₹ 5000 D. ₹ 10000
9. A man buys mangoes at ₹ 5 a dozen and an equal number at ₹ 4 a dozen. He sells them at ₹ 5.50 a dozen and makes a profit of ₹ 50. How many mangoes does he buy?
   A. 30 dozens B. 40 dozens
   C. 50 dozens D. 60 dozens
10. How many for a rupee must a shopkeeper sell to gain 25%, if he bought toys at 10 for a rupee?
    A. 10 B. 9
    C. 8 D. 6
11. Suppose the ratio of two investment be 3 : 2. What is the gain or loss on the two investments taken together if a man loses 20% on an investment but gains 25% on another investment.
    A. 2.5% B. 0.2%
    C. 2% D. 3%

12. A shopkeeper gives 12% additional discount after giving an initial discount of 20% on the labelled price of a T.V. If the sale price of the T.V. is ₹ 704. What is the labelled price of the T.V?

A. ₹ 844.80　B. ₹ 929.28
C. ₹ 1000　D. ₹ 900

13. By selling 12 oranges for a rupee, a man loses 10%. How many oranges for a rupee be sold to gain 20%?

A. 5　B. 4
C. 9　D. 12

14. A dishonest shopkeeper professes to sell pulses at his cost price but uses a false weight of 950 gm for each kilogram. His gain per cent is :

A. $5\frac{5}{19}\%$　B. 19%
C. $4\frac{5}{19}\%$　D. 95%

15. Sushil bought two boxes for ₹ 1300. He sold one box at a profit of 20% and the other box at a loss of 12%. If the selling price of both boxes is the same. Then the cost price of each box is :

A. ₹ 850, ₹ 650　B. ₹ 750, ₹ 750
C. ₹ 550, ₹ 750　D. ₹ 750, ₹ 650

16. A producer sells his articles to a wholesaler at 10% profit. The wholesaler sells it to a retailer at 20%. The retailer sells it to a customer at ₹ 41.25 making 25% profit. Then the cost of production is :

A. ₹ 52　B. ₹ 132
C. ₹ 110　D. ₹ 25

17. A bought two oxen for ₹ 1080. He sold one at a loss of 5% and the other at a gain of 7%. He neither gained nor lost in this transaction. C.P. of each is:

A. ₹ 630, ₹ 450
B. ₹ 680, ₹ 400
C. ₹ 600, ₹ 480
D. ₹ 540, ₹ 540

18. A businessman makes a profit of 20% in the first year. In the subsequent year, he had a loss of 25% on the capital which he had at the beginning of the second year. His overall gain or loss per cent in the capital is:

A. 120%　B. 90%
C. 100%　D. 10%

19. A co-operative society manufactures note books. It makes a profit of ₹ 9.00 when it sells 100 copies to a local shop. The local shop, in turn, makes a profit of ₹ 2 on selling 50 copies at 69 paisa per copy. How much did it cost the society to manufacture 100 note books?

A. ₹ 65　B. ₹ 55
C. ₹ 56　D. ₹ 32.50

20. A man marks his goods at a price that would give him 40% profit. He sells three-fourths of his goods at the marked price. For the remaining, he has to lower the marked price by 40%. His per cent profit on the entire transaction is:

A. 21%　B. 84%
C. 52%　D. 26%

21. By reducing the selling price of an article by ₹ 80 a gain of 5% turns into a loss of 5%. Then the original selling price of the article is:

A. ₹ 1050　B. ₹ 525
C. ₹ 510　D. ₹ 515

22. A man bought a horse and a carriage for ₹ 3000. He sold the horse at a gain of 20% and carriage at a loss of 10%, thereby gaining 2% on the whole. Then the cost of the horse is:

A. ₹ 3060　B. ₹ 1200
C. ₹ 2100　D. ₹ 3000

23. If 20% more would be gained by selling a price of cloth for ₹ 45.50 than by selling it for ₹ 39. What per cent would be gained by selling if for ₹ 42.25?

A. 32%　B. 42%
C. 30%　D. 35%

24. There would be 10% loss if rice is sold at ₹ 5.40 per kg. At what price per kg should it be sold to earn a profit of 20%?

A. ₹ 6
B. ₹ 6.48
C. ₹ 7.02
D. ₹ 7.20

25. A fruitseller buys lemons at 2 for a rupee and sells them at five for three rupees. His gain per cent is:

A. 10%　B. 15%
C. 20%　D. 25%

ANSWERS

1	2	3	4	5	6	7	8	9	10
A	B	A	C	B	C	A	D	C	C
11	12	13	14	15	16	17	18	19	20
C	C	C	A	C	D	A	D	C	D
21	22	23	24	25					
B	B	C	D	C					

SOME SELECTED EXPLANATORY ANSWERS

1. S.P. of the item $= 5600 \times \frac{3}{4} =$ ₹ 4200

$\therefore$ Loss % $= \frac{5600-4200}{5600} \times 100 = 25$

2. Let $x\%$ must the cost price be raised

$\therefore$ S.P. $= (100 + x)$

$\because (100+x)\frac{90}{100} = 120$

$\Rightarrow 3x = 100$

$\therefore x = 33\frac{1}{3}\%$.

3. Let A's C.P. = ₹ 100

A's S.P. $= 100 \times \frac{90}{100}$;

B's S.P. $= 100 \times \frac{90}{100} \times \frac{110}{100}$

C paid = B's S.P. $= 100 \times \frac{90}{100} \times \frac{110}{100}$

$= 99$

If A had sold at ₹ 99

Then, his loss = $(100 - 99)\% = 1\%$.

4. Let the C.P. of 1st cycle = ₹ x

and C.P. of 2nd cycle = ₹ $(1600 - x)$

Total S.P. in 1st case

$= x \times \frac{110}{100} + (1600 - x) \times \frac{120}{100}$

$= \frac{12 \times 1600 - x}{10}$

Total S.P. in 2nd case

$= x \times \frac{120}{100} + (1600 - x) \times \frac{110}{100}$

$= \frac{11 \times 1600 + x}{10}$

$\because \frac{11 \times 1600 + x}{10} - \frac{12 \times 1600 - x}{10} = 5$

$\therefore x = \frac{1650}{2} = 825$

C.P. of 1st cycle = 825

C.P. of 2nd cycle = 1600 − 825 = 775.

5. Let new S.P. be ₹ x

Then (100 + Gain%) : (1st S.P.)

= (100 + Gain%) : (2nd S.P.)

$125 : 35.50 = 140 : x$

$\Rightarrow x = \frac{35.50 \times 140}{125} =$ ₹ 39.76

$\therefore$ Increased in S.P. = ₹ (39.76 − 35.50)

= ₹ 4.26.

6. Let original C.P. be ₹ x

S.P. = 80% of $x = \frac{80x}{100} = \frac{4x}{5}$

New C.P. = 70% of $x = \frac{70x}{100} = \frac{7x}{10}$

New S.P. = 150% of $\frac{7x}{10} = \frac{21x}{20}$

$\therefore \frac{21x}{20} - \frac{4x}{5} = 60$

$\Rightarrow \frac{x}{4} = 60$

$x = 240$

7. Let C.P. of each article be ₹ 1

Then C.P. of 10 article = ₹ 10

S.P. of 10 article = ₹ 15

Gain % $= \left(\frac{15-10}{10} \times 100\right)\% = \left(\frac{5}{10} \times 100\right)\%$

$=$ 50%.

8. Let the labelled price be x

$\therefore$ S.P. = 80% of $x = \frac{4x}{5}$

New S.P. = 75% of $x = \frac{3x}{4}$

$\therefore \frac{4x}{5} - \frac{3x}{4} = 500$

$\Rightarrow x =$ ₹ 10000.

9. C.P. of 2 dozens of mangoes = ₹ (5 + 4)

= ₹ 9

S.P. of 2 dozens of mangoes = ₹ 11

2 dozens of mangoes are bought at a profit of ₹ 2.

If profit is ₹ 50, mangoes bought $= \frac{2}{2} \times 50$

= 50 dozens.

10. C.P. of 10 toys = ₹ 1

Gain = 25%

S.P. of 10 toys $= \frac{125}{100} \times 1 =$ ₹ $\frac{5}{4}$

Thus S.P. of 10 toys is ₹ $\frac{5}{4}$

$\therefore$ For ₹ 1, Number of toys $= 10 \times \frac{4}{5} = 8$

So he must sell 8 toys for a rupee.

11. Let the investments are $3x$ and $2x$

Then total investment = $5x$

$$\text{Receipt} = (80\% \text{ of } 3x + 125\% \text{ of } 2x)$$
$$= (2.4x + 2.5x) = 4.9x$$

$$\therefore \quad \text{loss} = \left(\frac{0.1x}{5x}\times 100\right)\% = 2\%$$

12. Let the labelled price of the T.V be ₹ x

$$\text{Initial S.P.} = 80\% \text{ of } x = \frac{80x}{100}$$

$$\text{New S.P.} = 88\% \text{ of } \frac{80x}{100}$$

$$= \frac{88}{100}\times\frac{80x}{100}$$

$$= \frac{704x}{1000}$$

From question,

$$\frac{704x}{1000} = 704$$

$$704x = 704 \times 1000$$

$$\Rightarrow \quad x = 1000$$

∴ The labelled price of the T.V. = ₹ 1000.

14. Let C.P. of 1 gm pulses be ₹ 1

∴ C.P. of 950 gm pulses = ₹ 950

S.P. of 950 gm = C.P. of 1 kg

= C.P. of 1000 gm = ₹ 1000

∴ Gain = ₹ (1000 – 950) = ₹ 50

$$\therefore \quad \text{Gain } \% = \frac{50}{950}\times 100 = 5\frac{5}{19}\%.$$

17. From question,

∴ Loss on one = Gain on other

∴ 5% of the C.P. of one = 7% of the C.P. of the other

$$\Rightarrow \quad \frac{\text{C.P. of 1st}}{\text{C.P. of 2nd}}$$

$$= \frac{7\%}{5\%} = \frac{7}{5}$$

or, C.P. of 1st : C.P. of 2nd = 7 : 5

Divide ₹ 1080 in the ratio of 7 : 5

$$\therefore \text{ C.P. of the 1st} = \frac{7}{12}\times 1080 = ₹\ 630.$$

$$\text{and C.P. of the 2nd} = ₹\ \frac{5}{12}\times 1080 = ₹\ 450.$$

18. Let his capital at the beginning of first year be ₹ 100

Profit during first year = 20% of ₹ 100 = ₹ 20

∴ Capital at the beginning of the second year

= ₹ (100 + 20) = ₹ 120

Loss during second year = 25% of ₹ 120

$$= ₹\left(120\times\frac{25}{100}\right) = ₹\ 30$$

∴ Capital at the end of second year

= ₹ (120 – 30) = ₹ 90

∴ Loss = ₹ (100 – 90) = ₹ 10

$$\text{Overall Loss \% on his capital} = \left(\frac{10}{100}\times 100\right)\%$$

= 10%.

19. The local shop sells 50 copies @ 69 paisa per copy

= ₹ (50 × 0.69) = ₹ 34.50

His profit = ₹ 2

∴ The local shop purchases 50 copies for

= S.P. – Profit = ₹ (34.50 – 2) = ₹ 32.50

∴ The local shop purchases 100 copies for

$$= ₹\left(\frac{32.50}{50}\times 100\right) = ₹\ 65$$

∴ Co-operative society sells 100 copies for ₹ 65

Profit = ₹ 9

∴ Co-operative society manufactures 100 copies for

= ₹ (65 – 9) = ₹ 56.

23. Let C.P. of cloth be ₹ x. Then $x\times\frac{20}{100}$

= ₹ (45.50 – 39) = ₹ 6.50

$$\Rightarrow \quad x = \frac{6.50\times 100}{20} = ₹\ 32.50$$

Gain = ₹ (42.25 – 32.50) = ₹ 9.75

$$\therefore \text{ Gain\%} = \frac{9.75}{32.50}\times 100 = 30\%.$$

24. 90 : 5.40 :: 120 : x

$$\therefore x = \frac{5.40\times 120}{90} = 7.20.$$

So, the rice must be sold at ₹ 7.20 per kg.

25. Suppose he buys 10 lemons.

$$\text{C.P.} = ₹\left(\frac{10}{2}\right) = ₹\ 5,\ \text{S.P.} = ₹\left(\frac{3}{5}\times 10\right) = ₹\ 6.$$

$$\text{Gain\%} = \left(\frac{1}{5}\times 100\right)\% = 20\%.$$

❑❑❑

7 MIXTURE & ALLIGATION

Alligation deals with calculation of values or properties of a mixture. Alligation is the rule that enables us—

(1) to find the proportion in which the two or more ingredients at the given prices must be mixed to yield a mixture at the given price. This is termed as "Alligation Alternate".

(2) to calculate the average or mean value of a mixture when the prices of two or more ingredients which are to be mixed together and proportion in which they are to be mixed are given. This is termed as "Alligation Medial".

1. Rule of Alligation:

$$\frac{\text{A of Cheap mixture}}{\text{A of Dearer mixture}} = \frac{\text{CP of Dearer} - \text{Mean Price}}{\text{Mean Price} - \text{CP of Cheaper}}$$

Here cost price of unit quantity of the mixture is called the *Mean Price.*

The above rule may be represented schematically as under:

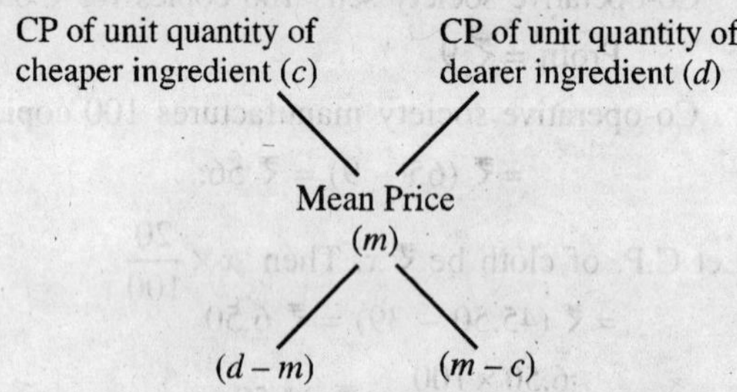

(Cheaper quantity) : (Dearer quantity) $= (d - m) : (m - c)$

This relationship is very helpful in solving problems on mixture involving percentage values, rates, prices, speeds etc.

2. m gm of sugar solution has x % sugar in it. To increase the sugar content in the solution to y %,

quantity of sugar need to be added $= \dfrac{m(y-x)}{100-y}$

3. A vessel contains x litres of liquid A. y litres are withdrawn and replaced by liquid B. Next y litres of the mixture is withdrawn and again replaced by liquid B. This operation is repeated n times.

$$\frac{\text{Quantity of liquid A left after } n\text{th operation}}{\text{Whole quantity of liquid A initially present}} = \left(\frac{x-y}{x}\right)^n \text{ or } \left(1-\frac{y}{x}\right)^n$$

SOLVED EXAMPLES

Example 1: Find the quantities of two types of wheat, one @ ₹ 6 per kg and the other @ ₹ 4 per kg. to get 20 kgs. of wheat mixture worth ₹ 4.5 per kg.

Solution:

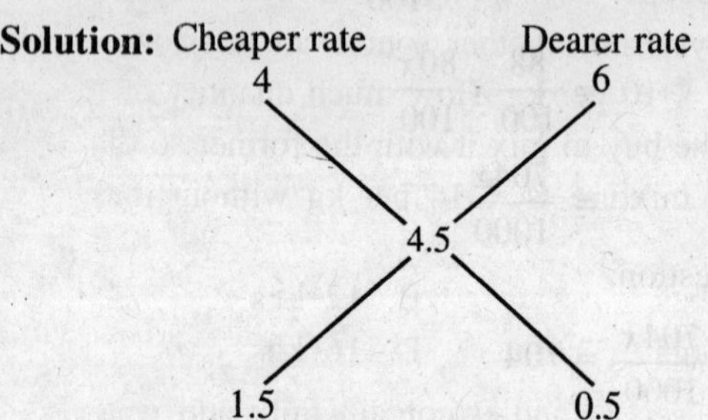

$$\frac{\text{Quantity of cheaper wheat}}{\text{Quantity of dearer wheat}} = \frac{1.5}{0.5} = \frac{3}{1}$$

Quantity of cheaper wheat $= \dfrac{3}{3+1} \times 20 = 15$ kgs

Quantity of dearer wheat $= \dfrac{1}{3+1} \times 20 = 5$ kgs.

Example 2: In what proportion water be mixed with pure milk in order to make a profit of 20% by selling it at cost price?

Solution: Let cost price of pure milk be Re. 1 per litre.

The SP of mixture = ₹ 1 per litre

Profit = 20%

So, CP of 1 litre of mixture $= ₹\left(1 \times \dfrac{100}{120}\right) = ₹\ \dfrac{5}{6}$

We assume that CP of 1 litre of water is zero.

(Water) Re. 0 (Pure Milk) Re. 1

(Mixture) Re. $\frac{5}{6}$

$\frac{1}{6}$ $\frac{5}{6}$

Using the rule of alligation on 1 litre,

$$\frac{\text{Quantity of water}}{\text{Quantity of pure milk}} = \frac{\frac{1}{6}}{\frac{5}{6}} = \frac{1}{5}$$

or, Ratio of water to pure milk in the mixture = 1 : 5.

MULTIPLE CHOICE QUESTIONS

1. In what proportion must tea at ₹ 62 per kg be mixed with tea at ₹ 72 per kg in order to obtain the mixture worth ₹ 65 per kg?

A. 4 : 6 B. 7 : 3
C. 2 : 3 D. 4 : 7

2. Find the quantity of rice @ ₹ 10 per kg. which should be mixed with 25 kgs of rice @ ₹ 8 per kg, so that on selling the mixture @ ₹ 15 per kg there is 80% profit.

A. 6 kgs B. 7 kgs
C. 3 kgs D. 5 kgs

3. A shopkeeper buys 26 kgs of milk @ ₹ 16 per kg. He also buys from another source an inferior quality of milk @ ₹ 10 per kg. How much quantity of the latter should he buy to mix it with the former so that he can sell the mixture @ ₹ 14 per kg without making any loss?

A. 13 kgs B. 12 kgs
C. 14 kgs D. 16 kgs

4. Two vessels A and B contain milk and water in the ratio 7 : 5 and 17 : 7 respectively. In what ratio mixtures from two vessels should be mixed to get a new mixture containing milk and water in the ratio 5 : 3?

A. 1 : 2 B. 2 : 1
C. 2 : 3 D. 3 : 2

5. Two vessels A and B contain mixture of milk and water in the ratio 4 : 1 and 9 : 11 respectively. They are mixed in the ratio of 3 : 2. Find the ratio of milk : water in the resulting mixture.

A. 34 : 16 B. 33 : 17
C. 16 : 34 D. 17 : 33

6. A person has two solutions of sugar with 30% and 50% concentration respectively. In what proportion should he mix two solutions to get 45% concentration in the resulting mixture?

A. 1 : 3 B. 3 : 1
C. 2 : 3 D. 3 : 2

7. 6 litres of milk and water mixture has 75% milk in it. How much milk should be added to the mixture to make it 90% pure?

A. 8 litres B. 9 litres
C. 10 litres D. 12 litres

8. In what ratio must water be added to spirit to gain 25% by selling it at cost price?

A. 1 : 4 B. 4 : 1
C. 3 : 4 D. 4 : 3

9. A shopkeeper has 50 kgs of rice. He sells a part of it at 20% profit and the rest at 40% profit. If he gains 25% on the whole, find the quantity of each part.

A. 12.5 kgs and 37.5 kgs
B. 37.5 kgs and 12.5 kgs
C. 23.5 kgs and 21.5 kgs
D. 21.5 kgs and 23.5 kgs

10. A shopkeeper has 100 kgs of tea. He sells a part of it at 20% profit and the rest at 5% loss. If his overall profit is 10%, find the quantity for each part.

A. 20 kgs B. 25 kgs
C. 30 kgs D. 40 kgs

ANSWERS

1	2	3	4	5	6	7	8	9	10
B	D	A	B	B	A	B	A	A	D

SOME SELECTED EXPLANATORY ANSWERS

1.

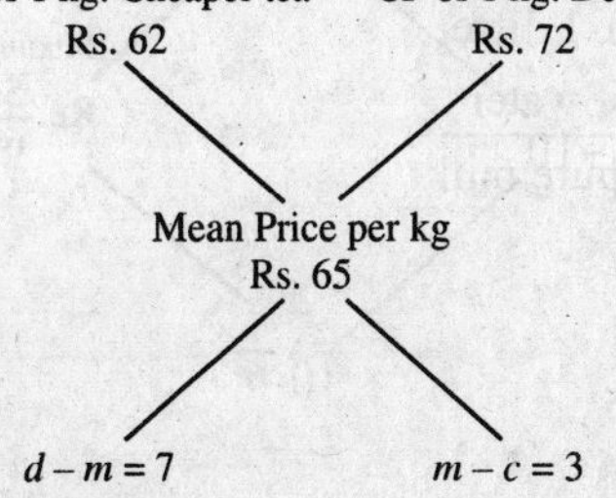

Using Alligation rule,

$$\frac{\text{Quantity of cheaper tea}}{\text{Quantity of dearer tea}} = \frac{d-m}{m-c} = \frac{7}{3}$$

Therefore, they must be mixed in the ratio of 7 : 3.

2. Cost price of the mixture $= 15 \times \frac{100}{180}$

$= ₹\ \frac{25}{3}$ per kg

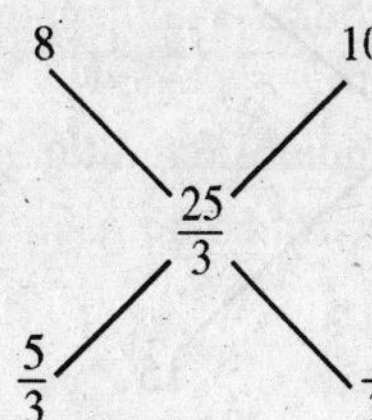

$$\frac{\text{Quantity of rice @ ₹ 8 per kg}}{\text{Quantity of rice @ ₹ 10 per kg}} = \frac{5/3}{1/3} = \frac{5}{1}$$

Quantity of rice @ ₹ 10 per kg = $25 \times \frac{1}{5}$
= 5 kgs.

3. 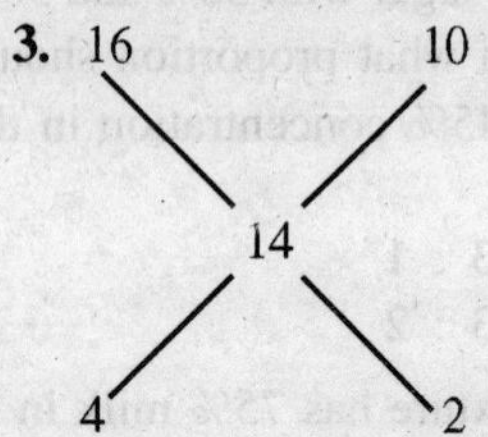

or 2 : 1, $\frac{\text{Quantity of milk @ ₹ 10 per kg}}{\text{Quantity of milk @ ₹ 16 per kg}} = \frac{1}{2}$

So, quantity of milk @ ₹ 10 per kg. = $\frac{26}{2}$ = 13 kgs.

4. First of all we write the fraction of milk present in three mixtures.

In A : $\frac{7}{12}$ In B : $\frac{17}{24}$

In combination of A and B : $\frac{5}{8}$

We now apply alligation rule on these fractions.

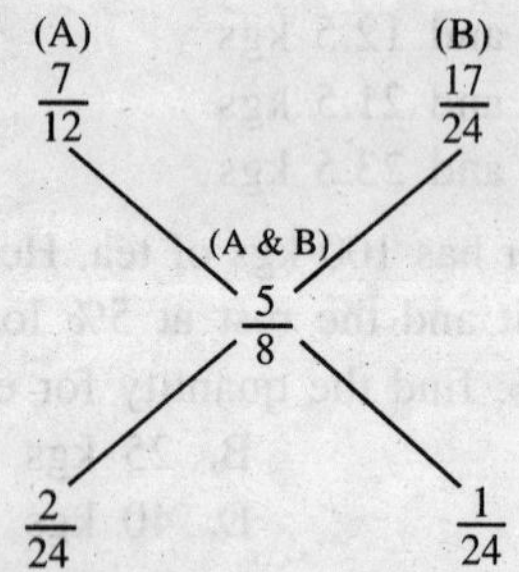

or, 2 : 1

So, Ratio of A : B = 2 : 1.

5. Fraction is *Milk* *Water*

A : $\frac{4}{5}$ $\frac{1}{5}$

B : $\frac{9}{20}$ $\frac{11}{20}$

(3A + 2B) = A and B : $\left(\frac{12}{5}+\frac{9}{10}\right)\left(\frac{3}{5}+\frac{11}{10}\right)$ $\frac{33}{10}$ $\frac{17}{10}$

So, Ratio of milk : water in the resulting mixture = 33 : 17.

6. 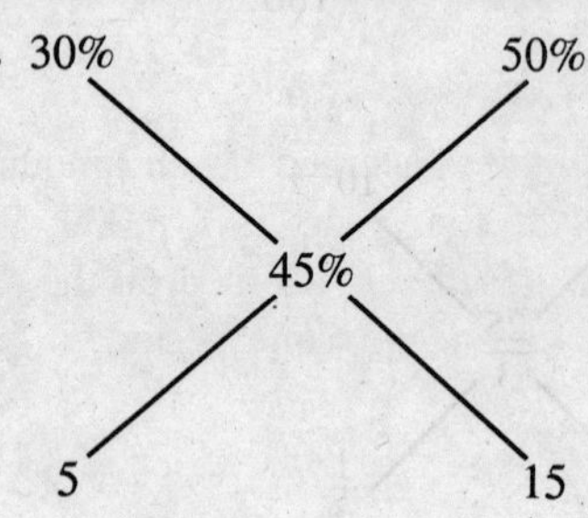

He should mix 30% and 50% in the ratio 5 : 15 or 1 : 3.

$\frac{\text{30\% Solution}}{\text{50\% Solution}} = \frac{1}{3}$ or 1 : 3

7. The given solution has 75% milk.
Milk to be added has 100% milk.

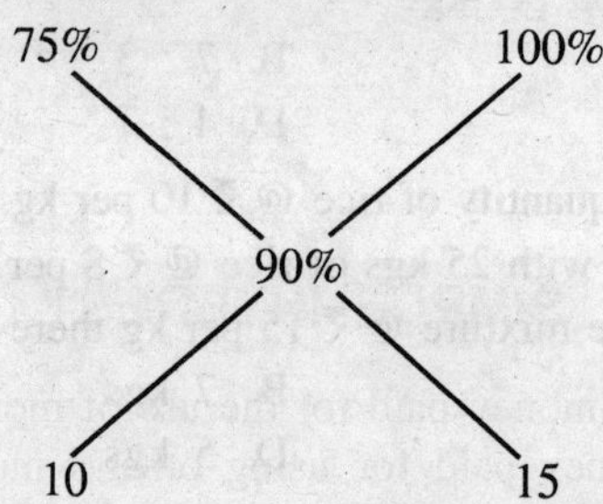

Milk should be added to the given mixture in the ratio 15 : 10 or 3 : 2.

∴ Quantity of milk to be added = $\frac{3}{2} \times 6$ = 9 litres.

8. Let cost price of spirit be Re. 1 per litre.
Then SP of mixture = Re. 1 per litre
Gain = 25%

So, CP of mixture $= 1 \times \frac{100}{125}$ = Re. $\frac{4}{5}$

We assume that CP of water is zero.
Using alligation rule on cost price,

Water should be mixed to spirit in the ratio $\frac{1}{5} : \frac{4}{5}$ or 1 : 4.

9. 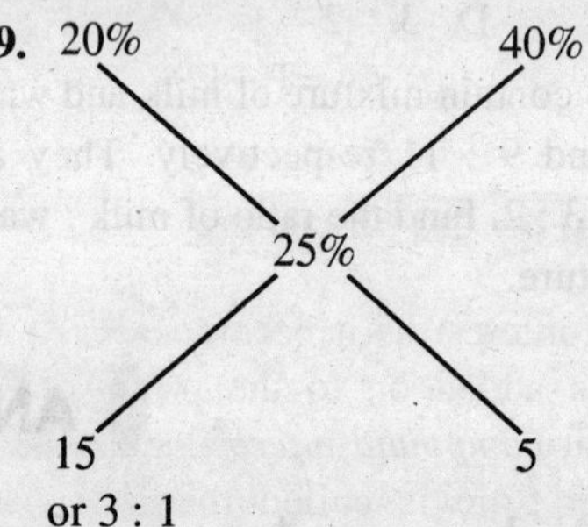

or 3 : 1

Quantity sold at 20% profit = $\frac{3}{3+1} \times 50$ = 37.5 kgs.

Quantity sold at 40% profit = (50 – 37.5) = 12.5 kgs.

10. 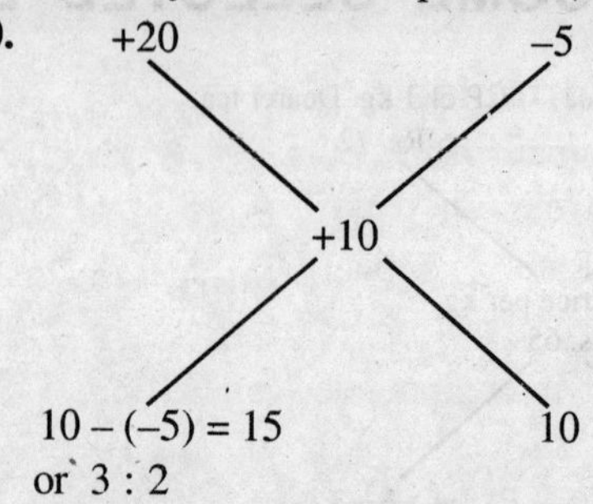

or 3 : 2

Quantity sold at 20% profit = $\frac{3}{3+2} \times 100$ = 60 kgs.

Quantity sold at 5% loss = (100 – 60) = 40 kgs.

❑❑❑

8 SIMPLE & COMPOUND INTERESTS

SIMPLE INTEREST

Interest is the money paid for the use of money borrowed, *i.e.*, extra money paid for using other's money is called *interest*.

The sum borrowed is called the principal. The sum of interest and principal is called the *Amount*.

If the interest on a certain sum borrowed for a certain period is reckoned uniformly, then it is called simple interest, denoted by S.I.

Thus, if A = Amount, P = Principal,
I = Interest, T = Time (in year),
R = Rate per cent per annum, then

(*a*) $I = \frac{P \times R \times T}{100}$ (*b*) $P = \frac{100 \times I}{R \times T}$

(*c*) $T = \frac{100 \times I}{P \times R}$ (*d*) $R = \frac{100 \times I}{P \times T}$

(*e*) $P = \frac{100\,A}{100 + RT}$ (*f*) $A = P + I.$

COMPOUND INTEREST

In business transaction if interest as it becomes due is not paid to the lender but is added on to the principal, the money is said to be lent at *compound interest* and the total sum owed after a given time is called the amount at compound interest for that time.

After a certain period, the difference between the amount and the original principal is called the compound Interest (C.I.).

Some Important Formulae :

Let Principal = P
Time = *n* years
Rate = *r*% p.a.

then, the amount,

(*a*) when interest is compounded annually:

$$\text{then, Amount} = P\left(1 + \frac{r}{100}\right)^n$$

(*b*) when interest is compounded half yearly:

$$\text{then, Amount} = P\left(1 + \frac{r/2}{100}\right)^{2n}$$

(*c*) when interest is compounded quarterly :

$$\text{then, Amount} = P\left(1 + \frac{r/4}{100}\right)^{4n}$$

(*d*) when time is fraction of a year, say $4\frac{1}{3}$ years,

$$\text{then, Amount} = P\left(1 + \frac{r}{100}\right)^4 \times \left(1 + \frac{\frac{1}{3}r}{100}\right)$$

(*e*) when rates are r_1%, r_2% and r_3% for Ist, IInd and IIIrd year respectively;

$$\text{then, Amount} = P\left(1 + \frac{r_1}{100}\right)\left(1 + \frac{r_2}{100}\right)\left(1 + \frac{r_3}{100}\right)$$

SOLVED EXAMPLES

Example 1: A man gets a simple interest of ₹ 1,000 on a certain principal at the rate of 5% p.a. in 4 years. What compound interest will the man get on twice the principal in two years at the same rate?

Solution: $\because$ Principal $= \frac{1000 \times 100}{4 \times 5} =$ ₹ 5000

$\therefore$ Required C.I. $= 1000\left[\left(1 + \frac{5}{100}\right)^2 - 1\right]$

$= 1000\left[\frac{441 - 400}{400}\right]$

$= 1000 \times \frac{41}{400}$

= ₹ 102.5.

Example 2: The simple interest accrued on an amount of ₹ 25,000 at the end of four years is ₹ 8,000. What would be the compound interest accrued on the same amount at the same rate in the same period?

Solution: Rate = $\frac{8000 \times 100}{25000 \times 4}\% = 8\%$

$\therefore$ C.I. $= 25000\left[\left(1+\frac{8}{100}\right)^4 - 1\right]$

$= 25000\left(\frac{27^4 - 25^4}{25^4}\right)$

$= 25000\left[\frac{531441 - 390625}{390625}\right]$

$=$ ₹ 9012.224

Example 3: The difference between the amount of compound interest and simple interest accrued on an amount of ₹ 26,000 at the end of 3 years is ₹ 2994.134. What is the rate of interest p.c.p.a.?

Solution: $\because$ $2994.134 = \frac{26000r^2}{(100)^2}\left(\frac{r}{100}+3\right)$

$= \frac{26r^2}{10}\left(\frac{r+300}{100}\right)$

$\Rightarrow$ $2994134 = 26r^3 + 7800r^2$

$\Rightarrow$ $115159 = r^3 + 300r^2$

$\therefore$ $r = 19$

Example 4: What would be the compound interest accrued on an amount of ₹ 45,400/- at the end of two years at the rate of 15% p.a.?

Solution: C.I. $= 45400\left[\left(1+\frac{15}{100}\right)^2 - 1\right]$

$= 45400\left[\frac{23}{20}\times\frac{23}{20} - 1\right]$

$= 45400 \times \frac{129}{400}$

$= \frac{29283}{2} =$ ₹ 14641.5

MULTIPLE CHOICE QUESTIONS

1. Anshul borrowed some money at the rate of 4% p.a. for the first three years, at the rate of 8% p.a. for the next two years and at the rate of 9% p.a. for the period beyond 5 years. If he pays a total simple interest of ₹ 19,550 at the end of 7 years, how much money did he borrow?
A. ₹ 39,500 B. ₹ 42,500
C. ₹ 41,900 D. ₹ 43,000

2. The simple interest accrued on an amount at the end of five years @ 12.5% p.a. ₹ 1,575. What is the amount?
A. ₹ 2,050 B. ₹ 2,550
C. ₹ 2,250 D. ₹ 2,520

3. Siyaram invested equal sum of money in two schemes. Under scheme X, the compound interest rate was 10% p.a. and under scheme Y, the compound interest rate was 12% p.a. The interest after two years on the sum invested in Scheme X was ₹ 63. How much is the interest earned under Scheme Y after two years?
A. ₹ 79.0272 B. ₹ 70.56
C. ₹ 76.32 D. Cannot be determined

4. What would be the compound interest accrued on an amount of ₹ 15,000 at the rate of 15% at the end of three years?
A. ₹ 7813.125 B. ₹ 7762.50
C. ₹ 7762.125 D. ₹ 11235.09375

5. If the difference between the simple interest and compound interest earned on an amount @ 15% p.a. at the end of 3 years is ₹ 595.35, what is the amount?
A. ₹ 8,400 B. ₹ 9,200
C. ₹ 6,800 D. Cannot be determined

6. What will be the simple interest earned on an amount of ₹ 988 @ 18% p.a., at the end of 5 years?
A. ₹ 711.36 B. ₹ 898.2
C. ₹ 799.25 D. None of these

7. The simple interest accrued on a sum of certain principal is ₹ 1,200 in four years at the rate of 8% p.a. What would be the simple interest accrued on thrice of that principal at the rate of 6% p.a. in 3 years?
A. ₹ 2,025 B. ₹ 3,025
C. ₹ 2,250 D. ₹ 2,150

8. What amount of compound interest can be obtained on an amount of ₹ 18,000 at the rate of 10% p.a. at the end of three years?
A. ₹ 5,628 B. ₹ 5,400
C. ₹ 5,940 D. None of these

9. Shrivastava invests ₹ 14500 for 6 years at the certain rate of simple interest. After 6 years his invested sum becomes ₹ 21460. Find out the rate of interest per annum—
A. 4% p.a. B. 10% p.a.
C. 6% p.a. D. 8% p.a.

10. A sum of ₹ 12,500 amounts to ₹ 15,500 in 4 years at the rate of simple interest. What is the rate of interest?
A. 3% B. 4%
C. 5% D. 6%

11. A sum fetched a total simple interest of ₹ 4016. 25 at the rate of 9% p.a. in 5 years. What is the sum?
A. ₹ 4462.50 B. ₹ 8032.50
C. ₹ 8900 D. ₹ 8925

12. ₹ 800 becomes ₹ 956 in 3 years at a certain rate of simple interest. If the rate of interest is increased by 4%, what amount will ₹ 800 become in 3 years?

A. ₹ 1020.80 B. ₹ 1025
C. ₹ 1052 D. Data inadequate

13. A certain amount earns simple interest of ₹ 1750 after 7 years. Had the interest been 2% more, how much more interest would it have earned?

A. ₹ 35
B. ₹ 245
C. ₹ 350
D. Cannot be determined

14. Neelam borrowed some money at the rate of 6% p.a. for the first three years, 9% p.a. for the next five years and 13% p.a. for the period beyond eight years. If the total interest paid by him at the end of eleven years is ₹ 8160, how much money did he borrow?

A. ₹ 8000 B. ₹ 10,000
C. ₹ 12000 D. Data inadequate

15. The simple interest on a sum of money will be ₹ 600 after 10 years. If the principal is trebled after 5 years, what will be the total interest at the end of the tenth year?

A. ₹ 600 B. ₹ 900
C. ₹ 1200 D. ₹ 1500

16. Simple interest on a certain sum at a certain annual rate of interest is $\frac{1}{9}$ of the sum. If the numbers representing rate percent and time in years be equal, then the rate of interest is :

A. $3\frac{1}{3}\%$ B. 5%

C. $6\frac{2}{3}\%$ D. 10%

17. A borrowed some money from B at 12% p.a. S.I. for 3 years. He then added some more money to the borrowed sum and lent it to C for the same period at 14% p.a. rate of interest. If A gains ₹ 93.90 in the whole transaction, how much money did he add from his side?

A. ₹ 35 B. ₹ 55
C. ₹ 80 D. ₹ 105

18. A sum of ₹ 725 is lent in the beginning of a year at a certain rate of interest. After 8 months, a sum of ₹ 362.50 more is lent but at the rate twice the former. At the end of the year, ₹ 33.50 is earned as interest from both the loans. What was the original rate of interest?

A. 3.6% B. 4.5%
C. 5% D. None of these

19. The difference between the simple interest received from two different sources on ₹ 1500 for 3 years is ₹ 13.50. The difference between their rates of interest is:

A. 0.1% B. 0.2%
C. 0.3% D. 0.4%

20. Priya invested an amount of ₹ 12,000 at the rate of 10% p.a. simple interest and another amount at the rate of 20% p.a. simple interest. The total interest earned at the end of one year on the total amount invested became 14% p.a. Find the total amount invested.

A. ₹ 20,000 B. ₹ 22,000
C. ₹ 24,000 D. ₹ 25,000

21. If the rate increases by 2%, the simple interest received on a sum of money increases by ₹ 108. If the time period is increased by 2 years, the simple interest on the same sum increases by ₹ 180. The sum is:

A. ₹ 1800 B. ₹ 3600
C. ₹ 5400 D. Data inadequate

22. A sum of ₹ 2600 is lent out in two parts in such a way that the interest on one part at 10% for 5 years is equal to that on another at 9% for 6 years. The sum lent out at 10% is:

A. ₹ 1150 B. ₹ 1250
C. ₹ 1350 D. ₹ 1450

23. A sum of 1550 was lent partly at 5% and partly at 8% p.a. simple interest. The total interest received after 3 years was ₹ 300. The ratio of the money lent at 5% to that lent at 8% is :

A. 5 : 8 B. 8 : 5
C. 16 : 15 D. 31 : 6

24. Deepak invested certain amount in three different schemes A, B and C with the rate of interest 10% p.a., 12% p.a. and 15% p.a. respectively. If the total interest accrued in one years was ₹ 3200 and the amount invested in Scheme C was 150% of the amount invested in Scheme A and 240% of the amount invested in Scheme B, what was the amount invested in Scheme B?

A. ₹ 5000
B. ₹ 6500
C. ₹ 8000
D. Cannot be determined

25. Shyam invested ₹ 15,000 @ 10% per annum for one year. If the interest is compounded half-yearly, then the amount received by Shyam at the end of the year will be :

A. ₹ 16,500
B. ₹ 16,525.50
C. ₹ 16,537.50
D. ₹ 18,150

ANSWERS

1	2	3	4	5	6	7	8	9	10
B	D	C	A	A	D	A	D	D	D
11	**12**	**13**	**14**	**15**	**16**	**17**	**18**	**19**	**20**
D	C	D	A	C	A	D	D	C	A
21	**22**	**23**	**24**	**25**					
D	C	C	A	C					

SOME SELECTED EXPLANATORY ANSWERS

2. Required amount $= ₹\dfrac{1575 \times 100}{12.5 \times 5} = ₹\ 2520.$

3. Suppose Sriram invested ₹ P in each scheme.

$$\therefore \quad 63 = P\left[\left(1+\frac{10}{100}\right)^2 - 1\right]$$

$$\Rightarrow \quad 63 = P\left(\frac{121}{100} - 1\right) = \frac{21P}{100}$$

$$\therefore \quad P = \frac{63 \times 100}{21} = ₹\ 300$$

Compound interest of 2 years under scheme Y

$$= 300\left[\left(1+\frac{12}{100}\right)^2 - 1\right]$$

$$= \frac{300 \times 159}{625} = ₹\ 76.32.$$

5. $\because$ Required Difference $= \dfrac{P \times r^2}{(100)^2}\left(\dfrac{r}{100} + 3\right)$

$$\Rightarrow \quad 595.35 = \frac{P \times 15 \times 15}{100 \times 100}\left(\frac{15}{100} + 3\right)$$

$$= \frac{225P}{10000} \times \frac{315}{100}$$

$$\therefore \quad P = \frac{595.35 \times 1000000}{225 \times 315} = ₹\ 8400$$

6. S.I. $= \dfrac{988 \times 18 \times 5}{100} = ₹\ 889.20$

7. Principal $= \dfrac{1200 \times 100}{4 \times 8} = ₹\ 3750$

$$\therefore \quad \text{S.I.} = \frac{3750 \times 3 \times 3 \times 6}{100} = ₹\ 2025$$

9. From question,

$$(21460 - 14500) = \frac{14500 \times r \times 6}{100}$$

$$\Rightarrow \quad \frac{6960}{145 \times 6} = r$$

$$\therefore \quad r = 8$$

Hence the rate of interest per annum = 8%.

10. S.I. = ₹ (15500 – 12500) = ₹ 3000.

$$\text{Rate} = \left(\frac{100 \times 3000}{12500 \times 4}\right)\% = 6\%.$$

11. Principal $= ₹\left(\dfrac{100 \times 4016.25}{9 \times 5}\right)$

$$= ₹\left(\frac{401625}{45}\right) = ₹\ 8925.$$

12. S.I. = ₹ (956 – 800) = ₹ 156.

$$\text{Rate} = \left(\frac{100 \times 156}{800 \times 3}\right)\% = 6\frac{1}{2}\%.$$

$$\text{New rate} = \left(6\frac{1}{2} + 4\right)\% = 10\frac{1}{2}\%.$$

$$\text{New S.I.} = ₹\left(800 \times \frac{21}{2} \times \frac{3}{100}\right) = ₹\ 252.$$

$\therefore$ New amount = ₹ (800 + 252) = ₹ 1052.

13. We need to know the S.I., principal and time to find the rate. Since the principal is not given, so data is inadequate.

14. Let the sum be ₹ x. Then,

$$\left(\frac{x \times 6 \times 3}{100}\right) + \left(\frac{x \times 9 \times 5}{100}\right) + \left(\frac{x \times 13 \times 3}{100}\right) = 8160$$

$$\Rightarrow \quad 18x + 45x + 39x = (8160 \times 100)$$

$$\Rightarrow \quad 102x = 816000 \quad \Rightarrow \quad x = 8000.$$

15. Let the sum be ₹ x. Now, S.I. = ₹ 600, T = 10 years.

$$\text{Rate} = \left(\frac{100 \times 600}{x \times 10}\right)\% = \left(\frac{6000}{x}\right)\%.$$

$$\text{S.I. for first 5 years} = ₹\left(\frac{x \times 5 \times 6000}{x \times 100}\right) = ₹\ 300.$$

$$\text{S.I. for last 5 years} = ₹\left(3x \times 5 \times \frac{6000}{x \times 100}\right) = ₹\ 900.$$

$\therefore$ Total interest = ₹ 1200.

16. Let sum = x. Then, S.I. = $\frac{x}{9}$.

Let rate = R% and time = R years.

$\therefore \left(\frac{x \times R \times R}{100}\right) = \frac{x}{9} \Rightarrow R^2 = \frac{100}{9}$

$\Rightarrow R = \frac{10}{3} = 3\frac{1}{3}$.

Hence, rate = $3\frac{1}{3}\%$.

17. Let the money added be ₹ x Then,

$\frac{(830 + x) \times 14 \times 3}{100} - \frac{830 \times 12 \times 3}{100} = 93.90$

$\Rightarrow$ 830 × 42 + 42x − 830 × 36 = 9390

$\Rightarrow$ 42x + 830 × (42 − 36) = 9390

$\Rightarrow 42x = 9390 - 4980 \Rightarrow x = \frac{4410}{42} = 105.$

$\therefore$ Money added = ₹ 105.

18. Let the original rate be R%. Then, new rate = (2R)%.

$\therefore \left(\frac{725 \times R \times 1}{100}\right) + \left(\frac{36250 \times 2R \times 1}{100 \times 3}\right) = 33.50$

$\Rightarrow$ (2175 + 725) R = 33.50 × 100 × 3 = 10050

$\Rightarrow R = \frac{10050}{2900} = 3.46.$

$\therefore$ Original rate = 3.46%.

19. $\left(\frac{1500 \times R_1 \times 3}{100}\right) - \left(\frac{1500 \times R_2 \times 3}{100}\right) = 13.50$

$\Rightarrow 4500 (R_1 - R_2) = 1350$

$\Rightarrow R_1 - R_2 = \frac{1350}{4500} = 0.3\%.$

20. Let the second amount be ₹ x. Then,

$\left(\frac{12000 \times 10 \times 1}{100}\right) + \left(\frac{x \times 20 \times 1}{100}\right) = \left[\frac{(12000 + x) \times 14 \times 1}{100}\right]$

$\Rightarrow$ 120000 + 20x = 168000 + 14x

$\Rightarrow 6x = 48000 \Rightarrow x = 8000.$

$\therefore$ Total investment = ₹ (12000 + 8000)

= ₹ 20000.

21. Let the sum be ₹ x, rate be R% p.a. and time be T years.

Then, $\left[\frac{x \times (R + 2) \times T}{100}\right] - \left(\frac{x \times R \times T}{100}\right) = 108$

$\Rightarrow$ 2xT = 10800 ...(*i*)

And, $\left[\frac{x \times R \times (T + 2)}{100}\right] - \left(\frac{x \times R \times T}{100}\right) = 180$

$\Rightarrow$ 2xR = 18000 ...(*ii*)

Clearly, from (*i*) and (*ii*), we cannot find the value of x. So, the data is inadequate.

22. Let the sum lent at 10% be ₹ x and that lent at 9% be ₹ (2600 − x). Then,

$\left(\frac{x \times 10 \times 5}{100}\right) = \frac{(2600 - x) \times 9 \times 6}{100}$

$\Rightarrow$ 50x = (2600 × 54) − 54x

$\Rightarrow x = \left(\frac{2600 \times 54}{104}\right) = 1350.$

$\therefore$ Sum lent at 10% = ₹ 1350.

23. Let the sum lent at 5% be ₹ x and that lent at 8% be ₹ (1550 − x). Then,

$\left(\frac{x \times 5 \times 3}{100}\right) + \left[\frac{(1550 - x) \times 8 \times 3}{100}\right] = 300$

$\Rightarrow$ 15x − 24x + (1550 × 24) = 30000

$\Rightarrow 9x = 7200 \Rightarrow x = 800.$

$\therefore$ Required ratio = 800 : 750 = 16 : 15.

24. Let x, y and z be the amounts invested in schemes A, B and C respectively. Then,

$\left(\frac{x \times 10 \times 1}{100}\right) + \left(\frac{y \times 12 \times 1}{100}\right) + \left(\frac{z \times 15 \times 1}{100}\right) = 3200$

$\Rightarrow$ 10x + 12y + 15z = 320000 ...(*i*)

Now, z = 240% of $y = \frac{12}{5}y$ ...(*ii*)

And, z = 150% of $x = \frac{3}{2}x$

$\Rightarrow x = \frac{2}{3}z = \left(\frac{2}{3} \times \frac{12}{5}\right)y = \frac{8}{5}y$ ...(*iii*)

From (*i*), (*ii*) and (*iii*), we have :

16y + 12y + 36y = 320000 $\Rightarrow$ 64y = 320000

$\Rightarrow y = 5000.$

$\therefore$ Sum invested in Scheme B = ₹ 5000.

25. P = ₹ 15000; R = 10% p.a. = 5% per half-year; T = 1 year = 2 half-years.

$\therefore$ Amount = ₹$\left[15000 \times \left(1 + \frac{5}{100}\right)^2\right]$

= ₹$\left(15000 \times \frac{21}{20} \times \frac{21}{20}\right)$

= ₹ 16537.50.

❑❑❑

9 TIME & WORK

IMPORTANT FACTS

1. If A can do a piece of work in n days, then work done by A in 1 day $= \frac{1}{n}$.
2. If work done by A in 1 day $= \frac{1}{n}$; then A can finish the whole work in n days.
3. If A is twice as good a workman as B then; Ratio of work done by A and B = 2 : 1
   Ratio of times taken by A and B to finish a work = 1 : 2.
4. If a pipe can fill a tank in x hours, then the part filled in 1 hour $= \frac{1}{x}$.
5. If a pipe can empty a tank in y hour, then the part of the tank emptied in 1 hour $= \frac{1}{y}$.
6. If two pipes can fill a tank in x and y hours respectively and both the pipes are opened simultaneously, then the part filled in 1 hour $= \frac{1}{x} + \frac{1}{y}$.
7. (*a*) A tap fills a cistern in x hours and the other can empty the cistern in y hours. If both the taps are opened simultaneously, then the net part of the tank filled in 1 hour $= \frac{1}{x} - \frac{1}{y}$; when $y > x$.

   (*b*) A tap can fill a tank in x hours and other can empty in y hours. If both the taps are opened simultaneously, then the net part of tank emptied in 1 hour $= \frac{1}{y} - \frac{1}{x}$; when $x > y$.

SOLVED EXAMPLES

Example 1: A and B together can complete a piece of work in 4 days. If A alone can complete the same piece of work in 5 days, in how many days will B alone complete it?

Solution: (A + B)'s 1 day's work $= \frac{1}{4}$

A's 1 day's work $= \frac{1}{5}$

$\therefore$ B's 1 day work $= \frac{1}{4} - \frac{1}{5} = \frac{5-4}{20} = \frac{1}{20}$

$\therefore$ B alone will complete the work in 20 days.

Example 2: Four examiners can examine a certain number of answer papers in 10 days by working for 5 hours a day. For how many hours in a day would 2 examiners have to work in order to examine twice the number of answer papers in 20 days?

Solution:

No. of exam	Hrs. per day	No. of papers	Days
4	5	1	10
↓	↓	↓	↓
2	x	2	20

$$\left.\begin{array}{l} 2 : 4 \\ 1 : 2 \\ 20 : 10 \end{array}\right\} :: 5 : x$$

$$\therefore \quad x = \frac{4 \times 2 \times 10 \times 5}{2 \times 20} = 10 \text{ hrs./day}$$

Example 3: 6 women and 6 men together can complete a piece of work in 6 days. In how many days can 15 men alone complete the piece of work if 9 women alone can complete the work in 10 days?

Solution: $\because$ Work of 1 woman for 1 day

$$= \frac{1}{9 \times 10} = \frac{1}{90}$$

$\Rightarrow$ Work of 6 women for 6 days

$$= \frac{1}{90} \times 6 \times 6 = \frac{2}{5}$$

$\Rightarrow$ Work of 6 men for 6 days

$$= 1 - \frac{2}{5} = \frac{3}{5}$$

$\Rightarrow$ Work of 1 man for 1 day

$$= \frac{3}{5 \times 6 \times 6} = \frac{1}{60}$$

∴ Work of 15 men for 1 day

$$= \frac{1}{60} \times 15 = \frac{1}{4}.$$

Hence, 15 men will complete the work in 4 days.

Example 4: Six boys or four men can complete a piece of work in 24 days. In how many days will 3 boys and 10 men together complete the same piece of work?

Solution: 4 men = 6 boys

∴ 10 men $= \frac{6}{4} \times 10$

= 15 boys

∴ 10 men + 3 boys = 15 + 3

= 18 boys

∴ Required number of days $= \frac{6 \times 24}{18} = 8.$

MULTIPLE CHOICE QUESTIONS

1. 24 men can complete a piece of work in 16 days. The same work can be completed by 8 women in 72 days, whereas 24 children take 32 days to complete it. If 10 men, 15 women and 24 children work together, in how many days can the work be completed?

A. 18 B. 8
C. 22 D. 12

2. 18 Men alone can complete a piece of work in 24 days. 54 Women alone can complete the same piece of work in 12 days and 16 children alone can complete the same piece of work in 54 days. In how many days can 3 men, 9 women and 6 children together complete the piece of work?

A. 18 B. 36
C. 27 D. Cannot be determined

3. If 80 persons can finish a work within 16 days by working 6 hours a day then how many hours per day should 64 persons work to complete that very job within 15 days?

A. 7 hrs B. 8 hrs
C. 6 hrs D. 5 hrs

4. A and B can do a piece of work in 12 days. B and C in 15 days and C and A in 20 days. In how many days A, B and C together can do the work?

A. 8 days B. 12 days
C. 10 days D. 14 days

5. 5 labourers can make 5 mats in 5 hours. How many mats will 10 labourers make in 10 hours?

A. 10 B. 20
C. 30 D. 35

6. A can do $\frac{1}{2}$ of a work in 9 days while B can do $\frac{1}{3}$ of the same work in 6 days. How long would it take for A and B together to complete the work?

A. 18 B. 6
C. 12 D. 9

7. A can do a piece of work in 40 days. He works on it for 5 days and then B completes it in 21 days. How long will A and B together take to complete the work?

A. 20 days B. 15 days
C. 30 days D. 10 days

8. A, B and C can complete a work separately in 24, 36 and 48 days respectively. They started together but C left after 4 days of start and A left 3 days before the completion of work. In how many days will the work be completed?

A. 15 days B. 18 days
C. 10 days D. 12 days

9. A and B can do a piece of work in 12 days. B and C together can do it in 15 days. If A is twice as good a work man as C, find in what time B alone can do it?

A. 12 days B. 15 days
C. 20 days D. 24 days

10. If 4 men or 6 boys can finish a piece of work in 20 days, in how many days can 6 men and 11 boys finish it?

A. 20 days B. 12 days
C. 8 days D. 6 days

11. 5 men and 2 boys together in 1 hour do 4 times work as 1 man and 1 boy do in an hour. Determine the ratio of the specified times of works of a man and a boy.

A. 4 : 1 B. 1 : 4
C. 3 : 4 D. 2 : 1

12. 75 boys finish a work in 24 days. How many men will complete twice the work in 20 days while 2 men do in a day same work as 3 boys do in a day?

A. 50 B. 24
C. 60 D. 120

13. If 3 men and 4 boys together earn ₹ 264 in 8 days and 2 men and 3 boys together earn ₹ 184 in the same time, then in how many days will 6 men and 7 boys together earn ₹ 315?

A. 5 days B. 6 days
C. 9 days D. 10 days

14. Pipes A and B can fill a tank in 36 and 48 hours respectively. Both pipes are opened together to fill the tank. After some time pipe B is closed and the tank is full in 24 hours. For how much time was the pipe B opend?

A. 20 hrs. B. 16 hrs.
C. 48 hrs. D. 36 hrs.

15. A tank is normally filled in 9 hours. But because of a leak in its bottom it takes 3 hours more to fill. How much time will it take the leak to empty the full tank?

A. 12 hrs. B. 24 hrs.
C. 36 hrs. D. 48 hrs.

16. Three pipes A, B and C are connected to a tank. A and B can fill it in 20 and 30 minutes respectively, while C can empty it in 15 minutes. If A, B and C are kept open successively for 1 minute each, how soon will the tank be filled?

A. 176 min B. 167 min
C. 180 min D. 170 min

17. Two pipes A and B can separately fill a cistern in $7\frac{1}{2}$ minutes and 5 minutes respectively and a waste pipe C can carry off 14 litres per minute. If all the pipes are opened when the cistern is full, it is emptied in 1 hour. How many litres does it hold?

A. 40 litres
B. 20 litres
C. 36 litres
D. 30 litres

18. Two workers A and B are engaged to do a work. A working alone takes 8 hours more to complete the job than if both worked together. If B worked alone, he would need $4\frac{1}{2}$ hours more to complete the job than they both working together. What time would they take to do the work together?

A. 4 hours B. 5 hours
C. 6 hours D. 7 hours

19. Savita can do a piece of work in 20 days. Tripti is 25% more efficient than Savita. The number of days taken by Tripti to do the same piece of work is :

A. 15 B. 16
C. 18 D. 25

20. A machine P can print one lakh books in 8 hours, machine Q can print the same number of books in 10 hours while machine R can print them in 12 hours. All the machines are started at 9 a.m. while machine P is closed at 11 a.m. and the remaining two machines complete the work. Approximately at what time will the work be finished?

A. 11:30 a.m. B. 12 noon
C. 12:30 p.m. D. 1 p.m.

ANSWERS

1	2	3	4	5	6	7	8	9	10
D	B	B	C	B	D	B	A	C	D
11	**12**	**13**	**14**	**15**	**16**	**17**	**18**	**19**	**20**
D	D	A	B	C	B	A	C	B	D

SOME SELECTED EXPLANATORY ANSWERS

1. In 16 days the work is completed by 24 men

∴ In 1 day the work is completed by

$= 24 \times 16 = 384$ men

Similarly in 1 day the work is completed by

$= 72 \times 8 = 576$ women

and in 1 day the work is completed by

$= 24 \times 32 = 768$ children

∵ 384 men = 768 children

∴ 10 men $= \frac{768 \times 10}{384} = 20$ children

and 576 women = 768 children

∴ 15 women $= \frac{768 \times 15}{576} = 20$ children

∴ (20 + 20 + 24) = 64 children

∵ 24 children complete the work in 32 days

∴ 64 children complete the work in $= \frac{32 \times 24}{64}$

$= 12$ days.

2. Work done by 3 man + 9 women + 6 children in 1 day

$$= \frac{3\times1}{24\times18} + \frac{9\times1}{12\times54} + \frac{6\times1}{54\times16}$$

$$= \frac{1}{144} + \frac{1}{72} + \frac{1}{144} = \frac{1}{36}$$

∵ $\frac{1}{36}$ work is done in 1 day.

∴ 1 work is done in $= \frac{1\times36}{1} = 36$ days.

3. 80 persons can do the job in 16 days by working = 6 hrs daily

1 person can do the job in 16 days by working

$= 6 \times 80$ hrs daily

1 person can do the job in 1 day by working

$= 6 \times 80 \times 16$ hrs daily

64 persons can do the job in 15 days by working

$= \frac{6\times80\times16}{64\times15}$ hrs = 8 hr.

5. 5 labourers in 5 hrs. can make = 5 mats

1 labourer in 5 hrs. can make = $\frac{5}{5}$ mats

1 labourer in 1 hrs. can make = $\frac{5}{5\times5}$ mats

10 labourers in 10 hrs. can make

$$= \frac{5\times10\times10}{5\times5} = 20 \text{ mats.}$$

6. A's 9 day's work = $\frac{1}{2}$

∴ A's 1 day's work = $\frac{1}{2\times9} = \frac{1}{18}$

B's 6 day's work = $\frac{1}{3}$

∴ B's 1 day's work = $\frac{1}{3\times6} = \frac{1}{18}$

∴ (A + B)'s 1 day's work = $\frac{1}{18}+\frac{1}{18}$

$$= \frac{2}{18} = \frac{1}{9}$$

∴ A and B both together will complete the work in 9 days.

8. Let the work be completed in x days. Therefore, A worked for $x - 3$ days, B for x days and C for 4 days.

A's 1 day's work = $\frac{1}{24}$

B's 1 day's work = $\frac{1}{36}$

and, C's 1 day's work = $\frac{1}{48}$

$$\therefore (x-3)\times\frac{1}{24}+x\times\frac{1}{36}+4\times\frac{1}{48} = 1$$

$$\Rightarrow \frac{x-3}{24}+\frac{x}{36}+\frac{1}{12} = 1$$

$$\Rightarrow \frac{3x-9+2x+6}{72} = 1$$

$$\Rightarrow 5x - 3 = 72$$

$$\Rightarrow 5x = 75$$

$$\Rightarrow x = \frac{75}{5} = 15$$

Hence, the work was completed in 15 days.

11. Work of (5 men + 2 boys) = 4 (work of 1 man + 1 boy)

= Work of 4 men + 4 boys

⇒ Work of (5 men – 4 men)

= Work of (4 boys – 2 boys)

⇒ Work of 1 man = Work of 2 boys

∴ Required ratio = 2 : 1

12. Work of 3 boys = Work of 2 men

∴ Work of 1 boy = Work of $\frac{2}{3}$ man

∴ Work of 75 boys = Work of $\frac{2}{3}\times 75$

= 50 men

∵ 1 work is completed in 24 days by 50 men

∴ 1 work is completed in 1 day by 50 × 24 men

∴ 2 works are completed in 20 days by

$$\frac{50\times24\times2}{20} = 120 \text{ men.}$$

13. Let men be denoted by m and boys by b.

$3m + 4b$ earn in 8 days = ₹ 264

∴ $3m + 4b$ earn in 1 day = $\frac{264}{8}$ = ₹ 33 ...(*i*)

And, $2m + 3b$ earn in 8 days= ₹ 184

∴ $2m + 3b$ earn in 1 day = $\frac{184}{8}$ = ₹ 23 ...(*ii*)

By (*ii*) × 3 – (*i*) × 2, we have

$6m + 9b - 6m - 8b = 69 - 66$

⇒ $1b$ = ₹ 3

∴ $3m + 4b = 33$

$3m = 33 - 4 \times 3 = 21$

$1m = 7$

∴ Wages for 1 day of 6 men and 7 boys

= 6 × 7 + 7 × 3

= 42 + 21 = ₹ 63

∴ ₹ 63 are wages for 1 day

∴ ₹ 315 are wages for = $\frac{315}{63}$ = 5 days.

15. Without the leak, in 1 hour $\frac{1}{9}$ of the tank is filled.

∴ In extra 3 hrs, the pipe fills $\frac{3}{9} = \frac{1}{3}$ of the tank more.

In (9 + 3) = 12 hours, the leak empties this extra $\frac{1}{3}$ of the tank.

∴ The leak will empty the full tank in $12\times\frac{3}{1}$ = 36 hrs.

16. $\left(\frac{1}{20}+\frac{1}{30}-\frac{1}{15}\right) = \frac{1}{60}$ of the tank is filled in first 3 minutes

$$\frac{1}{20}+\frac{1}{30} = \frac{5}{60}$$

$$1-\frac{5}{60} = \frac{55}{60}$$

This $\frac{55}{60}$ part of the tank will be filled in 3 × 55 = 165 minutes.

The last $\frac{5}{60}$ part will be filled in 2 minutes, successively by A and B.

Total time = 165 + 2 = 167 minutes.

17. Cistern filled by (A + B) in 1 minute

$$= \left(\frac{2}{15}+\frac{1}{5}\right) = \frac{1}{3}$$

Net emptying work done by (A + B + C) in 1 minute

$$= \frac{1}{60}$$

Work done by C in 1 minute = $\left(\frac{1}{60}+\frac{1}{3}\right)=\frac{7}{20}$

∴ C alone can empty the cistern in $\left(\frac{20}{7}\right)$ minutes

Water thrown out by C in 1 minute = 14 litres

Water thrown out by C in $\left(\frac{20}{7}\right)$ minutes

$$= \left(14\times\frac{20}{7}\right) = 40 \text{ litres}$$

∴ Capacity of the cistern = 40 litres.

18. Let A and B together take x hours to complete the work. Then

A alone takes (x + 8) hrs and B alone takes $\left(x+\frac{9}{2}\right)$ hrs to complete the work. Then

$$\frac{1}{(x+8)}+\frac{1}{\left(x+\frac{9}{2}\right)} = \frac{1}{x}$$

$$\Rightarrow \quad \frac{1}{(x+8)}+\frac{2}{(2x+9)} = \frac{1}{x}$$

$$\Rightarrow \quad x\,(4x + 25) = (x + 8)\,(2x + 9)$$

$$\Rightarrow \quad 2x^2 = 72$$

$$\Rightarrow \quad x^2 = 36$$

$$\Rightarrow \quad x = 6.$$

19. Ratio of times taken by Savita and Tripti

= 125 : 100

= 5 : 4.

Suppose Tripti takes x days to do the work.

$5 : 4 :: 20 : x \Rightarrow x = \left(\frac{4\times20}{5}\right)$

$\Rightarrow x = 16$ days.

Hence, Tripti takes 16 days to complete the work.

❑❑❑

10 TIME & DISTANCE

IMPORTANT FORMULAE

1. Speed = Distance ÷ Time
2. Distance = Time × Speed
3. Time = Distance ÷ Speed
4. x km/hr = $\left(x\times\frac{5}{18}\right)$ m/sec
5. x m/sec = $\left(x\times\frac{18}{5}\right)$ km/hr.
6. If the speed of a body is changed in the ratio $m : n$, then the ratio of the time taken changes in the ratio $n : m$.
7. When a man covers a certain distance with a speed of x km/h and another equal distance at the rate of y km/h, then for the whole journey, the average speed is given by

   Average speed = $\frac{2xy}{x+y}$ km/h.
8. The time taken by a train in passing a signal post or a telegraph pole or a man standing near a railway line $= \frac{\text{Length of the train}}{\text{Speed of the train}}$
9. The time taken by a train of length x passing a railway bridge or a platform or a tunnel or a train of length y at rest $= \frac{x+y}{\text{Speed}}$
10. (*a*) Time taken by faster train of length x and speed u to pass the slower train of length y and speed v in the same direction $= \frac{x+y}{u-v}$

    (*b*) Time taken by the trains in passing each other while moving in opposite direction $= \frac{x+y}{u+v}$
11. (*a*) Time taken by the train of length x and speed u to cross a man moving with speed y in same direction $= \frac{x}{u-v}$

    (*b*) Time taken by the train to cross a man moving in the opposite direction $= \frac{x}{u+v}$
12. If two trains start at the same time from two points A and B towards each other and after crossing, they take a and b hours in reaching B and A respectively. Then, A's speed : B's speed = $(\sqrt{b}:\sqrt{a})$

SOLVED EXAMPLES

Example 1: Distance between two railway stations A and B is 1536 kms. A train covers a journey between A to B at the uniform speed of 60 km/hr and returns from B to A at the uniform speed of 40 km/hr. What is the average speed of the train during the whole journey?

Solution: Average speed of train = $\frac{2\times 40\times 60}{40+60}$

$= \frac{2\times 40\times 60}{100}$ = 48 km/hr.

Example 2: A car covers the first 39 km of its journey in 45 minutes and covers the remaining 25 km in 35 minutes. What is the average speed of the car?

Solution: Total time = $\frac{45}{60}+\frac{35}{60}=\frac{4}{3}$ hrs.

and total distance = 39 + 25 = 64 km

∴ Average speed = $\frac{64\times 3}{4}$ = 48 km/hr.

Example 3: A train covered a distance of 1235 km in 19 hours. Also, the average speed of a car is four-fifth the average speed of the train. How much distance will the car cover in 22 hours?

Solution: Speed of the train = $\frac{1235}{19}$ = 65 km/hr

∴ Speed of the car = $65\times\frac{4}{5}$ = 52 km/hr

∴ Reqd. distance = 52 × 22 = 1144 km.

Example 4: A 320 metre long train moving with an average speed of 120 km/hr crosses a platform in 24 seconds. A man crosses the same platform in 4 minutes. What is the speed of man in metre/second?

Solution: Let the length of the platform be x metre. Then,

∵ Speed of the train = 120 km/hr = $120\times\frac{5}{18}$

$= \frac{100}{3}$ m/sec.

From question,

$\because \quad 320 \text{ m} + x = \frac{100}{3} \times 24$

$\therefore \quad x = 800 - 320$

$= 480$ metre.

$\therefore$ Reqd. speed of man $= \frac{480 \text{ m}}{4 \times 60 \text{ sec}} = 2$ m/sec.

Example 5: A 260 metre long train crosses a platform thrice its length in 80 seconds. What is the speed of the train in km/hour?

Solution: Speed of the train

$= \frac{(260+780)}{80} \times \frac{18}{5}$ km/hr.

$= 46.8$ km/hr.

MULTIPLE CHOICE QUESTIONS

1. A boat while travelling upstream covers a distance of 18 km at the speed of 3 km/hr, whereas while travelling downstream it covers the same distance at a speed of 9 km/hr. What is the speed of the boat in still waters?

A. 3 km/hr
B. 5 km/hr
C. 7 km/hr
D. None of these

2. The speed of a car is 1.5 times the speed of a bus. If the car travels at the speed of 60 km/hr what will be the difference in the time taken by the bus and the time taken by the car to cover 720 km?

A. 5 hours B. 6 hours
C. 4 hours D. 8 hours

3. A car covers a distance of 540 km in 9 hours. Speed of a train is double the speed of the car. Two-third the speed of the train is equal to the speed of a bike. How much distance will the bike cover in 5 hours?

A. 450 km B. 360 km
C. 400 km D. 500 km

4. A train travels at a speed of 30 km per hour for 12 minutes and then for the next 8 minutes at a speed of 45 km per hour. What is the average speed for the journey?

A. 40 km/hr B. 36 km/hr
C. 43 km/hr D. 46 km/hr

5. The ratio of the speeds of two trains is 7 : 8. If the second train runs 400 km in 5 hrs., find the speed of the first train.

A. 60 km/hr B. 55 km/hr
C. 70 km/hr D. 75 km/hr

6. A train travels from Dehradun to Delhi at a speed of 40 km/hr and returns at 60 km/hr. Find the average speed for the entire journey—

A. 50 km/hr B. 45 km/hr
C. 48 km/hr D. 52 km/hr

7. A car runs at 60 km per hr. A man runs at one-third the speed of the car and reaches office from his house in 15 minutes. How far is his office from his house?

A. 20 km B. 10 km
C. 5 km D. 4 km

8. Two men A and B start walking simultaneously from P to Q, a distance of 21 kms, at the speeds of 3 km and 4 km an hour respectively. B reaches Q, returns immediately and meets A at R. Then the distance from P to R is:

A. 6 km B. 12 km
C. 18 km D. 24 km

9. A monkey climbing up a greased pole ascends 12 metres and slips down 5 metres in alternate minutes. If the pole is 63 metres high, how long will it take him to reach the top?

A. $12\frac{7}{16}$ B. $7\frac{12}{16}$
C. $16\frac{7}{12}$ D. $10\frac{7}{12}$

10. A carriage driving in a fog passed a man who was walking at the speed of 6 km/hr. in the same direction. He could see the carriage for 4 minutes and it was visible to him up to a distance of 200 metres. The speed of the carriage is:

A. 9 km/hr B. 4 km/hr
C. 6 km/hr D. 8 km/hr

11. A train met with an accident 3 hours after starting, which detains it for one hour, after which it proceeds at 75% of its original speed. It arrives at the destination 4 hours late. Had the accident taken place 150 km further along the railway line, the train would have arrived only $3\frac{1}{2}$ hours late. Find the length of the trip:

A. 1200 km B. 1000 km
C. 2100 km D. 1050 km

12. Two places A and B are 162 kms apart. A train leaves A for B and at the same time another train leaves B for A. The two trains meet at the end of 6 hours. If the train travelling from A to B travels 8 km per hr. faster than the other. Then the speed of the faster train is:

A. $9\frac{1}{2}$ km/h B. 27 km/hr
C. $17\frac{1}{2}$ km/hr D. 19 km/hr

13. A train takes 18 seconds to pass completely through a station 162 metres long and 15 seconds to pass completely through another station 120 metres long. The length of the train is:

A. 60 m B. 75 m
C. 90 m D. 100 m

14. A man covered a distance of 3990 km partly by air, partly by sea and remaining by land. The time spent in air, on sea and on land is in the ratio 1 : 16 : 2 and the ratio of average speeds is 20 : 1 : 3 respectively. If total average speed is 42 km per hr, Then the distance covered by sea is :

A. 1502 kms B. 2520 kms
C. 1520 kms D. 1500 kms

15. A man is walking at a speed of 10 km/hr. After every kilometre, he takes rest for 5 minutes. How much time will he take to cover a distance of 5 km?

A. 1 hr B. 50 min
C. 20 min D. 30 min

16. Walking $\frac{5}{6}$ of his usual speed, a man reaches the station 10 min late. His usual time to reach the station is :

A. 30 min B. 40 min
C. 50 min D. 60 min

17. A is four times as fast as B and B is six times as fast as C. A certain distance is covered by B in 28 minutes. Then the time taken by C to cover the same distance is :

A. 2 : 48 hrs
B. 2 : 40 hrs
C. 2 : 28 hrs
D. 3 hrs

18. It takes eight hours for a 600 km journey, if 120 km is done by train and the rest by car. It takes 20 minutes more, if 200 km is done by train and the rest by car. The ratio of the speed of the train to the speed of the car is :

A. 2 : 3
B. 6 : 9
C. 3 : 4
D. 4 : 3

19. A bus takes two hours less for a journey of 300 km if its speed is increased by 5 kmph from its normal speed. The normal speed is

A. 30 kmph B. 25 kmph
C. 35 kmph D. 50 kmph

20. A boy goes to school with a speed of 3 km/hr and returns to the village with a speed of 2 km/hr. If he takes 5 hours in all, the distance between the village and the school is :

A. 6 km B. 7 km
C. 8 km D. 9 km

21. Rahim covers a certain distance in 14 hrs 40 min. He covers one half of the distance by train at 60 km/hr and the rest half by road at 50 km/hr. The distance travelled by him is :

A. 960 km B. 720 km
C. 1000 km D. 800 km

22. Two men start together to walk to a certain destination, one at 3.75 km an hour and another at 3 km an hour. The former arrives half an hour before the latter. The distance is:

A. 9.5 km B. 8 km
C. 7.5 km D. 6 km

23. A thief steals a car at 1.30 p.m. and drives it at 40 km an hour. The theft is discovered at 2 p.m. and the owner sets off in another car at 50 km an hour. He will overtake the thief at:

A. 3.30 p.m. B. 4 p.m.
C. 4.30 p.m. D. 6 p.m.

24. A man travels 35 km partly at 4 km/hr and at 5 km/hr. If he covers former distance at 5 km/hr and later distance at 4 km/hr, he could cover 2 km more in the same time. The time taken to cover the whole distance at original rate is :

A. 9 hours B. 7 hours
C. $4\frac{1}{2}$ hours D. 8 hours

25. A certain distance is covered at a certain speed. If half of this distance is covered in double the time, the ratio of the two speeds is :

A. 4 : 1 B. 1 : 4
C. 2 : 1 D. 1 : 2

ANSWERS

1	2	3	4	5	6	7	8	9	10
D	B	C	B	C	C	C	C	C	A
11	**12**	**13**	**14**	**15**	**16**	**17**	**18**	**19**	**20**
A	C	C	C	B	C	A	C	B	A
21	**22**	**23**	**24**	**25**					
D	C	B	D	A					

SOME SELECTED EXPLANATORY ANSWERS

1. Speed of boat in still water $= \frac{9+3}{2} = 6$ km/hr.

2. Speed of bus $= 60 \times \frac{1}{1.5} = 40$ km/hr.

Hence, required difference $= \frac{720}{40} - \frac{720}{60}$

$= 18 - 12 = 6$ hrs.

3. Speed of the car $= \frac{540}{9} = 60$ km/hr.

$\therefore$ Speed of train $= 60 \times 2 = 120$ km/hr.

and speed of bike $= 120 \times \frac{2}{3} = 80$ km/hr.

$\therefore$ Reqd. distance $= 80 \times 5 = 400$ km.

4. In 12 minutes, the train with 30 km per hour speed goes

$= 30 \times \frac{5}{18} \times 60 \times 12$ m

$= \frac{5 \times 5 \times 20 \times 12}{1000}$ km $= 6$ km

In 8 minutes, the train with 45 km per hr. speed goes

$= 45 \times \frac{5}{18} \times 60 \times \frac{8}{1000}$ km $= 6$ km

Average speed $= \frac{12 \text{ km}}{20 \text{ min}} = \frac{12}{20} \times 60$ km/hr

$= 36$ km/hr.

5. $x : \frac{400}{5} = 7 : 8$

$\Rightarrow x \times \frac{5}{400} = \frac{7}{8}$ $\therefore$ $x = 70$ km/hr.

6. Reqd. average speed $= \frac{2 \times 40 \times 60}{(40+60)}$

$= \frac{2 \times 2400}{100} = 48$ km/hr.

8. Let A and B meet after time t hours.

Distance covered by A in t hours $= 3t$ km.

Distance covered by B in t hours $= 4t$ km.

Total distance covered by A and B $= (3t + 4t)$ km

$= 7t$ km.

From the diagram we can see that the total distance covered by A and B is equal to twice the distance between P and Q.

$\therefore$ $7t = 2 \times 21$

$t = \frac{2 \times 21}{7} = 6$ hours

Distance (PR) $= 6 \times 3 = 18$ kms.

9. From question,

In 2 minutes the net ascending of the monkey is $12 - 5 = 7$ metres. So, to cover 63 metres to above process is repeated $\frac{63}{7} = 9$ times. Since on 9th time, it will climb to the top.

Hence, Time taken to cover 56 metres $= \frac{56 \times 2}{7}$

$= 16$ minutes

Remaining distance $= 63 - 56 = 7$ metres

Time taken to ascend 7 metres $= \frac{7}{12}$ minutes

$\therefore$ Total time taken $= 16 + \frac{7}{12} = 16\frac{7}{12}$ minutes.

10. The distance covered by man in 4 minutes

$= \frac{6 \times 1000 \times 4}{60} = 400$ metres

The distance coverd by carriage in 4 minutes $= 200 + 400 = 600$ metres

$\therefore$ Sepeed of carriage $= \frac{600}{4} \times \frac{60}{1000}$ km/hr.

$= 9$ km/hr.

12. Both trains meet after 6 hours.

$\therefore$ The relative speed of two trains $= \frac{162}{6} = 27$ km/hr.

The speed of the slower train starting from B $= \frac{27-8}{2}$

$= \frac{19}{2} = 9\frac{1}{2}$ km/hr.

$\therefore$ The speed of the faster train $= 9\frac{1}{2} + 8 = 17\frac{1}{2}$ km/hr.

13. Let the length of the train $= x$ metres

Then, in 18 sec. the train travels $(x + 162)$ metres ...(*i*)

and in 15 sec. the train travels $(x + 120)$ metres

$\therefore$ In $(18 - 15) = 3$ sec. the train travels $(x + 162) - (x + 120) = 42$ m

$\therefore$ In 1 sec the train travels $= \frac{42}{3} = 14$ metes ...(*ii*)

$\therefore$ In 18 sec. the train travels $= 14 \times 18$

$= 252$ metres ...(*iii*)

From equations (*i*) and (*iii*)

$\therefore$ $x + 162 = 252$

$\Rightarrow$ $x = 252 - 162 = 90$

$\therefore$ Length of the train $= 90$ metres.

14. Total distance travelled = 3990 km

Ratio of time spent = 1 : 16 : 2

$\therefore$ Ratio of time × speeds = 20 × 1 : 16 × 1 : 2 × 3

= 20 : 16 : 6

Sum of the ratios = 20 + 16 + 6

= 42

$\therefore$ Distance covered by sea = $\frac{3990}{42} \times 16$

= 1520 kms.

15. Total time = walking time + rest time

Walking time = $\frac{5}{10}$ hour = $\frac{1}{2}$ hour = 30 min

Rest time = 4 × 5 min = 20 min

$\therefore$ Required time taken = 30 min + 20 min

= 50 min.

17. Let the speed of C be x kmph

$\therefore$ B's speed = $6x$ kmph

and A's speed = 4 × $6x$ kmph = $24x$ kmph

The distance covered by B in 28 minutes

$= 6x \times \frac{28}{60}$ km

$= \frac{28x}{10}$ km $= \frac{14x}{5}$ km

The time taken by C to cover the same distance

$= \frac{\frac{14x}{5}\text{ km}}{x\text{ kmph}} = \frac{14}{5}$ hrs

$= 2\frac{4}{5}$ hours = 2 hrs 48 minutes

19. Let s be the normal speed and t be the normal time taken by the bus

$\therefore$ $s \times t = 300$ ...(1)

new speed = $s + 5$

new time = $t - 2$

$\therefore$ $(s + 5)(t - 2) = 300$

$(s+5)\left(\frac{300}{s} - 2\right) = 300$ (from (1))

$(s + 5)(300 - 2s) = 300s$

$300s - 2s^2 + 1500 - 10s = 300s$

$\Rightarrow$ $2s^2 + 10s - 1500 = 0$

$\Rightarrow$ $2s^2 + 60s - 50s - 1500 = 0$

$\Rightarrow$ $2s(s + 30) - 50(s + 30) = 0$

$\Rightarrow$ $(s + 30)(2s - 50) = 0$

$\therefore$ $s = 25$

$\therefore$ The normal speed of the bus is 25 kmph.

20. Let the required distance be x km. Then

$\frac{x}{3} + \frac{x}{2} = 5$

$\Rightarrow$ $2x + 3x = 30$

$\Rightarrow$ $x = 6.$

21. Let the total distance be x km. Then

$\frac{x}{2} \times \frac{1}{60} + \frac{x}{2} \times \frac{1}{50} = \frac{44}{3}$

or $\frac{x}{120} + \frac{x}{100} = \frac{44}{3}$

or $5x + 6x = 8800$

or $x = 800.$

$\therefore$ Required distance = 800 km.

22. Let the distance be x km. Then

$\frac{x}{3} - \frac{x}{3.75} = \frac{1}{2}$

or $\frac{3.75x - 3x}{3 \times 3.75} = \frac{1}{2}$

or $1.5x = 3 \times 3.75$

or $x = \frac{3 \times 3.75}{1.5} = 7.5$ km

23. Distance covered by thief in (1/2) hour = 20 km.

Now, 20 km is compensated by the owner at a relative speed of 10 km/hr in 2 hours.

So, he overtakes the thief at 4 p.m.

24. Suppose the man covers first distance in x hrs and second distance in y hrs. Then

$4x + 5y = 35$

and $5x + 4y = 37.$

Solving these equations, we get $x = 5$ and $y = 3$.

$\therefore$ Total time taken = (5 + 3) hrs = 8 hrs.

25. Let x km be covered in y hrs. Then

1st speed = $\left(\frac{x}{y}\right)$ km/hr.

2nd speed = $\left(\frac{x}{2} \div 2y\right)$ km/hr = $\left(\frac{x}{4y}\right)$ km/hr.

$\therefore$ Ratio of speed = $\frac{x}{y} : \frac{x}{4y} = 1 : \frac{1}{4} = 4 : 1.$

❑❑❑

11 MENSURATION

Triangle

1. Perimeter = sum of three sides
2. Area = $\frac{1}{2} \times \text{base} \times \text{height}$, or

   Area = $\sqrt{s(s-a)(s-b)(s-c)}$

   where *a, b, c*, are the lengths of the sides of triangle and

   $s = \frac{a+b+c}{2}$

Right Angled Triangle : It is one whose one of the angles is right angle, *i.e.*, 90°.

1. $(\text{Hypotenuse})^2 = (\text{Perpendicular})^2 + (\text{Base})^2$
2. Area = $\frac{1}{2} \times \text{Base} \times \text{Perpendicular}$

Equilateral Triangle : All three sides are equal in length and all three angles are equal to 60°.

1. Area = $\frac{\sqrt{3}}{4} \times (\text{Side})^2$
2. Area = $\frac{(\text{Height})^2}{\sqrt{3}}$
3. Height = $\frac{\sqrt{3}}{2} \times \text{side}$
4. Perimeter = 3 × side

Isosceles Triangle : Two sides are equal in lengths.

1. Area = $\frac{b}{4}\sqrt{4a^2 - b^2}$

   where a = lengths of equal sides

   b = length of unequal side
2. In an isosceles right triangle,

   (*a*) Hypotenuse = $\sqrt{2} \times$ congruent side (*a*)

   (*b*) Area = $\frac{1}{2} \times a^2$

   (c) Perimeter = $\sqrt{2} \times a(\sqrt{2}+1)$

Rectangle :

1. Area = length(l) × breadth(b)
2. Perimeter = $2(l + b)$
3. Diagonal = $\sqrt{l^2 + b^2}$

Square :

1. Area = $(\text{Side})^2$
2. Perimeter = 4 × side
3. Diagonal = side $\times \sqrt{2}$

Parallelogram: Area = Base × Height.

Trapezium : Area = $\frac{1}{2} \times \text{Height} \times$ (Sum of parallel sides).

Here, height is the distance between the two parallel sides.

Rhombus :

1. Area = $\frac{1}{2} \times$ Product of diagonals
2. Side = $\sqrt{\left(\frac{d_1}{2}\right)^2 + \left(\frac{d_2}{2}\right)^2}$, where d_1 and d_2 are diagonals
3. Perimeter = 4 × side

Quadrilateral : Area = $\frac{1}{2} \times$ One diagonal × (Sum of perpendicular to it from the opposite vertices)

$$= \frac{1}{2} \times d \times (a+b)$$

Circle :

1. Diameter = 2 × Radius
2. Area = $\pi r^2 = \frac{\pi}{4} d^2$; where d = diameter = $\sqrt{\frac{4A}{\pi}}$
3. Circumference = $2\pi r = \pi d$
4. Radius = $\frac{\text{Circumference}}{2\pi} = \frac{\sqrt{\text{Area}}}{\pi}$
5. Length of an Arc = $\frac{\theta}{360°} \times 2\pi r$
6. Area of sector = $\frac{\theta}{360°} \times \pi r^2 = \frac{1}{2} \times \text{Arc} \times r$

Polygon :

1. Interior angle + Exterior angle = 180°
2. Each interior angle = $\left(\frac{2n-4}{n}\right) \times 90°$

   where n = number of sides

3. Sum of Exterior angles = 360°
4. Perimeter = Number of sides × Length of side.
5. For an equilateral triangle of side 'a'

(a) radius of inscribed circle $= \frac{a}{2\sqrt{3}}$

and side of the triangle $= 2\sqrt{3}r$,

(b) radius of circumcircle $= \frac{a}{\sqrt{3}}$

6. Area of regular polygon $= \frac{1}{2}$(No. of sides) (Radius of the inscribed circle)

7. Area of regular hexagon $= \frac{3\sqrt{3}}{2}(\text{side})^2$
$= 2.598\ (\text{side})^2$

8. Area of a regular octagon
$= 2(\sqrt{2}+1)(\text{side})^2 = 4.828\ (\text{side})^2$

9. Area of quadrilateral, A
$= \sqrt{s(s-a)(s-b)(s-c)(s-d)}$

where, $s = \frac{a+b+c+d}{2}$

VOLUME AND SURFACE AREA OF SOLIDS

Cuboid : A cuboid has six faces, each one a ractangle. It has 12 edges. For example, a rectangular brick.

Let Length = l, Breadth = b and Height = h, then,

1. Volume = (Length × Breadth × Height)
2. Whole Surface Area = $2(lb + bh + lh)$
3. Diagonal = $\sqrt{l^2+b^2+h^2}$
4. Area of 4 walls of a room = $2 \times h\ (l + b)$

Cube : In a cube, Length = Breadth = Height

1. Volume = $(l)^3$
2. Length = $\sqrt[3]{\text{Volume}}$
3. Whole Surface Area = $6\ l^2$
4. Diagonal = $l \times \sqrt{3}$
5. Lateral Surface Area = $4\ l^2$

Cylinder :

1. Volume = $\pi r^2 h$
2. Curved Surface Area = $2\pi rh$
3. Total Surface Area = $2\pi r(r + h)$
where r = radius, h = height

Spherical Cell :

1. Volume $= \frac{4}{3}\pi(R^3 - r^3)$
2. Total Surface Area= $4\pi(R^2 - r^2)$
where R = Outer radius
r = Inner radius

Sphere :

1. Volume $= \frac{4}{3}\pi r^3$
2. Surface Area = $4\pi r^2$

Semi-sphere :

1. Volume $= \frac{2}{3}\pi r^3$
2. Curved surface area = $2\pi r^2$
3. Total surface area = $3\pi r^2$

Cone :

1. Slant height $(l) = \sqrt{r^2+h^2}$
2. Volume $= \frac{1}{3}\pi r^2 h$
3. Curved surface area = πrl
4. Total surface area = $\pi r\ (l + r)$
5. If the depth of the frustum of a cone be k and the radii of its ends are r_1 and r_2, then
(i) Slant height of the frustum of a cone
$= \sqrt{k^2+(r_1-r_2)^2}$
(ii) Curved surface of the frustum
$= \pi(r_1 + r_2)\ l.$
(iii) Volume $= \frac{\pi k}{3}(r_1^2 + r_1 r_2 + r_2^2)$

SOLVED EXAMPLES

Example 1: What is the longest rod that can be placed in a room which is 7 m long, 9 m broad and $\sqrt{39}$ m high?

Solution: Required length of rod

$= \sqrt{7^2+9^2+(\sqrt{39})^2} = \sqrt{49+81+39}$

$= \sqrt{169} = 13$ m.

Example 2: The total area of a circle and a square is equal to 5450 sq. cm. The diameter of the circle is 70 cms. What is the sum of the circumference of the circle and the perimeter of the square?

Solution: Let side of the square = x cm

Also $\pi \times 35 \times 35 + x^2 = 5450$

$\Rightarrow \frac{22}{7} \times 35 \times 35 + x^2 = 5450$

$\Rightarrow x^2 = 5450 - 3850 = 1600$

$\therefore x = 40$ cm

$\therefore$ Required sum = $\pi \times d + 4x$

$= \left(\frac{22}{7} \times 70 + 4 \times 40\right) = 380$ cm.

Example 3: Perimeter of a circle is equal to the prmimeter of a square whose area is 484 cm^2. What is the radius of the circle?

Solution: Side of a square = $\sqrt{\text{Area}} = \sqrt{484} = 22$ cm.

Perimeter of square = 4 × side = 4 × 22 = 88 cm.

$\therefore \quad 2\pi r = 88$

$\Rightarrow \quad 2\times\frac{22}{7}\times r = 88$

$\Rightarrow \quad r = \frac{88\times7}{2\times22} = 14$ cm.

Example 4: The perimeter of a square is equal to twice the perimeter of a rectangle of length 8 cm and breadth 7 cm. What is the circumference of a semicircle whose diameter is equal to the side of the square? (Rounded off to the two decimal place)

Solution: $\because$ Perimeter of the square

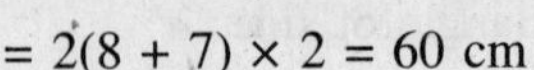

= 2 × Perimeter of rectangle

= 2(8 + 7) × 2 = 60 cm

One side of the square = 15 cm

Radius of the semicircle (R) = $\frac{15}{2}$ cm

$\therefore$ Perimeter of the semicircle = πR + 2R

$= \frac{22}{7}\times\frac{15}{2}+15 = 23.57 + 15$

= 38.57 cm

MULTIPLE CHOICE QUESTIONS

1. What is the area of a circle whose radius is equal to the side of a square whose perimeter is 112 metres?
A. 176 sq m B. 2504 sq m
C. 284 sq m D. None of these

2. The sum of the circumference of a circle and the perimeter of a rectangle is 132 cm. The area of the rectangle is 112 sq cm and breadth of the rectangle is 8 cms. What is the area of the circle?
A. 616 sq cm B. 540 sq cm
C. 396 sq cm D. Cannot be determined

3. The total area of a circle and a rectangle is equal to 1166 sq cm. The diameter of the circle is 28 cm. What is the sum of the circumference of the circle and the perimeter of the rectangle if the length of the rectangle is 25 cm?
A. 186 cm B. 182 cm
C. 184 cm D. Cannot be determined

4. What would be the cost of laying a carpet on a floor which has its length and breadth in the respective ratio of 32 : 21 and where its perimeter is 212 feet, if the cost per square foot of laying the carpet is ₹ 2.5?
A. ₹ 6,720 B. ₹ 5,420
C. ₹ 7,390 D. Cannot be determined

5. A triangle's perimeter is 25 cms. Which of the following may be true or is a possibility?
(*a*) The sides are 7 cms., 7 cms. and 11 cms.
(*b*) It is an equilateral triangle.
(*c*) The value of sides can be in integer only.
A. Only (*a*) B. Only (*a*) and (*b*)
C. Only (*c*) D. Only (*b*) and (*c*)

6. What will be the cost of building a fence around a circular field with area equal to 18,634 sq. metres; if the cost of building the fence per metre is ₹ 365?
A. ₹ 1,76,660 B. ₹ 68,01,410
C. ₹ 2,43,250 D. ₹ 56,60,220

7. The area of a square is 196 sq cms whose side is half the radius of a circle. The circumference of the circle is equal to breadth of a rectangle. If perimeter of the rectangle is 712 cm. What is the length of the rectangle?
A. 196 cm B. 186 cm
C. 180 cm D. 190 cm

8. The circumference of a circular plot is 484 metres. Find out the area of that circular plot—
A. 15246 m^2 B. 18634 m^2
C. 20328 m^2 D. 13552 m^2

9. A room measures 22 dm by 16 dm. I wish to buy a carpet for the floor leaving an uncarpeted margin 2 dm wide along each of the shorter sides of the room and a margin 0.5 dm wide along each of the longer sides of the room. If the price of the carpet is ₹ 500 per sq. metre, what is the cost of the whole carpet required?
A. ₹ 500 B. ₹ 2700
C. ₹ 2000 D. ₹ 1350

10. A paper is in the form of a rectangle ABCD where AB = 22 cm and BC = 14 cm. A semi-circular portion with segment BC as a diameter is cut off. Find the area of remaining paper.
A. 231 cm^2 B. 213 cm^2
C. 321 cm^2 D. 200 cm^2

11. How many plants can be put in a circular flower bed whose circumference is 880 dm allowing 35 dm^2 for each plant?
A. 880 B. 1760
C. 1000 D. 1500

12. An athletic track 14 m wide consists of two straight sections 120 m long joining semi-circular ends whose inner radius is 35 m. Calculate the area of the track :
A. 5670 m^2 B. 7065 m^2
C. 5607 m^2 D. 7056 m^2

13. A square park has each side of 100 m. At each corner of the park, there is a flower bed in the form of a quadrant of radius 14 m. Then the area of the remaining part of the park is :
A. 9384 m^2 B. 9834 m^2
C. 9000 m^2 D. 8900 m^2

∴ Area swept in one minute = Area of sector with central angle 6°

$= \frac{\theta}{360} \times \pi r^2 = \frac{6}{360} \times \frac{22}{7} \times 14 \times 14$

$= \frac{154}{15} = 10.26 \text{ cm}^2.$

15. Let R be the radius of outer circle and r the radius of inner circle.

Circumference of outer circle = 77 cm

∴ $2\pi R = 77$

$\Rightarrow R = \frac{77}{2\pi} = \frac{77 \times 7}{2 \times 22} = \frac{49}{4}$ cm

Circumference of inner circle = 55 cm

∴ $2\pi r = 55 \Rightarrow r = \frac{55}{2\pi} = \frac{55 \times 7}{2 \times 22} = \frac{35}{4}$ cm

∴ Area of ring = $\pi(R^2 - r^2)$

$= \frac{22}{7} \times \left(\frac{49}{4} + \frac{35}{4}\right)\left(\frac{49}{4} - \frac{35}{4}\right) = 231 \text{ cm}^2$

16. Volume of water that flows in one second

$= (18 \times 0.075 \times 0.045) \text{ m}^3$

Volume of water that flows in 30 minutes

$= 18 \times 0.075 \times 0.045 \times 30 \times 60$

$= 109.35 \text{ m}^3.$

Area of the base of the reservoir = $10.8 \times 3.75 \text{ m}^2$

∴ Height of water = $\frac{109.35}{10.8 \times 3.75} = 2.7$ metres.

17. Let r cm be the radius of the base and h cm be the height. Then, $h = 18$ cm.

Now, circumference of the base = Length of the Sheet

⇒ Circumference = 44 cm

⇒ $2\pi r = 44$

⇒ $2 \times \frac{22}{7} \times r = 44$

⇒ $r = 7$ cm

Volume of the cylinder = $\pi r^2 h$ cm³

$= \frac{22}{7} \times (7)^2 \times 18 \text{ cm}^3$

$= 2772 \text{ cm}^3$

18. Slant height, $l = \sqrt{r^2 + h^2}$

$= \sqrt{7^2 + 24^2} = 25$ metres

Curved Surface area of cone = πrl

$= \frac{22}{7} \times 7 \times 25 = 550 \text{ m}^2$

∴ Area of the cloth required = 550 m²

∴ Length of the cloth = $\frac{550}{5} = 110$ metres.

21. Volume of the metallic rod = $19 \times 4 \times 2$

= 152 cu. cm.

Volume of the cube = $4^3 = 64$ cu. cm.

Total volume of both after melting them

= 152 + 64 = 216 cu. cm.

∴ Volume of new cube = 216 cu. cm.

⇒ Side = 6 cm.

23. Let S_1 and S_2 be the two squares. Let the side of the square S_1 be x cm. Then the side of the square S_2 = $(x + 4)$ cm.

∴ Area of square $S_1 = x^2$

and, Area of square $S_2 = (x + 4)^2$

∴ According to the question,

$x^2 + (x + 4)^2 = 400$

Solving the equation, we get

$x = -16$ and 12

But x cannot be negative

∴ Side of the square S_1 = 12 cm

and that of square $S_2 = x + 4 = 12 + 4$

= 16 cm.

❑❑❑

12 PERMUTATION & COMBINATION

IMPORTANT RESULTS

(*i*) Number of permutations of n distinct things taken r at a time, $0 \le r \le n$

$= n(n-1)(n-2)... (n-r+1)$

$= n!/(n-r)! = {}^nP_r$.

This is equivalent to filling r places by r objects taking from n distinct objects.

(*ii*) The number of permutations of n distinct objects taken all at a time $= n!$

(*iii*) The number of combinations of n objects taken r at a time, $0 \le r \le n$. $= {}^nC_r$

$$= \frac{n!}{(n-r)!.r!}.$$

(*iv*) The number of permutations of n dissimilar things taken r at a time when each thing can be repeated any number of times $= n^r$.

(*v*) The number of combinations of n distinct objects taken r at a time when any object may be repeated any number of times

= coefficient of x^r in $(1 + x + x^2 + ... + x^r)^n$

= coefficient of x^r in $(1-x)^n = {}^{n+r-1}C_r$.

(*vi*) Number of combinations of n distinct things taken r at a time when p particular things always occur $= {}^{(n-p)}C_{(r-p)}$.

(*vii*) The number of permutations of n distinct things taken r at a time when p particular things always occur $= {}^{(n-p)}C_{(r-p)}.r!$.

(*viii*) Number of combinations of n distinct things taken r at a time when p particular things never occur $= {}^{(n-p)}C_r$.

(*ix*) Number of permutations (arrangements) of n distinct things taken r at a time when p particular things never occur $= {}^{(n-p)}C_r.r!$.

(*x*) Number of permutations of n things, taken all at a time when p_1 are alike of one kind, p_2 are alike of second kind, ..., p_r of them are alike of the r-th kind $p_1 + p_2 + ... + p_r \le n$, and remaining things are all different $= n!/\{p_1!p_2! ... p_r!\}$.

(*xi*) If $3n$ things are to be divided into three equal groups, then the number of ways $= \frac{(3n)!}{n!.n!.n!.3!}$.

(*xii*) If $3n$ things are to be divided equally between 3 persons (*i.e.*, division of $3n$ things into 3 equal groups with permutation of groups) then the number of ways $= \frac{(3n)!}{(n!)^3}$.

(*xiii*) Greatest value of ${}^nC_r$

${}^nC_r$ is greatest when $r = n/2$ if n is even

$r = (n-1)/2$ or $(n+1)/2$ if n is odd.

(*xiv*) ${}^nC_r = {}^nC_{n-r}$.

(*xv*) ${}^nC_r + {}^nC_{r+1} = {}^{n+1}C_{r+1}$.

(*xvi*) ${}^nC_r = {}^nC_s \Rightarrow r = s$ or $r + s = n$.

(*xvii*) The number of circular permutations of n different things taken all at a time $= (n-1)!$

(*xviii*) The number of arrangements of n persons on a round table $= (n-1)!$.

(*xix*) The number of arrangements of n flowers to make a garland $= \frac{1}{2}(n-1)!$.

SOLVED EXAMPLES

Example 1: In how many different ways can the letters of the word 'PRIDE' be arranged ?

Solution: Required number of arrangements

$$= {}^5P_5 = 5! = 120$$

Example 2: In how many different ways can the letters of the word 'PRAISE' be arranged ?

Solution: Required number of ways

$$= {}^6P_6 = 6! = 720$$

Example 3: On a shelf there are 4 books on Economics, 3 books on Management and 4 books on Statistics. In how many different ways can the books be arranged so that the books on Economics are kept together ?

Solution: Required number of different ways

$= {}^{8}P_8 \times {}^{4}P_4 = \underline{|8} \times \underline{|4}$

$= 40320 \times 24 = 967680$

Example 4: In how many different ways can the letters of the word 'PRETTY' be arranged?

Solution: Required ways $= \frac{\underline{|6}}{\underline{|2}} = 360$

Example 5: In how many different ways can the letters of the word 'PEANUT' be arranged ?

Solution: Required ways $= {}^{6}P_6 = \underline{|6}$

$= 6 \times 5 \times 4 \times 3 \times 2 \times 1 = 720.$

MULTIPLE CHOICE QUESTIONS

1. How many seven digit numbers can be made from the number 3428651, using each digit only once ?

A. 49 B. 180
C. 5040 D. 2520

2. How many words can be formed from the letters of the word 'DIRECTOR' so that the vowels are always together?

A. 2106 B. 1206
C. 360 D. 2160

3. In how many ways a committee of 5 members can be selected from 6 men and 5 ladies, consisting of 3 men and 2 ladies?

A. 120 B. 220
C. 200 D. 320

4. In how many ways can the letters of the word 'APPLE' be arranged?

A. 720 B. 120
C. 60 D. 180

5. How many words can be formed by using all the letters of the word. 'ALLAHABAD'?

A. 3780 B. 1890
C. 7560 D. 2520

6. How many words can be formed from the letters of the word 'SIGNATURE' so that the vowels always come together?

A. 720 B. 1440
C. 2880 D. 17280

7. In how many different ways can the letters of the word 'BANKING' be arranged so that the vowels always come together?.

A. 120 B. 240
C. 360 D. 720

8. In how many ways can a group of 5 men and 2 women be made out of a total of 7 men and 3 women?

A. 63 B. 90
C. 126 D. 45

9. In a group of 6 boys and 4 girls, four children are to be selected. In how many different ways can they be selected such that at least one boy should be there?

A. 159 B. 194
C. 205 D. 209

10. A box contains 2 white balls, 3 black balls and 4 red balls. In how many ways can 3 balls be drawn from the box, if at least one black ball is to be included in the draw?

A. 32 B. 48
C. 64 D. 96

11. In how many ways can a team of 3 boys and 3 girls be selected from 5 boys and 4 girls?

A. 14 B. 40
C. 18 D. 140

12. The number of ways of selecting 9 balls from 6 red, 5 white and 5 blue if each selection consists of 3 balls of each colour is :

A. 1200 B. 20000
C. 2200 D. 2000

13. In how many ways can we select 4 red balls and 3 blue balls from 8 red balls and 9 blue balls?

A. 8550 B. 5850
C. 5880 D. 8580

14. Find the number of diagonals of a decagon

A. 45 B. 35
C. 55 D. 25

15. In how many ways can a student choose a programme of 5 courses if 9 courses are available and 2 specific courses are compulsary for every student?

A. 53 B. 14
C. 35 D. 28

16. Seven different lecturers are to deliver lectures in seven periods of a class on a particular day. A, B and C are three of the lecturers. The number of ways in which a routine for the day can be made such that A delivers his lecuture before B, and B before C, is

A. 420 B. 120
C. 210 D. 840

17. The number of words that can be made by rearranging the letters of the word APURBA so that vowels and consonants alternate is

A. 18
B. 35
C. 36
D. 24

18. The number of ways in which the letters of the word ARTICLE can be rearranged so that the even places are always occupied by consonants is
A. 576
B. $^4C_3 \times (4!)$
C. 2(4!)
D. 288

19. The number of ways in which a couple can sit around a table with 6 guests if the couple take consecutive seats is
A. 1440
B. 720
C. 5040
D. 2880

20. The number of ways in which 20 different pearls of two colours can be set alternately on a necklace, there being 10 pearls of each colour, is
A. $9! \times 10!$
B. $5(9!)^2$
C. $(9!)^2$
D. $(18!)^2$

ANSWERS

1	2	3	4	5	6	7	8	9	10
C	D	C	C	C	D	D	A	D	C
11	**12**	**13**	**14**	**15**	**16**	**17**	**18**	**19**	**20**
B	D	C	B	C	D	C	A	A	B

SOME SELECTED EXPLANATORY ANSWERS

1. Required number of ways = $^7P_7 = \lfloor 7 = 5040$.

2. In the given word, we treat the vowels IEO as one letter.
Thus, we have DRCTR (IEO).
This group has 6 letters of which R occurs 2 times and others are different.

Number of ways arranging these letters $= \frac{6!}{2!} = 360$.

Now 3 vowels can be arranged among themselves in 3! = 6 ways.
∴ Required number of ways = (360 × 6) = 2160.

3. (3 men out of 6) and (2 ladies out of 5) are to be chosen.
∴ Required number of ways
$= (^6C_3 \times {^5C_2})$

$= \left(\frac{6\times5\times4}{3\times2\times1}\times\frac{5\times4}{2\times1}\right) = 200.$

4. The word 'APPLE' contains 5 letters, 1A, 2P, 1L and 1E.
∴ Required number of ways

$= \frac{5!}{(1!)(2!)(1!)(1!)} = 60.$

5. The word 'ALLAHABAD' contains 9 letters, namely 4A, 2L, 1H, 1B and 1D.
∴ Required number of words

$= \frac{9!}{(4!)(2!)(1!)(1!)(1!)} = 7560.$

6. The word 'SIGNATURE' contains 9 different letters. When the vowels IAUE are taken together, they can be supposed to form an entity, treated as one letter.

Then, the letters to be arranged are SGNTR (IAUE). These 6 letters can be arranged in $^6P_6 = 6! = 720$ ways. The vowels in the group (IAUE) can be arranged amongst themselves in $^4P_4 = 4! = 24$ ways.
∴ Required number of words = (720 × 24)
= 17280.

7. In the word 'BANKING', we treat the two vowels AI as one letter. Thus, we have BNKNG (AI).
This has 6 letters of which N occurs 2 times and the rest are different.
Number of ways of arranging these letters

$= \frac{6!}{(2!)(1!)(1!)(1!)(1!)} = 360.$

Now, 2 vowels AI can be arranged in 2! = 2 ways.
∴ Required number of ways = (360 × 2) = 720.

8. Required number of ways
$= (^7C_5 \times {^3C_2})$

$= (^7C_2 \times {^3C_1}) = \left(\frac{7\times6}{2\times1}\times3\right) = 63.$

9. We may have (1 boy and 3 girls) or (2 boys and 2 girls) or (3 boys and 1 girl) or (4 boys).
∴ Required number of ways
$= (^6C_1 \times {^4C_3}) + (^6C_2 \times {^4C_2}) + (^6C_3 \times {^4C_1}) + (^6C_4)$
$= (^6C_1 \times {^4C_1}) + (^6C_2 \times {^4C_2}) + (^6C_3 \times {^4C_1}) + (^6C_2)$

$= (6\times4)+\left(\frac{6\times5}{2\times1}\times\frac{4\times3}{2\times1}\right)+\left(\frac{6\times5\times4}{3\times2\times1}\times4\right)+\left(\frac{6\times5}{2\times1}\right)$

= (24 + 90 + 80 + 15) = 209.

10. We may have (1 black and 2 non-black) or (2 black and 1 non-black) or (3 black)

$\therefore$ Required number of ways
$= (^3C_1 \times {}^6C_2) + (^3C_2 \times {}^6C_1) + (^3C_3)$

$= \left(3\times\frac{6\times5}{2\times1}\right)+\left(\frac{3\times2}{2\times1}\times6\right)+1 = (45 + 18 + 1) = 64.$

13. 4 red balls from 8 red balls can be selected in ${}^8C_4$ ways 3 blue balls from 9 balls can be selected in ${}^9C_3$ ways

$\therefore$ Total number of selection $= {}^8C_4 \times {}^9C_3$

$= \frac{8\times7\times6\times5}{1\times2\times3\times4}\times\frac{9\times8\times7}{1\times2\times3}$

$= 70 \times 84 = 5880.$

14. A decagon has 10 vertices

Join any two vertices in ${}^{10}C_2$ lines 10 lines will be sides.

$\therefore$ Number of diagonals $= {}^{10}C_2 - 10$

$= \frac{10\times9}{1\times2} - 10$

$= 45 - 10 = 35.$

16. As the order of A, B and C is not to change they are to be treated identical in arrangement. So, the required Number of ways $= \frac{7!}{3!}$.

$= \frac{7\times6\times5\times4\times3\times2\times1}{3\times2\times1} = 840.$

18. The number of ways to fill the three even places by 4 consonants $= {}^4P_3$.

After filling the even places, remaining places can be filled in ${}^4P_4$ ways.

So, the required number of words

$= {}^4P_3 \times {}^4P_4$

$= 4! \times 4! = 24 \times 24 = 576.$

19. A couple and 6 guests can be arranged in $(7 - 1)!$ ways. But the two people forming the couple can be arranged among themselves in 2! ways.

$\therefore$ The required number of ways $= 6! \times 2!$

$= 720 \times 2 = 1440.$

❑❑❑

13 PROBABILITY

1. **Random Experiment:** If the result of an experiment is not certain and is any one of the several possible outcomes, the experiment is called a trial or a random experiment.
2. **Sample Space:** The set of all possible outcome of an experiment is called the sample space provided no two or more of these outcomes can occur simultaneously and exactly one of these outcomes must occur whenever the experiment is conducted.
3. **Events:** The outcomes of an experiment, *i.e.*, sample points of the sample space are usually known as simple events and any subset of the sample space 'S' is called an event.

   Thus throwing of a dice is an experiment, S = {1, 2, 3, 4, 5, 6} is the sample space, {1}, ... {6} are simple events and {1, 2}, etc., are events. The empty set ϕ is also an event as $\phi \subset S$ and it is called an impossible event. The sample space S is also a subset of S and so it is also an event. S represents the sure event, *i.e.*, certainty.
4. **Equally Likely Events:** A set of events is said to be equally likely if taking into consideration all the relevant factors there is no reason to expect one of them in preference to others.

   For example, when a fair coin is tossed, the occurrence of a tail or a head are equally likely.
5. **Exhaustive Events:** A set of events is said to be exhaustive if the performance of the experiment always results in the occurrence of atleast one of them.

   For example, if we throw a dice, then the events A_1 = {1, 2}, A_2 = {2, 3, 3} are not exhaustive as we can get 5 as outcome of the experiment which is not the member of any of the events A_1 and A_2. If we consider the events E_1 = {1, 2, 3} and E_2 = {2, 4, 5, 6}, then the set E_1, E_2, is exhaustive.
6. **Mutually Exclusive Events:** A set of events is said to be mutually exclusive if they have no point in common, *i.e.*, happening of one of them eliminates the happening of any of the remaining events. Thus E_1, E_2, E_3, ... are mutually exclusive iff $E_i \cap E_j = \phi$ for $i \neq E_1$ and E_2 are mutually exclusive.
7. **Complement of An Events:** The complement of an event A, denoted by $\overline{A}$, A' or A^c, is the set of all sample points of the space other than the sample points in A.

   e.g., In the experiment of throwing a fair dice, S = {1, 2, 3, 4, 5, 6}. If A = {1, 3, 5, 6}, then $\overline{A}$ = {2, 4}

   Note that $A \cap \overline{A} = S$.
8. **Classical Definition of Probability:** If there are *n* exhaustive mutually exclusive and equally likely outcomes of an experiment and *m* of them are favourable to an event A, the probability of the happening of A is defined as the ratio *m*/*n*.

   Thus, denoting the probability of the happening of an event A by *p*, we have $p = m/n$.

   Clearly *p* is a positive number not greater than unity, so that $0 \leq p \leq 1$.

   Since the number of cases in which the event A will not happen is $n - m$, the probability *q* that the event will not happen is given by $q = \frac{(n-m)}{n} = 1 - \frac{m}{n}$ $= 1 - p. \therefore p + q = 1$

   If probability of happening of an event A is 1, then A is certain event and if probability of happening of an event A is 0, then A is impossible event.
9. **Odds in Favour and Odds against an Event:** As a result of an experiment if *a* of the outcomes are favourable to an event E and *b* of the outcomes are against it, then we say that odds are *a* to *b* in favour of E or odds are *b* to *a* against E.

   Thus, odds in favour of an event E

   $$= \frac{\text{number of favourable cases}}{\text{number of unfavourable cases}}.$$

   Similarly, odds against an event E

   $$= \frac{\text{number of unfavourable cases}}{\text{number of favourable cases}}.$$

   If odds in favour of an event are *a* : *b* then the probability of the occurrence of that event is $\frac{a}{a+b}$

and the probability of the non-occurrence of that event is $\frac{b}{(a+b)}$.

Addition Theorem:

(*a*) If 'A' and 'B' are any two events in a sample space S, then $P(A \cup B) = P(A) + P(B) - P(A \cap B)$.

(*b*) If 'A' and 'B' are mutually exclusive then $P(A \cap B) = 0$ so that $P(A \cup B) = P(A) + P(B)$.

(*c*) If A is any event in S, then $P(A') = 1 - P(A)$.

Total Probability Theorem:

The probability that one of several mutually exclusive events $A_1, A_2, ..., A_n$ will happen, is the sum of the probabilities of the separate events. In symbol,

$P(A_1 + A_2 + ... + A_n) = P(A_1) + P(A_2) + ... + P(A_n)$.

Conditional Probability:

The probability of B under the assumption that A has occurred is called the conditional probability of B under the condition that the event A has taken place and is denoted by P(B/A). P(B/A) is read as "probability at the event B given A^B."

Conditional Probability Theorem:

If A and B are any two events in the sample space S, the conditional probability of B relative to A is given by P(B/

$$A) = \frac{P(B \cap A)}{P(A)} = \frac{n(B \cap A)}{n(A)}, A \neq \phi.$$

Some Important Remarks about Coins, Dice and Playing Cards:

(*a*) **Coins:** A coin has a head side and a tail side. If an experiment consist of more than a coin, coins are considered to be distinct if not otherwise stated.

(*b*) **Dice:** A die (cubical) has six faces marked 1, 2, 3, 4, 5, 6. We may have tetrahedral (having four faces 1, 2, 3, 4) or pentagonal (having five faces 1, 2, 3, 4, 5) die. As in the case of dice, if we have more than one die, all dice are considered to be distinct if not otherwise stated.

(*c*) **Playing Cards:** A pack of playing cards usually contain 52 cards.

There are 4 suits (spade, heart, diamond and club) each having 13 cards. There are two colours — red (heart and diamond) and black (spade and club) each having 26 cards.

In thirteen cards of each suit, there are 3 face cards namely king, queen and jack, so there are in all 12 face cards (4 kings, 4 queens and 4 jacks).

Also there are 16 honours cards, 4 of each suit namely ace, king, queen and jack.

SOLVED EXAMPLES

Example 1: A bag contains 7 Red balls, 4 Green balls and 5 Yellow balls. What is the probability that 3 balls drawn at random are either Green or Yellow?

Solution: Total ways = ${}^{16}C_3 = \frac{\lfloor 16}{\lfloor 13 \lfloor 3} = 560$

Favourable ways = ${}^4C_3 \times {}^5C_3 = \frac{\lfloor 4}{\lfloor 3 \lfloor 1} \times \frac{\lfloor 5}{\lfloor 3 \lfloor 2}$
$= 4 \times 10 = 40$.

$\therefore$ Reqd. Probability = $\frac{40}{560} = \frac{1}{14}$.

Example 2: A basket contains three Red and four Green balls. If four balls are drawn at random from the basket, what is the probability that two are Red and two are Green?

Solution: Reqd. Probability = $\frac{{}^3C_2 \times {}^4C_2}{{}^7C_4} = \frac{3 \times 6}{35}$

$= \frac{18}{35}$.

Example 3: A box contains 8 Red, 16 Blue, 4 Yellow and 12 Black bolls. Two balls are picked up randomly. What is the chance that both are Red?

Solution: Total results = ${}^{40}C_2 = \frac{40 \times 39}{2} = 780$

and favourable results = ${}^8C_2 = \frac{\lfloor 8}{\lfloor 2 \lfloor 6} = \frac{8 \times 7}{2}$

$= 28$.

$\therefore$ Required probability = $\frac{28}{780} = \frac{7}{195}$

Example 4: A bag contains 8 Red, 16 Blue, 12 Black and 4 Yellow marbles. One marbles is picked up randomly. What is the probability that it is not Blue?

Solution: Total results = ${}^{40}C_1 = 40$

Favourable results when it is Blue = ${}^{16}C_1 = 16$.

$\therefore$ Favourable results when it is not Blue

$= 40 - 16 = 24$

$\therefore$ Reqd. probability = $\frac{24}{40} = 0.6$.

MULTIPLE CHOICE QUESTIONS

Directions (Qs. 1 to 3) : *Study the information carefully to answer the questions that follow.*

A bucket contains 8 Red, 3 Blue and 5 Green marbles.

1. If 4 marbles are drawn at random, what is the probability that 2 are Red and 2 are Blue?

A. $\frac{11}{16}$ B. $\frac{3}{16}$

C. $\frac{11}{72}$ D. $\frac{3}{65}$

2. If 2 marbles are drawn at random, what is the probability that both are Green?

A. $\frac{1}{12}$ B. $\frac{5}{16}$

C. $\frac{2}{7}$ D. None of these

3. If 3 marbles are drawn at random, what is the probability that none is Red?

A. $\frac{3}{8}$ B. $\frac{1}{16}$

C. $\frac{1}{10}$ D. None of these

Directions (Qs. 4 to 5) : *Study the information and answer the questions that follow.*

A basket contains 3 Red balls, 5 Blue balls and 2 Green balls.

4. If three balls are drawn at random, what is the probability that none is Blue?

A. $\frac{1}{6}$ B. $\frac{1}{12}$

C. $\frac{1}{5}$ D. $\frac{3}{10}$

5. If four balls are drawn at random, what is the probability that at least one is Green?

A. $\frac{2}{3}$ B. $\frac{1}{2}$

C. $\frac{1}{3}$ D. $\frac{2}{5}$

6. If two balls are drawn at random, what is the probability that both are Red?

A. $\frac{1}{5}$ B. $\frac{3}{10}$

C. $\frac{3}{5}$ D. $\frac{1}{15}$

7. A dice is thrown once. Find the probability of getting a number greater than 3.

A. $\frac{2}{3}$ B. $\frac{1}{3}$

C. $\frac{1}{2}$ D. $\frac{3}{2}$

8. A bag contains 5 Red balls, 8 White balls, 4 Green balls and 7 Black balls. If one ball is drawn at random, find the probability that it is Black.

A. $\frac{7}{24}$ B. $\frac{5}{24}$

C. $\frac{5}{6}$ D. $\frac{1}{4}$

9. Find the probability that a number selected from the numbers 1 to 25 is not a prime number when each of the given number is equally to be selected.

A. $\frac{9}{25}$ B. $\frac{16}{25}$

C. $\frac{21}{25}$ D. $\frac{14}{25}$

10. A bag contains 3 Red balls and 5 Black balls. A ball is drawn at random from the bag. What is the probability that the ball drawn is not Red?

A. $\frac{3}{8}$ B. $\frac{5}{8}$

C. $\frac{1}{8}$ D. $\frac{7}{8}$

11. A die is thrown once. Find the probability of getting an odd number.

A. $\frac{1}{2}$ B. $\frac{3}{2}$

C. $\frac{2}{3}$ D. $\frac{1}{3}$

12. A letter is chosen at random from the word REED the probability of choosing an E is –

A. $\frac{3}{4}$ B. $\frac{1}{2}$

C. $\frac{1}{4}$ D. $\frac{2}{3}$

13. A card is drawn at random from a well-shuffled deck of playing cards. Find the probability that the card drawn is a card of spade or an ace.

A. $\frac{11}{13}$ B. $\frac{1}{26}$

C. $\frac{4}{13}$ D. $\frac{9}{13}$

14. If a letter is chosen at random from the word TRIANGLE.
What is the probability that it a vowel?

A. $\frac{3}{8}$ B. $\frac{5}{8}$

C. $\frac{1}{4}$ D. $\frac{3}{4}$

15. What is the chance that a leap year, selected at random, will contain 53 Sundays?

A. $\frac{52}{365}$ B. $\frac{52}{366}$

C. $\frac{2}{7}$ D. $\frac{5}{7}$

16. In a book of 300 pages, if a page is opened at random; find the probability that the sum of the digits in its number is 10.

A. $\frac{8}{15}$ B. $\frac{9}{15}$

C. $\frac{7}{75}$ D. $\frac{14}{15}$

17. A die is thrown once. Find the probability of getting an even number.

A. $\frac{1}{3}$ B. $\frac{1}{2}$

C. $\frac{1}{4}$ D. $\frac{1}{6}$

18. Two friends were born in the year 2000. What is the probability that they have the same birthday?

A. $\frac{1}{500}$ B. $\frac{1}{730}$

C. $\frac{1}{365}$ D. $\frac{1}{366}$

19. A number is chosen at random from among the first 30 natural numbers. The probability of the number chosen being prime is :

A. $\frac{1}{3}$ B. $\frac{3}{10}$

C. $\frac{1}{30}$ D. $\frac{11}{30}$

20. The probability that a number selected at random from the set of numbers {1, 2, 3, 4, ..., 100} is a cube is:

A. $\frac{1}{25}$

B. $\frac{2}{25}$

C. $\frac{3}{25}$

D. $\frac{4}{25}$

ANSWERS

1	2	3	4	5	6	7	8	9	10
D	A	A	B	A	D	C	A	B	B
11	**12**	**13**	**14**	**15**	**16**	**17**	**18**	**19**	**20**
A	B	C	A	C	C	B	D	A	A

SOME SELECTED EXPLANATORY ANSWERS

1. Total number of ways = ${}^{16}C_4 = \frac{\lfloor 16}{\lfloor 12 \lfloor 4}$

$= 1820$

And favourable number of ways = ${}^{8}C_2 \times {}^{3}C_2$

$= \frac{\lfloor 8}{\lfloor 6 \lfloor 2} \times \frac{\lfloor 3}{\lfloor 1 \lfloor 2} = 84$

$\therefore$ Reqd. probability = $\frac{84}{1820} = \frac{3}{65}$.

2. Total number of ways = ${}^{16}C_2 = \frac{\lfloor 16}{\lfloor 14 \lfloor 2} = 120$

And favourable number of ways = ${}^{5}C_2$

$= \frac{\lfloor 5}{\lfloor 3 \lfloor 2} = 10$

$\therefore$ Reqd. probability = $\frac{10}{120} = \frac{1}{12}$.

3. Total number of ways = ${}^{16}C_3 = \frac{\lfloor 16}{\lfloor 13 \lfloor 3} = 560$

Total number of ways when all the marbles are Red

$= {}^{8}C_3 = \frac{\lfloor 8}{\lfloor 5 \lfloor 3} = 56$

∴ Probability when all the three are Red

$$= \frac{56}{560} = \frac{1}{10}$$

∴ And probability when none is Red $= 1 - \frac{1}{10}$

$$= \frac{9}{10}.$$

4. Probability that none is blue

$$= \frac{^5C_3}{^{10}C_3} = \frac{10}{120} = \frac{1}{12}.$$

5. Probability that none is green

$$= \frac{^8C_4}{^{10}C_4} = \frac{70}{210} = \frac{1}{3}.$$

∴ Probability that at least one is green

$$= 1 - \frac{1}{3} = \frac{2}{3}.$$

6. Probability that both are red

$$= \frac{^3C_2}{^{10}C_2} = \frac{3}{45} = \frac{1}{15}.$$

7. Sample space S = {1, 2, 3, 4, 5, 6} ; $n(S) = 6$
Let A = "getting a number grater than 3" then
A = {4, 5, 6} ; $n(A) = 3$

$$P(A) = \frac{n(A)}{n(S)} = \frac{3}{6} = \frac{1}{2}.$$

9. We are given numbers from 1 to 25.
$n(S) = 25$.
Prime numbers from 1 to 25 are 2, 3, 5, 7, 11, 13, 17, 19, 23.
These are 9 prime numbers.
Let E denote the event 'Number drawn is not prime'.

∴ $n(E) = 25 - 9 = 16$

$$p(E) = \frac{n(E)}{n(S)} = \frac{16}{25}.$$

10. Total number of balls in the bag = 3 + 5 = 8
Let E denote the event 'ball drawn is red'.

∴ $n(E) = 3$ and $n(S) = 8$.

(*i*) $p(E) = \frac{n(E)}{n(S)} = \frac{3}{8}$

(*ii*) $p(\text{not red}) = p(\bar{E})$

$$= 1 - p(E) = 1 - \frac{3}{8} = \frac{5}{8}.$$

11. Sample S = {1, 2, 3, 4, 5, 6} ; $n(S) = 6$
Let F denote the event 'getting an odd number'.
F = {1, 3, 5} ; $n(S) = 3$

∴ $P(F) = \frac{n(F)}{n(S)} = \frac{3}{6} = \frac{1}{2}.$

12. The sample space is $\{R, E_1, E_2, D\}$
There are 2 ways to choose the letter E from the four letters

∴ $P(E) = \frac{2}{4} = \frac{1}{2}.$

13. There are 52 cards in a deck of 52 playing cards.
There are 13 spades and 4 aces in 52 playing cards.
Out of 13 spades there is one ace.
∴ Favourable no ways for the card drawn to be spade or an ace = 13 spades + 3 aces = 16.

∴ P(a card of spade or an ace) $= \frac{16}{52} = \frac{4}{13}.$

14. Since there are 3 vowels out of a total of 8 letters, the probability of choosing a vowel is 3/8.

15. A Leap year has 366 days. In a leap year, here are 52 complete weeks (52 Sundays) and 2 days over these two days can be as follows.
Sunday and Monday, Monday and Tuesday, Tuesday and Wednesday, Wednesday and Thursday, Thursday and Friday, Friday and Saturday, Saturday and Sunday.
Out of these 7 possibilities, only two (Saturday and Sunday; Sunday and Monday) are favourable for having 53 Sundays)

Required chance $= \frac{2}{7}.$

17. A die is thrown once. Its sample space is
S = {1, 2, 3, 4, 5, 6}, $n(S) = 6$
Let E : an even number, then E = {2, 4, 6} Number of favourable cases = $n(E) = 3$

∴ $P(E) = \frac{n(E)}{n(S)} = \frac{3}{6} = \frac{1}{2}.$

18. Year 2000 is a leap year. There are 366 days in the year 2000. Total number of cases in which two friends can be born on the same day are 366.
Out of 366 days, number of favourable ways in which two friends have the same birthday = 1

∴ Required probability $= \frac{1}{366}.$

19. The prime numbers from first 30 natural numbers are 2, 3, 5, 7, 11, 13, 17, 19, 23, 29.
We find that there are 10 prime numbers from 1 to 30.
∴ Probability that the number chosen being prime is

$$= \frac{10}{30} = \frac{1}{3}.$$

20. From the natural numbers 1 to 100 the four number 1, 8, 27 and 64 are cubes

∴ Required Probability $= \frac{4}{100} = \frac{1}{25}.$

❑❑❑

14 DATA INTERPRETATION

TABLES

Tables are often used in reports, magazines and newspaper to present as set of numerical data. It is one of the easiest and most accurate ways of presenting data. One of the main purposes of tables is to make complicated information easier to understand. Hence, the advantage of presenting data in a table is that one can see the information at a glance. We present below an example of tabular presentation of annual expenditure of 5 families for last 4 years.

Annual Expenditure of 5 families (in ₹ Thousands)

Years → Families ↓	2005	2006	2007	2008
A	35	50	55	60
B	40	60	65	75
C	45	50	70	80
D	30	40	45	50
E	50	55	60	70

Essentials of a Tables:

(i) **Title:** Heading of the table
(ii) **Stub:** The section of the table containing row headings in called Stub.
(iii) **Column Captions :** The heading of each column is designated as column caption.
(iv) **Body**
(v) **Footnotes**
(vi) **Source**

Example 1. Directions: *Study the folloiwng table and answer the questions given below:*

Categories of students according to their enrolment in various courses in a vocational college.

Courses	*Categories (Faculty)*			
	Arts		*Science*	
	Boys	*Girls*	*Boys*	*Girls*
1. Business Management	45	25	65	25
2. Typewriting	186	23	32	20
3. Stenography	120	25	58	12
4. Typewriting and Stenography	100	12	5	3

1. If 60% boys and 70% girls pass in their respective courses, then total pass percentage is:
A. 58% B. 66% C. 54% D. 62%

2. The total number of students who have opted the course of Business Management and the course of Stenography exceeds the number of students studying in typewriting course by:
A. 44% B. 66% C. 33% D. 55%

3. In which of the following courses, percentage of girls is the highest?
A. Stenography
B. Business Management
C. Typewriting
D. Typewriting and Stenography

4. In the art faculty number of students who have opted the course of stenography is how much per cent of the total student in the faculty?
A. 27% B. 10% C. 18% D. 15%

5. Total number of boys studying in the college exceeds the total number of girls in the college by:
A. 321% B. 280% C. 308% D. 250%

Solution 1. $\because$ Total boys = 45 + 186 + 120 + 100 + 65 + 32 + 58 + 5 = 611

$\therefore$ Number of boys who pass in their respective courses = 60% of 611 = $611 \times \frac{60}{100} = 366.60$

Total number of girls = 25 + 23 + 25 + 12 + 25 + 20 + 12 + 3 = 145

Number of girls who pass in their respective courses = 70% of 145 = $\frac{145 \times 70}{100} = 101.50$

$\therefore$ Combined pass per cent = $\frac{(366.6 + 101.5) \times 100}{611 + 145} = \frac{46810}{756} = 61.92 \simeq 62\%$

Solution 2. $\because$ Number of students in Business Management course = 160
Number of students in typewriting course = 261
Number of students in stenography corse = 215

$\therefore$ Required per cent = $\left(\frac{160 + 215 - 261}{261}\right) \times 100 \approx 44\%$

Solution 3. Percentage of girls in Business Management course = $\frac{(25 + 25) \times 100}{160} = 31.25$

Percentage of girls in typewriting course = $\frac{(23 + 20) \times 100}{261} = 16.47$

Percentage of girls in stenography course = $\frac{(25 + 12) \times 100}{215} = 12.56$

And percentage of girls in typewriting and stenography course = $\frac{(12 + 3) \times 100}{120} = 12.50$

Hence, it is clear from the above that percentage of girls in Business Management course is the highest.

Solution 4. Required percentage = $\frac{(25 + 120) \times 100}{536} \times 100 \simeq 27$

Solution 5. Total number of boys = 45 + 65 + 186 + 32 + 120 + 58 + 100 + 5 = 611
Total number of girls = 25 + 23 + 25 + 12 + 25 + 20 + 12 + 3 = 145

$\therefore$ Required percentage = $\left(\frac{611 - 145}{145}\right) \times 100 \simeq 321\%$

Example 2. Directions: *Figures of biscuit exports from a country during various years are given in the following table. Study the table carefully and answer the questions that follows:*

VOLUME OF EXPORT OF BISCUITS FROM A COUNTRY

Year	*Quantity (in lakh tins)*	*Price (in crores ₹)*
2004	100	150
2005	75	150
2006	150	330
2007	160	400
2008	200	500

1. During which year per tin export price remained at lowest level?

A. 2007 B. 2006 C. 2005 D. 2004

2. During which years price per tin remained at the same level?

A. 2006 and 2008 B. 2006 and 2007 C. 2007 and 2008 D. 2006 and 2004

3. The export price of biscuit increased from 2004 to 2008 by how much per cent?

A. 100 B. $116\frac{2}{3}$ C. $233\frac{1}{3}$ D. 350

4. The difference between the number of biscuit tins exported in 2008 and that in 2007 is:

A. 40 B. 40,000 C. 4,00,000 D. 40,00,000

Solution 1. Export price per tin in 2004 = $\frac{₹\ 150 \text{ crores}}{₹\ 100 \text{ lakhs}} = ₹\ 150$

Export price per tin in 2005 = $\frac{₹\ 150 \text{ crores}}{₹\ 75 \text{ lakhs}} = ₹\ 200$

Export price per tin in 2006 = $\frac{₹\ 330 \text{ crores}}{₹\ 150 \text{ lakhs}} = ₹\ 220$

Export price per tin in 2007 = $\frac{₹\ 400 \text{ crores}}{₹\ 160 \text{ lakhs}} = ₹\ 250$

Export price per tin in 2008 = $\frac{₹\ 500 \text{ crores}}{₹\ 200 \text{ lakhs}} = ₹\ 250$

Hence, it is clear that per tin export price was at lowest level in 2004.

Solution 2. From the explanation given in the answer of Q.No. 1, it is clear that per tin export price was same in 2007 and 2008.

Solution 3. From the level of 2004 percentage increase in export price in 2008 = $\left(\frac{500-150}{150}\right) \times 100 = 233\frac{1}{3}\%$

Solution 4. Required difference = 200 – 160 = 40 lakh tins = 40,00,000 tins.

Example. 3. Directions: *Study the following table carefully and answer the questions given below:*

Number of Employees Working in Various departments of a Factory

Year	*Production Deptt.*	*Sale Deptt.*	*Procurement Deptt.*	*Administration & Accounts Deptt.*	*Research & Development Deptt.*
2003	150	25	50	45	75
2004	225	40	45	62	70
2005	450	65	30	90	73
2006	470	73	32	105	70
2007	500	80	35	132	74
2008	505	75	36	130	75

1. During which of the following years number of employees working in production deptt. of the factory was less than 50% of the total employees of the factory?

A. 2003 B. 2005 C. 2006 D. 2007

2. During which year the number of employees working in each department was more than those in the previous year and nearly equal to next year?

A. 2007 B. 2006 C. 2005 D. 2004

3. In which department of the factory number of employees remained nearly same during the years from 2003 to 2008?

A. Production B. Sale
C. Research and Development D. Administration and Accounts
E. Procurement

4. In which department of the factory number of employees are maximum from 2003 to 2008?

A. Production
B. Sale
C. Research and Development
D. Administration and Accounts
E. Sale and Procurement

5. During which year number of employees in the factory became nearly double the total number of employees working in the factory during 2003.

A. 2008
B. 2007
C. 2006
D. 2005

Solution 1. Number of total employees in 2003 = 150 + 25 + 50 + 45 + 75 = 345

$\therefore$ Percentage number of employees working in producton deptt. = $\dfrac{150 \times 100}{345} = 43.48\%$

Number of total employees in 2004 = 225 + 40 + 45 + 62 + 70 = 442

$\therefore$ Percentage number of employees working in production deptt. = $\dfrac{225 \times 100}{442} = 50.9\%$

Number of total employees in 2005 = 450 + 65 + 30 + 90 + 73 = 708

$\therefore$ Percentage number of employees working in proudction deptt. = $\dfrac{450 \times 100}{708} = 63.56\%$

Total number of employees in 2006 = 470 + 73 + 32 + 105 + 70 = 750

$\therefore$ Percentage number of employees working in production deptt. = $\dfrac{470 \times 100}{750} = 62.67\%$

Total number of employees in 2007 = 500 + 80 + 35 + 132 + 74 = 821

$\therefore$ Percentage number of employees working in production deptt. = $\dfrac{500 \times 100}{821} = 60.9\%$

Total number of employees in 2007 = 505 + 75 + 36 + 130 + 75 = 821

$\therefore$ Percentage number of employees working in production in deptt. = $\dfrac{505 \times 100}{821} = 61.51\%$

Hence, it is clear that percentage number of employees working in production deptt. was less than 50% in 2003.

Solution 2. It is clear from the table that it was the year 2007 when the number of employees working in each department was more than that in the previous year and nearly equal to next year.

Solution 3. According to the table in the research and development department number of employees remained nearly same during the year from 2003 to 2008.

Solution 4. Production.

Solution 5. Total number of employes in 2003 = 345
Total number of employees in 2005 = 708
Hence, it was the year 2005 when total number of employees in the factory became nearly double the total number of emplyees working in the factory during 2003.

Example. 4. *Study the table carefully to answer the questions that follow.*

Number of students studying in six different classes of six different schools.

Class → School ↓	V	VI	VII	VIII	IX	X
P	152	160	145	156	147	144
Q	148	166	150	155	157	143
R	161	152	140	145	143	165
S	159	142	149	140	142	168
T	147	144	158	163	154	150
U	150	160	162	160	161	140

1. What is the respective ratio of students studying in class IX of schools Q and R together to those studying in class VI of schools S and T together?
A. 143 : 150 B. 150 : 143 C. 127 : 181 D. 181 : 127

2. Number of students studying in class X from school P forms approximately what per cent of the total number of students studying in class X from all schools together?
A. 9 B. 12 C. 16 D. 24

3. Total number of students studying in school T from all classes together forms what per cent of total number of students studying in school S from all classes together?
A. 100.26 B. 101.78 C. 102.64 D. 103.52

4. The number of students studying in class VII from school U forms what per cent of the total number of students from all the classes together from that school?
A. 15.93 B. 16.14 C. 17.36 D. 18.28

5. Which class has the maximum number of students from all schools together?
A. V B. VI C. VII D. X

Solution 1. Number of students of class IX of schools Q and R = 157 + 143 = 300
Number of students of class VI of schools S and T = 142 + 144 = 286
Hence, required ratio = 300 : 286 = 150 : 143

Solution 2. Total number of students of class X from all schools = 144 + 143 + 165 + 168 + 150 + 140 = 910

Required percentage = $\frac{144}{910} \times 100 = 15.82 \simeq 16\%$

Solution 3. Total number of students of school T from all classes = 147 + 144 + 158 + 163 + 154 + 150 = 916
Total number of students of school S from all classes = 159 + 142 + 149 + 140 + 142 + 168 = 900

Required percentage = $\frac{916}{900} \times 100 = 101.78\%$

Solution 4. Total number of students of school U from all the classes = 150 + 160 + 162 + 160 + 161 + 140 = 933

Required percentage = $\frac{162}{933} \times 100 = 17.36\%$

Solution 5. Total number of students of class V from all the schools = 152 + 148 + 161 + 159 + 147 + 150 = 917
Total number of students of class VI from all the schools = 160 + 166 + 152 + 142 + 144 + 160 = 924
Total number of students of class VII from all the schools = 145 + 150 + 140 + 149 + 158 + 162 = 904
Total number of students of class VIII from all the schools = 156 + 155 + 145 + 140 + 163 + 160 = 919
Total number of students of class IX from all the schools = 147 + 157 + 143 + 142 + 154 + 161 = 904
Total number of students of class X from all the schools = 144 + 143 + 165 + 168 + 150 + 140 = 910
Hence, the class VI has maximum number of students.

BAR GRAPHS

Given quantity of a bar graph can be compared by the height or length. A bar graph can have either vertical or horizontal bars. You can compare different quantities or the same quantity at the different times. The bars may be placed adjacent to each other or may be separated from each other by spaces depending upon the problem.

For Example: **Registration of New Vehicles in Delhi (in thousands)**

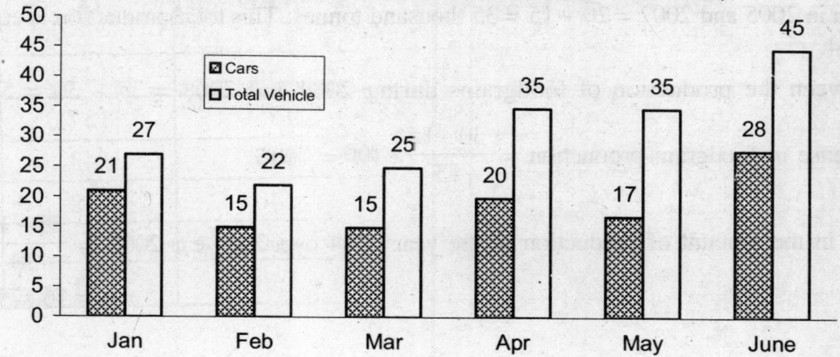

CUMULATIVE GRAPH

These are usually bar or line graphs where the height of the bar or line is divided up proportionally among various quantities presented in the graph. The representation of quantities may be done in terms of either percentage of the total or in absolute figures. These are also called sub-divided graphs. Thus, cumulative graph may be conveniently used for making comparisons.

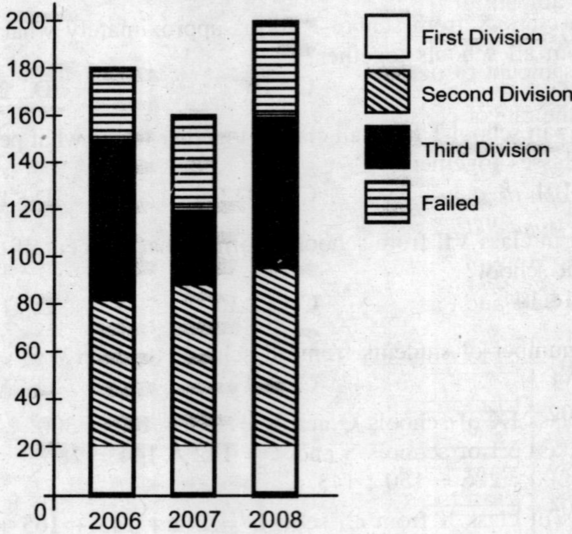

Example 1: Directions: *The following bar graph shows the production of food grains in India during certain year. Study the graph carefully and answer the questions given below:*

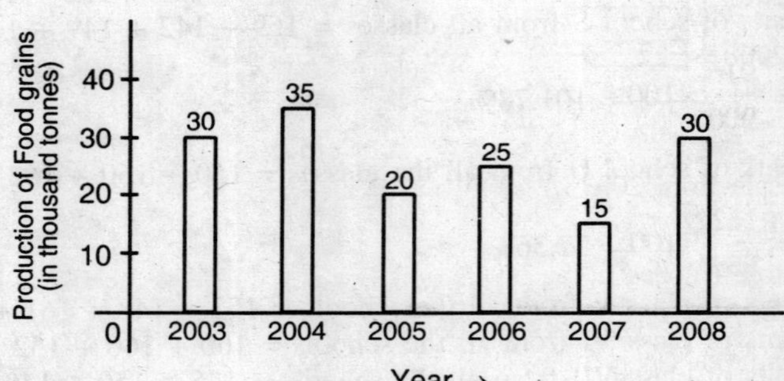

1. Total food grain production in 2005 and 2007 is equal to the production during which of the following years?
A. 2003 B. 2004 C. 2006 D. 2008

2. The difference between the foodgrain productions of 2004 and 2008 is:
A. 500 tonnes B. 1000 tonnes C. 5000 tonnes D. 10000 tonnes

3. Percentage increase in the production of foodgrains in the year 2008 over the year 2007 is:
A. 15% B. 30% C. 50% D. 100%

4. Rate of change in quantity of production in which of the following two consecutive years is at the minimum level?
A. 2003 and 2004 B. 2005 and 2006 C. 2007 and 2008 D. 2006 and 2007

Solution 1. Total production in 2005 and 2007 = 20 + 15 = 35 thousand tonnes. This total production is equal to the production in the year 2004.

Solution 2. Difference between the production of foodgrains during 2004 and 2008 = 35 – 30 = 5 thousand tonnes.

Solution 3. Percentage increase in foodgrain production = $\frac{30-15}{15} \times 100 = 100\%$

Solution 4. Rate of change in the amount of production in the year 2004 over the year 2003 = $\frac{35-30}{30} \times 100$

$= 16.67\%$

Rate of change in the amount of production in the year 2006 over the year 2005 = $\frac{(25-20)}{20} \times 100 = 25\%$

Rate of change in the amount of production in the year 2008 over the year 2007 = $\frac{(30-15)}{15} \times 100 = 100\%$

Rate of change in the amount of production in the year 2007 over the year 2006 = $\frac{(25-15)}{15} \times 100 = 66.67\%$

Hence, it is clear that the rate of change in the amount of production during the consecutive years 2007 and 2008 is at the highest level.

Example 2: Directions: *The bar graph as shown below gives information about the sale and profit details of a departmental store during the years from 2001–2008. Study the graph carefully and answer the questions asked here under.*

Sale and Profit details (2001-08)

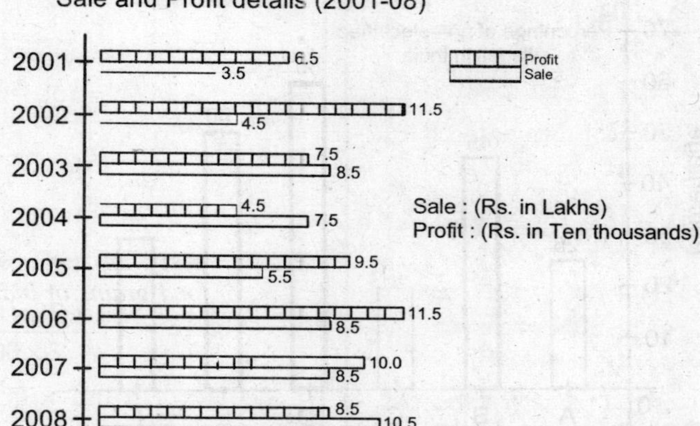

1. Mean of annual increase in sale from 2003 to 2008 (rupees in lakhs) is:

A. 0.1 B. 0.2 C. 0.3 D. 0.4

2. Annual mean profit of the store (rupees in ten thousands) is approximately:

A. 8.5 B. 8.6 C. 8.7 D. 9.0

3. During which of the following years percentage of profit earned by the store on the total sale was at the highest level?

A. 2001 B. 2002 C. 2003 D. 2005

4. Assuming the profit earned during the year 2001 as base (100), the profit made by the store during the year 2008 was:

A. 76 B. 105 C. 121 D. 131

5. During which year between 2001 to 2006 profit made by the store as compared to the previous year was more than 100%?

A. 2008 B. 2007 C. 2005 D. 2003

Solution 1. Mean of annual increase in sale from 2003 to 2008 = $\frac{10.5-8.5}{5} = .4$

Solution 2. Annual mean profit of the store (rupees in ten thousands)

$$= \frac{(6.5+11.5+7.5+4.5+9.5+11.5+10.0+8.5)}{8} = \frac{69.5}{8} = 8.7 \text{ (approx.)}$$

Solution 3. Percentage of profit on the total sale in 2001 = $\frac{6.5 \times 10000 \times 100}{3.5 \times 100000} = 18.57$

Percentage of profit on the total sale in 2002 = $\frac{11.5 \times 10000 \times 100}{4.5 \times 100000} = 25.56$

Percentage of profit on the total sale in 2003 = $\frac{7.5 \times 10000 \times 100}{8.5 \times 100000} = 8.82$

And percentage of profit on the total sale in 2005 = $\dfrac{9.5 \times 10000 \times 100}{5.5 \times 100000}$ = 17.27

∴ Percentage of profit on the total sale in 2002 was the highest level.

Solution 4. Required profit = $\dfrac{100 \times 8.5}{6.5}$ = 131

Solution 5. Profit per cent during the year 2005 as compared to the previous year = $\dfrac{(9.5-4.5)\times 100}{4.5}$ = 111.11%

Hence, profit in the year 2005 was more than 100% as compared to the previous year.

Example 3: Directions: *Study the graph given below and answer the questions asked there under.*

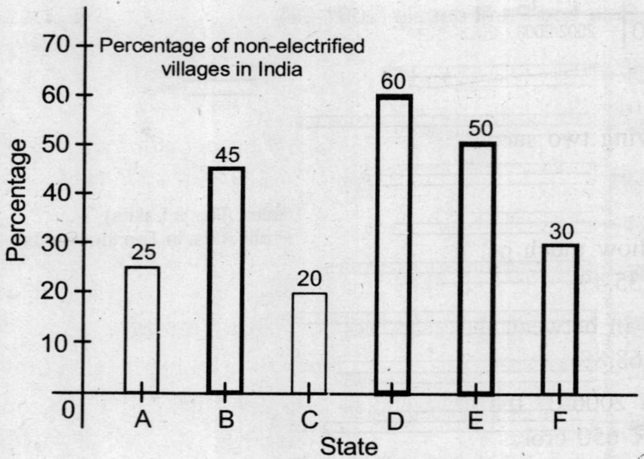

1. According to the table given below which state of India has the highest percentage of electrified villages?
   A. A B. B C. C D. D E. E
2. If central govt. decides to extend financial assistance for prompt electrification and begins with the state having the least electrified villages, then in the order of preference which of the following states will be fourth?
   A. C B. B C. A D. E E. F
3. How many states have at least 60% or more electrified villages?
   A. Five B. Three C. Four D. Two E. One
4. In which of the following states percentage of electrified villages is double the percentage of electrified villages in state (D)?
   A. C B. F C. A D. B E. E
5. What is the percentage of electrified villages in the state (A)?
   A. 65% B. 25% C. 35% D. 75% E. None of these

Solution 1. In the state (C) percentage of non-electrified villages is the least. It means the percentage of electrified villages for the state (C) is the highest.

Solution 2. The order of preference of the least electrified villages is given as: D, E, B, F, A, C.

Solution 3. In A, C and F states, percentage of non-electrified villages are 25, 20 and 30 per cent respectively. Hence, percentages of electrified villages for these three states are 75, 80 and 70 per cent respectively.

Solution 4. Percentage of electrified villages in state D = 100 – 60 = 40
Percentage of electrified villages in state C = 100 – 20 = 80
Hence, the percentage of electrified villages in the state C is double the percentage of electrified villages in state D.

Solution 5. Percentage of electrified villages in the state A = 100 – 25 = 75%

Example 4: Directions: *The following bar chart shows the amount accrued from additional taxation by the government during certain successive years. Study the chart carefully and answer the questions that follow:*

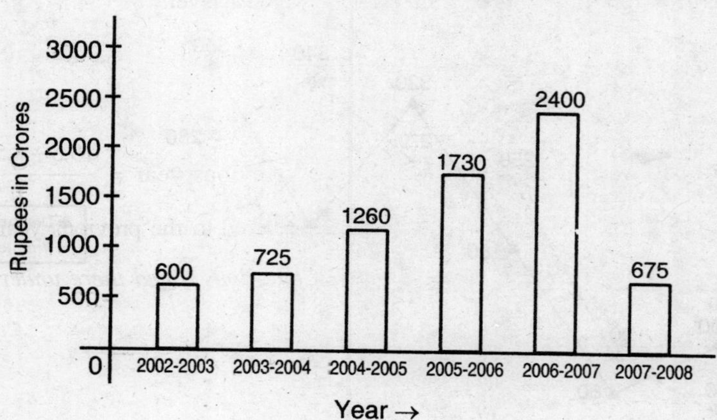

1. In between which of the following two successive financial years increase in taxation was at the highest level?
A. 2002-2003 and 2003-04
B. 2005-06 and 2006-07
C. 2006-07 and 2007-08
D. 2004-05 and 2005-06

2. Total increase in taxation was how much per cent between the years 2004-05 and 2005-06?
A. 37.3% B. 35.4% C. 38.5% D. 36.6%

3. Percentage decrease in taxation in between the years 2006-07 and 2007-08 was:
A. 71.8% B. 68.8% C. 72.6% D. 75%

4. Between the years 2005-06 and 2006-07 the taxation was increased by:
A. ₹ 670 crores B. ₹ 650 crores C. ₹ 700 crores D. ₹ 715 crores

5. What is the average amount of taxation during all these years?
A. ₹ 1233.7 crores B. ₹ 1433.5 crores C. ₹ 1231.7 crores D. ₹ 1400 crores

Solution 1. Between the financial years 2005-06 and 2006-07, maximum increase of ₹ 670 crores had been registered in taxation.

Solution 2. Percentage of total increase $= \dfrac{(1730-1260)}{1260}\times 100 = \dfrac{470\times 100}{1260} = 37.3\%$

Solution 3. Percentage of total decrease in taxation between the years 2006-07 and 2007-08

$$= \frac{(2400-675)}{2400}\times 100 = \frac{1725\times 100}{2400} = 71.8\%$$

Solution 4. Increase in taxation in between the financial years 2005-06 and 2006-07

= ₹ (2400 – 1730) = ₹ 670 crores

Solution 5. Average of the total taxation during the years $= \dfrac{600+725+1260+1730+2400+625}{6}$

$= \dfrac{7390}{6} =$ ₹ 1231.7 crores

LINE GRAPHS

Line graphs are used to show how a quantity changes continuously. If the line goes up, the quantity is increasing; if the line goes down, the quantity is decreasing; if the line is horizontal, the quantity is not changing.

For Example:

Demand and Production of rubber (in thousand tons) in various years

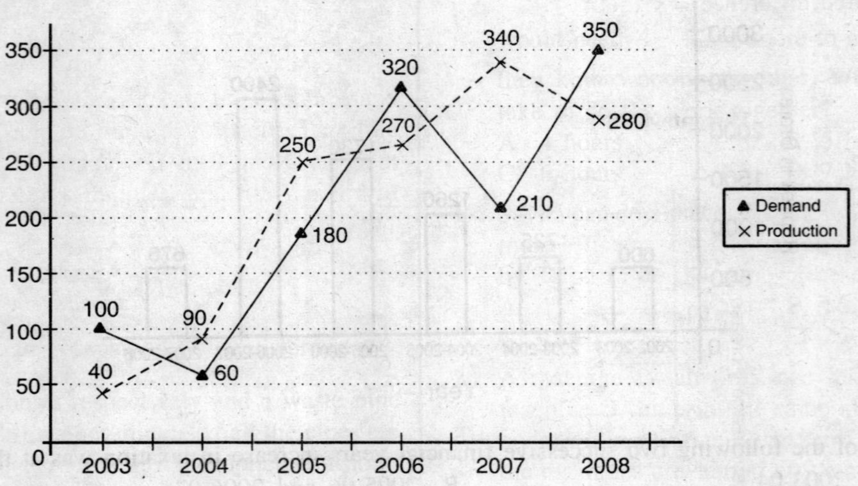

Example 1: Directions: *Study carefully the graph given below and answer the questions that follow:*

1. Price of a machine during 2005 was:

A. ₹ $5\frac{1}{3}$ thousand B. ₹ 50 thousand C. ₹ 5103 D. ₹ 3 thousand

2. The percentage decrease in the production in 2007 over the previous year 2006 was:

A. 5% B. 20% C. 25% D. 30%

3. The difference in revenue collection from the sale of machines during 2007 and 2008 was:

A. ₹ 10 lakhs B. ₹ 1 crore C. ₹ 4 crores D. ₹ 6 crores

4. Had the company sold its machines in 2008 at 25% inhanced price of 2007, what would have been the total selling price of machines produced during the year?

A. ₹ 35 crores B. ₹ 20 crores C. ₹ 12.5 crores D. ₹ 15.5 crores

5. Difference between the price of a machine in the year 2006 and that in the year 2007 was:

A. ₹ 1500 B. ₹ 2500 C. ₹ 1800 D. ₹ 3200

Solution 1. No. of machines produced during the year 2005 = 15000

And price of the machines = ₹ 8,0000000

$$\therefore \text{ Price of 1 machine in 2005} = ₹\ \frac{80000000}{15000} = ₹\ 5\frac{1}{3} \text{ thousand}$$

Solution 2. Percentage decrease in production of machines during 2007 over the previous year 2006

$$= \frac{(25-20)\times 100}{25} = 20\%$$

Solution 3. Difference in revenue collected from sale of machines during 2007 and 2008

= 16 – 10 = ₹ 6 crores.

Solution 4. On enhancing price by 25% in 2008, total price of the machines produced during the years 2008

$$= \frac{10\times 125}{100} = ₹\ 12.5 \text{ crores}$$

Solution 5. Price of 1 machine in 2006 = $\frac{80000000}{25000}$ = ₹ 3200

Price of 1 machine in 2007 = $\frac{100000000}{20000}$ = ₹ 5000

∴ Required difference = ₹ (5000 – 3200) = ₹ 1800

Example 2: Directions: *Study the graph carefully to answer the questions that follow:*

Percentage Increase in profit of two companies over the years

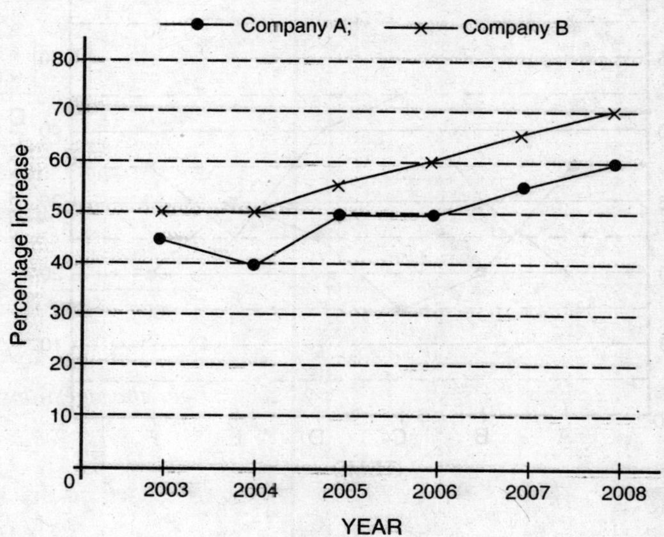

1. What is the per cent increase in profit of company A in the year 2007 from the previous year?
A. 5 B. 10 C. 45 D. 60

2. What is the per cent increase in profit of company A in the year 2008 from the previous year?
A. 7.64 B. 9.09 C. 8.12 D. 10.11

3. What is the per cent increase in profit of company A in the year 2005 from the previous year?
A. 10 B. 15 C. 20 D. 25

4. If the profit of company B in the year 2003 was ₹ 6,79,995, what would its profit have been in the year 2002?
A. ₹ 4,24,530 B. ₹ 4,53,330 C. ₹ 5,01,500 D. ₹ 5,53,330

5. Based on the graph, which of the following statements is True?
A. Company B has made the highest profit in the year 2008
B. Company A has made the lowest profit in the year 2004
C. Company B has made more amount of the profit than company A over the years
D. There is no increase in the profit of company B in the year 2005 from the previous year.

Solution 1. Required percentage = $\frac{55-50}{50} \times 100 = 10\%$

Solution 2. Required percentage = $\frac{60-55}{55} \times 100 = 9.09\%$

Solution 3. Required percentage = $\frac{50-40}{40} \times 100 = 25\%$

Solution 4. Required profit = $\frac{100}{150} \times 6{,}79{,}995$ = ₹ 4,53,330

Solution 5. It is clear from the graph that company B has made the highest profit in the year 2008, i.e., 70%

Example 3: Directions: *Study the following graph carefully to answer these questions:*

Quantity of Various items sold and price per kg

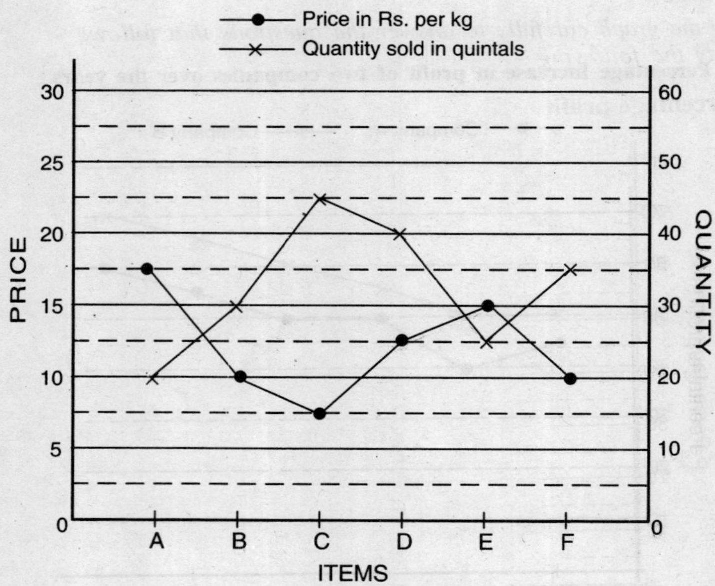

1. If the quantity sold of item D increased by 50% and the price reduced by 10%, what was the total value of the quantity sold for Item D?

A. ₹ 675 B. ₹ 6750 C. ₹ 67500 D. ₹ 67550

2. What is the ratio between the total values of quantity sold for items E and F respectively?

A. 3 : 2 B. 5 : 7 C. 7 : 5 D. 15 : 14

3. If the price as well as the quantity sold is increased by 20% for item A, what is the total value of quantity sold for item A?

A. ₹ 42000 B. ₹ 48500 C. ₹ 49000 D. ₹ 50400

4. What is the average price per kg. of items A, B and C?

A. ₹ 7.50 B. ₹ 9 C. ₹ 9.50 D. ₹ 11.67

5. Total value of quantity sold for item C is what per cent of the total value of the quantity sold for item E?

A. 85 B. 87.5 C. 90 D. 111

Solution 1. New quantity of item D = $\frac{150}{100} \times 40 = 60$ quintal

New price per kg of item D = $\frac{90}{100} \times 12.50 =$ ₹ 11.25

Since, total value = ₹ (60 × 100 × 11.25) = ₹ 67500

Solution 2. Required ratio = (25 × 100 × 15) : (35 × 100 × 10) = 15 : 14

Solution 3. New price of item A per kg = $\frac{120}{100} \times 17.50 =$ ₹ 21

New quantity of item A = $\frac{120}{100} \times 20 = 24$ quintal

Since, total value = ₹ (24 × 100 × 21) = ₹ 50400

77

Solution 4. Average price per kg of items A, B and C = $\frac{17.50+10+7.50}{3}$ = ₹ 11.67

Solution 5. Required percentage = $\frac{45 \times 100 \times 750}{25 \times 100 \times 15} \times 100 = 90\%$

Example 4: Directions: *Study the following graph carefully and answer the questions that follow:*

Percentage profit earned by two companies over the given years

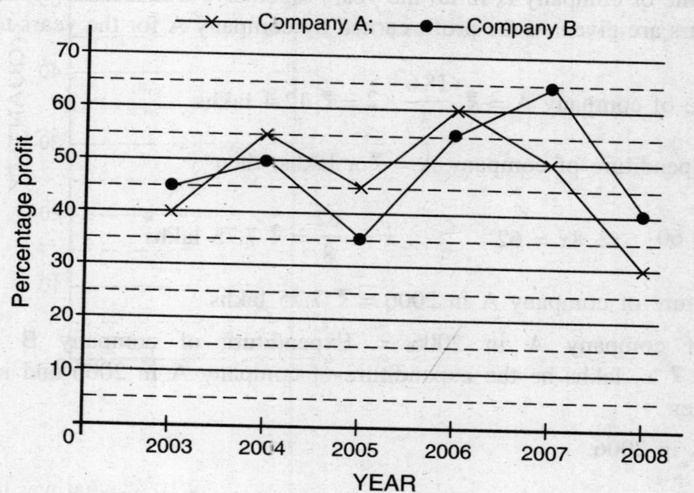

1. If the income of company A in 2005 was equal to its expenditue in 2007, what was the ratio between company's expenditure in the years 2005 and 2007 respectively?
   A. 19 : 20 B. 20 : 19 C. 20 : 29 D. 29 : 20
2. If the total expenditure of the two companies in 2008 was ₹ 18 lakhs and expenditure of companies A and B in that year in the ratio of 4 : 5 respectively, then what was the income of company B in that year (in lakh ₹)?
   A. 8 B. 10 C. 10.4 D. 14
3. If the total income of company A in all the years together was equal to the total expenditure of company B in all the years together, which was ₹ 265 lakhs, then what was the total percentage profit earned by Company A for all the years together?
   A. 37 B. 45 C. 52 D. Cannot be determined
4. If the income of company B in 2006 was ₹ 18.6 lakhs and ratio of incomes of company A and B in 2006 was 2 : 3, what was the expenditure of company A in 2006 (in lakhs)?
   A. 7.75 B. 9.75 C. 12 D. 12.4
5. If the income of company A in 2006 was equal to the total expenditure of company B in 2007, then what was the ratio of expenditure of company A in 2006 to the income of company B in 2007?
   A. 10 : 13 B. 13 : 10 C. 25 : 66 D. 66 : 25

Solution 1. Let income of company A in 2005 = Expenditure of Company A in 2007 = ₹ x and also expenditure of company A in 2005 = ₹ x_1; then

For company A in 2005,

$$\frac{x - x_1}{x_1} \times 100 = 45 \quad \Rightarrow 29x_1 = 20x \quad \therefore \; x_1 = \frac{20x}{29}$$

Since, required ratio = $\frac{20x}{29} : x = 20 : 29$

Solution 2. In 2008, expenditure of company B = $\frac{5}{4+5} \times 18$ lakhs = ₹ 10 lakhs.

Let, income of company B in 2008 = ₹ x lakhs; then

$$\frac{x-10}{10} \times 100 = 40 \quad \Rightarrow x - 10 = 4 \quad \therefore \; x = ₹ \; 14 \text{ lakhs}$$

Hence, income of company B in 2008 = ₹ 14 lakhs

Solution 3. Here, total income of company A in all the years together = ₹ 265 lakhs, while individual profit percentages for different years are given so the profit earned by company A for the years together can not be determined.

Solution 4. In 2006, income of company A = ₹ $\frac{18.6}{3} \times 2$ = ₹ 12.4 lakhs

Let in 2006, expenditure of company A = ₹ x lakhs, then

$$\frac{12.4 - x}{x} \times 100 = 60 \quad \Rightarrow 8x = 62 \quad \therefore \; x = \frac{62}{8} = ₹ \; 7.75 \text{ lakhs}$$

Hence, expenditure of company A in 2006 = ₹ 7.75 lakhs

Solution 5. Let income of company A in 2006 = Expenditure of company B in 2007 = ₹ x lakhs also ₹ x_1 lakhs, and ₹ x_2 lakhs be the expenditure of company A in 2006 and income of company B in 2007 respectively; then

For company A in 2006,

$$\frac{x - x_1}{x_1} \times 100 = 60 \quad \Rightarrow 8x_1 = 5x \quad \therefore \; x_1 = ₹ \; \frac{5x}{8} \text{ lakhs}$$

For company B in 2007,

$$\frac{x_2 - x}{x} \times 100 = 65 \quad \Rightarrow 20x_2 = 33x \quad \therefore \; x_2 = ₹ \; \frac{33x}{20} \text{ lakhs}$$

Since, required ratio = $\frac{5x}{8} : \frac{33x}{20} = \frac{5x}{8} \times 40 : \frac{33x}{20} \times 40 = 25 : 66$

PIE CHARTS

These are used to show the share of various sectors in the total. They usually show the percentage share of each sector in the whole (taken as 100%). In such representation the total quantity in question is distributed over a total angle of 360°. The area of each sector is proportional to the relative frequency of the class represented by the sector.

$$\text{Sector angle} = \frac{\text{Class frequency}}{\text{Total frequency}} \times 360°$$

For Example: ***Distribution of Expenditure of a family***

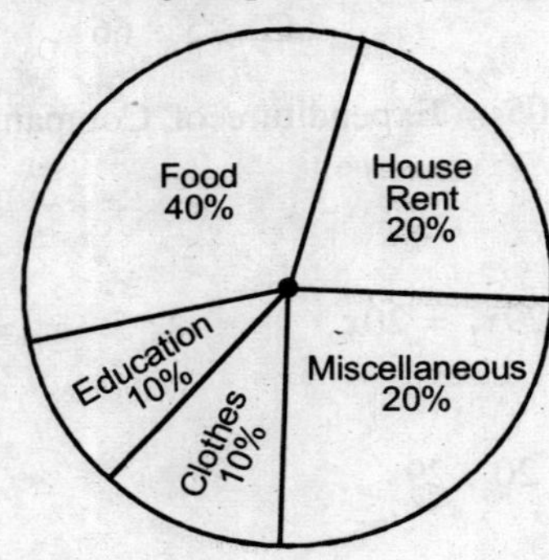

Example 1: Directions: *The pie-chart given below shows the household expenditure of a family on different items. Study the chart carefully and answer the questions that follows:*

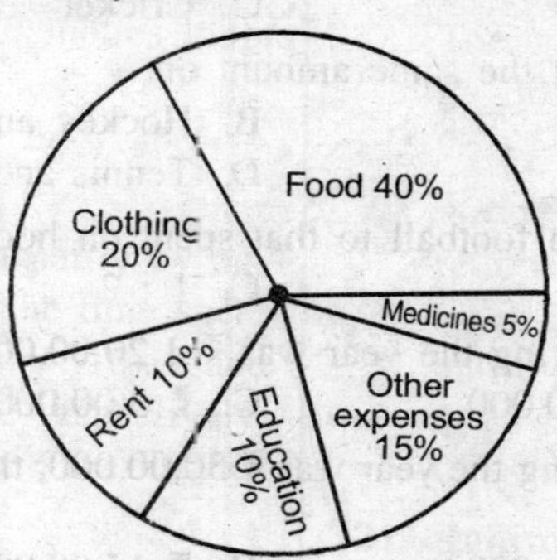

1. If the family's expenditure on education is ₹ 375 then the same amount is being expent by this family on which of the following items?
   A. Medicines B. Other expenses C. Rent D. Clothing
2. If the family expends ₹ 750 per month on food, what is the annual expenditure of this family on education?
   A. ₹ 2150 B. ₹ 1022.50 C. ₹ 2250 D. ₹ 1400
3. If total expenditure of this family is ₹ 4500, find the expenditure of the family on clothing?
   A. ₹ 800 B. ₹ 900 C. ₹ 840 D. ₹ 950
4. What is the angle subtended on the centre by the segment representing other expenses?
   A. 64° B. 54° C. 36° D. 15°
5. What is the ratio of total expenses on rent and clothing to the total expenses on medicines and other expenses of this family?
   A. 2 : 3 B. 3 : 4 C. 3 : 5 D. 3 : 2

Solution 1. Both segments representing education and rent respectively are each 10%. Hence, family's expenditure on these two items will be equal, *i.e.*, ₹ 375 will be expent on rent.

Solution 2. Here, 40% = ₹ 750

$\Rightarrow 10\% = \frac{750}{40} \times 10 =$ ₹ 187.50

∴ Annual expenditure of the family on education = 187.50 × 12 = ₹ 2250

Solution 3. Expenditure on clothing $= \frac{20}{100} \times 4500 =$ ₹ 900

Solution 4. Central angle for 15% $= \frac{15}{100} \times 360° = 54°$

Solution 5. Expenditure on rent and clothing = 10% + 20% = 30%
Expenditure on medicine and other expenses = 5% + 15% = 20%
∴ Ratio of the two = 30% : 20% = 3 : 2

Example 2: Directions: *The pie chart, drawn here, shows the spending of a country on various sports during a particular year. Study the graph carefully and answer the questions that follow:*

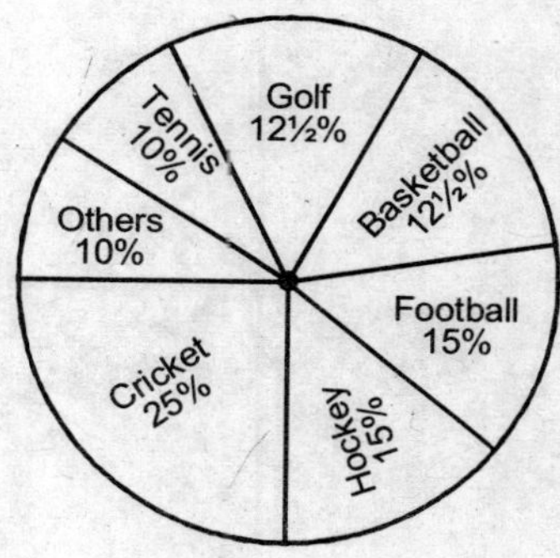

1. Graph shows that the most popular game of the country is:
   A. Football B. Hockey C. Cricket D. Tennis
2. Out of the following the country spent the same amount on:
   A. Hockey and Cricket B. Hockey and Football
   C. Hockey and Golf D. Tennis and Golf
3. The ratio of the total amount spent on football to that spent on hockey is:
   A. 2 : 1 B. 1 : 1 C. 1 : 2 D. 3 : 2
4. If the total amount spent on sports during the year was ₹ 1,20,00,000, how much was spent on basketball?
   A. ₹ 16,00,000 B. ₹ 18,00,000 C. ₹ 3,00,000 D. ₹ 15,00,000
5. If the total amount spent on sports during the year was ₹ 30,00,000, the amount spent on cricket and hockey together was:
   A. ₹ 18,00,000 B. ₹ 12,00,000 C. ₹ 15,00,000 D. ₹ 20,00,000

Solution 1. According to the graph, expenditure on cricket is the maximum. Therefore cricket is the most popular game.

Solution 2. According to the graph, equal amount has been spent on Hockey and Football.

Solution 3. Expenditure on the game of Football = 15% of total amount spent
Expenditure on the game of Hockey = 15% of total amount spent.
Therefore, the ratio of the expenditure on the two games = 1 : 1

Solution 4. 100% = ₹ 1,20,00,000
∴ Expenditure on the game of Basketball = 12½% of 1,20,00,000

$$= \frac{25 \times 1{,}20{,}00{,}000}{100} = ₹\ 15{,}00{,}000$$

Solution 5. 100% = ₹ 30,00,000
∴ Expenditure on the games of Cricket and Hockey = 25% + 15% = 40%
∴ Total expenditure on the games of Cricket and Hockey = 20% of 30,00,000

$$= \frac{40 \times 30{,}00{,}000}{100} = ₹\ 12{,}00{,}000.$$

❑❑❑

GENERAL INTELLIGENCE & REASONING ABILITY

1 LETTER SERIES

In letter series, the letters follow a definite order. The given series of letters can be in natural order or in reverse order or combination of both. The letters may be skipped or repeated or consecutive. The given series may be single or may even comprise of two different series merged at alternate positions. While attempting questions on letter series one should note the pattern of alphabet series.

Alphabets in natural series are :

A B C D E F G H I J K L M N O P Q R S T U V W X Y Z

A ↓ 1st, E ↓ 5th, J ↓ 10th, O ↓ 15th, T ↓ 20th, Y ↓ 25th

Alphabets in reverse series are :

Z Y X W V U T S R Q P O N M L K J I H G F E D C B A

Z ↓ 1st, V ↓ 5th, Q ↓ 10th, L ↓ 15th, G ↓ 20th, B ↓ 25th

Note : On reaching Z, the series restarts from A and on reaching A, it restarts from Z.

EXERCISE

Directions : *In each of the following series determine the order of the letters. Then from the given options select the one which will complete the given series.*

1. B Y C X D W E ?
(*a*) S (*b*) T
(*c*) U (*d*) V

2. B A F E J I P O ? U
(*a*) V (*b*) T
(*c*) S (*d*) Q

3. B A D C ? H G J I
(*a*) E F (*b*) F E
(*c*) F G (*d*) D F

4. ADG, XVT, BEH, WUS, ?
(*a*) VTR (*b*) CFI
(*c*) DFJ (*d*) STU

5. GMSY, IOUA, KQWC, ?
(*a*) MSYE (*b*) NSYE
(*c*) MTYE (*d*) MSYF

6. ADG, GJM, ?, SVY
(*a*) MPS (*b*) MQR
(*c*) MQS (*d*) SPM

7. XYZ, UVW, ?, OPQ
(*a*) RST (*b*) STU
(*c*) QRS (*d*) TUV

8. JOBS, KMEO, LKHK, ?, NGNC
(*a*) MJLH (*b*) LIKG
(*c*) MIKG (*d*) MNGM

9. AZ, GT, MN, ?, YB
(*a*) KF (*b*) TS
(*c*) RX (*d*) SH

10. BMY, DNW, FOU, ?
(*a*) HPT (*b*) HPS
(*c*) HQS (*d*) GPS

11. AZ, CX, EV, ?
(*a*) HU (*b*) GS
(*c*) GT (*d*) HT

12. DMP, FLN, HKL, JJJ, ?
(*a*) MIH (*b*) III
(*c*) LIH (*d*) MII

13. ECA, JHF, OMK, ?, YWU
(*a*) TRP (*b*) LNP
(*c*) QPN (*d*) RPT

14. ABP, CDQ, EFR, ?
(*a*) GHS (*b*) HGS
(*c*) GHR (*d*) GHT

15. BEH, KNQ, TWZ, ?
(*a*) IJL (*b*) BDF
(*c*) CFI (*d*) ADG

EXPLANATORY ANSWERS

1. (*d*) : There are two alternate series.

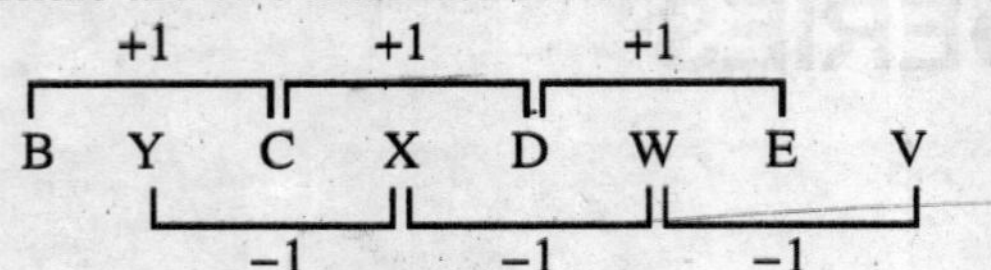

Series I : BCDE (natural order)
Series II : YXWV (reverse order)

2. (*a*) : Each vowel (AEIOU) is preceded by the letter that comes next to it in the natural alphabetical series.

B A F E J I P O V U

3. (*b*) : The letters in natural series are divided into sections of two letters each. The letters in each section are written backward.

BA DC FE HG JI

4. (*b*) : There are two alternate series.

ADG XVT BEH WUS CFI

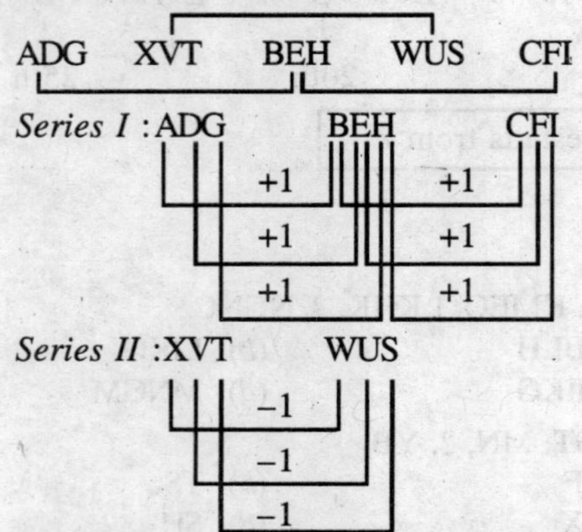

5. (*a*) : The series is formed by moving each letter two steps forward from one group to the next.

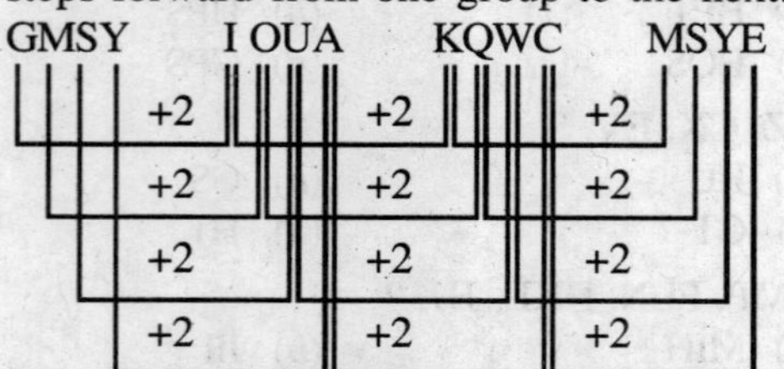

(The series restarts from A on reaching Z)

6. (*a*) : In each group of three letters the alphabet is in the succession of +3. The next group begins with the last alphabet of the previous group.

A D G G J M M P S S V Y
+3 +3 +3 +3 +3 +3 +3 +3

7. (*a*) : The alphabet from one group to the next are in recession of –3, *i.e.,*

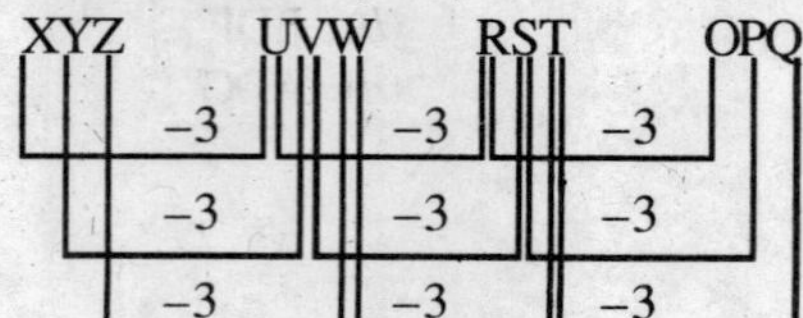

8. (*c*) : The alphabets in each group follow the pattern +1, –2, +3 and –4 respectively from one group to the next group.

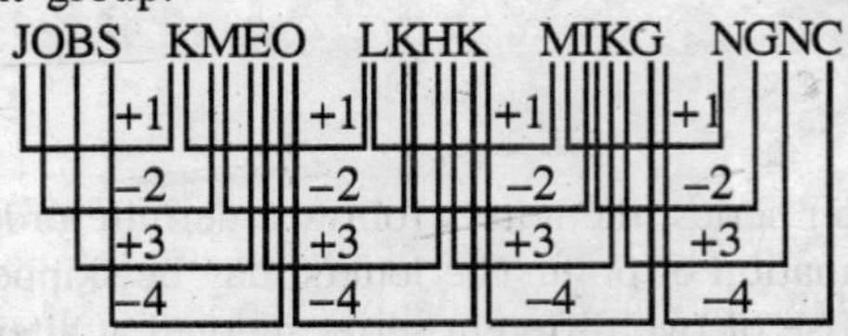

9. (*d*) : The letters in one group correspond to the letters in the next group in the manner +6, –6 respectively, *i.e.,*

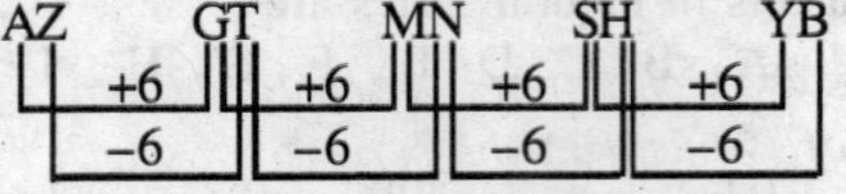

10. (*b*) : The letters in one group correspond to the letters in the next group in the manner +2, +1, –2 respectively, *i.e.,*

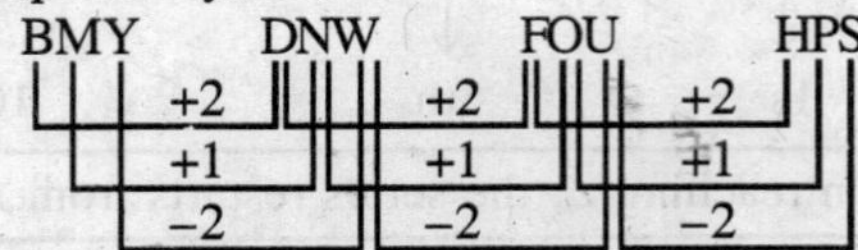

11. (*c*) : The letters in each group correspond to the letters in the next group in the manner +2, –2 respectively, *i.e.,*

AZ CX EV GT
+2 +2 +2
–2 –2 –2

12. (*c*) : The alphabets in each group correspond to the alphabets in the next group in the manner +2, –1, –2 respectively, *i.e.,*

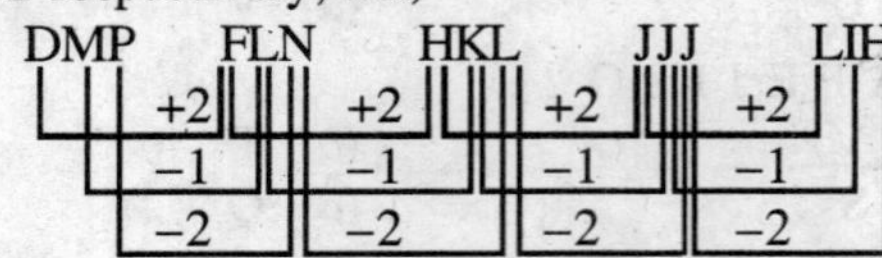

13. (*a*) : The alphabets in each group are moved five steps forward, *i.e.,*

ECA JHF OMK TRP YWU
+5 +5 +5 +5
+5 +5 +5 +5
+5 +5 +5 +5

14. (*a*) : The letters in one group correspond to the letters in the next group in the manner +2, +2, +1 respectively, *i.e.,*

ABP CDQ EFR GHS
+2 +2 +2
+2 +2 +2
+1 +1 +1

15. (*c*) : All the letters in each group are moved nine steps forward.

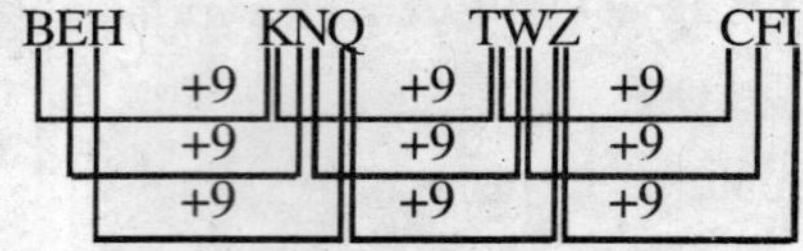

❑❑❑

2 WRONG LETTER SERIES

In this type of series, the candidates are not required to find the letter or group of letters which will complete the given series but, they have to identify the letter or number which is wrong or misfit in the given series.

EXERCISE

Directions : *Which letter(s) in each of the following series is wrong or is misfit in the series?*

1. A E H O U
(*a*) U (*b*) O (*c*) H (*d*) E

2. C H M S W B
(*a*) C (*b*) S (*c*) B (*d*) W

3. X S N I C Y
(*a*) Y (*b*) C (*c*) S (*d*) I

4. Z A W B X C
(*a*) D (*b*) C (*c*) X (*d*) W

5. M L O N Q P R
(*a*) R (*b*) O (*c*) Q (*d*) L

6. D K R Y F L
(*a*) L (*b*) D (*c*) R (*d*) Y

7. L N Q T W Z C F
(*a*) C (*b*) Q (*c*) L (*d*) F

8. XW, DC, CB, NM, PQ
(*a*) NM (*b*) CB (*c*) PQ (*d*) XW

9. B E I N S A I
(*a*) A (*b*) E (*c*) S (*d*) I

10. Z T P K H F
(*a*) Z (*b*) P (*c*) T (*d*) F

EXPLANATORY ANSWERS

1. (*c*) : The series is made with vowels only. AEIOU. I should be in place of H.

2. (*b*) : The letters in the series are moved five steps forward.

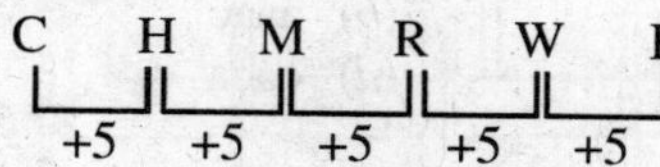

R should be in place of S
(The series restarts from A on reaching Z)

3. (*b*) : The pattern in the series is –5, *i.e.*,

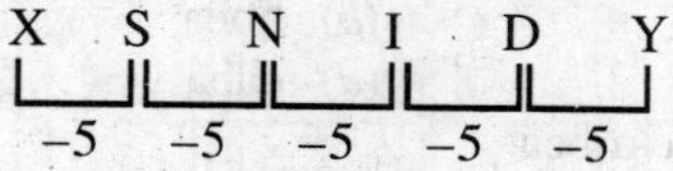

D should be in place of C.

4. (*d*) : There are two alternate series

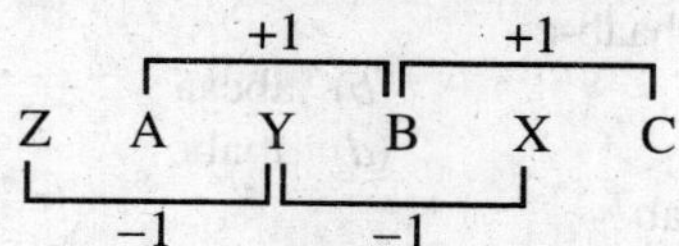

Series I : ZYX (reverse series)
Series II : ABC (natural series)
Y should be in place of W.

5. (*a*) : Two consecutive letters are written backwards.

ML ON QP SR

S should be in place of R.

6. (*a*) : The pattern in this series in moving the letters seven steps forward.

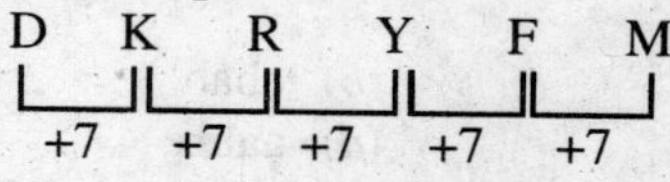

M should be in place of L.

7. (*c*) : The pattern in the series is +3

K N Q T W Z C F
+3 +3 +3 +3 +3 +3 +3

K should be in place of L.

8. (*c*) : The series is made with any two consecutive letters written backwards.

XW DC CB NM QP
← ← ← ← ←

Q should come before P in the series.

9. (*c*) : The difference between the letters is increased by one at each step.

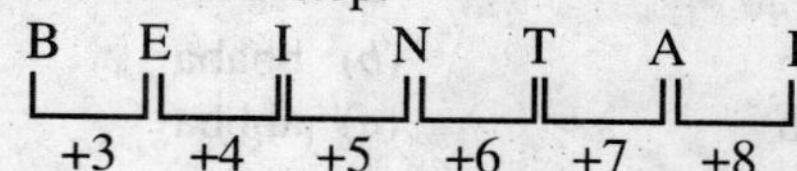

T should be in place of S.

10. (*b*) : The difference between the letters is decreased by one at each step.

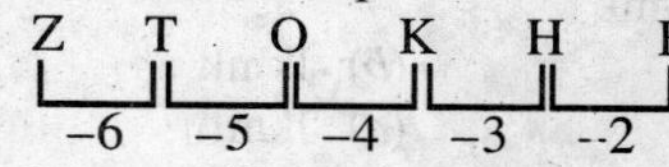

O should be in place of P.

❑❑❑

3 REPEAT SERIES

In this type of series, small letters of the alphabet are used to make a set of letters which are repeated. The candidate has to find the set of letters which will fit the blanks left in the given series in such a manner that one section of the series is further repeated in the same manner.

SOLVED EXAMPLE

1. Which of the following groups of letters will complete the given series?
ba-b-aab-a-b
(*a*) baab (*b*) abba (*c*) abaa (*d*) babb

Ans. (*b*) : The series is baab, baab, baab. Here the section 'baab' is repeated in the series.

***Solving steps* :** The candidate has to look for clues to solve such series pattern. 'aab' in the Series indicates that 'b' in this series is preceded by two 'a' so, the first blank and the last blank will be filled by 'a'. Now the first set is formed, *i.e.,* 'baab' in the beginning. This set is repeated, so the second and third blanks will have 'b' filling them. Now, solve the exercise given below to know the different ways in which these series are formed.

EXERCISE

Directions : *Which of the following groups of letters will complete the given series?*

1. ab---b-bbaa-
(*a*) babba (*b*) abaab
(*c*) abbab (*d*) baaab

2. aa-ab--aaa-a
(*a*) baaa (*b*) abab
(*c*) aaab (*d*) aabb

3. -baa-aab-a-a
(*a*) baab (*b*) abab
(*c*) aaba (*d*) aabb

4. -a cca-ccca-acccc-aaa
(*a*) ccaa (*b*) acca
(*c*) caac (*d*) caaa

5. c-bbb--abbbb-abbb-
(*a*) abccb (*b*) bacbb
(*c*) aabcb (*d*) abacb

6. ac-cab-baca-aba-acac
(*a*) bcbb (*b*) aacb
(*c*) babb (*d*) acbc

7. --aba--ba-ab
(*a*) abbab (*b*) bbaba
(*c*) baabb (*d*) abbba

8. --babbba-a--
(*a*) bbaba (*b*) babbb
(*c*) baaab (*d*) ababb

9. k-mk-lmkkl-kk-mk
(*a*) lklm (*b*) lkmk
(*c*) lkmm (*d*) lkml

10. abc-d-bc-d-b-dd
(*a*) decdb (*b*) dadac
(*c*) cdabe (*d*) bacde

11. b-abbc-bbca-bcabb-ab
(*a*) acba (*b*) acaa
(*c*) cacc (*d*) cabc

12. aca-ac--a-ac
(*a*) babc (*b*) aaac
(*c*) cacc (*d*) caca

13. ba-cb-b-bab-?
(*a*) acbb (*b*) bcaa
(*c*) cabb (*d*) bacc

14. ab-aa-caab-aab-a
(*a*) bcbc (*b*) bbca
(*c*) cbcc (*d*) caba

15. -bbcaa-bcaa-bc-a-bca
(*a*) bacab (*b*) abbab
(*c*) abcba (*d*) bcaab

16. a-bccb-ca-cca-baab-c
(*a*) accab (*b*) abcaa
(*c*) bacaa (*d*) ababc

17. b-dabbcd-b-c-ab
(*a*) cabd (*b*) bcad
(*c*) dcba (*d*) acbd

18. a-ba-caacb-bc-
(*a*) acbb (*b*) cbab
(*c*) cbaa (*d*) cbba

19. c-baa-aca-cacab-acac-bca
(*a*) acbaa (*b*) cbaac
(*c*) bccab (*d*) bbcaa

20. -bcc-ac-aabb-ab-cc
(*a*) bacab (*b*) abaca
(*c*) aabca (*d*) bcaca

21. ab-ccca-bccc-bbcc-
(*a*) abbc (*b*) bbac
(*c*) bbca (*d*) cabc

22. -cbc-a-bcaac-ca
(*a*) aaba (*b*) caab
(*c*) bcab (*d*) aacb

23. ab-ba--ba-
(*a*) abba (*b*) baab
(*c*) baba (*d*) abab

24. yx-yx-yxz-xzy-zyxz
(*a*) zzyx (*b*) xxzy
(*c*) yyzx (*d*) yzxz

25. xxxy-y-xxy-yxx-
(*a*) xyxy (*b*) yxyx
(*c*) yyxx (*d*) xxyy

EXPLANATORY ANSWERS

1. (*d*) : The series is abbaab, abbaab.
2. (*c*) : The series is aaaaba, aaaaba.
3. (*b*) : The series is aba, aba, aba, aba.
4. (*d*) : The series is c,a,cc,aa, ccc, aaa, cccc, aaaa.
5. (*a*) : The series is cabbbb, cabbbb, cabbbb.
6. (*b*) : The series is acac, abab, acac, abab, acac.
7. (*a*) : The series is ab, ab, ab, ab, ab, ab.
8. (*b*) : The series is bababb, bababb.
9. (*d*) : The series is klmk, klmk, klmk, klmk.
10. (*b*) : The series is abcdd, abcdd, abcdd.
11. (*d*) : The series is bcab, bcab, bcab, bcab, bcab.
12. (*c*) : The series is ac, ac, ac, ac, ac, ac.
13. (*d*) : The series is babc, babc, babc.
14. (*c*) : The series is abca, abca, abca, abca.
15. (*b*) : The series is abbca, abbca, abbca, abbca.
16. (*d*) : The series is aabcc, bbcaa, ccabb, aabcc.
17. (*a*) : The series is bcdab, bcdab, bcdab.
18. (*c*) : The series is acbabca, acbabca.
19. (*a*) : The series is cabaac, acabca, cabaac, acabca.
20. (*a*) : The series is bbccaa, ccaabb, aabbcc.
21. (*b*) : The series is abbccc abbccc.
22. (*d*) : The series is acbca acbca acbca.
23. (*d*) : The series is ab ab ab ab ab.
24. (*a*) : The series is yxz yxz yxz yxz yxz yxz.
25. (*b*) : The series is xxx yyy xxx yyy xxx.

❑❑❑

4 NUMBER SERIES

In this type of series, the set of given numbers in a series are related to one another in a particular pattern or manner. The relationship between the numbers may be

(*i*) consecutive odd/even numbers;
(*ii*) consecutive prime numbers;
(*iii*) squares/cubes of some numbers with/without variation of addition or subtraction of some number;
(*iv*) sum/product/difference of preceding numbers;
(*v*) addition/subtraction/multiplication/division by some number; and
(*vi*) many more combinations of the relationships given above.

EXERCISE

Directions : *In the following questions, select the number(s) from the given options for completing the given series.*

1. 7776, 1296, 216, 36, 6, ?
(*a*) 6 (*b*) 0
(*c*) 3 (*d*) 1

2. 29282, 2662, 242, 22, ?
(*a*) 1 (*b*) 2
(*c*) 0 (*d*) 11

3. 1, 2, 2, 4, 16, ?, 65536
(*a*) 276 (*b*) 64
(*c*) 256 (*d*) 198

4. 3, 5, 9, 15, 23, ?, 45
(*a*) 37 (*b*) 35
(*c*) 31 (*d*) 33

5. 7, 21, 35, 49, 63, ?
(*a*) 70 (*b*) 77
(*c*) 81 (*d*) 108

6. 10, 14, 23, 39, 64, ?, 149
(*a*) 78 (*b*) 128
(*c*) 103 (*d*) 100

7. 6, 24, 29, 116, 121, ?, 489
(*a*) 468
(*b*) 484
(*c*) 243
(*d*) 363

8. 5, 50, 45, 450, 445, ?, 4445
(*a*) 4450
(*b*) 4600
(*c*) 4550
(*d*) 4500

9. 6.25, 9, 12.25, 16, 20.25, 25, 30.25?
(*a*) 36 (*b*) 32
(*c*) 28.25 (*d*) 40.25

10. 243, 5, 81, 15, 27, 45, 9, ?
(*a*) 5 (*b*) 15
(*c*) 135 (*d*) 27

11. 2, 7, 14, 23, ?, 47
(*a*) 31 (*b*) 38
(*c*) 28 (*d*) 34

12. 0, 1, 8, 27, 64, ?
(*a*) 125 (*b*) 128
(*c*) 256 (*d*) 121

13. 37, 47, 58, ?, 79, 95
(*a*) 71 (*b*) 69
(*c*) 68 (*d*) 67

14. 4, –8, 14, –22, 32, ?
(*a*) –44 (*b*) 42
(*c*) –42 (*d*) 44

15. 6, 7, 9, 11, 15, 15, 24, 19, ?
(*a*) 32 (*b*) 34
(*c*) 36 (*d*) 37

EXPLANATORY ANSWERS

1. (*d*) : The numbers in this sequence are divided by 6 each time.

2. (*b*) : The numbers in the series are divided by 11 at each step.

3. (*c*) : The number in the series is product of all the numbers preceding it.

1 2 2 4 16 256 65536

(1×2)
(1×2×2)
(1×2×2×4)
(1×2×2×4×16)
(1×2×2×4×16×256)

4. *(d)* : The difference between consecutive numbers increases by 2 at each step.

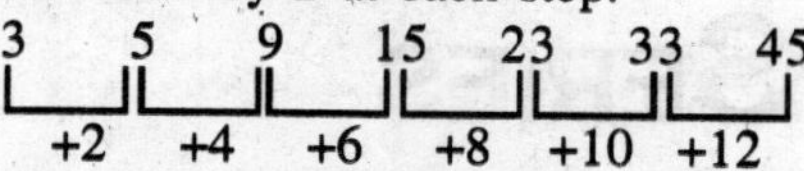

5. *(b)* : The series is multiplication of 7 by odd numbers starting from 3.

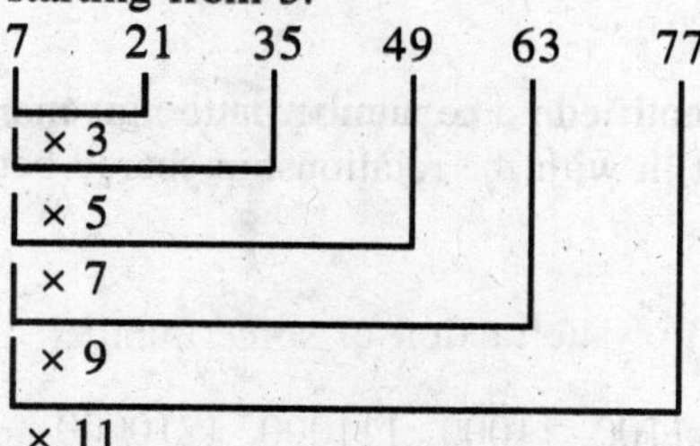

6. *(d)* : The number plus the square of numbers in natural order starting from 2 gives the next number in the series.

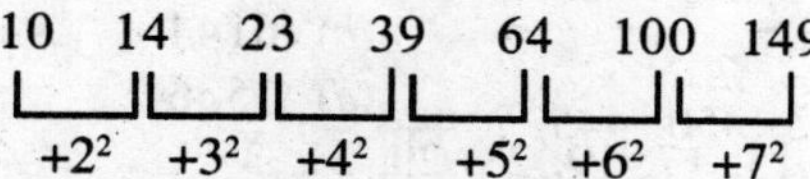

7. *(b)* : The sequence in the series is ×4, +5, which is repeated.

8. *(a)* : The sequence in the series is ×10, –5, which is repeated.

9. *(a)* : There are two alternate series :

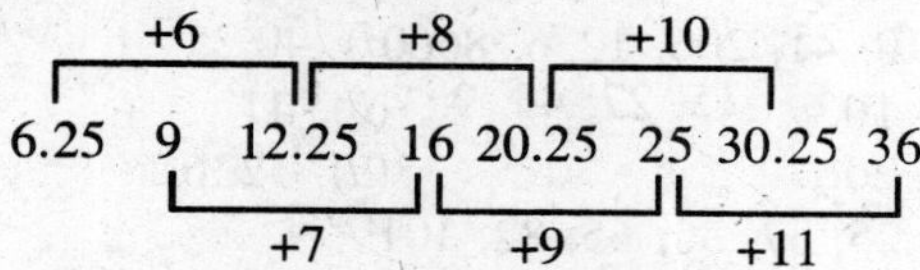

Series I : 6.25, 12.25, 20.25, 30.25 (sequence is +6, +8, +10)

Series II : 9, 16, 25, 36 (sequence is +7, +9, +11)

10. *(c)* : There are two alternate series :

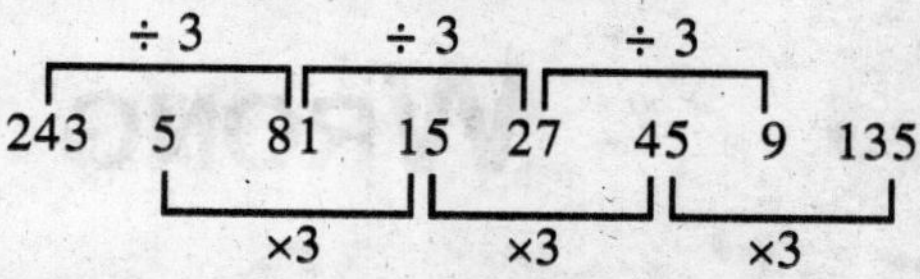

Series I : 243, 81, 27, 9 (division by 3)

Series II : 5, 15, 45, 135 (multiplication by 3)

11. *(d)* : The difference between two consecutive numbers is increasing by 2 starting from 5.

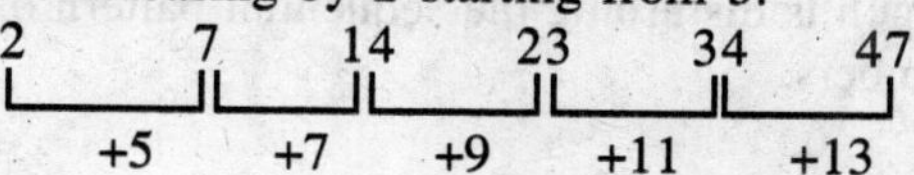

12. *(a)* : The numbers are cubes of numbers in natural order.

13. *(a)* : The sum of the digits of the number is added to the number to obtain the next number in the series.

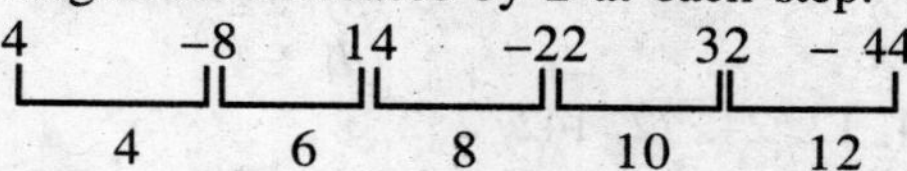

14. *(a)* : Alternate numbers are marked positive and negative, but the difference between their magnitude increases by 2 at each step.

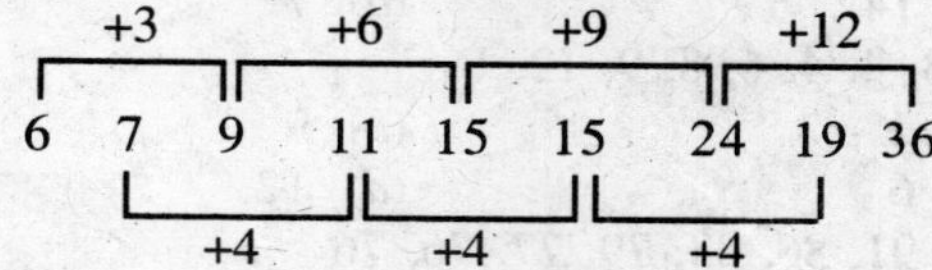

15. *(c)* : There are two alternate series :

+3 +6 +9 +12

6 7 9 11 15 15 24 19 36

+4 +4 +4

Series I : 6, 9, 15, 24, 36 (sequence is +3, +6, +9, +12)

Series II : 7, 11, 15, 19 (addition of 4 at each step)

❑❑❑

5 WRONG NUMBER SERIES

In this type of series, the given series may be complete but what needs to be identified is the number in the given completed series which is disturbing the sequential pattern of that series and does not fit in with the relationship shared between the other numbers.

EXERCISE

Directions : *In the given series find the number which is wrong.*

1. 5, 25, 120, 625, 3125, 15625
(*a*) 15625
(*b*) 625
(*c*) 120
(*d*) 5

2. 4, 8, 11, 22, 18, 36, 24, 50
(*a*) 8 (*b*) 22
(*c*) 36 (*d*) 24

3. 2, 4, 12, 24, 72, 142, 432
(*a*) 432 (*b*) 12
(*c*) 142 (*d*) 72

4. 2, 3, 4, 4, 6, 8, 9, 12, 16
(*a*) 3 (*b*) 9
(*c*) 6 (*d*) 12

5. 97, 91, 86, 83, 79, 77, 76, 76
(*a*) 86 (*b*) 76
(*c*) 91 (*d*) 83

6. 7, 11, 11, 9, 15, 7, 19, 5, 23, 1
(*a*) 5 (*b*) 7
(*c*) 1 (*d*) 9

7. 3, 7, 12, 28, 48, 118, 192, 448
(*a*) 12 (*b*) 118
(*c*) 28 (*d*) 7

8. 10, 100, 1100, 11000, 111000, 1210000
(*a*) 1210000 (*b*) 11000
(*c*) 100 (*d*) 111000

9. 24576, 6144, 1536, 386, 96, 24
(*a*) 386 (*b*) 6144
(*c*) 96 (*d*) 1536

10. 11, 13, 15, 17, 19, 23, 29, 31, 37
(*a*) 13 (*b*) 23
(*c*) 15 (*d*) 31

11. 36, 43, 49, 54, 60, 61, 63, 64
(*a*) 60 (*b*) 63
(*c*) 54 (*d*) 43

12. 3, 10, 41, 206, 1236, 8660
(*a*) 10 (*b*) 41
(*c*) 206 (*d*) 1236

13. 17, 25, 37, 50, 65, 82, 101
(*a*) 25 (*b*) 17
(*c*) 101 (*d*) 65

14. 12, 20, 38, 42, 56, 72
(*a*) 20 (*b*) 38
(*c*) 56 (*d*) 72

15. 5, 6, 11, 22, 42, 88, 176
(*a*) 5 (*b*) 42
(*c*) 176 (*d*) 11

EXPLANATORY ANSWERS

1. (*c*) : The numbers in the series are multiplied by 5 to get the next number.
∴ 125 should be in place of 120.

2. (*d*) : Two numbers form a pair. The first number increases by 7 for the next pair and the second number is the double of first number.

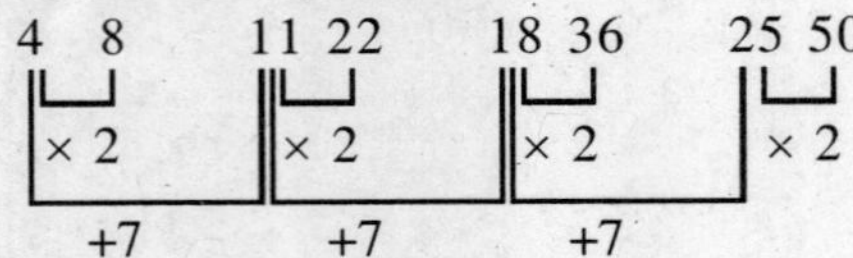

∴ 25 should be in place of 24.

3. (*c*) : There are two alternate series and in each series, the numbers are multiplied by 6 to get the next number.

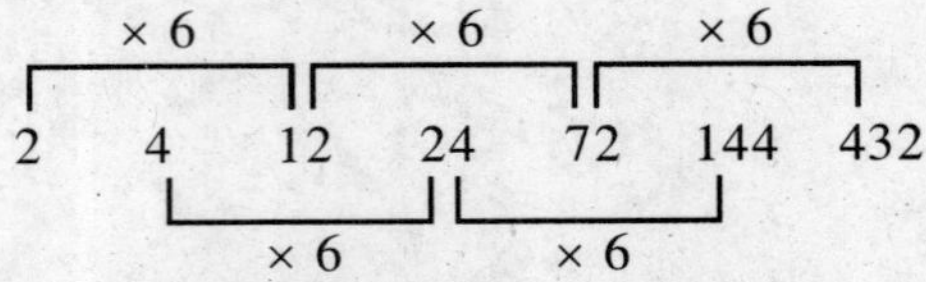

∴ 144 should be in place of 142.

4. (*b*) : There are three alternate series and in each series, the numbers are multiplied by 2 to get the next number.

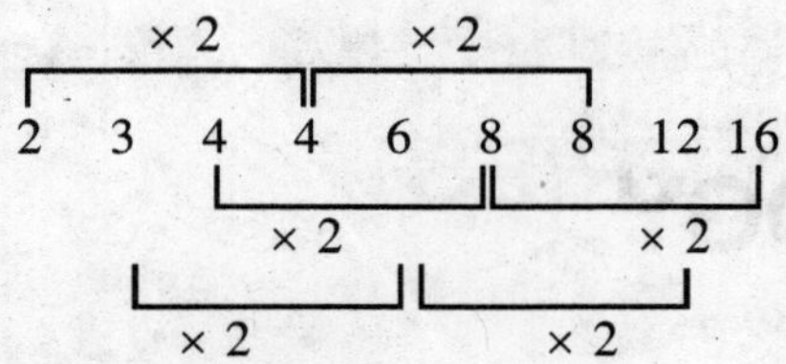

Series I : 2, 4, 8
Series II : 3, 6, 12
Series III : 4, 8, 16
∴ 8 should be in place of 9.

5. (*d*) : The difference between the consecutive numbers in the series decreases by 1 at each step.

97 91 86 82 79 77 76 76

−6 −5 −4 −3 −2 −1 −0

∴ 82 should be in place of 83.

6. (*c*) : There are two alternate series :

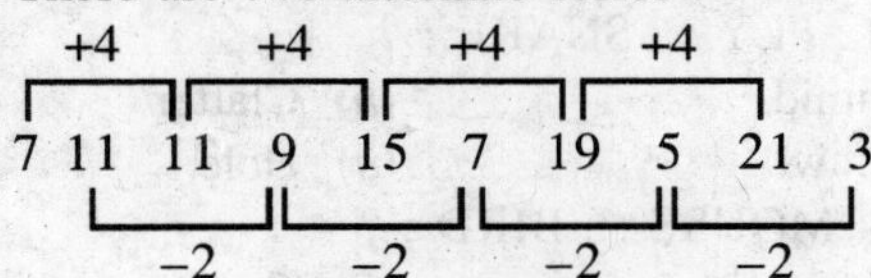

Series I : 7, 11, 15, 19, 23 (addition of 4)
Series II : 11, 9, 7, 5, 3 (subtraction of 2)
∴ 3 should be in place of 1.

7. (*b*) : There are two alternate series and in each series, the numbers are multiplied by 4 to get the next number.

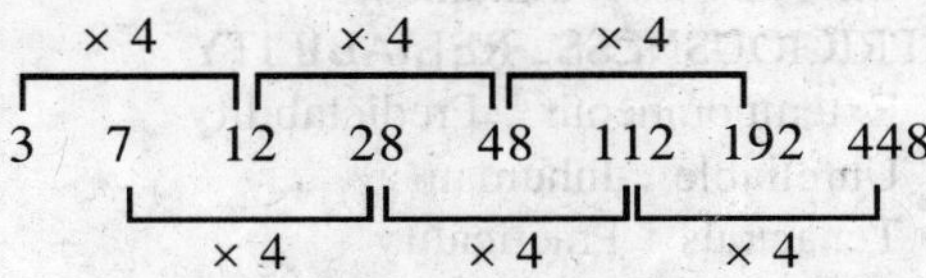

∴ 112 should be in place of 118.

8. (*d*) : The numbers in this series are multiplied by 10 and 11 alternately is, *i.e.*, × 10, × 11.

10 100 1100 11000 121000 1210000

× 10 × 11 × 10 × 11 × 10

∴ 121000 should be in place of 111000.

9. (*a*) : The numbers in this series are divided by 4 to get the next number.

24576 6144 1536 384 96 24

÷ 4 ÷ 4 ÷ 4 ÷ 4 ÷ 4

∴ 384 should be in place of 386.

10. (*c*) : The series comprises of prime numbers in increasing order. Only 15 is an exception.

11. (*a*) : The difference between two consecutive numbers is decreasing by 1 at each step.

36 43 49 54 58 61 63 64

+7 +6 +5 +4 +3 +2 +1

∴ 58 should be in place of 60.

12. (*d*) : The sequence followed in this series is :
3 × 3 + 1 = 10, 10 × 4 + 1 = 41
41 × 5 + 1 = 206, 206 × 6 + 1 = 1237; and
1237 × 7 + 1 = 8660
∴ 1237 should be in place of 1236.

13. (*a*) : The numbers in the series are 1 plus the squares of numbers in natural order starting from 4.

17 26 37 50 65 82 101

↓ ↓ ↓ ↓ ↓ ↓ ↓

$4^2 + 1$ $5^2 + 1$ $6^2 + 1$ $7^2 + 1$ $8^2 + 1$ $9^2 + 1$ $10^2 + 1$

∴ 26 should be in place of 25.

14. (*b*) : The sequence followed in this series is :
3 × 4 = 12, 4 × 5 = 20, 5 × 6 = 30,
6 × 7 = 42, 7 × 8 = 56, 8 × 9 = 72
∴ 30 should be in place of 38.

15. (*b*) : The numbers in the series are the sum of all the numbers preceding them.

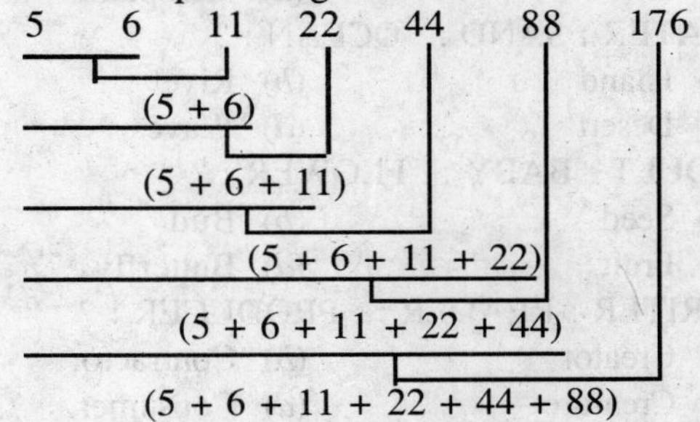

∴ 44 should be in place of 42.

❑❑❑

6 WORD ANALOGY

In Analogy Tests, the relationship between two given words is established and then applied to the other words. The type of relationship may vary, so while attempting such questions the first step is to identify the type of relationship, which can be any one of the following.

EXERCISE

Directions : *In the questions given below one term is missing. Based on the relationship of the two given words find the missing term from the given options.*

1. HUNGER : FOOD : : THIRST : ?
(*a*) Water (*b*) Drink
(*c*) Tea (*d*) Coffee

2. HUNTER : GUN : : WRITER : ?
(*a*) Book (*b*) Pen
(*c*) Poem (*d*) Page

3. WOOL : SHEEP : : SILK : ?
(*a*) Saree (*b*) String
(*c*) Silkworm (*d*) Moth

4. FOOD : STOMACH : : FUEL : ?
(*a*) Engine (*b*) Automobile
(*c*) Rail (*d*) Aeroplane

5. WATER : SAND : : OCEAN : ?
(*a*) Island (*b*) River
(*c*) Desert (*d*) Waves

6. ADULT : BABY : : FLOWER : ?
(*a*) Seed (*b*) Bud
(*c*) Fruit (*d*) Butterfly

7. WRITER : READER : : PRODUCER : ?
(*a*) Creator (*b*) Contractor
(*c*) Creature (*d*) Consumer

8. ENTRANCE : EXIT : : LOYALTY : ?
(*a*) Treachery (*b*) Patriotism
(*c*) Fidelity (*d*) Reward

9. MOTHER : MATERNAL : : FATHER : ?
(*a*) Eternal (*b*) Detrimental
(*c*) Paternal (*d*) Formidable

10. PEARL : NECKLACE : : FLOWER : ?
(*a*) Plant (*b*) Garden
(*c*) Petal (*d*) Bouquet

11. ALPHABET : WORD : : WORD : ?
(*a*) Sound (*b*) Music
(*c*) Sentence (*d*) Dictionary

12. LIFE : DEATH : : HOPE : ?
(*a*) Cry (*b*) Pain
(*c*) Despair (*d*) Sad

13. GOOD : BAD : : VIRTUE : ?
(*a*) Blame (*b*) Sin
(*c*) Despair (*d*) Vice

14. BIRD : FLY : : SNAKE : ?
(*a*) Timid (*b*) Clatter
(*c*) Crawl (*d*) Hole

15. CAT : MOUSE : : BIRD : ?
(*a*) Cage (*b*) Trap
(*c*) Eagle (*d*) Worm

16. STATE : EXILE
(*a*) Police : Arrest
(*b*) Judge : Convict
(*c*) Constitution : Amendment
(*d*) Church : Excommunicate

17. CAPRICIOUSNESS : RELIABILITY
(*a*) Extemporaneous : Predictability
(*b*) Unreliable : Inhuman
(*c*) Tenacious : Practicality
(*d*) Arbitrary : Whimsical

18. LOATH : COERCION
(*a*) Detest : Caressing
(*b*) Irritate : Caressing
(*c*) Irate : Antagonism
(*d*) Reluctant : Persuasion

19. SCALES : FISH
(*a*) Lady : Dress
(*b*) Tree : Leaves
(*c*) Bird : Feather
(*d*) Skin : Man

20. TREE : SAPLING
(*a*) Hut : Mansion
(*b*) Giant : Dwarf
(*c*) Horse : Foal
(*d*) Ant : Elephant

21. CHALK : BLACKBOARD
(*a*) Door : Handle
(*b*) Table : Chair
(*c*) Ink : Paper
(*d*) Type : Paint

14. The length of minute hand of a clock is 14 cm. Then the area swept by the minute hand in one minute is:
A. 10 m^2 B. 12.26 m^2
C. 20.26 m^2 D. 10.26 m^2

15. Find the area of ring between two concentric circles whose circumference are 77 cm and 55 cm.
A. 770 cm^2 B. 321 cm^2
C. 231 cm^2 D. 230 cm^2

16. A rectangle water reservoir is 10.8 metres long and 3.75 metres wide at base. Water flows into it at the rate of 18 m per sec. through the pipe having the cross section 7.5 cm × 4.5 cm. Then the height to which the water will rise in the reservoir in 30 minutes is :
A. 7.2 m B. 2.7 m
C. 3.7 m D. 7.3 m

17. A rectangular sheet of 44 cm × 18 cm is rolled along its length and a cylinder is formed. Then the volume of cylinder is :
A. 7227 cm^3 B. 7272 cm^3
C. 2727 cm^3 D. 2772 cm^3

18. How many metres of cloth 5 metre wide will be required to make a conical tent, the radius of whose base is 7 metre and height is 24 metre?
A. 100 m B. 110 m
C. 550 m D. 55 m

19. The surface area of a sphere whose volume is 4851 cubic metres is :
A. 1386 m^2 B. 1380 m^2
C. 1286 m^2 D. 3186 m^2

20. A hollow sphere of external and internal diameter 4 cm and 2 cm respectively, is melted into a cone of base diameter 8 cm. Then the height of the cone is :
A. 12 cm B. 14 cm
C. 20 cm D. 24 cm

21. The diamensions of a metallic rod are 19 cm × 4 cm × 2 cm and each side of a metallic cube is 4 cm. Both are melted and recast into a new cube. Find the length of edge of cube so formed.
A. 4 cm B. 5 cm
C. 6 cm D. 7 cm

22. An agricultural field is in the form of a rectangle of length 35 metres and width 15.4 metres. A pit 5.5 metres long, 4 metres wide and 2.5 metres deep is dug in the corner of the field and the earth taken out of the pit is spread uniformly over the remaining area of the field. The extent to which the level of the field has been raised is :
A. 16.6 cm B. 10.6 cm
C. 16.1 cm D. 6.10 cm

23. The side of a square exceeds the side of the another square by 4 cm and the sum of areas of two squares is 400 sq. cm. Find the dimensions of the square.
A. 8 cm, 12 cm B. 10 cm, 14 cm
C. 12 cm, 16 cm D. 14 cm, 18 cm

24. The cost of levelling a rectangular field at the rate of 85 paise per square metre is ₹ 624.75. Then the perimeter of the field if its sides are in the ratio of 5 : 3 is :
A. 35 m B. 21 m
C. 112 m D. 49 m

25. The diagonal of a rectangular field is 15 m and its area is 108 sq. m. What will be the total expenditure in fencing the field at the rate of ₹ 5 per metre?
A. ₹ 441 B. ₹ 420
C. ₹ 210 D. ₹ 120

ANSWERS

1	2	3	4	5	6	7	8	9	10
D	A	B	A	A	A	C	B	D	A
11	**12**	**13**	**14**	**15**	**16**	**17**	**18**	**19**	**20**
B	D	A	D	C	B	D	B	A	B
21	**22**	**23**	**24**	**25**					
C	B	C	C	C					

SOME SELECTED EXPLANATORY ANSWERS

1. $\because$ Radius of the circle $= \frac{112}{4} = 28$ m

$\therefore$ Area of the circle $= \frac{22}{7}\times 28\times 28 = 2464\ m^2$.

2. Length of the rectangle $= \frac{112}{8} = 14$ cm.

$\therefore$ Perimeter of the rectangle $= 2(14 + 8)$
$= 44$ cm.

$\therefore$ Circumference of the circle $= 132 - 44$
$= 88$ cm.

$\therefore$ $r = \frac{88\times 7}{2\times 22} = 14$ cm

$\therefore$ Area of the circle

$$= \frac{22}{7} \times 14 \times 14 = 616 \text{ sq cm.}$$

3. From question—

$\because$ Diameter of the circle = 28 cm.

$\Rightarrow$ Area of the circle = $\frac{22}{7} \times (14)^2 = 616 \text{ cm}^2$

$\therefore$ Area of the rectangle = 1166 – 616 = 550 cm^2

$\Rightarrow$ Breadth of the rectangle = $\frac{550}{25} = 22$ cm.

$\therefore$ Required sum = $2 \times \frac{22}{7} \times (14) + 2(25 + 22)$ = 88 + 94 = 182 cm.

4. Length of the floor = $\frac{212 \times 32}{2 \times (32 + 21)} = 64$ ft.

and breadth the floor = $\frac{64 \times 21}{32} = 42$ ft.

$\therefore$ Area of the floor = 64 × 42 = 2688 sq. ft.

$\therefore$ Reqd. cost = ₹ 2688 × 2.5 = ₹ 6720.

5. Only statement A may be true or possibility.

6. Area of the circular field = 18634 m^2

$\because$ $\pi r^2 = 18634$

$\Rightarrow$ $r^2 = 18634 \times \frac{7}{22} = 5929$

$\Rightarrow$ $r = 77$ m

$\because$ Length of the fence = $2 \times \frac{22}{7} \times 77$ = 484 m

$\therefore$ Total cost = 484 × 365 = ₹ 176660.

7. One side of the square = $\sqrt{196} = 14$ cm

$\therefore$ Radius of the circle = 28 cm

$\therefore$ Circumference of the circle = $2 \times \frac{22}{7} \times 28$ = 176 cm

$\therefore$ Breadth of the rectangle = 176 cm

$\therefore$ Length of the rectangle = $\frac{712}{2} - 176$ = 356 – 176 = 180 cm.

8. Let r be the radius of the circular plot then from problem,

$\because$ The circumference of the circular plot = 484 m

$\Rightarrow$ $2\pi r = 484$

$r = 484 \times \frac{7}{22} \times \frac{1}{2} = 77$ metres

$\therefore$ Area of the circular plot = $\pi r^2 = \frac{22}{7} \times (77)^2$ = 18634 m^2.

10. Area of the whole paper ABCD = 22 × 14 = 308 cm^2

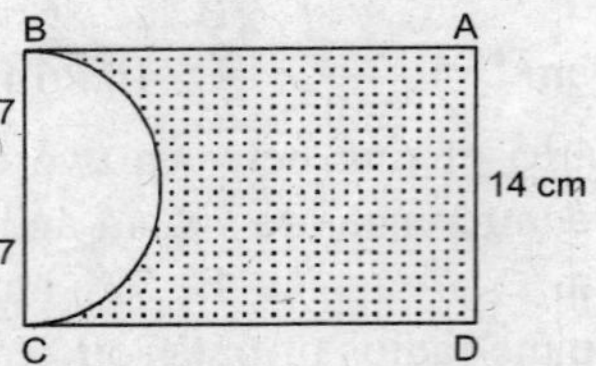

Radius of the semi-circle = $\frac{1}{2} \times 14 \text{ cm} = 7$ cm

$\therefore$ Area of the semi-circle = $\frac{1}{2}\pi r^2$

$= \frac{1}{2} \times \frac{22}{7} \times 7 \times 7$

$= 77 \text{ cm}^2$

$\therefore$ Area of the remaining part of the paper = 308 cm^2 – 77 cm^2 = 231 cm^2.

11. Circumference of flower bed = 880 dm

$\Rightarrow$ $2\pi r = 880$ dm

$\Rightarrow$ $r = \frac{880}{2\pi}$ dm $= \frac{880 \times 7}{2 \times 22} = 140$ dm

Area of flower bed = $\pi r^2 = \frac{22}{7} \times (140)^2 \text{ dm}^2$

$\therefore$ Required number of plants

$$= \frac{\frac{22}{7} \times 140 \times 140}{35} \text{dm}^2$$

$$= \frac{22}{7} \times \frac{140 \times 140}{35} = 1760.$$

13. Area of each quadrant = $\frac{\theta}{360} \times \pi r^2$

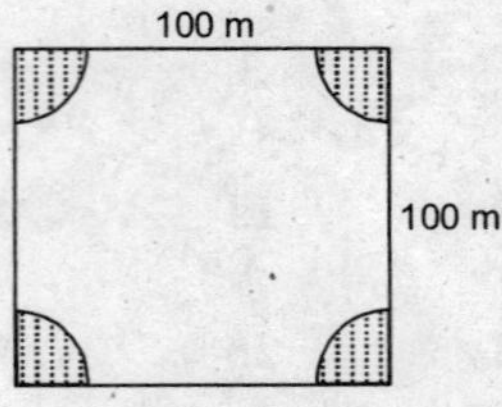

$= \frac{90}{360} \times \frac{22}{7} \times 14 \times 14 \text{ m}^2 = 154 \text{ m}^2$

$\therefore$ Area of 4 quadrants = 154 × 4 m^2 = 616 m^2

Area of park = $(100)^2$ = 10,000 m^2

Hence area of the remaining part of the park = 10,000 – 616 = 9,384 m^2.

14. Length of minute hand of clock = r = 14 cm

Central angle covered in 1 minute = $\frac{360}{60} = 6°$

22. PRIMEVAL : MEDIEVAL
(*a*) Dinosaur : Dragon
(*b*) Gorilla : Soldier
(*c*) Evolution : Revelation
(*d*) Thorn : Rose

23. TRILOGY : NOVEL
(*a*) Rice : Husk
(*b*) Milk : Cream
(*c*) Fabric : Weaving
(*d*) Serial : Episode

24. PEDANT : ERUDITION
(*a*) Prude : Modesty
(*b*) Blunt : Politician
(*c*) Diplomats : Tactless
(*d*) Enemy : Friendly

25. FURY : IRE
(*a*) Convulsion : Spasm
(*b*) Amusement : Happiness
(*c*) Joke : Laugh
(*d*) Dispassion : Emotion

EXPLANATORY ANSWERS

1. (*a*) : Hunger is satiated by food, thirst by water.

2. (*b*) : Weapon of a hunter is a gun, weapon of a writer is a pen.

3. (*c*) : Wool is obtained from sheep, silk is obtained from silkworm.

4. (*a*) : Food is consumed in stomach, fuel is consumed in engine.

5. (*c*) : The related words are near opposites.

6. (*b*) : The youngone of an adult is a baby and that of a flower is a bud.

7. (*d*) : A writer aims to please the readers by his writings, a producer aims to please the consumers by his products.

8. (*a*) : The related words are opposites.

9. (*c*) : Relations on the mother's side are maternal and on the father's side paternal.

10. (*d*) : Many pearls make a necklace, many flowers make a bouquet.

11. (*c*) : More than one alphabet make a word, more than one word make a sentence.

12. (*c*) : The related words are opposites.

13. (*d*) : The related words are opposites.

14. (*c*) : Birds fly, snakes crawl.

15. (*d*) : Cat chases the mouse, bird chases the worm.

16. (*d*) : Punishment of leaving the State is exile, punishment of leaving the Church is excommunication.

17. (*c*) : The related words are antonyms.

18. (*d*) : Loathing is the result of constant coersion, reluctance is the result of constant persuasion.

19. (*d*) : Covering of the fish is scales, covering of man is skin.

20. (*c*) : Young tree is a sapling, young horse is a foal.

21. (*c*) : Chalk is used to write on blackboard, ink is used to write on paper.

22. (*a*) : The related words represent almost the same time period and answer option represents almost the same sized creatures.

23. (*d*) : Trilogy is section of a novel, episode is a section of a serial.

24. (*a*) : The related words are synonyms.

25. (*b*) : Fury causes ire, amusement causes happiness.

❑❑❑

7 NUMBER ANALOGY

In number analogy also, the relationship between the given numbers is detected and then applied to the second part to find the missing numbers. This relationship between the numbers can be based on any of the following patterns :

(i) numbers can be odd/even/prime numbers;
(ii) numbers can be multiples of one number;
(iii) numbers can be squares/cubes of different numbers;
(iv) some numbers can be added to/subtracted from/multiplied to/divided into the first number to get the second number;
(v) the second number can be the sum/product/difference of the digits of first number; and
(vi) combinations of any mathematical calculations given above can apply to the relationship between the two given numbers.

EXERCISE

Directions : *In the following questions, select the number from the given options which follows the same relationship as shared between the first two numbers.*

1. 1 : 11 : : 2 : ?
(*a*) 20 (*b*) 22
(*c*) 24 (*d*) 44

2. $\frac{1}{7} : \frac{1}{14} :: \frac{1}{9} : ?$
(*a*) $\frac{1}{88}$ (*b*) $\frac{1}{80}$
(*c*) $\frac{1}{81}$ (*d*) $\frac{1}{18}$

3. 0.16 : 0.0016 : : 1.02 : ?
(*a*) 10.20
(*b*) 0.102
(*c*) 0.0102
(*d*) 1.020

4. 663 : 884 : : 221 : ?
(*a*) 332
(*b*) 554
(*c*) 773
(*d*) 442

5. 16 : 0.16 : : ?
(*a*) 2 : 0.02
(*b*) 7 : 0.007
(*c*) 1.3 : 0.13
(*d*) 0.01 : 0.001

6. $3 : \frac{1}{3} :: ?$
(*a*) 6 : 12 (*b*) 5 : 2/15
(*c*) 8 : 1/8 (*d*) 9 : 27

7. 65 : 13 : : 180 : ?
(*a*) 93
(*b*) 36
(*c*) 133
(*d*) 102

8. 125 : 27 : : 343 : ?
(*a*) 729
(*b*) 64
(*c*) 216
(*d*) 512

9. 357 : 73 : : ?
(*a*) 429 : 94
(*b*) 201 : 21
(*c*) 138 : 38
(*d*) 93 : 39

10. 731 : 902 : : 655 : ?
(*a*) 646 (*b*) 800
(*c*) 793 (*d*) 556

11. 162 : 9 : : 310 : ?
(*a*) 33 (*b*) 27
(*c*) 16 (*d*) 4

12. 13 : 17 : : 15 : ?
(*a*) 19 (*b*) 11
(*c*) 21 (*d*) 16

13. 225 : 15 : : 256 : ?
(*a*) 26 (*b*) 16
(*c*) 20 (*d*) 28

14. 46 : 48 : : 54 : ?
(*a*) 59 (*b*) 40
(*c*) 67 (*d*) 62

15. 33 : 36 : : 21 : ?
(*a*) 9 (*b*) 18
(*c*) 25 (*d*) 32

EXPLANATORY ANSWERS

1. *(b)* : The first number is repeated to obtain the second number.

2. *(d)* : The first fraction is multiplied by half to obtain the second fraction.

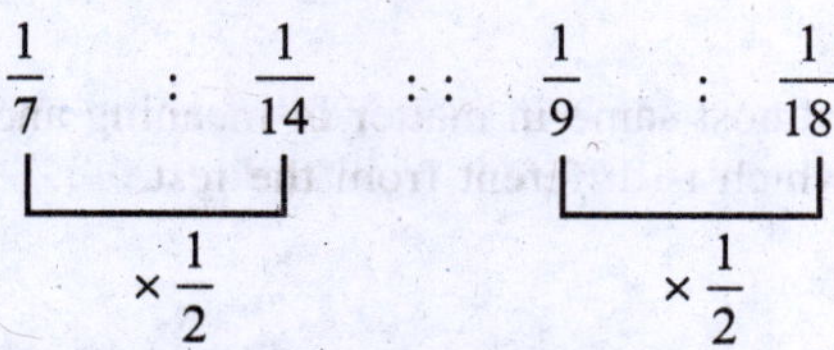

3. *(c)* : The decimals are divided by 100.

0.16 : 0.0016 : : 1.02 : 0.0102

÷ 100 ÷ 100

4. *(d)* : The digits at tens and hundreds place is same but the digit at the units place is half the other identical digits.

66 3 : 88 4 : : 22 1 : 44 2

5. *(a)* : Of the two related numbers, the second number is the result of first number divided by 100.

16 : 0.16 : : 2 : 0.02

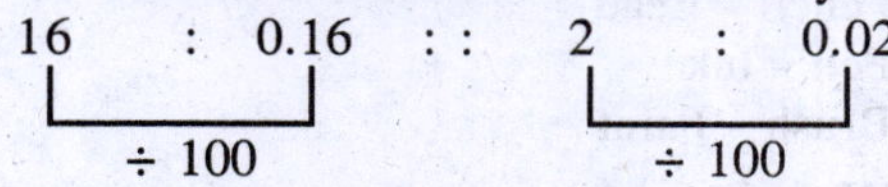

6. *(c)* : Of the two related numbers, the second number is the part fraction of the first number, *i.e.,* 3 is related to one-third $\left(\frac{1}{3}\right)$. Similarly, 8 will be related to one-eighth $\left(\frac{1}{8}\right)$.

7. *(b)* : The first number is divided by 5 to get the second number.

65 : 13 : : 180 : 36

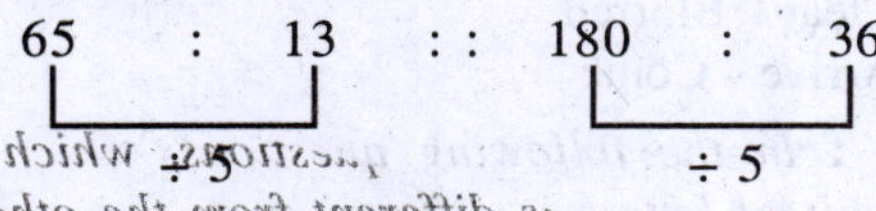

8. *(a)* : The numbers are cubes of different odd numbers.

125 : 27 : : 343 : 729

↓ ↓ ↓ ↓

5^3 3^3 7^3 9^3

9. *(a)* : The central digit of the first number is left out and the corner digits written in reverse order to get the second number.

357 : 73 : : 429 : 94

10. *(a)* : The sum of the digits of both the numbers is same.

731 : 902 → 7 + 3 + 1

= 9 + 0 + 2, *i.e.,* 11 = 11

655 : 646 → 6 + 5 + 5

= 6 + 4 + 6, *i.e.,* 16 = 16

11. *(d)* : The sum of the digits of the first number is the second number.

162 : 9 : : 310 : 4

1 + 6 + 2 3 + 1 + 0

12. *(a)* : First number plus 4 gives the second number.

13 : 17 : : 15 : 19

+4 +4

13. *(b)* : The root of first number is the second number.

225 : 15 : : 256 : 16

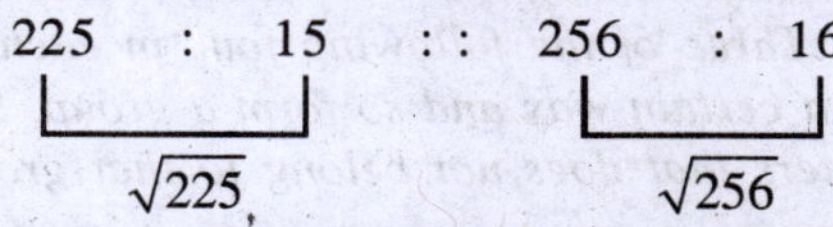

14. *(b)* : The product of the digits of first number is multiplied by 2 to get the second number.

46 : 48 : : 54 : 40

(4 × 6) 2 (5 × 4) 2

15. *(a)* : The square of the sum of the digits of the first number is the second number.

33 : 36 : : 21 : 9

$(3 + 3)^2$ $(2 + 1)^2$

❑❑❑

8 ODD ONE OUT

In this type of classification, four words are given out of which three are almost same in matter or meaning and only one word is different from the common three. One has to find out the word which is different from the rest.

EXERCISE

Directions : *In each of the following questions, three words are alike in some manner. Spot the odd one out.*

1. (*a*) Green (*b*) Red
(*c*) Colour (*d*) Orange

2. (*a*) Stable (*b*) Hole
(*c*) Canoe (*d*) Sty

3. (*a*) Nose (*b*) Eyes
(*c*) Skin (*d*) Teeth

4. (*a*) Venus (*b*) Moon
(*c*) Pluto (*d*) Mars

5. (*a*) Happy (*b*) Gloomy
(*c*) Lively (*d*) Cheerful

Directions : *Three of the following four in each question are alike in a certain way and so form a group. Select the group of letters that does not belong to that group.*

6. (*a*) ACE (*b*) LOR
(*c*) GIK (*d*) VXZ

7. (*a*) TSR (*b*) LKJ
(*c*) PQO (*d*) HGF

8. (*a*) EF LM (*b*) KJ SR
(*c*) XW HG (*d*) ED YX

9. (*a*) JOPK (*b*) BOPC
(*c*) QOPR (*d*) TOPS

10. (*a*) DfH (*b*) MoQ
(*c*) UwY (*d*) lnO

Directions : *In each of the following questions, there are four options. Three numbers, in these options, are alike in certain manner. Only one number does not fit in. Choose the one which is different from the rest.*

11. (*a*) 1948 (*b*) 2401
(*c*) 966 (*d*) 1449

12. (*a*) 182 (*b*) 169
(*c*) 130 (*d*) 158

13. (*a*) 129 (*b*) 130
(*c*) 131 (*d*) 132

14. (*a*) 3215 (*b*) 9309
(*c*) 4721 (*d*) 2850

15. (*a*) 1776 (*b*) 2364
(*c*) 1976 (*d*) 3776

Directions : *In the following questions select the pair which is different from the other three.*

16. (*a*) Chair - Furniture
(*b*) Shirt - Garment
(*c*) Necklace - Jewellery
(*d*) Bogie - Engine

17. (*a*) Crayon - Paper
(*b*) Pencil - Lead
(*c*) Pen - Ink
(*d*) Brush - Paint

18. (*a*) War - Peace
(*b*) Real - Natural
(*c*) Premiere - First
(*d*) Wrath - Anger

19. (*a*) Finger - Thimble
(*b*) Head - Cap
(*c*) Waist - Tiara
(*d*) Foot - Shoe

20. (*a*) Day - Night
(*b*) Clever - Foolish
(*c*) Clear - Blurred
(*d*) Arrive - Come

Directions : *In the following questions, which of the following pair of letters is different from the other three?*

21. (*a*) FGH - HIJ
(*b*) PQR - RST
(*c*) MNO - OPQ
(*d*) CDE - DEF

22. (*a*) JuM - jUm (*b*) iLo - Ilo
(*c*) PSa - psA (*d*) ZeX - zEx

23. (*a*) NQT - JMP (*b*) CFI - RUX
(*c*) ADG - FGH (*d*) SVY - ORU

24. (*a*) DXD - XDX (*b*) KUK - UKU
(*c*) FHF - EHE (*d*) RSR - SRS

25. (*a*) AYT - BZU (*b*) FNG - EMF
(*c*) RWO - QVN (*d*) HJD - GIC

EXPLANATORY ANSWERS

1. *(c)* : All others are types of colour.
2. *(c)* : Canoe is a boat. Others are resting places of birds/ animals.
3. *(d)* : All others are sense organs.
4. *(b)* : All others are planets.
5. *(b)* : All others are expressions of joy.
6. *(b)* : The sequence in each group is +2. Only option *(b)* has sequence in +3, *i.e.,*

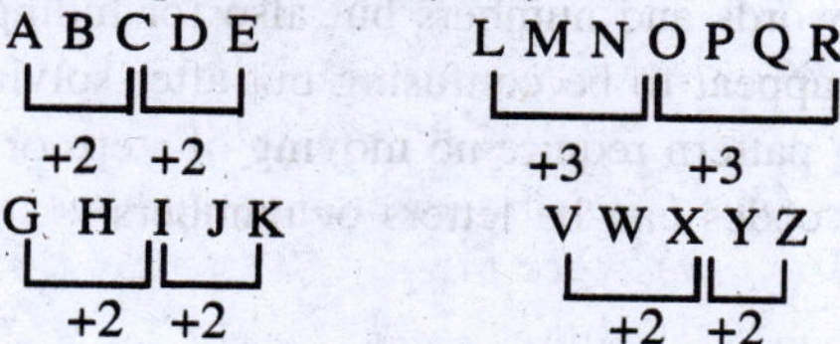

7. *(c)* : The sequence of alphabet in each group is in reverse order. Only option *(c)* has sequence in disturbed order.
8. *(a)* : Two consecutive alphabet in each group are in reverse sequence (–1), *i.e.,*

KJ SR ; XW HG ; ED YX
–1 –1 –1 –1 –1 –1

Only in option *(a)* the sequence is in natural order (+1), *i.e.,*

9. *(d)* : In each group, letters 'OP' are common. The two corner alphabet are in natural order (+1); *i.e.,*

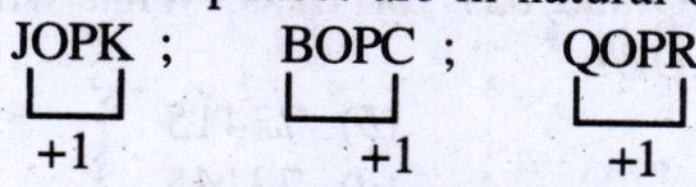

Only in option *(d)* they are in reverse order (–1); *i.e.,*

TOPS
–1

10. *(d)* : In other groups, only the alphabet in the centre is of lower case. In this option letter 'L' on the left is also in lower case.
11. *(a)* : Other numbers are divisible by 7.
12. *(d)* : Other numbers are multiples of 13.
13. *(c)* : 131 is a prime number.
14. *(b)* : In other numbers, no digit is repeated.
15. *(b)* : In other numbers, the last two digits are same.
16. *(d)* : Bogie is a part of train which is a type of conveyance. Chair, Shirt and Necklace are types of furniture, garment and jewellery respectively.
17. *(a)* : The medium used for writing with pencil is lead, with pen it is ink and with brush, it is paint. With crayon it should be wax.
18. *(a)* : The pair of words are opposite. Other pairs are synonyms.
19. *(c)* : Tiara is worn on the head.
20. *(d)* : Other words are opposite to each other.
21. *(d)* : In all other groups, the letters are in natural series and the last letter of first part is the first letter of the second part.
22. *(b)* : In all other groups, only the vowel is in lower case in the first part and in second part the case is reversed.
23. *(c)* : In all other groups, the letters jump two letters in between them.
24. *(c)* : In all other groups, the single letter in first part is repeated in the second and vice versa.
25. *(a)* : In all other groups, the letters in the first part are one step forward than the corresponding letters in the second part.

❑❑❑

9 CODING AND DECODING

Coding is a secretive language which is used to change the representation of the actual term/word/value. This coded language can be framed by *(i)* moving the letters one or more steps forward or backward; *(ii)* substituting numbers for letters and vice–versa; *(iii)* writing the letters of the given word in reverse order in part or in whole; and *(iv)* replacing the letters in their natural series by the same positioned letters in their reverse series.

There is variety in ways of coding. Coding language is not only for words and numbers but also for hiding a group of words, statements or even sentences. This form of coding pattern may appear to be confusing but after solving only a few questions it is very easy to understand. Questions based on this coding pattern require no moving of steps or straining efforts of calculations, but only quick tallying or comparing ability. The codes can be letters or numbers.

EXERCISE

Directions : *In the following questions select the right option which indicates the correct code for the word or letter given in the question.*

1. If MUSK is coded as 146816, then ZERO will be coded as :
(*a*) 113811 (*b*) 122912
(*c*) 15915 (*d*) 2651815

2. If BAD is coded as 7, HIS as 9, LOW will be coded as:
(*a*) 50 (*b*) 8
(*c*) 23 (*d*) 5

3. In a certain code LIBERATE is written as 56403170, TRIBAL will be written in the same code as :
(*a*) 734615 (*b*) 736415
(*c*) 136475 (*d*) 034615

4. In certain military code, SYSTEM is written as SYSMET, and NEARER as AENRER, what will be the code for FRACTION?
(*a*) CRAFNOIT (*b*) FRCAITNO
(*c*) CARFNOIT (*d*) FRACNOIT

5. If CRUDE is written as BSTED, then MOIST will be coded as :
(*a*) NNJRU (*b*) LNHRS
(*c*) NPJTU (*d*) LPHTS

6. In a certain code ALPACA is written as ACAPLA. How will ANIMAL be written in that code?
(*a*) LAMINA (*b*) ALAMIN
(*c*) LAMNIA (*d*) AAMLIN

7. In a certain code FINGER is written as DGLECP. What will be the code for KIDNEY?
(*a*) IGBLCW
(*b*) IGCLBW
(*c*) IBCGLE
(*d*) IGBKCV

8. In a certain code QUESTION is written as NXBVQLLQ. How will REPLY be coded?
(*a*) YHMOV (*b*) OBMVI
(*c*) VHSOB (*d*) OHMOV

9. If in a certain code SKEW is coded as PNCY, then what will JXQV will stand for?
(*a*) MUTS (*b*) MUST
(*c*) MTSU (*d*) STUM

10. In a certain code LONDON is written as MPOEPO. What will IVOHSZ mean in the same code?
(*a*) HUNGRY (*b*) HUNDRY
(*c*) GRUNHY (*d*) HONDUS

11. In a certain code language 8514 is a code for HEAD, 3945 for RIDE and 057 for BEG. What will be the code for GRADE?
(*a*) 71345 (*b*) 73415
(*c*) 74135 (*d*) 73145

12. If MOTHERLAND is coded as 9501623748, how will DREAM be coded?
(*a*) 82697 (*b*) 86297
(*c*) 82769 (*d*) 82679

13. If OATH is coded in a certain language as TEYL, then how will WORD be coded?
(*a*) BWRH (*b*) HRWB
(*c*) BSWH (*d*) CSXI

14. If FINANCE is coded as GKQESIL, then how will BANK be coded in the same manner?
(*a*) CBOL (*b*) CDRP
(*c*) CCQO (*d*) CCPN

15. PLANNING is coded in a certain language as UFFHSCSA. How will AUTHORITY be coded in the same language?
(*a*) FOYBTLNND (*b*) FYOTBNNLT
(*c*) FBOYTLNTN (*d*) FBOYTNLTN

EXPLANATORY ANSWERS

1. ***(b)*** **:** The coded number signifies the position of the alphabet in its reverse order of the alphabetical series (ZYXW...)

M U S K → MUSK
↓ ↓ ↓ ↓
14th 6th 8th 16th → 146816

Similarly,

Z E R O → ZERO
↓ ↓ ↓ ↓
1st 22nd 9th 12th → 122912

2. ***(d)*** **:** The coded number is the sum of number digits signifying the position of the alphabet in the natural order.

B A D
↓ ↓ ↓
2nd 1st 4th *i.e.,* 2 + 1 + 4 = 7

Similarly,

H I S
↓ ↓ ↓
8th 9th 19th *i.e.,* 8 + 9 + 19 = 36
further, 3 + 6 = 9

Also,

L O W
↓ ↓ ↓
12th 15th 23rd *i.e.,* 12 + 15 + 23 = 50
further, 5 + 0 = 0

3. ***(b)*** **:** The letters of the word TRIBAL are picked from LIBERATE. So will be the coded numbers.

L I B E R A T E → given word
5 6 4 0 3 1 7 0 → codes

Similarly,

T R I B A L → word to be coded
7 3 6 4 1 5 → answer codes

4. ***(c)*** **:** The word is divided into two equal parts and the letters of each part are written in reverse order.

SYS TEM SYS MET NEA RER AEN RER

Similarly,

5. ***(d)*** **:** The code is formed by moving the letters one step backwards and one step forward alternately.

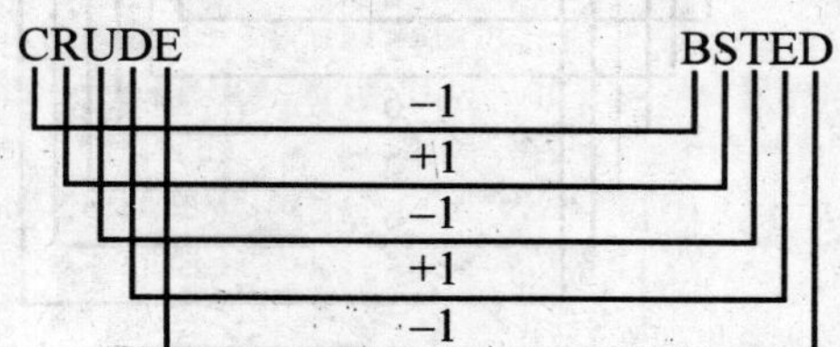

Similarly,

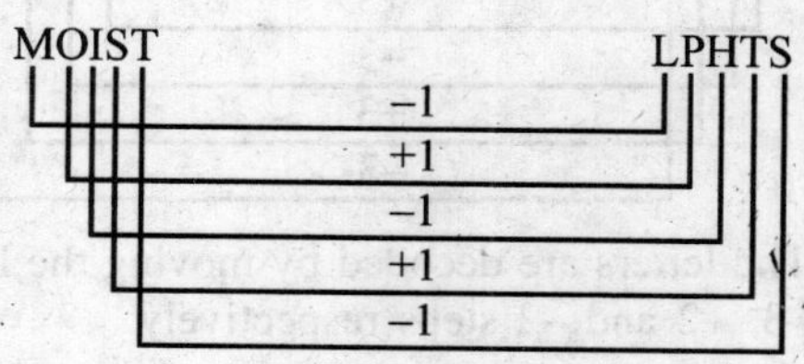

6. ***(a)*** **:** The letters of the word are written backwards.

Similarly,

7. ***(a)*** **:** The word is coded by moving the letters two steps backwards.

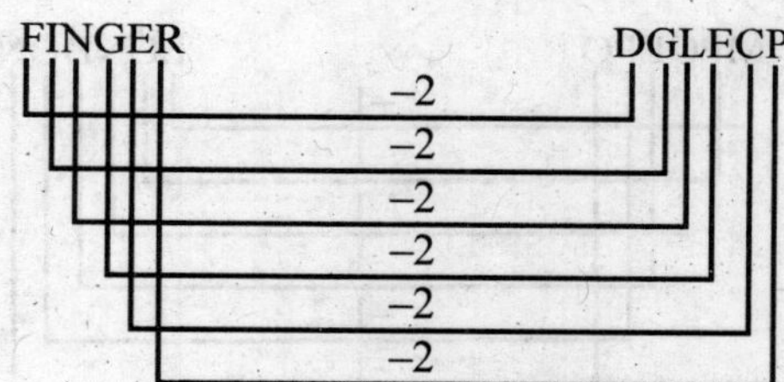

Similarly,

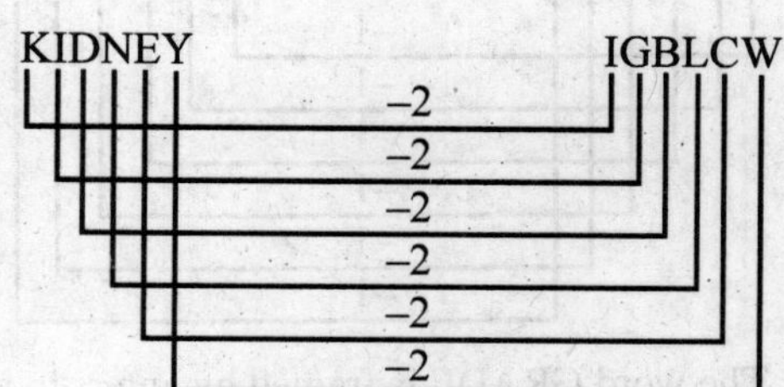

8. ***(d)*** **:** The letters of the word are coded by moving three steps backward and three steps forward alternately.

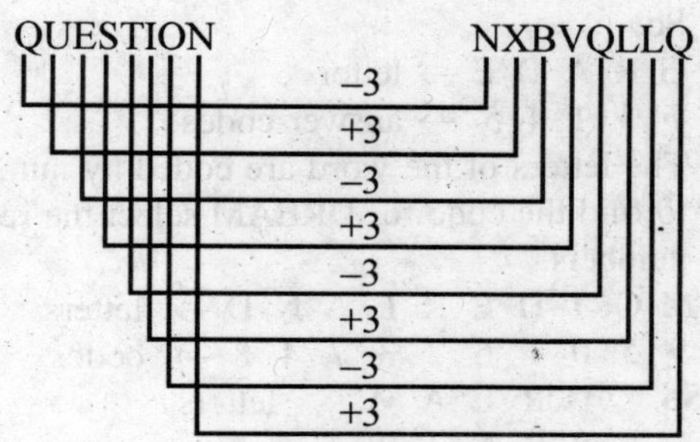

Similarly,

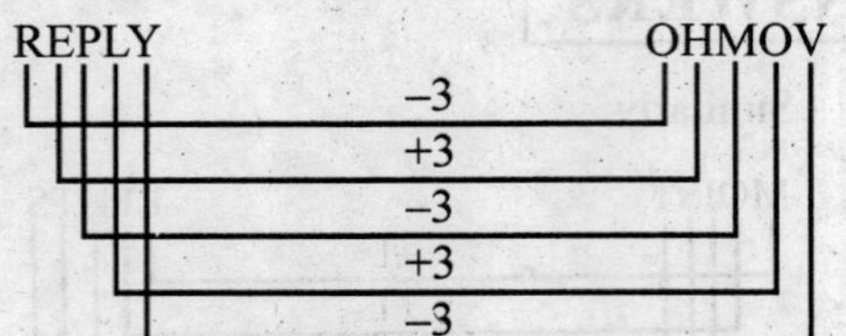

9. *(b)* **:** The letters are decoded by moving the letters +3, –3, +2 and –2 steps respectively.

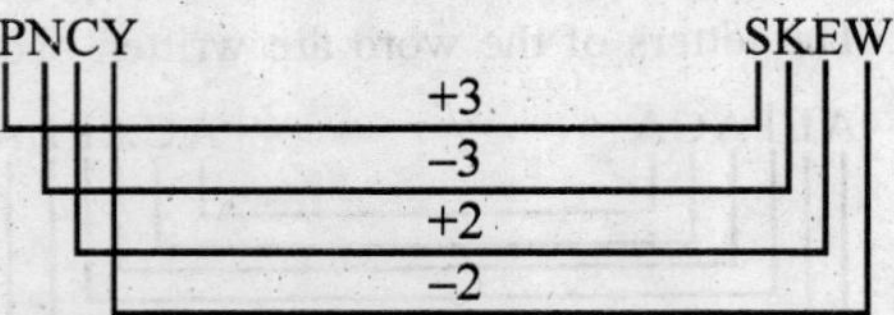

Similarly,

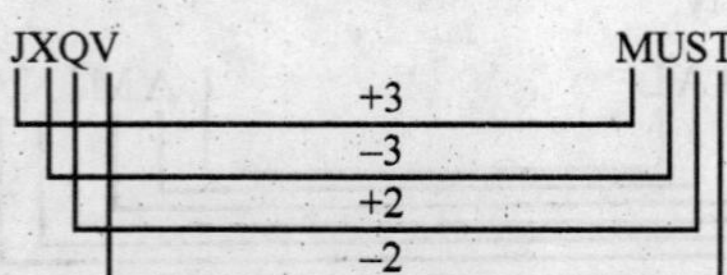

10. *(a)* **:** The letters of the coded word are moved one step backward.

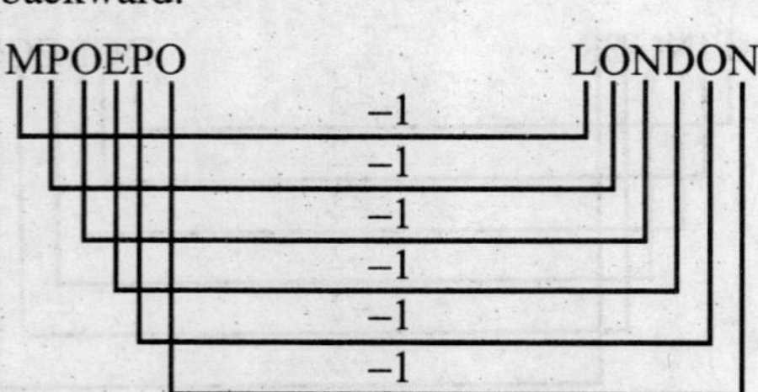

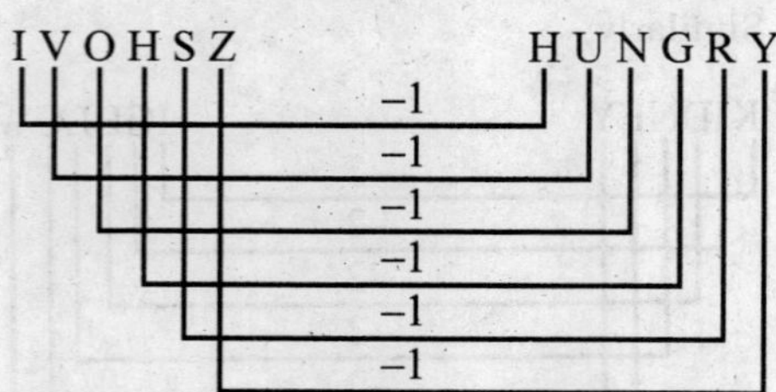

11. *(d)* **:** The word GRADE is framed by letters in the given words. So, in order to find the code for GRADE select the respective number codes.

H E A D R I D E B E G → letters
8 5 1 4 3 9 4 5 0 5 7 → codes

So,

G R A D E → letters
7 3 1 4 5 → answer codes

12. *(d)* **:** The letters of the word are coded by numbers. So to find the code for DREAM select the respective numbers.

M O T H E R L A N D → letters
9 5 0 1 6 2 3 7 4 8 → codes

So, D R E A M → letters
8 2 6 7 9 → answer codes

13. *(c)* **:** The letters are coded by moving five and four steps forward alternately.

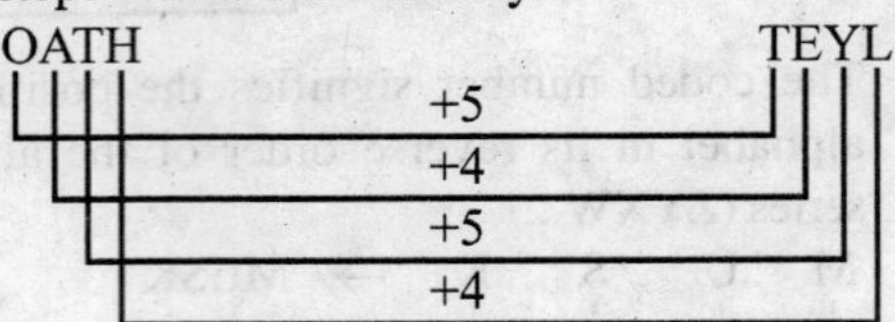

Similarly,

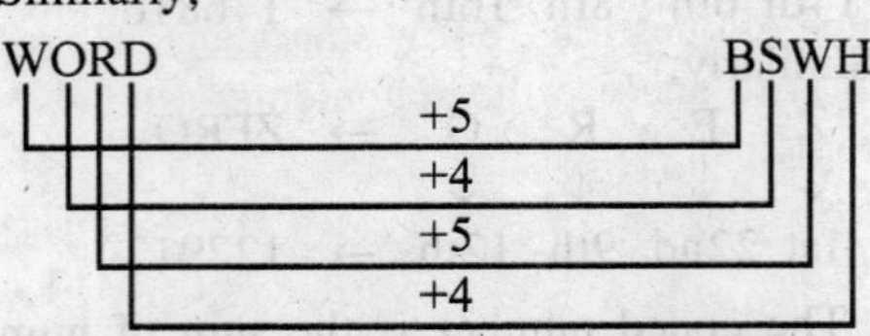

14. *(c)* **:** The letters of the word are coded by moving one step ahead and increasing the difference by one.

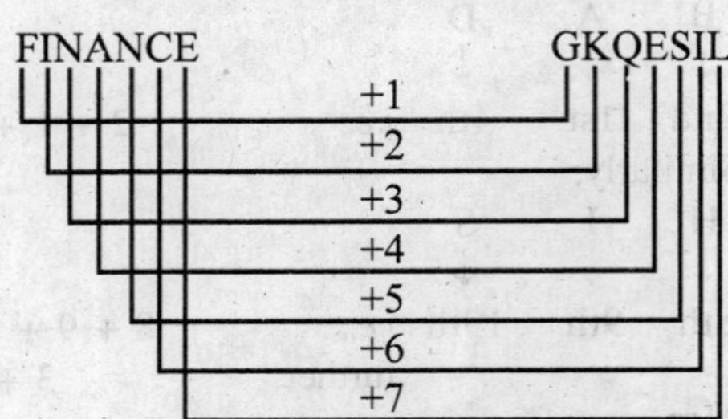

Similarly,

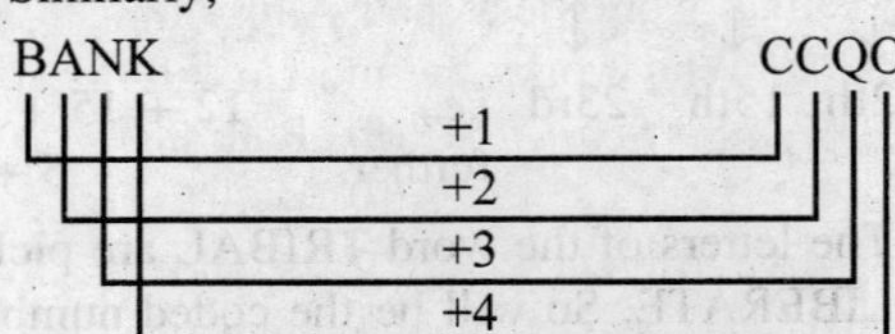

15. *(a)* **:** The letters of the word are coded by moving five steps forward and six steps backward alternately.

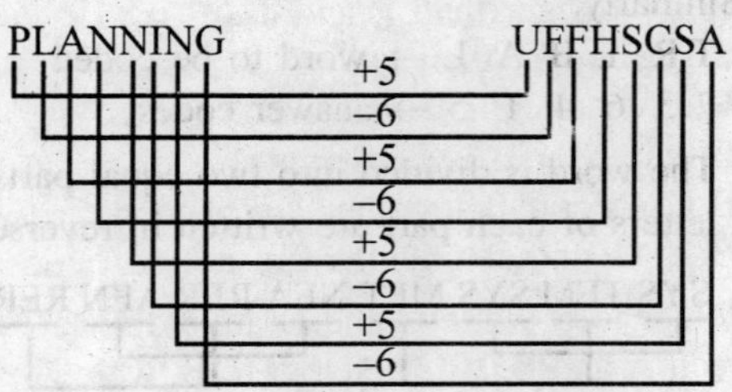

Similarly,

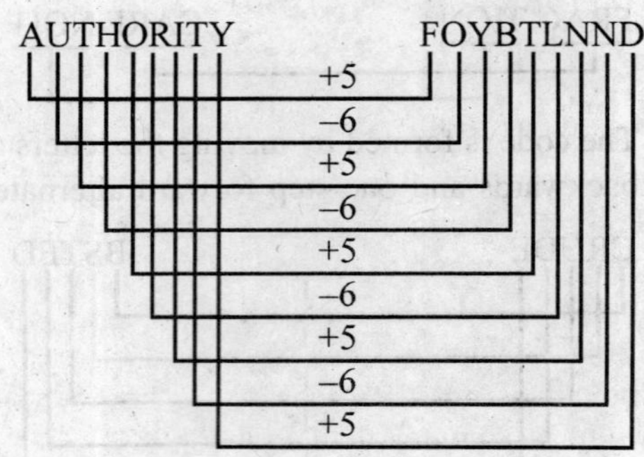

❑ ❑ ❑

10 STATEMENT ANALYSIS

In these type of questions, a few statements are given. Certain facts are broken up and mentioned in these statements. What is required is to analyse the statements, arrange and sort out the given facts and then answer the questions related to the given statements.

EXERCISE

1. Among five friends, A is heavier than B; C is lighter than D; B is lighter than D but heavier than E. Who among them is the heaviest?
(*a*) B (*b*) C
(*c*) A (*d*) Can't say

2. Pune is bigger than Jhansi, Sitapur is bigger than Chittor. Raigarh is not as big as Jhansi, but is bigger than Sitapur. Chittor is not as big as Sitapur. Which is the smallest?
(*a*) Jhansi (*b*) Pune
(*c*) Chittor (*d*) Sitapur

3. Ajay works more than Ram. Alok works as much as Raju. Pankaj works less than Alok. Ram works more than Alok. Who works the most of all?
(*a*) Ajay (*b*) Ram
(*c*) Alok (*d*) Raju

4. Among five friends P, Q, R, S and T, who is the youngest? To arrive at the answer which of the following information given in the statements (A) and (B) is sufficient?
(A) R is younger than P and T.
(B) S is younger than Q.
(*a*) Only A alone is sufficient
(*b*) Either A or B is sufficient
(*c*) Both A and B together are needed
(*d*) Both A and B together are not sufficient

5. A is elder to B while C and D are elder to E who lies between A and B. If C be elder to B, which one of the following statements is necessarily true?
(*a*) E is elder to B
(*b*) A is elder to C
(*c*) C is elder to D
(*d*) D is elder to C

6. Suresh is as much older than Kamal as he is younger than Prabodh. Navin is as old as Kamal. Which of the following statements is wrong?
(*a*) Suresh is older than Navin
(*b*) Kamal is younger than Suresh
(*c*) Prabodh is not the oldest
(*d*) Navin is younger than Prabodh

Directions (Qs. 7 to 9) : *Ram, Sohan and Mohan play football, hockey and cricket. Ram, Ramesh and Mohan play hockey, cricket and basketball. Ram, Sohan, Rahim and Mohan play football and cricket. Now answer the following questions based on the above statements :*

7. Which game is played by all the boys?
(*a*) Football (*b*) Hockey
(*c*) Cricket (*d*) Basketball

8. Which two boys play all the games?
(*a*) Ram, Sohan (*b*) Ram, Ramesh
(*c*) Sohan, Mohan (*d*) Ram, Mohan

9. Who does not play football?
(*a*) Ramesh (*b*) Sohan
(*c*) Rahim (*d*) Mohan

Directions (Qs. 10 to 12) : *Read the following directions and answer the questions given below :*

There are five persons in a group. Out of these two are men. Only three persons know swimming, of which one is a man. There is a couple, of which the husband knows swimming. A is the younger sister of D and B is the husband of E. C is a swimming champion.

10. Who is the other man in the group?
(*a*) C (*b*) B
(*c*) A (*d*) D

11. The two women who know how to swim are:
(*a*) A and C (*b*) C and D
(*c*) D and E (*d*) A and E

12. The two persons who do not know how to swim are :
(*a*) B and D (*b*) D and E
(*c*) A and E (*d*) A and D

Directions (Qs. 13 to 15) : *Read the following statements and answer the questions given below :*

Rajat, Sushil and Nagesh play football, hockey and cricket. Rajat, Ramu and Nagesh play hockey, cricket and basketball. Rajat, Sushil, Mayank and Nagesh play football and cricket.

13. Which game is played by all the boys?
(*a*) Hockey (*b*) Basketball
(*c*) Football (*d*) Cricket

14. Who does not play football?
(*a*) Rajat (*b*) Nagesh
(*c*) Sushil (*d*) Ramu

15. Which of the following two boys play all the games?
(*a*) Nagesh, Rajat (*b*) Mayank, Ramu
(*c*) Ramu, Nagesh (*d*) Sushil, Mayank

EXPLANATORY ANSWERS

1. ***(d)*** **:** The five friends in descending order of weight are : A/D, B/C, E or A/D, B, C/E. Either A or D is the heaviest.

2. ***(c)*** **:** The order of cities in descending order of size is : Pune, Jhansi, Raigarh, Sitapur, Chittor.

3. ***(a)*** **:** On the basis of doing work, the descending order will be : Ajay, Ram, Alok/Raju, Pankaj.

4. ***(d)*** **:** Statements are not inter-related.

5. ***(a)*** **:** The order in descending seniority will be : A/C/D, E, B.

6. ***(c)*** **:** On the basis of age the descending order will be : Prabodh, Suresh, Kamal/Navin.

Chart for Answers 7 to 9

Boy	*Games Played*
Ram	Football, Hocky, Cricket, Basketball
Sohan	Football, Hockey, Cricket
Mohan	Football, Hockey, Cricket, Basketball
Ramesh	Hockey, Cricket, Basketball
Rahim	Football, Cricket.

7. ***(c)*** **8.** ***(d)*** **9.** ***(a)***

For Answers 10 to 12 the information chart will be :

A. Woman ((younger sister of D); knows swimming.
B. Man (husband of E); knows swimming
C. Woman; Swimming champion
D. Man (brother of A)
E. Woman (wife of B)

From the couple B & E, B (husband) knows swimming. C is a swimming champion. Three persons know how to swim of which only B is a man. So, the two women who know how to swim are C and A (the younger sister of D). There are two men in the group of five. One is B and the other will be D.

10. ***(d)*** **11.** ***(a)*** **12.** ***(b)***

Chart for Answers 13 to 15

Boy	*Games Played*
Rajat	— Football, Hockey, Cricket, Basketball
Sushil	— Football, Hockey, Cricket, Basketball
Nagesh	— Football, Hockey, Cricket, Basketball
Ramu	— Hockey, Cricket, Basketball
Mayank	— Football, Cricket

13. ***(d)*** **14.** ***(d)*** **15.** ***(a)***

❑ ❑ ❑

11 Place Arrangement

Place arrangement generally refers to the positioning of persons or objects in a manner indicated by set of information given. One has to understand the order of placement and then attempt questions following the given information.

EXERCISE

Directions : *In the following questions, understand the arrangement pattern and then select the right answer from the given options :*

1. Five boys are sitting in a row. Raghu is not adjacent to Shyam or Amit. Ajay is not adjacent to Shyam. Raghu is adjacent to Mayank. If Mayank is at the middle in the row, then Ajay is adjacent to whom out of the following?
(*a*) Amit (*b*) Raghu
(*c*) Mayank (*d*) Shyam

2. Mini is to the right of Rajni but to the left of Ananta. Saya is to the right of Mini but to the left of Jaya. Who is on the extreme left if all the girls are facing North?
(*a*) Jaya (*b*) Mini
(*c*) Rajni (*d*) Saya

3. O, P, Q, R, S and T are standing on a bench according to their height. P is taller than O but shorter than S. Only S is taller than T. R is shorter than P but taller than Q. Who is the shortest?
(*a*) O
(*b*) Q
(*c*) P
(*d*) Cannot be said

4. Five personalities are living in a multistoried building. Mr. Effortless lives in a flat above Mr. Active, Mr. Charge lives in a flat below Mr. Diligent, Mr. Active lives in a flat above Mr. Diligent and Mr. Behaved lives in a flat below Mr. Charge. Who lives in the topmost flat?
(*a*) Mr. Charge
(*b*) Mr. Diligent
(*c*) Mr. Effortless
(*d*) Mr. Behaved

5. Six friends are sitting in a circle and playing cards. Kenny is to the left of Danny. Michael is in-between Bob and John. Roger is in between Kenny and Bob. Who is sitting to the right of Michael?
(*a*) Danny (*b*) John
(*c*) Kenny (*d*) Bob

6. Four girls A, B, C and D are sitting in a circle. B and C are facing each other. Which of the following is definitely true?
(*a*) A is to the left of C
(*b*) D is to the left of C
(*c*) A and D are facing each other
(*d*) A is not between B and C

7. Brijesh, Jayesh, Amar and Praveer are playing a game of cards. Amar is to the right of Jayesh who is to the right of Brijesh. Who is to the right of Amar?
(*a*) Brijesh
(*b*) Praveer
(*c*) Brijesh or Praveer
(*d*) Jayesh

8. In a pile of 10 books there are 3 of History, 3 of Hindi, 2 of Maths, and 2 of English. Taking from above there is an English book between a History and Maths book, a History book between a Maths and an English book, a Hindi book between an English and a Maths book, a Maths book between two Hindi books, and two Hindi books between a Maths and a History book. Book of which subject is at the sixth position from the top?
(*a*) English
(*b*) Hindi
(*c*) History
(*d*) Maths

9. Five persons A, B, C, D and E are sitting in a row facing you such that D is on the left of C and B is on the right of E. A is on the right of C and B is on the left of D. If E occupies a corner position, then who is sitting in the centre?
(*a*) A (*b*) B
(*c*) C (*d*) D

10. Six friends A, B, C, D, E and F are standing in a circle. B is between F and C; A is between E and D; F is to the left of D. Who is between A and F?
(*a*) C (*b*) B
(*c*) D (*d*) E

EXPLANATORY ANSWERS

1. (b) : The order of sitting is :

Amit, Shyam, Mayank, Ajay, Raghu

or

Ajay, Raghu, Mayank, Amit, Shyam

2. (c) : The order in which the girls are positioned is :

Rajni, Mini, Ananta, Saya, Jaya

or

Saya, Jaya, Ananta

or

Saya, Ananta, Jaya

3. (d) : In descending order of height, the standing positions are :

S		S
T		T
P	*or*	P
R		R
O		Q
Q		O

Either O or Q is the shortest. The information given is not enough to clarify the answer.

4. (c) : The personalities living in flats in multi-storied building are in order given below :

Mr. Effortless
Mr. Active
Mr. Diligent
Mr. Charge
Mr. Behaved

5. (d) : The order in which the friends are sitting is :

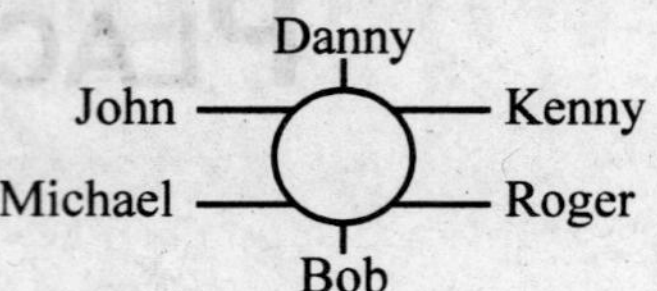

6. (c) : The sitting positions are :

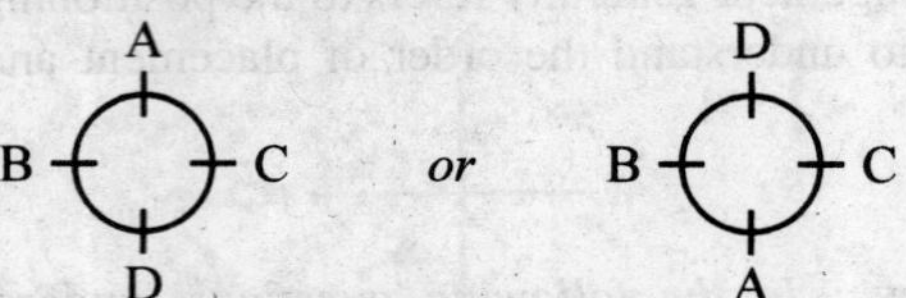

7. (b) : The order from left to right is :
Brijesh, Jayesh, Amar, Praveer

8. (b) : The pile of books is in the order :

1st — History
English
Maths
History
English
6th — Hindi
Maths
Hindi
Hindi
10th —History

9. (d) : Sitting order while facing us is :

A, C, D, B, E

10. (c) : The pattern of standing is :

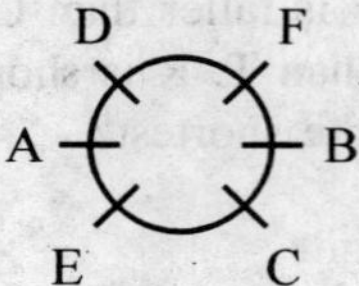

❑❑❑

12 DIRECTION SENSE

In these type of tests, the directions in questions needs to be perceived. Such questions are based on the direction chart.

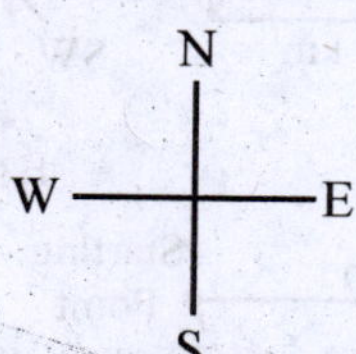

N = North S = South E = East W = West

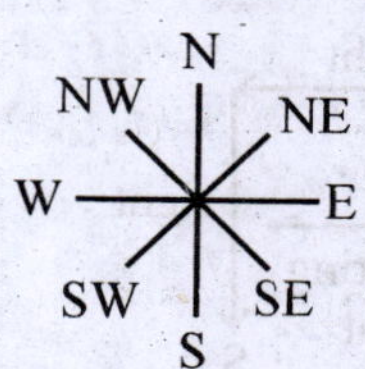

The sense of the different directions are guided by the left and right turns or angular turns.

EXERCISE

Directions : *In the following questions, select the right answer from the given options to depict the correct direction/ distance.*

1. Kittu walks towards East and then towards South. After walking some distance he turns towards West and then turns to his left. In which direction is he walking now?
(*a*) North (*b*) South
(*c*) East (*d*) West

2. A person is driving towards West. What sequence of directions should he follow so that he is driving towards South?
(*a*) left, right, right
(*b*) right, right, left
(*c*) left, left, left
(*d*) right, right, right

3. Richa drives 8 km to the South, turns left and drives 5 km. Again, she turns left and drives 8 km. How far is she from her starting point?
(*a*) 3 km (*b*) 5 km
(*c*) 8 km (*d*) 13 km

4. Dingi runs 40 km towards North then turns right and runs 50 km. He turns right and runs 30 km, and once again turns right and runs 50 km. How far is he from his starting point?
(*a*) 90 km (*b*) 50 km
(*c*) 10 km (*d*) 5 km

5. If North is called North-West, North-West is called West, West is called South-West and so on. What will South-East be called?
(*a*) East
(*b*) West
(*c*) North-East
(*d*) South-East

6. A man travels 100 km towards South. From there he turns right and travels 100 km and again turns right to travel 50 km. Which direction is he in from his starting point?
(*a*) North (*b*) North-East
(*c*) East (*d*) South-West

7. A train runs 120 km in West direction, 30 km in South direction and then 80 km in east direction before reaching the station. In which direction is the station from the train's starting point?
(*a*) South-West (*b*) North-West
(*c*) South-East (*d*) South

8. Facing the West direction, Priya jogs for 20 m, turns left and goes further 40 m. She turns left again and jogs for 20 m. Then she turns right to go 20 m to reach the park. How far is the park from her starting point and in which direction?
(*a*) 20 m South (*b*) 40 m West
(*c*) 60 m South (*d*) 100 m East

9. If all the directions are rotated, *i.e.*, if North is changed to West and East to North and so on, then what will come in place of North-West?
(*a*) South-West (*b*) North-East
(*c*) East-North (*d*) East-West

10. A and B start together from one point. They walk 10 km towards North. A turns left and covers 5 km whereas B turns right and covers 3 km. A turns left again and covers 15 km whereas B turns right and covers his 15 km. How far is A from B?
(*a*) 18 km
(*b*) 10 km
(*c*) 5 km
(*d*) 8 km

EXPLANATORY ANSWERS

1. *(b)* :

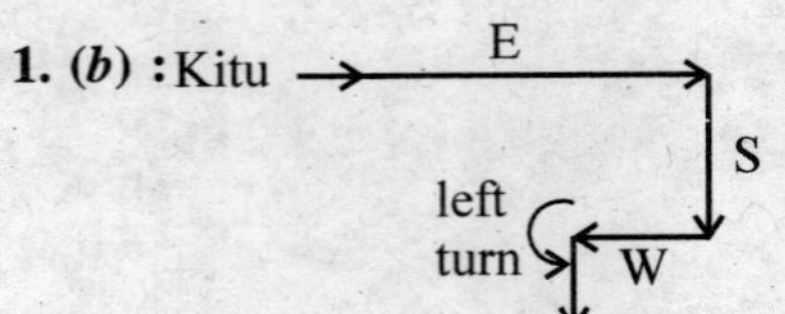

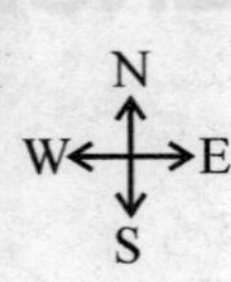

2. *(d)* :

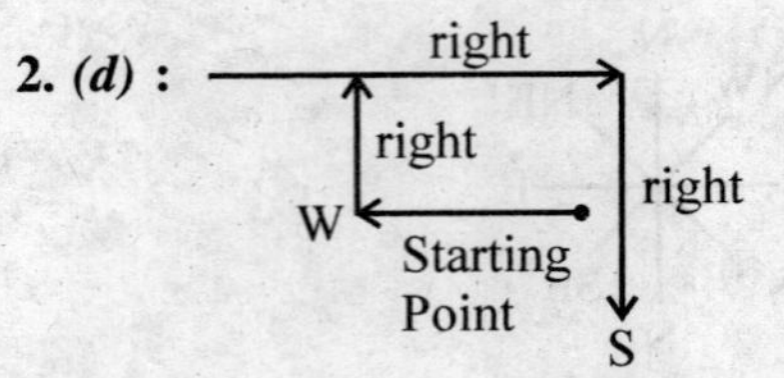

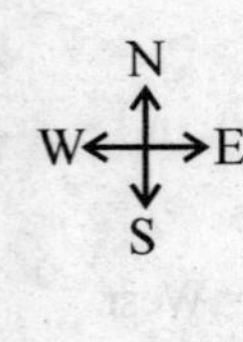

3. *(b)* :

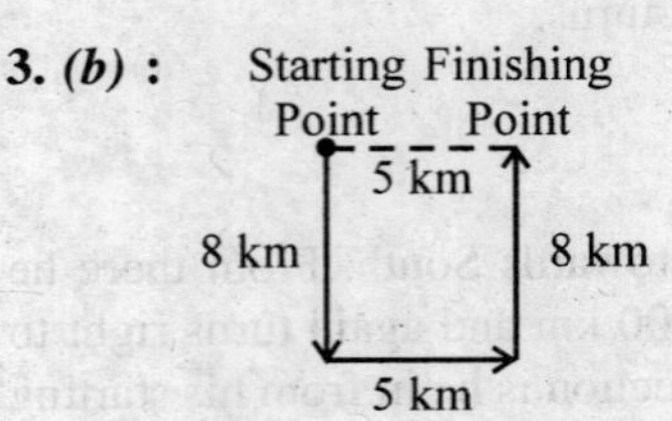

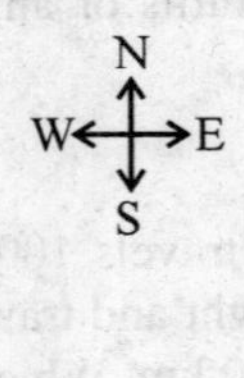

4. *(c)* :

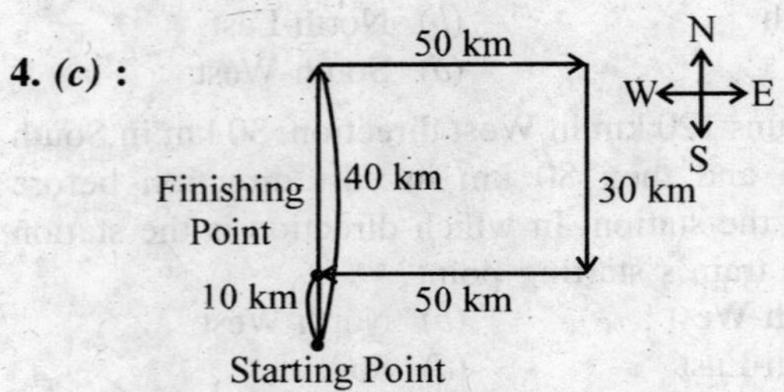

5. *(a)* : **Original Directions**

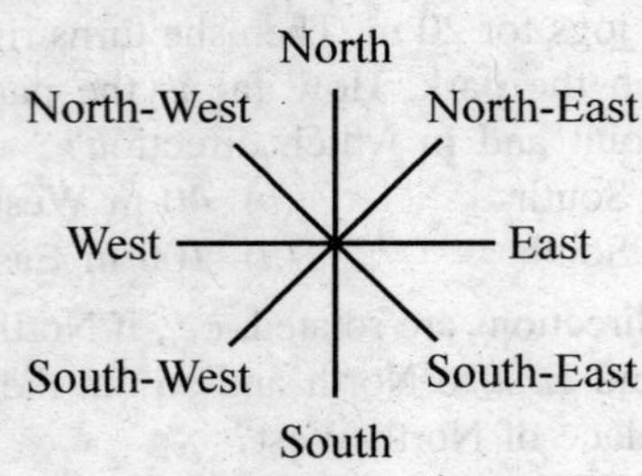

Changed Directions

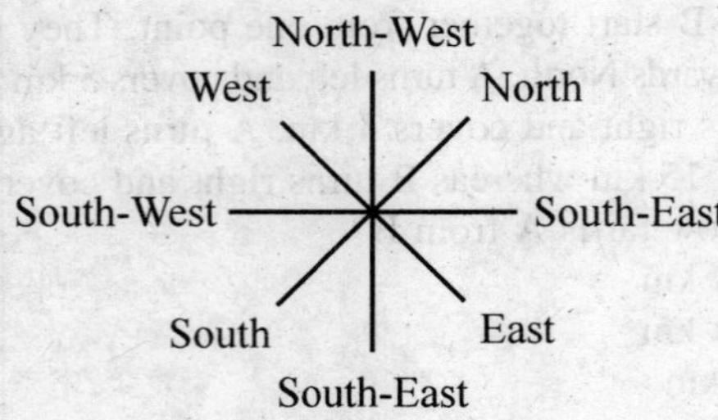

6. *(d)* :

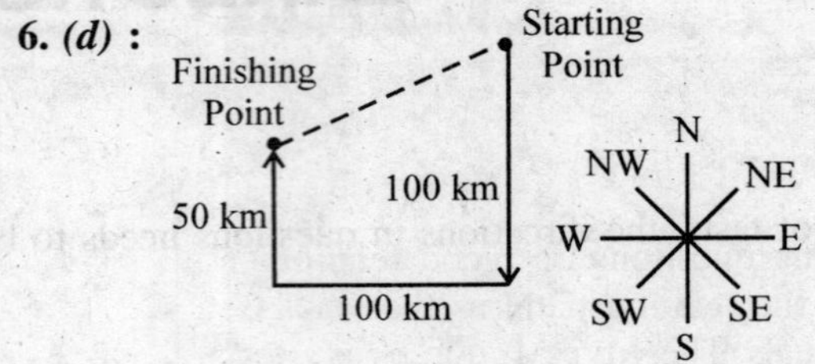

7. *(a)* :

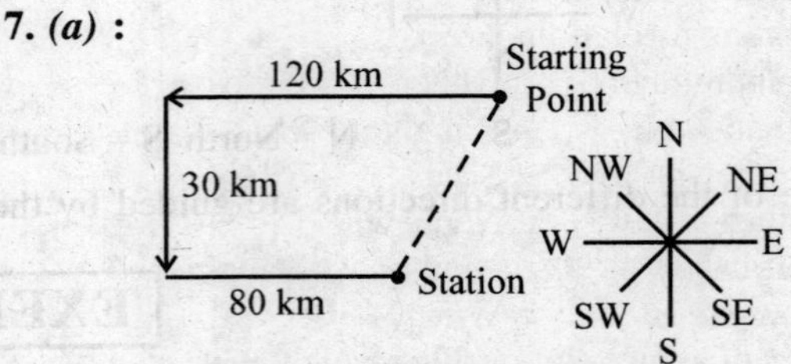

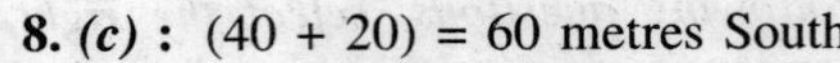

8. *(c)* : (40 + 20) = 60 metres South

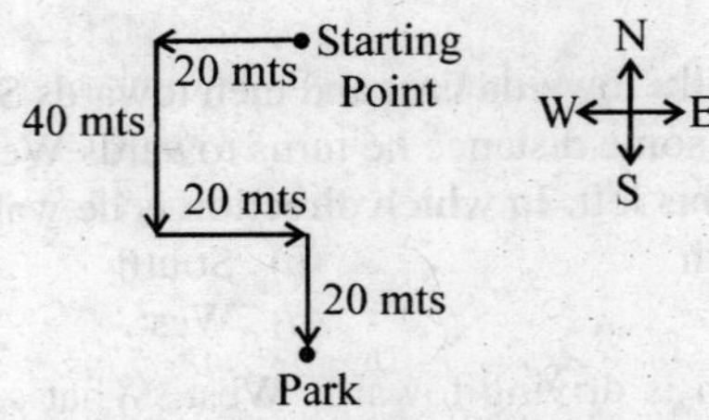

9. *(a)* : **Original Directions**

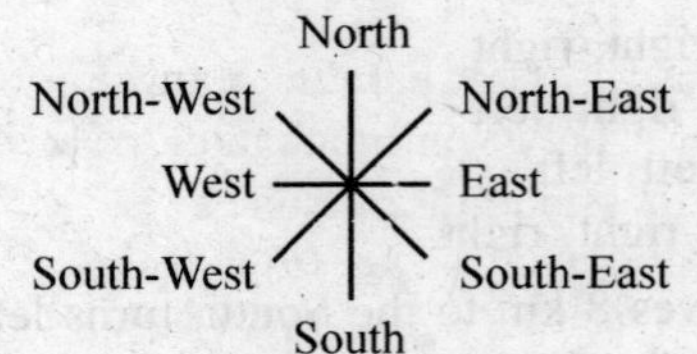

Changed Directions

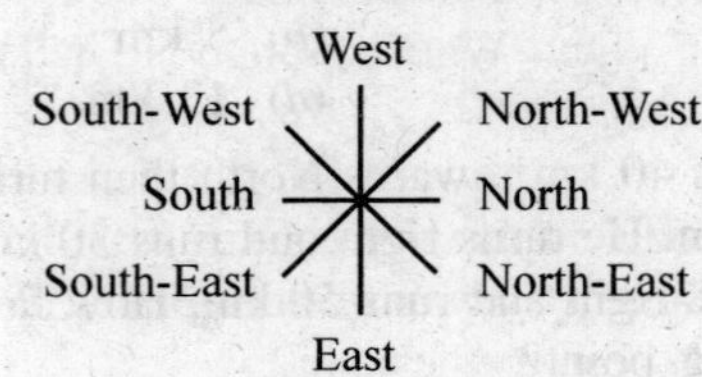

10. *(d)* :

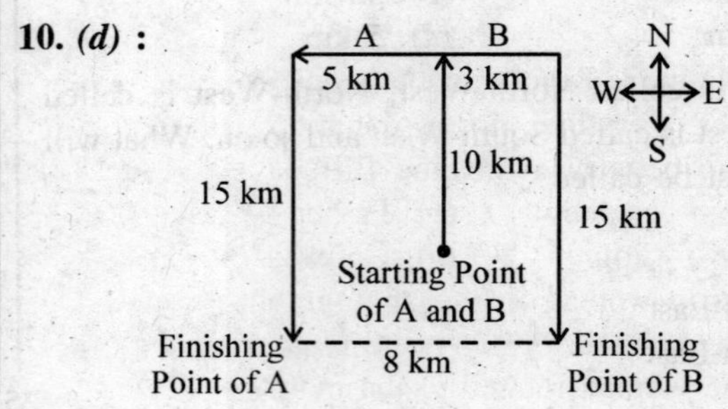

❑❑❑

13 BLOOD RELATIONSHIPS

While attempting questions on blood relations, one should be clear of all the relation patterns that can exist between any two individuals. These type of questions are given mainly to test one's relationship ability.

Very well-known relations are :

Mother	Grandmother	Father	Grandfather
Son	Grandson	Daughter	Granddaughter
Brother	Brother-in-law	Sister	Sister-in-law
Niece	Father-in-law	Nephew	Mother-in-law
Uncle	Son-in-law	Aunt	Daughter-in-law
Husband	Cousin	Wife	

The patterns of some relationships which help in solving questions in these tests are :

Father's *or* Mother's Father	— Grandfather (Paternal *or* Maternal)
Father's *or* Mother's Mother	— Grandmother (Paternal *or* Maternal)
Father's *or* Mother's Son	— Brother
Father's *or* Mother's Daughter	— Sister
Father's Brother	— Paternal Uncle
Father's Sister	— Paternal Aunt
Mother's Brother	— Maternal Uncle
Mother's Sister	— Maternal Aunt
Uncle *or* Aunt's Son *or* Daughter	— Cousin
Son's Wife	— Daughter-in-law
Daughter's Husband	— Son-in-law
Husband's *or* Wife's Brother	— Brother-in-law
Husband's *or* Wife's Sister	— Sister-in-law
Brother's Wife	— Sister-in-law
Sister's Husband	— Brother-in-law
Brother's Son	— Nephew
Brother's Daughter	— Niece

EXERCISE

Directions : *In each of the following questions keenly study the relationship mentioned between the persons, and then from the given options select the right relationship as the answer.*

1. A lady said, "The person standing there is my grandfather's only son's daughter". How is the lady related to the standing person?
(*a*) Sister (*b*) Mother
(*c*) Aunt (*d*) Cousin

2. Ajay is the brother of Vijay. Mili is the sister of Ajay. Sanjay is the brother of Rahul and Mehul is the daughter of Vijay. Who is Sanjay's Uncle?
(*a*) Rahul (*b*) Ajay
(*c*) Mehul (*d*) Data inadequate

3. A man introduced the boy coming with him as "He is son of the father of my wife's daughter". What relation did the boy bear to the man?
(*a*) Son-in-law (*b*) Son
(*c*) Brother (*d*) Father

4. If Amit's father is Billoo's father's only son and Billoo has neither a brother nor a daughter, what is the relationship between Amit and Billoo?
(*a*) Uncle — Nephew (*b*) Father — Daughter
(*c*) Father — Son (*d*) Cousins

5. Pointing to a woman in the photograph a man said, "She is the daughter of my grand-mother's only son." How is the woman related to the man?
(*a*) Mother (*b*) Daughter
(*c*) Sister-in-law (*d*) Sister

6. Pointing to a photograph, a woman said, "She is the only daughter of my mother's father." How is the woman related to the person in the photograph?
(*a*) Mother (*b*) Grandmother
(*c*) Daughter (*d*) Cannot be determined

7. Ram is the brother of Shyam and Mahesh is the father of Ram. Jagat is the brother of Priya and Priya is daughter of Shyam. Who is the uncle of Jagat ?
(*a*) Shyam (*b*) Mahesh
(*c*) Ram (*d*) Data insufficient

8. Introducing a man, a woman said, "His wife is the only daughter of my father". How is the man related to the woman?
(*a*) Husband (*b*) Father
(*c*) Father-in-law (*d*) Brother

9. If Maya is the only daughter of Richa's grandmother's brother, how is Maya's daughter related to Richa?
(*a*) Niece (*b*) Cousin
(*c*) Aunt (*d*) Mother

10. Pointing to a woman, a man said, "Her husband's mother is the wife of my father's only son". How is the man related to the woman?
(*a*) Son (*b*) Brother-in-law
(*c*) Uncle (*d*) Father-in-law

EXPLANATORY ANSWERS

1. (*a*) : Grandfather

Father
(only son)

Daughter ⟶ Lady
(standing person) (sister)

Lady's grandfather's son is lady's father and father's daughter will only be lady's sister.

2. (*d*) : 1. Mili ⟶ Ajay ⟶ Vijay ↓ Mehul
(sister) (brother) (daughter)

2. Sanjay ⟶ Rahul
(brother)

There are two sets of relationship. Information given is incomplete and no relation can be established between the two sets.

3. (*b*) : The relationship chart based on problem is :

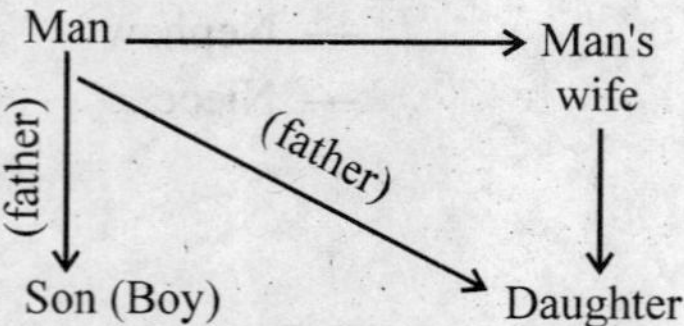

'Father of the man's wife's daughter' is the man himself and the boy in question is the man's son.

4. (*c*) : The relationship chart based on problem is :

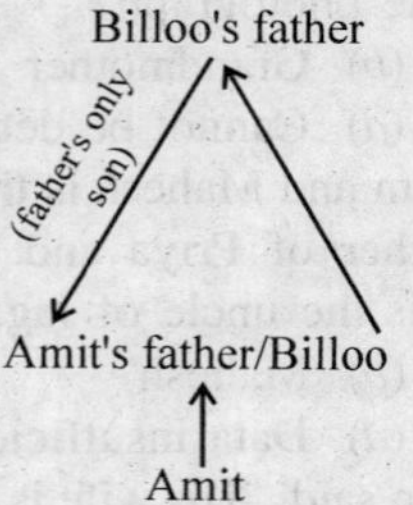

Amit's father is Billoo's father's only son means Billoo is the only son in question also, he is the father of Amit. It must be noted that Billoo has no brother which means he is single and also, when he has no daughter, Amit is his only son.

5. (*d*) : Man's Grandmother

Grandmother's only son

A

Man ⟵ (sister) Daughter

'My grandmother's only son' is the father of the man, and 'daughter of my grand-mother's only son' is the sister of the man.

6. (*c*) : Woman's mother's father
↕
Person in photograph
(woman's mother/only daughter)
↑ (daughter)
Woman

'Only daughter of my mother's father' is the person in the photograph and she is also the mother of the woman. So, the woman is the daughter of the person in the photograph.

7. (*c*) : Mahesh
(father)
Ram ⟶ (brother) Shyam
(uncle) (father) (daughter)
Jagat ⟶ Priya'
(brother)

Jagat is brother of Priya and Priya is daughter of Shyam. So Shyam is also the father of Jagat. Ram is the brother of Shyam. So, Jagat's father's brother Ram is the uncle of Jagat.

8. (*a*) : Woman's Father
↕
Man ⟶ (husband) Man's wife
(only daughter)

'Only daughter of my father' is the woman herself and the man is her husband.

9. (*b*) : Richa's Grandmother's Brother ⟵ Richa's Grandmother
Maya
(only daughter)
(granddaughter) (granddaughter)
Maya's Daughter ⟶ (cousin) Richa

Both Maya's Daughter and Richa are granddaughters of a brother and a sister respectively. So Maya's daughter is the cousin of Richa.

10. (*d*) :

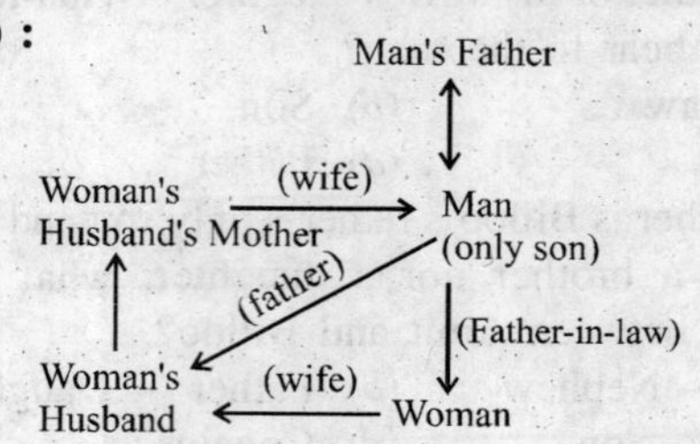

'My father's only son' is the man himself. 'Her husband's mother' is the wife of the man and so the man is the father of the woman's husband. As the woman is the wife of man's son, the man is the father-in-law of the woman.

❑ ❑ ❑

14 Rows and Ranks

These type of problems need easy calculations to find out the number of objects in a row, lane or queue or to find a person's rank in a class of certain number of students; or to find the total number of students.

EXERCISE

1. In a row of trees, one tree is fifth from either end of the row. How many trees are in the row?
(*a*) 11 (*b*) 8
(*c*) 10 (*d*) 9

2. Jaya ranks 5th in a class of 53. What is her rank from the bottom in the class?
(*a*) 49th (*b*) 48th
(*c*) 47th (*d*) 50th

3. Mohan ranks twenty-first in a class of sixty-five students. What will be his (Mohan's) rank if the lowest candidate is assigned rank 1?
(*a*) 44th
(*b*) 45th
(*c*) 46th
(*d*) Data inadequate

4. If Rahul finds that he is 12th from the right in a line of boys and 4th from the left, how many boys should be added to the line such that there are 28 boys in the line?
(*a*) 12 (*b*) 14
(*c*) 20 (*d*) 13

5. In a row of boys, Rajan is tenth from the right and Suraj is tenth from the left. When Rajan and Suraj interchange their positions, Suraj will be twenty-seventh from the left. Which of the following will be Rajan's position from the right?
(*a*) Tenth
(*b*) Twenty-sixth
(*c*) Twenty-ninth
(*d*) None of these

6. Mahesh and Suresh are ranked 11th and 12th respectively from the top in a class of 41 students. What will be their respective ranks from the bottom?
(*a*) 32nd and 33rd (*b*) 29th and 30th
(*c*) 30th and 31st (*d*) 31st and 30th

7. Uma ranked 8th from the top and 37th from bottom in a class. How many students are there in the class?
(*a*) 47 (*b*) 46
(*c*) 45 (*d*) None of these

8. In a queue, Sadiq is 14th from the front and Joseph is 17th from the end, while Jane is in between Sadiq and Joseph. If Sadiq be ahead of Joseph and there be 48 persons in the queue, how many persons are there between Sadiq and Jane?
(*a*) 5 (*b*) 6
(*c*) 7 (*d*) 8

9. Rohan ranked eleventh from the top and twenty-seventh from the bottom among the students who passed the annual examination in a class. If the number of students who failed in the examination was 12, how many students appeared for the examination?
(*a*) 48
(*b*) 49
(*c*) 50
(*d*) Cannot be determined

10. Some boys are sitting in a row. P is sitting fourteenth from the left and Q is seventh from the right. If there are four boys between P and Q, how many boys are there in the row?
(*a*) 19 (*b*) 21
(*c*) 25 (*d*) 23

EXPLANATORY ANSWERS

1. (*d*):

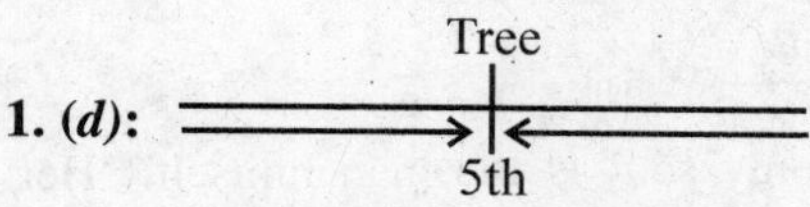

Total number of trees in the row are :
(5 + 5) −1 = 9.

2. (*a*) :

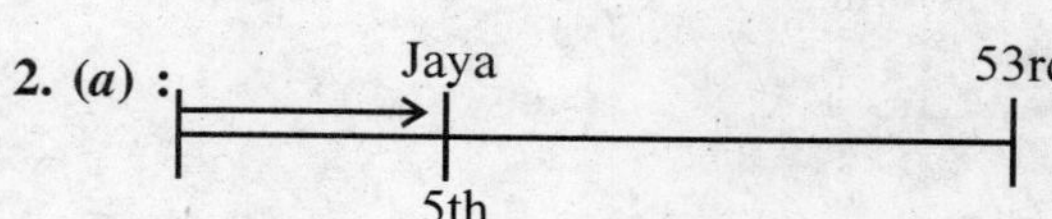

Jaya's rank from the bottom is :
(53 − 5) +1 = 49th.

3. (*b*) :

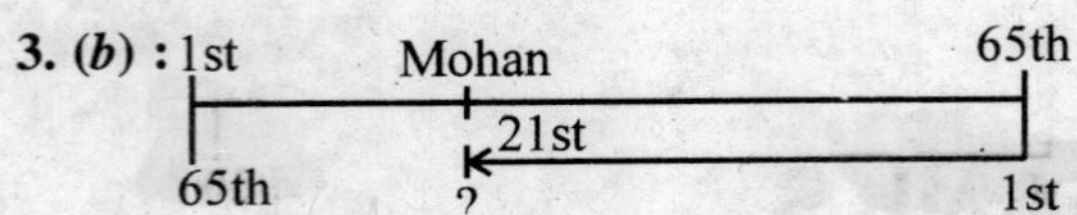

Note : Mohan's rank from the last or the question asked means the same.

Mohan's rank is (65 – 21) +1 = 45th.

4. (*d*) :

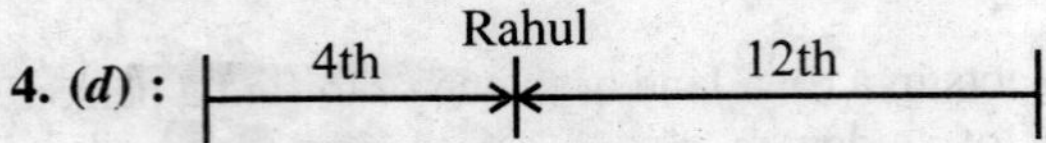

The number of boys in the line are :
(4 + 12) – 1 = 15
To make a line of 28 boys, (28 –15), *i.e.,* 13 more boys are needed.

5. (*d*) :

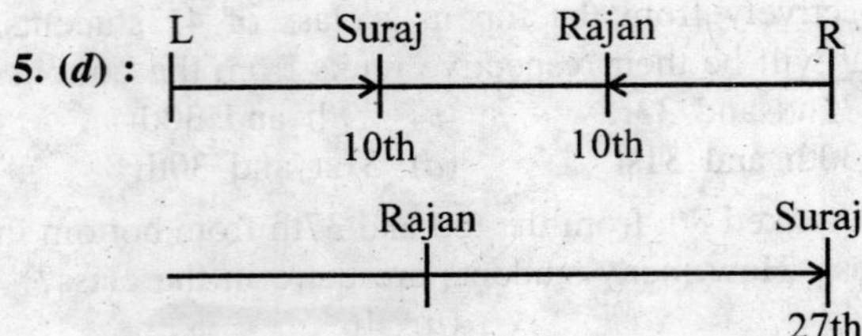

As the position of boys is equal from both ends, Rajan will also be 27th from the right after changing positions.

6. (*d*) :

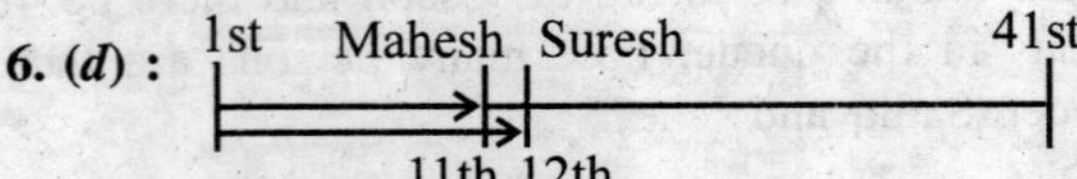

Mahesh's position from bottom is :
(41 – 11) + 1 = 31st
Suresh's position from bottom is :
(41 – 12) +1 = 30th.

7. (*d*) :

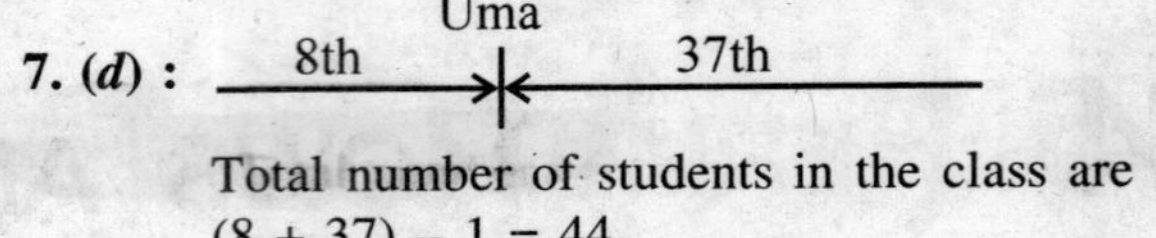

Total number of students in the class are :
(8 + 37) – 1 = 44.

8. (*d*) :

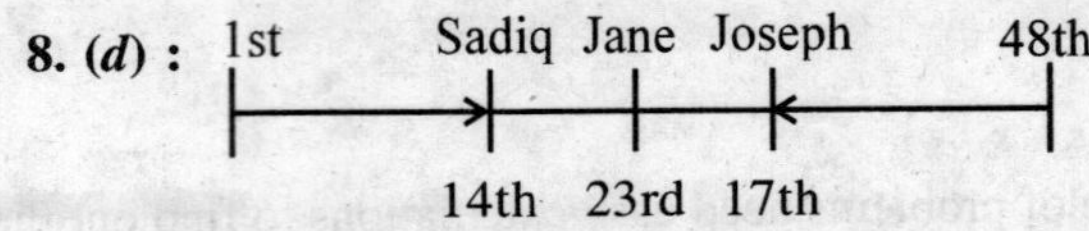

Sadiq's position from front : 14th
Joseph's position from last :
17th or 48 – 17 + 1 = 32nd from front.
Middle postion between Sadiq & Joseph

$$= \frac{(32-14)}{2} + 14 = 23 \text{ rd.}$$

Hence, Jane position is 23rd from front
Person between Sadiq & Jane
= 23 – 14 – 1 = 8.

9. (*b*) :

Rohan

11th 27th

Number of students who passed the examination
(11+ 27) – 1 = 37
Those who failed = 12
Total number of students who appeared in the examination = 37 + 12 = 49.

10. (*c*) :

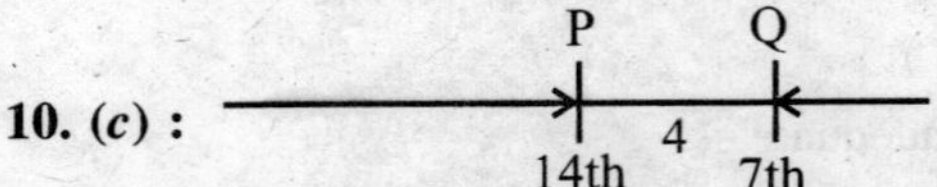

The number of boys in the row are :
(14 + 4 + 7) = 25.

❑ ❑ ❑

15 PERMUTATIONS AND COMBINATIONS

In these type of questions, the only factor essential is alertness. In every question, a word is given. By using the letters of this given word the options are formed. The candidates are required to find from the given options the word *(i)* which cannot be formed by using the letters of the given word or *(ii)* which can be formed by using the letters of the given word.

EXERCISE

Directions : *Find out the one word among the options which cannot be formed by using the letters of the word as given in each question.*

1. ROTATION
(a) TORN *(b)* NOTE
(c) TART *(d)* RAIN

2. PHILOSOPHY
(a) SOIL *(b)* SHIP
(c) SOLO *(d)* SPIN

3. SLAVATION
(a) SNORT *(b)* LATVIA
(c) SALIVA *(d)* AVAIL

4. ACADEMY
(a) DEMY *(b)* MACE
(c) DIRE *(d)* MADE

5. INCOGNITO
(a) GOING *(b)* INACTION
(c) IGNITION *(d)* TONGO

6. JUDICIARY
(a) INJURY *(b)* CADDY
(c) DICY *(d)* ACRID

7. DOCTRINE
(a) CRUST *(b)* DOCTOR
(c) TIRED *(d)* CREED

8. EDUCATED
(a) DATE *(b)* CUTE
(c) EAST *(d)* DUCT

9. INSUFFICIENT
(a) ENTICE *(b)* SCENT
(c) SUFFICE *(d)* THENCE

10. DECEMBER
(a) REDEEM *(b)* DECREE
(c) BRACED *(d)* MEMBER

11. FUGITIVE
(a) EXIT *(b)* FIVE
(c) GIVE *(d)* GIFT

12. CATASTROPHE
(a) TASTE *(b)* CHEAP
(c) POUCH *(d)* STARE

13. TORRENTIAL
(a) TRAIL *(b)* MENTAL
(c) LEARN *(d)* RETAIL

14. INFRASTRUCTURE
(a) RAPTURE *(b)* INSECURE
(c) CRAFTS *(d)* STRUCTURE

15. RECOMMEND
(a) MEND *(b)* ROME
(c) CANE *(d)* OMEN

ANSWERS

1	2	3	4	5	6	7	8	9	10
(b)	*(d)*	*(a)*	*(c)*	*(b)*	*(a)*	*(a)*	*(c)*	*(d)*	*(c)*
11	**12**	**13**	**14**	**15**					
(a)	*(c)*	*(b)*	*(a)*	*(c)*					

❑❑❑

16 SYMBOL SUBSTITUTION

Questions in these category are easy to attempt. Candidates must be quick in substituting symbols and calculations. The common pattern of questions asked are given below.

EXERCISE

1. If "+" means "–"; "–" means "×"; "×"means "÷" and "÷" means "+", then what will be the value of
$15 \times 5 \div 10 + 5 - 3 = ?$
(a) 9.5
(b) 0
(c) –2
(d) 24

2. If "+" means "×"; "–" means "÷"; "÷"means "+" and "×" means "–", then what will be the value of
$20 \div 40 - 4 \times 5 + 6 = ?$
(a) 60
(b) 1.67
(c) 150
(d) 0

3. If $\times$ stands for addition, $<$ for subtraction, $+$ stands for division, $>$ for multiplication, $-$ stands for equal to, $\div$ for greater than, and $=$ stands for less than, state which of the following is true?
(a) $5 \times 3 < 7 \div 8 + 4 \times 1$
(b) $3 \times 4 > 2 - 9 + 3 < 3$
(c) $5 > 2 + 2 = 10 < 4 \times 8$
(d) $3 \times 2 < 4 \div 16 > 2 + 4$

4. If $\rightarrow$ stands for subract, $\leftarrow$ stands for add, $\downarrow\uparrow\uparrow$ stands for multiply, $\downarrow\downarrow$ stands for divide, $\leftrightarrow$ for greater than, $\longleftrightarrow$ stands for equal to, then which of the following alternatives is true?
(a) $4 \leftarrow 6 \uparrow\uparrow 2 \longleftrightarrow 3 \rightarrow 12 \leftarrow 12$
(b) $10 \downarrow\downarrow 5 \uparrow\uparrow 5 \longleftrightarrow 9 \rightarrow 3 \leftarrow 4$
(c) $15 \uparrow\uparrow 2 \rightarrow 5 \longleftrightarrow 12 \downarrow\downarrow 4 \leftarrow 3$
(d) $13 \downarrow\downarrow 13 \leftarrow 1 \leftrightarrow 20 \rightarrow 5 \uparrow\uparrow 2$

5. If Δ denotes $=$; $+$ denotes $>$, $-$ denotes $<$, $\square$ denotes $\neq$, $\times$ denotes $>$ and $\div$ denotes $<$ then $a + b - c$ denotes
(a) $b \; \Delta \; c \; \square \; a$
(b) $b \; \square \; a \div c$
(c) $a \div b \times c$
(d) $b - a + c$

6. If '$\ast$' denotes '×', 'Δ' denotes '÷', '□' denotes '–', '●' denotes '+', 'α' denotes '=' and 'β' denotes ≠, then which of the following euations is correct?
(a) $2 \; \square \; 10 \ast 4 \; \Delta \; 5 \; \alpha \; 5 \bullet 12 \; \Delta \; 6$
(b) $27 \; \Delta \; 9 \bullet 6 \; \beta \; 3 \ast 6 \; \square \; 9$
(c) $4 \; \Delta \; 2 \ast 0 \; \alpha \; 7 \; \Delta \; 1 \ast 0$
(d) $5 \bullet 6 \; \Delta \; 3 \; \square \; 2 \; \alpha \; 8 \; \Delta \; 4 \ast 3$

7. If $\downarrow$ stands for '÷', $\uparrow$ stands for '×', $\rightarrow$ stands for '+' and $\leftarrow$ stands for '–', then
$25 \downarrow 5 \rightarrow 3 \uparrow 6 \leftarrow 8 = ?$
(a) 9
(b) 12
(c) 16
(d) 15

8. If the + and × signs of the following equations are interchanged, which will be the correct equation?
(a) $7 \times 5 + 3 = 20$
(b) $4 + 9 \times 1 = 42$
(c) $6 \times 5 + 8 = 46$
(d) $2 + 11 \times 4 = 28$

9. If '+' stands for multiplication, '×' stands for addition, '÷' stands for subtraction and '–' stands for division, then what will be the result of the following equation?
$7 \times 4 \div 10 \times 2 + 5 = ?$
(a) 7 *(b)* 0
(c) 11 *(d)* 15

10. If 'A' means '÷', 'B' means '+', 'C' means '×' and 'D' means '–', then
12 C 4 A 24 D 10 B 1 = ?
(a) $11\frac{1}{3}$
(b) 23
(c) – 7
(d) $16\frac{4}{5}$

EXPLANATORY ANSWERS

1. *(c)* : $15 \div 5 + 10 - 5 \times 3$

$3 + 10 - 15 = -2$

2. *(d)* : $20 + 40 \div 4 - 5 \times 6$

$20 + 10 - 30 = 0$

3. *(c)* : *(a)* $5 + 3 - 7 > 8 \div 4 + 1$

$1 > 3$

(b) $3 + 4 \times 2 = 9 \div 3 - 3$

$11 = 0$

(c) $5 \times 2 \div 2 < 10 - 4 + 8$

$5 < 14$

(d) $3 + 2 - 4 > 16 \times 2 \div 4$

$1 > 8$

4. *(b)* : *(a)* $4 + 6 \times 2 = 3 - 12 + 12$

$16 = 3$

(b) $10 \div 5 \times 5 = 9 - 3 + 4$

$10 = 10$

(c) $15 \times 2 - 5 = 12 \div 4 + 3$

$25 = 6$

(d) $13 \div 13 + 1 > 20 - 5 \times 2$

$2 > 10$

5. *(d)* : What is given is $a > b < c$

The equations are :

(a) $b = c \neq a$ which is wrong

(b) $b \neq a < c$ which is wrong

(c) $a < b > c$ which is wrong

(d) $b < a > c$ which is correct

Therefore, *(d)* is the answer.

6. *(c)* : The solved equations will be :

(a) $2 - 10 \times 4 \div 5 = 5 + 12 \div 6$

$2 - 8 = 5 + 2$

$-6 = 7$ which is wrong

(b) $27 \div 9 + 6 \neq 3 \times 6 - 9$

$3 + 6 \neq 18 - 9$

$9 \neq 9$ which is wrong

(c) $4 \div 2 \times 0 = 7 \div 1 \times 0$

$2 \times 0 = 7 \times 0$

$0 = 0$ which is correct

(d) $5 + 6 \div 3 - 2 = 8 \div 4 \times 3$

$5 = 6$ which is wrong

7. *(d)* : $25 \div 5 + 3 \times 6 - 8$

$5 + 18 - 8 = 15$

8. *(c)* : After interchanging the signs the equations are :

(a) $7 + 5 \times 3 = 22$ which is wrong

(b) $4 \times 9 + 1 = 37$ which is wrong

(c) $6 + 5 \times 8 = 46$ which is correct

(d) $2 \times 11 + 4 = 26$ which is wrong

9. *(c)* : $7 + 4 - 10 + 2 \times 5$

$7 + 4 - 10 + 10 = 11$

10. *(c)* : $12 \times 4 \div 24 - 10 + 1$

$2 - 10 + 1 = -7$

❑❑❑

17 MISSING NUMBERS

Playing with numbers and mathematical skills are needed to attempt these type of tests. The candidates have to work out the right combination of arithmetical symbols to arrive at the answer options which will take the place of the interrogation sign in the given questions.

EXERCISE

Directions: *In each question given below which one number can be placed at the sign of interrogation?*

1.

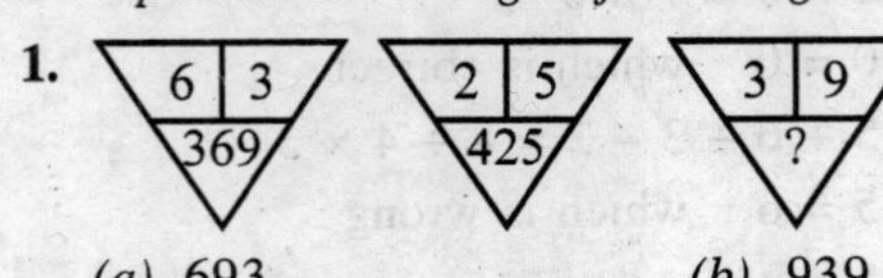

(*a*) 693 (*b*) 939
(*c*) 981 (*d*) 993

2.

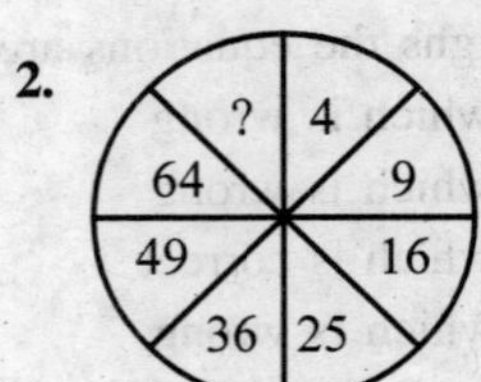

(*a*) 68 (*b*) 100
(*c*) 72 (*d*) 81

3.

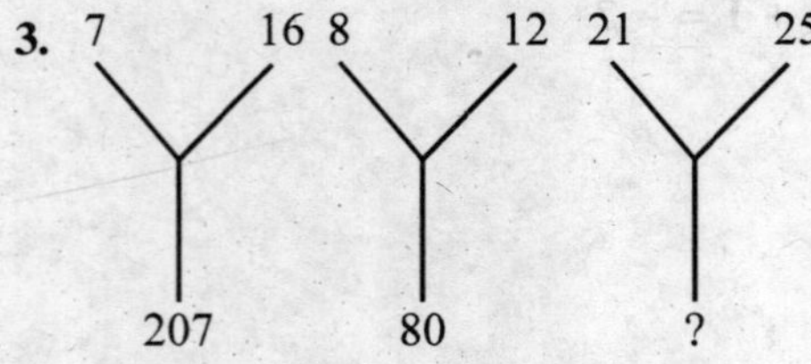

(*a*) 425 (*b*) 184
(*c*) 241 (*d*) 210

4.

3 5 / 39 / 6 3 4 7 / 51 / 5 4 3 5 / ? / 5 4

(*a*) 35 (*b*) 37
(*c*) 45 (*d*) 48

5.

7 5 / 6 5 21 / 13 24 4 / ?

(*a*) 4
(*b*) 8
(*c*) 20
(*d*) 14

6.

14	9	4
12	7	2
10	5	0
16	11	?

(*a*) 9
(*b*) 6
(*c*) 3
(*d*) 7

7.

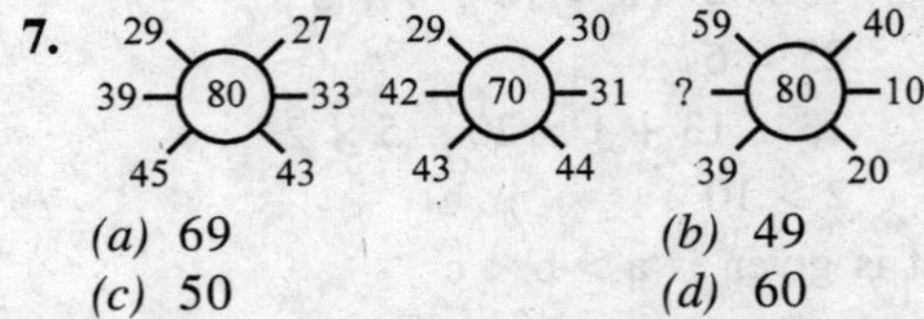

(*a*) 69 (*b*) 49
(*c*) 50 (*d*) 60

8.

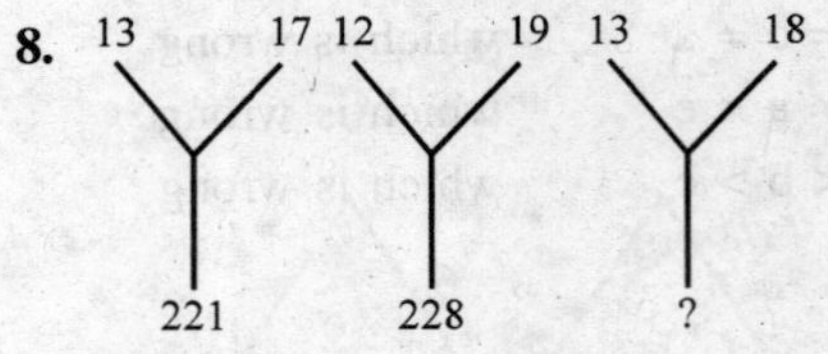

(*a*) 31
(*b*) 229
(*c*) 234
(*d*) 312

9.

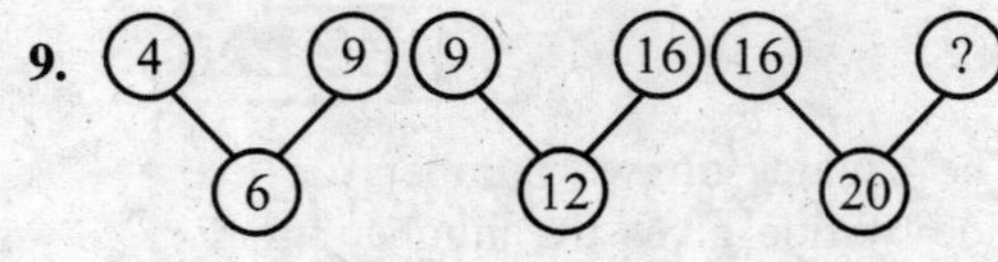

(*a*) 21
(*b*) 25
(*c*) 50
(*d*) 60

10.

51	(11)	61
64	(30)	32
35	(?)	43

(*a*) 25 (*b*) 27
(*c*) 32 (*d*) 37

11. 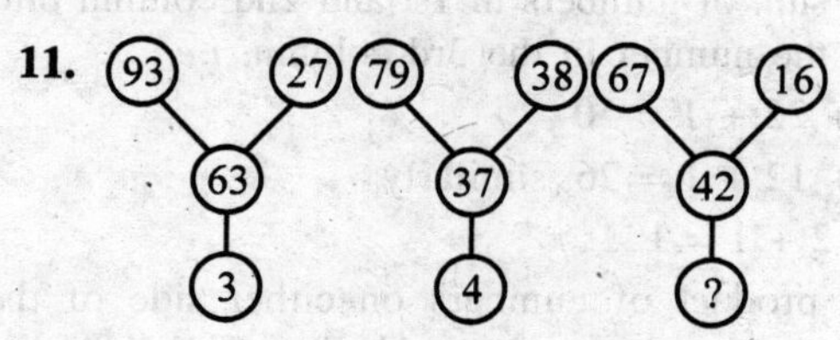

(a) 5 (b) 6
(c) 8 (d) 9

12. 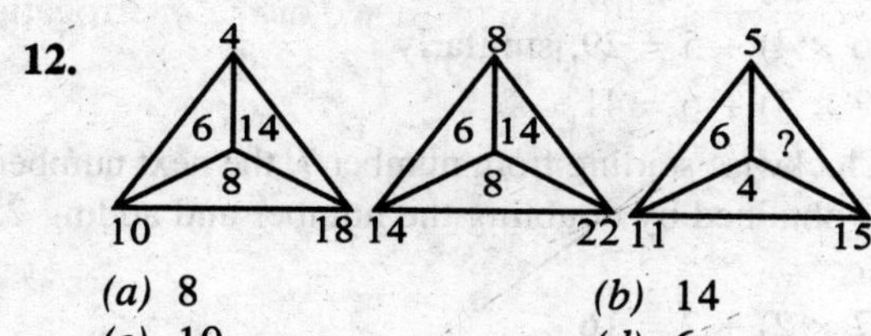

(a) 8 (b) 14
(c) 10 (d) 6

13. 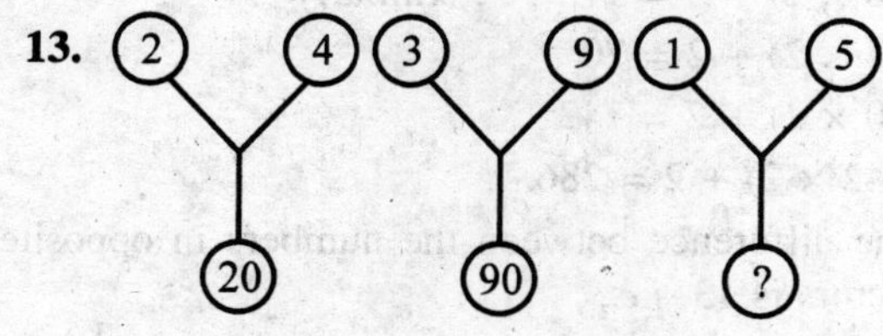

(a) 20 (b) 25
(c) 26 (d) 75

14.

27	22	50
13	12	26
9	2	?

(a) 12 (b) 39
(c) 18 (d) 24

15. 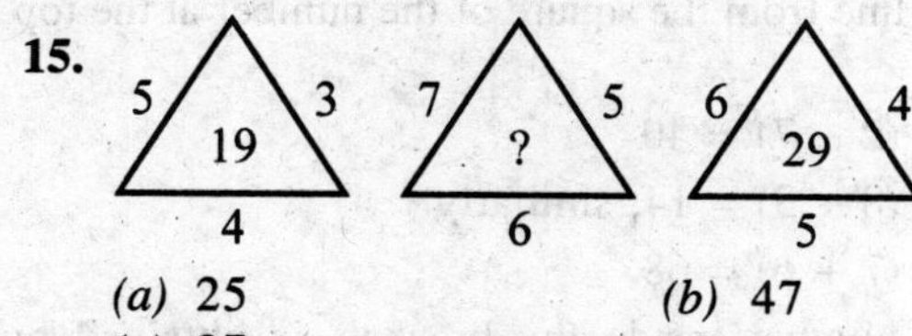

(a) 25 (b) 47
(c) 37 (d) 41

16. 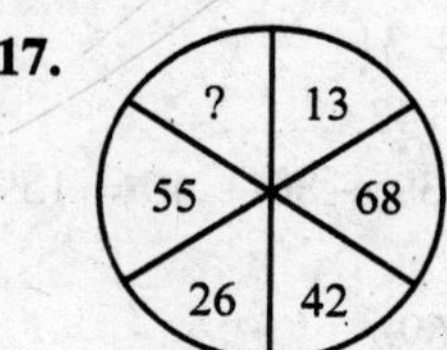

(a) 70 (b) 68
(c) 56 (d) 92

17.

? 13
55 68
26 42

(a) 41 (b) 37
(c) 29 (d) 25

18. 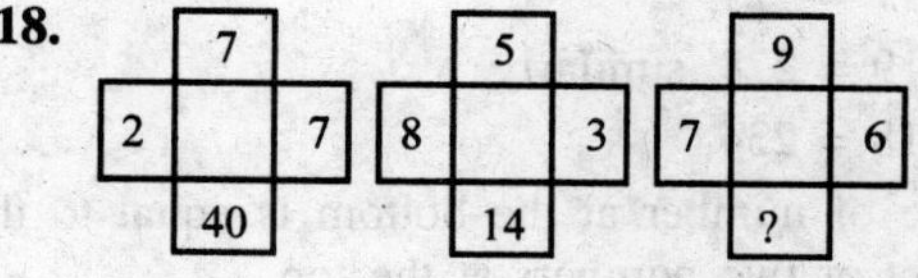

(a) 72 (b) 68
(c) 82 (d) 96

19.

42	(21)	22
78	(?)	84
162	(18)	99

(a) 12 (b) 13
(c) 60 (d) 72

20.

16, 107, 7, 10   25, 209, 20, 4   19, ?, 2, 17

(a) 68 (b) 93
(c) 175 (d) 217

EXPLANATORY ANSWERS

1. (c) : The squares of two numbers on the top placed side-by-side gives the number inside the bottom triangle, *i.e.*,

6^2 and 3^2 = 369

2^2 and 5^2 = 425, similarly

3^2 and 9^2 = 981.

2. (d) : Starting from number 4 the numbers are the squares of numbers in natural order, *i.e.*,

$2^2 = 4$, $3^2 = 9$, $4^2 = 16$ . . . . . $9^2 = 81$.

3. (b) : The number at the bottom is the difference of the squares of two numbers at the top, *i.e.*,

$16^2 - 7^2 = 256 - 49 = 207$

$12^2 - 8^2 = 144 - 64 = 80$, similarly

$25^2 - 21^2 = 625 - 441 = 184$.

4. (b) : The number in the centre is the sum of the products of diagonal numbers, *i.e.*,

$(3 \times 3) + (5 \times 6) = 39$

$(4 \times 4) + (7 \times 5) = 51$, similarly

$(3 \times 4) + (5 \times 5) = 37$.

5. (d) : Sum of two numbers on the top divided by 2 gives the third number, *i.e.*,

$(7 + 5) \div 2 = 6$

$(5 + 21) \div 2 = 13$, similarly

$(24 + 4) \div 2 = 14$.

6. (b) : The numbers in 2nd and 3rd columns are 5 less than the nunbers in 1st and 2nd columns respectively, *i.e.,*
$14 - 5 = 9$ and $9 - 5 = 4$
$12 - 5 = 7$ and $7 - 5 = 2$, . . . similarly
$16 - 5 = 11$ and $11 - 5 = 6$.

7. (a) : The sum of 3 numbers in each line in one figure is same, *i.e.,*
$29 + 80 + 43$ or $39 + 80 + 33$
or $45 + 80 + 27 = 152$
$29 + 70 + 44$ or $42 + 70 + 31$
or $43 + 70 + 30 = 143$,
similarly $59 + 80 + 20$ or $39 + 80 + 40 = 159$.
The missing number is :
$159 - (80 + 10) = 69$.

8. (c) : The number at the bottom is the product of two numbers at the top, *i.e.,*
$13 \times 17 = 221$
$12 \times 19 = 228$, similarly
$13 \times 18 = 234$.

9. (b) : Square of number at the bottom is equal to the product of two numbers at the top, *i.e.,*
$6^2 = 4 \times 9$, *i.e.,* 36
$12^2 = 9 \times 16$, *i.e.,* 144, similarly
$20^2 = 16 \times ?$, *i.e.,* 400. The missing number is $400 \div 16 = 25$.

10. (b) : The sum of the products of the digits of numbers in 1st and 3rd columns is the number in the 2nd column, *i.e.,*
$(5 \times 1) + (6 \times 1) = 11$
$(6 \times 4) + (3 \times 2) = 30$, similarly
$(3 \times 5) + (4 \times 3) = 27$.

11. (d) : The sum of numbers on right and centre subtracted from the number on the left gives the number at the bottom, *i.e.,*
$93 - (27 + 63) = 3$
$79 - (38 + 37) = 4$, similarly
$67 - (16 + 42) = 9$.

12. (c) : The number inside each triangle is the difference of the numbers at its base, *i.e.*
$10 - 4 = 6$, $18 - 4 = 14$ and $18 - 10 = 8$
$14 - 8 = 6$, $22 - 8 = 14$ and $22 - 14 = 8$, similarly
$11 - 5 = 6$, $15 - 5 = 10$ and $15 - 11 = 4$.

13. (c) : The sum of squares of two numbers at the top gives the third number below, *i.e.,*
$2^2 + 4^2 = 20$
$3^2 + 9^2 = 90$, similarly
$1^2 + 5^2 = 26$.

14. (a) : The sum of numbers in 1st and 2nd column plus 1 is the number in the 3rd column, *i.e.,*
$27 + 22 + 1 = 50$
$13 + 12 + 1 = 26$, similarly
$9 + 2 + 1 = 12$.

15. (d) : The product of numbers on either side of the triangle plus the number at the base is the number inside the triangle, *i.e.,*
$(5 \times 3) + 4 = 19$
$(6 \times 4) + 5 = 29$, similarly
$(7 \times 5) + 6 = 41$.

16. (a) : Clockwise starting from number 7, the next number is obtained by doubling the number and adding 2, *i.e.,*
$(7 \times 2) + 2 = 16$
$(16 \times 2) + 2 = 34$ . . . , similarly
$(34 \times 2) + 2 = 70$
$(70 \times 2) + 2 = 142$
$(142 \times 2) + 2 = 286$.

17. (c) : The difference between the numbers in opposite sectors is 13, *i.e.,*
$26 - 13 = 13$
$68 - 55 = 13$,
similarly
The missing number is $42 - 13 = 29$
($42 + 13 = 55$ is not given as option).

18. (b) : The number at the bottom is obtained by subtracting the sum of two numbers in the centre grid line from the square of the number at the top, *i.e.,*
$7^2 - (2 + 7) = 40$
$5^2 - (8 + 3) = 14$, similarly
$9^2 - (7 + 6) = 68$.

19. (b) : The number inside the brackets is obtained by multiplying the number on the left by 2 and then dividing the product by the sum of digits of number on the right, *i.e.,*
$(42 \times 2) \div (2 + 2) = 21$
$(162 \times 2) \div (9 + 9) = 18$,
similarly
$(78 \times 2) \div (8 + 4) = 13$.

20. (a) : Subtracting the sum of squares of two numbers at the base from the square of number at the apex gives the number inside the triangle, *i.e.,*
$16^2 - (7^2 + 10^2) = 107$
$25^2 - (20^2 + 4^2) = 209$,
similarly
$19^2 - (2^2 + 17^2) = 68$.

❑❑❑

18 ALPHABET PROBLEMS

Alphabet problems are fun to attempt. They are based on alphabetical series in natural as well as reverse order.

Natural Order

A B C D E F G H I J K L M N O P Q R S T U V W X Y Z

Reverse Order

Z Y X W V U T S R Q P O N M L K J I H G F E D C B A

Note : The series starts from A on reaching Z and from Z on reaching A. Of these A E I O U are vowels and the rest are consonants.

EXERCISE

1. Which letter should be ninth letter to the left of ninth letter from the right if the first half of the alphabet is reversed?

(a) I (b) D
(c) F (d) E

2. Starting from the fifth letter from the left, if twelve letters are written in reverse order, then which letter will be the seventh to the left of the fourteenth letter from the right?

(a) N (b) H
(c) L (d) O

3. What letter will come in the centre of sixth letter from the right and thirteenth letter from the left?

(a) Q (b) R
(c) P (d) S

4. If in the word "DISTURBANCE", the first letter is interchanged with the last letter, the second letter is interchanged with the tenth letter and so on, which letter would come after the letter "T" in the newly formed word?

(a) I (b) U
(c) N (d) S

5. If it is possible to make a meaningful word with the third, the fifth, the seventh and the tenth letters of the word PROJECTION. If no such word can be made, give 'O' as the answer. If more than one such word can be made, give 'M' as the answer.

(a) T (b) N
(c) O (d) M

6. A meaningful word is made if we take the first, fourth, fifth, seventh, tenth, eleventh and the twelfth letters of the word "FELICITATIONS". Which of the following will be the fifth letter of that word from the right end of that word?

(a) T (b) C
(c) N (d) I

7. On rearranging the jumbled spelling of the word SKARTINS, a language is obtained. What is the fifth letter from the right of the rearranged word?

(a) N (b) K
(c) R (d) S

8. If the 1st, 3rd, 5th, 7th, 10th and 13th letters of the word "ENTERTAINMENT" are used to make a meaningful word, then what two letters will come in the centre?

(a) A M (b) T T
(c) R E (d) N A

9. On rearranging the jumbled spelling of the word GRUBY a sport is obtained. What is the letter in the centre?

(a) R (b) B
(c) G (d) U

10. If the letters 'ERVSECI' can be rearranged to form a meaningful word what will be the fifth letter from the right?

(a) R (b) V
(c) E (d) None of these

11. From the word HASTEN how many independent meaningful English words can be made without changing the order of the letters and using each letter only once?

(a) 1 (b) 2
(c) 3 (d) 4

EXPLANATORY ANSWERS

1. *(d)* : MLKJIGHFEDCBANOPQRSTUVWXYZ

9th 9th

2. *(d)* : ABCDPONMLKJIHGFEQRSTUVWXYZ

7th 14th

3. *(a)* :

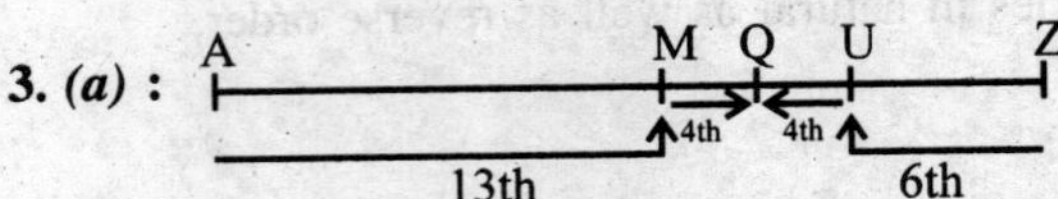

13th letter from left is 'M' and 6th letter from right is 'U'. The letter in the centre of 'M' and 'U' is 'Q'.

4. *(d)* : E C N A B R U T S I D

5. *(d)* : P R O J E C T I O N

The 3rd, 5th, 7th and 10th letters are OETN.

The words formed are TONE and NOTE.

6. *(b)* : F E L I C I T A T I O N S

The 1st, 4th, 5th, 7th, 10th, 11th and 12th lettes are FICTION.

The word is FICTION and 5th letter from right is 'C'.

7. *(d)* : The word is SANSKRIT and 5th letter from right is 'S'.

8. *(b)* : E N T E R T A I N M E N T

The 1st, 3rd, 5th 7th, 10th and 13th letters are ETRAMT.

The word formed is MATTER.

9. *(c)* : The sport is RUGBY. The letter in the centre is 'G'.

10. *(a)* : The word is SERVICE and fifth letter from right is 'R'.

11. *(b)* : The words formed are : HAS, TEN.

❑❑❑

19 LOGICAL DIAGRAM

In these type of questions, a set of five different figures is given as options. Each figure represents a logical pattern of certain groups of related words wherein each word represents a class. One has to identify the most appropriate logical figure for the set of words given. Some of the relationships represented by these diagrams are given below. Understand the relationship patterns and then attempt the exercise following the explanation.

EXERCISE

Directions : *From the five logical Diagrams, select one which best illustrates the relationship among three given classes in the questions 1 to 10.*

(a) *(b)*

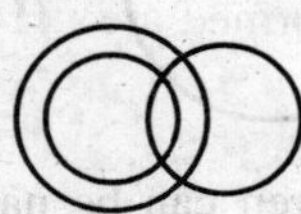

(c) *(d)*

(e)

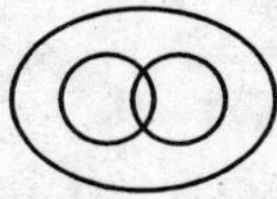

1. Birds, fruits, mangoes
2. Criminals, lawyers, bandits
3. Swimmers, bachelors, men
4. Smart, engineers, women
5. Vegetables, potatoes, brinjals
6. Grapes, sweet, fruit
7. Doctors, architects, humans
8. Scholars, people, Indians
9. Children, naughty, studious
10. Pens, pencils, stationery

Directions : *From the five logical diagrams select one which best illustrates the relationship among three given classes in questions 11 to 20.*

(a) *(b)*

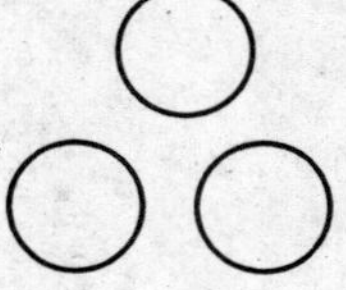

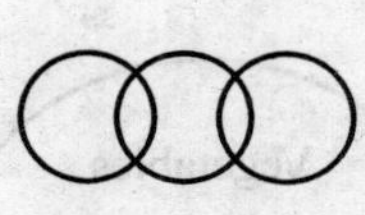

(c) *(d)*

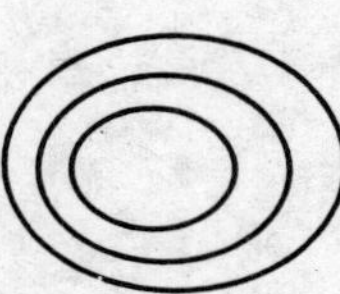

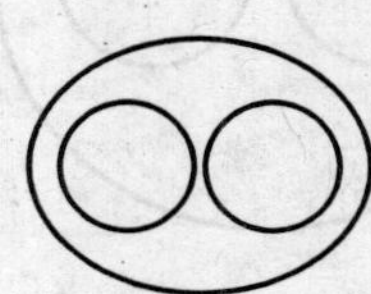

(e)

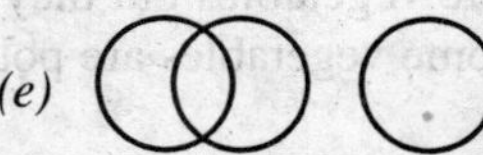

11. Ink, crayons, red
12. Canines, dogs, pups
13. Table, chair, stool
14. Ripe, mangoes, basket
15. Scholars, studious, illiterates
16. Cars, ships, means of conveyance
17. Age, number, thirteen
18. Country, state, continent
19. Father, parent, mother
20. Iron, metal, mercury

EXPLANATORY ANSWERS

1. *(a)* :

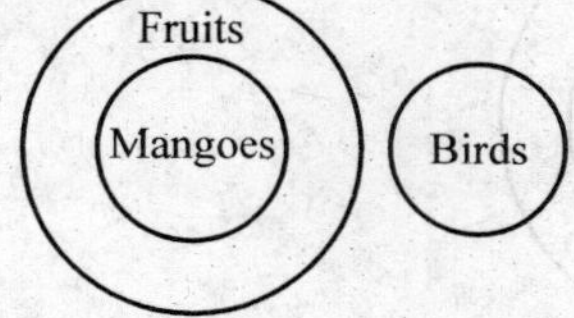

All mangoes are fruits, but neither fruits, nor mangoes can be birds.

2. *(a)* :

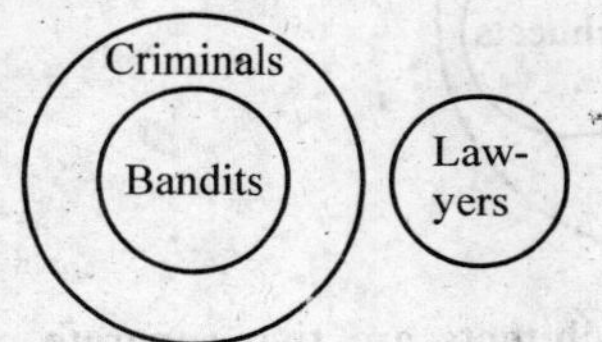

All bandits are criminal, but neither criminals nor bandits can be lawyers.

3. ***(b)*** **:**

Men
Bache-lors
Swim-mers

All bachelors are men and some men and bachelors can be swimmers.

4. ***(c)*** **:**

Smart
Women
Engineers

Some women can be smart and some women can be engineers and vice–versa. Some engineers can be women and some engineers can be smart and vice–versa.

5. ***(d)*** **:**

Vegetables
Potatoes
Brinjals

Potatoes and brinjals are vegetables but they have nothing in common. Some vegetables are potatoes and some are brinjals.

6. ***(b)*** **:**

Fruit
Grapes
Sweet

Some grapes are sweet and all grapes are fruit. But not all that is sweet is fruit.

7. ***(d)*** **:**

Humanbeings
Doctors
Architects

Doctors and architects are two separate classes, but all doctors and architects are humans and some humans are either doctors or architects.

8. ***(e)*** **:**

People
Scholars
Indians

Some Indians can be scholars and some scholars can be Indians. All scholars and Indians are people.

9. ***(c)*** **:**

Children
Naughty
Studious

Some children can be naughty and some can be studious, some studious can be children and some naughty. Some naughty can be studious and some children.

10. ***(d)*** **:**

Stationery
Pens
Pencils

Pens and pencils both are items of stationery and some stationery is pens and pencils, but pens and pencils are two separate classes.

11. ***(b)*** **:**

Inks
Red
Crayons

Some ink and some crayons can be red and some red units can be inks and crayons, but ink and crayon have nothing in common.

12. ***(c)*** **:**

Canines
Dogs
Pups

All pups are dogs and all dogs are canines. Some canines are dogs, of which some are pups.

13. *(a)* :

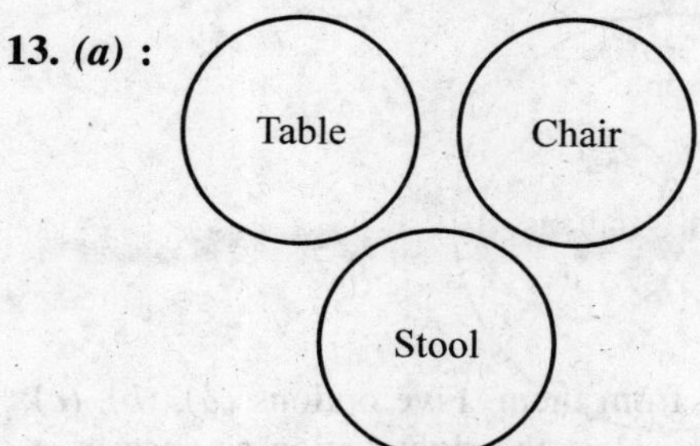

All three are different classes.

14. *(e)* :

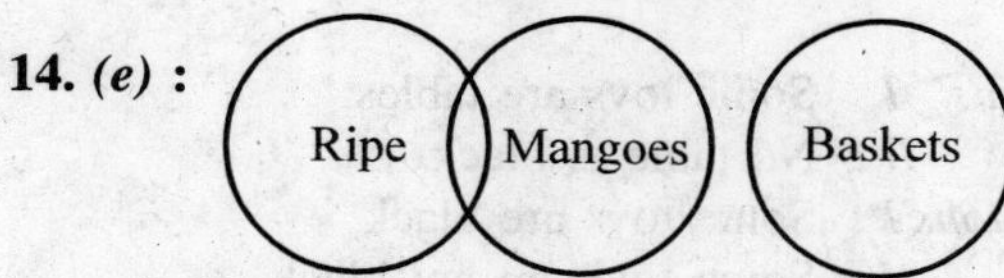

Some mangoes are ripe and some ripe units are mangoes, but neither ripe units nor mangoes can be baskets.

15. *(e)* :

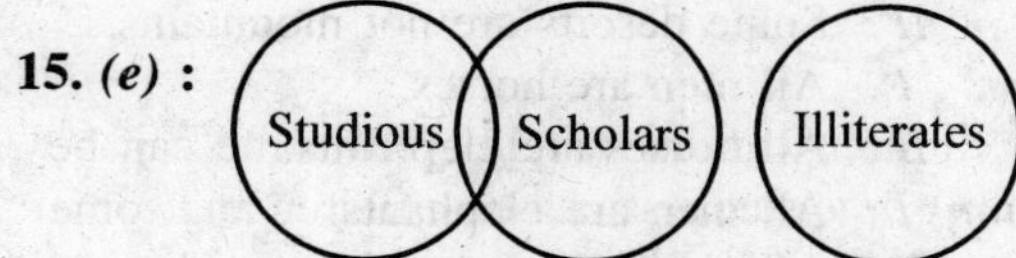

Some studious can be scholars and some scholars can be studious, but neither studious nor scholars can be illiterates.

16. *(d)* :

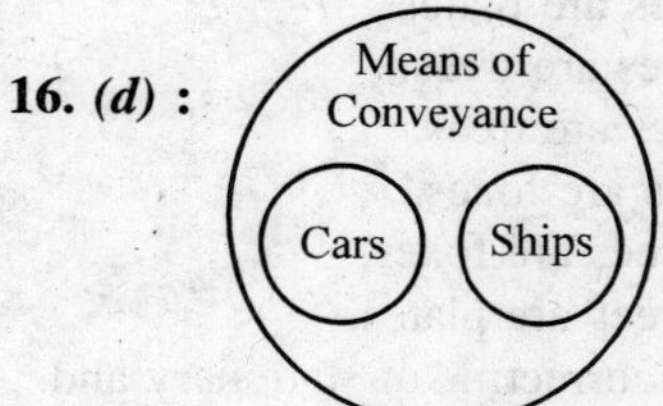

All cars and all ships are means of conveyance, but neither is contained in the other. Some means of conveyance are cars and some ships.

17. *(b)* :

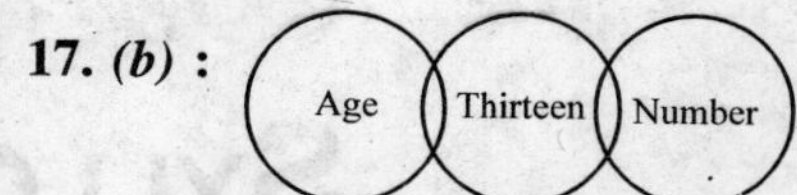

Some are aged thirteen and some numbers are thirteen. Some thirteen units are numbers and some ages. Age and number have nothing in common.

18. *(c)* :

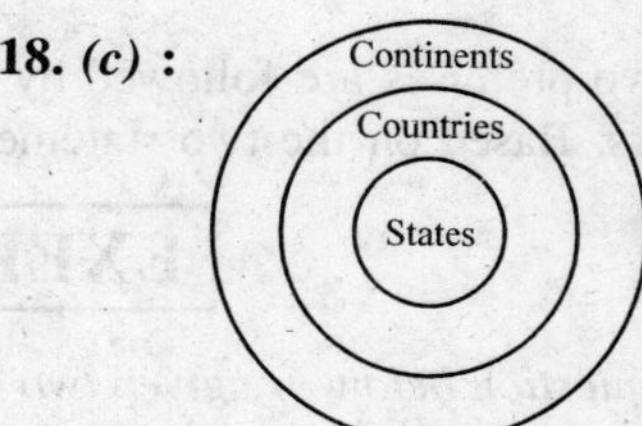

All continents contain countries within it and each country contains states within it.

19. *(d)* :

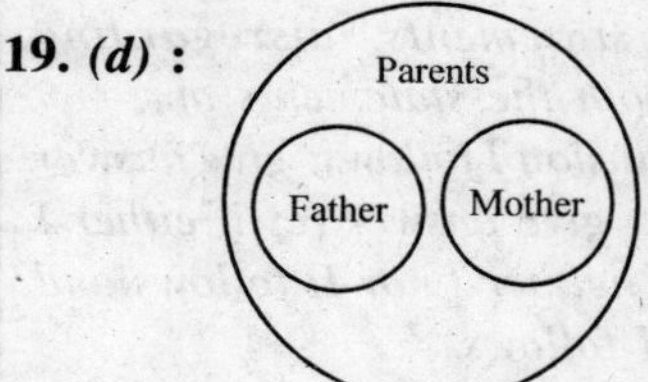

All fathers and mothers are parents, but they are two separate classes. Some of the parents are fathers and some are mothers.

20. *(d)* :

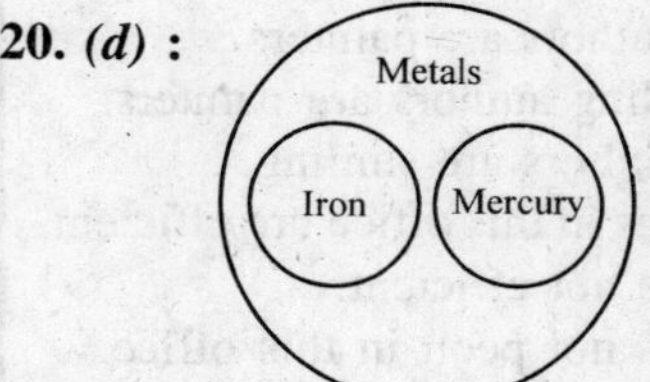

Iron and mercury are metals, but they have nothing in common. Some metals are iron and some mercury.

❑ ❑ ❑

20 SYLLOGISM

In this reasoning pattern, the two premises are followed by two conclusions drawn from them. Five options *(a)*, *(b)*, *(c)*, *(d)* and *(e)* are given as answers. Based on the two statements the candidate has to select the right option as answer.

EXERCISE

Directions (Qs. 1-10): *In each question below are given two statements followed by two conclusions numbered I and II. You have to take the two given statements to be true even if they seem to be at variance from commonly known facts and then decide which of the given conclusions logically follows from the two given statements, disregarding commonly known facts. Read both the statements and—*

Give answer (a) if only conclusion I follows; give answer (b) if only conclusion II follows; give answer (c) if either I or II follows; give answer (d) if neither I nor II follows and give answer (e) if both I and II follows.

1. *Statements* *I :* All tomatoes are red.
   II : All grapes are tomatoes.
   Conclusions I : All grapes are red.
   II : Some tomatoes are grapes.
2. *Statements* *I :* All painters are smiling.
   II : Some authors are painters.
   Conclusions I : All smiling authors are painters.
   II : Some authors are smiling.
3. *Statements* *I :* All peons in this office are efficient.
   II : Ramu is not efficient.
   Conclusions I : Ramu is not peon in this office.
   II : Ramu should be more efficient.
4. *Statements* *I :* All weavers are hard working.
   II : No hard working men are foolish.
   Conclusions I : No weavers are foolish.
   II : Some foolish are weavers.
5. *Statements* *I :* All fishes are cars.
   II : All cars are vegetables.
   Conclusions I : Some vegetables are cars.
   II : Some vegetables are fishes.
6. *Statements* *I :* Some dogs are pups.
   II : All horses are pups.
   Conclusions I : Some dogs are horses.
   II : Some horses are dogs.
7. *Statements* *I :* All beautiful women are mothers.
   II : All mothers are understanding.
   Conclusions I : All beautiful women are understanding.
   II : All mothers are beautiful women.
8. *Statements* *I :* Some toys are tables.
   II : No table is black.
   Conclusions I : Some toys are black.
   II : Some toys are not black.
9. *Statements* *I :* All rivers are mountains.
   II : Some rivers are deserts.
   Conclusions I : Some mountains are deserts.
   II : Some deserts are not mountains.
10. *Statements* *I :* All men are horses.
    II : All horses are elephants.
    Conclusions I : All men are elephants.
    II : All elephants are men.

Directions (Qs. 11-15): *In the following questions, select the set of conclusion which logically follows from the given statements.*

11. *Statements* *I :* All foxes are plates.
    II : All plates are trees.
    Conclusions I : All foxes are trees.
    II : All trees are foxes.
    III : Some trees are foxes.
    IV : Some trees are plates.
    (a) All conclusions are correct.
    (b) Only conclusions I, III, and IV follow.
    (c) Only conclusions II, III, and IV follow.
    (d) Only conclusions I and IV follow.
    (e) None of the above.
12. *Statements* *I :* Some cubes are squares.
    II : All squares are circles.
    Conclusions I : All cubes are circles.
    II : Some circles are cubes.
    III : Some circles are squares.
    IV : All squares are cubes.
    (a) Only conclusion I follows.
    (b) Only conclusion I, II and III follow.
    (c) All conclusions are correct.
    (d) Only conclusions II and III follow.
    (e) None of the above.
13. *Statements* *I :* All cups are goats.
    II : All goats are tins.
    Conclusions I : All goats are cups.

II : All tins are goats.
III : No cups are tins.
IV : No tins are cups.
(*a*) Only conclusions III and IV follow.
(*b*) Only conclusios I and II follow.
(*c*) Only conclusions I, II and III follow.
(*d*) All conclusions are correct.
(*e*) None of the above.

14. *Statements I :* All bombs are bags.
II : Some bags are jets.
Conclusions I : All bombs are jets.
II : All jets are bombs.
III : Some jets are bombs.
IV : Some bombs are jets.
(*a*) Only conclusion III follows.
(*b*) Only conclusions I and II follow.
(*c*) All conclusions are correct.
(*d*) Only conclusions III and IV follow.
(*e*) None of these.

15. *Statements I :* Some thorns are jackets.
II : Some jackets are boats.
Conclusions I : No thorns are boats.
II : All jackets are boats.
III : Some boats are thorns.
IV : No jackets are thorns.
(*a*) Either conclusion I or IV follows.
(*b*) Either conclusion I or II follows.
(*c*) Either conclusion I or III follows.
(*d*) No conclusion is correct.
(*e*) All conclusions are correct.

EXPLANATORY ANSWERS

1. (*e*) : When all tomatoes are red and all grapes are tomatoes, then all grapes are also red. When all grapes are tomatoes, then some tomatoes must be grapes. Therefore, both conclusions I and II are correct.

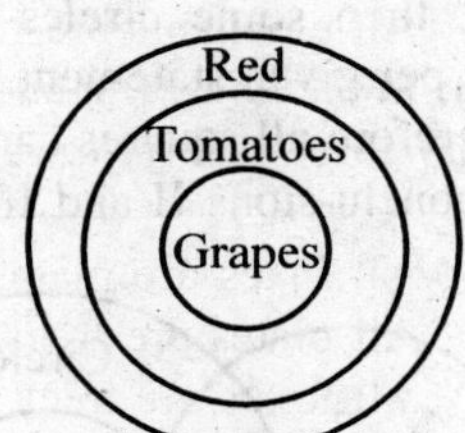

2. (*b*) : When all painters are smiling and some authors are painters, then some authors are smiling. Therefore, only conclusion II is correct.

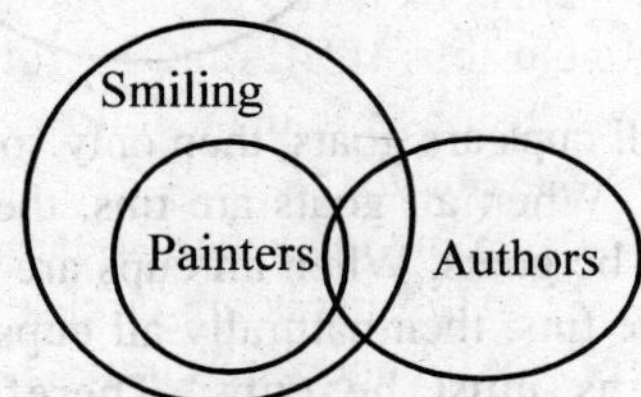

3. (*a*) : When all the peons of the office are efficient, then Ramu cannot be a peon in this office. Therefore, only conclusion I is correct.

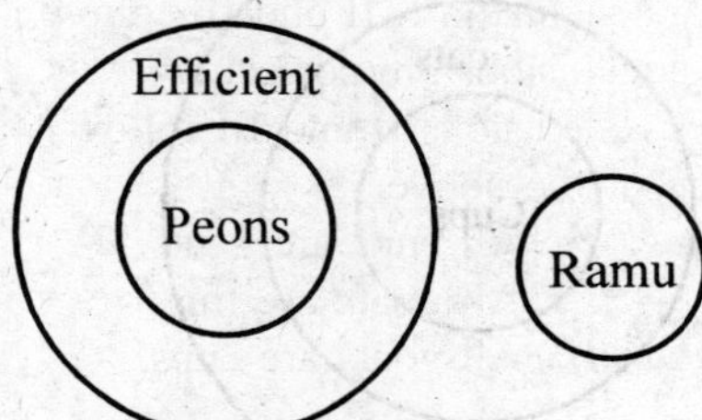

4. (*a*) : When all weavers are hardworking and no hardworking men are foolish, then no weavers are foolish. Therefore, only conclusion I is correct.

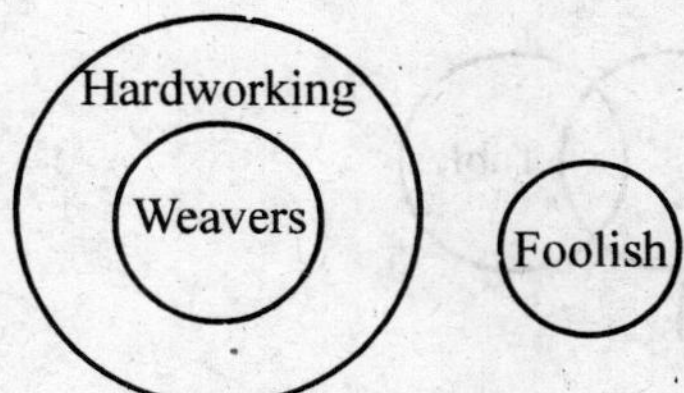

5. (*e*) : When all fishes are cars and all cars are vegetables, then all fishes will naturally be vegetables. This means that some vegetables are fishes. And when all cars are vegetables, then some vegetables will be cars naturally. Therefore, both the conclusions I and II are correct.

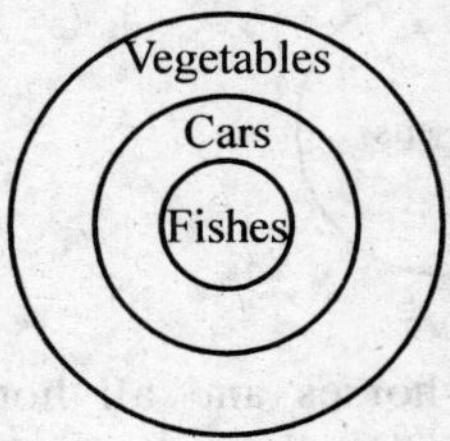

6. (*d*) : No relationship can be established between the two statements. Therefore, neither conclusion I nor conclusion II is correct.

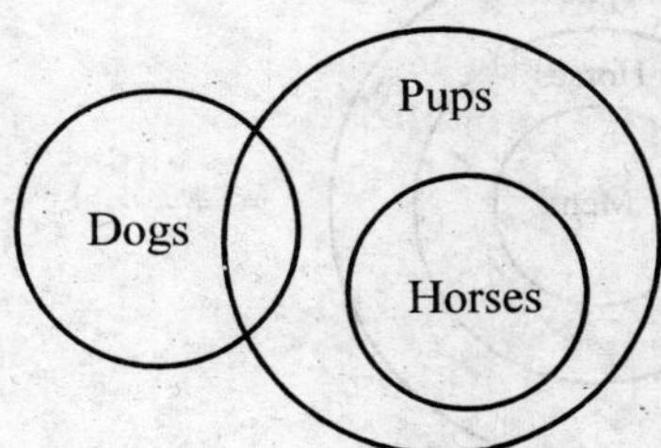

7. *(a)* : When all beautiful women are mothers and all mothers are understanding, then naturally all beautiful women are understanding. All mothers need not be beautiful women. Therefore, only conclusion I is correct.

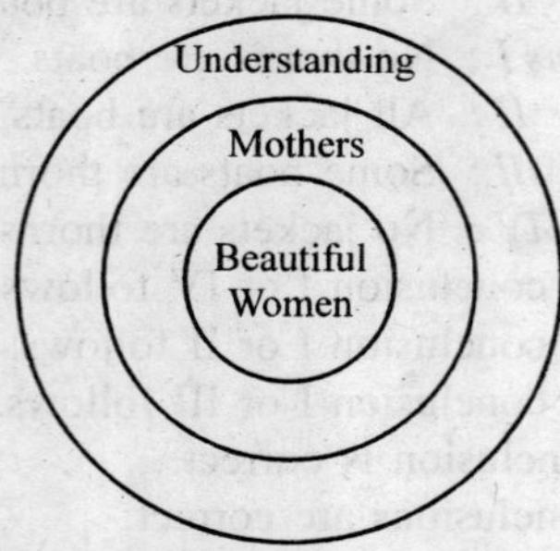

8. *(c)* : When some toys are tables and no table is black, then it is indicated that some toys can be black, as all toys are not tables. On the other hand, some toys may not be black. Therefore, there is a possibility that some toys may or may not be black. As such, either conclusion I or conclusion II can be correct.

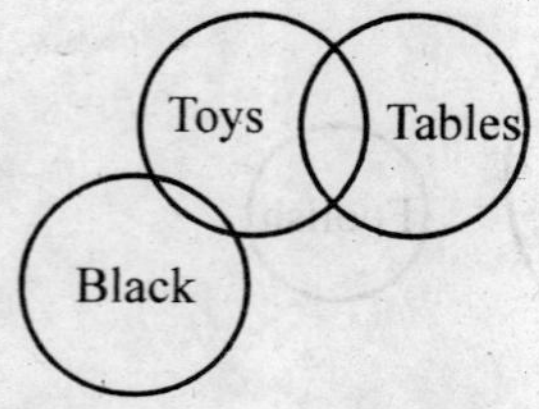

9. *(e)* : When all rivers are mountains and some rivers are deserts, then some deserts cannot be mountains and also, some mountains need not be deserts. Therefore, both conclusion I and conclusion II are correct.

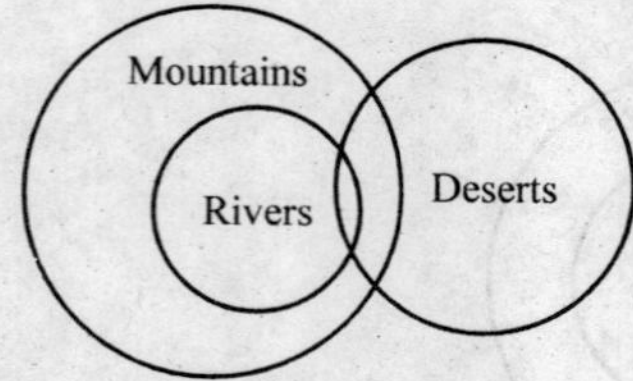

10. *(a)* : When all men are horses and all horses are elephants then, naturally all men are elephants, but all elephants need not be men. Therefore, only conclusion I is correct.

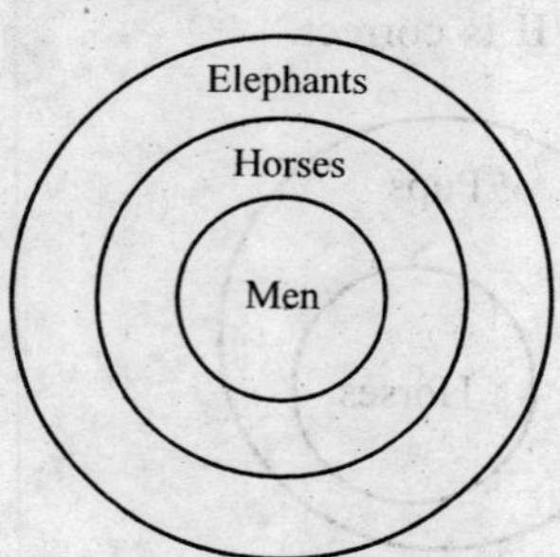

11. *(b)* :

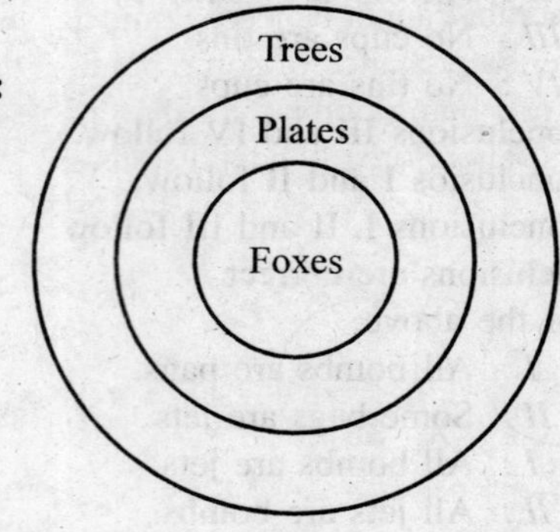

When all foxes are plates and all plates are trees, then naturally all foxes will be trees and some trees will then have to be foxes. And when all plates are trees then some trees will have to be plates. Therefore, only conclusions I, III and IV are correct.

12. *(d)* : When it is given that some cubes are squares and all squares are circles, then some cubes will naturally be circles, though all cubes cannot be circles. When some cubes are circles, then some circles will have to be cubes. And when all squares are circles, then some circles will have to be squares. As per given statement II, all squares are circles. Therefore all squares cannot be cubes. As such only conclu-sions II and III are correct.

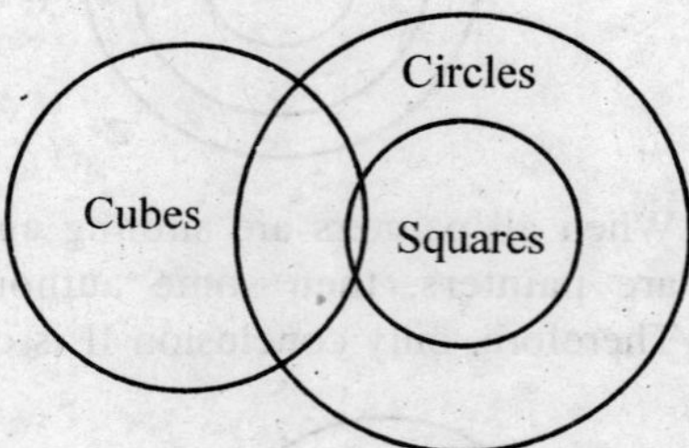

13. *(e)* : When all cups are goats, then only some goats can be cups. When all goats are tins, then only some tins can be goats. When all cups are goats and all goats are tins, then naturally all cups are tins and some tins must be cups. Therefore, all the conclusions are incorrect.

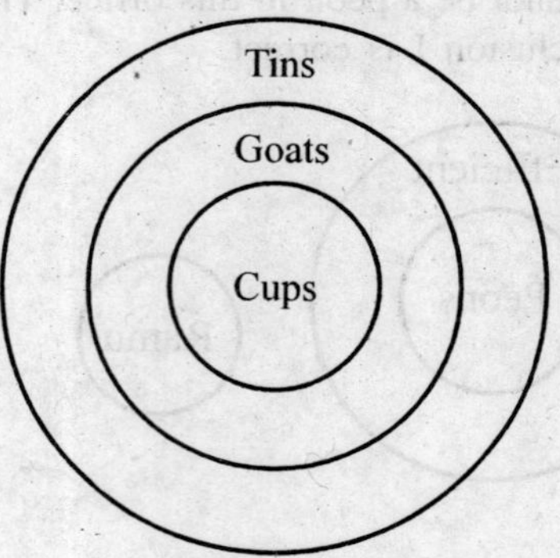

14. ***(e)*** **:** When all bombs are bags and some bags are jets then all bombs cannot be jets. 'Some bags' indicate that there is no chance of some bombs being jets, or some jets being bombs. Further all jets cannot be bombs. Therefore, all conclusions are incorrect.

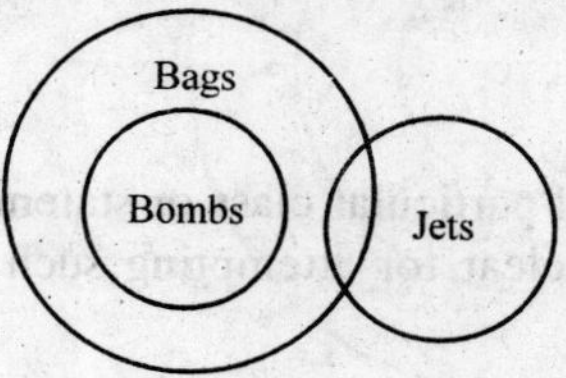

15. ***(d)*** **:** When some thorns are jackets and some jackets are boats, then some thorns may be boats but some boats cannot be thorns. As per Statement I, some thorns are jackets, some jackets need to be thorns. When Statement II conveys that some jackets are boats, then it is clear that all jackets cannot be boats. Therefore, no particular given conclusion can be drawn from the given statements.

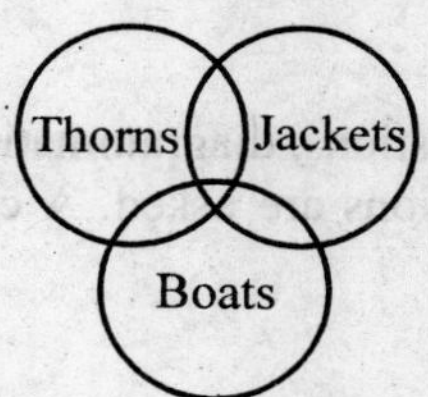

❑ ❑ ❑

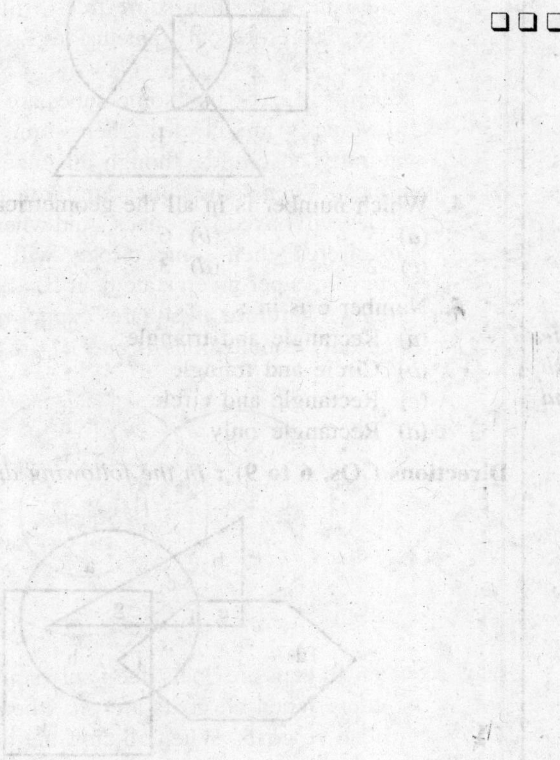

21 VENN DIAGRAMS

In these type of questions, diagrammatic representation presents a logical illustration of particular class or statements based on which the questions are asked. A clear view of the diagram makes the concepts clear for attempting such questions.

EXERCISE

1. What is the number which is common to only two geometrical figures?

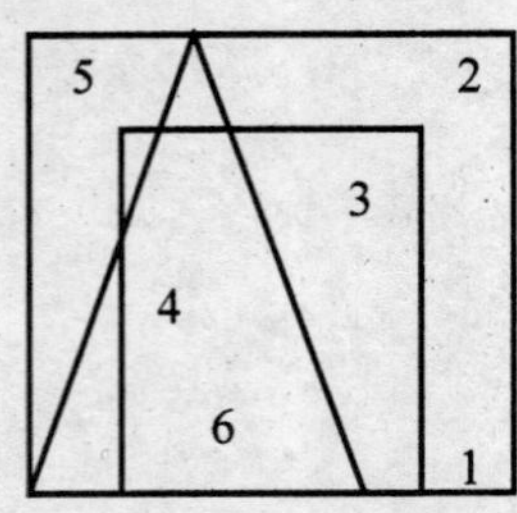

(*a*) 4 (*b*) 3
(*c*) 5 (*d*) 2

Directions (Qs. 2 and 3) : *In the following diagram, rectangle represents Hindi Announcers, circle represents English Announcers, square represents French Announcers, and triangle represents German Announcers.*

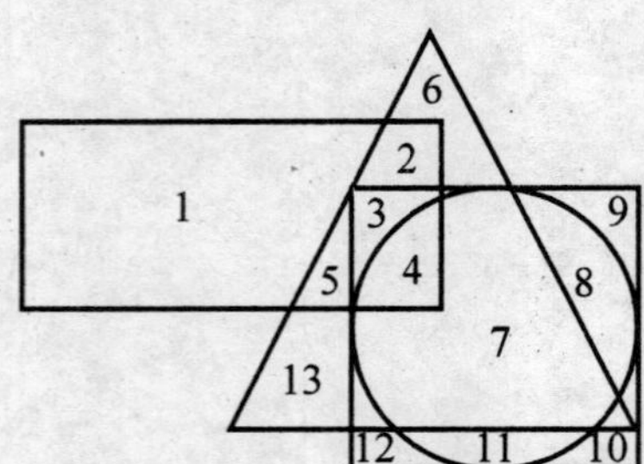

2. Which area represents those announcers who can present programmes in Hindi, French and German only?
(*a*) 1
(*b*) 2
(*c*) 3
(*d*) 4

3 Which area represents those announcers who can present programmes in French and English only?
(*a*) 7
(*b*) 9
(*c*) 11
(*d*) 13

Directions (Qs. 4 and 5) : *Study the diagram to answer these questions.*

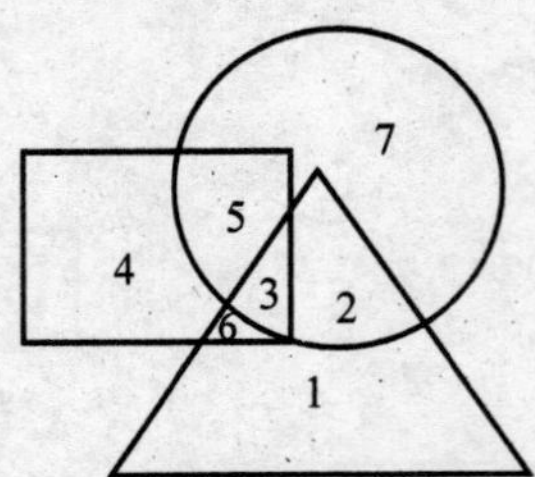

4. Which number is in all the geometrical figures?
(*a*) 5 (*b*) 6
(*c*) 2 (*d*) 3

5. Number 6 is in :
(*a*) Rectangle and triangle
(*b*) Circle and traingle
(*c*) Rectangle and circle
(*d*) Rectangle only

Directions (Qs. 6 to 9) : *In the following diagram*

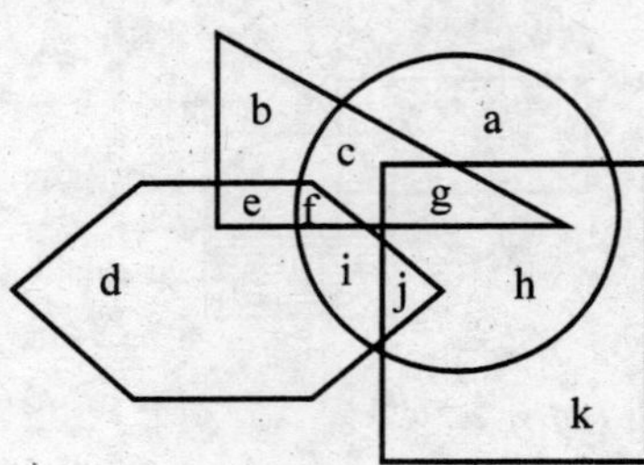

The Circle represents players
The Triangle represents outdoor games
The Hexagon represents indoor games and
The Square represents national level players
Study the diagram and answer the questions given below:

6. The letter in the section representing the players who play indoor games at national level is :
(*a*) f
(*b*) i
(*c*) j
(*d*) g

7. The letter representing the section of outdoor as well as indoor game players who do not play at the national level is :

(*a*) c (*b*) f
(*c*) e (*d*) i

8. The section representing national level players who do not play either outdoor or indoor games but still come under the category of players is :

(*a*) k (*b*) g
(*c*) c (*d*) h

9. Persons who play outdoor games but do not come under the category of players are represented in the section marked :

(*a*) b
(*b*) c
(*c*) a
(*d*) d

Direction (Q. 10) : *Study the diagram given below.*

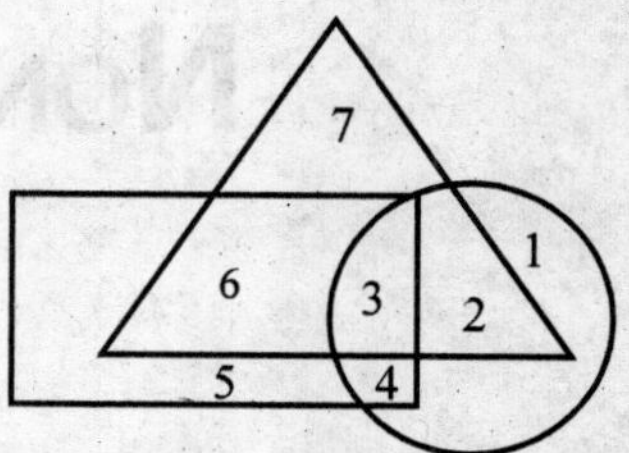

A college provides three different activities, students union represented by triangle, literary society represented by rectangle and social service league represented by circle.

10. Those who take part in both literary society and social service league but not in students union are represented by :

(*a*) 3 & 4 (*b*) 5 & 6
(*c*) 5 & 1 (*d*) 4

EXPLANATORY ANSWERS

1. *(b)* :

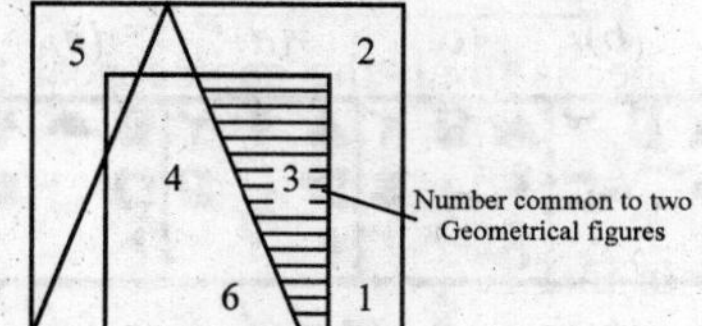

Note : Numbers 4 and 6 are common to all three geometrical figures.

2. *(c)*, **3.** *(c)* :

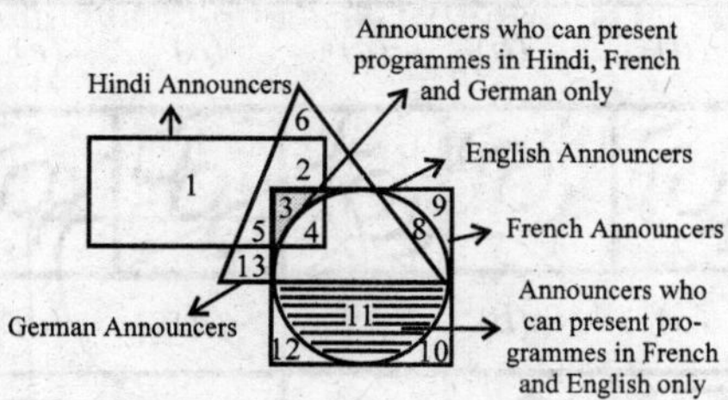

4. *(d)*, **5.** *(a)* :

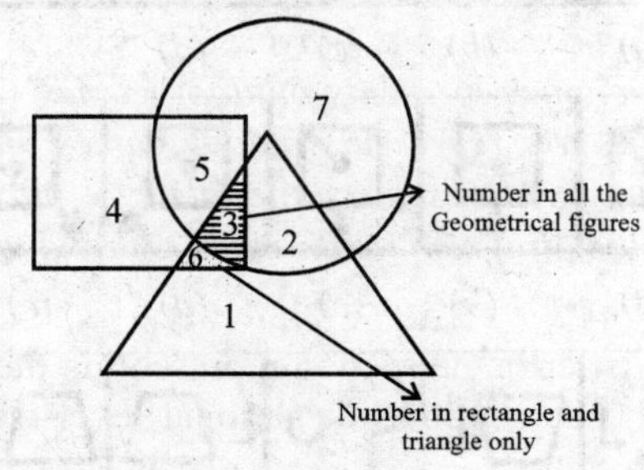

6. *(c)*, **7.** *(b)*, **8.** *(d)*, **9.** *(a)* :

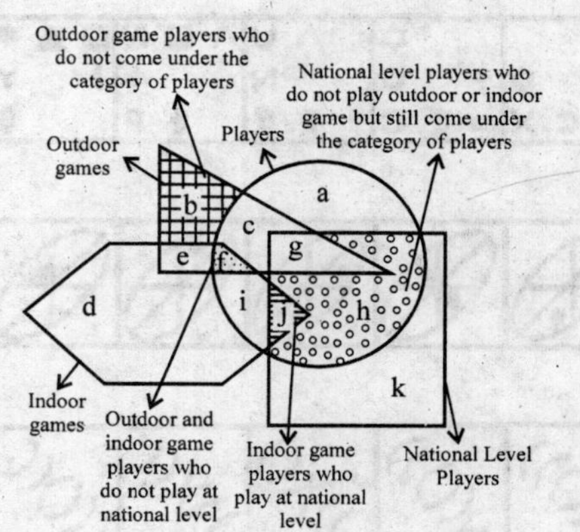

10. *(d)*

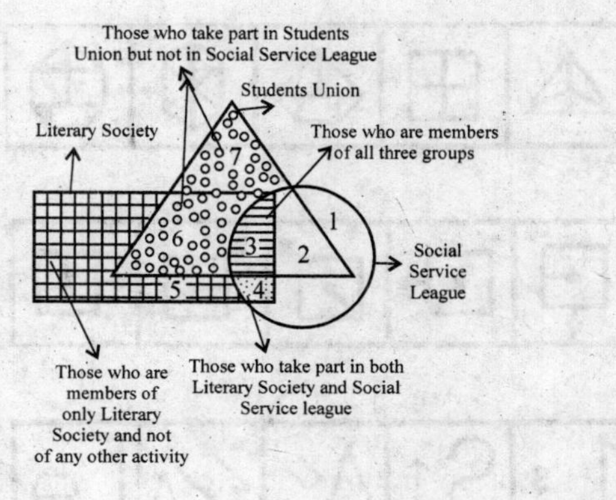

❑ ❑ ❑

22 NON-VERBAL SERIES

EXERCISE

Directions (Qs. 1–10) : *In each of the following questions which one of the five answer figures given below should come after the problem figures if the sequence are continued?*

Problem Figures

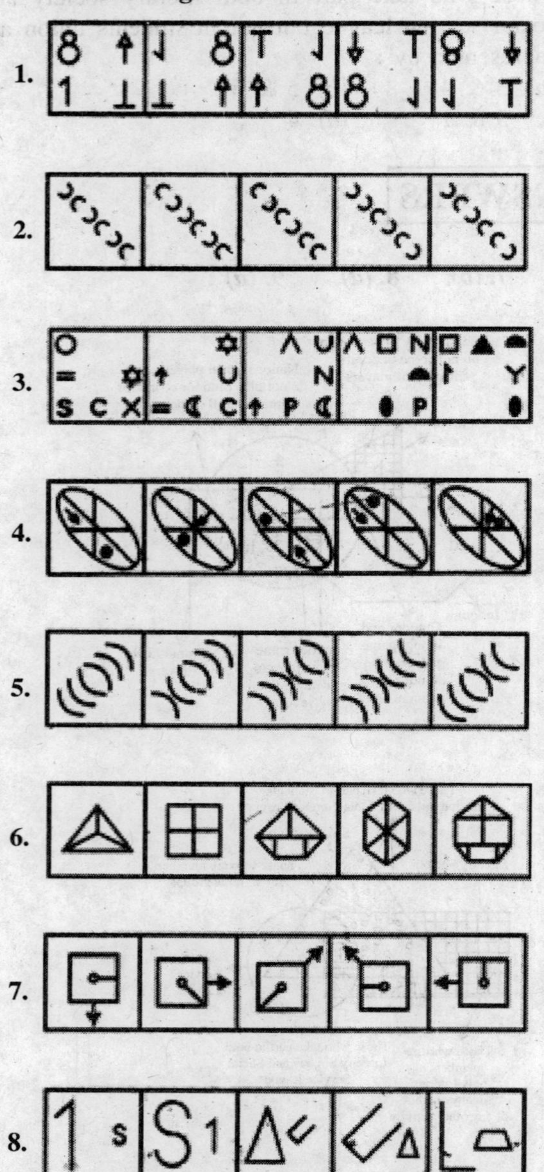

Answer Figures

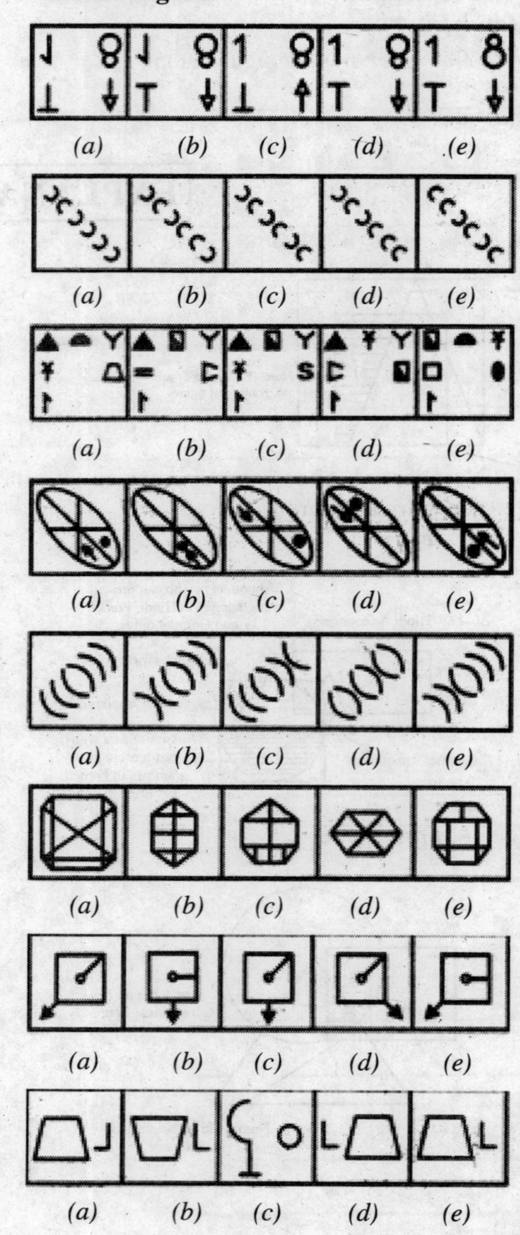

Problem Figures **Answer Figures**

9. 

10. 

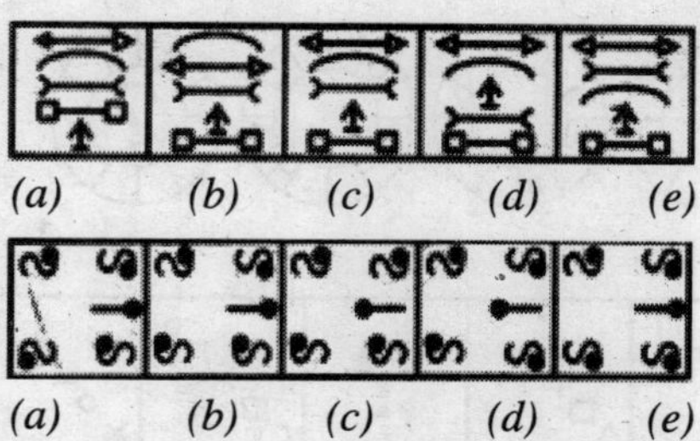

(a) (b) (c) (d) (e)

Directions (Qs. 11-20) : *In each of these questions, a series begins with an unmarked figure on the extreme left in the row of figures. One and only one of the five lettered figures in the series does not fit into the series. The two unmarked figures, one on the extreme left and the other on the extreme right fit into the series. Take as many aspects into account as possible of the figures in the series and find out the one and only of the five marked figures which does not fit into the series. The letter of that figure is the answer.*

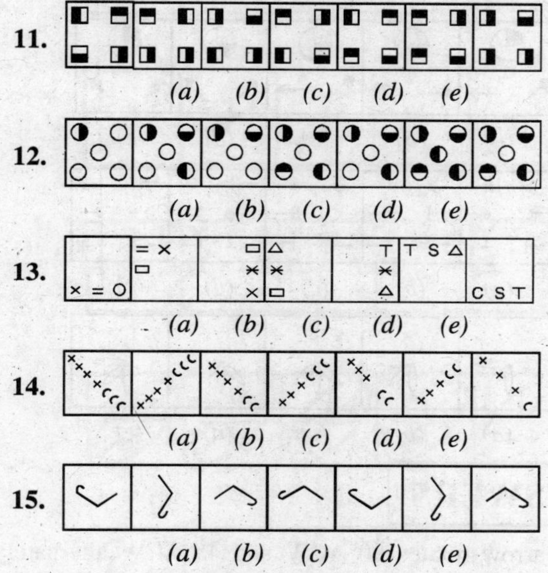

11. (a) (b) (c) (d) (e)

12. (a) (b) (c) (d) (e)

13. (a) (b) (c) (d) (e)

14. (a) (b) (c) (d) (e)

15. (a) (b) (c) (d) (e)

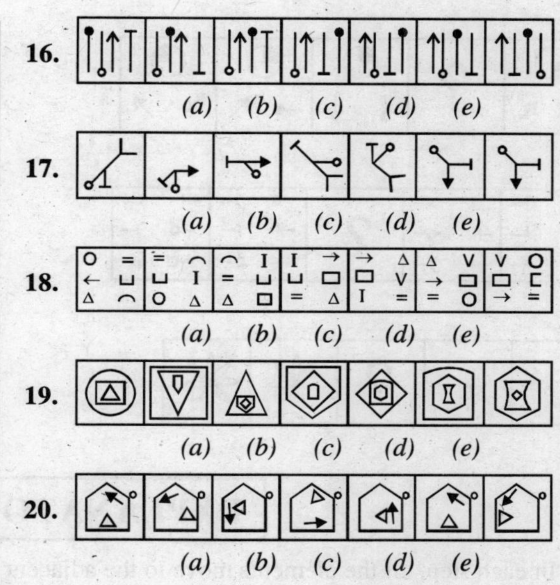

16. (a) (b) (c) (d) (e)

17. (a) (b) (c) (d) (e)

18. (a) (b) (c) (d) (e)

19. (a) (b) (c) (d) (e)

20. (a) (b) (c) (d) (e)

Directions (Qs. 21–30) : *Each of the following questions consist of problem figures followed by answer figures. Select a figure from amongst the answer figures which will continue the same series or pattern as established by the problem figures.*

Problem Figures **Answer Figures**

21. 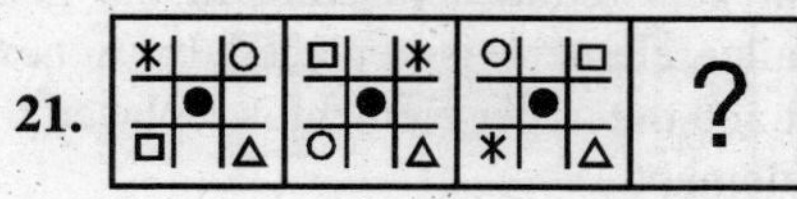

22. 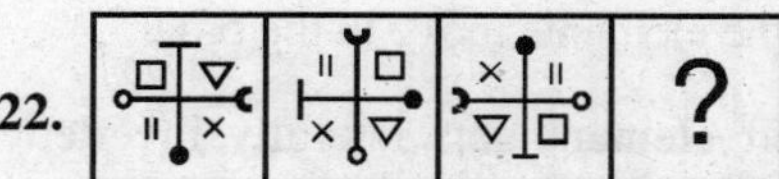

23. 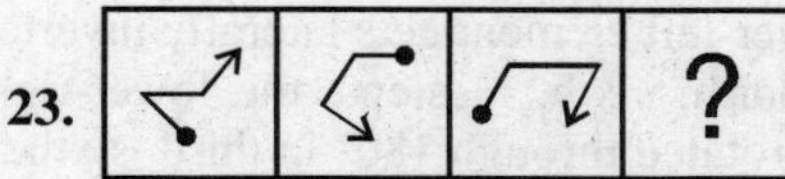

24. 

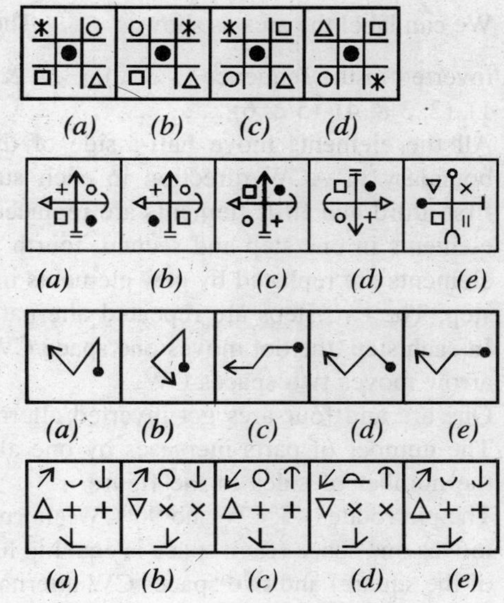

(a) (b) (c) (d)

(a) (b) (c) (d) (e)

(a) (b) (c) (d) (e)

(a) (b) (c) (d) (e)

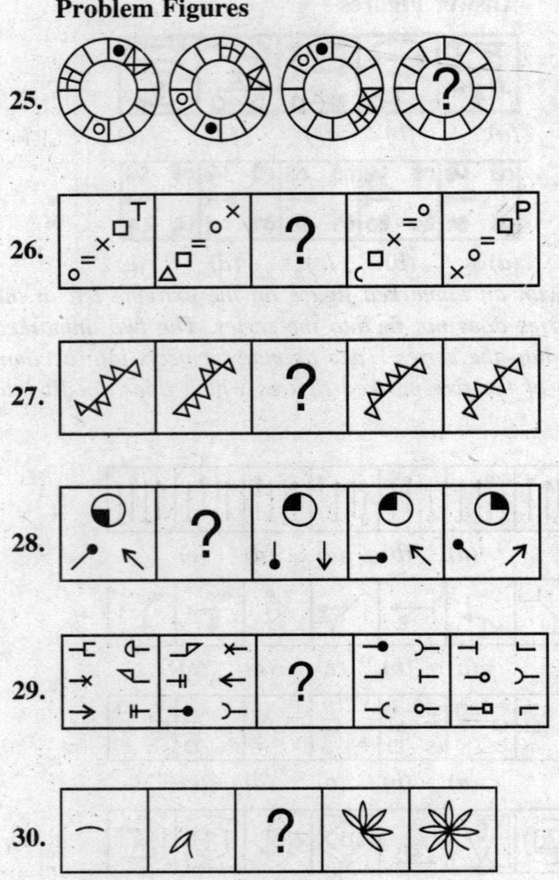

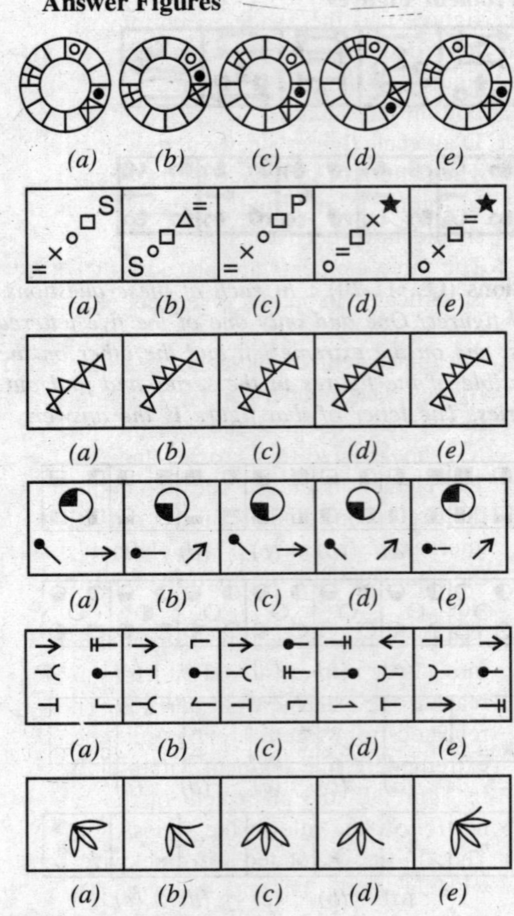

EXPLANATORY ANSWERS

1. *(d)* : In each step, all the elements move to the adjacent corner (of the square boundary) in a CW direction and the element that reaches the upper-left corner gets vertically inverted.

2. *(c)* : We can label the arcs as shown . The arcs get inverted in the sequence (1 & 2), (3, 4 & 5), (6 & 1), (2, 3 & 4), (5 & 6), ...

3. *(d)* : All the elements move half-a-side of the square boundary in ACW direction in each step. Also, first, third and fifth elements are replaced by new elements in one step and second, fourth and sixth elements are replaced by new elements in the next step. The two steps are repeated alternately.

4. *(a)* : In each step, the dot moves one space CW and the arrow moves two spaces CW.

5. *(c)* : One arc and four arcs get inverted alternately.

6. *(e)* : The number of parts increases by one along with the number of sides in the figure.

7. *(c)* : The pin rotates 45°CW and 90°CW alternately and moves one space (each space is equal to half-a-side of the square) and two spaces CW alternately. The arrow rotates 90°ACW and 45°ACW alternately and moves two spaces and one space.

8. *(e)* : In one step, the two elements interchange positions and the smaller element gets enlarged while the larger element gets reduced in size. In the next step, the smaller element is replaced by a new small element and the larger element is replaced by a new large element.

9. *(c)* : In each step, the elements move in the order .

10. *(b)* : The upper-left element gets laterally inverted in first, third, fifth. .... steps; the upper-right element gets rotated through 180° is first, fourth, seventh,.... steps; the lower-left element gets laterally inverted in second, fourth, sixth, ... steps; the lower-right element gets rotated through 180° in third, sixth,... steps and the pin at the middle-right position gets laterally inverted in every second step.

11. *(a)* : The shade in the top left square is moved one step clockwise till figure B and then reversed, the process is repeated. The shade in the top right square is moved one step anticlockwise till figure

D and then reversed. The shade in the bottom left square is moved one step clockwise in alternate figures and the shade in bottom right square is moved one step clockwise after two figures. In figure 'A' the rule is isolated by the shade in the bottom left square.

12. (e) : In alternate figures a new circle is shaded clockwise. The pattern of the shade is also moved clockwise. In figure 'E' right half of the circle in the centre should have been shaded.

13. (a) : The three elements are placed either horizontally or vertically. In option 'A' neither of the placements can be applied.

14. (c) : The placement of elements is same in alternate figures. The number and type of elements is same in two subsequent figures. In this manner, figure 'C' should have four crosses and two C shapes.

15. (c) : The element is moved one step anticlockwise and the arc at one end is turned outside and inside alternately. In figure 'C' the element should be on the right side with the arc turned outside on the top side.

16. (e) : The left most element, line segment with the dot is moved one step towards right till figure C where it reaches the extreme right position. This process is repeated from figure D where the element on the extreme left, line segment with a circle, is moved. In figure 'E' the placement of the elements does not follow the rule of the series.

17. (e) : The 'T' line is rotated 45° clockwise and the line with the circle 45° anticlockwise. The 'Y' shape and the arrow are repeated twice after two figures. In option E, the 'T' shape and the line with the circle are rotated by 90°.

18. (e) : First the elements in the four corners are moved one step anticlockwise, next the four elements from the top are moved one step anticlockwise and then the four elements from the bottom are moved one step anticlockwise. Of the remaining two elements, the one on the left is made new each time and then their places are interchanged. This process is repeated from figure D. In option 'E' open square should have been in place of circle to continue the series.

19. (a) : At each step the outermost figure is removed and a new figure is placed right in the centre of other two figures. In option 'A' the triangle is turned upside down, which violates the rule of the series.

20. (a) : The arrow is moved one step anticlockwise and the triangle one step clockwise. In figure 'A' the triangle should have been on the left side of the figure.

21. (a) : The places of star, circle and square are moved one step clockwise at each step.

22. (e) : The elements in the four quadrants are moved one step clockwise and the elements at the ends of the cross are moved one step anticlockwise in this series.

23. (a) : In alternate figures, the line with the dot is turned 90° clockwise and the arrow 180° clockwise.

24. (e) : In alternate figures, the element in the top left position is horizontally inverted and moved one and half steps anticlockwise, the top middle element is turned 90° clockwise and moved one step anticlockwise, the top right element is turned 135° clockwise and moved one step anticlockwise, the element at the bottom is replaced by a new element and moved to the top middle position, and the two identical elements are replaced by two new identical elements.

25. (a) : The cross and the circle move one and two steps clockwise respectively (at each step), the plus moves 3, 4 and 5 steps clockwise, and the dot 6, 5 and 4 steps clockwise.

26. (a) : At first step, the fifth or the bottom most element is moved to the second place from top, the second element moved to the fourth place, the fourth element is moved to the third place, the third element is moved to the first or the topmost place and the element on the top, which is made new, is moved to the last or the fifth place. At second step i.e., from second problem figure to third problem figure the above process is reversed. The bottom most element is the first and the top most element is the last or fifth. Hereafter, the process is repeated from the beginning. Option 'A' is the right answer.

27. (c) : Starting from the bottom, one triangle is moved to the opposite side at each step in upward order. Option 'C' fits into the question marked space.

28. (c) : The shade inside the circle is rotated clockwise in alternate figures; the line segment with a dot is rotated 135° clockwise in alternate figures and the arrow is rotated 135° anticlockwise in alternate figures. By this process answer figure 'C' completes the series.

29. (a) : At each step the elements are moved diagonally upward and then laterally inverted, and the top two elements are made new and placed at the bottom line. By this process, option figure 'A' completes the series.

30. (a) : The number of arcs making the petals of the flower are increased by one, one and half, two, two and half respectively at each step. Also, the flower is turned 45° anticlockwise. By this process, option 'A' is the right answer.

❑❑❑

23 NON-VERBAL ANALOGY

EXERCISE

TYPE-I

Directions (Qs. 1-15): *The second figure in the first unit of the Problem Figures bears a certain relationship to the first figure. Similarly, one of the figures in the Answer Figures bears the same relationship to the first figures in the second unit of the Problem Figures. Locate the figure which would fit the questions marks.*

Problem Figures | **Answer Figures**

1. 1 2 3 4 (a) (b) (c) (d) (e)

2. 1 2 3 4 (a) (b) (c) (d) (e)

3. 1 2 3 4 (a) (b) (c) (d) (e)

4. 1 2 3 4 (a) (b) (c) (d) (e)

5. 1 2 3 4 (a) (b) (c) (d) (e)

6. 1 2 3 4 (a) (b) (c) (d) (e)

7. 1 2 3 4 (a) (b) (c) (d) (e)

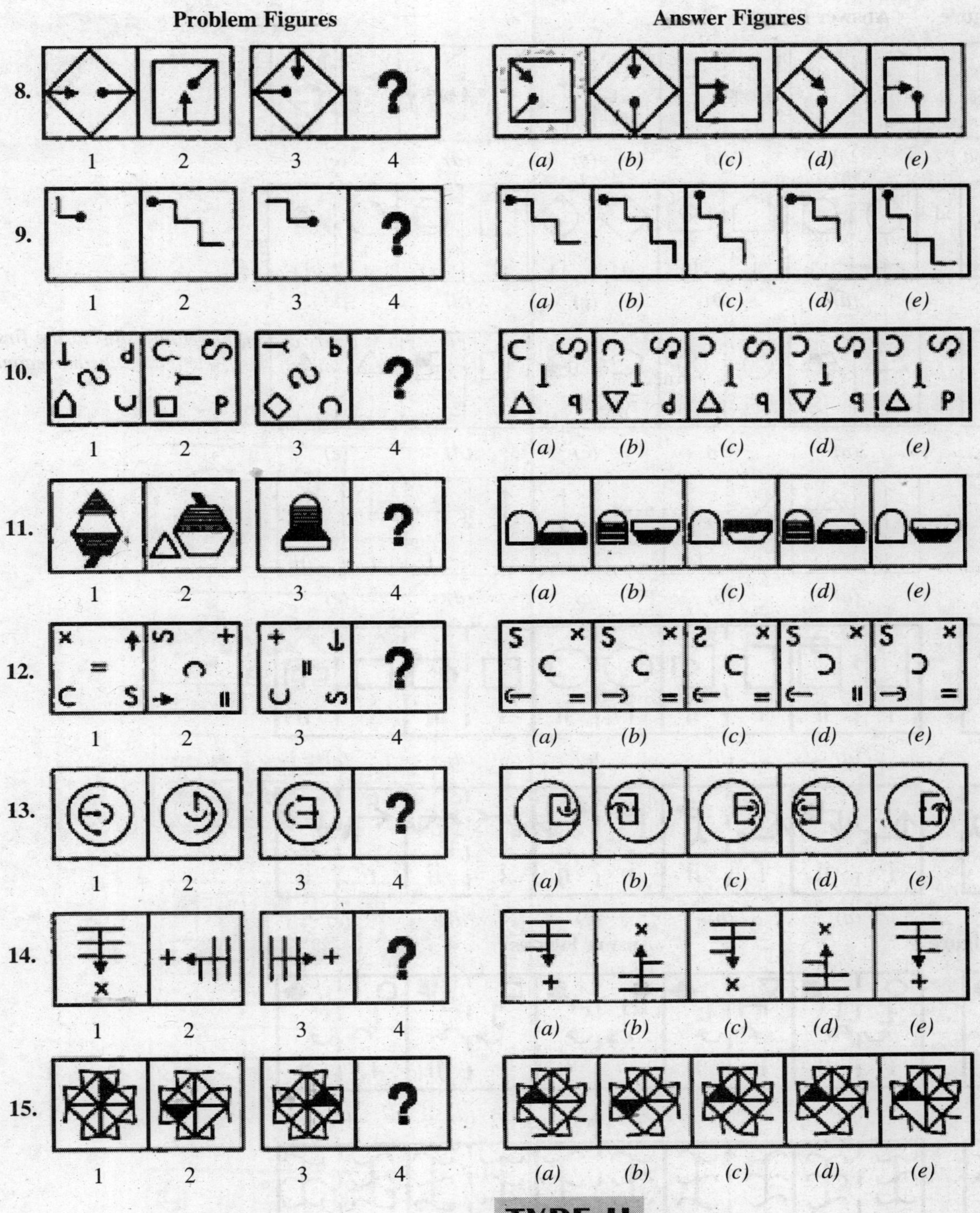

TYPE-II

Directions (Qs. 16–30): *In each of the following questions, a related pair of figures is followed by five numbered pairs of figures. Select the pair that has a relationship* ***similar*** *to that in the unnumbered pair.*

Problem Figure **Answer Figures**

16. I II I II I II I II I II I II

(a) (b) (c) (d) (e)

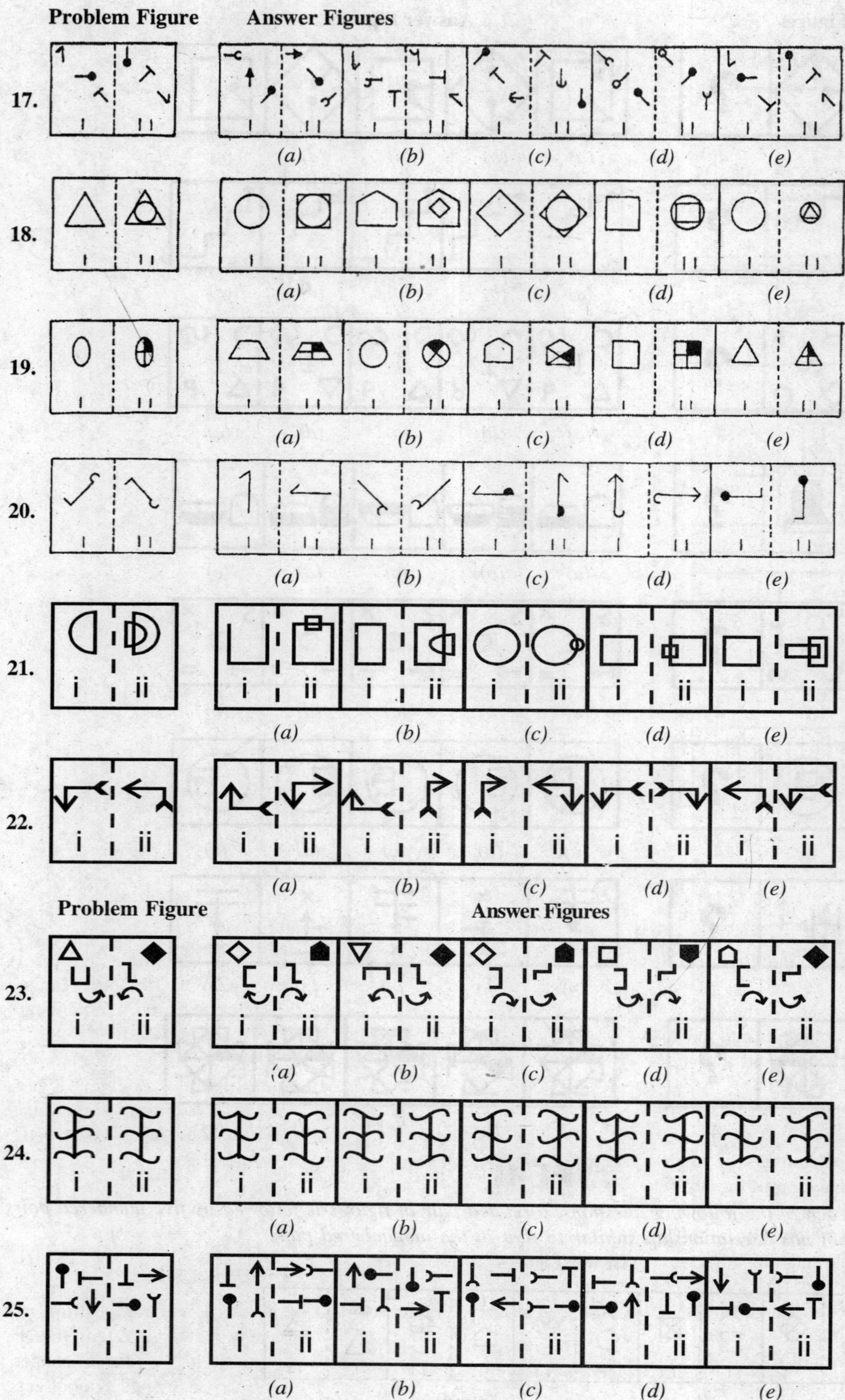

Problem Figure
Answer Figures
17.
18.
19.
20.
21.
22.
Problem Figure
Answer Figures
23.
24.
25.
(a)
(b)
(c)
(d)
(e)
i
ii

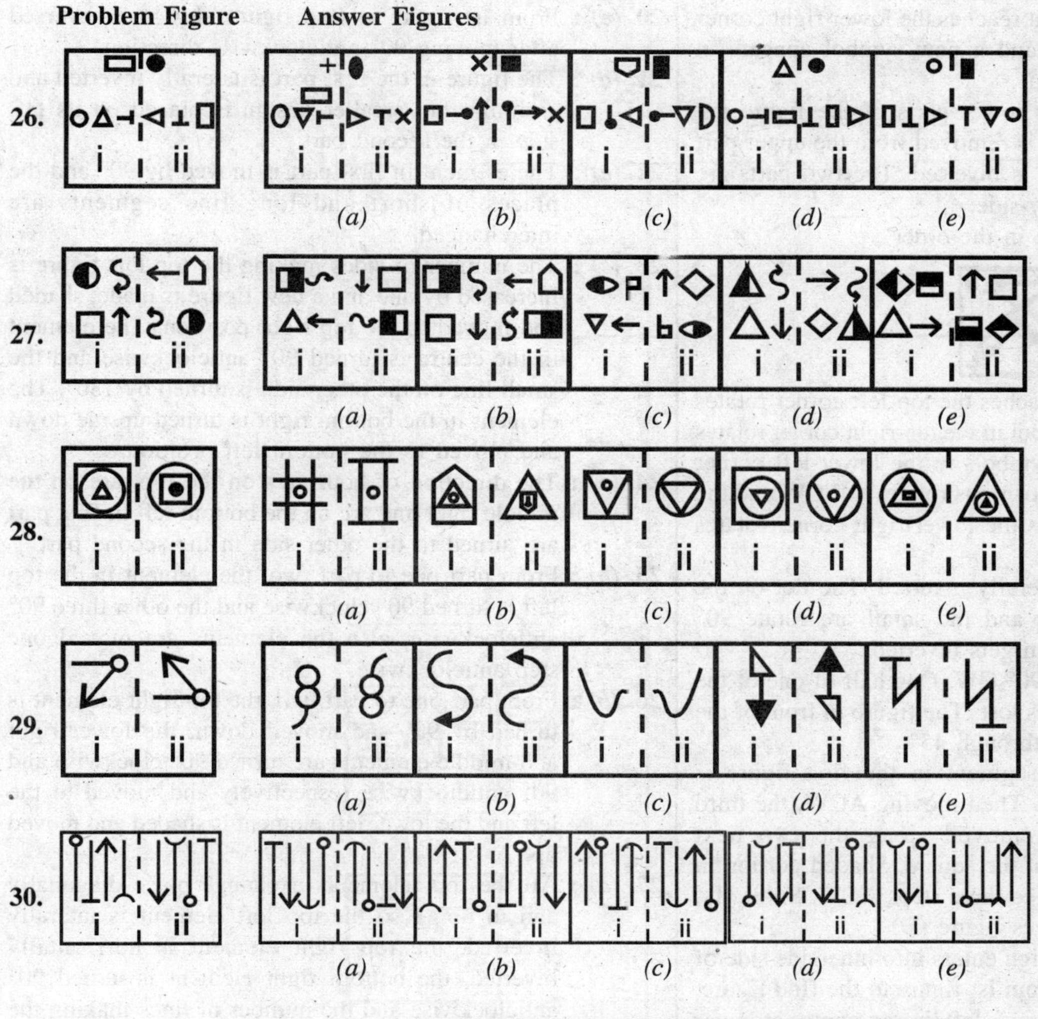

EXPLANATORY ANSWERS

1. *(b)* : The R.H.S. figure is fitted into the L.H.S. figure and the resulting figure is rotated 90° CW.

2. *(b)* : The figure rotates 45° ACW, the arrow changes to a curved line with dotted ends and the curved lines with dotted ends get converted to arrows.

3. *(d)* : The top left symbol rotates 90° ACW while all other symbols rotate 90° CW.

4. *(e)* : The black portion in top layer moves one step to the right; the black portions in the middle and the lower layers move one step to the left and the dot moves one step upwards.

5. *(d)* : The first and second symbols from the left interchange positions and the other two symbols also interchange positions. The symbol that reaches the first position from the left gets laterally inverted; the symbol that reaches the second position gets inverted, the third symbol rotates 90° CW and the fourth symbol gets replaced by a new one.

6. *(d)* : The single figure is replaced by a figure similar to the double figures and the double figures are replaced by figures similar to the single figure.

7. *(e)* : The figure rotates 135° ACW; a 'T' appears diagonally opposite to the black leaf and a 'Y' appears diagonally opposite to the white leaf.

8. *(c)* : The square rotates through 45°. The arrow moves 90° ACW and the pin moves 45° ACW.

9. *(b)* : The figure rotates through 180° and three lines forming a zig-zag, get attached to its lower end.

10. *(d)* : The symbols move in the order

The symbol that reaches the central position rotates 90° CW and its arc gets inverted; the 'P' shaped symbol rotates through 180°; the 'C' shaped symbol rotates 90° CW; the 'S' Shaped symbol gets laterally inverted and the fifth symbol gets replaced by a new one.

45°, the symbol that reaches the lower right corner rotates 90° ACW and a new symbol appears in middle-left position.

11. *(e)* : The upper and the lower parts of the figure get separated. Shading is removed from the upper part and the lower part is inverted. The two parts are then placed side-by-side.

12. *(a)* : The symbols move in the order

The symbol that reaches the top-left corner rotates 90° ACW; the symbol in the top-right corner rotates through 45°; the symbols in the lower-left corner and in the central positions rotates 90° CW and the symbol that reaches the lower-right corner rotates through 90°.

13. *(e)* : The figure gets laterally inverted. The dot on the larger arc, the pin and the small arc rotate 90° ACW. Also, the pin gets inverted.

14. *(c)* : The figure rotates 90° CW. One half of one of the lines on the arrow is lost. The figure in front of the arrowhead rotates through 45°.

15. *(d)* : The missing line segment in the first figure is replaced in second. Then moving ACW, the third line segment is removed along the two next consecutive sides of the square. Shaded portion in the first figure moves three steps ACW. Similarly, the third figure gives figure (D).

16. *(b)* : The uppermost design enters into innerside side of the lower design from Ist figure to the IInd figure.

17. *(a)* : In element I to II upper left design comes at lower right rotating 135° C.W. Middle design goes to upper left and rotates 90° CW. While lower right design goes to middle and it also rotates 90° C.W. The same changes occur in option A.

18. *(e)* : In element I to II and ellipse is put in the triangle. Similarly in option E a triangle is put in the ellipse.

19. *(d)* : From first figure to IInd figure, design is divided into four equal parts and right side of the upper portion becomes shaded.

20. *(e)* : From Ist figure to IInd figure, design is reversed after moving 90° anticlockwise direction.

21. *(d)* : The figure in the first part is laterally inverted and a similar but smaller design is placed on its left side in the second part.

22. *(e)* : The element in first part is moved by 90° and the places of short and long line segments are interchanged.

23. *(c)* : The number of sides making the top left figure is increased by one and a new figure is made, shaded and moved to the top right position. The element in the centre is turned 90° anticlockwise and the small line on the other side is turned by 180°. The element in the bottom right is turned upside down and moved to the bottom left position.

24. *(a)* : The direction of both arcs on the top, are on the middle right and arc on the bottom left in first part are turned to the other side in the second part.

25. *(b)* : From part one to part two, the element in the top left is turned 90° clockwise and the other three 90° anticlockwise, also the elements are moved one step anticlockwise.

26. *(b)* : From part one to part two, the top right element is turned by 90° and moved down, the lower right and middle elements are turned 90° clockwise and 90° anticlockwise respectively and moved to the left and the lower left element is shaded and moved up.

27. *(a)* : All the four elements exchange place diagonally and in doing so the top left element is laterally inverted, the top right element is horizontally inverted, the bottom right element is turned 90° anticlockwise and the number of lines making the element in bottom left is increased by one.

28. *(e)* : The innermost figure is removed and the new innermost figure also encloses the other two figures. The innermost and smallest figure is then shaded.

29. *(b)* : The design in the first part is horizontally inverted in the second.

30. *(b)* : All the elements in the first part are turned upside down and then 1st, 2nd, 3rd and 4th positioned elements become 3rd, 4th, 1st and 2nd elements in the second part.

❑❑❑

24 ODD MAN OUT

In this type of reasoning a statement is followed by inferences drawn from it. From these inferences only one definitely follows which is the hidden proposition of the sentence and it is the right answer to the question.

EXERCISE

Directions (Qs. 1–10) : *In each question below five figures are given. Four are similar in a certain way and so form a group. The question is— which one of the figures* ***does not*** *belong to that group?*

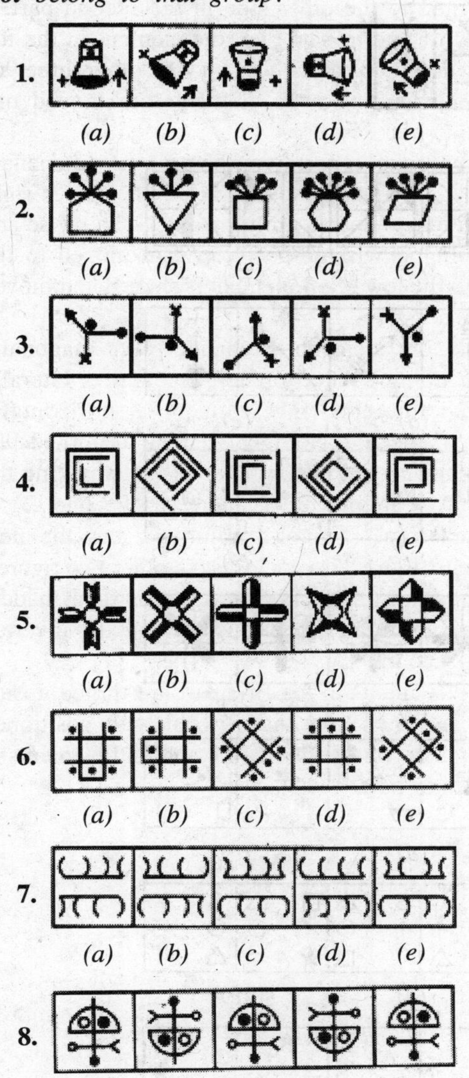

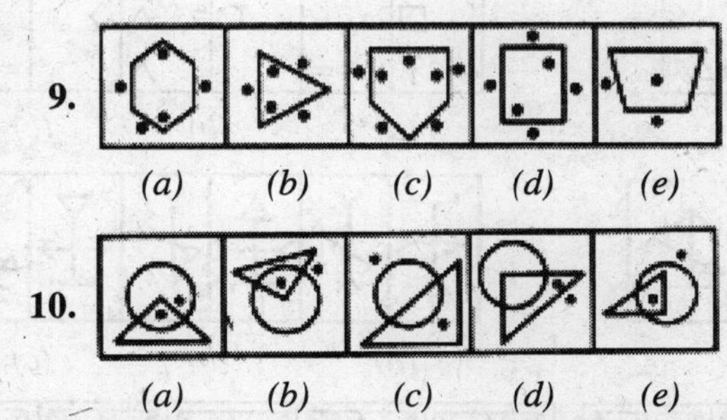

Directions (Qs. 11–20) : *In each of the following questions, in four out of the five figures, element I is related to element II in the same particular way. Find out the figure in which the element I is* ***not*** *so related to element II.*

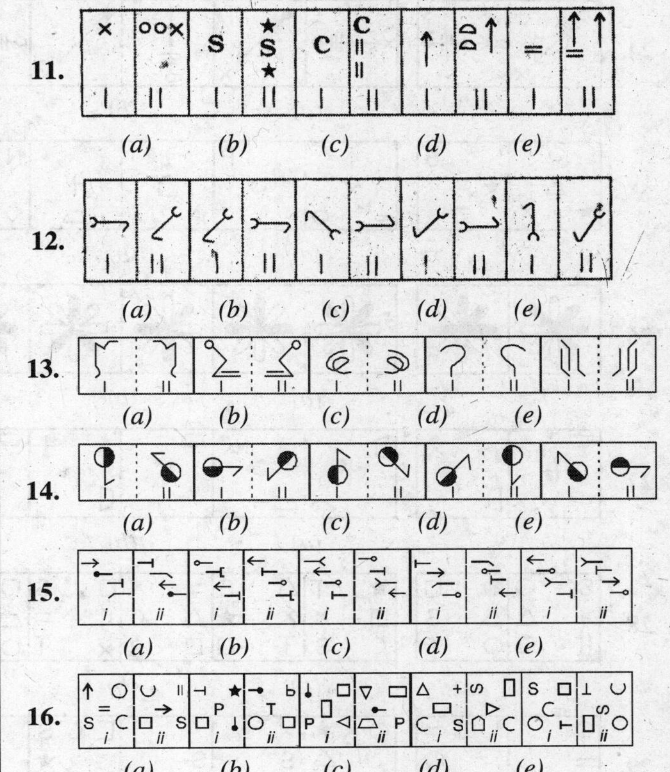

17.

(a) (b) (c) (d) (e)

18.

(a) (b) (c) (d) (e)

19.

(a) (b) (c) (d) (e)

20.

(a) (b) (c) (d) (e)

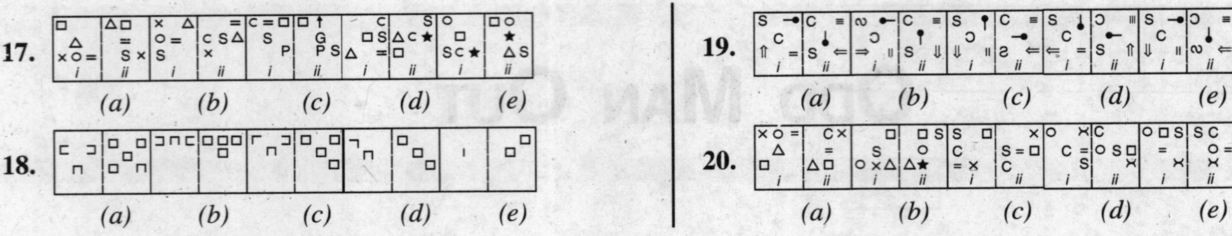

Directions (Qs. 21–30) : *In each of the following questions, a related pair of figures (unnumbered) is followed by five numbered pairs of figures. Out of these five, four have relationship similar to that in the unnumbered pair. Only one pair of figures does not have similar relationship. Select that pair of figures which does not have a similar relationship to that in the unnumbered pair. Number of that pair is your answer.*

21.

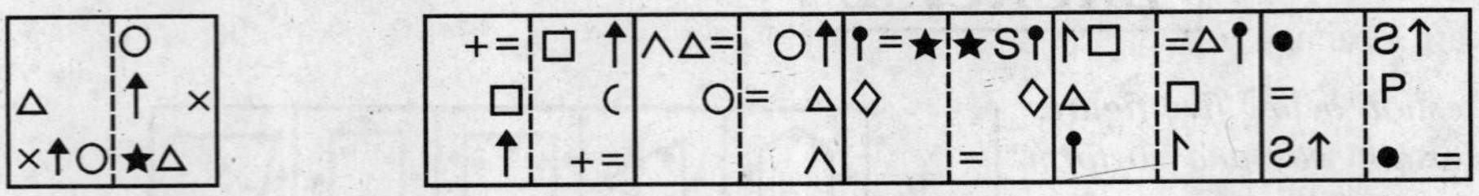

(a) (b) (c) (d) (e)

22.

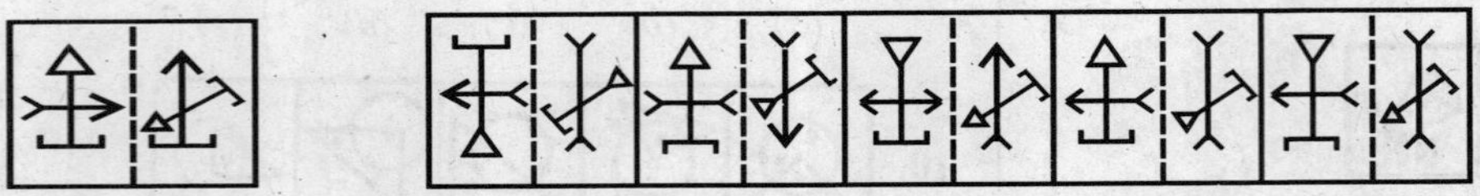

(a) (b) (c) (d) (e)

23.

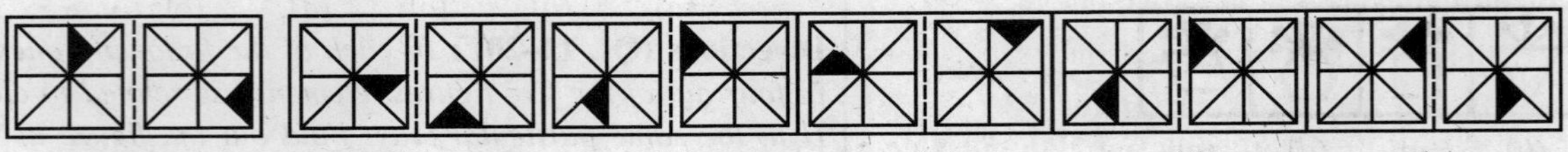

(a) (b) (c) (d) (e)

24.

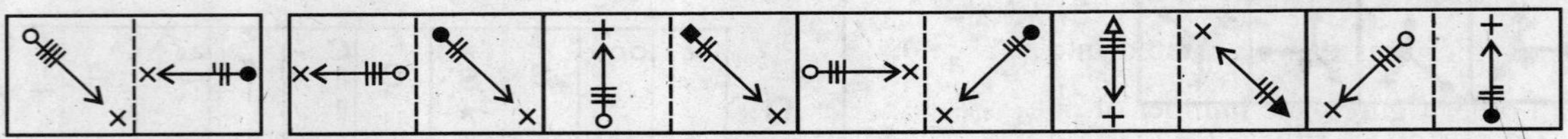

(a) (b) (c) (d) (e)

25.

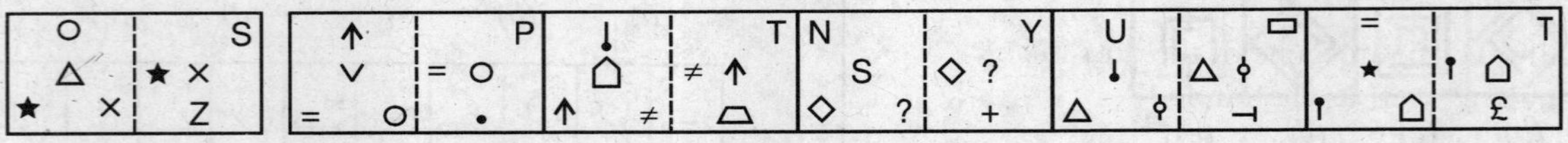

(a) (b) (c) (d) (e)

26.

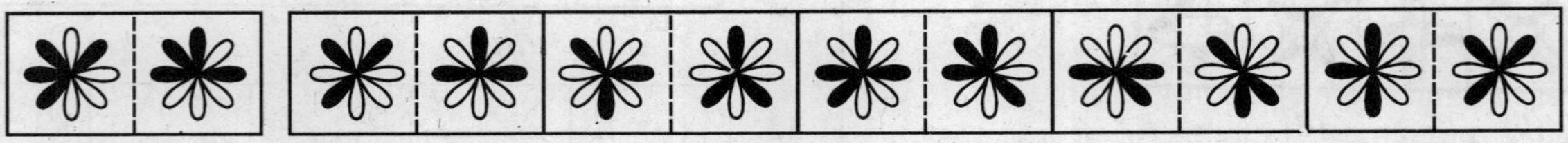

(a) (b) (c) (d) (e)

27.

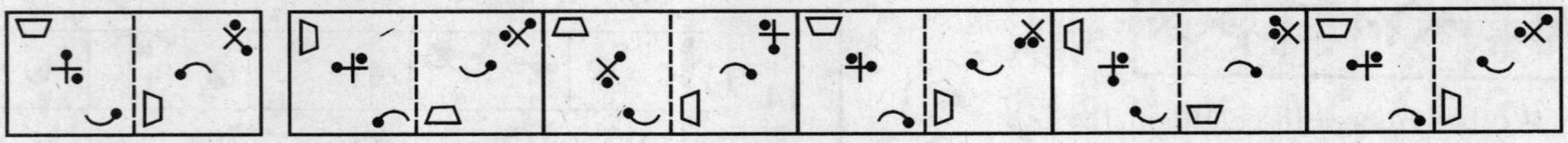

(a) (b) (c) (d) (e)

28.

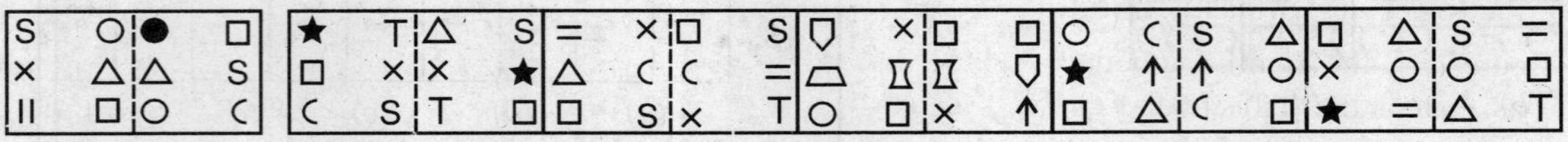

(a) (b) (c) (d) (e)

29.

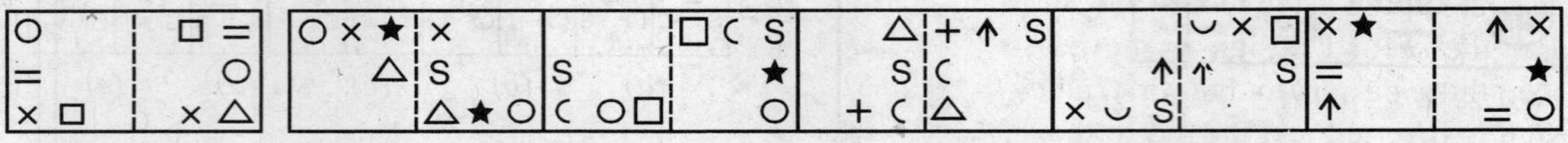

(a) (b) (c) (d) (e)

30. 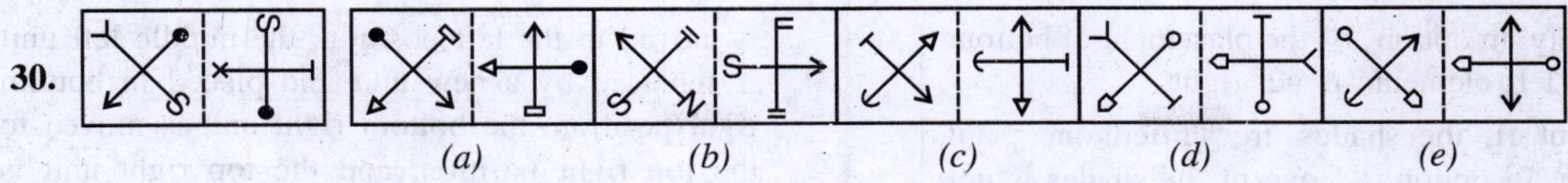

EXPLANATORY ANSWERS

1. *(d)* : In all other figures, the arrow and the + sign lie towards the black end of the main figure.

2.*(a)* : The pins, equal in number of sides in the main figure are attached to the midpoint of a side of the main figure in case of figures (B), (C), (D) and (E). In figure (A), these pins are attached to a vertex of the main figure.

3.*(c)* : In all other figures, the dot appears in the angle formed between the arrow and the pin.

4.*(a)* : All other figures can be rotated into each other. (In each figure except figure (A), the middle element is obtained by rotating the outer element through 90° CW and the inner element is obtained by rotating the middle element through 90° CW).

5.*(c)* : All other figures have at least one line of symmetry.

6.*(c)* : All other figures can be rotated into each other.

7.*(e)* : In each one of the other four figures, four arcs are curved towards the left and four other arcs are curved towards the right.

8.*(c)* : All other figures can be rotated into each other.

9.*(d)* : In all other figures, the number of dots outside the main figure is one more than the number of dots inside the main figure.

10.*(a)* : In all other figures, one of the dots lies outside the triangle as well as the circle.

11.*(e)* : Except in figure (B), in all other figures, from element I to II two new designs are added in one side of the main design.

12.*(c)* : In each figure from element I to II the main design rotates through 135° clockwise or anticlockwise. Except in figure (C), in all other figures, the smaller line segment moves to other side from element I to II.

13.*(a)* : In all other figures the element II can be obtained by the lateral inversion of the element I. In figure (A), the lower design has not been inverted.

14.*(b)* : In figure (B), the small segment is on the same side as that of the half shaded circle in both the elements.

15.*(d)* : The first design is inverted and moved to third place, the second design is moved to the fourth place, third design to the first place and fourth design is inverted and moved to the second place. Option (D) violates this.

16.*(b)* : In all other options the top-left element is moved to the centre with 90° clockwise rotation. Here, it is rotated anticlockwise.

17.*(d)* : All the designs are shifted in a set pattern one behind the other. The fourth design in all others is changed and placed in the last. Here, the fifth and last designs are changed.

18.*(a)* : In all other pair of figures, all incomplete squares in the first elements are completed and an extra square is added in the second element.

19.*(a)* : From element I to element II, the 'S' shape is turned 90° clockwise and moved down, the double arrow shape '⇒' is turned 90° clockwise and moved to the right, the two parallel lines one turned by 90°; one parallel line is added and all three lines are moved up, the line with a dot is turned 90° clockwise and moved to the centre and the 'C' shape in the centre is turned by 180° and moved to top left position. Here, the double arrow is turned anticlockwise.

20.*(c)* : Starting from one unit, all units are moved in a set pattern, the places of last two units moved are interchanged and the last unit is then made new. Here, no changes are made in the last two units.

21.*(d)* : From element I to element II clockwise the first unit is moved 2 steps forward, the second unit 1 step forward, the third unit 2½ steps forward and the fourth unit 3 steps forward. In option 'D' the third unit violates the rule.

22.*(e)* : From element I to element II, the horizontal bar is turned 135° anticlockwise and the unit at the lower end is turned by 180°. The vertical bar is turned 90° anticlockwise and the unit at the lower end is turned by 180°. In option 'E' one more unit at the top is turned by 180°.

23.*(e)* : In element II, the shade is moved two sections clockwise and shifted from the centre to the base. In option 'E' it is not so.

24.*(a)* : In element II, the arrow is turned 135° clockwise. In option 'A' it is turned anticlockwise.

25.*(b)* : From element I to element II, the bottom right unit and bottom left unit are moved to the centre and middle left position respectively. The other two units are removed and two new elements are placed in the top right and bottom centre position respectively. In option 'B' the placement of bottom right and left elements is not right.

26.(c) : In element II, the shades are shifted one petal clockwise. In option 'C' one of the shades is not moved.

27.(b) : From element I to element II, the unit on the top left is turned 90° anticlockwise and moved to the bottom right corner position, the unit in the centre is turned 135° anticlockwise and moved to the top right position, and the unit in the bottom right is turned by 180° and moved to the centre. In option 'B', the middle unit is turned 135° clockwise.

28.(a) : From element I to element II, a new unit is placed in the top left position, the top left unit is moved to the middle right position, the middle right unit is moved to the left position, the middle left unit is replaced by a new unit and placed in bottom right position, the bottom right unit is moved to the top right position, and the top right unit is moved diagonally to replace the bottom left unit. In option 'A', the middle left unit is not changed when moved to the bottom right position.

29.(e) : From element I to element II starting anticlockwise, the first and second units are moved 1½ steps clockwise respectively, the third unit ½ step anticlockwise, the fourth unit 2 steps clockwise, and a new unit is placed ahead of the first unit. Option 'E' violates the rules.

30.(e) : In element II, the cross is turned 135° clockwise and then the positions of left and top units on the cross are interchanged. In option 'E' it is not so.

❑❑❑

ENGLISH LANGUAGE

1 COMPREHENSION PASSAGES

ENGLISH LANGUAGE COMPREHENSION

The objective of language comprehension test is to ascertain the ability of the candidates to understand the passage properly. Therefore candidates are required to take notice of the following points:

1. Read the full passage very attentively and intelligently.
2. Try to comprehend the gist of it.
3. Make a mental note of all the important details and points given in the passage.
4. Read the passage for the second time in case you have not been able to understand it satisfactorily.
5. Divide the time proportionately for all the passages.
6. Answer the questions on the basis of facts, as given in the paragraph.
7. Don't waste much time in answering the questions of any one passage.
8. Check all the answers once again, very carefully, to see whether any question is left unanswered by mistake.

MODEL QUESTIONS (FOR PRACTICE)

Directions: *Each of the following passages is followed by five questions. Read the passage carefully and then answer the questions that follow each. For each question, four probable answers A, B, C and D are given. Only one out of these is correct. Choose the correct answer.*

PASSAGE-1

The use of words like 'welcome', 'thank you', 'please', etc., at the right moment reflects a polite nature. The civic sense also lies within the scope of good manners. We should not shout or talk loudly in public places like hospitals and libraries and create disturbance. We should not cheat people or make fun of them. Cleanliness is also necessary. We must not throw the waste on roads and make use of dustbins. We should not harm the public property as it belongs to all of us. While in a queue, discipline should be maintained. We must give fair chance to others.

1. Expressions like 'welcome' 'thank you' and 'please' reflect
   A. happiness B. discipline
   C. civic sense D. polite nature
2. While in a library, we should
   A. respect others B. avoid arguments
   C. talk in low tone D. be courteous
3. A public property belongs to
   A. nobody
   B. all of us
   C. government
   D. one who maintains it
4. Discipline is
   A. the rule of proper conduct or action
   B. the rule of road sense
   C. making use of dustbins
   D. forming a queue
5. The most appropriate title for this passage would be
   A. Polite Nature B. Courtesy
   C. Good Manners D. Civic Sense

PASSAGE-2

There is an old proverb 'Early to bed and early to rise makes a man healthy and wise.' I am in the habit of getting up early in the morning and have formed the habit of taking long morning walks in the past two years. It is a light exercise and best for physical fitness. The morning air which is fresh and pure is beneficial for the lungs. The early rays of the rising sun are good for healthy skin. 'Health is wealth' and doctors also recommend morning walk to their patients for gaining sound health and freshness of energy.

1. What is good for lungs?
   A. Sunrays B. Fresh air
   C. Sound sleep D. Light exercise
2. What is a light exercise?
   A. Early to bed B. Early to rise
   C. Morning walk D. Gaining sound health
3. What is good for skin?
   A. Fresh air
   B. Morning air
   C. Morning walk
   D. Rising sun's rays
4. What is best for physical fitness?
   A. Light exercise
   B. Long morning walk
   C. Early to rise
   D. Fresh and pure air
5. Long morning walk
   A. bring sound sleep
   B. ensures physical fitness
   C. ensures healthy skin
   D. keeps healthy, wealthy and wise

PASSAGE-3

Mahatma Gandhi lived a splendid long life and has set great moral standards before us. He showed to the world the true way to peace. He wished to see India prosper but he became a martyr for the noble cause of Hindu-Muslim unity at the time of partition when a religious fanatic, Nathuram Godse, shot him dead on January 30, 1948. His last words were 'Hey Ram'. He lived and died for his country and countryman.

1. Mahatma Gandhi showed the world the true way to
A. prosperity B. love
C. truth D. peace

2. Mahatma Gandhi became a martyr for the noble cause of
A. truth
B. non-violence
C. freedom of India
D. Hindu-Muslim unity

3. Mahatma Gandhi was shot dead
A. before India achieved independence
B. by a mad man
C. by an intolerant religious person
D. by a non-religious person

4. Mahatma Gandhi set great moral standards. It means
A. he was a great religious teacher
B. he was a great moralist
C. he made India morally stronger
D. moral was everything to him

5. Gandhiji lived and died for his country and countryman. It means
A. he was born in India and died in India
B. he was a patriot
C. he was a great moralist
D. he sacrified his life for India and her people

PASSAGE-4

On one hot day a crow felt very thirsty. He flew from one place to another in search of water. After long hours of labour he found a pitcher. Eagerly, he perched on the mouth of the pitcher. He found that the water was at the bottom of the vessel. He tried his best to dip his beak but did not succeed. He did not know what to do. Suddenly some pebbles lying nearby gave him an idea. One by one he dropped the pebbles with his beak into the pitcher. The level of water slowly came up to the mouth of the pitcher. The crow then drank the water and quenched his thirst.

1. The crow found a pitcher
A. as it flew
B. after many hours of labour
C. full of water
D. which was empty

2. What is the moral of the passage?
A. No pains, no gains
B. God helps those who help themselves
C. Necessity is the mother of invention
D. Try and try again, you will succeed at last

3. The crow flew from place to place
A. in search of pitcher
B. in search of pebbles
C. in search of water
D. in search of a vessel

4. The pitcher, the crow found
A. was full of water
B. was dry
C. had little water in the bottom
D. had water up to its mouth

5. As the crow dropped pebbles into the pitcher, what happend?
A. The pitcher broke down
B. The water leaked one of the pitcher
C. The level of water into the pitcher rose up slowly
D. Water level immediately rose to the mouth of the pitcher

PASSAGE-5

Once upon a time a crane and a fox lived in a forest. They were good friend. One day the fox invited the crane to a feast. He made a tasty food and served it before the crane on a plate. The crane could not eat anything because of the long beak. But the fox licked all his food. The crane felt insulted. He decided to teach the fox a lesson. Next day he invited the fox. He prepared the same tasty food and placed it in front of the fox inside a narrow glass. The crane ate easily while the fox looked on. Now, it was the fox's turn to remain hungry.

1. What is the moral of the passage?
A. Beware of the wicked
B. One good turn deserves another
C. Be contented with what you have
D. Tit for tat

2. The crane could not eat tasty food because the
A. food was served in a shallow plate
B. food was very hot
C. food was served in a long jar
D. crane was not hungry

3. The fox had to remain hungry because
A. the food served was not enough in quantity
B. the food was served inside a narrow glass
C. the food served was not tasty
D. the food was all liquid

4. Why did the crane feel insulted?
A. Because he was invited to feast but he could not eat anything
B. Because the food was served in a shallow plate and he could not eat
C. Because the food was too hot
D. Because the fox gulped all the food quickly

5. The crane successfully taught a lesson to the fox when he invited the fox to a feast and served the food
A. in a narrow glass
B. in a large plate
C. in a broken plate
D. in a long jar

PASSAGE-6

The family set down at the table and began to talk about the summer holidays. They had to decide a place to visit during the vacation. Should they go to their village or to a hill station? The parents preferred the village while the children wished to go the hill station. After few moments of discussion the elders decided to visit both the places. First they shall go to the village for a week and then stay at the hill station for the remaining days. For the first time the family shall be together during the holidays. The children were happy with the holiday plan.

1. The purpose for which the family set down at the table was
   A. to decide a place to visit during the vacation
   B. to educate the children how to carry articles during a visit to a hill station
   C. to decide the date when they should start their journey
   D. to tell the children that they will visit a hill station during this vacation
2. The final plan was to visit
   A. their village
   B. a hill station
   C. their village as well as a hill station
   D. their home town
3. The final decision was made by
   A. the boys B. the girls
   C. the women D. the elders
4. They decided first to go to their village and stay there for
   A. a day B. a week
   C. ten days D. a fortnight
5. Why were children happy?
   A. Because a hill station was included in their holiday plan
   B. Because a visit to their village was excluded from their holiday plan
   C. Because their choice prevailed
   D. Because they were going all alone to the hill station

PASSAGE-7

Once Govind intended to go on pilgrimage with his family. He asked Mirind to accompany. But for his trade's reason, he did not go with him. So Govind thought it safe to leave the box of his jewellery with him, as it was dangerous to leave it in a lone house or take it on the journey. So he went to him with the box. He took him to a lonely place under a tree and handed it over to him. He told Mirind, "Keep it safe with you. I shall return from the journey after six month then I shall take it back from you." Mirind said, "Don't worry, I shall keep it as safe as own."

1. Govind intended to go
   A. for a business trip
   B. to a hill station
   C. on a long journey to a sacred place
   D. to his home town for a long period
2. Why did Govind leave his box of jewellery with Mirind?
   A. Because it was not safe to take the box with him on a long journey
   B. Because Mirind was his fast friend
   C. Because the box was very heavy
   D. Because his house was unsafe
3. Why did Govind take Mirind to a lonely place?
   A. To tell him that the box contained valuable jewellery
   B. So that no third person could see box
   C. To show him what was within the box
   D. To tell him that the box will remain with him
4. Where did Govind hand over the box of jewellery to Mirind?
   A. At Mirind's house
   B. At his own house
   C. In a lonely place
   D. In a lonely place under a tree
5. It was not safe to leave the box in a lone house. Here the word 'lone house' means
   A. a house in a deserted place
   B. a house where none lives
   C. a house without door and lock
   D. a house near the forest

PASSAGE-8

Zahir-ud-din Babar was the first Mughal emperor of India. A descendent of Timur on father's side and Changez Khan on his mother's side, Babar was a brave warrior. After defeating Ibrahim Lodhi in the First Battle of Panipat in 1526 he entered Delhi and soon gained control over Agra. After many more battles with Rajputs he extended his empire over Punjab, Uttar Pradesh and north Bihar. He died at a young age of 48 years in 1530 at his capital Agra without getting much time to consolidate his victories.

1. Zahir-ud-din Babar was the first
   A. Muslim ruler of India
   B. Mughal ruler of India
   C. Afghan ruler of India
   D. Turk ruler of India
2. Babar was born in the years
   A. 1480 B. 1482
   C. 1492 D. 1962
3. Babar first occupied
   A. Punjab B. Agra
   C. Delhi D. Panipat
4. Babar was a brave warrior. Here brave warrior means
   A. courageous soldier
   B. a kind hearted soldier
   C. a clever fighter
   D. a victorious general
5. Babar extended his empire over Punjab and Uttar Pradesh after many more battles with the
   A. Afghans B. Rajputs
   C. Mughals D. Lodhies

PASSAGE-9

Our National Flag is tricolour. It has three equal horizontal strips. The strip at the top is saffron, in the middle is white and at the bottom is green. The ratio of width to length of the flag is 2 : 3. In the centre of the white strip is a wheel in navy blue. The wheel represents the *chakra.* Its design is similar to the wheel which appears on the abacus of the Sarnath Lion Capital of Ashoka. Its diameter approximates to the width of the white strip. The wheel has 24 spokes. It was adopted by Constituent Assembly on July 22, 1947. We love our national flag. We respect it. We are ready to sacrifice our life to protect its honour. It represents the nation. So it is a symbol of national honour.

1. In our national flag the wheel is located in the centre of
- A. saffron strip
- B. white strip
- C. green strip
- D. blue strip

2. In our national flag which of the strips is at the bottom in our national flag
- A. blue
- C. saffron
- B. white
- D. green

3. Why do we love our national flag?
- A. Because it is tricolour
- B. Because it has three strips
- C. Because it has a wheel at the centre
- D. Because it is a symbol of national honour

4. Our national flag was approved by
- A. President
- B. Lok Sabha
- C. Parliament
- D. Constituent Assembly

5. The diameter approximates to the width of the white strip. Here the word 'approximates' means
- A. is more or less equal
- B. is exactly equal
- C. is not equal
- D. is related

PASSAGE-10

Distance in large cities are long. All the people do not have their own means of transport. They have to depend upon the state or private buses. The number of bus users is very large. Every bus stop is, therefore, crowded. The number of buses is not adequate. Thus people suffer the torture of long wait at the bus stop. Some bus stops are quite orderly. People form queues and get into the buses turn by turn. However, often this order is forgotten and confusion spreads when the bus comes and the law of jungle prevails.

1. Why are the bus stops crowded?
- A. Because they are small is size
- B. Because the number of passengers is very large
- C. Because they are situated at some busy centre
- D. Because people do not form queues

2. Long wait at the bus stop is the result of
- A. over-crowding in the buses
- B. late running of buses
- C. shortage of buses
- D. slow speed of buses

3. Some bus stops are quite orderly where
- A. there is no crowd
- B. the number of buses is adequate
- C. people do not have to wait for long
- D. people form queues and enter the buses one by one

4. Most of the people who travel by buses are
- A. non-working
- B. do not have their own vehicles
- C. have to go a long distance
- D. live in large cities

5. What happens when people do not have their own transport?
- A. They have to wait for a bus at a bus stop
- B. They have to depend upon the state or private buses
- C. They have to travel long distances
- D. They form queues and get into buses one by one

ANSWERS

	1	2	3	4	5
Passage 1.	D	C	B	A	C
Passage 2.	B	C	D	B	B
Passage 3.	D	D	C	B	D
Passage 4.	B	C	C	C	C
Passage 5.	D	A	B	B	A
Passage 6.	A	C	D	B	A
Passage 7.	C	A	B	D	B
Passage 8.	B	B	C	A	B
Passage 9.	B	D	D	D	A
Passage 10.	B	C	D	B	B

●●●

2 ENGLISH GRAMMAR

PARTS OF SPEECH

Part of speech	Definition or Function	Examples
Noun	Name of a person, place, animal, quality or thing	Ram, boy, dog pen, sun, Delhi, truth, honesty
Pronoun	Used in place of a noun	I, you, he she, they
Articles & Determiners	Points out indefinite and definite nouns	a, an, the, few, some
Adjective	Describes a noun or pronoun	big, honest, wooden valuable, quiet, deep, soft, narrow
Adverb	Describes a verb, an adjective or another adverb	silently, widely, softly, quietly, very, carefully
Verb	Tells about action or state of something or someone	is, am, was, have, do, like, walk, work, make, throw, tell
Conjuction	Joins words, clauses or sentences	and, but, when, yet, while, else
Preposition	Links a noun or pronoun to another word	at, to, after, on for, under, over, with
Interjection	Expresses sudden feelings or emotions	Ah!, Alas!, oh!, ouch!, hi!, well!, Hurrah!

NOUNS

A word which denotes a person, a thing, an animal or a place is said to be a noun.

There are two noun numbers in English — the *Singular* and the *Plural*.

Singular Numbers : A noun that denotes one person or one thing, is said to be in the Singular number. For example — book, pencil, bird, dog, hen etc. are in singular number.

Plural Number : A noun that denotes more than one person or one thing is said to be in plural number. For example — boys, pens, lions, girls, men etc. are in plural number.

REMEMBER

Singular	*Plural*
Cat	Cats
Book	Books
Pen	Pens
Room	Rooms
Tree	Trees
Bus	Buses
Bush	Bushes
Box	Boxes
Glass	Glasses
Dish	Dishes
Judge	Judges
Tax	Taxes
Watch	Watches
Calf	Calves
Thief	Thieves
Knife	Knives
Scarf	Scarves
Wife	Wives
Leaf	Leaves
Wolf	Wolves
Half	Halves
Monarch	Monarchs
Roof	Roofs
Hoof	Hoofs
Gulf	Gulfs
Staff	Staffs
Radio	Radios
Bamboo	Bamboos
Folio	Folios
Hero	Heroes
Volcano	Volcanoes
Mango	Mangoes
Potato	Potatoes
Photo	Photos
Piano	Pianos
Baby	Babies
Fly	Flies

Singular	*Plural*
Country	Countries
Lady	Ladies
Boy	Boys
Monkey	Monkeys
Ox	Oxen
Child	Children
Man	Men
Woman	Women
Tooth	Teeth
Axis	Axes
Basis	Bases
Foot	Feet
Goose	Geese
Englishman	Englishmen
Radius	Radii
Vertex	Vertices
Stimulus	Stimuli

1. Note the plurals of the following nouns:

Singular	*Plural*	*Singular*	*Plural*
copy	copies	cry	cries
baby	babies	duty	duties
body	bodies	country	countries
family	families	diary	diaries
fly	flies	fairy	fairies
city	cities	spy	spies
army	armies	storey	storeys
bay	bays	monkey	monkeys

2. The following nouns do not undergo any change in plural form, in general.

Singular	*Plural*	*Singular*	*Plural*
deer	deer	sheep	sheep
thousand	thousand	pair	pair
hundred	hundred	score	score
dozen	dozen	gross	gross

Note: We can write—

(*a*) thousands of men; (*b*) two pairs of shoes; (*c*) dozens of mangoes; (*d*) scores of people etc. But—
(*a*) two thousand rupees; (*b*) three hundred men; (*c*) five dozen eggs, etc.

3. The following nouns are usually used in plural forms. They take a plural verb after them—

eatables	fetters	surroundings
riches	alms	spectacles
trousers	pants	scissors
premises	thanks	annals
congratulations	goods	shorts
tongs	pains	arms
breeches	(for troubles)	

4. The following are the nouns which are plural in appearance but are usually used in singular number. They are followed by a singular verb—

news	politics	physics
mathematics	economics	ethics
politics	classics	gallows
statistics	athletics	innings
mechanics	summons	mumps

5. Collective nouns often used as plurals—

public	police	cattle
audience	clergy	folk
people	poultry	nation
elite	gentry	glitterati

6. The nouns that are usually used in singular forms—

advice	hair	rice
fuel	alphabet	machinery
offspring	issue	furniture
mischief	stationery	luggage
bedding	information	abuse

7. Material nouns are always used in singular number—

gold	copper	milk
water	silk	wool

Note: They may be used in plural with a different meaning. copper coins (coppers), chains or fetters (irons), cans made of tin (tins).

GENDERS

The difference in sex is denoted by Gender in grammar. The various genders are as follows :

1. **Masculine Gender :** A noun that denotes a male is said to be of the masculine gender, as man, uncle, ox, boy etc.
2. **Feminine Gender :** A noun that denotes a female is said to be of feminine gender, as woman, aunt, princess, cow etc.
3. **Common Gender :** Nouns which denote both males and females are said to be of the common gender, as friend, cousin, person, parent, baby etc.
4. **Neuter Gender :** A noun that denotes the name of object without life is said to be of neuter gender, as file, table, pencil.

REMEMBER

Masculine	*Feminine*
Boy	Girl
Son	Daughter
Brother	Sister
Murderer	Murderess
Sorcerer	Sorceress
Son-in-law	Daughter-in-law
Father-in-law	Mother-in-law
Man-servant	Maid-servant
Land-lord	Land-lady
Bachelor	Maid
Gentleman	Lady
Monk	Nun
Earl	Countess
Lad	Lass
Sir	Madam
Duke	Dutchess

Masculine	*Feminine*
Emperor	Empress
Milk-man	Milk-maid
Pea-cock	Pea-hen
Step-father	Step-mother
Hero	Heroine
Viceroy	Vicerine
Mr.	Mrs.
Governor	Governess
Master	Mistress
Wizard	Witch
Heir	Heiress
Host	Hostess
Lion	Lioness
Mayor	Mayoress
Actor	Actress
Buck	Doe
Colt	Filly
Dog	Bitch
Horse	Mare
Count	Countess
Hunter	Huntress
Prince	Princess
Abbot	Abbess
God	Goddess
Author	Authoress
Ox	Cow
Widower	Widow
Grand-father	Grand-mother
He-goat	She-goat
Milk-man	Milk-woman
Bridegroom	Bride
Tiger	Tigress
Priest	Priestess
Poet	Poetess
Shepherd	Shepherdess
Nephew	Niece
Stag	Hind

PRONOUNS

The repetition of a noun in a sentence or a set of sentences is really boring. So, instead of repeating the noun, we can use a word (for that noun) called the pronoun.
"A pronoun is a word that we use instead of a noun".

Example:
This is *Sachin. He* plays cricket.
Note: *He* is the pronoun used in place of *Sachin.*

Kinds of Pronouns

1. **Personal pronouns :** A pronoun which is used instead of the name of a person is known as a 'Personal Pronoun'. A list of the 'Personal pronouns' is listed below :

I, my, mine, me, we (First Person)
You, your, yours (Second Person)
He, his, him, she, her, hers, it,
its, they, their, theirs, them (Third Person)

2. **Demonstrative, Indefinite and Distributive Pronouns:**

(a) Demonstrative Pronouns : Pronouns used to point out the objects to which they refer are called Demonstrative Pronouns.

Examples :
(i) *This* is a present from my uncle.
(ii) *These* are merely excuses.
(iii) Bembay mangoes are better than *those* of Bangaluru.

(b) Indefinite Pronouns : All pronouns which refer to persons or things in a general way and do not refer to any particular person or thing are called Indefinite Pronouns.

Examples :
(i) *Somebody* has stolen my watch.
(ii) *Few* escaped unhurt.
(iii) Did you ask *anybody* to come?

(c) Distributive Pronouns : Each, either, neither are called distributive pronouns because they refer to persons or things one at a time. For this reason they are always singular and followed by the verb in singular.

Examples :
(i) *Each* of the men received a reward.
(ii) *These* men received *each* a reward.
(iii) *Either* of you can go.

3. **Relative Pronouns :** A relative pronoun refers or relates to some noun going before, which is called its Antecedent.

Examples :
(i) I met Hari *who* used to live here.
(ii) I have found the pen *which* I had lost.
(iii) Here is the book *that* you lent me.

4. **Interrogative Pronouns :** These pronouns, are used for asking questions.

Examples :
(i) *Whose* book is this?
(ii) *What* will all the neighbours say?
(iii) *Which* do you prefer, tea or coffee?

Note : Interrogative pronouns can also be used in asking indirect questions. Consider the following examples :
(i) I asked *who* was speaking.
(ii) Tell me *what* you have done.
(iii) Say *which* you would like best.

Behaviour of the Pronouns

1. If three pronouns are used together in the same sentence they are arranged in the following order :

2	+	3	+	1
↓		↓		↓
Second Person		Third Person		First Person

Examples :

I, you and he must help *that* poor man. (Incorrect)

You, he and I must help *that* poor man. Correct)

2. When two or more singular nouns are joined by and, the pronoun used for them should be plural.

Examples :

Mohan and Sohan are friends. *They* play football. *They* live at Lajpat Nagar.

3. But if these nouns joined by and refer to the same person or thing, the pronoun used should be singular.

Examples :

(i) Delhi, the beautiful city and the capital of India, is famous for *its* historical monuments.

(ii) The manager and owner of the firm expressed *his* views on the demands of the workers.

4. When two nouns are used with as well as, the pronoun agrees with the first subject.

Examples :

(a) Mohan as well as his friends is doing *his* work.

(b) The students as well as their teachers are doing *their* work.

5. When two singular nouns joined by 'and' are preceded by *each* or *every,* the pronoun used must be singular and should agree in gender with the second noun.

Examples :

(a) Every man and every woman will do *her* best for the nation.

(b) Each boy and each girl went to *her* house.

6. When two nouns are joined by using 'with', the pronoun agrees with the noun coming before 'with'.

Examples :

(a) The boy with *his* parents has gone to see a movie.

(b) The children with *their* parents have gone to picnic.

7. When two different nouns are joined by either......... or; neither .... nor, the pronoun is used according to the number and gender of the second noun.

Examples :

(a) Either your sister or you have done *your* work.

(b) Neither the students nor the teacher was in *his* class.

8. The pronoun coming after '*than*' must be in the same case as that coming before '*than*'.

Examples :

(a) She plays better than *me.* (Incorrect)

She plays better than *I.* (Correct)

(b) His elder brother is more intelligent than *him.* (Incorrect)

His elder brother is more intelligent than *he.* (Correct)

9. 'Many a' always takes a singular pronoun and singular verb.

Example :

Many a soldier has met *his* death in the battle field.

10. 'Who', 'Whose', 'Whom' are used only for persons.

Examples :

(a) *Who* is knocking at the door?

(b) *Whose* pen is this?

(c) *What* do you want?

11. 'Which' is used for things.

Example : *Which* game do you like?

MULTIPLE CHOICE QUESTIONS

Directions: *In the following questions choose the correct options to fill the blanks.*

1. The place was so dirty that ..... wished to run away from there.

A. everybody B. anybody
C. few D. some

2. ..... was there to help me.

A. Somebody B. Anything
C. Anybody D. Nobody

3. Is there .... to eat?

A. some B. something
C. any D. few

4. ..... of the students were making a great noise.

A. Anyone B. Somebody
C. Many D. Nobody

5. ..... of the students can solve this sum.

A. Someone B. Anybody
C. Somebody D. None

6. ..... of us should try our best to make India a heaven.

A. Any B. Somebody
C. Anybody D. All

7. ..... of us do not know the real meaning of our lives.

A. Any B. Something
C. Several D. Many

8. My .... black.

A. hairs are B. hair is
C. hairs shall D. hair will

9. She saw two .... on the last Sunday.

A. thiefs B. theifs
C. thieves D. theives

10. My sister is a ....

A. bacheloress B. bachelor
C. unmaried D. spinster

11. One is supposed to do ....

A. our duty B. their duty
C. one's duty D. his duty

12. Take anything .... you want.
A. that B. which
C. than D. then

13. I cannot tolerate ....
A. separated you
B. your separation
C. separation from you
D. you separated

14. He is .... faithful partner.
A. Yours B. You
C. Your D. Your's

15. Ajay is more smart than ....
A. her B. hers
C. herself D. she

16. Vivek works harder than ....
A. me B. I
C. her D. his

17. They should help ....
A. the poor people B. the poor
C. the poor persons D. the poor peoples

18. .... are mad.
A. All his sons B. His all sons
C. Sons all his D. All sons his

19. The poor fellow .... to fate.
A. resigned
B. resigned himself
C. resigned itself
D. resigned themselves

20. Nobody will help you but ....
A. I B. me
C. ours D. his

21. It is a good chance, You must avail .....this opportunity.
A. of B. yourself of
C. for D. from

22. The person who is elected .... my relative.
A. is B. he is
C. his D. him

23. He made ....
A. yours mention B. mention of you
C. mention for you D. mention about you

24. .... I know, he is quite faithful.
A. As far as B. So far as
C. So far this D. So far so

25. It is a duty of a person to take .... for his family.
A. pain B. pains
C. pain-killers D. pained

26. She does not love .... husband.
A. his B. her
C. its D. their

27. Let .... work together.
A. him and me B. he and I
C. he and him D. I and me

28. Copper, Silver and Gold ....
A. each will do B. either will do
C. any one will do D. any will do

29. Jessica and Roma are very irregular .... habits.
A. in her B. in their
C. in its D. in every

30. One likes to enjoy .... who was a great poet.
A. The sonnets of Shakespeare
B. Shakespeare's sonnets
C. Sonnets
D. Shakespeare

ANSWERS

1	2	3	4	5	6	7	8	9	10
A	D	B	C	D	D	D	B	C	D
11	12	13	14	15	16	17	18	19	20
C	A	C	C	D	B	B	A	B	B
21	22	23	24	25	26	27	28	29	30
B	A	B	A	B	B	A	C	B	A

ARTICLES

The family of the articles has only three members. They are : A, An and The. However, they fall under two groups :
(a) Definite Article *(b)* Indefinite Article

'The' is known as definite article whereas 'a' and 'an' are known as indefinite articles.

Use of the Definite Article 'The'

'The' is used before

1. The superlative degree :
   He is the ablest man of the town.
   (ablest is a superlative degree)
2. The name of states, countries etc. having a descriptive name :
   (i) The J & K is a small state. (J & K is a descriptive name)
   (ii) He lives in the U.S.A. (U.S.A. is a descriptive name)
   (But the Delhi and the America are wrong because neither Delhi nor America is a descriptive name)
3. The names of the scriptures :
   The Gita is a holy book. (Gita is a scripture)

4. Name of newspapers :
The Tribune is published from Chandigarh.
5. Name of rivers, canals, seas, oceans, bays, gulfs, groups of islands etc. :
(i) The Ganga is a holy river.
(ii) The Indian Ocean is the deepest ocean.
(iii) The Persian Gulf is a narrow gulf.
6. The name of famous buildings :
The Taj is one of the best buildings in India.
7. The names of nationals, sects and communities:
(i) The English defeated the Germans in the World War.
(ii) The rich should help the poor.
(iii) The Hindus believe in the caste system.
8. Proper nouns used as common nouns :
(i) Kalidas is the Shakespeare of India.
(ii) Delhi is the London of India.
9. Famous historical events :
The Industrial Revolution changed the face of England.
10. The directions and the celestial bodies:
The sun rises in the east.
11. Titles : Akbar, the Great was loved by his subjects.

Do not use 'the'

1. Before languages :
The English is an international language. (Incorrect)
English is an international language. (Correct)
2. Before the names of games :
The hockey is a popular game. (Incorrect)
Hockey is a popular game. (Correct)

Use of the Indefinite Articles 'A' and 'An'

'A' is used before :

1. All singular common nouns beginning with a consonant :
(i) A boy sings a song.
(ii) A black and a white cow were grazing in the field.
2. If a word begins with a vowel but gives the sound of a consonant, 'a' should be used before it :
(i) He was helped in his work by a European.
(ii) He is a one-eyed man.
(iii) It is a useful work.

'An' is used as follows :

1. All singular common nouns beginning with a vowel (*i.e.*, a, e, i, o, u) :
(i) He is an artist.
(ii) He is an old man.
(iii) I intend to buy an umbrella.
2. If a word starts with a consonant but gives the sound of a vowel, "an" should be used before it :
(i) Brutus is an honourable man.
(ii) He is an honour to his profession.
(iii) He is an L.L.B.
(iv) He is an M.A.
(v) You will reach there in an hour.

Demonstratives, that, these and those

1. The demonstrative adjectives and pronouns are for objects nearby the speaker:
this (singular) those (plural)
and for objects far away from the speaker.
That (singular) those (plural)
2. Demonstratives are the only adjectives that agree in number with their nouns.
That hat is nice.
Those hats are nice.
3. When there is the idea of selection, the pronoun "one" (or "ones") often follows the demonstrative.
I want a book. I'll get this (one).
If the demonstrative is followed by an adjective, "one"(or "ones") must be used.
I want a book. I'll get this big one.

MULTIPLE CHOICE QUESTIONS

Directions: *In the following questions choose the correct options to fill the blanks.*

1. .... will have to be paid for this material.
A. Half rupee B. Half a rupee
C. A half rupee D. An half rupee

2. .... is taking keen interest in India.
A. The USA B. USA
C. An USA D. A USA

3. Only .... can save our country.
A. the Hitler B. a Hitler
C. Hitler D. an Hitler

4. I can run for ....
A. hundred miles B. the hundred miles
C. a hundred miles D. an hundred miles.

5. .... man-eater has been killed.
A. The B. A
C. An D. Either A or B

6. What .... fine idea!
A. the B. an
C. a D. No article

7. .... earth is moving around the sun.
A. An B. A
C. The D. No article

8. This is .... first example while I got.
A. the B. a
C. an D. No article

9. This is .... house which was built during earthquake.
A. a B. an
C. the D. No article

10. .... America is a rich country.
A. The B. An
C. A D. No article

11. .... U.S.A. is a developed country.
A. A B. An
C. The D. No article

12. .... Bible is a holy book.
A. A B. The
C. An D. No article

13. .... rich should help the poor.
A. The B. A
C. An D. No article

14. .... Gold is a costly metal.
A. The B. A
C. An D. No article

15. Kalidas is .... Shakespeare of India.
A. a B. an
C. the D. No article

16. I cannot do .... difficult work.
A. a such B. the such
C. such the D. such a

17. How foolish .... plan it is!
A. a B. an
C. the D. No article

18. An ink is .... useful article.
A. an B. a
C. the D. No article

19. There are .... husband and wife.
A. a B. an
C. the D. No article

20. He is learning .... French
A. the B. a
C. an D. No article

ANSWERS

1	2	3	4	5	6	7	8	9	10
B	A	B	C	D	C	C	A	C	D
11	**12**	**13**	**14**	**15**	**16**	**17**	**18**	**19**	**20**
C	B	A	D	C	D	A	B	D	D

ADJECTIVES & ADVERBS

An Adjective is a word which adds something to the meaning of a noun or a pronoun.

Mridula is an *intelligent* girl.
He has a *black* goat.
He is a *brilliant* student.
She is a *clever* girl.
It is a *beautiful* picture.

In the sentences given above, the words in italics are adjectives.

An Adverb is a word which qualifies the meaning of a Verb, an Adjective or another Adverb.

(*i*) He talks *slowly.*
(*ii*) He is a *very* good student.
(*iii*) He talks *very* slowly.

In sentence (*i*), *slowly* qualifies the verb *talks.*
In sentence (*ii*), *very* qualifies the adjective *good.*
In sentence (*iii*), *very* qualifies the adverb *slowly.*

Adjectives have three degrees of comparison :

1. **Positive Degree :** It expresses the common form of an adjective.
   Example :
   Ram is a *tall* boy.
   In the above sentence *tall* is an adjective and expresses the common form.
2. **Comparative Degree :** It expresses the more of the same form.
   Example :
   Ram is *taller* than Mahesh.
   In the above sentence *taller* is an adjective that expresses the more of the common form of the adjective *tall.*

"When and How to Use" Comparative Degree?

(a) Comparative Degree is used when two persons or two groups of persons or things are compared.
Examples :
(a) He is *wiser* than his younger brother.
(b) This glass is *cleaner* than the other.

(b) When two different qualities in the same person are compared, more is used instead of 'er' to form the comparative. The formula used in this case should be :
More + Positive Degree
She is *fairer* than polite. (Incorrect)
She is *more fair* than polite. (Correct)

(c) When selection of one out of two persons or things is meant, the degree of comparison is followed by of and *the.* is used before it.
Example :
Zia is abler of *the* two sisters.

(d) If two comparatives are used in the same sentence to impress upon an idea, both should be preceded by the definite article.
Examples :
(i) The higher you go, the cooler it is.
(ii) The more we get, the more we desire.

(e) When one person or thing is compared with another of the same kind, other is used after the comparative degree. In such sentences other is normally preceded by any or all.
Examples :
(i) Kalidas is greater than any dramatist.
(Incorrect)

Kalidas is greater than any other dramatist. (Correct)

(ii) Lead is heavier than all metals. (Incorrect)
Lead is heavier than all other metals. (Correct)

(f) Senior, junior, superior, inferior, prior, anterior (earlier than) and posterior (later than) are always followed by 'to'.

Examples :

(i) Ram is senior *to* Mohan by three years.
(ii) That pen is inferior *to* that.
(iii) He is junior *to* me in rank.
(iv) This event was posterior *to* that.

Note: Never use *than* after the above mentioned adjectives.

Important Information

(a) 'Preferable' is also used as an adjective of the comparative degree. As such, it is always followed by *to* and not *a*.
Death is preferable than dishonour. (Incorrect)
Death is preferable *to* dishonour. (Correct)

(b) To intensify the Degree of comparison, we use *far* or *much* before the comparative.

Examples :

(i) This book is *far* better than that.
(ii) His performance was *much* better than Mohan's.

Warning : Always avoid the use of double comparatives.

Don't say : Ram is more cleverer than his younger brother.

Say: Ram is cleverer than his younger brother.

3. **Superlative Degree :** It expresses the most of the common form of an adjective.

Example :

He is the ablest man of the town.

How and when to use the Superlative Degree?

(a) The Superlative Degree is used when more than two persons or things are compared.

(b) The Superlative Degree is generally preceded by 'the' and followed by 'of' in most of the cases or otherwise.

(c) When an adjective of the superlative degree is preceded by a Possessive Adjective or a Noun in the Possessive case, 'the' should not be used before it.

Example :

Which is Kalidas' best play?
It will be a blunder to use 'the' before the Superlative Degree in such cases.

Don't say : Which is Kalidas' the best play.

(d) To intensify the degree of comparison, *by far* is used before the superlative degree.

Example :

India is *by far* the most beautiful country of the world.

Note: Always avoid the use of double superlatives.

Don't say : He is the most strongest boy in the class.

Say : He is the strongest boy in the class.

Use of some Important Adjectives

1. (a) **'Some'** is used as follows :

(i) With countable nouns where it means— a little, a small quantity.
(ii) In a question which shows some request.

Examples :

(i) There is some water in the bottle.
(ii) Some of the students were absent yesterday.
(iii) Will you have some milk?
(iv) Will you buy some fruit for me?

(b) **'Any'** is used as follows :

(i) In negative sentences.
(ii) In interrogative sentences.
(iii) After 'Hardly', 'Scarcely' and 'Barely'.
(iv) After 'If'.

Examples :

(i) There is not any sugar in the pot.
(ii) We haven't any rice in the house.
(iii) I have hardly any money.
(iv) There are scarcely any plants in this field.
(v) If there is any danger, blow the whistle.

2. (a) **Older :** Older (and oldest) are used for persons animals and things. But 'Older' and 'Oldest' refer to the persons who do not belong to the same family.

Examples :

(i) Radha is older than Shyama.
(ii) John is the oldest member of the staff.
'Older' and 'Oldest' refer to the persons who do not belong to the same family.

(b) **Elder** (and **eldest**) are used in respect of the members of the same family like sons, daughters, brothers, sisters.

Examples :

(i) My elder sister is a lecturer.
(ii) Meenakshi is the eldest of the three sisters.

Note :

(i) 'Elder' is not followed by 'than'.
(ii) 'Elder' and 'Eldest' cannot be used for things.

3. (a) **'Few'** is negative and is the opposite of 'Many'. It means 'not many'.

(b) **'A few'** is positive and means 'some at least'. It is the opposite of 'None'.

(c) **'The few'** means 'minority' and suggests 'whether there is'.

Examples :

(i) We have few holidays in school.
(ii) Only a few boys will fail in the examination.

(iii) The few poems that he wrote are very popular.

4. (a) **Further** means 'something additional'.
(b) **Farther** means 'a greater distance'.
Examples :
(i) Further discussion will be held in the office of the principal.
(ii) Amritsar is farther from Delhi than Ambala.

5. (a) **Little** is negative. It means, 'not much', or 'hardly any'.
(b) **A little** is positive. It means 'some quantity'.
(c) **The little** denotes quantity. It means, 'not much but all that is, or whatever quantity there is'.
Examples :
(i) There is little hope of his success.
(ii) He knows a little of everything.
(iii) I have spent the little money I had.
(iv) The little knowledge of shoe-making proved very useful to me.

6. (a) **'Much'** expresses 'quantity'.
(b) **'Many'** expresses 'number'.
(c) **'Many a'**—'Singular noun' and 'Singular verb' are used with 'many a'.
Examples :
(i) There is not *much* water in the jug.
(ii) *Many* boys are absent today.
(iii) *Many* a battle has been fought on the soil of India.

7. (a) **'Less'** denotes 'in a small degree'.
(b) **'Fewer'** denotes 'number'.
Examples :
(i) He devotes less time to his studies.
(ii) There are no fewer than ten chairs in this room.

8. (a) **'Each'** is used for a single number of 'two persons' or 'things'.
(b) **'Every'** is used for a single number of 'many persons' or 'things'.
Examples :
(i) Each boy must take part in games.
(ii) There are only two poets. Each poet recited his poem.
(iii) Every man dies in this world.
(iv) Every man is expected to do his duty.

9. (a) **'Either'** means one of the two or both.
(b) **'Neither'** is negative of the either.
Examples :
(i) You may buy either of these two chairs.
(ii) Neither of them could speak on the stage.

10. (a) **'Later'** expresses 'late in time'.
(b) **'Latter'** means 'second in position or order'.
Examples :
(i) My father reached later than I expected.
(ii) The latter position was better than the former.

Use of some Important Adverbs

1. (a) Also, too, enough:
(i) He taught English. Also, he edited the school magazine
(ii) He is a writer and also he is a painter.
(iii) He is too obstinate to listen to any reason.
(iv) This is too difficult a piece for the junior students.
(v) Sarla was kind enough to help the poor.
(vi) He is brave enough to help the truth.
Note: 'Too' is used in a negative sense, but enough is used in a positive sense.

(b) Fairly and rather: Both suggest the meaning 'moderately'. But, mainly 'fairly' is used with the words that denote a positive meaning and rather is used with the words that denote a negative meaning:
(i) Rita did fairly well in that competition, but her performance was rather poor in sports.
(ii) Mona is fairly rich, but she is rather stingy.
Note: 'Rather' can also be used in a positive sense.
(i) This is a rather interesting job.
(ii) That boy is rather smart.

(c) Hardly, barely, scarcely: These words mostly convey the negative suggestions and are almost similar.
(i) I have hardly any strength now.
(ii) There was barely any supply to the township,
(iii) There were scarcely a hundred guests present.
Note: With slight variance in the meaning, the words given above convey the idea of 'very little', 'not enough', 'lack of quantity and number'.

(d) Yet, Still: These adverbs can often be used to connect the sentence units:
(i) He has been defeated many times in the contest; still he wants to be a competitor.
(ii) Mona was sick; yet she went on doing her work.

(e) Alone:
(i) He alone (none else) is capable of handling that fire,
(ii) He hunted all alone in the forest. (not in any company)

Special Note:
(a) Apart from their conventional positions the adverbs might be used in different positions with different meanings and angles.
(i) He had only four books.
(ii) John only contacted his friend in need.
(iii) He greeted me only.
(iv) Only he greeted me there.

(b) Inversion: Some adverbs can be inverted *i.e.* placed in the beginning of the sentence and then be followed by an interrogative form. The most common of these adverb are: so, seldom, never, nowhere, under no circumstances, hardly, scarcely etc.
(i) So big was the bus that it could not enter the narrow lane.
(ii) Hardly had he reached the station when he received the message.

MULTIPLE CHOICE QUESTIONS

Directions: *In the following questions choose the correct options to fill the blanks.*

1. The girl whom you met is the .... sister of Ravi.
A. eldest B. elder
C. older D. oldest

2. The historical place is ....
A. seeing worth B. worthy of seeing
C. worth seeing D. worthy seeing

3. These flowers smell ....
A. sweet B. sweetly
C. more sweetly D. sweetest

4. .... aspirant cannot pass the entrance examination.
A. Each B. Every
C. All D. No

5. Harivansh Rai .... second Shakespeare.
A. is a B. is
C. is the D. is an

6. .... student in the class got prizes.
A. Each and every B. Every and each
C. Every D. Never

7. It is .... picture than the one we saw last Monday.
A. interesting B. much interesting
C. more interesting D. most interesting

8. She is clever ....
A. that her mother is
B. as her mother is
C. to her mother is
D. than her mother is

9. They will get ....
A. Red, green and black paper
B. Red, green black paper
C. Red and green and black paper
D. Red green black paper

10. Health is .... wealth.
A. preferable to
B. more preferable than
C. more preferable to
D. most preferable then

11. .... water that was in the jug evaporated.
A. Little B. The little
C. Small D. A small

12. He has not sung .... songs.
A. much B. most
C. more D. many

13. Srishti has searched .... office.
A. whole the B. the whole
C. a whole D. some whole

14. Premchand was .... best and .... famous writer.
A. a, the most B. the, a most
C. the, more D. the, the most

15. William Shakespeare is famous as ....
A. a poet and a dramatist
B. a poet and dramatist
C. the poet and the dramatist
D. a poet and the dramatist

16. What does .... leader suggest?
A. other B. another
C. others D. anothers

17. He .... money.
A. has few B. have few
C. has little D. have little

18. The .... boys are rewarded.
A. first two B. two first
C. firsts two D. two's first

19. He is .... brave.
A. stronger than
B. stronger then
C. more strong then
D. more strong than

20. No sooner said ....
A. so done B. and done
C. then done D. but done

21. She returned .... than I had thought.
A. quickly B. more quicker
C. more quickly D. quicker

22. He is .... foolish person.
A. rather the B. a rather
C. rather a D. rather

23. This pen .... rupees.
A. costs twenty B. twenty costs only
C. costs only twenty D. only costs twenty

24. It is .... pride.
A. nothing else but
B. nothing else than
C. else nothing than
D. but

25. This tea is .... to drink.
A. too hot B. very hot
C. enough hot D. much hot

ANSWERS

1	2	3	4	5	6	7	8	9	10
A	C	A	B	A	C	C	C	A	A
11	**12**	**13**	**14**	**15**	**16**	**17**	**18**	**19**	**20**
B	D	B	D	B	B	C	A	D	C
21	**22**	**23**	**24**	**25**					
C	C	C	A	A					

DETERMINERS

Determiners are actually Adjectives. They are always followed by nouns.

Determiners are of the following kinds:

1. Demonstrative Determiners

this, that, these, those

2. Possessive Determiners

my, our, your, his, her, its, their

3. Quantitative Determiners

some, any, much, enough, sufficient, whole, a little, the little, little, all, both

4. Numerical Determiners

a few, some, few, the few, any, several, many, no, etc.

One, two, three ... (Cardinals)

First, second, third ... (Ordinals)

5. Distributive Determiners

either, neither

6. Articles

Indefinite: a, an

Definite: the

MULTIPLE CHOICE QUESTIONS

Directions: *In the following questions choose the correct options to fill the blanks.*

1. Give me .... rice.
A. some B. few
C. a few D. any

2. .... sheep grazing on the slope of the hill had gone away.
A. Any B. The few
C. This D. Much

3. Have you got .... magazines to read?
A. all B. much
C. some D. little

4. I have .... money that I want to spend on shares.
A. any B. much
C. less D. some

5. There is .... owl on the branch of the tree.
A. a B. the
C. an D. some

6. My brother is .... MBA.
A. a B. an
C. the D. any

7. Have you got .... cheese?
A. some B. many
C. a few D. few

8. No, I have not got .... cheese.
A. many B. few
C. any D. some

9. There is only .... milk left in the bottle.
A. enough B. few
C. much D. a little

10. There is .... hope of his recovery.
A. any B. little
C. many D. few

11. .... dogs were barking at the strangers.
A. Some B. Any
C. Much D. Less

12. The girl bought her father .... juice.
A. few B. some
C. any D. many

13. You should take .... honey everyday.
A. any B. many
C. a little D. a few

14. .... boy was punished by the teacher.
A. Either B. All
C. Any D. Many

15. .... girl was asked to join the army.
A. None B. Neither
C. All D. Any

16. .... water in the jug has been drunk by Mohan.
A. The little B. The few
C. A few D. Few

17. I shall play .... piano at the party.
A. some B. any
C. the D. few

18. .... labourers were found dead in the mine.
A. Any B. Fewer
C. Many D. Less

19. Could I borrow .... umbrella?
A. our B. your
C. yours D. my

20. My brother is standing in the .... row.
A. any B. many
C. some D. first

ANSWERS

1	2	3	4	5	6	7	8	9	10
A	B	C	D	C	B	A	C	D	B
11	**12**	**13**	**14**	**15**	**16**	**17**	**18**	**19**	**20**
A	B	C	A	B	A	C	C	B	D

THE VERB

A Verb is a word that tells something about the action or state of or happening to a person or thing.

A Verb tells the following:

1. What a person or thing does.
Sachin goes to school daily.
The bell *rang* loudly.
Many birds fly in the sky.
She *sang* a song.

2. What a person or thing is.
India *is* the biggest democracy in the world.
Ram Mehar *is* very rich.
They *are* happy.

3. What is done to a person or thing.
You *are liked* by all.
Two thieves *were arrested.*
Four students *were punished* by the teacher.

4. What happens to a person or thing.
His maternal uncle *died* last week.
Two ships *sank* yesterday.
Leaves *turn* yellow in autumn.

5. What a person or thing has, had, and so on.
I *have* a new car.
He *had* a scooter last year.
He *has* several cows and goats.

It goes without saying that a verb is the most important part of a sentence. No sentence is complete without a Verb.

Important Information

1. If two or more singular nouns are joined by 'and' the verb used will be plural.
Example:
(i) He and I were going to the market.
(ii) Ram and Mohan are friends.

2. If two singular nouns joined by 'and' points out to the same thing or person, the verb used must be singular.
Example:
(i) Rice and curry is the favourite food of the Punjabis.
(ii) The Collector and District Magistrate is away.

3. In case two subjects are joined by 'as well as' the verb agrees with the first subject.
Example :
(i) Kanta as well as her children is playing.
(ii) Children as well as their mother are playing.
In the case of first sentence the verb (is) agrees with Kanta and in the case of second sentence the verb (are) agrees with the children.

4. 'Neither', 'Either', 'Every', 'Each', 'Everyone', and 'Many a' are followed by a singular verb. **Example :**
(i) Either of the plans is to be adopted.
(ii) Neither of the two brothers is sure to pass.
(iii) Every student is expected to be obedient.
(iv) Everyone of them desires this.
(v) Many a person is drowned in the sea.

5. If two subjects are joined by 'Either .... or' / 'Neither .... nor', the verb agrees with the subject near to it.
Example :
(i) Either my brother or I am to do this work.
(ii) Neither he nor they are prepared to do this work.

6. 'A great many' is always followed by a 'plural noun' and a 'plural verb'. For example :
A great many students have been declared successful.

7. Similarly if two subjects are joined by 'with', 'together with', 'no less than', in addition to 'and not', etc. the verb agrees with the first subject.
Example :
(i) The boy with his parents has arrived.
(ii) He, no less than I, is to blame.

8. Nouns, plural in form, but singular in meaning, take a singular verb.
Example :
This news was broadcast from television yesterday.

MULTIPLE CHOICE QUESTIONS

Directions: *In the following questions choose the correct options to fill the blanks.*

1. The bus with all its passengers .... lost.
A. were B. was
C. are D. would

2. You as well as I .... responsible for this work.
A. am B. are
C. was D. is

3. Raghava like all his companions .... a spoiled child.
A. are B. were
C. is D. will be

4. Pen and ink .... required for me.
A. are B. were
C. is D. has required

5. Every girl and every boy .... attended the seminar.
A. have B. has
C. is D. are

6. Not only she but all her sisters ...... been married.
A. has B. have
C. is D. are

7. There .... nothing but miseries in life.
A. is B. are
C. were D. will be

8. Neither prose nor poem .... given.
A. were B. was
C. has D. have

9. Either he or I .... wrong.
A. is B. are
C. am D. were

10. Either Sulekha or Rekha .... coming here.
A. are B. is
C. were D. have

11. .... the child or his parents to blame?
A. Is B. Are
C. Were D. Has

12. You and I .... neighbours.
A. am B. are
C. was D. has

13. The house with all its belongings ..... sold away.
A. were B. are
C. was D. must

14. Either water or juice .... required.
A. is B. are
C. were D. has

15. There were not as many tables as .... required.
A. was B. were
C. is D. are

16. They each .... a book.
A. have B. are
C. has D. is

17. He and I .... class friends.
A. is B. am
C. was D. are

18. She as well as I .... guilty.
A. is B. are
C. am D. must be

19. Purushottam .... not read more on this chapter.
A. needs B. has been need
C. need D. had been need

20. He came .... to his aunt.
A. run B. running
C. to run D. in run

ANSWERS

1	2	3	4	5	6	7	8	9	10
B	B	C	C	B	B	A	B	C	B
11	**12**	**13**	**14**	**15**	**16**	**17**	**18**	**19**	**20**
A	B	C	A	B	A	D	A	C	B

CONJUNCTIONS

A conjunction is a word which connects words, clauses or sentences.

Look at the following sentences.

(i) He bought apples *and* mangoes.

(ii) God made the country *and* man made the town.

(iii) The door was open *but* there was no one in the house.

(iv) He knows that I am here *and* that I want to see him.

In the sentence (i), *and* connects two words—*apples* and *mangoes.*

In the sentence (ii), *and* connects two sentences—*God made the country* and *man made the town.*

In the sentence (iii), *but* connects two sentences— *The door was open* and *there was no one in the house.*

In the sentence (iv), *and* connects two clauses—*that I am here* and *that I want to see him.*

The main coordinating conjunctions are:

and, but, for, or, nor, also, either ..... or, neither ..... nor.

There are some conjunctions which are used in pairs. They are:

either .... or, ... neither .... nor, both .... and, though .... yet, whether .... or, not only .... but also.

Example: *Either* take it *or* leave it.

It is *neither* useful *nor* ornamental.

They *both* like *and* respect me.

Though he is suffering from high fever, *yet* he does not cry.

He does not care *whether* you go *or* stay.

He is *not only* doltish, *but also* obstinate.

The conjunctions which are used in pairs in this way, are called correlative conjunctions, or merely correlatives.

Use of Important Conjunctions

1. **As soon as :** As soon as denotes simultaneous time.
   Example : As soon as he saw his enemy, he took to his heels.
2. **No sooner .... than :**
   (a) 'No sooner' is always followed by 'than'.
   (b) Please remember that 'No sooner' is always followed by do/does/did. As such only first form of the verb should be used after the subject.

   Example :
   No sooner did he see his enemy than he took to his heels.
3. **Hardly :** Hardly is followed by when.
   Examples :
   (i) Hardly had I left the house when it started raining.
   (ii) We had hardly come into the room when his father began chastising him.

   Note :
   A. Hardly is never followed by than.
   B. 'Scarcely' can also be used in the sense and manner of 'Hardly'.
4. **Lest :** Lest is used in the sense of so that .... not. It is always followed by should. Lest is negative in sense. Hence 'not' should never be used with it.
   Example :
   Work hard lest you should fail.
   Note : 'Lest' is always followed by 'should' and not 'may'.
5. **Unless :** Unless expresses condition. It is also used in

the negative sense. Use of 'not' is not allowed with unless because unless is already in the negative sense.

Example :

Unless you labour hard you will not pass.

6. **Until :** 'Until' expresses time. It means 'till not'.

Example :

Wait here until I return.

Note : Until is in the negative sense. So 'not' should not be used with it. Example :

Wait here until I do not return. (Incorrect)

Wait here until I return. (Correct)

7. **As well as :** When two subjects are joined by 'as well as', the verb always agrees with the first subject.

Examples :

(i) The teacher as well as students is playing.

(ii) Students as well as the teacher are playing.

Note : 'Both' and 'as well as' cannot be used together in the same sentence.

Examples :

Both Sita as well as Kanta are beautiful. (Incorrect)

Sita as well as Kanta is beautiful. (Correct)

Both Sita and Kanta are beautiful. (Correct)

8. **As if :** 'As if' is used in the sense of pretension. While using 'as if' in a sentence, we should see that even the third person singular subject gets 'were'.

Example :

He talks as if he were mad.

9. **Till :** Till expresses time. Till is always used in the affirmative.

Example :

We did not come back till sunset.

10. **Rather than :** 'Rather than' is used in the sense of 'preference'. 'Rather' is always followed by 'than'.

Example :

I would rather die than submit.

11. **As long as/so long as :** Both express time during which an action or event takes place.

Example :

As long as there is life, there is hope.

12. **However :** It is both a subordinate and co-ordinate clause.

Examples :

(a) Mala worked hard, she however, failed.

(b) However hard he may work, he cannot pass.

13. **Such as :** 'Such as' gives us the sense of 'like'. Such is always followed by 'as'.

Example :

Life is such a puzzle as cannot be solved.

MULTIPLE CHOICE QUESTIONS

Directions: *In the following questions choose the correct options to fill the blanks.*

1. Neither he .... his friend is good.
   A. or B. and
   C. but D. nor
2. The officer asked the peon .... why he was late.
   A. that B. if
   C. but D. No word needed
3. Both Ajay .... Vijay are intelligent.
   A. or B. nor
   C. and D. No word needed
4. No Sooner did the thief see the public ..... he ran away.
   A. then B. and
   C. but D. than
5. Abhinav .... his brothers was going to Mumbai.
   A. but B. yet
   C. No word needed D. together with
6. He behaves .... he were the captain of the team.
   A. as if B. as
   C. No word needed D. that
7. Either Rupali .... Sonali is going to attend the meeting.
   A. and B. but
   C. nor D. or
8. Neither Nirmal .... Ashwinee is going to listen the speech.
   A. and B. but
   C. nor D. or
9. Ravi .... Prakash are going to Kolkata.
   A. or B. nor
   C. but D. and
10. Rice .... curry is my usual breakfast.
    A. and B. but
    C. then D. than
11. Hardly had he left .... his brother came.
    A. then B. than
    C. when D. that
12. I would rather have a copy .... a book.
    A. then B. than
    C. when D. that
13. He is no other .... my friend.
    A. then B. than
    C. when D. but
14. He saw a snake ....he awoke.
    A. then B. when
    C. than D. No word needed
15. Ten years have passed .... my grandmother died.
    A. since B. when
    C. then D. than
16. She is .... good .... bad.
    A. either, not B. neither, or
    C. neither, nor D. neither, than

17. The cellphone is both cheap .... best.
A. than B. and
C. then D. or

18. No sooner did the rogue see the police ... he disappeared.
A. then B. than
C. so D. because

19. Srishti will go .... Sanju goes.
A. if B. than
C. then D. although

20. She is wise .... timid.
A. and B. yet
C. but D. however

ANSWERS

1	2	3	4	5	6	7	8	9	10
D	D	C	D	D	A	D	C	D	A
11	**12**	**13**	**14**	**15**	**16**	**17**	**18**	**19**	**20**
C	B	B	B	A	C	B	B	A	C
21	**22**	**23**	**24**	**25**	**26**	**27**	**28**	**29**	**30**
B	B	B	A	B	C	A	C	D	D

PREPOSITIONS

A *Preposition* is a word which is placed before a noun or a pronoun to show its relation to some other word in the sentence.

1. I saw a goat *in* the field.
2. I am fond *of* hot coffee.

In sentence 1, the word *in* shows the relation between two things—*goat* and *field.*

In sentence 2, the word *of* shows the relation between the attribute expressed by the adjective *found* and *tea.*

The words *in* and *of* are here used as prepositions.

The noun or pronoun which is used with a preposition is called its object. The noun or pronoun is in the objective case. It is governed by the preposition. Now it is absolutely clear that in sentence 1, the noun *field* is in the objective case. The word *field* is governed by the preposition *in.*

A preposition may have two or more objects.

The road runs over *hill* and *plain.*

Here, the words *hill* and *plain* are used as objects.

Use of Important Prepositions

1. Among, Between

'**Among**' is used for more than two persons or things; '**Between**' is used only for two.

Examples :

(i) Distribute these sweets *among* the poor students of the class.

(ii) Distribute these books *between* Ram and Shyam.

2. Among, In

'**Among**' is used before collective plural nouns. '**In**' is used before collective singular nouns.

Examples :

(i) I found him standing *among* the crowd.

(ii) I saw him in the crowd.

3. Beside, Besides

'**Beside**' means 'by the side of'. '**Besides**' means 'in addition to'.

Examples :

(i) The daughter was sitting *beside* her mother.

(ii) *Besides* his relatives, he invited his friends also.

4. In, Within

'**In**' means at the expiry of a period of time in future, '**Within**' means before the expiry of a period of time in any tense.

Examples :

(i) She will return *in* a week.

(ii) I shall finish my work *within* a weak.

5. On, Upon

'**On**' is used for things at rest; '**Upon**' is used for things in motion.

Examples :

(i) He is sitting *on* the floor.

(ii) The dog sprang *upon* the table.

6. By, With

'**By**' denotes the agent or doer, '**With**' denotes the instrument with which anything is done.

Examples :

(i) The bird was killed *by* the hunter with an arrow.

(ii) He beat the dog *with* a stick.

(iii) I shall reach here *by* five o'clock.

7. After, In

'**After**' means at the end of a period of time in the past. '**In**' means at the end of a period of time in future.

Examples :

(i) I shall return your book *in* a week.

(ii) He returned the book *after* a week.

8. For, From, Since

'**For**' is used before a noun denoting a period of time with all the tenses. '**From**' is used before a noun or phrase denoting a point of time, it is used in all the tenses. '**Since**' is used before a noun or phrase denoting some point of time and is always produced by a verb in the perfect continuous tense or third form of a verb.

Examples :

(i) We have been playing cards *for* two hours.

(ii) She stayed with her uncle *from* the 15th of March to the 15th of May.

(iii) I have been reading this book *since* morning.

9. Above, Over

'Above' means 'higher from', **Over** is used in the following four senses :

(i) In the sense of 'above' :
At noon, the sun is *over* our heads.

(ii) In the sense of 'beyond' :
I cannot get *over* my disappointment.

(iii) In the sense of 'Superiority' :
God *over* all blesses for ever more.

(iv) In the sense of 'Conclusion' :
It is all *over* with me.

10. At, Towards

'At' denotes the idea of aim, **'Towards'** denotes the idea of destination.

Examples :

(i) He threw the stone *at* the cat.

(ii) He went *towards* the house.

11. At, In, On

'At' is used as follows :

(i) **'At'** is used with small towns and villages. **Examples :**

(a) He was born *at* Sonepat.

(b) He lives *at* village Bangra. (Bangra is a village)

(ii) **'At'** is used before a noun denoting a definite point of time.

Example :

He called on me *at* 9 p.m. yesterday.

'In' is used as follows :

(iii) **'In'** is used with the names of big cities, provinces and countries.

Examples :

(a) His father lives *in* England.

(b) His younger brother lives *in* Calcutta.

(iv) **'In'** is used before the names of months and years.

Example :

His elder sister was born *in* 1972 *in* the month of May.

'On' is used with dates and names of days. **Examples:**

(a) I joined college *on* the 26th April.

(b) He will leave for Kolkata *on* Wednesday next.

Important Information

1. **'In'** is also used in the following phrases :
In the morning; In the evening, In winter, In summer.
2. **'In'** also denotes a place inside anything.
He travelled *in* a crowded bus.
3. **'At'** is used in the following phrases :
At home, *At* the station, *At* work, *At* play.

12. Below, Beneath

Below means 'of lower level in position, dignity and expectation' etc. *Beneath* means 'under'.

Examples :

(i) It is *below* my dignity to talk to her.

(ii) They rested *beneath* the shade of a tree.

13. In, Into, To

'In' expresses Rest or Motion inside anything. **'Into'** expresses Motion towards the inside of anything or change from one medium to another. **'To'** denotes motion from one place to another.

Examples :

(i) The boys are *in* the room.

(ii) Translate this passage from English *into* Hindi.

(iii) Every morning he goes *to* the temple.

14. Till, By, Of, Off

- 'Till' means upto or not earlier than.
- 'By' means not later than.
- 'Of' shows cause, source, separation, quality, contents, possession, apposition, point of reference, space in time etc.
- 'Off' shows separation at a near distance, and detached condition.

Consider the following examples:

(i) I shall work *till* 5 a.m.

(ii) Madhu died *of* cancer.

(iii) The nib *of* the pen is made *of* gold.

(iv) He presented me a bottle *of* perfume.

(v) Our principal is a man *of* principle.

(vi) He lived in the house *of* his friend.

(vii) *By* this time tomorrow, I'll have finished my job.

(viii) My house is *off* the road.

(ix) The book fell *off* the table.

MULTIPLE CHOICE QUESTIONS

Directions: *Tick the correct preposition for the blank in each of the following sentences.*

1. He applied ...... the manager.
A. for B. to
C. with D. by

2. Trust ...... God and do the right.
A. in B. for
C. to D. with

3. She is worthy ...... a prize.
A. with B. for
C. to D. of

4. Mr. Gomes has no taste ...... music.
A. of B. for
C. with D. to

5. You are hard ...... hearing.
A. at B. of
C. with D. for

6. He is sure ...... his success
A. for B. with
C. on D. of

7. Preeti was warned ...... the danger ahead.
A. for B. at
C. of D. about

8. I am thankful ...... you for a good advice.
A. for B. with
C. to D. of

9. Deepak would not surrender ...... the police.
A. with B. to
C. for D. on

10. The small plant in your lawn is very sensitive ...... touch.
A. on B. with
C. to D. about

11. Divya was sure to succeed ..... the examination.
A. for B. in
C. to D. with

12. Geeta was jealous ...... Ravina's beauty.
A. to B. with
C. for D. of

13. He was ignorant ..... what was happening there.
A. for B. of
C. to D. with

14. Your pen is inferior ...... mine.
A. than B. with
C. from D. to

15. Reenu is no match ...... Meenu.
A. to B. for
C. with D. upon

16. It is necessary ...... you to apply for this job.
A. on B. with
C. for D. to

17. Be loyal ...... your country.
A. for B. to
C. on D. with

18. Mukesh is junior ...... me.
A. than B. to
C. from D. of

19. Deepika was innocent ...... the crime.
A. of B. with
C. from D. to

20. I am desirous.... joining the Indian cricket team.
A. for B. of
C. to D. on

ANSWERS

1	2	3	4	5	6	7	8	9	10
B	A	D	B	B	D	D	D	B	D
11	**12**	**13**	**14**	**15**	**16**	**17**	**18**	**19**	**20**
B	D	B	D	B	D	B	B	A	B

SYNONYMS

A synonym is a word which conveys a meaning similar to the given word.

REMEMBER

Words	*Synonyms*
Add	Increase
Adequate	Enough
Adjust	Adapt
All	Aggregate
Allow	Permit
Abode	Dwelling
Apt	Proper
Assess	Appraise
Accuse	Calumniate
Abashed	Timid
Annoy	Displease
Ample	Enough, Sufficient
Amplify	Increase
Apathetic	Unenthusiastic
Accost	Address
Authentic	True
Adjust	Fit
Approve	Assent, Allow, Accept

Words	*Synonyms*
Adapt	Conform
Adversary	Opponent, Rival, Competitor
Beat	Whack
Benign	Kind
Breeze	Zephyr
Baffle	Puzzle
Booty	Spoil
Beauty	Charm
Beast	Animal
Bandit	Robber
Blaze	Shine
Bond	Tie
Bend	Twist
Bate	Diminish
Beg	Plead
Barbaric	Wild, Savage
Bashful	Shy, Reserved
Begin	Start
Blend	Mix, Mingle
Bizarre	Funny
Below	Under

Words	Synonyms
Bedevil	Confuse
Bemoan	Lament
Babble	Nonsense
Blame	Fault
Behaviour	Demeanour
Call	Accost
Copy	Imitate
Close	Shut
Caress	Love
Camp	Stay
Connect	Attach
Cut	Injure, Curtail
Cling	Stick
Conical	Funny
Convey	Carry
Conspicuous	Prominent
Cheerful	Happy, Pleasant
Curtail	Decrease
Cheerless	Sad, Dejected
Curious	Strange
Circumstance	Factor, Situation, Condition
Competent	Capable
Congruent	Overlapping
Cope	Deal, Endure
Confident	Sure
Complex	Intricate
Cajole	Coax, Flatter
Cunning	Crafty
Delectable	Joyful, Delightful
Devilish	Diabolical
Delicate	Soft
Devil	Fiend
Delay	Postpone
Dislike	Repugnance
Destroy	Ruin
Dwell	Live, Dilate
Declare	Pronounce
Drunk	Flushed
Deficient	Lacking
Damn	Condemn, Curse
Decrease	Diminish
Destruction	Devastation
Efficient	Competent
Ethnic	Racial
Enthral	Enslave
Earnest	Serious
Envious	Jealous
Ending	Final
Egg	Incite
Extempore	At once
Extensive	Far-ranging
Extra	Surplus
Existence	Life

Words	Synonyms
Exceed	Overstep
Enormous	Vast
Excessive	Superfluous
Free	Unhindered
Frigid	Cold
Feed	Cater
Fame	Reputation
Frame	Make
First	Initial
Frighten	Terrorise, Intimidate
Fervent	Fervid
Fall	Decline
Feeble	Frail
Fickle	Changeable
Finish	Conclude
Fraud	Deception
Forgiving	Placable
Grow	Develop
Greed	Avidity
Greet	Welcome
Grave	Serious
Group	Constellation
Given	Bestowed
Gratitude	Thankfulness
Have	Possess
Hire	Rent
Hit	Strike
Handsome	Beautiful
Hinder	Prevent
Heap	Pile
Hope	Expect
Hard	Harsh
Help	Aid
Hymn	Song
Henpecked	Enslaved
Hoodwink	Mystify, Cheat
Humble	Polite, Urbane, Modest
Harass	Vex, Trouble
Impart	Instil
Intact	Untouched
Instal	Establish
Indict	Impeach
Imitate	Ape
Instigate	Incite
Initiate	Start, Introduce
Inimical	Unfriendly
Insufferable	Intolerable
Impartiality	Justice
Jolly	Merry
Joyful	Delectable
Join	Conjoin
Kind	Benign
Kill	Murder

Words	Synonyms
Kindred	Similar
Kinship	Relationship
Keen	Sharp
Knowledge	Scholarship
Lazy	Slothful
Large	Substantial, Gargantuan
Listless	Careless, Lackadaisical
Lax	Loose
Little	Small
Lifelike	Realistic
Lofty	High
Lenient	Soft, Gentle
Lacking	Deficient, Wanting
Lessen	Decrease
Middleclass	Bourgeois
Mitigate	Lessen, Abate
Modesty	Humility, Lowliness
Mix	Mingle, Blend
Mixture	Mingling
Mixed	Assorted
Modify	Decrease
Mean	Imply
Multifarious	Varied
Miscarry	Abort
Note	Notice
Noble	Stately
Native	Indigenous
Needful	Necessary
Notify	Declare
Nervous	Shaky, Tremulous, Timid
Natural	Spontaneous
Near	Close
Normal	Natural
Offend	Displease
Oppress	Persecute, Tyrannize
Opponent	Adversary
Obstruct	Hinder, Check
Offence	Fault
Offender	Villain
Overstep	Exceed
Overlapping	Congruent
Occult	Mystic
Profane	Unholy
Patience	Forbearance
Pornographic	Obscene
Plenitude	Abundance
Prominent	Important
Prodigal	Spender
Procrastinate	Postpone
Promote	Develop, Honour
Persecute	Tyrannise
Profess	Claim
Pliant	Flexible

Words	Synonyms
Plebian	Common
Polished	Sophisticated
Quake	Shake
Quit	Leave
Queer	Eccentric
Quell	Suppress
Quantify	Allot
Reply	Answer
Relinquish	Retire
Read	Peruse
Relation	Reference
Render	Do
Remainder	Residuals
Repeat	Reiterate
Repentant	Contrite
Retaliative	Retaliatory
Rumour	Hearsay
Reveal	Divulge
Ritualistic	Ceremonious
Soft	Delicate
Sort	Kind, Choose, Select
Selfish	Egoistic
Sensual	Earthly
Suppress	Quell, Check
Stimulate	Provoke
Tasteless	Insipid
Travel	Journey
True	Authentic, Faithful, Truthful
Turbulence	Turmoil
Tragedy	Calamity
Tasteful	Tasty, Delicious
Touching	Painful
Thankful	Grateful
Tremendous	Great, Huge
Tough	Strong
Terminate	Conclude, End
Theory	Doctrine
Tell	Relate
Tremble	Shake, Shiver
Urge	Spur
Unbeaten	Unsubdued
Use	Utilize, Practise
Underhand	Unfair, Undue
Unfair	Unjust
Unravel	Reveal, Divulge
Unimportant	Common
Unconcerned	Apathetic
Unimitated	Inimitable
Unfortunate	Unlucky
Understand	Perceive, Comprehend
Vain	Proud, Haughty, Conceited, Shameless
Vale	Valley, Dale, Dell

Words	Synonyms
Vice	Fault
Virtue	Quality
Veracity	Reality
Value	Price, Prize
Vex	Tease
Vibrate	Quiver, Shake
Violent	Excessive
Vivid	Clear, Lucid
Victory	Triumph
Vulgar	Indecent
Virtuous	Honest
Variegated	Varied, Multifarious
Well	Good
Yell	Cry, Shout
Yonder	There
Yearn	Wish, Desire
Yoke	Slavery
Zest	Earnestness, Enthusiasm

ANTONYMS

A antonym is a word which conveys a meaning opposite to the given word.

REMEMBER

Words	Antonyms
Abhor	Love
Abnormal	Normal
Able	Unable
Acceptable	Unacceptable
Adequate	Inadequate
Amusing	Boring
Angry	Calm
Apex	Bottom
Attract	Repel
Bad	Good
Barren	Fertile
Beautiful	Ugly
Bitter	Sweet
Brave	Cowardly
Brief	Lengthy
Bright	Dull
Calm	Violent
Careful	Careless
Clear	Vague, Cloudy
Cold	Hot
Cruel	Kind
Dear	Cheap
Deep	Shallow
Difficult	Easy
Direct	Indirect
Dishonest	Honest
Disobey	Obey
Encourage	Discourage
Enormous	Tiny
Excellent	Bad
Expensive	Cheap
Eat	Fast
Fair	Unfair
Fake	Authentic
False	True
Famous	Notorious
Fool	Genius
Generous	Miserly
Genius	Fool
Genuine	Unauthentic
Gigantic	Tiny
Glad	Depressed
Good	Bad
Great	Little
Happy	Sad
Hard	Soft
Hate	Love
Honest	Dishonest
Idle	Busy
Immoral	Moral
Include	Exclude
Incorrect	Correct
Intelligent	Unintelligent
Kind	Cruel
Like	Dislike
Long	Short
Lucid	Vague
Major	Minor
Naive	Experienced
Nadir	Apex
Neat	Clumsy
Obedient	Disobedient
Obscure	Clear
Oppose	Support
Optimistic	Pessimistic
Out	In
Patience	Impatience
Peaceful	Belligerent
Pious	Impious
Polite	Impolite
Potent	Impotent
Prominent	Unimportant
Proper	Improper
Pure	Impure
Quick	Slow
Quiet	Disturbance
Real	False, Unreal

Words	Antonyms
Reject	Select, Choose
Reliable	Unreliable
Respect	Disrespect
Right	Wrong
Robust	Feeble, Weak
Sad	Happy
Secret	Open
Sensible	Insensible
Severe	Mild
Sharp	Blunt
Simple	Complex
Sociable	Unsociable
Tall	Short

Words	Antonyms
Tidy	Untidy
Uncanny	Canny
Violent	Calm
Vivid	Vague
Strong	Weak
Big	Small
Easy	Difficult
Fast	Slow
High	Low
Catchy	Unattractive
Ugly	Handsome, Beautiful, Tidy
Tasty	Insipid
Sonorous	Harsh

MULTIPLE CHOICE QUESTIONS

Directions (Qs. 1 to 20): *In the following questions choose the word which best expresses the meaning of the given word.*

1. ABSURD
A. Foolish B. Simple
C. Courageous D. Silly

2. ABANDON
A. Lose B. Profit
C. Vacate D. Foil

3. CAJOLE
A. Pause B. Lenient
C. Blast D. Lure

4. COMBAT
A. Fight B. Conflict
C. Shoot D. Quarrel

5. LAMENT
A. Condone B. Console
C. Complain D. Contribution

6. DEBACLE
A. Disgrace B. Defeat
C. Collapse D. Decline

7. SHIVER
A. Fear B. Tremble
C. Shake D. Ache

8. TORTURE
A. Terror B. Harassment
C. Torment D. Tranquility

9. LAUDABLE
A. Lovable B. Commendable
C. Profitable D. Oblivious

10. FIXED
A. Sterile B. Static
C. Stubborn D. Parennial

11. QUEER
A. Unfamiliar B. Cute
C. Curious D. Strange

12. SUFFICIENT
A. Fit B. Proper
C. Adequate D. Vast

13. GLOSS
A. Brightness B. Soothing
C. Rubbing D. Miracle

14. LONGING
A. Prune B. Apathy
C. Curtail D. Craving

15. JEER
A. Applaud
B. Magnanimity
C. Avoid
D. Scoff

16. ZENITH
A. Minimum
B. Nadir
C. Plant
D. Peak

17. GARB
A. Distort B. Dress
C. Trivial D. Rage

18. ABHOR
A. Rude B. Reconcile
C. Crave D. Detest

19. YIELD
A. Shum B. Incisive
C. Retain D. Surrender

20. YOKE
A. Twist B. Release
C. Link D. Extra

Directions (Qs. 21 to 38): *In the following questions choose the word which best expresses the opposite of the given word.*

21. TRAGIC
A. Dramatic B. Strong
C. Gentle D. Comic

22. ORAL
A. Verbal B. Sane
C. Minor D. Written

23. ADMIRE
A. Hate B. Unlike
C. Dislike D. Enough

24. VIOLENT
A. Gentle B. Savage
C. Haughty D. Decline

25. ADVERSITY
A. Windfall B. Inprosperity
C. Prosperity D. Slave

26. GENUINE
A. Spurious B. Obscure
C. Countless D. Apathetic

27. GRUDGE
A. Essence B. Guile
C. Goodwill D. Ill-will

28. STIFF
A. Soft B. Courteous
C. Lively D. Flexible

29. VANITY
A. Conceit B. Pride
C. Ostentious D. Humility

30. FRONT
A. Upper B. Unusual
C. Back D. Rear

31. ATTRACT
A. Lured B. Longing
C. Repel D. Disguise

32. COMFORT
A. Discomfort B. Discontent
C. Uncomfort D. Miscomfort

33. WELCOME
A. Repel B. Accept
C. Resist D. Fight

34. TACTFUL
A. Naive B. Loose
C. Strict D. Uncivilized

35. DUTIFUL
A. Harmful B. Watchful
C. Forgetful D. Remiss

36. RIGID
A. Flux B. Adoptable
C. Yielding D. Adaptable

37. RARE
A. Petty B. Poor
C. Small D. Common

38. ZEAL
A. Despair
B. Calmness
C. Passiveness
D. Indifference

ANSWERS

1	2	3	4	5	6	7	8	9	10
D	C	D	A	C	C	B	C	B	B
11	**12**	**13**	**14**	**15**	**16**	**17**	**18**	**19**	**20**
D	C	A	D	D	D	B	D	D	C
21	**22**	**23**	**24**	**25**	**26**	**27**	**28**	**29**	**30**
D	D	C	A	C	A	C	D	D	D
31	**32**	**33**	**34**	**35**	**36**	**37**	**38**		
C	A	C	A	D	D	D	D		

●●●

3 SENTENCE COMPLETION

It is such an exercise which starts with the primary schools and continues in the highest level of competitive examinations. One must practise it regularly to score well.

Directions (Qs. 1 to 15): *Pick out the most effective word(s) from the given words to fill in the blanks to make the sentence meaningfully complete.*

1. The student ...... that book from the library to study at home.
A. issued B. borrowed
C. hired D. lent

2. I wish I ...... a king.
A. was B. am
C. should be D. were

3. He ...... to listen to my arguments and walked away.
A. denied B. disliked
C. objected D. refused

4. The flow of blood was so ...... that the patient died.
A. intense B. adequate
C. profuse D. extensive

5. When I met her yesterday, it was the first time I ...... her since Christmas.
A. saw B. have seen
C. had seen D. have been seing

6. Can you pay ...... all these articles?
A. for B. of
C. off D. out

7. I ...... you to be at the party this evening.
A. expect B. hope
C. look forward to D. desire

8. ...... being a handicapped person, he is very cooperative and self-reliant.
A. Because B. Although
C. Since D. Despite

9. The child broke ...... from his mother and ran towards the painting.
A. away B. after
C. down D. with

10. With his ...... income, he finds it difficult to live a comfortable life.
A. brief B. sufficient
C. meagre D. huge

11. He could ...... a lot of money in such a short time by using his intelligence and working hard.
A. spend B. spoil
C. exchange D. accumulate

12. Though the brothers are twins, they look ......
A. alike B. handsome
C. indifferent D. different

13. Unfavourable weather conditions can ..... illness.
A. cure B. detect
C. treat D. enhance

14. No sooner did the bell ring, ... the actor started singing.
A. when B. than
C. after D. before

15. If I ...... realised it, I would not have acted on his advice.
A. was B. had
C. were D. have

Directions (Qs. 16 to 20): *In each question, an incomplete statement (Stem) followed by four fillers is given. Pick out the best one which can complete the incomplete stem correctly and meaningfully.*

16. Unless you work harder you will fail, means .....
A. if you fail you will work harder.
B. you must at least plan well than you will not fail.
C. hardly you will fail if you do not desire so.
D. if you do not put more efforts, then you will fail.

17. Even if it rains I shall come, means .....
A. if I come it will not rain.
B. if it rains I shall not come.
C. I will certainly come whether it rains or not.
D. whenever there is rain I shall come.

18. Dinesh is as stupid as he is lazy means .....
A. Dinesh is stupid because he is lazy.
B. Dinesh is lazy because he is stupid.
C. Dinesh is either stupid or lazy.
D. Dinesh is equally stupid and lazy.

19. He is so lazy that he .....
A. cannot depend on others for getting his work done.
B. cannot delay the schedule of completing the work.
C. can seldom complete his work on time.
D. dislike to postpone the work that he undertakes to do.

20. He always stammers in public meetings, but his today's speech .....
A. was fairly audible to everyone present in the hall.
B. was not received satisfactorily.
C. could not be understood properly.
D. was free from that defect.

ANSWERS

1	2	3	4	5	6	7	8	9	10
B	D	D	C	C	A	A	D	A	C
11	**12**	**13**	**14**	**15**	**16**	**17**	**18**	**19**	**20**
D	D	D	B	B	D	C	D	C	D

4 SPOTTING ERRORS

The most common errors in English are of spellings, grammar and usage of words. By regular practice, the errors can be easily spotted and minimised.

MULTIPLE CHOICE QUESTIONS

Directions: *In the following questions some of the sentences have errors and some are correct. Find out which part of a sentence has an error, the number of that part is your answer. If a sentence is free from errors, then your answer is D i.e., No error.*

1. (A) Either Ram or/(B) you is responsible/(C) for this action./(D) No error.

2. (A) The student flatly denied/(B) that he had copied/(C) in the examination hall./(D) No error.

3. (A) By the time you arrive tomorrow/(B) I have finished/(C) my work./(D) No error.

4. (A) The captain with the members of his team/(B) are returning/(C) after a fortnight./(D) No error.

5. (A) After returning from/(B) an all-India tour/(C) I had to describe about it./(D) No error.

6. (A) The teacher asked his students/(B) if they had gone through/(C) either of the three chapters included in the prescribed text./(D) No error.

7. (A) Do you know/(B) how old were you/(C) when you came here?/(D) No error.

8. (A) Beware of/(B) a fair-weather friend/(C) who is neither a friend in need nor a friend indeed./(D) No error.

9. (A) Copernicus proved/(B) that Earth/(C) moves round the Sun./(D) No error.

10. (A) The property/(B) was divided/(C) among the two brothers./(D) No error.

11. (A) I am quite certain/(B) that the lady is not only greedy/(C) but miserly./(D) No error.

12. (A) The brilliant success in the examination/(B) as well as his record in sports/(C) deserves high praise./(D) No error.

13. (A) I cannot find/(B) where has he gone/(C) though I have tried may best./(D) No error.

14. (A) If I was/(B) the Prime Minister of India/(C) I would work wonders/(D) No error.

15. (A) If it weren't/(B) for you,/(C) I wouldn't be alive today./(D) No error.

16. (A) He looked like a lion/(B) baulked from/(C) its prey./(D) No error.

17. (A) Widespread flooding/(B) is affecting/(C) large areas of the villages./(D) No error.

18. (A) If we really set to/(B) we can get the whole house/(C) cleaned in an afternoon./(D) No error.

19. (A) It's arrogant for you/(B) to assume you'll/(C)win every time./(D) No error.

20. (A) The two books are the same/(B) except for the fact that this/(C) has an answer in the back./(D) No error.

ANSWERS

1	2	3	4	5	6	7	8	9	10
B	D	B	B	C	C	D	D	B	C
11	**12**	**13**	**14**	**15**	**16**	**17**	**18**	**19**	**20**
C	D	B	A	C	C	C	A	A	C

EXPLANATORY ANSWERS

1. Replace 'is' by 'are'.
2. No error.
3. Replace 'have' by 'would have'.
4. Replace 'are' by 'is'.
5. Replace 'had to describe' by 'described'.
6. Replace 'either' by 'any'.
7. No error.
8. No error.
9. Omit 'that'.
10. Replace 'among' by 'between'.
11. Add 'also'.
12. No error.
13. Replace 'has he' by 'he has'.
14. Replace 'was' by 'were'.
15. Replace 'wouldn't be' by 'would not have been'.
16. Replace 'its' by 'his'.
17. Replace 'areas' by 'area'.
18. Replace 'set to' by 'set on'.
19. Replace 'for' by 'of'.
20. Replace 'in' by 'on'.

●●●

5 ONE WORD SUBSTITUTION

There are many single words in English language which can be perfectly used for a number of words. These words help in expressing ideas in a short and correct manner for the right occasion. Such words not only increase the vocabulary but also enable you to economise in the use of words to a great extent.

Multiple Word Expression	*Substitution*
One who always looks towards the bright side of things	Optimist
One who always looks towards the dark side of things	Pessimist
The time when one develops from a child into an adult	Adolescence
The process of growing more plants in order to form a forest.	Afforestation
The science which deals with farming	Agriculture
From some other country or place etc.	Alien
A term, etc. giving more than one meaning	Ambiguous
A vehicle which is used to carry sick persons	Ambulance
An animal which can live both in water and on land	Amphibian
A lawless situation when there is no government	Anarchy
Belonging to the history of thousands of years old	Ancient
Once a year	Annual
A very old object but still valuable	Antique
Words of opposite meanings	Antonyms
Words of similar meanings	Synonyms
Signatures of a famous person	Autograph
A government led by one person with absolute authority	Autocracy
A written work of one's own life history	Autobiography
A person who has never been married	Bachelor
A person usually having no hair on his head	Bald
A place where one can deposit money and get interest	Bank
A person who cuts our hair	Barber
A building/group of buildings where soldiers live	Barracks
A person who makes buns and biscuits	Baker
A person who lives by asking people for food and money without doing any useful job	Beggar
The crime of having married to two persons at the same time	Bigamy
The branch of science which deals with the study of plants	Botany
Able to speak two languages	Bilingual
Able to speak more than two languages	Polyglot
The branch of science which deals with the living organisms	Biology
A powerful snow storm	Blizzard
A great successful book or movie	Blockbuster
A short news on the radio or TV	Bulletin
A system in which the most important works are organised by the government officials	Bureaucracy
A person who has no vision in his eyes	Blind
A page or a series of pages on which the information of days, weeks, months, etc. is given	Calendar
A person who eats human flesh	Cannibal
A complete list of items often arranged alphabetically	Catalogue
A sudden disaster	Catastrophe
A period of 100 years	Century
A branch of science which deals with chemicals	Chemistry

Multiple Word Expression	Substitution
A printed leaf usually issued by banks that we sign to carry certain financial deal	Cheque
A person who makes or mends shoes	Cobbler
A group of people who has been chosen by others to make decisions on their own	Committee
A building in which nuns live	Convent
An animal which feeds on other animals	Carnivorous
A person who does criticism	Critic
A person who cannot hear	Deaf
A condition in which one loses a lot of water from one's body because of vomiting, etc.	Dehydration
A system of government in which the people cast their votes to elect their leaders	Democracy
The study of skin problems	Dermatology
A long piece of land covered with sand	Desert
The art of managing relationships between countries	Diplomacy
A piece of information about the words in a book form	Dictionary
A piece of information about the telephone numbers of the people in a book from	Directory
A person in charge of a newspapers, magazine etc.	Editor
A person who thinks he is better than the others	Egoist
To leave your country and settle in some other country	Emigrate
A book or series of books giving almost all knowledge about an area or some persons etc.	Encyclopaedia
Study of insects	Entomology
Time when day and night are of the same duration	Equinox
To sell things out of the country	Export
To purchase things from some other country	Import
A plant or animal no longer in existence	Extinct
A situation when there is a shortage of food for a long period of time	Famine
An amount of money that we pay for some action or services	Fee
Related to women	Feminine
An animal strong and aggressive	Ferocious
A piece of land where plants grow easily from the soil that is favourable to them	Fertile
A work of literature having some imaginary events	Fiction
A large amount of water covering certain area	Flood
A person who sells flowers	Florist
A religious ceremony for burying or cremating a dead person	Funeral
A substance which kills fungus	Fungicide
A person studying or having studied the diseases and the related things of female reproductory system	Gynaecologist
The murder of the person of the same group race or country	Genocide
A substance which kills germs	Germicide
A situation in which many people die because of fire during war	Holocaust
The act of killing a person deliberately	Homicide
A word having the pronunciation as the other one does but it differs in meaning	Homophone
A word having the same spelling as the other one does but it is pronounced in some other way	Homonym
A person who is attracted towards the person of the same sex	Homosexual
Go across and parallel to the ground	Horizontal
A substance which kills the insects	Insecticide
That cannot be corrected	Incorrigible
That cannot be defeated	Invincible
That cannot be eaten	Inedible
That cannot be seen	Invisible
A place in a school or college where books are kept for the benefit of students, teachers etc.	Library

Multiple Word Expression	*Substitution*
A place in a school or college where scientific experiments are performed	Laboratory
An official who is a judge in the lowest court	Magistrate
A piece of music or a book before it is printed	Manuscript
Related to men	Masculine
One who believes in the existence of God	A theist
One who does not believe in the existence of good	An atheist
That can be believed	Credible
That cannot be believed	Incredible
That which dissolves in a solvent	Soluble
That which does not dissolves in a solvent	Insoluble
Hard writing that can be read	Legible
Hard writing that cannot be read	Illegible
A person who does jobs beneficial to mankind	Philanthropist
A person who goes on foot	Pedestrian
A person who fights for his own country	Patriot
An act of killing oneself	Suicide
A woman whose husband is dead	Widow
A man whose wife is dead	Widower
A person who eats vegetarian and non-vegetarian diets	Omnivorous
Something which is everywhere at the same time	Omnipresent
One who knows everything	Omniscient
A child who does not have parents	Orphan
An award etc. given after the death of the person	Posthumous
The place where animals are kept for amusement and to increase the knowledge of the public	Zoo
The science which deals with the study of animals	Zoology

MULTIPLE CHOICE QUESTIONS

Directions: *In questions given below, out of the four alternatives, choose the one which can be substituted for the given words/sentences.*

1. Something that relates to everyone in the world
A. General B. Common
C. Usual D. Universal

2. An expression of mild disapproval
A. Warning B. Denigration
C. Impertinence D. Reproof

3. One who is not easily pleased by anything
A. Maiden B. Medieval
C. Precarious D. Fastidious

4. Murder of a king
A. Infanticide B. Matricide
C. Genocide D. Regicide

5. A remedy for all diseases
A. Stoic B. Marvel
C. Panacea D. Recompense

6. A dramatic performance
A. Mask B. Mosque
C. Masque D. Mascot

7. Study of birds
A. Orology B. Optology
C. Ophthalmology D. Ornithology

8. Ready to believe
A. Credulous B. Credible
C. Creditable D. Incredible

9. Incapable of being seen through
A. Ductile B. Opaque
C. Obsolete D. Potable

10. One who eats everything
A. Omnivorous B. Omniscient
C. Irresistible D. Insolvent

11. A place where bees are kept is called
A. An apiary B. A mole
C. A hive D. A sanctuary

12. One who cannot be corrected
A. Incurable B. Incorrigible
C. Hardened D. Invulnerable

13. One who is in charge of a museum
A. Curator B. Supervisor
C. Caretaker D. Warden

14. Continuing fight between parties, families, clans, etc.
A. Enmity B. Feud
C. Quarrel D. Skirmish

15. A voice loud enough to be heard
A. Audible B. Applaudable
C. Laudable D. Oral

16. A paper written by hand
A. Handicraft B. Manuscript
C. Handiwork D. Thesis

17. Habitually silent or talking little
A. Serville B. Unequivocal
C. Taciturn D. Synoptic

18. To slap with a flat object
A. Chop B. Hew
C. Gnaw D. Swat

19. A person who speaks many languages
A. Linguist B. Monolingual
C. Polyglot D. Bilingual

20. A light sailing-boat built specially for racing
A. Canoe B. Yacht
C. Frigate D. Dinghy

21. A fixed orbit in space in relation to earth
A. Geological B. Geo-synchronous
C. Geo-centric D. Geo-stationary

22. A style in which a writer makes a display of his knowledge
A. Pedantic B. Verbose
C. Pompous D. Ornate

23. A religious discourse
A. Preach B. Stanza
C. Sanctorum D. Sermon

24. A place that provides refuge
A. Asylum B. Sanatorium
C. Shelter D. Orphanage

25. Detailed plan of a journey
A. Travelogue B. Travelkit
C. Schedule D. Itinerary

26. A person who insists on something
A. Disciplinarian B. Stickler
C. Instantaneous D. Boaster

27. A drawing on transparent paper
A. Red print B. Blue print
C. Negative D. Transparency

28. One who believes that all things and events in life are predetermined is a
A. Fatalist B. Puritan
C. Egoist D. Tyrant

29. A school boy who cuts classes frequently is a
A. Defeatist B. Sycophant
C. Truant D. Martinet

30. The act of violating the sanctity of the church is
A. Blasphemy B. Heresy
C. Sacrilege D. Desecration

31. A place where monks live as a secluded community
A. Cathedral B. Diocese
C. Convent D. Monastery

32. One who is fond of fighting
A. Bellicose B. Aggressive
C. Belligerent D. Militant

33. Tending to move away from the centre or axis
A. Centrifugal B. Centripetal
C. Axiomatic D. Awry

34. Words inscribed on tomb
A. Epitome B. Epistle
C. Epilogue D. Epitaph

35. Leave or remove from a place considered dangerous
A. Evade B. Evacuate
C. Avoid D. Exterminate

36. Original inhabitants of a country
A. Abroge B. Aborger
C. Aborgory D. Aborigins

37. Government by the officials
A. Theocracy B. Plutocracy
C. Bureaucracy D. Democracy

38. Incapable of being exhausted
A. Inexhaustible
B. Inaexhaustible
C. Exhaustable
D. Non-tired

39. A person of good understanding, knowledge and reasoning power
A. Expert B. Intellectual
C. Snob D. Literate

40. One absorbed in his own thoughts and feelings rather than in things outside
A. Scholar B. Recluse
C. Introvert D. Intellectual

ANSWERS

1	2	3	4	5	6	7	8	9	10
D	D	D	D	C	C	D	A	B	A
11	**12**	**13**	**14**	**15**	**16**	**17**	**18**	**19**	**20**
A	B	A	B	A	B	C	D	A	B
21	**22**	**23**	**24**	**25**	**26**	**27**	**28**	**29**	**30**
D	A	D	A	D	B	D	A	C	C
31	**32**	**33**	**34**	**35**	**36**	**37**	**38**	**39**	**40**
D	A	A	D	B	B	C	A	B	C

●●●

6 SPELLING ERRORS

There are thousands of words in English language. It is difficult to remember the spellings and meanings of all at once. Try to learn as many as you can. Use a dictionary regularly.

Directions: *Find the correctly spelt words.*

1. A. Damage B. Dammage C. Damaige D. Dammege

2. A. Efficiant B. Effecient C. Efficient D. Eficient

3. A. Schedule B. Schdule C. Schedale D. Schedeule

4. A. Occurad B. Occurred C. Ocurred D. Occured

5. A. Grieff B. Grief C. Grieef D. Grrief

6. A. Guarantee B. Garuntee C. Guaruntee D. Gaurantee

7. A. Meddicine B. Medicine C. Medicene D. Medicinne

8. A. Benefeted B. Benefitted C. Benifited D. Benefited

9. A. Acommodation B. Acomodation C. Accomodation D. Accommodation

10. A. Querrelsome B. Quarrelsame C. Quarrelsome D. Querralsome

11. A. Sympathetic B. Smypathetic C. Sympothetic D. Sympethetic

12. A. Prograssive B. Progressive C. Progresive D. Prograsive

13. A. Uncivilized B. Uncevilized C. Uncivillized D. Uncevelized

14. A. Extravagant B. Extreragent C. Extreregant D. Extravegent

15. A. Missunderstood B. Miesunderstood C. Misunderstood D. Misunderstod

16. A. Belligerent B. Beligirent C. Belligarant D. Belligerrent

17. A. Astonished B. Astronished C. Astoneshed D. Asstonished

18. A. Sincerely B. Sencerely C. Sincerelly D. Sincerrely

19. A. Rigourous B. Rigerous C. Rigorous D. Regerous

20. A. Satellite B. Sattellite C. Satelite D. Sattelite

21. A. Pesanger B. Passenger C. Pessenger D. Pasanger

22. A. Humurous B. Humorous C. Humoreus D. Humorrous

23. A. Exeggerate B. Exaggerate C. Exadgerate D. Exagerate

24. A. Fariegn B. Forein C. Foriegn D. Foreign

25. A. Excesive B. Excessive C. Exccessive D. Exccesive

26. A. Forcaust B. Forcast C. Forecast D. Forecaste

27. A. Paralleted B. Paralelled C. Parralleled D. Parallelled

28. A. Ocasion B. Occassion C. Occasion D. Ocassion

29. A. Boquet B. Bouquet C. Bouquete D. Bouquette

30. A. Chettering B. Chaterring C. Chattering D. Chatering

31. A. Discourage B. Disscourage C. Discourege D. Discaurage

32. A. Curageous B. Courageous C. Courrageous D. Couregeous

33. A. Abandon B. Abanddon C. Abendon D. Abbandon

34. A. Embarassment B. Emberrassement C. Embarrassment D. Embbaresment

35. A. Eccintric B. Eccentrie C. Eccentric D. Eccintrie

36. A. Occasional B. Occassional C. Occesional D. Occessional

37. A. Querrel B. Querral C. Quarrel D. Quarel

38. A. Contrebution B. Contribution C. Contributtion D. Conterbution

39. A. Desgrace B. Disgrece
C. Disgrice D. Disgrace

40. A. Harassment B. Herassment
C. Harasment D. Harassmient

41. A. Imaginative B. Imeginative
C. Imagenative D. Imaginetive

42. A. Suficient B. Suficiant
C. Sufficient D. Sufficiant

43. A. Adequate B. Edequate
C. Adaquete D. Edaquete

44. A. Experienced B. Experianced
C. Experienced D. Experrienced

45. A. Flatering B. Fletering
C. Flattering D. Fletaring

46. A. Cuttiveted B. Culltrivated
C. Cultivated D. Caltivated

47. A. Praiceworthy B. Peiseworthy
C. Praiseworthy D. Praisaworthy

48. A. Profesional B. Professionel
C. Professional D. Profissional

49. A. Ameteur B. Amateur
C. Amataur D. Amateor

50. A. Unfevourable B. Unfevaurable
C. Unfavourable D. Unfivourable

ANSWERS

1	2	3	4	5	6	7	8	9	10
A	C	A	B	B	A	B	B	D	C
11	**12**	**13**	**14**	**15**	**16**	**17**	**18**	**19**	**20**
A	B	A	A	C	A	A	A	C	A
21	**22**	**23**	**24**	**25**	**26**	**27**	**28**	**29**	**30**
B	B	B	D	B	C	A	C	B	C
31	**32**	**33**	**34**	**35**	**36**	**37**	**38**	**39**	**40**
A	B	A	C	C	A	C	B	D	A
41	**42**	**43**	**44**	**45**	**46**	**47**	**48**	**49**	**50**
A	C	A	C	A	C	C	C	B	C

● ● ●

हिन्दी भाषा

• अनुच्छेद आधारित प्रश्नोत्तर •

निर्देशः निम्नलिखित प्रत्येक अनुच्छेद पर आधारित प्रश्न दिए गए हैं। प्रश्नों के उत्तर देने से पहले अनुच्छेदों को ध्यानपूर्वक पढ़ें।

प्रत्येक प्रश्न के लिए A, B, C एवम् D विकल्प वाले चार सम्भावित उत्तर दिए गए हैं। इनमें से केवल एक ही उत्तर सही है। आपको सही उत्तर का चयन करना है।

अनुच्छेद-1

मनुष्य के विकास में शिक्षा का एक महत्वपूर्ण स्थान है। शिक्षा द्वारा मनुष्य का मानसिक एवम् बौद्धिक विकास होता है। शिक्षा के बिना मनुष्य पशु के समान है। यह अत्यन्त आवश्यक है कि पुरूष और स्त्रियाँ दोनों ही समान रूप से शिक्षा-प्राप्त करें। यदि स्त्रियाँ शिक्षित नहीं की गईं तो हमारा आधा समाज पिछड़ा ही रहेगा। आजकल संसार के अनेक भागों में स्त्रियों की शिक्षा के अच्छे परिणाम हम देख सकते हैं। इसका ही परिणाम है कि अनेक बुरे रीति-रिवाज और अन्ध-विश्वास समाज में बहुत तेजी से दूर होने लगे हैं। राष्ट्रीय विकास के हर क्षेत्र में स्त्रियाँ पुरूषों के कन्धों से कन्धा मिलाकर काम कर रही हैं और बराबर की जिम्मेदारी निभा रही हैं।

1. शिक्षा मनुष्य के लिए महत्वपूर्ण हैं, क्योंकि–
- A. यह पशु को मनुष्य बनाती है
- B. यह राष्ट्र को विकसित करती है
- C. इससे मनुष्य की मानसिक और बौद्धिक शक्ति का विकास होता है
- D. यह स्त्रियों के लिए आवश्यक है

2. स्त्रियों का शिक्षित होना आवश्यक है, क्योंकि–
- A. स्त्रियों को काम करना पसन्द है
- B. स्त्रियाँ अकेले ही समाज की बुराइयों को दूर कर सकतो हैं
- C. स्त्रियाँ स्वभाव से ही अन्धविश्वासी होती है
- D. पूरे समाज के शिक्षित होने पर ही उन्नति हो सकती है

3. शिक्षा के बिना मनुष्य पशु के समान है, क्योंकि–
- A. वह कठिन परिश्रम नहीं करता
- B. उसकी मानसिक शक्तियाँ विकसित नहीं हो पातीं
- C. यह अपनी जीविका पैदा नहीं कर सकता
- D. वह अन्ध-विश्वासी बना रहता है

4. स्त्री शिक्षा के कौन से अच्छे परिणाम हैं?
- A. स्त्रियों को नौकरियाँ मिल रही हैं
- B. स्त्रियाँ बहुत सारा धन कमा रही हैं
- C. लड़कियाँ स्कूलों में जा रही हैं
- D. अन्धविश्वासों और बुरे रीति-रिवाजों का तेजी से सफाया हो रहा है

5. स्त्रियाँ पुरूषों के साथ बराबर की जिम्मेदारी निभा रही हैं, क्योंकि।

A. वे शिक्षित हैं	B. वे बहुत सारा धन कमा रही हैं
C. वे पुरूषों के बराबर हैं	D. वे अन्धविश्वासी हैं।

अनुच्छेद-2

एक मन्त्री जब जेल का निरीक्षण कर रहे थे, तो उन्होंने वहाँ जेल की कोठरी में एक जवान अपराधी को देखा। मन्त्री ने कैदी से पूछा कि उसने कौन-सा अपराध किया है। कैदी ने बताया, "मैं तो खाली गली में घूम रहा था कि मैने जमीन पर एक रस्सी का टुकड़ा देखा, मैने सोचा वह किसी के काम का नहीं है। मैने उसे उठा लिया और अपने घर ले गया।" मन्त्रीजी उसकी बात को सुन कर आश्चर्य में पड़ गए। उनको उस पर दया आ गई। उन्होंने जेल अधीक्षक से पूछा, "क्या इस जवान को कैद करना ठीक है? उसने तो केवल एक पुरानी रस्सी का टुकड़ा उठा लिया था।" जेल अधीक्षक ने उत्तर दिया "कृपया आप उससे पूछें कि रस्सी से क्या बंधा हुआ था?" बदकिस्मती से उस रस्सी से एक गाय बंधी हुई थी, महोदय", उस जवान ने उत्तर दिया।

1. जवान आदमी ने रस्सी को क्यों उठाया?
- A. उसे रस्सी बहुत पसन्द थी
- B. उसे गाय को बाँधने के लिए रस्सी चाहिए थी
- C. रस्सी से एक गाय बंधी थी
- D. रस्सी किसी की नहीं थी

2. "बदकिस्मती से उस रस्सी से एक गाय बंधी हुई थी, महोदय" इस वाक्य से हमें ज्ञात होता है कि कैदी–

A. चालाक था	B. झूठा था
C. निर्दोष था	D. ईमानदार था

3. मन्त्री महोदय ने जवान कैदी को कब देखा?
- A. गली में घूमते समय
- B. जवान आदमी को रस्सी का टुकड़ा उठाते समय
- C. जवान आदमी को गाय ले जाते समय
- D. जेल का निरीक्षण करते समय

4. कैदी का पहला उत्तर सुनकर मन्त्रीजी–

A. आश्चर्य में पड़ गए	B. प्रसन्न हो गए
C. भड़क उठे	D. चिढ़ गए

5. मन्त्रीजी ने जेल अधीक्षक से पूछा–
- A. क्या रस्सी का टुकड़ा कैदी का था
- B. क्या जवान आदमी को छोड़ना है
- C. रस्सी से क्या गाय बंधी थी
- D. क्या जवान आदमी को कैद करना ठीक था

अनुच्छेद-3

अमेरिका के एक प्रसिद्ध जीवन-शास्त्री का कहना है कि जिन्दगी संघर्ष से भरी हुई है। एक के बाद एक खींचतान लगी ही रहती है और चैन नहीं मिल पाता, इसलिए जीवन में उन क्षणों की बहुत क़ीमत है जो जीवन को गुदगुदा दें और खींचतान की तेजी को भुला दें।

इस जीवन-शास्त्री ने लोगों को एक बड़ा दिलचस्प मशविरा दिया है कि जब तुम अपने किसी मित्र-दोस्त से बात करने बैठो, तो घड़ी का मुँह दीवार की तरफ कर दो।

जब उससे पूछा गया कि बातचीत और घड़ी का क्या सम्बन्ध है तो उत्तर मिला कि वह कम्बख्त याद दिलाती रहती है कि इतनी देर हो गई-इतनी देर हो गई और इस तरह वह आनन्द-क्षण खण्डित हो जाता है, जो मित्र की बातचीत से मिलता है।

1. जीवन-शास्त्री ने किसे कम्बख्त कहा है?
A. अपने को B. मित्र को
C. घड़ी को D. जीवन-शास्त्री को

2. लेखक के अनुसार आज का जीवन कैसा है?
A. तनावपूर्ण B. संघर्षमय
C. आनन्दपूर्ण D. शान्तिपूर्ण

3. जीवन में वे क्षण मूल्यवान हैं जो–
A. जिन्दगी में खींचतान ला दे
B. जिन्दगी में चैन से बैठने न दें
C. जिन्दगी को संघर्ष से भर दें
D. जिन्दगी की खींचतान को तेजी से भूला दें

4. मित्रतापूर्ण गपशप में प्रायः आ जाता है–
A. जोश B. आनन्द
C. तनाव D. अमित्रता

5. जीवन को गुदगुदाने वाले क्षणों की कीमत है, क्योंकि–
A. उनसे जीवन में तेजी आती हैं
B. उनसे जीवन में संघर्ष बढ़ता हैं
C. उनसे शान्तिपूर्ण जीवन में खींचतान बढ़ती हैं
D. उनसे तनावपूर्ण जीवन में चैन मिलता हैं

अनुच्छेद-4

हिन्दी के प्रसिद्ध कवि दिनकर एक बार रिक्शा पर बैठ कर कहीं जा रहे थे। उन्हें तभी अपनी कविता की एक पुस्तक पर हजार रुपए मिले थे। उन्होंने देखा कि एक औरत सड़क के किनारे बैठ कर भीख माँग रही थी। दिनकर जी ने रिक्शा रुकवाया और उसके पास गए।

"आज तुम्हें कितनी भीख मिली?"

"सवेरे से कुछ नहीं मिला बेटा"

दिनकर जी सोचने लगे, अगर इस औरत को मेरी तरह कोई बेटा होता, तो क्या इसे इस तरह भीख माँगनी पड़ती। उन्होंने उसे एक रुपया दिया ओर बोले, माँ! अब तुम्हें कितने दिन भीख नहीं माँगनी पड़ेगी?

"तीन दिन बेटे"

"मान लो यदि मैं तुम्हें 10 रुपए दे दूँ तो?"

"20 या 25 दिन"

"मान लो मैं तुम्हें एक सौ रुपए दे दूँ तो?"

"चार या पाँच महीने"

सूरज की भीषण गर्मी में दिनकर जी प्रश्न करते रहे और वह बुढ़िया उन्हें उत्तर देती रही। रिक्शा चालक भौंचक्का सा देखता रहा। जब दिनकर जी ने अपना अन्तिम रुपया भी बुढ़िया के भिक्षा पात्र में डाल दिया, तो वह खुशी से चिल्ला उठी, "बेटा, अब मुझे भीख नहीं माँगनी पड़ेगी।"

दिनकर जी ने राहत की साँस ली। उन्होंने उस औरत के पाँव छुए और रिक्शा पर बैठ कर अपने घर चले गए।

1. दिनकर सन्तुष्ट हो गए थे क्योंकि–
A. उन्होंने अपना पैसा भीख में दे दिया था
B. उन्हें उनकी माँ मिल गई थी
C. उन्होंने बुढ़िया को भीख माँगने से बचा लिया था
D. उन्होंने एक बुढ़िया के पाँव छुए थे

2. उस बुढ़िया को दिनकर जी ने कितने रुपए दिए?
A. एक रुपया B. दस रुपये
C. एक सौ रुपए D. एक हजार रुपये

3. निम्नलिखित में से इस कहानी का सबसे उपयुक्त शीर्षक कौन सा हैं?
A. एक लालची भिखमंगा
B. एक आज्ञाकारी पुत्र
C. भीख माँगना लाभदायक
D. उदार हदयी दिनकर

4. दिनकर जी रुककर उस बुढ़िया से बातें करने लगे, क्योंकि–
A. वे भीख माँगने वाली औरत की मदद करना चाहते थे
B. वे उसके पुत्र थे
C. उनके पास एक हजार रुपये थे
D. वे जानना चाहते थे कि भीख माँगने वाली औरत प्रतिदिन कितना पा जाती है

5. रिक्शा चालक को बहुत आश्चर्य हुआ क्योंकि–
A. दिनकर ने भीख माँगने वाली औरत के पाँव छुए
B. दिनकर ने बहुत सारा धन उस भीख माँगने वाली औरत को दे दिया
C. एक प्रसिद्ध कवि एक भीख माँगने वाली औरत से बात कर रहा था
D. दिनकर सूरज की भीषण गर्मी में खड़े थे

अनुच्छेद-5

जिन महापुरुषों ने भारतीय समाज की दुर्व्यवस्था एवम् गलत नीतियों को दूर करने में अपने जीवन के अमूल्य क्षणों का सदुपयोग किया, उनमें राजा राममोहन राय का नाम प्रमुख है। उन्होंने सती-प्रथा और बाल विवाह जैसी कुरीतियों को बन्द कराने का आन्दोलन चलाया जो आगे चलकर सफल हुआ। वे 'नए भारत के पिता' के नाम से हमारे देश में लब्धप्रतिष्ठ थे। राजा राममोहन राय ने समाज की कुरीतियों को हटाने के लिए पुस्तकें लिखीं, लेख लिखे और निर्भय होकर बुराइयों का भण्डाफोड़ किया। उन्होंने 'ब्रह्मसमाज' की स्थापना की। उनके चलते बंगाल के हिन्दू नवयुवक समझने लगे कि हिन्दू ठोस हैं और ढोंगियों ने इनमें बुराइयाँ फैला रखी हैं। राममोहन राय के समय

बंगाल में अंग्रेजी शासन था। उन्होंने शासन की ओर से ऐसे कानून बनवाने की कोशिशें की जिनसे भारतवासियों में फैली बुराइयाँ दूर हों। उन्होंने देखा कि अंग्रेजी सरकार हुकूमत के लिए अंग्रेजी में कागज-पत्र लिखती है। कानून की किताबें अंग्रेजी में लिखी जाती है। भारत के लोग अंग्रेजी पढ़ना-लिखना नहीं जानते और इसलिए सिर्फ चपरासी बनाए जाते हैं। उस समय अंग्रेज नहीं चाहते थे कि भारतीय अंग्रेजी पढ़ें, उनको डर था कि अंग्रेजी पढ़ जाने से वे हुकूमत में टांग अड़ाएंगें और अंग्रेजों की पोल खुल जाएगी। राममोहन राय अंग्रेजों की चाल समझ गए थे। उन्होंने आन्दोलन किया। दो-चार अंग्रेजों ने भी उनका समर्थन किया। लाचार होकर अंग्रेजी सरकार ने भारतीयों को अंग्रेजी पढ़ने के लिए शिक्षा-विभाग खोला।

1. राममोहन राय के समय भारतीय किस नौकरी में लिए जाते थे?

A. दारोगा B. चपरासी

C. किरानी D. सिपाही

2. सती-प्रथा और बाल-विवाह राममोहन राय के जमाने की क्या थी?

A. रीतियाँ B. संस्कार

C. प्रथाएँ D. कुरीतियाँ

3. राममोहन राय को किस नाम से प्रतिष्ठा प्राप्त थी?

A. नए भारत के पिता

B. नए भारत के निर्माता

C. नए भारत के संत

D. नए भारत के आन्दोलन कर्त्ता

4. हुकूमत के लिए अंग्रेजी सरकार कागज-पत्र किस भाषा में लिखती थी?

A. हिन्दी में

B. अंग्रेजी में

C. लैटिन में

D. हिन्दी एवम् अंग्रेजी दोनों में

5. राजा राममोहन राय ने किस समाज को स्थापित किया?

A. हिन्दू समाज B. वैष्णव समाज

C. ब्रह्मसमाज D. आर्य समाज

अनुच्छेद-6

टेलीफोन ने समय और दूरी के फासले में परिवर्तन कर दिखाया है। मैदान में खड़े होकर हम जोर से चिल्लाएँ, तो हमारी आवाज ज्यादा से ज्यादा एक सौ गज तक पहुँच पाएगी। लेकिन टेलीफोन पर धीरे से बोलें तो हजारों मील की दूरी तक आवाज आसानी से पहुँच जाती है। दरअसल टेलीफोन की आवाज बिजली की लहरों के जरिए भेजी जाती है। लहरों की रफ्तार आवाज की रफ्तार से लाख गुना ज्यादा है। टेलीफोन ने हमारी आवाज में मानों पंख लगा दिए हैं। टेलीफोन के अविष्कार की कहानी बड़ी मनोरंजक हैं इसे समझने के लिए आवाज के बारे में थोड़ी जानकारी हासिल कर लेनी जरूरी है, चोट करने पर नगाड़े के चमड़े का पर्दा कम्पन करने लगता है और तभी आवाज पैदा होती है। थाली में डण्डे से चोट करने पर थाली में कंपकंपी पैदा होती है और आवाज सुनाई पड़ती है। सितार के तार पर जब मिजराब से चोट करते हैं तब तार भी काँपने लगता है और उससे आवाज पैदा होती है। इस कंपकंपी से हवा में कम्पन्न पैदा होती हैं, जिसे आवाज की लहरें कहते है। हवा में उत्पन्न होने वाली ये लहरें जब कान के पर्दे पर चोट करती हैं तो पर्दे में हरकत पैदा होती है और हमें आवाज सुनाई पड़ने लगती है।

1. टेलीफोन ने हमारी आवाज में मानो क्या लगा दिए हैं?

A. घोड़े B. पंख

C. बिजली D. हवाई जहाज

2. हवा में उत्पन्न होने वाली लहरें हमारे कानों के पर्दे पर चोट करती हैं तो पर्दे में क्या पैदा होती है?

A. हरकत B. पीड़ा

C. खुजली D. जलन

3. मैदान में चिल्लाने से हमारी आवाज ज्यादा से ज्यादा कितने गज दूर पहुँचेगी?

A. चार सौ गज B. तीन सौ गज

C. दौ सौ गज D. एक सौ गज

4. सितार के तार पर किस वस्तु से चोट की जाती है?

A. जुराब से B. उंगली से

C. मिजराब से D. डण्डा से

5. थाली में डण्डे से चोट करने पर थाली में क्या पैदा होती है?

A. कंपकंपी B. लहरें

C. आवाज D. रफ्तार

अनुच्छेद-7

हमारा राष्ट्रीय झण्डा 'तिरंगा' है। यह हमारी राष्ट्रीय अस्मिता का प्रतीक है। हमारा तिरंगा झण्डा 3:2 के अनुपात में एक आयताकार कपड़े पर बना होता है। केसरिया, सफेद व हरी पट्टियों के बीच 24 तीलियों वाला एक चक्र होता है। यह चक्र अशोक स्तम्भ से लिया गया है। तीनों पट्टियाँ समान चौड़ाई की होती हैं। केसरिया रंग वाली पट्टी झण्डे के ऊपरी भाग में, सफेद रंग की पट्टी बीच में और हरे रंग की पट्टी नीचे होती है। चक्र बीच की सफेद पट्टी में बीचों-बीच होता हैं। चक्र हमारी गति का प्रतीक है। केसरिया रंग हमारे शौर्य का प्रतीक है। सफेद रंग हमारी शान्तिप्रियता एवम् हरा रंग हमारी धरती माँ की हरियाली का प्रतीक है। 15 अगस्त व 26 जनवरी को तिरंगा झण्डा फहराया जाता है। सभी भारतवासियों को अपने राष्ट्रीय झण्डे पर गर्व है। उन्हें यह प्राणों से भी प्यारा है।

1. तिरंगे झण्डे को कब फहराया जाता है?

A. 26 जनवरी को प्रतिवर्ष

B. 15 अगस्त को प्रतिवर्ष

C. प्रतिदिन प्रातः काल

D. 15 अगस्त व 26 जनवरी को प्रतिवर्ष

2. चक्र तिरंगे झण्डे में–

A. हरे रंग की पट्टी के बीचों-बीच होता है

B. केसरिया रंग की पट्टी में होता है

C. सफेद पट्टी के बीचों-बीच होता है

D. बीच में होता है

3. केसरिया रंग हमारे–

A. गति का प्रतीक है

B. शान्ति का प्रतीक है

C. शौर्य का प्रतीक है

D. हरियाली का प्रतीक है

4. हमारा तिरंगा झण्डा है–

A. आयताकार   B. गोलाकार
C. वर्गाकार   D. त्रिभुजाकार

5. तिरंगे झण्डे का अनुपात होता है–

A. 3 : 1   B. 4 : 2
C. 3 : 2   D. 3 : 4

अनुच्छेद-8

हैदराबाद आन्ध्र प्रदेश की राजधानी है। मुगल शासकों ने बहुत समय तक हैदराबाद पर शासन किया। इस कारण यहाँ की सभ्यता पर मुस्लिम संस्कृति का प्रभाव पड़ा। यह प्रभाव यहाँ की इमारतों व महत्वपूर्ण स्थलों में देखा जा सकता है। हैदराबाद का उस्मानिया विश्वविद्यालय शिक्षा के क्षेत्र में सुविख्यात है। हैदराबाद के निवासियों की मुख्य भाषा उर्दू मिश्रित तेलगू है। हैदराबाद के समीप फैली विशाल झील हुसैन सागर इस शहर की सुन्दरता में चार चाँद लगा देती है। हैदराबाद के पास एक पहाड़ी पर श्वेत मन्दिर स्थित है। पहाड़ी की दूसरी तरफ काली चट्टानों वाला नौबत पहाड़ स्थित है। हैदराबाद शहर के आठ किलोमीटर पश्चिम में स्थित गोलकुण्डा दुर्ग है। गोलकुण्डा को 'कोहिनूर की धरती' कहते हैं, क्योंकि इस हीरे को यहीं तराशा गया था।

1. मुस्लिम संस्कृति का प्रभाव हैदराबाद के–

A. लोगों के पहनावे में देखा जा सकता है
B. इमारतों व महत्वपूर्ण स्थलों में देखा जा सकता है
C. गोलकुण्डा में देखा जा सकता है
D. हुसैन सागर झील में देखा जा सकता है

2. गोलकुण्डा को कोहिनूर की धरती कहते हैं क्योंकि–

A. यहाँ कोहिनूर हीरा दुर्ग में रखा गया था
B. यहाँ कोहेनूर हीरा दुर्ग में रखा गया था
C. यहाँ के धनाढ्य व्यक्तियों के पास कोहिनूर हीरे हैं
D. यहाँ कोहिनूर हीरा तराशा गया था

3. हैदराबाद के निवासियों की मुख्य भाषा–

A. हिन्दी है   B. तेलगू है
C. मलयालम है   D. उर्दू मिश्रित तेलगू है

4. उस्मानिया विश्वविद्यालय

A. शिक्षा के क्षेत्र में प्रसिद्ध है
B. में 'कोहिनूर' रखा हुआ है
C. क्रिकेट के खेल के लिए प्रसिद्ध है
D. तकनीकी शिक्षा का केन्द्र है

5. हैदराबाद शहर से कितनी दूरी पर गोलकुण्डा दुर्ग है?

A. दस किलोमीटर   B. आठ किलोमीटर
C. पाँच किलोमीटर   D. अठारह किलोमीटर

अनुच्छेद-9

जब हम साफ रात्रि में आकाश की ओर देखते हैं तो हमें दूर-दूर तक हजारों तारें टिमटिमाते हुए दिखाई देते हैं। उन्हें देख कर लगता है जैसे किसी ने उन्हें आकाश की काली पृष्ठभूमि पर चिपका रखा है। कई बार अचम्भा होता है **कि वे हर रात एक ही जगह पर कैसे बने रहते हैं, गिर क्यों नहीं जाते।** रोचक **तथ्य तो यह है कि तारे वास्तव में एक जगह स्थिर नहीं रहते हैं।** जिस प्रकार पृथ्वी तथा अन्य आठ ग्रह सूर्य के चारों ओर अपने-अपने पथ पर चलते रहते हैं, वे भी उसी प्रकार अपने पथ पर धीरे-धीरे चलते रहते हैं। ऐसा लगता है कि तारे एक ही जगह स्थिर रहते हैं, क्योंकि हम उन्हें चलते हुए नहीं देख सकते हैं। इसका कारण यह है कि वे हमसे हजारों-हजार किलोमीटर दूर हैं। जब वे चलते हुए भी होते हैं तब भी ऐसा लगता है कि वे एक ही जगह पर हैं। इसके अतिरिक्त एक शक्ति है जिसे हम गुरुत्वाकर्षण शक्ति कहते हैं जिसके कारण चलते समय भी तारे अपने पथ पर बने रहते हैं। यह उनको एक-दूसरे से टकराने से भी बचाती है।

1. हम तारों को चलते हुए नहीं देख सकते क्योंकि–

A. वे टिमटिमाते हैं
B. रात्रि को आकाश साफ नहीं होता है
C. वे हमसे बहुत दूर है
D. गुरुत्वाकर्षण शक्ति ने उन्हें अपने स्थान पर स्थिर कर दिया है।

2. 'यह उनको एक-दूसरे से टकराने से भी बचाती है।' इस वाक्य में "यह" से तात्पर्य है–

A. आकाश से   B. सूर्य से
C. विशाल दूरी से   D. गुरुत्वाकर्षण शक्ति से

3. साफ रात्रि में आकाश की ओर देखने पर हमें दिखाई देता है कि–

A. दूर आकाश में तारे टिमटिमा रहे हैं
B. तारे एक पथ पर धीरे-धीरे चल रहे हैं
C. तारे एक-दूसरे के बहुत पास दिखाई दे रहे हैं
D. ग्रह अपने पथ पर चल रहे हैं

4. तारों के चलते समय अपने पथ पर बने रहने का कारण है–

A. उनकी धीमी गति   B. गुरुत्वाकर्षण शक्ति
C. उनका न गिरना   D. उनकी बहुत दूरी

5. उपरोक्त अनुच्छेद में किस रोचक तथ्य का उल्लेख किया गया है?

A. तारे एक जगह स्थिर नहीं रहते हैं
B. ग्रह सूर्य के ईर्द-गिर्द घूमते हैं
C. गुरुत्वाकर्षण शक्ति तारों को अपने स्थान पर स्थिर रखती हैं
D. तारे आकाश में चिपका दिए गए हैं

अनुच्छेद-10

एक व्यापारी को एक दिन तीसरे पहर अपने रसोईघर में एक साँप दिखाई दिया। उसे साँप मारना नहीं आता था। इसलिए उसने साँप को एक बरतन से ढक दिया। फिर वह अपने मित्रों से मिलने चला गया। उस रात उसके घर कुछ चोर आए। रसोईघर में रखे हुए उस बरतन को देखकर वे खुशी से चिल्ला कर बोले, "ओहो! व्यापारी ने इस बरतन में कोई मूल्यवान वस्तु छिपा रखी है। क्यों न हम इसे ले जाएँ।" यह सोचकर जैसे ही उन्होने वह बरतन उठाया साँप उन्हे डसने के लिए दौड़ते हुए आगे बढ़ा। चोर घबरा कर घर से भाग निकले। वे कुछ भी नहीं चुरा पाए। व्यापारी का सब धन उस साँप की वजह से बच गया।

1. चोर घर से भाग निकले क्योंकि–

A. वे कुछ भी चुराना नहीं चाहते थे
B. रसोईघर में खाने को कुछ नहीं था
C. वे साँप से डर गये थे
D. व्यापारी जाग गया था

2. उस रात घर में कौन आए?

A. साँप B. चोर

C. मित्र D. व्यापारी

3. व्यापारी को अपने घर में क्या मिला?

A. घर B. बरतन

C. साँप D. चोर

4. व्यापारी ने साँप को बरतन से ढक दिया था क्योंकि–

A. उसने सोचा कि वह उपयोगी रहेगा

B. उसे साँप मारना नहीं आता था

C. वह साँप को पालना चाहता था

D. वह चोरों को डराना चाहता था

5. चोरों ने बरतन को इसलिए उठाया कि

A. वे साँप को लेना चाहते थे

B. उनके विचार से उसमें कोई मूल्यवान वस्तु थी

C. वह उन्हे दिखाई दे गया था

D. वे उसे लेना चाहते थे

अनुच्छेद-11

माँ और बहन की मृत्यु के कुछ दिन बाद ही राजेन्द्र ने अपने कस्बे को छोड़ दिया। मेरठ में आकर उसने एक धनी महाजन के यहाँ नौकरी कर ली। महाजन की उस पर विशेष कृपा थी जिसके कारण वह सुखपूर्वक जीवन व्यतीत करने लगा था। संध्या समय काम समाप्त हो जाने के बाद वह कभी-कभी अपने मालिक के ऊँचे मकान की छत पर खड़ा होकर चारों ओर मकानों की लम्बी कतारों की ओर देखता रहता था। उन मकानों में रहने वाले सुखी परिवारों का चित्र उसकी आँखों के सामने खिंच जाता तथा उसे परिवार की याद ताजा होने लगती। वह एकदम उदास हो जाता उसे लगता जैसे इस संसार में वह अकेला है। उसका अपना कोई नहीं है।

1. छत पर खड़ा होकर राजेन्द्र क्या देखा करता था?

A. हरियाली के दृश्य

B. सुखी परिवार के सुखी लोगों को

C. मकानों की लम्बी कतारों को

D. भाई-बहन को खेलते हुए

2. माँ और बहन की मृत्यु के कुछ दिन बाद राजेन्द्र कस्बा छोड़ कर–

A. मारा-मारा फिरता रहा

B. मेरठ में नौकरी करने लगा

C. तीर्थ यात्रा पर निकल गया

D. मेरठ में एक फैक्टरी में नौकरी करने लगा

3. राजेन्द्र एकाएक उदास हो जाता था, क्योंकि–

A. वह नौकरी से ऊब गया था

B. उसे अपनी माँ और बहन की याद आ जाती थी

C. उसके न बहन है और न ही माँ

D. उसे लगता कि संसार में वह अकेला है

4. राजेन्द्र सुखपूर्वक रहने लगा, क्योंकि–

A. उसको बहुत बड़ा वेतन मिलता था

B. उसको बहुत कम काम करना पड़ता था

C. उसकी नौकरी आराम की थी

D. उसका मालिक उस पर विशेष कृपा करता था

5. काम समाप्त होने पर राजेन्द्र कभी-कभी–

A. पुस्तक पढ़ने लगता था

B. पड़ोसियों से बात करने लगता था

C. मकान की छत पर चढ़ जाता था

D. टहलने चला जाता था

अनुच्छेद-12

मोती राजा राघवेन्द्र प्रताप की सवारी का खास हाथी था। यों तो वह बहुत सीधा और समझदार था, पर कभी-कभी उसका मिजाज गर्म हो जाता था। एक बार पागलपन में उसने अपने महावत को मार डाला। राजा राघवेन्द्र प्रताप ने यह खबर सुनी, तो उन्हे बहुत क्रोध आया। उन्होंने मोती को राज सवारी की श्रेणी से निकाल कर उसकी पदवी छीन लेने का आदेश दिया। मोती की पदवी छिन गई। अब उसे कुलियों की तरह लकड़ियाँ ढोनी पड़तीं, पत्थर लादने पड़ते और शाम को वह पीपल के नीचे मोटी जंजीरों से बांध दिया जाता।

1. मोती एक सीधा हाथी था, परन्तु कभी-कभी–

A. पागलपन करने लगता

B. बाजार की ओर घूमने निकल जाता

C. वह उधम मचाने लगता

D. उसका मिजाज गर्म हो जाता

2. मोती को कुलियों की तरह काम करना पड़ता था, क्योंकि–

A. उसकी पद्वी छिन गई थी

B. वह पागल हो गया था

C. वह कामचोर हो गया था

D. उसने महावत को मार डाला था

3. राजा की सवारी में आने वाला मोती–

A. एक ऊँट था B. एक रथ था

C. एक घोड़ा था D. एक हाथी था

4. शाम के समय मोती को–

A. जंजीरों से बाँध दिया जाता

B. जंगल में भेज दिया जाता

C. खाना न दिया जाता

D. पीपल के नीचे लिटा दिया जाता

5. राजा साहब को बहुत क्रोध आया, क्योंकि–

A. मोती ने महावत को मार डाला

B. मोती के भोजन का कुछ भाग महावत खा लेता था

C. महावत मोती को बहुत सताता था

D. मोती पागल हो गया था

अनुच्छेद-13

अधिकांश गाँव वाले गरीब और अज्ञानी होते हैं। किसान उत्तम बीज और खाद नहीं खरीद सकता, क्योंकि उसे हमेशा पैसे की तंगी रहती है। उसे साहूकार से रुपया उधार लेना पड़ता है जो उसकी गरीबी का फायदा उठाता है और भारी ब्याज वसूलता है। इस प्रकार किसान की जिन्दगी कर्ज के बोझ के नीचे दब जाती है। अपनी अज्ञानता के कारण किसान खेती के नए-नए तौर-तरीके नहीं सीख पाता। इसलिए वह अपने खेतों की उपज नहीं बढ़ा पाता। नतीजा यह होता है कि उसकी आमदनी कम रहती है। अतः इन

आर्थिक समस्याओं को हल करने के लिए सख्त मेहनत करनी चाहिए। परस्पर सहयोग और मिलजुल कर काम करने की भावना इन समस्याओं को सुलझाने में बहुत सहायक हो सकती है। यदि लोग खुशी-खुशी सहयोग करें तो कोई ऐसी चीज नहीं है जिसे प्राप्त नहीं किया जा सकता है।

1. गाँव वालों की समस्या काफी हल हो सकती है, यदि–
A. लोग खुशी-खुशी परस्पर सहयोग करें
B. साहूकार भारी ब्याज नहीं वसूले
C. सरकार उनकी सहायता करे
D. उन्हें उत्तम बीज और खाद दिलवाए जाएँ

2. किसान की आमदनी कम रहती है क्योंकि–
A. वह अपनी उपज नहीं बढ़ा पाता
B. उसके ऊपर भारी कर्ज चढ़ा रहता है
C. उसे उत्तम बीज और खाद नहीं मिलते
D. साहूकार भारी ब्याज वसूलता है

3. उपरोक्त गद्यांश का सबसे अधिक उपयुक्त शीर्षक है–
A. खेती के नए तौर-तरीके
B. किसान की आर्थिक समस्याएँ
C. किसानों का ऋण
D. किसान सख्त मेहनत करें

4. किसानों को खेती के नए तौर-तरीकों का ज्ञान नहीं होता–
A. अज्ञानता के कारण
B. आलस्य के कारण
C. कर्ज के कारण
D. खेती की कम पैदावार के कारण

5. किसान उत्तम बीज और खाद नहीं खरीद सकता क्योंकि–
A. उसे साहूकार से खरीदना पड़ता है।
B. उसके पास पर्याप्त रुपया नहीं होता
C. उत्तम बीज व खाद आसानी से नहीं मिलते
D. सरकार उनकी समस्याओं को हल नहीं करती

अनुच्छेद-14

बादशाह अलाउद्दीन अपनी उदारता और अपने नम्र स्वभाव के लिए बहुत प्रसिद्ध थे। बादशाह होने पर भी अपने निजी खर्च के लिए उन्होंने शाही खजाने से कभी एक पैसा भी नहीं लिया। वह बच्चों को पढ़ाया करते थे और उससे अपनी रोजी कमाते थे।

एक दिन खाना बनाते समय उनकी बेगम का हाथ जल गया। असह्य पीड़ा होने लगी। वह भागी हुई अलाउद्दीन के पास गई और चीख कर बोली, "देखो तो मेरा हाथ जल गया। क्या आप जैसा बड़ा बादशाह एक रसोइया भी नहीं रख सकता?" बादशाह मुस्कराए और धीरे से बोले, "बेगम साहिबा! यह न भूलें कि यह शाही खजाना मेरा नहीं है। यह मेरी प्रजा का है। अपने लिए इसमें से एक पैसा भी लेना पाप होगा।" यह सुन कर बेगम चुप हो गईं और चुपचाप रसोई में चली गईं।

1. बेगम अलाउद्दीन के आगे इसलिए चीख पड़ी, क्योंकि–
A. उनका हाथ जल गया था
B. वे अच्छा खाना नहीं बनाती थी
C. वे चाहती थीं कि उनके पास कई नौकर रहें
D. शाही खजाने में ढेर सारा धन था

2. अलाउद्दीन बच्चों को इसलिए पढ़ाया करते, क्योंकि वे चाहते थे–
A. अपनी प्रजा को प्रसन्न करना
B. अपने लोगों को शिक्षित करना
C. बच्चों के साथ आनन्द लेना
D. अपनी निजी खर्च के लिए पैसा कमाना

3. अलाउद्दीन मानते थे कि शाही खजाने का धन–
A. उन्हीं का है
B. उनकी प्रजा का है
C. रानी का है
D. शाही परिवार का है

4. अलाउद्दीन के उत्तर को सुन कर बेगम इसलिए चुप हो गईं क्योंकि–
A. उन्होंने सोचा कि बादशाह नाराज हो गए थे
B. वे आश्चर्य में पड़ गयीं
C. उनके पास कोई उत्तर नहीं था
D. वे बादशाह के उच्च विचारों से बहुत प्रभावित हो गई थीं

5. अलाउद्दीन शाही खजाने से कुछ भी धन नहीं लेते थे, क्योंकि वे–
A. डरते थे
B. ईमानदार थे
C. एक बादशाह थे
D. एक कंजूस आदमी थे

अनुच्छेद-15

लक्ष्मी बाई एक साधारण परिवार में पैदा हुई थीं, लेकिन उनकी शादी झाँसी के राजा गंगाधर राव के साथ हुई थी। अभी लक्ष्मी बाई 18 वर्ष की ही थीं कि राजा चल बसे। उनके बाद वही राज करने लगीं। प्रजा उन्हे प्यार करती थी। उस समय अंग्रेजों ने भारत के लिए एक सरकार बना रखी थी, किन्तु भारत के अनेक भागों में अलग-अलग भारतीय शासक थे। अंग्रेजों को यह बात अच्छी नहीं लगती थी। वे चाहते थे कि ये शासक भी उनके अन्तर्गत आ जाएँ।

अंग्रेजों ने एक कानून बनाया कि यदि कोई राजा निस्संतान मरता है तो उसका राज्य अंग्रेजों के शासन में शामिल कर लिया जाएगा, किन्तु भारत की परम्परा है कि ऐसी स्थिति में राजा किसी बालक को गोद ले लेता है और वही दत्तक पुत्र आगे चल कर राजा की मृत्यु के बाद राजा बनता है। रानी लक्ष्मी बाई ने भी एक बालक को गोद ले लिया था और उसी की ओर से राजकाज देख रही थीं। अंग्रेजों ने उस व्यवस्था को नकारते हुए रानी के अधिकार को मान्यता देने से इन्कार कर दिया।

1. लक्ष्मी बाई पुत्री थीं–
A. एक भारतीय शासक की
B. एक अंग्रेज शासक की
C. एक राजा की
D. एक मामूली आदमी की

2. अंग्रेज अपने शासन के अन्तर्गत लाना चाहते थे–
A. किसी भी भारतीय राज्य को नहीं
B. केवल झाँसी के राज्य को
C. भारतीयों द्वारा शासित सभी राज्यों को
D. केवल उन राज्यों को जिनके राजा निस्संतान थे

3. शासन करने के रानी के अधिकार को मान्यता देने से अंग्रेजों ने मना कर दिया, क्योंकि–
A. वह एक मामूली परिवार की थीं
B. वह एक स्त्री थीं
C. उन्होंने किसी भी भारतीय शासक को मान्यता नहीं दी
D. उन्होंने उनके दत्तक पुत्र को मान्यता नहीं दी थी

4. लक्ष्मी बाई के जमाने में अंग्रेज शासन करते थे–
A. पूरे भारत पर
B. झाँसी राज्य पर
C. भारत के कुछ भागों पर
D. झाँसी के अलावा शेष भारत पर

5. अपने पति की मृत्यु के बाद लक्ष्मी बाई झाँसी की शासक बनीं; यह बात पसंद नहीं की गई–
A. अंग्रेजों द्वारा B. झाँसी की प्रजा द्वारा
C. उनके दत्तक पुत्र द्वारा D. भारतीय शासकों द्वारा

अनुच्छेद-16

रेडक्रॉस की स्थापना को 100 वर्ष से ऊपर हो गए हैं। सन् 1859 ई. में इटली में सोलफरीनों की लड़ाई में घायल सैनिकों की दर्दनाक हालत देख कर जियां हेनरी ड्यूनैट नामक स्विट्जरलैण्ड निवासी एक बैंकर को इसके लिए प्रेरणा मिली। ड्यूनैट ने युद्ध में घायल सैनिकों की देखभाल के लिए एक संस्था बनाने का निश्चय किया। उसे लगा कि सैनिक चाहे किसी भी पक्ष के हों, उनकी चिकित्सा अवश्य होनी चाहिए। ड्यूनैट ने इसी उद्देश्य से सन् 1864 ई. में स्विट्जरलैण्ड के जेनेवा नामक नगर में एक समिति बनाई। उसे 1901 ई. में शान्ति के लिए प्रथम नोबेल पुरस्कार दिया गया। रेड्क्रॉस का झण्डा, जिसमें सफेद पृष्ठभूमि पर लाल क्रॉस बना है, स्विट्ज़रलैण्ड के झण्डे का उल्टा है।

1. स्विट्ज़रलैण्ड के झण्डे में है–
A. लाल पृष्ठभूमि पर सफेद क्रॉस
B. लाल पृष्ठभूमि पर लाल क्रॉस
C. सफेद पृष्ठभूमि पर लाल क्रॉस
D. सफेद पृष्ठभूमि पर सफेद क्रॉस

2. जियां हेनरी ड्यूनैट–
A. डॉक्टर था
B. इटली का सैनिक था
C. स्विट्जरलैण्ड का बैंकर था
D. स्विट्जरलैण्ड का सैनिक था

3. ड्यूनैट को नोबेल पुरस्कार किस बात के लिए मिला?
A. युद्ध के लिए
B. सोलफरीनों की लड़ाई के लिए
C. रेडक्रॉस के लिए
D. शान्ति के लिए

4. सोलफरीनों की लड़ाई हुई थी?
A. सन् 1959 ई. में B. सन् 1864 ई. में
C. सन् 1901 ई. में D. सन् 1859 ई. में

5. रेडक्रॉस की स्थापना का उद्देश्य था–
A. नोबेल शान्ति पुरस्कार के लिए धन एकत्र करना
B. घायल सैनिकों की चिकित्सा की व्यवस्था करना
C. विजयी पक्ष के सैनिकों के लिए चिकित्सा की व्यवस्था करना
D. गरीब लोगों को चिकित्सा की सुविधा प्रदान करना

उत्तरमाला

अनुच्छेद-1

1	2	3	4	5
C	D	B	D	A

अनुच्छेद-2

1	2	3	4	5
C	A	D	A	D

अनुच्छेद-3

1	2	3	4	5
C	B	D	B	D

अनुच्छेद-4

1	2	3	4	5
C	D	A	A	D

अनुच्छेद-5

1	2	3	4	5
B	D	A	B	C

अनुच्छेद-6

1	2	3	4	5
B	A	D	C	A

अनुच्छेद-7

1	2	3	4	5
D	C	C	A	C

अनुच्छेद-8

1	2	3	4	5
B	D	D	A	B

अनुच्छेद-9

1	2	3	4	5
C	D	A	B	A

अनुच्छेद-10

1	2	3	4	5
C	B	C	B	B

अनुच्छेद-11

1	2	3	4	5
C	B	D	D	C

अनुच्छेद-12

1	2	3	4	5
D	A	D	A	A

अनुच्छेद-13

1	2	3	4	5
A	A	B	A	B

अनुच्छेद-14

1	2	3	4	5
A	D	B	D	B

अनुच्छेद-15

1	2	3	4	5
D	C	D	C	A

अनुच्छेद-16

1	2	3	4	5
C	C	D	D	B

वाक्य-क्रम व्यवस्थापन

निर्देशः *नीचे चार वाक्य दिए गए हैं जिन्हें 1, 2, 3, 4 क्रम दिया गया है। इन वाक्यों को उचित क्रमानुसार व्यवस्थित कर दिए गए विकल्पों में से उचित क्रम वाले विकल्प को चुनकर उत्तर चिह्नित करें।*

1. 1. जब मरण शय्या पर अंतिम सांस गिन रहा था
2. कि गरीब परिवार में जन्म लेकर वैभव के जिस शिखर पर आप पहुंचे हैं वहाँ तक कोई महान भाग्यशाली व्यक्ति ही पहुँच पाता है
3. मैंने सुना है कि अमेरिका का धन-कुबेर रथचाइल्ड
4. उस समय उसके एक मित्र ने उससे कहा

A. 1, 2, 3, 4 B. 2, 3, 1, 4
C. 3, 1 4, 2 D. 4, 1, 3, 2

2. 1. तो मैं जानना चाहता हूँ
2. प्रभु कृपा से आपकी हर इच्छा पूरी हुई है और आज जबकि आप
3. कि आप अपने मन में कोई अधूरी इच्छा लेकर तो यहां से नहीं जा रहे हैं
4. इस संसार से विदा हो रहे हैं

A. 2, 4, 1, 3 B. 1, 4, 2, 3
C. 3, 2, 1, 4 D. 4, 2, 1, 3

3. 1. कि केवल एक इच्छा मैं अपने मन में लेकर जा रहा हूँ
2. और मैं सौ अरब डालर का स्वामी बनकर इस संसार से विदा लेता
3. कि अपने दस अरब डालर पर एक बिंदी लग जाती
4. अरे ! इच्छाएं पूर्ण होने की बात, इसके बारे में इतना ही कहना चाहता हूँ

A. 3, 2, 4, 1 B. 1, 3, 4, 2
C. 1, 4, 3, 2 D. 4, 1, 3, 2

4. 1. और माया से मोड़कर
2. सूरज की ओर कर देता है
3. गुरु का महत्व इसलिए बताया गया है कि वह शिष्य का मुख छाया से मोड़कर
4. दिव्य ज्योति की ओर ले आता है पर यह कोई समर्थ गुरु ही कर पाता है

A. 3, 4, 1, 2 B. 3, 2, 1, 4
C. 2, 4, 3, 1 D. 1, 2, 3, 4

5. 1. ललक रहती है, परंतु प्रतिस्पर्धा में
2. परस्पर सहयोग की भावना में ईर्ष्या रहित भावना से स्वयं आगे
3. यदि मैं न बढ़ सकूं तो दूसरा भी न बढ़े की भावना प्रबल रूप से प्रधान होती है
4. बढ़ने और दूसरों को आगे बढ़ाने की

A. 2, 4, 1, 3 B. 1, 2, 3, 4
C. 3, 1, 2, 4 D. 4, 1, 2, 3

6. 1. ऊपर से आरोपित व्यवहार की भांति प्राणहीन निषेधों का संकायमात्र बन कर रह गई है
2. जो बौद्धिक विचारधारा के रूप में
3. अहिंसा को आचार-सूत्र बना देने से अहिंसा भी एक शास्त्र बन गई है
4. मनोविलास का साधन बनकर

A. 2, 4, 1, 3 B. 4, 2, 1, 3
C. 3, 2, 4, 1 D. 1, 2, 4, 3

7. 1. जिससे उसकी अद्वितीय औद्योगिक प्रगति
2. बाहर के देशों से मंगाना पड़ता है
3. केवल एशिया के लिए ही नहीं संपूर्ण विश्व के लिए अजीब चुनौती बन गई है
4. सभी जानते हैं कि जापान में कच्चा माल नहीं मिलता जो इस भूकंप बहुल देश में

A. 1, 3, 4, 2 B. 2, 4, 3, 1
C. 1, 4, 3, 2 D. 4, 2, 1, 3

8. 1. प्रायः जप-सुमिरन के समय हमारा अपना मन ही होता है
2. जो कहीं-का-कहीं चक्कर लगाता रहता है पर होठों पर नाम जप चलता रहता है
3. न बनने में सबसे बड़ी बाधा
4. नाम व मंत्र के चिनगारी

A. 1, 3, 4, 2 B. 2, 4, 3, 1
C. 1, 4, 3, 2 D. 4, 2, 1, 3

9. 1. अगर मुझमें लिखने की ताकत होती
2. लोग मृत्यु के नाम से घबराते हैं परंतु मृत्यु के अनुसंधानी प्रसिद्ध प्राणी-शास्त्री
3. तो विस्तारपूर्वक संसार को बतला देता कि मृत्यु स्वयं कितनी सरल और सुखद होती है
4. डॉ. विलियम ने अपने अंतिम क्षणों में कहा

A. 1, 3, 4, 2 B. 2, 4, 1, 3
C. 4, 1, 2, 3 D. 3, 4, 2, 1

10. 1. सामाजिक जीवन को सौन्दर्यमय बनाकर उसे आनंद से परिपूरित करें
2. जनता की इच्छाओं और आकांक्षाओं को प्रतिफलित होने दें और
3. उन्हें प्रोत्साहित करेंगे कि वे अपनी कलाकृतियों में
4. जों कलाकार नाटक, संगीत, नृत्य और चित्रकारी में लगे हैं, हम उन्हें एकत्र करेंगे और

A. 1, 2, 3, 4 B. 4, 3, 2, 1
C. 3, 2, 4, 1 D. 4, 1, 3, 2

11. 1. रोता व छाती पीटता हुआ आया
2. पर वह बेसुध दहाड़ें मार-मार कर रो रहा था हाय! मेरी करोड़ों की सम्पत्ति जल गई
3. लोगों की भीड़ उसे घेरे हुए थी

4. स्वामी रामतीर्थ बाजार में घूम रहे थे कि अचानक सामने से एक व्यक्ति

A. 4, 3, 2, 1 B. 3, 2, 1, 4
C. 4, 2, 3, 1 D. 4, 1, 3, 2

12. 1. यह निजी प्रशासन की अपेक्षा सरकारी प्रशासन पर अधिक ध्यान के लिए एक स्पष्ट अनुरोध है कि वह सरकार के द्वारा लिए गए/लिए जाने वाले सभी निर्णयों के रिकॉर्ड को तैयार स्थिति में रखें
2. यह सरकारी प्रशासन के राजनीतिक वातावरण से उत्पन्न विशेषता है दूसरी ओर निजी प्रशासन इस प्रकार के दबावों से मुक्त होता है
3. यह एक रिकॉर्ड रखने तथा बढ़े हुए कागज-कार्य के विषय में सरकारी निर्णय की देरी को स्पष्ट करता है
4. जैसे सरकार को आवश्यक रूप से अपने कार्यों के औचित्य को संसदीय समिति के समक्ष सिद्ध करना होता है, यह सरकारी कार्यकताओं को लक्ष्य प्राप्ति के स्थान पर नियमबद्धता को अधिक ध्यान में रखने पर जोर देता है

A. 1, 3, 4, 2 B. 2, 1, 3, 4
C. 1, 2, 4, 3 D. 3, 1, 4, 2

13. 1. मूल रूप में ऐसा लगा कि सरकार अस्त-व्यस्तताओं में सुधार करने के लिए विविध घातकी व्यूह का सहारा लेगी
2. वास्तव में यह इनके अन्तिम के साथ सर्वाधिक उल्टे सीधे (उबड़-खाबड़) मार्गों से गुजरा है नियंत्रित आयात के लिए निर्धारित निःशुल्क (मुक्त) विदेशी मुद्रा घटाने के सूचित निर्णय में परिणत हुआ
3. भारत की भुगतान सन्तुलन अच्छी हो गई है। इन असन्तुलनों को सुधारने का कार्य उस सरकार का था, जिसके पास कार्य को हाथ में लेने के लिए सहमति नहीं थी
4. इसने बजटीय घाटा को कम करने के लिए कहा, जो आवश्यक सामग्री में वृद्धि तथा अनावश्यक आयात पर रोक लगाने का आश्वासन प्रदान कर सके

A. 3, 1, 4, 2 B. 3, 4, 1, 2
C. 1, 3, 4, 2 D. 1, 4, 2, 3

14. 1. उद्घाटन करते हुए राजेन्द्र बाबू ने भारत को
2. अपनी सेनाएँ विघटित कर दें, तो इससे संसार को एक नया रास्ता मिल सकता है
3. यह सुझाव दिया था कि यह देश
4. आण्विक अस्त्रों के विरोध में दिल्ली में जो सार्वभौम समारोह हुआ था, उसका

A. 2, 4, 3, 1 B. 3, 1, 2, 4
C. 4, 1, 3, 2 D. 1, 3, 4, 2

15. 1. और नवयुग की चेतना लेकर निबन्ध के
2. एवं विचारात्मक कोटियों में रखे जा सकते हैं, जो इनके व्यक्तित्व की छाप लिए हुए हैं
3. आचार्य हजारी प्रसाद द्विवेदी प्राचीन सांस्कृतिक परम्परा का गम्भीर ज्ञान
4. क्षेत्र में अवतरित हुए तथा इनके निबंध भावात्मक

A. 4, 2, 3, 1 B. 1, 3, 4, 2
C. 2, 4, 1, 3 D. 3, 1, 4, 2

16. 1. साहित्यिक मूल्यांकन प्रस्तुत करेंगे तो
2. सामयिक आवश्यकता-रागात्मक एकता से दूर जा सकेंगे
3. साहित्य के मूल उद्देश्य तथा
4. जाति, देश और काल की सीमाओं में बँधे रहकर यदि हम

A. 3, 2, 1, 4 B. 4, 1, 3, 2
C. 4, 2, 3, 1 D. 1, 3, 2, 4

17. 1. वह अपना मनोरंजन संगीत और अभिनय जैसे
2. सच्ची बात तो यह है कि किसी भी युग का प्राणी ऐसा नीरस
3. आनन्ददायक साधनों के द्वारा नहीं करता
4. और हृदयहीन नहीं होता कि

A. 2, 1, 3, 4 B. 1, 3, 4, 2
C. 2, 4, 1, 3 D. 3, 4, 2, 1

18. 1. बहुत दिनों की इच्छा अभी तक पूरी नहीं हुई
2. ठीक जिसके चरित में नायकत्व प्रधान हो
3. कि एक जीवन-चरित लिखूँ,
4. चरितनायक नहीं मिल रहा था,

A. 1, 3, 4, 2 B. 1, 4, 3, 2
C. 3, 1, 4, 2 D. 3, 4, 1, 2

19. 1. स्वप्न में देखा, आकाश की नीली लता में सूर्य, चन्द्र और ताराओं के फूल
2. पृथ्वी की लता पर पर्वतों के फूल
3. हाथ जोड़े खिले हुए एक अज्ञात शक्ति की समीर से हिल रहे हैं,
4. हाथ जोड़े आकाश को नमस्कार कर रहे हैं

A. 2, 3, 1, 4 B. 3, 1, 2, 4
C. 2, 4, 1, 3 D. 1, 3, 2, 4

20. 1. समुदाय से चलता है तब उसे समाज कहते हैं,
2. तब उसे जीवन कहते हैं
3. प्राणों से चलता है
4. मनुष्य पाँव से चलता है तब उसे यात्रा कहते हैं,

A. 2, 3, 4, 1 B. 1, 3, 4, 2
C. 4, 3, 2, 1 D. 4, 1, 2, 3

21. 1. अनायास ही मानव-जीवन की सर्वोपयोगी वस्तुओं को प्राप्त कर सकते हैं
2. सरस साधन काव्य ही है, जिसका
3. संक्षेप में कहा जा सकता है कि चारों पदार्थों की प्राप्ति का सुलभ तथा
4. अनुशीलन करने पर अल्पबुद्धि वाले प्राणी भी

A. 3, 2, 4, 1 B. 4, 3, 2, 1
C. 1, 2, 4, 3 D. 3, 2, 1, 4

22. 1. हमारे दिमाग को इतना भोथरा,
2. सुकुमार दुनिया हमारी पथराई आँखों के सामने आकर भी नहीं आ पाती
3. बना दिया है कि संस्कृति की
4. गत अस्सी वर्षों के राजनीतिक-आर्थिक संघर्षों ने

A. 4, 3, 2, 1 B. 1, 4, 2, 3
C. 1, 2, 3, 4 D. 4, 1, 3, 2

23. 1. जहाँ एक ओर हास्य-कविता की लोकप्रियता बढ़ी है
2. कि उसमें घटिया और भोंडी बातों के समावेश से सूक्ष्म और परिष्कृत हास्य का स्तर गिर गया है
3. मनोविनोद की क्षमता से युक्त और कवि-सम्मेलनों के आश्रय में विकसित होने के कारण
4. वहीं एक हानि यह भी हुई है

A. 1, 3, 2, 4 B. 2, 4, 3, 1
C. 3, 1, 4, 2 D. 4, 1, 2, 3

24. 1. समाज सुधार के वर्तमान आंदोलनों के बीच जिस प्रकार सच्ची अनुभूति
2. द्वारा प्रेरित साहसी और स्वार्थी भी बहुत मिलते हैं
3. से प्रेरित उच्च आशय और गम्भीर पुरुष
4. पाए जाते हैं उसी प्रकार तुच्छ मनोवृत्तियाँ

A. 1, 2, 4, 3 B. 3, 2, 1, 4
C. 3, 1, 2, 4 D. 1, 3, 4, 2

25. 1. करना कि हमारा सामाजिक जीवन
2. हमारा उद्देश्य होगा, जीवन के हर सांस्कृतिक पहलू का इस प्रकार विकास
3. पुनर्गठित हो और वह सौन्दर्य एवं आनन्द को पूर्ण रूप से प्राप्त कर सके
4. स्वतंत्रता, समता और मानवता के आधार पर

A. 4, 2, 1, 3 B. 2, 1, 4, 3
C. 2, 1, 3, 4 D. 4, 2, 3, 1

26. 1. अर्थ देने वाले भाग
2. सार्वभौम रचनात्मकता को पहचानने वाले कला समीक्षक कहलाते हैं
3. मिथकीय आवरणों को हटा उसे तथ्यानुयायी
4. मनोवैज्ञानिक कहलाते हैं और आवरणों की

A. 1, 2, 4, 3 B. 3, 2, 4, 1
C. 3, 1, 4, 2 D. 1, 3, 4, 2

27. 1. प्रकृति स्वयं उस शक्ति का निर्माण करती है, जो
2. नाना प्रकार के दाहक और पाचक रसों के रूप में
3. वैसे देखा जाए तो उदर के भीतर कोई अग्नि की ज्वाला नहीं है, किन्तु
4. नाना भाँति के खाद्य पदार्थों अर्थात् भोज्य को पचा सकती है

A. 2, 1, 4, 3 B. 3, 2, 1, 4
C. 1, 2, 4, 3 D. 3, 1, 2, 4

28. 1. सन्त लोग चिल्लाकर थक गए कि
2. म्यान के मोलभाव से बाजार गर्म है
3. मगर तलवार बंद ही रह गई
4. 'मोल करो तलवार का पड़ा रहने दो म्यान'

A. 1, 3, 4, 2 B. 1, 4, 2, 3
C. 1, 4, 3, 2 D. 4, 1, 3, 2

29. 1. धर्म और उदारता के उच्च
2. ही एक ऐसा दिव्य आनंद भरा रहता है कि
3. कर्मों के विधान में
4. कर्त्ता को वे कर्म के ही फलस्वरूप लगते हैं

A. 3, 2, 1, 4 B. 1, 3, 2, 4
C. 1, 4, 3, 2 D. 3, 4, 2, 1

30. 1. सूर्य भगवान की अविश्राम तप्त किरणें, लू की सन्नाटा
2. शुष्क होते हुए मंद प्रवाह धरणी तल पर की अविरल शून्यता, विचित्र प्रभाव उत्पन्न करती है
3. निदाध कुसुमावतीपूरित वृक्षों का मुरझाना, नदी का
4. मारते हुए झपट, तेजपूरित उष्णता

A. 3, 2, 1, 4 B. 3, 2, 4, 1
C. 1, 4, 3, 2 D. 1, 4, 2, 3

31. 1. गम्भीर तामवृत्त संसार का गम्भीर रूप, झिल्लियों
2. के चमकने के साथ घोर वज्रपात शब्द, वर्षा
3. की झंकार के साथ-साथ बारम्बार जुगनू
4. मेघाछन्न आकाश में सौदामनी का चमकना हृदय को अधीर किए देता है

A. 1, 3, 2, 4 B. 3, 2, 4, 1
C. 2, 3, 4, 1 D. 4, 2, 1, 3

32. 1. सम्पूर्ण चराचर विश्व में
2. इस प्रकार जानना और प्रत्यक्ष देखना ही सब प्राणियों में स्थित भगवान् का भजन करना है
3. एक भगवान् ही परिपूर्ण है
4. जैसे वाष्प, बादल, कुहरा, बूँद बर्फ आदि में सर्वत्र जल भरा है, वैसे ही

A. 1, 3, 4, 2 B. 4, 3, 1, 2
C. 4, 1, 3, 2 D. 1, 3, 2, 4

33. 1. अमरीकी प्रजातंत्र की अथवा पुश्किन का काव्य साम्यवादी रूस की
2. भूमिका है, जिस प्रकार वाल्ट ह्विटमैन का काव्य
3. निराला का कृतित्व प्रजातांत्रिक भारतवर्ष की उसी प्रकार
4. अदम्य आशावाद, अपराजित पौरुष तथा अप्रतिम सौन्दर्य-चेतना का पूँजीभूत काव्य-प्रतिरूप

A. 1, 3, 2, 4 B. 4, 2, 3, 1
C. 3, 4, 1, 2 D. 4, 3, 2, 1

34. 1. धन की पूजा सदैव नहीं होती
2. इस संसार में धन ही सब कुछ नहीं है
3. उन व्यक्तियों की कीर्ति अक्षय है जिन्होंने केवल धनोपार्जन में अपना जीवन नहीं बिताया वरन् ऐसे कार्य किए हैं जिनसे मानव समाज का कल्याण हुआ
4. इतिहास साक्षी है कि

A. 1, 2, 3, 4
B. 2, 1, 4, 3
C. 1, 4, 2, 3
D. 2, 4, 1, 3

35. 1. भलाई की और
2. उसके कल्याण क्षेत्र में योग
3. पूजा उन्हीं की की गई है जिन्होंने मानव-समाज की
4. दिया, जिन्होंने धन को सब कुछ समझा, किसी ने जाना तक नहीं, वे कौन थे और कहाँ गए

A. 1, 2, 3, 4 B. 2, 1, 3, 4
C. 3, 1, 2, 4 D. 4, 3, 1, 2

36. 1. विद्यार्थी जीवन हँसने-हँसाने का
2. समय है खेल-खेल में
3. पढ़ाई का अभ्यास
4. इसी उम्र में होता है

A. 1, 2, 3, 4 B. 4, 2, 1, 3
C. 2, 1, 3, 4 D. 4, 3, 2, 1

37. 1. और यह निश्चय
2. आज हम इस असमंजस में पड़े हैं
3. नहीं कर पाए हैं
4. कि हम किस ओर चलेंगे और हमारा ध्येय क्या है

A. 1, 2, 3, 4 B. 1, 2, 4, 3
C. 2, 1, 3, 4 D. 4, 3, 2, 1

38. 1. में भले ही आकर्षक दिखाई दें उसका अन्तिम परिणाम अहितकर होता है
2. इसके विपरीत प्रेय आरम्भ
3. वह कठिन और श्रम-साध्य हो
4. प्रेय और श्रेय में से हमें एक को चुनना है, श्रेय ही हितकर है भले ही

A. 4, 3, 2, 1 B. 1, 2, 3, 4
C. 1, 4, 2, 3 D. 2, 3, 4, 1

39. 1. ने अनेक बहुधंधी
2. परियोजनाओं की शुरूआत की
3. स्वतंत्रता के बाद देश के बहुमुखी विकास के लिए सरकार
4. भारत में अनेक नदियाँ हैं, इन नदियों के जल का उपयोग करने के लिए बहुधंधी योजनाएँ बनाई गईं

A. 3, 1, 2, 4 B. 1, 2, 3, 4
C. 1, 3, 4, 2 D. 4, 3, 2, 1

40. 1. यह बहुत ही दुर्भाग्यपूर्ण है कि हम अभी
2. भी विदेशी भाषा
3. से चिपके हुए हैं और वे
4. भाषाएं जिनमें इस देश की संस्कृति की महक आती है, अभी भी उपेक्षित है

A. 1, 4, 2, 3 B. 4, 3, 2, 1
C. 1, 2, 3, 4 D. 2, 3, 4, 1

41. 1. शासन ही उत्तम होता है
2. गांधीजी का कहना था अपने लोगों द्वारा चलाया जाने वाला
3. इसलिए उन्होंने यहाँ उसका मतलब
4. स्वराज बताया और उन्होंने कहा कि किसी भी देश का आर्थिक विकास तभी सम्भव है जब वह देश स्वतंत्र हो

A. 1, 2, 3, 4 B. 2, 1, 3, 4
C. 4, 3, 2, 1 D. 2, 3, 4, 1

42. 1. लोगों में भावों की एकता होने पर ही
2. कहने की आवश्यकता नहीं है कि भावों की एकता भाषा और साहित्य द्वारा उत्पन्न की जाती है
3. एकता के लिए कई तत्व आवश्यक हैं इनमें सर्वाधिक महत्वपूर्ण है आपसी एकता
4. अन्य प्रकार की एकताएँ स्थापित होती हैं

A. 1, 2, 3, 4 B. 4, 3, 2, 1
C. 3, 1, 2, 4 D. 3, 1, 4, 2

43. 1. एक व्यवस्थित ढाँचा न होने पर भी
2. समाज में मान्यता न मिलने पर तथा
3. अपेक्षा अधिक हो रहे हैं और इनके विरोध की गहनता भी छँट रही है
4. आज अंतर्जातीय विवाह पहले की

A. 2, 1, 4, 3 B. 1, 2, 3, 4
C. 4, 2, 3, 1 D. 3, 1, 4, 2

44. 1. अब भी वह याद दिला देती है कि
2. अब भी प्रकृति मनुष्य को उसके भीतर वाले अस्त्र से वंचित नहीं कर रही है
3. नखधर मनुष्य अब एटम बम पर भरोसा करके आगे की ओर चल पड़ा है पर उसके नाखून अब भी बढ़ रहे हैं
4. तुम्हारे नाखून को भुलाया नहीं जा सकता तुम वही लाख वर्ष पहले के नखदन्तालम्बी जीव हो–पशु के साथ एक सतह पर विचरने वाले और चरने वाले

A. 1, 3, 4, 2 B. 4, 3, 2, 1
C. 2, 1, 4, 3 D. 3, 2, 1, 4

45. 1. जब हम साहित्य के स्वर में बोलते हैं तब वे स्वर दुस्तर समुद्रों पर सेतु बाँध कर मनुष्य तक अनायास पहुँचा देते हैं
2. और साहित्य को जानना मानव एकता की स्वानुभूति है
3. भाषा को सीखना उसके साहित्य को मानना है दुर्लब्य पर्वतों को राजपथ बना कर
4. मनुष्य की सुख-दुःख की कथा

A. 2, 1, 3, 4 B. 3, 2, 4, 1
C. 4, 2, 1, 3 D. 1, 3, 4, 2

46. 1. ईमानदारी के प्रति आग्रहशील होना चाहिए
2. कला के सम्बन्ध में हमारा दृष्टिकोण वस्तुतः कलात्मक सौन्दर्य केवल कल्पना-विलास
3. आदर्श अथवा यथार्थ सम्बन्धी पूर्वाग्रहों के स्थान पर अनुभूति की
4. अथवा यथार्थ के प्रत्यांकन में निहित न होकर इन दोनों के समन्वय में निहित होना चाहिए

A. 4, 2, 3, 1 B. 2, 3, 1, 4
C. 3, 1, 2, 4 D. 1, 4, 3, 2

47. 1. साहस और आत्मविश्वास के साथ जीना ही सच्चा जीवन है ऐसे व्यक्ति के सामने पहाड़ भी अपना सिर झुका लेते हैं
2. एक बार असफल होने पर भी नई उमंग, नए विश्वास व नए साहस से फिर प्रयत्न करता है ऐसे व्यक्ति ही अपने राष्ट्र व समाज के नेता होते हैं
3. और दुराशा उसके पास तक नहीं फटकती
4. साहसी व्यक्ति कभी भी अपना कर्म नहीं छोड़ता

A. 3, 1, 2, 4 B. 1, 4, 3, 2
C. 4, 2, 1, 3 D. 2, 3, 4, 1

48. 1. जो कभी हमारे थे, पुनजीर्वित-सा कर जाती हैं,
2. पर वे अपनी मूक भाषा में एक संदेश हमें दे जाती हैं
3. और उन क्षणों को,
4. मानस-सिंधु में उठने वाली स्मृति तरंगें काल के विषम तट से टकराकर भले ही विलीन हो जाएँ

A. 3, 1, 2, 4 B. 2, 3, 4, 1
C. 4, 2, 3, 1 D. 1, 4, 2, 3

49. 1. भूधर और सागर के बीच अपनापन खोजने में सरिता को जो कठिनाई होती है वह बेचारी बार-बार अपने गंतव्य को भूलती-सी है
2. वह पछाड़ें खाकर लौट-लौट जाना चाहती है
3. मरुस्थल की अनन्त प्यास बुझाने के लिए पर स्वयं अपनी ही बनाई तटों की कारा में बहने के लिए विवश है
4. इसे आज तक कोई जान नहीं पाया

A. 4, 1, 3, 2 B. 1, 4, 2, 3
C. 2, 3, 1, 4 D. 3, 2, 4, 1

50. 1. यदि वह संस्कृत का आचार्य या शास्त्री है
2. किन्तु दोनों दूसरों का उपकरण ही बन सकते हैं और समाज और राजनीति के संचालन में वह अपने को असमर्थ पाते हैं
3. यदि वह विज्ञान का विद्यार्थी है तो वह कुशल शिल्पी बन सकता है,
4. तो वह पौरोहित्य या अध्यापन का कार्य कर सकता है,

A. 2, 3, 4, 1 B. 1, 2, 3, 4
C. 3, 1, 4, 2 D. 4, 2, 1, 3

उत्तरमाला

1	2	3	4	5	6	7	8	9	10
C	A	D	B	A	C	D	C	B	B
11	**12**	**13**	**14**	**15**	**16**	**17**	**18**	**19**	**20**
D	A	B	C	D	B	C	A	D	C
21	**22**	**23**	**24**	**25**	**26**	**27**	**28**	**29**	**30**
A	D	C	D	B	C	D	C	B	C
31	**32**	**33**	**34**	**35**	**36**	**37**	**38**	**39**	**40**
A	C	B	B	C	A	C	A	A	C
41	**42**	**43**	**44**	**45**	**46**	**47**	**48**	**49**	**50**
B	D	A	D	B	B	B	C	B	C

●●●

शुद्ध वाक्य की पहचान

निर्देश : *निम्नलिखित में शुद्ध वाक्य का चयन कीजिए।*

1. A. हेम नरेश की पुस्तक दी
B. हेम ने नरेश को पुस्तक दी
C. हेम नरेश का पुस्तक देगा
D. हेम ने नरेश का पुस्तक दिया

2. A. मन्त्री ड्राइवर से कार चलवाता है
B. मन्त्री ड्राइवर की कार चलवाता है
C. मन्त्री ड्राइवर के लिए कार चलवाता है
D. मन्त्री ड्राइवर पर कार चलवाता है

3. A. जीवन और साहित्य का धोर सम्बन्ध है
B. जीवन और साहित्य का निकट सम्बन्ध है
C. जीवन और साहित्य का घनिष्ठ सम्बन्ध है
D. जीवन और साहित्य का गहरा सम्बन्ध है

4. A. सूर्य पश्चिम को अस्त होता है
B. मुझे विद्यालय जाना है
C. मैं तो आप के ऊपर निर्भर हूँ
D. लड़ाई में लोगों ने खूब कमाया

5. A. यह अध्यापक बहुत श्रेष्ठ पढ़ाता है
B. आज गोपाल उसके अपने काम से शहर गया
C. यह गाय बहुत प्यासी है
D. मानव ईश्वर की सबसे उत्कृष्टतम कृति है

6. A. रमेश के अन्दर बहुत विद्वता है
B. रमा विदुषी महिला है
C. सभी श्रेणियों के लोग वहाँ उपस्थित थे
D. धन्यवाद देता हूँ मैं उन्हें

7. A. आवश्यकता आविष्कार की जननी है
B. आविष्कार की जननी आवश्यकता है
C. आविष्कार आवश्यकता की जननी है
D. जननी है आविष्कार की आवश्यकता

8. A. मैं आपसे कुछ नहीं कह सकता हूँ
B. कुछ हीं कह सकता हूँ मैं आपसे
C. आपसे मैं कुछ नहीं कह सकता हूँ
D. आपको मैं कुछ नहीं कह सकता हूँ

9. A. गंगा का उद्गम स्थल गंगोत्री में है
B. गंगा का उद्गम स्थल गंगोत्री पर है
C. गंगा का उद्गम स्थल गंगोत्री से है
D. गंगा का उद्गम स्थल गंगोत्री है

10. A. मुझे आज की बैठक का समाचार नहीं था
B. मैंने अभी लखनऊ जाना है
C. पाप को डरो, पानी से नहीं
D. एक कप चाय मुझे भी देना

11. A. विष्णु के अनेकों नाम हैं
B. कन्या पराया धन होती है
C. वह पढ़ता-पढ़ता सो गया
D. मैं रोज गाने की कसरत करता हूँ

12. A. आज हमारी सौभाग्यवती कन्या का विवाह है
B. उसने गीत की दो-चार लड़ियाँ ही सुनाई
C. देखो, कहीं उसकी नींद न खुल जाए
D. यह कार्य आप पर निर्भर करता है

13. A. मैं बता तुझको दूँगा
B. मैं तुम्हें बता दूँगा
C. मैं तुझको बता दूँगा
D. सभी वाक्य सही हैं

14. A. पेड़ पर कोयलें बोल रही थीं
B. पेड़ पर कोयल बोल रही थी
C. पेड़ों पर कोयल थी
D. सभी वाक्य सही हैं

15. A. मुझे बहुत दुःख हुआ
B. मुझे दुःखी हुआ
C. मुझे ज्यादा दुःख हुआ
D. सभी वाक्य सही हैं

16. A. वह एकदम उत्तीर्ण हो गया
B. वह उत्तीर्ण हो गया
C. वह एकदम पास हो गया
D. सभी वाक्य सही हैं

17. A. एक गीतों की पुस्तक ला दो
B. गीतों की एक पुस्तक ला दो
C. पुस्तक एक गीतों की ला दो
D. पुस्तक गीतों की एक ला दो

18. A. बन्दर को काटकर चाकू से फल खिला दो
B. चाकू से बन्दर को काटकर फल खिला दो
C. चाकू से फल काटकर बन्दर को खिला दो
D. फल काटकर चाकू से बन्दर को खिला दो

19. A. बाघ और बकरी एक घाट पर पानी पीती हैं
B. बाघ और बकरी एक घाट पर पानी पीते हैं
C. यह मेरा पुस्तक है
D. सीता ने रोटी खाया

20. A. मैं गाने की कसरत कर रहा हूँ
B. मैं गाने का अभ्यास कर रहा हूँ
C. मैं गाने का शौक कर रहा हूँ
D. मैं गाने का व्यायाम कर रहा हूँ

21. A. उसकी अवस्था चालीस वर्ष की है
B. उसकी आयु चालीस वर्ष की है
C. उसका बात मत करो
D. आपका पत्र सधन्यवाद मिला

22. A. मैं जाते-जाते रुक गया
B. मैं जा रहा था पर रुक गया
C. मैं जा रहा था और रुक गया
D. अचानक जाते-जाते रुक गया

23. A. उसे जाने दो, रोको मत
B. रोको मत, उसे जाने दो
C. मत रोको, उसे जाने दो
D. उसे जाने ही दो, रोको नहीं

24. A. रात दस बजे गाड़ी आएगी
B. दस बजे रात में गाड़ी आएगी
C. रात में दस बजे गाड़ी आएगी
D. गाड़ी रात में दस बजे आएगी

25. A. रामचन्द्रजी को दशरथ ने चौदह वर्ष का वनवास दिया
B. दशरथ ने राम को चौदह वर्षों के लिए वनवास दिया
C. चौदह वर्षों का वनवास दशरथ ने राम को दिया
D. दशरथ ने राम को चौदह वर्षों का वनवास दिया

26. A. सम्भवतः कल तक वर्षा हो जाएगी
B. सम्भवतः कल तक अवश्य वर्षा हो जाएगी
C. कल तक निश्चित रूप से वर्षा होने की संभावना है
D. सम्भावना है कि कल तक निश्चय ही वर्षा होगी

27. A. हिन्दी के विकास के मुख्य तीन काल हैं, केवल
B. हिन्दी के विकास के तीन ही मुख्य काल हैं
C. तीन मुख्य काल हिन्दी के विकास के हैं
D. हिन्दी के विकास के तीन काल मुख्य हैं

28. छात्र द्वारा अवकाश के प्रार्थना-पत्र के अन्त में लिखा जाना चाहिए
A. आपका शिष्य
B. आपका आज्ञाकारी शिष्य
C. आपका छात्र
D. आपका स्नेही

29. A. जो जैसा कभी बोता है वैसा काटता है
B. वह जैसा कभी बोएगा है वैसा काटेगा
C. जो जैसा बोएगा वैसा ही काटेगा
D. जिसने जब जैसा बोया उसने तब वैसा काटा

30. A. मेरे को घर जाना चाहिए
B. मैंने घर जाना चाहिए
C. मुझे घर जाना चाहिए
D. मुझको घर को जाना चाहिए

31. प्रत्येक व्यक्ति कविता नहीं कर सकते
A. प्रत्येक व्यक्ति कविता कर सकते हैं
B. प्रत्येक व्यक्ति कविता नहीं कर सकते हैं
C. प्रत्येक व्यक्ति कविता नहीं कर सकता
D. हर व्यक्ति कविता कर सकते हैं

32. A. हमारे यहाँ तरुण नवयुवकों को काम सिखाया जाता है
B. पंडित जी की मृत्यु का हमें खेद है
C. यही नहीं, बल्कि वे वहाँ से चले भी आए
D. मुझसे यह काम सम्भव नहीं हो सकता

33. A. वहाँ भारी-भरकम भीड़ जमा थी
B. जो धन का भूखा है, वह साधु नहीं है
C. मुझे इस अधिवेशन का समाचार नहीं मिला था
D. मेरी कविता मुद्रित हो रही है

34. A. देश सदा महात्मा गांधी का ऋणी रहेगा
B. महात्मा गांधी का देश सदा ऋणी रहेगा
C. महात्मा गांधी का सदा देश ऋणी रहेगा
D. देश महात्मा गांधी का सदा ऋणी रहेगा

35. A. परिवर्तन का यह अर्थ नहीं कि कदापि अतीत की सर्वथा उपेक्षा की जाए
B. परिवर्तन का अर्थ यह कदापि नहीं कि अतीत की सर्वथा उपेक्षा की जाए
C. परिवर्तन का अर्थ यह कदापि नहीं कि अतीत की सर्वथा अपेक्षा की जाए
D. परिवर्तन का यह अर्थ कदापि नहीं कि अतीत की सर्वथा उपेक्षा की जाए

36. A. जानते हैं किसी को कि इस बात को सताया न जाए
B. जानते हैं इस बात को किसी को सताया न जाए
C. इस बात को जानते हैं किसी को कि सताया नहीं जाए
D. इस बात को जानते हैं कि किसी को सताया न जाए

37. A. सीटी की आवाज जिधर से आ रही थी मैं उधर ही दौड़ पड़ा
B. बस सीटी की आवाज जिधर से आ रही थी मैं उधर ही दौड़ पड़ा
C. सीटी की आवाज जिधर से आ रही थी बस उधर ही मैं दौड़ पड़ा
D. जिधर से सीटी की आवाज आ रही थी मैं उधर ही दौड़ पड़ा

38. A. अधिकारियों ने कागजात का निरीक्षण किया
B. अधिकारियों ने कागजात का परीक्षण किया
C. अधिकारियों ने कागजात की जाँच की
D. अधिकारियों ने कागजात का अन्वेषण किया

39. A. भारत में अनेकों जातियाँ हैं
B. भारत में अनेक जातियाँ हैं
C. भारत में अनेकों जाति हैं
D. भारत में अनेक जाति हैं

40. A. वह दण्ड देने योग्य है
B. वह दण्ड के योग्य है
C. वह दण्ड लेने योग्य है
D. वह दण्ड पाने योग्य है

41. A. फल बच्चे को काटकर खिलाओ
B. बच्चे को काटकर फल खिलाओ
C. बच्चे को फल काटकर खिलाओ
D. काटकर फल बच्चे को खिलाओ

42. A. उसे अनुत्तीर्ण होने की आशा है
B. उसे अनुत्तीर्ण होने की आशंका है
C. उसे अनुत्तीर्ण होने का शक है
D. उसे अनुत्तीर्ण होने का संशय है

43. A. कल पाठ पढ़कर आइए
B. पाठ पढ़कर कल आएं
C. पाठ पढ़कर आइए कल
D. कल पाठ पढ़कर आइए

44. A. जो मिठाई पसन्द हों आप खा लो
B. जो मिठाई पसन्द हो तुम खा लो
C. जो मिठाइयाँ पसन्द हों तुम खा लो
D. जो मिठाइयाँ पसन्द हों उन्हें आप खाइए

45. A. हम बचपन मं वहाँ जाएंगे
B. हम बचपन में वहाँ जाते रहे हैं
C. मैं बचपन से वहाँ जाता रहा हूँ
D. मैं बचपन में वहाँ जाऊँगा

उत्तरमाला

1	2	3	4	5	6	7	8	9	10
B	A	C	B	C	B	A	A	D	D
11	12	13	14	15	16	17	18	19	20
B	C	C	B	A	B	B	C	B	B
21	22	23	24	25	26	27	28	29	30
A	A	B	A	D	A	A	B	C	C
31	32	33	34	35	36	37	38	39	40
C	D	D	A	D	D	D	C	B	B
41	42	43	44	45					
C	B	B	D	C					

●●●

• रिक्त स्थानों के लिए उचित शब्द का चयन •

निर्देशः *निम्नलिखित वाक्यों में रिक्त स्थान की पूर्ति के लिए दिए हुए शब्दों में से सबसे उपयुक्त शब्द चुनिए और अपनी उत्तर पुस्तिका में सही उत्तर अंकित कीजिए।*

1. अदालतों में न्याय पाना बड़ा ...... हो गया है।
A. खर्चीला B. सरल
C. कठिन D. असम्भव

2. समाचार पत्रों में भी अब ...... समाचार कम छपते हैं।
A. धार्मिक B. जनहित के
C. अपराधियों के D. अमीरों के

3. अब नेताओं की सभा में उनके...... की ही भीड़ अधिक होती है।
A. बन्धुओं B. साथियों
C. चमचों D. बुजुर्गों

4. मंदिरों में पुजारी केवल..... ही देखते हैं।
A. चढ़ावा B. फूलमाला
C. भक्ति D. कपड़े

5. शिक्षा संस्थाओं में अध्यापकों का ध्यान प्रायः अपने ... पर ही रहता है।
A. छात्रों B. विषय
C. वेतन D. सौन्दर्य

6. न जाने आज गाय का ......दूध क्यों फट गया।
A. कुछ B. बहुत
C. सारा D. थोड़ा

7. कितने मन के ...... ढहे तब खड़ी हुई यह मधुशाला।
A. शहर B. गाँव
C. भूखंड D. महल

8. सखि पतंगा तो ...... ही है दीपक भी जलता है।
A. मरता B. जीता
C. जलता D. उड़ता

9. कश्मीर की समस्या अब शीघ्र ...... योग्य हो गई है।
A. विचारने B. समाधान
C. सुधारने D. हटाने

10. संस्कृत एक ...... भाषा के रूप में मानी जाती है।
A. देव B. मृत
C. प्राचीन D. श्रेष्ठ

11. राष्ट्रपति ने लोक सभा ...... कर दी।
A. भँग B. खत्म
C. समाप्त D. स्थगित

12. देश की ...... बनाए रखना हमारा प्रथम दायित्व है।
A. व्यवस्था B. एकता
C. सरकार D. आजादी

13. धैर्यवान व्यक्ति विपत्ति में भी ...... नहीं होता।
A. दुःखी B. चलायमान
C. अधीर D. विचलित

14. दीन-दुःखी की सहायता करना ही मानव का ...... होना चाहिए।
A. कर्म B. धर्म
C. फर्ज D. आभूषण

15. लोकतंत्र की सफलता के लिए जनता को ...... होना चाहिए।
A. शिक्षित B. अनुशासित
C. जागृत D. सभ्य

16. सभी धर्मों में ...... धर्म श्रेष्ठ है।
A. मानव B. हिन्दू
C. विश्व बंधुत्व D. भातृत्व

17. ...सबका भला चाहने वाला होता है
A. नेता B. संत
C. समाज-सेवी D. गुरु

18. हाथ से लिखी पुस्तक को ...कहते हैं।
A. हस्तलिखित B. हस्तलेखन
C. पाण्डुलिपि D. आलेख

19. वस्तुतः ...... मनुष्य वही है जो मानवता का आदर करता है।
A. सच्चा B. सम्पूर्ण
C. चरित्रवान D. यथार्थ

20. आणविक भट्टियाँ असीमित शक्ति का ...... हैं।
A. साधन B. स्रोत
C. उपकरण D. माध्यम

21. जैसे-जैसे अंधेरा ...... हमें आगे बढ़ने में कठिनाई होने लगी।
A. निकलता गया B. चढ़ता गया
C. फैलता गया D. आता गया

22. आपका उपकार जीवन ...... याद होगा।
A. तक B. से लेकर
C. भर D. के अन्दर

23. आप गेंद को जितनी ताकत से जमीन पर दे मारेंगे वह उतनी ही ऊँची ......।
A. झपटेगी B. आयेगी
C. निकलेगी D. उछलेगी

24. आज मानव पूजास्थलों का अपनी राजनीतिक स्वार्थ-सिद्धि के लिए ...... कर रहा है।
A. सदुपयोग B. सुप्रयोग
C. बल प्रयोग D. दुरुपयोग

25. मदिरापान मानव के विवेक को ...... कर देता है।
A. उन्नत B. जागृत
C. कुंठित D. उत्कृष्ठ

26. जिन लोगों की करनी-कथनी में अंतर है, वे जीवन में कभी... नहीं पाते।
A. यश B. सम्मान
C. महत्व D. उन्नति

27. जुआ खेलना सबसे बड़ा ...... है।
A. पाप B. दुर्व्यसन
C. लत D. अपराध

28. स्वाभिमान मनुष्य का अमूल्य ...... है।
A. संपत्ति B. पूंजी
C. कोष D. धन

29. अंधे को क्या चाहिए ......।
A. रोटी-कपड़ा B. मकान
C. दो आँखें D. दो रोटियाँ

30. चाटुकारिता आज के मानव की सफलता का सबसे घटिया ...... है।
A. अस्त्र B. शस्त्र
C. बल D. साधन

31. गीता भक्ति, ... और कर्म का संदेश देती है।
A. भोग B. ज्ञान
C. वियोग D. संयोग

32. ...... मृत्यु से बढ़कर है।
A. कीर्ति B. अपकीर्ति
C. मोह D. अहंकार

33. माता-पिता की सेवा करना मानव का ...... है।
A. श्रम B. भ्रम
C. धर्म D. कर्म

34. हमारी शिक्षा प्रणाली में खेलों की स्थिति ...... है।
A. स्मरणीय B. शोचनीय
C. विचारणीय D. अकथनीय

35. आजकल के राजनेता अपने कर्त्तव्यों से ...... हैं।
A. उदास B. विमुख
C. पीड़ित D. संलिप्त

36. कई दिन वहां रहने पर मुझे साध्वी की ...... के बारे में बहुत कुछ मालूम हो गया।
A. परिचर्या B. दिनचर्या
C. परिचर्चा D. परिक्रमा

37. प्रातःकाल उसके आश्रम से निरन्तर आती हुई तुलसीदास के भजनों की स्वर लहरी मेरी सोई हुई आत्मा को ...... कर देती थी।
A. विचलित B. चंचल
C. उदास D. जागृत्

38. कितने दिनों से मैं रेल-पेल व भागमभाग से ...... वातावरण से दूर जाने की बात सोच रहा था।
A. अचेत B. संलग्न
C. दूषित D. प्रभावित

39. इस युग में भविष्य के प्रति ..... बनी रहती है।
A. आशा B. हताशा
C. आशंका D. निश्चिन्तता

40. हमें जल्दी निर्णय लेने से रोकती रहती है फिर भी भीड़ से दूर निकलने की बलवती ...... किसके मन में रह-रह कर नहीं जाग उठती है?
A. लालसा B. तृष्णा
C. इच्छा D. उत्सुकता

41. पृथ्वी ...... सूर्य की परिक्रमा करती है।
A. अभिराम B. अविराम
C. अक्सर D. ज्यादातर

42. केन्द्र सरकार राज्यों को ......देती है।
A. प्रतिदिन B. दान
C. अनुदान D. अविरल

43. लोकतंत्र में सबको .... अधिकार होते हैं।
A. सामान B. असीम
C. निरन्तर D. समान

44. राम चौदह वर्ष की ...... के पश्चात् वन से अयोध्या लौटे।
A. समय B. अवधी
C. अवधि D. कालचक्र

45. राजा दशरथ के चार ..... थे।
A. सूत B. सुत
C. तनया D. तनुजा

46. भारत व पाकिस्तान के युद्ध में सेना ने ..... थे।
A. हाथ दिखाए B. हाथ पसारे
C. हाथ लगाए D. हाथ छोड़े

47. रात ..... 2 बजे थे।
A. को B. से
C. में D. के

48. सहकारी संस्था शीघ्र ही सदस्यता ..... प्रारम्भ कर रही है।
A. कार्यक्रम B. उपक्रम
C. आंदोलन D. भर्ती

49. अतिथि ने भोजन करने की ..... व्यक्त की।
A. कामना B. उत्कंठा
C. इच्छा D. आकांक्षा

50. आपका आचरण दूसरों के लिए ..... हो सकता है।
A. दृष्टान्त B. उदाहरण
C. उद्धरण D. अनुकरण

उत्तरमाला

1	2	3	4	5	6	7	8	9	10
C	B	C	A	C	C	D	C	B	C
11	12	13	14	15	16	17	18	19	20
A	B	D	B	A	A	B	B	A	D
21	22	23	24	25	26	27	28	29	30
C	C	D	D	C	B	B	D	C	D
31	32	33	34	35	36	37	38	39	40
B	B	C	B	B	B	D	D	C	C
41	42	43	44	45	46	47	48	49	50
B	C	D	C	B	A	D	A	C	B

●●●

समानार्थक शब्द

परिचय :

हिंदी भाषा में भी अन्य भाषाओं की तरह शब्दों का संसार अर्थ व प्रयोग की दृष्टि से अत्यन्त विलक्षण है। देखने व सुनने में सदृश होते हुए भी उनका अर्थ बिल्कुल ही भिन्न होता है।

निर्देश : *निम्नलिखित शब्दों के आगे चार-चार शब्द दिए गए हैं। इनमें से उचित समानार्थक पर्याय चुनकर चिह्नित करें।*

1. वक्त्र
A. कपोल B. सिर
C. मुख D. नेत्र

2. ब्रह्मा
A. देवता B. प्राचीन
C. विधाता D. अनादि

3. सरस्वती
A. वाणी B. विद्या
C. बुद्धि D. सरोवर

4. समीर
A. अग्नि B. पानी
C. हवा D. ठंडा

5. दिन
A. घाम B. दिवस
C. प्रकाश D. सफेद

6. मोक्ष
A. निर्वाण B. मूँछ
C. प्रस्थान D. स्वर्ग

7. गंगा
A. नदी B. धारा
C. मंदाकिनी D. सूर्यपुत्री

8. सूर्य
A. मार्त्तण्ड B. देवता
C. किरण D. प्रकाश

9. लक्ष्मी
A. पद्मा B. सुन्दरी
C. बड़ी D. माता

10. वृक्ष
A. आम B. पादप
C. बाग D. घास

11. वलय
A. वृक्ष की छाल B. मृग छाल
C. घेरा D. आवरण

12. सम्पुट
A. मिश्रण B. बंधी हुई अंजलि
C. पिटारी D. मन्जूषा

13. प्रभंजन
A. अंजन B. तोड़-फोड़
C. खण्ड-खण्ड D. तेज वायु

14. पुष्कल
A. जायफल B. पुण्यफल
C. बहुत-सा D. हरा-भरा

15. प्रत्यागमन
A. परिक्रमा करना B. प्रतिरोध करना
C. बार-बार आना D. वापस आना

16. परिवाद
A. विवाद B. सम्वाद
C. निन्दा D. परिवारवाद

17. शबनम
A. शीत B. ओस
C. पाला D. कोहरा

18. नैसर्गिक
A. प्राकृतिक B. स्वर्गिक
C. पारस्परिक D. स्वर्णिम

19. अस्मिता
A. आत्म प्रशंसा B. अहंता
C. स्वार्थ D. स्वाभिमान

20. अतीत
A. आने वाला B. बीता हुआ
C. आगम D. आरम्भ

21. प्रष्टव्य
A. पाने योग्य B. पूजने योग्य
C. देखने योग्य D. पूछने योग्य

22. आजीवन
A. जीवन-भर B. मरण तक
C. असीम D. आज-कल

23. आन्दोलन
A. आरोहण B. उद्वेलन
C. अभियान D. उच्छूलन

24. अनुज्ञा
A. अजा B. अवज्ञा
C. प्रज्ञा D. अनुमति

25. तूणीर
A. असंग B. निषंग
C. उत्संग D. निःसंग

26. फिजूल खर्ची
A. अव्यय B. मितव्यय
C. परिव्यय D. अपव्यय

27. कमल
A. पारिजात B. रजनी
C. विभावरी D. भामिनी

28. कलानिधि
A. नीर B. हिमाँशु
C. अम्बु D. आगार

29. तुंग
A. उन्नत B. प्रचण्ड
C. नारियल D. पुन्नाग

निर्देश : *नीचे प्रत्येक शब्द समूह में चार-चार शब्द दिए गए हैं। इनमें से तीन के अर्थ समान हैं। एक शब्द बेमेल है। बेमेल शब्द का चयन करें।*

30. A. अमृत B. पीयूष
C. सुधा D. लोचन

31. A. समझ B. बुद्धि
C. सोम D. अक्ल

32. A. जानशीन B. राजगद्दी
C. तख्त D. सिंहासन

33. A. आत्मजा B. सुता
C. सूनू D. मेदिनी

34. A. अमर B. अमर्त्य
C. वेदना D. दिव्य

35. A. शकुन B. सरित
C. शकुन्त D. पतंग

36. A. मेरू B. आर्या
C. उमा D. रुद्राणी

37. A. भूसुर B. महीसुर
C. विप्र D. भूरि

38. A. तड़ाग B. पुष्करिणी
C. सर D. मयंक

39. A. अक्षि B. कृशानु
C. रोहिताश्र D. वायुसखा

40. A. अंधा B. प्रारब्ध
C. भाग्य D. नसीब

41. A. क्रोध B. नयन
C. वक्षु D. नेत्र

42. A. व्योम B. नभ
C. अम्बर D. नरभि

43. A. इन्द्र B. सुरेश
C. धनाधिप D. सुरेन्द्र

44. A. सरस्वती B. वाचा
C. धनद D. शारदा

45. A. आतुरता B. आकुलता
C. भार्या D. उत्सुकता

46. A. सारंग B. शिखी
C. विशिख D. मयूर

47. A. तुरंग B. मृगेन्द्र
C. मृगराज D. व्याघ्र

48. A. पावक B. अनिल
C. अनल D. कृशानु

49. A. गौतमी B. अहिल्या
C. व्योम D. दुर्गा

50. A. गोपाल B. श्रीकृष्ण
C. अथर्ववेद का ब्राह्मण D. ग्वाला

51. A. सुमन B. कुसुम
C. चमन D. पुष्प

52. A. गुलामी B. गुलशन
C. दासत्व D. परतंत्रता

53. A. सीमा B. सागर
C. पारावार D. जलधि

54. A. दोष B. परिवाद
C. निन्दा D. बुराई

55. A. अन्याय B. धांधली
C. परायण D. अन्धेर

56. A. तख्त B. राजगद्दी
C. सिंहासन D. जानशीन

57. A. वित्त B. धन
C. विरति D. भत्ता

58. A. आभूषण B. नागर
C. जेवर D. अलंकार

59. A. सौरभ B. जलज
C. पंकज D. कंज

60. A. सज्जन B. सत्कार
C. सद्भावना D. सजीव

उत्तरमाला

1	2	3	4	5	6	7	8	9	10
C	C	A	C	B	A	C	A	A	B
11	**12**	**13**	**14**	**15**	**16**	**17**	**18**	**19**	**20**
C	B	D	C	D	C	B	A	B	B
21	**22**	**23**	**24**	**25**	**26**	**27**	**28**	**29**	**30**
D	A	C	D	B	D	A	B	A	D
31	**32**	**33**	**34**	**35**	**36**	**37**	**38**	**39**	**40**
C	A	D	C	B	A	D	D	A	A
41	**42**	**43**	**44**	**45**	**46**	**47**	**48**	**49**	**50**
A	D	C	C	C	C	A	B	C	D
51	**52**	**53**	**54**	**55**	**56**	**57**	**58**	**59**	**60**
C	B	A	B	C	D	C	B	D	D

●●●

अनेक शब्दों के लिए एक शब्द

परिचय :
अनेक शब्दों के लिए एक सार्थक शब्द के प्रयोग से कथन अत्यन्त प्रभावशाली व रोचक हो जाता है। वाक्यों में ऐसे शब्दों का प्रयोग करने से जहाँ बहुत सारी बातों को बहुत कम वाक्यों के द्वारा व्यक्त किया जा सकता है वहीं दूसरी ओर जगह और समय की भी बचत होती है अर्थात् ऐसे शब्दों के प्रयोग को गागर में सागर भरने की बात कही जाए तो कोई अतिशयोक्ति नहीं होगी। अनेक शब्दों के लिए एक शब्द का निर्माण समास बनाकर अथवा उपसर्ग या प्रत्यय जोड़कर किया जाता है। संक्षेपण की कला को विकसित करने में इसका विशेष महत्व है।

निर्देश : *नीचे दिए गए प्रत्येक वाक्यांश के लिए एक शब्द दीजिए इसके लिए चार-चार विकल्प दिए गए हैं। उचित विकल्प का चुनाव कीजिए।*

1. जो लौकिक न हो
A. पारलौकिक B. इहलौकिक
C. अलौकिक D. ऐहिक

2. वह स्थान जहाँ पृथ्वी और आकाश मिलते हुए से दिखाई पड़ते हैं
A. क्षितिज B. सरसिज
C. अन्तरिक्ष D. नीहारिका

3. जो पुरुषों के अनुरूप हो
A. पुरुषोचित B. पौरुषेय
C. पौरुष D. पुरुष

4. जो ऊपर से मिलाया गया हो
A. प्रक्षिप्त B. विक्षिप्त
C. संक्षिप्त D. विलुप्त

5. किसी कथा के अन्तर्गत आने वाली कोई अन्य कथा
A. दृष्टांत B. अन्तर्कथा
C. अंतःकथा D. अंतर्दृष्टांत

6. गुरु के समीप रहने वाला विद्यार्थी
A. अंतेवासी B. बटुक
C. ब्रह्मचारी D. शिष्य

7. हाथी की पीठ पर रखी जाने वाली चौकी
A. मचान B. हौदा
C. तख्त D. गद्दी

8. फाल्गुन की पूर्णिमा को होने वाला हिंदुओं का प्रसिद्ध त्यौहार
A. गुरु पूर्णिमा B. वसंतोत्सव
C. दीपावली D. होली

9. यज्ञ में आहुति देने वाला
A. पुरोहित B. हवि
C. होता D. समिधा

10. फेंककर चलाया जाने वाला हथियार
A. वाण B. शस्त्र
C. अस्त्र D. वर्म

11. काम से जी चुराने वाला
A. कामचोर B. बेकार
C. आलसी D. निकम्मा

12. किसी बात को करने का निश्चय
A. विकल्प B. संकल्प
C. कल्प D. अत्यल्प

13. जिस बीमारी का ठीक होना सम्भव न हो
A. असाध्य B. विकट
C. भयानक D. घातक

14. जिस पर विजय प्राप्त कर ली गई हो
A. आक्रान्त B. अजेय
C. विजित D. पराजित

15. सूर्य के उदय होने का स्थान
A. उदयाचल B. सूर्यादय
C. प्रभात स्थान D. गंधमादन

16. जो कहा न जा सके
A. अकथित B. अकथनीय
C. अकथ्य D. नामुमकिन

17. जिसे बहुत बातें करनी आती हों
A. वाचाल B. गम्भीर
C. समालोचक D. मुनि

18. जो स्त्री के वशीभूत हो
A. स्त्रीदास B. गुलाम
C. स्त्रैण D. प्रेमी

19. जो समान न हो
A. बराबर B. जटिल
C. अविषम D. विषम

20. जिसे पढ़ना-लिखना आता हो
A. अल्पज्ञानी B. शिक्षित
C. बुद्धिजीवी D. साक्षर

21. जो खाना मुफ्त में मिलता हो
A. भण्डार B. लंगर
C. खुराक D. राशन

22. जो अपने कर्तव्य को न जानता हो
A. अनजान B. अज्ञानी
C. किंकर्त्तव्यविमूढ़ D. कर्त्तव्यहीन

23. जो कानून के अनुकूल न हो
A. अवैध B. जघन्य
C. अवध्य D. आवेग

24. कामना पूरी होने का विश्वास
A. प्रत्याशा B. दुराशा
C. विभावना D. सम्भावना

25. परंपरा से प्राप्त होने वाला
A. लकीर का फकीर B. रूढ़ि
C. प्राचीनकालीन D. परंपरागत

26. जिसे किसी से लगाव न हो
A. नश्वर B. लिप्सु
C. निर्लिप्त D. अलगाववादी

27. जो कुछ जानने की इच्छा रखता हो
A. जिज्ञासु B. जननी
C. जानकी D. नीतिज्ञ

28. जो बात लोगों से सुनी गई हो
A. अश्रुति B. सर्वप्रिय
C. लोकोक्ति D. किंवदन्ती

29. सबके समानाधिकार पर विश्वास
A. अधिकारी B. समाजवाद
C. प्रगतिवाद D. अधिकारवाद

30. रजोगुण वाला
A. तामसिक B. राजसिक
C. वाचिक D. सात्विक

31. जो आयु में बड़ा हो
A. गुरु B. अग्रज
C. वरिष्ठ D. सहोदर

32. जिस तर्क का कोई जवाब न हो
A. जोरदार B. तीखा
C. सटीक D. अकाट्य

33. जो दूसरों की सहायता की अपेक्षा न करे
A. आत्मनिर्भर B. पुरुषार्थ
C. आत्मविश्वासी D. स्वाभिमानी

34. मर्म का स्पर्श करने या प्रभाव डालने का भाव
A. मर्मस्पृर्शिता B. मर्मस्पृशी
C. मर्मान्वेषी D. मर्मान्वेषण

35. जो आँख के समक्ष न हो
A. अनदेखा B. परोक्ष
C. अपरोक्ष D. अज्ञात

36. जिसका इन्द्रियों से अनुमान न हो सके
A. जितेन्द्रिय B. अतीन्द्रिय
C. कालजयी D. सर्वजयी

37. जो किसी नियम का पालन न करे
A. अभद्र B. दुष्ट
C. अनुशासनहीन D. उच्छृंखल

38. जिसको माता-पिता का आश्रय न मिला हो
A. पराश्रित B. निराश्रित
C. अनाथ D. अकिंचन

39. जिस स्त्री का पति जीवित होता है
A. कामिनी B. सुभगा
C. सधवा D. मधवा

40. अनुचित व्यय करने वाला
A. अतिव्ययी B. मितव्ययी
C. दुर्व्ययी D. अपव्ययी

41. जिसके पास कुछ न हो
A. निर्धन B. त्यागी
C. अकिंचन D. संन्यासी

42. जिस पर अभियोग लगाया गया हो
A. प्रतिवादी B. अभियोगी
C. अभियुक्त D. याची

43. मोक्ष प्राप्त करने की इच्छा रखने वाला
A. मोक्षेसु B. ममुक्ष
C. मुमुक्ष D. मुमुक्षु

44. जिसकी पत्नी मर गई है
A. विदुर B. विधवा
C. विधुर D. विधाता

45. जो किसी धर्म या व्यक्ति में आस्था न रखे
A. निशान्त B. धर्मनिरपेक्ष
C. धर्मभीरू D. नास्तिक

46. किए गए अहसानों को जानने, समझने व मानने वाला
A. सुविज्ञ B. कृतज्ञ
C. कृतघ्न D. विज्ञ

47. वह वस्तु जो छूने लायक न हो
A. त्याज्य B. अखाद्य
C. अदृश्य D. अस्पृश्य

48. एक ही माँ की कोख से जन्मा
A. सहोदर B. अग्रज
C. अनुज D. साथी

49. जो बिना वेतन कार्य करता हो
A. निःशुल्क B. अवैतनिक
C. वैतनिक D. इनमें से कोई नहीं

50. जिसकी स्त्री मर गई हो
A. पुश्चल B. जरठ
C. विधुर D. विसृत

उत्तरमाला

1	2	3	4	5	6	7	8	9	10
C	A	A	A	B	A	B	D	C	C
11	**12**	**13**	**14**	**15**	**16**	**17**	**18**	**19**	**20**
A	B	A	C	A	B	A	C	D	D
21	**22**	**23**	**24**	**25**	**26**	**27**	**28**	**29**	**30**
B	A	A	A	D	C	A	D	B	A
31	**32**	**33**	**34**	**35**	**36**	**37**	**38**	**39**	**40**
B	D	C	A	B	B	D	C	C	D
41	**42**	**43**	**44**	**45**	**46**	**47**	**48**	**49**	**50**
C	C	D	C	D	B	D	A	B	C

●●●

अनेकार्थी शब्द

परिचय :

अनेकार्थी शब्द वे शब्द कहे जाते हैं जिनके अनेक अर्थ होते हैं। हिन्दी भाषा में कई ऐसे शब्द हैं जिनके पूरे अर्थ शब्दकोश देख कर ही जाने जा सकते हैं। सूरदास के पदों में से उनके दृष्टकूटों में प्रयुक्त शब्द अपने अनेकार्थी होने के कारण प्रहेलिका बन जाते हैं किन्तु वे कौतूहलकारी भी हैं। पर्यायवाची शब्द तथा अनेकार्थी शब्दों में अन्तर यह होता है कि एक वस्तु को जब अनेक नामों से पुकारा जाता है तो उसे पर्यायवाची कहा जाता है जैसे—मयंक, शशि, कलाधर, हिमांशु, उडुपति आदि चन्द्रमा के लिए प्रयुक्त हुए हैं, इसलिए ये चन्द्रमा के पर्यायवाची शब्द हैं जबकि अनेकार्थी शब्द उस शब्द को कहा जाता है जब एक ही शब्द अनेक वस्तुओं के लिए अलग-अलग प्रयोग में आता है जैसे द्विजराज, कनक, सारंग आदि। यहाँ द्विजराज का अर्थ ब्राह्मण, चन्द्रमा, गरुड़ आदि है।

अनेकार्थी शब्द जहाँ हमारे ज्ञान में वृद्धि करते हैं वहीं किसी कविता अथवा कथन का आशय समझने में सहायक भी होते हैं। कवियों की पैनी दृष्टि तथा उक्ति को हृदयंगम करने के लिए अनेकार्थी शब्दों का विशेष महत्त्व माना जाता है। हिन्दी भाषा में अनेकार्थी शब्दों का प्रयोग लघु छन्दों, दोहा, सोरठा आदि में विशेष रूप से किया गया है।

निर्देश : *इन प्रश्नों में प्रत्येक में चार शब्द दिए गए हैं जिनमें से तीन अनेकार्थी शब्द की श्रेणी में आते हैं। जो शब्द इस श्रेणी में नहीं आता है, वही आपका उत्तर है।*

1. अंक
A. गोद B. नाटक का विभाजन
C. संख्या D. गणित

2. अर्थ
A. पाप B. धन
C. आशय D. प्रयोजन

3. आश्रय
A. आधार B. मैदान
C. सहायता D. तरकश

4. खग
A. मन B. तीर
C. पक्षी D. आकाश

5. चपला
A. लक्ष्मी B. चंचल
C. पुष्प D. तड़ित

6. नाग
A. साँप B. पर्वत
C. जवाहर D. बादल

7. पुर
A. गाँव B. घर
C. किला D. नगर

8. बक
A. बगुला B. ढोंगी
C. आँधी D. ठग

9. मृग
A. कस्तूरी B. मुर्गा
C. हरिण D. चन्द्रमा का कलंक

10. मूल
A. वंश B. जड़
C. औषध D. पूँजी

11. अक्षर
A. आत्मा B. वर्ण
C. अक्षत D. स्थिर

12. अक्रूर
A. मित्र B. शत्रु
C. कृष्ण के चाचा D. विनम्र

13. अचल
A. पहाड़ B. स्थिर
C. अटल D. चंचल

14. अपेक्षा
A. आशा B. निराशा
C. आवश्यकता D. इच्छा

15. अमूल्य
A. अनमोल B. जन
C. दूध D. अमर

16. अर्क
A. सर्प B. बुध
C. ताँबा D. सत्य

17. अधर
A. अंतरिक्ष
B. निचला होंठ
C. धरती और आसमान के मध्य
D. अब्धि

18. कनक
A. सोना B. गेहूँ
C. धतूरा D. कमल

19. वर्ण
A. अक्षर B. स्वर
C. जाति D. रंग

20. शिखी
A. मोर B. पर्वत
C. क्षत्रित D. अग्नि

21. सारंग
A. सर्प B. सिंह
C. भौंरा D. वादक

22. अंक
A. चिह्न B. लेख
C. अक्षर D. प्रकृति

23. अंकुर
A. आँख B. कोंपल
C. गरुड़ D. रक्त

24. अंग
A. शरीर B. भेद
C. गोद D. प्रकृति

25. अंगज
A. पुत्र B. पसीना
C. जल D. कामदेव

26. अक्ष
A. सोहागा B. शरीर
C. बछेड़ा D. गरुड़

27. अज
A. साँप B. बकरा
C. शिव D. शक्ति

28. अनन्त
A. असीम B. शेषनाग
C. बादल D. अभ्रक

29. अनी
A. माया B. माथा
C. झुण्ड D. नाव

30. अन्वय
A. संयोग B. मेल
C. अभ्रक D. खानदान

31. अपेक्षा
A. इच्छा B. आश्रय
C. अतिथि D. अनुरोध

32. अक्षर
A. सत्य B. मोक्ष
C. जल D. आँवला

33. अतिथि
A. अभ्यागत B. मुनि
C. अपरिचित D. जल

34. अधिष्ठान
A. नगर B. जनपद
C. सहारा D. नाव

35. अन्न
A. अनाज B. चाँद
C. पृथ्वी D. प्राण

36. अयन
A. सत्य B. स्थान
C. आश्रम D. अंश

37. अर्क
A. सूर्य B. रविवार
C. अन्न D. घोंसला

38. अर्थ
A. अभिप्राय B. काम
C. धन D. रस

39. अर्ह
A. योग्य B. तुच्छ
C. इन्द्र D. सोना

40. हेम
A. हिम B. सोना
C. नाग D. शेर

41. अवग्रह
A. अनावृष्टि B. वेद
C. संधिविच्छेद D. नीच

42. अहि
A. सर्प B. अग्नि
C. पृथ्वी D. सूर्य

43. अलि
A. कोयल B. फूल
C. बिच्छू D. सखी

44. अरुण
A. सूर्य B. कमल
C. अफीम D. सिंदूर

45. अशोक
A. एक वृक्ष का नाम B. पारा
C. एक सम्राट का नाम D. अपशकुन

उत्तरमाला

1	2	3	4	5	6	7	8	9	10
D	A	D	A	C	D	A	C	B	C
11	12	13	14	15	16	17	18	19	20
D	B	D	B	A	B	D	D	B	C
21	22	23	24	25	26	27	28	29	30
D	D	C	C	C	B	A	C	A	C
31	32	33	34	35	36	37	38	39	40
C	D	D	D	B	A	D	B	B	D
41	42	43	44	45					
D	B	B	B	D					

●●●

पर्यायवाची शब्द

परिचय :

पर्यायवाची शब्द प्रत्येक भाषा के शब्द भण्डार को सूचित करते हैं। कविता अथवा गद्य लेखन में ही नहीं वरन् साधारण बोलचाल में भी एक वस्तु के लिए अथवा एक भाव के लिए प्रसंगानुकूल विविध शब्दों का प्रयोग कथन को जोरदार तथा प्रभावशाली बनाता है। हिंदी एक सशक्त तथा जीवंत भाषा है जिसमें पर्यायवाची शब्दों की विपुलता पायी जाती है। यह भाषा एक विशाल भूखण्ड की भाषा होने के साथ-साथ राजकाज की भी भाषा है। अपनी जननी संस्कृत से इसे अक्षय शब्द भण्डार की उपलब्धि हुई है। इसके अतिरिक्त प्राकृत, पाली, अपभ्रंश, फारसी, तुर्की, अंग्रेजी तथा दक्षिण भारत की भाषाओं से भी इसने यथा अपेक्षित शब्द ग्रहण किए हैं जिसके कारण इस भाषा की शब्द सामर्थ्य काफी बढ़ गई है।

निर्देश : *नीचे दिए गए चार विकल्पों में से सही पर्यायवाची शब्द ज्ञात कीजिए।*

1. अनन्त
A. विष्णु B. अतिशय
C. असंख्य D. आकाश

2. आडम्बर
A. ढोंग B. तम्बू
C. दर्प D. आवाज

3. कपाल
A. अदृष्ट B. खप्पर
C. भाग्य D. माथा

4. छंद
A. आवरण B. पद
C. बंधन D. आचरण

5. ऐश्वर्य
A. बड़ाई B. विलास
C. सुख D. सम्पदा

6. खर
A. रावण B. कुंठित
C. गधा D. मूर्ख

7. पक्षी
A. नीरज B. नभ
C. विहग D. सरसिज

8. कमल
A. कुसुम B. पुष्प
C. प्रसून D. पुंडरीक

9. चतुरानन
A. ब्रह्मा B. इन्द्र
C. विष्णु D. देवता

10. जल
A. घटा B. नीर
C. दिनकर D. सुधाकर

11. अमृत
A. सुधा B. कौमुदी
C. मन्मथ D. सुधाकर

12. इच्छा
A. अमिय B. हर्ष
C. आकांक्षा D. रश्मि

13. उद्यान
A. धाम B. कुसुमाकर
C. आलय D. वाटिका

14. अन्त्य
A. समाप्त B. अन्तिम
C. नीच D. कुलीन

15. घर
A. सदन B. उपवन
C. पंचशर D. हुताशन

16. व्योम
A. आकाश B. किरण
C. अग्नि D. ब्रह्मा

17. कानन
A. मधुकर B. पुष्प
C. विहिप D. वन

18. दास
A. पादप B. तात
C. भृत्य D. श्रमिक

निर्देश : *निम्नलिखित प्रत्येक प्रश्न में पर्यायवाची शब्द के सर्वाधिक उपयुक्त युग्म को चुनिए।*

19. अंतरिक्ष
A. पृथ्वी, आकाश B. व्योम, आकाश
C. सुरपथ, सिद्दपथ D. अनन्त, गगन

20. अम्बुज
A. कमल, शंख B. कमला, ब्रह्मा
C. बज्र, बेंत D. मीन, जलकुंभी

21. खल
A. विश्वासघाती, निर्लज्ज
B. नीच, दुर्जन
C. दुष्ट, धोखेबाज
D. खली, खरल

22. तृण
A. तुच्छ, अल्प B. घास, पत्ता
C. तिनका, घास D. लता, द्रुम

23. क्षुद्र
A. कंजूस, कृपण B. निर्धन, दरिद्र
C. अल्प, मामूली D. नीच, अधम

24. उग्र
A. तीव्र, रौद्र B. प्रचण्ड, क्रोधी
C. उत्कट, घोर D. शिव, सूर्य

25. वटोही
A. दटमार, एकाकी B. असहाय, दुर्गम
C. पथिक, राहगीर D. पाथेय, मेघ

26. विरद
A. यश, ख्याति B. बीज, मूल
C. वृक्ष, पौधा D. विरही, वियोगी

27. यातु
A. पथिक, कष्ट B. काल, हवा
C. यातना, हिंसा D. राक्षस, निशाचर

28. विभु
A. सर्वव्यापक, नित्य B. ब्रह्म, आत्मा
C. महान, ईश्वर D. चिरस्थायी, दृढ़

निर्देश : *निम्नलिखित विकल्पों में से कौन-सा दिए गए शब्द का सही पर्यायवाची नहीं है?*

29. देवता
A. सुर B. असुर
C. अमर D. निर्जर

30. तारा
A. अम्बु B. तारक
C. नक्षत्र D. नखत

31. बेटा
A. पुत्र B. सुत
C. आत्मज D. अग्रज

32. मनुष्य
A. नर B. महीपाल
C. मनुज D. मानव

33. गणेश
A. गणपति B. गौरीसुत
C. मतंग D. गजानन

34. अनुरोध
A. आग्रह B. विनती
C. निवेदन D. याचना

35. द्विज
A. केश B. दाँत
C. ब्राह्मण D. दो

36. हवा
A. अनल B. अनिल
C. वायु D. पवन

37. अंकुश
A. प्रतिबन्ध B. रोक
C. अखुआ D. दबाव

38. अकृत
A. ईश्वर B. परमात्मा
C. अन्तर्यामी D. उपेक्षित

39. अक्षि
A. धुरी B. चक्षु
C. लोचन D. नेत्र

40. अगाध
A. गहना B. गहन
C. अथाह D. गम्भीर

41. अवधि
A. अचल B. पृथ्वी
C. इला D. धरती

42. राजा
A. क्षपाकर B. नृप
C. नरेश D. भूपति

43. पहाड़
A. पर्वत B. भूधर
C. भूप D. गिरि

44. सूर्य
A. रवि B. इन्दु
C. दिनेश D. भास्कर

45. पंकज
A. अम्बुज B. जलज
C. जलद D. सरोज

46. सोना
A. हेम B. हिरण्ये
C. रमणीक D. हाटक

47. अग्नि
A. अनल B. धूमकेतु
C. अम्बक D. कृशानु

48. नाहर
A. केशरी B. वनराज
C. मृग D. सिंह

49. जिस विकल्प में पर्यायवाची शब्द नहीं है, उसे चुनिए
A. आग–अनिल B. पद्म–जलज
C. फूल–पुष्प D. पेड़–विटप

50. जिस विकल्प में पर्यायवाची शब्द नहीं है उसे चुनिए
A. पृथ्वी–मही B. रात–राकेश
C. रास्ता–मार्ग D. बर्फ–हिम

उत्तरमाला

1	2	3	4	5	6	7	8	9	10
C	A	D	B	D	C	C	D	A	B
11	**12**	**13**	**14**	**15**	**16**	**17**	**18**	**19**	**20**
A	C	D	C	A	A	D	C	B	A
21	**22**	**23**	**24**	**25**	**26**	**27**	**28**	**29**	**30**
B	C	D	D	C	A	D	A	B	A
31	**32**	**33**	**34**	**35**	**36**	**37**	**38**	**39**	**40**
D	B	C	D	A	A	C	D	A	A
41	**42**	**43**	**44**	**45**	**46**	**47**	**48**	**49**	**50**
A	A	C	B	C	C	C	C	A	B

●●●

विलोम शब्द

परिचय :

विलोम शब्द को विपरीतार्थक, विलोमार्थी अथवा विरोधी शब्द कहा जाता है जो किसी शब्द के ठीक विपरीत अर्थ प्रकट करते है। अंग्रेजी में जिन शब्दों को एण्टानिम्स कहा जाता है, हिंदी में वही शब्द विलोमार्थी अथवा प्रातिकूल अर्थ के बोधक कहे जाते हैं। अतएव विलोमार्थी शब्दों को यदि हम परिभाषाबद्ध करना चाहें तो कह सकते हैं कि–''किसी एक शब्द के ठीक विपरीत अर्थ प्रकट करने वाले शब्द विलोम कहे जाते हैं।'' इन शब्दों को दिपर्याय के रूप में भी जाना जाता है।

निर्देश : *नीचे दिए गए शब्दों के विलोम के लिए चार-चार विकल्प दिए गए हैं। उनमें से उचित विकल्प का चयन कीजिए।*

1. कृपण
A. अधम B. दानी
C. कृतघ्न D. कनिष्ठ

2. क्षणिक
A. शाश्वत B. संक्षेप
C. विरह D. क्षुद्र

3. स्वदेश
A. गाँव B. नगर
C. परदेश D. स्वर्ग

4. स्तुति
A. सेवक B. निवेदन
C. प्रार्थना D. निन्दा

5. सर्दी
A. गर्मी B. धूप
C. उष्ण D. शीतल

6. शान्त
A. लघु B. चंचल
C. डरपोक D. बहादुर

7. भीगा
A. सूखा B. नरम
C. उष्ण D. गरम

8. कुसुम
A. वज्र B. नारी
C. खिन्न D. ठंडा

9. तम
A. सम B. कृश
C. नम D. प्रकाश

10. नख
A. शिख B. अनित्य
C. श्याम D. निन्दा

11. भौतिक
A. पाश्चात्य B. दैविक
C. दैहिक D. आध्यात्मिक

12. अवनि
A. आकाश B. अम्बर
C. गगन D. आसमान

13. कर्कशा
A. कोमल B. निर्मल
C. विह्वल D. व्याकुल

14. अवनत
A. बढ़ना B. उत्कर्ष
C. ऊँचा D. उन्नत

15. अति
A. न्यून B. कम
C. अल्प D. नगण्य

16. अद्‌भुत
A. सामान्य B. लौकिक
C. संसारी D. सुगम

17. दरिद्र
A. सम्पन्न B. समृद्धशाली
C. भूपति D. श्रीपति

18. ब्रह्म
A. जीव B. माया
C. जगत D. अज्ञान

19. बहिरंग
A. अंतरंग B. रंगारंग
C. जलतरंग D. रामरंग

20. दिवस
A. विभावरी B. अरविन्द
C. प्रवाहिणी D. विचक्षण

21. निर्मल
A. पवित्र B. शुद्ध
C. मलिन D. मृदु

22. उद्यम
A. प्रवीण B. आलस्य
C. नीरज D. नृप

23. अग्नि
A. पवन B. समीर
C. जल D. जलधि

24. अग्र
A. पश्च B. शांत
C. मध्यम D. अधम

25. अच्युत
A. अधम B. पतित
C. द्रवित D. च्युत

26. कटु
A. मधुर B. पटु
C. मृदु D. मीठा

27. नीरस
A. रसीला B. सरस
C. विरस D. अरस

28. ओजस्विनी
A. तेजस्विनी B. निर्जस्वी
C. तपस्विनी D. तपस्वी

29. अर्पण
A. ग्रहण B. तर्पण
C. समर्पण D. प्रत्यर्पण

30. सामिष
A. निरामिष B. वैष्णव
C. शाकाहारी D. मांसरहित

31. व्यय
A. धनागम B. आमदनी
C. धनोपार्जन D. आय

32. संयोग
A. विप्रलम्भ B. विरह
C. वियोग D. पार्थक्य

33. रूक्ष
A. पिच्छल B. चिक्कण
C. स्निग्ध D. सरस

34. सूक्ष्म
A. बड़ा B. मोटा
C. विशाल D. स्थूल

35. विघटन
A. सामूहिकता B. संगठन
C. समष्टि D. एकीकरण

36. विकास
A. उल्लास B. ह्रास
C. विनाश D. परिहास

37. अनायास
A. सायास B. विपर्यास
C. प्रयास D. आभास

38. गरिमा
A. कालिमा B. लघुमा
C. अरुणिमा D. लालिमा

39. उपेक्षा
A. वीक्षा B. उत्प्रेक्षा
C. अपेक्षा D. परीक्षा

40. अंगीकरण
A. तिरस्कार B. उपेक्षा
C. अनंगीकरण D. घृणा

41. अज्ञ
A. प्रज्ञ B. प्रवीण
C. चतुर D. समझदार

42. सामंजस्य
A. विवाद B. कलह
C. सन्ताप D. द्वेष

43. अमर
A. चेतन B. जर
C. अमृत D. मर्त्य

44. पराक्रम
A. भीरूता B. दुविधा
C. आलस्य D. दुर्बलता

45. गुरु
A. विस्तृत B. बड़ा
C. विशाल D. लघु

46. रंक
A. बलवान B. धनवान
C. किसान D. मजदूर

47. जन्म
A. मृत्यु B. मरण
C. अंत D. सुषुप्ति

48. संक्षेपण
A. स्फीति B. विस्तारण
C. विस्तीर्ण D. विस्तारीकरण

49. तिक्त
A. नमकीन B. मधुर
C. तीखा D. कड़ुवा

50. प्रीति
A. वैर B. दोस्ती
C. मदद D. सहायता

उत्तरमाला

1	2	3	4	5	6	7	8	9	10
B	A	C	D	A	B	A	A	D	A
11	**12**	**13**	**14**	**15**	**16**	**17**	**18**	**19**	**20**
D	B	A	D	C	A	B	A	A	A
21	**22**	**23**	**24**	**25**	**26**	**27**	**28**	**29**	**30**
C	B	C	A	D	A	B	D	A	A
31	**32**	**33**	**34**	**35**	**36**	**37**	**38**	**39**	**40**
D	C	C	D	B	B	A	B	C	B
41	**42**	**43**	**44**	**45**	**46**	**47**	**48**	**49**	**50**
D	A	D	C	D	B	A	B	B	A

●●●

उपसर्ग एवं प्रत्यय

परिचय :

उपसर्ग–एक ऐसी भाषिक इकाई है जिसका भाषा में स्वतंत्र प्रयोग प्रायः नहीं होता किंतु इन्हें शब्दों के आरम्भ में जोड़कर नया शब्द बनाया जाता है। हिन्दी में तीन प्रकार के उपसर्गों का प्रयोग किया जाता है जो इस प्रकार हैं–

तत्सम उपसर्ग : ऐसे उपसर्ग जो संस्कृत से यथावत् ले लिए गए हैं उन्हें तत्सम उपसर्ग कहा जाता है। जैसे–अति, उत्, अधि, अप, आ, उप, दुः, निः, परा, परि, प्र, प्रति, बहु, वि, स, सु आदि।

तद्भव उपसर्ग : वे उपसर्ग जो संस्कृत के उपसर्गों तथा ध्वनियों से कुछ परिवर्तित होकर आए हैं तथा जिनका हिन्दी में स्वतंत्र प्रयोग नहीं होता किन्तु शब्द रचना के लिए उनका प्रयोग किया जाता है। उदाहरण के लिए अ, औ, क, दु, नि, पर, स आदि।

विदेशी उपसर्ग : जो उपसर्ग भाषाओं से लिए गए हैं तथा हिन्दी ने उन्हें स्वीकार कर लिया है उन्हें विदेशी उपसर्ग कहा जाता है। हिन्दी में प्रयुक्त होने वाले उपसर्ग ज्यादातर अरबी तथा फारसी से लिए गए हैं जैसे–अल, दर, ब, बा, बे, ला आदि।

परिचय :

प्रत्यय–प्रत्यय ऐसी भाषिक इकाई है जिसका प्रयोग स्वतंत्र रूप से नहीं किया जाता वरन् इसे किसी अन्य भाषिक इकाई के साथ जोड़कर किया जाता है। प्रत्यय चार प्रकार के होते हैं–

तत्सम : अनीय, आ, आलु, इ, इमा, इष्ठ, ई, ए, जीवी, तः, ता।

तद्भव : आइन, आई, आहट, आलू, एरा, नी आदि।

देशज : अंक, अक्कड़, अड़, आटा, पन आदि।

विदेशी : आना, इयत, खीर, मन्द आदि।

निर्देश : *नीचे एक शब्द दिया गया है। दिए गए विकल्प से आपको शब्द में प्रयुक्त उपसर्ग ज्ञात करना है।*

1. विज्ञान
A. विज्ञ B. चिर
C. वि D. अन

2. चिरायु
A. चि B. चिर
C. यु D. आयु

3. अवनत
A. नत B. अ
C. अव D. अवन

4. अत्याचार
A. अ B. अत्या
C. अति D. चार

5. अध्यात्म
A. अध्य B. अधि
C. आत्म D. अ

निर्देश : *निम्नलिखित शब्दों में प्रत्यय लगाने से बनने वाले सही विकल्प को चुनिए।*

6. शरीर + इक
A. शारीरक B. शारिरीक
C. शारीरिक D. शरीरिक

7. वर + इष्ठ
A. वरीष्ठ B. वरेष्ठ
C. वरिष्ट D. वरिष्ठ

8. बहन + ओई
A. बहनौई B. बहनोई
C. बहनुई D. बहनौयी

9. आध्यात्मक + इक
A. आध्यात्मिक B. अध्यात्मिक
C. अधिआत्मिक D. अध्यात्मक

10. लड़का + पन
A. लड़कापन B. लड़पन
C. लड़कपन D. लड़कापन

निर्देश : *नीचे एक शब्द दिया गया है। दिए गए विकल्प से आपको शब्द में प्रयुक्त प्रत्यय ज्ञात करना है।*

11. पागलपन
A. पागल B. पा
C. पन D. इनमें से कोई नहीं

12. सावधानी
A. ई B. इ
C. धानी D. साव

13. धुंधला
A. धुं B. धुंध
C. ला D. इनमें से कोई नहीं

14. प्रत्यय रहित शब्द है
A. पराभव B. कवित्व
C. कुख्यात D. लघुत्व

निर्देश : *तत्सम शब्द का चुनाव कीजिए।*

15. A. अँगरखा B. अंगरक्षक
C. अंगरच्छक D. अंरक्षक

16. A. अँधेरा B. अंधाधुंध
C. अंधकार D. अंधड़

17. A. आँवला B. आँवलक
C. आमलक D. अँवला

18. A. आश्चर्य B. आम
C. इज्जत D. अचरज

19. A. आलस्य B. उबटन
C. अमोल D. ऊँट

20. A. पुस्तक B. अंगूठी
C. आमोल D. अचरज

निर्देश : *निम्नलिखित में से कौन-सा शब्द नीचे दिए गए तद्भव का सही तत्सम शब्द है?*

21. नमक
A. लावण्य B. नौन
C. लवण D. लौन

22. सतसई
A. सप्तपदी B. षट्शती
C. सप्तशती D. सत्यशती

23. तुरन्त
A. त्वरित B. त्वरन्त
C. तुवरन्त D. तवरन्त

24. साखी
A. सखी B. साक्षी
C. साक्ष्य D. शाखा

25. तिगुना
A. तीन गुना B. तिन गुणा
C. त्रयगुण D. त्रिगुण

निर्देश : *नीचे लिखे प्रत्येक वर्ग में दिए गए विकल्पों में से तद्भव शब्द का चयन कीजिए।*

26. A. कान B. नासिका
C. परीक्षण D. कटक

27. A. पीड़ा B. केरा
C. पर्याप्त D. शिल्प

28. A. पक्षी B. नृत्य
C. अँधेरा D. पश्य

29. A. बालिका B. बेत
C. आज्ञा D. सिद्धि

30. A. रक्षा B. तमंचा
C. विरोध D. शान्ति

उत्तरमाला

1	2	3	4	5	6	7	8	9	10
C	B	C	C	B	C	D	B	A	C
16	17	18	19	20					
11	12	13	14	15	16	17	18	19	20
C	A	C	C	B	C	C	A	A	A
21	22	23	24	25	26	27	28	29	30
C	C	A	B	D	A	A	C	C	A

●●●

● मुहावरे एवं लोकोक्तियां ●

परिचय :

मुहावरा : मुहावरा अरबी शब्द है तथा संस्कृत और हिन्दी में इसका सही पर्याय नहीं मिलता। प्रयुक्तता, वाग्रीति, वाग्धारा और भाषा सम्प्रदाय को हम मुहावरे का पर्याय मान सकते हैं किन्तु इन शब्दों में 'मुहावरे' जैसी प्रभावोत्पादकता नहीं है। हिन्दी में मुहावरे की जगह वाग्धारा चलाने का प्रयास किया गया था, किन्तु हिन्दी जगत में वह ग्राह्य नहीं हुआ तथा मुहावरा, मुहावरा ही बना रहा।

परिचय :

लोकोक्ति : लोकोक्ति शब्द लोक तथा उक्ति दो शब्दों के मेल से बना है। इसका अर्थ होता है कोई ऐसा पूर्ण या अपूर्ण वाक्य जिसमें कोई अनुभव, सारकथन अथवा कोई कथा छिपी होती है। जैसे—'का बरखा जब कृषि सुखाने' इसका अर्थ है कि यदि कोई काम समय पर नहीं हुआ तो असमय में उसके होने का कोई महत्व नहीं रह जाता।

निर्देश : *नीचे मुहावरे दिए गए है। प्रत्येक मुहावरे का अर्थ बताने के लिए चार विकल्प दिए गए हैं। इनमें एक अर्थ सही है। आपको इसी का चयन करना है।*

1. अंगारे उगलना
A. आग लगाना
B. क्रोध में कठोर वचन बोलना
C. आग बुझाना
D. जले हुए कोयले को इकट्ठा करना

2. इधर की दुनिया उधर करना
A. जिद पर अड़े रहना
B. असम्भव को सम्भव करना
C. दहेज कम करना
D. धनी व्यक्ति का निर्धन होना

3. ऊँचा-नीचा सुनाना
A. प्रेरक प्रसंग सुनाना
B. उपदेश देना
C. भला बुरा कहना
D. प्रवचन करना

4. काला नाग
A. विषधर सर्प
B. खोटा या घातक व्यक्ति
C. तीव्र बुद्धि वाला व्यक्ति
D. काला धन रखने वाला व्यक्ति

5. ठन-ठन गोपाल
A. बना ठना नवयुवक B. खोखला
C. धनवान D. शक्तिशाली

6. अंग-अंग ढीला होना
A. परेशान होना B. शिथिल गात होना
C. पिटाई होना D. बीमार होना

7. अंधे के हाथ बटेर लगना
A. किसी वस्तु का अनायास मिलना
B. अपात्र को बहुत बड़ी सफलता मिलना
C. अप्राप्य को प्राप्त करना
D. मुसीबत पर मुसीबत आना

8. घी का लड्डू टेढ़ा भी भला
A. गुणी व्यक्ति की आलोचना
B. उपयोगी वस्तु का रूप-रंग नहीं देखा जाता
C. घी का लड्डू स्वादिष्ट होता है
D. घी का लड्डू महंगा होता है

9. कोढ़ में खाज
A. परवाह नहीं करना
B. बराबर समझना
C. एक दुःख पर दूसरा दुःख होना
D. निपट मूर्ख

10. गुल खिलाना
A. मौज करना B. बहुत गुस्सा आना
C. व्यवधान पड़ना D. कोई बखेड़ा खड़ा करना

11. नाक का बाल होना
A. बहुत कष्ट झेलना B. किसी का प्रिय व्यक्ति होना
C. अपमान होना D. अनुभवी होना

12. सिक्का जमाना
A. झूठे आश्वासन देना B. बहुत सम्मान देना
C. सही व्यवहार करना D. प्रभाव स्थापित करना

13. पर निकलना
A. अभिमान करना B. व्यर्थ इतराना
C. बड़ा हो जाना D. शीघ्रता से काम करना

14. दूध का धुला होना
A. निर्दोष होना B. स्वस्थ होना
C. शाकाहारी होना D. स्वच्छ होना

15. दाँत खट्टे करना
A. हराना B. दाँत दुखना
C. चखना D. दाँत कमजोर होना

16. ओखली में सिर देना
A. सोच-समझकर कार्य करना
B. जानबूझ कर मुसीबत मोल लेना
C. बिना सोचे कार्य करना
D. अनजाने गड्ढे में गिरना

17. घोड़े बेच कर सोना
A. दुःखी होकर सोना B. अकेले सोना
C. खुश होकर सोना D. निश्चिंत होकर सोना

18. मुँह धो रखना
A. आशा न रखना B. आशा करना
C. इज्जत लेना D. कुछ खा लेना

19. हाथोंहाथ
A. सहयोग करना
B. खूब पीटना
C. किसी काम को शीघ्र कर देना
D. खतरा मोल लेना

20. सिर आँखों पर होना
A. सहर्ष स्वीकार करना
B. शोख करना
C. अच्छा बुरा सबको एक समझना
D. बुरा हाल होना

निर्देश : *प्रत्येक पंक्ति में एक लोकोक्ति दी गई है। उसके अर्थ स्वरूप चार विकल्प दिए गए हैं। इनमें से एक विकल्प सही है। आपको उसी का चयन करना है।*

21. अन्धा बाँटे रेवड़ी फिर-फिर अपनों को देय
A. उच्च पद पाकर अपने ही लोगों को लाभान्वित करना
B. न्याय की अवहेलना करके स्वजनों को लाभान्वित करना
C. अन्धा आदमी स्वजनों का ख्याल रखता है
D. स्वार्थी व्यक्ति पक्षपात करता है

22. अकल बड़ी कि भैंस
A. शारीरिक बल की अपेक्षा बौद्धिक बल श्रेष्ठ होता है
B. अक्ल अमूर्त और भैंस मूर्त रूप हैं
C. भैंस शारीरिक दृष्टि से बड़ी होती है
D. भैंस बुद्धिमान होती है

23. होनहार विरवान के होत चीकने पात
A. चिकने पत्तों वाला पौधा सुन्दर लगता है
B. बागवानी का शौक अच्छी बात है
C. होनहार बालक के लक्षण बचपन में ही प्रकट होने लगते हैं
D. चिकने पत्तों से पता लगता है कि यह पौधा वृक्ष बन जाएगा

24. सच्चे का बोलबाला, झूठे का मुँह काला
A. झूठ बोलना पाप है
B. झूठ बोलने वाला अपमानित होता है
C. असत्य बोलने वालों पर व्यंग्य
D. सत्य की सर्वत्र विजय होती है

25. शेर भूखा रह जाए, पर घास नहीं खाता
A. श्रेष्ठ व्यक्ति संकट में भी मर्यादा नहीं तोड़ता है
B. शेर केवल मांसाहारी होता है
C. शेर स्वयं शिकार होता है
D. स्वावलम्बी व्यक्ति किसी का सहारा नहीं तकता

26. हथेली पर सरसों नहीं जमती
A. सरसों के लिए जमीन चाहिए हथेली नहीं
B. हर काम में मनमानी नहीं चल सकती
C. काम के लिए समय चाहिए, जब चाहो, तभी काम नहीं हो सकता
D. सफलता समय पर आती है

27. आग लगे पर पानी कहाँ
A. कलह में कभी सुख नहीं होता
B. मुसीबत आने पर सहज नहीं टलती
C. वक्त पर अभीष्ट वस्तु नहीं मिलती
D. इनमें से कोई नहीं

28. घर में नहीं दाने, अम्मा चली भुनाने
A. झूठा आडम्बर
B. अधिक दिखावा करना
C. डींगें हाँकना
D. मुश्किल से गुजारा करना

29. ऊँची दुकान फीका पकवान
A. ऊँचे पर बनी दुकान के पकवान मीठे नहीं होते
B. ऊँची दुकान महँगी होती है
C. दिखावटी वस्तु में गुणवत्ता कम होती है
D. दिखावट में आकर्षण अधिक रहता है

30. न ऊधो का लेन, न माधो का देन
A. दूसरे के झंझट में दखल देना
B. किसी झंझट में न पड़ना
C. किसी से उधार न लेना
D. नगद लेन-देन करना

31. तीन लोक से मथुरा न्यारी
A. मथुरा सबसे श्रेष्ठ तीर्थ है
B. मथुरा नगर विशिष्ट है
C. सबसे श्रेष्ठ व सुन्दर
D. सबसे निराला

32. अधजल गगरी, छलकत जाए
A. निर्धन द्वारा अधिक खर्च करना
B. अज्ञानी द्वारा उपदेश देना
C. अल्पज्ञानी द्वारा अधिक प्रदर्शन करना
D. गगरी को पूरा भरना ही श्रेष्ठ

33. अपनी करनी, पार उतरनी
A. स्वयं के प्रयास से सफलता मिलती है
B. अपने कर्मों का फल भोगना
C. अपने साधन से ही नदी पार करनी चाहिए
D. अपने का हित करना

34. आये थे हरि भजन को ओटन लगे कपास
A. अच्छे कार्य न करके बुरे कार्य करना
B. पूजा-पाठ छोड़कर व्यापार करना
C. साधारण मनुष्य बनकर रहना
D. उच्च लक्ष्य छोड़कर साधारण कार्य में शक्ति लगाना

35. आगे नाथ न पीछे पगहा
A. पूर्ण स्वतन्त्र
B. अपने मन की करना
C. बन्धन रहित होना
D. इधर-उधर भागना

36. जस दूल्हा तसि बनी बराता
A. अच्छा दूल्हा और अच्छे साथी
B. अच्छा दूल्हा और खराब बाराती
C. सभी लोगों का अच्छा होना
D. जैसे व्यक्ति वैसे साथी

37. कहे से कुम्हार गधे पर नहीं चढ़ता
A. सरलता से न मानना
B. हठी व्यक्ति समझाने से नहीं मानता
C. किसी की न सुनना
D. भय दिखाने से ही काम बनता है

38. अधजल गगरी छलकत जाए
A. सीमित ज्ञान पर घमण्ड करना
B. आधी गगरी भरना
C. मूर्खता के कार्य करना
D. किसी कार्य को ठीक से न करना

39. ऊँट चढ़े पर कुत्ता काटे
A. अपना काम निकालना
B. कोई काम पूरा न हो पाना
C. दुस्साहस करके पछताना
D. विपत्ति सब जगह पीछा करती है

40. तन पर नहीं लत्ता, पान खायें अलबत्ता का अर्थ है
A. बुरी आदत में पड़ना
B. झूठा दिखावा करना
C. रौब डालना
D. रईस मिजाज होना

उत्तरमाला

1	2	3	4	5	6	7	8	9	10
B	B	C	B	B	B	A	B	C	D
11	12	13	14	15	16	17	18	19	20
B	D	B	A	A	B	D	A	C	A
21	22	23	24	25	26	27	28	29	30
D	A	C	D	A	C	C	A	C	B
31	32	33	34	35	36	37	38	39	40
D	C	A	D	C	D	B	A	D	B

●●●

General Awareness

Our India

INDIA : AT A GLANCE

Population (2011)	:	1,21,08,54,977
Capital	:	New Delhi
Area	:	32,87,263 sq km
Geographic Location	:	Between 8°4' and 37°6' north latitudes
	:	Between 68°7' and 97°25' east longitudes
Coastline Length	:	11,098.81 km including the coastline of Lakshadweep, Andaman & Nicobar Islands.
Major Languages	:	22
National Anthem	:	Jana Gana Mana
National Currency	:	Rupee (₹)
National Animal	:	Tiger
National Aquatic Animal	:	Dolphin
National Bird	:	Peacock
National River	:	Ganga
Characteristics of Indian	:	Socialist, Secular, Democratic, Republic
Legislature	:	Bicameral Legislature at the Centre Uni/Bicameral Legislatures in States
Executive	:	President, Vice-President and Council of Ministers at the Centre Governor and Council of Ministers in States
Judiciary	:	Independent from Executive with Supreme Court at the apex of the hierarchy
Total Road Length	:	66.71 lakh kilometres (March 2024)

India: States & Union Territories

States/Union Territories	*Capital*	*Area in (Sq. Km.)*	*Language*
Andhra Pradesh	Amaravati	1,60,205	Telugu
Arunachal Pradesh	Itanagar	83,743	Nyishi, Miji, Wancho etc.
Assam	Dispur	78,438	Assamese
Bihar	Patna	94,163	Hindi, Maithili
Chhattisgarh	Raipur	1,35,192	Hindi
Goa	Panji	3,702	Marathi and Konkani
Gujarat	Gandhinagar	1,96,024	Gujarati

contd...

States/Union Territories	Capital	Area in (Sq. Km.)	Language
Haryana	Chandigarh	44,212	Hindi
Himachal Pradesh	Shimla	55,673	Hindi and Pahari
Jharkhand	Ranchi	79,714	Hindi, Santhali
Karnataka	Bengaluru	1,91,791	Kannada
Keralam	Thiruvananthapuram	38,863	Malayalam
Madhya Pradesh	Bhopal	308,000	Hindi
Maharashtra	Mumbai	307,713	Marathi
Manipur	Imphal	22,327	Manipuri
Meghalaya	Shillong	22,429	Khasi, Garo and English
Mizoram	Aizawl	21,081	Mizo and English
Nagaland	Kohima	16,579	Sema, English
Odisha	Bhubaneswar	155,707	Odiya
Punjab	Chandigarh	50,362	Punjabi
Rajasthan	Jaipur	3,42,239	Hindi and Rajasthani
Sikkim	Gangtok	7,096	Bhutia, Nepali, Lepcha and Limbu
Tamil Nadu	Chennai	1,30,058	Tamil
Telangana	Hyderabad	1,12,077	Telugu
Tripura	Agartala	10,491	Bengali, Kakborak, Manipuri
Uttar Pradesh	Lucknow	2,40,928	Hindi and Urdu
Uttarakhand	Dehradun	53,483	Hindi
West Bengal	Kolkata	88,752	Bengali
Andaman & Nicobar Island	Shri Vijaya Puram	8,249	Bengali, Hindi, Nicobarese, Tamil, Telugu, and Malayalam
Chandigarh	Chandigarh	114	Hindi, Punjabi
Dadra & Nagar Haveli and Daman & Diu	Daman	603	Gujarati and Hindi
Delhi	Delhi	1483	Hindi, Punjabi and Urdu
Jammu & Kashmir	Srinagar (Summer) Jammu (Winter)	2,22,236*	Kashmiri, Urdu, Dogri
Ladakh	Leh	—	Ladakhi
Lakshadweep	Kavaratti	32	Malayalam
Puducherry	Puducherry	490	Tamil, Telugu, Malayalam, English and French

** Including areas of Ladakh and illegally occupied by China and Pakistan.*

POPULATION

As per the Census of India 2011, the population of India stood at 121.09 crore comprising 62.33 crore males and 58.76 crore females. Out of this 83.38 crore (68.9 per cent) lived in rural areas and the rest 37.71 crore (31.1 per cent) lived in urban areas. With a population of 102.87 crore in 2001, the decadal growth rate of population in India between 2001 and 2011 was 17.7 per cent. With such a huge population to support on so small an area, the country finds herself in great difficulty in making any significant dent on its poverty and economic backwardness. India's national income, which is barely 2 per cent of the total global income, clearly shows the tremendous strain of population on her economy.

2011 Census Highlights

Population of India–Total Indian population is 17.7% of total world population	:	1,21,08,54,977 (Male: 62,32,70,258; Female: 58,75,84,719)
Decadal Growth (2001-2011)	:	17.7 per cent (Males: 17.1 per cent; Females: 18.3 per cent)
Hightest Decadal Growth (State-wise)	:	Meghalaya (27.9 per cent)
Lowest Decadal Growth (State-wise)	:	Nagaland (–0.6 per cent)
Most populous State	:	Uttar Pradesh (16.50 per cent of National Population)
Density of population	:	382 persons per sq. km.
Most densly populated State	:	Bihar : 1106 per sq. km

Sex Ratio	:	943 females per 1000 males
Total Literacy Rate	:	73% (Males – 80.9%), (Females – 64.6%)
Highest Literacy (State-wise)	:	Kerala (94%)
Lowest Literacy (State-wise)	:	Bihar (61.8%)

OTHER DETAILS

(a) Population of India

1951	36,10,88,090
1961	43,92,34,771
1971	54,81,59,652
1981	68,33,29,097
1991	84,64,21,039
2001	1,02,87,37,436
2011	1,21,08,54,977

(b) Density of Population (Persons per square kilometre)

1951	113
1961	138
1971	177
1981	216
1991	267
2001	324
2011	382

(c) Annual Compound Rate of Growth

1941-1951	1.25 per cent
1951-1961	1.96 per cent
1961-1971	2.22 per cent
1971-1981	2.20 per cent
1981-1991	2.14 per cent
1991-2001	1.95 per cent
2001-2011	1.63 per cent

2011 CENSUS OF INDIA : POPULATION DISTRIBUTION, POPULATION DENSITY AND LITERACY RATE

S. No.	State/ Union Territories*	Population 2011			Population Density (per sq. km.)	Literacy Rate 2011		
		Persons	Males	Females	2011	Persons	Males	Females
	INDIA	1,21,08,54,977	62,32,70,258	58,75,84,719	382	73.0	80.9	64.6
1.	Jammu and Kashmir	1,25,41,302	66,40,662	59,00,640	124	67.2	76.8	56.4
2.	Himachal Pradesh	68,64,602	34,81,873	33,82,729	123	82.8	89.5	75.9
3.	Punjab	2,77,43,308	1,46,39,465	1,31,03,873	551	75.8	80.4	70.7
4.	Chandigarh	10,55,450	5,80,663	4,74,787	9,258	86.0	90.0	81.2
5.	Uttarakhand	1,00,86,292	51,37,773	49,48,519	189	78.8	87.4	70.0
6.	Haryana	2,53,51,462	1,34,94,734	1,18,56,728	573	75.6	84.1	65.9
7.	Delhi	1,67,87,941	89,87,326	78,00,615	11,320	86.2	90.9	80.8
8.	Rajasthan	6,85,48,437	3,55,50,997	3,29,97,440	200	66.1	79.2	52.1
9.	Uttar Pradesh	19,98,12,341	10,44,80,510	9,53,31,831	829	67.7	77.3	57.2
10.	Bihar	10,40,99,452	5,42,78,157	4,98,21,295	1,106	61.8	71.2	51.5
11.	Sikkim	6,10,577	3,23,070	2,87,507	86	81.4	86.6	75.6
12.	Arunachal Pradesh	13,83,727	7,13,912	6,69,815	17	65.4	72.6	57.7
13.	Nagaland	19,78,502	10,24,649	9,53,853	119	79.6	82.8	76.1
14.	Manipur	25,70,390	12,90,171	12,80,219	115	79.2	86.1	72.4
15.	Mizoram	10,97,206	5,55,339	5,41,867	52	91.3	93.3	89.3
16.	Tripura	36,73,917	18,74,376	17,99,541	350	87.2	91.5	82.7
17.	Meghalya	29,66,889	14,91,832	14,75,057	132	74.4	76.0	72.9
18.	Assam	3,12,05,576	1,59,39,443	1,52,66,133	398	72.2	77.8	66.3
19.	West Bengal	9,12,76,115	4,68,09,027	4,44,67,088	1,028	76.3	81.7	70.5
20.	Jharkhand	3,29,88,134	1,69,30,315	1,60,57,819	414	66.4	76.8	55.4
21.	Odisha	4,19,74,218	2,12,12,136	2,07,62,082	270	72.9	81.6	64.0
22.	Chhattisgarh	2,55,45,198	1,28,32,895	1,27,12,303	189	70.3	80.3	60.2
23.	Madhya Pradesh	7,26,26,809	3,76,12,306	3,50,14,503	236	69.3	78.7	59.2
24.	Gujarat	6,04,39,692	3,14,91,260	2,89,48,432	308	78.0	85.8	69.7
25.	Daman and Diu	2,43,247	1,50,301	92,946	2,191	87.1	91.5	79.5
26.	Dadra & Nagar Haweli	3,43,709	1,93,760	1,49,949	700	76.2	85.2	64.3
27.	Maharashtra	11,23,74,333	5,82,43,056	5,41,31,277	365	82.3	88.4	75.9
28.	Andhra Pradesh	4,93,86,799	2,47,38,068	2,46,48,731	308	67.4	74.8	60.0
29.	Karnataka	6,10,95,297	3,09,66,657	3,01,28,640	319	75.4	82.5	68.1
30.	Goa	14,58,545	7,39,140	7,19,405	394	88.7	92.6	84.7
31.	Lakshadweep	64,473	33,123	31,350	2,149	91.8	95.6	87.9
32.	Kerala	3,34,06,061	1,60,27,412	1,73,78,649	860	94.0	96.1	92.1
33.	Tamil Nadu	7,21,47,030	3,61,37,975	3,60,09,055	555	80.1	86.8	73.4
34.	Puducherry	12,47,953	6,12,511	6,35,442	2,547	85.8	91.3	80.7
35.	Andaman & Nicobar Island	3,80,581	2,02,871	1,77,710	46	86.6	90.3	82.4
36.	Telangana	3,51,93,978	17,704,078	17,489,900	310	66.5	75.0	57.9

*****

National Symbols

State Emblem: State Emblem of India is an adaptation from the Sarnath Lion Capital of Ashoka. It was adopted by the Government of India on January 26, 1950. In the adapted form, only three lions are visible, the fourth being hidden from the view. The wheel (Dharma Chakra) appears in relief in the centre of the abacus with a bull on the right and a horse on the left. The bell-shaped lotus has been omitted. The words "Satyameva Jayate" meaning "Truth alone triumphs" are inscribed below the Emblem in Devanagari script.

National Flag: The National Flag of India is a horizontal tricolour of deep saffron (Kesari), white and dark green in equal proportion. In the centre of the white band there is a wheel in navy blue colour. It has 24 spokes. The ratio of the length and the breadth of the flag is 3 : 2. Its design was adopted by the Constituent Assembly of India on July 22, 1947.

National Anthem: Rabindranath Tagore's song 'Jana-gana-mana' was adopted by the Constituent Assembly as the National Anthem of India on January 24, 1950.

Jana-gan-mana-adhinayaka jaya he, Bharata-bhagya-vidhata
Punjab-Sindh-Gujarat-Maratha-Dravida-Utkala-Banga
Vindhya-Himachala-Yamuna-Ganga Uchhala-jaladhi-taranga.
Tava subha name jage, Tava subha asisa mange, Gahe tava jaya gatha,
Jana-gana-mangala-dayak, jaya he Bharata bhagya vidhata,
Jaya he, jaya he, jaya he, Jaya jaya jaya, jaya he.

National Song: Bankim Chandra Chatterji's 'Vande Mataram' which was a source of inspiration to the people in their struggle for freedom, has been adopted as National Song. It has an equal status with the National Anthem.

Vande Mataram
Sujalam, suphalam, malayaja-shitalam,
Shasya shyamalam, Mataram
Shubhrajyotsna,pulkita yaminim,
Phulla kusumita drumadalashobhinim,
Subhasinim sumadhura—bhashinim,
Sukhadam, Varadam, Mataram.

National Bird and Animal of India: Peacock and Tiger; **National Aquatic Animal:** Dolphin; **National Flower:** Lotus; **National Calendar:** It was adopted on March 22, 1957. It has 365 days in the year and the first month of the year is Chaitra.

Months of the National Calender

(1) Chaitra, (2) Vaishakha, (3) Jaishtha, (4) Ashadha, (5) Shravan, (6) Bhadra, (7) Ashvina, (8) Kartika, (9) Marga-Shirsha, (10) Pausha, (11) Magha, (12) Phalguna.

*****

3

The Universe

The Solar System: Some Facts

Number of Planets: 8—Mercury, Venus, Earth, Mars, Jupiter, Saturn, Uranus and Neptune.

Largest most

Massive planet	Jupiter
Brightest planet	Venus
Brightest star	Sirius
Fastest orbiting planet	Mercury
Longest (Synodic) day	Mercury
Planet with largest moon	Jupiter
Greatest average density	Jupiter
Tallest mountain	Earth
Strongest magnetic fields	Jupiter
Most circular orbit	Venus
Shortest (synodic) day	Jupiter
Hottest planet	Venus
No moons	Mercury, Venus
Planet with moon with most eccentric orbit	Neptune
Lowest average density	Saturn
Greatest amount of liquid on the surface	Earth

The Earth: Facts and Data

Composition of the Earth: Aluminium (0.4%), Sulphur (2.7%), Silicon (13%), Oxygen (28%), Calcium (1.2%), Nickel (2.7%), Magnesium (17%), Iron (35%)

Surface area	:	510100500 sq km
Land Surface	:	148950800 sq km (29.1%)
Ocean Surface	:	361149700 sq km (70.9%)
Type of water	:	97% salt, 3% fresh
Total area of water	:	382672000 sq km
Equatorial diameter	:	12753 km
Equatorial Circumference	:	40066 km
Polar Circumference	:	39992 km
Polar diameter	:	12710 km
Equatorial radius	:	6376 km
Polar radius	:	6335 km
Mass (estimated weight)	:	594×10^{19} metric tons
Mean distance from the Sun	:	149407000 km
Earth's orbit speed (around sun)	:	107320 kmph
Period of Revolution (round the sun)	:	365 days 5 hrs 48 min. 45.51 seconds
Time of Rotation (on its axis)	:	23 hrs 56 min. 4.09 seconds
Inclination of the axis (to the plane of the eclipitc)	:	23°27'

Solar Statistics

Distance from the Earth	:	149.8 million km
Absolute Visual Magnitude	:	4.75
Diameter Core	:	13,84,000 km
Temperature	:	15000000 K
Photosphere Temperature	:	5770 K
Rotation as seen from the Earth (at the equator)	:	25.38 days
Rotation as seen from the Earth (near the poles)	:	33 days
Chemical Composition	:	Hydrogen 71% Helium 26.5% Other elements 2.5%
Age	:	About 4.5 billion years
Expected lifetime of a normal star	:	About 10 billion years

Oceans of the World

Pacific	16,62,41,000 sq km
Atlantic	8,65,57,000 sq km
Indian	7,34,27,000 sq km
Arctic	94,85,000 sq km

Longest Rivers

Name	*Country/ Continent*	*Length in Kilometres*
Nile	Africa	6690
Amazon	S. America	6437
Mississippi-Missouri	USA	6020
Yangtze-Kiang	China	5494
Ob-Irtysh	Russia	5410
Lena	Russia	4400
Hwang Ho	China	4344
Niger	Africa	4180
St. Lawrence	Canada (USA)	4023
Murray-Darling	Australia	3780
Volga	Russia	3690
Indus	Asia	2900
Danube	Europe	2850
Orinoco	S. America	2575

Major Riverside Cities

City	*River*	*Country*
Alexandria	Nile	Egypt
Amsterdam	Amsel	Netherland
Ankara	Kizil	Turkiye
Baghdad	Tigris	Iraq
Bangkok	Menam	Thailand
Belgrade	Danube	Serbia
Berlin	Spree	Germany
Budapest	Danube	Hungary
Cairo	Nile	Egypt
Chittagong	Karnaphuli	Bangladesh
Karachi	Indus	Pakistan
Khartoum	Blue & White Nile	Sudan
Lahore	Ravi	Pakistan
Lisbon	Tagus	Portugal
Liverpool	Mersey	England
London	Thames	England
Moscow New	Moskva	Russia
Orleans	Mississipi	USA
New York	Hudson	USA
Paris	Seine	France
Yangon	Irawadi	Myanmar
Rome	Tiber	Italy

Major Gulfs of the World

Names	*Areas (Sq. Kms.)*
Gulf of Mexico	15,44,000
Gulf of Hudson	12,33,000
Arabian Gulf	2,38,000
Gulf of St. Lawrence	2,37,000
Gulf of California	1,62,000
English Channel	89,900

Major Mountain Ranges of the World

Range	*Location*	*Length (km)*
Andes	South America	7,200
Himalayas-Karakoram-Hindukush	South Central Asia	5,000
Rockies	North America	4,800
Great Dividing Range	East Australia	3,600
Atlas	North West Africa	1,930
Western Ghats	Western India	1,610
Caucasus	Europe	1,200
Alaska	USA	1,130
Alps	Europe	1,050

Largest Deserts of the World

Subtropical	
Sahara, North Africa	94,00,000 sq. km.
Kalahari, Southern Africa	5,82,727 sq. km.
Thar, India/Pakistan	2,00,000 sq. km.
Great Sandy, Australia	4,00,000 sq. km.
Cool Coastal	
Atacama, Chile S.A.	1,40,000 sq. km
Cool Winter	
Gobi, China	13,00,000 sq. km.
Colorado, Western USA (also called the painted desert)	3,37,000 sq. km.

Atmosphere

Composition of Gases in Atmosphere

Nitrogen	78.03%
Oxygen	20.99%
Argon	0.93%
Carbon dioxide	0.03%
Hydrogen	0.01%
Neon	0.0018%
Helium	0.0005%
Crypton	0.0001%
Xenon	0.000,005%
Ozone	0.000,0001%

World Important Local Winds

Chinoon: A warm day wind frequently experienced on the eastern side of the Rocky Mountains.
Fohn: A warm dry wind descending a mountain, as on the north side of the Alps.
Haboob: A sand storm or a dust storm in north and north-east Sudan near Khartoum.
Bagrrio: It is the tropical cyclone of the Philippine Island.
Loo: A hot wind which blows in summer season in Indian sub-continent.
Papasago: A cold northerly wind sometimes felt on the Mexico plateau.
Bora: It is the name given to the cold dry wind experienced particularly in winter along the eastern coast of the Atlantic Ocean and in northern Italy.
Black Toller: A hot dust wind which blows in the vast plain of North America.

Principal Mountain Peaks of the World

Mountains	*Height in Metres*	*Range*	*Date of First Ascent*
1. Mount Everest	8,848	Himalayas	May 29, 1953
2. K-2 (Godwin Austen)	8,611	Karakoram	July 31, 1954
3. Kanchenjunga	8,597	Himalayas	May 25, 1955
4. Lhotse	8,511	Himalayas	May 18, 1956
5. Makalu I	8,481	Himalayas	May 15, 1955
6. Dhaulagiri I	8,167	Himalayas	May 13, 1960
7. Mansalu I	8,156	Himalayas	May 9, 1956
8. Chollyo	8,153	Himalayas	Oct. 19, 1954
9. Nanga Parbat	8,124	Himalayas	July 3, 1953
10. Annapurna I	8,091	Himalayas	June 3, 1950
11. Gasherbrum I	8,068	Karakoram	July 5, 1958
12. Broad Peak I	8,047	Karakoram	June 9, 1957
13. Gasherbrum II	8,034	Karakoram	July 7, 1956
14. Shisha Pangma (Gosainthan)	8,014	Himalayas	May 2, 1964
15. Gasherbrum III	7,952	Karakoram	Aug. 11, 1975

Types of World Agriculture

Viticulture: The cultivation of the vine for production of grapes and wine.
Pisciculture: The breeding, rearing and transplantation of fish by artificial means.
Sericulture: The raising of silk worms for the production of raw silk.
Horticulture: To grow flower front, vegetables on small plots.
Apiculture: Bee keeping on a commercial scale for the sale of honey.
Floriculture: The cultivation of flowers or flowering plants.
Mariculture: Sea farming, or the cultivation of marine plants and animals for commercial purposes.
Olericulture: The cultivation of vegetables and kitchen herbs.

Famous Straits of the World

Strait	*Between*	*Country*
Malacca Strait	Andaman Sea and South China Sea	Indonesia
Palk Strait	Mannar and Bay of Bengal	India-Sri Lanka
Magellan Strait	Pacific and South Atlantic Ocean	Chile
Dover Strait	English Channel and North Sea	England-France
Berring Strait	Berring Sea and Chukasi Sea	Alaska-Russia
Sugaroo Strait	Japan Sea and Pacific Ocean	Japan
Sunda Strait	Java and Indian Ocean	Indonesia
Gibralter Strait	Mediterranean Sea and Atlantic Ocean	Spain
Harmuj Strait	Persia and Bay of Oman	Oman-Iran
Hudson Strait	Bay of Hudson and Atlantic Ocean	Canada

World's Famous Official Documents

White Paper: India; **Orange Book:** Netherlands; **Yellow Book:** France; **Green Book:** Italy and Iran; **White Book:** Portugal, China and Germany; **Grey Book:** Japan and Belgium.

Famous Newspapers of the World

Newspaper	*Place of Publishing*	*Language*
Daily News	New York (America)	English
Guardian	London (Britain)	English
Pravada	Moscow (Russia)	Russian
Al-Ahram	Cairo (Egypt)	Arabic
Merdeca	Jakarta (Indonesia)	Indonesian
Times	London (Britain)	English
People's Daily	Beijing (China)	Chinese
New Statesman	Britain	English
Daily Mirror	Britain	English
Hindu, Hindustan Times, Times of India, Tribune, Statesman, Indian Express, Economic Times	India	English
Hindustan, Nav Bharat Times, Rashtriya Sahara, Dainik Jagaran, Punjab Kesari	India	Hindi

Important Boundary Lines

Boundary Line	*Countries*
Hindenberg Line	Germany-Poland
Maginot Line	France and Germany
Mannerhein Line	Russia-Finland
Mc Mahon Line	India and China
Order Niesse Line	Germany-Poland
Radcliff Line	India-Pakistan
Seigfrid Line	Germany-France
Durand Line	Pakistan and Afghanistan
17th Parallel	The line which defined the boundary between North Vietnam and South Vietnam before the two were united.
38th Parallel	North Korea and South Korea
49th Parallel	U.S.A. and Canada

Areawise 10 Big and Small Countries

10 Big Countries

S. No.	*Country*	*Area (Sq. km)*
1.	Russia (Europe-Asia)	17,098,242
2.	Canada	99,84,670
3.	China (Asia)	95,96,961
4.	U.S.A. (N. America)	93,72,614
5.	Brazil (S. America)	85,14,877
6.	Australia (S. Pacific)	77,41,220
7.	India (Asia)	32,87,263
8.	Argentina (S. America)	27,80,400
9.	Kazakhstan (Europe-Asia)	27,24,900
10.	Algeria (Africa)	23,81,741

10 Small Countries

S.N.	*Country*	*Area (Sq. km)*
1.	Vatican City (Europe)	0.44
2.	Monaco (Europe)	1.95
3.	Nauru (Southern Pacific)	21.10
4.	Tuvalu	26.00
5.	San Marino (Europe)	61.00
6.	Liechtenstein (Europe)	160.00
7.	Marshall Island (Central Pacific)	181.00
8.	St. Kitts and Nevis (Eastern Caribbean)	261.00
9.	Grenada (Eastern Caribbean Sea)	344.00
10.	Seychelles (Indian Ocean)	455.00

Populationwise 10 Big and Small Countries

10 Big Countries

S. No.	*Country*	*Population (2021) (In million)*
1.	China (Asia)	1,397.898
2.	India (Asia)	1,339
3.	U.S.A. (North America)	334.998
4.	Indonesia (Asia)	275.122
5.	Pakistan (Asia)	238.181
6.	Nigeria (Africa)	219.464
7.	Brazil (South America)	213.445
8.	Bangladesh (Asia)	164.099
9.	Russia (Europe-Asia)	142.321
10.	Japan (Asia)	124.687

10 Small Countries

S. No.	Country	Population (2021)
1.	Vatican City (Europe)	1,000
2.	Tuvalu	11,448
3.	Palau (Western Pacific)	21,613
4.	Monaco (Europe)	31,223
5.	San Marino (Europe)	34,467
6.	Liechtenstein (Europe)	39,425
7.	St. Kitts and Nevis (Eastern Caribbean)	54,149
8.	Northern Mariana Islands	56,660
9.	American Samoa	59,380
10.	Marshall Island (Central Pacific)	78,831

National Emblems of Important Countries

Country	National Emblem
America	Golden Rod
Australia	Kangaroo
Ireland	Shamrock
Italy	White Lily
Israel	Candelabrum
Iran	Rose
Canada	White Lily
Great Britain	Rose
Chile	Candor and Huemul
Germany	Corn Flower
Japan	Chrysanthemum
Zimbabwe	Zimbabwe Bird
Denmark	Beach
Turkiye	Crescent and Star
The Netherlands	Lion
New Zealand	Kiwi, Fern Southern Cross
Norway	Lion
Nepal	Kukri
Pakistan	Crescent
Poland	Eagle
France	Lily
Belgium	Lion
Bangladesh	Water Lily
Mongolia	The Soyombo
Russia	Double headed eagle
Lebanon	Cedar Tree
Sudan	Secretary Bird
Syria	Eagle
India	Lioned Capital

The Continents of the World

There are seven major continents. These are separated by large water bodies. These continents are - Asia, Europe, Africa, North America, South America, Australia and Antarctica.

Asia is the largest continent. It covers about onethird of the total land area of the earth. The continent lies in the Eastern Hemisphere. The Tropic of Cancer passes through this continent. Asia is separated from Europe by the Ural mountains on the west. The combined landmass of Europe and Asia is called the Eurasia (Europe + Asia).

Europe is much smaller than Asia. The continent lies to the west of Asia. The Arctic Circle passes through it. It is bound by water bodies on three sides.

Africa is the second largest continent after Asia. The Equator or 0° latitude runs almost through the middle of the continent. A large part of Africa lies in the Northern Hemisphere. It is the only continent through which the Tropic of Cancer, the Equator and the Tropic of Capricorn pass.

The Sahara Desert, the world's largest hot desert, is located in Africa. The continent is bound on all sides by oceans and seas. The world's longest river the Nile, flows through Africa.

North America is the third largest continent of the world. It is linked to South America by a very narrow strip of land called the Isthmus of Panama. The continent lies completely in the Northern and Western Hemisphere. Three oceans surround this continent.

South America lies mostly in the Southern Hemisphere. The Andes, world's longest mountain range, runs through its length from north to south. South America has the world's largest river, the Amazon.

Australia is the smallest continent that lies entirely in the Southern Hemisphere. It is surrounded on all sides by the oceans and seas. It is called an island continent.

Antarctica, completely in the Southern Hemisphere, is a huge continent. The South Pole lies almost at the centre of this continent. As it is located in the South Polar Region, it is permanently covered with thick ice sheets. There are no permanent human settlements. Many countries have research stations in Antarctica. India also has research stations there. These are named as and Dakshin Gangotri, Maitri and Bharti.

International Date Line

It roughly corresponds to 180°E or W meridian of longitude which falls on the opposite side of the Greenwich meridian and the date changes by one day (i.e. 24 hours), as this line is crossed. On crossing this line from east to west a day is added, and a day is subtracted on crossing it from west to east.

* * * * *

United Nations Organisation

- **Origin:** UN Charter was signed by 50 members on June 26, 1945. It officially came into existence on October 24, 1945.
- **UN Charter:** The Charter is the Constitution of the UNO and contains its aims and objectives and rules and regulations for its functioning.
- **Aims and Objectives:** They are security, welfare and human rights.
- **Headquarters:** New York.
- **Flag:** The flag is light blue in colour, and emblazoned in white, in its centre is the UN symbol—a polar map of world embraced by twin olive branches open at the top.
- **Official Languages:** The official languages of the UN are: English, French, Chinese, Russian, Arabic and Spanish. However, working languages are English & French only.

Secretary General of the U.N.O.

Name	*Country*	*Tenure*
Trygve Lie	Norway	(1946-53)
Dog Hammarsk-joeld	Sweden	(1953-61)
U. Thant	Myanmar	(1961-71)
Kurt Waldheim	Austria	(1972-81)
Javier Perez de Cuellar	Peru	(1982-91)
Dr. Boutros Ghali	Egypt	(1992-96)
Kofi Annan	Ghana	(1997-2006)
Ban Ki-moon	South Korea	(2007-2016)
Antonio Guterres	Portugal	(2017- —)

- **Main Organs of the UNO:** There are six main organs:
  1. General Assembly
  2. Security Council
  3. Economic and Social Council
  4. Trusteeship Council
  5. International Court of Justice, and (6) Secretariat.

1. **General Assembly:** It consists of representative of all members of the UN. Each member country has only one vote. It meets once a year and passes UN Budget.
2. **Security Council:** It is the Executive body of the UN and is mainly responsible for maintaining international peace and security. It has 15 members, 5 of which (USA, UK, France, Russia and China) are permanent members. The 10 non-permanent members are elected by General Assembly for two-year term and are not eligible for immediate re-election.
3. **Economic and Social Council:** It has 54 members elected by General Assembly.
4. **Trusteeship Council:** It looks after interest of the people in areas not yet independent and leads them towards self-government.
5. **International Court of Justice:** It has 15 judges, no two of whom may be nationals of the same state. They are elected by General Assembly and Security Council for a term of 9 years. The Court elects its President and Vice-President for a 3-year term.
6. **Secretariat:** It is the Secretariat of the UN and is headed by the Secretary General.

Years Observed by United Nations Organisation

1967 : International Tourism Year
1968 : Human Rights Year
1970 : International Education Year
1972 : International Book Year
1973 : Copernicus Year
1974 : World Population Year
1975 : International Women's Year
1979 : International Year of the Child
1981 : International Year of Disabled
1983 : World Communication Year
1985 : International Youth Year
1986 : International Year of Peace
1987 : International Year of Shelter for the Homeless
1990 : International Literacy Year
1992 : International Space Year
1993 : International Year for World's Indigenous People
1994 : International Year of Family
1995 : International Year of Tolerance
1996 : International Year for Eradication of Poverty
1998 : Human Rights Year
1999 : Year of Older Persons
2000 : Year of the Culture of Peace
2001 : International Year of Volunteer
2002 : International Year of Eco-tourism
2003 : International Year of Fresh Water
2004 : International Rice Year
2005 : International Year of Sports and Physical Education
2006 : International Year of Deserts and Desertification
2008 : International Year of Potato

2009: International Year of Astronomy
2010: International Year of Bio-diversity
2011: International Year of Forest
2012: International Year of Cooperatives
2013: International Year of Water Cooperation
2014: International Year of Family Farming
2015: International Year of Soils.
2016: International Year of Pulses
2017: International Year of Sustainable Tourism for Development
2019: International Year of Indigenous Languages
2020: International Year of Plant Health
2021: International Year of Peace and Trust
2022: International Year of Artisanal Fisheries and Aquaculture
2023: International Year of Millets
2024: International Year of Camelids
2025: International Year of Glaciers Preservation; International Year of Quantum Science and Technology; International Year of Cooperatives; International Year of Peace and Trust.
2026: International Year of the Woman Farmer; International Year of Volunteers for Sustainable Development; International Year of Range-lands and Pastoralists

- **Present Membership:** At present 193 countries are members of the UN. South Sudan is the latest entrant to this world organisation.

Famous International Organisations, Headquarters and Year of Establishment

International Organisations	Headquarters	Year of Establishment
United Nations (U.N.)	New York	1945
International Monetary Fund (I.M.F.)	Washington	1945
World Health Organisation (W.H.O.)	Geneva	1948
Food & Agricultural Organisation (FAO)	Rome	1945
International Labour Organisation (ILO)	Geneva	1919
UNESCO	Paris	1946
International Court of Justice	The Hague	1945
Universal Postal Union (UPU)	Berne	1874
International Civil Aviation Organisation (ICAO)	Montreal	1947
UNIDO	Vienna	1966
International Atomic Energy Agency (IAEA)	Vienna	1957
International Finance Corporation (IFC)	Washington	1956
United Nations Development Programme (UNDP)	New York	1965
UNICEF	New York	1946
International Maritime Organisation (IMO)	London	1948
World Meteorological Organisation (WMO)	Geneva	1950
International Telecommunication Union (ITU)	Geneva	1865
Arab League	Cairo	1945
Commonwealth of Nations	London	1931
World Trade Organisation (WTO)	Geneva	1995
International Development Association (IDA)	Washington D.C.	1960
International Bank for Reconstruction and Development (IBRD)	Washington D.C.	1944
World Intellectual Property Organisation (WIPO)	Geneva	1967
Organisation of Islamic Conference (OIC)	Jeddah (Saudi Arabia)	1969
Red Cross	Geneva	1863
Interpol	Lyons	1923
Asian Development Bank (ADB)	Manila	1966
North Atlantic Treaty Organisation (NATO)	Brussels	1949
Association of South East Asian Nations (ASEAN)	Jakarta	1967
South Asian Association for Regional Cooperation (SAARC)	Kathmandu	1985
Asia-Pacific Economic Cooperation (APEC)	–	1989
Organisation for Economic Cooperation and Development (OECD)	Paris	1961
Organisation of Petroleum Exporting Countries (OPEC)	Vienna	1960
Common Wealth of Independent States (CIS)	Minsk	1991
International Olympic Committee (IOC)	Switzerland	1894
European Union (EU)	Brussels	Changed form of EEC Established in 1958
Amnesty International (AI)	London	1961
Shanghai Cooperation Organisation (SCO)	Beijing	2002

*****

5 Indian Constitution & Polity

Indian Constitution is a comprehensive document and it is the lengthiest written Constitution in the World.

The Preamble of the Constitution: "We the people of India, having solemnly resolved to Constitute India into a Sovereign, Socialist, Secular Democratic Republic and to secure to all its citizen."

Justice: Social, economic and political.

Liberty: Of thought, expression, belief, faith and worship.

Equality: Of status and of opportunity, and to promote among them all.

Fraternity: Assuring the dignity of the individual and the unity and integrity of the nation. In our Constituent Assembly, this twenty-sixth day of November, 1949, do hereby adopt, enact and give to ourselves this constitution."

SCHEDULES TO THE CONSTITUTION

The Constitution of India originally contained only eight schedules. Presently there are 12 schedules in the constitution.

First Schedule: It consists the list of the States and Union territories.

Second Schedule: This Schedule is related to salary and allowances of the President, Governors, Speaker, Supreme Court and High Court Judges etc.

Third Schedule: Contains forms of oath and affirmation.

Fourth Schedule: Contains allocation of seats to each State and Union territory in the Council of States.

Fifth Schedule: Provides for administration and control of scheduled areas and scheduled tribes.

Sixth Schedule: Provides for administration of Tribal Areas in Assam, Meghalaya and Mizoram.

Seventh Schedule: Distribution of powers and functions between the centre and state governments under three lists.

Eighth Schedule: The languages recognised by Parliament.

Ninth Schedule: It contains laws passed by the Union or States which cannot be taken to courts.

Tenth Schedule: Provisions as to disqualification on the ground of political defection.

Eleventh Schedule: Provisions regarding powers, authority etc. of Panchayati Raj institutions.

Twelfth Schedule: Provisions regarding powers, authority etc. of Municipalities etc.

Foreign Sources of Indian Constitution

Foreign Sources	*Subject*
Britain	Parliamentary system, collective responsibilities of Cabinet
America	Fundamental right, Independent Judiciary, Judicial review
Canada	Division of powers
Ireland	Directive principles
Germany	Emergency provisions
Russia	Fundamental duties
Australia	Concurrent list

THE SUPREME COURT

The Supreme Court of India consists of the Chief Justice and other Judges whose number is prescribed by the Parliament from time to time. In 1950 there was a Chief Justice and there were 7 Judges. But the number of Judges continued increasing as per the need. The Supreme Court, at present, consists of the Chief Justice and 37 Judges.

The Chief Justice and other Judges of the Supreme Court are appointed by the President of India. For appointing the Chief Justice of India, the other Judges of the Supreme or High Courts may be consulted. Usually, the senior-most Judge in the Supreme Court is appointed as the Chief Justice. For the appointment of other Judges of the Supreme Court, the Chief Justice has to be consulted. Usually, the Chief Justice himself consults a collegium of the four senior-most Judges, and all of them need to agree for any candidate to be recommended for the appointment of a judge.

A person can be appointed as a Judge of the Supreme Court only if he/she:

I. is a citizen of India;

II. must have been at least a Judge of a High Court or of two or more such Courts in succession for at least five years; or

III. must have been an advocate of a High Court or of two or more such Courts in succession for at least ten years; or

IV. is, in the opinion of the President, a distinguished jurist.

Judges of the Supreme Court hold office till they attain the age of 65 years. But they may be removed from office by an order of the President, passed after an address by each House of Parliament supported by a special majority on the ground of proved misbehaviour or incapacity.

The Jurisdiction and Powers of the Supreme Court

The Supreme Court of India is a powerful judiciary. The Constitution of India has defined its jurisdiction and powers in detail, it has Original. Appellate and Advisory Jurisdictions Besides these jurisdictions, it has a few other important functions.

(i) **Original Jurisdiction:** The Supreme Court alone has the authority to hear directly certain cases. These are:
- *(a)* Disputes between the Union government and one or more State governments,
- *(b)* Disputes between two or more States,
- *(c)* Disputes between the Government of India and one or more States on the one side and one or more States on the other side.

(ii) **Appellate Jurisdiction:** The power of a superior or higher court to hear and decide appeals against the judgment of the lower court is called appellate jurisdiction. The Supreme Court is a court of appeal for constitutional, civil and criminal cases. It can hear appeals against the judgments of the High Courts. It also has the power to review its own judgment. It may in its own discretion grant special lease to appeal against any judgment or order delivered or passed by any court or tribunal within the territory of India.

Moreover, an Appeal may come to the Supreme Court in any criminal case, if the High Court certifies that the case is fit for appeal to the Supreme Court. The special appellate power has become a handy weapon in the hands of the Court to review the decisions pertaining to elections and Labour and Industrial Tribunals.

(iii) **Advisory Jurisdiction:** The Supreme Court has a special advisory jurisdiction in matters which may specifically be referred to it by the President of India. If at any time, it appears to the President that a question of law or fact has arisen or is likely to arise, which is of such public importance that it is urgent to obtain the opinion of the Supreme Court on it, he/she may refer it to the Supreme Court. The Supreme Court may, after such hearing as it thinks fit, report to the President its opinion thereon. The report or the opinion of the Supreme Court is of course, not binding on the President. Similarly, there is no compulsion for the Court to give its advice.

(iv) **Judicial Review:** The Supreme Court of India has the power to examine the validity of laws or executive orders. The Supreme Court has the powers to interpret the Constitution, and through this it has assumed the power of judicial review.

(v) **Guardian of the Constitution:** As the interpreter of the Constitution, the Supreme Court has the power to protect and defend the Constitution. If the Court finds that any law or executive order is against the Constitution, the same can be declared unconstitutional or invalid. Similarly the Supreme Court also acts as the custodian and protector of Fundamental Rights.

PARLIAMENT

Parliament is the national legislature of the Indian Union. It consists of two Houses known as the Council of States or the Rajya Sabha and the House of People or Lok Sabha. The President is an integal part of Parliament.

Rajya Sabha: The Rajya Sabha is the Upper House of the Parliament and it is constituted of representatives from the States or the Constituent units of the Indian Union. It is a permanent body, one third of its members retiring after every two years. Its maximum strength is 250. Out of these, twelve members are nominated by the President from well-known personalities in the realm of Science, Art, Literature and Social Service. Rest of 238 representatives of the States and Union Territories are elected. At present Rajya Sabha have 245 members.

Lok Sabha: The Lok Sabha whose life is five years, is the Lower House of Parliament and comprises of members directly elected by the people. The House of the people (Lok Sabha) at present consists of 543 members directly elected from the states and Union Territories. (By the 104th amendment of the Constitution the reservation of two members of Anglo Indian Community by President have been abolished). The House of the People shall continue for five years (unless sooner dissolved) from the date of its meeting and no longer and the expiry of the said period of 5 years shall operate as dissolution of the House.

Parliamentary Committees: There are several Parliamentary Committees to assist the Parliament in its deliberations. These are appointed or elected by the respective Houses of Lok Sabha and Rajya Sabha on a motion made or are nominated by their presiding officers, i.e., the Speaker of Lok Sabha and the Chairman of Rajya Sabha respectively. Broadly, Parliamentary Committees are of two kinds–standing committees and ad-hoc committees. Among the Standing Committees, three are financial Committees: (i) Public Account Committee; (ii) Estimate Committee; (iii) Public undertaking Committee.

Ad-hoc Committees are appointed as the need arises and cease to exist when the work is over.

Speaker of Lok Sabha:

- The Lok Sabha elects two of its members as its speaker and Deputy speaker respectively.
- The Speaker is the presiding officer of the House and his office is of great dignity, prestige and authority.
- In the order of precedence he is placed sixth and is bracketed with the Chief Justice of India.
- The office of the speaker has political importance as well. He is the head of the democratically elected representatives of the people.
- He does not resign when the House is dissolved unless and until the new House is formed and it elects another person to be the Speaker.
- When the President resigns, the fact of his resignation is comm-unicated to the Speaker and the House is informed by him of the President's resignation.

Functions of the Speaker:

Some of the powers and functions of the speaker are given below :

1. The basic function of the Speaker is to preside over the house and conduct the meetings of the House in orderly manner. No member can speak in the House without his/her permission. He/she may ask a member to finish his speech and in case the member does not obey he/she may order that the speech should not be recorded.
2. All the Bills, reports, motions and resolutions are introduced with Speaker's permission. He/she puts the motion or bill to vote. He/she does not participate in the voting but when there is a tie i.e. equal number of votes on both sides, he/she can use his casting vote. But he/she is expected to caste her vote in a manner so that her impartiality and independence is retained.
3. His/her decisions in all parliamentary matters are final. She also rules on points of order raised by the members and her decision is final.
4. He/she is the custodian of rights and privileges of the members.
5. He/she disqualifics a member of his/her membership in case of defection. He/she also accepts the resignation of members and decides about the genuineness of the resignation.
6. In case of joint sitting of Lok Sabha and Rajya Sabha, the Speaker presides over the meeting.

Indian States & Union Territories: Allocation of Seats

S. No.	State /UTs	Seats of Lok Sabha	Seats of Rajya Sabha	Legislative Assembly	Legislative Council
1.	Andhra Pradesh	25	11	175	58
2.	Arunachal Pradesh	2	1	60	
3.	Assam	14	7	126	
4.	Bihar	40	16	243	75
5.	Chhattisgarh	11	5	90	
6.	Goa	2	1	40	
7.	Gujarat	26	11	182	
8.	Haryana	10	5	90	
9.	Himachal Pradesh	4	3	68	
10.	Jharkhand	14	6	81	
11.	Karnataka	28	12	224	75
12.	Keralam	20	9	140	
13.	Madhya Pradesh	29	11	230	
14.	Maharashtra	48	19	288	78
15.	Manipur	2	1	60	
16.	Meghalaya	2	1	60	
17.	Mizoram	1	1	40	
18.	Nagaland	1	1	60	

S. No.	State/UTs	Seats of Lok Sabha	Seats of Rajya Sabha	Legislative Assembly	Legislative Council
19.	Odisha	21	10	147	
20.	Punjab	13	7	117	
21.	Rajasthan	25	10	200	
22.	Sikkim	1	1	32	
23.	Tamil Nadu	39	18	234	
24.	Telangana	17	7	119	40
25.	Tripura	2	1	60	
26.	Uttar Pradesh	80	31	403	100
27.	Uttarakhand	5	3	70	
28.	West Bengal	42	16	294	
29.	Jammu & Kashmir	5	4	—	—
30.	Andaman & Nicobar Islands	1	—	—	—
31.	Chandigarh	1	—	—	—
32.	Dadra & Nagar Haveli and Daman & Diu	2	—	—	—
33.	Delhi	7	3	70	—
34.	Lakshadweep	1	—	—	—
35.	Puduchery	1	1	30	—
36.	Ladakh	1	—	—	—

Table of Precedence

1. President
2. Vice-President
3. Prime Minister
4. Governors of States within their respective states
5. Former Presidents

5A. Deputy Prime Minister

6. Chief Justice of India, Speaker of Lok Sabha
7. Cabinet Ministers of the Union, Chief Ministers of States within their respective States Deputy Chairman NITI Aayog.

   Leaders of opposition in Rajya Sabha and Lok Sabha

7A. Holders of the Bharat Ratna Decoration

8. Ambassadors Extraordinary and Plenipotentiary and High Commissioners of Commonwealth Countries accredited to India

   Chief Ministers of States outside their respective States
9. Judges of the Supreme Court
10. Deputy Chairman Rajya Sabha, Deputy Chief Minister of States

    Deputy Speaker Lok Sabha, Members of the NITI Aayog, Minister of State of the Union and Other Minister in the Ministry of Defence.

PRESIDENT

The President is the Constitutional head of the Republic of India. He is more or less the titular head of the executive. Really speaking, he is the constitutional head but not the real executive. The real power is vested in the hands of the Council of Ministers.

Qualifications: (i) Indian citizen, (ii) age not less than 35 years, (iii) should have qualification for election to Lok Sabha, (iv) should not hold any office of profit, (v) should not be a Member of Parliament or State Legislature.

Powers: He makes appointments to all the constitutional posts. He can address either House of Parliament and dissolve Lok Sabha. All Bills passed by Parliament must receive his assent to become an Act. He issues ordinances when Parliament is not in session. No Money Bill can be introduced in Lok Sabha without his recommendation. He can grant pardon, reprieve or remit punishment and he can commute death sentences, can declare national emergency, state emergency and financial emergency.

Term and Emolument: The President holds the office for a period of five years. He is eligible for re-election. He draws a fix salary per month with various allowances. He is also entitled to rent free official residence called Rashtrapati Bhawan.

VICE-PRESIDENT

The Vice-President acts as the ex-officio Chairman of the Council of States (Rajya Sabha). He is elected by an electoral college consisting of the members of both Houses of Parliament in accordance with the system of proportional representation by means of the single transferable vote. He must be a citizen of India, not less than 35 years of age, and should be eligible for election as a member of the Council of States. Disputes in connection with election of a president or a vice-president are to be a dealt with in accordance with Article-71. Such disputes shall be decided by the Supreme Court.

PRIME MINISTER

The Constitution lays down that there shall be a Council of Ministers headed by the Prime Minister to aid and advise the President in the exercise of his functions. The Prime Minister is the head of the Cabinet. Other Ministers are appointed by the President on his advice. He is the leader of the majority party in the Lok Sabha.

FUNDAMENTAL RIGHTS

Following fundamental rights are enjoyed by every Indian citizen, irrespective of caste, colour, creed and sex:

1. Right to Equality: No special privileges, no distinction on grounds of religion, caste, creed and sex.

2. Right to Freedom: The right to freedom of expression and speech, the right to choose one's own profession, the right to reside in any part of the Indian Union.

3. Right to Freedom to Religion: Except when it is in the interest of public order, morality, health or other conditions, everybody has the right to profess, practice and propagate his religion freely.

4. Cultural and Educational Rights: The Constitution provides that every community can run its own institutions to preserve its own culture and language.

5. Right against Exploitation: Traffic in human beings and forced labour and the employment of children under 14 years in factories or mines, are punishable offences.

6. Rights to Constitutional Remedies: When a citizen finds that any of his fundamental rights has been encroached upon, he can move the Supreme Court, which has been empowered to safeguard the fundamental rights of a citizen (Article 32).

Jurisdiction and Seat of High Courts

Name	*Territorial Jurisdiction*	*Seat*
Allahabad	Uttar Pradesh	Prayagraj (Bench at Lucknow)
Andhra Pradesh	Andhra Pradesh	Amaravati
Bombay	Maharashtra, Goa, Dadar and Nagar Haveli and Daman and Diu	Mumbai (Benches at Nagpur, Panaji and Aurangabad)
Calcutta	West Bengal and Andaman & Nicobar Islands	Kolkata (Circuit Benches at Port Blair and Jalpaiguri)
Chhattisgarh	Chhattisgarh	Bilaspur
Delhi	Delhi	Delhi
Gauhati	Assam, Nagaland, Mizoram and Arunachal Pradesh	Guwahati (Benches at Kohima, Aizawl and Itanagar)
Gujarat	Gujarat	Ahmedabad
Himachal Pradesh	Himachal Pradesh	Shimla
Jammu & Kashmir and Ladakh	Jammu & Kashmir, Ladakh	Srinagar and Jammu
Jharkhand	Jharkhand	Ranchi
Karnataka	Karnataka	Bengaluru (Circuit Benches at Dharwar and Gulbarga)
Kerala	Kerala & Lakshadweep Islands	Kochi
Madhya Pradesh	Madhya Pradesh	Jabalpur (Benches at Gwalior and Indore)
Madras	Tamil Nadu & Puducherry	Chennai (Bench at Madurai)
Orissa	Odisha	Cuttack
Patna	Bihar	Patna
Punjab and Haryana	Punjab, Haryana and Chandigarh	Chandigarh
Rajasthan	Rajasthan	Jodhpur (Bench at Jaipur)
Sikkim	Sikkim	Gangtok
Uttarakhand	Uttarakhand	Nainital
Tripura	Tripura	Agartala
Meghalaya	Meghalaya	Shillong
Manipur	Manipur	Imphal
Telangana	Telangana	Hyderabad

FUNDAMENTAL DUTIES

The fundamental duties for the Indian citizens have been incorporated in the Constitution through the Constitution (42nd) Amendment Act, 1976. These duties are: (*i*) to abide by the Constitution and respect its ideals and institutions, the National Flag and the National Anthem; (*ii*) to cherish and follow the noble deeds which inspired our national struggle for freedom; (*iii*) to uphold and protect the sovereignty, unity and integrity of India; (*iv*) to defend the country and render national service when called upon to do so; (*v*) to promote harmony and the spirit of common brotherhood amongst all the people transcending religious, regional or sectional diversities and to renounce practices derogatory to the dignity of women; (*vi*) to value and preserve the rich heritage of our composite culture; (*vii*) to protect and improve natural environment including forests, lakes, rivers and wildlife, and to have compassion for living creatures; (*viii*) to develop the scientific temper, humanism and the spirit of inquiry and reform; (*ix*) to safeguard public property and to abjure violence; (*x*) to strive towards excellence in all spheres of individual and collective activity so that the nation constantly rises to higher levels of endeavour and achievement. (*xi*) who is parent or guardian to provide opportunities for education to his child or, as the case may be, ward between age of six and fourteen years.

DIRECTIVE PRINCIPLES OF STATE POLICY

The Directive Principles of State Policy are contained in Article 36 to 51 in Part IV of the constitution. Directive principles are not enforceable through courts. Main aim of Directive principles is to provide social and economic base of a genuine democracy.

Some Important Directive Principles:

- Provisions for adequate means of livelihood for all citizens (Art. 39).
- Right to work (Art. 41).
- Right to human condition of work and maternity relief (Art. 42).
- Right to a living wage and condition of work ensuring decent standard of life of worker (Art. 43).
- Common Civil Code (Art. 44).
- Prohibit consumption of liquor (Art. 47).
- Prevent slaughter of useful cattle (Art. 48).
- Organise Panchayati Raj (Art. 40).
- Separate the judiciary from the executive (Art. 50).
- Protect and maintain places of historic monuments (Art. 49).
- International peace (Art. 51).

Voting Age: The voting age in the election to the Lok Sabha and State Legislative Assemblies has been reduced from 21 to 18 years by the Constitution (61st) Amendment Act, 1989.

GOVERNOR

The Governor is appointed by the President and holds office during the pleasure of the President. Apart from the power to appoint the council of ministers, if the governor finds that the government of state cannot be carried on in accordance with the provisions of the constitution (Art. 356), he may send his report to the President who may assume to himself the functions of the government of the state. (This is popularly known as 'President's Rule').

THE ATTORNEY GENERAL OF INDIA

The Attorney General of India is the first law officer of the Government of India. Though he is not a member of cabinet he has the right to speak in the House of Parliament, but he has no right to vote. The Attorney General of India shall be appointed by the President and shall hold office during his pleasure. His duty shall be to give advice on such legal matter from time to time as may be referred to him by the President.

COMPTROLLER & AUDITOR GENERAL OF INDIA (CAG)

The Comptroller and Auditor General of India is guardian of the public purse and it is his duty to see that not a *paisa* is spent out of consolidated fund of India or of a state without the authority of the appropriate legislature. He is appointed by President of India.

Status

- Appointed by the President.
- A person with long administrative experience & knowledge of accounts is appointed.
- Holds office for 6 yrs or till 65 yrs of age.
- The President can remove him only on the recommendation of the 2 houses of Parliament (as in case of judge of Supreme Court).

INTER-STATE COUNCILS

Article 263 provides for inter-state councils. The power of the President to set up Inter-State Councils not only for advising upon disputes but also for investigating and discussing subjects in which some or all of the states, or the Union and one or more of the states have common interest.

UNION PUBLIC SERVICE COMMISSION (UPSC)

This Commission is responsible for (i) recruitment to all civil services and posts, under the Union Government by written examinations, interviews and promotions, and (ii) advising the Government on all matters relating to methods of recruitment, principles to be followed in making promotions and transfers. Its Chairman is appointed by the President.

STAFF SELECTION COMMISSION

The Union Government has constituted the Staff Selection Commission for recruitment to non-technical Group C and some of Group B posts in the central departments and in subordinate offices. The Administrative Reforms Commission had recommended the setting up of such a Commission.

IMPORTANT AMENDMENTS TO THE CONSTITUTION

First Amendment, 1951	:	Added Ninth Schedule.
Twenty-second Amendment, 1969	:	Formation of Meghalaya within the state of Assam was facilitated.
Twenty-sixth Amendment, 1971	:	The privy and privileges of the former rulers of Indian States were abolished.
Thirty-first Amendment, 1973	:	The upper limit of representation of states was raised from 500 to 525. The upper limit for representation of the UTs was reduced from 25 to 20.
Thirty-sixth Amendment, 1975	:	Sikkim was made a full-fledged state of Indian Union and it was included in the First Schedule.
Thirty-eight Amendment, 1975	:	This act led to the amendment of Article 123, Article 213 and Article 352 which stated that the satisfaction of President or of Governor contained in these Articles would be called in question in any court of law.
Forty-second Amendment, 1976	:	This amendment was done in accordance with the recommendations of Swaran Singh Committee and included a number of amendments.
Forty-third Amendment, 1977	:	It provided for the restoration of the Jurisdiction of the Supreme Court and High Courts, curtailed by the enactment of the Constitution (Forty-Second Amendment) Act, 1976.
Forty-fourth Amendment, 1978	:	The right to property was deleted as Fundamental Right and was made a legal right.
Fifty-third Amendment, 1986	:	The Act grants statehood to the Union Territory of Mizoram, thus making it the 23rd State of the Indian Unions.
Fifty-sixth Amendment, 1987	:	The UT of Goa converted into Goa state through this amendment whereas Daman and Diu were organised under a new UT.
Seventy-third Amendment, 1992	:	It is concerning Panchayati Raj.
Seventy-fourth Amendment, 1992	:	It is regarding Municipal Boards and Corporations.
Eighty-ninth Amendment, 2003	:	It provides for constitution of a separate National Commission for Scheduled Tribes. (Earlier, there was a combined National Commission for both SC/STs).
Ninety-first Amendment, 2003	:	It is regarding restricting the total number of Ministers including Prime Minister/ Chief Minister in Lok Sabha and State Legislatures to 15% of the total number of the Union or State Legislatures.
Ninety-sixth Amendment, 2011	:	Amendment of 8th Schedule, it replaces 'Orissa' with 'Odisha'.
Ninety-ninth Amendment, 2015	:	The amendment is in toto quashed by Supreme Court on 16 October, 2015.
One hundredth Amendment, 2015	:	Exchange of certain enclave territories with Bangladesh and conferment of citizenship rights to residents of enclaves consequent to signing of Land Boundary Agreement (LBA) Treaty between India and Bangladesh.
One hundredth and first Amendment, 2016	:	The act amends the Constitution to introduce "The Goods and Services Tax (GST)."
One hundredth and Third Amendment, 2019	:	The Act providing 10 per cent reservation in government jobs and educational institutions to Economically Weaker Sections (EWS) of General Category, came into effect on January 14, 2019.
One hundredth and Fourth Amendment, 2019	:	This Act ceased the reservation of seats for Anglo-Indians in the Lok Sabha and State Legislative assemblies and extended resevations for SCs and STs for up to ten years.
One hundredth and Fifth Amendment, 2021	:	This Act restores the power of State Government to identify and specify Socially and Economically Backward Classes (SEBCs).
One hundredth and Sixth Amendment, 2023	:	The Act povides 33 per cent reservation to women in the Lok Sabha and State Assemblies.

*****

6

Planning In India

The National Institution for Transforming India, also called NITI Aayog, was formed via a resolution of the Union Cabinet on January 1, 2015. NITI Aayog is the premier policy 'Think Tank' of the Government of India, providing both directional and policy inputs. While designing strategic and long term policies and programmes for the Government of India, NITI Aayog also provides relevant technical advice to the Centre and States.

The Government of India, in keeping with its reform agenda, constituted the NITI Aayog to replace the Planning Commission instituted in 1950. This was done in order to better serve the needs and aspirations of the people of India. An important evolutionary change from the past, NITI Aayog acts as the quintessential platform of the Government of India to bring States to act together in national interest, and thereby fosters Cooperative Federalism.

Five Year Plans in India

Plans	Period	Investment (₹ Crore)	Objectives
First Plan	April 1, 1951–March 31, 1956	1,960	Priority to agriculture, electricity and irrigation.
Second Plan	April 1, 1956–March 31, 1961	4,672	Development of basic and heavy industries.
Third Plan	April 1, 1961–March 31, 1966	8,577	Long term development of India's economy.
Annual Plan	April 1, 1966–March 31, 1967	2,137	
Annual Plan	April 1, 1967–March 31, 1968	2,205	
Annual Plan	April 1, 1968–March 31, 1969	2,283	
Fourth Plan	April 1, 1969–March 31, 1974	15,779	Enlarge the income of rural population and supply of goods of mass consumption.
Fifth Plan	April 1, 1974–March 31, 1979	39,426	Attain increased self reliance and employment avenues.
Annual Plan	April 1, 1979–March 31, 1980	12,176	
Sixth Plan	April 1, 1980–March 31, 1985	1,09,292	Removal of unemployment
Seventh Plan	April 1, 1985–March 31, 1990	2,18,730	Food work and productivity were the basic priorities.
Eighth Plan	April, 1992–March 31, 1997	4,95,670	Raising employment
Ninth Plan	April 1, 1997–March 31, 2002	9,41,041	Agriculture and rural development
Tenth Plan	April 1, 2002–March 31, 2007	14,91,610	Growth rate 7.8 percent per annum.
Eleventh Plan	April 1, 2007–March 31, 2012	36,44,718	Literacy, Employment, Rural development & Transport development.
Twelfth Plan	April 1, 2012–March 31, 2017	43,33,739	Long term development of India's economy.

INDIA'S AMBITIOUS 15-YEAR VISION PLAN

NITI Aayog has come forward with a draft 15-year vision plan to catapult the country's economy to more than three times as compared to the present day. The new plan is set to replace the centralised five-year plans the country has been following for decades.

The new plan is accompanied by shorter sub-plans—a seven-year strategy for 2017-24, and a three-year 'Action Agenda' from 2017-18 to 2019-20. No less than 300 specific action points covering a wide range of sectors have been drawn up as part of the 15 year vision.

The salient features of 15-year vision plan are :

- India aims to more than triple the size of its economy in 15 years with gross domestic product (GDP) expected to rise to ₹ 469 lakh crores from ₹ 137 lakh crore in 2015-16. Per capita GDP is expected to rise by three times to ₹ 3,14,667 in 2015-2016.
- NITI Aayog plans to work closely with states to boost infrastructure and services, including regions that require special attention. The government made a big push for Goods and Services Tax (GST), urging the state governments to speed up the legislation of state GST bills.
- India's urban population is expected to increase by 22 crores by 2031. The plan is likely to lay emphasis on urban development, taking a note from China's elaborate long-term development agenda.

- The plan envisages a central body for overseeing the implemention of sustainable development goals. Specific goals will cover clean water, removing hunger, climate efforts, responsible consumption, clean energy, quality education, reduced inequality and gender equality, among others.
- The NITI Aayog will work as a "collaborative federal body whose strength is in its ideas, rather than in administrative or financial control."

FINANCE COMMISSION

Article 280 of the Constitution provides for the appointment of a finance commission every five year. President appoints chairman and members of this commission. Finance commission are to recommend to President the basis for the distribution of the net proceeds of taxes between the centre and the states and the principles which should govern the grants-in-aid to be given to the states out of the consolidated funds of India.

Finance Commission of India

S. No.	Year of Constitution	Name of Commissioner	Years of Execution
1st	1951	K.C. Niyogi	1952–1957
2nd	1956	K. Santhanam	1957–1962
3rd	1960	A.K. Chanda	1962–1966
4th	1964	Dr. P.V. Rajamannar	1966–1969
5th	1968	Mahavir Tyagi	1969–1974
6th	1972	Brahmanand Reddy	1974–1979
7th	1977	J.M. Shallot	1979–1984
8th	1983	Y.V. Chavan	1984–1989
9th	1987	Dr. K.P. Salve	1989–1995
10th	1992	K.C. Pant	1995–2000
11th	1998	A.M. Khusro	2000–2005
12th	2002	Dr. C. Rangrajan	2005–2010
13th	2007	Dr. V.L. Kelkar	2010–2015
14th	2013	Y.V. Reddy	2015–2020
15th	2017	N.K. Singh	2020–2026
16th	2023	Arvind Panagariya	2026–2031

NITI AAYOG

The government on January 1, 2015 replaced the 65-year-old Planning Commission—a relic of the Socialist era—with a Niti Aayog or National Institution for Transforming India (NITI), marking a major shift in policy making by involving states. The Aayog will recommend a national agenda, including strategic and technical advice on elements of policy and economic matters. It will also develop mechanisms for village-level plans and aggregate these progressively at higher levels of government. It will work towards fostering co-operative federalism for providing a national agenda to the Centre and states.

NATIONAL DEVELOPMENT COUNCIL

The National Development Council, set-up in 1952, consists of representatives of the Central Government as well as the State governments. It is the supreme body insofar as planning is concerned and it determines policies, issues guidelines, reviews working of the plan and finally approves the plan. The Council consists of the Prime Minister (Chairman), all Union Cabinet Ministers, Chief Ministers of all States and Union Territories and the Chairman and members of the NITI Aayog. For matters relating to Plans and planning, the Union Minister of Planning is responsible to the Parliament.

RESERVE BANK OF INDIA

- It is the Central Bank of the country.
- It was established on April 1, 1935 with a capital of ₹ 5 crore. This capital of ₹ 5 crore was divided into 5 lakh equity shares of ₹ 100 each. In the beginning, the ownership of almost all the share capital was with the non-government share-holders.
- It was nationalized on Jan 1, 1949 as government acquired the private share holdings.
- **Governors:** Ist Governor - Sir Smith (1935-37)
  Ist Indian Governor - C.D. Deshmukh (1948-49)

Other Financial Institutions

Industrial Credit & Investment Corporation of India Bank (ICICI Bank)	• Established in 1955 as a public limited company to encourage and assist industrial units of the nation. It has been converted into a bank with effect from May 3, 2002.
Small Industries Development Bank of India (SIDBI)	• Established in 1990; promotes small scale sector.
National Bank of Agriculture & Rural Development (NABARD)	• Established on Nov 5, 1982; gives credit facilities to farmers.
Export-Import Bank of India (EXIM)	• Set-up on Jan 1, 1982; grants deferred credit to Indian exporters in order to operate in the International market.
Industrial Development Bank of India (IDBI)	• Established in 1964; to provide financial assistance to industrial enterprises.
Industrial Reconstruction Bank of India (IRBI)	• Set-up in 1971 with the objective of reviving and revitalizing sick industrial units in public and private sectors.

* * * * *

7 General Science

INVENTIONS AND DISCOVERIES

Important Inventions

Name of Invention	*Inventor*	*Nationality*	*Year*
Aeroplane	Orville & Wilbur Wright	U.S.A.	1903
Ball-Point Pen	John J. Loud	U.S.A.	1888
Barometer	Evangelista Torricelli	Italy	1644
Bicycle	Kirkpatrick Macmillan	Britain	1839-40
Bifocal Lens	Benjamin Franklin	U.S.A.	1780
Car (Petrol)	Karl Benz	Germany	1888
Celluloid	Alexander Parkes	Britain	1861
Cinema	Nicolas & Jean Lumiere	France	1895
Clock (mechanical)	I-Hsing & Liang Ling-Tsan	China	725
Diesel Engine	Rudolf Diesel	Germany	1895
Dynamo	Hypolite Pixii	France	1832
Electric Lamp	Thomas Alva Edison	U.S.A.	1879
Electric Motor (DC)	Zenobe Gramme	Belgium	1873
Electric Motor (AC)	Nikola Tesla	U.S.A.	1888
Electro-magnet	William Sturgeon	Britain	1824
Electronic Computer	Dr. Alan M. Turing	Britain	1943
Film (moving outlines)	Louis Prince	France	1885
Film (musical sound)	Dr. Le de Forest	U.S.A.	1923
Fountain Pen	Lewis E. Waterman	U.S.A.	1884
Gramophone	Thomas Alva Edison	U.S.A.	1878
Helicopter	Etienne Oehmichen	France	1924
Jet Engine	Sir Frank Whittle	Britain	1937
Laser	Charles H. Townes	U.S.A.	1960
Lift (Mechanical)	Elisha G. Otis	U.S.A.	1852
Locomotive	Richard Trevithick	Britain	1804
Machine Gun	James Puckle	Britain	1718
Microphone	Alexander Graham Bell	U.S.A.	1876
Microscope	Z. Janssen	Netherlands	1590
Motor Cycle	G. Daimler	Germany	1885
Photography (on film)	John Carbutt	U.S.A.	1888
Printing Press	Johann Gutenberg	Germany	c.1455
Razor (safety)	King C. Gillette	U.S.A.	1895
Refrigerator	James Harrison & Alexander Catlin	U.S.A.	1850
Safety Pin	Walter Hunt	U.S.A.	1849
Sewing machine	Barthelemy Thimmonnier	France	1829
Ship (steam)	J.C. Perier	France	1775
Ship (turbine)	Hon. Sir C. Parsons	Britain	1894
Skyscraper	W. Le Baron Jenny	U.S.A.	1882
Slide Rule	William Oughtred	Britain	1621

Name of Invention	Inventor	Nationality	Year
Steam Engine (condenser)	James Watt	Britain	1765
Steel Production	Henry Bessemer	Britain	1855
Steel (stainless)	Harry Brearley	Britain	1913
Submarine	David Bushnell	U.S.A.	1776
Tank	Sir Ernest Swinton	Britain	1914
Telegraph	M. Lammond	France	1787
Telegraph Code	Samuel F.B. Morse	U.S.A.	1837
Telephone (perfected)	Alexander Graham Bell	U.S.A.	1876
Television (mechanical)	John Logie Baird	Britain	1926
Television (electronic)	P.T. Farnsworth	U.S.A.	1927
Thermometer	Galileo Galilei	Italy	1593
Transformer	Michael Faraday	Britain	1831
Transistor	Bardeen, Shockley & Brattain	U.S.A.	1948
Washing Machine (elec.)	Hurley Machine Co.	U.S.A.	1907
Zip-Fastener	W.L. Judson	U.S.A.	1891

Important Discoveries

Discovery	Discoverer	Nationality	Year
Aluminium	Hans Christian Oerstedt	Denmark	1827
Atomic number	Henry Moseley	England	1913
Atomic structure of matter	John Dalton	England	1803
Chlorine	C.W. Scheele	Sweden	1774
Electromagnetic induction	Michael Faraday	England	1831
Electromagnetic waves	Heinrich Hertz	Germany	1886
Electromagnetism	Hans Christian Oersted	Denmark	1920
Electron	Sir Joseph Thomson	England	1897
General theory of relativity	Albert Einstein	Switzerland	1915
Hydrogen	Henry Cavendish	England	1766
Law of electric conduction	Georg Ohm	Germany	1827
Law of electromagnetism	Andre Ampere	France	1826
Law of falling bodies	Galileo	Italy	1590
Laws of gravitation & motion	Isaac Newton	England	1687
Laws of planetary motion	Johannes Kepler	Germany	1609-10
Magnesium	Sir Humphry Davy	England	1808
Neptune (Planet)	Johann Galle	Germany	1846
Neutron	James Chadwick	England	1932
Nickel	Axel Cronstedt	Sweden	1751
Nitrogen	Daniel Rutherford	England	1772
Oxygen	Joseph Priestly C.W. Scheele	England Sweden	1772
Ozone	Christian Schonbein	Germany	1839
Pluto (Planet)	Clyde Tombaugh	U.S.A	1930
Plutonium	G.T. Seaborg	U.S.A	1940
Proton	Ernest Rutherford	England	1919
Quantum Theory	Max Planck	Germany	1900
Radioactivity	Antoine Bacquerel	France	1896
Radium	Pierre & Marie Curie	France	1898
Silicon	Jons Berzelius	Sweden	1824
Special theory of relativity	Albert Einstein	Switzerland	1905
Sun as centre of solar system	Copernicus	Poland	1543
Uranium	Martin Klaproth	Germany	1789
Uranus (Planet)	William Herschel	England	1781
X-rays	Wilhelm Roentgen	Germany	1895

Geographical Explorations/Discoveries

Place	Explorer/Discoverer	Nationality	Year
America	Christopher Columbus	Italy	1492
Hawaii Islands (Sandwich Islands)	Captain James Cook	England	1778
Newfoundland	John Cabot	England	1497
New Zealand	Abel Janszoon Tasman	Holland	1642
North Pole	Robert Peary	USA	1909
Sea Route to India (via Cape of Good Hope)	Vasco da Gama	Portugal	1498
South Pole	Roald Amundsen	Norway	1911

Scientific Instruments

Name of Instrument	Used for
Altimeter	measuring altitude
Ammeter	measuring strength of an electric current
Anemometer	measuring the velocity of wind
Audiometer	measuring level of hearing
Barometer	measuring atmospheric pressure
Callipers	measuring the internal and external diameters of tubes
Calorimeter	measuring quantity of heat
Compass	finding out direction
Dynamo	converting mechanical energy into electrical energy
Eudiometer	measuring volume changes during chemical reactions between gases
Galvanometer	detecting and determining the strength of small electric currents
Hydrometer	measuring specific gravity of a liquid
Hygrometer	measuring the humidity in the atmosphere
Lactometer	measuring the purity of milk
Manometer	measuring the gaseous pressure
Micrometer	measuring minute distances, angles, etc.
Microscope	seeing magnified view of very small objects
Periscope	with the help of this instrument an observer in a submarine can see what is going on the surface of the sea
Photometer	measuring intensity of light from distant stars
Pyrometer	measuring high temperatures
Radar	detecting and finding the presence and location of moving objects like aircraft, missile, etc.
Radiometer	measuring the emission of radiant energy
Rain Gauge	measuring the amount of rainfall
Seismograph	measuring and recording the intensity and origin of earthquake shocks
Sextant	measuring altitude and angular distances between two objects or heavenly bodies
Spectrometer	measuring the refractive indices
Spherometer	measuring the curvature of spherical objects/surface
Sphygmomanometer	measuring blood pressure
Stethoscope	ascertaining the condition of heart and lungs by listening to their function
Stroboscope	viewing objects that are moving rapidly with a periodic motion as if they were at rest
Tachometer	measuring the rate of revolution or angular speed of a revolving shaft
Telescope	viewing magnified images of distant objects
Theodolite	measuring the horizontal and vertical angles
Thermocouple	measuring the temperature inside furnaces and jet engines
Thermometer	measuring human body temperature
Thermostat	regulating constant temperature
Ultrasonoscope	measuring utrasonic sounds
Viscometer	measuring the viscosity of a fluid
Voltmeter	measuring potential difference between two points.

Diseases and the Parts of Body they Affect

Disease	Part of body affected
AIDS	Immune system of body
Arthritis	Inflammation of joints
Asthma	Lungs
Cataract	Eyes
Conjunctivitis	Eyes
Diabetes	Pancreas
Diphtheria	Throat
Glaucoma	Eyes
Eczema	Skin
Goitre	Front of the neck (due to enlargement of thyroid gland)
Gout	Joints of bone

Disease	Part of body affected
Jaundice	Liver
Meningitis	Brain or spinal cord
Pleurisy	Pleura (inflammation of)
Polio	motor neurons
Pneumonia	Lungs
Pyorrhoea	Sockets of teeth
Tuberculosis	Lungs
Typhoid	Intestine
Malaria	Spleen
Leukaemia	Blood
Rickets	Bones

❋❋❋❋❋

8

Space Research

First in Space

First creator of rules regarding space research	—	Isaac Newton
First artificial satellite launched in space	—	Sputnik-1 (1957)
First living being sent in space	—	Louika (a dog)
Firstever manned spacecraft	—	Vostok-I
First man in space	—	Yuri Gagarin U.S.S.R. (1961)
First woman in space	—	Valentina Tereshkova U.S.S.R. (June 1963)
First man who moved in space out of the spacecraft	—	Alexi Livonov U.S.S.R. (June 1965)
First person to land on moon	—	Neil Armstrong, America (21st July, 1969)
First fourwheeled carriage without human being on moon	—	Leunokhev-I U.S.S.R. (1970)
First space lab in orbit	—	Skylab (America, 1973)
First space shuttle	—	Columbia (America, 1981)
First Indian (man) in space	—	Squadron leader—Rakesh Sharma (13th April, 1984)
First Indian (Woman) in space	—	Kalpana Chawla (19th Nov., 1997)
First American woman in space	—	Sailyride (1983)
First spacecraft on Mars	—	Pathfinder (6 July, 1997)
First woman who lead spacecraft	—	Allin Collis (America)
First spacecraft without man	—	Shenzoo, China (20th Nov. 1999)

Indian Space Programme : At a Glance

Satellite	*Date*	*Type*	*Launch Vehicle*	*Result*
Aryabhatta	19-04-75	Scientific	Cosmos	successful
Bhaskara I	07-06-79	Geosurvey	Cosmos	successful
Rohini	10-08-79	Geosurvey	S.L.V.3	unsuccessful
Rohini D-1	18-07-80	Geosurvey	S.L.V.3	successful
Rohini	31-05-81	Scientific	S.L.V.3	successful
Apple	19-06-81	Communication	Ariane	successful
Bhaskara II	20-11-81	Geosurvey	Cosonos	successful
INSAT-1A	10-04-82	Multipurpose	Delta	unsuccessful
Rohini	17-04-83	Scientific	S.L.V.3	successful
INSAT-1B	30-08-83	Multipurpose	Space Shuttle	successful
SROSS I	24-03-87	Technical	ASLV-D1	unsuccessful
IRS-1A	17-03-88	Remote sensing	Vostok	successful
SROSS II	17-07-88	Technical	ASLV-D2	unsuccessful
INSAT-1C	21-07-88	Multipurpose	Ariane-4	unsuccessful
INSAT-1D	12-06-90	Multipurpose	Delta	successful
IRS-1B	29-08-91	Remote sensing	Vostok	successful
INSAT-2A	10-07-92	Multipurpose	Ariane	successful
INSAT-2B	23-07-93	Multipurpose	Ariane	successful

Satellite	Date	Type	Launch Vehicle	Result
IRS-1C	28-12-95	Remote sensing	PSLV-D3	successful
IRS-ID	29-09-97	Remote sensing	PSLV	successful
MAT SAT	12-09-2002	Meteorology	PSLVC-4	successful
INSAT-3E	28-09-2003	Communication	Ariane-5	successful
CARTOSAT-1 & HAMSAT	05-05-2005	Maping and Communication	PSLV-C6	successful
CARTOSAT-2	10-01-2007	Communication	PSLV-C7	successful
INSAT-4B	12-03-2007	Communication	Ariane-5	successful
CARTOSAT-2A	28-04-2008	Communication	PSLV-C9	successful
Chandrayaan-I	22-10-2008	Maping and Scientific	PSLV-C11	successful
RISAT-2 & ANUSAT	20-04-2009	Maping and Communication	PSLV-C12	successful
CARTOSAT-2B	12-07-2010	Communication	PSLV-C15	successful
RESOURCESAT-2	20-04-2011	Remote Sensing	PSLV-C16	successful
Megha-Tropiques	12-10-2011	Maping and Scientific	PSLV-C18	successful
RISAT-1	26-04-2012	Remote Sensing	PSLV-C19	successful
Spot-6	09-09-2012	Remote Sensing	PSLV-C21	successful
Mangalyan	05-11-2013	Maping and Scientific	PSLV-C25	successful
GSAT-14	05-01-2014	Communication	GSLV-D5	successful
IRNSS-IB	04-04-2014	Maping and Scientific	PSLV C-24	successful
Spot 7	30-06-2014	Remote Sensing	PSLV C-23	successful
Astrosat	28-09-2015	Mapping and Scientific	PSLV-C30	successful
IRNSS-1E	20-01-2016	Mapping and Scientific	PSLV-C31	successful
IRNSS-1F	10-03-2016	Mapping and Scientific	PSLV-C32	successful
IRNSS-1G	28-04-2016	Mapping and Scientific	PSLV-C33	successful
CARTOSAT-2 & others	22-06-2016	Mapping and Scientific	PSLV-C34	successful
INSAT-3DR	08-09-2016	Meteorology	GSLV-F05	successful
SCATSAT-1 & others	26-09-2016	Multipurpose	PSLV-C35	successful
RESOURCESET-2A	07-12-2016	Earth Sciences	PSLV-C36	successful
CARTOSAT-2D	17-02-2017	Earth Sciences	PSLV-C37	successful
CARTOSAT-2F	10-01-2018	Earth Sciences	PSLV-C40	successful
CARTOSAT-2 & 103	15-02-2017	Multipurpose	PSLV-C37	successful
GSAT-9	06-05-2017	Communication	GSLVMK-II	successful
CARTOSAT-2E	23-06-2017	Earth Sciences	PSLV-C38	successful
GSAT-6A	29-03-2018	Communication	GSLV-F08	successful
GSAT-7A	19-12-2018	Military Satellite	GSLV-MKII-F11	successful
GSAT-31	06-02-2019	Communication	Ariane-5	successful
CARTOSAT-3	27-11-2019	Earth Imaging	PSLV-C47	successful
GSAT-30	17-01-2020	Communication	Ariane-5	successful
EOS-01	07-11-2020	Earth Observation	PSLV-C49	successful
Amezonia & 19 others	28-02-2021	Communication	PSLV-C51	successful
EOS-04	14-02-2022	Earth Observation	PSLV-C52	successful
GSAT-24	23-06-2022	Communication	Ariane-5	successful
DS-E0 and others	30-06-2022	Mapping	PSLV-C53	successful
Oceansat-3 & 8 others	26-11-2022	Earth Observation	PSLV-C54	successful
EOS-07	10-02-2023	Earth Observation	SSLV-02	successful
TeLEOS-2 & LUMILITE-4	22-04-2023	Earth Observation	PSLV-C55	successful
NVS-01	29-05-2023	Navigation	GSLV-F12	successful
Chandrayann-3	14-07-2023	Lunar Observation	LVM-3	successful
DS-SAR and 6 other	30-07-2023	Earth Observation	PSLV-C56	successful
XPoSat	01-01-2024	Earth Observation	PSLV-C58	successful
INSAT-3DS	17-02-2024	Meteorological	GSLV-F14	successful
EOS-08	16-08-2024	Earth Observation	SSLV-D3	successful
Proba-3	05-12-2024	Earth Observation	PSLV-C59	successful
NVS-02	29-01-2025	Navigation	GSLV-F15	successful
NISAR	30-07-2025	Earth Observation	GSLV-F16	successful
CMS-03	02-11-2025	Communication	LVM3-M5	successful
BlueBird Block-2	24-12-2025	Communication	LVM3-M6	successful

* * * * *

9

Indian History

Famous Sites of Indus Valley Civilization

Name of Site	*Year of Excavation*	*River/ Sea coast*	*Discoverer*
Harappa (Montgomery–Pakistan)	1921	Ravi River	Dayaram Sahney
Mohanjodaro (Larkana–Pakistan)	1922	Indus River	Rakhal Das Banerjee
Chanhudaro (Sindh–Pakistan)	1931	Indus River	N.G. Mazumdar
Alamgir pur (Meerut – U.P.)	1952-55	Hindan River	Yagyadatta Sharma
Ropar (Punjab)	1953	Sutlej River	Yagyadatta Sharma
Rangpur (Kathiabar–Gujarat)	1953	Bhabar River	Madho Swaroop Vatsa, Rang Nath Rao
Kotdigi (Sindh–Pakistan)	1953	Indus River	Fazal Ahmed Khan
Lothal (Ahmedabad-Gujarat)	1954	Bhogwa River	Rang Nath Rao
Kalibanga (Ganganagar–Rajasthan)	1961	Ghaggar	Brajwasi Lal
Surkotara (Kutch–Gujarat)	1967	Ghaggar River	Ravindra Singh Vishta
Banawali (Hissar Haryana)	1973	Ghaggar River	Ravindra Singh Vishta
Balakote	1979	Arabian Sea	George F. Dales
Dhaulavira (Gujarat)	1963-68	—	J.P. Joshi
	1990-91	—	Dr. R.S. Vishta

Wellknown Quotations

"Swarajya is My Birthright"	— Bal Gangadhar Tilak
"Give me blood, I shall give you freedom"	— Netajee Subhash Chandra Bose
"Inqalab Zindabad"	— Bhagat Singh
Saare Jahan Se Achcha, Hindustan Hamara"	— Dr. Mohammed Iqbal
"Dilli Chalo"	— Subhash Chandra Bose
"Sarfaroshi ki tamanna, Ab Hamare Dil Mein Hai."	— Ram Prasad Bismil
"I am socialist by nature".	— Jawahar Lal Nehru
"Go to Vedas"	— Swami Dayanand
"Aaram Haram Hai"	— Jawahar Lal Nehru
"Jai Jawan, Jai Kisan"	— Lal Bahadur Shastri
"Jai Jawan, Jai Kisan, Jai Vigyan"	— Atal Bihari Vajpayee
"Speak less, work more"	— Sanjay Gandhi
"Vijayee Vishwa Tiranga Pyara"	— Shyam Lal Gupta
"Quit India"	— Mahatma Gandhi
"Hindi, Hindu, Hindustan"	— Bhartendu Harishchandra
"Purna Swarajya"	— Jawahar Lal Nehru
"Every lathi blow inflicted on my body will prove a nail in British coffin"	— Lala Lajpat Rai

"Jai Hind"	— Subhash Chandra Bose
"Do or die"	— Mahatma Gandhi
"Who lives if India dies"	— Jawahar Lal Nehru
"Vande Mataram"	— Bankim Chandra Chatterjee
"Jana Gana Mana Adhinayaka Jai Hai"	—Rabindranath Tagore
"Hate sin, not the sinner."	— Mahatma Gandhi
"Service of the people is the service of God"	— Swami Vivekananda
"Truth and non-violence are my God."	— Mahatma Gandhi

Battles and Wars In India

War	Year	Result
Battle of Kalinga	(261 B.C.)	Ashoka defeated the king of Kalinga
Second battle of Tarain	(1192 A.D.)	Muhammad Gori defeated Prithviraj Chauhan
First battle of Panipat	(1526 A.D.)	Babar defeated Ibrahim Lodi
Battle of Khanwa	(1527 A.D.)	Babar defeated Rana Sanga
Battle of Chausa	(1539 A.D.)	Shershah Suri defeated Humayun and became ruler of Delhi
Second Battle of Panipat	(1556 A.D.)	Akbar defeated Hemu
Battle of Talikota	(1565 A.D.)	Allied forces of Bijapur, Bidar, Golkunda and Ahamadnagar defeated the King of Vijay Nagar
Battle of Haldighati	(1576 A.D.)	The battle of Haldighati was fought between Rana Pratap of Mewar and Mughal army led by Man Singh and Asif Khan. Some historian say that this battle was indecisive but some say that Rana Pratap was defeated.
Battle of Palasey	(1757 A.D.)	British forces defeated Nawab of Bengal Sirajudoulla
Battle of Wandiwash	(1760 A.D.)	British forces defeated the French
Third battle of Panipat	(1761 A.D.)	Maratha were defeated by Ahmad Shah Abadali
Battle of Buxar	(1764 A.D.)	British forces defeated the combined forces of Mir Quasim, Shah Alam Mughal empire and Awadh's Nawab
Third Anglo-Maratha War	(1792 A.D.)	Maratha were conclusively defeated
Fourth Anglo-Mysore War	(1799 A.D.)	Tipu Sultan died fighting the British forces
Second Anglo-Sikh War	(1848 A.D.)	British forces annexed Punjab from Sikh rulers
Indo-China War	(1962 A.D.)	China attacked India unilaterally and annexed some area
Indo-Pak War	(1965 A.D.)	Pakistan attacked India but had to suffer severe setbacks
Indo-Pak War	(1971 A.D.)	Pak declare war against India.

* * * * *

10

World Geography

Earth: The earth constitutes land, water and air. Land is made up of rocks and soil. It is distributed in continents and islands. The water found in oceans, seas, lakes, etc. occupies about 2/3 of the earth's surface. The earth is surrounded by a cover of air, called atmosphere, which extends up to several hundred kilometres above its surface.

Shape: In ancient times people believed that the earth was flat in shape. Greek philosopher Pythagoras (6th century BC) was the first person to declare that the earth was round. After careful measurement, the scientists have found that the earth is slightly oblate (flattened at poles) and not exactly round.

Motions: The earth has two motions: *(i) Rotation:* Earth makes a complete round on its axis once each 24 hours (more exactly 23 hours, 56 minutes and 4.09 seconds). It causes days and night on the earth. *(ii) Revolution:* The earth makes a complete round of the Sun in one year. This revolution of earth produces alternate seasons.

Some Facts: **(1)** Equal Day and Night — March 21 and September 23. **(2)** Longest Day — June 21. **(3)** Shortest Day — December 22. **(4)** The sunlight takes eight minutes in travelling from the Sun to the Earth. **(5)** Average speed of the earth in orbit — 66,600 miles (107,220 km) per hour. **(6)** Earth's equatorial diameter is about 7926 miles (12,756 km). **(7)** Water (oceans, seas, lakes and rivers) occupies nearly 75 per cent of the surface of the earth. **(8)** Earth's average distance from the Moon — 2,38,857 miles (3,84,400 km). **(9)** Earth's average distance from the Sun — 93 million miles (149.4 million km).

Greenwich Time: It is the local time of the Greenwich observatory in London on 0° meridian. Greenwich time is international standard time.

International Date Line: Half way round the earth from the Greenwich is International Date Line on 180° longitude. It runs down mid-Pacific. It is one day earlier on the east of this line than it is on the west of the line. When it is Monday east of the line, it is Tuesday west of the line.

Zones: On the basis of temperature and distribution of solar heat on the surface of the earth, the earth has been divided into five zones: (1) Torrid Zone, (2) North Temperate Zone, (3) South Temperate Zone, (4) Arctic Zone, and (5) Antarctic Zone.

Continents: Large land masses forming large geographical divisions are called continents. There are seven continents: (1) Asia (29.5%), (2) Africa (20%), (3) Europe (6.5%), (4) North America (16.3%), (5) South America (11.8%), (6) Australia (5.2%), and (7) Antarctica (9.6%).

Highest Mountain Peaks: (1) Everest (Asia-8848 metres), (2) Aconcagua (South America-6960 metres), (3) Mckinley (North America-6194 metres), (4) Kilimanjaro (Africa-5895 metres), (5) Elbrus (Europe-5642 metres), (6) Vinson Massif (Antarctica-5140 metres), (7) Kosciusko (Australia-2228 metres).

Largest Oceans: (1) Pacific Ocean (The largest, covers almost 1/3 of the earth's total area, and the deepest about 6.8 miles at Mariana Trench in western Pacific); (2) Atlantic Ocean, and (3) Indian Ocean. Other seas and gulfs are — the Mediterranean Sea, South China Sea, Bering Sea, Caribbean Sea, East China Sea, Sea of Japan, North Sea, Baltic Sea, Hudson Bay and Gulf of Mexico.

Longest Rivers: (1) Nile (6690 km-Africa), (2) Amazon (6437 km-South America), (3) Mississippi-Missouri (6020 km-North America), (4) Yangtze Kiang (5494 km-Asia), (5) Ob Irtysh (5410 km-Europe), (6) Congo (4666 km-Africa).

Great Deserts: (1) Sahara (94 lakh sq km-North Africa), (2) Libyan (11.65 lakh sq km-North Africa), (3) Australian (16 lakh sq km-Australia), (4) Gobi (13 lakh sq km-Mongolia), (5) Great Victoria (6,47,000 sq km-Australia), (6) Syrian (5,20,000 sq km-Arabia), (7) Arabian (23,30,000 sq km Arabia).

Largest Islands: (1) Greenland (21,75,600 sq km) (2) New Guinea (7,77,000 sq km), (3) Borneo (7,25,545 sq km), (4) Malagasy (5,90,000 sq km), (5) Baffin Island (4,76,070 sq km).

Highest Waterfalls: (1) Angel (807 m-Venezuela), (2) Mongefossen (774 m-Norway), (3) Kukenaam (610 m-Venezuela), (4) Ribbon (491 m-USA), (5) King George VI (487 m-Guyana), (6) Upper Yosemite (435 m-USA).

Major Producers of Crops, Minerals and Industrial goods

Coal	—	China, USA, India, Australia, Indonesia, Russia
Cocoa	—	Cote d'Ivaire, Ghana, Indonesia, Nigeria
Coffee	—	Brazil, Vietnam, Columbia, Indonesia
Copper	—	Chile, Peru, China, USA
Cotton	—	China, India, USA, Pakistan, Brazil
Gold	—	China, Australia, Russia, USA, Canada
Grapes	—	China, Italy, USA, France, Spain
Iron ore	—	Australia, Brazil, China, India
Jute	—	India, Bangladesh, China
Manganese	—	China, South Africa, Australia
Petroleum	—	USA, Saudi Arabia, Iraq
Rice	—	China, India, Indonesia, Bangladesh
Rubber	—	Thailand, Indonesia, Malaysia, Vietnam, India
Silk	—	China, India, Uzbekistan, Thailand
Silver	—	Mexico, Peru, China, Chili
Steel	—	China, Japan, India, USA
Tea	—	China, India, Kenya, Sri Lanka
Wheat	—	China, India, USA, France, Russia
Diamond	—	Russia, Australia, Congo, Botswana
Tobacco	—	China, Brazil, India, USA, Indonesia

The Highest, Biggest and Longest in the World

Airport	*Largest*	King Fahd International Airport, Dammon (Saudi Arabia)
Animal	*Tallest*	Giraffe (Average height 6.09 m)
	Largest and Heaviest	Blue Whale (190 tonnes)
	Longest recorded	Boot lace Worm (55 m)
	Fastest	Cheetah (Approximately 100 km/hr)
Bay	*With max. shore line*	Hudson Bay (Canada: 12268 km)
	With maximum area	Bay of Bengal (India: 217 million hc)
Building	*Tallest*	Burj Khalifa (Dubai, 818 meter)
Canal	*Big ship (longest)*	Suez Canal (160 km)
	Busiest	Kiel Canal (North Sea)
Canyon/Gorge	*Deepest*	Hells Canyon, Snake River (Idaho : 7900 ft)
	Largest	Grand Canyon (Colarado River; USA; 446 km)
Church	*Largest*	Basilica of St. Peter (Vatican City Rome — Area 23000 sq. m.)

City	*Largest in Area*	Jiuquan Gansu, China (Area 1,67,996 Sq km)
Continent	*Biggest*	Asia (31,845,872 km^2)
	Smallest	Australia Mainland (Area 76,17,930 km^2)
Country	*Largest in Area*	Russia (17,098,242 sq. km)
	With largest electorate	India (over 90 crores)
	Smallest independent	State of Vatican City (0.44 km^2)
	With most land frontiers	China
Delta	*Largest*	Sundarban's Ganga-Brahmaputra delta (1,05,000 sq. km)
Desert	*Largest*	Sahara (N. Africa; maximum length 5,150 km EW; maximum width 3,200 km NS)
Dome	*Largest*	Singapore National Stadium (310 m)
Epic	*Longest*	Mahabharata
Fish	*Largest fresh water*	Plabeuk (China, Laos and Thailand)
	Most abundant	Bristle mouth
	Most venomous	Stone Fish (Indo-Pacific Waters)
Film	*Most Oscars*	Ben Hur (11 Oscars–1959); Titanic (11 Oscars–1998); The Lord of Rings : The Return of the King (11 Oscars—2003).
Fountain	*Tallest*	King Fahd's Fountain (Jeddah, Saudi Arabia)
Fruit	*Most nutritive*	Avocado (Vitamins A, C, E and Proteins; Central and South America)
	Least nutritive	Cucumber
Gulf	*Largest*	Gulf of Mexico (1,544,000 sq. km)
Island	*Biggest*	Greenland (2,175,000 sq km)
Lake	*Largest*	Caspian Sea (Azerbaijan, Russia, Iran border: 37.18 lakh km^2)
	Deepest	Baikal (Siberia)
	Largest (fresh water)	Superior Lake (USA—Canada border: 82,350 km^2)
Library	*Biggest*	United States Library of Congress (Washington D.C. founded in 1800, contains 101 million items)
	Biggest non-statutory	New York Public Library
Mountain	*Highest peak*	Mt. Everest (8848 m; Nepal)
	Highest range	Himalayas, Asia (upto 4200 m)
	Greatest mountain range	Himalaya-Karakoram (96 out of 109 peaks over 7315 m are here)
Museum	*Largest*	American Museum of Natural History, New York
Ocean	*Largest and Deepest*	The Pacific (Area: 166,240,000 km^2; Depth: 10,924 m)
Peninsula	*Largest*	Arabia (3.25 million sq. km)
Places	*Rainiest (annual mean)*	Mowsyrnam near Cherapunji (Meghalaya; India; 11873 mm)
Planet	*Biggest*	Jupiter (equatorial diameter 142984 km)
	Brightest, hottest and nearest to Earth	Venus
	Nearest to Sun	Mercury

Plateau	*Highest*	Tibetan Plateau (Central Asia: 4900 m)
Platform	*Longest (rail)*	Shree Siddharoodha Swamiji Railway Station, Hubballi. (Karnataka, India, 1507 m. long)
Railway Line	*Longest*	Trans-Siberian Railway (Moscow-Nakhodka: 9438 km)
Railway Station	*Largest*	Grand Central Terminal (New York City; 19 hc)
Religion	*Oldest*	Hinduism
Religion	*Largest*	Christianity
Rivers	*Longest*	(i) Nile (6650 km) (ii) Amazon (6437 km)
Road	*Longest*	Pan American Highway (from Alaska-Brasila: 24140 km)
Stadium	*Largest*	Strahov stadium at Prague (Czech Republic 240,000 spectators)
Star	*Brightest*	Sirius A (also called Dog Star)
Statue	*Tallest*	Statue of Unity (182 m)
Swimming course	*Longest recognised*	English Channel
Telescope	*Largest (radio)*	Five Hundred meter Apertune Spherical Telescope (FAST), China.
	Largest (solar)	Kitt Peak National Observatory, (Arizona; USA)
	Largest refractor	At Yerkes observatory (Wisconsin; USA; 18.9 m)
Temple	*Largest*	Angkor Vat (Cambodia: 402 acres)
Tunnel	*Longest (railway)*	Gotthard Base Rail Tunnel (Switzerland; 57.1 km)
	Largest (road)	Laerdal, Norway (24.51 km)
Waterfall	*Highest*	Salto-Angel (in Venezuela on a branch of river Carrao, depth 807 m.)
	Largest	Khone Falls (Laos; width 10.8 km)

First in the World

First Chinese visitor to India	Fahien
First foreign invader of India	Alexander, the Great (Greek)
First person to climb Mt. Everest	Tenzing Norgay (Indian) and Edmund Hillary (Newzealand) May 29, 1953
First atom bomb dropped at	Hiroshima (Japan): Aug 6, 1945
First man in the space	Yuri Gagarin (former USSR): April, 1961
First woman in the space	Valentina Tereshkova (former USSR): June 1963
First person to walk in the space	Alexei Leonov (former USSR)
First person to land on the moon	Neil Armstrong (USA): July 21, 1969
First and the only woman to have climbed Mt. Everest twice	Santosh Yadav (Indian; May 1992; May 1993)
First person on Mt. Everest without oxygen	Phu Dorjee (Indian; May 9, 1984)
First person to climb Mt. Everest twice	Nawang Gombu
First President of the USA	George Washington
First woman Prime Minister	Sirimavo Bandaranaike (Sri Lanka)
First person to swim across English Channel	Mathew Webb
First woman to swim across English Channel	Gertrude Caroline Ederle

First woman to climb Mt. Everest	Junko Tabei (Japan): May 16, 1975
First woman to climb Mt. Everest alone and without oxygen supplies	Alison Hargreaves (Britain: May 13, 1995)
First Aeroplane to fly around the world without refuelling	Voyager (Dec. 1986)
First test-tube Baby	Louise Brown (UK; 1978)
First all-talking Film	Jaz Singer (1927)
First Secretary-General of the UN	Trygve Lie (Norway: 1946-53)
First woman President of the UN General Assembly	Vijayalakshmi Pandit (India: 1953)
First woman to reach North Pole	Ann Bancroft (1986)
First person to reach North Pole	Robert Peary
First person to reach South Pole	Amundsen

Popular Names

Popular Name	*Real Name*
Badshah Khan	Abdul Ghaffar Khan
Bapu, Father of Nation	M.K. Gandhi
Bard of Avon	William Shakespeare
Chachaji *or* Panditji	Jawaharlal Nehru
Desert Fox	Gen. Rommel (Germany)
Desh Bandhu	C.R. Das
Father of English Poetry	Geoffrey Chaucer
Fuhrer	Adolf Hitler
Grand Old Man of India	Dadabhai Naoroji
Grand Old Man of Britain	W.E. Gladstone
Gurudev	Rabindra Nath Tagore
Guruji	M.S. Golwalkar
Grand Commoner	Pitt, the younger
Iron Man of India	Sardar Patel
Lady with the Lamp	Florence Nightingale
Lal, Bal, Pal	Lala Lajpat Rai, Bal Gangadhar Tilak, Bipin Chandra Pal
Li-Kwan	Pearl Buck
Little Corporal *or* Man of Destiny	Napoleon Bonaparte
Lokmanya	Bal Gangadhar Tilak
Lok Nayak	Jayaprakash Narain
Mahamana	Pt. Madan Mohan Malaviya
Maid of Orleans	Joan of Arc
Maiden Queen	Queen Elizabeth I
Man of Blood and Iron	Prince Bismark
Netaji	Subhash Chandra Bose
Nightingale of India	Sarojini Naidu
Priyadarshini	Indira Gandhi
Punjab Kesari	Lala Lajpat Rai
Wizard of the North	Walter Scott

Geographical Surnames

Geographical Surname	*Real Name*
Bengal's Sorrow	Damodar River
Blue Mountains	Nilgiri Hills
China's Sorrow	Hwang-Ho
City of Palaces	Kolkata
City of Skyscrapers *or* Empire City	New York

Geographical Surname	Real Name
City of Dreaming Spires	Oxford
Cockpit of Europe	Belgium
Dark Continent	Africa
Emerald Isle	Ireland
Eternal City	Rome
Forbidden City	Lhasa (Tibet)
Gateway of India	Mumbai
Gate of Tears	Strait of Bab-el-mandab
Gift of the Nile	Egypt
Granite City	Aberdeen (Scotland)
Hermit Kingdom	Korea
Holy Land	Jerusalem (Israel)
Island of Pearls	Bahrain (Persian Gulf)
Island of Cloves	Zanzibar
Key to the Mediterranean	Gibraltar
Land of Five Rivers	Punjab
Land of Golden Pagoda	Myanmar
Land of Kangaroo	Australia
Land of Maple Leaf/Lillies	Canada
Land of Midnight Sun	Norway
Land of Morning Calm	Korea
Land of the Rising Sun	Japan
Land of Thousand Lakes	Finland
Land of Thunderbolt	Bhutan
Land of the White Elephants	Thailand
Manchester of the Orient	Osaka (Japan)
Pearl of the Antilles *or* Sugar Bowl of the World	Cuba
Pink City	Jaipur
Playground of Europe	Switzerland
Queen of the Adriatic	Venice (Italy)
Roof of the World	Pamirs
Sick Man of Europe	Turkiye
Venice of the North	Stockholm (Sweden)
Windy City	Chicago
Whiteman's Grave	Guinea Coast of Africa
World's Loneliest Island	Tristan de Cunha

Countries'/Cities' Names—Old and New

Old Name	New Name	Old Name	New Name
Abyssinia	Ethiopia	Leningrad	St. Petersburg
Basutoland	Lesotho	Leopoldville	Kinshasa
Bechuanaland	Botswana	Mesopotamia	Iraq
British Honduras	Belize	North Rhodesia	Zambia
Burma	Myanmar	Nyasaland	Malawi
Ceylon	Sri Lanka	Peking	Beijing
Zaire	Congo (Democratic Republic)	Persia	Iran
Constantinople	Istanbul	Rangoon	Yangon
Dahomey	Benin	Salisbury	Harare
Dutch East Indies	Indonesia	Siam	Thailand
East Pakistan	Bangladesh	South West Africa	Namibia
Formosa	Taiwan	Southern Rhodesia	Zimbabwe
Gold Coast	Ghana	Turkey	Turkiye

IMPORTANT RESIDENCES

• **Buckingham Palace (London):** King/Queen of Britain • **10, Downing Street (London):** Prime Minister, Britain • **Elysee Palace (Paris):** President, France • **Rashtrapati Bhawan (New Delhi):** President, India • **White House (Washington):** President, USA • **Vatican (Rome):** Pope

Important towns situated on the River Banks

Town	River	Town	River
Agra	Yamuna	Karachi	Indus
Ahmedabad	Sabarmati	Lahore	Ravi
Prayagraj	Confluence of the Ganga and the Yamuna	Leh	Indus
Ayodhya	Saryu	London	Thames
Baghdad	Tigris	Lucknow	Gomati
Berlin	Spree	Nasik	Godavari
Cairo	Nile	New York	Hudson
Kolkata	Hooghly	Paris	Seine
Cuttack	Mahanadi	Patna	Ganga
Delhi	Yamuna	Rome	Tiber
Dibrugarh	Brahmaputra	Srinagar	Jhelum
Dublin	Liffey	Surat	Tapti
Hardwar	Ganga	Sydney	Murray-Darling
Hyderabad	Musi	Varanasi	Ganga
Jabalpur	Narbada	Vienna	Danube
Kanpur	Ganga	Washington	Potamac
		Yangon	Irawadi

Books and Authors

FOREIGN

Book	Author	Book	Author
Aesop's Fables	Aesop	Iliad	Homer
Adventure of Robinson Crusoe	Daniel Defoe	Inferno	A. Dante
Adventures of Sherlok Holmes	Arthur Conan Doyle	In Memoriam	Lord Tennyson
Alice in Wonderland	Lewis Carrol	Ivanhoe	Walter Scott
Apple Cart	G.B. Shaw	Julius Caesar	William Shakespeare
Arabian Nights	Sir Richard Burton	Lady Chatterley's Lover	D.H. Lawrence
As You Like It	William Shakespeare	Lajja	Taslima Nasreen
A Tale of Two Cities	Charles Dickens	Les Miserable	Victor Hugo
A Tale of Two Gardens	Octavio Paz	Leviathan	Thomas Hobbes
A Thousand Suns	Dominique Lapierre	Lolita	V. Nobokov
August Coup	Mikhail S. Gorbachev	Lycidas	John Milton
Ben Hur	Lewis Wallace	Mein Kampf	Adolf Hitler
Candida	G.B. Shaw	Merchant of Venice	William Shakespeare
Das Kapital	Karl Marx	Midnight's Children	Salman Rushdie
David Copperfield	Charles Dickens	Moor's Last Sigh	Salman Rushdie
Divine Comedy	A. Dante	Mother	Maxim Gorky
Doctor's Dilemma	G.B. Shaw	Mother India	Katherine Mayo
Famished Road	Ben Okri	Nana	Emile Zola
Freedom From Fear	Aung San Suu Kyi	Ninteen Eighty Four	George Orwell
Gulistan Bostan	Sheikh Saadi	Odyssey	Homer
Gulliver's Travels	Jonathan Swift	Origin of Species	Charles Darwin
Hamlet	William Shakespeare	Othello	William Shakespeare
		Paradise Lost	John Milton

Book	Author	Book	Author
Paradise Regained	John Milton	The Tempest	William Shakespeare
Path to Power	Margaret Thatcher	Time Machine	H.G. Wells
Pickwick Papers	Charles Dickens	Tom Sawyer	Mark Twain
Pride and Prejudice	Jane Austen	Treasure Island	R.L. Stevenson
Razor's Edge	Somerset Maugham	Twelfth Night	William Shakespeare
Republic	Plato	Uncle Tom's Cabin	H.B. Stowe
Romeo and Juliet	William Shakespeare	Unto This Last	John Ruskin
Round the World in Eighty Days	Jules Verne	Utopia	Thomas More
Rubaiyat-i-Omar Khayyam	Edward Fitzgerald (Translator)	Universe Around Us	James Jeans
Shape of Things to Come	H.G. Wells	Vicar of Wakefield	Oliver Goldsmith
The Satanic Verses	Salman Rushdie	War and Peace	Leo Tolstoy
The Social Contract	Rousseau	Wealth of Nations	Adam Smith
		Wonder That was India	A.L. Basham
		Wuthering Heights	Emily Bronte

INDIAN

Book	Author	Book	Author
Abhigyan Shakuntalam	Kalidas	Chand ka Munh Terha Hai	Muktibodh
Ain-i-Akbari	Abul Fazal	Kapalkundala	Bankim Chandra Chatterjee
Anand Math	Bankim Chandra Chatterjee	Kadambari	Bana Bhatta
Arthashastra	Kautilya	Kagaz Te Kanwas	Amrita Pritam
A Suitable Boy	Vikram Seth	Kamayani	Jai Shankar Prasad
Bhagwat Gita	Ved Vyas	Kankaal	Jai Shankar Prasad
Chidambara	Sumitranandan Pant	Kumar Sambhav	Kalidas
Devdas	Sarat Chandra Chatterjee	Mahabharata	Ved Vyas
Diwan-i-Ghalib	Mirza Ghalib	Malgudi Days	R.K. Narayan
Discovery of India	Jawaharlal Nehru	Manvini Bhavai	Pannalal Patel
Essays on Gita	Aurobindo Ghosh	Mati Matal	Gopi Nath Mohanty
Eternal India	Indira Gandhi	Meghdoot	Kalidas
Faces of Everest	Major H.P.S. Ahluwalia	Meri Ekyavan Kavitain	Atal Bihari Vajpayee
Ganadevata	Tarashankar Bandopadhyaya	Meri Sansadiya Yatra	Atal Bihari Vajpayee
Geet Govind	Jaya Dev	Mritunjaya	B.K. Bhattacharya
Geetanjali	R.N. Tagore	Mudrarakshasa	Vishakhadatta
Glimpses of World History	Jawaharlal Nehru	My Experiments with Truth	M.K. Gandhi
Godaan	Prem Chand	My Own Boswell	M. Hidayatullah
Gul-e-Nagma	Firaq Gorakhpuri	My Presidential Years	R. Venkataraman
Gunahon ka Devta	Dharmveer Bharti	Nisheeth	Uma Shankar Joshi
Harsh Charita	Bana Bhatta	'No, Sir'	P.G. Mavlankar
Hindu View of Life	S. Radhakrishnan	One Day Wonders	Sunil Gavaskar
Idols	Sunil Gavaskar	Panchtantra	Vishnu Sharma
India Divided	Dr. Rajendra Prasad	Passage to England	Nirad C. Chaudhuri
The Judgement	Kuldip Nayyar	Prison Diary	Jaya Prakash Narayan
Juhi ki Kali	Surya Kant Tripathi 'Nirala'	Raghuvansha	Kalidas
Justice of Peace ke Aansu	Janardan Prasad Singh	Rajtarangini	Kalhana
		Ramayana	Balmiki

Book	Author	Book	Author
Ramcharit Manas	Tulsidas	The God of Small Things	Arundhati Roy
Rukh Te Rishi	Harbhajan Singh	Urvashi	Ram Dhari Singh 'Dinkar'
Satyarth Prakash	Swami Dayanand	Yama	Mahadevi Verma
Sur Sagar	Surdas	My Country : My Life (Autobiography)	L.K. Advani
The Guide	R.K. Narayan	The Test of My Life	Yuvraj Singh
The Insider	P.V. Narasimharao	Twenty Years in a Decade	Shah Rukh Khan
The Post Office — *Dak Ghar*	Rabindra Nath Tagore		

IMPORTANT BOOKS WRITTEN IN JAIL

Book	Author	Book	Author
My Experiments with Truth	Mahatma Gandhi	Pilgrim's Progress	John Bunyan
Glimpses of World History	Jawaharlal Nehru	Bible (in German language)	Martin Luther
Discovery of India		Les Miserables	Victor Hugo
Gita Rahasya	Lokmanya Bal Gangadhar Tilak	Long Walk to Freedom	Nelson Mandela

❋❋❋❋❋

11

First in India

First in India

The first Indian to get the Nobel Prize for Literature	Rabindra Nath Tagore
The first Indian to get the Nobel Prize for Physics	C.V. Raman
The first Indian to get the Nobel Prize for Peace	Mother Teresa
The first Indian to get the Nobel Prize for Economics	Amartya Sen
The first Indian to get Special Oscar award (1992)	Satyajit Ray
The first and the last Indian Governor-General of free India	C. Rajagopalachari
The first woman to become the Governor of a State	Smt. Sarojini Naidu
The first Indian Commander-in-Chief	General K.M. Cariappa
The first ever woman to become the Chief Minister of a State	Smt. Sucheta Kripalani
The first Indian woman President of United Nations General Assembly	Smt. Vijaylakshmi Pandit
The first Indian to become the President of International Court of Justice	Dr. Nagendra Singh
The first Indian girl to became Miss World	Miss Reita Faria
The first Indian woman to swim across the English Channel	Ms. Aarti Gupta
The first Indian girl to become Miss Universe	Miss Sushmita Sen
The first Indian to swim across the English Channel	Mihir Sen
The first Field Marshal	S.H.F.J. Manekshaw
The first Indian recipient of Victoria Cross	Khudadad Khan
The first Indian to conquer Mt. Everest	Sherpa Tenzing, May 29, 1953
The only woman in the world to climb Mount Everest twice	Santosh Yadav (May 1992 and May 1993)
The first Indian Cosmonaut	Rakesh Sharma
The first Indian woman Cosmonaut	Kalpana Chawla
The first woman to climb Mt. Everest	Miss Bachendri Pal, May 23, 1984
The first women Foreign Secretary	Chokila Iyer
The first ICS	Satyendranath Tagore
The first Indian to address the UN General Assembly in Hindi	Atal Behari Vajpayee
The first Newspaper	Bengal Gazette, Jan 27, 1780
The first Postage Stamp issued	In 1852
The first Telegraph line laid	In 1851, Kolkata; Diamond Harbour
The first Railways run	April 16, 1853; Mumbai-Thane
The first Electric Train run	1925: Mumbai-Kurla
The first Atomic Power Station	Tarapore (Maharashtra)
The first passenger-cum-cargo ship made in India	Harshavardhan
The first Satellite	Aryabhatta (1975)
The first Rocket	Rohini (1967)

The first Atomic Reactor	Apsara (1956)
The first Indian to climb Everest without oxygen	Phu Dorjee (1987)
The first film (movie)	Raja Harishchandra
The first film (talkie)	Alam Ara
The first Metro Railway	Kolkata Metro Railway
The first Test-tube baby, scientifically documented	Born on August 6, 1986 at K.E.M. Hospital, Mumbai
The first TV Centre	At Delhi
The first Indian to get an Oscar	Bhanu Athaiya
The first woman flies in IAF	Ms Harita Kaur Deol

First Important Officials of India

The Governor-General of free India	Lord Mountbatten
President	Dr. Rajendra Prasad
President (Female)	Pratibha Patil
Vice-President	Dr. S. Radhakrishnan
Prime Minister	Jawahar Lal Nehru
Prime Minister (Female)	Indira Gandhi
Deputy Prime Minister	Sardar Vallabhbhai Patel
Chief Justice	Harilal J. Kania
First Female Judge in Supreme Court	Smt. Meera Sahib Fatima Bibi
Speaker, Lok Sabha	Ganesh Vasudeo Mawlankar
Woman Speaker of Lok Sabha	Meira Kumar
Chief Election Commissioner	Sukumar Sen
Indian Commander-in-Chief	General K.M. Cariappa
Chief of Army Staff	General Maharaj Rajendra Sinhji
Indian Chief of Air Staff	Air Marshal S. Mukherjee
Indian Chief of Naval Staff	Vice Admiral Ramdas Katari
Chief of Defence Staff (CDS)	General Bipin Rawat
Female Minister	Raj Kumari Amrit Kaur (Health Minister)
Female Governor	Sarojini Naidu (U.P.)
Female Chief Minister	Sucheta Kripalani (U.P. 1963)
Finance Commissioner	K.C. Niyogi
Leader of Opposition in Lok Sabha (Recognised)	Y.V. Chavan (Congress)
Leader of Opposition in Rajya Sabha (Recognised)	Kamalapati Tripathi (Congress)

Highest, Biggest, Largest & Longest in India

Award for Gallantry, highest	Param Vir Chakra
Award, highest civilian	Bharat Ratna
Bank, with largest number of branches	State Bank of India
Road Bridge, Longest	Bhupen Hazarika Setu Lohit River, Assam (9.15 km)
Cattle fair, largest	Sonepur (Bihar)
Cellular Phone, First	Kolkata, August 1, 1995
City, Most Populous	Mumbai
Corridor, Longest	Rameshwaram Temple corridor (4,000 ft.)
Desert, Largest	Thar (Rajasthan)
Dam, Longest	Hirakud Dam (Odisha)
Delta, Largest	Sunderban's Delta
Dome, Largest	Gol Gumbaj (Bijapur)

Dam, Highest	Tihri Dam 261 m. (855 ft.)
Gateway, Highest	Buland Darwaja at Fatehpur Sikri (176 ft.)
Lake, Largest (Fresh Water)	Wular Lake (Kashmir)
Literacy, Highest	Keralam (94%)
Museum, Largest	Indian Museum (Kolkata)
Mosque, Biggest	Jama Masjid (Delhi)
Peak, Highest*	K-2 (Pak-Occupied Kashmir)
Platform, Longest	At Shree Siddharoodha Swamiji Railway Station, Hubballi, Karnataka (1507 m. long)
Railway Bridge, Longest	Vembanad Bridge, Keralam (4.6 km)
River, Longest**	The Ganges (2525 Km)
Rainfall, Highest (annual mean)	Mowsynram near Cherrapunji (1178 cm)
Road, Longest	NH-44 (3,745 km)
Road-Rail Longest Bridge	Bogibeel Bridge, Assam (4.94 km)
State, (Largest population)	Uttar Pradesh
State, Largest (in area)	Rajasthan
State, with maximum forest cover	Madhya Pradesh
State, with maximum density of population (2011)	Bihar
Telescope, Largest in Asia	Vainu Bappu telescope (at Kavalur : Chennai) 2.34 m.
Tiger State	Madhya Pradesh
Tunnel, Longest (Road)	Dr. Shyama Prasad Mukherjee Tunnel (9.28 kms, J&K)
Tunnel, Longest (Railway)	T-50 Tunnel, Between Khari and Sumber sections in J&K (12.77 km long)
Minar, Highest	Qutub Minar (Delhi, 72.5 m.)
Waterfall, Highest	Kunchikal Waterfall (Karnataka: 455 m)
Zoo, Largest	Arignar Anna Zoological Park, Chennai, Tamil Nadu

* *Highest peak in the world is Mount Everest, which is in Nepal, K-2 is the second highest peak in the world. It is 8,611 metres high.*

** *Indus and Brahmaputra (each 2800 Km). Both of them, however, cover a long distance outside India.*

Indian Banks

- **Reserve Bank of India:** It was established in 1935 and nationalised in 1949. It is the Central Bank of the country and issues all currency notes 10, 20, 50, 100, 200 and 500. It acts as a banker to the Government and exercises control over other commercial banks in the country. Headquarters of Reserve Bank of India is in Mumbai.
- **The State Bank of India:** Largest commercial bank, alongwith its seven other associate banks was nationalised in 1955. All associate banks of SBI have been merged in it.
- **Nationalisation of Banks:** The Government of India on July 19, 1969, took over 14 biggest commercial banks incorporated in the country. On April 15, 1980, six more banks were nationalised. In March 1994, the Parliament passed the Banking Regulation (Amendment) Bill, 1994 which inter alia provided for establishment of private sector banks.

Insurance

- **Life Insurance Corporation of India:** Since September 1, 1956, when the L.I.C. of India was established, life insurance business in India is transacted by the Corporation and, in a restricted sphere by the Posts and Telegraphs Department of the Government of India and by some State Governments.
- **General Insurance Corporation of India:** It was established in November, 1972 and with effect from January, 1974 the erstwhile 107 Indian and Foreign insurers were grouped by this corporation into four operation companies, namely National Insurance, New India Assurance, Oriental Insurance and United India Insurance.

*****

12 Cultural Activities

AKADEMIES

There are three akademies for promotion of creative art.

1. **Lalit Kala Akademi, New Delhi:** Established in 1954, the Lalit Kala Akademi strives for the popularisation of Indian art within the country and in various countries of the world through exhibitions, publications, workshops and camps. Every three year it organises the Triennale India, an international exhibition. It publishes research papers on Indian arts. Besides organising seminars, it honours eminent artists. The Akademi has set up regional centres called Rashtriya Lalit Kala Kendras at Lucknow, Kolkata, Chennai and Bhubaneswar and a small office at Mumbai.
2. **Sangeet Natak Akademi, New Delhi:** The Sangeet Natak Akademi, set-up in 1953, aims at the promotion and development of dance, drama and music. It holds seminars and festivals, presents awards to the eminent artists and extends financial assistance to traditional teachers and scholarships to students. It also operates a scheme of exchange of troupes.
3. **Sahitya Akademi, New Delhi:** The Sahitya Akademi, established in 1954, has the main functions of development of Indian letters, setting up high literary standards, translation of literary works of one Indian language into other Indian languages, publication of books on history of literature and criticism, bibliographies and reference books. The Akademy has regional offices at Mumbai, Kolkata, Bengaluru and Chennai.
4. **National School of Drama:** It is one of the top theatre training institutes in the world and only one of its kind in India. It was set up in 1959 under Sangeet Natak Akademi but was later made autonomous organisation in 1975.

SCULPTURE

Archaeological Survey of India, set up in 1861, is responsible for preservation and maintenance of sculptures and historical monuments and manages a number of archaeological museums. National Archives of India, established in 1891, it is the official custodian of all non-current records of permanent value of the Government of India and its predecessor bodies.

MUSEUMS

They are repositories of the cultural heritage and conserve and preserve historical technical and other materials against decay and transmit them to posterity as records of history.

MUSIC

Main Schools of Classical Music: There are two main schools of classical music, namely, the Hindustani and the Carnatic. The Hindustani school of classical music is in vogue in north-western India, eastern India and northern parts of the South India.

Musical Instruments: They are: Tabla, Mridangam, Pakhawaj, Chandai, Dholak, Veena, Sitar, Sarod, Gootuvadhyam, Sarangi, Flute, Nadaswaram, Shehnai, Shringi and Turahi.

DANCE

India has a very rich tradition of tribal, folk and classical dances.

Classical Dance

Dance	*State*	*Famous Artists*
Bharat Natyam	Tamil Nadu	Yamini Krishnamurthy, Rukmini Devi Arundale, Swapna Sundari, Sonal Mansingh, Vaijanti Mala, Mrinalini Sarabhai, Chandralekha, Indrani, Ram Gopal, Bal Saraswati
Kathakali	Keralam	Gopinath, K.K. Nayar, Kunju-Kurup, T.K. Chandu
Kuchipudi	Andhra Pradesh	Sapna Sundari, Raja Reddy, Shobha Nayar, Radha Reddy, Vedantam Satyanarayan, Vimpanti Chinna Satyam.
Kathak	North India	Birju Maharaj, Gopi Krishna, Shambhu Maharaj, Sitara Devi, Vishnu Sharma, Durga Lal, Shobhana Narayan
Odissi	Odisha	Kelucharan Mahapatra, Indrani Rehman, Madhavi Mudgal, Pratima Bedi, Samyukta Panigrahi, Sonal Mansingh, Debudas
Manipuri	Manipur	Uday Shankar, Bipin Singh, Suryamukhi, Darohra Jhaveri

Famous Folk-Dance

State/UT	Folk Dance
Andhra Pradesh	Dandari, Banjara
Assam	Bihu, Keli Gopal, Sataria
Bihar	Chhau, Magahi, Durga dance
W. Bengal	Kirtan, Kalatri, Asweabadh, Brita, Kalidance
Chhattisgarh	Saila, Karama, Bhagoria
Gujarat	Garba, Rasalila, Tippani, Dandia,
Haryana	Damyal, Lahoor
Himachal Pradesh	Dussehra dance, Hikat, Notio
Jammu & Kashmir	Dumhal
Jharkhand	Jhau, Ghumakudia, Jadur, Sarhul, Soharai, Karama, Vaima, Loojhari, Jat-Jatin, Vidayat
Karnataka	Yakṣhagan, Dolu Kunitha
Keralam	Mohini Attam, Padayuni

State	Folk Dance
Madhya Pradesh	Lota Nritya, Jawara
Maharashtra	Tamasha, Dahi Handi, Gof, Deepak Dindi
Manipur	Dhol Cholam
Meghalaya	Nongakarem
Nagaland	Bamboo dance
Odisha	Chhau, Maya Shabari, Dalachai
Punjab	Gidda, Bhangra, Panihari
Rajasthan	Thumar, Kathaputali, Tera Tali
Tamil Nadu	Terukalathu, Kabalatam, Kargam, Pulivesham
Tripura	Hazagiri
Uttar Pradesh	Rasalila, Nautanki, Thali, Dhurang, Jhumela, Huraka, Bol.
Uttarakhand	Kajari, Karan
Goa	Dhode Modini

Musical Instruments and Artists

Musical Instrument	Artists
Flute	Hari Prasad Chaurasia, Panna Lal Ghosh, T.R. Mahalingam, N. Ramani, Vijaya Raghava Rao
Tabla	Allah Rakha, Gudai Maharaj, Latif Khan, Zakir Hussain
Violin	Lalgudi Jayaraman, L. Subramaniam, M.S. Gopal Krishnan, S. Subrahmaniam, V.G. Jog, N. Rajan
Shehnai	Bismilla Khan, Imrat Khan
Sarod	Ali Akbar Khan, Amjad Ali Khan, Alauddin Khan , Saren Rani, Brij Narayan

Musical Instrument	Artists
Sitar	Pandit Ravishankar, Vilayat Khan
Santur	Shiv Kumar Sharma
Rudraveena	Zia Mohiuddin Dagar
Pakhawaj	Govind Rao, Anokhe Lal, Kanthi Maharaj
Mridanga	Palghat R. Raghu, U.S. Burman
Harmonium	Purushottam Walawakar, M. Dhaulpuri
Guitar	Pt. Vishnu Mohan Bhatt, Brij Bhushan Kalra
Ghatam	T.H. Vinayakaram
Janjira	V. Nagarajan
Symphony	Jubin Mehta

Wild Life Sanctuary in India

India is rich in flora and fauna. However, due to increasing population and industrial and commercial activities, there has been acute pressure on forests. The Government has taken several steps to check the sharp fall in the number of these species. Among the measures are declaration of certain habitats as national parks and sanctuaries. 107 national parks and 574 sanctuaries have been established till August, 2025, important ones being given below:

Assam : Kaziranga National Park (know for one-horn Rhinoceroses); Manas Sanctuary.

Jharkhand : Hazaribagh National Park; Betla Tiger Reserve Palamau.

Cujarat : Valvadar National Park, Bhavnagar; Marine National Park, Gir Forests.

Himachal Pradesh : Rohla National Park; Motichur Sanctuary.

Jammu & Kashmir : Dachigam Sanctuary.

Karnataka : Bandipur National Park; Bannargheta National Park, Bangalore; Nagorhole National Park, Coorg; Ranganthitto Bird Sanctuary.

Keralam : Eravikulam Rajmallay National Park, Idduki; Periyar Game Sanctuary.

Madhya Pradesh : Kanha National Park; Bandhavgarh National Park, Shahdol, Shivpuri National Park.

Maharashtra : Taloba National Park, Chandrapur; Panch National Park, Nagpur; Borivali National Park, Mumbai;

	Nawagaon National Park, Bandara; Melghat National Park.
Manipur	: Keibul Lamjao National Park.
Odisha	: Simlipal, Tiger Sanctuary.
Rajasthan	: Sariska Sanctuary; Ghana Bird Sanctuary, Ranthambhor Sanctuary.
Sikkim	: Khangchandzenda National Park, Gangtok.
Tamil Nadu	: Vedanthangal Bird Sanctuary; Guindy National Park, Chennai; Mudumalai Sanctuary; Kalakad-Munden Thurai Reserve.
Uttar Pradesh	: Chandraprabha Sanctuary; Dudhwa National Park, Lakhimpur.
West Bengal	: Jaldapara Sanctuary; Sunderbans.
Uttarakhand	: Corbett National Park; Nainital.

Biosphere Reserves in India

S. No.	Name of the Biosphere Reserve	Area in Km^2	Date of Establishment	Location in the State (s)/Union Territory
1.	Nilgiri*	5520	01.08.1986	Part of Wynad, Nagarhole, Bandipur and Madumalai, Nilambur, Silent Valley and Siruvani hills in Tamil Nadu, Keralam and Karnataka.
2.	Nanda Devi*	6407.03	18.01.1988	Part of Chamoli, Pithoragarh and Almora districts in Uttarakhand.
3.	Nokrek*	820	01.09.1988	Part of East, West and South Garo Hill districts in Meghalaya.
4.	Manas	2837	14.03.1989	Part of Kokrajhar, Bongaigaon, Barpeta, Nalbari, Kamprup and Darang districts in Assam.
5.	Sunderban*	9630	29.03.1989	Part of delta of Ganges & Brahamaputra river system in West Bengal.
6.	Gulf of Mannar*	10500	18.02.1989	India part of Gulf of Mannar extending from Rameswaram island in the North to Kanyakumari in the South of Tamil Nadu.
7.	Great Nicobar*	1038.7	06.01.1989	Southern most island of Andaman and Nicobar Islands.
8.	Similipal*	5569	21.06.1994	Part of Mayurbhanj district in Odisha.
9.	Dibru-Saikhova	765	28.07.1997	Part of Dibrugarh and Tinsukia districts in Assam.
10.	Dehang-Dibang	5111.5	02.09.1998	Part of Upper Siang, West Siang and Dibang Valley districts in Arunachal Pradesh.
11.	Pachmarhi*	4981.72	03.03.1999	Part of Betul, Narmadapuram and Chhindwara districts in Madhya Pradesh.
12.	Khangchendzonga*	2931.12	07.02.2000	Part of North and West districts in Sikkim.
13.	Agasthyamalai*	3500	12.11.2001	Part of Thirunelveli and Kanyakumari districts in Tamil Nadu and Thiruvanthapuram, Kollam and Pathanmthitta districts in Keralam.
14.	Achanakmar-Amarkantak*	3,835. 51	30.03.2005	Part of Anuppur and Dindori districts of Madhya Pradesh and Bilaspur district of Chhattisgarh.
15.	Great Rann of Kutch	12,454	29.01.2008	Part of Kutch, Rajkot, Surendranagar and Patan districts in Gujarat.
16.	Cold Desert*	7,770	28.08.2009	Pin Valley National Park and surroundings; Chandratal & Sarchu; and Kibber Wildlife sanctuary in Himachal Pradesh.
17.	Seshachalam	4755.58	20.09.2010	Seshachalam hill ranges in Eastern Ghats encompassing part of Chittoor and Kadapa districts in Andhra Pradesh.
18.	Panna*	2998.98	25.08.2011	Part of Panna and Chhattarpur districts in Madhya Pradesh

* Recognised by UNESCO on World Network of Biosphere Reserves

*****

13 Awards

NATIONAL AWARDS

Bharat Ratna

This is India's highest civilian award. It is given for exceptional work on art, literature, science, sports and recognition of public service of the highest order. Government servants are not eligible for it.

Padma Vibhushan

The **Padma Vibhushan** is the second-highest civilian award of the Republic of India, preceded by Bharat Ratna and followed by Padma Bhushan. Instituted on 2 January 1954, the award is given for "exceptional and distinguished service", without distinction of race, occupation, position, or sex. The award criteria include "service in any field including service rendered by Government servants" including doctors and scientists, but excludes those working with the public sector undertakings.

During 1 May and 15 September of every year, the recommendations for the award are submitted to the Padma Awards Committee, constituted by the Prime Minister of India. The recommendations are received from all the state and the union territory governments, the Ministries of the Government of India, the Bharat Ratna and previous Padma Vibhushan award recipients, the Institutes of Excellence, the Ministers, the Chief Ministers and the Governors of State, and the Members of Parliament including private individuals. The committee later submits their recommendations to the Prime Minister and the President of India for the further approval. The award recipients are announced on Republic Day.

Padma Bhushan

The **Padma Bhushan** is the third-highest civilian award in the Republic of India, after the Bharat Ratna and the Padma Vibhushan, but coming before the Padma Shri. It is announced on the occasion of Republic Day of India every year. It is conferred by the President of India at a function held at Rashtrapati Bhavan sometime around March or April. The award was established on 2 January 1954 by the president of India. It is awarded to recognize distinguished service of a high order to the nation, in any field.

Padma Shri

Padma Shri (also Padmashree) is the fourth highest civilian award in the Republic of India, after the Bharat Ratna, the Padma Vibhushan and the Padma Bhushan. Awarded by the Government of India, it is announced every year on India's Republic Day. Padma Awards were instituted in 1954 to be awarded to citizens of India in recognition of their distinguished contribution in various spheres of activity including the Arts, Education, Industry, Literature, Science, Sports, Medicine, Social Service and Public Affairs. It has also been awarded to some distinguished individuals who were not citizens of India but did contribute in various ways to India. The selection criteria have been criticized in some quarters with the claim that many highly deserving artists have been left out in order to favor certain individuals.

On its obverse, the words "Padma", meaning lotus in Sanskrit, and "Shri", a Sanskrit-derived honorific equivalent to 'Mr.' or 'Ms.', appear in Devanagari above and below a lotus flower. The geometrical pattern on either side is in burnished bronze. All embossing is in white gold.

GALLANTRY AWARDS

Param Vir Chakra

The highest award for bravery or some daring and pre-eminent act of valour or self-sacrifice in the presence of the enemy, whether on land, at sea or in the air.

Mahavir Chakra

It is the second highest decoration and is awarded for acts of conspicuous gallantry in the presence of the enemy, whether on land, at sea or in the air.

Vir Chakra

It is the third in order of awards given for acts of gallantry in the presence of enemy, whether on land, at sea or in the air.

Ashok Chakra

This medal is awarded for the most conspicuous bravery or some daring or pre-eminent act of valour or self-sacrifice on land, at sea or in the air but not in the presence of enemy.

Vishishta Sewa Medal

It is awarded to personnel of all the three Services in class I, II and III in recognition of distinguished service of the "most exceptional" and "exceptional" and a "high" order respectively. Prefixes *Parma* and *Ati* are added before first two categories of medals respectively.

Jeewan Raksha Padak

Awarded for meritorious acts or a series of acts of a human nature displayed in saving life from drowning, fire and rescue operations in mines etc.

OTHER NATIONAL AWARDS

Jamnalal Bajaj Awards

In 1977, the Jamnalal Bajaj Foundation was established for promoting Gandhian constructive programmes and assisting constructive workers who devoted themselves to the national cause. The foundation has instituted four annual awards each carrying a cash prize of ₹ 10 lakh for its equivalent in foreign currency a citation and a trophy. The awards are intended to recognise outstanding contribution in:

- Constructive work
- Application of science and technology for rural development
- Upliftment and welfare of women and children and/or Gandhian constructive work by women workers
- Promotion of Gandhian values outside India by individuals other than Indian citizens

Dada Saheb Phalke Award

Instituted in 1969 the Dada Saheb Phalke Award is awarded by the Government of India for outstanding contribution to the cause of cinema. The award is named after Dhundiraj Govind Phalke, the father of Indian cinema, who made India's first feature film Raja Harishchandra in 1913. The award comprises a Swarna Kamal, a cash prize of ₹ 15 lakh and a shawl. The award was first given to Devika Rani in 1969 who became the first lady recipient of the award. Prithviraj Kapoor was the first to be honoured posthumously with the Dada Saheb Phalke Award.

Saraswati Samman

The award is given by K.K. Birla Foundation to an outstanding author for his literary work in any Indian language mentioned in the Eighth Schedule of the Constitution and published during the last 10 years. The award carries a cash prize of ₹ 15 lakh.

Bharatiya Jnanpith Award

The Bhartiya Jnanpith Award has been sponsored by Bharatiya Jnanpith, a cultural-literary society, founded in 1944 by the noted industrialist, Shanti Prasad Jain, with the twin object of rediscovering the neglected treasures of Indian philosophy and of encouraging creative writing in various modern Indian languages. The award carries with it a cash prize of ₹ 11 lakh, a citation and a replica of the Vagdevi, the symbol of outstanding literary achievement.

Vyasa Samman

This is awarded by KK Birla Foundation for outstanding Hindi Literary work by an Indian citizen that was published in the past decade. This carries a cash prize of ₹ 4 lakh.

Sahitya Akademi Awards

These prizes are awarded annually to the authors of the most outstanding books of literary merit published in each of the 22 languages which are specified in the Eighth Schedule of the Constitution. There are also two awards for Rajasthani and English. The award, inform of a casket containing an inscribed copper plate and a cheque of ₹ 1 lakh is given to the author or his/her heir.

Kabir Samman

The award is conferred annually on a person of literature of very high order on the basis of his or her superb creativity and consistent commitment to the most recent and latest trends of literary creation in any of the Indian languages. The award carries ₹ 3 lakh and a letter of citation.

Kalidas Samman

Instituted by the Madhya Pradesh Government, the award is of the value of ₹ 2 lakh.

Indira Gandhi Award

The award has been instituted for promoting national integration and understanding amongst the religious groups, communities and ethnic groups of India.

Rajiv Gandhi National Sadbhavana Award

Instituted in 1992 to mark the golden jubilee of the Quit India Movement, the award carries a cash prize of ₹ 10 lakh and a citation.

Dhyanchand Khel Ratna Award

It was launched in the year 1991-92 with the objective of honouring sports persons to enhance their dignity and place of honour in society. Under this, an amount of ₹ 25 lakhs is given as award for the most spectacular and outstanding performance in the field of sports by an individual sports person or a team. This award was previously known as Rajiv Gandhi Khel Ratna Award.

Arjuna Award

Instituted in 1961 this award is given to a sportsman who has displayed outstanding performance for three years (prior to the year of award) both at national and international levels. The award comprises a cheque of ₹ 15 lakhs a small statue of the great archer from the epic Mahabharata and a citation.

Arjuna Award (Lifetime)

The objective of Arjuna Award (Lifetime) is to honour those Sports persons who have contributed to sports by their performance and continue to contribute to promotion of sports even after retirement from their active sporting career. This award carries an amount of ₹ 10 lakhs.

Dronacharya Award

Instituted in 1985 the award was named after Dronacharya—the legendary guru of the epic age of Mahabharata who taught archery and sports to Kauravas and Pandavas. The Dronacharya (Lifetime) awardees get 15 lakh and Dronacharya (Regular) awardees gets 10 lakhs a plaque, a blazer and a citation.

Shanti Swaroop Bhatnagar Prizes

The Shanti Swaroop Bhatnagar (SSB) Prizes are awarded annually by the Council of Scientific & Industrial Research (CSIR) to outstanding Indian research workers in seven disciplines of science and technology. The SSB Prizes are awarded to scientists for their outstanding scientific contributions made primarily in India during last 5 years preceding the year of the award are eligible for the Prize.

Gujar Mal Modi Award

The award carries ₹ 2.01 lakh as cash prize, apart from a silver shield and a scroll and is given to the best scientist of the year who makes an outstanding contribution to research resulting in new innovative technology.

INTERNATIONAL AWARDS

Nobel Prize

Nobel Prizes are awarded each year under the will of Alfred Bernhard Nobel (1833-96), Swedish chemist and engineer. The interest of the fund is divided annually among the persons who have made the most outstanding contribution in various fields. In all, there are six prizes. The prizes are awarded to persons who have made outstanding contributions in the fields of physics, chemistry, and physiology or medicine, Literature and World Peace. The sixth prize, that is The Nobel Prize for economic sciences was established in 1967 by risk bank, the Swedish bank, in celebration of its 300th anniversary and was awarded for the first time in 1969. Other awards were started in 1901.

Indians Honoured with Nobel Prize: So far, following Indians have been honoured with these prizes. Their names are (*i*) Rabindra Nath Tagore for Literature, for his book 'Gitanjali', in 1913, (*ii*) Dr. C.V. Raman for Physics in 1930, for his discovery of 'Raman Effect', (*iii*) Mother Teresa for Peace in 1979, (*iv*) Prof. Amartya Sen in 1998 for Economics and (*v*) Kailash Satyarthi for Peace in 2014.

In addition, four non-resident Indians have also been awarded the Nobel Prize. They are:

(*i*) Hargobind Khurana for Medicine in 1968
(*ii*) Subramanian Chandrasekhar for Physics in 1983
(*iii*) Venkatraman Ramkrishnan for Chemistry in 2009.
(*iv*) Abhijit Banerjee for Economics in 2019.

Pulitzer Prize

Instituted in 1970 and named after the US publisher Joseph Pulitzer (1847-1911). It is conferred annually in the United States for accomplishment in journalism, literature and music under the management to the Pulitzer Prize Board at Columbia University.

Ramon Magsaysay Award

The Raman Magsaysay Award, named after a Philippines President, who died in an air crash in 1957, is given annually to Asian nationals or institutions who have made worthy contributions to public service, community leadership, journalism, literature and the creative arts and international understanding. It carries a gold medal, a certificate and US$ 50,000. It is awarded on August 31, every year.

Mahatma Gandhi Peace Prize

This award, which carries an amount of ₹ 1 crore and a citation, was instituted by the Government of India in 1994, during the 125th birth anniversary celebrations of Mahatma Gandhi. The first person to receive this award in 1995, was Dr. Julius K. Nyerere, former President of Tanzania.

Jawaharlal Nehru Award for International Understanding

The Government of India instituted the Jawaharlal Nehru Award for International Understanding in 1965 as a tribute to the memory of the late Prime Minister for his lifelong dedication to the cause of world peace and international understanding. The award, which is given away annually to an eminent person for outstanding contribution towards the promotion of international understanding, goodwill and friendship among the people of the world, carries an amount of ₹ 25 lakh (convertible into foreign currency) and a citation. The award is administered by the Indian Council for Cultural Relations and is made by a seven-member independent jury which includes the Vice-President and the Chief Justice of India.

Man Booker Prize

Instituted in 1968, it is the highest literary award set up by the Booker Company and the British Publishers Association along the lines of the Pultizer Prize, of USA, worth £ 20,000 (1992). Since 2002, it has been known as the 'Man Booker Prize', reflecting the sponsorship by an investment company, the Man Group plc. The winner receives £ 50,000 and both the winner and the shorlisted authors are guaranteed a world wide readership plus a dramatic increase in book sales.

Templeton Award

Instituted in 1972, this award is conferred by the Templeton Foundation for progress in religion. It was inaugurated in 1972 by John M. Templeton, a presbyterian of Nassau Bahamas. The prize is a sum in amount of £ 795,000 Sterling, more than $1.4 million, and it is the world's largest annual monetary prize given to an individual.

Right Livelihood Award

Instituted in 1980, by Jakob Von Uexkull, a Swedish-German writer and philatetic expert after selling his stamp collection. This award is known as the 'Alternative Nobel Prize'. The Pro-ecology Right Livelihood Society, based in Britain's Isle of Man, but with a staff in Stockholm, awards this prize annually for practical and exemplary solutions to real problems of today. Earlier, India received this coveted award in 1987 for the 'Chipko' movement.

Oscar Awards

The annual Oscar presentation has been held since 1929. After three-quarters of a century of recognizing excellence in cinema achievement, the annual presentation of the Oscars has become the Academy of Motion Picture Arts and Sciences' most famous activity.

World Food Prize

The Prize recognizes contributions in any field involved in the world food supply — food and agriculture science and technology, manufacturing, marketing, nutrition, economics, poverty alleviation, political leadership and the social sciences. The prize was created in 1986 by Nobel Peace Prize Laureate Norman Borlaug and since 1990 has been sponsored by business man and Philanthropist John Ruan.

Grammy Awards

The Grammy Foundation was established in 1989 to cultivate an awareness, appreciation and advancement of the contribution of recorded music. The Grammy Foundation works in partnership with its founder, the Recording Academy, to bring national attention to important issues such as the value and impact of music and arts education and the urgency of preserving our rich cultural legacy.

Sydney Peace Prize

The Sydney Peace Prize is the only International Peace Prize awarded in Australia. This Prize has global significance in terms of the support and recognition given to leaders for peace.

Goldman Environmental Prize

The Goldman Environmental prize is the world's largest prize program honouring grass roots environmentalists and is known as the noble prize for environment. Awards are given to activists in six regions-Africa, Asia, Europe, Island Nation, North America and South/Central America and each recipient receives $ 25,000.

International Simon Bolivar Prize

The purpose of the International Simon Bolivar Prize is stated in its statutes as being to reward activity of outstanding merit which, in accordance with the ideals of Simon Bolivar, has contributed to the freedom, independence and dignity of people.

Highest Honours of Some Countries

Country	*Highest Honour*
India	Bharat Ratna
Pakistan	Nishan-e-Pakistan
Kuwait	Mubarak-Al-kabir Medal
Saudi Arabia	Shah Abdul Aziz Medal
Argentina	The Order of Sona Martin
Nicaragua	Augusto-Caesar Sandino Order
Vietnam	The order of the Golden Star
Hungary	The Order of Banner
Britain	Member of British Empire, Victoria Cross
Japan	Order of Moulovenice Sun
Denmark	Order of Diana Brog
France	Legend of Honour
America	Presidential Medal of Freedom
Germany	Pore Lee Merit Iron Cross
The Netherlands	Netherlands Lion

* * * * *

14

Sports

Important Cups & Trophies

International

• *American Cup*	:	Yacht Racing	• *Walker Cup*	:	Golf
• *Ashes*	:	Cricket	• *Westchester Cup*	:	Polo
• *Benson and Hedges*	:	Cricket	• *Wightman Cup*	:	Lawn Tennis
• *Canada Cup*	:	Golf	• *World Cup*	:	Cricket
• *Colombo Cup*	:	Football	• *World Cup*	:	Hockey
• *Corbitton Cup*	:	Table Tennis (Women)	• *Reliance Cup*	:	Cricket
• *Davis Cup*	:	Lawn Tennis	• *Rothman's Trophy*	:	Cricket
• *Derby*	:	Horse Race	• *William's Cup*	:	Basketball
• *Grand National*	:	Horse Streple Chase Race	• *European Champions Cup*	:	Football
• *Jules Rimet Trophy*	:	World Soccer Cup	• *Eisenhower Cup*	:	Golf
• *King's Cup*	:	Air Races	• *Essande Champions Cup*	:	Hockey
• *Merdeka Cup*	:	Football	• *Rene Frank Trophy*	:	Hockey
• *Ryder Cup*	:	Golf	• *Grand Prix*	:	Table Tennis
• *Swaythling Cup*	:	Table Tennis (Men)	• *Edgbaston Cup*	:	Lawn Tennis
• *Thomas Cup*	:	Badminton	• *Grand Prix*	:	Lawn Tennis
• *Uber Cup*	:	Badminton (Women)	• *World Cup*	:	Weightlifting
• *U. Thant Cup*	:	Tennis			

National

• *Agarwal Cup*	:	Badminton	• *Dhyan Chand Trophy*	:	Hockey
• *Agha Khan Cup*	:	Hockey	• *Dr. B.C. Roy Trophy*	:	Football (Junior)
• *All India Women's Guru Nanak Championship*	:	Hockey	• *Ezra Cup*	:	Polo
• *Bandodkar Trophy*	:	Football	• *F.A. Cup*	:	Football
• *Bangalore Blues Challenge Cup*	:	Basketball	• *G.D. Birla Trophy*	:	Cricket
• *Barna-Bellack Cup*	:	Table Tennis	• *Ghulam Ahmed Trophy*	:	Cricket
• *Beighton Cup*	:	Hockey	• *Gurmeet Trophy*	:	Hockey
• *Bombay Gold Cup*	:	Hockey	• *Guru Nanak Cup*	:	Hockey
• *Burdwan Trophy*	:	Weightlifting	• *Gyanvati Devi Trophy*	:	Hockey
• *Charminar Trophy*	:	Atheletics	• *Holkar Trophy*	:	Bridge
• *Chadha Cup*	:	Badminton	• *Irani Trophy*	:	Cricket
• *C.K. Naidu Trophy*	:	Cricket	• *I.F.A. Shield*	:	Football
• *Chakola Gold Trophy*	:	Football	• *Indira Gold Cup*	:	Hockey
• *Divan Cup*	:	Badminton	• *Jawaharlal Challenge*	:	Air Racing
• *Deodhar Trophy*	:	Cricket	• *Jaswant Singh Trophy*	:	Best Services Sportsman
• *Duleep Trophy*	:	Cricket	• *Kuppuswamy Naidu Trophy*	:	Hockey
• *D.C.M. Cup*	:	Football	• *Lady Rattan Tata Trophy*	:	Hockey
• *Durand Cup*	:	Football	• *MCC Trophy*	:	Hockey
			• *Moinuddaula Gold Cup*	:	Cricket
			• *Murugappa Gold Cup*	:	Hockey
			• *Modi Gold Cup*	:	Hockey

- *Narang Cup* : Badminton
- *Nehru Trophy* : Hockey
- *Nixan Gold Cup* : Football
- *Obaidullah Gold Cup* : Hockey
- *Prithi Singh Cup* : Polo
- *Rani Jhansi Trophy* : Cricket
- *Ranji Trophy* : Cricket
- *Rangaswami Cup* : Hockey
- *Ranjit Singh Gold Cup* : Hockey
- *Rajendra Prasad Cup* : Tennis
- *Ramanujan Trophy* : Table Tennis
- *Rene Frank Trophy* : Hockey
- *Radha Mohan Cup* : Polo
- *Raghbir Singh Memorial* : Football
- *Rohinton Baria Trophy* : Cricket
- *Rovers Cup* : Football
- *Sanjay Gold Cup* : Football
- *Santosh Trophy* : Football
- *Sir Ashutosh Mukherjee* : Football
- *Subroto Cup* : Football
- *Scindia Gold Cup* : Hockey
- *Sahni Trophy* : Hockey
- *Sheesh Mahal Trophy* : Cricket
- *Todd Memorial Trophy* : Football
- *Tommy Eman Gold Cup* : Hockey
- *Vittal Trophy* : Football
- *Vizzy Trophy* : Cricket
- *Vijay Merchant Trophy* : Cricket
- *Wellington Trophy* : Rowing
- *Wills Trophy* : Cricket

Sports Measurements

- *Badminton Courts:* 44 ft. by 20 ft. (doubles) 44 ft. by 17 ft. (singles)
- *Boxing Ring:* 12 ft. by 28 ft. Sq.
- *Cricket Pitch:* 22 yards (distance)
- *Derby Course:* 1½ miles. (2.4 km)
- *Football Field:*
  (a) Length : 100 – 120 yards.
  [Breadth: 50 – 56 yards.
  (b) Rugby : 100 yards by 75 yards
- *Hockey Ground:* 100 yards by 55 to 60 yards
- *Lawn Tennis Court:* 78 ft. by 36 ft. (double), 78 ft. by 28 ft. (single)
- *Marathon Race:* 26 miles, 385 yards
- *Polo Ground:* 300 yards by 200 yards (if boarded)
- *Golf:* Hole 4½ inches in diameter.

Sports Terms

- **Badminton:** Mixed doubles; Deuce; Drop; Smash; Let; Foot work; Setting.
- **Base Ball:** Pitcher; Put out, Strike; Home; Bunt.
- **Billiards:** Cue; Jigger; Pot; Break; In Baulk; In Off; Cannons.
- **Boxing:** Upper cut; Round; Punch; Bout; Knock down; Hitting below the belt; Ring.
- **Bridge:** Finesse; Dummy; Revoke; Grand Slam; Little Slam; No Trump; Rubber.
- **Chess:** Bishop, Gambit; Checkmate; Stalemate.
- **Cricket:** L.B.W. *(leg before wicket)*; Creases, Popping-creases; Stumped; Bye; Leg-Bye; Googly; Hattrick; Maiden over; Drive; Bowling; Duck; Follow-on; No ball; Leg Break; Silly point; Cover point; Hit-wicket; Late-cut; Slip; Off-spinner; In-swing.
- **Football:** Off Side; Block; Drop-kick; Penalty-kick (or *goal kick*); Corner-kick; Free-kick; Dribble; Thrown-in; Foul.
- **Golf:** Boggy; Foursome; Stymic; Tee; Put; Hole; Niblic; Caddie; Links; The green; Bunker.
- **Hockey:** Carried; Short Corner; Bully; Sticks; Off side; Roll in; Striking Circle; Under-cutting; Dribble.
- **Horse racing:** Jockey; Punter.
- **Polo:** Bunker; Chukker; Mallet.
- **Tennis:** Back hand drive; Volley; Smash; Half-volley; Deuce; Service; Let; Grand Slam.

Name of Playing Compound of Different Games

Name of Compound	*Related Sports*	*Name of Compound*	*Related Sports*
Court	Lawn Tennis, Badminton, Netball, Hand ball, Volleyball, Squash, Kho-Kho, Kabaddi	Pool	Swimming
		Alley	Bowling
		Mat	Judo, Karate II
		Arena	Horse Riding
Diamond	Baseball	Vellodrum	Cycling
Ring	Boxing, Skating, Wrestling, Circus, Riding display	Field	Polo, Football, Hockey
		Track	Athletics
Course	Golf	Pitch	Cricket, Rugby
Board	Table Tennis	Rink	Ice Hockey

Number of Players in Some Games/Sports

Sports	No. of Players	Sports	No. of Players	Sports	No. of Players
Badminton	1 or 2	Cricket	11	Football (Rugby)	15
Baseball	9	Croquest	13 or 15	Table	1 or
Basketball	5	Football (Soccer)	11	Tennis	2
Billiards (Snooker)	1	Hockey	11	Lawn	1 or
Boxing	1	Lacrosse	12	Tennis	2
Bridge	2	Netball	7	Volleyball	6
Chess	1	Polo Rugby	4	Water Polo	7

OLYMPIC GAMES

First of all these games were held by the Greeks in 776 B.C. on Mount Olympus in honour of the Greek God Zeus. In this way, the history of Olympic Games is about twenty eight hundred years old.

These games continued to be held every four years until 394 A.D. When these games were stopped by a royal order of the emperor of Rome. The modern Olympic Games which started in Athens in 1896, are the result of the devotion and dedication of a French educator Baron Pierre de Coubertin and the first Olympic meet in the modern series was held in 1896 in Athens, the Capital of Greece. Since then, they are being held every four years except for breaks during world wars.

The Olympic flag is white in colour with five coloured rings, each ring symbolic of a continent. Summer as well as winter Olympics are held in the same year.

ASIAN GAMES

After the Second World War, most of the Asian Countries gained independence. On the lines of Olympic Games, Asian Games were planned every four years. India hosted the first Asian Games in 1951.

COMMONWEALTH GAMES

The Commonwealth Games are held every four years, in the year in which Asian Games are held. All the Commonwealth Countries (former colonies of Britain) can take part in it. The first Commonwealth Games were held in 1930 at Hamilton (Canada).

CRICKET WORLD CUP

The first Cricket World Cup was organised in England in 1975. A separate women's Cricket World Cup has been held every 4 years since 1973. Australia is the winner of 2023 Cricket World Cup.

HOCKEY WORLD CUP

The first Hockey World Cup was organised in Barcelona (Spain) in 1971. Women's Hockey World Cup has been held since 1974.

FOOTBALL WORLD CUP

The Football World Cup is organised by FIFA (Federation of International Football Association). The World Cup is called 'Jules Rimet Cup' named after the name of FIFA President Jules Rimet. The first Football World Cup was organised in Uruguay in 1930.

Stadia in Various Cities of India

- **Delhi:** Ambedkar Stadium, Arun Jaitley Stadium, Jawaharlal Nehru Stadium, Indira Gandhi Indoor Stadium, Shivaji Stadium, National Stadium.
- **Mumbai:** Brabourne Stadium, Wankhede Stadium.
- **Kolkata:** Eden Gardens, Salt Lake Stadium, Ranjit Stadium, Subhas Sarovar.
- **Chennai:** Nehru Stadium, Chidambaram Stadium, Chepauk.
- **Cuttack:** Barabati Stadium.
- **Kanpur:** Green Park.
- **Jamshedpur:** Keenan Stadium.
- **Nagpur:** Vidarbha CA Ground
- **Jaipur:** Swai Mansingh Stadium
- **Gwalior:** Roop Singh Stadium
- **Pune:** Nehru Stadium
- **Vadodara:** Moti Bagh Stadium
- **Patna:** Moin-ul-Haq Stadium
- **Hyderabad:** Lal Bahadur Stadium
- **Patiala:** Yaduvindra Stadium.
- **Bengaluru:** Chinnaswami Stadium.
- **Siliguri:** Kanchenjunga Stadium.
- **Faridabad:** Mayur Stadium.
- **Vishakhapatnam:** Indira Priyadarshini Stadium.

✱✱✱✱✱

15

Computer

The computer is the system of that electronic device through which various informations are processed on the basis of a definite set of instructions called program and mathematical (numerical) and non-mathematical both types of informations are processed. The first mechanical computer was composed or fabricated by Blaise Pascal in 1642 and it is called Pascalene. But in 1833, Charles Babbage first time conceived an automatic calculator or computer. Charles Babbage is called the father of modern computer. Herman made an electronic tabulating machine based on punch cards which operates automatically. In 1937, first mechanical computer mark-I was fabricated by Howard Akeen. The most outstanding contribution in the development of modern computer goes to John Wan Newmaan who brought the 2nd revolution in the area of computer in 1951. He discovered EDVAC (Electronic Discrete Variable Automatic Computer) and utilised the stored program and the binary number system in the computer.

Functions of Computer

1. Collection and composition (input) of datas;
2. Storage of datas.
3. Processing of datas.
4. Retrieval or output of the proccessed informations and datas.

Units of Computer

1. Input unit.
2. Central processing unit–CPU.
3. External Memory unit.
4. Output unit.

The CPU of the computer is called brain of the computer and sometimes CPU is also called Micro Processor of the computer. The data is entered through the input unit in the computer and through the central processing unit with the help of External Memory Unit datas are arranged and processed. Ultimately by the output unit these datas or informations are issued or released.

Parts of Computer

- **Monitor :** The monitor of the computer is like a television in which the picture appears in the form of doted points on the screen and these are called pixcels.
- **Hard Disc and Floppy Disc :** The Hard Disc is the permanent disc in the computers while the Floppy Disc is the disc utilised when datas or informations are to be transferred from one computer to another.
- **Mouse :** The mouse of the computer is like the remote control of TV through which computer is directly regulated or controlled without utilising the key-board.
- **Printer :** The printer is a device which prints any documents or processed informations of the computer.

Some high level languages

- **FORTRAN :** This language was developed for solving the mathematical formulae very quickly and conveniently.
- **COBOL :** This language was developed for the commerical purposes. For the processing of this language a group of sentences is selected called paragraph and all paragraphs composed are called a section, while all sections composed are called a division.
- **BASIC :** In basic a definite part of the prescribed instruction is only inserted in the computer.
- **ALGOL :** This was basically fabricated and designed for the complex algebraic calculations.
- **PASCAL :** It is an amplified and modified form of ALGOL.
- **COMAL :** This computer language is used for the students of secondary level.
- **LOGO :** This language is used for children and kids for drawing Graphic line diagrams.

- **PROLOG :** This language is developed in 1973 in France and this language is used for Artificial Intelligence which is capable and equivalent to the logical program.
- **FORTH :** This language was invented by Charles Mure which is frequently used in all types of the works in the computer.

Computer Virus

The computer virus is an electronic code which is used to abolish or erradicate the inclusive informations or programs of the computer. Some important computer viruses are Micheleanjalo, Dork Avangor, kilo, filip, Macmug, Scores, Casecade, Jeruslem, Date crime, Coloumbs crime, Internet virus, Pachcom, Pach EXE, COM-EXE, Marizuana, C-brain, bloody, Chenge Mungu and Desi etc.

Computer Networking

There are two types of networkings which are usually occur— Local Area Networking (LAN) and Wide Area Networking (WAN). By LAN all the computers of the same buildings are connected like the computers of university premises, computers of offices etc. By WAN all the comptuers of a large area are connected like the computers of all the offices of a city or town etc. In India a very large computer network namely INDONET has been installing through which all the main towns and cities has to be interlinked.

Computer Terminology

- **Bit :** The bit is a unit of measurement of the electronic data. One bit is either 0 or 1 but not both. On composing 8 bits, 1 byte is formed.
- **Bug :** The Bug is the error in the computer program or system and its eradication is called Debug.
- **Byte :** Total eight bits compose a byte. Thus 8 bits = 1 byte.
- **CD-ROM :** A CD like of music CD in which data can be stored substantially called CD-ROM. In a CD with comparison to floppy extremely more datas can be stored but one problem in it is that one time recorded data can not be deleted or modified.
- **Chip :** It is a thin slice on which by a special mechanism a circuit is designed which is normally made from Silicon.
- **Memory System :** The place where computer data and program are temporarily kept is called Memory system. Usually memory is implied from RAM.
- **Modem :** The device which converts digital signals into analogue signals and vice-versa is called Modem.
- **RAM :** It is Random Access Memory (a place) where datas to be processed are kept temporarily and it is unstable memory.
- **ROM :** It is Read Only Memory and it is stable or Non-valatile memory which doesn't ended after power off.
- **Scanner :** It is a device through which graphic image is transformed to digital image and the scanners are of usually two types one desktop and another hand operating.

Programing

Computers perform phenomenal feats of calculation, but they do not do so in a complicated way. They actually carry out very simple operations, such as addition and subtraction. They achieve their fantastic computing power by carrying out these operations at incredible speed.

The programme, or set of instructions for operating the computer, is therefore written as a sequence of very simple steps. (See box below) Several computer languages have been developed for different applications, including BASIC, COBOL, FORTRAN and PASCAL.

Writing programmes is very skilled and time-consuming work. But for most typical computer applications ready-written programmes are available, called "packages".

* * * * *

Multiple Choice Questions

GENERAL AWARENESS

1. The part of the Sun, which is visible during eclipses only, is known as
A. photosphere
B. chromosphere
C. corona
D. all the parts are visible with naked eye
2. Sphygmomanometer is used for
A. measuring the brain pulse of a patient
B. measuring the systolic and diastolic blood pressures of man
C. measuring the amount of blood in a human body
D. measuring the haemoglobin count in a human body
3. The most abundant gas in air is
A. nitrogen B. hydrogen
C. oxygen D. ozone
4. The most commonly found acid in nature is
A. hydrochloric acid B. sulphuric acid
C. lactic acid D. acetic acid
5. This bomb is used to destroy living beings but would not damage the buildings and other property
A. napalm bomb B. neutron bomb
C. hydrogen bomb D. None of the above
6. Electrical energy is measured in terms of units which are also termed as
A. KW B. KWH
C. WH D. KVAR
7. In cold countries, the radiator water of cars is mixed with glycerol. This is done to
A. increase the specific heat of water
B. reduce the freezing point of water
C. improve the engine efficiency
D. glycerol is not added in radiator water
8. If the Richter scale shows a value of 7.2, then the seismograph indicates
A. an earthquake of low intensity
B. an earthquake of very high intensity
C. an earthquake of moderate intensity
D. either A or C
9. The theory of origin of species is based primarily on
A. the process of biological evolution
B. the process of natural selection
C. the evolution of life from the oceans
D. the evolution of man from apes
10. Common coal used in our households is
A. Anthracite B. Bituminous coal
C. Lignite D. All of the above
11. Some recent findings on moon, which point out towards the possibility of settlement of man on moon, include
A. nil atmospheric gases
B. ice reserves on the poles
C. micro-organisms
D. None of the above
12. Viagra is a medicine for
A. treatment of AIDS
B. treatment of female fertility
C. treatment of male impotency
D. treatment of Lukaemia
13. Rickets is a disease which is caused by the deficiency of
A. Vitamin A B. Riboflavin
C. Vitamin C D. Vitamin D
14. When a ship enters waters of the sea from a river, then its level
A. rises as the sea water is saline and hence bouyancy force is more
B. decreases as ocean is a large mass of water
C. remains the same as water is the same for the river and the sea
D. None of the above
15. The major constituent of pearl is
A. calcium carbonate
B. calcium oxide and ammonium chloride
C. organic mass
D. calcium carbonate and silica
16. A healthy person needs ..... calories per day.
A. 2200 B. 2400
C. 2500 D. 1800
17. The value of one (marine) Naut is
A. 1951 metre per hour
B. 1852 metre per hour
C. 2305 metre per hour
D. 1860 metre per hour

18. Acid and base combine to form
 A. salt and nitrogen
 B. nitrogen and oxygen
 C. salt and water
 D. acid and alkali
19. Cellulose could be obtained from
 A. wood and cotton B. silk and cotton
 C. paper and silk D. wood and silk
20. ELISA test is done for the detection of
 A. cancer B. AIDS
 C. diabetes D. None of the above
21. Triple Antigen, prevents
 A. small pox, malaria, whooping cough
 B. tetanus, diphtheria, small pox
 C. whooping cough, tetanus, polio
 D. diphtheria, tetanus, whooping cough
22. A freely falling body
 A. would fall towards the surface of the earth
 B. would have no weight
 C. would have one half of its original weight
 D. None of the above
23. If the motor neurons of the spinal cord of a child are damaged, then he would develop the following disease.
 A. Rickets B. Polio
 C. Diphtheria D. Jaundice
24. Which one of the following is not a part of the balanced diet?
 A. Vitamins B. Carbohydrate
 C. Proteins D. Alcohol
25. Which statement is not correct in connection with human physiology?
 A. The length of the small intestine is 7 metres and its diameter is 2.5 cm.
 B. There are 639 muscles in a human body
 C. An infant breathes 45 times per minute whereas a six year old child breathes 25 times per minute
 D. The weight of the adult human brain is nearly 700 gms
26. The bottles of beer are not kept in the deep freezer because
 A. beer is an alcohol which could burst under conditions of low temperature
 B. alcohol could damage the deep freezer due to its corrosive action if the bottles break accidently
 C. water content in beer gets converted into ice which expends (after change of state from water to ice) and this could lead to bursting of beer bottles
 D. the low temperature could degrade the beer and hence, it may not good remain for consumption
27. Rocket works on the basis of
 A. principle of conservation of momentum
 B. principle of relativity
 C. principle of conservation of mass
 D. principle of conservation of energy
28. Which one of the following groups is more closely related from the viewpoint of taxonomy?
 A. silverfish, starfish, cuttlefish
 B. earthworm, seahorse, hookworm
 C. housefly, dragonfly, butterfly
 D. None of the above
29. Red blood corpuscles are produced in
 A. liver B. spleen
 C. bone marrow D. kidneys
30. The disease for which the first oral drug has been developed for treatment.
 A. Cancer B. Pneumonid
 C. Small pox D. Plauge
31. E-comm is a short form of
 A. Engineering Commercial
 B. Electronic Commercial
 C. Electronic Commerce
 D. None of the above
32. High AC voltages are used for transmitting electric power because
 A. at high voltages, current is low and hence, losses are low
 B. the transmission of power is quicker
 C. the high voltages a consume lesser materials for transmission
 D. None of the above
33. There is a hole in the boat through which, water is seeping into the boat. Just before the boat capsizes
 A. water level would decrease
 B. water level would increase
 C. water level would remain the same
 D. None of the above
34. During which month, the rate of rotation of the earth on its axis is the fastest?
 A. December
 B. May
 C. the rate of rotation is fixed
 D. It is fastest when the earth is closest to the Sun.
35. The time taken by the Sun rays to reach the earth is
 A. 9 minutes B. 10 minutes
 C. 7 minutes D. 8 minutes
36. The outer planets are
 A. Moon, Earth, Mercury, Venus
 B. Jupiter, Saturn, Uranus, Earth, Mars
 C. Jupiter, Uranus, Saturn, Neptune
 D. None of the above
37. According to the astrophysicists
 A. the universe is mobile and expanding
 B. the universe is heading for a collision with another universe
 C. the universe is stationary
 D. the doomsday of universe is near due to the formation of many new black holes
38. Which is popular as the White City?
 A. New York B. Belgrade
 C. Bangalore D. Bab-el-mandab

39. The national currency of Haiti is
A. Rupiah B. Gourde
C. Quetzal D. Dong

40. Which one is not a news agency of India?
A. UNI
B. PTI
C. Hindustan Samachar
D. Reuters

41. The abundant element of the earth's atmosphere is:
A. Oxygen B. nitrogen
C. hydrogen D. CO_2

42. The first talking movie of India was ..... and the first silent movie of India was .....
A. Aan, Aawara
B. Raja Harish Chandra, Alamara
C. Alamara, Raja Harish Chandra
D. Purana Mandir, Raja Harish Chandra

43. Hair becomes grey because
A. rays of the Sun force it to become grey
B. the quantity of melanin is reduced in human body with growing age
C. there is a lack of vitamins in the body due to growing age
D. None of the above

44. Salaries of Supreme Court judges are drawn from:
A. Law Ministry Grants
B. Consolidated Fund of India
C. Home Ministry Grants
D. Parliamentary Grants

45. The term "Paper-gold" is associated with
A. deficit budgeting
B. loans from the World Bank
C. Special Drawing Rights (SDRs) from the IMF
D. None of the above

46. TRAI refers to
A. Terresteral Remote Sensing Authority of India
B. Telecommunication Research Authority of India
C. Transport Regulatory Authority of India
D. Telecom Regulatory Authority of India

47. NSDL is an organisation in India which
A. provides security to depositors
B. accepts deposits from recognised bodies
C. provides data security for on-line computer systems
D. None of the above

48. The enzyme pepsin converts
A. proteins into peptones
B. fats to amino acids
C. carbohydrates to sugars
D. proteins to amino acids

49. Who among the following is not a winner of the PVC?
A. Bana Singh
B. Nirmal Jeet Singh Sekhon
C. Somnath Sharma
D. Shanti Swaroop Rana

50. Which one of the following pairs is not correct?
A. Narmada – Betul district
B. Krishna – near Mahabaleshwar
C. Chambal – near Mhow
D. Godavari – Nashik district

51. The Japanese art of flower arrangement is known as
A. Bonsai B. Ongami
C. Ikebota D. None of the above

52. The meaning of the Latin word *Vive Rex* is
A. Long live the king!
B. Let the Nation Live
C. A middle course
D. Nothing wrong here

53. The permanent station of India in Antarctica is known as
A. *Vikalp* B. Antarctica India Station
C. *Maitri* D. *Dakshin Yamunotri*

54. A man dies due to electrocution because
A. electric current passes through his body to earth which leads to sudden contraction and expansion of muscles (including heart muscles) and this, alongwith development of heat in the body, leads to heart failure.
B. there is no resistance offered by the body
C. the body allows the current to flow through the blood which cannot circulate any longer
D. None of the above

55. "Blue Dwarfs" are
A. members of the Russian circus
B. warriors of Mongolia
C. young stars of the universe
D. naval officers in the high seas

56. What is a fly leaf?
A. thin paper sheet for making packaging material
B. a blank page at the beginning or end of a book
C. a marker in a book
D. a sheet of paper next to the main title of the book

57. Who is associated with the theory of inheritance of acquired characters?
A. Spencer B. Mandeleev
C. Lamarck D. All of the above

58. Ligaments and tendons in the body are made up of
A. skeletal tissue B. muscular tissue
C. connective tissue D. epithelial tissue

59. A cell membrane is
A. completely permeable
B. impermeable
C. semi-permeable
D. None of the above

60. The tenure of the non-permanent members of the UN Security Council is
A. one year B. three years
C. two years D. there is no fixed tenure

61. Why proper earthing is necessary?
A. It reduces the consumption of electricity

B. It allows the current to flow through the earth wire and into the earth, thus protecting the person
C. It allows the appliance to operate efficiently
D. None of the above

62. Which one of the following items has not been included in the minimum needs programme?
A. unemployment allowance
B. rural water supply
C. rural electrification
D. adult education

63. This is not the principle organ of digestion and absorption in the human body.
A. small intestine B. stomach
C. large intestine D. Both A and B

64. Which are the two stars which appear as morning stars in the Eastern sky and evening stars in the Western sky?
A. Jupiter and Mars
B. Mars and Venus
C. Saturn and Mercury
D. Mercury and Venus

65. Which planet rotates on its axis from East to West?
A. Mercury B. Jupiter
C. Earth D. Venus

66. The chemical compound present in the stone of human kidney is
A. calcium phosphate B. calcium carbonate
C. silica D. calcium oxalate

67. Which one of the following diseases would be caused by bacterial infection?
A. tetanus B. rabies
C. cancer D. malaria

68. India On-line Limited is
A. an advertising agency
B. a reservation office
C. an information service
D. an internet services provider

69. CTBT is related to
A. economic sanctions imposed by the USA on India
B. the codename of Pokharan-II blasts
C. the nuclear test ban treaty which India is being forced to adhere to
D. codename of Pakistani nuclear arsenal

70. The disagreement between Lok Sabha and Rajya Sabha is solved by:
A. setting up Joint Select Committee
B. dissolving Lok Sabha
C. setting up adjudication committee
D. calling a joint session

71. The national anthem was written by ..... and was translated into English by .....
A. Bankim Chandra Chatterji, Aurobindo Ghosh
B. Rabindra Nath Tagore, Aurobindo Ghosh
C. Bankim Chandra Chatterji, Rabindra Nath Tagore
D. the national anthem was originally written in English and was translated later

72. The tear in human body is a solution of :
A. Sodium hydroxide and sodium chloride
B. Calcium bicarbonate and sodium chloride
C. Magnesium bicarbonate and sodium hydroxide
D. Sodium bicarbonate and Magnesium chloride

73. The drug seroxat is
A. a new medicine for treating the lepers.
B. a new medicine developed by British scientists and is used for the treatment of shyness and social phobia
C. is anti-AIDS therapy developed by France
D. is an antacid developed in India under guidance of WHO

74. What is "Bermuda Triangle" sometimes referred to as the "Grakeyard of ships", located?
A. in the South Pacific ocean
B. in the North Atlantic ocean
C. in the Indian ocean
D. in the Arctic ocean

75. The theory propounded by Nobel laurate Professor Amartya Sen–is commonly known as
A. The Famine Economics
B. The Theory of Economic Divide
C. The Amartya Sen Shift
D. The Amartya Sen Divide

76. Which is known as the Electronics City of India?
A. Tumkoor B. Secunderabad
C. Bhopal D. None of the above

77. The main objective behind the creation of concept of *Navratnas* in the public sector was
A. to increase the control of the PSUs over economy
B. to boost local manufacturing and exports in the core sectors
C. to improve the functional autonomy
D. to improve their image and efficiency by giving them high status

78. The North American seaport on the Pacific side is
A. Baltimore B. Boston
C. New York D. Seattle

79. The old name of Harare was
A. Sam B. Rhodesia
C. Salisbury D. Batavia

80. The famous Prince of Wales Museum is located in
A. Mumbai B. Kolkata
C. Vadodara D. Bangalore

81. Who invented Atom Bomb (Uranium Fission)?
A. A W Haffmann B. Otto Hahn
C. A Einstein D. None of the above

82. The first ever woman to go into space was
A. Kalpana Chawla B. Valentina Tereshkova
C. Mary Pierce D. None of the above

83. The highest mountain peak in India is
A. K-2 B. Everest
C. Kanchanjunga D. Makalu-I

84. The "Garden City" of England is
A. Portsmouth B. Manchester
C. Kent D. Warwickshire

85. *Habeas Corpus* is
A. an order of the International Court of Justice
B. a type of writ issued by a High Court or Supreme Court against illegal detention of a person.
C. the petition of a lawyer in the Supreme Court on behalf of his client for bail against the orders of any other court in India
D. None of the above

86. If impeachment motion is passed by the American Senate against the US President, he would have to
A. leave office and all his assets created by him during Presidency
B. leave office, lose his pensions, security cover and all those benefits that are accorded to a retired US President
C. jailed for five years and will not get any benefits.
D. retire honourably with all his benefits, compensations, assets and pensions remaining intact

87. Who appoints the non-permanent members of the UN Security Council?
A. the permanent members
B. the General Assembly
C. the International Court of Justice
D. None of the above

88. The Preamble of the Constitution was amended by:
A. 1st amendment B. 26th amendment
C. 42nd amendment D. 44th amendment

89. Angora wool is extracted from which of the following animals?
A. Sheep B. Goat
C. Rabbit D. Fox

90. The official airline of Australia is
A. SIA B. Lufthansa
C. Modiluft D. None of the above

91. Which one of the following types of coal contains a higher percentage of carbon than the rest?
A. Bituminous Coal B. Lignite
C. Anthracite D. Peat

92. Ten Commandments were revealed by God to:
A. Abraham B. Moses
C. Jesus D. Peter

93. Kalinga in older days, is now known as:
A. Odisha B. Kohima
C. Karnataka D. Maharashtra

94. Bihu festival is celebrated in:
A. Gujarat B. Assam
C. Bihar D. West Bengal

95. Milk is an example of
A. gel B. emulsion
C. suspension D. mixture

96. The President can dissolve the Lok Sabha before expiry of its term, on the advice of:
A. Prime Minister B. Speaker
C. Vice-President D. Election Commissioner

97. In a landmark judgement, the Allahabad High Court ruled that
A. Capital Sentence is not to be imposed upon the rapists
B. pension is the fundamental right of the government employees
C. the Supreme Court should not be bothered for cases of financial compensation
D. None of the above

98. Tughlaq dynasty occupied Delhi throne after decline of:
A. Suri dynasty B. Slave dynasty
C. Lodhi dynasty D. Khilji dynasty

99. Governors of states are:
A. appointed by Chief Ministers
B. appointed by the President
C. elected by members of Legislative Assembly
D. elected by people

100. The partition of Bengal was carried out by:
A. Lord Curzon B. Lord Minto
C. Lord Canning D. Lord Ripon

101. The Air Force Day falls on
A. October 10 B. October 9
C. September 5 D. October 8

102. MAD stands for
A. Most Active Disease
B. Mica Aluminium Duo
C. Mutually Assured Death
D. Mutually Assured Destruction

103. "Disguised Unemployment" means
A. more persons employed for a job that only a few could accomplish
B. people without any technical jobs
C. woman without jobs in rural areas
D. employment of children in factories

104. In India, an active volcano is situated at
A. Lakshadweep
B. Chhotanagpur Plateau
C. Andaman and Nicobar
D. Malawa Plateau

105. The first country to establish trade relationships with India was
A. England B. France
C. The Netherlands D. Portugal

106. Which has the highest share of electrical power generation in India?
A. thermal power
B. nuclear power
C. hydro-power
D. naphtha-based and gas-based power

107. The great ocean liner, known to be the best and luxurious during her times, sank in the year

A. 1902 B. 1912
C. 1908 D. 1889

108. Who among the following is known as the Indian Napoleon?
A. Chandra Gupta Maurya
B. Bindusar
C. Samudra Gupta
D. Harshvardhana

109. Time gap between two sessions of Parliament cannot exceed:
A. 3 months B. 6 months
C. 1 year D. no fixed gap

110. In which state, Panchayati Raj was introduced for the first time?
A. Bihar B. Punjab
C. Rajasthan D. Andhra Pradesh

111. Which one is not a national duty?
A. Respect the Constitution
B. Respect the President
C. Defend the country
D. Protect natural environment

112. Treaty of Seringapatam was signed between:
A. Tipu Sultan and Nawab of Hyderabad
B. Tipu Sultan and English
C. Tipu Sultan & Rani of Jhansi
D. Tipu Sultan and French

113. NHRC stands for
A. National Hydro Research Committee
B. National Handicapped Rahabilitation Council
C. National Human Rights Commission
D. None of the above

114. "Water wàter everywhere but not a drop to drink" who stated these lines in a poem?
A. John Milton
B. Samuel Taylor Coleridge
C. Lord Byron
D. P.B. Shelley

115. Rabindranath Tagore gave up his knighthood after:
A. Jallianwala Bagh Tragedy
B. Introduction of separate electorates
C. Bengal faminine
D. Bengal Partition

116. Which country is known as the land of golden wool?
A. India B. Turkey
C. Australia D. Myanmar

117. BIFR stands for
A. Bilateral and International Foreign Regulation
B. Board of Industrial Financial Resurrection
C. Board of Industrial and Financial Reconstruction
D. None of the above

118. Pinaca is a
A. drug for curing AIDS
B. multi-barrel rocket system
C. fighter aircraft developed by HAL
D. codename of the nuclear test operation carried out on May 11, 1998

119. Vice-President is ex-officio:
A. Member of Rajya Sabha
B. Chairman of Rajya Sabha
C. Member of Lok Sabha
D. Speaker of Lok Sabha

120. Vitamin C is not available in this food in sufficiently large quantities.
A. lemon B. tomato
C. cod liver oil D. fresh fruits

121. This book was not written in a jail
A. *Glimpses of World History* – J L Nehru
B. *The Bible* (German) – Martin Luther
C. *Les Miserables* – Victor Hugo
D. *Yama* – Mahadevi Verma

122. Who among the following can be removed from office through impeachment by Parliament?
A. Speaker of Lok Sabha
B. Prime Minister
C. President of India
D. Vice-President of India

123. The following is not the function of the liver.
A. to store excesssive sugar in the form of glycogen
B. the produce an antidote for neutralising poison
C. to manufacture red blood corpuscles
D. to purify the blood through bile

124. A fascist is a person whose views are extremely
A. left-winged B. rational
C. right-winged D. liberal

125. The famous mathematician and a professor of Astronomy designed this building in London
A. Westminister Abbey
B. St Paul's Cathedral
C. Stock Exchange
D. Tower of London

126. Which one of the following sounds cannot be heard by a human ear?
A. 30,000 vibrations per second
B. 10,000 vibrations per second
C. 1,000 vibrations per second
D. 300 vibrations per second

127. A weather balloon may not be inflated completely on the ground because
A. it cannot withstand the atmospheric pressure if inflated fully
B. if the balloon is inflated fully on ground, fuel consumption would be higher
C. the air inside the balloon expands as it rises and hence, the balloon could get burst
D. None of the above

128. Which one of the following vitamins is stored in the liver?
A. Vitamin C
B. Vitamin B_{12}
C. Vitamin A
D. Vitamin K and Vitamin A

129. All of the following are plant products except
A. silk B. cork
C. hemp D. linen

130. Which one of the following organs in the human body is known as "Adam's Apple?"
A. thyroid B. liver
C. thymus D. adrenal

131. Insecticides or medicines could be harmful
A. to the insects and weeds as they kill them instantaneously upon consumption
B. to the habitat as the environment could become polluted due to excessive usage of chemicals in our crop management processes
C. to the human beings and animals who consume the food adulterated by the insecticides and weedicides
D. to the transporters and movers of the crops who could inhale noxious fumes of insecticides and weedicides

132. Name the assassin of John Lennon
A. Art Buchwald
B. Lee Oswald
C. Mark David Chapman
D. None of the above

133. Which one of the following is not a sprinter?
A. Marion Jones
B. Florence Griffith Joyner
C. Ben Johnson
D. Susie O' Neill

134. Which of the following is called the "Gateway to the Pacific"?
A. Suez Canal B. Bering Sea
C. Panama Canal D. Gulf of Alaska

135. Which one of the following statements is true regarding the treaty on banning the landmines?
A. the USA does not want to sign the CTBT
B. the treaty was kept open for signatures in Ottawa in December, 1997.
C. India has already signed it
D. A and B are true

136. The Chief Election Commissioner can be removed by:
A. Prime Minister B. President
C. Supreme Court D. Parliament

137. The famous Gandhian, who was also known as the "Frontier Gandhi," is
A. Liaqat Ali Khan
B. Yusuf Khan
C. Khan Abdul Ghaffar Khan
D. Abdul Wali Khan

138. Which one of the following is an alloy?
A. copper B. lanthanum
C. bronze D. uranium

139. World Environment Day is celebrated on
A. June 4 B. June 5
C. June 7 D. March 5

140. This country is the largest producer of cotton in the world.
A. India B. China
C. Egypt D. the USA

141. Which is 'Country of Golden Fleece'?
A. Scotland B. Denmark
C. Australia D. Thailand

142. The temples of Khajuraho were built by
A. Chalukyas B. Pallavas
C. Rashtrakutas D. Chandelas

143. National Remote Sensing Agency (NRSA) is located at:
A. Hyderabad
B. Bangalore
C. Thiruvananthapuram
D. Gadanki, near Tirupati

144. The Tomb of Salim Chisti is built at:
A. Ajmer B. Nagaur
C. Lahore D. Fatehpur Sikri

145. AWWA stands for
A. All Women Welfare Association
B. Army Wives Welfare Association
C. Airport Weather and Welfare Authority
D. None of the above

146. The popular book *The Gift of Time* by Jonathan Schell, deals with
A. the lewid affair of Bill Clinton and Monica Lewinsky
B. the elimination of nuclear weapons from the world
C. Indo-US relationships
D. the deteriorating environment in industrial America

147. How can a person move on a hard icy surface?
A. he should use roller skates
B. he should hop, sneeze, jump and step in the direction which is opposite to the direction of his required movement
C. he should hop, sneeze, jump and step in the direction in which the movement is required
D. he should skid on his knees and hands

148. Which states are deriving benefits from the Tungbhadra project?
A. Tamil Nadu, Karnataka, Kerala
B. Tamil Nadu only
C. Andhra Pradesh and Tamil Nadu
D. Tamil Nadu, Andhra Pradesh, Karnataka

149. Solar Calendar based on 365 days was developed by ....
A. Greek B. Egyptian
C. Chinese D. Roman

150. Pyroclastics are
A. non-toxic gases
B. lava flows
C. fragments of hot rock and spattering lava
D. pollutant chemicals from a leather factory

151. Which one of the following is not a sedimentary rock?
A. slate B. limestone
C. clay D. sandstone

152. Oketa is
A. used to define human-induced climatic changes
B. used to describe increasing drought periods of high magnitudes
C. a unit to describe the prevailing cloudiness
D. None of the above

153. The following state produces the maximum quantities of raw silk in India
A. Kerala B. Jammu and Kashmir
C. Karnataka D. Tamil Nadu

154. Salal Hydro Electric Project is situated on the river
A. Beas B. Jhelum
C. Chenab D. Sutlej

155. Which is the largest island sea in the world?
A. Caribbean Sea B. Mediterranean Sea
C. Red Sea D. Beaufort Sea

156. What is the name of the bell used at the Lloyds in London?
A. The Great Bell B. The Charmer
C. The Tower Bell D. Lutine

157. What are "The Hagiographs?"
A. These are the poems written by Lord Byron
B. These are the holy writings of Jewish scriptures
C. These are the geographical lines representing same rainfall levels
D. None of the above

158. Which one of the following forms would provide the lowest protection?
A. Patent B. Trademark
C. Copyright D. Logo

159. The twenty-fifth State of India is
A. Goa B. Nagaland
C. Mizoram D. Delhi

160. What does the 17th Parallel line separate?
A. South and North America
B. North and South Korea
C. South and North Yemen
D. South and North Vietnam

161. Operation Flood-II, the prestigious milk products revolution of India, was initiated on
A. October 1, 1979 B. October 2, 1979
C. January 26, 1979 D. October 2, 1978

162. After World War I, the peace treaty was signed in:
A. Geneva B. Versailles
C. Paris D. Venice

163. Potassium chloride is given to the patient for
A. curing his bleeding gums
B. reducing his cholestrol level
C. reducing his blood pressure
D. alleviating his arthiritis pain

164. What is notation?
A. It is another word for "Mutually Assured Destruction"
B. It is the Latin deformation of the phrase "to swim"
C. It is a term used to denote the growth of illeterate masses
D. None of the above

165. The hideout of Adolf Hitler in the mountains was
A. Stuttgart B. Heidelberg
C. Berchtesgaden D. Both A and C

166. Who stated, "Where wealth accumulates decay?"
A. J M Keynes B. Adam Smith
C. Frederic Engels D. Oliver Goldsmith

167. Who was the national leader who wrote History of India on the walls of the Andaman Cellular Jail?
A. Ambedkar B. Vir Savarkar
C. Nandlal Bose D. Jyotiba Phule

168. The USA does not possess the following space shuttle
A. Columbia B. Atlantis
C. Challenger D. Discovery

169. The term "White Elephant" is used to denote
A. very bright and white item
B. very costly and expensive item
C. an item or a head that is very costly to maintain
D. an item or a head that is a part of the national economic budget of a country

170. Kolar Gold Mines are in this state.
A. Karnataka B. Bihar
C. Odisha D. Madhya Pradesh

171. Which is the morning star?
A. Pluto B. Venus
C. Neptune D. None of the above

172. Which one of the following is not an alkali?
A. sodium hydroxide
B. calcium carbonate
C. magnesium hydroxide
D. sodium sulphate

173. Polar ice is melting due to greenhouse effect. This would lead to
A. more melting of the polar glaciers and hence, subsequent submerging of land areas of earth
B. increasing temperatures on polar caps
C. reduction in temperature of ocean waters and rise in temperature of the Arctic circle waters as well as those of the Antartic circle waters
D. no impact

174. *India 2020* is a book written by
A. Trilok Gurtu
B. Khushwant Singh
C. P Chidambaram
D. A P J Abdul Kalaam

175. The Panama Canal connects:
A. The Pacific and Atlantic Oceans
B. The Pacific and Arctic Oceans
C. The Atlantic and Arctic Oceans
D. The Atlantic and Indian Oceans

176. The following are single cell structures
A. Paramaecium B. Amoebia
C. Both A and B D. None of A or B

177. 'The Last Supper' was painted by:
A. Picasso B. Francis Bacon
C. Michaelangelo D. Raphael

178. The plants, which can resist high temperatures, are known as
A. thermophilic B. thermophobic
C. thermoduric D. Both A and B

179. Which one of the following vaccines is used for controlling tuberculosis among the cattle?
A. Cell Culture Vaccine
B. Goat Tissue Adapted Vaccine
C. Adjuvant Vaccine
D. BCG Vaccine

180. Which one of the following chemicals is carcinogenic if inhaled?
A. carbon dioxide
B. suspended particulate matter
C. lead oxide
D. sulphur dioxide

181. What is a "Tenurial System?"
A. It is a system that identifies the ownership of land and the relationship of the land owner with the actual cultivator
B. It identities the land size and the *modus-operandi* of its usage
C. It identifies the ownership of the land
D. None of the above

182. Pulses are deficient in
A. methionine B. lysine
C. leusine D. iso-leusine

183. Which types of roses are grown in India for industrial applications?
A. R Centripetala and Bushra Rose
B. R Damascena Var Bifera
C. Rosa Damascena
D. A, B and C

184. Why sprinkler irrigation is preferred over other methods of irrigation?
A. It is a cheap method and does not require canal-digging and canal maintenance
B. It uses water effectively and water resolves are optimally utilised
C. It does not require well-digging measures which are costly
D. It supplies water only to those fields where the same is required

185. The size of clay particles is
A. greater than 0.2 mm
B. 0.02 mm – 0.2 mm
C. 0.002 mm – 0.02 mm
D. less than 0.002 mm

186. Which one of the following plants is of great medicinal value?
A. Ranwolfia Serpentiana
B. Thea Sinesis
C. Coffea Robusta
D. Ficus Religiosa

187. Biological control agents of soil borne plant pathogens act by
A. rapidly repleting nutrients and thereby, causing starvation and death of the pathogen
B. secreting toxic metabolitics
C. direct parastism or predation on the pathogens
D. All of the above

188. Nearly 80 percent of sugarcane in India is planted during
A. July – December B. May – August
C. June – August D. December – April

189. Soluble salt content of soil is determined by measuring its
A. pH Value
B. organic matter content
C. Sulphur content
D. electrical conductivity

190. Operation Flood is related to ..... whereas development of fisheries is related to .....
A. white revolution, black revolution
B. white revolution, blue revolution
C. green revolution, blue revolution
D. blue revolution, green revolution

191. An upper air wind system with very high velocities in certain parts of the atmosphere is called
A. Cyclone B. Anticyclone
C. Jet stream D. Tsunami

192. "Mixed Farming" refers to
A. farming by traditional and modern methods
B. agriculture and dairy farming clubbed together
C. farming without synthetic fertilisers but with traditional manure
D. farming with synthetic fertilisers and with traditional manure

193. The main constituent of *Gobar Gas* is
A. butane B. carbon monoxide
C. methane D. octane

194. Speed of sound waves is maximum in
A. solids B. liquids
C. gases D. vacuum

195. When a body gets positively charged, it actually
A. gains electrons
B. loses electrons
C. becomes a donor of ions
D. becomes a receptor of ions

196. Which type of nerves carries impulses from the sense organs in response to the stimulus?
A. sensory B. motor
C. secretory D. None of the above

197. Which gas does not pollute air (for human and animal consumption)?
A. carbon monoxide B. nitrogen dioxide
C. sulphur dioxide D. carbon dioxide

198. The human brain sends and receives signals as
- A. electrical impulses
- B. chemical impulses
- C. motor movements
- D. either A or B

199. "Foot and Mouth" disease attacks
- A. cattle
- B. pigs and cattle
- C. sheep and pigs
- D. cattle, sheep and pigs

200. While returning to earth, the spacecraft has a total communication blackout. The reason is
- A. during the re-entry period, the density of the plasma generated by the intense functional heat is so high that the operational frequencies used for communication become much lesser than the plasma cut-off frequency, thus resulting in a total blackout
- B. the electromagnetic waves present in the space above the earth temporarily overpower the communication system of the aircraft, thus completely crippling its operation and transmission
- C. the force of gravity counters the radiowaves emitted by the aircraft
- D. None of the above

ANSWERS

1	2	3	4	5	6	7	8	9	10
C	B	A	D	B	B	B	B	B	A
11	**12**	**13**	**14**	**15**	**16**	**17**	**18**	**19**	**20**
B	C	D	A	A	C	B	C	A	B
21	**22**	**23**	**24**	**25**	**26**	**27**	**28**	**29**	**30**
D	B	B	D	D	C	A	C	C	C
31	**32**	**33**	**34**	**35**	**36**	**37**	**38**	**39**	**40**
C	A	A	C	D	C	A	B	B	D
41	**42**	**43**	**44**	**45**	**46**	**47**	**48**	**49**	**50**
B	C	B	B	C	D	A	A	D	A
51	**52**	**53**	**54**	**55**	**56**	**57**	**58**	**59**	**60**
D	A	C	A	C	B	C	A	C	C
61	**62**	**63**	**64**	**65**	**66**	**67**	**68**	**69**	**70**
B	A	C	B	D	D	A	C	C	D
71	**72**	**73**	**74**	**75**	**76**	**77**	**78**	**79**	**80**
B	B	B	B	C	D	C	D	C	A
81	**82**	**83**	**84**	**85**	**86**	**87**	**88**	**89**	**90**
B	B	A	C	B	B	B	C	C	D
91	**92**	**93**	**94**	**95**	**96**	**97**	**98**	**99**	**100**
C	B	A	B	B	A	B	D	B	A
101	**102**	**103**	**104**	**105**	**106**	**107**	**108**	**109**	**110**
D	D	A	C	D	A	B	C	B	C
111	**112**	**113**	**114**	**115**	**116**	**117**	**118**	**119**	**120**
B	B	C	B	A	C	C	B	B	C
121	**122**	**123**	**124**	**125**	**126**	**127**	**128**	**129**	**130**
D	C	D	C	B	A	C	C	A	A
131	**132**	**133**	**134**	**135**	**136**	**137**	**138**	**139**	**140**
C	C	D	C	D	D	C	C	B	B
141	**142**	**143**	**144**	**145**	**146**	**147**	**148**	**149**	**150**
C	D	A	D	B	B	B	D	B	C
151	**152**	**153**	**154**	**155**	**156**	**157**	**158**	**159**	**160**
A	C	C	C	B	D	B	A	A	D
161	**162**	**163**	**164**	**165**	**166**	**167**	**168**	**169**	**170**
B	B	C	B	C	D	B	C	C	A
171	**172**	**173**	**174**	**175**	**176**	**177**	**178**	**179**	**180**
B	D	A	D	A	C	C	C	D	C
181	**182**	**183**	**184**	**185**	**186**	**187**	**188**	**189**	**190**
A	A	D	B	D	A	D	D	D	B
191	**192**	**193**	**194**	**195**	**196**	**197**	**198**	**199**	**200**
C	B	C	A	B	A	D	B	D	A

SPORTS

1. The first winning stroke in Lawn Tennis gives the player:
A. 2 points B. 1 point
C. 10 points D. 15 points

2. Which of the following game is played for stipulated period of 70 minutes?
A. Hockey B. Football
C. Rugby D. Basketball

3. Neeraj Chopra is associated with which game.
A. Polo B. Javelin Throw
C. Tennis D. Cricket

4. Arjuna Award has been instituted for outstanding contribution in the field of
A. Social Service B. Games and Sports
C. Literature D. Art and Music

5. Murugappa Gold Cup is associated with:
A. Football B. Polo
C. Hockey D. Bridge

6. Jimmy Connors and Geoff Boycott are related with following games respectively:
A. Tennis, Football
B. Tennis, Cricket
C. Chess, Cricket
D. Football, Hockey

7. Which of the following is the first Indian player to achieve 'Bharat Ratna'?
A. Marry Kom
B. Dhanraj Pillay
C. Sachin Tendulkar
D. Sunil Gavaskar

8. Which Indian player won gold medal in Tokyo Olympic–2020?
A. S. Mirabai Chanu B. Neeraj Chopra
C. P.V. Sindhu D. Manika Batra

9. The term 'Steeple Chase' is associated with which of the following games
A. Polo B. Tennis
C. Horse Racing D. Cricket

10. With which game is the term 'butterfly stroke' associated?
A. Swimming B. Cricket
C. Gliding D. Skiing

11. The first Olympic games were revived by ..... in 1896 at Athens
A. Lord Welsley
B. Queen Elizabeth-I
C. Baron Piere de Cubertin
D. None of the above

12. The national game of the USA is
A. swimming B. baseball
C. athletics D. None of the above

13. Jules Rimmet Cup is associated with
A. hockey B. archery
C. football D. table tennis

14. The approximate weight of a cricket ball is
A. 5.25 Oz B. 6.30 Oz
C. 7.20 Oz D. 8.25 Oz

15. The number of players on each side in a basketball match is
A. 10 B. 6
C. 5 D. 8

16. The first woman in the history of US open Championship to have played 100 matches, is:
A. Martina Navaratilova
B. Chris Evert
C. Steffi Graf
D. Helena Sukova

17. Swaythling Cup is associated with
A. World Table Tennis Tournament (men)
B. World Table Tennis Tournament (university)
C. World Table Tennis tournament (women)
D. World Hockey Tournament (university)

18. Which one of the following is not a cricket - playing nation?
A. West Indies B. Zimbabwe
C. Kenya D. Columbia

19. The first recipient of Major Dhyanchand Khel Ratna Award (1991-92) was:
A. Geet Sethi B. N Kunjurani Devi
C. V Anand D. P K Garg

20. The first Olympic Games were held at Olympia (Greece) in the year:
A. 300 BC B. 776 BC
C. 500 BC D. 394 AD

21. Which of the following is the National Game of Spain?
A. Bull fighting B. Baseball
C. Rugby D. Golf

22. 'Ashes' is the name of a series between ..... and ..... and it relates to .....
A. Pakistan, Australia, Hockey
B. India, England, Cricket
C. England, Australia, Cricket
D. New Zealand, Australia, Cricket

23. The term "Butterfly Stroke" is associated with
A. Kabaddi B. Wrestling
C. Polo D. Swimming

24. Which is the national sport of Canada?
A. Field Hockey
B. Cricket
C. Lacrosse/Ice Hockey
D. Volleyall

25. 'Gambit' is a term normally associated with
A. Bridge B. Chess
C. Billiards D. Polo

26. 'Bunker' and 'Chukker' are the two terms associated with
A. Polo B. Rowing
C. Bungey Jumping D. Ice Hockey

27. A Lawn Tennis court measures
A. 78 feet by 28 feet
B. 79 feet by 29 feet
C. 76 feet by 26 feet
D. 70 feet by 24 feet

28. Who scored the fastest timing (in case of an under-13 swimmer) for crossing the English Channel?
A. Arati Saha
B. Uday Shenoy
C. Rihen Mehta
D. Rupali Ramdas Ropal

29. Which one of the following has been entrusted with the responsibility of training coaches in various disciplines of sports?
A. Tata Football Academy
B. Ministry of Human Resource Development
C. Netaji Subhash Institute of Sports
D. Lakshmibai National College of Physical Education

30. Name the first oldest person to climb the Mount Everest:
A. Santosh Yadav
B. Sundare Sherpa
C. Ramon Balanco Saurez
D. Ang Rita Sherpa

31. Archery is the National Sport of which country?
A. Afghanistan B. India
C. Japan D. Bhutan

32. Who was the first deaf & dumb swimmer in the world to swim 30 km Gibralter strait?
A. Des Renford B. Mihir Sen
C. Arti Pradhan D. Taranath Shenoy

33. The height of the net in the centre of the tennis court is
A. 3 feet, 5 inches B. 3 feet, 2 inches
C. 2 feet, 8 inches D. 2 feet, 6 inches

34. 'Canon' is a sports term associated with the following game.
A. Billiards B. Volleyball
C. Shot-Put D. Table Tennis

35. The Himalayan Mountaineering Institute is located in
A. Leh B. Darjeeling
C. Kohima D. Dispur

36. The diameter of a golf hole is
A. 4.36 inches B. 4.50 inches
C. 5.63 inches D. 4.75 inches

37. The total distance of a Marathon Race is ..... miles and ..... yards.
A. 29, 388 B. 26, 380
C. 26, 385 D. 25, 372

38. The first woman, who won six gold medals in a single Olympics tournament, was
A. Evelyn Ashford
B. Florence Griffth Joyner
C. Kristin Otto
D. Susi Susanti

39. In which year on account of a decree issued by Roman Emperor the Olympic Games were ceased to be played?
A. 350 AD B. 394 AD
C. 300 BC D. 384 AD

40. Putney (UK) is a place most frequently associated with
A. swimming B. horse racing
C. boat rowing D. polo

41. ________ has Cricket as its national sports.
A. Jamaica B. India
C. Sri Lanka D. United States

42. The term 'Finesse' is normally associated with this game.
A. Chess B. Bridge
C. Snooker D. Rowing

43. The following trophy is not associated with cricket.
A. Ranji Trophy
B. Rohintan Baria Trophy
C. Singer-Akai-Nidahas Trophy
D. Asia Cup

44. Tonya Harding is a controversial athlete and has been associated with the following game.
A. Rowing B. Table Tennis
C. Figure Skating D. Boxing

45. When and where the first Asian Games were held?
A. 1955, Seoul B. 1951, New Delhi
C. 1954, Manila D. 1970, Bangkok

46. Olympic Games were first started by which country and in which year?
A. France (1924) B. Greece (1896)
C. Greece (1890) D. France (1894)

47. What is the measurement of a Golf Hole?
A. 3½ inch in diameter
B. 4½ inch in diameter
C. 7½ centimeter in diameter
D. 10 inch in diameter

48. Bandy is national sport of which country?
A. Latvia B. Peru
C. Russia D. Lithuania

49. K Sasikaran is well known as a
A. table tennis player
B. swimmer
C. chess player
D. football player

50. If we are using the following words in a game. Which game are we playing?
Break, Cannons, Cue, In off, Jigger, Scratch
A. Polo B. Bridge
C. Billiards D. Baseball

ANSWERS

1	2	3	4	5	6	7	8	9	10
D	A	B	B	C	B	C	B	C	A
11	12	13	14	15	16	17	18	19	20
C	B	C	A	C	B	A	D	C	B
21	22	23	24	25	26	27	28	29	30
A	C	D	C	B	A	A	D	C	C
31	32	33	34	35	36	37	38	39	40
D	D	B	A	B	B	C	C	B	C
41	42	43	44	45	46	47	48	49	50
A	B	D	C	B	C	B	C	C	B

HONOURS AND AWARDS

1. In which of the following years 'Nobel Prizes' were instituted?
A. 1910 B. 1905
C. 1901 D. 1911

2. The writer who refused the Nobel Prize for Literature was:
A. Winston Churchill
B. Prem Chand
C. Jean Paul Sartre
D. None of the above

3. Which country awards the Noble Prize?
A. USA B. India
C. Russia D. Sweden

4. In which of the following years Arjuna Awards were instituted
A. 1951 B. 1971
C. 1961 D. 1965

5. National Awards for Popularising Science was instituted in the year
A. 1981 B. 1985
C. 1987 D. 1988

6. The Government of which state has instituted the 'Tansen Samman'?
A. Madhya Pradesh
B. Uttar Pradesh
C. Gujarat
D. Maharashtra

7. Gujarmal Modi Award is given in the field of
A. Dance
B. Science
C. Cinema
D. Literature

8. Who returned the award of 'Sir' given by the British government in protest against the "Jallianwala Bagh Massacre" on April 13, 1919?
A. Prem Chand
B. Thomas Roe
C. Rabindra Nath Tagore
D. Dada Bhai Naoroji

9. Nobel Prize is not awarded in the following disciplines
A. Chemistry and Physics
B. Literature and Peace
C. Economics and Medicine
D. Geography and Space Research

10. In which year Nehru Award for International Understanding instituted?
A. 1965 B. 1969
C. 1974 D. 1964

11. Which of the following Indians was awarded Legion D award, the highest civilian awards of France?
A. Jawahar Lal Nehru
B. Satyajit Ray
C. Mother Teresa
D. Shahrukh Khan

12. 'Pulitzer' prizes are awarded to Americans for excellence in
A. Films B. Journalism
C. Medicine D. Social Work

13. C.V. Raman received Nobel Prize in the year
A. 1934 B. 1931
C. 1932 D. 1930

14. Saraswati Samman is awarded by
A. Government of India
B. Sahitya Academy
C. K.K. Birla Foundation
D. Lalit Kala Akademi

15. On which day every year National Awards for Teachers are announced?
A. August 15 B. September 5
C. November 19 D. November 14

16. The National Award given to the distinguishec sportsmen/women in India is known as
A. Dronacharya Award
B. Param Vir Chakra
C. Arjun Award
D. Nehru Award

17. The prestigious Ramon Magsaysay Award was instituted in the memory of Mr Ramon Magsaysay who was
    A. the Secretary – General of UN
    B. the Commander of NATO in Europe
    C. the President of the Philippines
    D. the President of Cambodia
18. The Kalinga Prize is awarded by UNESCO but it was founded by an Indian. His name is
    A. Biju Patnaik B. Sharad Pawar
    C. C V Raman D. Piloo Modi
19. Who was the first Indian to receive the World Food Prize?
    A. Dr. M.S. Swaminathan
    B. Dr. Amrita Patel
    C. Dr. Verghese Kurien
    D. None of these
20. Jesse Owens Global award is given in the field of:
    A. Literature B. Sports
    C. Science D. Journalism
21. B.C. Roy Award is given in the field of:
    A. Music B. Journalism
    C. Medicine D. Environment
22. Grammy Awards are given in the field of
    A. painting B. architecture
    C. music D. rock dance
23. The highest civilian award of India is
    A. *Padma Vibhushan* B. *Padma Shri*
    C. *Bharat Ratna* D. *Param Vir Chakra*
24. The highest military award of India is
    A. Shaurya Chakra
    B. Param Vishisht Sewa Medal
    C. Param Vir Chakra
    D. Kirti Chakra
25. The first ever B.R. Ambedkar National Award was given to
    A. Baba Amte
    B. T Shiv Shankar Pillai
    C. International Red Cross
    D. National Institute for Social Work and Social Sciences
26. 'Victory Medal' is awarded in:
    A. UK B. USA
    C. Russia D. France
27. Which one of the following is not a Shram Award?
    A. Shram Bhushan B. Shram Dev
    C. Shram Devi D. Shram Vir
28. Dr Shanti Swaroop Bhatnagar Awards are given in any field of science by
    A. Indian Council of Applied Economic Research
    B. Defence Research and Development Organisation
    C. National Institute for Social Work and Social Sciences
    D. Tata Institute of Fundamental Research
29. Abel Prize is associated with:
    A. Film
    B. Mathematics
    C. Music
    D. Creative Writing
30. First Miss World Competition was established by 'Miss World Incorporation' in the year
    A. 1941 B. 1950
    C. 1951 D. 1957
31. The size of an Olympic medal is ..... mm and thickness is ..... mm.
    A. 50, 2.5 B. 60, 3.0
    C. 60.5, 3.5 D. 55.2, 2.5
32. "Dhanwantari Award" is given in the field of
    A. swimming B. Bharata Natyam
    C. cinema D. medicine
33. In which year was Pulitzer Prize established?
    A. 1912 B. 1916
    C. 1917 D. 1922
34. Which is the second Highest Civilian award in India?
    A. Padma Vibushan
    B. Padma Shri
    C. Bharat Ratna
    D. Ashok Chakra
35. Who is the first Asian winner of Nobel prize?
    A. C.V. Raman
    B. Rabindranath Tagore
    C. Mother Teresa
    D. Hargobind Khurana
36. The second highest gallantry award in India is:
    A. Padma Bhushan
    B. Vir Chakra
    C. Mahavir Chakra
    D. Ashok Chakra
37. 'Mubarak-Al-Kabir' medal is the highest honour of
    A. Kuwait B. Iran
    C. Afghanistan D. Iraq
38. Bharatendu Harish Chandra awards are given annually for:
    A. best local self administration
    B. showing kindness and generosity of unusual kind
    C. promoting original writing in Hindi
    D. None of the above
39. Tulsi Samman is given in the field of ....
    A. Folk Arts B. Cinema
    C. Creative Writing D. Sports
40. Liberty Medal is the highest honour of which government?
    A. India B. UK
    C. USA D. Australia
41. Nobel Prizes are not given for which of the following fields?
    A. Physics B. Chemistry
    C. Peace D. Music

42. Oscar award is related to
A. books
B. politics
C. European Community
D. films

43. Feroz Gandhi Memorial Award is associated with
A. Sports B. Literature
C. Journalism D. Cinema

44. Out of the Gallantry awards — PVSM, AVSM and VSM — the most exceptional medal is
A. PVSM
B. AVSM
C. VSM
D. All have equal recognition status

45. *Jeewan Raksha Padak* is awarded for
A. bravery in the battle front
B. fine display of vocal music skills
C. saving the life of human beings
D. None of the above

46. Who is not eligible for Bharat Ratna?
A. A government official
B. A sportsperson
C. A film actress
D. A Prime Minister

47. Jamnalal Bajaj award is given in the field of
I. Social Work
II. Fine Arts
III. Application of Science and Technology
IV. Literature
A. I and II B. I, II and III
C. II and IV D. I and III

48. In which year Indira Gandhi Peace Prize was instituted?
A. 1985 B. 1984
C. 1986 D. 1987

49. Borlaug Award was instituted for recognising outstanding contribution in the field of:
A. Ecology B. Medicine
C. Agriculture D. Journalism

50. Except Dr. Nelson Mandela, who is the other non-Indian so far honoured with Bharat Ratna?
A. Dr. Julius Nyerere
B. Helen Hint
C. Hideki Yuka
D. Khan Abdul Ghaffar Khan

ANSWERS

1	2	3	4	5	6	7	8	9	10
C	C	D	C	C	A	B	C	D	D
11	**12**	**13**	**14**	**15**	**16**	**17**	**18**	**19**	**20**
B	B	D	C	B	C	C	A	C	B
21	**22**	**23**	**24**	**25**	**26**	**27**	**28**	**29**	**30**
C	C	C	C	D	B	B	C	B	C
31	**32**	**33**	**34**	**35**	**36**	**37**	**38**	**39**	**40**
B	D	C	A	B	C	A	C	A	C
41	**42**	**43**	**44**	**45**	**46**	**47**	**48**	**49**	**50**
D	D	C	A	C	A	D	C	C	D

BOOKS AND AUTHORS

1. The book "*The Insider*" is written by
A. Madhav Rao Scindia
B. Nana Patekar
C. Shobha De
D. P V Narasimha Rao

2. *India Wins Freedom* was written by
A. Dadabhai Nauroji
B. Ashfaqulla Khan
C. Sarojini Naidu
D. Maulana Abul Kalam Azad

3. *A Tale of Two Cities* is, in fact, the story of two famous cities. Those cities are
A. Paris and New York
B. London and New York
C. London and Paris
D. Stockholm and New York

4. *Ben Hur* was penned by
A. Lewis Wallace
B. Lord Byron
C. William Shakespeare
D. None of the above

5. *Panchatantra* was written by
A. R K Narayan B. R K Laxman
C. Vishnu Sharma D. None of the above

6. Arundhati Roy has been awarded the prestigious
A. Booker's Prize – 1997
B. Jnanpeeth Award – 1997
C. Sahitya Akademi Award – 1998
D. None of the above

7. Who wrote *Odyssey?*
A. George Orwell B. Homer
C. Dom Moraes D. None of the above

8. Which one of the following was not written by Shakespeare?
A. *As You Like It* B. *Mcbeth*
C. *Hamlet* D. *A Farewell to Arms*

9. Lewis Carol wrote a masterpiece. What is its name?
A. *Don Quixote*
B. *Alice in Wonderland*
C. *Adventures of Robinson Crusoe*
D. *Great Expectations*

10. The *Tamil Ramayana* is the work of
A. Tulsidas B. Jayangondar
C. Kambar D. Veda Vyas

11. In *Shrimad Bhagwat Geeta,* Lord Krishna teaches his disciple Arjuna to
A. rise to the occasion and fight with his near and dear ones
B. withdraw from the battlefield
C. do his duty and not to expect anything in return
D. attack the enemy in a planned and meticulous approach

12. Who wrote *Origin of Species?*
A. Charles Darwin B. Alexander Flaming
C. G.B. Shaw D. D.H. Lawrence

13. The poet and the well-known friend of Prithvi Raj Chauhan, who wrote *Prithvi Raj Raso,* was
A. Harisena B. Vishnu Datt
C. Chand Bardai D. None of the above

14. The first book was printed in India in the year 1561. Its name was
A. *The spiritual Compendium of the Christian Life*
B. *Aain-e-Akbari*
C. *Babur Nama*
D. *Ram Charit Manas*

15. The famous book *Runs and Ruins* was written by
A. Sir Donald Bradman
B. Sunil Gavaskar
C. Kapil Dev
D. Richard Hadlee

16. Adam Smith wrote the following famous book
A. The Wreck
B. Dr Zhivago
C. The Wealth of Nations
D. Tarzan of the Apes

17. H G Wells is known as a
A. poet
B. science-fiction writer
C. thriller-fiction writer
D. essay writer and critic

18. Tukaram wrote his devotional songs in this language
A. Urdu B. Gujarati
C. Hindi D. Marathi

19. Our ancient scholars and writers used this language for their social, religious and political books and works
A. Tamil B. Sanskrit
C. Urdu D. Hindi *(Devanagari)*

20. *Gora* is the hero of a book written by Rabindra Nath Tagore. What is the name of the book?
A. *Geetanjali* B. *Patanjali*
C. *Gora* D. *Twelfth Night*

21. Shylock is
A. the villain *in A Pound of Flesh* by William Shakespeare
B. an old Jew who is a famous hero of the Israeli nation
C. the hero of *Miranda,* written by William Shakespeare
D. the comic character of *Alice In the Wonderland* by Lewis Caroll

22. The following was a famous Hindi author and story-writer
A. Shobha De B. Aruna Asaf Ali
C. Mahadevi Verma D. Amrita Pritam

23. *Mudrarakshasa* was composed by
A. Vishakhadatta B. Bhavabhuti
C. Sivananda D. Jayadeva

24. *Razor's Edge* was written by
A. Toni Morrison
B. Saul Bellow
C. W Somerset Maugham
D. None of the above

25. *Sakharam Binder* is a famous play written by
A. Anil Barve B. Vijay Tendulkar
C. V S Naipaul D. Tasleema Nasreen

26. The major work of Sir Isaac Newton is
A. *Principia*
B. *Heritage*
C. *Human knowledge*
D. *I Dare*

27. The hero of *The Jungle Book,* written by Rudyard Kipling, is
A. the lion
B. Mowghuli
C. the father of Mowghuli
D. there is no hero

28. Who stated, "Peace hath her victories, no less renowned than war?"
A. Alfred Lord Tennyson
B. William Shakespeare
C. John Milton
D. None of the above

29. Macawber is a character who was created by
A. Thomas Hardy B. P G Wodehouse
C. Charles Dickens D. J W Von Goethe

30. *Pride and Prejudice* was written by
A. Anton Chekhov B. Maxim Gorky
C. Jane Austen D. Anthony West

31. *In the Afternoon Time* is the English translation of the autobiography of the famous poet, Harivansh Rai Bachchan. The autobiography was translated into English by

A. Vikram Seth B. Dr Rupert Snell
C. William Faulkner D. P D Tandon

32. Who is the author of the book *The Celestine Vision?*

A. Paul Hockins B. Salman Rushdie
C. Joseph Conrad D. James Redfield

33. The author of the famous book *Blue Mountain Revisited* is

A. Charles Kingsley B. Virginia Woolf
C. Arthur Koestler D. Peter Topkins

34. Homer was the great poet of the following language

A. italian B. Greek
C. Arabic D. French

35. The controversial author – Salman Rushdie – was awarded the European Union Literary Award fcr one of his novels on November 13, 1996, in Copenhagen. What is the name of the novel?

A. *Shame*
B. *Mid-night's Children*
C. *The Moor's Last Sigh*
D. None of the above

36. *Godaan* was written by Munshi Prem Chand and it depicts

A. the methodology for taking adequate care of the cows
B. exploitation of simple rural folk by the rich landlords of rural India
C. the mutiny of 1857 in which, Indians refused to bite the *Kartoos* made with cow beef
D. None of the above

37. Manu wrote a book during ancient times in which, he divided the Aryan society into four distinct classes. What was the name of the book?

A. *Arthashastra* B. *Manusmriti*
C. *Moti Mahal* D. *My Truth*

38. R. Venkataraman wrote *My Presidential Years.* What was the main theme of the book?

A. It described the aristocratic procedures being followed in the *Rashtrapati Bhawan* during his tenure as President
B. It described the power equations and ploys in the centre and in the states during his term
C. It described how he felt caged while he was President due to a load of procedures and formalities
D. It explained the machinations of the political party which was in power during his tenure as President

39. The hero of the play cried in the end, "Et Tu, Brute!" and died. Which is the play and who is the author?

A. The Wealth of Nations — Adam Smith
B. Mein Kempf — Adolf Hitler
C. Julius Caesar — William Shakespeare
D. None of the above

40. Don Veto Corleone was the undisputed king of the underworld in this novel. This masterpiece was also converted into a film in which Al Pacino played the role of the Don. What is the name of the novel and that of the author?

A. *A Farewell to Arms* — E Hemingway
B. *The Godfather* — Mario Puzo
C. *From Here to Eternity* — James Jones
D. *Dialogue with Death* — Arthur Koestler

41. *Gypsy Camp Vanishes Into the Blue* was a famous blockbuster movie made by the erstwhile USSR. The original story was written by a famous author. His name is

A. Leo Tolstoy B. Anton Chekhov
C. Maxim Gorky D. Leon Uris

42. The total number of *Puranas* written during the Vedic age is

A. 22 B. 9
C. 18 D. 25

43. He was a poet, playwright and the first President of the Czech Republic. He received the Indira Gandhi Prize for Peace, Disarmament and Development in 1983. His name is

A. Lech Walesa B. Vaclav Havel
C. Seymour M Hersh D. None of the above

44. W B Yeats won the Nobel Prize for literature in 1923 and Samuel Backet won the same prize in 1969. Both were Irish. The third Irish to have won the Nobel Prize for literature (1995) was

A. Alison Hargreaves B. Bobby Sands
C. Paul Crutzen D. Seamus Heaney

45. According to *The Ramayana,* who received the last teaching lessons from the knowledgeable Ravana while he was on his death-bed?

A. Rama B. Sugreeva
C. Laxmana D. Both A and C

46. He was a German but he saved many a Jew from the cruel hands of the Nazis. A movie was made on this theme which won the coveted Oscar Prize. The book and the author are

A. *Operation Shylock* — Philip Roth
B. *Schindler's List* — Thomas Keneally
C. *The Rescue* — Joseph Conrad
D. *The Slave* — Isaac Bashevis Singer

47. He was the favourite assistant of Sherlock Holmes, the famous character created by Arthur Conan Doyle. His name is

A. Zhivago B. Watson
C. Hawkins D. Hector

48. Who wrote the famous book—"We the People"?

A. Nani Palkhivala B. T.N. Kaul
C. Khushwant Singh D. Arundhati Roy

49. He wrote *Sharmili*, *Gaylord* and *Kati Patang*. His novels were written in Hindi and some of them have been converted into films also. His name is
A. Gita Mehta B. B N Mullick
C. Nirad C Chaudhary D. Gulshan Nanda

50. Who wrote the line 'A thing of beauty is joy forever'?
A. A. William wordsworth
B. P.B. Shelley
C. Robert Browing
D. John Keets

ANSWERS

1	2	3	4	5	6	7	8	9	10
D	D	C	A	C	A	B	D	B	C
11	12	13	14	15	16	17	18	19	20
C	A	C	A	B	C	B	D	B	C
21	22	23	24	25	26	27	28	29	30
A	C	A	C	B	A	B	C	C	C
31	32	33	34	35	36	37	38	39	40
B	D	D	B	C	B	B	C	C	B
41	42	43	44	45	46	47	48	49	50
C	C	B	D	C	B	B	A	D	D

ECONOMY, BUSINESS AND COMMERCE

1. The Policy of Economic reforms in India was adopted due to:
A. 1985 B. 1989
C. 1991 D. 1996

2. The currencies has the highest value in terms of rupee is:
A. Dollar B. Kuwaiti Dinar
C. Pound D. Euro

3. The economies of the Oriental countries depend upon the growth or decline of
A. the American economy
B. the Japanese economy
C. the Korean economy
D. the Thai economy

4. The difference between the monetary policy and the fiscal policy is
A. fiscal policy tries to control aggregate demand through budgetary means whereas monetary policy controls the same through the quantity of money and the rate of interest
B. monetary policy is related to the money supply whereas the fiscal policy is related to the rate of interest
C. monetary policy is automatic whereas the fiscal policy is discretionary
D. both the policies are similar and have similar objectives

5. Which one of the following is a *Navratna* Company?
A. Delhi Vidyut Board
B. National Textiles Corporation
C. Mahanagar Telephone Nigam Ltd
D. Electronics Corporation of India Ltd

6. Which country holds the dubious distinction of becoming the biggest user of anti-dumping duty (ADD) since the Uruguay Round?
A. China B. Japan
C. US D. India

7. Find the odd city with the viewpoint of Indian Railways
A. Chittaranjan B. Chennai
C. Kapurthala D. Trombay

8. Which company released the slogan "Redefining the value of Rupee?"
A. Toshiba B. Samsung
C. Akai D. Panasonic

9. 'KUSUM' Scheme launched by Government of India is associated with:
A. Female Child Protection
B. Flower Production
C. Solar Power Plants
D. Promoting Plantation

10. The major field of research of the Nobel laureate, Amartya Sen, is
A. mixed economy
B. welfare economics
C. the Amartya Sen Shift
D. capitalistic economy

11. Which of the following days has been declared as 'National Handloom Day' by the Government?
A. August 01 B. August 17
C. August 23 D. August 07

12. Which one of the following is not a chief characteristic of FEMA?
A. Current account transactions are permitted unless there are RBI restrictions
B. Capital accounts transactions are permitted unless there are RBI transactions
C. Treatment for violations is harsh and is deemed to be a congnisable and non-bailable offence
D. Enforcement Directorate can arrest the accused in case of violations

13. The current market trends are
A. recession oriented
B. inflation oriented
C. recession oriented with inflation
D. boom oriented

14. Which company is manufacturing the brand name 'Indica'' which is an automobile?
A. Tata Steel B. SIEL
C. Telco D. HM

15. This company does not deal in consumer durables
A. Samsung B. Akai
C. Godrej D. Nestle

16. Find the odd one out.
A. Lintas B. HTA
C. Contract D. LML

17. E-com does not require
A. Internet connectivity
B. Technological inputs
C. Negotiations through E-mail
D. Knowledge about entertainment groups

18. Which one of the following is not an infrastructure related project?
A. Narmada Valley Project
B. North-South and East-West Corridors
C. Software exports
D. Railway modernisation

19. When the stock markets crash, then
A. stocks sell at lower prices than anticipated
B. scrips sell at higher prices than anticipated
C. the sellers are not very keen to sell in anticipation of sudden rise in values of stocks
D. None of the above

20. What is 'Dumping?'
A. It is the term given by the economists to excavation and digging activities of the MNCs that deal in earth moving equipment
B. It is the sale of the products and services by foreign nations and firms at very low prices so that they could find firm markets in India
C. It is the excessive supply of fast moving consumer goods by a developed country to an under-developed country
D. It is a series of measures taken by Government of India to facilitate international trade

21. Varishtha Pension Bima Yojna has been launched by
A. National Insurance Co.
B. LIC of India
C. Oriental Insurance Co.
D. United India Insurance Co.

22. Which company is the manufacturer of the product brand name 'Spectra?'
A. Telco B. Kinetic
C. LML D. None of the above

23. Who wrote the General Theory of Employment, Interest and Money?
A. Kaldor B. Marx
C. Keynes D. Marshall

24. Which one of the following is not an electronics products manufacturer?
A. Samsung B. Matsushita
C. Motorola D. Ford

25. PARAM-1000 supercomputer was developed by
A. DoT
B. CDAC
C. Department of Electronics
D. None of the above

26. Which of the following taxes in India is also known as the 'Google Tax'?
A. Import Duty
B. Securities Transaction Tax
C. Equalisation Levy
D. Anti-dumping Duty

27. The spirit of JIT is to
A. produce that much which could be sold and acquire that much of material inputs that could justify the sales
B. produce less but buy still lesser
C. collect orders from the markets and then produce
D. keep your inventory levels just equal to the market demand for the products

28. US-64 Scheme was launched by
A. LIC B. UTI
C. ICICI D. IDBI

29. Who among the following was first among the European nations to trade with India?
A. Britain B. Spain
C. Portugal D. France

30. GTX Extra is a brand name associated with
A. MRF B. HP
C. IOL D. Castrol

31. In India, the first bank of limited liability managed Indians and founded in 1881 was
A. Hindustan Commercial Bank
B. Oudh Commercial Bank
C. Punjab and Sind
D. Bank of India

32. In the new millennium, the industries related to ..... would be facing maximum growth rates?

A. manufacturing
B. FMCGs
C. information technology
D. consumer non-durables

33. Which one of the following items is not exported from India?
A. gold ornaments
B. leather items
C. software products
D. nuclear weapons

34. The stock value index of the registered companies of a stock exchange is known as
A. Nikkei B. Dow-Jones
C. Sensex D. None of the above

35. India has her only OTCEI in
A. Kolkata B. Indore
C. Mumbai D. New Delhi

36. Estimates of National Income in India are prepared by
A. Ministry of Finance
B. Planning Commission
C. Reserve Bank of India
D. Central Statistical Organisation

37. If the Rupee becomes stronger vis-a-vis the US Dollar, then
A. exports would rise
B. imports would remain stagnant
C. exports would decline
D. None of the above

38. Economy reforms in India is designed by:
A. IMF B. World Bank
C. GoI D. All the above

39. Which one of the following is not a core operation of L & T group?
A. Electricals
B. Construction Machinery
C. Shipping
D. Cement

40. The famous breakfast cereal Kellogg was started as ..... during its early days of inception.
A. medicine
B. diet for patients in a nursing home
C. breakfast food for some top businessmen of the USA
D. diet enriching ingredient for the school-going children in Europe

41. Who observed, "as the population increases, the economic means of supporting that population do not grow in the same proportion?"
A. Goldsmith B. Malthus
C. Frederic Engels D. Adam Smith

42. The eminent Nobel Laureate–Amartya Sen is known for his research in
A. welfare economics
B. draughts and famines
C. poverty elimination
D. free market system of economy

43. According to 16th Finance Commission, the share of states in the divisible pool of the Central taxes for the period of 2026-31 was:
A. 42% B. 40%
C. 41% D. 39%

44. Which was the first country in the world to introduce Goods and Service Tax (GST)?
A. Italy B. France
C. U.K. D. Japan

45. If supply of onions is reduced, then
A. the demand would rise and the prices of the existing stocks would jump up
B. the demand would rise but prices would remain unaffected
C. the demand would fall as the users would avoid taking onions because of the fear of a sharp price rise
D. None of the above

46. How could the government break the vicious cycle of poverty among the poor masses?
A. By providing them with money
B. By providing them with opportunities of employment and entreprenenrship
C. By educating them about family planning
D. By getting loans for them from global financial agencies

47. WTO is dedicated to
A. liberal trade terms between the member nations
B. removal of all the trade protection procedures by all the member nations
C. agreements on patents of agricultural commodities like rice etc.
D. None of the above

48. Which types of tax helps in reducing disparities of income?
A. Proportionate tax
B. Regressive tax
C. Progressive tax
D. None of the above

49. The basic objective of SIDBI is to
A. give more loans for infrastructure development to the corporate sector
B. grant loans to agricultural farmers for export of their commodities
C. solve the financial problems of small scale industries
D. assist IDBI and ICICI in the process of national industrial development

50. The major function of the Food Corporation of India is:
A. to control the demand side of foodgrains
B. to distribute high yielding variety seeds
C. to check the fluctuation in foodgrain price by controlling supply
D. to extend credit to farmers

ANSWERS

1	2	3	4	5	6	7	8	9	10
C	B	B	A	C	D	D	C	C	B
11	12	13	14	15	16	17	18	19	20
D	D	C	C	D	D	D	C	A	B
21	22	23	24	25	26	27	28	29	30
B	D	C	D	B	C	A	B	C	D
31	32	33	34	35	36	37	38	39	40
B	C	D	C	C	D	C	C	C	B
41	42	43	44	45	46	47	48	49	50
B	A	C	B	A	B	A	C	C	C

TECHNOLOGY AND ENVIRONMENT

1. What is the full form of E-Com?
A. Electrical Commercial Protocol
B. Electronic Commercial Syndicate
C. Electronic Commerce
D. Engineering Commercial

2. The new Internet Policy allowed the Internet Services Providers (ISPs) to allow a foreign equity of upto
A. 47 per cent
B. 51 per cent
C. 49 per cent
D. no foreign equity was to be allowed

3. Which of the following is not a Computer Language
A. Basic B. Tally
C. Pascal D. Fortran

4. Indian National Satellite System (INSAT) was commissioned in which year?
A. 1982 B. 1983
C. 1984 D. 1985

5. Which of the following is not an air pollutant?
A. Smoke B. Carbon Dioxide
C. Nitrogen Gas D. Sulphur Dioxide

6. Artificial Intelligence (AI) is not related to
A. development of robotics which could perform routine operations depending upon the environmental parameters
B. thinking machines which could tolerate environmental hazards like heat, smoke fire and acids
C. combination of biological organisms and robotics for thinking independently during the adverse circumstances
D. None of the above

7. A vitamin has been found to have great usage in cardio-vuscular diseases. In fact, it reduces the risk of the occurrence of these diseases. Its name is
A. Vitamin E B. Folic acid
C. Vitamin C D. Vitamin K

8. A unit of electrical energy is equivalent to
A. 1 KVA B. 1 KWH
C. 1 KV D. 1 V

9. ANSI stands for
A. African National System Information
B. American Non-Standard Information
C. American National Standard Institute
D. None of these

10. A computer has 32 MB of RAM. The programmer loads a programme through the CD-ROM which has an operational memory requirement of 32 MB. Would the software work?
A. no, it would not
B. yes, is would work comfortably
C. it would work but would have Delayed Execution Syndrome
D. the message would be displayed on the monitor regarding insufficient RAM in the system

11. Internet system belongs to
A. Rupert Murdoch
B. the US Administration
C. a few owners who are net-connected
D. nobody

12. The two most important constituents of the ecological system of the earth are
A. lithosphere and mesosphere
B. physical environment and various organisms living in it
C. plants only
D. human beings and animals

13. Which city in India is the first to use municipal wastes to generate power?
A. Kolkata B. Mumbai
C. Delhi D. Chennai

14. Which one of the following planets takes maximum time for one revolution on around the sun?
A. Jupiter B. Earth
C. Mars D. Venus

15. Which part of Plant evaporates water?
A. Fruit B. Stomala
C. Branch D. Root

16. SMPS, in computer terminology, refers to
A. Serial Mega-ports System
B. Switching Mode Power Supply
C. Static Modular Power System
D. Static Modular Power Supply

17. Which is more elastic—steel or rubber?
A. steel
B. rubber
C. both have same elasticity
D. the principle of elasticity is not applicable on steel

18. A computer virus can
A. multiply itself on the storage memory area like the HDD
B. destroy the application programmes and data stored in permanent memory
C. corrupt the OS
D. All of the above

19. Multimedia is not related to
A. graphics designing
B. audio and video effects
C. animation
D. AUTOCAD

20. FTP (in Internet terminology) is the abbreviated form of
A. File Texture Programme
B. Fumbled Transfer Programme
C. File Transfer Protocol
D. Fixed Time Penetration

21. A thick glass tumbler cracks more easily than a thin one, when hot water is poured into it, why?
A. Thick glass is more brittler than thin glass
B. The inner surface of the tumbler expands more than its outer surface
C. Thick glass is of inferior quality
D. The outer surface of the tumbler expands more than its inner surface

22. What is a nuclear fallout?
A. The nuclear fusion reaction going on in the Sun.
B. The spread in atmosphere and subsequent deposition of radioactive particles on the surface of the earth
C. The absorption of nuclear isotopes by the oceans
D. Explosion of fissile material in space and the subsequent spread of radio-activity in the atmosphere.

23. PHWR is a technique used in nuclear power generation. The expanded form of this technology is
A. Pressurised Heavy Water Reactor
B. Pre-Heating Water Reservoir
C. Post-Hydro Water Reactor
D. Pressurised Heat Water Reaction

24. The advantage of sub-critical nuclear tests is that
A. these tests escape the scrutiny of IAEA and the UNO
B. these tests do not lead to nuclear explosions and can be controlled in the laboratories
C. these tests can be used to make high-grade fissile materials
D. these tests are not hazards for those who conduct them

25. What is the role of heavy water in a nuclear reactor?
A. It absorbs the additional neutrons meant for a chain reaction and hence, controls the chain reaction
B. It gets heated up and transfers this heat to the water cycle for steam generation
C. It retards the speeds of fast moving neutrons so that
D. They could be slowed down to effect secondary fission

26. A thermonuclear test is related to
A. nuclear fusion
B. nuclear fission
C. missile test on a mock target
D. study of nuclear reduction

27. Which one of the following may not be used in the wars of future
A. satellites B. nuclear missiles
C. chemical weapons D. face-to-face combat

28. The most striking feature of the cloned sheep 'Dolly' is
A. she resembles her 'mother' from whom the basic cell structure was taken
B. she is sheep but her 'mother' is not a sheep
C. she has different habits from those of her 'mother'
D. None of the above

29. The Nano humming bird is
A. A new species of hitherto undiscovered humming bird.
B. An extremely small electric car that can take 360° turn.
C. A pocket sized unmanned spy plane developed in the USA.
D. A new variety of honey bee.

30. A rise in the level of SO_2 would lead to the increase in the incidence and severity of
A. asthma
B. TB
C. muscular weaknesses
D. lung cancer

31. PbO_2 is the chief causative factor of
A. TB
B. lung cancer
C. skin diseases
D. occular defects

32. What is a solar pond?

A. It is a panel made up of photovoltaic cells and is used to generate electrical energy (direct current) in Rajasthan

B. It is a collection of water mass in which salt has been added so that solar energy could be retained by it upto 85ºC. This pond has been made in Bhuj (Gujarat)

C. It is an artificial surface of a satellite that has solar cells and gold flaps that absorb the requisite amounts of solar energy for the operation of the satellite

D. None of the above

33. A painless injection was developed by a firm for administering the dosages of medicine to the patients. The disease is

A. asthma B. tuberculosis bacilus

C. diabetes D. arthiritis

34. Which one of the following is a computer language?

A. SYBASE B. PASCAL

C. COREL DRAW D. Quark Express

35. The technology of cloning could be used for

A. creating the look-alikes of those people who are dead

B. making new varieties of plants and seeds

C. developing new varieties of plants and seeds that would be immune to diseases, floods and other natural hazards

D. None of the above

36. HAIL-BOPP is a

A. satellite sent by the USA into space

B. space station being operated by NATO States

C. comet

D. dying star

37. If nuclear warheads are dumped in the seas or are buried underground, they contaminate our environment. What should be done to eliminate them?

A. Destroy them in remote area in outer space

B. Use the nuclear warheads in atomic reactors as such

C. Use the nuclear warheads in atomic reactors with some modifications, enrichment or moderations

D. None of the above

38. Viagra is a pill for

A. removing sterility among men

B. removing frigidity among women

C. treating AIDS patients during the initial stages of the disease

D. removing shyness and promoting socially acceptable manners among people

39. The credit of "Green Revolution" in India goes to a prominent agricultural technologist whose name is

A. Dr Verghese Kurien

B. Professor Norman E Bourloug

C. Jayant Narlikar

D. Sitakanta Mohapatra

40. The credit of "White Revolution" in India goes to

A. Professor Norman E Bourlong

B. Dr M C Modi

C. Dr Nafis Sadik

D. Dr Verghese Kurien

41. If water is purified, it would be free from ..... so that it becomes potable

A. salts of magnesium and calcium

B. SPM

C. chlorine

D. Both A and B

42. The latest video data storage and entertainment technology is

A. CD B. DVD

C. DIVX D. None of the above

43. India has developed the technology for sending satellites into space which could weigh as high as

A. 1,000 kgs

B. 3,000 kgs

C. 2,500 kgs

D. this technology is not related to satellite payloads.

44. Find the odd man out

A. Dr H J Bhabha

B. Sir C V Raman

C. Dr A P J Abdul Kalaam

D. C Rangarajan

45. Which famous author wrote about future technological progress to be made by man and also, other science fiction stories?

A. Bertrand Russel B. H G Wells

C. Johannes Kepler D. Graham Greene

46. Which could be the possible fuels for automobiles of the future?

A. Petrol and diesel

B. Gasohol and electricity (DC)

C. Benzene and LPG

D. CNG and diesel

47. Internet operations could transmit

A. voice B. data

C. text and graphics D. All of the above

48. Which one of the following tasks is not possible through LASER?

A. Removal of fat from the blood vessels of a human body

B. Digging of tunnels in the mountains

C. Annihilation of an atomic weapon that is on its way to the target

D. Thinking as a robot for performing AI operations

49. Which energy is converted into Electrical Energy by a Solar Cell?

A. Chemical Energy B. Solar Energy

C. Nuclear Energy D. Magnetic Energy

50. The advantage of using fibre-optic cables in the fields of medicine and technology is
A. that the optical-fibre cable could be burried underground
B. that the optical-fibre cable is flexible
C. that the optical-fibre cable is not harmed by high temperatures
D. that the signals (optical, electrical or electronic) can be transmitted through the optical-fibre cable without any deviations and distortions

ANSWERS

1	2	3	4	5	6	7	8	9	10
C	C	B	B	C	C	B	B	C	C
11	**12**	**13**	**14**	**15**	**16**	**17**	**18**	**19**	**20**
D	B	C	A	B	B	A	D	D	C
21	**22**	**23**	**24**	**25**	**26**	**27**	**28**	**29**	**30**
B	B	A	B	D	A	D	A	C	A
31	**32**	**33**	**34**	**35**	**36**	**37**	**38**	**39**	**40**
B	B	C	B	C	C	C	A	B	D
41	**42**	**43**	**44**	**45**	**46**	**47**	**48**	**49**	**50**
D	C	B	D	B	B	D	D	B	D

BANKING AND FINANCE

1. Which one of the following services is not provided by the mobile banking service?
A. Checking of balance of an account
B. Requesting for an accounts statement
C. Enquiring details of the fixed deposit
D. Asking for share prices of all the stocks at the BSE

2. Scheduled bank is that bank which is:
A. Nationalised
B. Not-nationalised
C. Based at foreign country
D. Included in the Second Schedule of R.B.I.

3. Grameen Bank and Micro Credit are asociated with:
A. Manmohan Singh B. Bill Gates
C. Md. Yunus D. Aung San Su Ki

4. ICICI Bank, prior to commencing its operations as a bank was a/an:
A. Market research group
B. Industrial finance corporation
C. Small-time player in consumer durables
D. Conduct for RRBs

5. If there is a capital flight from India:
A. Exchange rate of rupee will fall
B. Share prices will rise
C. Interest rate will fall
D. Exchange rate of rupee will rise

6. The headquarters of standard Chartered Bank are located at:
A. New York B. Hawai
C. London D. New Delhi

7. 'Shishu', 'Tarun' and 'Kishore' named enterprises are associated with:
A. SBI B. MUDRA Bank
C. IDBI D. NABARD

8. India's first floating ATM has been launched in Kerala by
A. Canara Bank B. Corporation Bank
C. HDFC Bank D. State Bank of India

9. Which are the three international credit card companies?
A. Amex, Citibank, Master
B. Master, Amex, HSBC
C. Amex, Master, Visa
D. Visa, Citibank, Standard Chartered

10. Name the first bank in India to start using PKI (Public Key Infrastructure) based digital signatures for electronic fund transfer.
A. Bank of Punjab B. Punjab National Bank
C. Canara Bank D. Bank of Baroda

11. Federal Reserves is the Central Bank of...
A. Britain B. U.S.A.
C. Japan D. Canada

12. Capital market means
A. Mutual funds B. Money market
C. Direct taxes D. Securities market

13. The World Bank has given a go-ahead to India on the Baglihar Hydro-electric Project being build on the river:
A. Jhelum B. Sutlej
C. Chenab D. Beas

14. Which state has maximum branches of public sector commercial banks?
A. U.P. B. Maharashtra
C. Karnataka D. Gujarat

15. The "Adhoc Treasury Bill System" of meeting budget deficit in India was replaced by 'Ways and Means Advances System' which has come into force on:
A. March 31, 1997 B. April 1, 1996
C. April 1, 1997 D. None of these

16. Plastic money relates to:
A. Plastic currency B. Paper currency
C. ATM cards D. Credit cards

17. The rate at which RBI gives short-term loan to commercial banks is called:
A. Reverse Repo Rate B. Repo Rate
C. Bank Rate D. Cash Reserve Rate

18. In the context of stock market, the abbreviation IPO stands for
A. Immediate Payment Order
B. Internal Policy Obligation
C. External Policy Obligation
D. Initial Public Offering

19. The Reserve Bank of India (RBI) keeps on modifying various rates/ratios to keep the flow of liquidity in the market in a balanced situation. Which of the following rates/ratios/indexes is not directly controlled by the RBI?
A. Cash Reserve Ratio (CRR)
B. Bank Rate
C. Repo Rate
D. Wholesale Price Index (WPI)

20. Which bank launched the first international credit card in India?
A. Hong Kong Bank B. Citibank
C. SBI D. Deutsche Bank

21. What is near money?
A. Money that is banked in nearby banks
B. Assets that are easily convertible into cash
C. Money held in local currency
D. Money that can be recalled easily

22. What is fiat money?
A. Money not backed by gold or any other valuable goods
B. Money issued by a government fiat
C. Money used to buy worthless assets
D. Assets that are easily convertible into cash

23. Which bank introduced the first Automatic Teller Machine (ATM) in India?
A. State Bank of India B. Citibank
C. Bank of America D. Hong Kong Bank

24. Bank of Rajasthan, belongs to which business family of India?
A. Hindujas B. Singhanias
C. Bangurs D. Modis

25. Which company launched the first electronic cash card in India?
A. Kotak Mahindra B. SBI
C. Bank of Baroda D. Escorts Finance

26. Where is the foreign exchange of India deposited?
A. Reserve Bank of India
B. State Bank of India
C. Both (A) and (B)
D. Union Finance Ministry

27. The apex institution in the field of industrial development banking in India is:
A. IFCI B. ICICI
C. LIC D. IDBI

28. Banking Sector will fall under which of the following sectors?
A. Agricultural Sector B. Service Sector
C. Manufacturing Sector D. Industrial Sector

29. Which of the following types of borrowings from the IMF has the softest servicing conditions?
A. Second Tranch Loan B. SAF
C. ESAF D. Oil facility

30. If the cash-reserve ratio is lowered by the Central Bank, what will be its effect on credit creation?
A. It will decrease credit creation
B. It will not decrease credit creation
C. It will increase credit creation
D. It will not change credit creation

31. "Conditionality" of an I.M.F. loan to a member country stands for:
A. Schedule of disbursement of loan instalments
B. Interest and repayment terms of the loan
C. The policy steps which the borrower country must take
D. An assessment of the credit-worthiness of the borrower

32. Credit is a:
A. Stock concept B. Flow concept
C. A stock-flow concept D. None of these

33. The IBRD aims at:
A. Promoting international monetary co-operation
B. Helping in reconstruction and development of economics
C. Helping children all over the world
D. Promoting the peaceful uses of atomic energy

34. People's Bank of India was founded in the year:
A. 1910 B. 1911
C. 1901 D. 1920

35. The RBI was established in the year:
A. 1935 B. 1936
C. 1940 D. 1945

36. Blank cheque is:
A. Without date
B. A cheque which has been signed and dated but in which the amount payable has not been filled in
C. Without signatures
D. None of the above

37. The United Commercial Bank was started by the Birlas in the year:
A. 1948 B. 1943
C. 1949 D. 1950

38. Financial Investment is:
A. Any investment
B. Investment which cannot be traded
C. Any investment which can be traded, such as shares, certificates of deposit, etc
D. None of the above

39. A Joint Account is:
A. A firm account
B. A bank account owned jointly by two or more people
C. A shop account
D. None of the above

40. The Foreign Investments Board was set up in the year:
A. 1960 B. 1968
C. 1969 D. 1970

41. The SBI floated its first Mutual Fund in the year:
A. 1987 B. 1988
C. 1989 D. 1990

42. Loan Shark is:
A. A person who lends money at a very high interest rate
B. Lending money at lower rates
C. Lending money without interest
D. None of the above

43. The IDBI started its operations in year:
A. 1964 B. 1965
C. 1966 D. 1967

44. Banking Companies Act was passed in the year:
A. 1947 B. 1948
C. 1949 D. 1950

45. Bearer Cheque is a cheque that is payable to:
A. A person whosoever present it to the banker
B. Only to the account person
C. Only to the account holder
D. None of the above

46. The Imperial Bank was converted to State Bank of India in the year:
A. 1950 B. 1955
C. 1956 D. 1957

47. The Unit Trust of India was launched in the year:
A. 1964 B. 1965
C. 1966 D. 1967

48. Treasury Bills are:
A. Taxes
B. Marketable financial bills of the central government
C. Acts
D. None of the above

49. CACS (Capital Adequacy, Asset Quality, Compliance and Systems) is a rating model used by RBI. This system is used by RBI to rate:
A. State run banks outside India
B. Foreign banks operating in India
C. Private banks in India
D. Co-operative banks

50. Name of the first Indian financial institution to be listed on the New York Stock Exchange (NYSE).
A. IFCI B. UTI
C. ICICI D. IDBI

ANSWERS

1	2	3	4	5	6	7	8	9	10
D	D	C	B	A	C	B	D	C	A
11	**12**	**13**	**14**	**15**	**16**	**17**	**18**	**19**	**20**
B	D	C	A	C	D	B	D	D	A
21	**22**	**23**	**24**	**25**	**26**	**27**	**28**	**29**	**30**
B	A	D	C	D	A	D	B	C	C
31	**32**	**33**	**34**	**35**	**36**	**37**	**38**	**39**	**40**
C	C	B	C	A	B	B	C	B	B
41	**42**	**43**	**44**	**45**	**46**	**47**	**48**	**49**	**50**
A	A	A	B	A	B	A	B	B	C

INDIAN CORPORATES

1. Pulsar is popular brand name of:
A. Scooters B. Motor cycles
C. Cars D. Trucks

2. Woven-gold is a brand name of:
A. Chandeliers B. Silk Clothes
C. Bath tubs D. None of these

3. Tagline 'Empowering People' is linked with which brand?
A. Acer B. Compaq
C. HCL D. Wipro

4. Voltas Limited is a:
A. Birla group firm B. Singhania group firm
C. Tata group firm D. None of these

5. Which of the following industries are the major beneficiaries of the Mumbai port?
A. Sugar and Cotton textile industry

B. Iron and Steel industry
C. Cotton textile and Petrochemical industry
D. Engineering and Fertilizer industry

6. To which State Nano Car product has been shifted from West Bengal?
A. Andhra Pradesh B. Karnataka
C. Gujarat D. Haryana

7. Economic Survey in India is published officially by
A. RBI B. NITI Aayog
C. Ministry of Industries D. Ministry of Finance

8. India's largest aluminium maker is:
A. Indalco B. Hindalco
C. Indian Rare Earths Ltd D. None of these

9. Which of the following is not one of the three fundamental methods of firm valuation?
A. Discounted Cash flow
B. Income of earnings–where the firm is valued on some multiple of accounting income or earnings.
C. Balance sheet–where the firm is valued in terms of its assets
D. Market Share

10. The Wipro group started its operations from a/an:
A. Software firm B. Oil mill
C. Toothpaste company D. All of these

11. The largest private sector firm of India is:
A. RIL B. HLL
C. ONGC D. Infosys

12. Shareholders wealth increases with the increase in:
A. EPS
B. Market value of the firm
C. Dividend & Market value of the firm
D. Market price of the equity share

13. Which city has been identified as the hottest (i.e., first ranking) outsourcing destination in the world?
A. Bangalore (India)
B. Dublin (Ireland)
C. Makati City (The Philippines)
D. Tokyo (Japan)

14. The well-known book "The Argumentative Indian" has been written by
A. Robin S. Sharma B. Vikram Seth
C. Amartya Sen D. Pavan K. Verma

15. Which one of the following is a reputed manufacturer of tractors in India?
A. PTL B. Escotel
C. SKF D. KG Khosla

16. The ad-line 'Life's Good' is associated with which company?
A. Nokia B. LG
C. Samsung D. Sony

17. CBDT stands for
A. Central Board of Direct Taxes
B. Central Bureau of Direct Tariffs
C. Central Board of Direct Trades
D. None of these

18. Which TV Channel has its slogan as 'Subse Tej'?
A. Zee New B. Aaj Tak
C. Star News D. NDTV India

19. Which one of the following firms/groups is not associated with textiles?
A. Reliance B. P&G
C. Vardhman D. None of these

20. Which firm, out of the following is associated with heavy electrical equipment?
A. Stamford B. Kirloskar Brothers Ltd
C. KG Khosla D. Vam Organics

21. Who was the founder of the Appollo group of companies?
A. Shiv Nadar B. AS Ganguly
C. GD Birla D. Raunaq Singh

22. What is common in Titan, Safari and Voltas?
A. All of these are owned by the Singhania clan
B. All of these are being questioned under the MRTP Ltd.
C. All of these belong to the Tata Group
D. All of these manufacture Fast Moving Consumer Goods (FMCGs)

23. Which of the following organisations has established the 'Indian Institute of Insurance Surveyors and Loss Assessors'?
A. ICICI Lombard General Insurance Co.
B. Insurance Regulatory and Development Authority (IRDA)
C. Reserve Bank of India (RBI)
D. Life Insurance Corporation of India (LIC)

24. Who is the founder of Videocon International?
A. K.L. Dhoot B. N.M. Dhoot
C. M.C. Mehta D. R.N. Gupta

25. What is the name of the group to which, Herbertsons belongs?
A. UB B. MRF
C. Lloyds D. BPL

26. The famous advertising firm, Enterprise Nexus, was set up in this year.
A. 1997 B. 1998
C. 1995 D. 2001

27. Skimming price relates to:
A. Charging competitive price
B. Charging high initial price
C. Charging low initial price
D. None of these

28. Cost of capital does not mean:
A. Rate of interest
B. Cut off rate decided by management
C. Expectations of investors for dividend
D. Money paid to SEBI for permission to acquire capital

29. Financial Leverage is intended to:
A. Increase return on capital employed
B. Increase net equity return
C. Increase return on capital employed and net equity
D. Decrease volatility in return

30. ONGC Videsh Limited was earlier known as:
A. OVL B. OEG
C. HIL D. None of the above

31. Induction means:
A. Training B. Introduction
C. Incentives D. Promotion

32. Workers participation in management in any organization is:
A. Democratic B. Institutional
C. Voluntary D. All of the above

33. Employee morale relates to—
A. Productivity B. Attitude
C. Empathy D. Skills

34. Which of the following is the latest buzzword among bankers?
A. Social Banking B. Financial inclusion
C. Mass Banking D. None of the above

35. The short term money market comprises:
A. The Call Money Market
B. The inter bank deposit market
C. The bills re-discounting market
D. All of the above

36. What is the value of the firm usually based on?
A. The value of debt and equity.
B. The value of equity.
C. The value of debt.
D. The value of assets plus liabilities.

37. DIGJAM Suiting is a product of:
A. Tata Enterprise B. Birla Enterprise
C. Reliance Enterprise D. Oswal Enterprise

38. 'Cosmopolitan' has been brought in India by:
A. The Times of India B. The Hindustan Times
C. Living Media D. The Tribune

39. Monte Carlo collections is marketed by:
A. Snowhite B. Raymonds
C. Oswal D. Zodiac

40. What is the purpose of the India Brand Equity Fund?
A. To organise trade fairs
B. To promote in-bound tourism
C. To make 'Made in India' a label of quality
D. To provide venture capital to IT Sector

41. Which company is the sole India licencee of the brand, Pringle of Scotland?
A. Oswal Knit India Ltd B. Vardhaman Industries
C. Raymonds D. None of the above

42. Arrange the companies in column 2 with the cars mentioned in column 1 and tick the right answer.

Column 1	*Column 2*
1. Matiz	*a.* Hyundai
2. Mistubishi Lancer	*b.* Daewoo
3. Santro	*c.* Tata
4. Indica	*d.* Hindustan Motors

A. *a b c d* B. *b a d c*
C. *b d a c* D. *b a c d*

43. What is 'Super 301'?
A. A French news channel
B. An American trade law
C. A British anti-aircraft missile
D. None of these

44. Which is not a product from the company Indian Oil?
A. Servo lubricants B. Xtra Premium Petrol
C. Xtra Mile Diesel D. High Speed Diesel

45. Aquaguard water purification systems are products from
A. Kenstar B. Voltas
C. Bluestar D. None of these

46. The leader in the market for zinc chloride batteries is:
A. Duracell B. Novino
C. Eveready D. Energizer

47. 'Real' juices are products of which company?
A. Nestle B. Dabur
C. ITC D. None of these

48. Hindustan Machine Tools (HMT) is a:
A. Private Sector Company
B. Joint Sector Company
C. Public Sector Company
D. None of these

49. Which one is not a product from Daburs?
A. Real Juice B. Vatika Shampoo
C. Hajmola D. Amla Hair Oil

50. What is cognitive dissonance?
A. Buying Behaviour
B. Pre-purchase Behaviour
C. Post-purchase Behaviour
D. Buying indifference

51. 'Fair and Lovely' range of products was launched by
A. Procter and Gamble B. Lakme
C. Hindustan Lever D. Godrej

52. Who is the father of principles of management?
A. Fleming B. Henry Fayol
C. F.W. Taylor D. Bavnard

53. Country's first energy exchange 'Indian Energy Exchange' (IEX) has become operational since–
A. June 27, 2008 B. June 30, 2008
C. July 1, 2008 D. July 10, 2008

54. Bisleri bottled water is a product from
A. Pepsi B. Parle
C. Coca Cola D. Nestle

55. Kelkar Committee dealt with
A. Industrial pollution B. Tax reforms
C. Babri Masjid issue D. Railway accidents

56. Whirlpool Home Appliances company is a company from
A. France B. Italy
C. UK D. USA

57. Haier, which is a major home appliances company, is a company from

A. North Korea
B. South Korea
C. China
D. Japan

58. Which city is known as Silicon Valley of India?
A. Bangalore (Bengaluru)
B. Mumbai
C. Hyderabad
D. Chennai

59. 'Servo' brand lubricants are from
A. Bharat Petroleum
B. Hindustan Petroleum
C. IBP
D. Indian Oil

60. India's first electric car is:
A. Enviro
B. Reva
C. Astra
D. Futura

61. Which company in India is the only manufacturer of Vitamin B_{12} in Asia:
A. Burroughs Wellcome
B. Sandoz
C. Cadila
D. Merind

62. The slogan 'Make Life Simple' is associated with
A. SBI Card
B. BOB Card
C. Standard Chartered Bank Card
D. None of these

63. SEZ stands for
A. Southern Economic Zone
B. South European Zone
C. Special Economic Zone
D. Special Eastern Zone

64. Which is India's largest Mutual Fund organisation?
A. GIC
B. SBI
C. UTI
D. ICICI

65. With what would you associate the brand name *Ruggers?*
A. Shoes
B. Jeans
C. Cigarettes
D. Casual Wear

66. 'Because you deserve to know' is the punchline used by
A. The Times of India
B. The Hindu
C. Indian Express
D. Hindustan Times

67. Which of the following is not an Ad agency?
A. Mudra
B. Contract
C. Andersen
D. Clarion

68. Which brand's byline is "Made for each other"?
A. Four Square
B. Wills
C. Gold Flake
D. Charms

69. Name the advertising agency that produces the famous Amul advertisements featuring a cartoon character.
A. HTA
B. Da Cunha
C. Avenues
D. None of the above

70. The tool adopted to change corporate culture is:
A. Span of Control
B. Hierarchy
C. Managerial Grid
D. Seven's Framework

71. Ashok Leyland, a company manufacturing trukcs is associated with:
A. Reliance
B. Tata
C. Birlas
D. Hindujas

72. Petroleum prices, in the world are determined by
A. IMF
B. IBRD
C. OPEC
D. None of these

73. The organisation arranging the India International Trade Fair (IITF) is
A. ITDC
B. ITPO
C. CII
D. FICCI

74. Which of the following is not a Godrej product?
A. Cinthol
B. Good Knight
C. Jumpin Drink
D. Close-up

75. The types of audit are:
1. Pre-audit
2. Post-audit
3. Regular-audit
4. Concurrent-audit

Select the correct answer from the codes given below:
Codes :
A. 1 and 2
B. 1, 2 and 3
C. 1, 2 and 4
D. 1 and 4

76. 'Madonna' range of fabrics are being produced in India by:
A. OCM
B. Vimal
C. Raymond
D. Praful

77. Which one of the following is not a brand of Liberty?
A. Force 10
B. Footfun
C. Windsor
D. Ambassador

78. Which one of the following is not an advertising agency?
A. Trikaya Grey
B. MICA
C. Rediffusion
D. HTA

79. Which was the first Indian company to be listed on NASDAQ?
A. Infosys
B. Satyam
C. Unicarp
D. TCS

80. Which one of the following agencies has the power to declare any industrial unit as a potentially sick unit?
A. BIFR
B. MRTPC
C. FICCI
D. IRBI

81. Name the first Indian businessman who found a place in the cover story of forbes globe.
A. Anil Ambani
B. Dr. Reddy
C. Azim Hashan
D. Narayan Murthy

82. CRISIL stands for
A. international aid
B. credit rating
C. crisis management
D. debt rate

83. Prime lending rate refers to
A. the interest rate to prime real estate holders
B. the interest rate set by RBI
C. the interest rate set by the primary markets
D. the interest rate for the bank's best client

84. Pick the odd man out:
A. OPEL
B. DAEWOO
C. NISSAN
D. MRF

85. The Tata Group's holding company is known as
A. Tata Ltd B. Tata Holding Co.
C. THC D. TISCO

86. Crop loan can be availed from any
A. Commercial Bank B. Rural Bank
C. Co-operative Bank D. All of these

87. Which one of the following is not correctly matched?
A. White Revolution — Dairy
B. Green Revolution — Agriculture
C. Blue Revolution — Fishery
D. Red Revolution — Wool

88. As per the guidelines issued by the SEBI the Permanent Account Number (PAN) is a must for which of the following?
A. Demat Accounts
B. All Saving Bank Accounts
C. All Housing Loan Accounts
D. All Current Accounts

89. NAFED is connected with:
A. Animal husbandry
B. Conservation of fuels
C. Agricultural marketing
D. Agricultural implements

90. Which one of the following refers to traditional Budgeting?
A. Performance Budgeting
B. Line-item Budgeting
C. Capital Budgeting
D. Zero-based Budgeting

91. Taj Majal Hotel was started in the year:
A. 1904 B. 1903
C. 1905 D. 1906

92. TISCO was set up in the year:
A. 1904 B. 1905
C. 1906 D. 1907

93. Premier Automobiles Ltd (PAL) was set up in the year:
A. 1944 B. 1945
C. 1947 D. 1948

94. Production of India's first Automotive Tyre of Dunlop was started in the year.
A. 1940 B. 1941
C. 1936 D. 1950

95. Usha Sewing Machine Factory was established in the year:
A. 1930 B. 1935
C. 1940 D. 1946

96. Mafatlal Spinning Mills was established in the year:
A. 1930 B. 1931
C. 1932 D. 1933

97. The Indian Chamber of Commerce was set up in the year:
A. 1920 B. 1922
C. 1923 D. 1926

98. The Imperial Tobacco Co. was founded in the year:
A. 1911 B. 1915
C. 1916 D. 1910

99. Country's first credit card was launched by the Diners's Club in the year:
A. 1969 B. 1970
C. 1971 D. 1980

100. Dunlop Rubber Co. was set up in the year:
A. 1926 B. 1930
C. 1935 D. 1936

ANSWERS

1	2	3	4	5	6	7	8	9	10
B	C	D	C	C	C	D	B	D	B
11	**12**	**13**	**14**	**15**	**16**	**17**	**18**	**19**	**20**
A	C	A	C	A	B	A	B	B	A
21	**22**	**23**	**24**	**25**	**26**	**27**	**28**	**29**	**30**
D	C	B	B	A	C	B	B	C	C
31	**32**	**33**	**34**	**35**	**36**	**37**	**38**	**39**	**40**
B	A	B	C	D	B	D	C	C	C
41	**42**	**43**	**44**	**45**	**46**	**47**	**48**	**49**	**50**
A	C	B	D	D	C	B	C	B	A
51	**52**	**53**	**54**	**55**	**56**	**57**	**58**	**59**	**60**
C	B	A	B	B	D	C	A	D	B
61	**62**	**63**	**64**	**65**	**66**	**67**	**68**	**69**	**70**
D	A	C	C	D	D	C	B	B	C
71	**72**	**73**	**74**	**75**	**76**	**77**	**78**	**79**	**80**
D	C	B	D	C	A	D	B	A	A
81	**82**	**83**	**84**	**85**	**86**	**87**	**88**	**89**	**90**
C	B	D	D	D	D	D	A	C	B
91	**92**	**93**	**94**	**95**	**96**	**97**	**98**	**99**	**100**
B	D	A	C	B	A	D	D	A	A

* * * * *

COMPUTER SCIENCE

with 1000+ MCQs

1 THE COMPUTER SYSTEM

THE BASIC COMPUTER

THE VON NEUMANN ARCHITECTURE

The term Von Neumann architecture is used in reference to a model of computer design that has only a single storage area used to contain both the set of instructions required for the performance of a transaction and the data required or produced by the transaction. The architecture takes its name from the Hungarian mathematician John Von Neumann, a man whose 1945 paper entitled First Draft Report on the EDVAC is widely onsidered to be one of the pioneering documented accounts on the topic of the broad purpose stored-program computer (known as an EDVAC). A computer that makes use of Von Neumann architecture has five components: a control circuitry, an arithmetic-logic unit, an input/output device, a memory, and a bus that ensures a data path connecting these components. Computers that use this type of architecture are often referred to as Von Neumann machines, but this can be a source of confusion, since the term is also used to refer to self-reproducing machines, a concept that Von Neumann devoted much time to during its very early stages and that he came to call universal constructors.

The name applied to it comes from John Von Neumann, who as author of two papers in 1945 [Goldstine and Von Neumann 1963, Von Neumann 1981] and co-author of a third paper in 1946 [Burks, et al. 1963] was the first to spell out the requirements for a general purpose electronic computer. The 1946 paper, written with Arthur W. Burks and Hermann H. Goldstine, was titled "Preliminary Discussion of the Logical Design of an Electronic Computing Instrument," and the ideas in it were to have a profound impact on the subsequent development of such machines.

Von Neumann's design led eventually to the construction of the EDVAC computer in 1952. However, the first computer of this type to be actually constructed and operated was the Manchester Mark I, designed and built at Manchester University in England [Siewiorek, et al. 1982]. It ran its first program in 1948, executing it out of its 96 word memory. It executed an instruction in 1.2 milliseconds, which must have seemed phenomenal at the time. Using today's popular "MIPS" terminology (millions of instructions per second), it would be rated at .00083 MIPS. By contrast, some current supercomputers are rated at in excess of 1000 MIPS. And yet, these computers, such as the Cray systems and the Control Data Cyber 200 models, are still tied to the Von Neumann architecture to a large extent.

The expectations for the fifth generation systems seem to require that substantially new architectures be evolved, and that both hardware and software be freed from the limitations of the Von Neumann architecture.

Von Neumann begins his "Preliminary Discussion" with a broad description of the general-purpose computing machine containing four main "organs." These are identified as relating to arithmetic, memory, control, and connection with the human operator. In other words, the arithmetic logic unit, the control unit, the memory, and the input-output devices that we see in the classical model of what a computer "looks like."

In a special purpose machine the computational procedure could be part of the hardware. In a general purpose one the instructions must be as changeable as the numbers they acted upon. This frequently is viewed as the principal contribution provided by Von Neumann's insight into the nature of what a computer should be.

INSTRUCTION EXECUTION

A microproccesor typically breaks the execution of an instruction into smaller operations. Each of these operations completes a portion of the entire instruction's execution. Typically the instruction is broken down into the following operations:

D–Decode: Looks at the decode in the instruction to determine the type of instruction to be executed.

A–Address: Generates the address for any memory based operands.

T–Translate: Modifies the address based on table values setup in memory. These tables typically are used by an operating system to change where data is stored. This allows multiple programs that do stores to the same address to really write to different locations of physical memory.

B–Buffer – Fetches operands needed to execute an instruction. These typically come from the general registers or for memory based operands, the cache (a.k.a. buffer).

E–Execute – Performs the ALU operation. These are simple mathematical operations such as addition, and subtraction. For execution of many instructions, the ALU performs an operation that has no effect, such as adding zero. This is used for instructions that have a result the same as the source operand. For example, a store instruction takes the value of a register and stores it, unmodified, at a specified memory location. For this instruction the ALU needs to perform an operation that produces a result equal to the source operand.

W–Write – Writes the result.

Example – Loading For this example, we will demonstrate the execution of the following instruction:

58204060 with the following assumptions:

- The CPU implements the S/370 architecture.
- Memory Locations 105060 - 105063 have the values 89, AB, BA, 98.
- General Purpose Register (GPR) 4 is equal to 00005000.
- The Operating System has "setup tables" so that the number 100000 (HEX) is added to all of the memory addresses specified by the program to determine the location in physical memory.

Instruction Cycle

The instruction cycle (also called fetch-and-execute cycle, fetch-decode-execute cycle (FDX)) can refer to either the time period during which one instruction is fetched from memory and executed when a computer receives a machine language instruction; or the sequence of actions that a CPU.

Interrupts

In computing, an interrupt is an asynchronous signal from hardware indicating the need for attention or a synchronous event in software indicating the need for a change in execution.

COMPUTERS: THEN AND NOW

Computer is a fast and accurate data manipulation device which works on the principle of give and take. Charles Babbage considered the father of Computers because he invented Diffence Engine and then Analytical Engine, which can store the information on Punched Cards during 1800's (Year). Storing of Information on Punched Cards is done by Charles Babbage on those days; this is the reason - why he is so called as "Father of Computers"

GENERATION OF COMPUTER

- **First Generation—1940-1956: Vacuum Tubes–** The first computers used vacuum tubes for circuitry and magnetic drums for memory, and were often enormous, taking up entire rooms. They were very expensive to operate and in addition to using a great deal of electricity, generated a lot of heat, which was often the cause of malfunctions.
- **Second Generation—1956-1963: Transistors–** Transistors replaced vacuum tubes and ushered in the second generation of computers. The transistor was invented in 1947 but did not see widespread use in computers until the late 50s. The transistor was far superior to the vacuum tube, allowing computers to become smaller, faster, cheaper, more energy-efficient and more reliable than their first-generation predecessors. Though the transistor still generated a great deal of heat that subjected the computer to damage.
- **Third Generation—1964-1971: Integrated Circuits** – The development of the integrated circuit was the hallmark of the third generation of computers. Transistors were miniaturized and placed on silicon chips, called semiconductors, which drastically increased the speed and efficiency of computers.
- **Fourth Generation—1971-Present: Microprocessors** – The microprocessor brought the fourth generation of computers, as thousands of integrated circuits were built onto a single silicon chip. What in the first generation filled an entire room could now fit in the palm of the hand. The Intel 4004 chip, developed in 1971, located all the components of the computer - from the central processing unit and memory to input/output controls - on a single chip.
- **Fifth Generation – Present and Beyond: Artificial Intelligence** – Fifth generation computing devices, based on artificial intelligence, are still in development, though there are some applications, such as voice recognition, that are being used today.

DATA REPRESENTATION

INTRODUCTION

The form in which data is stored in a particular operating environment. Different operating environments use different standards or conventions for storing floating-point numbers (for example, IEEE or IBM 390); for character encoding (ASCII or EBCDIC); for the ordering of bytes in memory (big Endian or little Endian); for word alignment (4-byte boundaries or 8-byte boundaries); and for data-type length (16-bit, 32-bit, or 64-bit).

NUMBER SYSTEMS

Binary Number System

The binary numeral system, or base-2 number system, is a numeral system that represents numeric values 0 using two symbois, usually 0 and 1. More specifically, the usual base-2 system is a positional notation with a radix of 2. Owing to its straightforward implementation in electronic circuitry, the binary system is used internally by virtually all modern computers.

Hexadecima Number System

Hexadecimal means 16. The base 16 numbering system is used as a shorthand for representing binary numbers. Each half byte (four bits) is assigned a hex digit as shown in the following chart with its decimal and binary equivalents. Hex values are identified with an "h" or dollar sign, thus $3E0, 3E0h and 3E0H all stand for the hex humber 3E0.

Octal

A numbering system that uses eight digits. It is used as a shorthand method for representing binary characters that use six-bits. Each three bits (half a character) is converted into a single octal digit. Okta is Greek for 8.

Ones' complement

Alternatively, a system known as **ones' complement** can be used to represent negative numbers. The ones' complement form of a negative binary number is the bitwise NOT applied to it — the complement of its positive counterpart. Like sign-and-magnitude representation, ones' complement has two representations of 0: 00000000 (+0) and 11111111 (-0).

Two's complement

The problems of multiple representations of 0 and the need for the end-around carry are circumvented by a system called **two's complement**. In two's complement, negative numbers are represented by the bit pattern which is one greater (in an unsigned sense) than the ones' complement of the positive value.

DATA REPRESENTATION FOR COMPUTATION

Binary number Representation

A binary number can be represented by any sequence of bits (binary digits), which in turn may be represented by any mechanism capable of being in two mutually exclusive states. The following sequences of symbols could all be interpreted as the same binary numeric value of 666:

1 0 1 0 0 1 1 0 1 0

| – | – – | | – | –

x o x o o x x o x o

y n y n n y y n y n

Arithmetic Operations in binary Number

Arithmetic in binary is much like arithmetic in other numeral systems. Addition, subtraction, multiplication, and division can be performed on binary numerals.

Addition

The simplest arithmetic operation in binary is addition. Adding two single-digit binary numbers is relatively simple:

0 + 0 = 0

0 + 1 = 1

1 + 0 = 1

1 + 1 = 10 (carry:1)

Subtraction

Subtraction works in much the same way:

0 − 0 = 0

0 − 1 = 1 (with borrow)

1 − 0 = 1

1 − 1 = 0

One binary numeral can be subtracted from another as follows:

```
  *   * * *   (starred columns are borrowed from)
  1 1 0 1 1 1 0
−     1 0 1 1 1
= 1 0 1 0 1 1 1
```

Multiplication

Multiplication in binary is similar to its decimal counterpart. Two numbers *A* and *B* can be multiplied by partial products: for each digit in *B*, the product of that digit in *A* is calculated and written on a new line, shifted leftward so that its rightmost digit lines up with the digit in *B* that was used. The sum of all these partial products gives the final result.

Example –The binary numbers 1011 and 1010 are multiplied as follows:

COMPUTER SCIENCE

```
    1 0 1 1  (A)
  × 1 0 1 0  (B)
  ---------
    0 0 0 0  ← Corresponds to a zero in B
  + 1 0 1 1  ← Corresponds to a one in B
  + 0 0 0 0
 + 1 0 1 1
 -------------
 = 1 1 0 1 1 1 0
```

Division

Binary division is again similar to its decimal counterpart:

```
101 | 11011
```

Here, the divisor is 101_2, or 5 decimal, while the dividend is 11011_2, or 27 decimal. The procedure is the same as that of decimal long division; here, the divisor 101_2 goes into the first three digits 110_2 of the dividend one time, so a "1" is written on the top line. This result is multiplied by the divisor, and subtracted from the first three digits of the dividend; the next digit (a "1") is included to obtain a new three-digit sequence:

```
          1
101  | 1 1 0 1 1
     - 1 0 1
       -----
         0 1 1
```

The procedure is then repeated with the new sequence, continuing until the digits in the dividend have been exhausted:

```
          1 0 1
101  | 1 1 0 1 1
     - 1 0 1
       -----
         0 1 1
       - 0 0 0
         -----
           1 1 1
         - 1 0 1
           -----
             1 0
```

Thus, the quotient of 11011_2 divided by 101_2 is 101_2, as shown on the top line, while the remainder, shown on the bottom line, is 10_2. In decimal, 27 divided by 5 is 5, with a remainder of 2.

PRINCIPLES OF LOGIC CIRCUITS

LOGIC GATES: LOGIC COMBINATIONAL CIRCUITS

Sequential Circuits

We said that the output of a combinational circuit depends solely upon the input. The implication is that combinational circuits have no memory. In order to build sophisticated digital logic circuits, including computers, we need more a powerful model. We need circuits whose output depends upon both the input of the circuit and its previous state. In other words, we need circuits that have memory. For a device to serve as a memory, it must have three characteristics:

- the device must have two stable states
- there must be a way to read the state of the device
- there must be a way to set the state at least once.

The S-R Latch

The output of a NOR gate is true only when both inputs are false. Consider the circuit in Figure 1. The output of each NOR gate is fed back to the input of the other.

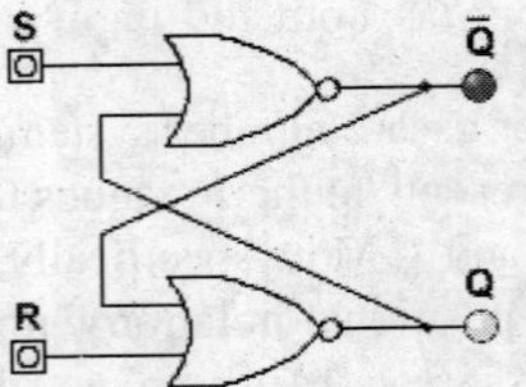

Fig. 1. The S-R Latch. S sets the latch, causing Q to become true, R resets the latch.

Fig. 2. The symbol the S-R latch

This means that if the output of one NOR gate is true, the output of the other must be false. Study the circuit for a moment before you push any buttons and convince yourself that this is the case. The output of the upper NOR gate, $\bar{Q}$ is true, or one. This means that one of the inputs of the lower NOR gate, **Q** is true, and the output of the lower NOR must be false. For the output of the upper NOR to be true, both its inputs have to be false. Examine the circuit and you will see that this is also correct. Now press the S button. The output of the upper NOR gate, $\bar{Q}$ is forced to false, allowing the output of the lower NOR to become true. Press S again to turn it off. The output of the circuit is unchanged. Examine the circuit to understand why. What has happened is that we have stored the value of S. Turning S on and off again does not change the output.

With S off, turn R on, then off again. What happens? Why. This circuit is an **S-R latch.** An S-R latch is also called a set-reset latch. An input on S sets the latch, making **Q** true and $\bar{Q}$ false. An input on R resets the latch; **Q** becomes false and $\bar{Q}$ becomes true. The output of the circuit is *stable* in either state with the inputs removed. We can remove the input that caused a particular output and the output will be unchanged. The state, and so the output, will only change when the complementary input is applied. Such a circuit is said to be **bistable** because it has two stable states.The symbol for the S-R latch is shown in Figure 1-B. Whether the $\bar{Q}$ output is available depends upon how the latch is packaged and whether an extra pin is available. The input S = R = 1 is not allowed. If both inputs are true, both outputs must be false. This implies **Q = $\bar{\mathbf{Q}}$** = 0, which is logically inconsistent. Further, the circuit is unstable in this state; when one of the inputs returns to the false state, the remaining input determines the stable state and the output changes. We use the word *latch* here to mean a circuit that can store one bit. A register that supplies data to the inputs of a combinational circuit is also called a latch; we will encounter this second meaning of the word later.

Note: The circuits above have been drawn with **S** and **$\bar{\mathbf{Q}}$** at the top to be consistent with Tanenbaum. Most other textbooks place **R** and **Q** at the top. Since the circuit is symmetrical, exchanging the labels makes no difference so long as both the input and output labels are exchanged.

TIMING CONSIDERATIONS

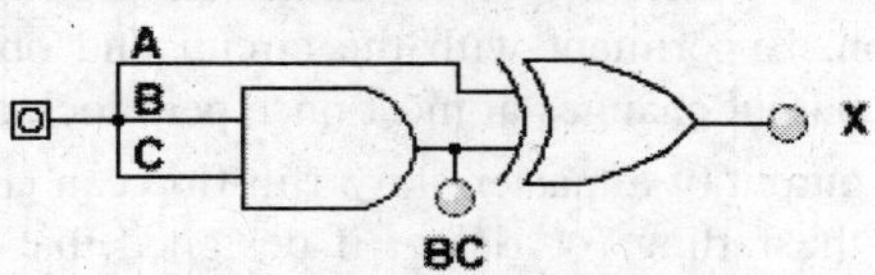

Fig. 3. This circuit can produce a *glitch*.

Figure 3 shows a combinational circuit adapted from [MURD00]; in ordinary circumstances, the three inputs A, B, and C would come from other circuits. We've wired them all to one pushbutton to make a point. If you study the circuit, you will see that the output should be zero or false regardless of the input. If the input is zero, both A and BC will be zero and the XOR gate will produce a zero. If the input is a one, A and BC will be ones, and the XOR gate will *still* produce an output of zero or false. Let's look at what happens in reality. With all inputs off, the AND gate produces an output of false, both inputs to the XOR gate are false, and the output of the circuit is false. Press the pushbutton and observe carefully what happens. (Cycle from off to on and back a few times if you need to.) The A input to the XOR gate becomes true, and the BC inputs to the AND gate also become true. However, the *output* of the AND gate remains false for a time equal to one gate delay. The XOR gate has inputs of true-false, and will produce an output of true one gate delay later.

After one gate delay has passed, the output of the AND gate is true and the input of the XOR gate is true-true. However, the output of the XOR gate remains true for one gate delay time. After the second gate delay time, the output of the XOR gate attains the correct value of false. The process reverses itself when the pushbutton is turned off. Experiment with the circuit until you are sure you understand what is happening.

A circumstance where timing dependencies can briefly cause incorrect output is called a **hazard.**

CLOCKING

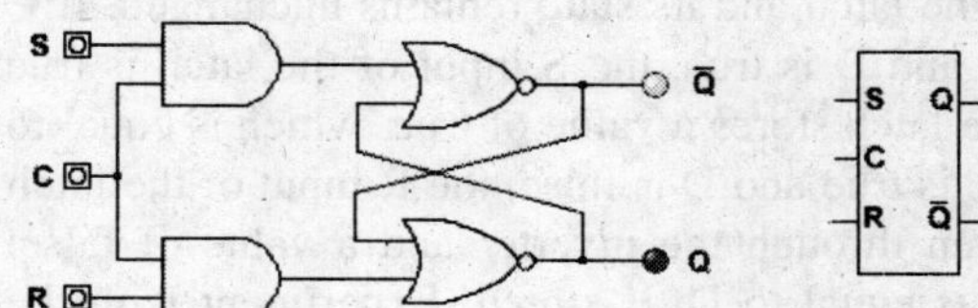

Fig. 4(a). A clocked S-R latch can change only when C is true

Fig. 4(b) The symbol for the clocked S-R latch.

One way to do that is to interpose AND gates between the S and R inputs and the latch circuit. The control signal drives the other input of each AND gate. When the control signal is false, the output of the two AND gates is always low and changes to S and R do not affect the bit stored by the latch.

When the control signal is true, the S and R signals are propagated through the AND gates and the stored value can change. Because the control input is generally driven by a regular train of pulses, it is often called a *clock* input. The circuit of Figure 4 is a clocked **S-R latch.** With the C input false, experiment with the S and R inputs. Now make the C input true by pressing the button and experiment again with S and R. Note that clocking does not help with the problem of S=R=1. In fact, it makes the problem worse. With S and R both true, turn C on and off several times. You cannot predict whether the latch will store **Q** or **$\bar{\mathbf{Q}}$** . When the S and R inputs are removed simultaneously, the latch settles into one of its two stable states at random.

THE CLOCKED D-LATCH

Once we have applied the idea of clocking to our S-R latch, we can get rid of the problem of what to do with S = R = 1 and also simplify the input to our circuit. Usually what we want to do with a storage device is store one bit of information. The need for explicitly setting and resetting the latch is added complexity. What we would really like is a circuit that has a data input D and a data output Q. When the clock signal is high, whatever appears on D should be stored in Q.

The circuit of Figure 5 is such a circuit. It has a data input, D, and a control input, C. The data input is connected through an AND gate to the S input of an S-R latch. It is also connected through

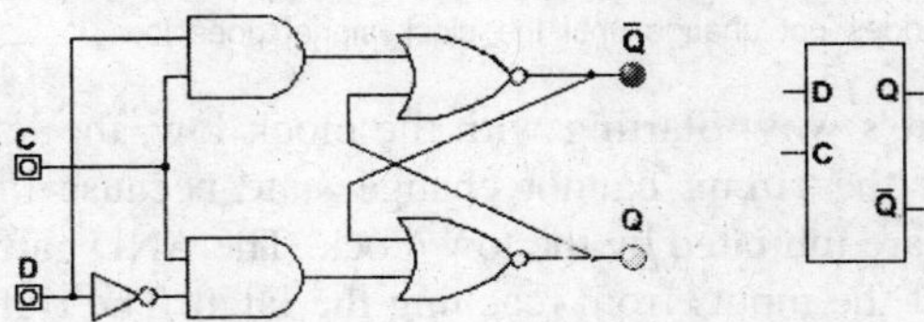

Fig. 5(a). A clocked D latch. When C (control) is true, the value at (D) (data) is stored in Q.

Fig. 5(b) The symbol for the clocked D latch.

an inverter and an AND gate to the R input. The other inputs of the two AND gates are connected to the C input of the circuit. If C is false, no signals reach the latch and its state remains unchanged. If C is true and D is true, the S input of the latch is true and the latch stores a value of true, which is equal to D. If C is true and D is false, the R input of the latch is driven through the inverter and a value of false, which is equal to D, is stored. Experiment with the circuit and observe what happens.

The clocked D-latch stores whatever is on the D input when C is true. If C is asserted (made true) only after the input circuits have settled, this circuit will store the correct value of D. Because there is only one data input, the case of S=R=1 cannot occur. Make C true by operating the push button, then change the value of D and watch what happens. As long as the C input is true, changes to D are reflected in the output of the circuit. The clocked D-latch is a level triggered device. Whether it stores data depends upon level at C.

MASTER-SLAVE FLIP-FLOPS

The clocked D-latch solves several of the problems of storing output from a combinational circuit, but not all of them. Particularly, if D changes while C is true, the new value of D will appear at the output. Generally this is not what is wanted. If the stored value can change state more than once during a single clock pulse, the result is a hazard that might introduce a glitch later in the circuit. We must design the circuit so that the state can change only once per clock cycle. This can be accomplished by connecting two latches together as shown in Figure 6. The left half of the circuit is the clocked D-latch from the previous section. The right half of the circuit is a clocked S-R latch; however, the clock signal for the output section is the input clock signal inverted. The output of this device can only change once per clock cycle. The change occurs shortly after the falling edge of the clock cycle.

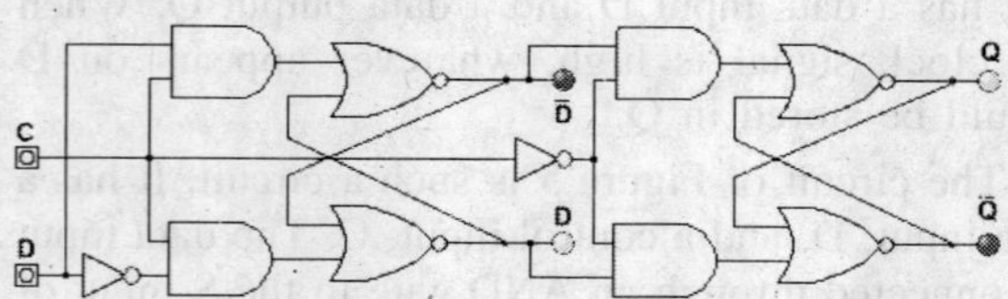

Fig. 6(a). A Master-Slave D Flip-Flop. The output of this device does not change until the clock signal goes low.

Here's why: Starting with the clock low, the left half of the circuit cannot change state because the inputs are inhibited by the low clock. The AND gates prevent the inputs from reaching the latch. The right half of the circuit could change because it "sees" a high clock, but its inputs come from the latch on the left, and they can't change. When the clock signal goes high, the D input can change the state of the left latch. One gate delay later, the clock input of the right latch goes low. Since there are at least two gate delays through the D latch that is the left half of the circuit, the right latch cannot change state before its clock signal goes low. With the clock signal high, D can change, and the left latch will change also. However, the output will not change.

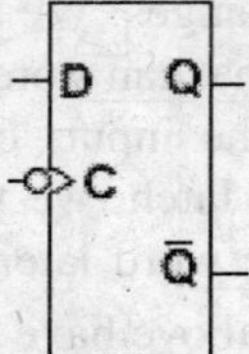

Fig. 6(b). The symbol for the D flip-flop.

When the clock returns low, the R and S inputs of the output latch will be driven by whatever value is stored by the first latch at that moment. The output of the circuit will change to reflect the value of D at the moment when the clock makes its high-to-low transition. Experiment with the circuit and observe that the output changes at most once per clock cycle.

The output of a master-slave flip-flop can change only at the falling (or rising, if designed that way) edge of the clock pulse. That's why we call it a flip-flop instead of a latch. Tanenbaum [TANE99] is careful to call level-triggered devices *latches* and edge-triggered devices *flip-flops*. Not all authors are as exacting in this distinction. The symbol for the D flop-flop is shown in Figure 6-B. The triangle at the clock input indicates that this device changes state only on clock transitions. The negation bubble indicates that the change is on the "negative" or falling edge of the clock.

The master-slave flip-flop is an adequate design for a D flip-flop. There are other types of flip-flops, not studied here, for which it doesn't work. The J-K flop-flop, for example, exhibits a phenomenon known as ones-catching in the master-slave configuration. A spurious one on the input will be latched and propagated to the output even if the input returns to zero before the end of the clock period.

EDGE TRIGGERED DEVICES

We could solve the problems of hazards and ones-catching if we could design a memory that would both sample its inputs and store data based on the transition of a clock pulse. If the combinational parts of a circuit could settle during the time the clock signal was true, and the storage part of the circuit sampled the input and saved the result when the clock changed from true to false, we would have no problems with hazards at the output nor with ones catching. A storage circuit like that is called a negative edge-triggered flip-flop. A circuit that stores a result on transition of the clock from false to true is a positive edge-triggered flip-flop.

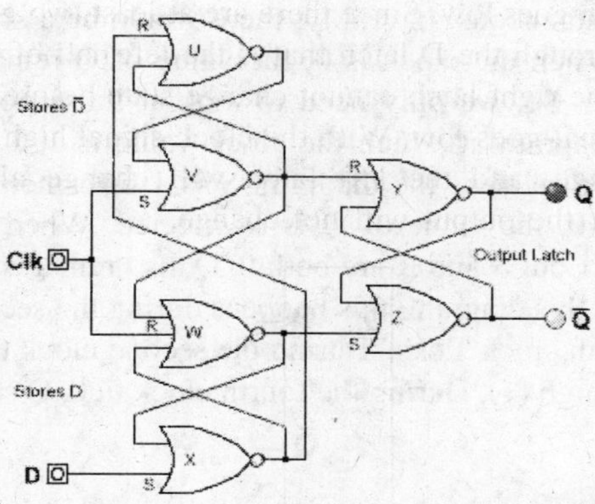

Fig. 7. This circuit is triggered by the falling edge of the clock.

The circuit in Figure 7 is a negative edge-triggered flip-flop. This circuit was adapted from Murdocca [MURD00]. It is effectively three S-R latches. Latch W-X stores D, and latch U-V stores the complement of D. Latch Y-Z prevents the output from changing except on a true-to-false transition of the clock. Here is how it works: When the clock is true, the S input of latch U-V and the R input of latch W-X are also true. This forces the S and R inputs of latch Y-Z to false, and the circuit cannot change state. When the clock changes from true to false, D appears on the S input of latch Y-Z and the complement of D appears on the R input. Output Q reflects the value of D.

When the clock is false, one of the inputs to Y-Z is true and the other is false. Latches U-V and W-X are stable in this state regardless of changes in D. Latch Y-Z, and therefore the output of the circuit, can only change on the true-to-false clock transition. Let's examine the assertion that the latches U-V and W-X are stable when the clock is low. At the falling edge of the clock, either Y's R must be true or Z's S, but not both. Consider the case that Y's R is true. This means V's inputs must both be false. That the clock is false is given. V's other input comes from U; U's lower input comes from V and is true from the assumption that Y's R is true. Therefore, U's output must be zero and the output of latch U-V is stable regardless of changes in D.

The alternative assumption is that Z's S is true, meaning that the ouptut of W is true. All three of W's inputs must be false. Clock is false by assumption.The upper input of W is false given the assumption that the output of V is false. If the output of W is true, the upper input of X is true, the output of X is false, and the lower input of W is false. The output of W is stable when the clock is low regardless of changes in D. By experimenting with the circuit, verify that changing D has no effect on the output regardless of whether the clock is high or low. The output changes to reflect the current state of D only when the clock changes from high to low.

COMBINATIONAL VS. SEQUENTIAL CIRCUITS

Sequential circuits have loops - these enable circuits to receive feedback. A simple example of a system dependent on feedback is a thermostat. It controls the temperature by receiving feedback in the form of a temperature reading. A diagram of this system is:

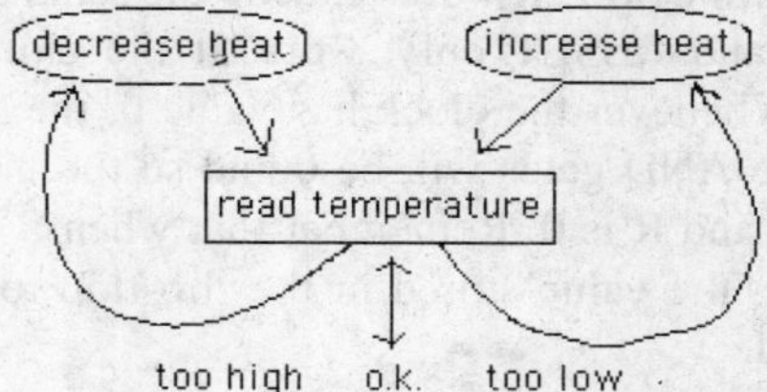

This system has loops. The output of the temperature changing functions affects the input of the temperature-checking function. Its output affects the operation of the temperature changing function(s).

S-R FLIP-FLOP

The S-R flip-flop has two input lines and one output line. The output, Q, is always whatever value is 'stored' in the flip-flop. The input lines specify whether a 0 or 1 should be stored in the flip-flop. If S is 1, the flip-flop is 'set' to 1. If R is 1, the flip-flop is 'reset' to 0. If S & R are both 0, the flip-flop should be neither set nor reset, so the bit that is currently stored in the flip-flop remains there. R and S are not allowed to both be 1 at the same time. (Logically, it doesn't make sense to try to both set and reset the flip-flop at the same time.)

Here is an implementation of an S-R flip-flop: (others exist)

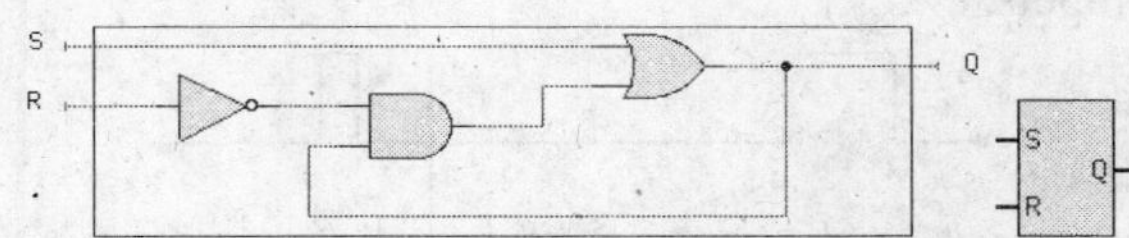

S	R	State	Output	
0	0	0	0	the output = S OR ((NOT R) AND state)
0	0	1	1	NOT R AND state => 1, so the output is 1
0	1	0	0	the input to the AND gate, R, is inverted. 0 AND 0 => 0
0	1	1	0	
1	0	0	1	
1	0	1	1	
1	1	0		x - these 2 states are officially undefined, b/c you dont' want
1	1	1	x	to set and reset at the same time!

THE CLOCK

For sequential circuits, we add the control of a clock. By using a clock, we can ensure that certain events occur in the correct order. A clock is just an alternating sequence of 0's and 1's that has a set frequency. In the diagram below, you can see the key aspects of a clock. When the clock is 'high', its value is 1; when it's 'low', its value is 0.

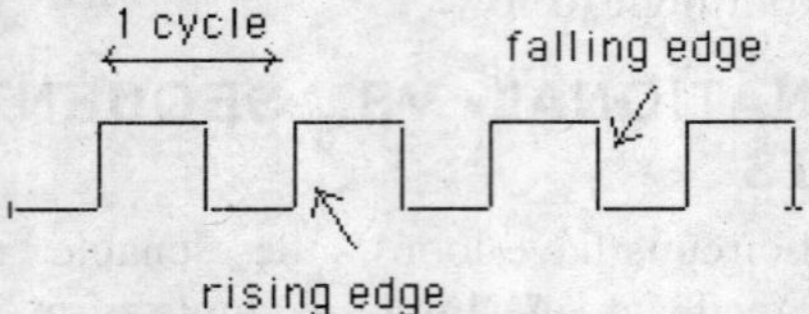

Often, the clock (wire) and the input it controls are combined with an AND gate. The input will only be activated if the clock has value 1. A clocked flip-flop is shown below. It works exactly the same except that SET and RESET only 'work' if the clock has value 1. Whenever the clock has value 0, the output of both the AND gates will be 0 and so the input to for both S and R is 0. Remember that when S and R are both 0, the value stored in the flip-flop remains unchanged.

Clocked SR flip flop

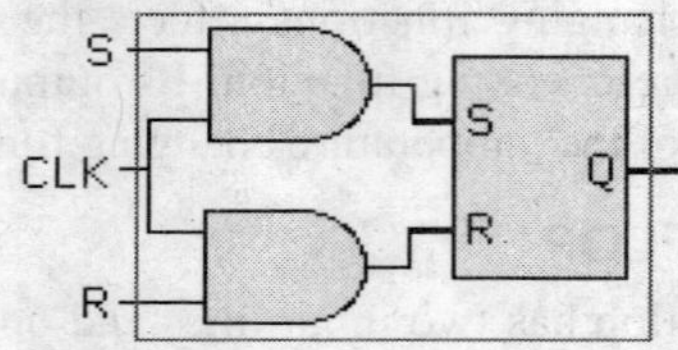

TIMING DIAGRAMS

Timing diagrams are used to better understand the operation of sequential functions. They are to sequential circuits what truth tables are to combinational circuits. They show the values of inputs over time and the resulting output. When the 'line' is raised, it corresponds to a value of 1; when it is flat, it corresponds to a value of 0. They are read from left to right, like a time-line. The sequence of each input value is given: in this case, S & R (and the clock). The output can be computed based on the values of the inputs.

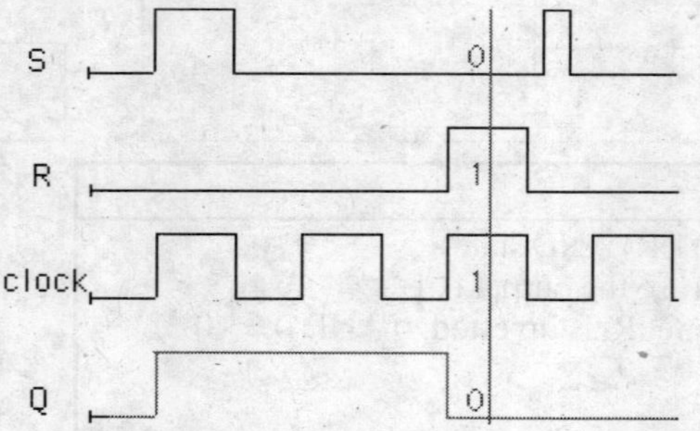

In this timing diagram, Q has the initial value of 0. During the first clock 'tick', the value of S is 1, so Q is set to 1. In this diagram, the transition from 0 to 1 is instantaneous. In reality, there would be a slight delay. When the clock is 0, the value of Q remains the same. So, we only need to look at those points in the diagram at which the clock value is 1. Look at the top right of the diagram. S is 1 but since the clock is 0, the value of Q is unaffected. When the clock is 1 but S and R are both 0, Q also remains the same. In this diagram, this happens during the second and fourth clock 'ticks.' During the second clock tick, Q stays high (1). During the fourth clock tick, Q stays low (0).

D flip flop

A D-type flip-flop uses a S-R flip-flop for its implementation. The input D controls what is written to the flip-flop. If the clock is active (value=1), then the flip-flop will get D's value (0 or 1). A timing diagram is given for a 0-1-1 sequence of D values.

Register

A register is just a sequence of flip flops. In TOY, we had 16-bit registers. A series of 16 flip-flops can be used to form one of these registers. The clock (and the extra control of a load line) is used to ensure that new values are loaded only when they are supposed to be. Here's how it works. If LOAD has value 0, all the AND gates have output 0, so neither S nor R (on any of the flip-flops) has value=1. The register is unchanged, which is what we want. If LOAD has value 1 and a bit, x, has value 1, then the AND gate connected to the S input of its flip-flop will have output 1. So, SET will be activated, and a 1 will be stored in that register. Alternatively, if bit x has value 0, the AND gate corresponding to its RESET input will have value 1, and a 0 will be stored in that flip-flop. All the values will be set in parallel. The slide mentions several applications for registers.

Register File

To implement memory, we need to have a control to handling reading in addition to writing. The SELECT control selects the desired flip-flop using a decoder. By connecting the SELECT lines to the input of the decoder, we can control which flip-flop we read. This slide demonstrates how computers are built up with components such as decoders and flip-flops. Each time we create a new 'system,' we can think of it abstractly, as a 'black box.' As long as we know how many inputs and outputs a circuit has and understand the function it performs, we can represent this component of the computer more abstractly. The Memory Bit 'black box' on the right of this slide is a good example of this.

It hides a lot. The Memory Bit consists of a Decoder and Flip-Flops. Decoders and Flip-Flops are built up of the primitive gates, like AND/OR/NOT, and these gates are built from transistors. Attempting to draw this Memory Bit system out of transistors alone would be extremely challenging, and it's likely that we would make a mistake.

2 THE CENTRAL PROCESSING UNIT

COMPUTABILITY: MODELS OF COMPUTATION

Modern computers are often viewed as having three main components: the central processing unit (CPU), memory, and input-output devices. The CPU is responsible for arithmetical computations and logical decisions based on particular data items. However, the amount of data the unit can handle at anyone time is fixed forever by its design; in order to deal with more than this predetermined, limited amount of information, it must ship data back and forth, over time, to and from the memory and input-output devices. The memory may be of several different kinds, such as magnetic core, semi-conductor, bubble, disks, and tapes.

The common feature is that the information capacity of the memory is vastly greater than what can be accommodated, at any one instant of time, in the CPU; therefore this memory is sometimes called auxiliary, to distinguish it from the limited storage that is part of the central processor. The memory can be expanded, in theory at least, without limit, by adding more core boxes, more tape drives, and so on. The input/output devices are the means by which information is communicated back and forth to the outside world: these are devices such as terminals, card readers, and lineprinters. Tapes could be used for this purpose as well; a tape unit might then be regarded as an input-output device rather than a memory device.

A severely restricted model of an actual computer called a finite automaton. It shares with a real computer the fact that its "central processor" is of fixed finite capacity, depending on its original design. A finite automaton has *no auxiliary memory* at all. It receives its input as a string; the input string is delivered to it on an input tape. It delivers no output at all, except an indication of whether the input is considered acceptable. A finite automaton is not really without memory; it simply has a memory capacity that is fixed "at the factory" and cannot thereafter be expanded. That capacity may, however, be quite large. So we may view machines with many large auxiliary memory units as finite automata, so long as we are content not to require expansion of this memory later on.

Finite automata are limited in strength, but they are a thoroughly understood subclass of more powerful computational models.

DETERMINISTIC FINITE AUTOMATA

In DFA, automation operation is completely determined by its input in a way described below. Deterministic finite automaton is a simple language recognition device. Strings are fed into the device by means of an input tape, which is divided into squares, with one symbol inscribed in each tape square. Each square contains a single symbol from the input alphabet. The main part of the machine itself is a "black box" with innards that can be, at any specified moment, in one of a finite number of distinct internal states. This black box–called the finite control–can sense what symbol is written at any position on the input tape by means of a movable reading head. Initially, the reading head is placed at the leftmost square of the tape and the finite control is set in a designated initial state.

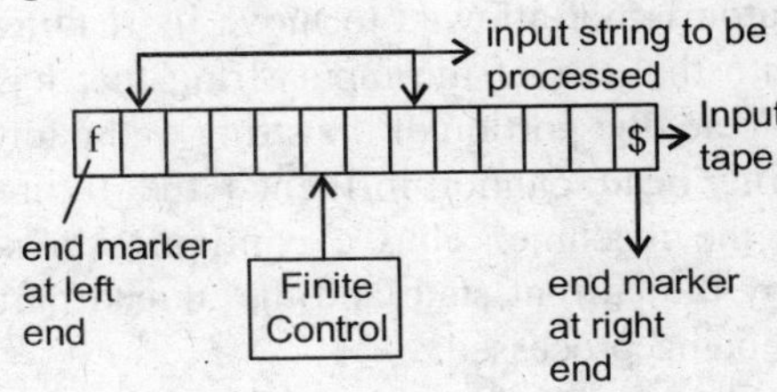

Fig. 2.1

At regular intervals the automaton reads one symbol from the input tape and then enters a new state that depends only on the current state and the symbol just read. It is very easy to determine whether a deterministic finite automaton accepts an input string since there is at most one path from the start state labeled by that string. After reading an input symbol, the reading head moves one square to the right on the input tape so that on the next move it will read the symbol in the next tape square. This process is repeated again and again; a symbol is read, the reading head moves to the right, and the state of the finite control changes. The input to the finite control will be usually : symbol under the R-head, say A, or the present state of the machine say *q* to give the following outputs (*a*) A motion of R-head along the tape to the next square (*b*) the next state of the finite state machine given by 8 (qA). Eventually, the reading head reaches the end of the input string. The automaton then indicates its approval or disapproval of what it has read by the state it is in at the end: if it winds up in one of the set of final states the input string is considered to be accepted. The language accepted by the machine is the set of strings it accepts.

When this informal account is boiled down to its mathematical essentials, the following formal version is obtained.

Definition: The mathematical version of DFA is as follows :

A deterministic finite automaton is a quintuple M = (K, Σ, δ, q_0, *f*)

K is a finite nonempty set of states,

Σ is a finite nonempty set if inputs called input alphabet

$q_0 \in$ K is the intial state.

$f \subseteq$ K is the set of final states. There may be more than one final state, and δ the transition function, is a function which maks K × Σ into K and generally called direct transition function.

The rules according to which the automaton *M* picks its next state are encoded into the transition function.

A sequence of *configurations* that represent the status of the finite control, reading head, and input tape at successive moments. But since a deterministic finite automaton is not allowed to move its reading head back into the part of the input string that has already been read, the portion of the string to the left of the reading head cannot influence the future operation of the machine. Thus a configuration is determined by the current state and the unread part of the string being processed.

Non-Deterministic Finite Automata

Non-determinism is an essential feature of finite automata: every non-deterministic finite automata is equivalent to a deterministic finite automaton. The ability to change states in a way that only *partially* determined by the current state and input symbol. Several possible "next states" for a given combination of current state and input symbol can be drawn. The automaton, as it reads the input string, may choose at each step to go into anyone of these legal next states; the choice is not determined by anything in our model, and is therefore said to be *non-deterministic*. On the other hand, the choice is not wholly unlimited either; only those next states that are legal from a given state with a given input symbol can be chosen. Though non-determinism is a feature we do not normally associate with real computer, it arises naturally as an extension of the behaviour of deterministic finite automata and in some cases greatly simplifies the description of these automata.

A NDFA (Non-Deterministic Finite Automata) is a mathematical model and can be a much more convenient device to design than a deterministic finite automaton. NDFA model consists of:

- a set of states
- a set of finite nonempty input symbol Σ (the input symbol alphabet)
- a transition function δ mapping from Q × Σ into 2q which is the power set of θ, the set of all subsets of θ.
- $q_0 \in$ Q is a initial state
- F ⊆ Q is the set of final states.

Definition 1: A non-deterministic finite automaton is a quintuple M = (θ, Σ, δ, q_0, F),

where θ is a finite set of states, Σ is an alphabet, $q_0 \in$ Q is the initial state, F ⊆ Q is the set of final states, δ the transition function mapping from θ × Σ into 2q which is the power set of θ, the set of all subsets of θ.

An NFA can be represented diagramatically by a labelled directed graph called transistion graph where nodes are states and labelled edges represent the transition function. This graph appears like a transition diagram, but the same character can label two or more transition out of one state and edges can be labelled by the special symbol ∈ as well as by input symbol.

The difference between the deterministic and non-deterministic automata is only δ. For deterministic automaton(DFA), the outcome is a state, i.e., an element of Q; for non-deterministic automaton the outcome is a subset of Q. NDFA appears to be more general than DFA they are nevertheless no more powerful in terms of languages they accept. A NDFA can always be converted into deterministic one.

Definition 2: *A string w* ∈ Σ* *is accepted by NDFA if* $\delta(q_o, w)$ *contains some final state.*

Definition 3: *The set accepted by an automaton M (deterministic or non-deterministic) is the set of* *all input strings accepted by M. It is denoted by T(M).*

The Equivalence of DFA and NDFA: *Finite automata M_1 and M_2 are said to be equivalent if $L(M_1)=L(M_2)$.*

Two automata are considered to be equivalent if they accept the same language, even though they may "use different methods" to do so. A DFA can simulate the behaviour of NDFA by increasing the number of states, or a DFA (θ, Σ, δ, q_0, F) can be viewed as an NDFA (θ, Σ, δ', q_0, F) by defining $\delta'(q, a) = \{b(q, a)\}$. Any NDFA is a more general machine without being more powerful.

Theorem. *For each non-deterministic finite automaton, there is an equivalent deterministic finite automaton which simulates the behaviour of* NDFA.

Conversion of Non-deterministic Systems to Deterministic Systems

Step 1 Convert the given transition system into state transition table in which each state corresponds to a row and each input symbol corresponds to a column.

Step 2 Construct the successor table which lists subsets of states reachable from the set of initial states.

Step 3 The transition graph given by the successor table is the required deterministic system. The final states contain some final state of NDFA. If possible, reduce the number of states.

CONVERSION OF AN NFA INTO DFA

The transition functions is multivalued, make it hard to simulate an NFA with computer programme.

Subset Construction: Following algorithms are useful for simulating an NFA by computer program.

- The general idea behind the NFA-to-DFA construction is that each DFA state corresponds to a set of NFA states. DFA uses its state to keep track of all possible states the NFA can be in after heading each input symbol.
- The DFA uses its state to keep track of all possible states the NFA can be in after reading each input symbol. After reading input a_1 a_2 ..., a_n, the DFA is in a state that represents the subset T of the states of the NFA that are reachable from the NFA's start state along some path labelled a_1 a_2 ..., a_n.
- The number of states of the DFA can be exponential in the number of states of the NFA, but in practice worst case occurs rarely.
- A state of deterministic finite automata is an accepting state if it is a set of NFA states containing at least one accepting state of N.

Example: NFA, N accepting the language $(a \mid b)^*abb$ is shown in figure 2.2

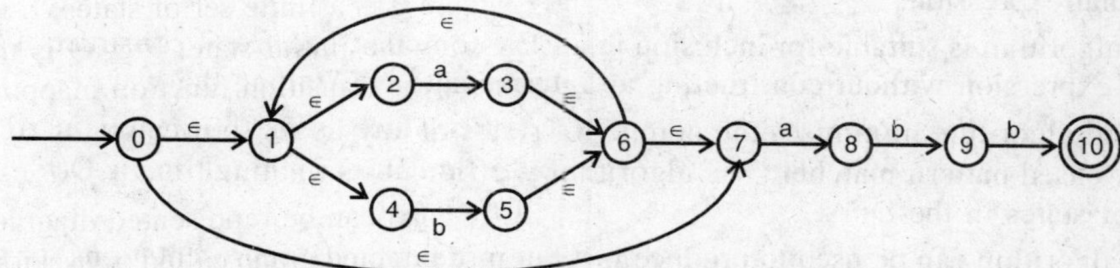

Fig. 2.2 : *NFA, N for (a | b)*abb.*

- The start state of the equivalent DFA is ∈-closure (O), which is A = {0, 1, 2, 4, 7}. Since these are exactly the states reachable from state 0 via a path in which every edge is labelled ∈. A path can have no edge, so 0 is reached from itself by such a path.
- The input symbol alphabet is {*a*, *b*}, then ∈ closure (move (A, *a*)). We first move (A, *a*), the set of states of N having transitions on *a* from members of A.

  ∈ – closure (move ({0, 1, 2, 4, 7}, *a*))

  = ∈ – closure ({3, 8})

  = {1, 2, 3, 4, 6, 7, 8}

  D tran [A, *a*] = B (let B is set)

Among the states in A, only 4 has a transition on *b* to 5; so the DFA has a transition on *b* from A to C = ∈ – closure ({5}) = {1, 2, 4, 5, 6, 7} thus

D tran [A, *b*] = C

The five different sets of states are actually to construct are:

A = {0, 1, 2, 4, 7}

B = {1, 2, 3, 4, 6, 7, 8}

C = {1, 2, 4, 5, 6, 7}

D = {1, 2, 4, 5, 6, 7, 9}

E = {1, 2, 4, 5, 6, 7, 10}

where A is start state and state E is the only accepting state

State	Input	Symbol
	a	*b*
A	B	C
B	B	D
C	B	C
D	B	E
E	B	C

Transition table D tran for DFA.

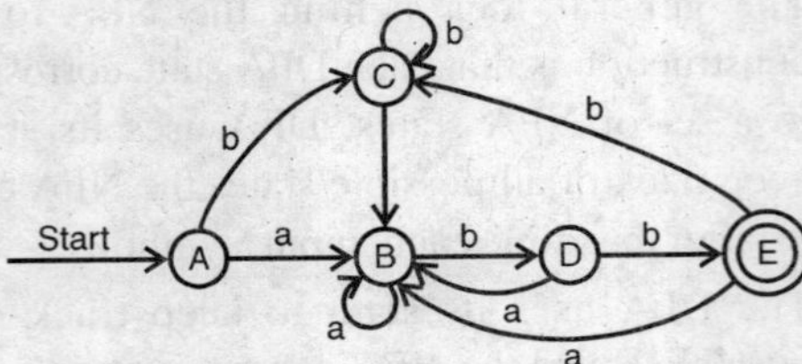

Fig. 2.3 : *Subset construction*

Q. 1: We make the NFA or DFA from syntax tree for $(a \mid b)$ * *abb*

Solution: Syntax tree for $(a \mid b)$ * *abb* ≠

- It is a regular expression, where • (Dot) is said, cat node.
- Leaves in syntax tree for a regular expression are labelled by alphabet; symbols or by ∈ to each leaf not labelled, by ∈ we attach a unique integer and refer to this integer as the position of the leaf and also as a position also its symbol.

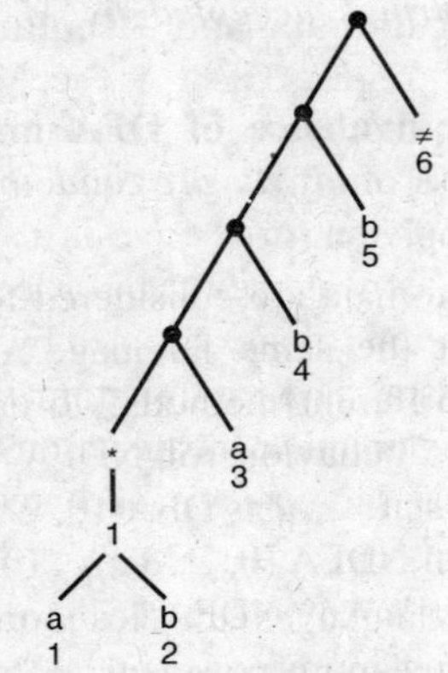

Fig. 2.4 : *Syntax tree for (a | b) * abb ¹ (Regular)*

Regular Expression to DFA

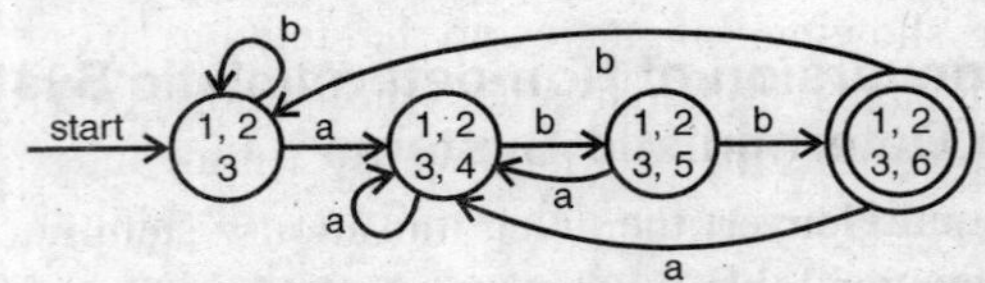

Fig. 2.5 : *Resulting DFA*

- Numbered states in the NFA correspond to the positions of the leaves in the syntax tree.
- The DFA can be obtained from the NFA if we apply the subset construction and identify subsets containing the same important states.

Optimisation of DFA Based Pattern Matchers

- There are three algorithms that have been used to implement and optimise pattern matchers constructed from regular expression.

1. The first algorithm is suitable for inclusion in a LEX compiler, because it constructs a DFA directly from a regular expression without constructing an intermediate NFA along the way.
2. The second algorithm minimises the number of states of any DFA, so it can be used to reduce the size of a DFA-based pattern matcher. The algorithm is efficient its running time is O(n log$n$) where n is the number of states in the DFA.
3. The first algorithm can be used to produce fast but more compact representations for the transition table of a DFA than a straight forward two dimensions.

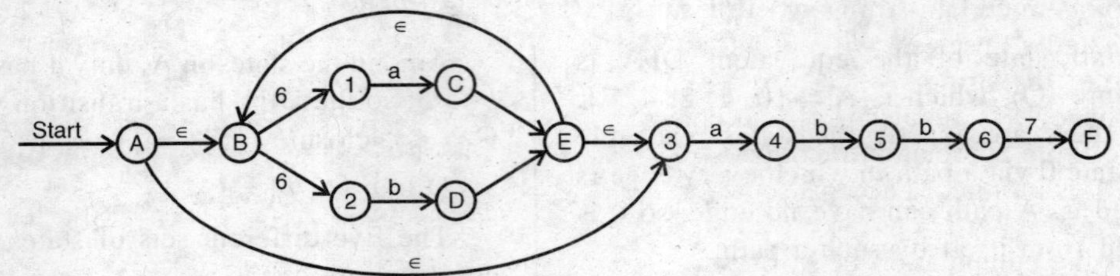

Fig. 2.6 : *NFA*

ASSEMBLY LANGUAGE

The class of languages accepted by finite automata has a sort of stability. Natural operations for constructing languages from others do not lead outside the class. These results are established by simulation.

The class of languages accepted by Finite Automata is closed under :

(i) Union

(ii) Concatenation

(iii) Kleen Star

(iv) Complementation

(v) Intersection

Finite Automata and Regular Expression: A language is regular if it is accepted by a finite automaton. The class of regular languages is the smallest class of languages containing the empty set ϕ and the singleton (σ)where σ is a symbol and closed under union, concatenation and Kleen star. Empty set (ϕ) and singleton (σ) are accepted by non-deterministic finite automata. The finite automaton languages are closed under union, concatenation and Kleene star. Every regular language is accepted by some finite automaton.

Regular languages are closed under a variety of operations and regular languages may be specified by regular expressions or by deterministic or non-deterministic finite automata. These facts used singly or in combinations, provide a variety of techniques for showing languages to be regular. Nonregular languages do exist since the number of regular expressions or the number of finite automata is countable whereas the number of languages is uncountable. But to demonstrate that any particular language is not regular requires special tools. Two properties shared by all regular languages, but not by certain non regular languages are as follows:

1. When a string is scanned left-to-right, the amount of memory that is needed in order to determine at the end whether or not the string is in the language must be bounded-fixed in advance and dependent on the language, not the particular input string.
2. Regular languages with an infinite number of strings have infinite subsets with a certain simple repetitive structure that arises from a star in a corresponding regular expression or a cycle in the state diagram of a finite automaton.

Theorem: *Let L be an infinite regular language. Then there are strings x, y, and z such that y = e and xy*z* belongs to *L for each* $n \geq$ O.

This theorem is one of a general class called pumping theorems, because they assert the existence of certain points in certain strings where a substring can be repeatedly inserted without affecting the acceptability of the string.

Proof: Since L is regular, L is accepted by a deterministic finite automaton M. Suppose M has n states. Since L is infinite, M accepts some string w of length n or greater. Let L= $|w|$, $w = \sigma_1 ... \sigma_1 > \sigma_1 \in \Sigma$ and consider the computation of M on w:

q_0 is the initial state of M and q_i is a final state of M. Since $1 \geq n$ and M has only n states, by the Pigeonhole principle, there exist i and j, $0 \leq i < j \leq l$, such that $q_i = q_j$'. M accepts $\sigma_1 ......\sigma_i$ $(\sigma_{iH} ......\sigma_j)^n$ $\sigma_{j+1} ..... \sigma_i$ for each $n \geq 0$

If $x = \sigma_1 .... \sigma_i$, $y = \sigma_{i+1} .....\sigma_j$, $z = \sigma_{j+1} .....\sigma_i$, then

$$(q_0, xy^n z)\, \phi * \mathrm{M}(q_i, y_z^n)\, \phi * \mathrm{M}\, (q_i, y^{n-1} z)\, \phi * \mathrm{M}$$

$$..........\phi * \mathrm{M}(q_i, z)\, \phi * \mathrm{M}(q_i, \rho)$$

Context-Free Grammars

The finite automata are formalised types of language recognisers. Nevertheless the idea of a language generator has some explanatory force in attempts to discuss human language. The theory of generators of formal, "artificial" languages, such as the regular languages and the important class of "context-free" languages introduced below.

Definition: A grammar is called a type 2 grammar if it consists only type 2 productions. It is also known as context-free grammar. A language generated by context free grammar is called a type 2 language or a context free language.

Definition: A type 2 production is a production of the form $A \to \alpha$, $A \in V_N$, $\alpha \in (V_N \cup \Sigma)^*$.

Definition: A grammar is called a type 3 or regular grammar if all its productions are type 3 productions. A production $S \to$ ^ is allowed in type 3 grammar. S does not appear or RHS of any production.

Computer programmes written in any programming language must satisfy some rigid criteria in order to be syntactically correct and therefore amenable to mechanical interpretation. The syntax of most programming languages can, unlike that of human languages, be captured by context free grammars. Context free is extremely helpful when it comes to parsing a programme, *i.e.*, analysing it to understand its syntax.

Definition: A context-free grammar G is a quadruple (V, Σ, R, S), where V is an alphabet,

Σ is the set of terminals, a subset of V,

R is the set of rules, a finite subset of $(V - \Sigma)$ X V*

S (the start symbol) is an element of $V - \Sigma$

The members of $V - \Sigma$ are called non-terminals. For any A belongs to $V - \Sigma$ and $U \in V^*$, we write $A \to u$ whenever $(A, u) \in R$. For any strings $u, v \in V^*$, we write $\to$ if and only if there are strings $x, y, v' \in V - \Sigma^*$

such that $u = xAy$, $v = xv'y$, and $A \to v'$.

Finally, L(G), the language generated by G, is $\{w \in \Sigma^*; S \to w\}$; we also say that G generates each string in L(G). A language L is said to be a context-free language if it is equal to L(G) for some context-free grammar G.

G is context free if every production is of the form $A \to \alpha$, $A \in V_N$, $\alpha \in (V_N \cup \Sigma)^*$.

Regular Languages and Context-Free Languages

Strings: A string over some alphabet is a finite sequence of symbols drawn from that alphabet. String is written in term of sentence and word. The length of string s, written as $|s|$.

Empty String: The empty string, denoted $\in$, is a special string of length zero, the empty string is identity element under concatenation, *i.e.*,

$$\in s = s\in = s.$$

Language: Any set of strings over some fixed alphabet is called language.

Abstract Language: The set of only the empty strings are called abstract language.

Example: ϕ, empty set, or $\{\in\}$.

Concatenation: Concatenation of string x and y written as xy.

Operation on Languages

In lexical analysis, union, concatenation and closure in operation on language.

Exponentation operator to language define by L^0 to be $\{\in\}$ and L^i and L^i to $L^i + L^0$. L^i is L concatenated with itself $i - 1$ times.

Example:

$$L = \{A, B, ..., Z, a, b, ..., z\}$$
$$D = \{0, 1, ..., 9\}$$

where L is the set of alphabet consisting of the set of upper and lower case letter and D is the set of alphabet of ten decimal, digits set L and D are finite language.

Here we can define L and D in different ways:

1. L $\cup$ D is the set of letter and digits.
2. LD is set of strings where letter is followed by digit.
3. L* is set of all strings of letter, including $\in$, the empty string. It is called Kleen closure of h, where $L^* = \bigcup_{i=0}^{\infty} L^i$.
4. D^+ is the set of all strings of one or more digits.

   L^+ denotes one or more concatenation of L.
5. Union of L and M, represented by LUM and LUM = $\{s|s,\ s \text{ is in L and } s \text{ is in M}\}$.
6. Concatenation of L and M represented by LM = $\{st|s\ s \text{ in L and } t \text{ in M}\}$.

Definition: A context-free grammar G = (V, Σ, R, S) is regular if and only if

$$R \subseteq (V - \Sigma) \times \Sigma^*((V - \Sigma) \cup \{e\}).$$

A regular grammar is a context-free grammar such that the right-hand side of every rule contains at most one nonterminal, which, if present must be the last symbol in the string. This nonterminal can be used for remembering the "state" of a derivation.

Theorem: A language is regular if and only if it is generated by a regular grammar.

Regular Sets and Regular Grammars

Regular Expressions: Regular expressions are the means of representing certain subsets of strings over Σ.

Regular expressions are useful for representing certain sets of strings in an algebraic fashion. These describe the languages accepted by finite state automata. We give a formal recursive definition of regular expressions over Σ as discussed below:

Regular Expression

An identifier is a letter followed by zero or more letters or digits; that is, an identifier is a member of the set defined in L and D.

Regular expression is defined like letter (letter digit)*, where | means 'OR' and parentheses are use to group subexpression; * means 'zero' or more instance of.

A regular expression is built up out of simple regular expression using a set of defining rules. Each regular expression r denotes a language $L(r)$.

Regular expressions define over alphabet Σ.

Specification of Regular Expression

1. $\in$ is a regular expression that denotes $\{\in\}$, *i.e.*, empty string.
2. If symbol a is in Σ, then a is regular expression that denotes $\{a\}$, *i.e.*, the set containing the string a.
3. If r and s are regular expression, denoted by languages $L(r)$ and $L(s)$, then
   (*i*) $(r) | (s)$ is a regular expression denoted by $L(r) \cup L(s)$.
   (*ii*) $(r)\ (s)$ is a regular language denoted by $L(r)\ L(s)$.
   (*iii*) (r) * is a regular expression denoted by $(L(r))^*$.
   (*iv*) (r) is a regular expression denoting $L(r)^2$.

A language denoted by a regular expression is said to be a regular set.

Unnecessary parentheses should be avoided in regular expression if we adopt some convention.

1. The unary operator * has the highest precedence and it is left associative.
2. Concatenation has the second highest precedence and is left associative.
3. Has the lowest precedence and is left associative.

Example:

$(a) | ((b) * (c))$ is equivalent to $a | b * c$.

Regular expression represented by following way

1. The regular expression $a | b$ denoted by the set $\{a, b\}$.

2. Regular expression a * denoted the set of all strings of zero or more a's, *i.e.*, {∈, a, aa, $aaaa$}.
3. The regular expression (a | b) (a | b) denotes {aa, ab, ba, bb}, the set of all strings of a's and b's of length two. This regular expression also represented by like aa | ab | ba | bb.
4. The regular expression (a | b)* denotes the set of all strings containing zero or more instances of an a or b, *i.e.*, the set of all strings a's and b's it also represented by in other way like (a* b*)*.
5. The regular expression a | $a0$ * b denotes the set containing the string a and all strings consisting of zero or more a's followed by ab.
6. If same language represented by two regular expression, then two language are equivalent and represented by (a | b) = (b | a).

Properties of Regular Expression

1. r | s = s | r, 1 is commutative.
2. r | (s | t) = (r | s) | t; | is associative.
3. (r s)t = r (st) concatenation is associative.
4. r(s | t) = rs | rt, concatenation distributes over.
5. ∈ r = r ∈ = r, ∈ is the identity element of concatenation.
6. r* = (r | ∈)*; it describe relation between * and ∈.
7. r** = r*, where * is idempotent.

REGULAR DEFINITIONS

Regular definitions is a sequence of definitions of the form.

$d_1 \to r_1$

$d_2 \to r_2$

....

....

$d_n \to r_n$

where d_i is distinct name and r_i is a regular expression over the symbols in $\Sigma \cup \{d_1, d_2, ..., d_i\}$.

The identifier are described in the form of regular definitions.

letter → A | B | .... |Z| | a | b | ... K

digit → 0 | 4 ... | 9

id → letter (letter | digit)*

NOTATIONAL SHORTHANDS

One or more instances: The unary post size operator '+' means 'one or more instances of'. If r is a regular expression that denotes the language L(r), then $(r)^+$ is a regular expression that denotes the language $(L(r))^+$. The regular expression denotes the set of all strings of one or more a's.

The operator + has the same precedence and associativity, as the operator *, *e.g.*,

$r^* = r^+ \mid \in$ and $r^+ = rr^*$ relate the Kleene and positive closure operators.

Zero or one instances: The unary postfix operator? means "zero or more instance of". The notation r ? is shorthand for r | ∈. If r is a regular expression, then (r)? is a regular expression that denotes the language L(r) ∪ {∈}. We write the regular definition with help of + and ? operators, *e.g.*,

digit → 0 | 1 | ... | 9

digits → digit +

Optional fraction → (digits)?

Optional – exponent → (E(+ | –)? digits)?

num → digits optional – fraction optional $(x)'$

Character Classes: The notation [abc] where a, b and c are alphabet symbols denotes the regular expression a | b | c. [a^{-2}] denotes the regular expression a | b |.

Non Regular Sets

1. Regular expressions cannot be used to describe balanced or nested constructs.
2. The set of all strings of balanced parentheses cannot be described by a regular expression.
3. Repeating strings cannot be described by regular expression, *e.g.*, {w c w | w is string of a's and b's} cannot be denoted by any regular expression, nor can it be described by a context free grammar.
4. Regular expressions can be used to denote only a fixed number of repetition s or an unspecified number of repetitions of a given construct.
5. Two arbitrary numbers cannot be compared to see whether they are the same, thus we cannot describe Hollerith strings of the form $n + 1\ a_1\ a_2\ .....\ a_n$ from early version of Fortran with a regular expression.

A programming language can be defined by describing what its programme look like or other way can say the syntax of the languages and what is programme means or other way can say the semantics of the language.

- For specifying the syntax of a language, we used notation called context free grammars or BNF (Back us Naur Form).
- Syntax of language context free language can be used to help guide the translation of programme. A grammar oriented compilation technique, known as syntax directed translation.

3 OPERATING SYSTEMS

OPERATING SYSTEMS

The earliest operating systems were developed in the late 1950s to manage tape storage, but programmers mostly wrote their own I/O routines. In the mid 1960s, operating systems became essential to manage disks, complex time sharing and multitasking systems.

OS consists of different software layers such as Non-Kernel modules, User Interface, Kernel. Structure of an operating system consists of User Interface,Policies, Mechanism. Although some operating systems still are device dependent, the trend today is toward device independent operating systems that will run on many manufacturer's computers. The advantage of this operating system is that even if you change computer models or vendors, you can retain existing application software and data files. New versions of an operating system are download compatible which recognises and work with application software.

Early computers were (physically) enormously large machines run from a *console*. The common input devices were card readers and tape drives. The common output devices were line printers, tape drives, and card punches. The users of such systems did not interact directly with the computer systems. Rather, the user prepared a job consisted of the programme, the data, and some control information about the nature of the job (control cards) and submitted it to the computer operator. The job would usually be in the form of punch cards. At some later time (perhaps minutes, hours, or days), the output appeared. The output consisted of the result of the programme, as well as a dump of memory and registers in case of programme error.

The operating system in these early computers was fairly simple. Its major task was to transfer control automatically from one job to the next. The operating system was always (resident) in memory (Figure 3.1).

To speed up processing, jobs with similar needs were *batched* together and were run through the computer as a group. Thus, the programmers would leave their programmes with the operator. The operator would sort programmes into batches with similar requirements and, as the computer became available, would run each batch. The output from each job would be sent back to the appropriate programmer.

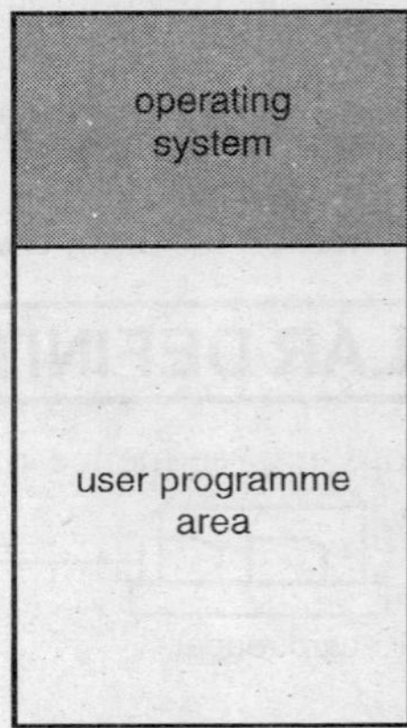

Fig. 3.1: *Operating system in early computers.*

A batch operating system, thus, normally reads a stream of separate jobs (from a card reader, for example), each with its own control cards that predefine what the job does. When the job is complete, its output is usually printed (on a line printer, for example). The definitive feature of a batch system is the *lack* of interaction between the user and the job while that job is executing. The job is prepared and submitted, and at some later time, the output appears. The delay between job submission and job completion (called *turnaround* time) may result from the amount of computing needed, or from delays before the operating system starts to process the job.

In this execution environment, the CPU is often idle. This idleness occurs because the speeds of the mechanical I/O devices are intrinsically slower than those of electronic devices. Even a slow CPU works in the microsecond range, with thousands of instructions executed per second. A fast card reader, on the other hand, might read 1200 cards per minute (17 cards per second). Thus, the difference in speed between the CPU and its I/O devices may be three orders of magnitude or more. Over time, of course, improvements in technology resulted in faster I/O devices. Unfortunately, CPU speeds increased even faster, so that the problem was not only unresolved, but also exacerbated.

The introduction of disk technology has helped in this regard. Rather than the cards being read from the card reader directly into memory, and then the job being processed, cards are read directly from the card rader onto the disk. The location of card images is recorded in a table kept by the operating system. When a job is executed, the operating system satisfies its requests for card-reader input by reading from the disk. Similarly, when the job requests the printer to output a line, that line is copied into a system buffer and is written to the disk. When the job is completed, the output is actually printed. This form of processing is called *spooling* (Figure 3.2); the name is an acronym for simultaneous peripheral operation on-line. Spooling, in essence, uses the disk as a huge buffer, for reading as far ahead as possible on input devices and for storing output files until the output devices are able to accept them.

Spooling is also used for processing data at remote sites. The CPU sends the data *via* communications paths to a remote printer (or accepts an entire input job from a remote card reader). The remote processing is done at its own speed, with no CPU intervention. The CPU just needs to be notified when the processing is completed, so that it can spool the next batch of data.

Spooling overlaps the I/O of one job with the computation of other jobs. Even in a simple system, the spooler may be reading the input of one job while printing the output of a different job. During this time, still another job (or jobs) may be executed, reading their "cards" from disk and "printing" their output lines onto the disk.

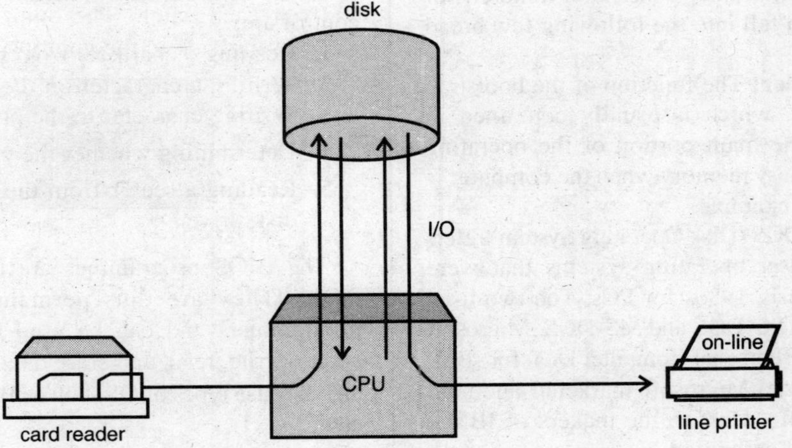

Fig. 3.2: *Spooling.*

Spooling has a direct beneficial effect on the performance of a system. For the cost of some disk space and a few tables, the computation of one job can overlap with the I/O of other jobs. Thus, spooling can keep both the CPU and the I/O devics working at much higher rates. Todays, all multi-purpose computers from micro to mainframe use an operating system. Special purpose devices (appliances, games, toys, etc.) generally do not use because they usually employ to single programme that performs all the required I/O and processing tasks. The operating system used on a computer sometimes is called the software platform. Applications that run identically on more than one operating system are referred to as cross platform. File maker pro for example runs on several operating system including several versions of microsoft windows and the macintosh operating system.

Functions of Operating System

An operating system (OS) is a set of programme containing instructions that co-ordinate all of the activities among computer hardware resources. The functions of the operating system are as follows :

- Recognises input from an input device such as the keyboard, mouse or microphone.
- Co-ordinates the display of output on the monitor.
- Instructs a printer how and when to print information; and manager data, instructions and information stored on disk.
- Contains instructions that allow you to run application software and also coordinate all of the activities of hardware devices.

The core of an operating system, called the Kernel is responsible for managing memory, files and devices; maintaining the computer's clock which contains the current data and time; starting applications; and assigning the computer's resources; such as hardware devices, software programmes, data and information.

Act as a user interface : The operating system may allow for different shells; for example, DOS and UNIX Private Command-driven interfaces but can host other shells that provide a menu-driven or graphical interface.

Perform Job management activities: It controls the running of programmes. In small computers, the operating system responds to interactive commands from the user and loads the requested application programme into memory for execution.

Perform Task management activities: It controls the simultaneous of execution of programmes. In single tasking computers, the operating system has virtually no task management to do, but in multitasking computers it is responsible for the concurrent operation of one or more programmes jobs.

Types of Operating System Programmes

An operating system usually consists of hundreds of programmes, which fall into the following few broad categories:

1. Booting Loader: The function of the bootstrap loader programme, which is usually contained in ROM, is to read the main portion of the operating system from secondary memory when the computer is first turned up. For example,

DOS: The term DOS (Disk Operating System) refers to several single user operating systems that were developed in the early 1980s for PCs. The two used versions of DOS are PC-DOS and MS-DOS. Microsoft developed PC-DOS (Personal Computer Dos) for IBM, and at the same time, Microsoft marketed and sold MS-DOS (Microsoft - Dos) to the makers of IBM - compatible personal computers.

The original version of MS-DOS defined a memory 'layout' which allocated specific ranges of addresses to the various elements which have to share the memory, such as the operating system itself, the ROM BIOS, video memory and user programme space. User programme space was assigned an area less than 640 Kbytes which, at that time, was considered more than enough for the purpose. Unfortunately, this limitations became a considerable inconvenience to later development and has prompted the appearance of various software devices such as expanded and extended memory.

Today DOS is out of practice due to non presence of GUI element and cannot take full advantage of modern 32 - bit microprocessors.

2. Diagnostic Tests: The operating system contains a number of diagnostic programmes that test the operation of the system components. For example, one diagnostic programme might check the operation of the disk drives, while another might check the operation of RAM. Some of these diagnostic programmes are contained within ROM and are run automatically when the system is first turned on. Other diagnostic programmes are loaded from secondary memory and are run on user request.

3. Operating System Executive: The operating system executive (also called *the monitor)* is a programme that controls the activities of the system, including executing programmes and assigning tasks to hardware devices. In response to user or operator requests, the operating system executive schedules the execution of programmes. It is the operating system executive that is read into RAM when the computer first starts. Some sophisticated operating system executives (mostly on minicomputers and mainframe computers) allow several programmes to be run simultaneously. This operating system feature is called **multitasking**.

4. BIOS: The basic Input/Output system (BIOS) programmes consists of the low level routines used to control the most rudimentary functions of the hardware devices. Some functions BIOS programmes control are:

1. Reading a character from the keyboard
2. Writing a character on the video display
3. Writing character to the printer
4. Determining whether the printer is busy or not
5. Reading a sector from the disk in a particular disk drive.

The BIOS programmes are usually recorded in ROM. They are thus permanently available to programmers and can be used by programmers to create, write, read, and erase data. For example, there are variouse types of OS such as Windows, Unix, NOS etc.

Windows 95 or WIN 95

Microsoft developed a multitasking operating system. One advantage of windows 95 was its improved graphical user interface which made working with files and programmes easier than the early versions. Most programmes ran faster under windows 95 because it was written to take advantage of 32 - bit processors (versus 16 - bit processors). Windows 95 also included support for networking. Plug and play technology, longer file names and e-mail.

Windows 3.x versions basically were not operating systems instead they were operating environments which is a graphical user interface that works in combination with an operating system to simplify its use.

Windows 2000

Microsoft Windows 2000 is an upgrade to the Windows 98 and Windows NT operating systems. Now latest version of Windows is Window 2000 and it is capable of handling some extra features. It is a complete multitasking operating system that has a graphical user interface. Two basic versions of windows 2000 exist. The windows 2000 server and windows 2000 professional.

UNIX

UNIX is a powerful operating system, capable of handling a high volume of transactions in a multiuser environment and working with multiple CPUs but it has a command-line interface and many of its commands are difficult to remember and use. Thus, it is a multiuser, multitasking operating system developed in the early 1970s by scientists at Bell Laboratories, Bell Labs (a subsidiary of AT&T) was prohibited from actively promoting UNIX in the commercial market place. After deregulation of the telephone companies in the 1980s, UNIX was licensed to many hardware and software companies. Today, a version of UNIX is available for most computers of all sizes.

A Unix OS consists of wide variety of programmes such as system programmes which include programme loader, command interpreter etc; Language processors such as compiler, assembler, linker; utilities such as text editor and filters document formatters etc. Subroutine libraries such as standard C library etc. all these items work together. For example, the text editor must produce a file which can be compiled by the compiler which must produce a module in a format acceptable to the linker and so on.

Network Operating System(NOS)

An operating system that includes the capability for connecting computers and devices to a local area network (LAN). Some standard operating systems such as UNIX and Mac OS, have in-built networking functions, but normally the term's reserved for additional software that provides the networking functionality. Examples are Novell Netware and Windows NT.

Essential Features and Some Mechanism of Modern OS

Multitasking Operating System is one of the mechanism that multiprogramming operating system employs in managing the totality of computer related resources like CPU, memory and I/O devices. Multitasking is the process of loading and running at least two programmes at the same time. Most current operating systems support multitasking which can be cooperative or preemptive. In cooperative multitasking, tasks give up control to the operating system and in preemptive multitasking, the operating system takes the decision.

Multiprogramming is a form of processing in which computer holds more than one programme in memory and works on them in round-robin fashion, that is by sharing out the processor's time so that each programme receives some attention some of the time. This way of working is in, contrast to using the processor to run one programme of a time.

Other operating system executives, called multiuser operating systems, allow for several users to have simultaneous access to system devices and data.

Batch Processing OS is a method of organising work for a computer in which items of work are queued up, and the operating system takes on job at a time from the queue and processes it. Each job must be entirely self-contained. It must not require any intervention from the person who submitted it.

This is because, the order in which the jobs are run is at the discretion of the operating system, which will take into account, the estimated time to run the job and its demand on resources such as main store or tape drives.

MULTI PROGRAMMED BATCHED SYSTEMS

Spooling provides an important data structure; a *job pool.* Spooling will generally result in several jobs that have already been read waiting on disk, ready to run. A pool of jobs on disk allows the operating system to select which job to run next, to increase CPU utilisation. When jobs come in directly on cards or even on magnetic tape, it is not possible to run jobs in a different order. Jobs must be run sequentially, on a first-come, first-served basis. However, when several jobs are on a direct-access device, such as a disk, *job scheduling* becomes possible.

The most important aspect of job scheduling is the ability to *multiprogramme.* Off-line operation and spooling for overlapped I/O have their limitations. A single user cannot, in general, keep either the CPU or the I/O devices busy at all times. Multiprogramming increases CPU utilisation by organising jobs such that the CPU always has one to execute. The idea is proceeding further.

The operating system keeps several jobs in memory at a time (Figure 3.3). This set of jobs is a subset of the jobs kept in the job pool (since the number of jobs that can be kept simultaneously in memory is usually much smaller than the number of jobs that can be in the job pool). The operating system picks and begins to execute one of the jobs in the memory. Eventually, the job may have to wait for some task, such as a tape to be mounted, or an I/O operation to complete. In a nonmultiprogrammed system, the CPU would sit idle. In a multiprogramming system, the operating system simply switches to and executes another job. When that job needs to wait, the CPU is switched to another job, and so on. Eventually, the first job finishes waiting and gets the CPU back. As long as there is always some job to execute, the CPU will never be idle.

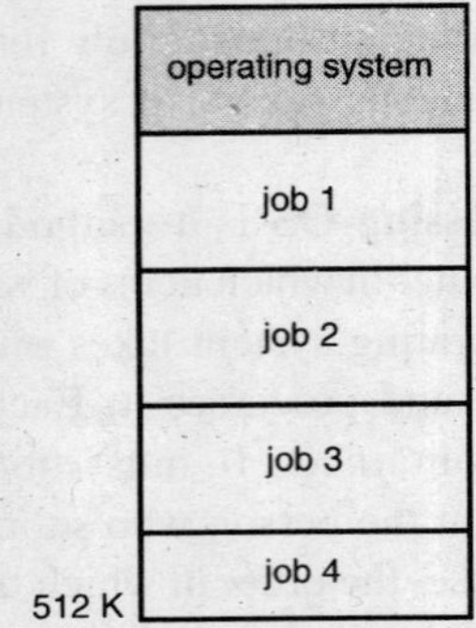

Fig. 3.3: *Memory layout for a multiprogramming system.*

This idea is common in other life situations. A lawyer does not have only one client at a time. Rather, several clients may be in the process of being served at the same time. While one case is waiting to go to trial or to have papers typed, the lawyer can work on another case. If he/she has enough clients, a lawyer never needs to be idle. (Idle lawyers tend to become politicians, so there is a certain social value in keeping lawyers busy).

Multiprogramming is the first instance where the operating system must make decisions for the users. Multiprogrammed operating systems are therefore fairly sophisticated. All the jobs that enter the system are kept in the job pool. This pool consists of all processes residing on mass storage awaiting allocation of main memory. If several jobs are ready to be brought into memory, and there is not enough room for all of them, then the system must choose among them. Making this decision is *job scheduling.* When the operating system selects a job from the job pool, it loads the job into memory for execution. Having several programmes in memory at the same time requires having some form of memory management. In addition, if several jobs are ready to run at the same time, the system must choose among them. Making this decision is *CPU scheduling.* Finally, multiple jobs running concurrently require that their ability to affect one another be limited in all phases of the operating system, including process schedulling, disk storage, and memory management. These considerations are discussed throughout the text.

Time Sharing OS

The lag between input and output time, must be sufficiently small for the effective operation of the system and can range from a few seconds to less than a microsecond. The system must be able to respond to some external event and able to perform calculations and control functions within a specified and very brief time limit. **Time sharing** is a use of a computer system by more than one individual at the same time. Time sharing runs separate programmes by inter leaving portion of processing time allotted to each programme. Time sharing allowed different clients to rent time on a large computer and pay for only the portion of time they used.

Time sharing, or *multitasking,* is a logical extension of multiprogramming. Multiple jobs are executed by the CPU switching between them, but the switches occur so frequently that the users may interact with each programme while it is running.

An *interactive,* or *hands-on,* computer system provides on-line communication between the user and the system. The user gives instructions to the operating system or to a programme directly, and receives an immediate response. Usually, a keyboard is used to provide input, and a display screen (such as a cathode-ray tube (CRT), or monitor) is used to provide output. When the operating system finishes the execution of one command, it seeks the next "control statement" not from a card reader, but rather from the user's keyboard. The user gives a command, waits for the response, and decides on the next command, based on the result of the previous one. The user can easily experiment, and can see results immediately. Most systems have an interactive text editor for entering programmes, and an interactive debugger for assisting in debugging programmes.

If users are to be able to access both data and code conveniently, an *on-line file system* must be available. A *file* is a collection of related information defined by its creator. Commonly, files represent programmes (both source and object forms) and data. Data files may be numeric, alphabetic, or alphanumeric. Files may be free-form, such as text files, or may be rigidly formatted. In general, a file is a sequence of bits, bytes, lines, or records whose meaning is defined by its creator and user. The operating system implements that abstract concept of a file by managing mass-storage devices, such as tapes and disks. Files are normally organised into logical clusters, or *directories,* which make them easier to locate and access. Since multiple users have access to files, it is desirable to control by whom and in what ways files may be accessed.

Early computers with a single user were interactive systems. That is, the entire system was at the immediate disposal of the programmer/operator. This situation allowed the programmer great flexibility and freedom in programme testing and development. But, as we saw, this arrangement resulted in substantial idle time while the CPU waited for some action to be taken by the programmer/operator. Because of the high cost of these early computers, idle CPU time was undesirable. Batch operating systems were developed to avoid this problem. Batch systems improved the system utilisation for owners of the computer systems.

Time-sharing systems were developed to provide interactive use of a computer system at a reasonable cost. A time-shared operating system uses CPU scheduling and multiprogramming to provide each user with a small portion of a time-shared computer. Each user has at least one separate programme in memory. A programme that is loaded into memory and is executing is commonly referred to as a *process.* When a process executes, it typically executes for only a short time before it either finishes or needs to perform I/O. I/O may be interactive; that is, output is to a display for the user and input is from a user keyboard. Since interactive I/O typically runs at people speeds, it may take a long time to complete. Input, for example, may be bounded by the user's typing speed; five characters per second is fairly fast for people, but is incredibly slow for computers. Rather than let the CPU sit idle when this interactive input takes place, the operating system will rapidly switch the CPU to the programme of some other user.

The idea of time sharing was demonstrated as early as 1960, but since time-shared systems are difficult and expensive to build, they did not become common until the early 1970s. As the popularity of time sharing has grown, researchers have attempted to merge batch and time-shared systems. Many computer systems that were designed as primarily batch systems have been modified to create a time-sharing subsystem. For example, IBM's OS/360, a batch system, was modified to support the Time-Sharing Option (TSO). At the same time, time-sharing systems have often added a batch subsystem. Today, most systems provide both batch processing and time sharing, although their basic design and use tends to be one or the other type.

The 'Process' Concept

A process /task is the basic unit for CPU scheduling in an operating system. The concept of a process, which was first used by the designers of Multitasking, is an essential part of the modern operating systems. The execution of a programme or "That which a processor executes" is called a process. The process may be independent of other processes in the system or may interact with some other processes. An interaction involves sharing of data or exchange of messages and control signals to coordinate its activities with the activities of other processes. The OS provides some means of process synchronisation to implement process interactions in a desired manner. A process is a dynamic entity. For example, in some programming languages *e.g.* Pascal, Ada, etc., different parts of a programme can execute concurrently. The OS is made aware of the existence and identities of these parts and considers them as separate entities for the purpose of scheduling.

A process is more than the programme code (sometimes known as the *text section*). It also includes the current activity, as represented by the value of the *programme counter* and the contents of the processor's registers. A process generally also includes the process *stack*, containing temporary data (such as subroutine parameters, return addresses, and temporary variables), and a *data section* containing global variables.

Although two processes may be associated with the same programme, they are nevertheless considered two separate execution sequences. For instance, several users may be running copies of the mail programme, or the same user may invoke many copies of the editor programme. Each of these is a separate process, and, although the text section are equivalent, the data sections will vary.

Process State

As a process executes, it changes *state*. The state of a process is defined in part by the current activity of that process. Each process may be in one of the following states:

- **New:** The process is being created.
- **Running:** Instructions are being executed.
- **Waiting:** The process is waiting for some event to occur (such as an I/O completion or reception of a signal).
- **Ready:** The process is waiting to be assigned to a processor.
- **Terminated:** The process has finished execution.

Process Control Block

Each process is represented in the operating system by a *process control block* (*PCB*) —also called a task control block.

A PCB is shown in Figure 3.4. It contains many pieces of information associated with a specific process, including these:

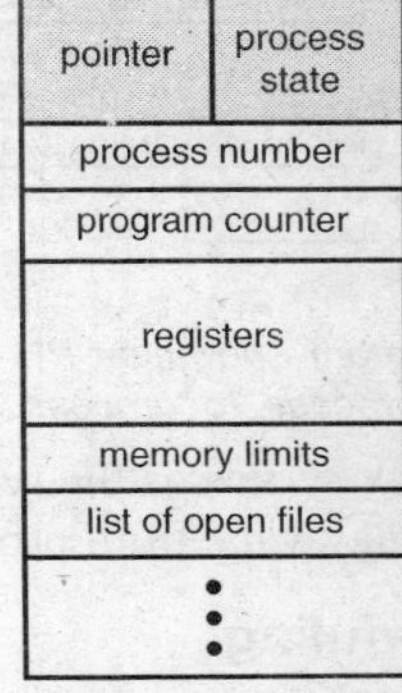

Fig. 3.4: *Process control block.*

COMPUTER SCIENCE

- **Process state:** The state may be new, ready, running, waiting, halted, and so on.
- **Programme counter:** The counter indicates the address of the next instruction to be executed for this process.
- **CPU registers:** The registers vary in number and type, depending on the computer architecture. They include accumulators, index registers, stack pointers, and general-purpose registers, plus any condition-code information. Along with the programme counter, this state information must be saved when an interrupt occurs, to allow the process to be continued correctly afterward (Figure 3.5).
- **CPU scheduling information:** This information includes a process priority, pointers to scheduling queues, and any other scheduling parameters.
- **Memory-management information:** This information may include such information as the value of the base and limit registers, the page tables, or the segment tables depending on the memory system used by the operating system.
- **Accounting information:** This information includes the amount of CPU and real time used, time limits, account numbers, job or process numbers, and so on.
- **I/O status information:** The information includes the list of I/O devices (such as tape drives) allocated to this process, a list of open files, and so on.

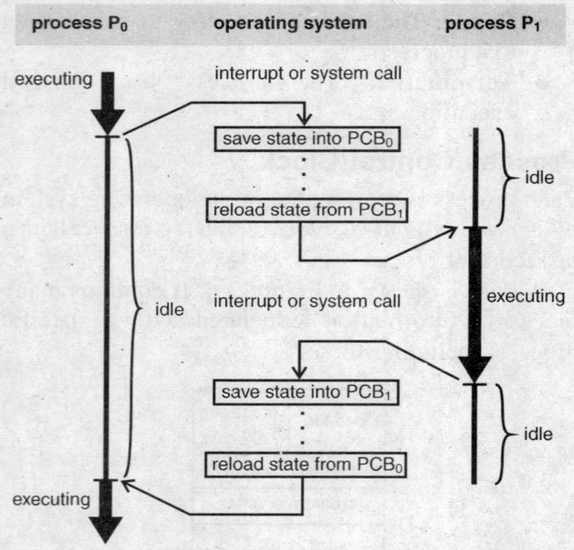

Fig. 3.5: *Diagram showing CPU switch from process to process.*

The PCB simply serves as the repository for any information that may vary from process to process.

Process Scheduling

The objective of multiprogramming is to have some process running at all times, to maximise CPU utilisation. The objective of time sharing is to switch the CPU among processes so frequently that users can interact with each programme while it is running. For a uniprocessor system, there will never be more than one running process. If there are more processes, the rest will have to wait until the CPU is free and can be rescheduled.

Scheduling Queues

As processes enter the system, they are put into a *job queue.* This queue consists of all processes in the system. The processes that are residing in main memory and are ready and waiting to execute are kept on a list called the *ready queue.* This queue is generally stored as a linked list. A ready-queue header will contain pointers to the first and last PCBs in the list. Each PCB has a pointer field that points to the next process in the ready queue.

A new process is initially put in the ready queue. It waits in the ready queue until it is selected for execution (or *dispatched*) and is given the CPU. Once the process is allocated the CPU and is executing, one of several events could occur:

- The process could issue an I/O request, and then be placed in an I/O queue.
- The process could create a new subprocess and wait for its termination.
- The process could be removed forcibly from the CPU, as a result of an interrupt, and be put back in the ready queue.

In the first two cases, the process eventually switches from the waiting state to the ready state, and is then put back in the ready queue. A process continues this cycle until it terminates, at which time it is removed from all queues and had its PCB resources deallocated.

MEMORY MANAGEMENT

Memory management means management of primary memories. OS responsibility in memory management includes memory allocation and deallocation, efficient utilisation of memory and protection of a programme's memory from interference by other programmes. The memory hierarchy of a computer system consists of

- Auxiliary/Secondary memories provides backup storage of data such as disks, tapes, etc. Management of secondary memory is under the control of file system. Main/Primary memories communicate directly with CPU.
- Buffer
- Cache memory : It is a special very high speed memory, used to increase the speed of processing by making current programmes and data available to CPU at rapid rate. It is employed in computer system to compensate for the speed differential between main memory access time and processor logic. A technique

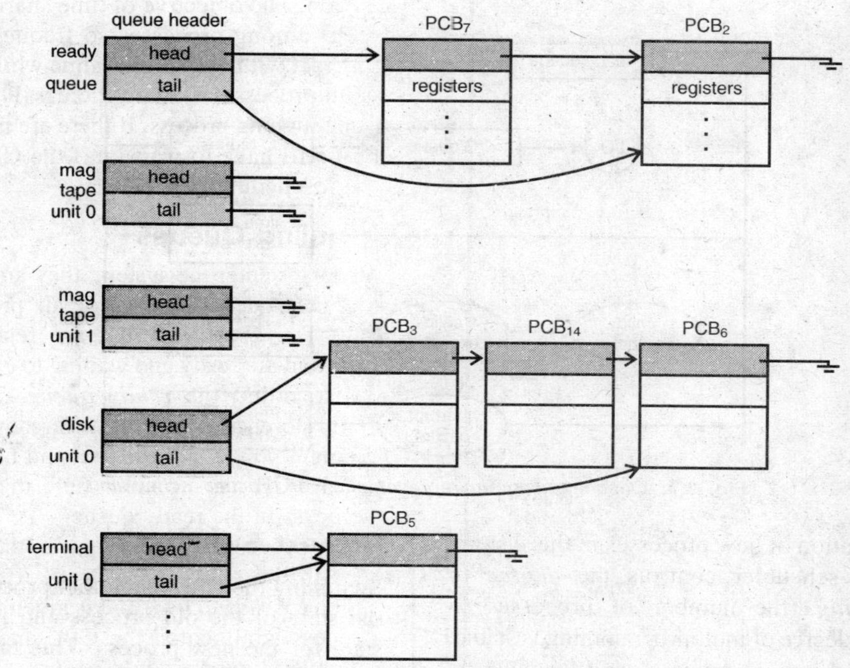

Fig. 3.6: *The ready queue and various I/O device queues.*

used to compensate for mismatch in operating speeds is to employ an extremely fast, small cache between the CPU and main memory whose access time is close to processor logic clock cycle time. The cache is used for storing segments of programmes currently being executed in the CPU and temporary data needed in present calculations. By making programmes and data available at a rapid rate, it is possible to increase the performance rate of the computer.

There are two types of memory management :

- **Contiguous memory management:** which assumes a programme's data and instructions to occupy a single contiguous memory area.
- Noncontiguous memory management:, wherein a programme's data and instructions may occupy many noncontiguous memory areas.

Virtual Memory

A virtual memory system is one that uses an ATU to implement noncontiguous memory allocation. In this system the logical address of an instruction or data word used in a programme instruction is likely to be different from its physical address. Two fundamental approaches used in implementing virtual memory system are—Paging and Segmentation. In paging, the demarcation between the programme components is determined by the architecture of computer system in a manner in which is transparent to the programme. Thus a programme continues to visualise itself as a single contiguous address space. In the segmentation, the programmer identifies the logical entities in his programme and declares them as programme components for the purpose of virtual memory implementation.

Schedulers

A process migrates between the various scheduling queues throughout its lifetime. The operating system must select, for scheduling purposes, processes from these queues in some fashion. The selection process is carried out by the appropriate *scheduler.* (Figure 3.7)

In a batch system, there are often more processes submitted that can be executed immediately. These processes are spooled to a mass-storage device (typically a disk), where they are kept for later execution. The *long-term scheduler* (or *job scheduler*) selects processes from this pool and loads them into memory for execution. The *short-term scheduler* (or *CPU scheduler*) selects from among the processes that are ready to execute, and allocates the CPU to one of them.

The primary distinction between these two schedulers is the frequency of their execution. The short-term scheduler must select a new process for the CPU quite frequently. A process may execute for only a few milliseconds before waiting for an I/O request. Often, the short-term scheduler executes at least once every 100 milliseconds. Because of the short duration of time between executions, the short-term scheduler must be very fast. If it takes 10 milliseconds to decide to execute a process for 100 milliseconds, then 10/(100 + 10) = 9 percent of the CPU is being used (wasted) simply for scheduling the work.

The long-term scheduler, on the other hand, executes much less frequently. There may be minutes

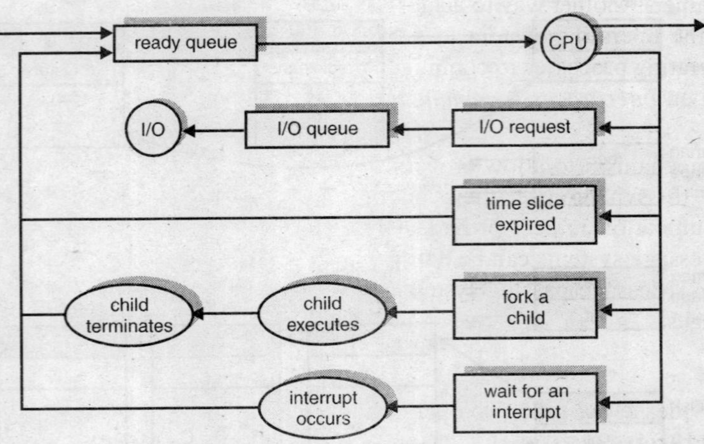

Fig. 3.7: *Queueing-diagram representation of process scheduling.*

between the creation of new processes in the system. The long-term scheduler controls the *degree of multiprogramming* (the number of processes in memory). If the degree of multiprogramming is stable, then the average rate of process creation must be equal to the average departure rate of processes leaving the system. Thus, the long-term scheduler may need to be invoked only when a process leaves the system. Because of the longer interval between executions, the long-term scheduler can afford to take more time to decide which process should be selected for execution. Some operating systems, such as time-sharing systems, may introduce an additional, intermediate level of scheduling. This *medium-term scheduler* is diagrammed in Figure 3.8. The key idea behind a medium-term scheduler is that sometimes it can be advantageous to remove processes from memory (and from active contention for the CPU), and thus to reduce the degree of multiprogramming. At some later time, the process can be reintroduced into memory and its execution can be continued where it left off. This scheme is called *swapping*. The process is swapped out and swapped in later by the medium-term scheduler. Swapping may be necessary to improve the process mix, or because a change in memory requirements has overcommitted available memory, requiring memory to be freed up.

Context Switch

Switching the CPU to another process rquires saving the state of the old process and loading the saved state for the new process. This task is known as a *context switch.* Context-switch time is pure overhead, because the system does no useful work while switching. Its speed varies from machine to machine, depending on the memory speed, the number of registers which must be copied, and the existence of special instructions (such as a single instruction to load or store all registers). Typically, the speed ranges from 1 to 1000 microseconds.

Context-switch times are highly dependent on hardware support. For instance, some processors (such as the DECSYSTEM-20) provide multiple sets of registers. A context switch simply includes changing the pointer to the current register set. Of course, if there are more active processes than there are register sets, the system resorts to copying register data to and from memory, as before. Also, the more complex the operating system, the more work must be done during a context switch.

Interprocess Communication

The scheme requires that these processes share a common buffer pool, and that the code for implementing the buffer be explicitly written by the

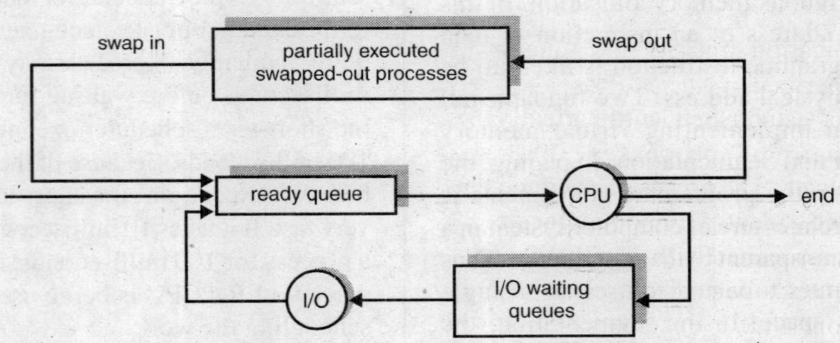

Fig. 3.8: *Addition of medium-term scheduling to the queueing diagram.*

application programmer. Another way to achieve the same effect is for the operating system to provide the means for cooperating processes to communicate with each other via an *interprocess-communication (IPC)* facility.

IPC provides a mechanism to allow processes to communicate and to synchronise their actions. Interprocess-communication is best provided by a message system. Message systems can be defined in many different ways. Message-passing systems also have other advantages.

Basic Structure

An IPC facility provides at least the two operations: **send** *(message)* and **receive** *(message).*

Messages sent by a process can be of either fixed or variable size. If only fixed-sized messages can be sent, the physical implementation is straight-forward. This restriction, however, makes the task of programming more difficult. On the other hand, variable-sized messages require a more complex physical implementation, but the programming task becomes simpler.

If processes *P* and Q want to communicate, they must send messages to and receive messages from each other; a *communication link* must exist between them. This link can be implemented in a variety of ways. We are concerned here not with the link's physical implementation (such as shared memory, hardware bus, or network).

The definition of *unidirectional* must be stated more carefully, since a link may be associated with more than two processes. Thus, we say that a link is unidirectional only if each process connected to the link can either send or receive, but not both, and each link has at least one receiver process connected to it.

Direct Communication: In the direct-communication discipline, each process that wants to communicate must explicitly name the recipient or sender of the communication. In this scheme, the **send** and **receive** primitives are defined as follows:
send*(P, message):* Send a message to process *P.*
receive*(Q, message):* Receive a message to process *Q.*

A communication link in this scheme has the following properties:

- A link is established automatically between every pair of processes that want to communicate. The processes need to know only each other's identity to communicate.
- A link is associated with exactly two processes.
- Between each pair of processes, there exists exactly one link.
- The link may be unidirectional, but is usually bidirectional.

The *producer* process is defined as

repeat
...
produce an item in *nextp*
...
send(*consumer, nextp);*
until *false;*

The consumer process is defined as

repeat
receive(*producer,nextc*);
...
consume the item in *nextc*
...
until *false;*

This scheme exhibits a symmetry in addressing; that is, both the sender and the receiver processes have to name each other to communicate. A variant of this scheme employs asymmetry in addressing. Only the sender names the recipient; the recipient is not required to name the sender. In this scheme, the **send** and **receive** primitives are defined as follows:

- **send**(*P, message*): Send a *message* to process *P.*
- **receive**(*id, message*): Receive a *message* from any process; the variable *id* is set to the name of the process with which communication has taken place.

The disadvantage in both of these schemes (symmetric and asymmetric) is the limited modularity of the resulting process definitions. Changing the name of a process may necessitate examining all other process definitions. All references to the old name must be found, so that they can be modified to the new name. This situation is not desirable from the viewpoint of separate compilation.

Indirect Communication: With indirect communication, the messages are sent to and received from *mailboxes* (also referred to as *ports*). A mailbox can be viewed abstractly as an object into which messages can be placed by processes and from which messages can be removed. Each mailbox has a unique identification. In this scheme, a process can communicate with some other process via a number of different mailboxes. Two processes can communicate only if the processes have a shared mailbox. The **send** and **receive** primitives are defined as follows:
send*(A, message):* Send a *message* to mailbox *A.*
receive*(A, message):* Receive a *message* from mailbox *A.*

In this scheme, a communication link has the following properties:

- A link is established between a pair of processes only if they have a shared mailbox.
- A link may be associated with more than two processes.
- Between each pair of communicating processes, there may be a number of different links, each link corresponding to one mailbox.

- A link may be either unidirectional or bidirectional.

Buffering

A link has some capacity that determines the number of messages that can reside in it temporarily. This property can be viewed as a queue of messages attached to the link. Basically, there are three ways that such a queue can be implemented:

- **Zero capacity:** The queue has maximum length 0; thus, the link cannot have any messages waiting in it. In this case, the sender must wait until the recipient receives the message. The two processes must be synchronised for a message transfer to take place. This synchronisation is called a *rendezvous* (prearranged meeting).
- **Bounded capacity:** The queue has finite length *n*; thus, at most *n* messages can reside in it. If the queue is not full when a new message is sent, the latter is placed in the queue (either the message is copied or a pointer to the message is kept), and the sender can continue execution without waiting. The link has a finite capacity, however. If the link is full, the sender must be delayed until space is available in the queue.
- **Unbounded capacity:** The queue has potentially infinite length; thus, any number of messages can wait in it. The sender is never delayed.

The zero-capacity case is sometimes referred to as a message system with no buffering; the other cases provide automatic buffering.

There are special cases that do not fit directly into any of the categories that we have discussed:

- The process sending a message is never delayed. However, if the receiver has not received the message before the sending process sends another message, the first message is lost. The advantage of this scheme is that large messages do not need to be copied more than once. The main disadvantage is that the programming task becomes more difficult. Processes need to synchronise explicitly, to ensure both that messsages are not lost and that the sender and receiver do not manipulate the message buffer simultaneously.
- The process of sending a message is delayed until it receives a reply. This scheme was adopted in the *Thoth* operating system. In this system, messages are of fixed size (eight words). A process P that sends a message is blocked until the receiving process has received the message and has sent back an eight-word reply by the **reply**(P, *message*) primitive. The reply message overwrites the original message buffer. The only difference between the **send** and **reply** primitives is that a **send** causes the sending process to be blocked, whereas the **reply** allows both the sending process and the receiving process to continue with their executions immediately.

This synchronous communication method can be expanded easily into a full-featured *remote procedure call* (RPC) system. An RPC system is based on the realisation that a subroutine or procedure call in a single-processor system acts exactly like a message system in which the sender blocks until it receives a reply. The message is then like a subroutine call, and the return message contains the value of the subroutine computed.

Exception Conditions

A message system is particularly useful in a distributed environment, where processes may reside at different sites (machines). In such an environment, the probability that an error will occur during communication (and processing) is much larger than in a single-machine environment. In a single-machine environment, messages are usually implemented in shared memory. If a failure occurs, the entire system fails. In a distributed environment, however, messages are transferred by communication lines, and the failure of one site (or link) does not necessarily result in the failure of the entire system.

Process Terminates

Either a sender or a receiver may terminate before a message is processed. This situation will leave messages that will never be received or processes waiting for messages that will never be sent. We consider two cases here:

1. A receiver process *P* may wait for a message from a process *Q* that has terminated. If no action is taken, *P* will be blocked forever. In this case, the system may either terminate *P* or notify *P* that *Q* has terminated.
2. Process *P* may send a message to a process *Q* that has terminated. In the automatic-buffering scheme, no harm is done; *P* simply continues with its execution. If *P* needs to know that its message has been processed by *Q*, it must programme explicitly for an acknowledgment. In the no-buffering case, *P* will be blocked forever. As in case 1, the system may either terminate *P* or notify *P* that *Q* has terminated.

There are three basic methods for dealing with this event:

1. The operating system is responsible for detecting this event and for resending the message.
2. The sending process is responsible for detecting this event and for retransmitting the message, if it wants to do so.

3. The operating system is responsible for detecting this event; it then notifies the sending process that the message has been lost. The sending process can proceed as it chooses.

CPU Scheduling

CPU scheduling is the basis of multiprogrammed operating systems. By switching the CPU among processes, the operating system can make the computer more productive.

Basic Concepts

The objective of multiprogramming is to have some process running at all times, to maximise CPU utilisation. For a uniprocessor system, there will never be more than one running process. If there are more processes, the rest will have to wait until the CPU is free and can be rescheduled.

The idea of multiprogramming is relatively simple. A process is executed until it must wait typically for the completion of some I/O request. In a simple computer system, the CPU would then just sit idle. All this waiting time is wasted; no useful work is accomplished. With multi-programming, we try to use this time productively. Several processes are kept in memory at one time. When one process has to wait, the operating system takes the CPU away from that process and gives the CPU to another process. This pattern continues. Every time one process has to wait, another process may take over the use of the CPU.

CPU–I/O BURST CYCLE

The success of CPU scheduling depends on the following observed property of processes. Process execution consists of a *cycle* of CPU execution and I/O wait. Processes alternate back and forth between

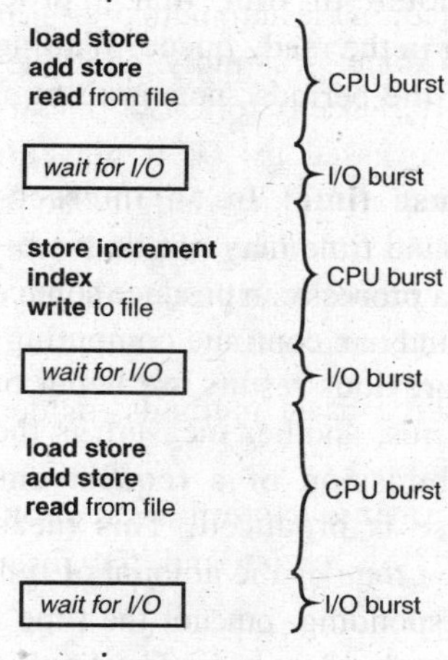

Fig. 3.9: *Alternating sequence of CPU and I/O bursts.*

these two states. Process execution begins with a CPU *burst*. That is followed by an I/O *burst*, which is followed by another CPU burst, then another I/O burst, and so on. Eventually, the last CPU burst will end with a system request to terminate execution, rather than with another I/O burst (Figure 3.9).

The durations of these CPU bursts have been extensively measured. Although they vary greatly from process to process and computer to computer, they tend to have a frequency curve similar to that shown in Figure 3.10. The curve is generally characterised as exponential or hyperexponential. There is a large number of short CPU bursts, and there is a small number of long CPU bursts. An I/O-bound programme would typically have many very short CPU bursts. A CPU-bound programme might have a few very long CPU bursts. This distribution can be important in the selection of an appropriate CPU scheduling algorithm.

CPU Scheduler

Whenever the CPU becomes idle, the operating system must select one of the processes in the ready queue to be executed. The selection process is carried out by the *short-term scheduler* (or CPU scheduler). The scheduler selects from among the processes in memory that are ready to execute, and allocates the CPU to one of them.

Preemptive Scheduling

CPU scheduling decisions may take place under the following four circumstances:

1. When a process switches from the running state to the waiting state (for example, I/O request, or invocation of wait for the termination of one of the child processes)
2. When a process switches from the running state to the ready state (for example, when an interrupt occurs)
3. When a process switches from the waiting state to the ready state (for example, completion of I/O)
4. When a process terminates

When scheduling takes place only under circumstances 1 and 4, we say the scheduling scheme is *nonpreemptive;* otherwise, the scheduling scheme is *preemptive.* Under nonpreemptive scheduling, once the CPU has been allocated to a process, the process keeps the CPU until it releases the CPU either by terminating or by switching to the waiting state. This scheduling method is used by the Microsoft Windows environment. It is the only method that can be used on certain hardware platforms, because it does not require the special hardware (for example, a timer) needed for preemptive scheduling.

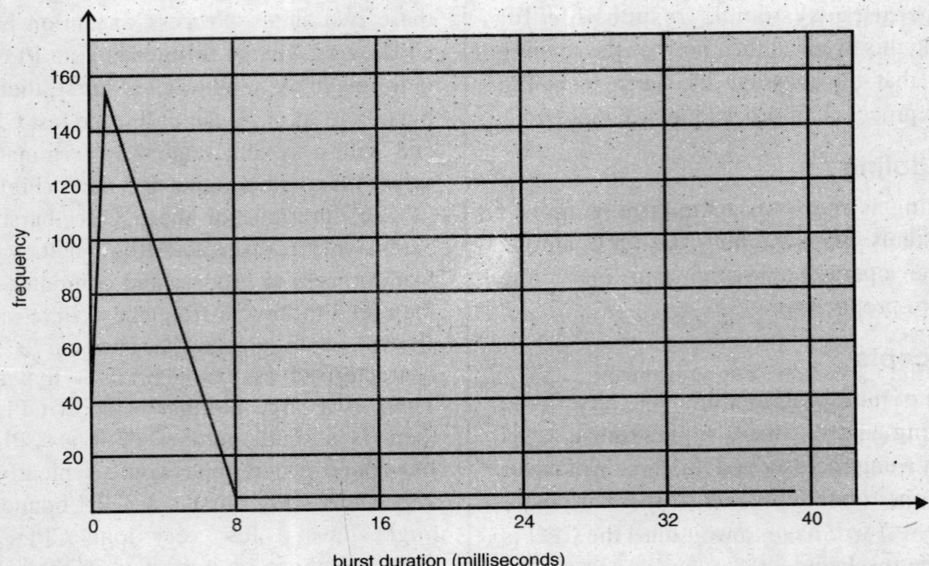

Fig. 3.10: *Histogram of CPU-burst times.*

Dispatcher

Another component involved in the CPU scheduling function is the *dispatcher.* The dispatcher is the module that gives control of the CPU to the process selected by the short-term scheduler. This function involves:

- Switching context
- Switching to user mode
- Jumping to the proper location in the user programme to restart that programme

The dispatcher should be as fast as possible, given that it is invoked during every process switch. The time it takes for the dispatcher to stop one process and start another running is known as the *dispatch latency.*

Scheduling Criteria

Different CPU scheduling algorithms have different properties and may favour one class of processes over another. In choosing which algorithm to use in a particular situation, we must consider the properties of the various algorithms.

Many criteria have been suggested for comparing CPU scheduling algorithms. Which characteristics are used for comparison can make a substantial difference in the determination of the best algorithm. Criteria that are used include the following:

- **CPU utilisation:** We want to keep the CPU as busy as possible. CPU utilisation may range from 0 to 100 per cent. In a real system, it should range from 40 per cent (for a lightly loaded system) to 90 per cent (for a heavily used system).
- **Throughput:** If the CPU is busy executing processes, then work is being done. One measure of work is the number of processes that are completed per time unit, called *throughput.* For long processes, this rate may be one process per hour; for short transactions, throughput might be 10 processes per second.
- **Turnaround time:** From the point of view of a particular process, the important criterion is how long it takes to execute that process. The interval from the time of submission of a process to the time of completion is the *turnaround time.* Turnaround time is the sum of the periods spent waiting to get into memory, waiting in the ready queue, executing on the CPU, and doing I/O.
- **Waiting time:** The CPU scheduling algorithm does not affect the amount of time during which a process executes or does I/O; it affects only the amount of time that a process spends waiting in the ready queue. Waiting time is the sum of the periods spent waiting in the ready queue.
- **Response time:** In an interactive system, turnaround time may not be the best criterion. Often, a process can produce some output fairly early, and can continue computing new results while previous results are being output to the user. Thus, another measure is the time from the submission of a request until the first response is produced. This measure, called *response time,* is the amount of time it takes to start responding, but not the time that it takes to output that response. The turnaround time is generally limited by the speed of the output device.

Scheduling Algorithms

CPU scheduling deals with the problem of deciding of the processes in the ready queue is to be allocated the CPU. There are many different CPU scheduling algorithms. In this section, we describe several of these algorithms.

First-Come, First-Served Scheduling

By far the simplest CPU scheduling algorithm is the *first-come, first-served scheduling (FCFS)* algorithm. With this scheme, the process that requests the CPU first is allocated the CPU first. The implementation of the FCFS policy is easily managed with a FIFO queue. When a process enters the ready queue, its PCB is linked onto the tail of the queue. When the CPU is free, it is allocated to the process at the head of the queue. The running process is then removed from the queue. The code for FCFS scheduling is simple to write and understand.

The average waiting time under the FCFS policy, however, is often quite long. Consider the following set of processes that arrive at time 0, with the length of the CPU-burst time given in milliseconds:

Process	***Burst Time***
P_1	24
P_2	3
P_3	3

If the processes arrive in the order P_1, P_2, P_3, and are served in FCFS order, we get the result shown in the following Gantt chart:

The waiting time is 0 milliseconds for process P_1, 24 milliseconds for process P_2, and 27 milliseconds for process P_3. Thus, the average waiting time is (0 + 24 + 27)/3 = 17 milliseconds. If the processes arrive in the order P_2, P_3, P_1, however, the results will be as shown in the following Gantt chart:

P_2	P_3	P_1
0–3	3–6	6–30

The average waiting time is now (6 + 0 + 3)/3 = 3 milliseconds. This reduction is substantial. Thus, the average waiting time under a FCFS policy is generally not minimal, and may vary substantially if the process CPU-burst times vary greatly.

Shortest-Job-First Scheduling

A different approach to CPU scheduling is the *shortest-job-first (SJF)* algorithm. This algorithm associates with each process the length of the latter's next CPU burst. When the CPU is available, it is assigned to the process that has the smallest next CPU burst. If two processes have the same length next CPU burst, FCFS scheduling is used to break the tie. Note that a more appropriate term would be the *shortest next CPU burst,* because the scheduling is done by examining the length of the next CPU-burst of a process, rather than its total length. We use the term SJF because most people and textbooks refer to this type of scheduling discipline as SJF.

As an example, consider the following set of processes, with the length of the CPU burst time given in milliseconds:

Process	***Burst Time***
P_1	6
P_2	8
P_3	7
P_4	3

Using SJF scheduling, we would schedule these processes according to the following Gantt chart:

P_4	P_1	P_3	P_2
0–3	3–9	9–16	16–24

The waiting time is 3 milliseconds for process P_1, 16 milliseconds for process P_2, 9 milliseconds for process P_3, and 0 milliseconds for process P_4. Thus, the average waiting time is (3 + 16 + 9 + 0)/4 = 7 milliseconds. If we were using the FCFS scheduling scheme, then the average waiting time would be 10.25 milliseconds.

The SJF scheduling algorithm is probably *optimal,* in that it gives the minimum average waiting time for a given set of processes. By moving a short process before a long one the waiting time of the short process decreases more than it increases the waiting time of the long process. Consequently, the *average* waiting time decreases.

The SJF algorithm may be either *preemptive* or *nonpreemptive.* The choice arises when a new process arrives at the ready queue while a previous process is executing. The new process may have a shorter next CPU burst than what is left of the currently executing process. A preemptive SJF algorithm will preempt the currently executing process, whereas a nonpreemptive SJF algorithm will allow the currently running process to finish its CPU burst. Preemptive SJF scheduling is sometimes called *shortest-remaining-time-first* scheduling.

As an example, consider the following four processes, with the length of the CPU-burst time given in milliseconds:

Process	***Arrival Time***	***Burst Time***
P_1	0	8
P_2	1	4
P_3	2	9
P_4	3	5

If the processes arrive at the ready queue at the times shown and need the indicated burst times, then the resulting preemptive SJF schedule is as depicted in the following Gantt Chart:

P_1	P_2	P_4	P_1	P_3
0–1	1–5	5–10	10–17	17–26

Process P_1 is started at time 0, since it is the only process in the queue. Process P_2 arrives at time 1. The remaining time for process P_1 (7 milliseconds) is larger than the time required by process P_2 (4 milliseconds), so process P_1 is preempted, and process P_2 is scheduled. The average waiting time for this example is ((10 – 1) + (1 – 1) + (17 – 2) + (5 – 3))/ 4 = 26/4 = 6.5 milliseconds. A nonpreemptive SJF scheduling would result in an average waiting time of 7.75 milliseconds.

Priority Scheduling

The SJF algorithm is a special case of the general *priority scheduling* algorithm. A priority is associated on each process, and the CPU is allocated to the process with the highest priority. Equal-priority processes are scheduled in FCFS order.

An SJF algorithm is simply a priority algorithm where the priority *(p)* is the inverse of the (predicted) next CPU burst. The larger the CPU burst, the lower the priority, and *vice versa.*

As an example, consider the following set of processes, assumed to have arrived at time 0, in the order P_1, P_2, ..., P_5, with the length of the CPU-burst time given in milliseconds:

Process	***Burst Time***	***Priority***
P_1	10	3
P_2	1	1
P_3	2	3
P_4	1	4
P_5	5	2

Using priority scheduling, we would schedule these processes according to the following Gantt Chart:

P_2	P_5	P_1	P_3	P_4

0 1 6 16 18 19

The average waiting time is 8.2 milliseconds.

Priorities can be defined either internally or externally. Internally defined priorities use some measurable quantity or quantities to compute the priority of a process.

A major problem with priority scheduling algorithms is *indefinite blocking* or *starvation*. A process that is ready to run but lacking the CPU can be considered blocked, waiting for the CPU. A priority scheduling algorithm can leave some low-priority processes waiting indefinitely for the CPU. In a heavily loaded computer system, a steady stream of higher-priority processes can prevent a low-priority process from ever getting the CPU.

Round-Robin Scheduling

The *round-robin (RR)* scheduling algorithm is designed especially for time-sharing systems. It is similar to FCFS scheduling, but preemption is added to switch between processes. A small unit of time, called a *time quantum* or time slice, is defined. A time quantum is generally from 10 to 100 milliseconds. The ready queue is treated as a circular queue. The CPU scheduler goes around the ready queue, allocating the CPU to each process for a time interval of up to 1 time quantum.

To implement RR scheduling, we keep the ready queue as a FIFO queue of processes. New processes are added to the tail of the ready queue. The CPU scheduler picks the first process from the ready queue, sets a timer to interrupt after 1 time quantum, and dispatches the process.

The average waiting time under the RR policy, however, is often quite long. Consider the following set of processes that arrive at time 0, with the length of the CPU-burst time given in milliseconds.

Process	***Burst Time***
P_1	24
P_2	3
P_3	3

If we use a time quantum of 4 milliseconds, then process P_1 gets the first 4 milliseconds. Since it requires another 20 milliseconds, it is preempted after the first time quantum, and the CPU is given to the next process in the queue, process P_2. Since process P_2 does not need 4 milliseconds, it quits before its time quantum expires. The CPU is then given to the next process, process P_3. Once each process has received time quantum the CPU is returned to process P_1 for an additional time quantum. The resulting RR schedule is

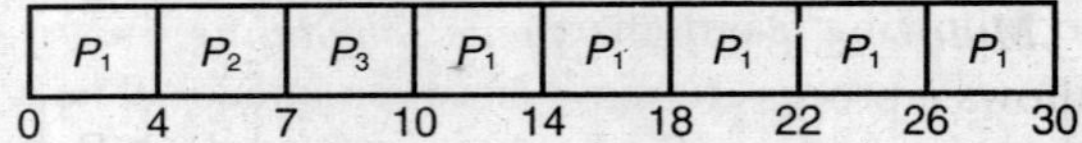

The average waiting time is 77/3 = 5.66 milliseconds.

In the RR scheduling algorithm, no process is allocated the CPU for more than 1 time quantum in a row. If a process CPU burst exceeds 1 time quantum, that process is *preempted* and is put back in the ready queue. The RR scheduling algorithm is preemptive.

MULTILEVEL QUEUE SCHEDULING

A *multilevel queue-scheduling algorithm* partitions the ready queue into several separate queues (Figure 3.11). The processes are permanently assigned to one queue, generally based on some property of the process, such as memory size, process priority, or process type. Each queue has its own scheduling algorithm. For example, separate queues might be used for foreground and background processes. The foreground queue might be scheduled by an RR algorithm, while the background queue is scheduled by an FCFS algorithm.

Let us look at an example of a multilevel queue scheduling algorithm with five queues:

1. System processes
2. Interactive processes
3. Interactive editing processes
4. Batch processes
5. Student processes

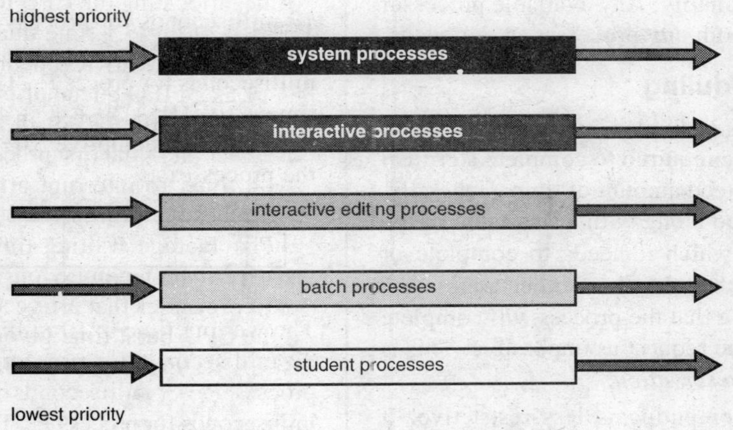

Fig. 3.11: *Multilevel queue scheduling.*

Multilevel Feedback Queue Scheduling

Normally, in a multilevel queue-scheduling algorithm, processes are permanently assigned to a queue on entry to the system. Processes do not move between queues. If there are separate queues for foreground and background processes, for example, processes do not move from one queue to the other, since processes do not change their foreground or background nature. This setup has the advantage of low scheduling overhead, but is inflexible.

Multilevel feedback queue scheduling, however, allows a process to move between queues. The idea is to separate processes with different CPU-burst characteristics. If a process uses too much CPU time, it will be moved to a lower-priority queue. This scheme leaves I/O-bound and interactive processes in the higher-priority queues. Similarly, a process that waits too long in a lower-priority queue may be moved to a higher-priority queue. This form of aging prevents starvation.

For example, consider a multilevel feedback queue scheduler with three queues, numbered from 0 to 2 (Figure 3.12). The scheduler first executes all processes in queue 0. Only when queue 0 is empty will it execute processes in queue 1. Similarly, processes in queue 2 will only be executed if queues 0 and 1 are empty. A process that arrives for queues 1 will preempt a process in queue 2. A process in queue 1 will in turn be preempted by a process arriving for queue 0.

This scheduling algorithm gives highest priority to any process with a CPU burst of 8 milliseconds or less. Such a process will quickly get the CPU, finish its CPU burst, and go off to its next I/O burst. Processes that need more than 8, but less than 24 milliseconds are also served quickly, although with

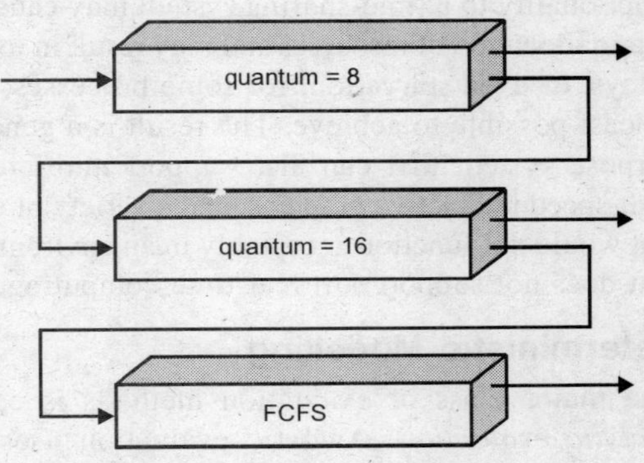

Fig. 3.12: *Multilevel feedback queues.*

lower priority than shorter processes. Long processes automatically sink to queue 2 and are served in FCFS order with any CPU cycles left over from queues 0 and 1.

In general, a multilevel feedback queue scheduler is defined by the following parameters:

- The number of queues
- The scheduling algorithm for each queue
- The method used to determine when to upgrade a process to a higher-priority queue
- The method used to determine when to demote a process to a lower-priority queue
- The method used to determine which queue a process will enter when that process needs service

Multiple-Processor Scheduling

Our discussion thus far has focused on the problems of scheduling the CPU in a system with a single processor. If multiple CPUs are available, the scheduling problem is correspondingly more complex. Many possibilities have been tried, and, as we saw with single-processor CPU scheduling there is no one best solution. In the following section, we discuss briefly some of the issues concerning multiprocessor scheduling. We concentrate on systems where the processors are identical (*homogeneous*) in terms of their functionality; Any available processor can then be used to run any processes in the queue.

Real-Time Scheduling

Real-time computing is divided into two types. *Hard real-time* systems are required to complete a critical task within a guaranteed amount of time. Generally, a process is submitted along with a statement of the amount of time in which it needs to complete or perform I/O. The scheduler then either admits the process, guaranteeing that the process will complete on time, or rejects the request as impossible. This is known as *resource reservation.*

Soft real-time computing is less restrictive. It requires that critical processes receive priority over less fortunate ones. Although adding soft real-time functionality to a time-sharing system may cause an unfair allocation of resources and may result in longer delays, or even starvation, for some processes, it is at least possible to achieve. The result is a general-purpose system that can also support multimedia, high-speed interactive graphics, and a variety of tasks that would not function acceptably in an environment that does not support soft real-time computing.

Deterministic Modelling

One major class of evaluation methods is called *analytic evaluation.* Analytic evaluation uses the given algorithm and the system workload to produce a formula or number that evaluates the performance of the algorithm for that workload.

One type of analytic evaluation is *deterministic modelling.* This method takes a particular predetermined workload and defines the performance of each algorithm for that workload. For example, assume that we have the workload shown below. All five processes arrive at time 0, in the order given, with the length of the CPU-burst time given in milliseconds.

Process	***Burst Time***
P_1	10
P_2	29
P_3	3
P_4	7
P_5	12

Consider the FCFS, SJF, and RR (quantum = 10 milliseconds) scheduling algorithms for this set of processes. Which algorithm would give the minimum average waiting time?

For the FCFS algorithm, we would execute the processes as

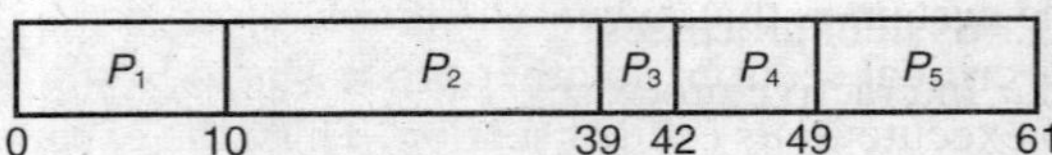

The waiting time is 0 milliseconds for process P_1, 10 milliseconds for process P_2, 39 milliseconds for process P_3, 42 milliseconds for process P_4 and 49 milliseconds for proces P_5. Thus, the average waiting time is (0 + 10 + 39 + 42 + 49)/5 = 28 milliseconds.

With nonpreemptive SJF scheduling, we execute the processes as

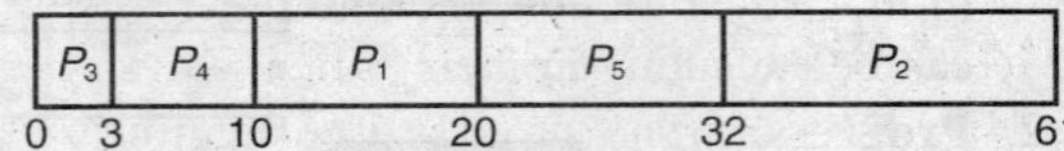

The waiting time is 10 milliseconds for process P_1, 32 milliseconds for process P_2, 0 milliseconds for process P_3, 3 milliseconds for process P_4, and 20 milliseconds for process P_5. Thus, the average waiting time is (10 + 32 + 0 + 3 + 20)/5 = 13 milliseconds.

With the RR algorithm, we start process P_2, but preempt it after 10 milliseconds, putting it in the back of the queue:

P_1	P_3	P_4	P_2	P_5
0	20	23	32	40

61

The waiting time is 0 milliseconds for process P_1, 32 milliseconds for process P_2, 20 milliseconds for process P_3, 23 milliseconds for process P_4, and 40 milliseconds for process P_5. Thus, the average waiting time is (0 + 32 + 20 + 23 + 40)/5 = 23 milliseconds.

Deterministic modelling is simple and fast. It gives exact numbers, allowing the algorithms to be compared. However, it requires exact numbers for input, and its answers apply to only those cases. The main uses of deterministic modelling are in describing scheduling algorithms and providing examples.

Simulations

To get a more accurate evaluation of scheduling algorithms, we can use *simulations.* Simulations involve programming a model of the computer system. Software data structures represent the major components of the system. The simulator has a variable representing a clock; as this variable's value is increased, the simulator modifies the system state to reflect the activities of the devices, the processes, and the scheduler. As the simulation executes, statistics that indicate algorithm performance are gathered and printed.

The Critical-Section Problem

Consider a system consisting of n processes $\{P_0, P_1, ..., P_{n-1}\}$. Each process has a segment of code, called a *critical section,* in which the process may be changing common variables, updating a table, writing a file, and so on. The important feature of the system is that, when one process is executing in its critical section, no other process is to be allowed to execute in its critical section. Thus, the execution of critical sections by the processes is *mutually exclusive* in time. The critical-section problem is to design a protocol that the processes can use to cooperate. Each process must request permission to enter its critical section.

A solution to the critical-section problem must satisfy the following three requirements:

1. **Mutual Exclusion:** If process P_i is executing in its critical section, then no other processes can be executing in their critical sections.
2. **Progress:** If no process is executing in its critical section and there exist some processes that wish to enter their critical sections, then only those processes that are not executing in their remainder section can participate in the decision of which will enter its critical section next, and this section cannot be postponed indefinitely.
3. **Bounded Waiting:** There exist a bound on the number of times that other processes are allowed to enter their critical sections after a process has made a request to enter its critical section and before that request is granted.

Synchronisation Hardware

As with other aspects of software, features of the hardware can make the programming task easier and improve system efficiency.

The critical-section problem could be solved simply in a uniprocessor environment if we could disallow interrupts to occur while a shared variable is being modified. In this manner, we could be sure that the current sequence of instructions would be allowed to execute in order without preemption. No other instructions would be run, so no unexpected modifications could be made to the shared variable.

Many machines therefore provide special hardware instructions that allow us either to test and modify the content of a word, or to swap the contents of two words, atomically.

The *Test-and-Set* instruction can be defined as shown in Figure 3.13. The important characteristic is that this instruction is executed atomically – that is, as one uninterruptible unit. Thus, if two *Test-and-Set* instructions are executed simultaneously (each on a different CPU), they will be executed sequentially in some arbitrary order.

```
begin
        Test-and-Set : = target;
        target : = true;
  end;
```

Figure 3.13: *The definition of the Test-and-Set instruction.*

If the machine supports the *Test-and-Set* instruction, then we can implement mutual exclusion by declaring a Boolean variable *lock,* initialised to *false*. The structure of process P_i is shown in Figure 3.14.

```
repeat
 while Test-and-Set(lock) do no-op;
     critical section
         lock : = false;
                    remainder section
     until false;
```

Fig. 3.14: *Mutual-exclusion implementation with Test-and-Set.*

The *Swap* instruction, defined as shown in Figure 3.15 operates on the contents of two words; like the *Test-and-Set* instruction, it is executed atomically.

If the machine supports the *Swap* instruction, then mutual exclusion can be provided as follows. A global Boolean variable *lock* is declared and is initialised **function** *Test-and-Set* **(var** *target: boolean): boolean;* **to** *false*. In addition, each process also has a local Boolean variable *key*. The structure of process P_i is shown in Figure 3.16.

These algorithms do not satisfy the bounded-waiting requirement. We present an algorithm that uses the *Test-and-Set* instruction in Figure 3.17. This algorithm satisfies all the critical-section requirements. The common data struture are

```
var waiting: array [0..n - 1] of boolean
       lock: boolean
```

These data structures are initialised to *false*.

```
procedure Swap (var a, b: boolean);
   var temp: boolean;
   begin
          temp := a;
          a := b;
          b := temp;
   end;
```

Fig. 3.15: *The definition of the Swap instruction.*

```
repeat
  key := true;
  repeat
  Swap(lock,key);
  until key = false;
          critical section
          lock := false;
          remainder section
until false;
```

Fig. 3.16: *Mutual-exclusion implementation with the swap instruction.*

```
var j: 0..n - 1;
  key: boolean;
repeat
  waiting[i] := true;
```

COMPUTER SCIENCE

```
    key := true;
    while waiting[i] and key do key := Test-
and-Set(lock);
    waiting[i] := false;
        critical section
    j := i + 1 mod n;
    while (j ¹ i) and (not waiting [j]) do
    j := j + 1 mod n;
    if j = i then lock := false
             else waiting [j] := false;
        remainder section
until false;
```

Fig. 3.17: *Bounded-waiting mutual exclusion with Test-and-Set.*

Semaphores

A semaphores *S* is an integer variable that, apart from initialisation, is accessed only through two standard *atomic* operations; *wait* and *signal.* These operations were originally termed *P* (for *wait;* from the Dutch *proberen,* to test) and V (for *signal;* from *verhogen;* to increment). The classical definitions of *wait* and *signal* are

```
wait(S); while S £ 0 do no-op;
             S := S - 1;
signal(S):     S : = S + 1;
```

Modifications to the integer value of the semaphore in the *wait* and *signal* operations must be executed indivisibly. That is, when one process modifies the semaphore value, no other process can simultaneously modify that same semaphore value. In addition, in the case of the *wait(S)*, the testing of the integer value of *S* (S ≤ 0), and its possible modification (S := *S* – 1), must also be executed without interruption.

Usage: We can use semaphores to deal with the *n*-process critical-section problem. The *n* processes share a semaphore, *mutex* (standing for mutual exclusion), initialised to 1. Each process P_i is organized as shown in Figure 3.18.

```
repeat
    wait(mutex);
                  critical section
    signal(mutex);
                  remainder section
until false;
```

Fig. 3.18: *Mutual-exclusion implementation with semaphores.*

Implementation

To overcome the need for busy waiting, we can modify the definition of *wait* and *signal* semaphore operations. When a process executes the *wait* operation and finds that the semaphore value is not positive, it must wait. However, rather than busy waiting, the process can *block* itself. The block operation places a process into a waiting queue associated with the semaphore, and the state of the process is switched to the waiting state. Then, control is transferred to the CPU scheduler, which selects another process to execute.

A process that is blocked, waiting on a semaphore *S*, should be restarted when some other process executed a *signal* operation. The process is restarted by a *wakeup* operation, which changes the process from the waiting state to the ready state. The process is then placed in the ready queue. (The CPU may or may not be switched from the running process to the newly ready process, depending on the CPU-scheduling algorithm.)

To implement semaphores under the definition, we define a semaphore as a record:

```
type semaphore = record
                 value: integer;
                 L: list of process;
                 end;
```

Each semaphore has an integer value and a list of processes. When a process must wait on a semaphore, it is added to the list of processes. A *signal* operation removes one process from the list of waiting processes, and awakens that process.

The semaphore operations can now be defined as

```
wait(S): S.value := S.value - 1;
        if S.value < 0
          then begin
                 add this process to
          S.L;
                block;
                end;
signal(S): S.value := S.value + 1;
      if S.value £ 0
          then begin
        remove a process P from S.L;
        wakeup(P);
        end;
```

The *block* operation suspends the process that invokes it. The *wakeup(P)* operation resumes the execution of a blocked process *P*. These two operations are provided by the operating system as basic system calls.

Deadlocks and Starvation

The implementation of a semaphore with a waiting queue may result in a situation where two or more processes are waiting indefinitely for an event that can be caused by only one of the waiting processes. The event in question is the execution of a *signal* operation. When such a state is reached, these processes are said to be *deadlocked.*

We consider a system consisting of two processes, P_0 and P_1, each accessing two semaphores, S and Q, set to the value 1:

```
     P0                 P1
  wait(S);           wait(Q);
  wait(Q);           wait(S);
     .                  .
     .                  .
     .                  .
  signal(S);         signal(Q);
  signal(Q);         signal(S);
```

Suppose that P_0 executes *wait(S)*, and then P_1 executes *wait(Q)*. When P_0 executes *wait(Q)*, it must wait until P_1 executes *signal(Q)*. Similarly, when P_1 executes *wait(S)*, it must wait until P_0 executes *signal(S)*. Since these signal operations cannot be executed, P_0 and P_1 are deadlocked.

Another problem related to deadlocks is *indefinite blocking* or *starvation,* a situation where processes wait indefinitely within the semaphore. Indefinite blocking may occur if we add and remove processes from the list associated with a semaphore in LIFO order.

Binary Semaphores

A *binary* semaphore is a semaphore with an integer value that can range only between 0 and 1. A binary semaphore can be simpler to implement than a counting semaphore, depending on the underlying hardware architecture. We will now show how a counting semaphore can be implemented using binary semaphores.

Let S be a counting semaphore. To implement it in terms of binary semaphores we need the following data structures:

```
var S1: binary-semaphore;
    S2: binary-semaphore;
    S3: binary-semaphore;
    C: integer;
```

Initially $S1 = S3 = 1$, $S2 = 0$, and the value of integer C is set to the initial value of the counting semaphore S.

The *wait* operation on the counting semaphore S can be implemented as follows:

```
wait(S3);
wait(S1);
C := C – 1;
if C < 0
then begin
        signal(S1);
        wait(S2);
     end
else signal(S1);
signal(S3);
```

The *signal* operation on the counting semaphore S can be implemented as follows:

```
wait(S1);
C := C + 1;
if C ≤ 0 then signal(S2);
signal(S1);
```

The $S3$ semaphore has no effect on *signal(S)*, it merely serialises the *wait(S)* operations.

The Bounded-Buffer Problem

The *mutex* semaphore provides mutual exclusion for accesses to the buffer pool and is initialized to the value 1. The *empty* and *full* semaphores count the number of empty and full buffers, respectively. The semaphore *empty* is initialised to the value n; the semaphore *full* is initialised to the value 0 as shown in Fig. 3.19.

```
repeat
          ...
      produce an item in nextp
          ...
      wait(empty);
      wait(mutex);
          ...
      add nextp to buffer
          ...
      signal(mutex);
      signal(full);
until false;
```

Fig. 3.19: *The structure of the produce process.*

The Readers and Writers Problem

A data object (such as a file or record) is to be shared among several concurrent processes. Some of these processes may want only to read the content of the shared object, whereas others may want to update (that is, to read and write) content of the shared object (Figure 3.20).

```
repeat
  wait(full);
  wait(mutex);
    ...
  remove an item from buffer to nextc
    ...
  signal(mutex);
  signal(empty);
    ...
  consume the item in nextc
    ...
until false;
```

Fig. 3.20: *The structure of the consumer process.*

The Dining-Philosophers Problem

The dining-philosophers problem is considered a classic synchronisation problem, neither because of its practical importance, nor because computer scientists dislike philosophers, but because it is an example for a large class of concurrency-control problems. It is a simple representation of the need to allocate several resources among several processes in a deadlock and starvation-free manner.

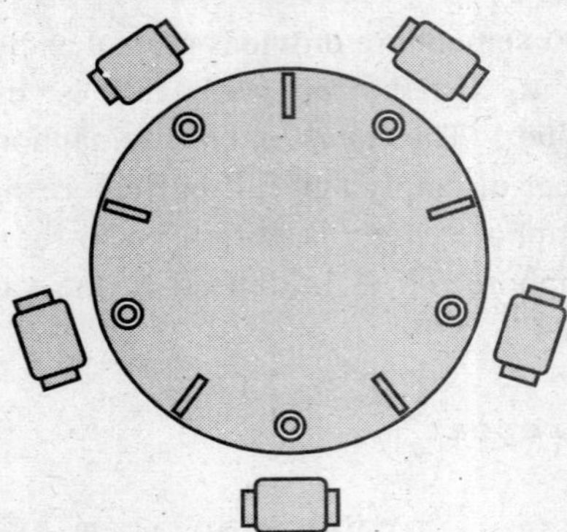

Fig. 3.21: *The situation of the dining philosophers.*

One simple solution is to represent each chopstick by a semaphore. A philosopher tries to grab the chopstick by executing a *wait* operation on that semaphore; she releases her chopsticks by executing the *signal* operation on the appropriate semaphores. Thus, the shared data are

var *chopstick:* **array** [0..4] **of** *semaphore;*

where all the elements of *chopstick* are initialized to 1. The structure of philosopher *i* is shown in Figure 3.22.

Although this solution guarantees that no two neighbours are eating simultaneously, it nevertheless must be rejected because it has the possibility of creating a deadlock. Suppose that all five philosophers become hungry simultaneously, and each grabs her left chopstick. All the elements of *chopstick* will now be equal to 0. When each philosopher tries to grab her right chopstick, she will be delayed forever.

```
repat
    wait(chopstick[i]);
    wait(chopstick[i + 1 mod 5]);
      ...
      eat
      ...
    signal(chopstick[i]);
    signal(chopstick[i + 1 mod 5]);
      ...
      think
      ...
until false;
```

Fig. 3.22: *The structure of philosopher i.*

Critical Regions

Although semaphores provide a convenient and effective mechanism for process synchronisation, their incorrect use can still result in timing errors that are difficult to detect, since these errors happen only if some particular execution sequences take place, and these sequences do not always occur.

Unfortunately, such timing errors can still occur with the use of semaphores. To illustrate how, let us review the solution to the critical-section problem using semaphores. All processes has a semaphore variable *mutex,* which is initialised to 1. Each process must execute *wait(mutex)* before entering the critical section, and *signal(mutex)* afterward. If this sequence is not observed, two processes may be in their critical sections simultaneously.

- Suppose that a process interchanges the order in which the *wait* and *signal* operations on the semaphore *mutex* are executed, resulting in the following execution:

  signal(mutex);

  ...

  critical section

  ...

  wait(mutex);

  In this situation, several processes may be executing in their critical section simultaneously, violating the mutual-exclusion requirement. This error may be discovered only if several processes are simultaneously active in their critical sections. Note that this situation may not always be reproducible.
- Suppose that a process replaces *signal(mutex)* with *wait(mutex)*. That is, it executes

  wait(mutex);

  ...

  critical section

  ...

  wait(mutex);

  In this case, a deadlock will occur.
- Suppose that a process omits the *wait(mutex)*, or the *signal(mutex),* or both. In this case, either mutual exclusion is violated or a deadlock will occur.

Monitors

Another high-level synchronisation construct is the *monitor* type. A monitor is characterised by a set of programmer-defined operators. The representation of a monitor type consists of declarations of variables whose values define the state of an instance of the type, as well as the bodies of procedures or functions that implement operations on the type.

Deadlocks

In a multiprogramming environment, several processes may complete for a finite number of resources. A process requests resources; if the resources are not available at that time, the process enters a wait state. It may happen that waiting processes will never again change state, because the resources they have requested are held by other waiting processes. This situation is called a *deadlock*.

System Model

A system consists of a finite number of resources to be distributed among a number of completing processes. The resources are partitioned into several types, each of which consists of some number of identical instances. Memory space, CPU cycles, files, and I/O devices (such as printers and tape drives) are examples of resource types. If a system has two CPUs, then the resource type CPU has two instances. Similarly, the resource type *printer* may have five instances.

If a process requests an instance of a resource type, the allocation of *any* instance of the type will satisfy the request. If it will not, then the instances are not identical, and the resource type classes have not been defined properly. For example, a system may have two printers. These two printers may be defined to be in the same resource class if no one cares which printer prints which output. However, if one printer is on the ninth floor and the other is in the basement, then people on the ninth floor may not see both printers as equivalent, and separate resource classes may need to be defined for each printer.

Under the normal mode of operation, a process may utilise a resource in only the following sequence:

1. **Request:** If the request can not be granted immediately (for example, the resource is being used by another process), then the requesting process must wait until it can acquire the resource.
2. **Use:** The process can operate on the resource (for example, if the resource is a printer, the process can print on the printer).
3. **Release:** The process releases the resource.

The request and release of resources are system calls. To illustrate a deadlock state, we consider a system with three tape drives. Suppose that there are three processes, each holding one of these tape drives. If each process now requests another tape drive, the three processes will be in a deadlock state. Each is waiting for the event "tape drive is released," which can be caused only by one of the other waiting processes. This example illustrates a deadlock involving processes competing for the same resource type.

Necessary Conditions

A deadlock situation can arise if the following four conditions hold simultaneously in a system:

1. **Mutual exclusion:** At least one resource must be held in a nonsharable mode; that is, only one process at a time can use the resource. If another process requests that resource, the requesting process must be delayed until the resource has been released.
2. **Hold and wait:** There must exist a process that is holding at least one resource and is waiting to acquire additional resources that are currently being held by other processes.
3. **No preemption:** Resources cannot be preempted; that is, a resource can be released only voluntarily by the process holding it, after that process has completed its task.
4. **Circular wait:** There must exist a set $\{P_0, P_1, ..., P_n\}$ of waiting processes such that P_0 is waiting for a resource that is held by P_1, P_1 is waiting for a resource that is held by P_2, ..., P_{n-1} is waiting for a resource that is held by P_n and P_n is waiting for a resource that is held by P_0.

Resource-Allocation Graph

Deadlocks can be described more precisely in terms of a directed graph called a *system resource-allocation graph.* This graph consists of a set of vertices V and a set of edges E. The set of vertices V is partitioned into two different types of nodes $P = \{P_1, P_2, ..., P_n\}$, the set consisting of all the active processes in the system, and $R = \{R_1, R_2, ..., R_m\}$, the set consisting of all resource types in the system.

A directed edge from process P_i to resource type R_j is denoted by $P_i \rightarrow R_j$; it signifies that process P_i requested an instance of resource type R_j and is currently waiting for that resource. A directed edge from resource type R_j to process P_i is denoted by $R_j \rightarrow P_i$; it signifies that an instance of resource type R_j has been allocated to process P_i. A directed edge $P_i \rightarrow R_j$ is called a *request edge;* a directed edge $R_j \rightarrow P_i$ is called an *assignment edge.*

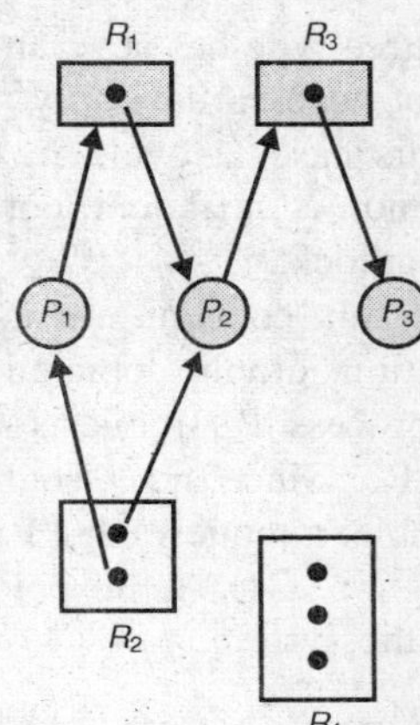

Fig. 3.23: *Resource-alloation graph.*

Pictorially, we represent each process P_i as a circle, and each resource type R_j as a square. Since resource type R_j may have more than one instance, we represent each such instance as a dot within the square. Note that a request edge points to only the square R_j,

COMPUTER SCIENCE

whereas an assignment edge must also designate one of the dots in the square.

When process P_i requests an instance of resource type R_j, a request edge is inserted in the resource-allocation graph. When this request can be fulfilled, the request edge is *instantaneously* transformed to an assignment edge. When the process no longer needs access to the resource it releases the resource, and as a result the assignment edge is deleted.

The resource-allocation graph shown in Figure 3.23 depicts the following situation.

- The sets P, R, and E:
  - $P = \{P_1, P_2, P_3\}$
  - $R = \{R_1, R_2, R_3, R_4\}$
  - $E = \{P_1 \rightarrow R_1, P_2 \rightarrow R_3, R_1 \rightarrow P_2, R_2 \rightarrow P_2, R_2 \rightarrow P_1, R_3 \rightarrow P_3\}$
- Resource instances:
  - One instance of resource type R_1
  - Two instances of resource type R_2
  - One instance of resource type R_3
  - Three instances of resource type R_4
- Process states:
  - Process P_1 is holding an instance of resource type R_2, and is waiting for an instance of resource type R_1.
  - Process P_2 is holding an instance of R_1 and R_2, and is waiting for an instance of resource type R_3.
  - Process P_3 is holding an instance of R_3.

If each resource type has exactly one instance, then a cycle implies that a deadlock has occurred. If the cycle involves only a set of resource types, each of which has only a single instance, then a deadlock has occurred. Each process involved in the cycle is deadlocked. In this case, a cycle in the graph is both a necessary and a sufficient condition for the existence of deadlock.

If each resource type has several instances, then a cycle does not necessarily imply that a deadlock occurred. In this case, a cycle in the graph is a necessary but not a sufficient condition for the existence of deadlock.

To illustrate this concept, let us return to the resource-allocation graph depicted in Fig. 8.23 Suppose that process P_3, requests an instance of resource type R_2. Since no resource instance is currently available, a request edge $P_3 \rightarrow R_2$ is added to the graph (Figure 3.24). At this point, two minimal cycles exist in the system:

$$P_1 \rightarrow R_1 \rightarrow P_2 \rightarrow R_3 \rightarrow P_3 \rightarrow R_2 \rightarrow P_1$$
$$P_2 \rightarrow R_3 \rightarrow P_3 \rightarrow R_2 \rightarrow P_2$$

Processes P_1, P_2 and P_3 are deadlocked. Process P_2 is waiting for the resource R_3, which is held by process P_3. Process P_3, on the other hand, is waiting for either process P_1 or process P_2 to release resource R_2. In addition, process P_1 is waiting for process P_2 to release resource R_1.

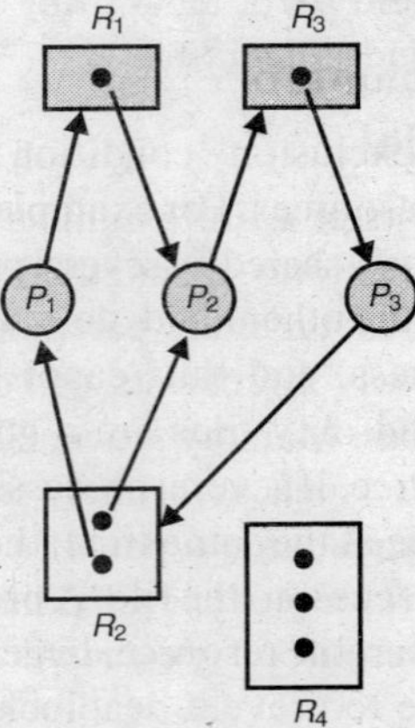

Fig. 3.24: *Resource-allocation graph with a deadlock.*

Now consider the resource-allocation graph in Figure 3.25. In this example, we also have a cycle.

$$P_1 \rightarrow R_1 \rightarrow P_3 \rightarrow R_2 \rightarrow P_1$$

However, there is no deadlock. Observe that process P_4 may relese its instance of resource type R_2. That resource can then be allocated to P_3, breaking the cycle.

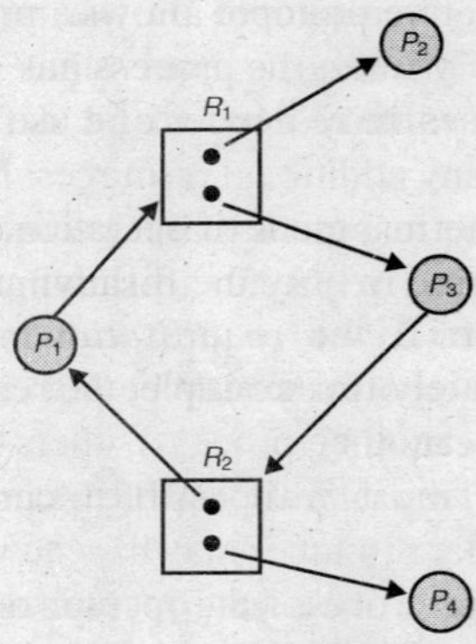

Fig. 3.25: *Resource-allocation graph with a cycle but no deadlock.*

Methods for Handling Deadlocks

Principally there are three different methods for dealing with the deadlock problem:

- We can use a protocol to ensure that the system will *never* enter a deadlock state.
- We can allow the system to enter a deadlock state and then recover.
- We can ignore the problem all together, and pretend that deadlocks never occur in the system. This solution is the one used by most operating systems, including UNIX.

Deadlock Prevention

For a deadlock to occur, each of the four necessary conditions must hold. By ensuring that at least one of these conditions cannot hold, we can *prevent* the occurrence of a deadlock. Let us elaborate on this approach by examining each of the four necessary conditions separately.

Mutual Exclusion

The mutual-exclusion condition must hold for nonsharable resources. For example, a printer cannot be simultaneously shared by several processes. Sharable resources, on the other hand, do not require mutually exclusive access, and thus canot be involved in a deadlock. Read-only files are a good example of a sharable resource. If several processes attempt to open a read-only file at the same time, they can be granted simultaneous access to the file. A process never needs to wait for a sharable resource. In general, however, it is not possible to prevent deadlocks by denying the mutual-exclusion con-dition. Some resources are intrinsically nonsharable.

Hold and Wait

One protocol that can be used requires each process to request and be allocated all its resources before it begins execution. We can implement this provision by requiring that system calls requesting resources for a process precede all other system calls.

An alternative protocol allows a process to request resources only when the process has none. A process may request some resources and use them. Before it can request any additional resources, however, it must release all the resources that it is currently allocated.

There are two main disadvantages to these protocols. First, *resource utilisation* may be low, since many of the resources may be allocated but unused for a long period.

Second, *starvation* is possible. A process that needs several popular resources may have to wait indefinitely, because at least one of the resources that it needs is always allocated to some other process.

No Preemption

The third necessary condition is that there be no preemption of resources that have already been allocated. To ensure that this condition does not hold, we can use the following protocol. If a process that is holding some resources requests another resource that cannot be immediately allocated to it (that is, the process must wait), then all resources currently being held are preempted. That is, these resources are implicitly released. The preempted resources are added to the list of resources for which the process is waiting. The process will be restarted only when it can regain its old resources, as well as the new ones that it is requesting.

Circular-Wait

One way to ensure that the circular-wait condition never holds is to impose a total ordering of all resource types, and to require that each process requests resources in an increasing order of enumeration.

Let $R = \{R_1, R_2, ..., R_m\}$ be the set of resource types. We assign to each resource type a unique integer number, which allows us to compare two resources and to determine whether one precedes another in our ordering. Formally, we define a one-to-one function $F : R \rightarrow N$, where N is the set of natural numbers. For example, if the set of resource types R includes tape drives, disk drives, and printers, then the function F might be defined as follows:

F(tape drive) = 1,
F(disk drive) = 5.
F(Printer) = 12.

Deadlock Avoidance

An alternative method for avoiding deadlocks is to require additional information about how resources are to be requested. For example, in a system with one tape drive and one printer, we might be told that process *P* will request first the tape drive, and later the printer, before releasing both resources. Process *Q*, on the other hand, will request first the printer, and then the tape drive. With the knowledge of the complete sequence of requests and releases for each process, we can decide for each request whether or not the process should wait.

Safe State

A state is *safe* if the system can allocate resources to each process (up to its maximum) in some order and still avoid a deadlock. More formally, a system is in a safe state only if there exists a *safe sequence.* A sequence of processes $<P_2, P_3, ..., P_n>$ is a safe sequence for the current allocation state if, for each P_i, the resources that P_i can still request, can be satisfied by the currently available resources plus the resources held by all the P_j, with $j < i$. In this situation, if the resources that process P_i needs are not immediately available, then P_i can wait until all P_j have finished. When they have finished, P_i can obtain all of its needed resources, complete its designated task, return its allocated resources, and terminate. When P_i terminates, P_{i+1} can obtain its needed resources, and so on. If no such sequence exists, then the system state is said to be *unsafe*.

A safe state is not a deadlock state. Conversely, a deadlock state is an unsafe state. Not all unsafe states are deadlocks, however (Figure 3.26). An unsafe state may lead to a deadlock. As long as the state is safe, the operating system can avoid unsafe (and deadlock) states. In an unsafe state, the operating system cannot prevent processes from requesting resources such that a deadlock occurs: the behaviour of the processes controls unsafe states.

To illustrate, we consider a system with 12 magnetic tape drives and 3 processes: P_0, P_1 and P_2. Process P_0 requires 10 tape drives, process P_1 may need as many as 4, and process P_2 may need up to 9 tape drives. Suppose that, at time t_0, process P_0 is holding 5 tape drives, process P_1 is holding 2, and process P_2 is holding 2 tape drives. (Thus, there are 3 free tape drives.)

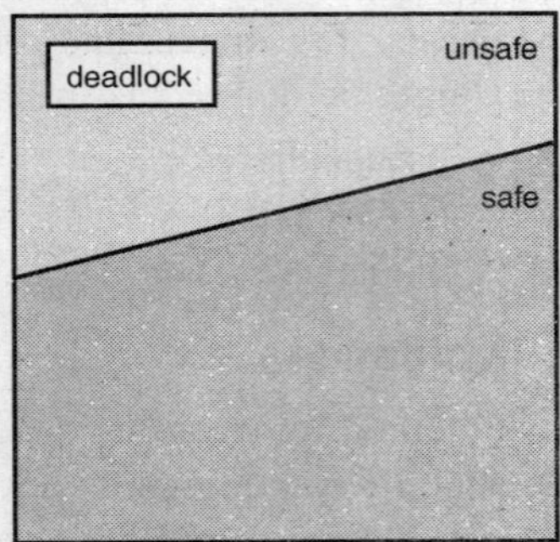

Fig. 3.26: *Safe, unsafe, and deadlock state spaces*

	Maximum Needs	*Current Needs*
P_0	10	5
P_1	4	2
P_2	9	2

At time t_0, the system is in a safe state. The sequence $<P_1, P_0, P_2>$ satisfies the safety condition, since process P_1 can immediately be allocated all its tape drives and then return them (the system will then have 5 available tape drives), then process P_0 can get all its tape drives and return them (the system will then have 10 available tape drives, and finally process P_2 could get all its tape drives and return them (the system will then have all 12 tape drives available).

Note that it is possible to go from a safe state to an unsafe state. Suppose that, at time t_1, process P_2 requests and is allocated 1 more tape drive. The system is no longer in a safe state. At this point, only process P_1 can be allocated all its tape drives. When it returns then, the system will have only 4 available tape drives. Since process P_0 is allocated 5 tape drives, but has a maximum of 10, it may then request 5 more tape drives. Since they are unavailable, process P_0 must wait. Similarly, process P_2 may request an additional 6 tape drives and have to wait, resulting in a deadlock.

Banker's Algorithm

The resource-allocation graph algorithm is not applicable to a resource-allocation system with multiple instances of each resource type. The deadlock-avoidance algorithm that we have same described is applicable to such a system, but is less efficient than the resource-allocation graph scheme. This algorithm is commonly known as the *banker's algorithm.* The name was chosen because this algorithm could be used in a banking system to ensure that the bank never allocates its available cash such that it can no longer satisfy the needs of all its customers.

Several data structures must be maintained to implement the banker's algorithm. These data structures encode the state of the resource-allocation system. Let *n* be the number of processes in the system and *m* be the number of resource types. We need the following data structures:

- *Available:* A vector of length *m* indicates the number of available resources of each type. If *Available*[*j*] = *k*, there are *k* instances of resource type R_j available.
- *Max:* An *n* × *m* matrix defines the maximum demand of each process. If *Max*[*i*, *j*] = *k*, the P_i may request at most *k* instances of resource type R_j.
- *Allocation:* An *n* × *m* matrix defines the number of resources of each type currently allocated to each process. If *Allocation*[*i*, *j*] = *k*, then process P_i is currently allocatd *k* instances of resource type R_j.
- *Need:* An *n* × *m* matrix indicates the remaining resource need of each process. If *Need*[*i*, *j*] = *k*, then P_i may need *k* more instances of resource type R_j to complete its task. Note that *Need*[*i*, *j*] = *Max*[*i*, *j*] – *Allocation*[*i*, *j*].

Safety Algorithm

The algorithm for finding out whether or not a system is in a safe state can be described as follows:

1. Let *Work* and *Finish* be vectors of length *m* and *n*, respectively. Initialise *Work* := *Available* and *Finish*[*i*] := *false* for i = 1, 2, . . . , *n*.
2. Find an *i* such that both
   a. *Finish*[*i*] = *false*
   b. $Need_i \le Work$

   If no such *i* exists, go to step 4.
3. *Work* := *Work* + $Allocation_i$
   Finish[*i*] := *true*
   go to step 2
4. If *Finish*[*i*] = *true* for all *i*, then the system is in a safe state.

This algorithm may require an order of $m \times n^2$ operations to decide whether a state is safe.

Resource-Request Algorithm

Let $Request_i$ be the request vector for process P_i. If $Request_i[j] = k$, then process P_i wants *k* instances of resource type R_j. When a request for resources is made by process P_i, the following actions are taken:

1. If $Request_i \le Need_i$, go to step 2. Otherwise, raise an error conditon, since the process has exceeded its maximum claim.
2. If $Request_i \le Available$, go to step 3. Otherwise, P_i must wait, since the resources are not available.

3. Have the system pretend to have allocated the requested resources to process P_i by modifying the state as follows:

   Available := *Available* – $Request_i$;
   $Allocation_i$:= $Allocation_i$ + $Request_i$;
   $Need_i$:= $Need_i$ – $Request_i$;

   If the resulting resource-allocation state is safe, the transaction is completed and process P_i is allocated its resources. However, if the new state is unsafe, then P_i must wait for $Request_i$ and the old resource-allocation state is restored.

An Illustrative Example

Consider a system with five processes P_0 through P_4 and three resource types *A, B, C*. Resource type *A* has 10 instances, resource type *B* has 5 instances, and resource type *C* has 7 instances. Suppose that, at time T_0, the following snapshot of the system has been taken:

	Allocation	*Max*	*Available*
	A B C	A B C	A B C
P_0	0 1 0	7 5 3	3 3 2
P_1	2 0 0	3 2 2	
P_2	3 0 2	9 0 2	
P_3	2 1 1	2 2 2	
P_4	0 0 2	4 3 3	

The content of the matrix *Need* is defined to be *Max* – *Allocation* and is

	Need
	A B C
P_0	7 4 3
P_1	1 2 2
P_2	6 0 0
P_3	0 1 1
P_4	4 3 1

We claim that the system is currently in a safe state. Indeed, the sequence $<P_1, P_3, P_4, P_2, P_0>$ satisfies the safety criteria.

Suppose now that process P_1 requests one additional instance of resource type *A* and two instances of resource type *C*, so $Request_1$ = (1,0,2). To decide whether this request can be immediately granted, we first check that $Request_1 \leq Available$ (that is, $(1,0,2) \leq (3,3,2)$), which is true. We then pretend that this request has been fulfilled, and we arrive at the following new state:

	Allocation	*Need*	*Available*
	A B C	A B C	A B C
P_0	0 1 0	7 4 3	2 3 0
P_1	3 0 2	0 2 0	
P_2	3 0 2	6 0 0	
P_3	2 1 1	0 1 1	
P_4	0 0 2	4 3 1	

Deadlock Detection

If a system does not employ either a deadlock-prevention or a deadlock-avoidance algorithm, then a deadlock situation may occur. In this environment, the system must provide:

- An algorithm that examines the state of the system to determine whether a deadlock has occurred
- An algorithm to recover from the deadlock

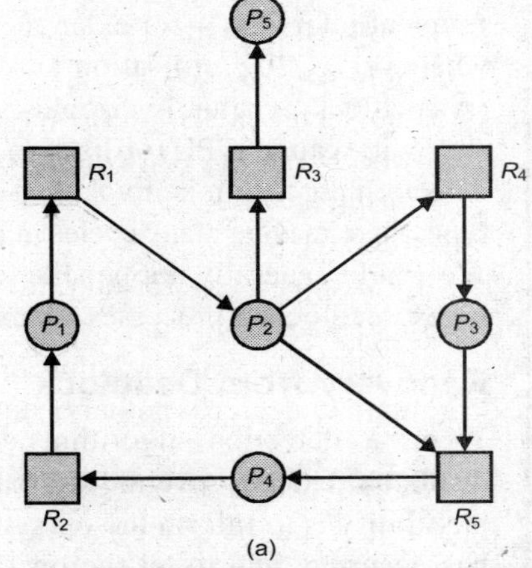

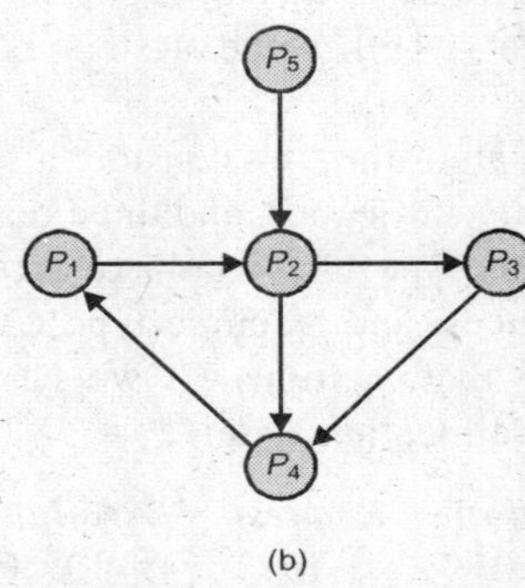

Fig. 3.27: *(a) Resource-allocation graph. (b) Corresponding wait-for graph.*

Single Instance of Each Resource Type

If all resources have only a single instance, then we can define a deadlock detection algorithm that uses a variant of the resource-allocation graph, called a *wait-for* graph. We obtain this graph from the resource-allocation graph by removing the nodes of type resource and collapsing the appropriate edges.

More precisely, an edge from P_i to P_j in a wait-for graph implies that process P_i is waiting for process P_j to release a resource that P_i needs. An edge $P_i \rightarrow$

COMPUTER SCIENCE

P_j exists in a wait-for graph if and only if the corresponding resource-allocation graph contains two edges $P_i \rightarrow R_q$ and $R_q \rightarrow P_j$ for some resource R_q. For example, in Figure 3.27, we present a resource-allocation graph and the corresponding wait-for graph.

Several Instances of Resource Type

The wait-for graph scheme is not applicable to a resource-allocation system with multiple instances of each resource type. The algorithm employs several time-varying data structures that are similar to those used in the banker's algorithm:

- *Available:* A vector of length m indicates the number of available resources of each type.
- *Allocation:* An $n \times m$ matrix defines the number of resources of each type currently allocated to each process.
- *Request:* An $n \times m$ matrix indicates the current request of each process. If $Request[i,j] = k$, then process P_i is requesting k more instances of resource type R_j.

Compare this algorithm with the *banker's algorithm*

1. Let *Work* and *Finish* be vectors of length m and n, respectively. Initialise *Work* := *Available*. For $i = 1, 2, \ldots, n$, if $Allocation_i \neq 0$, then $Finish[i]$:= *false;* otherwise, $Finish[i]$:= *true.*
2. Find an index i such that both
   a. $Finish[i] = false$.
   b. $Request_i \leq Work$.
   If no such i exists, go to step 4.
3. $Work := Work + Allocation_i$
   $Finish[i] := true$
   go to step 2.
4. If $Finish[i]$ = false, for some i, $1 \leq i \leq n$, then the system is in a deadlock state. Moreover, if $Finish[i]$ = *false,* then process P_i is deadlocked.

This algorithm requires an order of $m \times n^2$ operations to detect whether the system is in a deadlocked state.

To illustrate this algorithm, we consider a system with five processes P_0 through P_4 and three resource types *A, B, C.* Resource type *A* has 7 instances, resource type *B* has 2 instances, and resource type *C* has 6 instances. Suppose that, at time T_0, we have the following resource-allocation state:

	Allocation	*Request*	*Available*
	A B C	A B C	A B C
P_0	0 1 0	0 0 0	0 0 0
P_1	2 0 0	2 0 2	
P_2	3 0 3	0 0 0	
P_3	2 1 1	1 0 0	
P_4	0 0 2	0 0 2	

We claim that the system is not in a deadlocked state. Indeed, if we execute our algorithm, we will find that the sequence $<P_0, P_2, P_3, P_1, P_4>$ will result in $Finish[i]$ = true for all i.

Suppose now that process P_2 makes one additional request for an instance of type C. The *Request* matrix is modified as follows:

	Need
	A B C
P_0	0 0 0
P_1	2 0 2
P_2	0 0 1
P_3	1 0 0
P_4	0 0 2

We claim that the system is now deadlocked. Although we can reclaim the resources held by process P_0, the number of available resources is not sufficient to fulfill the requests of the other processes. Thus, a deadlock exists, consisting of processes P_1, P_2, P_3, and P_4.

Detection-Algorithm Usage

If deadlocks occur frequently, then the detection algorithm should be invoked frequently. Resources allocated to deadlocked processes will be idle until the deadlock can be broken. In addition, the number of processes involved in the deadlock cycle may grow.

Deadlocks can come into being only when some process makes a request that cannot be granted immediately. It is possible that this request is the final request that completes a chain of waiting processes.

Of course, invoking the deadlock-detection algorithm for every request may incur a considerable overhead in computation time. A less expensive alternative is simply to invoke the algorithm at less frequent intervals — for example, once per hour, or whenever CPU utilisation drops below 40%. (A deadlock eventually cripples system throughput and will cause CPU utilisation to drop). If the detection algorithm is invoked at arbitrary points in time, there may be many cycles in the resource graph. We would generally not be able to tell which of the many deadlocked processes "caused" the deadlock.

Recovery from Deadlock

When a detection algorithm determines that a deadlock exists, several alternatives exist. One possibility is to inform the operator that a deadlock has occurred, and to let the operator deal with the deadlock manually. The other possibility is to let the system *recover* from the deadlock automatically. There are two options for breaking a deadlock. One solution is simply to abort one or more process to break the circular-wait. The second option is to preempt some resources from one or more of the deadlocked processes.

Address Binding

Usually, a programme resides on a disk as a binary executable file. The programme must be brought into memory and placed within a process for it to be executed. Depending on the memory management in use, the process may be moved between disk and memory during its execution. The collection of processes on the disk that are waiting to be brought into memory for execution forms the *input queue*.

Addresses in the source programme are generally symbolic (such as COUNT). A compiler will typically *bind* these symbolic addresses to relocatable addresses (such as "14 bytes from the beginning of this module"). The linkage editor or loader will in turn bind these relocatable addresses to absolute addresses (such as 74014). Each binding is a mapping from one address space to another.

Classically, the *binding* of instructions and data to memory addresses can be done at any step along the way:

- **Compile time:** If it is known at compile time where the process will reside in memory, then *absolute* code can be generated. For example, if it is known a priority that a user process resides starting at location *R*, then the generated compiler code will start at that location and extend up from there. If, at some later time, the starting location changes, then it will be necessary to recompile this code. The MS-DOS.COM-format programmes are absolute code bound at compile time.
- **Load time:** If it is not known at compile time where the process will reside in memory, then the compiler must generate *relocatable* code. In this case, final binding is delayed until load time. If the starting address changes, we need only to reload the user code to incorporate this changed value.
- **Execution time:** If the process can be moved during its execution from one memory segment to another, then binding must be delayed until run time. Special hardware must be available for this scheme to work.

Dynamic Loading

To obtain better memory-space utilisation, we can use *dynamic loading.* The main programme is loaded into memory and is executed. When a routine needs to call another routine, the calling routine first checks to see whether the other routine has been loaded.

The advantage of dynamic loading is that an unused routine is never loaded. This scheme is particularly useful when large amounts of code are needed to handle infrequently occurring cases, such as error routines.

Dynamic loading does not require special support from the operating system.

Dynamic Linking

Most operating systems support only *static linking,* in which system language libraries are treated like any other object module and are combined by the loader into the binary programme image. The concept of dynamic linking is similar to that of dynamic loading (Fig. 3.28).

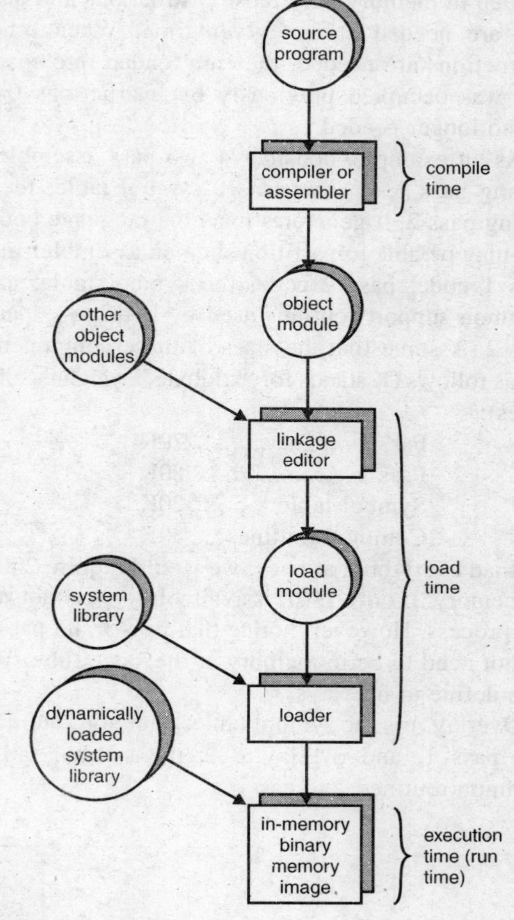

Fig. 3.28: *Multistep processing of a user programme*

This feature is usually used with system libraries, such as language subroutine libraries. Without this facility, all programmes on a system need to have a copy of their language library (or at least the routines referenced by the programme) included in the executable image. This requirement wastes both disk space and main memory. With dynamic linking, a *stub* is included in the image for each library-routine reference. This stub is a small piece of code that indicates how to locate the appropriate memory-resident library routine, or how to load the library if the routine is not already present.

Unlike dynamic loading, dynamic linking generally requires some help from the operating system. If the processes in memory are protected from one another, then the operating system is the only entity that can check to see whether the needed routine is in another processes memory space, and can allow multiple processes to access the same memory addresses.

Overlays

The size of a process is limited to the size of physical memory. So that a process can be larger than the amount of memory allocated to it, a technique called *overlays* is sometimes used. The idea of overlays is to keep in memory only those instructions and data that are needed at any given time. When other instructions are needed, they are loaded into space that was occupied previously by instructions that are no longer needed.

As an example, consider a two-pass assembler. During pass 1, it constructs a symbol table; then, during pass 2, it generates machine-language code. We may be able to partition such an assembler into pass 1 code, pass 2 code, the symbol table, and common support routines used by both pass 1 and pass 2. Assume that the sizes of these components are as follows (K stands for "kilobyte," which is 1024 bytes):

Pass 1 .... 70K
Pass 2 .... 80K
Symbol table 20K
Common routines..... 30K

To load everything at once, we would require 200K of memory. If only 150K is available, we cannot run our process. However, notice that pass 1 and pass 2 do not need to be in memory at the same time. We thus define to overlays:

Overlay *A* is the symbol table, common routines, and pass 1, and overlay *B* is the symbol table, common routines, and pass 2.

We add an overlay driver (10K) and start with overlay *A* in memory. When we finish pass 1, we jump to the overlay driver, which reads overlay *B* into memory, overwriting overlay *A*, and then transfers control to pass 2. Overlay *A* needs only 120K, whereas overlay *B* needs 130K (Figure 3.29). We can now run our assembler in the 150K of memory. It will load somewhat faster because fewer data need to be transferred before execution starts. However, it will run somewhat slower, due to the extra I/O to read the code for overlay *B* over the code for overlay *A*.

Logical Vs Physical Address Space

An address generated by the CPU is commonly referred to as a *logical address,* whereas an address seen by the memory unit (that is, the one loaded into the *memory address register* of the memory) is commonly referred to as a *physical address.*

The compile-time and load-time address-binding schemes result in an environment where the logical and physical addresses are the same. However, the execution-time address-binding scheme results in an environment where the logical and physical addresses differ. In this case, we usually refer to the logical address as a *virtual address.* We use *logical address* and *virtual address* interchangeably in the text. The set of all logical addresses generated by a programme is reffered to as a logical address space; the set of all physical addresses corres-ponding to these logical addresses is referred to as a *physical address space.* Thus, in the execution-time address-binding scheme, the logical and physical address spaces differ.

The run-time mapping from virtual to physical addresses is done by the *memory-management unit*

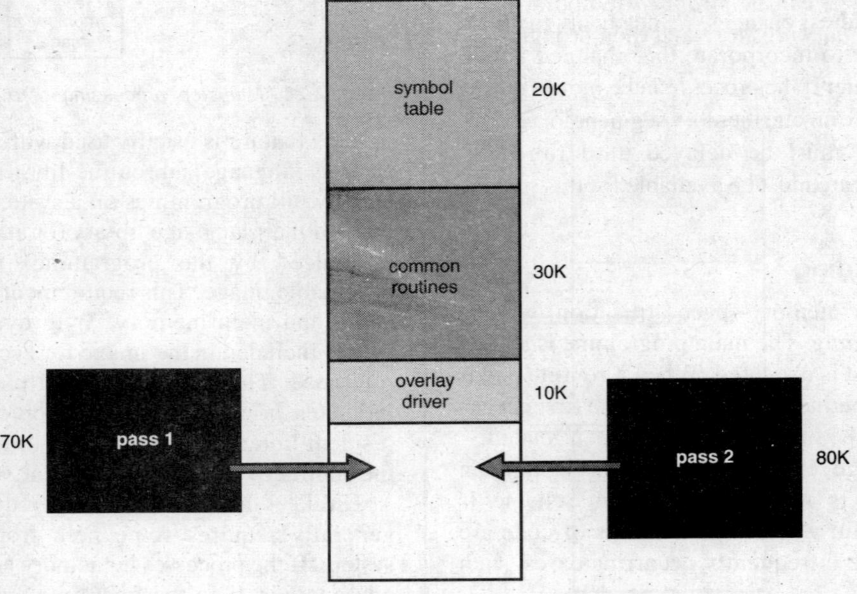

Fig. 3.29: *Overlays for a two-pass assembler.*

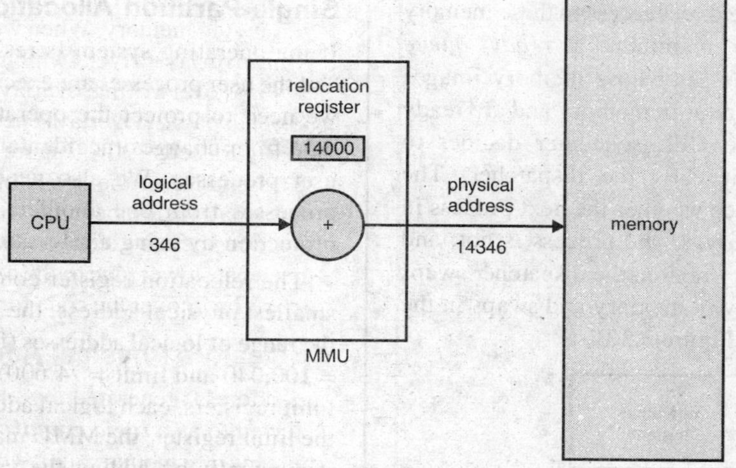

Fig. 3.30: *Dynamic relocation using a relocation register.*

(MMU), which is a hardware device. The base register is now called a *relocation* register (as shown in Figure 3.30). The value in the relocation register is added to every address generated by a user process at the time it is sent to memory. For example, if the base is at 14,000, then an attempt by the user to address location 0 is dynamically relocated to location 14,000; an access to location 346 is mapped to location 14,346. The MS-DOS operating system running on the Intel 80X86 family of processors uses four relocation registers when loading and running processes.

The concept of a *logical space* that is bound to a separate *physical address space* is central to proper memory management.

Swapping

A process needs to be in memory to be executed. A process, however, can be *swapped* temporarily out of memory to a *backing store* and then brought back into memory for continued execution (as shown in Figure 3.31). For example, assume a multiprogrammeming environment with a round-robin CPU-scheduling algorithm. When a quantum expires, the memory manager will start to swap out the process that just finished, and to swap in another process to the memory space that has been freed.

A variant of this swapping policy is used for priority-based scheduling algorithms. If a higher-priority process arrives and wants service, the memory manager can swap out the lower-priority process so that it can load and execute the higher-priority process. When the higher-priority process finishes, the lower-priority process can be swapped back in and continued. This variant of swapping is sometimes called *roll out, roll in.*

Swapping requires a *backing store.* The backing store is commonly a fast disk. It must be large enough to accommodate copies of all memory images for all

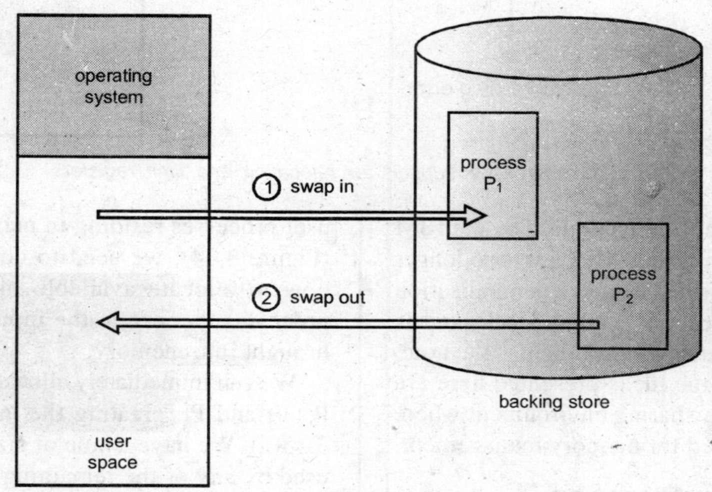

Fig. 3.31: *Swapping of two processes using a disk as a backing store.*

users, and must provide direct access to these memory images. The system maintains a *ready queue* consisting of all processes whose memory images are on the backing store or in memory and are ready to run. Whenever the CPU scheduler decides to execute a process, it calls the dispatcher. The dispatcher checks to see whether the next process in the queue is in memory. If the process is not, and there is no free memory region, the dispatcher swaps out a process currently in memory and swaps in the destored process (see Figure 3.32).

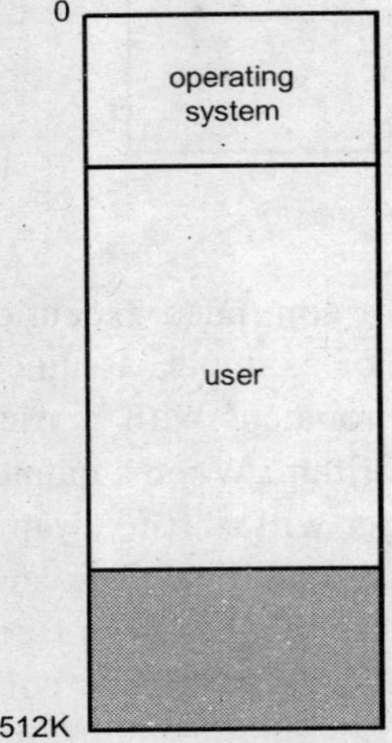

Fig. 3.32: *Memory partition.*

Single-Partition Allocation

If the operating system is residing in low memory and the user processes are executing in high memory, we need to protect the operating-system code and data from changes (accidental or malicious) by the user processes. We also need to protect the user processes from one another. We can provide this protection by using a relocation register.

The relocation register contains the value of the smallest physical address; the limit register contains the range of logical addresses (for example, relocation = 100,040 and limit = 74,600). With relocation and limit registers, each logical address must be less than the limit register; the MMU maps the logical address *dynamically* by adding the value in the relocation register. The mapped address is sent to memory (Figure 3.33).

Thus, using this code changes the size of the operating system during programme execution.

One of the simplest schemes for memory allocation is to divide memory into a number of fixed-sized *partitions.* Each partition may contain exactly one process. Thus, the degree of multiprogramming is bound by the number of partitions. When a partition is free, a process is selected from the input queue and is loaded into the free partition. When the process terminates, the partition becomes available for another

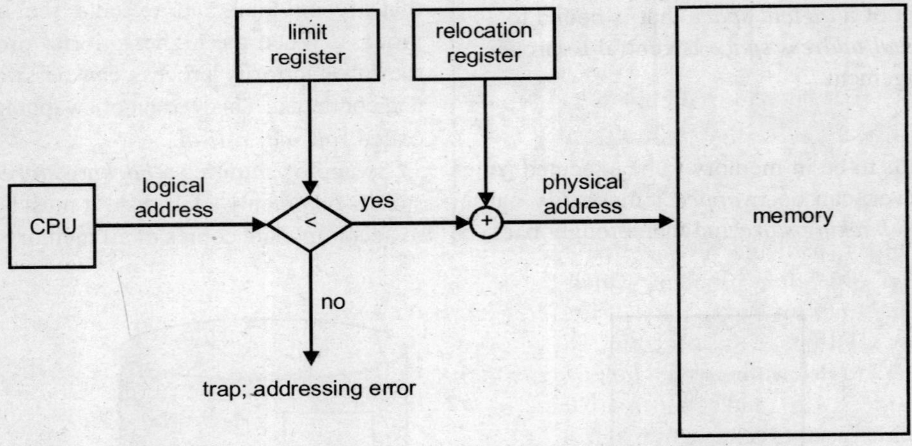

Fig. 3.33: *Hardware support for relocation and limit registers*

process. This scheme was originally used by the IBM OS/360 operating system (called MFT); it is no longer in use. The scheme described next is a generalisation of the fixed-partition scheme (called MVT) and is used primarily in a batch environment. We note, however, that many of the ideas presented here are also applicable to a time-sharing environment where pure segmentation is used for memory management.

Multipl72e-Partition Allocation

Because it is desirable, in general, that there be several user processes residing in memory at the same time (Figure 3.34), we need to consider the problem of how to allocate available memory to the various processes that are in the input queue waiting to be brought into memory.

We can immediately allocate memory to processes P_1, P_2 and P_3, creating the memory map of Figure 3.35(a). We have a hole of size 260K that cannot be used by any of the remaining processes in the input queue. Using a round-robin CPU-scheduling with a quantum of 1 time unit, process P_2 will terminate at

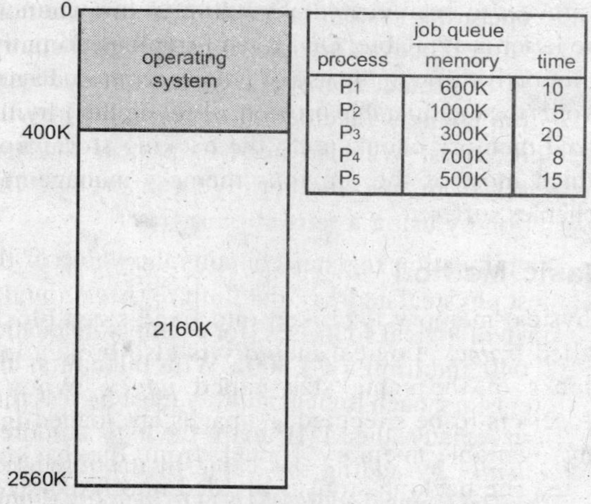

process	job queue memory	time
P_1	600K	10
P_2	1000K	5
P_3	300K	20
P_4	700K	8
P_5	500K	15

Fig. 3.34: *Scheduling example*

time 14, releasing its memory. This situation is illustrated in Figure 3.35 (b). We then return to our job queue and schedule the next process, process P_4, to produce the memory map of Figure 3.35 (c). Process P_1 will terminate at time 28 to produce Figure 3.35 (d); process P_5 is then scheduled, producing Figure 3.35 (e).

This example illustrates the general structure of the allocation scheme. As processes enter the system, they are put into an input queue. The operating system takes into account the memory requirements of each process and the amount of available memory space in determining which processes are allocated memory. When a process is allocated space, it is loaded into memory and it can then compete for the CPU. When a process terminates, it releases its memory, which the operating system may then fill with another process from the input queue.

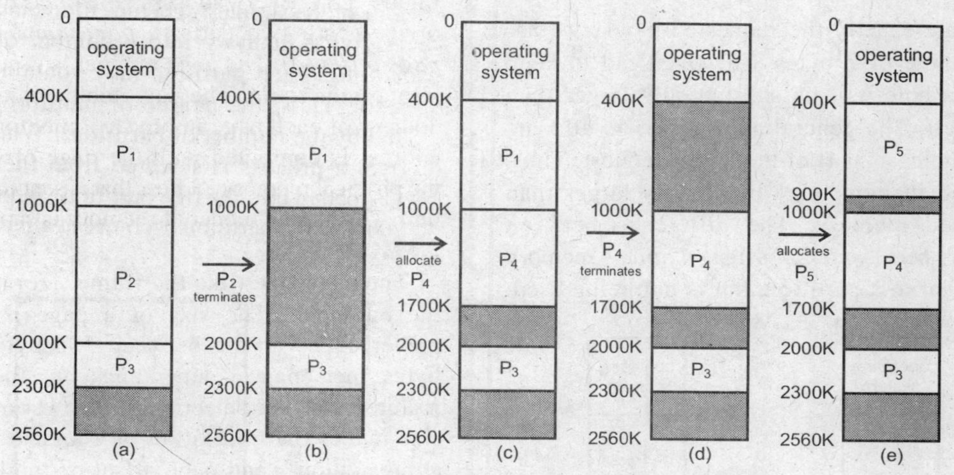

Fig. 3.35: *Memory allocation and long-term scheduling*

This procedure is a particular instance of the general *dynamic storage-allocation* problem, which is how to satisfy a request of size *n* from a list of free holes. There are many solutions to this problem. The set of holes is searched to determine which hole is best to allocate. *First-fit, best-fit,* and *worst-fit* are the most common strategies used to select a free hole from the set of available holes which are given below.

- **First-fit:** Allocate the *first* hole that is big enough. Searching can start either at the beginning of the set of holes or where the previous first-fit search ended. We can stop searching as soon as we find a free hole that is large enough.
- **Best-fit:** Allocate the *smallest* hole that is big enough. We must search the entire list, unless the list is kept ordered by size. This strategy produces the smallest leftover hole.
- **Worst-fit:** Allocate the *largest* hole. Again, we must search the entire list, unless it is sorted by size. This strategy produces the largest leftover hole, which may be more useful than the smaller leftover hole from a best-fit approach.

External and Internal Fragmentation

The algorithms described in above section suffer from *external fragmentation.* As processes are loaded and removed from memory, the free memory space is broken into little pieces. External fragmentation exists when enough total memory space exists to satisfy a request, but it is not contiguous; storage is fragmented into a large number of small holes.

Depending on the total amount of memory storage and the average process size external fragmentation may be either a minor or a major problem. Statistical analysis of first-fit, for instance, reveals that, even with some optimisation, given N allocated blocks, another 0.5 N blocks will be lost due to fragmentation. That is, one-third of memory may be unusable! This property is known as the 50% rule.

Another problem that arises with the multiple partition allocation scheme is illustrated by Figure 3.36. Consider the hole of 18,464 bytes. Suppose that the next process requets 18,462 bytes.

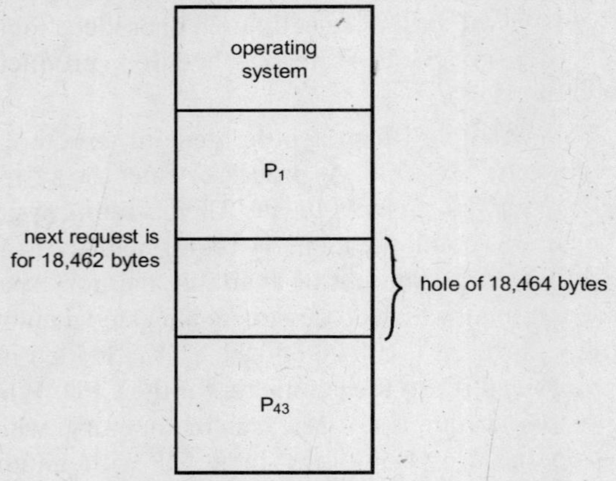

Fig. 3.36: *Memory allocation made in some multiple of bytes*

If we allocate exactly the requested block, we are left with a hole of 2 bytes. The overhead to keep track of this hole will be substantially larger than the hole itself. The general approach is to allocate very small holes as part of the larger request. Thus, the allocated memory may be slightly larger than the requested memory. The difference between these two numbers is *internal fragmentation* – memory that is internal to a partition, but is not being used.

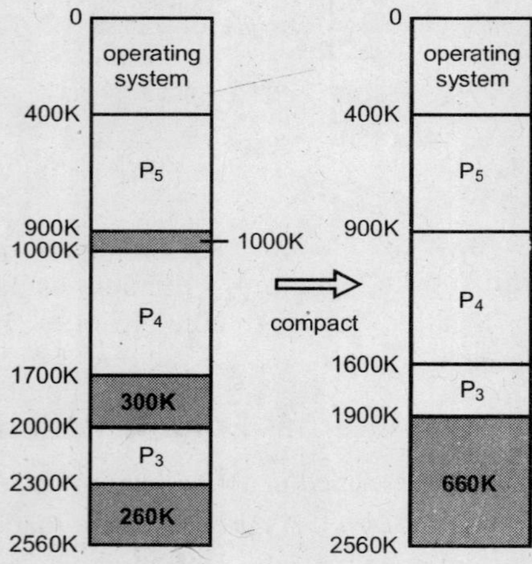

Fig. 3.37: *Compaction*

One solution to the problem of external fragmentation is *compaction.* The goal is to shuffle the memory contents to place all free memory together in one large block. For example, the memory map of figure can be compacted, as shown in Figure 3.37. The three holes of sizes 100K, 300K, and 260K can be compacted into one hole of size 660K.

Paging

Another possible solution to the external fragmentation problem is to permit the logical address space of a process to be noncontiguous, thus allowing a process to be allocated physical memory wherever the latter is available. One way of implementing this solution is through the use of *paging* scheme. Paging avoids the considerable problem of fitting the varying-sized memory chunks onto the backing store, from which most of the previous memory-management schemes suffered.

Basic Method

Physical memory is broken into fixed-sized blocks called *frames.* Logical memory is also broken into blocks of the same size called *pages.* When a process is to be executed, its pages are loaded into any available memory frames from the backing store. The backing store is divided into fixed-sized blocks that are of the same size as the memory frames.

The hardware support for paging is illustrated in Figure 3.38. Every address generated by the CPU is divided into two parts: a *page number (p)* and a *page offset (d).* The page number is used as an index into a *page table.* The page table contains the base address of each page in physical memory. This base address is combined with the page offset to define the physical memory address that is sent to the memory unit. The paging model of memory is shown in Figure 3.39.

The page size (like the frame size) is defined by the hardware. The size of a page is typically a power of 2 varying between 512 bytes and 8192 bytes per page, depending on the computer architecture. The selection of a power of 2 as a page size makes the translation of a logical address into a page number and page offset particularly easy. If the size of logical address space is 2^m, and a page size is 2^n addressing units (bytes or words), then the high order $m - n$ bits of a logical address designate the page number, and the n low-order bits designate the page offset. Thus, the logical address is as follows:

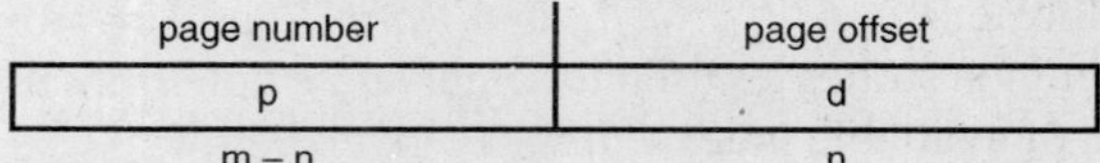

where p is an index into the page table and d is the displacement.

Hardware Support

The hardware implementation of the page table can be done in a number of different ways. In the simplest case, the page table is implemented as a set of dedicated registers. These registers should be built with very high-speed logic to make the paging address translation efficient. Every access to memory must go through the paging map, so efficiency is a major consideration. The CPU dispatcher reloads these registers, just as it

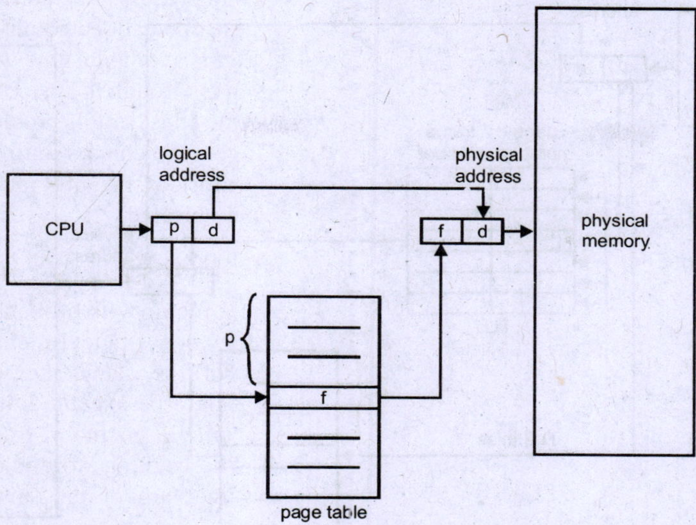

Fig. 3.38: *Paging hardware*

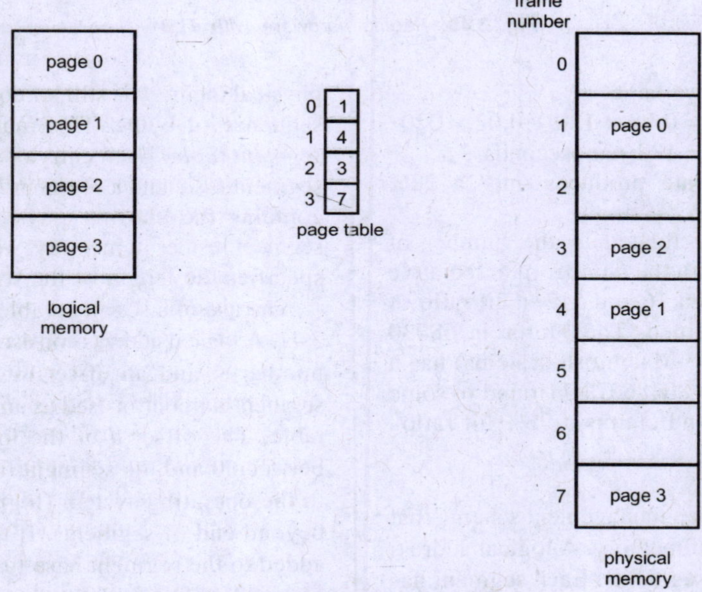

Fig. 3.39: *Paging model of memory.*

reloads the other registers. Instructions to load or modify the page-table registers are, of course, privileged (Figure 3.40).

The standard solution to this problem is to use a special, small, fast-lookup hardware cache, variously called *associative registers* or *translation look-aside buffers (TLBs)*. A set of associative registers is built of especially high-speed memory. Each register consists of two parts: a key and a value. When the associative registers are presented with an item, it is compared with all keys simultaneously. If the item is found, the corresponding value field is output. The search is fast; the hardware, however, is expensive. Typically, the number of entries in a TLB varies between 8 and 2048.

The percentage of times that a page number is found in the associative registers is called a *hit ratio.* An 80% hit ratio means that we find the desired page number in the associative registers 80% of the time. If it takes 20 nanoseconds to search the associative registers, and 100 nanoseconds to access memory, then a mapped memory access takes 120 nanoseconds when the page number is in the associative registers. If we fail to find the page number in the associative registers (20 nanoseconds), then we must first access memory for the page table and frame number (100 nanoseconds), and then access the desired byte in memory (100 nanoseconds), for a total of 220 nanoseconds. To find the *effective memory-access time,* we must weight each case by its probability:

$$\text{effective access time} = 0.80 \times 120 + 0.20 \times 220 = 140 \text{ nanoseconds.}$$

In this example, we suffer a 40% slowdown in memory access time (from 100 to 140 nanoseconds).

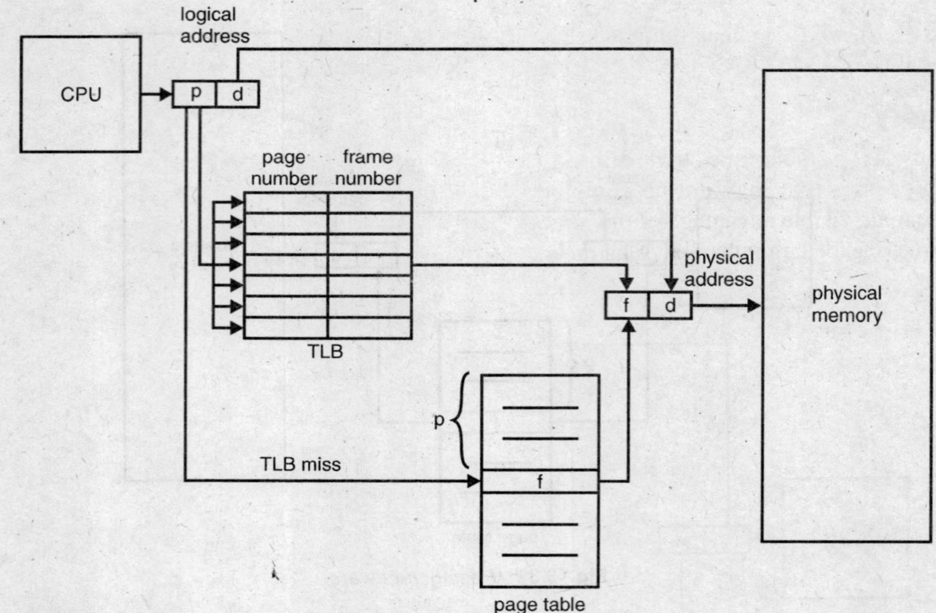

Fig. 3.40: *Paging hardware with TLB*

For a 98% hit ratio, we have

effective access time = 0.98 × 120 + 0.02 × 220
= 122 nanoseconds.

This increased hit rate produces only a 22% slowdown in memory access time.

The hit ratio is clearly related to the number of associative registers. With the number of associative registers ranging between 16 and 512, a hit ratio of 80 to 98% can be obtained. The Motorcla 68030 processor (used in Apple Macintosh systems) has a 22-entry TLB. The Intel 80486 CPU (found in some PCs) has 32 registers, and claims a 98% hit ratio.

Segmentation

Segmentation is a memory-management scheme that supports this user view of memory. A logical address space is a collection of segments. Each segment has a name and a length. The addresses specify both the segment name and the offset within the segment. The user therefore specifies each address by two quantities: a segment name and an offset.

Thus, a logical address consists of a two tuple:

$\langle$segment-number, offset$\rangle$

Normally, the user programme is compiled, and the compiler automatically constructs segments reflecting the input programme. A Pascal compiler might create separate segments for (1) the global variables; (2) the procedure call stack, to store parameters and return addresses; (3) the code portion of each procedure or function; and (4) the local variables of each procedure and function.

Hardware

Although the user can now refer to objects in the programme by a two-dimensional address, the actual physical memory is still, of course, a one-dimensional sequence of bytes. This mapping is effected by a *segment table.* Each entry of the segment table has a segment *base* and a segment *limit.* The segment base contains the starting physical address where the segment resides in memory, whereas the segment limit specifies the length of the segment.

The use of a segment table is illustrated in Figure 3.41. A logical address consists of two parts; a segment number *s*, and an offset into that segment *d*. The segment number is used as an index into the segment table. The offset *d* of the logical address must be between 0 and the segment limit. If it is not we trap to the operating system (logical addressing attempt beyond end of segment). If this offset is legal, it is added to the segment base to produce the address in physical memory of the desired byte. The segment table is thus essentially an array of base-limit register pairs.

Implementation of Segment Tables

Segmentation is closely related to the partition models of memory management presented earlier, the main difference being that one programme may consist of several segments. Like the page table, the segment table can be put either in fast registers or in memory. A segment table kept in registers can be referenced quickly; the addition to the base and comparison with the limit can be done simultaneously to save time.

A *segment-table base register (STBR)* points to the segment table. Also, because the number of segments used by a programme may vary widely, a *segment-table length register (STLR)* is used. For a logical address (s, d), we first check that the segment number s is legal (*i.e.*, $s <$ STLR).

Virtual Memory

Virtual memory is a technique that allows the execution of processes that may not be completely in memory. The main visible advantage of this scheme is that programmes can be larger than physical memory (Figure 3.42). Further, it abstracts main memory into an extremely large, uniform array of storage, separating logical memory as viewed by the user from physical memory. This technique frees programmers from concern over memory storage limitations. Virtual memory is not easy to implement, however, and may substantially decrease performance if it is used carelessly.

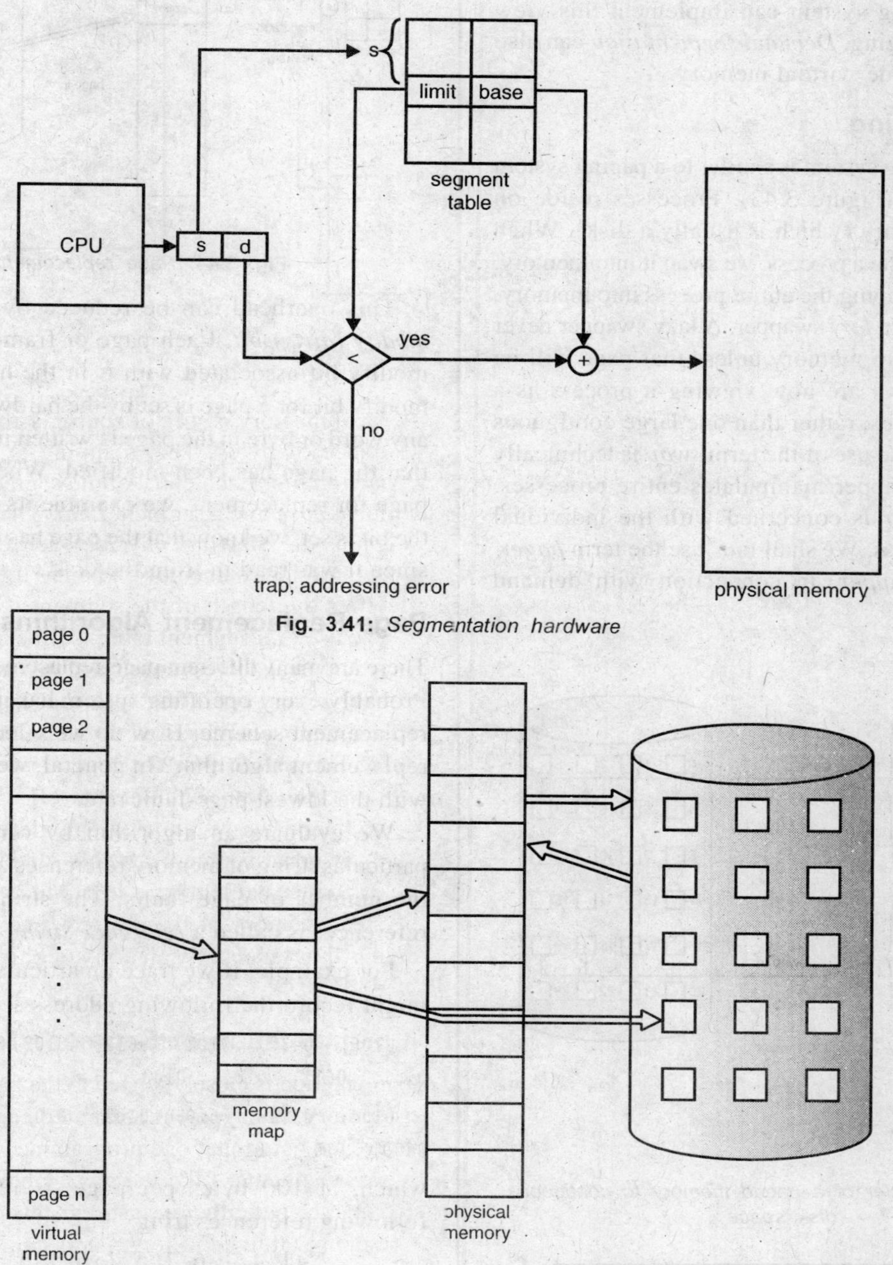

Fig. 3.41: *Segmentation hardware*

Fig. 3.42: *Diagram showing virtual memory larger than physical memory*

Thus, running a programme that is not entirely in memory would benefit both the system and the user.

Virtual memory is the separation of user logical memory from physical memory. This separation allows an extremely large virtual memory to be provided for programmers when only a smaller physical memory is available. Virtual memory makes the task of programming much easier, because the programmer no longer needs to worry about the amount of physical memory available, or about what code can be placed in overlays, but can concentrate instead on the problem to be programmed. On systems which support virtual memory, overlays have virtually disappeared.

Virtual memory is commonly implemented by *demanding paging.* It can also be implemented in a segmentation system. Several systems provide a paged segmentation scheme, where segments are broken into pages. Thus, the user view is segmenta-tion, but the operating system can implement this view with demand paging. *Demand segmentation* can also be used to provide virtual memory.

Demand Paging

A demand paging system is similar to a paging system with swapping (Figure 3.43). Processes reside on secondary memory (which is usually a disk). When we want to execute a process, we swap it into memory. Rather than swapping the entire process into memory, however, we use a *lazy* swapper. A lazy swapper never swaps a page into memory unless that page will be needed. Since we are now viewing a process as a sequence of pages, rather than one large contiguous address space, the use of the term *swap* is technically incorrect. A swapper manipulates entire processes, whereas a *pager* is concerned with the individual pages of a process. We shall thus use the term *pager,* rather than *swapper*, in connection with demand paging.

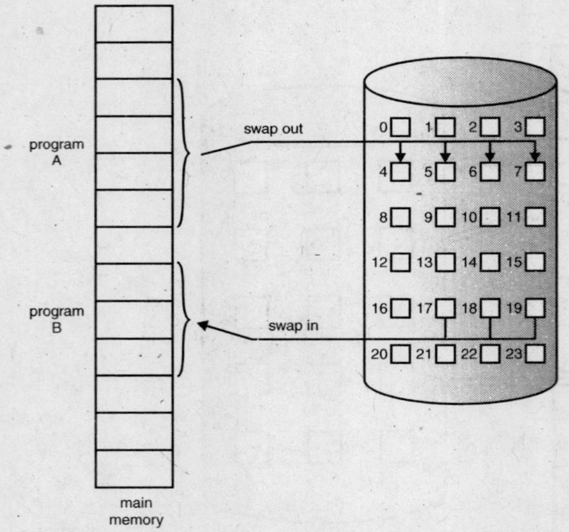

Fig. 3.43: *Transfer of a paged memory to contiguous disk space*

PAGE REPLACEMENT

Page replacement takes the following approach. If no frame is free, we find one that is not currently being used and free it. We can free a frame by writing its contents to swap space, and changing the page table (and all other tables) to indicate that the page is no longer in memory (Figure 3.44). The freed frame can now be use to hold the page for which the process faulted.

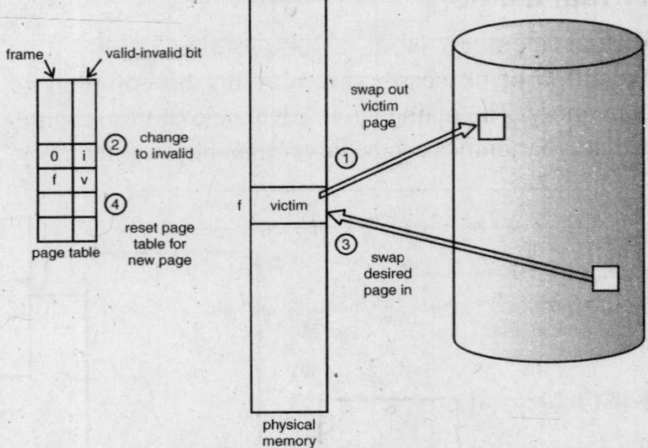

Fig. 3.44: *Page replacement.*

This overhead can be reduced by the use of a *modify (dirty) bit.* Each page or frame may have a modify bit associated with it in the hardware. The modify bit for a page is set by the hardware whenever any word or byte in the page is written into, indicating that the page has been modified. When we select a page for replacement, we examine its modify bit. If the bit is set, we know that the page has been modified since it was read in from the disk.

Page-Replacement Algorithms

There are many different page-replacement algorithms. Probably every operating system has its own unique replacement scheme. How do we select a particular replacement algorithm? In general, we want the one with the lowest page-fault rate.

We evaluate an algorithm by running it on a particular string of memory references and computing the number of page faults. The string of memory references is called a *reference string.*

For example, if we trace a particular process, we might record the following address sequence:

0100, 0432, 0101, 0612, 0102, 0103, 0104, 0101, 0611, 0102, 0103,

0104, 0101, 0610, 0102, 0103, 0104, 0101, 0609, 0102, 0105.

which, at 100 bytes per page, is reduced to the following reference string

1, 4, 1, 6, 1, 6, 1, 6, 1, 6, 1.

To determine the number of page faults for a particular reference string and page-replacement algorithm, we also need to know the number of page frames available. Obviously, as the number of frames available increases, the number of page faults will decrease (Figure 3.45).

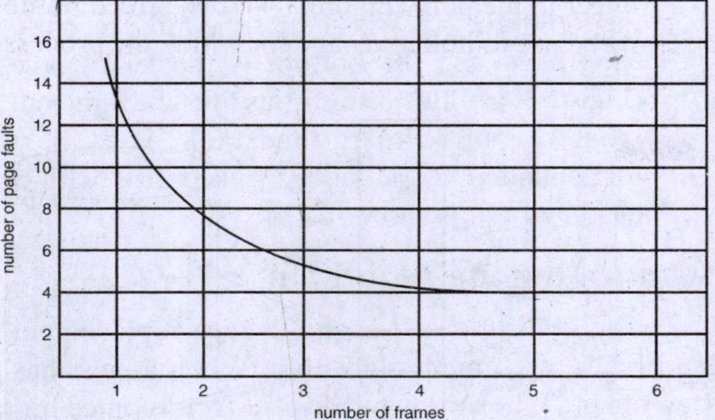

Fig. 3.45: *Graph of page faults versus the number of frames.*

FIFO Algorithm

The simplest page-replacement algorithm is a FIFO algorithm. A FIFO replacement algorithm associates with each page the time when that page was brought into memory. When a page must be replaced, the oldest page is chosen. Notice that it is not strictly necessary to record the time when a page is brought in. We can create a FIFO queue to hold all pages in memory. We replace the page at the head of the queue. When a page is brought into memory, we insert it at the tail of the queue.

For our example reference string, our three frames are initially empty. The first three references (7, 0, 1) cause page faults, and are brought into these empty frames. The next reference (2) replaces page 7, because page 7 was brought in first. Since 0 is the next reference and 0 is already in memory, we have no fault for this reference. The first reference to 3 results in page 0 being replaced, since it was the first of the three pages in memory (0, 1, and 2) to be brought in. This replacement means that the next reference, to 0, will fault. Page 1 is then replaced by page 0. This process continues as shown in Figure 3.46. Every time a fault occurs, we show which pages are in our three frames. There are 15 faults altogether.

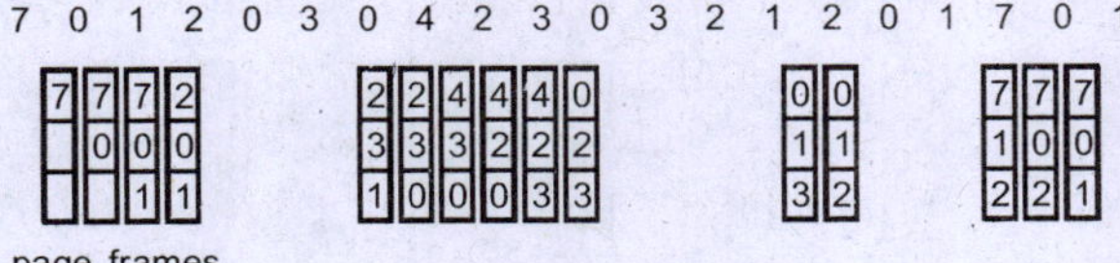

Fig. 3.46: *FIFO page-replacement algorithm.*

The FIFO page-replacement algorithm is easy to understand and programme. However, its performance is not always good. The page replaced may be an initialisation module that was used a long time ago and is no longer needed. The problems that are possible with a FIFO page-replacement algorithm, we consider the reference string

1, 2, 3, 4, 1, 2, 5, 1, 2, 3, 4, 5

Figure 3.47 shows the curve of page faults versus the number of available frames. We notice that the number of faults for four frames (10) is greater than the number of faults for three frames (nine)! This result is most unexpected and is known as *Belady's anomaly*. Belady's anomaly reflects the fact that, for some page-replacement algorithms, the page-faults rate may increase as the number of allocated frames increases. We would expect that giving more memory to a process would improve its performance. In some early research, investigators noticed that this assumption was not always true. Belady's anomaly was discovered as a result.

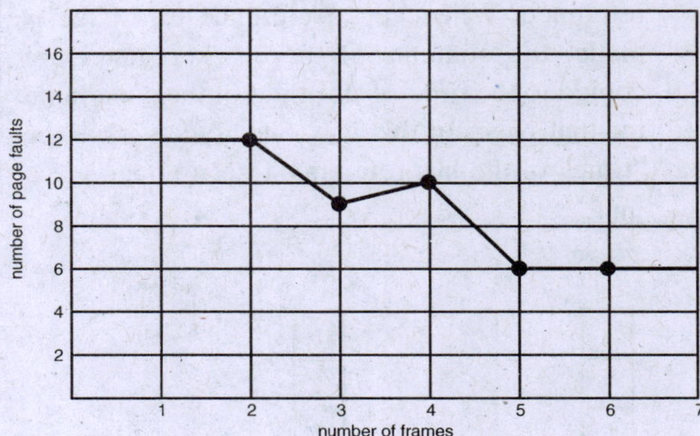

Fig. 3.47: *Page-fault curve for FIFO replacement on a reference string.*

Optimal Algorithm

One result of the discovery of Belady's anomaly was the search for an *optimal* page-replacement algorithm. An optimal page-replacement algorithm has the lowest page-fault rate of all algorithms. An optimal algorithm will never suffer from Belady's anomaly. An optimal page-replacement algorithm exists, and has been called OPT or MIN. It is simply "replace the page that will not be used for the longest period of time". Use of this page-replacement algorithm guarantees the lowest possible page-fault rate for a fixed number of frames.

LRU Algorithm

If we use the recent past as an approximation of the near future, then we will replace the pages that have not been used for the longest period of time (Figure 3.48). This approach is the *least recently used (LRU)* algorithm.

LRU replacement associates with each page the time of that page's last use. When a page must be replaced, LRU chooses that page that has not been used for the longest period of time.

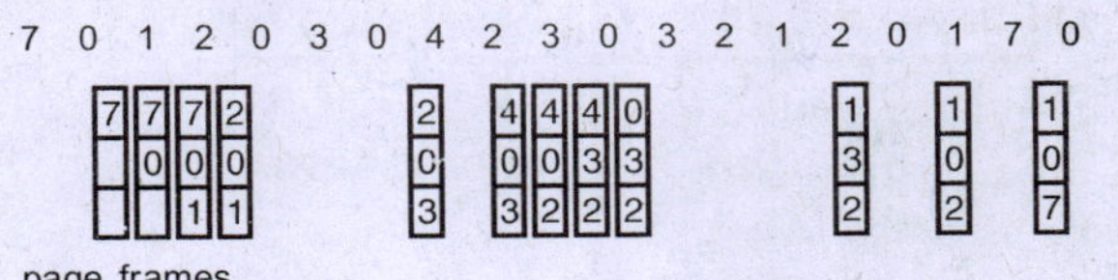

Fig. 3.48: *LRU page-replacement algorithm.*

COMPUTER SCIENCE

The LRU policy is often used as a page-replacement algorithm and is considered to be quite good. The major problem is how to implement LRU replacement. An LRU page-replacement algorithm may require substantial hardware assistance. The problem is to determine an order for the frames defined by the time of last use. Two implementations are feasible:

(i) **Counters:** In the simplest case, we associate with each page-table entry a time-of-use field, and add to the CPU a logical clock or counter. The clock is incremented for every memory reference. Whenever a reference to a page is made, the contents of the clock register are copied to the time-of-use field in the page table for that page. In this way, we always have the "time" of the last reference to each page.

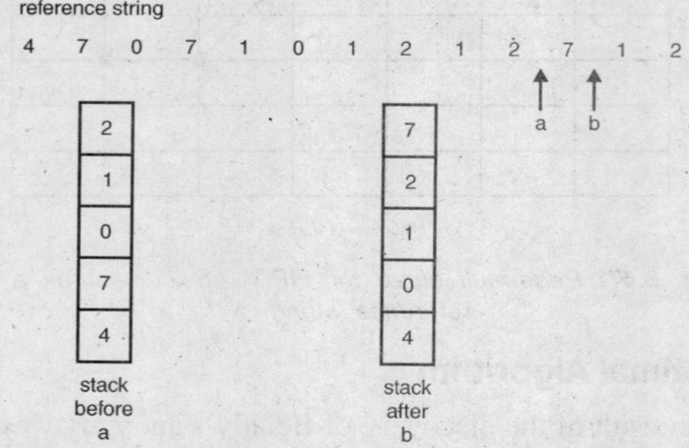

Fig. 3.49: *Use of a stack to record the most recent page references.*

(ii) **Stack:** Another approach to implementing LRU replacement is to keep a *stack* of page numbers. Whenever a page is referenced, it is removed from the stack and put on the top. In this way, the top of the stack is always the most recently used page and the bottom is the LRU page (Figure 3.49). Because entries must be removed from the middle of the stack, it is best implemented by a doubly linked list, with a head and tail pointer.

Second-Change Algorithm

The basic algorithm of second-chance replacement is a FIFO replacement algorithm. When a page has been selected, however, we inspect its reference bit. If the value is 0, we proceed to replace this page. If the reference bit is 1, however, we give that page a second chance and move on to select the next FIFO page. When a page gets a second chance, its reference bit is cleared and its arrival time is reset to the current time. Thus, a page that is given a second chance will not be replaced until all other pages are replaced (or given second chances). In addition, if a page is used often enough to keep its reference bit set, it will never be replaced.

One way to implement the second-chance (sometimes referred to as the clock) algorithm is as a circular queue. A pointer indicates which page is to be replaced next. When a frame is needed, the pointer advances until it finds a page with a 0 reference bit. As it advances, it clears the reference bits (Figure 3.50). Once a victim page is found, the page is replaced and the new page is inserted in the circular queue in that position. Notice that, in the worst case, when all bits are set, the pointer cycles through the whole queue, giving each page a second chance. It clears all the reference bits before selecting the next page for replacement. Second chance replacement degenerates to FIFO replacement if all bits are set.

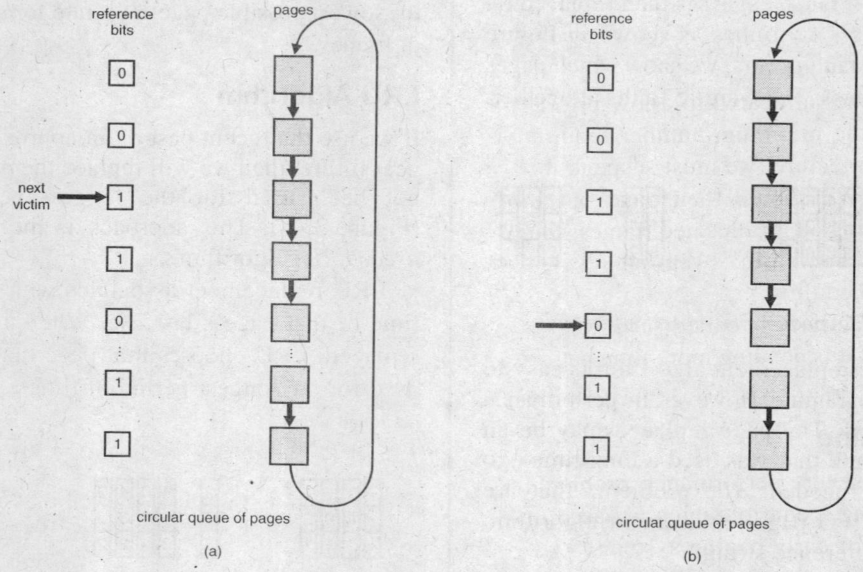

Fig. 3.50: *Second-chance (clock) page-replacement algorithm*

Counting Algorithms

There are many other algorithms that can be used for page replacement. For example, we could keep a counter of the number of references that have been made to each page, and develop the following two schemes.

- **LFU Algorithm:** The *least frequently used (LFU)* page-replacement algorithm requires that the page with the smallest count be replaced. The reason for this selection is that an actively used page should have a large reference count. This algorithm suffers from the situation in which a page is used heavily during the initial phase of a process, but then is never used again. Since it was used heavily, it has a large count and remains in memory even though it is no longer needed. One solution is to shift the counts right by 1 bit at regular intervals, forming an exponentially decaying average usage count.
- **MFU Algorithm:** The *most frequently used (MFU)* page-replacement algorithm is based on the argument that the page with the smallest count was probably just brought in and has yet to be used.

Global Versus Local Allocation

Another important factor in the way frames are allocated to the various processes is page replacement. With multiple processes competing for frames, we can classify page-replacement algorithms into two broad categories: *global replacement* and *local replacement.* Global replacement allows a process to select a replacement frame from the set of all frames, even if that frame is currently allocated to some other process; one process can take a frame from another. Local replacement requires that each process select from only its own set of allocated frames.

Thrashing

If the number of frames allocated to a low-priority process falls below the minimum number required by the computer architecture, we must suspend that process' execution. We should then page out its remaining pages, freeing all its allocated frames. This provision introduces a swap-in, swap-out level of intermediate CPU scheduling.

This high paging activity is called *thrashing.* A process is thrashing if it is pending more time paging than executing.

Cause of Thrashing

Thrashing results in severe performance problems. Consider the following scenario, which is based on the actual behaviour of early paging systems.

The operating system monitors CPU utilisation. If CPU utilisation is too low, we increase the degree of multiprogramming by introducing a new process to the system. A global page-replacement algorithm is used, replacing pages with no regard to the process to which they belong. Now suppose a process enters a new phase in its execution and needs more frames. It starts faulting and taking pages away from other processes. These processes need those pages, however, and so they also fault, taking pages from other processes. These faulting processes must use the paging device to swap pages in and out. As they queue up for the paging device, the ready queue empties. As processes wait for the paging device, CPU utilisation decreases.

This phenomenon is illustrated in Fig. 3.51. CPU utilisation is plotted against the degree of multiprogramming. As the degree of multiprogramming increases, CPU utilisation also increases, although more slowly, until a maximum is reached. If the degree of multi-programming is increased even further, thrashing sets in and CPU utilisation drops sharply. At this point, to increase CPU utilisation and stop thrashing we must *decrease* the degree of multiprogramming.

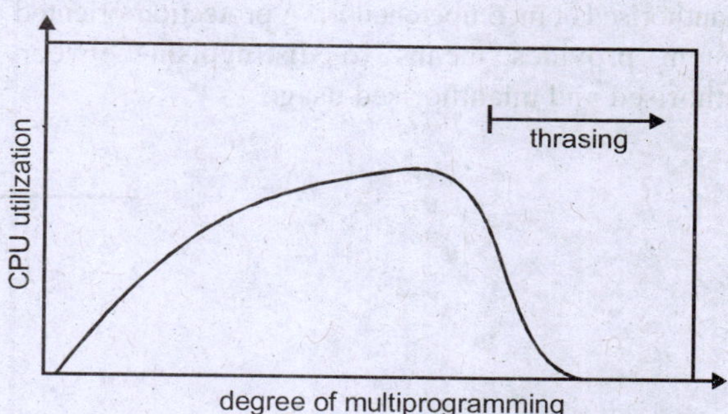

Fig. 3.51: *Thrashing*

The effects of thrashing can be limited by using a *local* (or *priority) replacement algorithm.* With local replacement, if one process starts thrashing, it cannot steal frames from another process and cause the latter to thrash also. Pages are replaced with regard to the process of which they are a part. However, if processes are thrashing, they will be in the queue for the paging device most of the time. The average service time for a page fault will increase, due to the longer average queue for the paging device. Thus, the effective access time will increase even for a process that is not thrashing.

Protection

The various processes in an operating system must be protected from one another's activities. For that purpose, various mechanisms exist that can be used to ensure that the files, memory segments, CPU, and other resources can be operated on by only those processes that have gained proper authorisation from the operating system.

Protection refers to a mechanism for controlling the access of programmes, processes, or users to the resources defined by a computer system. This mechanism must provide a means for specification of the controls to be imposed, together with some means for enforcement.

Goals of Protection

There are several reasons for providing protection. Most obvious is the need to prevent mischievous, intentional violation of an access restriction by a user. Of more general importance, however, is the need to ensure that each programme component active in a system uses system resources only in ways consistent with the staged policies for the uses of these resources. This requirement is an absolute one for a reliable system.

Protection can improve reliability by detecting latent errors at the interfaces between component subsystems. Early detection of interface errors can often prevent contamination of a healthy subsystem by a subsystem that is malfunctioning. An unprotected resource cannot defend against use (or misuse) by an unauthorised or incompetent user. A protection-oriented system provides means to distinguish between authorised and unauthorised usage.

The role of protection in a computer system is to provide a *mechanism* for the enforcement of the *policies* governing resource use. These policies can be established in a variety of ways. Some are fixed in the design of the system, whereas others are formulated by the management of a system.

Domain Protection

A computer system is a collection of processes and objects. By *objects,* we mean both hardware objects (such as the CPU, memory segments, printers, disks, and tape drives), and software objects (such as files, programmes, and semaphores).

Each object has a unique name that differentiates it from all other objects in the system, and each can be accessed only through well-defined and meaningful operations. Objects are essentially *abstract data types.*

The operations that are possible may depend on the object. For example, a CPU can only be executed on. Memory segments can be read and written, whereas a card reader can only be read. Tape drives can be read, written, and rewound. Data files can be created, opened, read, written, closed, and deleted; programme files can be read, written, executed, and deleted.

PROGRAMMING FUNDAMENTALS

ASSEMBLY LANGUAGE PROGRAMMING

An assembly language is a low level programming language for a computer system. It is machine dependent in nature i.e it is specific to a certain computer system (or a family of computer systems). Compared to a machine language, it provides three basic features which simplify programming:

1. **Mnemonic operation codes:** A *mnemonic* is a name associated with an entity. Use of mnemonic operation codes (also called *mnemonic opcodes)* for machine instructions, instead of numeric ones, provides some convenience in programme writing. It also enables indication of coding errors like misspelt operation codes.
2. **Symbolic operands:** Symbolic names can be associated with data or instructions. Use of symbolic names in operand references avoids the use of memory addresses in instructions.
3. **Data declarations:** Data can be declared in a variety of notations, including the decimal notation. This avoids manual conversion of constants into their internal machine representation, *e.g.* -5 into (11111010h or 10.5 into 41A80000h6.

Statement Format

An assembly language statement has the following format

```
[Label]
<Opcode>
<operand spec>[,<operand spec> ..j
```

where the notation [..] indicates that the enclosed specification is optional. If a label is specified in a statement, it is associated as a symbolic name with the memory word(s) generated for the statement. *<operand spec>* can have one of the following forms

```
AREA
AREA+5
AREA (4)
AREA+5(4)
```

The first specification refers to the memory word with which the name AREA is associated. The second specification refers to the memory word 5 words away from the word with the name AREA. Here '5' is called the *displacement* or *offset* from AREA. The third specification implies indexing with index register 4, *i.e.* the operand address is obtained by adding the contents of index register 4 to the address of AREA. The last specification is a combination of the previous two.

A Simple Assembly Language

In simple assembly language each assembly statement has two operands, the first operand is always a register which can be any one of AREG, BREG, CREG and DREG. The second operand refers to a memory word using the first or second operand specification form.

The mnemonic opcodes such as MOVE opcode moves a value between a memory word and a register. In this instruction the second operand is the source operand and the first operand is the target operand. All arithmetic is performed in a register (*i.e.* the result replaces the contents of the register) and sets a *condition code.* A comparison instruction sets a condition code analogous to a subtract instruction without affecting the values of its operands. The condition code can be tested by a Branch on Condition (BC) statement with the form

```
BC
<condition code spec>, <memory address>
```

ABC instruction transfers control to the memory word with the address spec *<memory address>* if the current value of condition code matches *<condition code spec>*.

Assembly Language Statements

An assembly programme contains three kinds of statements:

1. Imperative statements,
2. Declaration statements, and
3. Assembler directives.

Imperative Statements: An imperative statement indicates an action to be performed during the execution of the assembled programme. Each imperative statement translates into one machine instruction.

Declaration statements: Reserves areas of memory and associates names with them. The syntax of declaration statement is as follows :-

```
[Label] DS   <constant>
[Label] DC   <value>
```

The DC (short for *declare constant)* statement constructs memory words containing constants. The statement ONE DC '1' associates the name ONE with a memory word containing the value '1'. The programmer can declare constants in different forms, *e.g.* decimal, binary, hexadecimal, etc. The assembler would convert them to the appropriate internal form.

Constants as in a HLL can be used in one of two ways

1. As immediate operands; and
2. As literals

Immediate operands can be used in an assembly statement only if the architecture of the target machine supports it. For example the statement is translated into an instruction with two operands - AREG and the value '5' as an immediate operand.

A *literal* differs from immediate operand in that the architecture of the computer need not support immediate operands. A literal has the syntax ='*<value>*'.

Assembler directives: Instruct the assembler to perform certain actions during the assembly of a programme. For example

```
START  <constant>
```

This directive indicates that the first word of object programme generated by assembler should be placed in the memory word with address <constant>

```
END [<operand spec>]
```

This directive indicates the end of source programme to be assembled. The optional <operand spec> indicates the address of the memory word where the execution of the programme should begin.

Advantages of Assembly language:

- Due to operand specifications which are symbolic in nature, changes in addresses of the constants and reserved memory areas are not required in assembly programmes.
- Assembly language programming holds an edge over HLL programming in situations where it is necessary to use specific architectural features of a computer *e.g.* special instructions supported by CPU.

Data structure of the assembler :

The source programme would be read by pass I on a statement by statement basis. After processing a source statement can be written into a file for subsequent use in pass II. The IC generated for it would also be written into another file. The target code and the programme listings can be written out as a separate files by pass II. Since all these files are sequential in nature, it is beneficial to use appropriate blocking and bufferring of records.

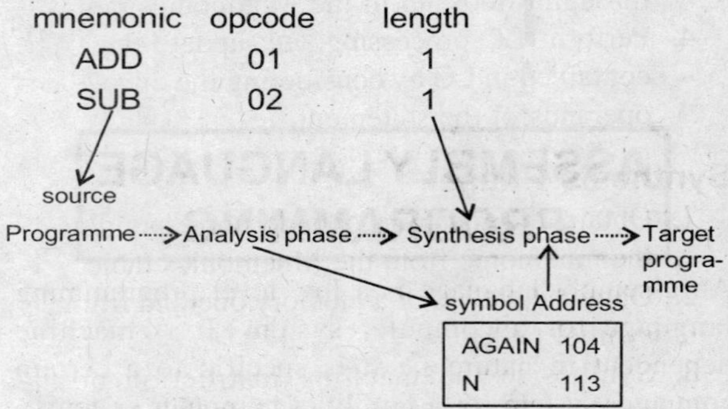

Fig. 4.1: *Symbol table*

Two Pass Translation

The key function performed by analysis phase is the building of symbol table in Fig. 4.1. For this purpose it must determine the addresses with which the various names used in the programme are associated. Two pass translation of an assembly language programme ,can take care of the problem of forward references. Location counter (LC) is a data structure which helps in implementing memory allocation.

LC processing is performed in the first pass and symbols defined in the programme are entered into the symbol table. The second pass synthesises the target form using the address information, found in the symbol table. In effect, the first pass performs analysis of the source programme while the second pass performs synthesis of the target programme. The first pass constructs an intermediate program representation for use by the second pass. This representation consists of two main components — data structures like the symbol table and a processed form of the source programme. The latter component is called *intermediate code* (IC).

Pass I

Analysis of source programme and synthesis if intermediate programme representation:

- seperate the symbol, mnemonic opcode and operand fields
- build the symbol table
- perform LC processing
- construct IC

Pass II

Processes the intermediate representation to synthesise the target programme.

Functions of the analysis and synthesis phases of the assembler

Analysis Phase

1. Isolate the label, mnemonic opcode and operand fields of a statement.
2. If a symbol is found in the label field, enter the pair
   `(symbol, <LC contents>)`
   in a new entry of symbol table.
3. Check the validity of the mnemonic opcode through a look-up in the Mnemonics table.
4. Perform LC processing, *i.e.* update the value contained in LC by considering the opcode and operands of the statement.

Synthesis Phase

1. Obtain the machine opcode corresponding to the mnemonic from the Mnemonics table.
2. Obtainad—class of a memory operand from the symbol table.
3. Synthesise the machine instruction or the machine form of the constant, as the case may be.

Single Pass Translation

Translation on a statement-by statement basis called single pass translation. Single pass translation would face a problem while assembling statements containing forward references. This problem can be tackled as follows - instructions containing forward references can be left incomplete, until address of the referenced symbol becomes known.

Macros and Macros Processors

Macros provided in assembly are of two kinds:

Lexical expansion : Involves replacement of character string by a corresponding character string during programme generation.

Semantic expansion: Facilitates generation of instructions tailored to the requirements of a specific usage; e.g., generation of type specific instructions for manipulation of byte and word operands.

A macro definition is enclosed between a macro header statement and a macro end statement. Macro definitions are located at the beginning of programme. A macro definition consist of a macro prototype statement: Declare the name of a macro and the names and kinds of its parameters. A macro prototype statement has the following syntax

`<macro name> [<formal parameter spec> [,...]]`

where macro name appears in the mnemonic field of an assembly statement and <formal parameter spec> is of the form

`&<parameter name>[<parameter kind>]`

- One or more model statements: A model statement is a statement from which an assembly language statement may be generated during macro expansion.
- Macro preprocessor statements: A preprocessor statement is used to perform auxiliary functions during macro expansion.

A macro definition is shown below :

```
MACRO
INCR &MEM_VAL, &INCR_VAL, &REG
MOVER   &REG,  &MEM- VAL
ADD     &REG, &INCR_VAL
 MOVEM   &REG,  &MEM_VAL
 MEND
```

The definition of macro INCR, MACRO and MEND are the macro header and macro end statements, respectively. The prototype statement indicates that three parameters called MEM3AL, INCR_VAL and REG exist for the macro. Since the kind of parameter is not specified for any of the parameters, they are all of the default kind "positional parameter".

Macro Call

A macro is called by writing the macro name in the mnemonic field of an assembly statement. The macro call has the syntax

`<macro name> [<actual parameter spec> [,..]]`

where an actual parameter typically resembls an operand specification in an assembly language statement.

MACROEXPANSION

A macro call leads to *macro expansion.* During macro expansion, the macro call statement is replaced by a sequence of assembly statements. To differentiate between the original statements of a programme and the statements resulting from macro expansion, we mark each expanded statement with a '+' preceding its label field.

Two key notions in macro expansion are

1. Flow of control during expansion, which determines the order in which model statements are visited during macro expansion, and
2. *Lexical substitution,* which is used to generate an assembly statement from a model statement.

Flow of Control During Expansion

The default flow of control during macro expansion is *sequential.* Thus, in the absence of preprocessor statements, the model statements of a macro are visited sequentially from the statement following the macro prototype statement to the statement preceding MEND statement.

A preprocessor statement can alter the flow of control during expansion such that some model statements are either (i) never visited during expansion and this results in *conditional expansion*, or (ii) repeatedly visited during expansion and the results in *expansion time loops.*

The flow of control during macro expansion is implemented using a *macro expansion counter*- (MEC).

Lexical Substitution

A model statement consists of 3 types of strings:

1. An ordinary string, which stands for itself,
2. The name of a formal parameter which is preceded by the character '&', and
3. The name of a preprocessor variable, which is also preceded by the character '&'.

Two kinds of parameters, *positional* and *keyword* parameters are described below.

Positional Parameters

A formal parameter of the positional kind is written *&<parameter name>, e.g.* & AMPLE where AMPLE is the name of a parameter.

`<parameter kind>` is omitted. The `<actual parameter spee>` is simply an `<ordinary string>`.

Default Specifications of Parameters

Default is a standard assumption in the absence of an explicit specification by the programmer. Default specification of parameters is useful in situations where a parameter has the same value in most calls. When the desired value is different from the default value, the desired value can be specified explicitly in a macro call. This specification overrides the default value of the parameter for the duration of the call.

Default specification of keyword parameters can be incorporated by extending the syntax for formal parameter specification, as follows

```
& < parameter-name> [< parameter kind> [< default value>]]
```

Mixed Parameter Lists

A macro may be defined to use both positional and keyword parameters but in that case one thing is important, that is all positional parameters must preceed all keyword parameters. The parameters can appear in operand fields of model statement. Parameters can also appear in the label and opcode field of model statements.

Nested macro calls: A model statement in one macro may constitute a call on another macro. Such calls are known as nested macro calls. We refer to macro containing the nested call as the outer macro and the called macro as the inner macro. Expansion of nested macro calls follows the lst-in-first-out rule(LIFO).

In a structure of nested macro calls, expansion of latest macro call (*i.e.* the innermost macro call in the structure) is completed first.

Design of a Macro-assembler

Use of a macro preprocessor followed by a conventional assembler (as shown in Fig. 4.2) is an expensive way of handling macros.

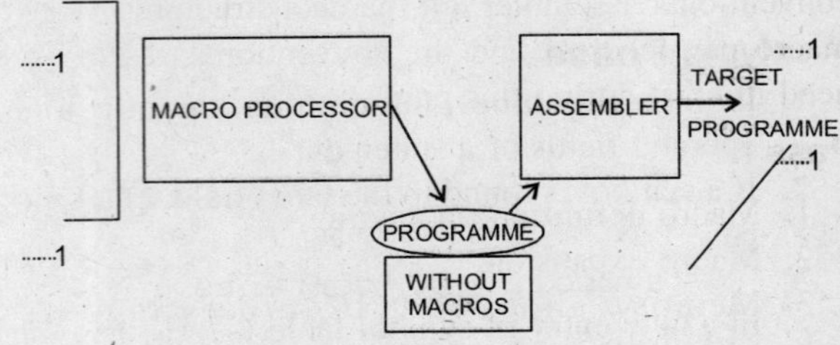

Fig. 4.2 : *A macro processor schematic*

The number of passes over the source programme is large and many functions get duplicated. For example, analysis of a source statement to detect macro calls requires us to process the mnemonic field. A similar function is required in the first pass of the assembler. Similar functions can be merged if macros are handled by a macro assembler which performs macro expansion and programme assembly simultaneously. Number of passes may be reduced.

Certain type of forward references in macros cannot be handled in single pass as shown below :-

```
         MACRO
         CREATE_CONST  &X, &y
         AIF      (T'&X EQ B) .BYTE
&Y       DW             25
         AGO            . OVER
. BYTE   ANOP
&Y       DB             25
. OVER   MEND
         CREATE_CONST  A, NEW -CON
A        DB                     ?
         END
```

In the above assembly programme the type attribute T'&X in macro CREATKCONST is a forward reference to symbol *A*. Processing of the type attribute cannot be postponed because it determines the nature of the constant defined by the macro. In turn, this affects memory allocation and hence the address of *A*!

This problem leads to the classical two pass organisation for macro expansion. The first pass collects information about the symbols defined in a programme and the second pass to macro expansion.

Pass I

1. Macro definition processing,
2. Collect names of declared symbols and information relating to their attributes.

Pass II

1. Macro expansion,
2. Memory allocation and LC processing;
3. Processing of literals; and
4. Intermediate code generation.

Pass III

Target code generation: Pass II is large in size since it performs many functions. Further, since it performs macro expansion as well as pass I of a conventional assembler, all the data structures of the macro preprocessor and the conventional assembler need to exist during this pass.

Pass I

1. Macro definition processing,
2. Macro expansion,
3. Memory allocation, IC processing and SYMTAB construction,
4. Processing of literals; and
5. Intermediate code generation.

Pass II

Target code generation: There is imbalance between the sizes of the two passes.

A 3-pass structure might be preferred for this reason.

Advanced Macro Facilities

The advanced macro facilities can be grouped into:

1. Facilities to alter the flow of control during expansion;
2. Expansion time variables; and
3. Attributes of parameters;
   writing of expansion time loops, and in semantic expansion.

Altering the flow of control during expansion

Alteration of the flow of control during expansion can be done through the use of:

1. Expansion time sequencing symbols,
2. Expansion time statements AIF, AGO and ANOP.

A sequencing symbol (SS), which has the syntax

`<ordinary string>`

is defined by putting it in the label field of a statement in the macro body. It is used in an AIF or AGO statement to designate the destination of an expansion time control transfer. It never comes in the expanded form of model statement.

An AIF statement has the syntax

AIF « *expression*» *<sequencing symbol>*

where *<expression>* is a relational expression involving ordinary strings, formal parameters and their attributes, and expansion time variables. If the Boolean condition evaluates to *true,* expansion time control is transferred to the statement containing *<sequencing symbol>* in its label field. An AGO statement has the syntax

`AGO` *<sequencing symbol>*

and conditionally transfers expansion time control to the statement is as follows :-

<sequencing symbol> `ANOP`

and has the effect of defining the sequencing symbol. /

Expansion Time Variables

Expansion time variables (EV's) are variables which can only be used during the expansion of macro calls. An EV can be *local* in scope, in which case it is created for use during a particular macro call, or *global,* in which case it exists across all macro calls situated in a programme and can be used in any macro which has a declaration for it. Local and global EV's are created through declaration statements with the following syntax

LCL *<EV specification>*[,*<EV specification>* ..]

GBL *<EV specification>* [,*<EV specification>* ..]

where *<EV specification>* has the syntax analogous to that of the formal parameters, *&<EV name>*

Values of EV's can be manipulated through the preprocessor statement SET. A SET statement has the following syntax

<EV spec> SET *<SET-expression>*

where *<EV specification>* appears in the label field and SET in the mnemonic field. A SET statement assigns the value of *<SETexpression>* to the EV specified in *<EV specification>*. The value of an EV can be used in any field of a model statement, and in the expression of an AIF statement.

Attributes of formal parameters: An attribute is written with the following syntax:-

<attribute name>'<formal parameter spec>

and represents information about the value of the formal parameter *i.e.* about corresponding actual parameter. The type, length, size attributes have names T, L, S.

Linkers

Execution of a programme written in a language L includes following steps :-

1. Translation of programme which is done by translator which produces an object code for a programme.
2. Linking of programme with other programmes required for its execution, is performed by a linker.
3. Relocation of the programme to execute from specific memory, is performed by linker. Linker process a set of object modules to produce a ready-to-execute programme-form called binary programme.
4. Loading of the programme in the memory for execution, is performed by loader. The loader load binary programme into memory for execution.

While compiling a programme P, a translator is given an origin specification for P known as translated origin of P. In assembly language Programmer can mention the origin in a START and ORIGIN statement. The translator uses the value of translated origin while performing memory allocation for symbols declared in P. This results in the assignment of a translation time address assigned to each symbol in the programme. The origin of the programme may be changed by linker or loader, this change the start address in the execution and in the address assigned to symbols.

Programme relocation is the process of modifying the addresses used in the address sensitive instructions of a programme sucn that the programme can execute correctly from a designated area of memory.

Linking is the process of binding an external reference to correct load time address. An external reference is said to be unresolved until linking is performed for it. It is said to be resolved when its linking is completed. To form a binary programme from a set of object modules, the programmer invokes the linker using the command

```
linker <load origin>, <object module name> [, <execution start address>]
```

where load origin specifies memory address to be given to the first word of binary programme. <execution start address> is usually a pair (programme name, offset in the programme). The linker converts this into linked start address. This is stored along with binary programme for use when the programme is to be executed. If specification of <execution start address> is omitted, the load origin is assumed to be the execution start address.

SELF-RELOCATING PROGRAMMES

The manner in which a programme can be modified, or can modify itself to execute from a given *load* origin can be used to classify programme into the following:

1. Non relocatable programmes;
2. Relocatable programmes; and
3. Self-relocating programmes

A non relocatable programme is a programme which cannot be executed in any memory area other than the area starting on its translated origin. Non relocatability is the result of address sensivity of a programme and lack of information concerning the address sensitive instructions in the programme. A non relocatable programme is made relocatable by maintaining information concerning the address sensitive instructions in it. Representative examples of non relocatable and relocatable programmes are a hand coded machine language programme and an object module, respectively.

A self-relocating programme is a programme which can perform the relocation of its own address sensitive instructions. It contains 2 provisions for this purpose

1. Information of address sensitive instructions in it, and
2. Code to perform the relocation of address sensitive instructions.

Number of passes to be used by assembler while deciding number of passes to be used by assembler, two factors should be in balance and taken care of - assembly speed—storage requirement of assembler. Due to this reason more than one assembler may be given for a system *e.g.* assembler 'E' and 'F' of the IBM/360 DOS. Assembler 'F' needs 44 K bytes of storage for its operation.

Assemblers, Compilers and Interperators

Aspects of Compilation: The main reason for the use of higher level languages for programming (HLLs) over the years are as follows :

- programming ease.
- Portability and maintainability of programmes, However, computers do not 'understand' HLLs. To execute HLL programme, it should be converted into the *machine language.* A compiler is a programme which translates from an HLL into the machine language of a computer. The important task of a compiler are:
  - *(i)* Translating the HLL programme input to it *(the source programme)* into an equivalent machine language programme.
  - *(ii)* Providing diagnostic messages wherever specifications of the HLL (the source language) are violated by the programmer.

Comparison between Assemblers and Compilers:

- Assemblers are translators for the lower level assembly languages of computers, while compilers are translators for HLLs.
- An assembly language is mostly peculiar family, while an HLL is generally machine-independent and thus portable.
- Assembly languages inherit the architecture of the computer for which they are devised. HLLs create their own feature-architecture.

In an assembly language programme, it is the programmer's responsibility to select and use appropriate machine instructions to manipulate data item of a particular type. This makes the programmer's job difficult, more so since there is no check by the assembler to verify whether the instructions used are compatible with the data type. In the case of an error, the programmer may simply get wrong results.

HLLs, on the other hand, guard the integrity of their data types. Compatibility of an operator with its operands is checked by the compiler and wherever necessary (and permissible), compatibility is forced by a type coercion operation. Thus, no invalid operations can be performed with the data items of different types.

Example 1:

```
a,b: real;
i,j: integer;
b: = 100
a:=b+i;
```

While executing the first assignment statement, the compiler must realise that *a* is a real variable, hence it must convert '100' from integer representation to floating point representation. Thus the compiler has to ensure that the value stored in *b* is always a real number. An assembler will not make such ckeck.

Data structures: HLL allows programmer to declare and use different data structures such as arrays, stacks, tables, records, lists etc. Records and tables contains heterogeneous data which lead to complex storage mappings and user defined types pose interesting problems in storage allocation and access. Thus compiler must figure out how to represent different values of programmer defined type and then develop appropriate mapping.

Scope rules: In HLL, the scope of data items normally associated with block structures of the language. Interaction between various name spaces is permitted and has to be provided for, by the compiler. Thus correspondence to be established during compilation time and during execution and compiler should have appropriate provisions to implement HLL rules governing especially procedure calls like call by value/reference/name etc. Access to non local variables is governed by rules of scope.

```
today:=Monday; info[i].id: =j;
if today = Monday then...
```

Here, info is an array of records. The reference info[i].id involves different kinds of mapping. The first one is the homogeneous mapping of an array reference. In the second mapping, the compiler has to provide for access to the field id from a collection of heterogeneous fields. Weekday is a programmer defined data type. A totally different mapping is involved here since the compiler must figure out how to represent the different values of the programmer defined type, and then develop an appropriate mapping.

Scope Rules and Control Structures

In an HLL, the scope of data item names is normally associated with the block structure of the language. Thus, in FORTRAN, the scope of a data item is the programme/ subprogramme in which the variable is declared. In ALGOL, PLiI or PASCAL, the scope is restricted to the programme block in which the data then is declared. Some HLLs even permit the programmer to dynamically control the scope of data items.

Interaction between the various name spaces is permitted, and has to be provided for, by the compiler. This has two aspects (*i*) correspondence to be established at compilation time, like for data items residing in COMMON blocks of different FORTRAN subprograms; and (*ii*) correspondence to be established during execution, *viz.* Parameters in procedure calls. The target language programme generated by the compiler should have appropriate provision to implement the HLL rules governing procedure calls, like call by value/reference/name etc. Control structures are the important part of HLL but they also leads to interesting problems for compilation technique. Since compiler is a system programme, its design is also based on which environment it has to function. The primary aim of compiler is to speedy compilation, generation of efficient code, good diagnostic support.

The Process of Translation

Analysis of source text + Synthesis of Target text = translation from source to target text.

In the analysis phase, we must know the grammar of the source code, rules of grammar called a syntax and how to determine of statement once its grammatical structure becomes known and rules of meaning known as semantics. In synthesis phase, address for the symbol should also be entered into the list. For this purpose, the analysis phase should keep track of how many machine words have been used up since the start of a programme so that if a symbol exists in the label field of a statement, its address can be readily determined.

Analysis Phase of compiler: The function of this phase is to perform Lexical analysis, syntax analysis and semantic analysis.

The Analysis phase: Compilation is a two step process. In source text analysis, it checks the grammar of source language or determines the syntactic structure of source statement and represents in an intermediate form from which semantic analysis can be performed. In semantic analysis, it determines the meaning of the statement. During syntax analysis, the individual lexical units namely identifiers/constants etc. of programming language are not important but information regarding the syntax categories to which these lexical units belong are important. A lexical analysis step is introduced prior to syntax analysis to filter out all the information from reaching the syntax analyser.

Lexical Analysis: It performs micro level examination of input text in order to identify the lexical units occuring in it and to determine their syntax categories and construct appropriate tables *e.g.* a table of identifiers, a table of constants etc.. The lexical phase look for delimeters (generally keywords/ operators in HLL) and this process is called scanning. After isolating a lexical constituent, it is first classified according to its syntax category and then checked for validity according to rules of that category. This can lead to detection and indication of certain lexical errors like invalid variable name etc. A descriptor/ token is built for lexical analysis which contains the category of lexical unit and an attribute that differentiates between different instances of the syntax category.The descriptor needs to contain sufficient information such that actual identifiers can be recalled when required. This is done by entering all identifiers encountered in source programme into a table(the symbol table).

Syntax analysis: It processes the string of descriptors synthesised by lexical analyser to determine the syntactic structure of an input statement and this process is known as parsing. Output of the parsing step is a representation of syntactic structure of a statement.

Semantic Analysis: Processing of declarative statement and processing executable *e.g.* imperative statements are performed during semantic analysis. Items of information are added to various lexical tables.

Synthesis phase: It performs two main functions: Storage .allocation and code generation (*e.g.* knowledge of instruction set, addressing modes etc). In storage allocation step, the storage requirment of a particular constituent is calculated from various information items like its length and dimensionality stored in the tables and constituent is allocated a machine address. The allocated address is now entered into a field of the table, so that reference to a particular constituent in the intermediate code can be readily converted into reference to the corressponding storage location in the target code.

LANGUAGE PROCESSOR DEVELOPMENT TOOLS (LPDT)

Two commonly used LPDT are — lexical analyser-Lex and the parser generator YACC.

Lex accepts input specification which consists of - specification of strings representing lexical unit in language L *e.g.,* ids, constants etc. This specification is in the form of regular expressions.

— Semantic actions aimed at IR, which consists of a set of tables of lexical units and sequence of tokens for lexical units occuring in a source statement. Accordingly, IR building actions makes new entries in tables and build tokens for lexical units.

YACC: Each string specification in the input to YACC resembles a grammar production. The parser generated by YACC performs reductions according to this grammar. The actions associated with a string specification are executed when a reduction is made according to the specification. An attribute is associated with every nonterminal symbol. The value of this attribute can be manipulated during parsing.The attribute can be given any user defined structure. A symbol '$n' in the action part of translation rule refers to the attribute of the symbol occupying position #n in RHS of string specification '$$' represents the attribute of LHS symbol of the string specification.

PROGRAMME RELOCATABILITY

Feasibility of relocating a programme and the manner in which relocation can be carried out characterises a programme into one of the following forms:

(i) Non-relocatable programme
(ii) Relocatable programme
(iii) Self-relocating programme

Non-Relocatable Programmes: A non-relocatable programmes is one which cannot be made to execute in any area of storage other than the one designated for it at the time of its coding or translation. Non-relocatability is the result of address sensitivity of code and lack of information regarding: (i) which parts of the Programme are address sensitive and (ii) in what manner.

Relocation is feasible only if relevant regarding the address-sensitivity of a programmes is available. A programme form which does not contain any such information is non-relocatable. According to this definition, a Programme phase is a non-relocatable programme form.

Relocatable Programmes: A relocatable programme form is one which consists of a Programme and relevant information for its relocation. Using this information, it is possible to relocate the programme to execute from a storage area other than the one designated for it at the time of its coding or tanslation. The relocation information would identify address-sensitive portions of code and indicate how they can be relocated. For example, in the case of Programme A assuming 'absolute address' kind of addressing mode for the instructions, the relocation information can be a table containing the addresses of those instructions which need to be relocated, or it could simply be the address of first and last instruction of the Programme, assuming all instructions to be contiguous.

It should be noted that in the relocatable form, the Programme is a passive object. Some other Programme must operate on it using the relocation information, in order to make it ready-to execute from its load area. The relocatable Programme form is called an object module and the agent which perform its relocation is obviously the linkage editor or linking loader. The object module is illustrated below. For, the target Programme produced by the translator which uses the translate -and-go schematic) should be an object module and not merely the code and data constituting the target Programme.

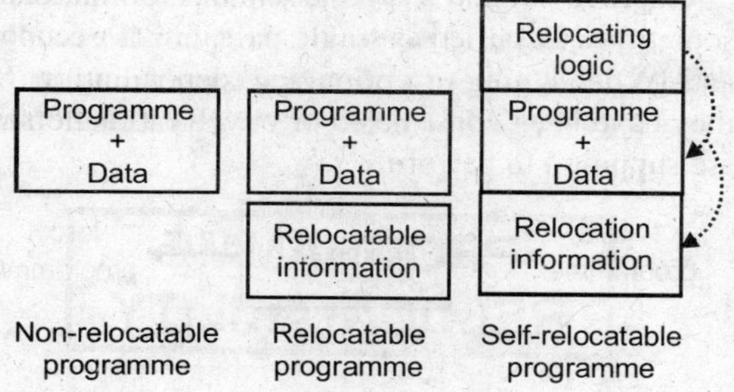

Fig. 4.3

Self-relocating Progammes: A self-relocating programme is one which can itself perform the relocation of its address-sensitive portions. Thus, it not only contains information regarding its address-sensitivity but also the code to make use of this information to relocate the address sensitive part of its code. Such a Programme does not need an external agency like the linkage editor to relocate it. It can be simply loaded into its load area and given control for execution. Prior to execution of its main code, the relocating, logic would be executed to adopt the Programme to its execution time storage addresses.

TEXT EDITORS

Line Editor: The line editor supports editing operations whose basic unit is a line. The basic limitations of such editors are that part of a line cannot be processed and that the text to be edited has to be explicitly addressed. It incorporates a context search, which permitted the user to indicate a position in the text by specifying a character string. The editor would search for the string and position itself at a line containing the character string. Another facility permitted a relative line specifications, viz +nm or – mm, whereby the current position in text would be incremented by nn lines, or decremented by mm lines before performing the next edit operation.

Stream Editor: The stream editor removed all restrictions of line editors. The editor looked upon the entire text as a single continuous stream of characters. Thus, context searches and editing operations could be performed uniformly through the text. One difficulty with stream editors was that the user would prefer to retain the line-oriented structure of the text, *viz.* a programme as a sequence of statement lines, manuscript as a sequence of lines, etc., while the editor would prefer not have end-of-line characters in the text.

The editor supports character, line and context-oriented commands, using the concept of a pointer into user text (the buffer pointer). The pointer can be manipulated by using some positioning or search commands. TECO also supports advanced features like iterative command sequences and Q-registers which can be manipulated like registers/accumulators in a computer.

Screen Editors: Even though stream editors remove most restrictions of line editors, they too can be quite difficult to use, especially in an online interactive environment.

Working Principle of Screen Editor

The text is conceptually split into screens. At any time, a screen is displayed on the terminal. The user has full control over the terminal and can perform any editing operation he desires. For example, he can overtype an existing string which he wishes to replace. The character would be deleted and characters to its right would move left to fill the vacancy. Pressing delete key once again will imply deleting the next character. The editors might also permit windowing over text so that any arbitrary piece of text could be viewed as a screen for editing purposes. This further extends the editing freedom given to the user.

Table 4.1: Some TECO Commands (DEC- 10 version)

Command Code	*Example*	*Explanation*
C	nC	Moves pointer forward by n characters
R	nR	Moves pointer backward by n characters
J	J	Initialises position of buffer pointer
ZJ	ZJ	Moves pointer to end of buffer
S	nSstring	Searches for n t' occurrence of string starting from current pointer position.
FS	FS string 1$ string 2$$	Searches for string I and replaces it by string 2
L	±nL	Moves Pointer forward/backward by n lines
D	nD	Deletes n characters
I	Istring	Inserts string at current position of pointer

Structure Editors

A stream editor helps to search but it is of little use unless a unique string can be indicated. A screen editor permits browsing, but in a strictly sequential manner. NLS (short form for online System) is the earliest structure editor [Engelbart, English 1968]. It is oriented towards document editing. Each document has a hierarchic structure, with different levels like group, plex, branch and statement. Within a section, we can talk of a paragraph, the preceding succeeding paragraph, first statement in the paragraph etc. Thus, editing can be in terms of structure of document and not merely its content.

Structural awareness by the editor has been found especially useful while editing Programme texts since, it eliminates the time consuming process of removing syntax errors. This had led to the development of many structure editors for Programme text, the so called syntax directed editors. Syntax editors are commonly used in programming environments.

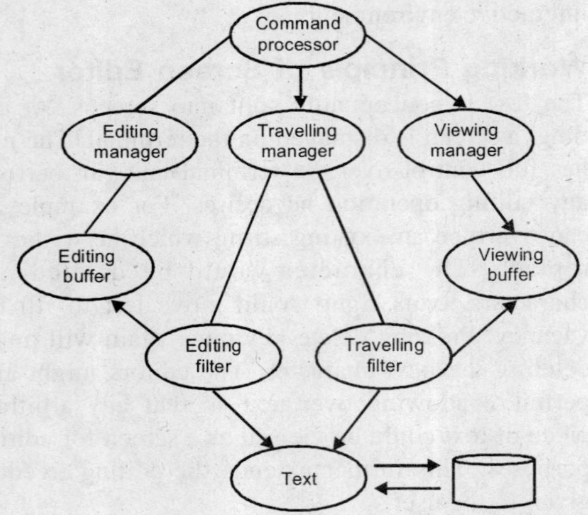

Fig. 4.4: *A schematic of editor structure.*

Most editors support the following four functions in one form or another - travelling, editing, viewing and display.

Travelling implies movement of the editing context to a new position within the text. This may be done explicitly by the user (*e.g.* the line number command of a line editor).

Viewing implies formatting the text in a manner desired by the user.

The display component may determine where on the screen a particular view is to appear. The distinction between viewing and display gives rise to interesting possibilities, like multiple views, *i.e.* windows, appearing on the same screen, multiple independent edit operations using the same display terminal, etc.

An important function of the editor is to maintain compatibility of the two views. This is implemented by using two filters, the edit filter and the viewing filter, both of which operate on the internal form of text.

Compilation and Compilers

A compiler is a proramme that reads a Programme written in one language, the source language and translate it into an equivalent Programme in another language—the target language. As an important part of this translation process, the compiler reports to its user the presence of errors in the source Programme.

There are thousands of source languages, ranging from traditional programming languages such as Fortran and Pascal to specialized languages that have arisen in virtually every area of computer application. Target languages are equally as varied; a target language may be another programming language, or the machine language of any computer between a microprocessor and a super computer. Compilers are sometimes classified as single-pass, multi-pass, load-and-go debugging or optimizing, depending on how they have been constructed or on what function they are supposed to perform.

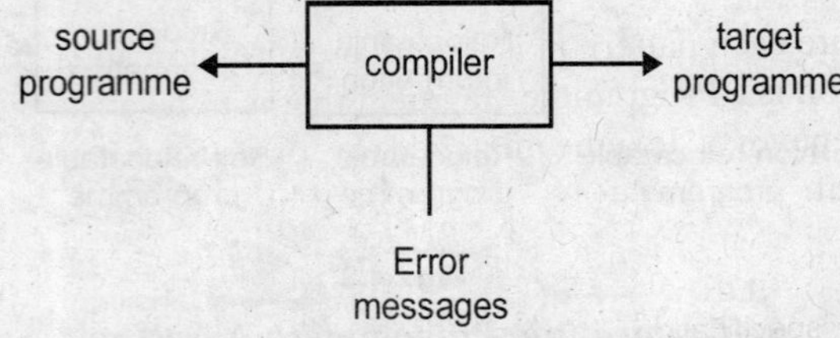

F ig. 4.5: *Compiler view*

BOOTSTRAP COMPILER

A compiler is a complex enough programme that we would like to write it in a friendlier language that assembly language. In the UNIX programming environment, compilers are usually written in C. Using the facilities offered by a language to compile itself is the essence of bootstrapping.

For bootstrapping, a compiler is characterised by 3 languages: the source language 'S' that compiles the target language 'T' that generates code for and the implementation language 'I' that it is written in.

Phases of a Compiler

Conceptually, a compiler operates in phases, each of which transforms the source Programme from one representation to another.

The first three phases form the bulk of the analysis portion of a compiler.

Lexical Analysis

In a compiler, linear analysis is called lexical analysis or scanning. For example, in lexical analysis the characters in the assignment statement

position: = initial + rate * 60

would be grouped into the following tokens

1. The identifier (position)
2. The assignment symbol (: =)
3. The identifier (initial)
4. The plus sign (+)
5. The identifier (rate)
6. The multiplication sign (*)
7. The number (60)

LEX PACKAGE ON UNIX

We consider the design of a software tool that automatically constructs a lexical analyzer from a Programme in the Lex language.

We assume that we have specification of a lexical analyzer of the form

P_1 {action}
P_2 {action2}
....
P_n {actions}

where each pattern pi is a regular expression and each action is a Programme fragment that is to be executed whenever a lexeme matched by pi is found in the input.

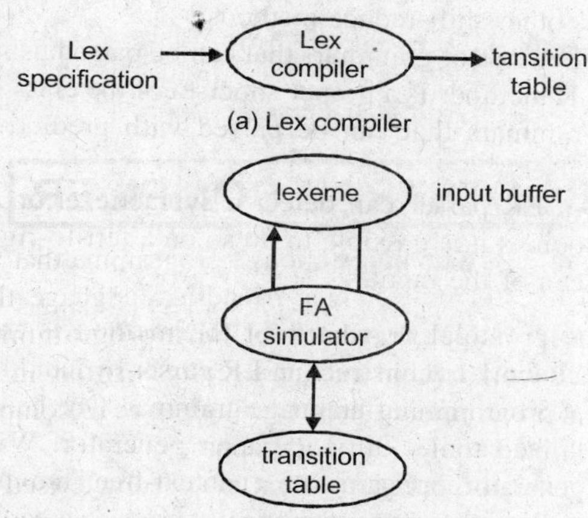

Fig. 4.6: *Schematic lexical analyzer*

If more than one pattern matches, the recognizer is to choose the longest. If there are two or more patterns that match the longest lexeme, the first-listed matching pattern is chosen.

A finite automation is a natural model around which to build a lexical analyzer and the one constructed by out Lex compiler. There is an input buffer with two pointers to it, a lexeme beginning and a forward pointer. The Lex compiler constructs a transition table for a finite automation from the regular expression patterns in the Lex specification.

CONTEXT FREE GRAMMAR

A context - free grammar is a finite set of variables (also called non-terminals or syntactic categories) each of which represents a language. The rules relating the variable are called productions. A typical production stages that the language associated with a given variable contains other variables, possibly along with some terminals.

A context- free grammar (CFG or just grammar) is denoted by G = (V, T, P, S), where V and T are finite sets of variables and terminals, respectively.

Example : Suppose we use E instead of <expression> for the variable in the grammar. Then we could formally express this grammar as ({E}, {+, *, (,), id}, P, E), where P consists of

$E \rightarrow E + E$
$E \rightarrow E * E$
$E \rightarrow (E)$
$E \rightarrow id$

Notational Conventions

To avoid always having to state that "these are the terminals", "these are the non-terminals", and so on, we shall employ the following notational conventions.

Symbols as Terminals

(i) Lower-case letters early in the alphabet such as a, b, c.
(ii) Operator symbols such as +, – etc.
(iii) Punctuation symbols such as parentheses, comma, etc.
(iv) The digits 0, 1, ..., 9.
(v) Boldface strings such as id or if.

Symbols as Non-terminals

(i) Upper-case letters early in the alphabet such as A, B, C.
(ii) The letter S, which when it appears, is usually the start symbol.
(iii) Lower-case italic names such as expr or stmt.

Upper-case letters late in the alphabet, such as X, Y, Z, represent grammar symbols as either non-terminals or terminals.

Lower-case letters late in the alphabet, chiefly u, v, ... z, represent strings of terminals.

Lower-case Greek letters, a, b, g, for example, represent strings of grammar symbols. Thus, a generic production could be written as $A \rightarrow \alpha$, indicating that there is a single nonterminal A on the left of the arrow (the left side of the production) and a string of grammar symbols *a* to the right of the arrow (the right side of the production).

If $A \rightarrow \alpha_1$ $A \rightarrow \alpha_2$,............ $A \rightarrow \alpha_k$ are all productions with A on left (we call them A productions) we may write $A \rightarrow \alpha_1 |\alpha_2|$ .... |ak. We call a1, α_2, ... α_k the alternatives for A.

Unless otherwise stated, the left side of the first production is the start symbol.

Derivation Trees (Parse Trees)

Derivations are displayed as trees. These pictures, called derivation (or parse) trees, superimpose a structure on the words of a language that is useful in applications such as the compilation of programming languages. The vertices of a derivation tree are labelled with terminal or variable symbols of the grammar or possibly with e. If an interior vertex n is labelled A, and the sons of n are labelled X_1, X_2, ..., X_k from the left, then $A \rightarrow X_1 X_2 .... X_k$ must be production. If we read the leaves in left - to - right order, we get the last line of (5.1), (id + id) & id.

<Expression> ⇒ <Expression> * <Expression>
⇒(<Expression>) * <Expression>

COMPUTER SCIENCE

⇒(<Expression>) * id
⇒(<Expression> + <Expression>) * id
⇒(<Expression> + id) * id
⇒(id + id) * id

More family, let G = (V, T, P, S) be a CFG. A tree is a derivation (or parse) tree for G if

(i) Every vertex has a label, which is a symbol of V U T U {S}.

(ii) The label of the root is S.

(iiii) If a vertex is interior and has label A, then A must be in V.

(iv) If n has label A and vertices n_1, n_2, ... nk are the sons of vertex n, in order from the left, with labels X_1, X_2, ... X_k, respectively, then $A \rightarrow X_1, X_2, ... X_k$ must be production in P.

(v) If vertex has label s, then n is a leaf and is the only son of its father.

Algorithm: Operator-precedence passing algorithm.

Input: An input string w and a table of precedence relations.

Output: If w is a well-formed, a skeletal parse tree, with a placeholder non terminal E labelling all interior nodes, otherwise an error detection.

Method: Initially, the stack contains $ and the input buffer the string w$. To parse we execute the following programme.

Steps

1. set ip to point to the first symbol of , w$;
2. repeat forever
3. if $ is on top of the stack and ip points to $ then
4. return
   else begin
5. let a be the topmost terminal symbol on the stack, and let b be the symbol pointed to by ip;
6. if $a < b$ or $a = b$ then begin
7. push b onto the stack;
8. advance ip to the next input symbol;
   end;
9. else if $a > b$ then more / * reduce * /
10. repeat
11. pop the stack
12. until the top stack terminal is related by <.
13. else error ()
    end

L.R. PARSERS

The technique that can be used to parse a large class of context-free grammars is called LR (k) parsing; the "L" is for left-to-right scanning of the input, the "R" for constructing a right most derivation in reverse and the k for the number of input symbols of lookahead that are used in making parsing decisions. When (k) is omitted, k is assumed to be 1. LR parsing is attractive for a variety of reasons.

1. LR parsers can be constructed to recognise virtually all programming language constructs for which context-free grammars can be written.
2. The LR parsing method is the most general non-backtracking shift-reduce parsing method known, yet it can be implemented as efficiently as other shift-reduce methods.
3. The class of grammars that can be parsed using LR methods is a proper superset of the class of grammars that can be parsed with predictive parsers.
4. An LR parser can detect a syntactic error as soon as it is possible to do so on a left-to-right scan of the input.

The principal drawback of the method is that too much work to construct an LR parser by hand for a typical programming-language grammar. One needs a specialized tool - an LR parser generator. With such a generator, one can write a context-free grammar and have the generator automatically produce a parser for that grammar. If the grammar contains ambiguities or other constructs that are difficult to parse in a left-to-right scan of the input, then the parser generator can locate these constructs and inform the compiler designer of their presence.

There are three techniques for constructing an LR parsing table for a grammar.

1. Simple LR (SLR) for short), is the easiest to implement, but the least powerful of the three. It may fail to produce a parsing table for certain grammars on which the other methods succeed.
2. Canonical LR, is the most powerful and the most expensive.
3. Look ahead LR (LALR for short), is intermediate in power and cost between the other two. The LALR method will work on most programming-language grammars and, with some effort, can be implemented efficiently.

Intermediate Code Generation

After syntax and semantic analysis, some compilers generate an explicity intermediate representation of the source programme. This intermediate representation should have two important properties; it should be easy to produce and easy to translate into the target programme.

The intermediate representation form called "three-address code", which is like the assembly language for a machine in which every memory location can act like a register. Three address code consists of a sequence of instructions, each of which has at most operands. The source programme might appear in three-address code as

temp 1: = *inttoreal* (60)

temp 2: = *id3* * *templ*

temp 3: = 02 + *templ*

idl: = *temp* 3

This intermediate form has several properties. First, each three-address instruction has at most one operator in addition to the assignment. Thus, when generating these instructions, the compiler has to decide on the order in which operations are to be done; the multiplication precedes the addition in the source programme. Secondly, the compiler must generate a temporary name to hold the value computed by each instruction. Third, some "three-address" instructions have fewer than three operands, *e.g.*, the first and last instructions in 4.

Code Optimisation

The code optimisation phase attempts to improve the intermediate code, so that faster-running machine code will result. Some optimisations are trivial. For example, a natural algorithm generates the intermediate code 4, using an instruction for each operator in the tree representation after semantic analysis, even though there is a better way to perform the same calculation, using the two instructions.

Code Generation

The final phase of any compiler is the generation of target code, consisting normally of relocatable machine code or assembly code. Memory locations are selected for each of the variables used by the programme. Then, intermediate instructions are each translated into a sequence or machine instructions that perform the same tasks. A crucial aspect is the assignment of variables to registers.

5 DATA STRUCTURES

DATA STRUCTURE

Data are represented by data values held temporarily within programme's data area or recorded permanently on a file. Often the different data values are related to each other. To enable programmes to make use of these relationships, these data values must be in an organised form. The organised collection of data is called a **data structure**. The programmes have to follow certain rules to access and process the structured data. We may, therefore, say data are represented as:

Data Structure = Organised Data + Allowed Operations

There are standard data structures which are often used in their own right and can form the basis for complex data structures. One such basic data structure called **Array**. Arrays are basic building block for more complex data structures. Designing and using data structures is an important programming skill.

VARIOUS DATA STRUCTURES

Linear and non-linear data structures: However, this is not the only way to classify data structures. In linear data structure the data items are arranged in a linear sequence like in an array. In a non-linear data structures,the data are not in sequence. An example of a non linear data structure is a *tree*. Data structures may also be classified as **homogeneous and nonhomogeneous data structures**. An Array is a homogeneous structure in which all elements are of same type. In non-homogeneous structures all elements are of different types. Another way of classifying data structures is as **static or dynamic data structures.** Static structures are ones whose sizes and structures associated memory location are fixed at compile time. Dynamic structures are ones, which expand or shrink as required during the programme execution and their associated memory locations change. Records are a common example of non-homogeneous data structures.

Array Declaration

Three things need to be specified to declare an array in most of the programming languages:

1. the array name
2. the type of data to be stored in array elements
3. the subscript range

In first declaration A, is the array name; the elements of A can hold integer data and the number of elements is 24 *i.e.* subscripts range from 0 to 23.

In the next declaration B is the array name; the data type of its elements is real and it is a 2-dimensional array with subscripts ranging from 0 to 99 and 0 to 24. It makes more sense to start the array at a value that corresponds to the context of your data. You may notice that the subscript may not always be positive. It can be negative or Zero or negative subscripts.

An array declaration tells the computer two major pieces of information about an array. First, the range of subscripts allow the computer to determine how many memory locations must be allocated. Second, the array type tells the computer how much space is required to hold each value.

Operations Arrays

The array is a homogeneous structure, *i.e.* the elements of an array are of the same type. Following set of operations is defined for this structure:

1. creating an array
2. initialising an array
3. storing an element
4. retrieving an element
5. inserting an element
6. deleting an element
7. searching for an element
8. sorting elements
9. printing an array

These operations apply to array of any dimension. The operation of searching for value in an array looks for a mark of value with the elements in the array. If found, it returns the index of such an element that matches the value. Otherwise it returns an appropriate message. Sorting means rearranging the array elements in a particular order.

Sparse Arrays

Sparse arrays are special arrays which arise commonly in applications. It is difficult to draw the dividing line between the sparse and non-sparse array. Loosely an array is called sparse if it has a relatively number of zero elements. For example in Figure 5.1, out of 49 elements, only 6 are non-zero This is a sparse array.

0	0	0	0	0	1	0
0	0	0	0	1	0	0
0	0	0	0	0	0	0
0	0	0	0	3	0	0
0	2	0	0	0	0	0
0	0	0	0	4	0	0
0	0	0	0	2	0	0

Fig. 5.1: *A Sparse Array*

To store those array, there would be much wasted space. Two alternative representations that will store explicitly only the non-zero elements:

1. Vector representation
2. Linked List representation

In vector representation each elements of a 2-dimensional array is uniquely characterised by its row and column position we may, therefore, store a sparse array in another array of the form

A[n+1] [3]

The sparse array given in Figure 5.1 may be stored in the array A[7] [3] as shown in Figure 5.2.

		1	2	3
A	0	7	5	6
	1	1	6	1
	2	2	5	1
	3	4	5	3
	4	5	2	2
	5	6	5	4
	6	7	5	2

Fig. 5.2: *Sparse Array Representation*

The elements A[0] [0] and A[0] [1] contain the number of rows and columns of the sparse array. A[0] [2] contains the number of non-zero elements of sparse array. The first and second element of each of the rows store the number of row and column of the non-zero term and the third element stores the value of non-zero term. In other words, each non-zero element in a 2-dimensional sparse array is represented as a triplet with the format (row subscript, column subscript, value).

If the sparse array was one-dimensional, each non-zero element would be represented by a pair. In general, for an N-dimensional sparse array, non-zero elements are represented by an entry with N+1 values.

Lists like arrays are used to store ordered data. A list is a linear of data objects of the same type. Real-life event such as people waiting to be served at a bank counter or at a railway reservation counter may be implemented using List structures. In computer science, Lists are extensively used in database management systems, in process management, in operating systems, in editors etc.

These lists also motivate a discussion of storage allocation in computers. Storage or space management is of vatal importance. The first step in this is the acquisition of adequate storage space. This is done by estimating the amount of space required for all the following categories of data:

- Operating system
- Special software
- User programme
- Data files
- Temporary files
- Scratch area

The storage thus acquired is managed by the operating system. This section will study storage management methods under the following heads:

- Storage allocation
- Storage pools
- Garbage collection
- Blocks, Retrieval, Fragmentation
- Block splitting, Compaction, Relocation

A linear list is an ordered set consisting of a variable number of elements to which addition and deletions can be made. A linear list displays the relationship of physical adjacency.

The first element of a List is called head of List and the last element is called the tail of List.

The first element to the head of the List is called its successor. The previous element to the tail (if it is not the head of the List) of the List is called its predecessor.

Clearly, a head does not have a predecessor, and a tail does not have a successor. Any other element of the List has both one successor and one predecessor.

The elements in a List are tied together by their successor-predecessor relationship.

Following are some of the basic operations that may be performed on a List :

- Create a List
- Check for an empty List
- Search for an element in a List
- Search for predecessor or a successor of an element of a List
- Delete an element from a List
- Add an element at a specified location of a List

- Retrieve an element from a List
- Update an element of a List
- Sort a List
- Print a List
- Determine the size or number of elements in a List
- Delete a List

More complex operations may be performed on a List, however a complex operation would generally turn out to be a combination of two or more of the above basic operations.

A List can be implemented statically or dynamically using an array index or pointers respectively.

Static Implementation Lists

It is the simplest implementation. Its size fixed and allocated at compilation time. A List can be implemented as an array as follows :

Let our List elements be names of all the colours, say BLUE, RED, YELLOW, GREEN and ORANGE.

We may have an array List declared as List [LIST _SIZE], and fix its size as 8. Therefore, we have something like as given in Figure 5.3.

	LIST	
LIST (0)	BLUE	
LIST (1)	RED	
LIST (2)	YELLOW	
LIST (3)	GREEN	
LIST (4)	ORANGE	
LIST (5)		allocated but not used
LIST (6)		
LIST (7)		

Fig. 5.3

The elements are sequentially stored in LIST[0], LIST [1].......LIST [4]. LIST [5] through LIST [7] are allocated but not used.

The predecessor of LIST [0] (or head) is NIL; LIST [4] is the tail of the LIST and has no successor. We may also tabulate the predecessors and successors of the other elements of the List as given in Table 5.1.

TABLE 5.1

	Data	*Array Index*	*Predecessor Index*	*Successor Index*
	BLUE	0	NIL	1
	RED	1	0	2
	YELLOW	2	1	3
	GREEN	3	2	4
	ORANGE	4	3	NIL
	--	--	--	--
Unused	--	--	--	--
locations	--	--	--	--

Since the elements are sequentially stored, we don't need to store the predecessor and successor indices. Any element in the List can be accessed through its index.

Now let us see an Insert operation. If we want to insert an element at k^{th} position *i.e.* after LIST [k-1].

To do this, we must shift elements LIST [K] through LIST[Last]to respectively LIST [K+1] through LIST [Last +1]. At the same time we must also check that LIST [Last +1] does not exceed the value of LIST [LISTsize -1].

LIST [Last] is nothing but the tail of the List.

Let us see the operations to be performed in an algorithmic form.

1. new_last =Last+1
2. If new_last>LIST_size-1, error:overflow
3. LIST[Last+1]=LIST[Last]
   LIST[Last]=LIST [Last-1] Shifting of elements from
   ....
   k+1through Last+ 1
   ....
   LIST[K+2]=LIST[K+1]
   LIST[K+1]=LIST[K]
4. LIST[K]= element Inserting element at K_{th} position
5. tail=new_last

In the delete operation, we need to shift element in upwards direction and also decrement the value of tail by 1.

You must have noticed that array implementations of a List has certain drawbacks. These are:

1. Memory storage space is wasted; very often the List is much shorter than the array size declared.
2. List can not grow in its size beyond the size of the declared array if required during programme execution.
3. Operations like insertion and deletion at a specified location in a List requires a lot of movement of data, therefore, leading to inefficient and time consuming algorithms.

POINTER IMPLEMENTATION OF LISTS

For the list elements BLUE, RED, YELLOW, GREEN and ORANGE, we can form a linked List using points. The structure of such a list may be as below:

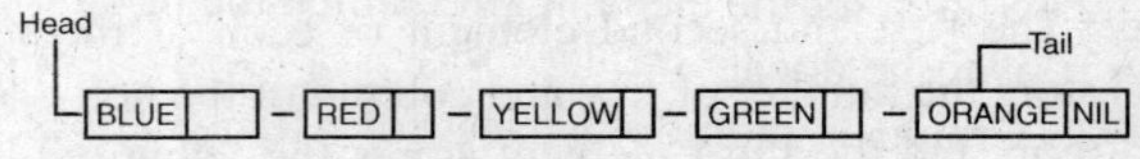

Fig. 5.4: *A Linked List*

The Head and Tail are also pointers to first and last element of the List respectively

This is a singly linked List structure *i.e.* each of its elements have

- data and
- a pointer pointing to next element of the Lists

For an empty List Head and Tail pointer have the value NIL. When the List has one element the head and Tail point to the same.

When the List has two elements the Head points to the first and the Tail points to the second element. The pointer of element points to second element and that of second element holds a value NIL.

The primary advantage of Linked Lists over arrays is that Linked Lists can grow and shrink in size during their lifetime. In particular, their maximum size need not be known in advance. In practical applications, this often makes it possible to have several data structures share the same space without paying particular attention to their relative size at any time.

A second advantage of Linked Lists is that they provide flexibility in allowing the items to be rearranged efficiently. This flexibility is gained at the expense of quick access to any arbitrary item in the List. This will become more apparent below after we have examined some of the basic properties of Linked Lists and some of the fundamental operations we perform on them.

Now, this explicit representation of the ordering allows certain operations to be performed much more efficiently than would be possible for arrays. For example, suppose that we want to move the GREEN to the beginning of the List. In an array, we would have to move every item to make room for the new item at the beginning in a linked list, we just change three links, as shown in Figure 5.5.

Fig. 5.5 : *Charges:Head puts to Green, Green to Blue, Yellow to Orange*

The two versions shown in Figure 5.4 are equivalent; they are just drawn differently. We make the node containing GREEN point to BLUE, the node containing YELLOW point to ORANGE, and head point to GREEN, Even if the List was very long, we could make this structural change by changing just three links.

Insertion in a List

Let see how an Insertion algorithm works for inserting an element in a linked List after a specified element.

1. Check if List is empty, return if yes
2. Search for the element after which the insertion is to be done.
3. Create a memory space for element to be inserted
4. Assign the data value to its data field
5. Assign its pointer to pointer of the element searched at step 2
6. Assign its pointer of the element searched at step 2 to this new element created

Let us consider a List as given in Figure 5.4.

We want to insert PINK before YELLOW, we must create space for element with data PINK *i.e.* we will have

PINK	NIL

NEW-ELEMENT

Now we need to assign the pointer of NEW_ELEMENT, which has a value NIL at present to the value stored in structure containing data yellow *i.e.*

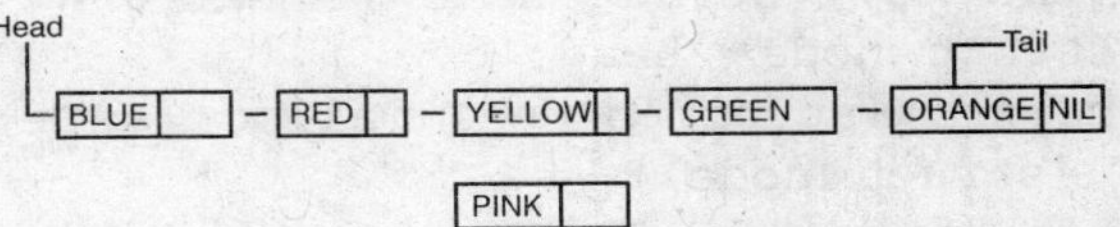

Fig. 5.6: *Insertion in a Linked List*

Now we need to delink YELLOW from RED and assign it to the new_element created.

Therefore, we will have

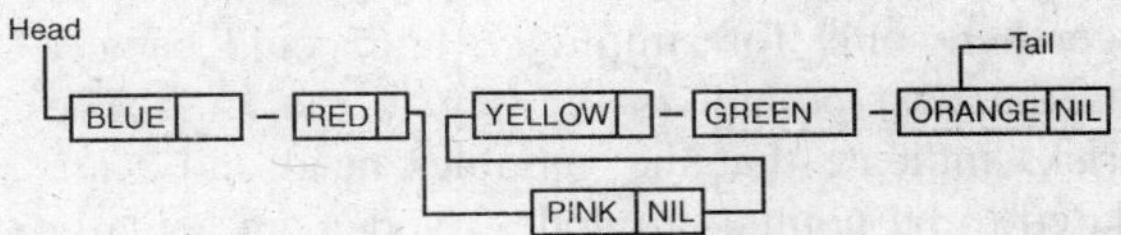

Fig. 5.7: *Insertion in a Linked List*

We may notice that no data is physically moved, as we had seen in array implementation. Only the pointers are readjusted.

Deletion from a List

Deletion of an element from a single linked List requires

1. List to be checked for empty List
2. Search for the element with key value same as the element to be deleted
3. Its pointer to next element be saved and later assigned to next element of predecessor of the element searched at step
4. Dispose the memory space held by the deleted element

There are other operations for which Linked Lists are not well-suited. The most obvious of these is "find the k^{th}item" (find an item given its index): in an array this is done simply by accessing a[k], but in a list we have to travel through *k* links. Another operation that is unnatural on Linked Lists is 'find the item before a given item'. If all we have is the link to GREEN in our sample list in Figure 5.2, then the only way we can find the link to YELLOW is to start at head and travel through the list to find the node that points to GREEN. As a matter of fact, this operation is necessary if we want to be able to delete a given node from a linked list: how else do we find the node whose link must be changed? In many applications, we can get around this problem, by re-designing the deletion

COMPUTER SCIENCE

operation to be "delete the next node". A similar problem can be avoided for insertion by making the insertion operation "insert a given item after a given node" in the List.

Implementation

To illustrate how basic linked List primitives might be implemented, we begin by precisely specifying the format of the List nodes and building an empty List, as follows :

```
struct node
{int key; struct node * next;};
struct node* head, *z;
head = (struct node*) malloc (size
of (struct node));
z = (struct node*) malloc (size of
(struct node);
head --->next =z; z-->next=z;
```

The struct declaration specifies that Lists are made up of nodes, each node containing an integer and a pointer to the next node on the List. The key is an integer here only for simplicity, and could be any type –the next pointer is the key to the LIST.The asterisks indicate that the variables head and *z* are declared to be pointers to nodes. Nodes are actually created only when the built-in function malloc is called. This hides a complex mechanism that is intended to relieve the programmer of the burden of "allocating" storage for the nodes as the List grows. We discuss this mechanism in some detail below. The "arrow" (minus sign follows by a reference to a link followed by this symbol to indicate a reference to the node pointed to by that link. Thus, the above code creates two new nodes referred to by head and z and sets both of them to point to z.

To insert a new node with key value v into a linked List at a point following a given node *t*, we create the node struct x=(struct node*) malloc (size of (struct node)); and put in the key value (x-->key =v), then copy t's link into it (x-->next =t -->next)and put in the key value (x-->key =v), then copy t's link into it (x-->next =t--> next) and made t's link point to the new node (t--> next =x).

To extract the node following a given node t from a linked List, we get a pointer to that node (x=t-next). copy its pointer into t to take it out of the List (t-next =x-next), and return it to the storage allocation system using the built-in procedure delete, unless the List was empty (if x!=z) delete x).

Storage of Sparse Arrays using Linked List

It is often necessary to deal with large arrays in which many of the element has a zero value. Such arrays are called *sparse arrays*.

One of the methods of storing these sparse arrays, is by using a 3-tuple for each element. Often non zero elements need to be added or deleted. That requires a lot of data movement in a static storage system. An improvement over this would be to store these non zero element as a linked List of 3 tuples instead of using an array.

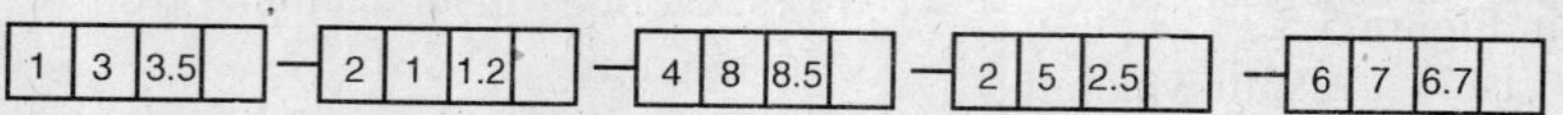

Fig. 5.8: *Linked List for sparse Array*

Doubly Linked Lists

In many applications it is required to traverse a List in both directions. This two-way traversal can be realised by maintaining two link fields in each node instead of one. We call such a structure a Doubly Linked List. Each element of a doubly linked list structure has three fields

- data value
- a link to its successor
- a link to its predecessor

The predecessor link is called the left link and the successor link is known as the right link.

Thus the traversal of the List can be in any direction. We have a structure as given in Fig. 5.9. Note that the left link of leftmost node and right link of rightmost node are NIL.

Inserting of a Node

To insert a node into a doubly linked List to the right of a specified node, we have to consider several cases. These are as follows :

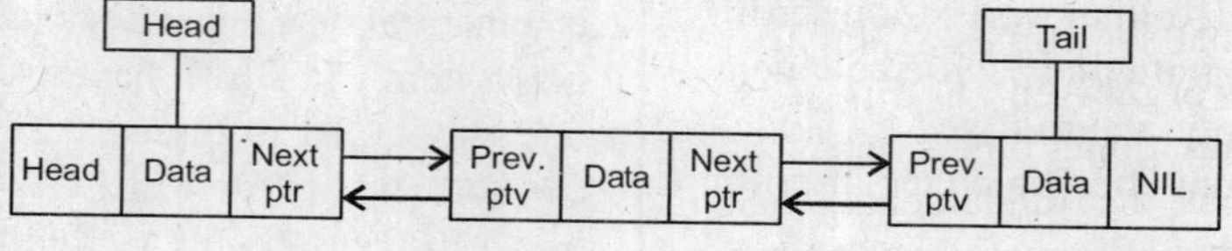

Fig. 5.9

1. If the List is empty, *i.e.* the left and right link of specified node pointed to by says variable HERE are nil. An insertion in this node is simply making left and right link point to the new node and left and right link of new node to be set to nil.
2. If there is a predecessor and a successor to the given node. In such a case we need to readjust

links of the specified node and its successor node. The procedure may be depicted as given in Figure 5.10.

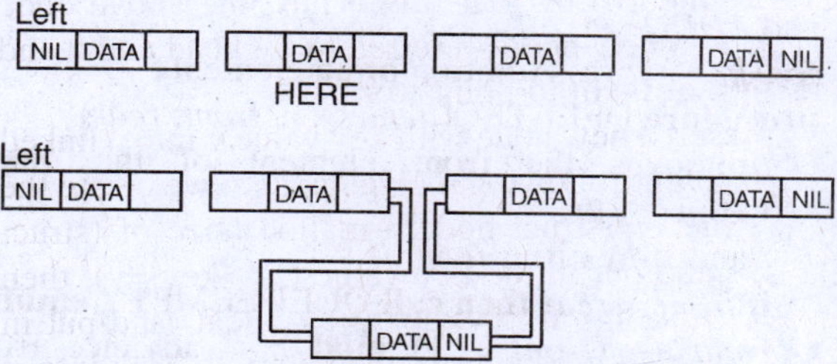

Fig. 5.10: *Insertion in Doubly Linked List*

3. If the insertion is to be done after the rightmost node in the List. In such a case only the right link of the specified node *i.e.* the rightmost node is to be changed.

Deletion of a Node

Similar to insertion of a node, we have to consider several cases for deletion of a node.

Circular Linked List

Another alternative to overcome the drawback of singly linked List structure is to make the last element point to the first of the List. The resulting structure is called a circularly linked List (Figure 5.10).

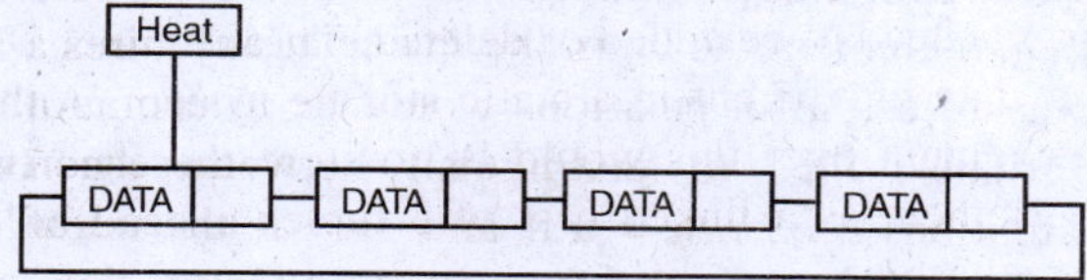

Fig. 5.12: *A Circular List*

A circularly linked List is a List in which the link field of the last element of the List contains a pointer to the first element of the List. The last element of the List no longer points to a NIL value.

Defining Stack and Queue

A stack is a linear data structure in which data is inserted and deleted at one end (same end) *i.e.* data is stored and retrieved in a Last In First Out (LIFO) order. The most recently arrived data object is the first one to depart from a stack. A stack operates somewhat like a busy executive's "in" box; work piles up on a stack, and whenever the bottom of the stack for some time, but a good executive would presumably manage to get the stack emptied periodically. It turns out that sometimes a computer programme is naturally organised in this way, postponing some tasks while doing others, and thus pushdown stacks appear as the fundamental data structure for many algorithms. We may draw a stack in any one of the forms as given in Figure 5.11.

Each one of the above has one open and one closed end. The data movement (*i.e.* storage and retrieval) takes place only at the open end, *i.e.* data is stored and retrieved in Last in First Out (LIFO) order. We generally use the form given in Figure 15.11(a), having the open end in up direction.

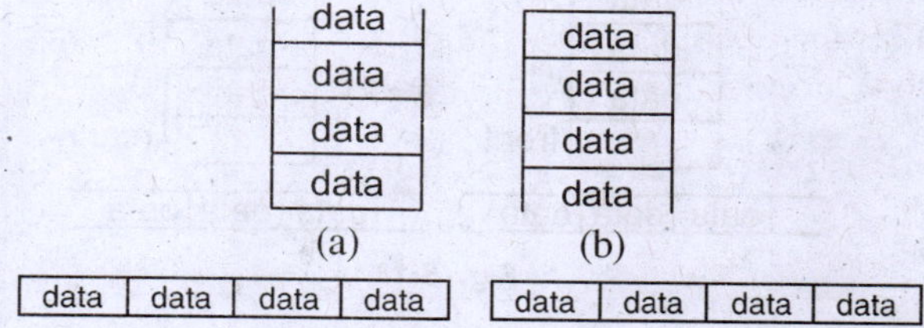

Fig. 5.11

The open end of the stack is called the top of the stack The store and retrieval operations for a stack are called *push* and *pop* respectively.

Another fundamental restricted-access data structure is called the Queue. A Queue is an ordered list in which all insertions take place at one end, the rear, while all deletions take place at the other end, the frong. Again, only two basic operations are involved : one can insert an item into the Queue at the beginning and remove an item from the end. Perhaps our busy executive's "in" box should operate like a Queue, since then work that arrives first would get done first. In a stack, something can get buried at the bottom, but in a Queue eveything is processed in the order received. Queues obey a "First In First Out (FIFO)"discipline. We may draw Queues in any one of the forms as given in Figure 5.12.

Queue is marked with two open ends called front and rear.

Basic operation on stack are as given below :

1. Create a stack
2. Check whether a stack is empty
3. Check whether a stack is full
4. Initialise a stack
5. Push an element onto a stack (if not full)
6. Pop an element from a stack (if not empty)
7. Read a stack top
8. Print the entire stack

Stack (a special case of List) can be implemented as one of the following data structures:

- Array
- Linked List

An efficient queue representation is obtained by taking an array, declared as Q(0:n – 1), and treating it as if it was circular. Elements are inserted by increasing the variable *rear* to the next free position. When *rear* = n – 1, the next element is entered at Q(0) in case that spot is free, *front* will always point one position counter clockwise from the first element in the queue. *front* = *rear* is and only if the queue is empty and initially we have *front* = *rear* = 0. Fig. 5.13 illustrates two of the possible configurations for a circular queue containing the four elements J_1 – J_4 with $n > 4$.

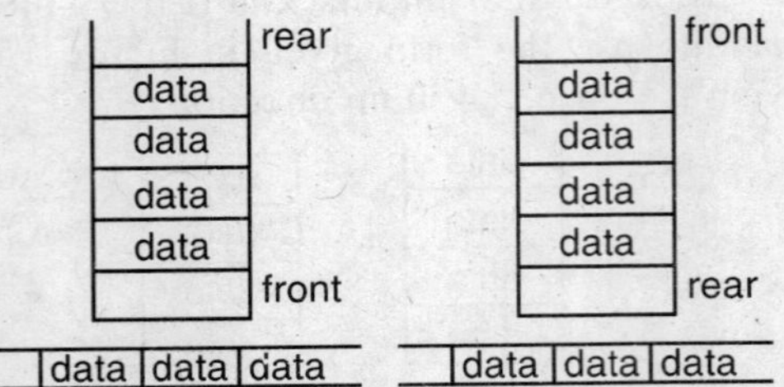

Fig. 5.13

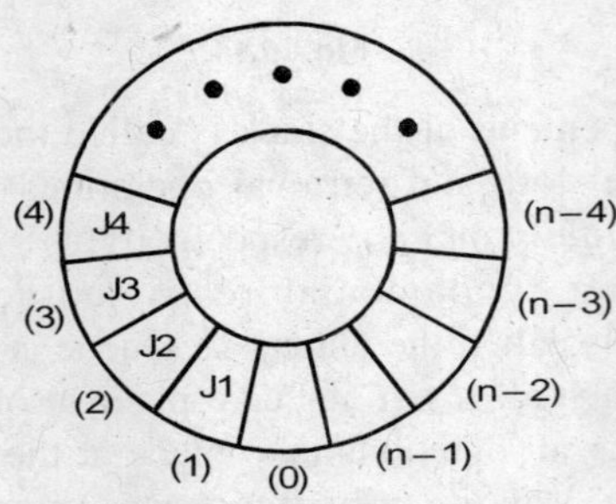

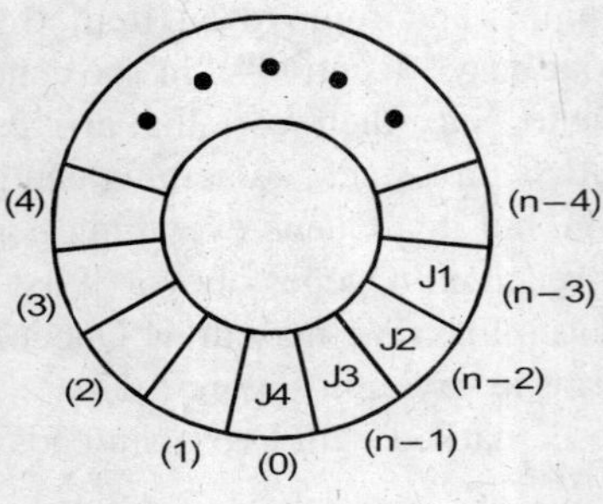

Fig. 5.14: *Circular queue of capacity* n *containing four elements J1, J2, J3, J4.*

In order to insert an element, it will be necessary to move *rear* one position clockwise. This can be done using the code:

if *rear* = *n* – 1 **then** *rear* ← 0
else *rear* ← *rear* + 1
endif.

A more elegant way to do this is to use the built-in modul operator which computers remainders. Before doing an insert we would increase the rear pointer by saying *rear* ← (*rear* + 1) **mod** *n*. Similarly, it will be necessary to move *front* one position clockwise each time a deletion is made. An examination of the algorithms (algorithm (a) and (b)) indicates that by treating the array circularly, addition and deletion for queues can be carried out in a fixed amount of time or $O(1)$.

procedure ADDQ(*item*, Q, *n*, *front*, *rear*)
//insert *item* in the circular queue stored in Q(0:*n* – 1);//
//*rear* points to the last item and *front* is one position//
//counterclockwise from the first item in Q//
rear ←(*rear* + 1)**mod** *n* // advance rear clockwise/
/
if *front* = *rear* **then call** QUEUEFULL **endif**
Q(*rear*) ← *item* //inset new item//
end *ADDQ*

(a) Addition of an element

procedure DELETEQ(*item*, Q, *n*, *front*, *rear*)
//removes the front element of the queue Q(0:*n* – 1)//
//and stores it in *item* .//
if *front* = *rear* **then call** QUEUEEMPTY **endif**
front ← (*front* + 1) **mod** *n* // advance front clockwise//
item ← Q(*front*)// set item to front of queue//
end *DELETEQ*

(b) Deletion of an element

Algorithm: *Basic Queue Operations*

One surprising feature in these two algorithms is that the test for queue full in ADDQ and the test for queue empty in DELETEQ are the same. In the case of ADDQ, however, when *front* = *rear* is actually one space free, Q(*rear*), since the first element in the queue is not at Q(*front*) but is one position clockwise from this point. However, if we insert an item there, then we will not be able to distinguish between the cases full and empty, since this insertion would leave *front* = *rear*. To avoid this, we signal queue full, thus permitting a maximum of *n* – 1 rather than *n* elements to be in the queue at any time. One way to use all *n* positions would be to use another variable, *tag*, to distinguish between the two situations, *i.e.*, *tag* = 0 if and only if the queue is empty. This would however slow down the two algorithms. Since the ADDQ and DELETEQ algorithms will be used many times in any problem involving queues, the loss of one queue position will be more than made up for by the reduction in computing time.

The procedures QUEUEFULL and QUEUE-EMPTY have been used without explanation, but they are similar to STACKFULL and STACK-EMPTY. Their function will depend on the particular application.

Another way to represent a queue would be by using links. Fig. 5.15 shows a queue with the four elements A, B, C, D, entered in that order.

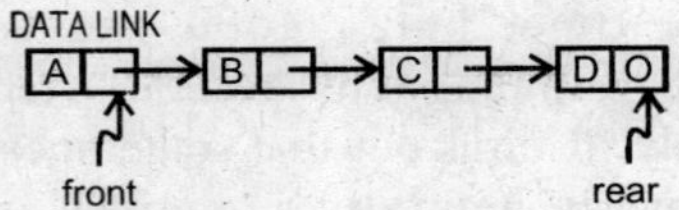

Fig 5.15: *A linked queue with 4 elements.*

As with the linked stack example each node of the queue is composed of the two fields DATA and LINK. A queue is pointed at by two variables, *front* and *rear*. Deletions are made at the front and insertions at the rear. When *front* = 0 that signals an empty queue. Again, when using linked allocation one assumes the existence of procedures GETNODE and RETNODE which operate as they did for stacks. The procedures for insertion and deletion of linked queues are left as exercises.

Heaps and Heapsort

In this section, we study a way of structuring data which permits one to insert elements into a set and also a find the largest element efficiently. A data structure which provides for these two operations is called a *priority queue*. Many algorithms need to make use of priority queues and so an efficient way to implement these operations will be very useful.

We might first consider using a queue since inserting new elements would be very efficient. But finding the largest element would necessitate a scan of the entire queue. A second suggestion would be to use a sorted list which is stored sequentially. But an insertion could require moving all of the items in the list. What we want is a data structure which allows both operations to be done efficiently.

Definition: A *heap* is a complete binary tree with the property that the value at each node is at least as large as the values at its children (if they exist).

This definition implies that a largest element is at the root of the heap. If the elements are distinct, then the root contains the largest item. The relation greater than or equal to may be reserved so that the parent node contains a value as small as or smaller than its children. In this case, the root contains the smallest element. But clinging the historical tradition we will assume that the larger values are closer to the root.

It is possible to take any binary tree containing values for which an ordering exists and move these values around so that the shape of the tree is preserved and the heap property is satisfied, see Fig. 5.16. However, it is more often the case that we are given n items, say n integers and we are free to choose whatever shape binary tree seems most desirable. In this case the complete binary tree is chosen and represented sequentially, see Fig. 5.16. This is why in the definition of heap we insist that a complete binary tree is used.

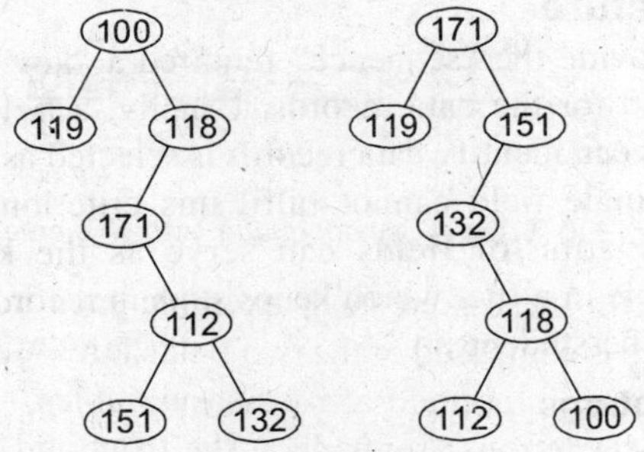

Fig. 5.16: *A binary tree and a heap that preserves the tree's shape.*

Now let us consider how to form a heap given n integers stored in A(1:n). One strategy is to determine how to insert one element at a time into an already existing heap. If we can do this then we can apply the algorithm n times, first inserting one element into an empty heap and continuing in that way until all n elements have been inserted. The solution is simple, one adds a new item "at the bottom" of the heap and then compares it with its parent, grandparent, greatgrandparent, etc. until it is less than or equal to one of these values. Procedure INSERT, Algorithm describes this process in full detail.

```
procedure INSERT(A,n)
  //inserts the value in A(n) into the heap which is
  storet//
  //at A(1) to A(n – 1)//
  integer i, j, n,;
  j ← n; i ← [n/2]; item ← A(n)
  while i > 0 and A(i) < item do
      A(j) ← A(i)        //move the parent down//
      j ← i; i ← [i/2]   //the parent of A(i) is at
                          A([i/2])//
  repeat
  A(j) item        //a place for A(n) is found//
end INSERT
```

Algorithm: *Heap creation by inserting one item at a time.*

Priority Queues 'e'

Many application involving queues require priority queues rather than the simple FIFO strategy. Each queue element has an associated priority value and the elements are served on a priority basis instead of using the order of arrival. For elements of same priority, the FIFO order is used. For example, in a multi-user system, there will be several programmes competing for use of the central processor at one time. The programmes have a priority value associated to them and are held in a priority queue. The programme with the highest priority is given first use of the central processor.

Scheduling of jobs within a time-sharing system is another application of queues. In such a system many users may request processing at a time and computer time divided among these requests. The simplest approach sets up one queue that store all requests for processing. Computer processes the request at the front of the queue and finished it before starting on the next. Same approach is also used when several users want to use the same output device, say a printer.

In a time-sharing system, another common approach used is to process a job only for a specified maximum length of time. If the programme is fully processed within that time, then the computer goes on to the next process. If the programme is not completely processed within the specified time, the intermediate value *s* are stored and the remaining part of the programme is put back on the queue. This approach is useful in handling a mix of long and short jobs.

Terminology

We will now define the term's of the hierarchical structure of computer stored data collections.

1. Field: It is an elementary data item characterised by its size, length and type.

For example:

Name : a character type of size 10

Age : a numeric type

2. Record: It is a collection of related fields that can be treated as a unit from an applications point of view.

For example:

A university could use a student record with the fields, University Enrolment Numbers, Name, Major subjects.

3. File: Data is organised for storage in files. A file is a collection of similar, related records. It has an identifying name.

For example: "STUDENT" could be a file Consisting of student records for all the pupils in a university.

4. Index: An index file corresponds to a data file. It's records contain a key field and a pointer to that record of the data file which has the same value of the key field.

Indexing will be discussed in detail later in the unit.

The data stored in files is accessed by software which can be divided into the following two categories:

5. User Programmes: These are usually written by a programmer to manipulate retrieved data in the manner required by the application.

6. File Operations: These deal with the physical movement of data in and out of files. User programmes effectively use file operations through appropriate programming language syntax. The File Management System manages the independent files and acts as the software interface between the user programmes and the file operations.

File operations can be categorised as:

(i) CREATION of the file,
(ii) INSERTION of records in the file
(iii) UPDATION of previously inserted records
(iv) RETRIEVAL of previously inserted records
(v) DELETION of records
(vi) DELETION of the file.

FILE ORGANISATION

File organisation can most simply be defined as the method of sorting storing data record in a file and the subsequent implications on the way these records can be accessed. The factors involved in selecting a particular file organisation for users are:

- Ease of retrieval
- Convenience of updates
- Economy of storage
- Reliability
- Security
- Integrity

Different file organisations accord the above factors differing weightages. The choice must be made depending upon the individual needs of the particular application in question.

We now introduce in brief the various commonly encountered file organisations.

1. **Sequential Files:** Data records are stored in some specific sequence e.g. order of arrival value of key field etc.
2. **Relative Files:** Each data record has a fixed place in a relative file. Each record must have associated with it in integer key value that will help identify this slot. This key, therefore, will be used for insertion and retrieval of the record. Random as well as sequential access is possible. Relative files can exist only on random access devices like disks.
3. **Direct Files:** These are similar to relative files, except that the key value need not be an integer. The user can specify keys which make sense to his application.
4. **Indexed Sequential Files:** An index is added to the sequential file to provide random access. An overflow area needs to be maintained to permit insertion in sequence.
5. **Indexed Files:** In this file organisation, no sequence is imposed on the storage of records in the data file, therefore, no overflow area is needed. The index, however, is maintained in strict sequence. Multiple indexes are allowed on a file to improve access.

SEQUENTIAL FILES

A sequentially organised file may be stored on either a serial-access or a direct-access storage medium.

Structure

To provide the "sequence" required a "key"must be defined for the data records. Usually, a field whose values can identify data records is selected as the key. If a single field cannot fulfil this criterion, then a combination of fields can serve as the key. For example in a file, which keeps student records, a key could be student no.

Operations

1. Insertion: Records must be inserted at the place dictated by the sequence of the keys. As is obvious, direct insertions into the main data file would lead to frequent rebuilding of the file. This problem could be mitigated by reserving overflow areas in the file for insertions. But this leads to wastage of space and also the overflow areas may also be filled.

The common method is to use transaction logging. This works as follows:

- collect records for insertion in a transaction file in their order of arrival
- when population of the transactions file has ceased, sort the transaction file in the order of the key of the primary data file
- merge the two files on the basis of the key to get a new copy of the primary sequential file.

Such insertions are usually done in a batch mode when the activity/programme, which populates the transaction file, have ceased. The structure of the transaction files records will be identical to that of the primary file.

2. Deletion: Deletion is the reverse process of insertion. The space occupied by the record should be freed for use. Usually, deletion (like-insertion) is not done immediately. The concerned record is written to a transaction file. At the time of merging the corresponding data record will be dropped from the primary data file.

3. Updation: Updation is a combination of insertion and deletions. The record with the new values is inserted and the earlier version deleted. This is also done using transaction files.

4. Retrieval: User programmes will often retrieve data for viewing prior to making decisions, therefore, it is vital that this data reflects the latest state of the data if the merging activity has not yet taken place.

Retrieval is usually done for a particular value of the key field. Before return in to the user, the data record should be merged with the transaction the record (if any) for that key value.

The other two operations "creation" and "deletion" of files are achieved by simple programming language statements.

Following are some of the disadvantages of sequential file organisation:

- Updates are not easily accommodated
- By definition, random access is not possible
- All records must be structurally identical. If a new field has to be added, then every record must be rewritten to provide space for the new field.
- Continuous areas may not possible because both the primary data file and the transaction file must be looked during merging.

Areas of Use

Sequential files are most frequently used in commercial batch oriented data processing where there is the concept of a master file to which details are added periodically. Example is payroll applications.

Direct File Organisation

It offers an effective way to organise data when there is a need to access individual records directly.

To access a record directly (or random access) a relationship is used to translate the key value into a physical address. This is called the mapping function RR. (key value) -- Address

Direct files are stored on DASD (Direct Access Storage Device)

A calculation is performed on the key value to get an address. This address calculation technique is often termed as *hashing*. The calculation applied is called a hash function.

Division-Remainder Hashing

According to this method, key value is divided by an appropriate number, generally a prime number, and the division of remainder is used as the address for the record.

Indexed Sequential File Organisation

When there is need to access records sequentially by some key value and also to access records directly by the same key value, the collection of records may be organised in an effective manner called Indexes Sequential Organisation.

You must be familiar with search process for a word in a language dictionary. The data in the dictionary is stored in sequential manner. However an index is provided in terms of thumb tabs. To search for word we do not search sequentially. We access the index that is the appropriate thumb tab, locate an approximate location for the word and then proceed to find the word sequentially.

To implement the concept of indexed sequential file organisations, we consider an approach in which the index part and data part reside on a separate file. The index file has a tree structure and data file has a sequential structure. Since the data file is sequenced, it is necessary for the index to have an entry for each record following Figure 5.17 shows a sequential file with a two-level index.

Level 1 of the index holds an entry for each three-record section of the main file. The level 2 indexes level 1 in the same way.

When the new records are inserted in the data file, the sequence of records need to be preserved and also the index is accordingly updated.

Two approaches used to implement indexes are static indexes and dynamic indexes.

As the main data file changes due to insertions and deletions, the static index contents may change but the structure does not change. In case of dynamic indexing approach, insertions and deletions in the main data file may lead to changes in the index structure.

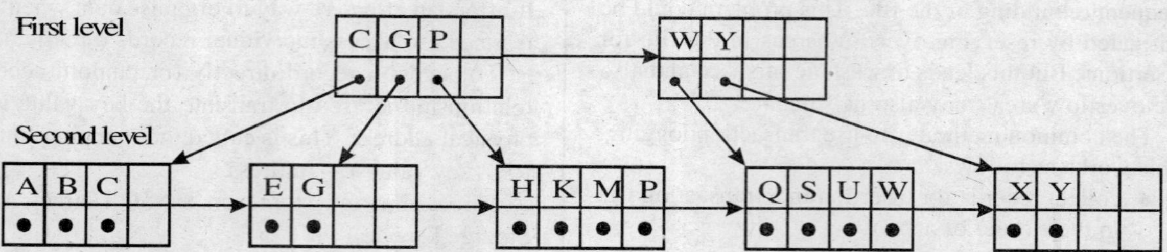

Fig. 5.17: *A sequential file with a two-level index*

Both dynamic and static indexing techniques are useful depending on the type of application.

Sequential File Organisation finds in use in application areas where batch processing is more common. Sequential Files are simple to use and can be stored on inexpensive media. They are suitable for applications that require direct access to only particular records of the collection. They do not provide adequate support for interactive applications.

In direct file organisation, there exists a predictable relationship between the key used and by programme to indentify a particular record and or programmer that record's location on secondary storage. A direct file must be stored on a direct access device. Direct files are used extensively in application areas where interactive processing is used.

An indexed sequential file supports both sequential access by key value and direct access to a particular record given its key value. It is implemented by building an index on top of a sequential data file that resides on a direct access storage device.

The B-tree has additional constraints that ensure that the tree is always balanced and that the space wasted by deletion, if any, never becomes excessive. The algorithms for insertion and deletion, though, become more complex in order to maintain these constraints. Nonetheless, most insertions and deletions are simple processes; they become complicated only under special circumstances-namely, whenever we attempt an insertion into a node that is already full or a deletion from a node that makes it less than half full.

B⁺ Trees

Most implementations of a dynamic multilevel index use a variation of the B-tree data structure called a **B⁺-tree.** In a B-tree, every value of the search field appears once at some level in the tree, along with a data pointer. In a B⁺-tree, data pointers are stored only at the leaf nodes of the tree; hence, the structure of leaf nodes differs from the structure of internal nodes. The leaf nodes have an entry for every value of the search field, along with a data pointer to the record (or to the block that contains this record) if the search field is a key field. For a nonkey search field, the pointer points to a block containing pointers to the data file records, creating an extra level of indirection.

The leaf nodes of the B⁺-tree are usually linked together to provide ordered access on the search field to the records. These leaf nodes are similar to the first (base) level of an index. Internal nodes of the B⁺-tree correspond to the other levels of a multilevel index. Some search field values from the leaf nodes are repeated in the internal nodes of the B⁺-tree to guide the search.

6 PROGRAMMING IN C AND C++

INTRODUCTION

The most power for any computer is its assembly language it provides instructions to exploit every feature of the machine's architecture. But assembly language is unwieldy to use, difficult to learn, and restricts the user to the particular computer for which it is designed. In contrast, languages such as Pascal, FORTRAN and COBOL, while easy to learn, cannot provide such control over the Machine's hardware as its assembly can. Thus, there had for long been a gap in the levels of capabilities provided to the programmer by HLL (High Level Languages) and LLL (Low Level Languages).

Assembly was a second generation programming language that uses simple phrasing in place of the complex series of switches used in machine language.

On the one hand there were the languages that were easy to programme in, and that are reportable across a variety of platforms, and on the other hand, there was assembly, difficult to programme in but which could provide vastly more facilities for control, on a generic, particular machine.

This gap was admirably filled by the advent of C, which offers all the advantages of the high level languages and many of the features that assembly alone can provide and are directly supported by most computers. C is not a "Large" language, in the sense that FORTRAN and COBOL are. But it has a wealth of operators, and a rich library of built in functions, that make for ease of programming and resulting in the construction of efficient programmes.

Early computer languages such as BASIC, COBOL and FORTRAN were not designed around structured principles. Instead, they relied upon the GOTO as a primary means of programmes control, jumps and conditional branches make a programme virtually impossible to understand. While languages like Pascal are structured, they were not designed for efficiency, and failed to include certain features necessary to make them applicable to a wide range of programmes.

The need for a structured effect, programmes invited and first implemented by Dennis Ritchie on a DEC ADP - 11 running the UNIX Operating System, (was the result of a development, process that started with an older language called BCPL, developed by Martin Richards). BCPL influenced a language called B, invented by Ken Thompson, which led to the developments, the *de facto* standard for C was the one supplied with the UNIX operating system and described in the C programming language as brain by Kernighan and Dennis Ritchie. C was formally standardised in December 1989, when the American National Standards Institute (ANSI) Standard for was adopted.

The creation of C is considered to be the beginning of the modern age of computer languages. It was powerful, efficient structure language that was relatively easy to learn. C is a language designed by and for programmers. It was independent of any particular machine architecture or operating system which makes it easy to write portable programmes.

C is a successful and useful language during late 1970s and early 1980s and still today also it is widely used. But the increasing complexity of a programme give the birth to C++. C++ is a response to that need. To managing programme complexity is the fundamental to the creation of C++.

Features of C Language

- Independent of any particular machine architecutre or OS which makes it easy to write portable programmes
- Modular language, each module is designed to perform its specific function.

- Supports recursion, functions can be defined recurively the function may directly or indirectly call itself in the course of its execution
- Its data types and control structures allow the development of well-structured programmes.

PROGRAMMING IN C

All high level languages support the concept of data type. A data type defines a set of values that a variable can store along with a set of operations that can be carried out on that variable. Common data types are integer, character, and real. Although C has five data types, it is not strong types language as other high level languages such as PASCAL, ADA, FORTRAN etc., but C supports direct manipulation of bits, bytes, words and pointers which makes it well suitable for system level programming where these operations are required. C has 32 keywords out of which 27 are given by Kernighan and Ritchie *de facto* standard and remaining 5 added by ANSI standardisation committee.

Structure of a 'C' Programme

The various components of 'C' programme are given below. All C programmes are made up of one or more functions, each performing a particular operation. The first line of C programme is # includes < stdio.h> tells the computer to include information about standard I/O library. This is known as preprocessor directive which should come first followed by global variable definitions, if any. After these the function follows.

Every programme has a special function named main (). It is called to be a special function because the execution of any programme starts at the beginning of its main function. The parentheses are used for passing parameters to a function. The keyword void enclosed with the parenthesis indicates that no ''parameters'' or ''arguments'' are expected by this routine.

Following main function, an open brace { and its parameters lists marks the beginning of function body. The closing brace } marks the end of a function body, is used at the end. If required, the variables declarations and statements are added. Variables are used to hold values during computation and statements specify the computing operation required to achieve the desired result.

Thus a typical 'C' programme has the following sections.

- Preprocessor directives
- Global variable declarations
- Functions

Example :

```
# include < stdio.h>
int main (void)
{
Printf (''A sample programme'');\*
a call to standard Library function
Printf*/
}
```

In the above example # include <stdio.h> is a preprocessor directive. All C compilers have a standard library, which is a collection of commonly used C functions for use by other C programmes. The prototypes for these functions are given in a standard set of header files.

The Print routine is a function in the C system that prints or displays its argument at the terminal. \n (backslash n) are together known as new line character. A new line character tells the C system to go to a new line. Any character printed after the new line character will then appear on the next line of the terminal or display.

* */ are called comments which are standard remarks used within a programme. They make you understand the concept of the programme, what a specific statement/s meant to accomplish. Any line of text bounded by asterisks and enclosed within slashes is a comment. Comments are ineffect from programme's execution point of view and can be placed anywhere within the programme.

Keywords in C

The keywords of C are as follows: *auto, break, case, char, const, continue, default, do, double, else, enum, extern, float, for, goto, if, int, long, register, return, short, signed, sized, static, struct, switch, typedef, union, unsigned, void, volatile, while.*

Constants

Constant is a name C compiler associates with a value that does not change. The constants can be classified into five categories:

1. Integer constants
2. Floating point constants
3. Character constants(Escape sequences)
4. Literal constants (Strings)
5. Enumeration constants

Const is a keyword in C to declare constant, with *const* keyword one requires to use prefixes/suffixes such as l, L used for long integer and double; f,F used for float constants, For Octal leading o is used, For hexadecimal *0x* is written in leading. For unsigned numbers *u*, U suffix is used, Character constant quoted in single quote.

Another method to create a constant in C is to use a **define** directive. The syntax is as follows :

define constant name size of the constant

When C preprocessor later encounters the constant name, the preprocessor will replace the constant name with its value.

Escapes Sequences

An escape sequence is denoted by backslash(\) followed by maximum of three digits (no leading zero is required). Some most commonly used escape characters are as follows:

\a used for bell and the short notation is BEL

\b used for back space and the short notation is BS

\f used for form feed and the short notation is FF

\n used for new line and the short notation is NL

\0 used for null character the short notation is NC

DATA TYPES IN C

There are four data types in: Integer, Floating point, double precision, and character data.

Integer: An integer values, also known as integer constant in C, is any positive or negative number without a decimal point. For example 5, –10, +23423.

Floating point and Double Precision Numbers

This is any signed or unsigned number having a decimal point. For example +10.876, –9.08, 0.0, 8.98, +2., +98.09 etc. The difference between floating point and double precision numbers is the amount of storage that a computer uses for each type. Most computers use twice the computer storage for double precision numbers than for floating point numbers, which allows a double precision number to have approximately twice the precision of a floating point number. Due to this fact floating point numbers are sometimes referred to single precision numbers. However, the actual storage allocation for each data type depends on the particular computer.

Scientific notation: Floating point and double precision number can be written as scientific notation which is commonly used to express either very large or very small numbers in a compact form. In scientific notation, letter *e* stands for exponent. The number following the *e* represents a power of 10 and indicates the number of places the decimal point should be moved to obtain the standard decimal value. The decimal point is moved to the right if the number after the *e* is positive, or moved to the left if the number after the *e* is negative. For example, 1625 can be written in scientific notation as 1.625e3

In the above example *e3* means move the decimal three places to the right so that the number comes 1625. Another example .00741 can be written in scientific notation as 7.41e-3. The *e-3* in this number means move the decimal point three places to the left, so that 7.41e-3 becomes .00741.

Character Type: Character are the letters of the alphabet, ten digits 0 to 9, special symbols such as @, !, $, # etc. A single character constant is any one letter, digit or special symbol enclosed by single quotes. Character constants are stored in a computer using either ASCII or EBCDIC codes. Each of these codes assign individual character to a specific pattern of 0's and 1's. For example, 'M' is a valid character constant which has an ASCII code 01001101.

Operators: Integers, floating point numbers and double precision numbers can be added, subtracted, divided or multiplied. The operators used for these arithmetic operations are known as arithmetic operators.The arithmetic operators are +, –, /, * respectively. Each of these arithmetic operators is a binary operator that requires two operands. A simple arithmetic expression consists of an arithmetic operator connecting two arithmetic operands. For example, 8+9, 87–9, .08*76, 8/4 etc. are arithmetic operands. An expression is a sequence of one or more operands seprated by operators. An operand is a constant, a variable or another expression. A value is associated with an expression. Expressions are evaluated according to precedence and associativity of the operators used in the expression. While evaluating an expression a computer follows these rules:

- If all operands are integers, the result is an integer;
- If any operand is a floating point or double precision value, the result is a double precision number.; and
- The result of an arithmetic expression is never a floating point number because the computer temporarily converts all floating point numbers to double precision numbers when arithmetic is being done.

Integer Division: If you divide integer 15 by integer 2, then you will get only number 7, which is incorrect, because integer cannot store the decimal part. But there are times you want to retain remainder of an integer division. To do this, modulus sign is used in C which captures the remainder when two integers are divided. This modulus symbol uses % symbol. The modulus operator is used only with integers. For example

9 % 4 is 1, 17 % 3 is 2

A Unary Operator: It uses (–) sign in front of a single numerical operand negates (reverse the sign of the number) the number.

Below table lists both the precedence and associativity of the operators.

Table 6.1

OPERATOR	ASSOCIATIVITY
Unary -	right to left
* / %	left to right
+ –	left to right

Expressions containing operators with the same precedence are evaluated according to their associativity. This means evaluation is either from left to right or from right to left as each operator is encountered. For example, 8 + 5 * 7 % 2 * 4, the multiplication and modulus operator are both of higher precedence than the addition operator and are evaluated first. Both of these operators are of equal priority. Therefore, these operators are evaluated according to their left to right associativity, yielding,

8 + 5 * 7 % 2 * 4 =
8+35 % 2 * 4 =
8 + 1 * 4 =
8 + 4 = 12

The assignment symbol = is an operator. Expression using this operator assign a value to a variable; additionally, its expression itself takes on a value. Since assignment is an operation in C, multiple uses of the assignment operator are possible in the same expression.

The increment ++ operator adds one to a variable, while the decrement operator -- subtracts one from a variable. Both of these operators can be used as prefixes or postfixes. In prefix operation, the variable is incremented or decremented before its value is used. In postfix operation, the variable is incremented or decremented after its value is used.

Variables and Declarations

All data used in a computer programme must be stored and retrieved computer's memory. Consider the four bytes of memory storage illustrated in Figure 6.1. For purposes of illustration assume that the two bytes with 1321 and 1322 are used to store one integer number and that the bytes with addresses 2649 and 2450 are used to store a second integer.

Before high-level languages such as C existed, actual memory addresses used to store and retrieve data. For example, storing the number 62 in first set of bytes illustrated in Figure 6.1 and 17 in the next set of bytes required instructions equivalent to put a 62 in location 1321 and put a 17 in location 2649.

Notice that only the address of the first byte in each set of locations was given. The computer needed only this first address to locate the starting storage or retrieval. Adding the two numbers just stored and saving in another set of memory locations, for example at location 45, required a statement comparable to add the contents of location 1321 to the contents of location 2649 and store the result into location 45,

This method of storage and retrieval was a cumbersome process. In high-level languages like C, symbolic names are used in place of actual memory addresses. These symbolic names are called *variables.*

Variable: A variable is simply a name given by the programmer to computer storage locations. A variable name is useful because it frees the programmer from concern over where data is physically stored inside the computer. The term variable is used because the value stored in the variable can change, or vary. For each name that the programmer uses, the computer keeps track of the actual addresses. All variables have an *l value* and an *r value*. The *l value* is the address of the variable and the *r value* is the contents of the variable. Programmer typically uses variable names to reference the variable's contents(its value) while computers uses a variable's name to reference its address(*l value*). The address operator (ampersand) can be used to obtain the variable's *l value*.

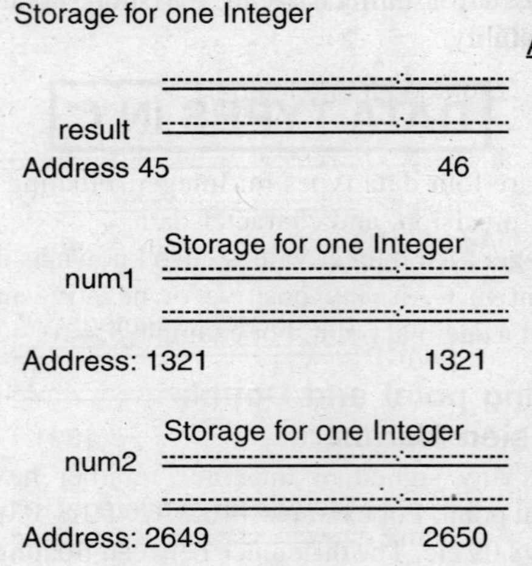

Fig. 6.1

Naming a variable is equivalent to putting a name on the door of a hotel room and referring to the room (or suite of rooms) by this name, such as the Blue Room, rather than using the actual room number.

The selection of variable names is left to the programmer, as long as the following rules are observed:

1. The variable name must begin with a letter or underscore (_), and may contain only letters, underscores, or digits. It cannot contain any blanks, commas, or special symbols, such as ( ) & , $ # . ! \ ? .
2. A variable name cannot be a reserved word
3. Only the first eight characters of a variable name are used by most computers that run C programmes.

These rules are very similar to those used to name functions. As with function names, variable names should be mnemonics that give some indication of the variable's use. For example, a variable named total indicates that this variable will probably be used to store a value that is the total of some other values. As with function names, all variable names are typed in lowercase letters. This again is traditional in C, although not required.

Using these variable names, storing 62 in location 1321, 17 in location 2649, and adding the contents of these two locations is accomplished by the C statements :-

numl = 62;
num2 = 17;
result = num1 + num2

These statements are called *assignment statements* because they tell the computer to assign (store) a value into a variable. Assignment statements always have an (==) equal sign and one variable name immediately to the left of this sign. The value on the right of the equal sign is determined first and this value is assigned to the variable on the left of the equal sign. The blank spaces are used in assignment statement to improve readability.

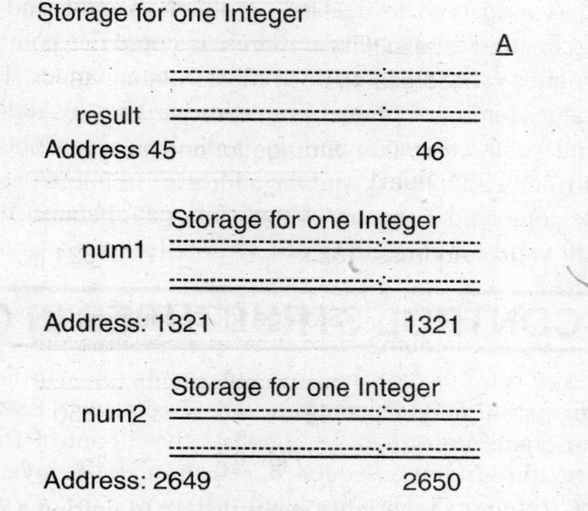

Fig. 6.2

Declaration of a Variable

Every variable in C programme must be declared as to the type of value it can store. We must tell in advance the names of the variable that will be used for characters, the names that will be used for integers and the names that will be used to store the other data types supported by C. Then, when the variable name is used, the computer will know how many bytes of storage to access. Naming and defining the data type that can be stored in each variable is accomplished by using declaration statements.

A simple C programme containing declaration statements has the form:

```
main()
 {
 Declaration statements;
 other statements;
 }
```

Declaration statements always plays software role of informing the compiler of a function's valid variable names. When a variable declaration also causes the computer to set aside memory locations for the variable, the declaration statement is also called a definition statement. The size of operator can be used to determine the amount of storage reserved for variables.

Declarations within a function must be placed as the first statements after a left brace. Variables may also be initialised when they are declared. Additionally, variables of the same type may be declared using a single declaration statement.

BITS, BYTES, ADDRESSES AND NUMBER CODES

It would have been very convenient if computers stored numbers and letter 0 to 8 the way that people do. The number 126, for example, would then be stored as 126, and the letter A stored as the letter A. Unfortunately, due to the physical components used in building a computer, this is not the case.

The smallest and most basic storage unit in a computer is called a *bit*. Physically, *a bit* is really a switch that can be either open or closed. By convention, till open and closed positions of each switch are represented as a 0 and a 1, respectively.

A single bit that can represent the values 0 and 1, by itself, has limited usefulness. All computers, therefore, group a set number of bits together. The grouping of eight bits to form a larger unit is an almost universal computer standard. Such groups are commonly referred to as *bytes*. A single byte consisting of eight bits, where each bit can be 0 or 1, can represent anyone of 256 different bit patterns. These consist of the pattern OOOOOOOO (all eight switches open) to the pattern 11111111 (all eight switches closed), and all possible combinations of 0s and 1s in between. Each of these patterns can be used to represent either a letter of the alphabet, other single characters, such as a dollar sign, comma etc., a single digit or numbers containing more than one digit. The patterns of 0s and 1s are used to represent letters, single digits and other single characters are called character codes. One such code is ASCII code. The patterns used to store numbers are called number codes (one such code, called two's complement). Two's complement numbers are the *most common* integer code using bit patterns is called the two's complement representation. Using this code, the integer equivalent of any bit pattern, such as 10001101, is easy to determine and can be found for either positive or negative numbers with no change in the conversion method.

WORDS AND ADDRESSES

One or more bytes may themselves be grouped into larger units called *words*. The advantage of combining bytes into words is that multiple bytes are stored or retrieved by the computer for each word access. For example, retrieving a word consisting of four bytes results in more information than that obtained by retrieving a word consisting of a single byte. Such a retrieval is also considerably faster than individual retrievals of four single bytes. The increase in speed, however, is achieved by an increase in *cost* and complexity of the computer.

Earlier Personal Computers, such as the Apple and Commodore machines, had words consisting of single bytes. AT&T and IBM Personal Computers, as well as Digital Equipment, Data General, and Prime minicomputers, had *words* consisting of two bytes each. Mainframe computers and advanced microprocessors had four-byte words.

The arrangement of words in a computer's memory can be compared to the arrangement of suites in a very large hotel, where each suite is made up of rooms of the same size. Just as each suite has a unique room number *to* locate and identify it, each word has a unique numeric address. In computers that allow each byte to be individually accessed, each byte has its own address. Like *room* numbers, *word* and byte addresses are always positive, whole numbers that are used for location and identification purposes. Also, like hotel rooms with connecting doors for forming larger suites, words can be combined to form larger units for the accommodation of different size data types.

Literals: Constants are also called literals because they are literally included directly in the statement. Additional examples of literals are contained in the following, C assignment statements. For example :

```
perimeter =', 2 * length * width;
      y = (5 * p) / 7.2;
salestax =005 * purchase;
```

The literals are the numbers 2, 5 and 7.2 and 0.5 in the first, second, and third statements, respectively.

Quite frequently, the same literal appears many times in the same programme.

For example, in a programme used to determine bank interest charges, the interest rate would typically appear in a number of different places throughout the programme. Similarly, in a programme used to calculate taxes and the tax rate .

Literal values that appear many times in the same programme are referred to programmers as *magic numbers.* C provides the programmer with the capability to store the value once, by equatinq the number to a *symbolic name.* Then, instead of using the number throughout the programme, the symbolic name is used in, if the number ever has to be changed, the change need only be made at the point where the symbolic name is equated to the actual number. Equating numbers to symbolic names is accomplished using a *#define* statement. Expressions can be made equivalent to a single identifier using the preprocessor define command. This command has the form *# define* identifier expression. For example, two such statements are:

```
#define SALESTAX 0.05
#define PJ 3.1416
```

(**Note :** no semicolon is used above)

Each compiled C programme is automatically passed through a preprocessor. Lines beginning with # the first column are recognised as commands to this preprocessor. Preprocessor commands are not terminated with a semi-colon. *#Define* command allows the identifier to be used instead of the expression anywhere in the programme after the command. Generally, this statement is placed at the top of the C programme.

Pointer: A pointer is a variable that is used to store the address of another variable. Pointers, like all C variables must be declared. The indirection operator *, is used both to declare a pointer variable and to access the variable whose address is stored in a pointer. Pointer variables like all variables contain values. The value stored in a pointer is an address. Thus by adding and subtracting numbers to pointers we can obtain different addresses. And the addresses in pointers can be compared using any of the relational operators that are valid for comparing other variables.

CONTROL STRUCTURES IN C

Flow of control means the order in which a programme's statements are executed. Every programming language supports three control flow structures namely sequence, selection and *Repetitive* or *Iterative*. Unless directed otherwise, the normal flow of control for all programmes is sequential *i.e.,* statement(s) executes in a sequential manner, one after another, in the order in which they are placed within the programme. Both selection and repetition statements allow the programmer to alter the normal sequential flow of control. Selection statements provide the ability to select which statement will be executed next, while repetition statements provide the ability to go back and repeat a set of statements. Selection requires choosing between alternatives. The expressions used to compare operands are called *relational expression.* A simple relational expression consists of a relational operator connecting two variable and/or constant operand. These relational operators may be used with integer, float, double or character data.

Relational expressions are used to compare operands. Relational expressions are sometimes called *conditions.* If a relational expression is true, the value of the expression is the integer 1. If the relational expression is false, it has an integer value of 0.

Table 6.2 shows a list of Relational operator and their meaning.

In addition to numeric operands, character data can be compared using relational operators.

Logical operators: Most complex conditions can be created using logical operators AND, OR, NOT. These operators are represented by the symbols &&,

| |, ! respectively. When the AND and & operator is used with two simple expressions, the condition is true only if both single expressions are true by themselves. When the OR | | operator is used with two simple expressions, the condition is true only if either one or both single expressions is true. The NOT operator is used to change an expression to its opposite state *i.e.*, if the expression has any non zero value(true) ! expression produces a zero value(false). If an expression is false to begin with (has a zero value), ! expression is true and evaluates to 1.

Table 6.2

OPERATOR	*Meaning*	*Example*
<	less than	age < 90
>	greater than	a > b
<=	less than or equal to	a<= b
>=	greater than or equal to	temp >= 98.6
=	equal to	grade == 100
!=	not equal to	num != 450

The relational and logical operators have a hierarchy of execution similar to arithmetic operators. Table 6.3 lists the precedence of these operators in relation to other operators.

Table 6.3 ***Relational and Logical Operators***

OPERATOR	*ASSOCIATIVITY*
! Unary – ++ – –	right to left
* / %	left to right
+ –	left to right
<<=>>=	left to right
= = !=	left to right
&&	left to right
| |	left to right
+= –= *= /=	right to left

Parentheses can be used to alter the assigned operator priority and improve the readability of relational expressions. For example:

(6 * 3 = = 36 / 2) | | (13 < 3 * 3 + 4) && ! (6 - 2 < 5)

(18 = = 18) | | (13 < 9 + 4) && ! (4 < 5)

1 | | (13 < 13) && ! 1

1 | | 0 && 0

1 | | 0

1

Selection Statement: The *if-else statements* are used to select between two alternative statements based on the value of an expression. Although relational expressions are used for tested expressions, any valid expression can be used. In testing an expression, *if-else statements* interpret a non-zero value as true and a zero value as false. *if-else* statements can contain other *if-else* statements. In the absence of braces, each else is associated with the closest unpaired *if-else* statements.

Compound Statement: A compound statement consists of any number of individual statements enclosed within the brace pair { }. Compound statements are treated as a single unit and can be used anywhere a single statement is called for.

Multi-directional decision branching: A switch statement provides a multi-directional decision branch equivalent to an *if-else* chain. For this statement, the value of an integer expression is compared to a number of integer or character constants or constant expressions. Programme execution is transferred to the first matching case and continues through the end of the Switch statement unless an optional break statement is encountered. Cases in switch statement can appear in any order and an optional default case can be included. The default case is executed if none of the other cases is matched.

Looping Or Repetitive statements: The real power of most computers programmes resides in their ability to repeat the same calculation or sequence of instructions many times over, each time using different data, without the necessity of rerunning the programme for each new set of data values. Some of these statements are *While Statement*, *The for Statement*, *The do Statement*. These statements create programme loops. These statements evaluates an expression and based on the resulting expression value, either terminate the loop or continue with it.

The *while statement* checks its expression before any other statement in the loop. This requires any variables in the tested expression, have values assigned before while is encountered. Within a while loop there must be a statement that alters the tested expression's value. The syntax is as follows :-

```
initialising statements
while (expressions)
{
loop statements ;
-------
--------
expression-altering statements;
}
 For example:-
 count = 1;
while (count <= 10)
{
printf("%d", count);
++count;
}
```

The *for statement* executes loop a fixed number of times. Initialising the expressions, the tested expression and expressions affecting the tested expression can all be included in parentheses at the top of a for loop. Any other loop statement can be included additionally within for's parentheses as part of its altering lists.The syntax is as follows:

for (initialising list; expression; altering list) statement ;

```
For example :-
for (count = 1; count <= 10;
++count;) printf("%d", count);
```

The *'break' statement* can be used to transfer the control to the end of the construct. In looping constructs, it transfers the control to the next statement after the construct. In nested loop constructs, the *break statement terminates* the inner most loop only.

The *'continue' statement* functions just the opposite way of the *'break' statement*. It forces the next iteration of the loop to take place, skimpping in any code in between. It transfers control to the beginning of loop construct. In the for-loop construct, 'continue' transfers control to the increment part of the loop which is evaluated. But in the case of do-while or in while construct, 'continue transfers control to the condition part of the loop', which is evaluated.

The *do statement* checks its expression at the end of the loop. This ensures that the body of a do loop is executed at least once. Within a do loop there must be at least one statement that alters the tested expression's value. The syntax is as follows :

```
do
  Statement;
  while (expression);
```

For example, the following programme requests for an identification number is repeated until a valid number is entered.

```
do
{
printf("\nEnter an identification
                          number: ");
scanf("%f", &id_num);
if (id_num < 1000 | | id_num >
                              1999)
{
printf("\n Invalid number
                          entered");
while (id_num < 1000 | | id_num >
                             1999);
```

Functions in C

1. A function is called by giving its name and passing any data parentheses following the name. If a variable is one of the argument function call the called function receives a copy of the variable 2. The general form of a user-written function is:

```
function_type  function_name
(argument list argument declarations;
{
variable declarations;
other C statements; return
(expression);
```

2. The first two lines of the function are referred to as the function. The opening and closing braces of the function and all statements in these braces constitute the function's body.
3. A function's type is the data type of the value returned by the f1 no type is declared the function is assumed to "return an integer value function does not return a value it should be declared as a *void*.
4. Argument declarations declare the data type of the values passed to function. They are placed before the opening brace that defines the function's body.
5. Functions can formally return only one value to their calling functions.
6. A function that returns a value must be declared in the calling function. This can be done either by physically placing the called function above the calling function in the programme or by including a function declaration within the calling programme.
7. A function can also be passed the address of a variable. This address must be stored in a pointer of the proper type and can be used to directly alter the value stored at the passed address. By passing addresses, a function has the capability of effectively returning many values.
8. Every variable used in a programme has a scope, which determines where in the programme the variable can be used. The scope of a variable is either local or global and is determined by where the variable's definition statement is placed. A local variable is defined within a function and can also be used within its defining function. A global variable is defined outside a function and can be used in any function following the variable's definition. All global variables (which are formally called external variables) are initialised to zero and can be shared between files using the keyword extern.
9. Every variable has a class. The class of a variable determines how long the value in the variable will be retained. Automatic variables are local variables that exist only while their defining function is executing. Register variables are similar to automatic variables but are stored in a computer's internal registers rather than in memory. Static variables can be either global or local and retain their values for the duration of a programme's execution. Static variables are also set to zero when they are defined.

Standard Library Functions: A set of preprogrammed functions for input, output, mathematical procedures and string handling are included in the standard library provided with each C compiler. To use one of these functions, you must obtain the name of the function, the arguments expected by the function, data type of the returned value (if any), and a description of what the function does.

NEED FOR ARRAYS IN PROGRAMMING

Each variable can store a single value at a time. These types of variables are called *scalar variables* because they cannot be further subdivided or seperated into a legitimate data type. A simple list consisting of individual items of the same scalar data type is called a single dimensional array or one dimensional array in computer language.

Each array has sufficient memory reserved for it to hold the number of data items given in the declaration statement. Each item in a list is called an element or component of an array. To access individual elements in one-dimensional array, requires some unique means of identifying each element. Any single item can be accessed by giving the name of the array and the position of the item in the array. The element's position is called *index* or *subscript value*. The first element has an index value of 0, the second element has an index of 1 and so on. The index or subscript value gives the position of the element in the array. The index gives the number of elements to move over, starting from the beginning of the array, to locate the desired element. In C, the array name and index are combined by listing the index in square brackets after the array name. Each individual element is called an indexed variable or subscripted variable, since both variable name and an index or subscript value must be used to reference the element.

Arrays can be declared either global or local arrays. Global array elements are automatically initialised to zero if no other explicit initialisation is given. Global static arrays and local static arrays are also initialised to zero. If no other explicit initialisation is given. Automatic local arrays cannot be initialised when they are declared and contain "garbage" values when they are created.

Arrays are passed to a function by passing the name of the array as an argument. The value actually passed is the address of the first array storage location. Therefore the called function receives direct access to the original array and not a copy of the array elements. Within the called function a formal argument must be declared to receive the passed array name. The declaration of the formal argument can omit the row size of the array.

In most respects an array name and pointer can be used interchangeably. A true pointer however is a variable and the address stored in it can be changed. An array name is a pointer constant and the address stored in the pointer can not be changed by an assignment statement. Elements of an array can be referenced using pointers, a pointer reference can always be replaced with a subscript reference. For example if num_ptr is declared as a pointer variable, the expression * (num_ptr + i) can also be written as num_ptr[i].

Arrays are passed to a function by reference. The called function always receives direct access to the originally declared array elements. When a single dimensional array is passed to a function, the argument declaration for the function can be either an array declaration or a pointer declaration. Thus the following argument declarations are equivalent:

```
float a[ ];
float *a;
```

Two dimensional arrays: They are declared by specifying both a row and a column size. For example, the declaration

```
float taxes [12][20] ;
```

reserves memory space for a table of 12 by 20 floating point values. Individual elements in a two dimensional array are identified by providing both a row and a column index. The element in the first row and first column has row and column subscripts of 0. All static arrays(local or global) and all global two-dimensional array elements are set to zero unless explicitly initialised.

Consider a two dimensional array [3] [4] which consists marks.

	0	1	2	3
0	5	50	11	90
1	12	60	18	10
2	9	10	76	20

Fig. 6.3

To define and initialise two dimensional array, declaration should be done in the following manner.

```
int marks [3] [4] =
{
{5, 50, 11, 90},
{12, 60, 18, 10},
{9, 10, 76, 20}
};
```

The C language allows one to define an array without specification *i.e.*, number of elements. If the number of elements not specified, the size of the array is determined automatically based on number of initialization elements.

String Manipulation: A string constant also known as string is any sequence of characters enclosed in double quotes. For example, "Hello". A

COMPUTER SCIENCE

string is stored as an array of characters terminated by a special end-of-string marker called the null character.

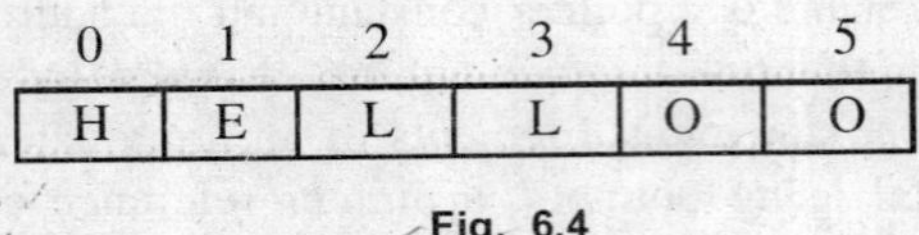

0	1	2	3	4	5
H	E	L	L	O	O

Fig. 6.4

The null character, represented by the escape sequence \0, is the sentinel marking the end of the string. The double quotes are not stored as a part of the string. Since a string is stored as an array of characters, the individual characters in the array can be input, manipulated or output using standard array-handling techniques utilising either subscript or pointer notations . The end of the string null character is useful for detecting the end of the strings when handling string in this fashion.

The gets(), scanf() and getchar() library functions can be used to input a string. The scanf() function tends to be of limited usefulness for string input because it terminates input when a blank is encountered. The puts(), printf(), and putchar() functions can be used to display strings. In place of subscripts, pointer notation and pointer arithmetic are especially useful for manipulating string elements. Many standard library functions exist for processing strings as a complete unit. Internally, these functions manipulate strings in a character by character manner, usually using pointers. String storage can be created by declaring an array of characters or a pointer to a character. A pointer to a character can be assigned a string directly. String assignment to an array of characters is invalid except when in a declaration statement. As with arrays only static and external character arrays can be initialised. These arrays can be initialised using a string assignment of the form

char *arr_name[ ] = "text";

This initialisation is similar to

char *arr_name [ ] = {'t','e','x','t','\0'};

Structures: In broadest sense, structures refers to the way individual elements of a group are arranged or organised. For example, a corporation's structure refers to the organisation of the people and departments in the company and a government's structure refers to its form or arrangement. In programming, a structure refers to the way individual data items are arranged to form a cohesive and related unit. For example, consider the data items used in preparingmailing labels shown below:

Typical mailing list components

Name:
Address:
City:
State:
Pin code:

The contents of a structure are as follows:

Rahul Khanna
89- Lal Road
New Delhi
110090

Note : *This common group of related data items in other languages are referred to as record but in C it is referred as a structure.*

The form of a structure consists of the symbolic names, data types and arrangement of individual data items in the structure. The content of a structure refers to the actual data stored in the symbolic names content

Assigning actual data values to the data items of a structure is called populating the structure which is a relatively straightforward procedure. Each member of a structure is accessed by giving both the structure name and individual data item name separated by a period.

The general form for declaring a structure is as follows:

```
struct
individual member declarations;
} structure_name;
For example :-
main ()
  {
      struct
        {
         int month;
         int day ;
         int year ;
        } birth;
birth.month = 11;
birth.day = 14;
birth.year = 75;
printf("My date of birth is %d/%d
% d", birth.month,birth.day,birth.
year);
}
Note: It can be defined in one
line also e.g
     struct         { int month; int
day ; int year ;} birth;
```

It creates two structures having same form. The members of first structure are referenced by the individual names birth.month , birth.day birth.year and members of DOB will refer as dob.month , dob.day, dob.year.

A tag name can be used to create a generalised structure template in the form and arrangement of elements in a structure. This tag can then be used to define specific structure variables. Structures are particularly useful as elements of arrays. Used in this manner, each structure becomes one record in a list of records.

Individual members of a structure are passed to a function in the manner appropriate to the data type of the member being passed. Some C constructs also allow complete structures to be passed, in which case the called function receives a copy of each element in the structure. The address of structure may also be passed, which provjides the called function with direct access to the structure.

Structure members can be any valid C data type, including structures, unions arrays, and pointers. When a pointer is included as a structure member a linked list can be created. Such a list uses the pointer in one structure "point to" (contain the address of) the next logical structure in the list.

Unions

Unions are declared in the same manner as structures. The definite union creates a memory overlay area, with each union member using same memory storage locations. Thus, only one member of a union may be active at a time.

Arrays of Structures: The real power of structures is realised as the data shown in Figure 6.5a and 6.5b.

Clearly, the employee numbers can be stored together in an array of long integers, the names in an array of pointers, and the pay rates in an array of either floating point or double precision numbers. In organising data in this fashion below is considered as a separate list which is stored in its own array. Using arrays, the correspondence between items for each individual employee is maintained by storing an employee's data in same array position in each array.

Fig. 6.5a. *A List of Employee Data*

Employee' number	*Employee name*	*Employee pay rate*
32479	Abrams, B.	6.7
33623	Bohm, P.	5.56
34145	Donaldson, S.	5.56
3598i'	Ernst, T.	5.43
3620	Gwodz, K.	8.72
36417	Hanson, H.	7.64
3.7634	Monroe, G.	5.29
38321	Price, S.	9.67
39435	Robbins, L.	8.50
39567	Williams, B.	7.20

Using a structure, the integrity of the data organisation as record can be maintained and reflected by the programme. Under this approach, the list illustrated in Figure 6.4 can be processed as a single array" of ten structures.

Declaring an array of structures is the same as declaring an array of any other variable type. For example, if the template pay_recis declared as struct pay_rec (long idnum; char name [20]; float rate;};

then an array of ten such structures can be defined as

```
struct pay_rec employee[10];
```

Fig. 6.5b. *List of Employee Data*

Employee' number	*Employee name*	*Employee pay rate*
32479	Abrams,B.	6.7 -- record1
33623	Bohm, P.	5.56 -- record2
34145	Donaldson, S.	5.56 -- record3
3598i'	Ernst, T.	5.43 -- record4
3620	Gwodz, K.	8.72 :
36417	Hanson, H.	7.64 :
3.7634	Monroe, G.	5.29 :
38321	Price, S.	9.67 :
39435	Robbins, L.	8,50 :
39567	Williams, B.	7.20 -- record10

This definition statement constructs an array of ten elements, each of which is structure of the type pay_rec. Notice that the creation of an array of ten structures has the same form as the creation of any other array. For example, creating an array of ten integers named `employee` requires the declaration

```
int employee[10];
```

This declaration of the data type is integer, while in the former declaration for employee the data type is a structure using the `pay_rec` template.

Once an array of structures is declared, a particular data item is referenced giving the position of the desired structure in the" array followed by a period and the appropriate structure member. For example, the variable employee [0]`.rate` references the `rate` member of the first `employee` structure in the `employee` array. Including structures as elements of an array permits a list of records, to be processed using standard array programmming.

Passing and Returning Structures

Individual structure numbers may be passed to a function in the same manner as any scalar variable. For example, given the structure definition

```
struct {

int id_num; double pay_rate;
                    double hours;
} emp;
```

the statement

```
display(emp.id_num);
```

passes a copy of the structure member emp. id_num to a function

`display ()`. Similarly, the statement

```
calc-pay(emp.pay_rate,emp.hours);
```

passes copies of the values stored in structure members emp.pay._.rate and

COMPUTER SCIENCE

emp.hours to the function calc-pay(). Both functions, display() and calc_pay ( ), must declare the correct data types of their respective. arguments.

On most compilers, complete copies of all members of a structure can also be passed to a function by including the name of the structure as an argument to the called function. For example, the function call

```
calc_net (emp);
```

passes a copy of the complete emp structure to calc_net (). Internal to calc_net ( ), an appropriate declaration must be made to receive the structure. Below programme declares a global template for an employee record. This template is then used by both the main( ) and calc_net( ) functions to define specific structures with the names emp and temp, respectively.

Programme

```
struct employee

/* declare a global template */

int id_num; double pay_rate; double
hours;
} ;
 main (). (

static struct employee emp = {6782,
8.93, 40.5};
double net pay, calc_net();
                          net_pay =
calc_net (empf;           > /* pass
copies -of the value_ in emp */
printf("The net pay for employee%d
1s "$%6..2f",emp.id_num,net-_pay);

}
,double calc__et (temp) struct employee
'temp;
{
return (temp .pay _rate * temp.hours);

/* temp is of data type struct
employee */

return(temp.pay_rate * temp.hours);
```

The output produced by programme is:

The net pay for employee 6782 is $361.66

In reviewing programme observe that both main () and calc_net () use the same global template to define their individual structures. The structure defined in main"( )" and the structure defined in calc_net( ) are two completely different structures. Any changes made to the local temp structure in 'calc _net () are not reflected in 'the emp structure of main ( ). In fact, since both structures are local to their respective functions, the same structure name could have been used in both functions with no ambiguity.

When calc_net. ( ) is called by main(), copies of emp's structure values are passed to the temp structure. calc_net 0, then uses two of the passed member values to calculate a number,' which is returned to main (). Since calc_net ( ) returns a non-integer number, the data type of the value returned must be included in all declarations for calc_net ( ).

Although the structures in both main ( ) and calc_net ( ) use the same globally defined template, this is not strictly necessary. For example, the structure in main ( ) could have been defined directly as:

```
static struct
iint id_num;
double pay_rate;
double,hours;
} emp = {6782, 8..93, 40.5};
```

Similarly, the structure in calc_net ( ) could have been defined as:

```
struct {,

int id_num; double pay_rate; double
hours;
```

In this call, an address is passed. To correctly store this address calc _net ( ) must declare the argument as a pointer. A suitable function definition calc_net () is

```
calc net(pt)
struct employee *pt;
```

Here, the declaration for pt declares' this argument as a pointer to a structure of type employee. The pointer- variable, pt, receives the starting address of a structure whenever calc_net ( ) is called. Within calc_net ( ), this pointer is used to directly reference any member in the structure. For example, (*pt) id_num refers to the id_num m_mber of the structure, (*pt) .pay_rate refers to the pay rate member of the structure, and (*pt) hours refers to the hours member of the structure. These relationships are illustrated in Figure 6.6.

Figure 6.6. A Pointer Can Be Used to Access Structure Members

pt: (*pt).pay_rate

Starting Address of emp-----------------------------

(*pt).pay_rate ------------------------: :

(*pt)id.num=*pt:

emp: id.num : pay-rate : hours :

Fig. 6.6

In the above figure the parentheses around the expression *pt are necessary to initially access "the structure whose address is in pt." This is followed by a reference to access the desired member within the structure. In the absence of the parentheses, the structure member operator takes precedence over the indirection operator. Therefore the expression *pt.hours in another way of writing *(pt. hours), which would refer to "the variable whose address is in the pt.hours variable." This last expression makes no sense because there is no structure named pt and hours does not contain an address. As shown above, the starting address of the emp structure is also the address of the first member of the structure. Thus the expression *pt and (*pt).id_num both refer to the id_num member of the emp structure. The use of pointers is so common with structures that a special notation exists for them. The general expression (*pointer).member can always be replaced with the notation pointer->member, where the -> operator is constructed using a minus sign followed by a right-facing arrow (greater than symbol). Either expression can be used to locate the desired member. For example, the following expressions act the same performance:-

(*pt).id_num can be replaced by pt->id_num

(*pt).pay_rate can be replaced by pt->pay_rate

(*pt).hours can be replaced by pt->hours

Below programme shows a passing a structure's address and using a pointer with the new notation to directly reference the structure.

Programme A1.

```
struct employee
{
int id_num;
employee pay_rate;
 double hours;
 );
    main ()
     (

static struct employee emp = {6782,
8.93, 40.5};
double net. pay  ,  calc_net()
net pay = calc_net(&emp)'
printf ("The net.pay for employee
%d is $%6.2f",emp.id_num,net_pay);
}

double calc_net(pt)
struct employee *pt;
{
return(pt->pay_rate * pt->hours);
}
```

In the above struct employee *pt statement *pt is used as a pointer to a structure of employee type. The name of 'the pointer argument declared in Programme A1\ Selected by the programmer. When calc_net () is called, emp's s1 dress is passed to the function. Using this address as a reference individual members of the structure are accessed by including their names with the pointer.

As with all C expressions that reference a variable, the increment operators can also be applied to structure references. For example, expression '++pt->hours adds one to' the hours member of the emp structure. Since the -> o_ a higher priority than the increment operator, the hours member is first and then the increment is applied.

Alternatively, the expression (pt++) ->hours uses the postfix i operator to increment the address in pt after the hours member. Similarly, the expression (++pt) ->hours, uses the prefix increment operator to increment the address in pt before the hours member is accessed, of these cases, however, there must be sufficient defined structures that the incremented pointers actually point to legitimate structures.

As an example, 'Figure 6.6 illustrates an array of three structure employee! Assuming that the address of emp[1] is stored in the pointer variable pt, the expression ++pt changes the' address in pt to the starting address, of emp [2] , while the expression—pt changes the address to-point to emp [0].

RETURNING STRUCTURES

In practice, most structure-handling functions receive direct access the value by passing the address of the structure to the function. Then any change can be made directly by the function using pointer references.

Figure 3.7 Changing Pointer Addresses

pt `

&emp[1]

The address in pt currently points to emp [1]

Decrementing the address in pt causes the pointer to point here

emp[0] .emp[0] .pay_rate emp[0] .hours
id.num

emp[1] . emp[1] .pay_rate emp[1] . hours
id num'

emp[2]'emp[2] .pay_rate emp[2] .hours
Id.num

Incrementing the 'address in pt causes the pointer to point here

If you have a function return a separate structure, however, and your compiler suit this option, you must follow the same procedures for returning,\complete structures as for returning scalar values. These include both declaring/the, function appropriately and alerting any calling function to the type of structure returned. For example)' the function get_vals ( ) in Programme A4 returns template structure to main ( ).

COMPUTER SCIENCE

Programme A4

```
struct employee

/* declare a global template*/

int id_num;
double pay_rate; double hours;
};
main ()
{
struct employee emp;
struct employee. get_vals () ;

emp= get_vals () ;
intf ("\nThe employee id n_er is
%d", emp. id—.num) ; dntf(n\nThe
employee pay rate. is $%5.2f"_
emp.pay__ate); idntf("\nThe employee
hours are %5.2f")' emp.hours);
}
struct employee get_vals ()
{
struct employee new;

new.id_num = 6189; w.payrate =
16.25; Iw.hours = 38.0;
return (new) ;
```

The following output is displayed when Programme 11-6 is run:

The employee id number is 6189 The employee pay rate is $16.25 The employee hours are 38.00,

Since the get_vals ( ) function returns a structure, the function header for get_vals () must contain the type of structure being returned. As get_val( ) does not receive any arguments, the function header has no argument declarations and consists of single line

struct employee get_vals()

Within get_vals(), the variable new is defined as a structure of the type to be returned. After values have been assigned to the new structure, the structure values are returned by including the structure name within the parentheses of the return statement. On receiving side, main() must be cautioned that the function get_vals() will be returning a structure. This is handled by including a function declaration for get_vals() in main().

Linked List

A classic data-handling problem is making additions or deletions to existing records that are maintained in a specific order. This is best illustrated by considering the alphabetical telephone list shown in Figure 6.7. Starting with this initial set of names and telephone numbers, we desire to add new records to list in the proper alphabetical sequence, and to delete existing records in such a way that the storage for deleted records is eliminated.

Although the insertion or deletion of ordered records can be accomplished by an array of structures, these arrays are not efficient representations for adding or deleting records internal to the array. Arrays are fixed and prespecified size. Deleting a record from an array creates an empty slot that requires either dial marking or shifting up. All elements below the deleted record to close .

Figure 6.7 *Telephone List in Alphabetical Order*

Acme, Sam (201) 898-2392
Dolan, Edith (213) 682-3104
Lanfrank, John (415) 718-4581
Mening, Stephen (914) 382-7070
Zemann, Harold (718)'219-9912

<u>(213) 682-3104</u>
Address of
Lanfrank structure
Dolan, Edith

Similarly, adding a record to the body of an array of structum requires that all elements below the addition be shifted down to make room for the new entry or the new element could be added to the bottom of the existing array and the array then resorted to restore the proper order of the records. Thus, either adding or deleting records to such a list generally requires restructuring and rewriting the list-a cumbersome, time-consuming, and inefficient practice.

A *linked list* provides a convenient method for maintaining a constantly changing list, without the need to continually reorder and restructure the complete list. A linked list is simply a set of structures in which each structure contains at least one member whose value is the address of the next logically ordered structure in the list. Rather than requiring each record to be physically stored in the proper order, each new record is physically added either to the end of the existing list, or wherever the computer has free space in its storage area. The records are "linked" together by including the address of the next record in the record logically preceding it. From a programming standpoint, the current record being processed contains the address of the next record, no matter where the next record is actually stored.

The concept of a linked list is illustrated in Figure 6.8. Although the actual data for the Lanfrank structure illustrated in the figure may be physically stored anywhere in the computer, the additional member included at the end of the Dolan structure maintains the proper alphabetical order. This member provides the starting address of the location where the Lanfrank record is stored. As you might expect, this member is a pointer!

Notice that the pointer in each structure simply points to the location of the next ordered structure, even if that structure is not physically located in the correct order. Removal of a structure from the ordered list is the reverse process of adding a record. The actual record is logically removed from the list by Figure

6.8 using pointers to Link Structures

Dolan, Edith	Lanfrank, John	Hagar, June
(213)682-3104	(415)718-4581	(718)467-1810
Address of Hagar structure	Address of Mening structure	Address of Lanfrank structure

Fig. 6.8

Figure 6.9 Adjusting Addresses to Point to Appropriate Records

Simply changing the address in the structure lure immediately following the deleted record.

Each structure in a linked list has the same format, the last record cannot have a valid pointer value that points to another record, since there is none. C provides a special pointer value called NULL that act as a sentinel or flag to indicate when the last record has been processed. The NULL pointer value, like its end-of-string counterpart, has a numerical value of zero.

Besides an end-of-list sentinel value, a special pointer must also be provided for storing the address of the first structure in the list. Below figure illustrates this the complete set of pointers and structures for a list consisting of three names. The inclusion of a pointer in a structure should not seem surprising. A structure can contain any C data type, *e.g.*

the structure declaration

```
struct test {
int id num;
 double *pt_pay
} ;
```

declares a structure template consisting of two members. The first member is an integer variable named id_num, and the second variable is a pointer named pt_pay, which is a pointer to a double precision number.

Figure 6.10 Use of the Initial and Final Pointer

Address of Acme structure Acme, Sam, Dolan, Edith Lanfrank John

(201) 898-2392	(213) 682-3104	(415)718-4581
Address of Dolan structure	Address of Lanfrank structure	Address of NULL

Below programme illustrates that the pointer member of a structure is used like any other pointer variable.

Programme D7

```
struct test {
int id_num;
double _ptpay;
}
 main () {
struct test emp;
double pay = 456.20;
emp.id_num = 12345;
emp.pt_pay = &pay;
printf("Employee number %d was paid $%6.2f",
emp.id_num, *emp.pt_pay);
}
```

The ouput is as follows :-

Employee number 12345 was paid $456.20

Dynamic Storage Allocation

An alternative to fixed or static allocation of memory storage location is the dynamic allocation of memory. In dynamic allocation method, storage is allocated to a programme and released back to the computer while the programme is running rather than being fixed at compile time. The dynamic allocation of memory is extremely useful when dealing with list of structures, because it allows the list of expand as new records are added and contract as records are deleted. For example, in constructing a list of names and phone numbers, the exact number of structures ultimately needed may not be known. Rather than creating a fixed array of structures, it is extremely useful to have a mechanism whereby the list can be enlarged and shrunk as necessary. Most standard C libraries provide functions that have this dynamic capability. Two of these function *malloc ()* and *free ()* are described below:

malloc (): It reserves the number of bytes requested by the argument passed to the function. Return the address of the first reserved location or NULL if sufficient memory is not available.

free()- Releases a block of bytes previously reserved. The address of the first reserved location is passed as an argument to the function.

In allocating storage dynamically, we do not know where the computer system will physically reserve the requested number of bytes and we have no explicit name to access the newly created storage locations. To provide access to these locations *malloc()* returns the address of the first location has been reserved. This address must, of course, be assigned to a pointer. The return of a pointer by *malloc()* is especially useful for creating a linked list of data structures. As each new structure is created, the pointer returned by *malloc()* to the structure can be assigned to a member of the previous structure in the list. Before illustrating the actual dynamic allocation of in a programme, we will consider one logistic problem created by *malloc()*. The *malloc ()* function always returns a pointer to the first byte of storage considers this first byte as a character. As such the function declaration of *malloc()* is `char` **malloc ()*. Any function that calls *malloc ()* must include this declaration in order to be alerted that a pointer to a character will be returned. This presents a slight problem when using *malloc()* to storage for a structure. Although *malloc* () will reserve the necessary number of bytes for a structure and return the correct address of the first reserved byte, this address will be interpreted as the address of a character to reference subsequent structure members, it must be reinterpreted as pointing to a structure.

The mechanism for converting one data type into another is called a *cast*. In this case, then we need to cast (or force) a pointer to a character into a pointer to a structure. The following programme illustatres using *malloc-()* to create a structure dynamically in response to a user-input request.

Programme

```
# include <stdio.h>
struct tel_typ
{name(30);
phone_no(15)
};
main()
{
char key;
char *malloc();
struct tel_typ * rec_point /* rec_
point is a pointer to a */
            /* structure of type
tel typ */
 printf("Do you wish to create a
new record y/n");
 key = getchar();
 if (key == 'y')
 {
 rec_point = (struct tel_typ
*)malloc(size of(struct tel_type));
  populate(recyoint);
 disp_one(rec_point);
 }
 else
      printf ("'nNo record has been
created.");
 }
 populate (record)     /* get a
name and phone. number */
 struct  tel_typ  *recotd;  /* a
pointer to a structure of type
tel__typ/
 printf ("Enter a name: ");
 gets(record->name);
 printf ("Enter the phone number:
");
  gets(record->phone_no);
 return;
 }
 disp_one(contents)  /* display the
contents of one record */
 struct ,tel_typ *contents; /* a
pointer- to a structure of type
tel_typ */

 printf ("'The contents of the
record just created is:");
printf("'nName: %s",contents->name);
  printf("'nPhone Number: %s",
contents->phone_no); return;
```

The output of the above programme may look like this :-

Do you wish to create a new record *y* or *n:* y
Enter a name: Mono, James
Enter the phone number: (617) 555-1817

The contents of the record just created is:
```
Name: Mono, James
Phone Number: (617) 555-1817
```

In the above programme notice that only, three declarations are made in main ( ). The variable key is declared as a character variable, the malloc() function is declared as providing a pointer to a character, and the variable `rec_point` is declared as being a pointer to a structure of the `tel_typ` type. Since the declaration for the template `tel_typ` is global, `tel_typ` can be used within `main` () to define `rec_point` as a pointer to a structure of the `tel_typ` type.

If a user enters *y* in response to the main(), a call to *malloc()* is made. The argument passed required structure. Although *`malloc()`* returns the address of the first reserved location, this address is considered as pointing to a character. To store the address in `rec_point,` which has been declared as a pointer to a structure the address returned by malloc () is coerced into the proper type by use of the expression `(struct tel_typ *)`.

Once `rec_point` has been loaded with proper address, this address can be used to access the newly created structure. The function populate() is used to prompt the user for data needed in filling the entered data in the correct members of the structure. The argument passed to `populate` () in `main` () is the pointer `rec_point`. The value contained in `rec_point` is passed to the function. Since the value in rec_point is an address, `populate` () actually receives the address of the newly created structure.

Within `populate` (), the value received by it is stored in the argument named `record`. Since the value to be stored, structure, `record` must be declared is the address of a structure, record must be declared as a pointer to a structure. This declaration is provided by the statement `struct` tel_type *record, the statements within `populate` () use the address in record to locate the respective members of the structure.

The `disp_one` () function in programme is used to display the contents of the newly created and populated structure. The address passed to the disp_one() is the same address that was passed to populate(). This passed value is the address of a structure, the argument name used to store the address of a structure, the argument named used to store the address is declared as a pointer to the correct structure type. disp _one () and populate() functions return no values to main (), because they were not declared in the main () [**Note :-**This was done in the above programme to make sure that the computer you are using.] If your compiler supports void data type then your declaration void populate (), disp_one should be included with main ()'s other declaration. Once you understand the mechanism of calling function to construct a linked list of structures. The structures used in a linked list must contain one pointer member. The address in the pointer member is the starting address of the next structure in the list. Additionally, a pointer must be reserved for the address of the first structure, and the pointer member of the last structure in the list is given to a NULL address to indicate that no more members are being pointed to.

The following programme construct a linked list of names and phone numbers.

Programme

```
#include <stdio.h>
 struct tel_typ
(

char name[25];
char phone_no[15]; struct tel_typ
*nextaddr;
) ; main () (

int i;
struct tel_typ *list, *current; I*-
two pointers to structures of type
tel_typ */
char *malloc{}; /* malloc{}
returns a pointer to a char */
/* get a pointer to the first
structure in the list */ list =
(struct tel_typ *) malloc{size
of(struct tel_type;
current = list;
/* populate the current structure
and create two more structures */
for (i -0; i < 2; ++i)
(
populate{current);
current->nextaddr = (struct tel_typ
*) malloc (size of (struct tel_typ));
 current = current->nextaddr;
}
populate(current); /* populate the
last structure */
current->nextaddr = NULL; /* set
the last address */ printf("\nThe
list consists of.the following
records:\n".);
display(list); /* display the
structures */
populate (record) /* get a name
and phone number */
struct tel_typ *record;
/* a pointer to a structure of,
type tel_typ */

(
printf("Enter a name: ");
gets(record_>name);
printf("Enter the phone number: ");
gets(record->phone_no);
return;
display (contents)
/* display till end of. linked list
*/
struct tel_typ *contents; /* a
pointer to a structure of type tel_typ
*/
{
while (contents != NULL)
{
printf("\n%-30s %-20s",contents-
>name, contents->phone_no);
contents = contents->follow;
return;
```

O-O Programming Concepts

Object-orientation is about representing 'objects' in software. Objects are the elements through which we observe the world around us. Our environments composed of 'things' which have recognisable identities and particular behaviours. The most common features of an object are as follows :-

- All objects have these characteristics of identity (what we call an object) and behaviour (what an object does) for recognising them as discrete things.
- Exhibit 'state', which means that we can describe what an object is, as well as what it does and what it is called.
- Objects can be classified into two types. It is instinctive to classify individual objects according to their common characteristics, *e.g.* all dogs are of a single 'type'. Although we may also identify individual differences between specific dogs, our perception is that all individual dogs belongs to a general 'class' which we call 'Dog'. We know about all dogs because we recognise what they have in common.
- Also some objects are composed of other objects, or contain other objects. e.g., a 'house' object is composed of objects such as bricks, windows, doors, tiles etc.

We can identify two kinds of objects:-

1. Those that directly represents the ideas used to describe the application.
2. Those that are artifacts of the implementation-objects used as programming tools to implement the code.

The basic philosophy of using objects in programmes is a simple one-that the world is composed of interacting, classifiable and identifiable objects, and therefore programmes, too can usefully be structured in this way. Since all software applications serve people living in the real world, then that software should mirror the real world as closely as possible, both in its workings and in its underlying design. Thus, object-oriented programing is a more natural way to programme and can be charcterised as data controlling access to code. Object Oriented programming develops a programme around its data and sets well-defined interfaces to that data. There is thus a distinction between objects that are part of an application such as banks, petrol pumps and customers, and others that rare programming tools such as data structures (stacks, queues etc.) which allow us to implement the application objects.

Object-orientation provides true 'modularity', in which software modules (objects) provide the ultimate.

1. **Low (data) Coupling:** *Coupling* is the extent to which different modules rely on one another and for external data in order to function.
2. **High (functional) Cohesion:** *Cohesion* is the extent to which a programming module makes sense as an entity. A module which exhibits 'low coupling' is not tied to a 'particular environment in order to function. The external interface of an object is clearly defined in terms of the operations that object call undergo, and any external inputs that affect the object' s behaviour. Its coupling to other objects is through flexible 'message passing' mechanism and it is only the uses of these message passing mechanisms that will tend to vary widely between applications. Therefore, object is easily 'decoupled' from a particular application and 'coupled' to another.

Cohesion is to some extent a matter of semantics-what the 'meaning' of a particular module is. A 'highly cohesive module is therefore one that has clearly defined role. The ideal type ot cohesion in functional decomposition is 'functional cohesion' by which a module performs one problem-related task. Object-orientation can go further than this and encapsulate together functions related to data representations of real world objects. The semantics of a module then becomes the same as the semantics of the real world-if we can understand something as an object in reality, then we can model it as a cohesive module in software. Not all objects have 'real world' parallels, but 'computational objects' such as stacks, queues and lists exhibit the same characteristics of' modularity as cars, stereos and dogs, since their role in an application is defined by their external behaviours, not by their internal workings.

In principle, OOP is all about 'abstraction' (unification of ideas) at one level and appropriate. 'specialisation' at another. The innate classification of data is the basis of data abstraction.

Data Abstraction: The object oriented model is based on three important concepts namely :

Encapsulation, Inheritance and Polymorphism. Encapsulation is nothing but a mechanism, which binds together code and the data it manipulates. It keeps both safe from outside interference and measure or mishandling. The process by which one object acquires the properties of another object is called inheritance. Polymorphism is a feature that allows one interface to be used for a general class of actions. OOP is a new dicipline based upon a combined data and code abstraction that will help solve a class of programming and associated problems in a less tedious manner than usual. ***Data abstraction helps you to tie data and functions together, which effectively defines a new data type with its own set of operations. Such a data type is called an abstract data type (ADT), also referred to as a class.***

Data abstraction is the process of defining a data type, often called user defined data types or an *abstract data type (ADT),* together with the principle of data hiding. The definition of an ADT involves specifying the internal representation of the ADT's data as well as the functions to be used by others to manipulate the ADT. Data hiding ensures that the internal structure of the ADT can be altered without any fear of breaking the programmes that call the functions provided for operations on that ADT. You can think of the ADT as a template from which specific instances of objects can be created as needed. The ADT is a template for objects in the sense that creating an object involves setting aside a block of memory for the variables of that object. (C ++ supports data abstraction through classes)

Essentially, an ADT is a collection of variables together with the functions necessary to operate on those variables. The variables represent the information contained in the object, whereas the functions define the operations that can be performed on that object. To build an abstract data type in a programme, we have to identify three things:

1. Things which we want to represent
2. Data which represents the state of that 'thing'
3. Behaviour of that 'thing'.

The 'thing' is the name of abstract data type. The 'thing' we are trying to define is not the object but a class of objects which we classify as being of a particular type. The class defines the common attributes and methods fo all objects of the class.

After deciding what our abstract data type is going to represent, we have to identify what elements go to make up its state. These are known as *attributes* in OO terminology, but in programming terms are variables and data structures(e.g arrays, lists etc.). When we identify *attributes* we are not specifying values for them. For example, we might decide that our data type must have the attribute of the 'colour', but we do not predetermine what the colour might be for any individual. For example : All animals have some common attributes such that all animals have a colour of some kind. They have two eyes, one tail, one nose, lips etc.

Basic Components of an Abstract Data Type

There are three basic components of an abstract data type. These are:

1. a unique name
2. attributes
3. methods

Inheritance

Data abstraction does not cover an important characteristic of objects. Real-world objects do not exist in isolation. Each object is related to one or more other objects. In fact, you can often describe a new kind of object by pointing out how the new object's characteristics and behaviour differ from that of a class of objects that already exists. This is what you do when you describe an object with a sentence such as: *B is just like A, except that B has. . ., and B does. . . .* Here you are defining objects of type *B* in terms of those of type *A*.

Inheritance enables us to organise the classes in a hierarchy so that you can place common data and functions in a base class from which other classes can inherit them. Inheritance involves the creation of a new type from an existing user-defined type in some hierarchical fashion. C++ supports inheritance through class derivation. An inheritance hierarchy defines a type/sub-type relationship between class types.

Multiple Inheritance

A real-world object often exhibits characteristics that it inherits from more than one type of objects. For instance, on the basis of eating habits, an animal may be classified as a carnivore; other ways of classification place it in a specific family, such as the bear family. When modelling a corporation, you may want to describe a technical manager as someone who is an engineer as well as a manager. An example from the programming world is a ***full-screen text editor***. It displays a block of text on the screen and also stores the text in an internal buffer so that you can perform operations such as insert a character and delete a character. Thus, you may want to say that a text editor inherits its behaviour from two classes: a *text buffer* class and a *text display* class that, for instance, manages an 80-character by 25-line text display area.

These examples illustrate *multiple inheritance*-the idea that a class can be derived from more than one base class. Many object-oriented programming languages do not support multiple inheritance, but C++ does.

Polymorphism

Polymorphism provides a common interface for several different classes so that objects of those classes can be manipulated identically by the programme. Virtual function mechanism support this concept. Polymorphism helps you keep your programme conceptually simple by enabling you to call the same function to perform similar tasks in all classes in a hierarchy. In a literal sense, polymorphism means the quality of having more than one form. In the context of OOP, polymorphism refers to the fact that a single operation can have different behaviour in different objects. In other words, different objects react differently to the same message. For example, consider the operation of addition. For two numbers, addition should generate the sum. In a programming language that supports OOP, you should be able to express the operation of addition by a single operator, say, +. When this is possible, you can use the expression $x+y$ to denote the sum of x and y, for many different types of x and y: integers, floating-point numbers, and complex numbers, to name a few. You can even define the + operation for two strings to mean the concatenation of the string.

Polymorphism helps by enabling you to simplify the syntax of performing the same operation on a collection of objects. For example, by exploiting polymorphism, you can compute the area of each geometrical shape in an array of shapes with a simple loop like this:

```
/* Assume "shapes" is an array of shapes
(rectangles, circles, * and so on) and "compute_area"
is a function that computes * the area of a shape
 */
 for (i = 0; i < number_ot_shapes;
i++)
    area_of_shape=shapes[i].compute_
area();
```

This is possible because regardless of the exact geometrical shape, each object supports the compute_area function and computes the area in a way appropriate for that shape.

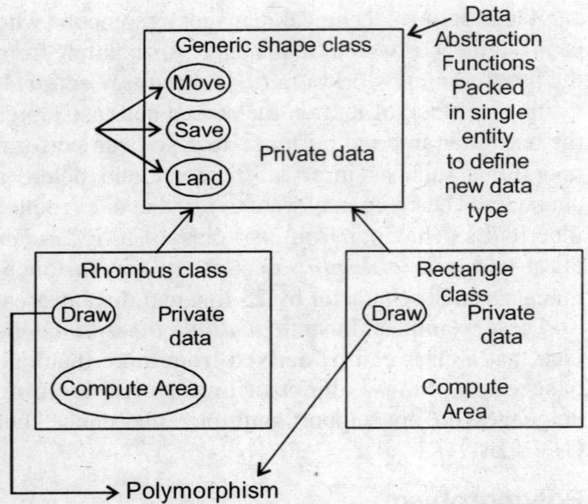

Fig. 6.11: *Polymorphism (same message functions differently in different classes)*

Figure: 6.11 Abstraction, inheritance and polymorphism in OOP. C++ includes these features.

ATTRIBUTES, OPERATION, OBJECTS, CLASSES, ABSTRACTION

Attributes

An attribute is a data value possessed by the objects in a class. Each attribute has a value for each object instance. For example, attribute title has value object book. We can say, the title of the book is the *Ramayan*. Different object instances may have the same or different clause for a given attribute. Each attribute name is unique within a class. Thus, class man and class driver may each have an attribute called *age*. An attribute has to be a pure data value and not an object.

Operation

An operation is a function or transformation that can be applied to or by objects in a class. For example cut, paste are the operation of class window. The same operation may be applied to different classes. Such an operation is polymorphic *i.e.* same operation takes on different forms in different classes. A method is the implimentation of an operation for a class. For example, the class file may have an operation print. Different methods could be implemented to print files, print binary files and print digitised picture files. All these methods logically perform the same task-printing a file, thus it can be reffered to a general term print. But you may implement each method by a different piece of code. An operation may have arguments apart from its target objects. Such arguments parameterise the operation but do not affect the choice of method.

Objects

In object-oriented terminology an object is simply something that makes sense in the common application. The term object is defined as a concept, abstraction, or a thing with defined boundaries and meaning for problem being attended. An object serves two basic purposes. They help in understanding the real world. They provide a practical basis for computer implementation.

Features of an Object:

1. Objects are instinctively classified in terms of types *i.e.* a type of pen, a type of magazine etc. based on the attributes and behaviours they have in common.
2. All objects belong to a particular class of object.
3. Common elements of a set of objects help us in classifying them in an abstract data type. C++ uses the word class to describe an abstract data type.
4. All objects have identity and are distinguishable. Two Maruti cars with same colour, shape are still separate cars, even through they may look the same. The term identity means objects are known by their inherent existence and not by descriptive properties that they may have.

Classes

A class describes a group of objects with similar properties (attributes), common behaviour (operations), common relationships to other objects, and common semantics. Person, team, animal, and door are all object classes. Objects in a class have the same attributes and behaviour patterns. They get their individuality from differences in their attribute values and relationships to other objects. However, objects with identical attributes values and relationships are also possible.

The objects in a class share a common semantic purpose, apart from common attributes and behaviour. Even though a car and a cycle both have a cost and age, they may belong to different classes. A car requires petrol but cycle does not, they would be modelled as distinct classes. The interpretation of semantics depends on the purpose of each application and is a matter of judgement.

Each object "knows" its class. OOP in general can decide an object's class at run time. An object class is an implicit property of the object. A C++ class has four associated components :

1. A set of instance variables (also called data members), the state of the class data members can be static or non static. There may be zero or more data members of any types in a class.

2. A collection of member functions– Member functions can be static or non-static functions. Non-static functions can be either normal functions or overloaded operator functions or conversion functions or constructors or a destructor.
3. Access specifiers—member of a class may be marked as private, protected or public
4. An associated class tag name.

Abstraction

The notion of abstraction is important in OOP. By grouping into classes, we abstract a problem. Abstraction gives modelling its power and ability to generalise from a few specific cases to many similar cases. Commom definitions (such as class name and attribute names) are stored once per class rather than once per instance. Operations can be written once for each class, so that all the objects in the class benefit from code reuse. For example, all triangles share the same procedures to draw them, compute their areas, or test for intersection with a line; polygons would have a separate set of procedures. Even special cases, such as a right angled triangles can use the general procedures, though better procedures are available.

Creation of an Object

In OOP, you create an *object* from an ADT. The term *class* is often used for this template. Consequently, class is synonymous with an ADT.

Method

The functions that operate on an object are known as *method.* This term comes from the object-oriented language *Smalltalk*.The methods define the behaviour of an object. In C++, methods are called the *member functions* of the class. A method is the implementation of an operation for a class. For example, the class Human have an operation eat. Various method could be implemented to eat food, fruits etc. Methods logically do the same eating the eatable, therefore they are all called by a generic operation-eat. However, each method of eating may be implemented by a different code.

An operation may have arguments in addition to its target object. These argument parameterise the operation but do not affect the choice metnod. The method depends only on the class of the target object.

Another common term of OOP originated in *Smalltalk* the idea of sending messages to an object, causing it to perform an operation by invoking one of the methods. In C++, you do this by calling the appropriate member function of the object. For objects implemented in C you can *send a message* by calling a function that accepts a pointer to a data structure representing the ADT's internal structure. Of course the function must be capable of handling the operation you want.

Encapsulation: The idea of combining data and code that go together with the data as a single concept known as object. Encapsulation deals with this unification.

Creating Objects in Object Oriented Language

Object-oriented languages create new objects in two ways. Some languages, such as *Smalltalk*, an operation applied to a class object (called class operation) creates a new of the class. Other languages, such as *C++* and *Eiffel* do not have class objects. These languages have special operations that create new objects.

When a new object is created, the language allocates storage for its attribute values and assigns it a unique object ID, either the address of the storage block or an index in a table. Object-oriented languages, also free the programmer from responsibility of allocating memory for objects.

These languages use one of two styles of destroying objects when they are no longer needed. In some languages, objects are destroyed by an explicit operation (e.g. *destroy*). The programmer should check that no references to a destroyed object remain, otherwise memory access errors may crop up. Explicit memory management is subject to errors. Smalltalk have automatic garbage collectors that destroy objects that are inaccessible, without requiring or allowing any explicit deal location.

Genericity

Parametric polymorphism (generacity)- The primary application of parametric list also termed *generacity*, is an object-oriented systems, since it is a means of handling all data types, defined types, in a generic way. Such methods are therefore applicable to a range of objects. There is an important distinction between functions which are simply overloaded by their parameters, and truly generic functions. An overloaded function name will execute different implementations of the function depending on the type(s) of parameter(s) it is passed. In contrast, however, a generic method will execute the same implementation but be able to accept a range of types as parameters. For example a function name may have different parameters list such as int, float, char, double etc. but it has a single implementation for all data types.

Overloading

Overloading means defining several functions with the same name but varying arguments. It also permits to redefine the meanings of operators such as + - * / % += -= for any class. In other words you can overload the meanings of operators. For example in C++ < <- to overload operator, first define a member function that prints the class members the way you want. Define the operator << function with a reference to an *ostream* and a reference to a class as its first and second arguments respectively. The function's return type should be ostream &. In the body of the function, call your class member function to do the printing and return the first argument, which happens to be the reference to the stream. Now use the << operator to print objects of your class on a stream.

For Example : Suppose you have defined a class for complex numbers, and the << operator to display objects of your class. In other words you code like this:

```
complex z (1 .1, 1.2);
.......
.......
cout << z;
```

You can do this easily by overloading the<< operator. Define the function operator << for your class. The arguments are passed by reference for efficiency, and the cout prefix in the second argument says that you do not want the operator to alter the complex number. The operator << function must return a reference to the stream-this is the key to being able to concatenate the << operators. For example, the following sample programme uses an abbreviated definition for a complex class and goes through the steps necessary to define and use the << operator:

```
#include <iostream.h>
class complex {

/* A simple class for complex numbers


float real, imag;
public:
complex()  { real  =  imag  =  0.0;}
complex(float a, float b) { real void
print(ostream& s) const
};
// requires this function so that
operator<< can do its job by calling
this one
void complex::print(ostream& s)
const
obs << real « . + " << imag;
}
// Overload the operator<< for use
with complex class
ostream& operator<<(ostream &s;
const complex& z) {

z.print(s);
 return s ;

}
// Testing the overloaded <<
operator. . .
main ( )
{
complex a(1.9, 2.4);
cout « " a = " << a << endl;
}
Output of the above programme :
 a = 1.9 + 2.4
```

PROGRAMMING IN C++

C++ was created by extending C with features that are designed to support oriented programming. C++s support for OOP comes through the class and struct constructs, the concepts of overloading functions and operators, and virtual functions. Many features of the C++ language, such as function prototypes, void and enum types, have been incorporated into ANSI standard C, officially known as ANSI X3.159 1989. Because many syntactical details of C+ + are similar to those of ANSI C.

A typical C++ programme would contain four sections:

1. Include files
2. Class declaration
3. Class functional definitions
4. Main function programme

Generally, a programme is organised into three separate files. The class declarations are placed in a header file and the definitions of member functions go into, another file. The approach enables the programmer to separate the abstract specification of the interface (class definition) from implementation details (member function definition). The main programme uses the class is placed in a third file which "includes" the previous two files as well as any other files required.

C++ programmes can be created using any text editor. The file name should have a proper file extension to indicate that it is a C++ programme file. C++ implemantations use extensions such as •C, •C, •CC, •CPP, •C××. Operating system manual should be consulted to determine the proper file name extensions to be used. The process of linking and compiling depends upon the operating system.

C++ programme is a collection of functions. Every C++ programme must have a main ( ). C++ is a free form language. With a few exceptions, the compiler ignores carriage returns and white spaces. C++ statements terminate with semi-colon. Comments starts with a double slash symbol and terminate at the end of the line. A comment may start anywhere in the line and whatever follow is ignored till the end of line. Comment symbol *, * are still valid in C++ and are more suitable for multiline comments.

The header file iostream.h should be included at the beginning of all programmes that use I/O statements. Appropriate header files should be included, depending on the contents of the programme. For example, the header file stdio.h should be included for printf ( ) and scanf ( ) operation.

Tokens

The smallest individual units in a programme are called tokens. C++ has the following tokens:

- **Keywords:** They are explicitly reserved identifiers and cannot be used as names for the programme variables or other user-defined program elements. For example, asm, auto, break, class, delete, inline etc. are keywords.
- **Indentifiers:** It refers to the names of variables, functions, array, classes etc. created by programmer. For naming these identifiers, following rules must be followed :
- Only alphabetic characters, digits and underscores are allowed
- Name cannot start with a digit
- Upper case and lower case letters are distinct
- A declared keyword cannot be used as a variable name.

Basically C++ places no limit on the length of variable name but some operating systems impose a restriction on the length of variable name.

How C++ Differs from C?

To support object-oriented programming, C++ introduced 15 new addition to those reserved by ANSI C. For Example :

asm, friend, private, this, catch, in line, protected, throw, class, new, public, virtual, delete, operator, template

Const Variables: *The const keyword used to prefix the name of a variable indicates that the contents of the variable must not be modified by the programme. Similarly, if a function's argument is pointer and if that pointer is declared to be const, the function cannot modify the contents of the location referenced by that pointer.*

By qualifying an argument to a function by the const keyword, you can inform the C++ compiler that the function should not modify the argument. The compiler will generate an error message if the function inadvertendly tries to alter that argument. The cout qualifier is significant only for arguments that are pointers or that are passed by reference. This is because changes made by a function to arguments passed by value cannot be seen in the calling programme.

C+ + requires you to initialise cout variables when you declare them; ANSI C not. Thus, you can use cout buflen;

// OK in ANSI C but not *in* C++
in ANSI C, but' in C++, you must write

Const buflen = 512; // OK in C++ as well as ANSI C

where 512 happens to be the value of buf len. Cout integers can be used as subscripts and in any expression. This is possible because C++ requires cout variables to be initialised during declaration. Thus, the compiler always knows the value of a cout integer.

This enables you to have the following:

cout buflen = 512;

char buffer [buflen]; // Allowed in C++ but not in *ANSI C*

Because const integers declared this way are full-fledged variables,

In C++ , instead of writing this

```
#define EOF -1
#define maxlen 128 #define Pi
3.14159
char one_line[maxlen];
```

you should write this:

```
const EOF = -1;
const maxlen = 128;
const double Pi = 3.14159;
char one_line[maxlen]; // Define
an array to hold a line
```

Names declared with #def line are not typed, but names declared with `const` have been typed. This information can help the compiler detect errors such as calling a with arguments of the wrong type.

Void *Pointers*

ANSI C allows pointers of type void * to be assigned to any other pointer and any pointer to be assigned to a pointer of type void *. C++ does not allow assignment of a pointer of type void * to any other pointer without an explicit cast. The following example illustrates the difference:

```
void *P_void;
 int i, *p_i;
p_void = &i;        /* Allowed in both
C and C++ */
p_i = P_voidj       /* Allowed ih C but
not in C++ */
p_i = (int *)P_void; /* Cast makes
it OK to use in C++ */
```

Initialisation of Character Arrays

In ANSI C, you can initialise an array of three characters with the following:

```
char name[3] = "You"; // Allowed in
ANSI C but not in C++
```

After the initialisation, the array elements name [0], name [1], and name [2] will be set to y, o, and u, respectively. However, C++ does not allow this type of initialisation, because the array does not have room for the terminating null character. In C++, if you need to set up the name array as you did in C, you have to rewrite the initialisation as follows:

```
char name[3] = {'Y', 'o', 'u'}; //
Allowed in both C and C++
```

COMPUTER SCIENCE

Of course, the following initialisation is valid in both C and C+ +, but this sets up a 4-byte array with the last byte set to a null character:

char name[] = `"You"; //` Allowed `in both C and C++`

`Size of Operator: In ANSI` C, the size of a character constant such as the expression size of ('Q') we evaluate to the same value as size of (int). But, C++ correctly evaluates this size of(char).

Also, in ANSI C, the size of an even variable is same as size of (int). In C++ it will be the `size of` an integral type, not necessarily `size of (int)`.

Scope of Enums

ANSI C, the list of constants appearing in an enum are known throughout the file. C++ considers the constants in an enum to be local to a `class` or a struct known only to member and friend functions of the class. For example, the following code is allowed in C++ but not in ANSI C:

```
struct finite_state_machine
{

enum state{init_ reset, end};
...
}

int init(int state);
// Another variable name state is allowed
```

`in C++ but not in ANSI C`. If a class declares an enum, functions outside the class can refer to the enumerated constants by explicitly qualifying the name using the scope resolution operator.

As an example, suppose you want to refer to the enumerated constant in it which is defined in the class named finite_state_machine, use notation finite_state_machine:: init to access this constant.

Restriction on goto: ANSI C enables you to jump into a block of code, skipping over the declarations and initialisations that may appear in the beginning of the block but C++ does not allow this. For example,

```
goto Start;
........
// OK in ANSI C but not in C++
{int a = 2, b = 4;
Node t1; // This could be a class
char bufI 10] ;
Start:
// . . .
} // Class destructors are called before leaving block
```

Although jumping into a block is a questionable practice in C, such jumps always bound to be fatal in a C++ programme. This is because C++ calls constructors for any class objects created at the beginning of a block, and it calls the corresponding destructors when the block ends. Allowing a jump into the middle of a block mean that there may be calls to destructors for which there were no matching calls to constructors. Typically, that would be a fatal error for the programme.

Defining Data Types in C++

In C++, we define new data types using the class or struct keyword. The term class refers to these user-defined data types created by class or struct. A class declaration specifies the variables in the class, the member functions that manipulate. These objects are a set of rules for controlling access to the member functions and member variables because class is at the heart of object-oriented programming.

DATA TYPES & LOOPS IN C++

Data types are used in all languages to declare variables or Constants) which will contain values when a programme is running. C++ has a range of data types. The data types to declare variables and constants in C++ are given in the Table 6.4 below. C++ allows the declaration of a variable anywhere in the scope. A variable can be declared right at the place of its first use

Table 6.4

Type	*Range*		*Bytes*	*Represent*
TO				
Chart / Short	-128	127	1	Characters
Unsigned Char	0	255	1	Characters
int	-32,768	32,767	2	Whole numbers
Unsigned int	0	65,535	2	Whole numbers
Long	-2,147,438,648	2,149,438,647	4	Whole numbers
Unsigned long	0	4,294,9678,295	4	Whole numbers
float	34×10^{-38}	1.7×10^{308}	8	Whole number
Double	1.7×10^{-383}	1.7×10^{308}	8	Fractional number
Long double	3.4×10^{-4932}	3.4×104932		Fractional number

Data types in C++ are shown below:

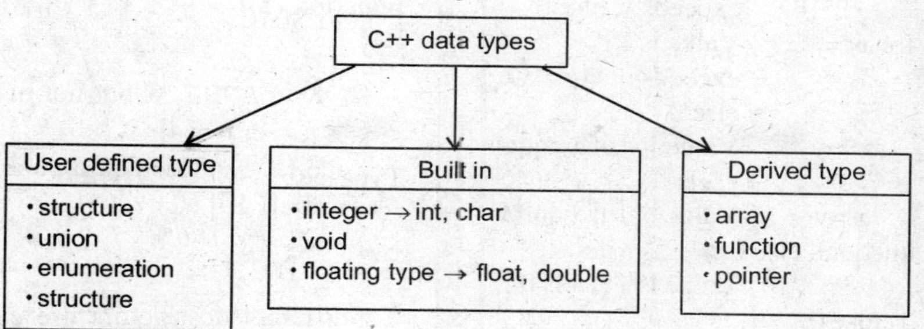

Fig. 6.12

There is also a data type called "void", which means no data type at all. There is no 'string' type in C++. Two normal uses of void are:

- To specify the return type of a funcion when it is not returning any value
- To indicate an empty argument list to a function

Pointers: Pointers are declared using the unary *Operator. The general form is

Type * qualifier - list object_name;

Where type is the name of a type, object_name is a list of qualifiers that apply of the pointer. The qualifiers can be const, volatile, or both. Here are some pointer declarations:

Const int *p - i; // P - i is constant

int * const P-C-1, // pointer P - C - I is constant

char * title = "Object - Oriented Programming in C++" ;

You can declare a pointer to a class member as follows.

class_name :- : * Optimal :- qualifier ptr - name;
where class_name is the name of the class and ptr_name is the name of the member pointer variable. The optional - qualifier is Const, variable, or both. Pointers in C++ are used for memory management and achieving poles morphism.

An array declaration is denoted by adding as suffix a pair of square brackets to one of the following :

1. A fundamental type except void
2. A pointer
3. Class
4. A pointer to a class members.
5. An enumeration.
6. Another array

The syntax for declaring an array is

```
a - type [integer_constant] ;
```

Where a type denotes one of the types of which arrays can be declared and integer_constant is an optional constant expressions that specifies the dimension of the array.

Expressions

An *expression* is a combination of variables, function calls and operators that results in a single value. For example, here is an expr... on whose value is the number of bytes, needed to store the null-terminated string (an array of char with a zero at the end), str:

(strlen(str) * sizeof(char) + 1)

This expression involves a function call, *strlen* (str), and the operator size of as well as a multiplication sign (*) and an addition symbol (+).

ANSI C has a large number of operators, and they are an impol expressions. Table 6.5 summarises the operators in ANSI C. C++ has some new operators such as :: scope resolution operator, ::* pointer to member declarator, →* pointers to member operator, l* pointer to member operator, delete memory release operator, new memory allocation operator, set w field width operator end Line feed operator etc. Several meanings can be given to operator.

Table 6.5 *Summary of ANSI C Operators*

Name of Operator	*Syntax*	*Result*
Arithmetic Operators		
Add	*x+y*	Adds *x* and *y*
Subtract	*x–y*	Subtracts *y* from *x*
Multiply	*x*y*	Multiplies *x* and *y*
Divide	*x/y*	Divides *x* by *y*
Remainder	*x%y*	Computes the remainder 0 by *y*
Preincrement	*++x*	Increments *x* before use.
Postincrement	*x++*	Increments *x* after use
Predecrement	*--x*	Decrements *x* before use.
Postdecrement	*x--*	Decrements *x* after use.
	-x	Negates the value of *x*
Plus	*+x*	Maintains value of *x* unchar
Relational and Logical operators		
Greater than	*x>y*	Value is 1 if *x* exceeds y, else 0
Greater than or equal to	*x>=y*	Value is 1 if *x* exceeds or equals y else 0
Less than	*x<y*	Value is 1 if *y*

COMPUTER SCIENCE

		exceeds x, else 0
Less than or equal to	$x<=y$	Value is 1 if y exceeds or equals x, else 0
Equal to	$x==y$	Value is 1 if x equals y, else 0
Not equal to	$x!=y$	Value is 1 if x and y are unequal, else 0.
Logical NOT	!x	Value is 1 if x is 0, else 0.
Logical AND	$x\&\&y$	Value is 0 if either x or y is 0.
Logical OR	x::y	Value is 0 if both x and y are 0.
Name of Operator	*Syntax*	*Result*
Assignment Operators		
Assignment	x=y	Puts value of y into x
Compound assignment	x 0= y	Equivalent to x = x 0 y where 0 is one of the +-* *1%* >>&
	A:	operators.
Data Access and Size operators		
Subscript	x[y]	Selects the y-th element of array x.
Member selection	$x.y$	Selects member y of structure (or union) x.
Member selection	x->y	Selects member named y from a structure or union whose address is x.
Indirection	*x	Contents of location whose address is x.
Address of object named	&x	Address of data x.
Size of	sizeof(x)	Size (in bytes) of data object named x.
Bitwise Operators		
Bitwise NOT	-x	Changes ll 1s to 0s and 0s to 1s.
Bitwise AND	x&y	Result is bitwise AND of x and y.
Bitwise OR	x | y	Result is bitwise OR of x and y.
Bitwise exclusive OR	x^y	Result _as 1s where corresponding bits of x and y differ.
Left shift	x<<y	Shifts the bits of x to the left by y bit positions. Fills 0s in vacated bit positions.
Right shift	x>>y	Shifts the bits of x to the right h positions. Fills 0s in vacated bit positions.
Miscellaneous Operators		
Function call	x (y)	Result is value returned (if any) by function x which is called with argument y.
Type cast	(type)x	Converts value of x to type whose name appears in parentheses
Conditional	z?x:y	If z is not 0, evaluates x, else evaluates y.
Comma	x,y	First evaluates x, then y

Operator Precedence

Operator Group	*Operator Name Subscript*	*Notation*	*Associativity*
Postfix			
	Function call	x[y]	Left to right
	Member selection	x(y)	
	Member selection	x.y	
	Postincrement	x->y	
	Postdecrement	x++	
	Preincrement	x—	
Unary	Predecrement	++x	Right to left
	Address of &x	—x	
	Indirection	*x	
	Plus	+x	
	Minus	-x	
	Bitwise NOT	-x	
	Logical NOT	Ix	
	Size of size of	x	
	Type cast (type)	x	
Multiplicative	Multiply	x*y	Left to right
	Divide	x/y	
	Remainder	x%y	
Additive	Add	x+y	Left to right
	Subtract	x-y	
Shift	Left shift	x<<y	Left to right
	Right shift	x<<y	
Relational	Greater than	x>y	Left to right
	Greater than or equal	x>=y	
	Less than	x<y	
	Less than or equal	x<=y	
Equality	Equal to	x==y	Left to right
	Not equal to	xl=y	
Bitwise AND	Bitwise AND	x&y	Left to right
Bitwise XOR	Bitwise exclusive	OR × Ay	Left to right
Bitwise OR	Bitwise OR	x:y	Left to right
Logical AND	Logical AND	x&&y	Left to right
Logical OR	Logical OR	x::y	Left to right
Conditional	Conditional	z?x:y	Right to left
Assignment	Assignment	x=y	Right to left
	Multiply assign	x *= y	
	Divide assign	x /= y	
	Remainder assign	x %= y	
	Add assign	x += y	
	Subtract assign	x -= y	
	Left shift assign	x <<= y	
	Right shift assign	x >>= y	
	Bitwise AND assign	x &= y	
Bitwise XOR	assign	x A= y	
	Bitwise OR assign	x := y	
Comma	Comma	x,y	Left to right

Symbolic Constants: There are two ways of creating symbolic constant in C++.

1. Using the qualifier const
2. Define a set of integers constants using enun keyword

In both C and C++, any value declared as const cannot be modified by the programme in any way : C++ requires a const to be initialised. ANSIC does not require an initialiser, if none is given, it initialises the const at 0. The scoping of const value differs. A const in C++ defaults to internal linkage and local to file where it is created. In ANSI C, const values are global in nature. They are visible outside the file in which they are declared. By declaring as static, they can be made local. To give a const value external linkage, so that it can be referred from another file, define as an extern in C++.

C++ combines the power of structured programming with the object oriented paradigm. The syntax for control statements in C++ are very much similar to C. Control statements are if statement (simple and if else), switch statement, do-while statement, the for statement.

Friend Functions

C++ introduces another new keyword-the friend specifier—to help you implement OOP techniques efficiently. The rules of data encapsulation in a class are such that only member functions can access the private data of a class. A class can provide special number functions that can return the values of its private variables, but this approach may be too inefficient in some cases. In that case, you may want to allow a nonmember function to directly access data private to the class. You can do this by declaring that nonmember function within the class with the friend access specifier.

For example, suppose you want to define a nonmember function two complex numbers. The following programme illustrates how to use friend functions to accomplish this.

```
#include <stdio.h>
class complex {
float real, imag;
public:
friend complex add (complex a,
complex b);
  friend void print(complex a);
  complex() { real = imag = 0.0;}
  complex(float a, float b) {real =
a; imag = b;}
};

complex add (complex a, complex b)
{
     complex z;
     z.real = a.real + b.real;
     z.imag = a.imag + b.imag;
     return z;
}
void print(complex a)
{
printf("  (%f  +  i  %f)\n", a.real,
a.imag)j
}main ( )
 {
complex a, b, c,
a = complex(1.6, 2.2);
 b = complex(1.1, 1.4)j
printf("Sum of ");
 print(a);
printf( "and") ;
print(b);

c = add(a,b);
printf (" = ") j print(c);
}
```

This programme uses the friend functions add and print to add two complex numbers and display the results. The output is as follows :-

Sum of (1.600000 + i 2.200000) and (1.100000 + i 1.400000) = (2.700000 + i 3.600000)

Reference Types as Arguments

To pass arguments by reference, just simply add an & after data types of the argument, thus changing all complex&(you can have a space between the type and &). Just add const prefix to the arguments to emphasise that the functions add and print must not alter their arguments.

Rewrite the above programme by using references is as follows :-

```
#include <stdio.h>
class complex {
float real, imag;
public:
friend complex add (const complex
&a, const complex &b);
 friend void print(const complex &a);
 complex() { real = imag = 0.0;}
 complex(float a, float b) {real =
a; imag = b;}
};
complex add (const complex &a, const
complex &b)
{
complex z;
z.real = a.real + b.real
z.imag = a.imag + b.imag;
return z;
}
```

Overloading

Overloading means defining several functions with the same name but varying arguments. It also permits

COMPUTER SCIENCE

to redefine the meanings of operators such as + – * / % += -= for any class. Several meanings can be given to an operator, depending upon the types of arguments used. This process is known as operator over loading. In other words you can overload the meanings of operators. For example, in C++ instead of writing an add function to add two complex variables, you can define the + operator to perform addition for the complex class shown above. By using friend function and const reference types, you might define the + operator as follows:

```
class complex {
float real, imag;
public:
friend complex operator+(const complex &a, const complex &b);
complex() {real = imag = 0.0}
complex(float a, float b) {real = a; imag = b;}
};
complex operator+ (const complex &a, const complex &b)
{
complex z;
z.real = a.real + b.real
z.imag = a.imag + b.imag;
return z;
}
```

Note : Overloading operator is same as complex operator except for a special syntax for the name of the function- the name is the symbol of the operator with the operator keyword as prefix. After defining a + operator for the complex class, you can use it just as would normally use the + operator for other data types.

complex a, b, c;
a = complex(1.6, 2.2);
b=complex(1.2, 1.4)
c = a+b; // Add two complex numbers a and b

In an object-oriented system, we can use this facility to define more than one method with the same name in a single class. This is particularly useful for example in overloading the constructor, so that we can objects with different sets of arguments.

Figure :Overloaded function 'function1'
Function1(..:)

Same function name:
Different parameter list
(int) (char) (char*) (int, float) (char, int)
Separate implementations for each version of the function

```
int x;
"float y;     absoluteValue(int)
absoluteValu&(x);
absoluteValue(y);
      absoluteValue(float)
```

Fig. 13: *The 'absolute value function implementation for different parameter types*

An overloaded constructor gives us different ways of creating objects, allowing us default behaviours to a given constructor and override other behaviours with parameters. Since we can overload the constructor as many times as we like, this is a more flexible mechanism than simply giving default parameter values to a single version of the constructor.

The Class Definition

A class definition has two components:

1. Class head, constituted of the keyword class, followed by the class tag name, normally referred to as class name.
2. Class body, inserted between a couple of curley brackets which should be followed by either a semicolon or a declaration list. Withing the class body, its data members, member functions, and levels of information hiding are specified.

Member Access Control

It is used to enforce information hiding in C++. It is specified by labeled public, private and protected compartments within the class body. A public member can be accessed by any function. Members of a struct or union are public by default. A private member can be accessed only by member functions and friends of the class in which it is declared class members are by default private. A protected member can be accessed by members functions and from the declared class. There may be any number of public, protected or private labeled sections. No particular order of access specifier is required.

Class Members: A class may declare data, functions, enums, bit-fields within its scope, these are referred to as class members. It may also declare type names within its scope; they are called nested types. A class member may be static. It may not be auto, extern, or register. A static data member, enum or hested type may not have the same name as its class.

Class Data Members: As like variable declarations, you can adopt same declaration technique except that initialiser is not permitted. A class can only be initialised by the use of a constructor which is a special non-static member function. The order of allocation of data members with separate access specifier label is implementation dependent. A class object can be declared as a data member only if its class definition has already been detected by the complier. If a class definition has not been discovered forward declaration of the class can be supplied which permits pointers and references do not cause creation of class objects.

Classes as Objects: Describe a new data type together with the functions that can manipulate that type. To represent a new data type, declare the data type in terms of some existing types.

An Example of Controlling Access to Class

Members

For complete support of data abstraction, you need control over who can access what is in a structure. C++ does introduce a new keyword, class, which you can use exactly like struct. Unlike a struct, however, the members of a class are not accessible to any outside functions. In other words, a struct is wide open, but a class is totally hidden. Because neither of these is a good solution, C+ + adds three new keywords to help specify access: private, public, and protected. You can explicitly mark sections of a class or a struct as private, public, and protected as follows:

```
.#include <stddef.h> // For size_t
type
 class String
 {
 public:
 size_t length(void); // Other
publicly accessible member functions

 protected:
 // Members accessible to derived
classes only II . . .

 private:
 // Members accessible to other
members of this class

 char *p_C;
  size_t _length;
  size t _maxlen;
```

The public section lists the members that are accessible to any function in the programme. Only member functions of the class can access the private section. The members in the protected section accessible to classes that are derived from this one.

Public Functions Can Return Private Values

The public section of a class usually declares all the member functions of the class that can be invoked from anywhere in the programme. These functions acts as the interface to the outside world.

To provide the value of a private variable to the outside world, you call a public member function.

Public Member Functions: They are the outside world's gateway to a class. For a class to be useful, it must include a complete set of public member functions. A minimal set should include the following categories of functions:-

Class management functions: Some standard set of functions that perform chores such as creating an instance of the class(constructor), destroying it(destructor), creating an instance and initializing it by copying from another instance(copy constructor), assigning one instance to another type (type conversion operator). They have a standard declaration syntax.

Class Implementation Functions: These functions implement the *behaviour* of the data type represented by the class. They are the workhorse of the class. For a string class, these functions might include operator for concatenating strings and comparison operators such as operator ==, operator>, and operator<.

Class Access Functions: These functions return information about internal variables of a class. The outside world can access the object internal state through these functions. The length function in the string class is a good example of this type of member function.

Class Utility Functions: These member functions, often declared to be private, are used internally within the class for miscellaneous tasks such as error-handling.

Member Functions: Users of a class may carry out a broad range of operations on the class objects. This collection of operations to use and handle an object is declared within the class body. These operations are termed as member functions of the class. Only the member functions of a class are permitted to access the class data members. Functions which are designed to implement the operations allowed on the data type represented by a class. For declaring a member function, place its prototype in the body of the class or struct. There is no need to define the function inside the class, the definition can be outside the class or even in separate file.

Inline Member Functions: Defining a function inside the body of a class has a special consequences. Such definitions are considered to be *inline,* and the entire body of an inline function in a class and often you call it function, you can end up using a large amount of memory for the programme. The main advantage of using inline function is that you avoid the overhead of a function call to execute the body of the function.Thus, you should make a function inline only if the overhead of calling function is a large proportion of the time needed to execute the body of the function. When you have a simple function, such as length in the String class, you can safely define the entire function inside the body of the class, thereby making it inline.

```
class String
{
public:
size_t length(void) { return
_length; }
/ / . . .

private: 1/ . . .
size_t _length;
};
```

COMPUTER SCIENCE

You do not have to define a function inside a class to make it inline. C++ provides the inline keyword that, when placed in front of a function's definition, make it inline. Note, however, that you can use an inline function only in the file in which it is defined. This is because the compiler needs the entire definition of an inline function in the same header file that declares a class to ensure that every programme that uses the class can also use its inline functions. Member functions larger than one or two lines are best defined outside the class body. They need an extra C++ syntax (class scope operator, ": :" to associate then with their class.

Inline junctions are like preprocessor macros without the pitfalls of macros. For example, the following macro

```
#define square(x)  x*x
```

gives you a wrong answer when it is used to evaluate an expression such as square(a+b), because it doesn't use. parentheses around the macro's argument. However, if you define square as an inline function:

in line double square(x) { return X*Xj }

You can safely use square(a+b) to evaluate the square of a+b, because inline functions work just like any C++ function.

Memory Management Operators: C uses malloc ( ) and calloc ( ) functions to allocate memory dynamically at run time. It uses the function free ( ) to free dynamically allocated memory. C++ also support this function; it also defines two unary operators *new* and *delete* that allocate and free the memory in a better and easier way. Since these operators manipulate memory on the free store, they are also known as *free store operators*. An object can be created by using new and destroyed by using delete as when required. A data object created inside a block with new will remain in existence until it is explicitly destroyed by using delete. The new operator can be used to create objects of any type and it has the syntax:

Pointer-variable = new date-type;

pointer of type date type allocates sufficient memory and returns address of object

Destroying Objects on the Free Store

In C++, the operator serves the same purpose as C's free. Like free, the delete expects a pointer to an object as its operand. Thus, if p_code is the point_ instance of Opcode created by the new operator, you can destroy it by the statement.

delete p_code; // Frees storage pointed to by p_code'

In addition to freeing up storage used by the object, if that object's destructor defined, delete calls it to ensure a proper clean-up.

Arrays of Objects on the Free Store

One use of *new* is to allocate an array of objects. The syntax for this is very much is same the way you define arrays. For example, you could define an array of string by writing:

String edit_buf[128];

To create the same array on the free store, you would use this:

String *edit_buf = new String[128] ;

You can use the array of Strings as you would any other array. The first String is edit_buf[0]' the second one is edit_buf[1], and so on. .

There is a special syntax for deallocatting the array of objects on free store. You have to specify the size of the array when deallocating it by using the operator as follows:

```
delete[128] edit_buf;
```

This ensures that the destructor of the String class is called for each element array. Each String object maintains an internal pointer to a character array allocated by the constructor and freed by the destructor. Thus, a call to the destructor of each String in the array takes care of properly deallocating the internal arrays used by the String objects.

Handling Errors in Memory Allocation

If you allocate many objects dynamically, chances are that sooner or later the space will be exhausted and the new operator will fail. When the new operator fails, it tests a fun pointer named _new_handler. If this pointer is zero, new returns a zero jt malloc and canoc do. However, if_new_handler is nonzero, new calls the fun whose address is in _new_handler. In other words, you can handle all mel allocation errors in a central function by setting _new_handler to the addres your error-handling function. The advantage of handling errors this way is thal no longer have to test each use of the new operator for a return value of zero.

You can install an error-handler for new in one of two ways:

The function pointer _new_handler pointer is defined ih the header

<new. h> as follows:

```
void (*_new_handler)();
```

Thus, you can simply include <new. h> and directly set the

_new_handler pointer as follows:

```
#include <new.h>
void my_new_handler(); // Our own error-
handler _new_handler = my_new_handler;
```

The second method is to use the set_new_handler function to install error-handling function as follows:

```
#include <new.h>
set_new_handler(my_new_handler);
```

Garbage Collection Strategies

Object-oriented languages use one of the two methods of destroying objects that are not needed. In some languages like C++ objects are destroyed by an explicit operation(by calling a destroyer). The programmer has to take care of not allowing any remains of the destroyed object in the memory space, but this involves human error element. In C++ garbage collector is not there. Delete operator is used to destroy garbage. Thus there is always a risk of loss of memory to inaccessible objects and their object references. The destructor only cleans up the object on C++. The programmer must see that no remains of object are there after delete operator is used.

Templates

Templates enable us to define generic classes. We can define templates for both classes and function. In C++ genericity is achieved by the use of templates. A template will operate on any data type for which the internal implementation is appropriate. For example, a template function which compares two objects using the '>' operator and returns the higher will operate on any data type for which the '>'symbol is applicable. Since, *through* operator overloading, we can explicitly overload the '>' operator to work with objects of any classes. Templates can be a very useful tool in object-oriented systems. A template can be considered as a kind of macro when an object of a specific type is defined for actual use, the template definition for that class is substituted with required data type. A template is defined with parameter that would be replaced by the specified data type at the time of actual use of the class or function. The templates are also sometimes known as parameteriol classes or functions. Template allows us to define generic classes. It is a simple process to create a generic class using a template with an anonymous type. The general format of a class template is :

```
Tempale < class T >
Class classname
{
      \\......
      \\ class member specification
      \\with anonynous type T
      \\ wherever appropriate
      \\ ....
      };
```

The class template definition is just similar to an ordinary class definition except the refix template <class T> and the use of type T. This prefix tells the compiler that a template is going to be declared and use T as a type name in the declaration. A class created from a class template is called a *template class*. The syntax for defining an object of a template class is as follows:

```
classname <type> objectname
(arglist);
```

This process is called instantiation (*i.e.*, creating a specific class from a class template). Error analysis is performed by compiler only when an instantiation takes place. Thus it is better to create and debug an ordinary class before converting it into a template.

A template can have multiple arguments *i.e.*, in addition to type argument T, we can also use other arguments such as strings, functions flames, constant expressions and built-in types.

Function Template: A function generated from a function template is called template function and like class templates, function templates can also be defined that could be used to create a family of functions with different argument types. The general format of a function template is :

```
template <class T>
return type functionname (arguments
of type T){
        \\...............
        \\ Body of function
        \\ with type T
        \\ whenever appropriate
        \\ ..........
        \\ ...............
}
```

We must use the template parameter T as and when necessary in the function body and in its argument list.

A template function may be overloaded either by template functions or ordinary functions of its name. In those cases overloading resolution is reached as follows:

- call ordinary function that has an exact match
- call a template function that could be created with an exact match.
- perform normal overloading resolution to ordinary functions and call the particulars which matches. If no match is founds, an error occur. No automatic conversions are applied to arguments on the template functions.

The differences between overloading by parameter list, and genericity are as follows :-

(i) We often need to perform a similar process on different data types.

(ii) The data type(s) being processed are passed to a method as parameters.

(iii) With parameter overloading, each type of parameter will cause the compiler to use a different (type specific) method.

(iv) With genericity, a single generic function is able to process all data types, including those

defined by the programmer (i.e objects) all data types are handled by one type generic method.

(v) Genericity can be seen as a more productive technique than overloading. Overloading requires a different implementation to be provided for all possible parameter types, it is not easily extensible to handle new types whereas a generic function only has one implementation which may be used for all parameter types, even those which may not be defined yet.

(vi) Genericity provides a much greater degree of reusability than overloading.

Defining Operations on Objects Arguments and Return Values

In C++, you manipulate objects using member functions and operators defined for the class of which the object is an instance. As a C programmer, you know that functions accept one or more arguments and return a value. C employs the *pass-byvalue* mechanism for providing a function with its arguments. In pass-by-value, functions receive their argument in a special area of memory called the *stack,* which is a last-in, first-out (LIFO) data structure. Before calling a function, the calling programme copies each argument's value onto the stack and passes control to the function. The function retrieves the arguments from the stack and uses them in the body of the function. If necessary, the function can return a single value to the calling programme. The net effect of this mechanism of passing arguments is that the function never accesses the actual storage locations of the arguments that its caller provides. Instead, it always works with a local copy of the arguments. On return from the function, the local copies of the arguments are discarded from the stack.

This *pass-by-value* approach is a good choice for argument passing it guarantees that a function never alters its arguments.

Pointers and References

Although a function that receives its arguments by value cannot alter the what if an argument is the address of a variable in other words, a *pointer to the* variable? In this case, the function can clearly alter the value of the variable through that pointer. For example, suppose you want to swap the contents of two integer variables. One way to do this is to write a function that accepts pointers to int variables, like this:

```
void swap_int(int *p_a, int *p_b)
{
int temp;
temp = *p_a;
*p_a = *p_b;
  *p_b = temp;
}You can- use this function to swap
integer variables as follows: int  x
int x = 12, Y =13;
  swap_int(&x, &y); 1* Now x = 13 and
y = 12 */
```

Although you can continue to use this type of function in C++. C++ introduces the concept of a reference, which makes it much easier to write this type of function. A reference is an alternate name for an object, and use it just as you would use the object itself. A reference is the address of an item except that unlike a pointer, a reference is not a real variable.

A reference is initialised when it is defined, and you cannot modify its value on. The syntax of a reference mimics that of a pointer except that a refe_ needs an ampersand (&) where the pointer declaration has an asterisk (*).

```
int  *p_i;  //  An  un- initialised
pointer to integer
```

defines an int pointer, whereas the following is a reference to an int named i:

int &r _i = i; //I Reference to i (an int variable)

Example - use of reference, here is the swap _int function with arguments passed by reference:

```
void swap_int(int &a, int &b)
{
int temp;
 temp = a;
 a = b;
b = temp;
}
```

Compare this version of the function with the one that uses pointers. You can see that the version that uses references looks cleaner. You no longer have to dereference pointers in each expression. It is also simpler to use the new version of the function, because there is no need to provide as arguments the address of the integers being swapped. Instead, you call the function as if the arguments were being passed by value:

```
void swap_int(int&, int&);
// Prototype of function

int x = 12, Y = 13;
swap_int(x, y);
// Now x = 13 and Y = 12
```

The compiler knows from the function's prototype that it has to pass references to the variables *x* and *y*.

As we can see from the examples in this section, you can think of a reference as a pointer with a constant value that the C++ compiler automatically dereferences whenever you use it. In other words, given the following:

```
int i;     // An integer variable
int &r_i = i; // A reference to "i"
int *p_i = &i; // A pointer to "i"
```

You can think of r - i as being equivalent to P - i, except that wherever you use the expression r - i, the compiler substitutes * P i for it. Because the value of a reference cannot change from its initial assignment the C++ compiler does not have to allocate storage for a reference. All it has to do is to implement the semantics of each reference.

Comparison of Passing by Value & Passing by Reference

When a function implement the pass-by-value semantics, the compiler has to copy the stack before the function is called. For large class objects, copying involves a penalty in space and time. These overheads of copying can be avoided by using reference to the object as the argument instead of using the object itself. If the function does not modify an argument, you can indicate this by using the const qualifier for that reference argument. Thus, passing argument by reference enhances the efficiency of object-based programming in C+ +.

Returning a Reference

Just as passing arguments by reference prevents unnecessary, copying to you can return an object by reference to avoid copying the returned object what happens when you return an object by value. Suppose you return a object from a function add_strings that returns the concatenation of two strings

```
String add_strings(const String& S1, const String& S2)
  {
String S;
// Append s1 and s2 to s
return S;
}
```

In this case, the return statement has to copy the String's to an area of memory provided by the calling programme. To do so properly, the return statement will call a special constructor, the *copy constructor,* which can create and initialise instance of an object from an existing one. After creating the copy, return calls the destructor of the String class to destroy String s before retuning to the programme.

Although returning by reference would save the time spent to copying the object, you cannot return a reference to String *s*, because *s* is a temporary object that exists only within the function add_string *s* and destroyed when the function returns. Thus, you have to be careful while using return by reference. Because a reference is like a pointer, you cannot return reference to anything that is temporary.

A common use of returning by reference is in an access function—a function that gives access to an internal element of an existing object. For example, suppose you want to write a member function named char _at_pos for the string class that gives access to the character at a specified location in an instance of String. In this case, you can safely return a reference to the character at the specified location. Thus, you might write the char _at_pos function as follows:

```
char& String::char_at_pos(int index)
  {
  // Check whether index goes beyond allocated length.
  // Return last element, if it does
  if (index > _maxlen-1) return p_c[_maxlen-1];
  else return p_c[index];
  }
```

Here is a typical use of the function:

```
String s1 = "Temp"; // . . .
//Print the second character of String s1
        cout « "3rd char = " « s1.char_at_pos(2) « endl;
// Change the first character of s1
s1.char_at_pos(0) = 'B'; /I Nows1 = "Bend"
```

You expect the first use of the char_at_pos function to get the character at a specific position in the string, but you may not have realised that you can even set a character to a new value. The second use of char_at_pos is possible only because the functior returns a reference to a char . A reference being exactly like the variable itself, you can assign a new value to the returned reference.

Rules for Using References

You should pass arguments to a function via reference when you want the function to modify the arguments.

The function is not going to modify the arguments. but you want to avoid copying the objects to the stack. In this case, use the const qualifier *r* to indicate that the argument being passed by reference will not be altered by the function.

As for return values, you should return a reference to an object whenever you want to use that return value as the left-hand side of an assignment. Of course you should return a reference to an object only when the object is guaranteed persist after the function returns.

CREATING AND DESTROYING OBJECTS

Although basic data types such as *int* and *float* are simply a chunk of memory holds a single value, a user-defined class can have many more components, Some of which may require additional work during creation besides setting aside a number of bytes of storage. For instance, the String class internally stores a pointer "array of characters that holds the null-terminated string. For proper functioning, newly created String object has to set this pointer to a properly allocated array of chars and, quite possibly, initialise that array to a specific string. If a string to be treated like any other type of variable, you have to be statements such as these:

```
String this_os = "UNIX";
String new_os = this_os;
```

For proper handling of this type of initialization, C++ allows each class special function called the *constructor,* which has the same name as the class and which does not have any return type. Thus, the constructor for the string class is a function named String. As with other functions, you can have one constructor, each with a unique list of arguments and each meant for a specific type of initialisation.

A constructor for a class like String will allocate extra memory for the null terminated string. This means that there must be a way to release this memory when the String is no longer needed. C++ handles this need through destructor, which is a function with the same name as the class but with a title (-) as prefix. Thus, the destructor of the String class is named -String. Destructor do not take any argument. Therefore, you cannot overload a destructor.

C++ does not have class objects or class operations to create instances of a class. It uses a special operation to initialise new objects. The name of the method for the class constructor has the same name as the class.

C++ allows multiple constructors for a single class to be defined, known by the number and types of their arguments called *overloading*.

A constructor is executed whenever a new object instance is allocated. At the time of allocation, programmer specifies the arguments for the constructor; the constructor with matching argument types is executed. If arguments are not specified, then the default constructor with no argument is executed. (A constructor that accepts no parameters is called default constructor.)

A constructor is a 'special' member function used to initialise the objects of its class. It is called constructor since it construct the values of data members of the class.

In C++ constructors and destructors simply initialise and clean up objects. Memory allocation and deallocation are invoked explicitly by the *new* and *delete* operators or implicitly by declaration of level variables.

C++ allows flexibility in memory allocation. The programmer can override the built-in memory allocator for a given class and use a new one. Operators like assignment and type conversion can also be overridden on a class-by-class basis. Hence, it is possible to completely control allocation and creation of objects.

The constructor functions have some special characteristics:

- Should be declared in the public section, when a constructor is declared for a class, initialisation of class objects becomes mandatory.
- Invoked automatically when the objects are created but they can not return values as they do not have return types, not even void.
- Can have default arguments.
- Can not be inherited, through a derived class can call the base class constructor.
- Cannot be virtual.
- Cannot refer to their addresses.
- Objects with a constructor/destructor cannot be used as a member of union.
- When the constructor is parameterised, provide appropriate arguments for the constructor.
- Can also be defined as inline functions.
- The parameters of a constructor can be of any type except that of the class to which it belongs but it can accept a reference to its own class as a parameter. For example (a) :

```
Class A
  {
     _
     _
     _
     _
     _
  Public;
     A (A);
  };
is not correct.
```

Example (b) :

```
Class A
  {
     _
     _
     _
     _
Public;
  A (A&);
  };
```

is correct and the constructor is called the copy constructor.

Multiple Constructors in a CLASS

To use multiple constructors in *e.g.* three constructors for integer object in a class, we define a class as follows:

```
Class integer
{
  int c, d;
  public:
  integer ( ) {C = 0; d = 0;}
                     // constructor 1
  integer (int a, int b)
   { C = a; d = b;}// constructor 2
  integer (integer & i)
  {C = i.c; d = i.d;} //constructor 3
  };
```

In the above, the 1st constructor receives no arguments, 2nd receives two integer arguments, third receives one integer object as an argument.

The statement Integer I1;

invoke the first constructor, both c and d of I1 will get to zero.

The statement Integer I1 920, 30) invoke the second constructor and data members c and d of I2 will set to 20 and 30 respectively. The statement I3 (I2); invoke the third constructor which copies the value of I2 into I3. This is called copy constructor.

Constructors/Destructors for the String Class

The declaration of a String class represents a text string data type, complete with its own operators and string manipulation functions. Based on the general description of the String class, a pointer to an array of bytes hold a null-terminated array of characters, which is the standard way of representing strings in C and C++. The variables _maxlen and length denote the size of the allocated array and the length of the string stored in the array, respectively. To allow for insertion of characters into the String, the size of the char array is rounded up to the next higher multiple of a specified chunk of bytes. For example, if the chunk is 8 bytes, the allocated size of array to hold a 10-character string will be 16 bytes-the nearest multiple of 8 that exceeds 10. This idea is useful if you plan to use the String objects in a text editor, for instance, where you will have to allow for insertion of characters into a String. Refresh your memory, here is a skeleton declaration ofthe String class showing the private members, the constructors, and the destructor:

```
class String
{
public:
 II Constructors with a variety of
arguments
 String ( ) ;
 String(size_t len);
 String(const      char     *str);
String(const String &s);

 II Destructor
    -String();

 /I . . .

 private:
 // Internal data members of this
class

 char *p_C;
  size_t _length;
  size_t _maxlen;

// Pointer to allocated space II
Current length of string // Number
of bytes allocated
};
```

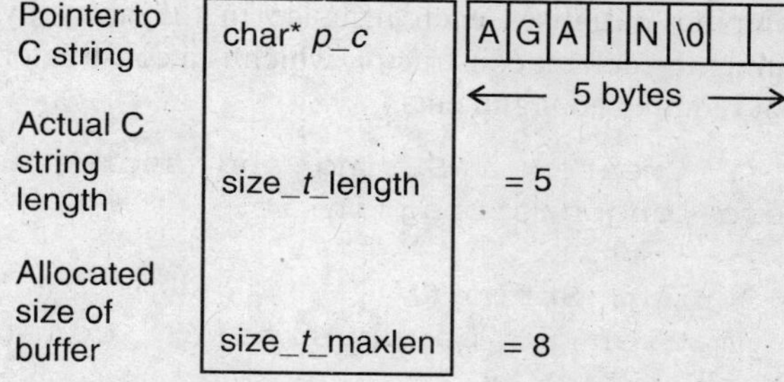

Fig. 6.14 *An instance of the String class.*

Which Constructor is Called Appropriate?

If a class defines constructors, the C++ compiler calls an appropriate constructor to initialise each instance of a class. The way you define the class instances controls the constructor that gets called. The constructor with no arguments is called when you define an instance but do not specify any initial value. For other cases, the type of initial value determines the constructor that the C++ compiler calls.

You can define and initialise a class instance in three ways:

1. Use the C-style syntax as illustrated by the following example for instance of the String class:
   String operating_system = "MS-DOS";
2. Use a function call syntax such as this:
   String operating_system("MS-DOS");

3. Use the new operator to allocate on the free store:

String *lines = new String[25];

In the first two cases, the C++ compiler calls the String (const char*) constructor because you are initialising the String object with a null-terminated character array. Thus, the compiler calls the constructor, which takes as an argument the type of value that you are using to initialise the class instance. In the last case, the compiler calls the constructor that takes no arguments-and it calls this constructor for each of the 25 string objects being created.

Because the String class defines a constructor that accepts a string length argument, the following is an initialisation.

string eight_blanks = `8; //` string with eight blanks

Based on the description of the String(size_ t) constructor, creates a String initialised with eight blank spaces.

Default Constructor

The *default constructor* is a constructor that takes no arguments. For the String class , you can define the default constructor as a function that allocates a single chunk of bytes and initialises it to a zero-length string.

If you define constructors for a class, you should always define a *default constructor* as well. When you define an array of instances of that class, the C++ compiler initialises each instance in the array by calling the default constructor, which is a constructor that requires no arguments.

```
// Creates a String and stores a
zero-length string in it

String::String() {
_maxlen = chunk_size;// const
chunk_size = 8;
p_c = new char[_maxlen];
_length = 0;
p_c[0] = '\0';

}
```

In case of a constructor with no arguments, the upcoming ANSI standard for C++ plans to allow the compiler to use as the default constructor—any constructor that has default values specified for all of its arguments. For a point class that represents point in the *x-y* plane, such a default constructor might be as follows:

```
Point::Point(int x = 0, int y = 0)
{
// Copy x and y coordinates into
internal variables of point }
```

The default constructor is called whenever you define an instance of the class without providing any explicit initial value. Thus, if you were to write:

`String s1; // s1 is initialised by calling default constructor` the String `s1` will be initialised by calling String': :String (), which is the deconstructor of the String class.

When you allocate an array of class instances, the C++ compiler automatically calls the default constructor for each element of the array. Thus if you were to write this:

`String edit_buf[24];` // Create an array of 24 Strings

The default constructor of String will be called to initialise each element array edit_buf.

Dynamic Constructors

Allocation of memory to objects at the time of their constructions is called dynamic constructions of objects. The new operator is used to allocate the memory. In the following programme main function ( ) concatenates three strings into one string. The member function join ( ) concatenates two strings and the system allocates memory for combined string. The function join ( ), length and name are members of the object that calls the function, while a length and a name are member of the argument object *a*.

Programme

```
# include <iostream.h>
# include <string.h>
class string
{
char * nam
int length;
Public;
string ( ) //empty constructor allow
to declare an array of strings.
{
Length = 0;
nam = new char [length + 1] // one
additional character space is
} // allocated to hold the end
of string
     // '\0
{ string (char * d) \ initialise
the length of string and allocates
needful space
     length = strlen (d).
     nam = new char [length +1];
     strcpy nam, d);
}
Void display (void)
{cout << nam << ''\n'';}
void join (string & a, string & b);
};
void string : : join (string & a,
string & b)
{
     Length = a.lenth + b.length;
     delete nam;
```

```
    nam = new char [length +1]; //
dynaic allocation
    strcpy (nam, b.nam);
    strcat (nam, b.nam);
    };
    main ( )
    {
    char * first = ''Ram'';
    string nam1 (first), nam2
(''kumar''), nam3 (''Malhotra''), d1,
d2;
    d1.join (nam1, nam2);
    d2.join (d1, nam3);
    d1.display ( );
    d2.display ( );
    }
```

Output of the programme

Ram Kumar

Ram Kumar Malhotra

Defining Other String Constructors

The String class has a few other constructors besides the default one. One of them takes a number of bytes as argument and creates a blank string with that many. Following is the definition of that constructor:

```
  // This version creates a blank
string of size "len"
  String::String(size_t len)
  {
  _length = len;
  // NOTE: const chunk_size =8;
    _maxlen = chunk_size*(_length /
chunk_size + 1);
  I p_c = new char[_maxlen];
  int i;
  for(i = 0; i < len; i++) p_c[i] = '
';
  p_c[i] = '\0';
  }
```

First the constructor computes - maxlen, the number of bytes to allocate. Then it uses the new operator to allocate the array of chars and initialise the array to a null terminated string containing the specified number of space characters. Another useful constructor for the String class is one that accepts a null terminated character array and creates a String from it. You might define this constructor as follows:

```
  // string
  // Creates a String object and
initialises it from a
  // null-terminated C string

  string::string(Const char *s)
  {
     _length = strlen(s);
  // NOTE: const chunk_size = 8;
     _maxlen = chunk_size*(_length/
chunk_size + 1);
     p_c = new char[_maxlen];
     strcpy(p_c, s);
  }
```

String Destructor

The function of destructor is to reverse anything that was done in the constructor *i.e.* releasing memory that was allocated by the constructor when it created the object. Destructor is used to destroy the objects that have been created by a constructor. Like a constructor, the destructor is a member function whose name is the same as the class name but is preceeded by tilde. A destructor never takes any argument nor does it mention any value. It will be invoked implicitly by compiler upon exit from programme (or block or function as the case may be) to free storage that is no longer used or accessible. Whenever new is used to allocate memory in the constructors, we use delete to free that memory. For the String class, the constructor allocates the array that holds the null-terminated string. The pointer to this array is stored in the private member variable p_c. Thus, the destructor string should free up the memory allocated for the character array:

```
// Destroy a String
String:: ~ String() {
delete p_c;
}
```

Copy Constructor: A copy constructor is a special type of constructor which is capable of creating new object as a replica of an existing one.

Need for Copy Constructor: Suppose you decide to pass a String object by value to a function append_space that, presumably, adds a space at the end of the string. The function should be declared and used as follows:

void append_space(string s);
string s1 = "Test is";
append_space(s1);

C++ compiler makes a copy of string s1 to append_space. The body of string object contains a pointer to the actual null-terminated string. The constructor of the string class takes care of allocating and initialising the memory. To make a copy of string s1 on the stack, the compiler copy each member of string s1 to the stack by default. Both the copy and the original string points to the same null-terminated string because the character pointers are identical. To create a complete copy, define a constructor for the string that takes a String reference as the argument. For the string class, implement copy constructor like shown below. The copy constructor allocates room for null-terminated string and copies into it the C string that was passed to it as an argument. When the copy constructor is used, you get a complete copy of the string.

```
// copy constructor

string::string(Const String &s)
{
      length = s._length;
_maxlen = s._maxlen;
      p_c = new char[_maxlen];
      strcpy(p_c, s.pc);
}
```

The copy constructor also can be written as follows :

String s1 = "Try";

String s2 = s1;

Here string s2 will be initialised by compiler the value of string s1. To do this, compiler looks for a copy constructor for string class.

String(const String&);

Because of the form of the declaration, books and manuals on C++ this as the X(const X&) constructor, where X denotes any class.

Tips : If your class does not include any pointers that have to be initialised properly, then there is no need to provide a copy constructor. The C++ compiler will use a default copy constructor that performs a memberwise copy of one class instance to another.

Provide a copy constructor only for classes with a pointer variable like the String class. If you do not, the result of copying will be as shown for the String objects. Both copies will hold pointers to a single array of characters.

Provide a copy constructor of the form X: : X(const X&) for any class that allocates memory in its constructor. The copy constructor ensures that instances of that class are copied correctly.

Initialise a class that contains an instance of an other class:

Member initialiser list, which is a list of member variable initialisations of the form

variable_name (value)

separated by commas. Here variable_name refers to a member variable of the class, and the value within parentheses denotes the value with which that variable is initialised. The member initialiser list appears between the function's argument list and its body and is guaranteed to be processed *before* the statements in the function's body are executed. You can use the initialiser list syntax for built-in types such as int, double, and char* as well.

```
class Name
{
public :
Name (const char *first, const char
*last);
Private:
String first_name;
String last_name;
};
```

Name: Name(const char *first, const char *last) : first_name(first), last_name(last) {}

Now the compiler can construct an instance of Name in a single step by processing the initialiser list:

1. The compiler calls the String(const char*) constructor of the String class to create the String first_name out of first and the String last_name out of last.

In this case, storage for character arrays is allocated only once for each String, and there are no unnecessary temporary objects. Thus, for reasons of efficiency, you should use initialiser lists to initialise member variables.

Can we Initialise const Member Variables and References?

Even if you were to ignore the efficiency of initialiser lists, on some occasions you must use member initialisers to create an instance of a class. This occurs when the class in question has one of the following:

- A const member variable
- A reference member variable

Both of these member variables, according to the rules of C++, must be initialised when they are defined. In otherwords, these member variables must have a constant value as soon as the class instance is created. In the following example, the integer argument to the constructor is used to initialise the const variable obj_id, and the int reference r_i is set to another integer variable within the class.

Use member initialiser lists to efficiently initialise class members that are instances of other classes. You must use member initialisers to initialise nonstatic const and reference members of a class.

The following fictitious class illustrates how to do this:

```
class TryClass {
public:
// Constructor uses member
initialiser list
TryClass(int id) : obj_id),
r_i(i){}
private:
```

```
const int obj_id;
int i;
int & r_i;
};
```

Functions and Operators

All I/O functions of C are supported by C++. In addition, C++ adds a few unique features of its own. It supports several functions that allow reading and writing of data in both formatted and unformatted forms. The member functions and operators model the behaviour of a class. They define how you use the objects represented by a class. The functions are defined like any other functions, except that you have to indicate the association of a function with a class by using the scope resolution operator (: :). To eliminate the cost of calls of small functions, C++ supports a concept known as *inline function*. These functions are specified with keyword inline. An inline function is inserted wherever a call to that function appears. This is known as *inline expansion*. All inline functions must be defined before they are called. Function names can be overloaded in C++ *i.e.* we can assign the same name to two or more distinct functions.

Example

int mul (int a, int b); // proto type
float mul (float c, float d); // proto type

The function name *mul* is overloaded which means it has more than one implementation. The execution of the correct implementation is decided by the compiler by matching the type of the arguments in the function call with the types in the function proto types.

The this Pointer

C++ uses 'this' to represent an object that invokes a member function. An important application of this is to return the object it points. Before you see how member functions and operators are defined, you need to know about this keyword. First, here is an observation about the member variables and member functions of a class. Although there is a unique copy of member variables for each instance of a class, all instances share a single set of member functions. Yet none of the member functions that you have seen thus far have any way of indicating the class instance whose member variables are being used in the function. Take, for instance, the length function of the String class. If you write this:

```
String s1 ("Hello"), s2("Hai");
   Len1 = s1.length();          // len1 = 5
lerl2 = s2.length(); // len2 = 3
```

each call to length returns a unique answer, yet the length function is defined as follows:

```
inline size_t String::length(void)
const
{
    return _length;
}
```

where _length is a member variable of the String class.

Note : - return the correct length for each string by a function, use this keyword in your programme.

This Points to Instance of Class

The C+ + compiler alters each member function in a class by making two changes:

- It passes an additional argument named this, which is a pointer to the specific object for which the function is being invoked. Thus, the call s1 length() will include an argument this set to the address of the String instance s1._
- It adds the this -> prefix to all member variables and functions. Therefore " the _length variable in the length function becomes this->_length, which refers to the copy of _length in the class instance whose address is in this.
- Typically, you do not have to use this explicitly in a member function but if required, refer to this. For example, if you have to return the object to the calling programme, you can do so with the return statement.

return *this;

The statement return *this; inside a member function will return the object that invoked the function.

You can return a *reference* to the object with the same statement.

You have to return references when defining certain operators such as the assignment operator (=).

The statement return * this; assumes importance when we want to compare two or more objects inside a member function and return the invoking object as a result. For example

```
man & man : : greater (man & x)
{
     if x.age > age
  return x;  // argument object
     else
     return * this;//   invoking
object
     }
```

Suppose we invoke this function by the call

mass = A.greater (B);

The function will return the argument object *i.e.*, object B, if the age of man B is greater than that of A, otherwise it will return invoking object ie object A using the pointer this.

Operators as Functions

Defining operators for a class is easy once you know how the application operator is translated to a function call. For a unary operator such as &, write the following:

&A

where X is an instance of some class, the C++ 'compiler applies the operator by calling this function:

A. operator&()

The compiler automatically passes a pointer to the class instance to the function . For binary operators such as +, an expression such as this:

A + b

where X and Y are class instances, the compiler calls the function:

A.operator+(B)

The C++ compiler reduces the application of operators to calls. Thus, you can overload an operator by defining a function whose name with the keyword operator followed by the symbolic notation of that operator.

Arguments to Operator Functions

Like all member functions, operator functions receive a pointer to the class instance in the hidden argument named this. Because this argument is implicit, unary operator functions are defined with no arguments at all. Binary operator functions that are members of the class take a single argument, which is the right-hand side of the operator expression.

However, you can define an operator function as a friend instead of as a member function of the class.

There are times when you need to define friend operator functions. When declared as a friend, the operator function requires all arguments explicitly. Thus, to declare operator+ as a friend function of class A, you would write the following:

friend A operator+(A&, A&);

// Assume A is a class

and thereafter, to evaluate the expression a1 + a2 for two instances of class X, the C++ compiler will call the function operator+ (a1, a2).

Every member function of a class implicitly receives a pointer to the current instance of the class in a pointer named this. Inside the body of a member function, you can use this to refer to the address of the class instance upon which the function is to operate. Thus, if a function has to return the instance or a reference to it, you can write the following:

return *this;

The dereference operator * produce the contents at the address contained in the pointer.

Note : You do not have to explicitly use the this pointer in the member functions. The C+ + compiler will automatically use the pointer behind the scenes during the process in which members of that instance of the class are accessed.

Operators That You Can Overload

Table 6.5 below lists the C++ operators that you are allowed to overload. You can overload almost all predefined operators in C++. The only ones that you may not overload are the following:

Table 6.5

Member access operator	x.y
Dereferencing pointer to member	x. *y
Scope resolution operator	x: :y
Conditional operator	x?y:z

Exception Handling

C++ lacks certain features such as *exception handling* and *templates.*

Exception handling will provide a uniform way to handle errors in C++ class libraries and programs. Templates will support the definition of parameter classes and functions. The American National Standards Institute (ANSI))X3J16 committee, which is developing a draft standard for the C++ programming language, plans to add templates and exception handling to the C++ language.

Now exception handling is added to ANSI C++.

Exceptions refers to unusual conditions in a programme. They can be outright errors that cause the programme to fail or conditions that can *lead* to errors. When a programmme encounters an exceptional condition it is important that is is dealt with. Exceptions are of two kinds—synchronous and asynchronous exceptions. Errors such as "out of range index" and "overflow" belong to synchronous type exceptions. You can always detect when certain types of errors, are about to occur. For instance, in implementing the subscript function (operator []) of the Array class, you could detect whether the index is beyond the range of valid values. Such errors which occur at a predictable time are called *synchronous exceptions,* because this type of error caused by the *array* index going out of bounds will occur only after executing a Statement where that out-of-bounds index is used.

Asynchronous exceptions, which are caused by events beyond the control of programme (such as keyboard interrupts). Therefore, programme cannot anticipate their time of occurrence . The proposed exception handling mechanism for C++ is meant to cope with synchronous exceptions only. The purpose of exception handling mechanism is to provide means to detect and report on "exceptional circumstance". So to take appropriate actions, the mechanism suggests a separate error handling code which consists of two segments, one to delete errors and to throw exceptions and the other to catch the exceptions and to take appropriate actions. C++ uses keywords throw, try and catch to handle exceptions. When a function returns using the exception handling mechanism, it is referred to as throwing an exception. The keyword throw implements this "return" activity. The keyword try prefaces a block of statements which may generate exceptions: A catch block defined by keyword catch 'catches' the exceptions 'thrown' by throw and handles them appropriately..

Benefits of Exception Handling

```
if ((line = (char *) malloc(MAXCHR))
== NULL) {
/* Failed to allocate mamory; print
message and exit */
fprintf(stperr, "Failed to allocate
memory.\n"); exit ( 1 ) ;
}
```

Whenever you call malloc in your programme, you essentially repeat similar blocks of code over and over again.

Now consider an alternative. Suppose malloc was written so that whenever it fails, it would *jump* (ANSI C's `setjmp` and `longjmp` functions provide the capability to jump from one function to another) to a function that you specify perhaps with an error code as an argument a code that indicates what went wrong. Such a function is typically called a *handler* or an *exception handler*. If you do not provide an exception handler, malloc could jump to a default handler that prints a message and exits. If you do provide a handler, you could handle the error condition anyway you wish. In certain applications, you may not even have to terminate the application. Best of all, with such an exception handler installed you could call malloc without worrying about an error return, because you know that, in case of any allocation failure, malloc will jump to the exception handler. Thus, if you know that there is an exception handler, you can avoid using all those extra lines of code that checks if `malloc` has returned a NULL pointer.

Like malloc, C++ class libraries will have many functions that will de_ error condition and will have to decide how to handle the condition. In fact, handling is an integral part of C++, all class libraries will have a uniform way to cope with all "exceptional conditions." That is why there is an ongoing effort to provide exception handling in C++.

Exception Handling using setjmp and longjmp

In C, you can use the pair of functions setjmp and longjmp to handle conditions. You can save the *state* or the *context* of the process by calling later on, call longjmp with the saved context to revert to a previous point in your programme. The context of a process refers to the information needed to reconstruct exactly the way the process is at a particular point in its flow of execution. ANSI C requires a compiler to define an array data type named. jmp - buf that can hold the information needed to restore a calling environment. This data type is defined in header file. The following example illustrates the use of setjump and longjmp:

```
./

/*- - - - -- - - - - - - - - - - - - -
- - - - - - - - - - - - - - - - - - - -
- - -'- - - - - - - — - - - - - - - -*/
/* Illustrate use of "setjmp" and
"longjmp. to
 * handle exceptions.
 */

#include <setjmp.h>
jmp_buf last_context;
void process_commands(void);
/*    —    *
void main(void)  , {
/*

Establish a context to which you
can return */ if (setjmp (last_context)
== 0)
 {

 process_commands();
 }
 else
 {
 /* This part executed when longjmp
is called
 / * Place code for handling error
here */

 }
 }
 /*- - —- - - - - - - - - - - - - - - -
- - - - - - - - - - - - - - - - - - - -
- - - - - - - - - - - - - - - - -*/ void
process_commands(void)
 {

 int error_flag;
 /* . . . * /
 /* In case of error, return to last
context */ if (error_flag)
longjmp(last_context , 1);
 }
```

The setjmp function saves the current context in the variable last_context text and returns a 0. In this case, the if statement in main is satisfied and process_commands is called. Assume that the integer error _flag is set to 1 when any error occurs in the process commands function. Then, you can handle the error by testing this flag and by calling the longjmp function with two arguments, of which the first one is the jmp but array that contains the context to which you want to return. When the calling environment reverts to this saved state, and longjmp returns, it will be exactly like returning from the call to setjmp that originally saved the buffer last_context. The second argument to longjmp specifies the value to be returned by the function. It should be non-zero so that the if statement in main branches to else clause when the return is induced by a longjmp.

It is tempting to use setjmp and longjmp to handle exceptions in C++ but the calls to constructors and destructors create some problems. All initialised up to the point error must be destroyed before you call longjmp to jump to an error-handling section of the programme. This can be done only if you keep track of all objects created in your programme. Still, at least one mail class library,3 the *NH Class Library,* uses setjmp and longjmp to exceptions.

However, you may not have to devise your own exception handling scheme using setjmp and longjmp, because the ANSI standard for C++ expected to include a well-defined method for handling exceptions in C++ programmes.

The Problem using witb setjmp *and* longjmp

In ANSI C, the pair of functions, setjmp and longjmlp, enables you to jump back from many levels of function calls to a specific location in your programme. In this abort what you were doing and get back to where you started. The setjmp saves the "state" or the "context" of the process; longjmp uses the saved context to revert to a previous point in the programme. The context (or "state") of a process refers to the information that will enable you to reconstruct exactly the way the process is at a particular point in its flow of execution. In ANSI C, an array data type named jmp_buf is used for storing information needed to restore a calling environment. This data type is defined in the header file <setjmp.h>. For example

```
#include <setjmp.h>
jmp_buf saved_context;
main()
{

if (setjmp(Saved_context) == 0)
{
// executed when the first time
set_jmp is called
process_commandS();
}
else
{
// This block is executed when
longjmp is called.
    handle__error();
}
}
process_commands()
{
int error_flag = 0;
// When an error occurs, errOr_flag
is set to 1
//. . .
if                (error_flag)
longjmp(Saved_context, 1);
}
```

When you call the setjmp *function,* it will save the current context in the jmp - buf variable named saved_context and return a zero. In this case, the first if statement in main is satisfied, and the process commands function is called. If there is any error in process_commands, the error _flag will be set to a non-zero value, and we will *call-1ongjmp* with the following arguments:

The first argument is the jmp_buf variable, which contains the context to
which *longjmp should* return.

The second argument specifies the return value to be used during this return.

The *longjmp* function will first revert the calling environment to this saved state; this amounts to "unrolling" or "unwinding" the stack back to where it was when setjmp was originally called. After reverting to the saved context, long jump returns. When the return statement in long j mp is executed it will be just like retuning from the call to setjmp that originally saved the buffersaved_context, beside that the returned value will be what you provide as the second argument to *longjmp.* Thus, calling *longjmp* causes the programme to "jump" into the else block of the first if statement in main. In this way, the setjmp and longjmp pair gives you the capability to jump unconditionally from one C function to another without using conventional return statements. Essentially, setjmp marks the destination of the jump and longjmp acts as a nonlocal goto that executes the jump.

When you first look at it, a combination of setjmp and longjmp appears to be the ideal way to handle exceptions in C++, but the problem is the following. In C++, class instances have to initialised by calling class constructors and destroyed by calling the corresponding destructors. Because longjmp abruptly jumps back to a previous point in the execution of the programme, there will be situations in which a constructor has been called, but a jump occurs before calling the destructor. In such cases, any memory allocated by a constructor will not be freed, because the call to the destructor is skipped. There may be other problems as well, because the internal state of some objects may be left in an unknown condition. Thus, if you use setjmp and longjmp to handle exceptions, there must be a way to call the destructors of all relevant objects before you call longj mp.

Proposed Exception-Handling Mechanism for C++

Andrew Koenig and Bjame Stroustrup have proposed an exception-handling mechanism for C++, which they describe in their recent paper, "Exception Handling for C++," in the journal a/Object-Oriented Programming 3, No.2 (July-August 1990), pp 16-33. In this paper, the authors outline a portable implementation of the proposed design based on C's setjmp/longjmp mechanism. In particular, they describe a scheme to solve the problem of ensuring that the destructors are called correctly before you "unwind" the stack.The general syntax of exception handling can be illustrated as follows:

```
//Exception classes
class IOException; class
MemAllocException;
 class MathErro;

// Place inside a "try_ block code
& that may throw exceptions
try
{

process_commands();
}
// Place the exception-handling code
inside "catch" b1 II for each type of
exception

catch(IOException io)
 {
// Errors in 1/0
/I/. . .
}
catch(MemAllocException mem)
{

// "Out of mel1lory" errors /I ...
}
catch(MathError math) {
// Handle math errors
/I . . .

}
catch(...) // Use .,. to mean any
exception
{
// Handle all other exceptions here
// . . .
}
```

As you can see, each try block can have a number of associated catch blocks that establish handlers for various exceptions. The catch blocks are tried in the order of appearance. You should place the catch (. . .) last, because block is meant for any type of exception. A function that detects errors and throws exceptions can indicate the specific exceptions that it might throw. Suppose a function named setup_data throws the exceptions IOException and MemAllocException. The function is as follows to indicate : void setup_data() throw(IOException, MemAllocException);

The list of possible exceptions is called the exception specification of the function.

Special Functions Meant for Handling Exceptions

There are two special functions that are meant for handling exceptions that occur during exception handling itself:

void terminate ( ); is called when you do not provide an exception handler for a thrown exception or when an error occurs during the stack unwinding. The terminate function, by default, calls the abort () function from the ANSI C library. You can, however have terminate call a function that you can set up by calling the set_terminate function which is declared as follows:

```
typedef void (*PtrFuncVoid)();
PtrFuncVoid set_terminate(PtrFuncVoid);
```

Write a function named handle_termination to handle the termination, you can have terminate () call it by doing the following:

```
PtrFuncVoid old_term_handler; //I To save old
handler
void handle_termination(); // New handler
old_term_handler = set_terminate(handle_
termination)j
```

void unexpected ( ) ; is called if a function throws an exception that is not in its exception specification-the list of exceptions that the function is supposed to throw. The default action of unexpected () is to call terminate ( ), which in turn calls abort () to exit the program. Like set_terminate, there is a set_unexpected function with which you specify a function that unexpected in the same manner as set_terminate:

```
typedef void (*PtrFuncVoid)();
PtrFuncVoid old_unexpected; // To save old
handler
        void handle_unexpected(); // New handler
old_unexpected = set_unexpected
(handle_unexpected);
```

7 RELATIONAL DATABASE MANAGEMENT SYSTEM

DBMS CONCEPTS

ADVANTAGES & DISADVANTAGES OF A DBMS

Using a DBMS to manage data has many advantages:

Data independence

Application programs should be as independent as possible from details of data representation and storage. The DBMS can provide an abstract view of the data to insulate application code from such details.

Efficient data access

A DBMS utilizes a variety of sophisticated techniques to store and retrieve data efficiently. This feature is especially important if the data is stored on external storage devices.

Data integrity and security

If data is always accessed through the DBMS, the DBMS can enforce integrity constraints on the data. For example, before inserting salary information for an employee, the DBMS can check that the department budget is not exceeded. Also, the DBMS can enforce access controls that govern what data is visible to different classes of users.

Data administration

When several users share the data, centralizing the administration of data can offer significant improvements. Experienced professionals who understand the nature of the data being managed, and how different groups of users use it, can be responsible for organizing the data representation to minimize redundancy and for fine-tuning the storage of the data to make retrieval efficient.

Concurrent access and crash recovery

A DBMS schedules concurrent accesses to the data in such a manner that users can think of the data as being accessed by only one user at a time. Further, the DBMS protects users from the effects of system failures.

Reduced application development time

Clearly, the DBMS supports many important functions that are common to many applications accessing data stored in the DBMS. This, in conjunction with the high-level interface to the data, facilitates quick development of applications. Such applications are also likely to be more robust than applications developed from scratch because many important tasks are handled by the DBMS instead of being implemented by the application.

Disadvantages

A DBMS is a complex piece of software, optimized for certain kinds of workloads (e.g., answering complex queries or handling many concurrent requests), and its performance may not be adequate for certain specialized applications. Examples include applications with tight real-time constraints or applications with just a few well-defined critical operations for which efficient custom code must be written. Another reason for not using a DBMS is that an application may need to manipulate the data in ways not supported by the query language. In such a situation, the abstract view of the data presented by the DBMS does not match the application's needs, and actually gets in the way. As an example, relational databases do not support flexible analysis of text data (although vendors are now extending their products in this direction). If specialized performance or data manipulation requirements are central to an application, the application may choose not to use a DBMS, especially if the added benefits of a DBMS (e.g., flexible querying, security, concurrent access, and crash recovery) are not required. In most situations calling for large-scale data management, however, DBMSs have become an indispensable tool.

DATABASE MANAGEMENT SYSTEM (DBMS)

- Collection of interrelated data
- Set of programs to access the data
- DBMS contains information about a particular enterprise
- DBMS provides an environment that is both convenient and efficient to use.
- Database Applications:
  1. Banking: all transactions
  2. Airlines: reservations, schedules
  3. Universities: registration, grades
  4. Sales: customers, products, purchases
  5. Manufacturing: production, inventory, orders, supply chain
  6. Human resources: employee records, salaries, tax deductions
- Databases touch all aspects of our lives

PURPOSE OF DATABASE SYSTEM

- In the early days, database applications were built on top of file systems
- Drawbacks of using file systems to store data:
- Data redundancy and inconsistency
- Multiple file formats, duplication of information in different files
- Difficulty in accessing data
- Need to write a new program to carry out each new task
- Data isolation — multiple files and formats
- Integrity problems
- Integrity constraints (e.g. account balance > 0) become part of program code
- Hard to add new constraints or change existing ones

DRAWBACKS OF USING FILE SYSTEMS (CONT.)

Atomicity of updates

- Failures may leave database in an inconsistent state with partial updates carried out E.g. transfer of funds from one account to another should either complete or not happen at all.
- Concurrent access by multiple users
- Concurrent accessed needed for performance
- Uncontrolled concurrent accesses can lead to inconsistencies E.g. two people reading a balance and updating it at the same time
- Security problems

DATABASE SYSTEMS OFFER SOLUTIONS TO ALL THE ABOVE PROBLEMS

Levels of Abstraction

- **Physical level** describes how a record (e.g., customer) is stored.
- **Logical level**: describes data stored in database, and the relationships among the data.

  Type customer = record
  name : string;
  street : string;
  city : integer;
  end;

View level

application programs hide details of data types. Views can also hide information (e.g., salary) for security purposes.

View of Data

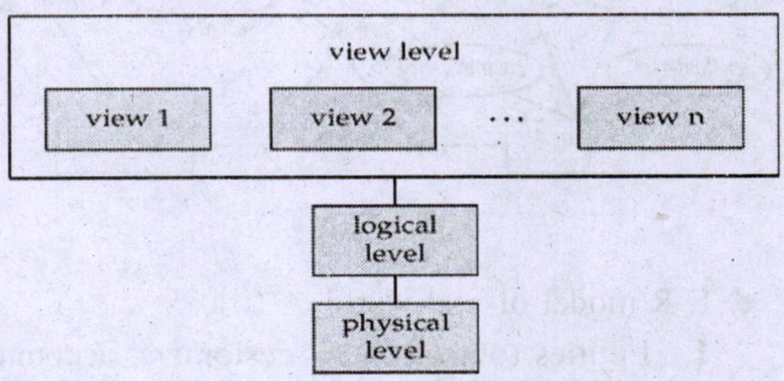

INSTANCES AND SCHEMAS

- Similar to types and variables in programm-ing languages
- Schema – the logical structure of the database. e.g., the database consists of information about a set of customers and accounts and the relationship between them
- Analogous to type information of a variable in a program
- **Physical schema**: database design at the physical level
- **Logical schema**: database design at the logical level
- **Instance** – the actual content of the database at a particular point in time
- Analogous to the value of a variable

PHYSICAL DATA INDEPENDENCE

The ability to modify the physical schema without changing the logical schema.

- Applications depend on the logical schema
- In general, the interfaces between the various levels and components should be well defined so that changes in some parts do not seriously influence others.

DATA MODELS

- A collection of tools for describing
- data
- data relationships
- data semantics
- data constraints
- Entity-Relationship model

- Relational model
- Other models
- object-oriented model
- semi-structured data models
- Older models: network model and hiera-rchical model

ENTITY-RELATIONSHIP DIAGRAM (E–R DIAGRAM)

ENTITY-RELATIONSHIP MODEL

Example of schema in the entity-relationship model

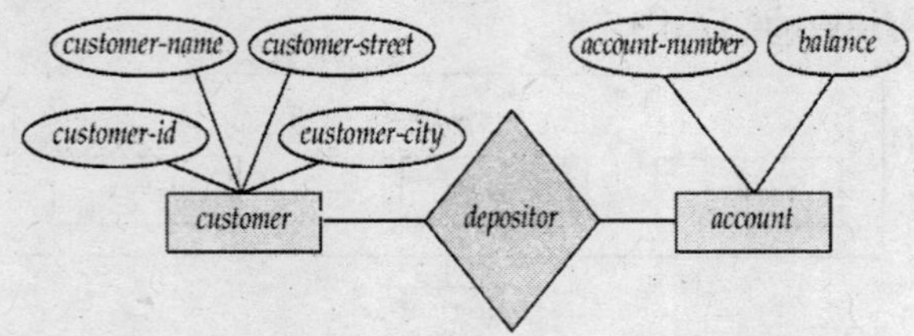

- E-R model of real world
  1. Entities (objects) *e.g.*. customers, accounts, bank branch
  2. Relationships between entities *e.g.*, Account A-101 is held by customer Johnson elationship set depositor associates customers with accounts
- Widely used for database design
- Database design in E-R model usually converted to design in the relational model (coming up next) which is used for storage and processing

DATA DEFINITION LANGUAGE (DDL)

- Specification notation for defining the database schema e.g., create table account (account-number char(10), balance integer)
- DDL compiler generates a set of tables stored in a data dictionary
- Data dictionary contains metadata (*i.e.*, data about data)
- database schema
- Data storage and definition language
  1. language in which the storage structure and access methods used by the database system are specified
  2. Usually an extension of the data definition language

DATA MANIPULATION LANGUAGE (DML)

- Language for accessing and manipulating the data organized by the appropriate data model
- DML also known as query language
- Two classes of languages
- Procedural – user specifies what data is required and how to get those data
- Nonprocedural – user specifies what data is required without specifying how to get those data
- SQL is the most widely used query language

NORMALIZATION

STRUCTURED QUERY LANGUAGE (SQL)

- SQL: widely used non-procedural language *e.g.*, find the name of the customer with customer-id 192-83-7465

```
select  customer customer-name
from    customer
where   customer customer-id = '192-83-7465'
```

e.g., find the balances of all accounts held by the customer with customer-id 192-83-7465

```
select  account balance
from    depositor, account
where   depositor customer-id = '192-83-7465'
        and depositor account-number =
        account account-number
```

Application programs generally access databases through one of

Language extensions to allow embedded SQL

Application program interface (*e.g.*, ODBC/ JDBC) which allow SQL queries to be sent to a database

DATABASE USERS

- Users are differentiated by the way they expect to interact with the system
- Application programmers – interact with system through DML calls
- Sophisticated users – form requests in a database query language
- Specialized users – write specialized database applications that do not fit into the traditional data processing framework
- Naïve users – invoke one of the permanent application programs that have been written previously

  E.g. people accessing database over the web, bank tellers, clerical staff

DATABASE ADMINISTRATOR

Coordinates all the activities of the database system; the database administrator has a good understanding of the enterprise's information resources and needs.

Database administrator's duties include:

1. Schema definition
2. Storage structure and access method definition
3. Schema and physical organization modification
4. Granting user authority to access the database
5. Specifying integrity constraints
6. Acting as liaison with users
7. Monitoring performance and responding to changes in requirements

TRANSACTION MANAGEMENT

A transaction is a collection of operations that performs a single logical function in a database application

Transaction-management component ensures that the database remains in a consistent (correct) state despite system failures (e.g., power failures and operating system crashes) and transaction failures.

Concurrency-control manager controls the interaction among the concurrent transactions, to ensure the consistency of the database.

STORAGE MANAGEMENT

Storage manager is a program module that provides the interface between the low-level data stored in the database and the application programs and queries submitted to the system.

The storage manager is responsible to the following tasks:

1. interaction with the file manager
2. efficient storing, retrieving and updating of data.

STRUCTURED QUERY LANGUAGES

NORMALIZATION

Normalization is a technique for producing a set of relations with desirable properties, given the data requirements of an enterprise. The process of normalization is a formal method that identifies relations based on their primary or candidate keys and the functional dependencies among their attributes.

Functional Dependencies

Functional dependency describes the relationship between attributes in a relation. For example, if A and B are attributes of relation R, and B is functionally dependent on A (denoted A B), if each value of A is associated with exactly one value of B. (A and B may each consist of one or more attributes.)

Main characteristics of functional dependencies in normalization

1. Have a one-to-one relationship between attribute(s) on the left- and right- hand side of a dependency
2. hold for all time
3. are nontrivial.

Identifying the primary key

Functional dependency is a property of the meaning or semantics of the attributes in a relation. When a functional dependency is present, the dependency is specified as a constraint between the attributes. An important integrity constraint to consider first is the identification of candidate keys, one of which is selected to be the primary key for the relation using functional dependency.

Inference Rules

A set of all functional dependencies that are implied by a given set of functional dependencies X is called closure of X, written X+. A set of inference rule is needed to compute X+ from X.

Armstrong's axioms

1. Reflexivity:	If B is a subset of A, then A → B
2. Augmentation:	If A → B, then A, C → B
3. Transitivity:	If A → B and B → C, then A→ C
4. Self-determination:	A → A
5. Decomposition:	If A → B,C then A → B and A→ C
6. Union:	If A → B and A → C, then A→ B,C
7. Composition:	If A → B and C → D, then A,C→ B

Minial Sets of Functional Dependencies

A set of functional dependencies X is minimal if it satisfies the following condition:

- Every dependency in X has a single attribute on its right-hand side
- We cannot replace any dependency A → B in X with dependency C → B, where C is a proper subset of A, and still have a set of dependencies that is equivalent to X.
- We cannot remove any dependency from X and still have a set of dependencies that is equivalent to X.

The Process of Normalization

- Normalization is often executed as a series of steps. Each step corresponds to a specific normal form that has known properties.
- As normalization proceeds, the relations become progressively more restricted in format, and also less vulnerable to update nomalies.
- For the relational data model, it is important to recognize that it is only first normal form (1NF) that is critical in creating relations. All the subsequent normal forms are optional.

FIRST NORMAL FORM (1NF)

Definition of 1NF

First Normal Form is a relation in which the intersection of each row and column contains one and only one value. There are two approaches to removing repeating groups from unnormalized tables:

1. Removes the repeating groups by entering appropriate data in the empty columns of rows containing the repeating data.
2. Removes the repeating group by placing the repeating data, along with a copy of the original key attribute(s), in a separate relation. A primary key is identified for the new relation.

SECOND NORMAL FORM (2NF)

Definition of 2NF

Second normal form is a relation that is in first normal form and every non-primary-key attribute is fully functionally dependent on the primary key. The normalization of 1NF relations to 2NF involves the removal of partial dependencies. If a partial dependency exists, we remove the function dependent attributes from the relation by placing them in a new relation along with a copy of their determinant.

THIRD NORMAL FORM (3NF)

Definition of 3NF

A relation that is in first and second normal form, and in which no non-primary-key attribute is transitively dependent on the primary key. The normalization of 2NF relations to 3NF involves the removal of transitive dependencies by placing the attribute(s) in a new relation along with a copy of the determinant.

Transitive dependency

A condition where A, B, and C are attributes of a relation such that if A à B and B à C, then C is transitively dependent on A via B (provided that A is not functionally dependent on B or C).

FOURTH NORMAL FORM (4NF)

Definition of 4NF

A relation that is in Boyce Codd normal form and contains no nontrivial multi-valued dependencies.

Multi-valued dependency (MVD)

Represents a dependency between attributes (for example, A, B and C) in a relation, such that for each value of A there is a set of values for B and a set of value for C. However, the set of values for B and C are independent of each other.

A multi-valued dependency can be further defined as being trivial or nontrivial.

A MVD A ® B in relation R is defined as being trivial if

n B is a subset of A Or n A U B = R

A MVD is defined as being nontrivial if neither of the above two conditions is satisfied.

FIFTH NORMAL FORM (5NF)

Definition of 5NF

A relation that has no join dependency.

Join dependency

Describes a type of dependency. For example, for a relation R with subsets of the attributes of R denoted as A, B, …, Z, a relation R satisfies a join dependency if, and only if, every legal value of R is equal to the join of its projections on A, B, …, Z.

Lossless-join dependency

A property of decomposition, which ensures that no spurious tuples are generated when relations are reunited through a natural join operation.

DISTRIBUTED DATABASE SYSTEM

DISTRIBUTED DATABASE SYSTEM

- A distributed database system consists of loosely coupled sites that share no physical component
- Database systems that run on each site are independent of each other
- Transactions may access data at one or more sites

HOMOGENEOUS DISTRIBUTED DATABASES

- In a homogeneous distributed database, all sites have identical software are aware of each other and agree to cooperate in processing user requests.
- Each site surrenders part of its autonomy in terms of right to change schemas or software appears to user as a single system. In a heterogeneous distributed database
- Different sites may use different schemas and software
  1. Difference in schema is a major problem for query processing
  2. Difference in software is a major problem for transaction processing
- Sites may not be aware of each other and may provide only limited facilities for cooperation in transaction processing

DISTRIBUTED DATA STORAGE

- Assume relational data model
- Replication
- System maintains multiple copies of data, stored in different sites, for faster retrieval and fault tolerance.
- Fragmentation
- Relation is partitioned into several fragments stored in distinct sites
- Replication and fragmentation can be combined
- Relation is partitioned into several fragments: system maintains several identical replicas of each such fragment.

1661 (CS)–17-II

DATA REPLICATION

A relation or fragment of a relation is **replicated** if it is stored redundantly in two or more sites. Full replication of a relation is the case where the relation is stored at all sites.

- Fully redundant databases are those in which every site contains a copy of the entire database.

Advantages of Replication

1. **Availability**: failure of site containing relation *r* does not result in unavailability of *r* is replicas exist.
2. **Parallelism**: queries on *r* may be processed by several nodes in parallel.
3. **Reduced data transfer**: relation *r* is available locally at each site containing a replica of *r*.

Disadvantages of Replication

1. Increased cost of updates: each replica of relation *r* must be updated.
2. Increased complexity of concurrency control: concurrent updates to distinct replicas may lead to inconsistent data unless special concurrency control mechanisms are implemented.
3. One solution: choose one copy as primary copy and apply concurrency control operations on primary copy.

DATA FRAGMENTATION

- Division of relation r into fragments $r_1, r_2, \ldots, r_n$ which contain sufficient information to reconstruct relation r.
- **Horizontal fragmentation**: each tuple of r is assigned to one or more fragments
- **Vertical fragmentation**: the schema for relation r is split into several smaller schemas
  1. All schemas must contain a common candidate key (or superkey) to ensure lossless join property.
  2. A special attribute, the tuple-id attribute may be added to each schema to serve as a candidate key.
- Example : relation account with following schema
- Account = (branch_name, account_number, balance)

Advantages of Fragmentation

- **Horizontal:** allows parallel processing on fragments of a relation, allows a relation to be split so that tuples are located where they are most frequently accessed
- **Vertical**: allows tuples to be split so that each part of the tuple is stored where it is most frequently accessed tuple-id attribute allows efficient joining of vertical fragments, allows parallel processing on a relation
- Vertical and horizontal fragmentation can be mixed.

RDBMS TOOLS : ORACLE

INTRODUCTION

Traditionally, the design and testing of application programmes has been considered to be more in the realm of the software engineering domain than in the database domain. There is some commonality between database design methodologies and software engineering design methodologies. As database design methodologies attempt to include more of the concepts for specifying operations on database objects, and as software engineering methodologies specify in more detail the structure of the databases that software programmes will use and access, it is certain that this commonality will increase. The goal of a relational database design is to generate a set of relation schemas that allows as to store information without unnecessary redundancy and allow us to easily retrieve the information.

ENTITY-RELATIONSHIP (ER) MODEL

This is a popular high-level conceptual data model. This model and its variations are frequently used for the conceptual design of database applications, and many database design tools employ its concepts.

The conceptual schema is a concise description of the data requirements of the users and includes detailed descriptions of the entity types, relationships, and constraints; these are expressed using the concepts provided by the high-level data model. Because these concepts do not include implemenatation details, they are usually easier to understand and can be used to communicate with nontechnical users. The high-level conceptual schema can also be used as a reference to ensure that all users data requirements are met and that the requirements do not include conflicts. This approach enables the database designers to concentrate on specifying the properties of the data, without being concerned with storage details.

During or after the conceptual schema design, the basic data model operations can be used to specify the high-level user operations identified during functional analysis.

The next step in database design is the actual implementation of the database, using a commercial DBMS. Most current commercial DBMSs use an implementation data model—such as the relational or the object database model— so the conceptual schema is transformed from the high-level data model into the implementation data model. This step is called **logical design** or **data model mapping,** and its result is a database schema in the implementation data model of the DBMS.

Finally, the last step is the **physical design** phase, during which the internal storage structures, access paths, and file orgnisations for the database files are specified. In parallel with these activities, application programmes are designed and implemented as database transactions corresponding to the high-level transaction specifications.The ER model describes data as entities, relationships, and attributes.

The basic object that the ER model represents is an **entity,** which is a "thing" in the real world with an independent existence. An entity may be an object with a physical existence — a particular person, car, house, or employee — or it may be an object with a conceptual existence — a company, a job, or a university course. Each entity has **attributes** the particular properties that describe it. Several types of attributes occur in the ER model: simple versus composite; single-valued versus multivalued; and stored versus derived.

Composite Versus Simple (Atomic) Attributes

Composite attributes can be divided into smaller subparts, which represent more basic attributes with independent meanings. Composite attributes can form a hierarchy; The value of a composite attribute is the concatenation of the values of its constituent simple attributes.

Composite attributes are useful to model situations in which a user sometimes refers to the composite attribute as a unit but at other times refers specifically to its components. If the composite attribute is referenced only as a whole, there is no need to subdivide it into component attributes.

Single-valued Versus Multivalued Attributes

Most attributes have a single value for a particular entity; such attributes are called **single-valued.** A multivalued attribute may have lower and upper bounds on the number of values allowed for each individual entity.

Stored Versus Derived Attributes

In some cases two (or more) attribute values are related for example, the Age and Birth Date attributes of a person. For a particular person entity, the value of Age can be determined from the current (today's) date and the value of that person's Birth Date. The Age attribute is hence called a **derived attribute** and is said to be **derivable** from the Birth Date attribute, which is called a **stored attribute.** Some attribute values can be derived from related entities; for example, an attribute Number of Employees of a department entity can be derived by counting the number of employees related to (working for) that department.

Null Values: In some cases a particular entity may not have an applicable value for an attribute. For example, the Apartment Number attribute of an address applies only to addresses that are in apartment buildings and not to other types of residences, such as single-family homes. For such situations, a special value called **null** is created. Null can also be used if we do not know the value of an attribute for a particular entity. The unknown category of null can be further classified into two cases. The first case arises when it is known that the attribute value exists but is missing-for example, if the height attribute of a person is listed as null. The second case arises when it is not known whether the attribute value exists--for example, if the HomePhone attribute of a person is null.

Complex Attributes: Notice that composite and multivalued attributes can be nested in an arbitrary way. We can represent arbitrary nesting by grouping components of a composite attribute between parentheses ( ) and separating the components with commas, and by displaying multivalued attributes between braces{ }. Such attributes are called **complex attributes.**

The main phases of database design are :

- requirements collection and analysis
- data requirements collection --result written user requirement
- functional "of the application --include user defined operations / transactions updation or retrieval and DFD, Scenario and other techniques
- Analysis of requirements
- Conceptual design
- Create a Conceptual Schema for database using high-level conceptual data model.

ENTITY TYPES AND ENTITY SETS

A database usually contains groups of entities that are similar. An **entity type** defines a collection (or set) of entities that have the same attributes. Each entity types, named database is described by its name and attributes. The collection of all entities of a particular entity type in the database at any point in time is called an **entity set,** which is usually referred to using the same name as the entity type. For example, l EMPLOYEE refers to both a type of entity as well as the current set of all employee entities in the database.

An entity type is represented in ER diagrams as a rectangular box enclosing the entity type name. Attribute names are enclosed in ovals and are attached to their entity by straight lines. Composite attributes are attached to their component attributes by straight lines. Multivalued attributes are displayed in double ovals.

An entity type describes the schema or intension for a set of entities that share the same structure. The collection of entities of a particular entity type are grouped into an entity set, which is also called the **extension** of the entity type.

Key Attributes of an Entity Type: An important constraint on the entities of an entity type is the **Key** or **uniqueness constraint** on attributes. An entity type usually has an attribute whose values are distinct for each individual entity in the collection. Such an attribute is called a **key attribute,** and its values can be used to identify each entity uniquely. For example, the Name attribute is a key of the COMPANY entity type.

Specifying that an attribute is a key of an entity type means that the preceding uniquenesss property must hold for every extension of the entity type. It is a constraint that prohibits any two entities from having the same value for the key attribute at the same time. It is not the property of a perticular extension; rather it is a constraint on all extensions of the entity type.

Some entity types have more than one key atribute. An entity type may also have no key, in this case it is called a weak entity type.

Value Sets (Domains) of Attributes: Each simple attribute of an entity type is associated with a **value set** (or **domain** of values), which specifies the set of values that may be assigned to that attribute for each individual entity. Value sets are not displayed in ER diagrams.

Mathematically, an attribute A of entity type E whose value set is V can be defined as a **function** from E to the power set.

We refer to the value of attribute A for entity *e* as A (*e*). A null value is represented by the empty set. For single-valued attributes, A(e) is restricted to being a singleton for each entity *e* in E whereas there is no restriction on multivalued attributes. For a composite atttribute A, the value set V is the Cartesian product of $P(V_1)$, $P(V_2)$,..., $P(V_n)$, where V_1, $V_{2,}$..., V_n are the value sets of the simple component attributes that form A:

$$V = P(V_1) \times P(V_2) \times ... \times P(V_n)$$

Whenever an attribute of one entity type refers to another entity type, some relationship exists. For example, the attribute Manager of DEPARTMENT refers to an employee who manages the department; the attribute Controlling Department of PROJECT refers to the department that controls the project; the attribute Supervisor of EMPLOYEE refers to another employee (the one who supervises this employee); the attribute Department of EMPLOYEE refers to the department for which the employee works; and so on. In the ER model, these references should not be represented as attributes but as **relationships.**

A relationship type R among *n* entity types E_1, E_2,..., E_N defines a set of associations-- or a relationship set -- among entities from these types. As for entity types and entity sets, a relationship type and its corresponding relationship set are customarily referred to by the same name R. Mathematically, the relationship set R is a set of **relationship instances** $_{ri,}$ where each $_{ri}$ associates n individual entities (e_1, $e_{2,}$..., e_n),and each entity e_j in r_i is a member of entity type E_j, $1 \geq j \geq n$. Hence, a relationship type is a mathematical relation on $E_{1,}$ $E_{2,}$..., $E_{n,}$ or alternatively it can be defined as a subset of the Cartesian product $E_1 E_2 \times ... \times E_n$. Each of the entity types $E_{1,}$ $E_{2,}$...,E_n is said to **participate** in the relationship type R, and similarly each of the individual entities e_1, e_2,..., e_n is said to relationship instance $r_i = (e_1, e_2, ..., e_n)$.

Informally, each relationship instance r_i in R is an association of entities, where the association includes exactly one entity from each participating entity type. Each such relationship instance r_i represents the fact that the entities participating in r_i are related in some way in the corresponding miniworld situation.

In ER diagrams, relationship types are displayed as diamond-shaped boxes, which are connected by straight lines to the rectangular boxes representing the participating entity types. The relationship name is displayed in the diamond-shaped box. This concept of representing relationship types as attributes is used in a class of data models called **functional data models.** In object databases relationships can be represented by reference attributes, either in one direction or in both directions as inverses. In relational databases, foreign keys are a type of reference attribute used to represent relationships.

Degree of a Relationship Type

The degree of a relationship type is the number of participating entity types. A relationship type of degree two is called binary, and one of degree three is called **ternary.**

Each entity type that participates in a relationship type plays a particular role in the relationship. The **role name** signifies the role that a participating entity from the type plays in each relationship instance, and helps to explain what the relationship means.

Role names are not technically necessary in relationship types where all the participating entity types are distinct, since each entity type name can be used as the role name. However, in some cases the same entity type participates more than once in a relationship type in different roles. In such cases the role name becomes essential for distinguishing the meaning of each participation. Such relationship types are called **recursive relationships**.

Relationship types usually have certain constraints that limit the possible combinations of entities that may participate in the corresponding relationship set. These constraints are determined from the miniworld situation that the relationships represents.

Cardinality Rations for Binary Relationships: The cardinality ratio for a binary relationship specifies the number of relationship instances that an entity can participate in. Cardinality ratios for binary ralationships are displayed on ER diagrams by displaying L, M, and N on the diamonds.The **participation constraint** specifies whether the existence of an entity depends on its being related to another entity via the relationship type. There are two types of participation constraints — total and partial. Total participation is also called **existence dependency.** Cardinality ratio and participation constraints, taken together, as the **structural constraints** of a relationship type.

In ER diagrams, total participation is displayed as a double line connecting the participating entity type to the relationship, whereas partial participation is represented by a single line.

Entity types that do not have key attributes of their own are called **weak entity types.** In contrast, **regular entity types** that do have a key attribute are sometimes called **strong entity types.** Entities belonging to a weak entity type are identified by being related to specific entities from another entity type in combination with some of their attribute values. We call this other entity type the **identifying** or **owner entity type,** and we call the relationship type that relates a weak entity type to its owner the **identifying relationship** of the weak entity type. A weak entity type always has a total participation constraint (existence dependency) with respect to its identifying relationship, because a weak entity cannot be identified without an owner entity. However, not every existence dependency results in a weak entity type.

Two dependents of two destinct employees may. by chance, have the same values for Name, Birth Date, Sex, and Relationship, but they are still distinct entities. They are identified as distinct entities only after determining the particular employee entity to which each dependent is related. Each employee entity is said to **own** the dependent entities that are related to it.

A weak entity type normally has a **partial key,** which is the set of attributes that can uniquely identify weak entities that are related to the same owner entity. In the worst case, a composite attribute of all the weak entities attributes will be the partial key. In ER diagrams, both a weak entity type and its identifying relationship are distinguished by surrounding their boxes and diamonds with double lines. The partial key attribute is underlined with a dashed or dotted line.

Weak entity types can sometimes be represented as complex (composite multivalued) attributes. The choice of which representation to use is made by the database designer. One criterion that may be used is to choose the weak entity type representation if there are many atributes. If the weak entity participates independently in relationship types other than its identifying relationship type, then it should not be modeled as a complex attribute.

In general, any number of levels of weak entity types can be defined; an owner entity type may itself be a weak entity type. In addition, a weak entity type may have more than one identifying entity type and an identifying relationship type of degree higher than two.

The choice of names for entity types, attributes, relationship types, and (particularly) roles is not always straightforward. One should choose names that convey, as much as possible, the meanings attached to the different constructs in the schema. We choose to use singular names for entity types, rather than plural ones, because the entity type name applies to each individual entity belonging to that entity type.

As a general practice, given a narrative description of the database requirements, the nouns appearing in the narrative tend to give rise to entity type names, and the verbs tend to indicate names of relationship types. Attribute names generally arise from additional nouns that describe the nouns that describe the nouns correponding to entity types.

Another naming consideration involves choosing relationship names to make the ER diagram of the schema readable from, left to right and from top to bottom. Some brief guidelines as to which construct should be chosen in particular situation.

In general, the schema design process should be considered an iterative refinement process, where an initial design is created and then iteratively refined until the most suitable design is reached. Some of the refinements that are often used include the following:

1. A concept may be first modelled as an attribute and then refined into a relationship because it is determined that the attribute is a reference to another entity type. It is often the case that a

pair of such attributes that are inverses of one another are refined into a binary relationship.

2. Similarly, an attribute that exists in several entity types may be refined into its own independent entity type.
3. An inverse refinement to the previous case may be applied.

The ER modeling concepts, for "traditional'' database applications, mainly include data processing applications in business and industry. Since the late 1970s, however, newer applications of database technology have become commonplace; these include databases for engineering design and manufacturing (CAD/CAM), telecommunications, images and graphics, multimedia, datamining, data warehousing, geographic information systems (GIS), and databases for indexing the World Wide Web, among many other applications. These types of databases have more complex requirements than do the more traditional applications. To represent these requirements as accurately and clearly as possible, designers of database applications must use additional semantic data modeling concepts. Various semantic data models have been proposed in the literature. The ER model can be enhanced to include these concepts, leading to the enhanced - ER or EER model.

Specialisation is the process of defining a set of subclasses of an entity type, this entity type is called the **superclass** of the specialisation.The set of subclasses that form a specialisation is defined on the basis of some distinguishing characteristic of the entities in the superclass. For example, the set of subclasses (SECRETARY, ENGINEEER, TECHNICIAN) is a specialisation of the superclass EMPLOYEE that distinguishes among EMPLOYEE entities based on the job type of each entity. We may have several specialisations of the same entity type based on different distinguishing characteristics. For example another specialisation of the EMPLOYEE entity type may yield the set of subclasses {SALARIED_EMPLOYEE, HOURLY_EMPLOYEE}; this specialisation distinguishes among employees based on the method of pay.

There are two main reasons for including class / subclass relationships and specialisations in a data model. The first is that certain attributes may apply to some but not all entities of the superclass. A *subclass* is defined in order to group the entities to which these attributes apply. The members of the subclass for example, the SECRETARY subclass may have an attribute Typing Speed, whereas the ENGINEER subclass may have an attribute Engineer Type, but SECRETARY and ENGINEER shares their other attributes as members of the EMPLOYEE entity type.

The second reason for using subclasses is that some relationship types may be participated in only by entities that are members of the subclass. For example, if only HOURLY_EMPLOYEES can belong to a trade union, we can represent that fact by creating the subclass HOURLY_EMPLOYEE of EMPLOYEE and relating the subclass to an entity type TRADE _UNION via the BELONGS_TO relationship type, the specialisation process allows us to do the following:

- Define a set of subclasses of an entity type
- Establish additional specific attributes with each subclass
- Establish additional specific relationship types between each subclass and other entity types or other subclasses

Generalisation refers to the process of defining a generalised entity type from the given entity types. The generalization processs can be viewed as being functionally the inverse of the specialisation process.

A diagrammatic notation to distinguish between generalisation and specialisation is used in some design methodologies. An arrow pointing to the generalised subclasses represent a specialisation.

In general, a superclass or subclass represents a collection of entities of the same type and hence also describes an entity type. That is why superclasses and subclasses are shown in rectangles in EER diagrams (like entity types).

The following four possible constraints on specialisation are:

- Disjoint, total
- Disjoint, partial
- Overlapping, total
- Overlapping, partial

Of course, the correct constraint is determined from the real-world meaning that aplies to each specialisation. However, a superclass that was identified through the generalisation process usually is total, because the superclass is derived from the subclass and hence contains only the entities that are in the subclasses.

Certain insertion and deletion rules apply to specialisation (and generalisation) as a consequence of the constraints specified earlier. Some of these rules are as follows:

- Deleting an entity from a superclass implies that it is automatically deleted from all the subclasses to which it belongs.
- Inserting an entity in a superclass implies that the entity is mandatorily inserted in all predicate -defined (or attribute-defined) subclasses for which the entity satisfies the defining predicate.
- Inserting an entity in a superclass of a total specialisation implies that the entity is mandatorily inserted in at least one of the subclasses of the specialisation.

The reader is encouraged to make a complete list of rules for insertions and deletions for the various types of specializations.

Specialisation/Generalisation Hierarchies and Lattices

A subclass itself may have further subclass specified on it, forming a hierarchy or a lattice of specialisations. A **specialisation hierarchy** has the constraint that every subclass participates as a subclass in only one class/subclass relationship. In contrast, for a **specialisation lattice** a subclass can be a subclass in more than one class /subclass relationship.

A subclass with more than one superclass is called a **shared subclass.** For example, if every ENGINEERING_MANAGER must be an ENGINEER but must also be a SALARIED_EMPLOYEE and a MANAGER, then ENGINEERING_MANAGER should be a shared subclass of all three superclasses. This leads to the concept known as **multiple inheritance,** since the shared subclass ENGINEERING _MANAGER directly inherits attributes and relationships from multiple classes. Notice that the existence of at least one shared subclasses leads to a lattice (and hence to multiple inheritance) if no shared subclasses existed, we would have a heirarchy rather than a lattice. If an attribute (or relationship) originating in the same superclass (PERSON) is inherited more than once via different paths (EMPLOYEE and STUDENT) in the lattice, then it should be included only once in the shared subclass.

Some inheritance mechanisms do not allow multiple inheritance (shared subclasses). In such a model, it is necessary to create additional subclasses to cover all possibie combinations of classes that may have some entity belong to all these classes simultaneously. Hence, any overlapping specialisation would require multiple additional subclasses.

Utilizing Specialisation and Generalisation in Conceptual Data Modeling

The specialisation and generalisation processes during conceptual database design. In the specialisation process, we typically start with an entity type and then define subclasses of the entity type by successive specialisation, *i.e.*, we repeatedly define more specific groupings of the entity type.

In structural terms, hierarchies or lattices resulting from either process may be identical; the only difference relates to the manner or order in which the schema superclasses and subclasses were specified. In practice, it is likely that neither the generalisation process nor the specialisation process is followed strictly, but a combination of the two processes is employed. In this case, new classes are continually incorporated into a hierarchy or lattice as they become apparent to users and designers.

FORMAL DEFINITIONS FOR THE EER MODEL CONCEPTS

A class is a set or collection of entities, this includes any of the EER schema constructs that group entities such as entity types, subclasses, superclasses, and categories. A **subclass** S is a class whose entities must always be a subset of the entities in another class, called the **superclass** C of the **superclass/subclass** (or IS - A) relationship. We denote such a relationship by C/S. For such a superclass/subclass relationship, we must always have

$$S \subseteq C$$

A **specialisation** $Z = \{S_1, S_2, \ldots, S_n\}$ is a set of subclasses that have the same superclass G; that is, G/ S_i is a superclass /subclass relationship for i= 1,2,..., n. G is called a generalised entity type (or the superclass of the specialisation, or a generalisation of the subclasses $\{S_1, S_2, \ldots, S_n\}$). Z is said to be total if always (at any point in time) have

$$\bigcup_{i=1}^{\pi} s_i = G$$

otherwise, Z is said to be overlapping.

A subclass S of C is said to be predicate-defined if a predicate p on the attributes of C is used to specify which entities in C are members of S; that is, S=C[p], where C[p], the set of entities in C that satisfy p. A subclass that is not defined by a predicate is called *user-defined.*

A specialisation Z (or generalisation G) is said to be attribute-defined if a predicate ($A=c_i$), where A is an attribute of G and c_i is a constant value from the domain of A, is used to specify membership in each subclass S_i in Z. Notice that, if c_i /= c_i for i =/ j, and A is a single-valued attribute, then the specialization will be disjoint.

A category T is a class that is a subset of the union of *n* defining superclasses $D_1, D_2, \ldots, D_n n > 1$, and is formally specified as follows :

$$T \subseteq (D_1 \cup D_2 \ldots \cup D_n)$$

A predicate p_i on the attributes of D_i can be used to specify the members of each D_i that are members of T. If a predicate is specified on every D_i we get

$$T=(D_1[p_1] \cup D_2[p_2] \ldots \cup D_n[p_n])$$

We should now extend the definition of **relationship type**. By allowing any class — not only any entity type — to participate in a relationship. Hence, we should replace the words entity type with class in that definition. The graphical notation of EER is consistent with ER because all classes are represented by rectangles.

Knowledge representation models allow multiple classification schemes in which one class is an instance of another class (called a **meta-class**). Notice that this cannot be represented directly in the EER model, because we have only two levels —classes and instances.The only relationship among classes in the EER model is a superclass /subclass relationship whereas in some KE schemas an additional class/ instance relationship can be represented directly in a class hierarchy. An instance may itself be another class, allowing multiple level classification schemas.

Indentification is the abstraction process whereby classes and objects are made uniquely identifiable by means of some **identifier.** For example, a class name uniquely identifies a whole class. An additional mechanism is necessary for telling distinct object instances apart by means of object identifiers. Moreover, it is necessary to identify multiple manifestations in the database of the same real-world object. Identification is needed at two levels:

1. To distinguish among database object and classes
2. To identify database objects and to relate them to their real -world counterparts

In the EER model, identification of schema constructs is based on a system of unique names for the constructs. For example, every class in an EER schema-whether it is an entity type, a subclass, a category, or a relationship type-must have a distinct name. The names of attributes of a given class must also be distinct. Rules for unambiguously identifying attribute name references in a specialisation or generalization lattice or hierarchy are needed as well.

At the object level, the values of key attributes are used to distinguish among entities of a particular entity type. For weak entity types, entities are identified by a combination of their own partial key values and the entities they are related to in the owner entity type(s). Relationship instances are identified by some combination of the entities that they relate, depending on the cardinality ratio specified.

Specialisation is the process of classifying class of objects into more specialised subclasses. Generalisation is the inverse process of generalising several classes into a higher level abstract class that includes the objects in all these classes. Specialisation is conceptual refinement, whereas generalisation is conceptual synthesis. Subclasses are used in the EER model to represent specialization and generalisation. We call the relationship between a subclass and its superclass an IS-A-SUBCLASS-OF relationship or simply an IS-A relationship.

Aggregation is an abstraction concept for building composite objects from their component objects. There are three cases where this concept can be related to the EER model. The first case is the situation where we aggregate attribute values of an object to form the whole object. The second case is when we represent an aggregation relationship as an ordinary relationship. The third case, which the EER model does not provide for explicitly, involves the possibility of combining object that are related by a particular relationship instance into a higher-level aggregate object. This is sometimes useful when the higherlevel aggregate object is itself to be related to another object. We call the relationship between the primitive objects and their aggregate object IS-A-PART-OF; the inverse is called IS-A -COMPONENT-OF UML provides for all three types of aggregation.

The abstraction of **association** is used to associate objects from several independent classes. Hence, it is somewhat similar to the second use of aggregation. It is represented in the EER model by relationship types and in UML by associations. This abstract relationship is called IS-ASSOCIATED-WITH.

RELATIONAL MODEL CONCEPTS

The relational model represents the database as a collection of relations. Informally, each relation resembles a table of values or, to some extent, a "flat" of records.

When a relation is thought of as a table of values, each row in the table represents a collection of related data values. In the relational model, each row in the table represents a fact that typically corresponds to a real-world entity or relationship.The table name and column names are used to help in interpreting the meaning of the values in each row.

In relational model terminology, a row is called a tuple, a column header is called an attribute, and the table is called a relation.The data type describing the types of values that can appear in each column is called a domain.

A domain D is a set of atomic values. By atomic value we mean that each value in the domain is indivisible as far as the relational model is concerned. A common method of specifying a domain is to specify a data type from which the data values forming the domain are drawn. It is also useful to specify a name for the domain, to help in interpreting its values.

- USA_ phone _numbers: The set of 10-digit phone numbers valid in the United States
- Local _phone_numbers: The set of 7-digit phone numbers valid within a particular area code in the United States

The preceding are called logical definitions of domains. A data type or format is also specified for each domain. For example, the data type for the domain USA_phone_numbers can be declared as a character string of the form (ddd)ddd-dddd, where each *d* is a numeric (decimal) digit and the first three digits form a valid telephone area code.

A relation schema R, denoted by R $(A_1, A_2,...,A_n)$, is made up of a relation name R and a list of attributes A_1, A relation schema is used to describe a relation; R is called the name of this relation. The degree of a relation is the number of attributes *n* of its relation schema.

A relation (or relation state) *r* of the relation schema R $(A_1,A_2,...,A_n)$, also denoted by r(R), is a set of n-tuples $r=\{t_1,t_2,...,t_m\}$. Each n-tuple t is an ordered list of *n* values $t=<v_1,v_2,...,v_n>$, where each value v_i, $1 \leq i \leq n$, is an element of dom(A_i)or is a special null value. The terms relation state r(R) are also commonly used.

The above definition of a relation can be restated as follows. A relation r(R) is a **mathematical relation** of degree *n* on the domains dom (A_1),dom (A_2),...,dom (A_n), which is a subset of the **Cartesian product** of the domains that define R:

$$r(R) \subseteq (\text{dom } (A_1) \text{ X... X dom } (A_n))$$

The Cartesian product specifies all possible combinations of values from the underlying domains. Hence, if we denote the number of values or **cardinality** of a domain D by | D |, and assume that all domains are finite, the total number of tuples in the Cartesian product is,

$$|\text{ dom } (A_1)| * |\text{ dom } (A_2)| * |\text{ dom } (A_n)|$$

Out of all these possible combinations, a relation state at a given time -the **current relation state** - reflects only the valid tuples that represent a particular state of the real world. In general, as the state of the real world changes, so does the relation, by being transformed into another relation state. However, the schema R is relatively static and does not change except very infrequently -for example, as a result of adding an attribute to represent new information that was not originally stored in the relation.

It is possible for several attributes to have the same domain. The attributes indicate different **roles,** or interpretations, for the domain. For example, in the STUDENT relation, the same domain Local _phone _numbers plays the role of Homephone, referring to the "home phone of a student, "and the role of OfficePhone, referring to the "office phone of the student."

A relation is defined as a set of tuples. Mathematically, elements of a set have no order among them; hence tuples in a relation do not have any particular order. However, in a file, records are physically stored on disk so there always is an order among the records. This ordering indicates first, second, $i^{th,}$ and last records in the file. Similarly, when we display a relation as a table, the rows are displayed in a certain order.

Tuple ordering is not part of a relation definition, because a relation attempts to represent facts at a logical or abstract level. Many logical orders can be specified on a relation.

An **alternative definition** of a relation can be given, making the ordering of values in a tuple unnecessary. In this definition, a relation schema $R = \{A_1, A_2,..., A_n\}$ is a set of attributes, and a relation r(R) is a finite set of **mappings** $r =\{t_1, t_2,..., t_m\}$, where each tuple t_i is a mapping from R to D, and D is the union of the attribute domains; that is, D=dom (A_1) U dom (A_2) U... U dom(A_n). In this definition, t[A_i]must be in dom (A_i) for $1 \leq i \leq n$ for each mapping *t* in *r*. Each mapping t_i is called a tuple.

According to this definition, a **tuple** can be considered as a **set** of (<attribute>,<value>) pairs, where each pair gives the value of the mapping from an attribute A_i to a value v_i from dom (A_i). The ordering of attributes is not important, because the attribute name appears with its value. By this definition, the two tuples shown in Figure 7.1 are identical. This makes sense at an abstract or logical level, since there really is no reason to prefer having one attribute value appear before another in a tuple.

t = < (Name, Rakesh Garg), (SSN, 466-12-2456), (HomePhone, null), (Address, 23 MG Road), (OfficePhone, 011-26767575), (Age, 24), (GPA, 64)>

t=<(Address, 23 MG Road), (Name, Rakesh Garg), (SSN, 466-12-2456), (Age, 24), (OfficePhone, 011-26767575), (GPA, 464), (HomePhone, null)>

Fig. 7.1: *Two Identical Tuples*

Values in the Tuples: Each value in a tuple is an **atomic** value, that is, it is not divisible into components within the framework of the basic relational model. Hence, composite and multivalued attributes are not allowed.

The values of some attributes within a particular tuple may be unknown or maynot apply to that tuple. A special value, called **null,** is used for these cases.

Interpretation of a Relation: The relation schema can be interpreted as a declaration or a type of **assertion.** An alternative interpretation of a relation schema is as a **predicate;** in this case, the values in each tuple are interpreted as values that *satisfy* the predicate. This interpretation is quite useful in the context of logic programming languages, such as PROLOG, because it allows the relational model to be used within these languages.

Entity Integrity, Referential Integrity, and Foreign Keys

The entity integrity constraint states that no primary key value can be null. This is because the primary key value is used to identify individual tuples in a relation having null values for the primary key implies that we cannot identify some tuples. For example, if two or more tuples had null for their primary keys, we might not be able to distinguish them.

Key constraints and entity integrity constraints are specified on individual relations. The **referential integrity constraint** is specified between two relations and is used to maintain the consistency among tuples of the two relations. Informally, the referential integrity constraint states that a tuple in one relation that refers to another relation must refer to an existing tuple in that relation. For example, the attribute DNO of EMPLOYEE gives the department number for which each employee works; hence, its value in every EMPLOYEE tuple must match the DNUMBER value of some tuple in the DEPARTMENT relation.

To define referential integrity more formally, we first define the concept of a *foreign* key. The conditions for a foreign key, given below, specify a referential integrity constraint between the two rela-tion schema R_1 and R_2. A set of attributes FK in relation schema R_1 is a **foreign key** of R_1 that references relation R_2 if it satisfies the following two rules:

1. The attributes in FK have the same domain(s) as the primary key attributes PK of R_2; the attributes FK are said to **reference** or **refer** to the relation R_2.
2. A value of FK in a tuple t_1 of the current state r_1 (R_1) either occurs as a value of PK for some tuple t_2 in the current state $t_2(R_2)$ or is null. In the former case, we have $t_1[FK] = t_2[PK]$, and we say that the tuple t_1 **references** or **refer** to the tuple t_2. R_1 is called the **referencing relation** and R_2 is the **referenced relation.**

In a database of many relation, there are usually many referential integrity constraints. To specify these constraints, we must first have a clear understanding of the meaning or role that each set of attributes plays in the various relation schemas of the database. Referential integrity constraints typically arise from the relationships among the entities represented by the relation schemas a foreign key can refer to its own relation.

All integrity constraints should be specified on the relational database schema if we want to enforce these constraints on the database states. Hence, the DDL includes provisions for specifying the various types of constraints so that the DBMS can automatically enforce them. Most relational DBMSs support key and entity integrity constraints, and make provisions to support referential integrity. These constraints are specified as a part of data definition.

The preceding integrity constraints do not include a large class of general constraints, sometimes called semantic integrity constraints, that may have to be specified and enforced on a relational database. Examples of such constraints are "the salary of an employee should not exceed the salary of the employee's supervisor" and "the maximum number of hours an employee can work on all projects per week is 56". Such constraints can be specified and enforced by using a general purpose **constraint specification language.** Mechanisms called **triggers** and **assertions** can be used.

Update Operations and Dealing with Constraint Violations

The operations of the relational model can be categorised into retrievals and updates. There are three basic update operations on relations: (1) insert, (2) delete, and (3) modify. **Insert** is used to insert a new tuple or tuples in a relatin; **Delete** is used to delete tuple; and **Update** (or **Modify**) is used to change the values of some attributes in existing tuple. Whenever update operations are applied, the integrity constraints specified on the relational database schema should not be violated.

The **Insert** operation provides a list of attribute values for a new tuple *t* that is to be inserted into a relation R. Insert can violate any of the four types of constraints. Domain constraints can be violated if an attribute value is given that does not appear in the corresponding domain. Key constraints can be violated if a key value in the new tuple *t* already exists in another tuple in the relation r (R). Entity integrity can be violated if the primary key of the new tuple is null. Referential integrity can be violated if the value of any foreign key in *t* refers to a tuple that does not exist in the referenced relation.

The **Delete** operation can violate only referential integrity, if the tuple being deleted is referenced by the foreign keys from other tuples in the database. To specify deletion, a condition on the attributes of the relation selects the tuple (or tuples) to be deleted.

The **Update** operation is used to change the values of one or more attributes in a tuple (or tuples) of some relation R. It is necessary to specify a condition on the attributes of the relation to select the tuple (or tuples) to be modified.

Basic Relational Algebra Operations

In addition to definning the database structure and constraints, a data model must include a set of operations to manipulate the data. A basic set of relational model operations constitute the **relational algebra.** These operations enable the user to specify basic retrieval requests. The result of a retrieval is a new relation, which may have been formed from one or more relations. The algebra operations thus produce new relations, which can be further manipulated using operations of the same algebra. A sequence of relational algebra operations forms a **relational algebra expression,** whose result will also be a relation.

The relational algebra operations are usually divided into two groups. One group includes set operations from mathematical set theory; these are applicable because each relation is defined to be a set of tuples. Set operations include UNION, INTERSECTION, SET DIFFERENCE, and CARTESIAN PRODUCT. The other group consists of operations developed specifically for relational databases; these include SELECT, PROJECT, and JOIN, among others. The SELECT and PROJECT operations are discussed first, because they are the simplest.

Some common database requests cannot be performed with the basic relational algebra operations, so additional operations are needed to express these requests.

Aggregate Functions and Grouping

The first type of request that cannot be expressed in the basic relational algebra is to specify mathematical **aggregate functions** on collections of values from the database. Examples of such functions include retrieving the average or total salary of all employees or the number of employee tuples. Common functions applied to collections of numeric values include SUM, AVERAGE, MAXIMUM, and MINIMUM. The function is used for counting tuples or values.

Another common type of request involves grouping the tuples in a relation by the value of some of their attributes and then applying an aggregate function independently to each group. An example would be to group employee tuples by DNO, so that each group includes the tuples for employees working in the same department. We can then list each DNO value along with, say, the average salary of employees within the department.

We can define an AGGREGATE FUNCTION operation, using the symbol ξ (pronouced "script F"), to specify these types of requests as follows:

<grouping attributes> ξ <function list> (R)

where <grouping attributes> is a list of attributes of the relation specified in R, and <function list> is a list of (<function> <attribute>) pairs. In each such pair, <function> is one of the allowed functions - such as SUM, AVERAGE, MAXIMUM, MINIMUM, COUNT- and <attribute> is an attribute of the relation specified by R. The resulting relation has the grouping attributes plus one attribute for each element in the function list. For example, to retrieve each deparment number, the number of employees in the department, and their average salary, while renaming the resulting attributes as indicated below, we write:

PR(DNO, NO_OF_EMPLOYEES, AVERAGE_SAL) (DNO ξ COUNT SSN, AVERAGE SALARY $_{\text{(EMPLOYEE)}}$)

In general, duplicates are not eliminated when an aggregate function is applied; this way, the normal interpretation of functions such as SUM and AVERAGE is computed. It is worth emphasising that the result of applying an aggregate function is a relation, not a scalar number even if it has a single value.

Recursive Closure Operations

Another type of operation that, in general, cannot be specified in the basic relational algebra is **recursive closure.** This operation is applied to a **recursive relationship** between tuples of the same type, such as the relationship between an employee and a supervisor. An example of a recursive operation is to retrieve all supervisers of an employee *e* at all levels-that is, all employees *e*' directly supervised by *e*; all employees *e*" directly supervised by each employee *e*" and so on. Although it is straightforward in the relational algebra to specify all employees supervised by *e* at a specific level, it is difficult to specify all supervised employees at all levels. For example, to specify the SSNs of all employees s' directly supervised at level one by the employee *e* whose name is 'James Borg' we can apply the following operation:

BORG_SSN ---- π_{SSN}(o$_{\text{FNAME='James'}}$ AND LNAME='Borg'$^{\text{(EMPLOYEE)}}$

SUPERVISION(SSN1,SSN2)——$\pi_{\text{SSN, SUPERSSN}}$(EMPLOYEE)

RESULT1 (SSN) ---- π_{SSN1} (SUPERVISION |X|$_{\text{ssn2=ssn}}$ BORG_SSN)

To retrieve all employees supervised by Borg at level 2-that is, all employees *e*" supervised by some employee *e*' who is directly supervised by Borg-- we can apply another JOIN to the result of the first query, as follows:

RUSULT 2 (SSN) ----- π_{SSN1}(supervision |X|$_{\text{SSN2=SSN}}$ RESULT1)

To get both sets of employees supervised at levels 1 and 2 by 'James Borg,' we can apply the UNION operation to the two results, as follows:

RESULT ---- RESULT 2 $\cup$ RESULT 1

Although it is possible to retrieve employees at each level and then take their UNION, we cannot, in general, specify a query such as "retrieve the supervisees of 'James Borg' at all levels" without utilising a looping mechanism. An operation called the transitive closure of relations has been proposed to compute the recursive relationship as far as the recursion proceeds.

Situations that lead to problematic relation schema, and we proposed informal guidelines for a good relational design. The problems we pointed out, which can be detected without additional tools of analysis, are as follows:

- Anomalies that imply additional work to be done during insertion into and modification of a relation, and that may cause accidental loss of information during a deletion from a relation.
- Waste of storage space due to nulls and difficulty of performing aggregation operations and joins due to null values.
- Generation of invalid and spurious data during joins on improperly related base relations.

Functional Dependencies

A functional dependency is a constraint between two sets of attributes from the database. Suppose that our relational database schema has *n* attributes $A_1, A_2, ... A_n$; let us think of the whole database as being described by a single **universal** relation schema $R=\{A_1, A_2,...,A_n\}$. We do not imply that we will actually store the database as a single universal table; we use this concept only in developing the formal theory of data dependencies.

A functional dependency, denoted by X ---> Y, between two sets of attributes X and Y that are subsets of R specifies a constraint on the possible tuples that can form a relation state r of R. The constraint is that, for any two tuples t_1 and t that have $t_1[X] = t_2 [X]$, we must also have $t_1[Y] =t_2[Y]$. This means that the values of the Y component of a tuple in r depend on, or are determined by, the values of the X component of a tuple uniquely (or functionally) determine the values of the Y component. We also say that there is a functional dependency in **FD** or **f.d.** The set of attributes X is called the left-hand of the FD, and Y is called the right-hand side.

Thus X functionally determines Y in a relation schema R if and only if, whenever two tuples of r(R) agree on their X -value, they must necessarily, agree on their Y-value. Notice the following:

- If a constraint on R states that there cannot be more than one tuple with a given X-value in any relation instance r (R) -that is, X is a candidate key of R -this implies that X→ Y for any subset of attributes Y of r (because the key constraint implies that no two tuples in any legal state r (R) will have the same value of X).
- If X→ Y in R, this does not say whether or not Y→ X in R.

A functional dependency is a property of the semantics or meaning of the attributes. The databases designers will use their understanding of the semantics of the attributes of R-that is, how they relate to one another to specify the functional dependencies that should hold on all relation states (extensions) r of R. Whenever the semantics of two sets of attributes in R indicate that a functional dependency should hold, we specify the depen-dencies a constraint relation extensions that satisfy the functional dependency constraints are called legal extensions (or legal relation states) of R, because they obey the functional dependency constraints. Hence, the main use of functional dependencies is to describe further a relation schema R by specifying constraints on its attributes that must hold at all times. Certain FDs can be specified without referring to a specific relation, but as a property of those attributes. For example, {State, Driver_license_number} $\rightarrow_{SSN}$ should hold for any adult in the United States. It is also possible that certain functional dependencies may cease to exist in the real world if the relationship changes.

A functional dependency is a property of the relation schema (intension) R, not of a particular legal relation state (extension) r of R. Hence, an FD cannot be inferred automatically from a given relation extension r but must be defined explicitly by someone who knows the semantics of the attributes of R. Each FD is displayed as a horizontal line. The left-hand side attributes of the FD are connected by vertical lines to the line representing the FD, while the right-hand-side attributes are connected by arrows pointing toward the attributes.

The reflexive rule (IR1) states that a set of attributes always determines itself or any of its subsets, which is obvious. Because IR1 generates dependencies that are always true, such dependencies are called trivial. Formally, a functional dependency X→Y is trivial if X # Y; otherwise, it is non-trivial. The augmentation rule (IR2) says that adding the same set of attributes to both the left-and right-hand sides of a dependency results in another valid dependency. According to IR3, functional dependencies are transitive. The decomposition rule (IR4) says that we can remove attributes from the right-hand side of a dependency applying this rule repeatedly can decompose the FD $X \rightarrow \{A_1,A_2,....,A_n\}$ into the set of dependencies $\{X\rightarrow A_1, X\rightarrow A_2,......, X\rightarrow A_n\}$. The union rule (IR5) allows us to do the opposite; we can combine a set of dependencies $\{X\rightarrow A_1, X\rightarrow A_2,..., X\rightarrow A_n\}$ into the single FD $X\rightarrow \{A_1, A_2,....,A_n\}$.

A set of functional dependencies E is covered by a set of functional dependencies f or alternatively, F is said to cover E -if every FD in E is also in F^+; that is, every dependency in E can be inferred from f. Two sets of functional dependencies E and F are equivalent if $E^+ = F^+$. Hence, equivalence means that every FD in E can be inferred from F, and every FD in F can be inferred from E; that is, E is equivalent to F if both the conditions E covers F and F covers E hold.

We can determine whether F covers E by calculating X^+ with respect to F for each FD X→Y in E and then cheking whether this X^+ includes the attributes in Y. If this is the case for every FD in E, then F covers E. We determine whether E and F are equivalent by checking that E covers F and F covers E.

A set of functional dependencies F is minimal if it satisfies the following conditions;

1. Every dependency in F has a single attribute for its right-hand side.
2. We cannot replace any dependency $X \rightarrow A$ in F with a dependency $Y \rightarrow A$, where Y is a proper subset of X, and still have a set of dependencies that is equivalent to F.
3. We cannot remove any dependency from F and still have a set of dependencies that is equivalent to F.

We can think of a minimal set of dependencies as being a set of dependencies in a standard or canonical form and with no redundancies. Condition 1 ensures that every dependency is in a canonical form with a single attribute on the right-hand side. Conditions 2 and 3 ensure that there are no redundancies in the dependencies either by having redundant attributes on the left-hand side of a dependency (Condition 2), or by having a dependency that can be inferred from the remaining FDs is F (Condition 3). A minimal cover of a set of functional depencies F is a minimal set of dependencies F_{min} that is equivalent to F. Unfortunately, there can be several minimal covers for a set of functional dependecies. We can always find at least one minimal cover G for any set of dependencies F using Algorithm.

Algorithm Finding a minimal cover G for F

1. Set G := F.
2. Replace each functional 1 dependency $X \rightarrow \{A_1, A_2, \ldots, A_n\}$ in G by the *n* functional dependencies $X \rightarrow A_1, X \rightarrow A_2, X \rightarrow A_n$.
3. For each functional dependency $X \rightarrow A$ in G for each attribute B that is an element of X if $((G - \{X \rightarrow A\}) \cup \{(X - \{B\}) \rightarrow A\})$ is equivalent to G,

   then replace $X \rightarrow A$ with $(X - \{B\}) \rightarrow A$ in G.
4. For each remaining functional dependency $X \rightarrow$ in G.

   if $(G - \{X \rightarrow A\})$ is equivalent to G, then remove $X \rightarrow A$ from G.

Introduction to Normalisation

The normalisation process, as first proposed by Codd (1972a), takes a relation schema through a series of tests to "certify" whether it satisfies a certain normal form. The process, which proceeds in a top-down fashion by evaluating each relation against the criteria for normal forms and decomposing relations as necessary, can thus be considered as relational design by analysis. Initially, Codd proposed three normal forms, which he called first, second, and third normal form. A stronger definition of 3NF-called Boyce-Codd normal form (BCNF) was proposed later by Boyce and Codd. All these normal forms are based on the functional dependencies among the attributes of a relation. Later, a fourth normal form (4 NF) and a fifth normal form (5NF) were proposed, based on the concepts of multivalued dependencies and join dependencies, respectively.

Normalisation of data can hence be looked upon as a process of analysing the given relation schemas based on their FDs and primary keys to achieve the desirable properties of (1) minimising redundancy and (2) minimising the insertion, deletion, and update anomalies. Unsatisfactory relation schemas that do not meet certain conditions —the normal form tests —are decomposed into smaller relation schemas that meet the tests and hence possess the desirable properties. Thus, the normalisation procedure provides database designers with:

- A formal framework for analyzing relation schemas based on their keys and on the functional dependencies among their attributes.
- A series of normal form tests that can be carried out an individual relation schemas so that the relational database can be normalised to any desired degree.

The normal form of a relational refers to the highest normal form condition that it meets, and hence indicates the degree to which it has been normalised. Normal forms, when considered in isolation from other factors, do not guarantee a good database design. It is generally not sufficient to check separately that each relation schema in the database is, say, in BCNF or 3NF. Rather, the process of normalisation through decomposition must also confirm the existence of additional properties that the relational schemas, taken together, should possess. These would include two properties:

1. The **lossless join** or **nonadditive join property,** which guarantees that the spurious tuple generation problem does not occur with respect to the relation schemas created after decomposition.
2. The **dependency preservation property,** which ensures that each functional depedency is represented in some individual relations resulting after decomposition.

The *nonadditive* join property is extremely critical and must be achieved at any cost, whereas the dependency preservation property, although desirable, is sometimes sacrificed.

Additional normal forms may be defined to meet other desirable criteria, based on additional types of constraints. However, the practical utility of normal forms becomes questionable when the constraints on which they are based are hard to understand or to detect by the database designers and users who must discover these constraints. Thus database disign as practiced in industry today pays particular attention to normal form known as **denormalisation.**

A **superkey** of a relation schema R = {A_1, A_2,...., A_n} is a set of attributes S $\subseteq$ R with the property that no two tuples t_1 and t_2 in any legal relation state *r* of *r* will have $t_1[S] = t_2[S]$. A key K is a superkey with the additional property that removal of any attribute from K will cause K not to be a superkey any more. The difference between a key and superkey is that a key has to be minimal; that is, if we havc a key K ={A_1, A_2,...,A_k} of R, then K{A_i}is not a key of R for any i, $1 \leq i \leq k$. {SSN}is a key for EMPLOYEE, whereas {SSN}, {SSN, ENAME}, {SSN, ENAME, BDATE }, etc., are all superkeys.

If a relation schema has more than one key, each is called a **candidate key.** One of the candidate keys is arbitrarily designated to be the **primary key,** and the others are called secondary keys. Each relation schema must have a primary key.

An attribute of relation schema R is called a **prime attribute** of R if it is a member of some candidate key of R. An attribute is called **nonprime** if it is not a prime attribute - that is, if it is not a member of any candidate key.

First Normal Form (INF)

INF disallows having a set of values, a tuple of values, or a combination of both as an attribute value for a single tuple. In other words, 1NF disallows "relations within relations" or "relations as attributes of tuples." The only attribute values permitted by 1NF are single atomic (or **indivisible-values.**

Second Normal Form (2NF)

Second normal form (2NF) is based on the concept of full functional dependency. A functional dependency X→Y is a full functional dependency if removal of any attribute A from X means that the dependency does not hold any more; that is, for any attribute A E X, (X--{A}) does not functionally determine Y. A functional dependency X →Y is a **partial dependency** if some attribute A E X can be removed from X and the dependency still holds; that is, for some attribute A E X (X--{A})→Y.

The test for 2NF involves testing for functional dependencies whose left-hand side attributes are part of the primary key. If the primary key contains a single attribute, the test need not be applied at all. A relation schema R is in 2NF if every nonprime attribute A in R is fully functionally dependent on the primary key of R.

If a relation schema is not in 2NF, it can be "Second normalised" or "2NF normalised" into a number if 2NF relations in which nonprime attributes are associated only with the part of the primary key on which they are fully functionally dependent.

Third Normal Form (3NF)

Third normal form (3NF) is based on the concept of transitive dependency. A functional dependency X→ Y in a relation schema R is a **transitive dependency** if there is a set of attributes Z that is neither a candidate key nor a subset of any key of R, and both X→ Z and Z→Y hold.

Table 7.1 : *Summary of Normal Forms Based on Primary Keys and Corresponding Normalisation.*

Normal	*Form Test*	*Remedy (Normalisation)*
First (1NF)	Relation should have no nonatomic attributes or nested relations.	Form new relations for each nonatomic attribute or nested relation.
Second (2NF)	For relations where primary key contains multiple attributes, no nonkey attribute should be functi-onally dependent on a part of the primary key.	Decompose and set up a new relation for each partial key with its dependent attribute(s). Make sure to keep a relation with the original primary key and any attributes that are fully functionally dependent on it.
Third (3NF)	Relation should not have a nonkey attribute functionally determined by another nonkey attribute (or by a set of nonkey attributes.) That is, there should be no transitive dependency of a nonkey attribute on the primary key.	Decompose and set up a relation that include the nonkey attribute(s) that functionally det-ermine(s) other nonkey attribute(s).

According to Codd's original definition, a relation schema R is in 3NF if it satisfies 2NF and no nonprime attribute of R is transitively dependent on the primary key.

We can state a **general alternative definition of 3NF** as follow: A relation schema R is in 3NF if every nonprime attribute of R meets both of the following terms:

- It is fully functionally dependent on every key of R.
- It is nontransitively dependent on every key of R.

Boyce-Codd Normal Form (BCNF)

Boyce-Codd normal form (BCNF) was proposed as a simpler form of 3NF, but it was found to be stricter than 3NF, because every relation in BCNF is also in 3NF; however, a relation in 3NF is not necessarily in BCNF.

The formal definition of BCNF differs slightly from the definition of 3NF. A relation schema R is in **BCNF** if whenever a nontrivial functional dependency X→ A holds in R, then X is a superkey of R. The only difference between the definitions of BCNF and 3NF is that condition (b) of 3NF, which allows A to be prime, is absent from BCNF.

SQL

The SQL language may be considered one of the major reasons for the success of relational databases in the commercial world. Because it became a standard for relational databases, users were less concerned about migrating their database applications from other types of database systems, —for example, network or hierarchical systems to relational systems. The reason is that even if the user became dissatisfied with the particular relational DBMS product they chose to use, converting to another relational DBMS would not be expected to be too expensive and time consuming, since both systems would follow the same language standards. In practice, of course, there are many differences between various commercial relational DBMS packages. However, if the user is diligent in using only those features that are part of the standard, and if both relational systems should be much simplified. Another advantage of having such a standard is that users may write statements in a database without having to change the database sub-language (SQL) if both relational DBMSs support standard.

The name SQL is derived from Structured Query Language. Originally, SQL was called SEQUEL (for Structured English Query Language) and was designed and implemented at IBM Research as the interface for an experimental relational database system called SYSTEM R. SQL is now the standard language for commercial relational DBMSs. A joint effort by ANSI (the American National Standards Institute) and ISO (the International Standards Organisation) has led to a standard version of SQL (ANSI 1986), called SQL-86 or SQL1. A revised and much expanded standard called SQL2 (also referred to as SQL-92) has subsequently been developed. Plans are already well underway for SQL3, which will further extend SQL with object-oriented and other recent database concepts.

SQL is a comprehensive database language; it has statements for data definition, query, and update. Hence, it is both a DDL and a DML. In addition, it has facilities for defining views on the database, for specifying security and authorisation, for defining integrity constraints, and for specifying transaction controls. It also has rules for embedding SQL statements into a general-purpose programming language such as C or PASCAL.

SQL users the terms table, row, and column for relation, tuple, and attribute, respectively. We will use the corresponding terms interchangeably. The SQL2 commands for data definition are CREATE, ALTER, and DROP.

Early versions of SQL did not include the concept of a relational database schema; all table (relations) were considered part of the same schema. The concept of an SQL schema was incorporated into SQL2 in order to group together tables and other constructs that belong to the same database application. An **SQLschema** is identified by a **schema name,** and includes an authorisation identifier to indicate the user or account who owns the schema, as well as descriptors for each element in the schema. Schema elements include the tables, constraints, views, domains, and other constructs (such as authorisation grants) that describe the schema. A schema is created via the CREATE SCHEMA statement, which can include all the schema elements 'definitions. Alternatively, the schema can be assigned a name and authorisation identifier, and the elements can be defined later.

SQL2 uses the concept of catalogue-a named collection of schema *s* in an SQL environment. A catalogue always contains a special schema called INFORMATION_SCHEMA, which provides information on all the element descriptors of all the schemas in the catalogue to authorised users. Integrity constraints such as referential integrity can be defined between relations only is they exist in schemas within the same catalogue. Schemas within the same catalogue can also share certain elements, such as domain definitions.

A referential integrity constraint can be violated when tuples are inserted or deleted or when a foreign key attribute value is modified. In SQL2, the schema designer can specify the action to be taken if a referential integrity constraint is violated upon deletion of a referenced tuple or upon modification of a referenced primary key value, by attaching a **referential triggered action** clause to any foreign key constraint. The options include SET NULL, CASCADE, and SET DEFAULT. An option must be qualified with either ON DELETE or ON UPDATE.

In general, the action taken by the DBMS for SET NULL or SET DEFAULT is the same for both ON

DELETE or ON UPDATE; the value of the affected referencing attributes is changed to NULL for SET NULL, and to the specified default value for SET DEFAULT. The action for CASCADE ON DELETE is to delete all the referencing tuples, whereas the action for CASCADE ON UPDATE is to change the value of the foreign key to the updated (new) primary key value for all referencing tuples. It is the responsibility of the database designer to choose the appropriate action and to specify it in the DDL. As a general rule, the CASCADE option is suitable for "relationship" relations such as WORKS_ON, for relations that represent multivalued attributes.

A constraint name is used to identify a particular constraint in case the constraint must be dropped later and replaced with another constraint.

The relations declared through CREATE TABLE statements are called **base tables** (or base relation); this means that the relation and its tuples are actually created and stored as a file by the DBMS. Base relations are distinguished from **virtual relations,** created through the CREATE VIEW statement. Which may or may not correspond to an actual physical file. In SQL the attributes in a base table are considered to be ordered in the sequence in which they are specified in the CREATE TABLE statement. However, rows (tuples) are not considered to be ordered within a relation.

If a whole schema is not needed any more, the DROP SCHEMA command can be used. There are two drop behaviour options: CASCADE and RESTRICT.

If the RESTRICT option is choosen in place of CASCADE, the schema is dropped only if it has no elements in it; otherwise, the DROP command will not be executed. If a base relation within a schema is not needed any longer, the relation and its definition can be deleted by using the DROP TABLE command.

If the RESTRICT option is chosen instead of CASCADE, a table is dropped only if it is not referenced in any constraints (for example, by foreign key definitions in another relation) or views with the CASCADE option, all such constraints and views that reference the table are dropped automatically from the schema, along with the table itself.

The definition of a base table can be changed by using the ALTER TABLE command, which is a **schema evolution** command. The possible alter table actions include adding or dropping a column (attribute), changing a column definition, and adding or dropping table constraints.

To drop a column, we must choose either CASCADE or RESTRICT for drop behaviour. If CASCADE is chosen, all constraints and views that reference the column are dropped automatically from the schema, along with the column. If RESTRICT is chosen, the commmand is successful only if no views or constraints reference the column.

BASIC QUERIES IN SQL

SQL has one basic statement for retrieving information from a database: the SELECT statement. The SELECT statement has no relationship to the SELECT operaion of relational algebra. There are many options and flavours to the SELECT statement in SQL.

SQL allows a table (relation) to have two or more tuples that are identical in all their attribute values. Hence, in general, an SQL table is not a set of tuples, because a set does not allow two identical members; rather it is a multiset (sometimes called a bag) of tuples. Some SQL relations are constrained to be sets because a key constraint has been declared or because the DISTINCT option has been used with the SELECT statement.

The SELECT-FROM -WHERE Structure of SQL Queries

The basic form of the SELECT statement, sometimes called a mapping or a select -from -where block, is formed of the three clauses SELECT, FROM, and WHERE and has the following form :

```
SELECT    <attribute list>
FROM      <table list >
WHERE     <condition>;
```

where:

- <attribute list > is a list of attribute names whose values are to be retrieved by the query.
- <table list> is a list of the relation names required to process the query.
- <condition> is a conditional (Boolean) expression that identifies the tuples to be retrieved by the query.

A simple SQL query with a single relation name in the FROM -claused is similar to a SELECT-PROJECT pair of relational algebra operations. The SELECT - clause of SQL specifies the projection attributes, and the WHERE-clause specifies the selection condition. The only difference is that in the SQL query we may get duplicate tuples in the result of the query, because the constraint is a set is not enforced.

Dealing with Ambiguous Attribute Names and Renaming (Aliasing)

In SQL the same name can be used for two (or more) attributes as long as the attributes are in different relations. If this is the case, and a query refers to two or more attributes with the same name, we must qualify the attribute name with the relation name, to prevent ambiguity. This is done by prefixing the relation name to the attribute name and separating the two by a period.

COMPUTER SCIENCE

A missing WHERE -clause indicates no condition on tuple selection; hence, all tuples of the relation specified in the FROM-clause qualify and are selected for the query result. If more than one relation is specified in the FROM-clause and there is no WHERE -clause, then the CROSS PRODUCT-all possible tuple combinations for these relations is selected.

To retrieve all the attribute values of the selected tuples, we do not have to list the attribute names explicitly in SQL; we just specify an asterisk (*), which stands for all the attributes.

Tables as Sets in SQL

SQL usually treats a table not as a set but rather as a **multiset;** duplicate tuples can appear more than once in a table, and in the result of a query. SQL does not automatically eliminate duplicate tuples in the results of queries, for the following reasons:

- Duplicate elimination is an expensive operation. One way to implement it is to sort the tuples first and then eliminate duplicates.
- The user may want to see duplicate tuples in the result of a query.
- When an aggregate function is applied to tuples, in most cases we do not want to eliminate duplicates.

An SQL table with a key is restricted to being a set, since the key value must be distinct in each tuple. If we do want to eliminate duplicate tuples from the result of an SQL query, we use the keyword DISTINCT in the SELECT-clause, meaning that only distinct tuples should remain in the result. In general, a query with SELECT DISTINCT eliminates duplicates whereas a query with SELECT ALL does not (specifying SELECT with neither ALL nor DISTINCT is equivalent to SELECT ALL).

SQL has directly incorporated some of the set operations of relational algebra. There is a set union operation (UNION), and in SQL2 there are also set difference (EXCPT) and set intersection (INTERSECT) operations. The relations resulting from these set operations are sets of tuples; that is, duplicate tuples are eliminated from the result. Because these set operations apply to union-compatible relations, we must make sure that the two relations on which we apply the operation have the same attributes and that the attributes appear in the same order in both relations.

In general, we can have several levels of nested queries. We can once again be faced with possible ambiguity among attribute names if attributes of the same name exist-once in a relation in the FROM-clause of the outer query, and the other in a relation in the FROM-clause of the nested query. The rule is that a reference to an unqualified attribute refers to the relation declared in the **innermost nested query.**

Correlated Nested Queries: Whenever a condition in the WHERE-clause of a nested query references some attribute of a relation declared in the outer query, the two queries are said to **correlate.** We can understand a correlated query better by considering that the nested query is evaluated once for each tuple (or combination of tuples) in the outer query.

The EXISTS and UNIQUE Functions in SQL

The EXISTS function in SQL is used to check whether the result of a correlated nested query is emply (contains no tuples) or not.

EXISTS and NOT EXISTS are usually used in conjunction with a correlated nested query.

Explicit Sets and NULLS in SQL

It is also possible to use an explicit set of values in the WHERE-clause, rather than a nested query. Such a set is enclosed in parentheses in SQL.

SQL allows queries that check whether a value is NULL--missing or undefined or not applicable. However, rather than using = or # to compare an attribute to NULL, SQL uses IS or IS NOT. This is because SQL considers each null value as being distinct from every other null value, so equality comparison is not appropriate. It follows that, when a join condition is specified, tuples with null values for the join attributes are not included in the result unless it is an OUTER JOIN.

Renaming Attributes and Joined Tables

It is possible to rename any attribute that appears in the result of a query by adding the qualifier AS followed by the desired new name. Hence, the AS construct can be used to assign both attribute and relation names, and it can be used in both the SELECT and FROM clauses.

The concept of a joined table (or joined relation) was incorporated into SQL 2 to permit users to specify a table resulting from a join operatin in the FROM -clause of a query. This construct may be easier to comprehend than mixing together all the select and join conditions in the WHERE -clause.

A query in SQL can consist of up to six clauses, but only the first two —SELECT and FROM —are mandatory. The clauses are specified in the following order, with the clauses between square brackets [....] being optional:

SELECT <attribute and function list>
FROM <table list >
[WHERE <condition>]
[GROUP By <grouping attribute(s)>]
[HAVING <group condition>]
[ORDER BY <attribute list>];

The SELECT -clause lists the attributes or functions to be retrieved. The FROM-clause specifies all relations (tables) needed in the query, including joined relations, but not those in nested queries. The WHERE -clauses specifies the conditions for selection of tuples from these relations, including join conditions if needed. GROUP BY specifies grouping attributes, whereas HAVING specifies a condition on the groups being selected rather than on the individual tuples. The built-in aggregate functions COUNT, SUM, MIN, MAX, and AVG are used in conjunction with grouping, but they can also be applied to all the selected tuples in a query without a GROUP BY clause. Finally, ORDER BY specifies an order for displaying the result of a query.

A query is evaluated conceptually by applying first the FROM -clause (to identify all tables involved in the query or to materialise any joined tables), followed by the WHERE - clause, and then GROUP BY and HAVING. Conceptually, ORDER BY is applied at the end to sort the query result. If none of the last three clauses (GROUP BY, HAVING, ORDER BY) are specified, we can think conceptually of a query as being executed as follows: for each combination of tuples —one from each of the relations specified in the FROM-clause; -evaluate the WHERE-clause; if it evaluates to TRUE, place the values of the attributes specified in the SELECT-clause form this tuple combination in the result of the query. Of course, this is not an efficient way to implement the query in a real system, and each DBMS has special query optimisation routines to decide on an execution plan that is efficient.

In general, there are numerous ways to specify the same query in SQL. This flexibility in specifying queries has advantages and disadvantages. The main advantage is that users can choose the technique they are most comfortable with when specifying a query. For example, many queries may be specified with join conditions in the WHERE- clause, or by using joined relations in the FROM -clause, or with some form of nested queries and the in-comparison operator. Some users may be more comfortable with one approach, whereas others may be more comfortable with another. From the programmer's and the system's query optimisation point of view, it is generally preferable to write a query with as little nesting and implied ordering as possible.

The disadvantage of having numerous ways of specifying the same query is that this may confuse the user, who may not know which technique to use to specify particular types of queries. Another problem is that it may more efficient to execute a query specified in one way than the same query specified in an alternative way. Ideally, this should not be the case: the DBMS should process the same query in the same way, regardless of how the query is specified. But this is quite difficult in practice, as each DBMS has different methods for processing queries specified in defferent ways. Thus, an additional burden on the user is to determine which of the alternative specifications is the most efficient. Ideally, the user should worry only about specifying the query correctly. It is the responsibility of the DBMS to execute the query efficiently. In practice, however, it helps if the user is aware of which types of constructs in a query are more expensive to process than others.

Views (Virtual Tables) in SQL

Concept of a View in SQL: A view in SQL terminology is a single table that is derived from other tables. These other tables could be base tables or previously defined views. A view does not necessarily exist in physical form; it is considered a **virtual table,** in contrast to base tables whose tuples are actually stored in the database. This limits the possible update operations that can be applied to views, but it does not provide any limitations on querying a view.

We can think of a view as a way of specifying a table that we need to reference frequently, even though it may not exist physically.

The command to specify a view is CREATE VIEW. The view is given a (virtual) table name (or view name), a list of attribute names, and a query to specify the contents of the view. If none of the view attributes result from applying functions or arithmetic operations, we do not have to specify attribute names for the view, as they would be the same as the names of the attributes of the defining tables in the default case. The views in V1 and V2 create virtual tables with schemas.

The same query would require the specification of two joins if specified on the base relations; one of the main advantages of a view is to simplify the specification of certain queries. Views are also used as a security and authorisation mechanism.

A view is always up to date if we modify the tuples in the base tables on which the view is defined, the view must automatically reflect these changes. Hence, the view is not realised at the time of view definition but rather at the same time we specify a query on the view. It is the responsibility of the DBMS and not the user to make sure that the view is up to date.

If we do not deed a view any more, we can use the DROP VIEW command to dispose of it.

8 BUSINESS COMPUTING

PARALLEL COMPUTING

PVM -Parallel Virtual Machine

Multi computers are of ten programmed using a mesage passing, *i.e.,* **PVM(Parallel Virtual Machine)**, is a public-domain message-passing system available on many multi computers. Initially it was designed to run on UNIX-based COWs. It has since been ported to many other platforms, including most commercial MPPs and remained *de facto* standard for years. It is a self-contained system, including process management and I/O support. PVM is easier to learn and simpler to use.

PVM consists of two parts: a **user-callable library** and a **daemon process** that runs all the time on each machine in the multi computer. When PVM is started, it finds out which machines are to be part of its virtual multicomputer by reading a configuration file. A PVM daemon is started on each of these. Machines can be added and removed by issuing commands on the PVM terminal.

PVM is a simple, straightforward, easy-to-use package available on most parallel computers and is very popular. PVM support library calls for sending and receiving messages, with many options. It run on top of existing operating systems. PVM allows *n* parallel processes to be started using the console command

```
spawn - count n prog
```

Each process will run *prog*. **PVM** decides where to place the processes, but a user can override these with arguments to the spawn command. Processes can also be started from a running process by calling Pvm_spawn. Processes can be organised into groups, with group membership changing dynamically during execution.

Communication in PVM is handled with explicit message-passing primitives and in such a way as to allow machines with different number representations to communicate, PVM supports point-to-point, broadcasting and multicasting.

Each PVM process has one active send buffer and one active receive buffer at any instant. To send a message, a process calls library procedures to pack values into the active send buffer in a self-describing way so that the receiver can recognise them and convert them to its native format.

Once the message has been assembled, the sender calls the library procedure pvm_send, which is a blocking send. Various options are available for the receiver such as pvm_recv, which blocks the receiver until a suitable message has arrived. When the call returns, the message will be in the active receive buffer. It can be unpacked and converted to values suitable for its machine using a set of unpack procedures. If a receiver is worried about potentially blocking forever, it can call pvm_trecv, which blocks the receiver for a certain time interval, but if no suitable message has arrived, times out and reports failure. Still another option is pvm_nrecv, which returns at once, either with a message or with an indication that no message has arrived. This call can be made repeatedly to poll for incoming messages.

Besides these primitives for point-to-point messages, PVM also supports broadcasting (pvm_bcast) which sends to all processes in a group; and multicasting (pvm_mcast) which sends to a specific list of processes.

Synchronisation between processes is done using pvm_barrier. When a process calls this procedure, it is blocked until a specified number of other **PVM** calls are available for host management, group management, buffer management, signaling, status checking, and miscellaneous functions.

MPI–MESSAGE-PASSING INTERFACE

For programming multicomputers, **MPI (Message-Passing Interface)** is a second communication package. It also run on top of operating system. MPI is a formal standard with a standardisation committee and an official defining document. MPI is better than PCM in the following manner. It is much richer and more complex than PCM, with many more library calls, extensive set of communication options, many more options, and many more parameters per call. The original version of MPI, now called MPI-1, was augmented by MPI-2 in 1997.

MPI-1 does not deal with process creation or management, as PVM does. It is up to the user to create processes using local system calls. Once they have been created, they are arranged into static, unchanging process groups. It is with these groups that MPI works.

Messages are typed and many data types are supported, including characters, short, regular, and long integers, single- and double-precision floating - point numbers, and so on. It is also possible to construct other types derived from these.

MPI support library calls for sending and receiving messages, with many options. It runs on top of existing operating systems. MPI is based on four orthogonal concepts: communicators, message data types, communication operations, and virtual topologies. A **communicator** is a process group plus a context. A context is a label that identifieds something, such as a phase of execution. When messages are sent and received, the context can be used to keep unrelated messages from interfering with one another. MPI supports an extensive set of communication operations. The most basic one is used to send messages as follows:

MPI_Send(buffer, count, data_type, destination, tag, communicator)

This call sends a buffer with count number of the specified data type to the destination. The tag field labels the message so the receiver can say it only wants to receive a message with that tag. The last field tells which process group the destination is in (the destination field is just an index into the list of processes for the specified group). The correspond call for receiving a message is

MPI_Recv(&buffer, count, data_type, source, tag, communicator, &status)

Which announces that the receiver is looking for a message of a certain type from which the sender may not begin sending until the receiver has called MPI_Recv. Mode 2 is buffered, in which this restriction does not hold. Mode 3 is standard, which is implementation dependent and can be either synchronous or buffered. Mode 4 is ready, in which the sender claims the receiver is available (as in synchronous), but no check is made. Each of these primitives comes in a blocking and a nonblocking version, leading to eight primitives in all. Receiving only has two variants: blocking and nonblocking.

MPI allows collective communication, including broadcast, scatter/gather, total exchange, aggregation, and barrier. For all forms of collective communication, all the processes in a group must make the call and with compatible arguments otherwise an error occur. A typical form of collective communication is for processes organised in a tree, in which values propagate up from the leaves to the root, undergoing some processing at each step, for example, adding up the values or taking the maximum.

Virtual topology is the fourth basic concept in MPI, in which the processes can be arranged in a tree, ring, grid, torus, or other topology. Such an arrangement provides a way to name communication paths and facilitates communication.

MPI-2 adds dynamic processes, remote memory access, nonblocking collective communication, scalable I/O support, real-time processing, and many new features.

ADVANCED ARCHITECTURES

The basic structural design of each chip is known as architecture, has grown steadily in sophistication and complexity. The architecture of 8086 contained only few thousand transistors, but today's powerful Pentium III Xeon processors contain 9.5 million. This increasingly complex architecture is basically responsible for continually increasing power and speed of Intel processor line.

Intel's first microprocessors were quite simple in contrast to today's standards 8086 has a good level of computing power never before seen in single processing chip. In 80286, more transistors were incorporated on to the surface of its chips which enabled processors to handle more instructions per second and access greater amounts of memory. Later some sophisticated techniques were used for processing. In 80386, this improvement called virtual 8086 mode. In this mode, a single 80386 chip could achieve the processing power of sixteen separate 8086 chips, each running a separate copy of opeating system. Different programmes can run at the same time. This technique is known as multitasking.

In 486, a 386 processor, a math coprocessor and a cache memory controller combined on a single chip. Because these chips were no longer separate, they no longer had to communicate through the bus which results in increased speed of the system dramatically. Later models of Pentium runs application programmes approximately five times faster than a 486 at the same clock speed. Part of the Pentium's speed comes from a super scalar architecture. This architecture allows the chips to process more than one instruction in a single clock cycle. Pentium Pro support dynamic execution *i.e.* it supports out of order execution means instructions that cannot be executed immediately are put aside while Pentium Pro begins processing other instructions. Pentium also supports MMX technology which includes three primary architectural design enhancements:

- New instructions
- SIMD process, enables one instruction to perform same function on multiple pieces of data, reducing number of loops required to handle vides
- Additional cache, graphical, audio, animation data.

MMX includes a set of 57 instructions resulting in increasing multimedia capabilities of a computer chip. In 1998 Intel expanded the Pentium II family by announcing two new processors Celeron and Xeon. In 2000 Pentium III includes seventy new built-in instructions and improved multimedia handling features. The Pentium IIII's major enhancement is streaming SIMD extensions (SSE). It results in faster video and graphics handling.

TODAY'S COMPUTERS

As software developers and users place ever increasing demands on micro computer systems, pocessor developers respond with chips of ever increasing speed and power. Chips makers such as Intel, Motorola, Advanced Micro Devices (AMD) etc are trying to prove that there seems to be no end to the potential power of personal computer. AMD proved that it could compete features for feature with many Intel's best selling product. AMD introduced k6 chips, feature MMX technology. In 1999, AMD's Athlon processor was the fastest microprocessor available operating at speeds upto 6590 MHz. In March 2000, the Athlon was the first PC-class CPU to reach on operating speed of 1GHz. Athlon includes a 64 kB level-1 cache and 512 KB of level-2 cache 164-bit registers.

An alternative approach is to use application-level shared memory such as a page-based DSM system, the Linda tuple space, or Orca or Globe objects. DSM simulates shared memory at the page level, making it similar to a NUMA machine, except with a much greater penalty for remote references. Linda, Orca, and Globe all provide the user with the illusion of a (restricted) shared memory model using tuples, local objects, and global objects, respectively.

MOBILE COMPUTING: MOBILE CONNECTIVITY

Today, wireless communiction is very flexible in terms of network layout. It competes with twisted pair, coaxial, fiber-optic cable. It relies on radio signals or infrared signals for transmitting data.

Wireless networks are of great value to fleets of trucks, taxies, delivery vehicles, and repairpersons for keeping in contact with home. Wireless networks are also important to the military.

Wireless networking and mobile computing are often related, they are not identical.

Some Wireless computers are not mobile.

As wireless technology becomes more widespread, numerous other applications are likely to emerge. For example, (*a*) office LANs can use signals to transmit data between nodes. (*b*) Wireless parking meters have advantages for both users and city governments. The meters could accept credit or debit cards with instant verification over the wireles link. When a meter expires, it could check for the presence of a car (by bouncing a signal off it) and report the expiration to the pólice. Wireless could save money in utility meter reading. If electricity, gas, water, and other meters in people's homes were to report usage over a wireless network, there would be no need to send out meter readers. Similarly, wireless smoke detectors could call the fire department instead of making a big noise (which has little value if no one is home). (*c*) There are other application areas. A whole different application area for wireless networks is the expected merger of cell phones and PDAs into tiny wireless computers. Tiny wireless PDAs could display stripped-down Web pages on their even tinier screens. This system, called **WAP1.0 (Wireless Application Protocol)** failed, mostly due to the microscopic screens, low bandwidth, and poor service. WAP 2.0 have used the devices very well in the area of **M-commerce (mobilecommerce)**. Wireless PDAs can be used for banking and shopping. It can be used as a kind of electronic wallet, authorizing payments in stores, as a replacement for cash and credit cards.

AMPS (ADVANCED MOBILE PHONE SYSTEM)

AMPS, invented by Bell Lebs and first installed in the United States in 1982. In England, it was called TACS, and in Japan, where it was called MCS-L1. In all mobile phone systems, a geographic region is divided up into cells, which is why the devices are typically 10 to 20 km across; in digital systems. the cells are smaller. Each cell uses some set of frequencies not used by any of its neighbors. The use of relatively small cells and the reuse of transmission frequencies in nearby (but not adjacent) cells gives cellular systems far more capacity than previous systems. Whereas an IMTS system 100 km across can have one call on each frequency, an AMPS system might have 100 10-km cells in the same area and be able to have 10 to 15 calls on each frequency, in widely separated cells, Thus, the cellular design increases the system capacity by at least an order of magnitude, more as the cells get smaller. Smaller cells mean that less power is needed, which leads to smaller and cheaper transmitters and handsets.

In an area where the number of users has grown to the point that the system is overloaded, the power is reduced, and the overloaded cells are split into smaller **microcells** to permit more frequency reuse.

As the center of each cell is a base station to which all the telephones in the cell transmit. The base station consists of a computer and transmitter/receiver connected to an antenna. In a small system, all the base station are connected to a single device called an **MTSO (Mobile Telephone Switching Office)** or **MSC (Mobile Switching Center)**. In a larger one several MTSOs may be needed, all of which are connected to a second-level **MTSO,** and so on. The MTSOs are essentially end offices as in the telephone system, and are, in fact, connected to at least one telephone system end office. The MTSOs communicate with the base stations, each other, and the PSTN using a packet-switching network. In a packet switching, messages are divided into short packets of fixed length and format and transmitting packets from long messages interspersed with pockets from short messages. The store and forward switching centres sort the packets from the various messages and transmitting them to their proper next destinations. At a final destination of a message, it must be reassembled from its constituent packets. This form of communication is called packet switching. Packet switching is used when very fast communication is needed.

Each mobile telephone is logically exist in one specific cell and under the control of that cell's base station. When a mobile telephone physically leaves a cell, its base station notices the telephone's signal fading away and asks all the surrounding base station then transfers ownership to the cell getting the strongest signal, that is, the cell where the telephone is now located. The telephone is then informed of its new boss, and if a call is in progress, it will be asked to switch to a new channel (because the old one is not reused in any of the adjacent cells). This process, called **handoff,** takes about 300 msec. Channel assignment is done by the **MTSO,** the nerve center of the system. The base stations are really just radio relays.

Handoffs can be done in two ways. In a soft handoff, the telephone is acquired by the new base station before the previous one signs off. In this way there is no loss of continuity. The telephone needs to be able to tune to two frequencies at the same time (the old one and the new one). First and second generation devices can not do this.

In a **hard handoff,** the old base station drops the telephone before the new one acquires it. If the new one is unable to acquire it (*e.g.*, because there is no available frequency), the call is disconnected abruptly. Users tend to notice this, but it is inevitable occasionally with the current design.

The first generation of mobile phones was analog; the second generation was digital. Four systems are in use now: D-AMPS, GSM, CDMA, and PDC.

On a D-AMPS mobile phone, the voice signals picked up by the microphone is digitisad and compressed using a model that is more sophisticated than the deltamodulation and predictive encoding schemes.

With mobile telephone there is great benefit from doing digitisation and compression in the handset, so much so that in D-AMPS, three users can share a single frequency pair using time division multiplexing. Each frequency pair supports 25 frames/sec of 40 msec each. Each frame is divided into six time slots of 6.67 msec each, Each frame holds three users who take turns using the upstream and downstream links. During slot 1 user 1 may transmit to the base station and user 3 is receiving from the base station. Each slot is 324 bits long, of which 64 bits are used for guard times, synchronisation, and control purposes, leaving 260 bits for the user payload. Of the payload bits, 101 are used for error correction over the noisy air link, so ultimately only 159 bits are left for compressed speech. With 50 slots/sec, the bandwidth available for compressed speech is just under 8 kbps, 1/7 of the standard PCM bandwidth.

Using better compression algorithms, it is possible to get the speech down to 4 kbps, in which case six users can be stuffed into a frame. The quality of speech at 4 kbps is not comparable to what can be achieved at 56 kbps.

The control structure of D-AMPS is fairly complicated, groups of 16 frames form a superframe, with certain control information present in each superframe a limited number of times. Six main control channels are used: **system configuration, real-time and nonreal-time control, paging, access response,** and **short messages**. But conceptually, it works like AMPS. When a mobile is switched on, it makes contact with the base station to announce itself and then listens on a control channel for incoming calls. Having picked up a new mobile, the MTSO informs the user's home-base where he is, so calls can be routed correctly.

One difference betweeen AMPS and D-AMPS is how handoff is handled. In AMPS, the MTSO manages it completely without help from the mobile devices.

D-AMPS is widely used in the U.S. and (in modified form) in Japan. Virtually, everywhere else in the world, and system called **GSM (Global System for Mobile communications)** is used, and it is even starting to be used in the U.S. on a limited scale. GSM is similar to D-AMPS. Both are cellular systems. In both systems, frequency division multiplexing is used, with each mobile transmitting one one frequency and receiving on a higher frequency (80 MHz higher for D-AMPS, 55 MHz higher for GSM). Also in both systems, a single frequency pair is split by time-division multiplexing into time slots shared by multiple mobiles. However, the GSM channels are much wider than the AMPS channels (200 kHz versus 30 kHz) and hold relatively few additional users (8 versus 3), giving GSM a much higher data rate per user than D-AMPS.

Each frequency band is 200 kHz wide. A GSM system has 124 pairs of simplex channels. Each simplex channel is 200 kHz wide and supports eight separate connections on it, using time division multiplexing. Each currently active station is assigned one time slot on one channel pair. Theoretically, 992 channels can be supported in each cell, but many of them are not available, to avoid frequency conflicts with neighbouring cells. Transmitting and receiving does not happen in the same time slot because the GSM radios cannot transmit and receive at the same time and it takes time to switch from one to the other. If the mobile station assigned to 890.4/935.4 MHz and time slot 2 wanted to transmit to the base station, it would use the lower four shaded slots (and the ones following them in time), putting some data in each slot until all the data had been sent.

The **broadcast control channel** is a continuous stream of output from the base station containing the base station's identity and the channel status.All mobile stations monitor their signal strength to see when they have moved into a new cell.

The **dedicated control channel** is used for location updating, registration, and call setup. In particular, each base station maintains a database of mobile stations currently under its jurisdiction. Information needed to maintain this base is sent on the dedicated control channel.

Finally, there is the **common control channel,** which is splot up into three logical subchannels. The first of these subchannels is the **paging channel,** which the base station uses to announce incoming calls. Each mobile station monitors it continuously to watch for calls it should answer. The second is the **random access channel,** which allows users to request a slot on the dedicated control channel. If two requests collide, they are garbled and have to be retried later. Using the dedicated control channel slot, the station can set up a call. The assigned slot is announced on the third subchannel, the **access grant channel.**

CDMA-CODE DIVISION MULTIPLE ACECSS

D-AMPS and GSM are fairly; conventional systems. They use both FDM and TDM to divide the spectrum into channels and the channels into time slots, but **CDMA (Code Division Multiple Access),** works completely differently. CDMA is completely different from AMPS, D-AMPS, and GSM. Instead of dividing the allowed frequency range into a few hundred narrow channels, CDMA allows each station to transmit over the entire frequency spectrum all the time. Multiple simultaneous transmissions are separated using coding theory. CDMA also relaxes the assumes that multiple signals add linearly.

In an ideal, noiseless CDMA system, the capacity (*i.e.*, number of stations) can be made arbitrarily large. In practice, physical limitations reduce the capacity considerably. The sender and receiver synchronise by having the sender trasmit a predefined chip sequence that is long enough for the receiver ot lock onto. All the other (unsynchronised) trasmissions are then seen as random noise. If there are not too many of them, however, the basic decoding algorithm still works fairly well.

CDMA is typically used for wireless systems with a fixed base station and many mobile stations at varying distances from it. The power levels received at the base station depend on how far away the transmitters are, a mobile station receiving a weak signal from the transmitters use more power than one getting a strong signal. The base station can also give explicit commands to the mobile stations to increase or decrease their transmission power.

Third-Generation Mobile Phones: Digital Voice and Data

Data traffic already exceeds voice traffic on the fixed network and is growing exponentially, whereas voice traffic is essentially flat. Many people are drooling over a lightweight, potable device that acts as a telephone, CD player, DVD player, e-mail terminal, Web interface, gaming machine, word processor, and more, all with worldwide wireless connectivity to the Internet at high bandwidth.

The basic services that the IMT-2000 network is supposed to provide to its users are:

1. High-quality voice transmission.

2. Messaging (replacing e-mail, fax, SMS, chat, etc.).
3. Multimedia (playing music, viewing videos films, television, etc.).
4. Internet access (Web surfing, including pages with audio and video).

Some other services might be video conferencing, telepresence, group game playing, and m-commerce (waving your telephone at the cashier to pay in a store). Furthermore, all these services are supposed to be available worldwide (with automatic connection via a satellite when no terrestrial network can be located) instantly (always on), and with quality-of-sservice guarantees.

The available time slots are divided into several logical channels, used for different purposes. The base station determines which logical channels are mapped onto which time slots. One logical channel is for downloading packets from the base station to some mobile station, with each packet indication who it is destined for. To send an IP packet, a mobile station requests one or more time slots by sending a request to the base station. If the request arrives without damage, the base station announces the frequency and time slots allocated to the mobile for sending the packet. Once the packet has arrived at the base station, it is transferred to the Internet by a wired connection. Since GPRS is just an overlay over the existing voice system, it is at best a stop-gap measure until 3G arrives.

For mobile applications, the fixed telephone system is not suitable. Mobile phones are currently in widespread use for voice and will soon be in widespread use for data. The first generation was analog, dominated by AMPS. The second generation was digital, with D-AMPS, GSM, and CDMA the major options. The third generation will be digital and based on broadband CDMA.

An alternative system for network access is the cable television system, which has gradually evolved from a community antenna to hybrid fibre coax. Potentially, it offers very high bandwidth, but the actual bandwidth available in practice depends heavily on the number of other users currently active and what they are doing.

To represent the two-dimensional image in front of it as a one-dimensional voltage as a function of time, the camera scans an electron beam rapidly across the image and slowly down it, recording the light intensity as it goes. At the end of the scan, called a **frame,** the beam retraces. This intensity as a function of time is broadcast, and receivers repeat the scanning process to reconstruct the image.

The simplest representation of digital video is a sequence of frames, each consisting of a rectangular grid of picture elements, or **pixels.** Each pixel can be a single bit, to represent either black or white.

The next step up is to use 8 bits per pixel to represent 256 gray levels. This scheme gives high-quality black -and-white video. For colour video, good systems use 8 bits for each of the **RGB** colours, although nearly all systems mix these into composite video for transmission. While using 24 bits per pixel limits the number of colours to about 16 million, the human eye cannot even distinguish these many colours, let alone more, Digital colour images are produced using three scanning beams, one per colour. To produce smooth motion, digital video, like analog video, must display at least 25 frames/sec.

Mobile Databases

Due to advancement in wireless technology, mobile computing is a new dimension in data communication and processing. The mobile computing environment will provide database applications with useful aspects of wireless technology. The mobile computing platform allows users to establish communication with other users and to manage their work while they are mobile. This feature is especially useful to geographically dispersed, organisations. Typical examples might include traffic police, taxi dispatchers, and weather reporting services, as well as financial market reporting and information brokering applications. However, there are a number of hardware as well as software problems that must be resolved before the capabilities of mobile computing can be fully utilized. Some of the software problems—which may involve data management, transaction management, and database recovery—have their origin in distributed database systems. In mobile computing however, these problems become more difficult to solve, mainly because of the narrow bandwidth of the wireless communication channels, the relatively short active of the power supply (battery) of mobile units, and the changing locations of required information (sometimes in cache, sometimes in the air, sometimes at the server). Mobile computing has its own unique architectural challenges.

MOBILE COMPUTING ARCHITECTURE

The general architecture of a mobile platform: It is a distributed architecture where a number of computers, generally referred to as Fixed Hosts (FS) and Base Stations (BS), are interconnected through a high-speed wired network. Fixed hosts are general purpose computers that are not equipped to manage mobile units but can be configured to do so. Base stations are equipped with wireless interfaces and can communicate with mobile units to support data access.

Mobile Units (MU) (or hosts) and base stations communicate through wireless, channels having bandwidths significantly lower than those of a wired network. A down-link channel is used for sending data from a BS to an MU and an uplink channel is used for sending data from an MU to its BS. Recent products for portable wireless have an upper limit of 1 Mbps (megabits per second) for infrared communication, 2 Mbps for radio communication, and 9.14 Kbps (kilobits per second) for cellular telephony. Ethernet, by comparison, provides 10 Mbps fast bandwidth and FDDl provides 100 Mbps and ATM (asynchronous transfer mode) provides 155 Mbps.

Mobil Units are battery-powered portable computers that move freely in a geographic mobility domain, an area that is restricted by the limited bandwidth of wireless communication channels. To manage the mobility of units, the entire geographic mobility domain is divided into smaller domains called cells. The mobile discipline requires that the movement of mobile unit be unrestricted within the goegraphic mobility domain (inter-cell movement), while having information access contiguity during movement guarantees that the movement of a mobile unit across cell boundaries will have no effect on the data retrieval process.

The mobile computing platform can be effectively described under the client-server paradigm, which means we may sometimes refer to a mobile unit as a client or sometimes as user, and the base station. Each cell is managed by base station which contains transmitters and receivers for responding to the information-processing needs of client located in the cell. We assume that the average query of shorter than the time required by the client to physically traverse a cell is much clients and servers communicate through 'wireless channels. The commuication link between a client and a server may be modeled as multiple data channels or as a single channel.

Characteristics of Mobile Environments: In mobile database environments, data generally changes very rapidly. Users often query servers to remain up-to-date. More specifically, they often want to track every broadcast for their data item of interest. Examples of this type of data are stock market information, weather data, and airline information. The database is updated asynchronously by an independent external process.

Users are mobile and randomly enter and exit from cells. The average duration of a user's stay in the cell is referred to as residence latency (RL), a parameter that is computed (and continually adjusted) by observing user residence times in cells. Thus each cell has an RL value. User reference behaviour tends to be localised-le., users tend to access certain parts of the database very frequently. Servers maintain neither client arrival and departure patterns nor client-specific data request information.

There is a difference between wireless networks and wired networks in many ways. Database users over a wired network remain connected not only to the network but also to a continuous power source. Thus, response time is the key performance metrics. In a wireless network, however, both the response time and the active life of the user's power source (battery) are important. While a mobile unit is listening or transmitting on-line, it is considered to be inactive mode. For current laptops with CD-ROM drives, estimated battery life in active mode is under 3 hours. In order to conserve energy and extend battery·life, clients can slip into a doze mode, where they are not actively listening on the channel and they can expend significantly less energy than they do in active mode. Clients can be woken up from the doze mode when the server needs to communicate with the client.

Types of Data in Mobile Applications

Applications that run on mobile hosts have different data requirements users either engage in personal communications or office activities or they simply receive updates on frequently changing information. Mobile applications can be categorise in two; *(1)* vertical applications and *(2)* horizontal applications. In vertical application users access data within a specified cell, and access is denied to user outside of that cell.

Data may be classified into three categories:

1. *Private data:* A single user owns this data and manages it. No other user may access it.
2. *Public data:* This data can be used by anyone who can read it. Only one source updates it. Examples include weather bulletins or stock prices.
3. *Shared data:* This data is accessed both in read and write modes by groups of users.

Examples include inventory data for products in a company.

Public data is primarily managed by vertical applications, while shared data is used by horizontal applications, possibly with some replication. Copies of shared data may be stored both in base and mobile stations. This presents a variety of difficult problems in transaction management consistency as well as integrity and scalability of the architecture.

Data Management Issues

From data management standpoint, mobile computing may be considered a variation of distributed computing. Mobile databases can be distributed under two possible scenarios: I. The entire database is distributed mainly among the wired components possibly. DBMS like functionality, with additional functionality for locating mobile units and additional query and transaction management features to meet the requirements of mobile environments.

2. The database is distributed among wired and wireless components data management responsibility is shared among base stations and mobile units.

Hence the distributed data management issues can be applied to mobile databases with the following additional considerations and variations.

1. **Data distribution and replication:** Data is unevenly distributed among the base stations and mobile units. The consistency constraints compound the problem of cache management. Caches attempt to provide the most frequently accessed and updated data to mobile units that process their own transaction and may be disconnected over long periods.
2. **Transaction models:** Issues of fault tolerance and correctness of transactions are aggravated in the mobile environment. A mobile transaction is executed sequentially through several base stations and possibly on multiple data sets depending upon the movement of the mobile unit. Central coordination of transaction execution is lacking, particularly in scenario (2) under Data Management Issues. Hence, traditional ACID properties of transactions may need to be modified and new transaction models must be defined.
3. **Query processing:** Awareness of where the data is located is important and affects the cost/ benefit analysis of query processing. The query response needs to be returned to mobile units that may be in transit or may cross cell boundaries yet must receive complete and correct query results.
4. **Recovery and fault tolerance:** The mobile database environment must deal with sete, media, transation, and communication failures. Site failure at an MU is frequently due to limited battery power. If an MU has a voluntary shutdown, it should not be treated as a failure. Transaction failures are more frequent during handoff when an MU crosses cells. MU failure causes a network partitioning and affects routing algorithms.
5. **Mobile database design:** The global name resolution problem for handling queries is compouned because of mobility and frequent shutdown. Mobile database design must consider many issues of metadata management - for example, the constant updation of location information.

E-TECHNOLOGIES

Digital Libraries and Data Warehousing : Digital libraries are an important and active research area. Conceptually, a digital library is an analog of a traditional library — a large collection of information sources in various media— coupled with the advantages of digital technologies. However, digital libraries differ from their traditional counterparts in significant ways; storage is digital, remote access is quick and easy, and materials are copied from a master version. Furthermore, keeping extra copies on hand is easy and is not hampered by budget and storage restrictions, which are major problems in traditional libraries. Thus, digital technologies overcome many of the physical and economic limitations of traditional libraries.

The Digital Library Initiative (DLI), jointly funded by NSF, DARPA, and NASA, has been a major accelerator of the development of digital libraries. This initiative provided significant funding to six major projects at six universities in its first phase covering a broad spectrum of enabling technologies. The magnitude of these data collections as well as their diversity and multiple formats provides challenges on a new scale. The future progression of the development of digital libraries is likely to move from the present technology of retrieval via the Internet, through net searches of indexed information in repositories, to a time of information, storing it, and organising it to support informational requirements learned in the decades of design and implementation of databases will provide the baseline for development of approaches appropriate for digital libraries. Search, retrieval, and processing of the many forms of digital information will make use of the lessons learned from database operations on those forms of information.

The Digital Libraries Initiative

The University of Illinois at Unbana-Champaign is coordinating national synchronisation of the six DLI projects underway at six participating universities. The projects illustrate major aspects of digital library development requirements. The participants and their focuses are as follows:

This project will implement a digital library as a collection of distributed information services, emphasizing automated indexing, intelligent retrieval, support by distributed databases, a better client-server retrieval protocol, better data acquisition technology, and a new interaction paradigm.

University of California at Santa Barbara : The Alexandria Project, spatially referenced map information. This project will develop distributed library services for spatially indexed and graphical information collections.

Carnegie Mellon University : Infomedia Digital Video Library. Using digital video libraries, this project will focus on full-content search and retrival.

University of Illinois at Urbana-Champaign: Federating Repositories of Scientific Literature. This project will scale up a digital library for thousands of users and documents.

University of Michigan: Intelligent Agents for Information location. The project will focus on agent technology, including use of user-interface agents, mediation agents to coordinate searches, and collection agents.

Stanford University: Interoperation Mechanisms Among Heterogeneous Services. This project will develop enabling technologies for an integrated digital library providing uniform access to novel services using networked information collections.

Geographic Information Systems (GIS) are used to collect, model, store, and analyse information describing physical properties of the geographical world. The scope of GIS broadly encompasses two types of data: *(1)* spatial data, originating from maps, digital images, administrative and political boundaries, roads, transportation networks; physical data such as rivers, soil characteristics, climatic regions, land elevations, and *(2)* nonspatial data, such as census counts, economic data, and sales or marketing information. GIS is a rapidly developing domain that offers highly innovative approaches to meet some challenging technical demands.

GIS Applications

Table 8.1 ***GIS Applications***

Cartographic	*Digital Terrain Modeling Applications*	*Geographic Objects Applications*
Irrigation	Earth science resource studies	Car navigation systems
Crop yield analysis	Civil engineering and military	Geographic market analysis
Land evaluation	Evaluation Soil surveys	Utility distribution and consumption
Planning and facilities management	Air and water pollution studies	Consumer product and services-economic analysis
Landscape studies	Flood control	
Traffic pattern analysis	Water resource	management

Data Management Requirements of GIS

The functional requirements of the GIS applications above translate into the following database requirements.

Data Modeling and Representation. GIS data can be broadly represented in two formats: vector and raster. Vector data represents geometric objects such as points, lines, and polygons. Thus a lake may be represented as a polygon, a river by a series of line segments. Rester data is characterised as an array of points, where each point represents the value of an attribute for a real-world location. Informally, raster images are n-dimensional arrays where each entry is a unit of the image and represents an attribute. Two dimensional units are called pixels, while three-dimensional units are called voxels. Three-dimensional elevation data is stored in a raster-based **digital elevation model (DEM)** format. Another raster format called **triangular irregular network (TIN)** is a topological vector-based approach that models surfaces by connecting sample points as vertices of triangles and has a point density that may vary with the roughness of the terrain. Rectangular grids (or elevation matrices) are two-dimensional array structures. In **digital terrain modeling (DTM),** the model also may be used by substituting the elevation with some attribute of interest such as population density or air temperature. GIS data often includes a temporal structure in addition to a spatial structure. For example, traffic density may be measured every 60 seconds at a set of points.

Data Analysis. GIS data undergoes various types of analysis. For example, in applications such as soil erosion studies, enviromental impact studies, or hydrological runoff simulation, DTM data may undergo various types of **geomorphometric analysis-** measurements such as slope values, gradients (the rate of change in altitude), aspect (the compass direction of the gradient), profile convexity (the rate of change of gradient), plan convexity (the convexity of contours and other parameters). When GIS data is used for decision support applications, it may undergo aggregation and expansion operations using data warehousing. Beside this, geometric operations (to compute distances, areas, volumes), topological operations (to compute overlaps, intersections, shortest paths), and temporal (to compute internal-based or eventbased queries) are involved. Analysis involves a number of temporal and spatial operations,

Data Integration. GISs must integrate both vector and raster data from a variety of sources. Sometimes edges and regions are inferred from a raster image to form a vector model, or conversely, raster images such as aerial photographs are used to update vector models. Several coordinate systems such as Universal Transverse Mercator (UTM), latitude/longitude, and local cadastral systems are used to identify locations. Data originating from different coordinate systems requires appropriate transformations. Major public sources of geographic data, including the TIGER files maintained by U.S. Department of commerce, are used for road maps by many web-based map drawing tools (*e.g.*, http://maps.yahoo.com). Often there are high-accuracy, atribute-poor maps that have to be merged with low-accuracy, attribute-rich maps. This is done with a process called "rubberbanding" where the user defines a set of control points in both maps and the transformation of the low accuracy map is accomplished to line up the control points. A major integration issue is to create and maintain attribute information (such as air quality or traffic density) which can be related to and integrated with appropriate geographical information over time as both evolve.

Data Capture. The first step in developing a spatial database for carographic modeling is to capture the two-dimensional or three-dimensional geographical information in digital form— a process that is sometimes impeded by source map characteristics such as resolution, type of projection, map scales, cartographic licensing, diversity of measurement techniques, and coordinate system differences. Spatial data can also be captured from remote sensors in satellites such as Landsat, NORA, and Advanced Very High resolution radiometer (AVHRR) as well as SPOT HRV (High Resolution Visible Range Instrument), which is free of interpretive bias and very accurate. For digital terrain modeling, data capture methods range from manual to fully automated. Groung surveys are the traditional approach and the most accurate, but they are time consuming. Other techniques include photogrammetric sampling and digitising cartographic documents.

Specific GIS Data Operations

GIS applications are conducted through the use of special operators such as the following :

Interpolation: This process derives elevation data for points at which no samples have been taken. It includes computation at single points, computation for a rectangular grid or along a contour, and so forth. Most interpolation methods are based on triangulation that uses the TIN method for interpolation elevations inside the triangle based on those of its vertices.

Interpretation: Digital terrain modeling involves the interpretaion of operations on terrain data such as editing, smoothing, reducing entails, and enhancing. Additional operations involve patching or zipping the borders of triangles (in TIN data), and merging, which implies combining overlapping models and resolving conflicts among attribute data. Among grid models, contour models, and TIN data are involved in the interpretation of the terrain.

Proximity analysis: Several classes of proximity analysis include computations of "zones of interest" around objects, such as the determination of a buffer around a car on a highway. Shortest path algorithms using 2D or 3D information is an important class of proximity analysis.

Raster image processing: This process can be divided into two categories *(1)* map algebra, which is used to integrate geographic features on different map layers to produce new maps algebraically; and *(2)* digital image analysis, which deals with analysis of a digital image for features such as edge detection and object detection. Detecting roads in a satellite image of a city is an example of the latter.

Analysis of networks: Networks occur in GIS in many contexts that must be analysed and may be subjected to segmentaions, overlays, and so on. Network overlay refers to a type of spatial join where a given network —for example, accident locations – to yield, in this case, a profile of high-accident roadways.

Other Database Functionality. The functionality of a GIS database is also subject to other considerations.

Extensibility: GISs are required to be extensible to accommodate a variety of constantly evolving applications and corresponding data types. If a standard DBMS is used, it must allows care set of data types with a provision for defining additional types and methods for those types.

Data quality control: As in many other applications, quality of source data is of paramount importance for providing accurate results to queries. This problem is particularly significant in the GIS context because of the variety of data, sources, and measurement techniques involved and the absolute accuracy expected by applications users.

Visualisation: A crucial function in GIS is related to visualisation —the graphical display of terrain information and the appropriate representation of application attributes to go with it. Major visualisation techniques include *(1)* contouring through the use of isolines, spatial units of lines or arcs of equal attribute values; (2) hillshading, an illumination method used for qualitative relief depiction using varied light intensities for individual facets of terrain model facets using perspective projection methods from computer graphics. These techniques impose cartographic data and other three-dimensional images of terrain data providing animated scene renderings such as those in flight simulations and animated movies.

Such requirements clearly illustrate that standard RDBMSs or ODBMSs do not meet the special needs of GIS. It is therefore necessary to design systems that support the vector and raster representations and the spationality as well as the required DBMS features. A popular GIS called ARC-INFO, which is not a DBMS but integrates RDBMS functionality in the INFO part of the system. More systems are likely to be designed in the future to work with relational or object databases that will contain some of the spatial and most of the nonspatial information.

Problems and Future Issues in GIS

GIS is an expanding application area of databases, reflecting an explosion in the number of end users using digitised maps, terrain data, space images, weather data, and traffic information suport data. As a consequence, an increasing number of problems related to GIS application have been generated and will need to be solved.

New architectures: GIS applications will need a new client-server architecture that will benefit from existing advances in RDBMS and ODBMS technology. One possible solution is to separate spatial from nonspatial data and to manage the latter entirely by a DBMS. Such a process calls for appropriate modeling and integration as both types of data evolve. Commercial vendors find that it is more viable to keep a small number of independent databases with an automatic posting of updates across them. Appropriate tools for data transfer, change management, and workflow management will be required.

Versioning and object life-cycle approach: Because of constantly evolving geographical features, GISs must maintain elaborate cartographic and terrain data —a management problem that might be eased by incremental updating coupled with update authorisation schemes for different levels of users. Under the object life-cycle approach, which covers the activities into permanent objects, a complete set of methods may be predefined to control these activities for GIS objects.

Data standards: Due to diversity of representation schemes and models, formalisation of data transfer standards is crucial for the success of GIS. The international standardisation body (ISO TC 211) and the European standards body (CEN TC278) are now in the process of debating relevant issues-among them conversion between vector and raster data for fast query performance.

Matching applications and data structures: A classification of GIS applications is based on the nature and organisation of data. In the future, systems covering a wide range of functions —from market analysis and utilities to car navigation —will need boundary-oriented data and functionality. On the other hand, applications in environmental science, hydrology, and agriculture will require more area - oriented and terrain model data. It is not clear that all this functionality can be supported by a single general -purpose GIS. The specialised needs of GISs will require that general purpose DBMSs must be enhanced with additional data types and functionality before full-fledged GIS applications can be supported.

Lack of semantics in data structures: This is evident especially in maps. Information such as highway and road crossings may be difficult to determine based on the stored data. One way streets are also hard to represent in the present GISs. Transportation CAD systems have incorporated such semantics into GIS.

Architecture of the Internet

The modem is a card within the PC that converts the digital signals the computer produces to analog signals that can pass unhindered over the telephone system. These signals are transferred to the ISP's **POP** (**Point of Presence**), where they are removed from the telephone system and injected into the ISP's regional network. From this point on, the system is fully digital and packed switched. If the ISP, is the local telco, the **POP** will probably be located in the telephone switching office where the telephone wire from the client terminates. If the ISP is not the local telco, the **POP** may be a few switching offices down the road.

The ISP's regional network consists of interconnected routers in the various cities the ISP serves. If the packet is destined for a host served directly by the ISP,the packet is delivered to the host. Otherwise, it is handed over to the ISP's backbone operator.

At the top of the food chain are the major backbone operators, companies like AT&T and Sprint. They operate large international backbone networks with thousands of routers connected by high-bandwidth fibre optics. Large corporations and hosting services that run server farms (machines that can serve thousands of Web pages per second) often connect directly to the backbone. Backbone operators encourage this direct connection by renting space in what are called **carrier hotels,** basically equipment racks in the same room as the router to allow short, fast connections between server farms and the backbone.

If a packet given to the backbone is destined for an ISP or company served by the backbone, it is sent to the closest router and handed of there. However, many backbones, of varying sizes, exist in the world, so a packet may have to go to a competing backbone. To allow packets to hop between backbones, all the major backbones connect at the NAPs. Basically, a NAP is a room full of routers, at least one per backbone. A LAN in the room connects all the router, so packets can be forwarded from any backbone to any other backbone. In addition to being interconnected at NAPs, the larger backbones have numerous direct connections between their routers, a technique known as **private peering.** One of the many paradoxes of the Internet is that ISPs who publicly compete with one another for customers often privately cooperate to do private peering.

Connection-Oriented Networks: X.25 Frame Relay, and ATM.

The connection-oriented camp comes from the world of telephone companies. In the telephone system, a caller must dial the called part's number and wait for a connection before talking or sending data. This connection setup establishes a route through the telephone, the same route. If a line or switch on the path goes down, the call is aborted.

And Frame Relay

Out first example of a connection-oriented network is **X.25,** which was the first public data network. It was deployed in the 1970s at a time when telephone service was a monopoly everywhere and the telephone company in each country expected their to be one data network per country these. To use X.25, a computer first established a connection to the remote computer, that is, placed a telephone call. This connection was given a connection number to be used in data transfer packets (because multiple connections of a 3-byte header and up to 128 bytes of data. The header consisted of a 12-bit connection number, a packet sequence works operated for about a decade with mixed success.

In the 1980s, the X.25 networks were largely replaced by a new kind of network called **frame relay.** The esssence of frame relay is that it is a connection-oriented network with no error control and no flow control. Because it was connection-oriented, packets were delivered in order (if they were delivered at all). The properties of in-order delivery, no error control, and no flow control make frame relay akin to a wide area LAN. Its most important application is interconnecting LANs at multiple company offices. Frame relay enjoyed a modest success and is still in use in places today.

ASYNCHRONOUS TRANSFER MODE (ATM)

ATM is a protocol designed by telecommunica-tions industry as a more efficient way to send voice, video, computer data over a single network. ATM is a network protocol, similar to Ethernet and Token Ring. DSL, ISDN, T1, T3 can all be used effectively to setup WANS as long as networks are used primarily for transferring the data files, e-mail messages etc. But for live video and sound, these facilities are not well suitable. To overcome this problem ATM services can be used. Thus ATM was designed to solve all the world's networking and telecommunications problems by merging voice, data, cable television, telex, telegraph, carrier pigeon, tin cans connected by strings, tom-toms, smoke signals, and everything else into a single integrated system that could do everything for everyone. It did not happen. In large part, the problems were similar concerning **OSI,** that is, bad timing, technology, implementation, and politics. ATM was much more successful than OSI, and it is now widely used deep within the telephone system, often for moving IP packets. Because it is now mostly used by carriers for internal transport, users are often unaware of its existence, but it is definitely alive and well.

Voice and data have different bandwidth requirement. Digital video signal also requires different bandwidth. ATM, take care of the needs of different kinds of communication by providing different kinds of connections and bandwidth on demand. Rather than reserving a fixed amount of bandwidth whether data is being transmitted or not.

ATM is based on cell switching. ATM networks transmits packet known as cells which include information of destination address, type of data order number of the packet. If required cells can be sent by different routes, even out of orders. Because, the volume of cells being transmitted can vary with the bandwidth of the incoming signal, ATM very well combine voice, data, video transmission on the same high bandwidth network. ATM is fast, flexible, well suited for all types of data and become a backbone in telecommunication branch offices.

ATM Virtual Circuits

Since ATM networks are connection-oriented, sending data requires first sending a packet to set up the connection. As the setup packet winds its way through the subnet, all the routers on the path make an entry in their internal tables noting the existence of the connection and reserving whatever resources are needed for it. Connections are often called **virtual circuits,** in analogy with the physical circuits used within the telephone system. Most ATM networks also support **permanent virtual circuits,** which are permanent connections between two (distant) hosts. They are similar to leased lines in the telephone world. Each connection, temporary or permanent, has a unique connection identifier.

Once a connection has been established, either side can begin transmitting data. The basic idea behind ATM is to transmit all information in small, fixed size packets called cells. ATM is based on cell switching. The cells are 53 bytes long, of which 5 bytes are header and 48 bytes are payload. Part of the header is the connection identifier, so the sending and receiving host and all the intermediate routers can tell which cells belong to which connections. This information allows each router to know how to route each incoming cell. Cell routing is done in hardware, at high speed. In fact, the main argument for having fixed-size cells is that it is easy to build hardware routers to handle short, fixed-length cells. Variable-length IP packets have to be routed by software, which is a slower process. Another advantage of ATM is that the hardware can be set up to copy one incoming cell to multiple output lines, a property that is required for handling a television programme that is being broadcast to many receivers. Finally, small cells do not block any line for very long, which makes guaranteeing quality of service easier.

All cells follow the same route to the destination. Cell delivery is not guaranteed, but their order is. If cells 1 and 2 are sent in that order, then if both arrive, they will arrive in that order never first 2 then 1. But either or both of them can be lost along the way. It is up to higher protocol levels to recover from lost cells. Note that although this guarantee is not perfect, it is better than what the Internet provides. There packets can not only be lost, but delivered out of order as well. ATM, in contrast, guarantees never to deliver cells out order.

ATM networks are organised like traditional WANs, with lines and switches (routers). The most common speeds for ATM networks are 155 Mbps and 622 Mbps, although higher speeds are also supported. The 155-Mbps speed was chosen because this is about what is needed to transmit high definition television. The exact choice of 155.52 Mbps was made for compatibility with AT&T's SONET transmission system. The 622 Mbps speed was chosen so that four 155-Mbps channels could be sent over it.

The ATM Reference Model

ATM has its own reference model, different from the OSI model and also different from the TCP/IP model. This model is consists of three layers, the physical, ATM, and ATM adaptation layers, plus whatever users want to put on top of that.

The physical layer deals with the physical medium: voltages, bit timing, and various other issues. ATM does not prescribe a particular set of rules but instead says that ATM cells can be sent on a wire or fibre by themselves, but they can also be packaged inside the payload of other carrier systems. In other words, ATM has been designed to be independent of the transmission medium.

The ATM layer deals with cells and cell transport. It defines the layout of a cell and tells what the header fields mean. It also deals with establishment and release of virtual circuits. Congestion control is also located here.

Because most applications do not want to work directly with cells (although some may), a layer above the ATM layer has been defined to allow users to send packets larger than a cell. The ATM interface segments these packets, transmits the cells individually, and reassembles them at the other end. This layer is the AAL layer (ATM Adaptation Layer).

The ATM layer manages cells, including their generation and transport. Most of the interesting aspects of ATM are located there. It is a mixture of the OSI data link and network layers; it is not split into sublayers.

The AAL layer is split into a **SAR (Segmentation And Reassembly)** sublayer and a **CS(Convergence Sublayer).** The lower sublayer breaks up packets into cells on the transmission side and puts them back together again at the destination. The upper sublayer makes it possible to have ATM systems offer different kinds of services to different applications (*e.g.*, file transfer and video on demand have different requirements concerning error handling, timing, etc.).

Data warehousing and data mining are the important means of preparing the government to face the challenges of new millenium. The increasing processing power and sophistication of analytical tools and techniques have resulted in the development of data warehouses. These data warehouses provide storage, functionality, and responsiveness to queries beyond the capabilities of transaction-orient databases. Accompanying this ever-increasing power has become a great demand to improve the data access performance of databases. A data warehouse, being a subject oriented, integrated and time variant collection of data, aims at supporting business decisions.

In modern organisations, users of data are often complelely removed from the data sources. Many people only need read-access to data, but still need a very rapid access to a larger volume of data that can conveniently be downloaded to the desktop. Often such data comes from multiple databases. Because many of the analyses performed are recurrent and predictable, software vendors and system support staff have begun to design systems to support these functions. At present great need to provide decision makers from middle management upward with information at correct level of detail to support decision making. Data warehousing, on-line analytical processing (OLAP), and data mining provide this functionality. Several types of applications—OLAP, DSS, and data mining applications–are supported OLAP (on line analytical processing), is a term used to describe the analysis of complex data warehouse. In the hands of skilled knowledge workers, OLAP are distributed computing capabilities for analyses that require more storage and processing power that can be economically and efficiently located on an individual desktop. DSS (Decision support systems) also known as EIS (executive information systems) support an organisation's leading decision makers with higher-level data for complex and important decisions. Traditional data bases support on line transaction processing (OLTP), which includes insertions, updates, and deletions, while also supporting information query requirements. Traditional relational databases are optimised to process queries that may touch a small part of the database and transactions that deal with insertions or updates of a few tuples per relation to process. Thus, they cannot be optimised for OLAP, DSS, or data mining where as, data warehouses are designed precisely to support efficient extraction, processing and presentation for analytic and decision-making purposes. Data warehouses generally contain very large amount of data from multiple sources that may include databases from different data models and sometimes files acquired from independent systems and platforms. As a data warehouse grows in complexity, the divercity of subject covered grows which adds more perspectives to access the data. Multifact star scheme can be utilised in the case.

Terminology and Definitions: A database is a collection of related data and a database system as a database and database software together. A datawarehouse is a collection of information as well as a supporting system. We can define datawarehouse as "A subject-oriented integrated, nonvolatile, time-variant collection of data in support of management's decision." Datawarehouse provide access to data for complex analysis, knowledge discovery, and decision making.

Datawarehouse is "a collection of decision support technologies, aimed at enabling the knowledge worker (executive, manager, analyst) to make better and faster decisions." A data warehouse is a repository of subjectively selected and adapted operational data which can answer any queries such as *ad hoc*, statitical.

Data Warehousing and Characteristics of Data Warehouses:

- Data warehouse is a store of integrated data from multiple sources, processed for storage in a multidimensional model.
- Information in the data warehouse changes far less often and may be regarded as non real time with periodic updating.
- Data warehouse information is much more coarse grained and is refreshed according to a careful choice of refresh policy, usually incremental.
- Data warehouse updates are handled by the warehouse's acquisition component that provides all required preprocessing.
- Data warehouses also have the following distinctive characteristics: multidimensional conceptual view, generic dimensionality, unlimited dimensions and aggregation levels, unrestricted cross-dimensional operations, dynamic sparse matrix handling.
- Data warehouse has a client-server architecture.
- Supports multi-user accessibility, transparency, intuitive data manipulation, consistent reporting performance, flexible reporting.
- Enterprise-wide data warehouses are huge projects requiring massive investment of time and resources.
- Virtual data warehouses provide views of operational databases that are materialised for efficient access.
- Data marts generally are targeted to a subset of the organisation such as a department, and are more tightly focused.

Acquisition of data for the warehouse involves the following steps:-

- The data must be extracted from multiple, heterogeneous sources.
- The data must be cleaned to ensure validity. Data cleaning is an involved complex process that has been identified as the largest labour-demanding components of data warehouse construction. For input data, cleaning must occur before the data are loaded into the warehouse. There is nothing about cleaning data that is specific to data warehousing and that could not be applied to a host database, but input data must be examined and formatted consistently, data warehouse builders should take this opportunity to check for validity and quality recognising erroneous and incomplete data is difficult to automate, and cleaning that requires automatic error correction can be even tougher. Some aspects, such as domain checking are easily coded into data cleaning routines, but automatic recognition of other data problems can be more challenging.
- The data must be fitted into the data model of the warehouse. Data from the various sources must be installed in the data model of the warehouse. Data may have to be converted from relational, object oriented or legacy databases(network and/or hierarchical) to a multidimensional model.
- The data must be loaded into the warehouse. The sheer volume of data in the warehouse makes loading the data a significant task. Monitoring tools for loads as well as methods to recover from incomplete or incorrect loads are required. Updation should be there.
- Data storage in a data warehousing reflects the following processes:-
- Storing the data according to the data model of the warehouse
- Creating and maintaining required data structures
- Creating and maintaining appropriate access paths
- providing for time-variant data as new data are added
- Supporting the updating of warehouse data
- Refreshing the data
- Purging data

Although adequate time can be devoted initially to constructing the warehouse, the sheer volume of data in the warehouse generally makes it impossible to simply reload the warehouse in its entirety later on. Alternatives include selective (partial) refreshing of data and separate warehouse versions (requiring double storage capacity for the warehouse). When the warehouse uses an incremental data refreshing mechanism, data may need to be periodically purged.

- Data warehouses must be designed with full consideration of the environment and organisational details.
- The architecture of the organisation's distributed computing environment is a major determining characteristic for the design of the warehouse. There are two basic distributed architectures: the distributed warehousee and the federated warehouse. For a distributed warehouse. all the issues of distributed databases are relevant, *e.g.*, replication, partitioning, communications, and consistency concerns. A distributed architecture can provide benefits particularly important to warehouse.

Functioning of Warehouses

Data warehouses exist to facilitate complex, data-intensive, and frequent *ad hoc* queries. Accordingly, data warehouses must provide far greater and more efficient query support that is demanded of transactional databases. The data warehouse access component Supports enhanced spreadsheet functionality, efficient query processing, structured queries, *ad hoc* queries, data mining, and materialised views. In particular, enhanced spreadsheet functionality includes support for state-of-the-art spreadsheet applications (*e.g.* MS-Excel) as well as for OLAP applications programmes. These offer preprogrammed functionalities such as the following:

- Roll-up: Data is summarised with increasing generalisation (*e.g.*, weekly to quarterly to annually).
- Dnll-down: Increasing levels of detail are revealed the complement of roll-up.
- Pivot: Cross tabulation (also referred as rotation) is performed.
- Slice and dice: Performing projection operations on the dimensions.
- Sorting: Data is sorted by ordinal value.
- Selection: Data is available by value or range.
- Derived (computed) attributes: Attributes are computed by operation on stored and derived values.
- Data warehouses are free from the restrictions of the transactional environment there is an increased efficiency in query processing.

From a data warehouse data flows to various departments for their customised DSS usage. These individual departmental components are called data marts. Data mart is a subset of a data warehouse and is much more popular than data warehouse. The data warehouse provides granular data and various data marts interpret and structure the granular data to suit their needs. Two types of data marts can be there—MBDB or MOLAP, relational OLAP (ROLAP). In multidimensional (MDDB) data mart, numeric data, which is muti dimensional in its original nature, can be sliced and died in a free form, *i.e.*, free from data modelling constraints of a DBMS. Meta data is an internal part of a data mart environment, enables different data marts to achieve a degree of, cohesiveness, allows end users to access data in a data mart. The software for datamart includes: a DBMS, access and analysis software, metadata management, software, purge and archival software, system management etc. Star schema is inadequate when a data warehouse grows in complexity. Further larger growth of datawarehouse leads to breakdown of star schema due to its over complexity and size. Then multifact star schema or snow flake schema technique can be utilised. This scheme provide aggregation at different levels of hierarchies in a given dimensions. This goal is achieved by normalising those hierarchical dimensions into more detailed data sets to facilitate the aggregation of fact date. Thus modelling the data warehouse into separate groups are possibles, through star scheme where each group addressed specific performance and trend analysis objective of a specific user.

Hybrid approaches also exists which integrate both ROLAP and MOLAP techniques and they are usually called multi-relational database systems. All these tools implement star schema or snow flake schema. Applications requiring iterative and comprehensive time series analysis of trends are well suited for MOLAP technology (*e.g.*, financial analysis and budgeting). ROLAP is the latest and fastest growing OLAP technology. All OLAP vendors position their products to be completely Web compliant. Server-centric tools, such as Information Advantage and Prodea Beacon from Platinum Technology and the multi dimensional OLAP tools—Arbor's Essbase, Oracle Express, Planning Sciences Gentia, Kenan Technologies Accumate ES, Pilot's Software's Pilot server—are conducting excellent position to take advantage of their architectures to provide easy access from a web browser. Client entric tools such as Business objects, Brio Technologies—Brio suite of products are developing and enhancing full-featured web-enabled versions of their products. The job become easier due to both Java and Active X are available for Web deployment.

Architecture of Data warehouse: Operational data and processing is completely separate from data warehouse processing. Data warehouse architecture is based on a RDMS (Relational Database Management

1661 (CS)–21-II

System) Server which acts as the central repostory for Information Data. Data warehouse can be viewed as an information server to its clients end users using front end tools. Two-tiered data warehouse architecture is based on the first generation of client/ server architecture but it lacks the scaleability and flexibility *e.g.*, multitiered model, multitiered data warehouse architecture reflects the multitiered client/ server model alternato options. Application servers can be data mart servers with all the advantages of a dependent data mart environment already integrated into a scaleable architecture. A client system is left with Data Access, Report Formatting, Query specification, GUI/Presentation logic, Data Analysis.

The data warehousing architecture contains eight components:

Data sourcing, cleanup, transformation, migration tools: The source data for the warehosue are the operational applications. As the data enters the data warehouse, it is transformed into an integrated structure and format. The transformation process may involve conversion, summarisation filtering and condensation of data.

- Metadata repository
- Data Marts
- Datawarehouse database Technology
- Data query, Report, EIS tools, OLAP tools, Datamining and Application tools
- Datawarehouse administration and management
- Information delivery system

Operational Data Store (ODS)

ODS can be used not only for decision support activities against the operational data but also as a staging area for the data acquisition into the data warehouse. ODS provide a consistent view of operational data for decision support and analysis.

Views and Data warehousing: Some people have considered data warehouses to be an extension of database views. Materialised views- one way of meeting requirements for improved access to data materialised views have been explored for their performance enhancement. Views, however provide only a subset of the functions and capabilities of data warehouses. Views and warehouses are alike in that they both have read-only extracts from databases and subject-orientation but data warehouses are different from views in the following manner:

- Data warehouses exist as persistent storage instead of being materialised on demand.
- Data warehouses are not usually relational, but rather multidimensional. Views of a relational database are relational.
- Data warehouses can be indexed to optimise performance. Views cannot be indexed independent from the underlying databases.
- Data warehouses characteristically provide specific support of functionality; views cannot.
- Data warehouses provide large amounts of integrated and often temporal data, generally more than is contained in one database, whereas views are an extract of a database.

Difficulties of Implementing Data Warehouses

Some operational issues arise with data warehousing: construction, administration and quantity control. Project management–the design, construction, and implementation of the warehouse–is an important and challenging consideration that should not be underestimated. The administration of a data warehouse is an intensive enterprise, propotional to the size and complexity of the warehouse. An organisation that a warehouse must realistically understand the complex nature of its administration. Although designed for read-access, a data warehouse is no more a stastic structure than any of its information sources. Source databases can be expected to evolve. The warehouses schema and acquistion component must be expected to be updated to handle these evolutions.

A significant issue in data warehousing is the quality control of data. Both quality and consistency of data are major concerns. Automating the data extraction and required frequency of updates needs to be the warehouse's responsibility. The warehouse should also be designed to accommodate additional changes if required of data sources without major redesign. Because there is continual rapid change in technologies, both the requirement and capabilities of the warehouse will change considerably over time. Additionally data warehousing technology itself will continue to evolve for some time so that component structures and functionalities will continually be upgraded. This certain change is motivation for having fully modular design of components.

Data Mining

Data mining refers to the mining or discovery of new information in terms of patterns or rules from vast amounts of data. Data mining is the process of extracting previously not known valid and actionable information from large data and then using the information so derived to make crucial business and strategic decisions. To be practically useful, data mining must be carried out efficiently on large files and databases. To data, it is not well-integrated with database management systems.

Approaches to Data Mining Problems:

- Discovery of sequential patterns
- Discovery of patterns in time series
- Discovery of classification rules
- Neural Networks

- Generic Algorithms
- Clustering and Segmentation

Data Mining and Data Warehousing. The goal of a data warehouse is to support decision making with data. The business problems solved by data warehousing and complementary technologies all have one common trend-they provide the organisations with a sustainable competitive advantage frequently provided by datamining. Data mining can be used in conjunction with a data warehouse to help with certain types of decisions. Data mining can be applied to operational databases with individual transactions. To make data mining more efficient, the data warehouse should have an aggregated or summarised collection of data.

Data mining helps in extracting meaningful new correlations, patterns that cannot be found necessarily by merely querying or processing data or metadata in the data warehouse. Data mining applications should therefore be strongly considered early, during the design of a data warehouse. Also, data mining tools should be designed to facilitate their use in conjunction with data warehouses. In fact, for very large databases runing into terabytes of data, successful use of database mining applications will depend first on the construction of a data warehouse.

The data warehousing and data mining technologies have extensive potential applications in govt. Data mining is the process of discovering new patterns, correlations, trends by mining large amounts of data stored in warehoused. It has a capability to build predicture rather than retrospective models. Data mining is not specific to any industry. Datamining tools are predictive and explains next month demand. It defnies concentrated micromarket to reduce future mailing costs and imporve success rates.

Data mining as a part of the Knowledge Discovery Process. Knowledge discovery in databases, frequently abbreviated as KDD, typically encompasses more than data mining. The knowledge discovery process comprises six phases: data mining, and the reporting and display of the discovered information.

The results of data mining may be reported in a variety of formats, such as listings, graphic outputs, summary tables, or visualisations.

Goals of Data Mining and Knowledge Discovery. Broadly speaking, the goals of data mining fall into the following classes: prediction, identification, classification, and optimisation.

Prediction: Data mining can show how certain attributes within the data will behave in the future. Examples of predictive data mining include the analysis of buying transactions to predict what consumers will buy under certain discounts, how much sales volume a store would generate in a given period, and whether deleting a product line would yield more profits or explain why some customers defect to our competitions. In such applications, business logic is used coupled with data mining. In a scientific context, certain seismic wave patterns may predict an earthquake with high probability.

Identification: Data patterns can be used to identify the existence of an item, an event, or an activity or some new patterns of customer behaviour. For example, intruders trying to break a system may be identified by the programmes executed, files accessed, and CPU time per session. In biological applications, existence of a gene may be identified by certain sequences of nucleotide symbols in the DNA sequence. The area known as authentication is a form of identification. It ascertains whether a user is indeed a specific user or one from an authorised class; it involves a comparison of parameters or images or signals against a database.

Classification: Data mining can partition the data so that different classes or categories can be identified based on combinations of parameters to find a clever say to display the data. For example, customers in a supermarket can be categorised into discount-seeking shoppers, shoppers in a rush, loyal regular shoppers, and infrequent shoppers. This classification may be used in different analyses of customer buying transactions as a post-mining activity. Sometimes classification based on common domain knowledge is used as an input to decompose the mining problem and make it simpler. For instance, health foods, party foods, or school lunch foods are distinct categories in the supermarket business. It makes sense to analyse relationships within and across categories as separate problems. Such categorisation may be used to encode the data appropriately before subjecting it to further data mining.

Optimisation: One eventual goal of data mining may be to optimise the use of limited resources such as time, space, money, or materials and to maximise output variables such as sales or profits under a given set of constraints. As such, this goal of data deals with optimisation under constraints. Data mining techniques can help identity and correct problems in the most consistent ways possible.

The term data mining is currently used in a very broad sense. In some situations it includes statistical analysis and constrained optimisation as well as machine learning. There is no sharp line separating data mining from these disciplines.

Types of Knowledge Discovered during Data Mining: The term "Knowledge" is very broadly interpreted as involving some degree of intelligence. Knowledge is often classified as inductive and deductive. Data mining addresses inductive knowledge which can be represented in many forms: in an unstructured sense, it can be represented in decision trees, semantic networks, neural networks, or hierarchies of classes or frames. The knowledge discovered during data mining can be described in four ways are discussed below, as follows.

1. **Association rules :** These rules correlate the presence of a set of items with another range of values for another set of variables. Examples: (*i*) When a female retail shopper buys a handbag, she is likely to buy shoes. (*ii*) An X-ray image containing characteristics *a* and *b* is likely to also exhibit characteristic *c*.
2. **Classification hierarchies:** The goal is to work from an existing set of events or transactions to create a hierarchy of class. Examples: (*i*) A population may be divided into five ranges of credit worthiness based on a history of previous credit transactions. (*ii*) A model may be developed for the factors that determine the desirability of location of a store on a 1-10 scale. (*iii*) Mutual funds may be classified based on performance data using characteristics such as growth, income, and stability.
3. **Sequential patterns:** A sequence of actions or events is sought. Example: If a patient underwent cardiac bypass surgerkly for blocked arteries and later developed high blood urea within a year of surgery, he or she is likely to suffer from kidney failure within the next 18 months. Detection of sequential patterns is equivalent to detecting among events with certain temporal relationships.
4. **Patterns within time series:** Similarities can be detected within positions of the time series. Three examples follow with the stock market price data as a time series: (*i*) Stocks of a utility company ABC Power and a financial company XYZ Securities show the same selling pattern during 2006 in terms of closing stock price. (*ii*) Two products show the same selling pattern in summer but a different one in winter. (*iii*) The web accesses made by a collection of users against a set of documents (say, in digital library) may be analysed in terms of the keywords of documents to reveal clusters or categories of users. For most applications, the desired knowledge is a combination of the above types.

Applications of Data Mining

Data mining technologies can be applied to a large variety of decision-making contexts in business. In particular, areas of significant payoffs are expected to include the following:

Marketing: Marketing depends heavily on accurate information to execute retention analysis, trending, targeted promotions etc. Applications include analysis of consumer behavior based on buying patterns; determination of marketing strategies including advertising, store location, and targeted mailing; segmentation of customers, stores, or products; and design of catalogs, store layouts, and advertising campaigns.

Finance: Applications include analysis of creditworthiness of clients, segmentation of account receivables, performance analysis of finance investments like stocks, bonds, and mutual funds; evaluation of financing options; and fraud detection. A bank can identify fiscally related companies that may be in financial zeopardy before extending loan to them.

Manufacturing: Applications involve optimisations of resources like machines, manpower, and materials; optimal design of manufacturing processes, shop-floor layouts, and product design, such as for automobiles based on customer requirements.

Health Care: Applications include an analysis of effectiveness of certain treatments; optimisation of processes within a hospital, relating patient wellness data with doctor qualifications; and analyzing side effects of drugs.

Sales and customer service : When information is properly aggregated and delivered to front line sales and service professionals, customer service is greatly enhanced. On availability of customer's information rule-based software can be employed to automatically recommend product.

State-of-the-Art of Commercial Data Mining Tools: All the tools for data mining are classified into following categories: commercial tools, public domain tools and research prototypes. At the present time, commercial data mining tools use several common techniques to extract knowledge. These include association rules, clustering, neural networks, sequencing, and statistical analysis. Also used are decision trees, which are a representation of the rules used in classification or clustering, and statistical analyses, which may include regression and many other techniques. Other commercial products use advanced techniques such as genetic algorithms, case-based reasoning, Bayesian networks, nonlinear regression, combinatorial optimisation, pattern matching, and fuzzy logic.

Most data mining tools use the ODBC (Open database Connectivity) interface. ODBC is and industry standard that works with databases; it enables access to data in most of the popular database programmes such as Access, dBASE, Informix, Oracle, and SQL Server. Some of these software packages provide interfaces to specific database programmes; the most common are Oracle, Access, and SQL Server.

Most of the tools work in the Microsoft Windows environment and a few work in the UNIX operating system. The trend is for all products to operate under the Microsoft Windows environment. One tool, Data Surveyor, mentions ODMG compliance.

In general, these programmes perform sequential processing in a single machine. Many of these products work in the client-server mode. Some products incorporate parallel processing in parallel computer architectures and work as a part of on-line analytical processing (OLAP) tools.

Public domain tools are largely freeware with just registration fees. Research prototypes are classified as single task and generic multi-task tools. The generic single task tools generally use neural networks or decision trees. They cover only data mining part and require extensive pre processing and post processing steps. Generic multitasking tools offer modules for preprocessing and post processing stages and also offer a broad selection of various data mining algorithms as clustering, deviction etc.

User Interface: Most of the tools run in a graphical user interface (GUI) environment. Some products include sophisticated visualisation techniques to view data and rules (*e.g.*, MineSet of SGI), and are even able to manipulate data this way interactively. Text interfaces are rare and are more common in tools available for UNIX, such as IBM's Intelligent Miner.

Application Programming Interface: Usually, the application programming interface (API) is an optional tool. Most products do not permit using their internal functions. However, some of them allow the application programmer to reuse their code. The most common interfaces are C libraries and Dynamic Link Libraries (DLLs). Some tools include proprietary database command languages.

Future Directions: Data mining tools are continully evolving, building on ideas from the latest scientific research. Many of these tools incorporate the latest algorithms taken from artificial intelligence (AI), statistics, and optimisation.

At present, fast processing is done using modern database techniques--such as distributed processing--in client -server architecture, in parallel database, and in data warehousing. For the future, the trend is toward developing Internet capabilities more fully. In addition, hybrid approaches will become commonplace, and processing will be done using all resources is available. Processing will take advantage of both parallel and distributed computing environments. This shift is especially important because modern databases contain very large amounts of information. Not only are multimedia databases growing, but image storage and retrieval are both slow operations. Also, the cost of secondary storage is decreasing, so massive information storage will be feasible, even for small companies. Thus, data mining programmes will have to deal with larger sets of data of more companies.

In the near future it seems that Microsoft Windows NT and UNIX will be the standard platforms, with NT being dominant. Most of data mining software will use the ODBC standard to extract data from business databases; proprietary input formats can be expected to disappear. There is a definite need to include nonstandard data, including images and other multimedia data, as source data for data mining. However, the algorithmic developments for nonstandard data mining have not reached a maturity level sufficient for commercialisation.

WINDOWS PROGRAMMING

Windows applications use the Win-32 functions and communicate with the Win32 subsystem to make system calls. The **Win 32 subsystem** accepts the Win 32 function calls and uses the **system interface** library module to make the necessary true NT system calls to carry them out.

Microsoft has define a set of calls called the **Win32 API (Application Programming Interface)** are library procedures that either make system calls to get the work done, or, in some case, do the work right in the user-space library procedure or in the Win32 subsystem. The Win32 API calls do not change with new releases, to promote stability. However, there are also NT API calls that may change between releases of NT. Although the Win32 API calls are not all NT system calls, it is better to focus on these here rather than the true NT system calls because the Win 32 API calls are well documented are more stable over time.

The Win 32 API philosophy is completely different from the UNIX philosophy. In the latter, the system calls are all publicly known and form a minimal interface: removing even one of them would reduce a very comprehensive interface, often with three or four ways of doing the same thing, and including many functions that clearly should not be (and are not) system calls, such as an API call to copy an entire file.

Many Win32 API calls create kernel objects of one kind or another, including files, processes, threads, pipes, etc. Every call creating a kernel object returns a result called a **handle** to the caller. This handle can be subsequently used to perform operations on the object. Handles are specific to the process that created the object referred to by the handle. They cannot be passed directly to another process and used there (just as UNIX file descriptors cannot be passed to other processes and used there). However, under certain circumstances, it is possible to duplicate a handle and pass it to other processes in a protected way, allowing them controlled access to objects belonging to other processes. Every object also has a security descriptor associated with it, telling in detail; who may and may not perform what kinds of operations on the object.

NT is sometimes said to be object-oriented because

the only way to manipulate kernel objects is by invoking methods (API function) on their handles. On the other hand, it lacks some of the most basic properties of object-oriented systems such as inheritance and polymorphism. But it allows files to be mapped directly onto regions of virtual address spaces & thereafter it can be read/write using ordinary memory references.

The Win32 API is also available on Windows 95/98 (as well as on the consumer electronics operating system, Windows CE), with a small number of exceptions. For example, Windows 95/98 do not have any security, so those API calls that relate to security just return error codes on Windows 95/98. Also, NTfile names use the Unicode character set, which is not available on Windows 95/98. There are also differences in parameters to some API function calls. On NT, for example, all the screen coordinates given in the graphics functions are true 32-bit number; on Windows 95/98, only the low-order 16 bits are used (for backward compatibility with Windows 3.1). The existence of the Win32 API on several different operating systems makes it easier to port programmes between them but also tells out more clearly that it is somewhat decoupled from the actual system calls.

Windows API

The microsoft windows operating system and its environment defines hundreds of individual functions that you can use in your visual basic programmes. These functions are available to you through the windows Application Programme Interface (API) third party vender less make thousands of additional functions available use in your basic programmes.

Windows NT Virtual Memory

In NT, every user process has its own virtual address space. Virtual addresses are 32 bits long, so each process has 4 GB of virtual address space. The lower 2 GB are available for the process code and data; the upper 2 GB allow (limited) access to kernel memory, except in Enterprise versions of NT in which the split can be 3 GB for the user and 1 GB for the kernel. The virtual address space is demand paged, with a fixed page size (4 KB on the Pentium II).

Each virtual page can be in one of three states: free, reserved, or committed. A **free page** is not currently use and a reference to it causes a page fault. When a process is started, all of its pages are in free state until the programme and initial data are mapped into its address space. Once code or data is mapped onto a page, the page is said to be **committed.** A reference to a comitted page is mapped using the virtual memory hardware and succeeds if the page is in main memory. If the page is not in main memory, a page fault occurs and the operating system finds and brings in the page from disk. A virtual page can also be in **reserved** state, which indicates it is not available for being mapped until the reservation is explicitly removed. In additional to the free, reserved, and commited attributes, pages also have other attributes. such as being readable, writable, and executable. The top 64 KB and bottom 64 KB of memory are always free, to catch pointer errors (uninitiased pointers are often 0 or –1).

Each committed page has a shadow page on the disk where it is kept when it is not in main memory. Free and reserved pages do not have shadow pages, so references to them cause page fauls (the system cannot bring in a page from disk if there is no page on disk). The shadow pages on the disk are arranged into one or more paging files. The operating system keeps track of which virtual page maps onto which part of which paging file. For (execute only) programme text, the excutable binary file contains the shadow pages; for data pages, special paging files are used.

NT, like System V, allows files to be mapped directly onto regions of the virtual address spaces (*i.e.*, runs of consecutive pages). Once a file has been mapped onto the address space, it can be read or written using ordinary memory references.

Memory-mapped files are implemented in the same way as other committed pages, only the shadow pages can be in the disk file instead of in the paging file.As a result, when a file is mapped in, the version in memory may not be identical to the disk version (due to recent writres to the virtual address space). However, when the file is unmapped or is explicitly flushed, the disk version is brought up to data.

NT explicitly allows two or more processes to map in the same file at the same time, possibly at different virtual addresses. By reading and writing memory words, the processes can now communicate with each other and pass data back and forth at very high bandwidth, since no copying is required. Different processes may have different accesss permissions. Since all the processes using a mapped file share the same pages, changes made by one of them are immediately visible to all the others even if the disk file has not yet been updated.

The Win32 API contains a number of functions that allow a process to manage its virtual memory explicitly.

The heart of any operating system is providing services to user programmes. mostly I/O services such as reading and writing files. Both UNIX and NT offer a wide variety of I/O services to user programmes. For most UNIX system calls, NT has an equivalent call, but the reverse is not true as NT has far more calls and each of them is far more complicated than its UNIX counterpart.

NT supports several file systems, the most important of which are **NTFS (NT File System)** and the **FAT (File Allocation Table)** file system. The former is a new file system developed specifically for NT; the latter is the old MS-DOS file system, which is also used on Windows 95/98 (albeit with support for longer file nemes). Since the FAT file system is basically obsolete (although several hundred million people are still using it). Starting with NT 5.0, the FAT32 file system used in later versions of Windows 95 and in Windows 98 was also supported.

File names in NTFS can be up to 255 characters long. File names are in Unicode, allowing people in countries not using the Latin alphabet (*e.g.*, Japan, India and Israel) to write file names in their native language. (Infact, NT uses Unicode throughout internally; versions starting with NT 5.0 have a single binary that can be used in any country and still use the local language because all the menus, error messages, etc., are kept in country-dependent configuration files). NTFS fully supports case - sensitive names (so foo is different from FOO). Unfortunately, the Win 32 API does not fully support case-sensitivity for file names and not at all for directory names, so this advantage is lost to programmes using Win 32.

As with UNIX, a file is just a linear sequence of bytes, although up to a maximum of $2^{64}–1$.File pointers also exist, as in UNIX, but are 64 bits wide rather than 32 bits, to handle the maximum length file. The Win 32 API function calls for file and directory manipulation are roughly similar to their UNIX counterparts, except most have more parameters and the security model is different. Opening a file returns a handle, which is then used for reading and writing the file. However, unlike in UNIX, handles are not small integers, and standard input, standard output, and standard error have to be acquired explicitly rather than being predefined as 0,1, and 2 (except in console mode, where they are preopened).

NT supports a hierarchical file system, similar to the UNIX file system. The separator between component names is \ however, instead of /, a fossil inherited from MS-DOS. There is a concept of a current working directory and path names can be relative or absolute. One significant difference with UNIX, however, is UNIX allows the file systems on different disks and machiners to be mounted together in a single naming tree, thus hiding the disk structure from all software. NT 4.0 does not have this property, so absolute file names must begin with a drive letter indication which logical disk is meant, as in C:\windows\system \foo.dll. Starting with NT 5.0, UNIX-style 5.0 mounting of file systems was added.

NT 4.0 did not support file links. At level of the graphical desktop, shortcuts were supported, but these constructions were internal to the desktop and had no counterpart in the file system itself. An application programme could not enter a file in a second directory without copying the entire file. Starting with NT 5.0 file linking was added to the file system proper.

NT has a much more elaborate security mechanism than UNIX, Although there are hundreds of API functions relating to security, the following brief description gives the general idea. When a user logs in, his or her initial process is given an **access token** by the operating system. The access token contains the user's **SID(Security ID),** a list of the security groups to which the user belongs, any special privileges available, and a few other items. The point of the access token is to concentrate all the security information in one easy-to-find place. All processes created by this process inherit the same access token.

One of the parameters that can be suplied when any object is created is its **security descriptor.** The security descriptor contains a list of entries called an **ACL (Access Control List).** Each entry permits or prohibits some set of the operations on the object by some SID or group. For example, a file could have a security descriptor specifying that Elinor has no access to the file at all, Ken can read the file's length but nothing else.

When a process tries to perform some operarion on an object using the handle it got when it opened the object, the security manager gets the process access token and goes down the list of entries in the ACL in order. As soon as it finds an entry that matches the caller's SID or one of the caller's groups, the access found there is taken as definitive. For this reason, it is usual to put entries denying access ahead of entries granting access in the ACK, so that a user who is specifically denied access cannot get in via a back door by being a member of group that has legitimate access. The security descriptor also contains information used for auditing accesses to the object.

The standard information field contains information such as the time stamps needed by POSIX, the hard link count, the read-only and archive bits, etc. It is a fixed-length field and always present. The file name is variable length, up to 255 Unicode characters. In order to make such files accessible to old 16-bit programmes, files can also have a MS-DOS name, which consists of 8 alphanumeric characters optionally followed by a dot and an extension of up to 3 alphanumeric characters. If the actual file name conforms to the MS-DOS 8+3 naming rule, a secondary MS-DOS name is not used.

Regarding the security information, in versions up to and including NT 4.0, the secutity field contained the actual security descriptor. Starting with NT 5.0, all the security information was centralised in a single file, with the security field simply pointing to the relevant part of this file.

For small files, the file data itself is actually contained in the MFT entry, saving a disk access to fetch it. This idea is called an **immediate file**. For somewhat larger files, this field contains pointers to the clusters containing the data, or more commonly, runs of consecutive clusters so a single cluster and a length can represent an arbitrary amount of file data. If a single MFT entry is insufficiently large to hold whatever information it is supposed to hold, one or more additional entries can be chained to it.

The maximum file size is 2^{64} bytes. To get an idea of how big a 264-byte file is, imagine that the file were written out in binary, with each 0 or 1 occupying 1 mm of space. The 267-mm listing would be 15 light -years long, reaching far beyond the solar system, to Alpha Centauri and back.

The NTFS file system has other important features such as data compression and fault tolerance using atomic transactions.

Declaring Windows API Functions

Declaration for API routines should be located in module-level code. For a list of predefined windows API function declaration consult the Win 32 API.txt file in the win API sub directory of visual basic (at the time of this writing the file is available only for the professional editor of visual basic). The file is more than 600 KB and growing instead, simply cut and paste the declaration you need into your programme. You can use the API viewer tool to import any declarations and programme constant you need.

(a) API Declaration Syntax The syntax used to declare an API function follows: [Public: Private] Declare function Name Lib "Library Name"--[Alias "Alias Name "] ([Argument List]) IS API function Type Specifier

The syntax follows the standard visual basic syntax, visual basic conventions where item surrounded by brackets ([ ]) are optional and might or might not be present in the declaration.

(b) The syntax for an API subroutine is slightly different.

[Public: Private] Declare sub API subroutine
Name
Lib. "Library Name "--
[Alias "Alias Name"] ([Argument List])

Note the subroutines do not return values, so a function type specifier is not added to the end of the API declaration for an API subroutine. These differences imply that you must pay close attention to the specifies of any API call made in your programmes and their associated declaration.

Passing Information to the Windows API Function

Many Windows API functions require a list of arguments. Each argument passed to the routine has four parts:

A Byval keyword

- The name of the variable being passed
- The As Visual Basic Keyword
- The data type being passed.

Retrieving Information from the Windows API Function

Windows API functions return a value (Declare as function) and some do not (Declare as sub).

Those that return a value can be used in the same manner as visual basic function. You might retrieve some system Information.

Dim heapsize as long.

heapsize =Getfree space **(f Flag %)**

This method to retrieve small amount of Information from a window API function.

E-COMMERCE

The act of conducting business online is called E-commerce. Any commercial activity that takes place directly between a business, its partners, or its customers through a combination of computing and communication technologies comes under E-commerce.

Electronic commerce is the general term used for a buying and selling process, which is carried out electronically. In this process, the selling companies describe their products and services on the net which can be searched by prospective customers and orders may be placed by the buyers using their credit cards. The product is then delivered physically to the buyer. Software can be sent electronically directly to the computer of the costomer.

The World Wide Web is playing a major role in enhancing E-business. The World Wide Web is expected to have an increasing impact on trade. At the consumer level, it is possible to buy a wide range of goods and services at websites. At corporate level, e-commerce technologies enables companies to form on line partnerships, conduct business transactions online and collaborate on projects. The web can provide a good picture, an eloquent description and even customer reviews or virtual reality displays. Although many of the early sites were mainly concerned with publicizing an organisation's products and providing contacts, there is now more emphasis on supporting trade. This requires two issues to be solved. The first is the technical one of providing the interfaces through which potential clients can place orders. Many organisations are now developing interfaces for searches for required products, followed by direct placement of orders for those products. Potential clients browsing the Web can read this information and, if they wish, either make an enquiry or directly place a request for service, or order a product, through the site. This inquiry is processed against a database and people who can fulfill the service or order notified about any actions that are needed. There is another kind of site, called electronic shopping malls, which can provide access to a variety of bussinesses through the one site.

The other problem is to manage the actual financial transactions, or what is often referred to as electronic commerce. An important problem to be solved in managing financial transactions is that of security of the messages and their exchange to prevent people making fraudulent entries, getting unauthorised access to accounts, or altering transactions either to get benefits or simply to interfare in the process. More and more techniques are evolving to provide the needed security, ranging from authentication using passwords or smart cards, to more complex crytographic techniques. Now many sites provide & secure environment for transactions.

Internet is revolutionising e-commerce which is entirely different way for companies to conduct business. It provides the first affordable and secure way to link people and computers spontaneously across organisational boundaries. This is spawning numerous innovative enterprises-virtual organisations, markets, and trading communities. But the internet's potential is imperilled by the rising spectre of digital anarchy: closed markets that cannot use each other's services, incompatible applications and frameworks that cannot interoperate or build upon each other; and an array of security and payment options that confuses consumers.

One solution to these problems is an object-oriented architectural framework for internet commerce. Several major vendors of electronic-commerce solutions have announced proprietary versions of such a framework. The major platforms are :

- IBM Commerce Point.
- Microsoft Internet Commerce Framework.
- Netscape ONE (Open Network Environment).
- Oracle NCA (Network Computing Architecture).
- Sun/Javasoft JECF (Java Electronic Commerce Framework).

Recently, four of these companies have agreed to support a common distributed object model based on CORBA IIOP (Common Object Request Broker Architecture Internet thrive, such systems must also interoperate at a business application level.

A consumer or business using one framework should be able to shop for, purchase, and pay for goods and services offered on a different framework. This is currently not possible. But CommerceNet is organising Eco System, a cross-industry effort to build a framework - of frameworks, involving both e-commerce vendors and end users. But technically this project is challenging because information technology is advancing day by days and there is seldom time for even de facto standards to emerge. Instead, we must deal with de facto interoperation-making incompatible products already in the market place to communicate. Protocols, formats, and the like should not create obstacles in business. All businesses operate within an external environment.

The success of this proccess clearly depends on market leaders in each area participating actively on their respective task forces.

CommerceNet is also developing a Common Business Language (CBL) that allows application agents communicate using messages and objects that model communications in the real business world. A network services architecture (protocols, APIs, and data formats) will insulate application agents from each other and from platform dependencies, while facilitating their interoperation. Functionally, Eco-System fills three distinct roles. These are:

- a layer of middleware that facilitates agent interoperation through services such as authentication, billing, payment, and directories;
- an object-oriented development environment that encourages the reuse of e-commerce modules (even modules that represent the product line of an entire company);
- an industry roadmap and interoperability example that promotes open standards and helps technology vendors communicate with the users about product features.

Framework of Frameworks

A framework is an almost complete application that users can customise or extend to address particular needs. EcoSystem is a framework for building internet markets. Specifically, it is a framework of frameworks that model key business processes and services. Since frameworks build on each other, the resulting applications are tightly linked through a shared - services infrastructure.

V-market services are those that serve an internet market. These are vertical markets of closely aligned businesses. Examples are real estate, securities tranding (buy, sell, and quote services), or any vertical supply chain.

Business services include generic business process and applications common to multiple V-markets. They include retail and business-to-business (procurement, order entry, inventory and supply chain management, and logistics) functions. Vendors may have initially developed such services for specific V-market and later generalised them for reuse. Marketware is a special sub-class of these services that links buyers to sellers.

Commerce services are basic e-commerce services, such as digital "wallets", that allow individuals and companies to authenticate their identities, make payments, locate vendors, collaborate, and otherwise participate in a V-market. Advanced, next -generation commerce services will include secure multimedia mail, smart-card-based security and payment, digital-content delivery, application billing and accounting, transaction management, and agent management.

Network services enhance the performance, reliability and security of the internet to accommodate mission-critical business needs. Examples include quality-of -service management, IP (Internet Protocol) multicast, delivery receipts, authenticated packets, and smart firewalls (those that pass packets only among authorised business partners).

Each framework specifies core services that all application objects belonging to that class (for example, payments and catalogues) must provide. They must also specify a network services interface (NSI). An NSI is a set of messages in an implementation -independent language (CORBA IDL, Interface Definition Language). The standard messages request services over a network and differ from APIs in that they are at a higher level and written in IDL. In addition, a framework must specify APIs for software modules involved in delivering services.

Every application under Eco System-whether a catalogue or an entire V-market –is a network-accessible service.Vendors will differentiate their products by providing additional services beyond those specified in the framework. But the defining characteristic of a payment, shipping, or catalogue object is its ability to respond to the associated framework. Modules can plug into frameworks via APIs; thus, some frameworks function as middleware, allowing access to several vendors modules through a common set of requests. Object wrappers transform stand alone and legacy applications (written before a relevant Eco service framework existed) into Eco services.

Application modules plug into e-commerce platforms via APIs, and other applications can access them using standard NSI requests. The JEPI framework is an example of a payment platform. When fully developed, it will define standard APIs and protocols that allow interoperability of many incompatible payment solutions already on the market.

Getting Frameworks To Talk

Eco System is based on CORBA 2.0, an emerging industry standard for distributed objects and networking. CORBA 2.0 includes the Internet Inter ORB Protocol (IIOP), which Netscape Communicator will support. Eco will also work with HTTP (hypertext transfer protocol), HTML (hypertext markup languge), and Java. The following design decisions conform to emerging industry trends:

Marketware

A special class of Eco applications and services brings together buyers and sellers. Marketware is based on a common platform that developers can customise by plugging in different application modules. These modules serve as building blocks to implement a variety of value - added markets and market services:

- Matchmaking is a trading post where buyers and sellers can exchange goods or services. This service matches buyers and sellers on the basis of product descriptions and personal or company profiles (like, for example, Sun's Matchmaker).
- Negotiation services allow buyers and sellers to post offers specifying price ranges, quantities, delivery dates, and other terms. The service notifies parties in real time or via e-mail of close matches. Parties can respond by modifying their offers if so desired (as in, for example, the Fast Parts system).
- Buy-sell brokering allows buyers to post requests for quotations, which the service forwards to registered sellers with appropriate interest profiles. Sellers can respond with bids, which the service collects, sorts, and forwards to the buyer. (Shopping agents such as Andersen Consulting's Bargain Finder are a special case of this service.)
- Referrals and directory services handle buyer requests for referrals. These services match requests against profile of registered sellers using buyer-supplied criteria.
- Aggregation allows buyers to submit requests for goods and services, which the service pools with similar requests to obtain quantity discounts.
- The marketware framework supports these applications by providing a common set of structures and functions.
- Standard profiles for buyers, sellers, and intermediaries. Profiles provide the information needed for a party to participate in market transactions. This information could include size and type of business, location and street address, terms, conditions, contracts supported, certificate information, credentials, credit rating, and references.
- Standard taxonomies of goods and services would allow parties to target particular transactions and filter out others. Taxonomies would use standard commercial classifications such as SIC (standard industrial classification) codes as well as custom ones. For example, a

three-level hierarchy would classify products by industry (for example, computer), subarea (peripherals), and type (disk drives). CommerceNet is working to develop an evolvable "Taxonomy of Everything" for products.

- Standard CBL commands to invoke market actions such as buy, sell, bid, post request for quote, and locate interested buyers or qualified vendors.
- Authentication and authorisation functions that use buyer and seller profiles to control what information a party can see or modify.
- Acccounting and reporting of transactions for buyers, sellers, and market administrators.
- A notification service allows buyers and sellers to register their interest in selected market events (a new -bid posting, for example) and receive a CBL notification message when they occut.

Object orientation

Every Eco System service is a network-accessible object. Objects respond to agents using CBL commands delivered over HOP and to browsers using HTTR HTML, and Java. This duality maintains compatibility with current websites and affords a graceful migration path. It's also compatible with emerging industry trends and anticipates the possibility that the next generation of HTTP and HOP may some day merge. If the industry does not widely accept CORBA, agents will still be able to access the web by using embedded semantic mark-up. Such embedded mark-up will let agents understand and respond to the information depicted graphically in a web page.

Microsoft and Netscape recently endoresed XML (Extended Mark-up Language), a simplified version of SGML used for embedding tags into HTML. Eco imposes a layer of middleware on top of leading Internet commerce platforms such as Netscape ONE and Oracle NCA. It uses the CORBA HOP accommodate CBL agents.

CORBA and HOP insulate .application developers from most implementation and runtime details. CORBA provides IDL, a neutral definition language not tied to any specific programming language. Compiling the IDL generates object-oriented code implementing APIs. This allows any vendor to provide application object(s) that actually implement the specification. Vendors can write such objects in any language, and the objects can reside on any internet - connected host. This architecture accommodates legacy applications by encapsulating them in an object wrapper and creating a corresponding IDL file as an interface.

CORBA standardises a CORBA-IDL-to C++ mapping. Java Soft and the OMG (Object Management Group) have released Java IDL alpha 2.2 for mapping IDL to Java. Object orientation allows developers to more quickly write and/or reuse applications to support changing business environments. Maintaining Eco's object orientation requires the use of an object-oriented language, CommerceNet has selected Java for this task. Java is an interpreted language developed specifically with heterogeneous distributed networks and applications in mind. Vendor-neutral bytecode can be securely downloaded from the network as an applet that runs on a virtual machine residing on the user's system, most likely a Java-enabled browser.

The Java runtime has built-in security features such as a bytecode verifier that enforces the Java security model for example, disallowing pointers and prevents malicious code from escaping the Java virtual machine (or "sandbox") and accessing the underlying operating system. Finally, Java Beans provides an architecture and platform-neutral API for creating and using dynamic Java components. Developers will be able to use a variety of development tools to assemble custom applications. These applications can draw on a rich variety of support services (such as event handling and persistence) that make Java Beans fully portable.

Protocol negotiation, mediators, and gateways

Application vendors are usually much more willing to agree on a metaprotocol than a standard. That's because a standard would require most to abandon rival technologies in which they have a substantial investment. Since today's computers can support multiple protocols, negotiation is a practical way of realising *de facto* interoperation.

Negotiation protocols, bridging gateways, and mediators (smart gateways) have a part in accomplishing interoperability. In JEPI, sellers provide buyers with a list of payment types they accept (analogous to merchants displaying credit card logos in their store windows). Buyers then select the form of payment they wish to use, which implicitly selects the appropriate protocols (SET or Mondex, for example).

An alternative to protocol negotiation is simply to translate between proprietary protocols using a gateway service. Gateways work well with functionally similar protocols that differ in syntactical details. Thus, gateways are often a good way for legacy database applications to communicate because the applications involved are reasonably well standardised at a functional level. Gateways can also complement protocol negotiation. Namely, one alternative can be for each party to adhere to their favourite protocol and employ gateway services. In effect, the parties agree to disagree.

Mediators are smart gateways, which can negotiate a mutually acceptable protocol with each of several sites, retrieve information from each site, and integrate it. Mediators were originally developed for advanced information retrieval tasks, but are well-suited to e-commerce tasks such as integrating the catalogues and business system of several cooperating firms.

Common Business Language

NSI messages, business objects, and product taxonomies will constitute a CBL for internet commerce. Eco extends HOP by adding two new levels of abstraction: CBL messages and CBL agents. A CBL message is an object-oriented alternative to the ad hoc text strings currently used in electronic data interchange. Each framework inherits the service requests and business objects of those frameworks upon which it builds, specialising and extending the inherited entities to provide new functions.

CBL agents provide a baseline set of common (Telescriptlike) services that all e-commerce applications can build on.They include basic authentication, authorisation, billing and accounting, micropayment, and directory services. Eco's agent platform provides an agent transport protocol and associated management and support services (creating and destroying agents, subcontrating tasks, delegating permissions and resources, and administering offers to buy or sell services). Using IDL, the CBL stub translates CBL messages into object requests to use HOP- provided interoperability services.

Future Developments

In December 1995, the World Wide Web Consortium (W3C) and CommerceNet co-sponsored the Joint Electronic Payment Initiative (JEPI) to bring key industry players together (Cyber Cash, IBM, Microsoft, Xerox, and British Telecom, among others) to ensure that multiple payment instruments, protocols, and transports will interoperate over the internet. JEPI is a metaprotocol built on top of two new Web protocols- PEP (Protocol Extension Protocol) and UPP (Universal Payment Preamble)–that let clients and merchant servers negotiate among and select payment mechanisms.

Clients and servers can ask each other what forms of payment they support and negotiate a mutually acceptable payment mechanism. PEP is protocol for extending HTTP so that it can dynamically deploy applications that require more facilities than those provided by HTTP's request-response model. PEP associates new extensions to HTTP with a URI and uses a new Protocol: header field to carry the extension identifier and other necessary information-including possibly an implementation of the extension-between clients and servers. Like Java's protocol handlers, PEP provides the capability to automatically and dynamically download software component interfaces, enabling sophisticated applications such as distributed authoring tools to interoperate over the web. PEP has been submitted to the IETF (Internet Engineering Task Force) for inclusion in HTTR Universal Payment Preamble has been built on top of PEP to provide added features.

UPP is intended to provide a minimal layer that lets customers use a multipayment wallet and easily move from payment to payment. It provides a uniform vocabulary and syntax for naming options common to many payment systems, enabling clients and servers to exchange the necessary information and denter a specific payment system. This approach redefines each proprietary payment system as an URI-identified, PEP protocol extension implemented by a generic UPP protocol and module.

UPP negotiations occur via exchange of PEP protocol headers before or during shopping. Negotiation requests available payment choice, presents multiple choices, demands or makes a selection, and accepts or rejects choices.The payment protocol guarantees security, not UPP.

JEPI completed phase 1 in April, 1997 with a JEPI implementation comprising two payment instruments, Cyber Cash and GCTech's GlobelD. Phase 2 strategies, include: validation/revision of UPP/PEP(JEPI used the August 1996 version of PEP, which was subsequently revised for consideration by IETF); incorporation of more payment systems (SET and micro-payments), smart card integration; waller and cash register APIs; and extension of HTML for micro -payments. CommerceNet has committed to phase 2 development, according to CommerceNet's Jim Galvin, project manager for JEPI.

AIMSNet

AIMSNet, a product of the Agile Infrastructure for Manufacturing Systems (AIMS) programme, is a working example of an I-market in the making. Using AIMSNet, an intercompany network (using the internet) links companies like Lockheed Martin and its suppliers, allowing multicompany project teams to exchange technical and business information, collaborate on design, post quotes and purchase orders, tender or accept bits, find potential suppliers and partners and track project milestones. More than 10 companies currently use AIMSNet and in future many more will join.

One of AIMSNet's powerful features is support for collaborative design. Its Multimedia Environment for Collaborative Engineering (MECE) is an online, shared notebook system developed by Lockheed Martin. This allows project team members to assemble and share information, such as design rationale and programme decisions, in the form of text, audio, video, and screen snapshots. It also accommodates 3D design and manufacturing information by using VRML. VRML provides a 3D model independent of any specific CAD programme. Virtual Reality modeling language (VRML) technology allow 3-D effect on the web. VRML is a special programming language that enables designers to create a 3D virtual envirnonment for use in www pages. Users with VRML enabled browsers can navigate through these environment with great freedom, entering and existing rooms, interfacing with objects, looking through windows soon.

Team members use these tools to review information, collect comments, and make recommendations and changes. Current AIMSNet users are large programmes within aerospace companies that develop complex systems such as satellites, rocket engines, missiles, and so on. This effort, funded by the US Defense Advanced Research Projects Agency, has also developed templates to standardise transactions between companies.

An important e-commerce concept, templates convey information between companies in a standard format easily accessed from anywhere through a HTML browser. Users can import information from legacy systems as well as through industry standard protocols. These templates also serve as simple front-end-to -remote databases that are network accessible. They serve to provide multiplier supply chain coordination and facilities for evaluating and selecting suppliers. The coordination agent enables team members to track events critical to a project's success. The agent filters, sorts, priorities, and presents status information coming from various sources to project members manage the project from their own perspective. The supplier selection agent provides a mechanism for rapidly identifying key partners that can meet a project's multiple criteria. AIMSNet offers users a preliminary version of these services. AIMSNet, an industrial commerce infrastructure, is currently piloted as an aerospace I-market but can be easily customised to several other V-markets including automotive, electronics, and construction.

Electronic Payment Systems—The ways of paying for e-commerce transactions can be classified as :

(*a*) Credit cards

(*b*) Debit cards

(*c*) Stored value cards

(*d*) e-cash or Network Money

(*e*) Delayed Payments

(*a*) Credit Cards :This is the most common way of paying e-commerce transactions. The customer types the credit card numebr, expiry data and billing address on the order form and the vendor can verify the details and be confident of payment. The details are generally recorded online or in most cases, rung through a telecast office. Credit cards used in a conventional retail application are recorded on a transaction slip and verified by the use of a signature. Telephone ordering is less secure than the conventional use of credit cards; there is no signature that can be checked and no possibility of assessing if the customer gives the impression of being genuine. For anonyonous customer, credit card payment is not the right choice since it is traceable. But credit cards are likely to continue for small to big transactions.

(*b*) Debit cards : They are also used as credit cards as used in e-commerce. Debit cards are not suitable for small transactions and do not afford anonymity.

(*c*) Stored value cards :This is the most common form of electronic payment. This is used in some public transport operation. Stored value cards are suitable for small transactions and afford anonymity.

(*d*) e-cash or Network money : This is the cheapest method on the net. The system functions by the user transferring money from a credit card or bank account into an e-cash accounts. Then e-cash can be used to make payment for e-commerce transactions.

(*e*) Delayed payments : Payment made through if line is another option.

Risks in Electronic Payment Systems : The privacy of personal details and security of financial transactions are a serious concern to many users and users of e-commerce. Concerns for the security of on line crdit card payments include:

- Fraudulent use of credit cards.
- Credit card details sent over the Internet could be intercepted.
- Remote storage of credit card details also create a risk that someone else might use that account or hack into the system and get the card details.

Electronic Data Interchange (EDI)

EDI provides a standardised system for coding trade transactions so that they can be communicated directly from one computer system to another without the need for printed orders, invoices, delays and errors occurs in paper handling.

It involves the electronic transmission of routine, business transactions data directly between the computer systems of different organisations doing business with each other. In EDI, formatted documents are transmitted over communication links directly between computers, without paper documents or manual data entry. Thus, EDI helps providing faster, consistent and complete information to organisations. EDI standards are to be followed for any new EDI application. Recently, Internet is used as an EDI VADS, Internet provide only the basic services of VADS such as store and forward facilities. Internet does not concern safe delivery of any data you sent in EDI standards provide a common language for the interchange of standard transactions. The EDI standard specifies the syntax for the coding of the electronic document, it does not specify the method of transmission: EDI messages can be encrypted or can include an electronics signature. EDI software is the element of EDI system is bought in from specialist supplier.

EDI interoperability Testing

EDIINT, the Internet Engineering Task Force (IETF) work-group has recommended standards for interoperable, secure electronic data interchange over the Internet. CommerceNet is sponsoring interoperability testing of these EDIINT recommen-dations among implementations from 10 vendors. These vendors include Actra Business Systems (a Netscape/ GEIS company). Atlas Products International, AT&T, CyberPath, DaNet, Digital Equipment Corp., EDS, Harbinger, Premenos, and Sterling Commerce. The vendors are checking the ability of their products to pass EDI securely among themselves. Recently, five vendors demonstrated the successful exchange of digitally signed data among their products.

The demonstration involved passing electronic documents over SMTP (Simple Mail Transport Protocol) using S/MIME standard, factors such as certificate version differences and S/MIME support for multipart /signed documents still caused short-term interoperability problems.

Setting up an E-commerce system

There are hundreds of consulting companies providing the internet based businesses with everything they need to establish an e-commerce system to fit their needs–from helping to designing websites to providing e-business courses. Thesse consulting companies help companies decide what they should do to ensure a successful online business. Often success and failure are determined by the same factors that contribute to the success or failure of any business. These are given below:

- Price
- Selection
- Advertising
- Customer
- Customer convenience
- Consumer satisfaction
- The total cost of business

A general idea about setting up an e-commerce system.

1. ***Configuring a shopping cart:*** To configure a shopping cart, you must specify parameters such as the shopping cart's dimensions and background image. You will need to specify the data that you want the shopping cart to display for each item purchased. Among other things, this data might include item descriptions and options such as size and colour.
2. ***Choosing languages and currency:*** With e-commerce software you can choose from a list of languages in which the shopping cart text can be displayed. You will probably be able to accept more than one kind of currency.
3. ***Establishing shipping costs:*** You should be able to choose how you would like your e-commerce system to calculate shipping costs.
4. ***Designing storefront and catalogue pages:*** Most e-commerce software includes instructions to build your online store front and catalogue pages. Your storefront should welcome people to your store, contain your company logo, have a professional appearance, and be organised so potential customers and business partners can easily navigate your company's site.
5. ***Configuring data paths:*** Your e-commerce software will capture the order information from the shopping cart. You will need to configure the path or paths. This captured information should take to enable the e-commerce system to fill the customer's order.
6. ***Building a database:*** You must also build the database that the shopping cart will access to obtain the information it displays to the customer. The format of this database will depend on the database server you are using. This database should contain all the information that applies to the products or services you sell.

Nowadays, electronic funds transfer is widely used in the banking industry. It is a very fast technique in capturing and processing of cash and credit transfers between businesses and customers. EFT eliminates delays associated with sending hard copy documents. However security being a serious issue with EFT, it should be used with utmost care and precautions.

Electronics in Commerce and Areas of Operation

Today, when commerce is responsible for more than 35 percent of all employment. The new electronic technologies dominate the mechanisation of financial institutions. In other commercial sectors non-electronic machines play a larger role.

Banks must cooperate with one another, and moreover they must have a considerable degree of uniformity in their basic procedures if cheque are to be a useful way to pay bills. Transportation companies, wholesalers, and warehouse operators must work together to ensure the flow of goods from factories to stores.

Banking

Among financial industries banking offers the widest scope for examining the nature and impact of mechanisation.

Standards for coding, the position of codes on cheques, an acceptable printing ink, and similar requirements were established. Essentially all banks employed MICR, MICR'S stream of machine - readable data speeded the development of computer - based record-keeping for virtually all cheking accounts records spread rapidly to other bank activities.

For ATM transaction the customer himself punches a set of codes into a terminal; thus provides his bank with machine-readable data. In effect, he is doing work for which the bank previously had to use its own staff. This type of "labour sharing" is becoming increasingly common.

Service to individuals is only part of a bank's operations; relations with business organisations are at least as important. In this regard a major factor in mechnisation has been the drive by businesses to improve their cash management. The business must know its cash position accurately and be able to move its cash around quickly and economically. In order to move the funds rapidly, banks in turn must be interconnected with one another by computer -to - computer telecommunications networks.

In a subtle way mechanisation has contributed to a change in the nature of banking. Because of government regulations that restrict the activities of banks, the banks have lost ground to other financial organisations as intermediaries between those who have money available and those who want to borrow money.

The loans are mediated by underwriting and securities companies. Moreover, money-market funds have replaced savings accounts for many individuals. Meanwhile, however, and partly as a result of high capacity, efficiency and low costs, the banks have increased their activity as movers of funds. In the process the operations of the financial intermediaries that now compete with banks have been supported and even facilitated. Employment in banking has not suffered from mechanisation. Much of the current flow of money through banks is a response to high inflation and volatile interest rates, and the flow may drop if a stabler economic environment returns. Regulatory reforms may remove the restrictions banks now face. The industry has none the less been restructured, and a complete return of banks to their traditional practices is unlikely.

Transportation

The mechanisation of transport, however clearly calls for more non-electronic equipment than banking does, although transport too makes intensive use of electronic systems. The combination of non-electronic and electronic equipment can be seen in the recent growth of containerised shipping. Containers themselves are an ancient form of technology, but their current level of service owes much to the availability of telecommunications and computers.

New electronic equipment is being applied in all forms of transportations. Computer-based systems are beginning to provide brokerage that bring together empty trucks and cargo awaiting movement.

Microprocessors installed in vehicles now analyse data they get from sensors to improve the performance of all types of engines. They will come to have a role in other forms of vehicle control. In one potential application microprocessors would be given information on the "consist "of a train (the order and weight of each car in the train) and use it to guide the train's breaking. The results would likely be lower fuel consumption and less wear and damage to both the train and its cargo.

The speed, accuracy, ease of use, and cost efficiency of electronic reservation systems is a great advantage.

Telecommunications

Telecommunications is an aspect of high importance. Telecommunications is one of the fastest growing industries in the world.

The dial systems took the labour of establishing a telephonic connection between two parties and transferred it from the operator to the caller. Over the years, the dialling system has been in geographic scope to both national and international operations has been enhanced by the installation of computer-based systems for recording calls and mechanising the preparation of telephone bills. Within the central telephone offices a series of technical advances has marked the transition from electromechanical switches to solid-state ones.

The newer switches have lower maintenance requirements, are faster, have better transmission characteristics, and more efficiently collect and maintain data for usage analysis and billing. Originally all telephone were "hard-wired", that is, the telephone lines were more or less permanently connected to the instruments. Then in the 1960s telephone be installed at each service number. More recently practice has changed further: the telephone wiring now put into houses has universal sockets that enable users to install their own telephones.

Although this last change reduced pressure from manufactures selling equipment designed to interconnect with telephone installation charges, many of the telephone companies have now developed computer databases that record the location of all the wiring and jack sockets in a home, so that people changing their residence can determine their needs in advance and arrange to pick up telephones at a telephone store and install the instruments themselves. A relatively simple set of changes in industry practice has thus allowed labour -sharing and a reduction in installation personnel.

Data warehousing and Digital Libraries

Typically, a data warehouse is a decision-support system which integrates at a single place a plethora of diverse data and record formats, stored in a range of different systems and platforms. A data warehouse is a repository of subjectively selected and adapted operational data, which can answer an *ad hoc*, complex, statistical or analytical queries. It is placed at the centre of DSS (Decision Support System) of an organisation (or corporation) and contains integrated historical data both summarised and detailed information which is common to whole organisation. This implies standardisation of data from a variety of sources to make it more easy to comprehend and apply. Executives need fast and reliable feedback about how the business is performing *vis-a-vis* plants, to measure success and adjust corporate strategy. Data warehousing is becoming essential, heralded as the solution to the management of information impasse, and a defence mechanism against trenchant competition. It has become one of the most used and abused terms in the IT vocabulary. Data warehousing enables easy organisation and maintenance of large data. To most IT solution providers, a data warehouse is virtually any large database, typically in the giga-byte to the tetra-byte range, containing data from more than one source, collected data for the purpose of providing management information and maintaining long-term online storage.

Data can be classified into three categories : reference and transaction data, derived data and denormalised data. Reference and transaction data originates from operational (source) systems and is generally kept in a conventional database system one put, the data cannot be modified. Derived data is derived from the reference and transaction data based on certain rules or computations. It can always be derived again on fresh or modified basis of derivation. Denormalised data is the data which is prepared periodically but is directly based on detailed reference (transaction) data. Denormalised data is the basis for online analytical processing tools (OLAP).

Some vendors of online analytical processing tools (OLAP), which gives the user the capability to perform multidimensional analysis of data define data warehouse as any collection of summarised data from various sources, structured and optimised for query-access.

Business intelligence begins with a top-down view of the key performance indicators or KPIs. The standard queries and reports that create the KPIs may include revenue and profit growth, quality of products and services, and customer satisfaction. The data warehouse provides a quick review of these broad measures and trends, along with departures from the expected results. This allows timely executive intervention to manage the digressions from the plan.

The development of a storage system to handle the growth of data is a major challenge in itself. Implementing data warehousing is an even bigger challenge. As the practice of sharing enormous amounts of information with customers and suppliers through data warehouses is gaining prevalence, a data warehouse or business intelligence application now requires a wide range of client interfaces and the ability to both query and analyse data interactively from a variety of different client platforms.

Managing a data warehouse successfully means optimising the data-storage space to ensure rapid delivery of the required information and to provide the users the right format, to access information in a manner such as a product-wise and region-wise review of sales. A successful data warehouse attracts more users and more data, thus requiring the availability of a more robust and scalable service.

To ensure rapid response time, the data storage aimed at effective integration of operational databases into an environment that enables the strategic use of data. Data storage has to be simplified and automated, based on the initial and usage-based data warehouse information. As new data sources are added, the old ones need to be changed. This is how a data warehouse evolves. For an IT manager, it is crucial to select a platform that provides integrated, easy-to-use tools for query, data analysis, and assessment from a wide variety of tools. A well-constructed data warehouse framework enables a wide range of client applications to be analysed and viewed interactively, whether it is through the corporate firewall, a web server, via e-mail, or a custom-built or purchased application. Data warehousing is a blend of technologies which include relational and multi-dimensional database management systems, client/server architecture, metadata modeling and repositories, GUI etc.

COMPUTER SCIENCE

The benefits of data warehousing can be easily extended to strategic decision making, which can yield very large and tangible benefits. Data warehousing is designed to provide an architecture that will make corporate data readily accessible and usable to knowledge workers and decision makers. It is a database designed for analytical tasks where data may be used from multiple applications. A data warehouse combines one or more tools to extract fields from any kind of structure (open or proprietary, flat, hierachical, object or relational or external data) and synthesis of data into integrated, nonvolatile, subject oriented database with a metadata ''catalog''.

The create database command now specifies the name and size of the data and log files associated with the database; the disk init statement that was used in previous versions to create the actual physical database file and the requirement to reference size in terms of the number of 2k datapages is no longer necessary (SQL Server 7 now uses 8k datapages). Now the database size reference is in terms that most users are familiar with: kilobytes, megabytes, and gigabytes. In addition to these changes in the storage structure, there are new disk formats for rows, extents, data files, and log files. These new formats will allow the desired scalability from low-end to high-end systems while improving performance. In an effort to improve space utilisation and image data can now be shared by multiple rows. In previous versions, if a column contained a few bytes of text or image data it would take up an entire 2k page. Now free space on the new 8k page will be used by data belonging to other rows.

There is also the provision of automatic database creation and alteration when a database is restored. Just the act of issuing a command to restore a database file will automatically create and/or alter the database. This way the database administrator won't have to figure out the size of the receiving database and then create it before restoration. This is merely one example of how SQL Server 7 is much easier to administer.

9 WEB DEVELOPMENT

Architecture of Access

Access is an RDBMS that has several components. One component is the underlying database engine, called the Microsoft Jet engine;16 which is responsible for managing the data. Another component is the user interface, which calls the engine to provide data services, such as storage and retrieval of data. The engine stores all the application data {tables,. indexes, forms, reports, macros, and modules} in a single Microsoft database file (.mdb file). The engine also provides advanced capabilities, such as heterogeneous data access through ODBC, data validation, concurrency control using locks, and query optimisation.

Access works like a complete application development environment, with the internal engine serving to provide the user with RDBMS capabilities. The Access user interface provides Wizards and Builders to aid the user in designing a database application. Builders are interactive programmes that help the user build syntactically correct expressions. The programming model used by Access is event-driven. The user builds a sequence of simple operations, called macros, to be performed in response to actions that occur during the use of the database application. While some applications can be written in their entitety using macros, others may require the extended capabilities of Access Basic, the programming language provided by Access.

There are different ways in which an application with multiple components that includes Access can be integrated. A component (in Microsoft terminology) is an application or development tool that makes its objects available to other applications. Using automation in Visual Basic, it is possible to work with objects from other components to costruct a seamless integrated application. Using the Object Linking and Embedding(OLE) technology, a user can include documents created in another component on a report or form within Access. Automation and OLE are distinct technologies, which are a part of Component Object Mode(COM), a standard proposed by Microsoft.

OLE is a windows feature that combines object embedding and linking functions. OLE allows the users to construct a document consisting data from a single point in time or one in which the data keeps on constantly uptated.

Active X: Microsoft's answer Java is Active X. Active X code creates self contained functions similar to Java applets. These functions may be accessed and executed by any other Active X compatible programme on any Active X system or network. Active X controls are Pentium binary programmes that can be embedded in Web pages. When one of them is encountered, a check is made to see if it should be executed, and if it passes the test, it is executed. It is not interpreted or sandboxed in any way, so it has as much power as any other user programme and can potentially do great harm. Thus, all the security is in the decision whether to run the ActiveX control. The method that Microsoft chose for making this decision is based on the idea of code signing. Each ActiveX control is accompanied by a digital signature–a hash of the code that is signed by its creator using public key cryptography. When an ActiveX control shows up, the browser first verifies the signature to make sure it has not been tampered with in transit. If the signature is correct, the browser then checks its internal tables to see if the programme's creator is trusted or there is a chain of trust back to a trusted creator. If the creator is trusted, the programme is executed; otherwise, it is not. The Microsoft system for verifying ActiveX controls is called Authenticode.

Comparison of Java and ActiveX Approaches

With the Java approach, no attempt is made to determine who wrote the applet. Instead, a run-time interpreter makes sure it does not do things the machine owner has said applets may not do. In contrast, with code signing, there is no attempt to monitor the mobile code's run-time behavior. If it came from a trusted source and has not been modified in transit, it just runs. No attempt is made to see whether the code is malicious or not. If the original programmer intended the code to format the hard disk and then erase the flash ROM so the computer can never again be booted, and if the programmer has been certified as trusted, the code will be run and destroy the computer (unless ActiveX controls have been disabled in the browser).

But there are other, absolutely fundamental differences, between Java and ActiveX, including portability and security. Java has security designed in right from the beginning, and ActiveX can make no such claim. Java applications are secured from both accidental and intentional attacks on system integrity. Active X can only offer the alternative of cryptographic certificates, whose protection is aimed at a completely different target. Sun's Java programming language is independent of both the underlying operating system and the basic hardware Computer, that it runs on. Java reflects unix approach and a similar fundamental philosophy. Java applets can run on any system for which there is a Java interpreter. Active X is available only on the Windows/ Intel, or *Intel* platform used in PCs.

ActiveX specification, which consists of three main elements:

ActiveX controls, which function just like conventional OLE controls (OLXs). They can be located on your browser or can be downloaded from the server and used for something as simple as a button all the way to something as complex as a whole report. ActiveX controls can also interact with one another. **ActiveX documents,** which allow you to view active documents as well as HTML pages, thus presenting you with a common interface for several tasks.

ActiveX scripting, which allows you to coordinate ActiveX controls on your Website using the two available scripting languages, JavaScript and the Visual Basic-based VBScript. Eventually, we may even see ActiveX scripting implementations of Sun's JavaScript and Perl. At this point, VBScript has a smaller runtime module, at 50K compared with the 1.2MB needed for Java.

ActiveX is a careful repackaging of Microsoft's COM (Common Object Model), the foundation that supported OLE. By adding network capabilities (and so creating DCOM or Distributed COM) and by reducing the scope of OLE to create ActiveX, Microsoft has created a comprehensive suite of component-based Internet and intranet-oriented applications. ActiveX controls are not completely incompatible with Java, and Microsoft has not only licensed Java from Sun, but also agreed to provide a wrapper to make Java applets behave just like ActiveX objects.

Microsoft has also announced a set of drop-in ActiveX controls for nonbrowser applications, including the following:

FTP ActiveX Control, which lets applications use FTP

HTML ActiveX Control, which lets applications launch their own simple \ browser

HTTP ActiveX Control, which lets applications behave like simple Web SE

NNTP ActiveX Control, which gives applications access to Usenet newsg and other NNTP news

SMTP/POP3 ActiveX Control, which lets applications use e-mail without need to start a separate programme

WinSock ActiveX Control, which provides an interface to the TCP/IP suite protocols in Windows 95 and Windows NT

These controls are all contained in Microsoft's Internet Control Pack (ICP) and jointly developed by NetManage, Inc. and Microsoft.

An ActiveX Control is a reusable software component that has been developed by Microsoft or by a third-party software vendor. As Table 9.1 shows, an ActiveX Control can be as small as a single button and as large as a Web Browser Control

Table 9.1: Active X controls

Web Browser control	Displays HTML pages, ActiveX controls, and ActiveX Documents and is based on Internet Explorer 3
Marque control at	Scrol/s an HTML page in any direction, a specified rate
ActiveMmovie control	Displays streaming and nonstreaming video and audio
Label	Creates a text label
Textbox	Creates a multiline text-entry and text-display box
Listbox Options	Creates a drop-down list box lets users choose among several options
Toggle button	Creates a *button* with two scrollbar states, such as On and Off creates horizontal and vertical scrollbars
Chart	Creates different kinds of charts
Menu	Creates a menu on a Web page

Currently more than 1,000 commercially ActiveX controls that you can access using MS's C, C++, Visual Basic or Visual J++ programming languages.

When Internet Explorer comes across a Web page containing an ActiveX control, it first checks the System Registry to see if that component is available on that machine. If it is, the Web page is displayed and the control is activated. If not, Internet Explorer finds the control in a location specified by the creator of the HTML page and installs it, automatically. When a component has to be downloaded, you'll see a message to this with effect, so you can choose to cancel or continue with the download. If the control has been digitally signed, you'll see a message that verifies the name of the software developer and that the control has not been tampered with. By default, all downloaded controls are placed in the directory \ WINDOWS \ OCCACHE.

ActiveX technical papers, downloadable software, tips and tricks can be found on Microsoft's Web site at

`http://www.microsoft.com/intdev/controls/controls-f.htm`

and on ActiveX Component Gallery at `http://www.microsoft.com/activex/gallery/`

The ActiveX Gallery includes a library of ActiveX applications, as well as instructions for downloading the software development kit (SDK) from

`http://www.microsoft.com/intdev/sdk/`

10 WEB SCRIPTING

JAVA SCRIPT

OBJECT-ORIENTED PROGRAMMING CONCEPTS

THE OBJECT MODEL

While the benefits of object-oriented software development are getting widely accepted there is no common understanding of how to define objects - neither on the specification or implementation level nor on the conceptual level, which is of outstanding importance for our point of view. Among the still increasing number of object-oriented design methodologies (in a survey we did last year we found more than forty approaches) we felt most inspired by the ones proposed by Booch. Nevertheless none of the two was satisfactory for our purpose. While Rumbaugh et al.' methodology suffers from being somewhat superficial and not consequently objectoriented (for instance: attributes are defined by data types and not by classes) Booch's approach seems to be overloaded by details of various programming languages - which, on our opinion, should not be part of a general methodology for the design of *conceptual* models (for a comprehensive comparison of both methodologies, for other comparisons. When we decided to develop yet another meta model for the design of object models we wanted to take advantage of the benefits provided by all three roots of object-oriented software development, namely programming languages, data modelling, and Artificial Intelligence. In particular we put special emphasis on requirements like integrity, event-handling, business-rules, and user-interface modelling.

CONCEPTUALIZING OBJECTS

While from a (re-)using programmer´s point of view it is sufficient to describe an object solely by the services it provides, analysis and design require a more detailed view. Within an object model one defines classes and associations between classes or between objects respectively. Like in most other methodo-logies the outstanding features of a class are attributes and services. An attribute is regarded as an object that is encapsulated within an object. We do not allow attributes to only hold references to external objects that have an existence of there own in the object space. An attributes semantics is primarily defined by its class. Furthermore a cardinality (using min-max notation) may be assigned: A costumer may have no or many telephone numbers, but he has exactly one date of birth. Assigning a default value allows for generating appropriate initialization operations. The authorization to access an attribute can be separately described for get- and put-access where each access type can be assigned one of three authorization numbers: private (0), protected (1) or public (2). It is not allowed to define write-permission to be greater than read-permission. Each attribute is also characterized by a history-flag. Setting it to true means that every update should be recorded somehow.

A DESIGN ENVIRONMENT TO SUPPORT THE METHODOLOGY

Designing enterprise models according to the proposed methodology can hardly be accomplished without appropriate tools: A complex model requires support for browsing and searching. Because of multiple integrity constraints maintenance that is solely done manually jeopardizes a model's consistency to an unacceptable extent. Finally it is impossible to do without tools when prototyping is to be accomplished. For these reasons we developed an environment that supports analysis, design and maintenance. It was implemented using Smalltalk-80 within the Objectworks 4.0 environment on Sun4-workstations. High productivity could be achieved by using additional class libraries.

MULTIPLE INHERITANCE

When a class extends another class, it inherits the data and methods of the class it extends. This is known as *single inheritance*. It is also possible for a class to extend classes on more than one branch of the class hierarchy tree, as shown in Figure 5.3. This is known as *multiple inheritance*. Multiple inheritance poses some difficulties for object-oriented programming. Most of these difficulties stem from the problem of determining which parent of a class to use under certain conditions. Numerous ambiguities arise when a class may have more than one immediate parent. For example, suppose a class X extends both a class Y and a class Z. Both class Y and class Z implement a unique print method. How does the compiler determine what method should be used to print objects of class X? What if the ambiguity arises during runtime for an object that inherits methods over several widely spaced branches of the class hierarchy? What's a poor compiler to do?

It is possible to design compilers and runtime systems that solve the ambiguities resulting from multiple inheritance, but these solutions tend to introduce a significant amount of processing overhead, adversely affecting program size and performance. The developers of Java have opted to support only single inheritance. This greatly simplifies the Java language, compiler, and runtime system. Java uses the interface construct to provide the benefits of multiple inheritance without the drawbacks resulting from parent ambiguity. You'll learn more about this construct in "Interfaces."

MESSAGES, METHODS, AND OBJECT INTERACTION

In a pure object-oriented programming model, such as that used by Smalltalk, objects interact by sending messages to each other. When an object receives a message, the object invokes a method to process the message. The method may change the state of the object, return information contained in the object, or cause objects to be created or deleted.

The object model used by Java is consistent with the concept of message passing, but does not emphasize it. In the Java model, objects interact by invoking each other's methods. *Methods* provide access to the information contained in an object. The type of access varies depending on the method.

ENCAPSULATION

One of the characteristics of object-oriented programming that is often touted in discussions of the subject is *encapsulation*. The term carries the connotation of an object being enclosed in some sort of container-and that is exactly what it means. Encapsulation is the combining of data and the code that manipulates that data into a single component-that is, an object. Encapsulation also refers to the control of access to the details of an object's implementation. Object access is limited to a well-defined, controlled interface. This allows objects to be self-contained and protects them from accidental misuse, both of which are important to reliable software design.

POLYMORPHISM

Polymorphism is the ability to assume different forms. In object-oriented programming, this refers to the ability of objects to have many methods of the same name, but with different forms. The compiler and runtime system support polymorphism by matching each method invocation to the correct method, class, and object. The ability to figure out which method to use, in complex situations, is the essence of polymorphism.

Luckily for us, polymorphism is implemented in the compiler and runtime system-we don't need to do anything to make it happen. We just need to know that it works.

DYNAMIC BINDING

Sometimes a program might need to interface with objects of many different classes. For example, consider a program that has the responsibility of sending out objects over a communication link. The program may not know what class an object belongs to until it is time to send it. The capability to defer until runtime decisions about what class an object belongs to and the methods for accessing the object is known as *dynamic binding*. Dynamic binding is important to object-oriented programming because it eliminates many potentially constraining assumptions about the classes that an object belongs to and enables objects to be designed in a more general and open manner.

Dynamic binding also provides capabilities that are necessary for the advanced network programming capabilities of Java applets. When a browser executes a Java applet, the applet could require the loading of classes located on other sites across the Internet. Furthermore, these classes could be in a continual state of modification and upgrade. Dynamic binding allows new and modified objects to be used by executing software without requiring recompilation. The compiler and interpreter work together to provide executable code with the capabilities needed to dynamically interface with unknown objects during program execution.

JAVA LANGUAGE BASICS

THE ORIGINS OF JAVA

At this point, you may wonder how Sun's engineers were able to develop such a powerful software development environment and surpass all known programming languages. The answer is they didn't-at least not directly. Java evolved from other research projects at Sun.

The development of Java wasn't as accidental or monumental as the discovery of penicillin, but it shares some of its characteristics. The origins of Java trace back to 1991, when Sun was investigating consumer electronics products. At this time, Mosaic and the World Wide Web were just interesting concepts.

James Gosling, the father of Java, was intent on building a low-cost, hardware-independent software platform using C++. For a number of technical reasons, C++ was dropped, and a new language, called Oak, was developed, based on C++, but eliminating its shortcomings. These shortcomings include problems associated with multiple inheritance, automatic type conversion, the use of pointers, and memory management.

Oak was used to develop a small electronics device called *7. This project resulted in the precursors of many of the components of Java: the development environment, runtime system, and API. The technology was explored in a number of consumer applications but was a little ahead of its time.

By 1994 the Web emerged, Oak was renamed Java, and the proverbial light bulb went on in the minds of the Java developers. Java was used as the basis for a Web browser, called WebRunner. WebRunner was successfully demonstrated, and the Java/HotJava project took off. HotJava, Java, and the Java documentation and source code were made available over the Web, as an alpha version, in early 1995. Initially Java was hosted on SPARC Solaris, and then on Windows NT. In the summer of 1995, Java was ported to Windows 95 and Linux. In the fall of 1995 the Java Beta 1 version was released through Sun's Web site, and Java support was introduced in the Netscape 2.0 browser.

The Java Beta 1 release led scores of vendors to license Java technology, and Java porting efforts were initiated for all major operating systems. In December 1995 the Java Beta 2 version was released, and JavaScript was announced by Sun and Netscape. Java's success became inevitable when, in early December, both Microsoft and IBM announced their intention to license Java technology. On January 23, 1996, Java 1.0 was officially released and made available for download over the Internet. JavaScript was also released. Netscape 2.0 now provides support for both Java and JavaScript.

JAVA PROGRAM STRUCTURE

A file containing Java source code is considered a compilation unit. Such a compilation unit contains a set of classes and, optionally, a package definition to group related classes together. Classes contain data and method members that specify the state and behavior of the objects in your program.

JAVA PROGRAM EXECUTION

The Java byte-code compiler translates a Java source file into machine independent byte code. The byte code for each publicly visible class is placed in a separate file, so that the Java runtime system can easily find it. If your program instantiates an object of class A, for example, the class loader searches the directories listed in your CLASSPATH environment variable for a file called A.class that contains the class definition and byte code for class A.

CLASSIFICATION AND INHERITANCE

Classification is a common way that we organize knowledge. When we encounter a new object in our daily experience, we try to fit that object in our hierarchical classification scheme. If it fits in an existing category, we know what kind of object it is. If it doesn't fit, we add a new category. Describes how we use classification to represent knowledge.

When we classify objects in this hierarchical fashion, the object categories at the top of the classification tree include all the object categories below them. If an object category appears in the classification tree, it satisfies the properties of all object categories above it in the tree presents a classification tree for vehicles. All categories in the tree below the category automobile, for example, share the common characteristics of being four-wheeled, self-powered, and designed for passenger transportation. The fact that a lower-level category shares the characteristics of the categories above it on the classification tree is known as *inheritance*. The lower-level categories are said to inherit the characteristics of the categories above them on the tree. At this point, you're probably wondering what any of this has to do with object-oriented programming in general, and Java software development in particular. We're almost there.

The classes you learned about in the previous section can also be organized in a hierarchical fashion. A class X is said to *extend* another class Y if it contains all the data contained in class Y and implements all the methods implemented by class Y. Class X is said to be a *subclass* of class Y, and class Y is said to be a *superclass*, or *parent class*, of class

X. Classes form a hierarchical classification tree under the subclass relationship. If a class X is a subclass of a class Y, it inherits the properties of Y. This means that all of the data and methods defined for class Y are available to class X. Most object-oriented programming languages, and Java in particular, allow you to easily define subclasses that automatically inherit the data and methods of the classes they extend. This is a very powerful feature for software reuse. Not only can you reuse classes as they are defined, but you can easily extend and tailor their definitions by adding additional data and access methods to their subclasses.

There are many times that you may have a class definition you can use in your program, but it would be better if it supported additional state information or access methods. Java's support of subclassing enables you to easily extend such classes by supplying only the additional data and methods that are unique to the subclass. This allows you to take advantage of all the features of the superclass without having to implement any of them.

MULTIPLE INHERITANCE

When a class extends another class, it inherits the data and methods of the class it extends. This is known as *single inheritance*. It is also possible for a class to extend classes on more than one branch of the class hierarchy tree, This is known as *multiple inheritance*. Multiple inheritance poses some difficulties for object-oriented programming. Most of these difficulties stem from the problem of determining which parent of a class to use under certain conditions. Numerous ambiguities arise when a class may have more than one immediate parent. For example, suppose a class X extends both a class Y and a class Z. Both class Y and class Z implement a unique print method. How does the compiler determine what method should be used to print objects of class X? What if the ambiguity arises during runtime for an object that inherits methods over several widely spaced branches of the class hierarchy? What's a poor compiler to do?

It is possible to design compilers and runtime systems that solve the ambiguities resulting from multiple inheritance, but these solutions tend to introduce a significant amount of processing overhead, adversely affecting program size and performance. The developers of Java have opted to support only single inheritance. This greatly simplifies the Java language, compiler, and runtime system. Java uses the interface construct to provide the benefits of multiple inheritance without the drawbacks resulting from parent ambiguity.

MESSAGES, METHODS, AND OBJECT INTERACTION

In a pure object-oriented programming model, such as that used by Smalltalk, objects interact by sending messages to each other. When an object receives a message, the object invokes a method to process the message. The method may change the state of the object, return information contained in the object, or cause objects to be created or deleted.

The object model used by Java is consistent with the concept of message passing, but does not emphasize it. In the Java model, objects interact by invoking each other's methods. *Methods* provide access to the information contained in an object. The type of access varies depending on the method.

ENCAPSULATION

One of the characteristics of object-oriented programming that is often touted in discussions of the subject is *encapsulation*. The term carries the connotation of an object being enclosed in some sort of container-and that is exactly what it means. Encapsulation is the combining of data and the code that manipulates that data into a single component-that is, an object. Encapsulation also refers to the control of access to the details of an object's implementation. Object access is limited to a well-defined, controlled interface. This allows objects to be self-contained and protects them from accidental misuse, both of which are important to reliable software design.

POLYMORPHISM

Polymorphism is the ability to assume different forms. In object-oriented programming, this refers to the ability of objects to have many methods of the same name, but with different forms. The compiler and runtime system support polymorphism by matching each method invocation to the correct method, class, and object. The ability to figure out which method to use, in complex situations, is the essence of polymorphism. Luckily for us, polymorphism is implemented in the compiler and runtime system-we don't need to do anything to make it happen. We just need to know that it works.

DYNAMIC BINDING

Sometimes a program might need to interface with objects of many different classes. For example, consider a program that has the responsibility of sending out objects over a communication link. The program may not know what class an object belongs to until it is time to send it. The capability to defer until runtime decisions about what class an object belongs to and the methods for accessing the object is known as *dynamic binding*. Dynamic binding is important to object-oriented programming because it eliminates many potentially constraining assumptions about the classes that an object belongs to and enables objects to be designed in a more general and open manner.

Dynamic binding also provides capabilities that are necessary for the advanced network programming capabilities of Java applets. When a browser executes a Java applet, the applet could require the loading of classes located on other sites across the Internet. Furthermore, these classes could be in a continual state of modification and upgrade. Dynamic binding allows new and modified objects to be used by executing software without requiring recompilation. The compiler and interpreter work together to provide executable code with the capabilities needed to dynamically interface with unknown objects during program execution.

JAVA CLASSES

The concepts of encapsulation, composition and reuse, classification and inheritance, polymorphism, and dynamic binding. CDrawApp will allow you to draw points, boxes, and text strings on a character-based grid that is displayed using the Java console window.

The program will be introduced as a series of Java classes that cover different aspects of class and object syntax. Each new class will make use of the capabilities provided by previous classes and will provide additional building blocks required for the program's development. It is important that you understand each class that is presented before moving on to subsequent classes.

You should create a ch05 directory, under c:\java\jdg, to store the Java source and bytecode files for this lesson. All classes will be developed in the jdg.ch05 package.

CLASS SYNTAX

The Java language is class and object oriented. Classes are templates for the creation of objects. They define the data contained in an object together with methods for accessing that data.

Classes are declared as follows:

ClassModifiers class ClassName ExtendsClause ImplementsClause ClassBody

The *ClassModifiers*, *ExtendsClause*, and *ImplementsClause* are optional. Interfaces and the *ImplementsClause* are covered in the next chapter. The *ClassBody* is enclosed by braces, and contains zero or more field declarations.

An example of a simple class declaration is

class SimpleClass { }

It declares a class, named SimpleClass, that is a subclass of Object, the highest-level class in the Java class hierarchy. SimpleClass declares no variables or methods of its own; it has only those that it inherits from Object.

THE POINT CLASS

The first class that you'll define for the CDrawApp program is the Point class. This class is used to identify a point on a grid by its x- and y-coordinates. The source code for the class declaration follows. (See Listing 5.1.) You should enter the code in a file named Point.java and store it in your c:\java\jdg\ch05 directory. Then compile it using the command javac Point.java.

CLASS MODIFIERS

The Point class is declared using the public class modifier. *Class modifiers* are keywords that are used to specify the properties of a class. Three class modifiers are supported: public, final, and abstract. If a class is declared as public, it can be accessed outside of its package; otherwise, it cannot. Because Point is declared as public, it can be accessed outside its package. Only one public class or interface is allowed in a compilation unit. Point is the only class in Point.java and, therefore, follows this rule.

If a class is declared as final, it cannot be extended. Final classes form the leaves of the class hierarchy tree.

An abstract class is used to define the general behavior for an intended set of subclasses. abstract classes are used to set the stage for subsequent subclass development. They are, by definition, incomplete and cannot be instantiated in terms of objects. abstract classes describe the behavior expected of their subclasses through the declaration of *abstract methods*. abstract methods must be redefined, or *overridden*, before they can be used. Only abstract classes are allowed to declare or inherit abstract methods. The CGObject class is an example of an abstract class. It is presented in the section "The CGObject class," later in this chapter.

EXTENDING SUPERCLASSES

When a class declaration does not contain an extends clause, the class is automatically made a subclass of the Object class. The Point class does not contain an extends clause and, therefore, is a subclass of Object. The Object class is at the top of the Java class hierarchy, being the *superclass* of all Java classes.

You can change a class's position in the class hierarchy by identifying its immediate super-class in the class declaration. The *immediate superclass* is the parent class directly above it in the class hierarchy. You identify the immediate superclass of a class using the extends clause in the class declaration. For example, you can place SimpleClass under ExampleClass in the class hierarchy as follows:

class SimpleClass extends ExampleClass { }

SimpleClass does not have any unique variables or methods of its own, but it inherits those of ExampleClass and all superclasses of ExampleClass.

ADDING BODY TO CLASSES

The body of the Point class consists of all declarations between the opening and closing braces. If a class is to add any features to its superclass, it does so in its class body. It is here that additional variables and methods are declared. These additional declarations are referred to as *field declarations*.

The field declarations are identified within the opening and closing braces ({ and }) of the class body. You need to supply the braces even if you don't intend to declare any fields, as you saw in the SimpleClass example.

VARIABLE DECLARATIONSN

Variables are the components of an object that store data and state information. They are declared as follows:

Variable Modifiers Type Variable Declarators

VariableModifiers are keywords that identify special properties of the variables being declared. *Type* is the Java type of the declared variables. It may be a primitive type, a class type, an interface type, or an array type. *VariableDeclarators* identify the names of the declared variables and can be used to specify the initial values of these variables. The Point class declares two integer variables: x and y. They are used to store the location of a point on a two-dimensional grid. These variables are declared with the private modifier. This modifier restricts access to the x and y variables to within the Point class. The Point class illustrates the principles of encapsulation. Data and methods are combined with a well-defined interface to provide maximum modularity. Access to the internal operation of the class is controlled.

Constructor Declarations

Constructors are special methods that are used to initialize newly created objects. They are used together with the new operator to create and initialize objects that are instances of a class. Constructors are declared in a slightly different manner than other methods. Their syntax is as follows:

AccessSpecifier Construct or Declarator ThrowsClause Construct or Body

AccessSpecifier identifies the type of access allowed to the constructor. *Construct or Declarat or* identifies a method with the same name as the class and specifies its parameter list. The parameter list is a comma-separated list of parameter declarations where each parameter declaration identifies the type and name of a parameter that is passed to the constructor upon invocation.

EXCEPTIONS

ELIMINATING SOFTWARE ERRORS

Programs are reliable, in part, because they are able to cope with errors and exceptions that occur during their execution. The development of reliable, error-tolerant software is a multiphase effort that spans program design, coding, compilation, loading, and execution. The most serious errors are those that are designed into a program. Many design errors can be eliminated by following a sound development approach, using modern software engineering methods, and making a firm commitment to software quality. The use of an object-oriented approach to software development helps to simplify software design, reduce errors, and promote software reliability.

Programming errors initially occur when a software design is translated into source code. Program verification, validation, analysis, and test activities help to eliminate design and programming errors. The implementation of coding standards and code walkthroughs also reduces the likelihood of undetected programming errors.

The Java language eliminates whole classes of errors that result from the use of dangerous programming constructs such as pointers and automatic type conversions. The simplicity and familiarity of the language also reduce the occurrence of programming errors.

The Java compiler and runtime environment help to keep errors from being introduced into executable Java code. The compiler performs extensive type checking to ensure that objects are correctly referenced and updated and that methods are properly invoked. The runtime system duplicates compile-time checks and implements additional checks to verify that executable code follows established rules for program correctness.

With all the error checking that takes place before a program is executed, you might think that it would be unlikely that errors could still creep into a program. They can and always do, in accordance with Murphy's Law. Runtime error and exception handling is used to identify error conditions and perform processing that minimizes their impact.

ERROR PROCESSING AND EXCEPTIONS

Java provides superior support for runtime error and exception handling, allowing programs to check for anomalous conditions and respond to them with minimal impact on the normal flow of program execution. This allows error- and exception-handling code to be added easily to existing methods.

Exceptions are generated by the Java runtime system in response to errors that are detected when classes are loaded and their methods are executed. The runtime system is said to *throw* these *runtime exceptions*. Runtime exceptions are objects of the class java.lang.RuntimeException or of its subclasses.

Exceptions may also be thrown directly by Java code using the throw statement. These exceptions are thrown when code detects a condition that could potentially lead to a program malfunction. The exceptions thrown by user programs are generally not objects of a subclass of RuntimeException. These non-runtime exceptions are referred to as *program* exceptions.

Throwing Exceptions – Exceptions are thrown using the throw statement. Its syntax is as follows:

throw *Expression;*

Expression must evaluate to an object that is an instance of a subclass of the java.lang.Exception class. The Exception class is defined in the Java API. When an exception is thrown, execution does not continue after the throw statement. Instead, it continues with any code that catches the exception. If an exception is not caught, the current thread of execution is terminated and an error is displayed on the console window.

For example, the following statement will throw an exception, using an object of class ExampleException:

throw new ExampleException();

The new operator is invoked with the ExampleException() constructor to allocate and initialize an object of class ExampleException. This object is then thrown by the throw statement

DECLARING EXCEPTIONS

A method's throws clause lists the types of exceptions that can be thrown during a method's execution. The throws clause appears immediately before a method's body in the method declaration. For example, the following method throws the ExampleException:

public void exampleMethod() throws Example Exception { throw new Example Exception();}

When more than one exception may be thrown during the execution of a method, the exceptions are separated by commas in the throws clause. For example, the following method can throw either the Test1Exception or the Test2Exception:

public void test Method(int i) throws Test1 Exception, Test2 Exception { if(i==1) throw new Test1Exception(); if(i==2) throw new Test2 Exception();}

The types identified in the throws clause must be capable of being legally assigned to the exceptions that may be thrown.

DECLARE OR CATCH

If a program exception can be thrown during the execution of a method, the method must either catch the expression or declare it in the throws clause of its method declaration. If an exception is not caught, it must be declared, even if it is thrown in other methods that are invoked during the method's execution.

For example, suppose that method A of object X invokes method B of object Y, which invokes method C of object Z. If method C throws an exception, it must be caught by method C or declared in method C's throws clause. If it is not caught by method C, it must be caught by method B or declared in method B's throws clause. Similarly, if the exception is not caught by method B, it must be caught by method A or declared in method A's throws clause. The handling of exceptions is a hierarchical process that mirrors the method invocation hierarchy (or *call tree*). Either an exception is caught by a method and removed from the hierarchy or it must be declared and propagated back through the method invocation hierarchy.

MULTIMEDIA AND AUTHORING TOOLS AND IMAGE FORMATS

INTRODUCTION TO COMPUTER GRAPHICS

Although computer graphics is a vast field that encompasses almost any graphical aspect, we are mainly interested in the generation of images of 3-dimensional scenes. Computer imagery has applications for film special effects, simulation and training, games, medical imagery, flying logos, etc. Computer graphics relies on an internal *model* of the scene, that is, a mathematical representation suitable for graphical computations. The model describes the 3D shapes, layout and materials of the scene. This 3D representation then has to be projected to compute a 2D image from a given viewpoint, this is the *rendering* step. Rendering involves projecting the objects (perspective), handling visibility (which parts of objects are hidden) and computing their appearance and lighting interactions. Finally, for animated sequence, the motion of objects has to be specified. We will not discuss animation in this document.

PIXELS

A computer image is usually represented as a discrete grid of picture elements a.k.a. pixels. The number of pixels determines the resolution of the image. Typical resolutions range from 320*200 to 2000*1500. For a black and white image, a number describes the intensity of each pixel. It can be expressed between 0.0 (black) and 1.0 (white). However, for internal binary representation reasons, it is usually stored as an integer between 0 (black) and 255 (white). For a color image, each pixel is described by a triple of numbers representing the intensity of red, green and blue. For example, pure red is (255, 0, 0) and purple is (255, 0, 255).

POLYGONS

The most classical method for modeling 3D geometry is the use of polygons. An object is approximated by a polygonal mesh, that is a set of connected polygons (see below). Most of the time, triangles are used for simplicity and generality.

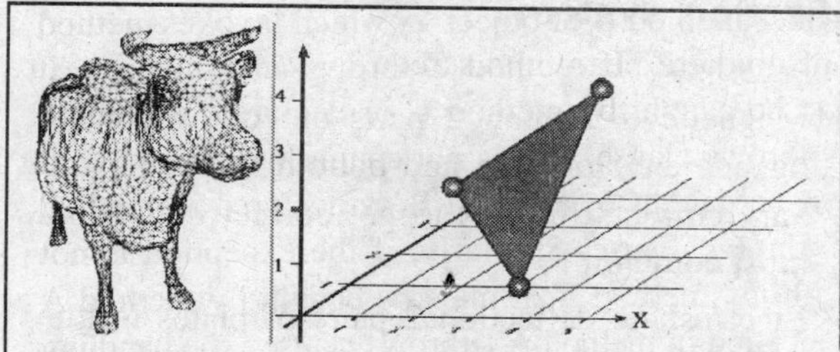

Left: A cow modeled as a mesh of triangles.
Right: This triangle can be stored using the coordinates of its vertices as [(2, 4, 2), (3, 1, 0), (1, 1, 2)].

PRIMITIVES

The most classical geometric entities can be directly used as *primitives*, e.g. cubes, cylinders, spheres and cones. A sphere for example can be simply described by the coordinates of its center and its radius.

SMOOTH PATCHES

More complex mathematical entities permit the representation of complex smooth objects. Spline patches and NURBS are the most popular. They are however harder to manipulate since one does not directly control the surface but so called *control points* that are only indirectly related to the final shape. Moreover, obtaining smooth junctions between different patches can be problematic. However, the recently popular *subdivision surfaces* overcome this limitation. They offer the best of both world and provide the simplicity of polygons and the smoothness of patches.

PROJECTION AND RASTERIZATION

The image projection of the 3D objects is computed using linear perspective. Given the position of the viewpoint and some camera parameters (*e.g.*, field of view), it is very easy to compute the projection of a 3D point onto the 2D image. For mathematics enthusiasts, this can be simply expressed using a 4*4 matrix. In most methods, the geometric entities are then *rasterized.* It consists in drawing all the pixels covered by the entity. In the example below, the projections of the 3 red points have been computed using linear perspective, and the triangle has then been rasterized by filling the pixels in black. For richer rendering, the color of each rasterized pixel must take into account the optical properties of the object, as we will discuss below.

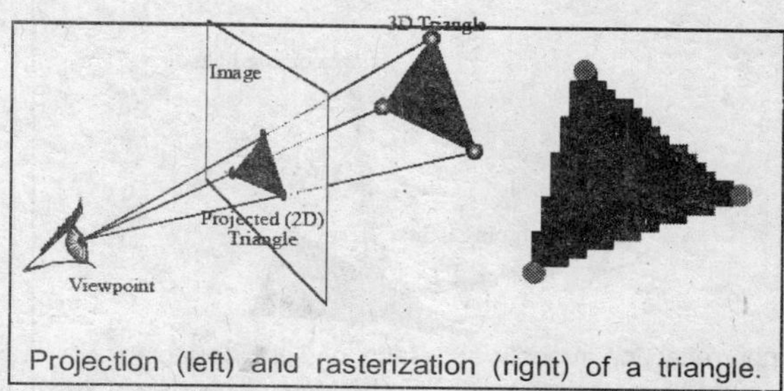

Projection (left) and rasterization (right) of a triangle.

VISIBILITY

If the scene contains more than one object, *occlusions* may occur. That is, some objects may be hidden by others. Only visible objects should be represented. *Visibility* techniques deal with this issue. One classical algorithm that solves the visibility problem is the so-called *painter's algorithm.* It consists in sorting the objects or polygons from back to front and rasterizing them in this order. This way, frontmost polygons cover the more distant polygons that they hide.

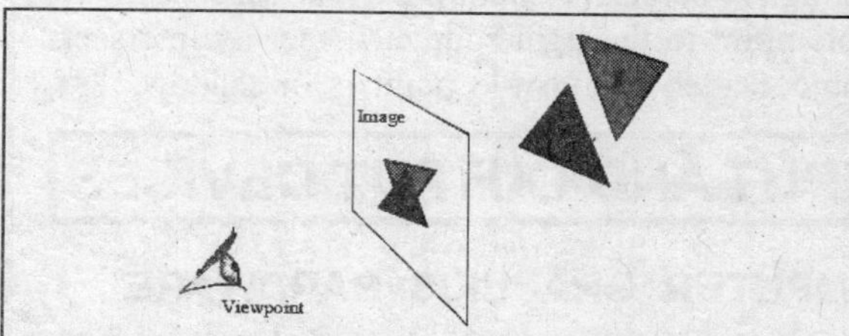

The Painter's algorithm. Triangle I is drawn first because it is more distant. Triangle 2 is drawn next and covers Triangle 1, which yields correct occlusion.

The *ray-tracing* algorithm does not use a rasterization phase. It sends one ray from the eye and through each pixel of the image. The intersection between this ray and the objects of the scene is computed, and only the closest intersection is considered.

The *z-buffer* method is the most common now a days (*e.g.*, for computer graphics cards). It stores the depth z) of each pixel. When a new polygon is rasterized, for each pixel, the algorithm compares the depth of the current polygon and the depth of the pixel. If the new polygon has a closer depth, the color and depth of the pixel are updated. Otherwise, it means that for this pixel, a formerly drawn polygon hides the current polygon.

SHADING AND MATERIALS

Augmenting the scene with light sources allows for better rendering. The objects can be *shaded* according to their interaction with light. Various shading models have been proposed in the literature. They describe how light is reflected by object, depending on the relative orientation of the surface, light source and viewpoint.

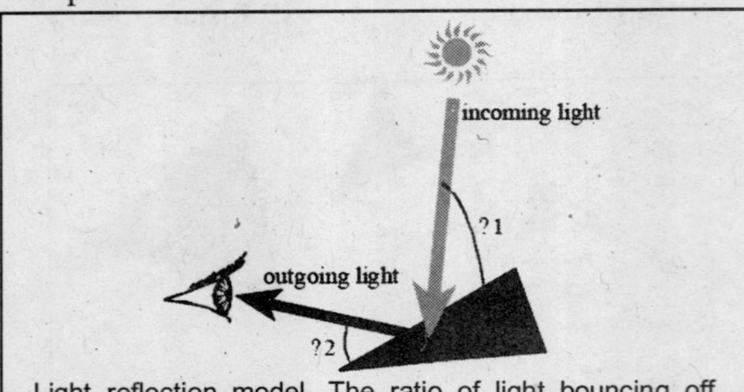

Light reflection model. The ratio of light bouncing off the surface in the direction of the eye depends on the two angle.

SHADOWS AND LIGHTING SIMULATION

Shading and material models only take into account the local interaction of surfaces and light. They do not simulate *shadows* that are harder to handle because they imply long-range interactions. A shadow is caused by the occlusion of light by one object. Ray-tracing, for example, can handle shadows, but requires a shadow computation for each pixel and each light source. A *shadow ray* is sent from the visible point to the light source. If the ray intersects an object, then the visible point is in shadow.

INPUT AND OUTPUT DEVICES

COMPUTER GRAPHICS HARDWARE

- Output Devices
- Display
- Vector
- Rastor
- Hardcopy
- Plotters
- Printers
- Input Devices
- Graphics Processors

VIDEO DISPLAY DEVICES

Video Monitor

CRT (cathode ray tube) was most common Storage CRT versus Refresh CRT Draw once and image remains on screen Constant refreshing of screen Refresh rates - 30 Hz, interlaced Basic CRT design.

Vacuum in a glass tube

Electron gun Cathode with coiled wire filament heat and it emits electrons very high voltages.

Deflection system

Phosphor coated screen.

Focusing system

Electrons repel each other-diverge

(*a*) Magnetic coil around outside of tube very small spot size flying spot scanners.

(*b*) Electrostatic most common in graphics monitors positively charged metal cylinder (electrostatic lens) focuses beam in middle of screen curved screen distance from "lens" to screen is constant flat screen distances increase from center additional electronic deflection dependent focusing.

Deflection system

Control where beam hits screen

(*a*) Magnetic deflection 2 pairs of coils mounted outside envelope top and bottom right and left vary currents in coils to get correct deflection most common.

(*b*) Electrostatic deflection 2 pairs of plates inside envelope vary charge.

Screen

A coated with phosphors electrons hit screen and loose energy heat most goes to electrons of phosphor jumps them to higher energy states when fall back to lower states - give off energy as light

Phosphor characteristics

Color of light - wavelength of energy persistence time taken to go from initial light level to 1/10th long persistence refresh less frequently what happens to image of moving objects? short persistence refresh more frequently less motion blur typical 10-60 microseconds.

Intensity

Control grid of electron gun the more negatively charged, more electrons get repelled the fewer make it through the control grid Intensity distribution of spot on screen.

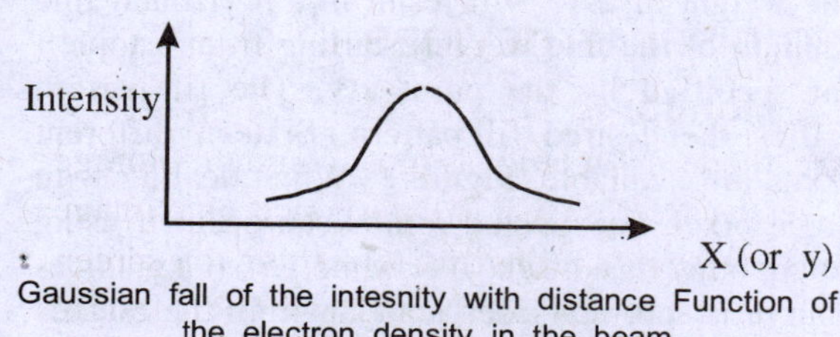

Gaussian fall of the intesnity with distance Function of the electron density in the beam

Resolution

Maximum number of dots that can be displayed without overlap on CRT (1K by 1K) independent of screen size **OR** Maximum number of dots that can be displayed per inch or cm (300 dpi).

Aspect ratio

Ratio of number of vertical points to horizontal points to produce equal length lines.

RASTOR SCAN VERSUS RANDOM SCAN

RANDOM SCAN: refresh is a function of the image complexity.

RASTOR SCAN: horizontal retrace and vertical retrace interlaced versus noninterlaced.

REFRESH RATE: 60 hz is typical how often refresh each "dot" on screen? once every 16667 microseconds compare to persistence (10-60 microseconds) "dot" is mostly dark!

FLICKER: when image appears to go on and off refresh rate not high enough.

CF: critical fusion frequency – freq at which flickering display just fuses into nonflickering what determines CFF? for given phosphor?

HORIZONTAL SCAN RATE: scan lines displayed per second approximately refresh rate times number of lines

COLOR CRTs: Beam penetration Random scan two layers of phosphor slow beam - outer layer (say red) faster beam - inner layer (say green)

SHADOW MASK: more colors better quality small patches of red, green and blue phosphors perceive as one colored patch 3 electron guns.

(*a*) delta-delta triad of patches shadow mask difficult to keep aligned high resolution

(*b*) precision in-line easier to align, lower resolution.

FLAT-PANEL DISPLAYS: Thinner, lighter, require less power.

PLASMA PANELS: mixture of gases between two glass plates vertical and horizontal conducting ribbons apply voltage to two ribbons to make plasma glow. Thin-film electroluminescent displays similar, but phosphor instead of gas.

LED's: matrix of diodes, one per pixel apply voltage and they produce light nonemissive.

LCD: LC substance flow like a liquid, but have crystalline molecular structure usually use nematic LC's (threadlike). Two polarizers, two conductors, reflector LC in normal state twists the light, so is reflected back to viewer apply voltage to conductors to turn off.

ACTIVE MATRIX LCD: transistor at each pixel (stores)

DOT MATRIX PRINTERS: Print head with matrix of wire pins retract some pins before printing to print specified pattern.

LASER PRINTERS: Drum coated with photoelectric material (*e.g.,* selenium) Laser beam creates charge distribution on drum. Toner applied to drum and sticks according to charge Toner.

INK-JET PRINTERS: Paper rolled on drum boiled ink squirted onto paper through little nozzles (jets) Charged ink stream deflected by electric field Electrostatic Printers negatively charge a row at a time on paper apply toner

ELECTRO THERMAL PRINTER: Heat sensitive paper Dot matrix print head applies heat.

GRAPHICS PRIMITIVES

Using HTML to create your projects at compile time allows you to make rich user interfaces quickly and easily. Sometimes, though, the ability to draw graphic primitives like lines, rectangles, filled rectangles and single pixels at runtime, is needed. Amulet's uHTML does not inherently give you the ability to do this. With the addition of a new communications protocol that allows the external processor to be the master and the Amulet to be the slave comes a way to send unsolicited graphic primitives to the Amulet. The drawing of these graphic primitives is independent of the uHTML that is currently being run on the Amulet. You do need to keep in mind that the uHTML will still be running, so any widgets or objects that write to the LCD might write over the graphics primitive you send to the LCD.

By default, the Amulet will respond to all graphic primitive commands with a response opcode (0xE9-0xEC) and an echo of all other bytes. If it is desired to have the Amulet respond with an ACK(0xF0) or no response at all, a META tag using SlaveAckRsp or Slave NoRsp can be used on the home page of the project. One thing to keep in mind is that the Amulet will use that attribute for all "Set" or "Draw" commands coming from your external processor. The line primitive draws a line from point 1(x and y coordinates) to point 2(x and y coordinates), that has a line weight of 1-15 and is one of 16 different patterns. The line primitive is drawn by sending out the "Draw line primitive" opcode(0xD9), followed by the x-coordinate of point 1, the y-coordinate of point 1, the x-coordinate of point 2, the y-coordinate of point 2, the line pattern and finally the line weight. The x and y coordinates are 16-bit numbers. The line pattern and line weight are both 4-bit numbers. Because Amulet uses an ASCII protocol, each coordinate that is sent to the Amulet is comprised of four different bytes. For example, if the x-coordinate of point 1 is 0x0020, the 4 bytes that would be sent to the Amulet for that particular coordinate would be 0x30,0x30,0x32,0x30. The line pattern and line weight, when sent to the Amulet, are one byte each. The line pattern byte specifies the desired line pattern. Sixteen different patterns are available, Figure 1. The line weight specifies the thickness of the line, range of 1-15. The entire line primitive message sent to the Amulet is a total of 19 bytes. The rectangle primitive draws a rectangle with a given starting top left point(x and y coordinates) and a delta x and delta y, plus a line weight and line pattern. The rectangle primitive is drawn by sending out the "Draw rectangle primitive" opcode(0xDA), followed by the x-coordinate of the topleft point, the y-coordinate of the topleft point, the delta x, the delta y, the line pattern and finally the line weight. The x and y coordinates and the delta x and delta y are all 16-bit numbers. The line pattern and line weight are both 4-bit numbers. The delta x is a 16-bit number specifying the length of the rectangle in the x direction and the delta y is a 16-bit number specifying the height of the rectangle in the y direction. The line weight specifies the thickness of the line, range of 1-15. The line pattern specifies the desired line pattern. Sixteen different patterns are available, Figure.

The fill rectangle primitive draws a solid rectangle with a given starting top left point(x and y coordinates) and a delta x and delta y, plus a line weight and line pattern. The fill rectangle primitive is drawn by sending out the "Draw fill rectangle primitive" opcode(0xDB), followed by the x-coordinate of the topleft point, the y-coordinate of the topleft point, the delta x, the delta y, the fill pattern and finally the line weight. The x and y coordinates and the delta x and delta y are all 16-bit numbers. The delta x is a 16-bit number specifying the length of the rectangle in the x direction and the delta y is a 16-bit number specifying the height of the rectangle in the y direction. The fill pattern and line weight are both 4-bit numbers. The line weight is not used by this primitive, but the parameter still must be included, range of 1-15. The fill pattern specifies the desired fill pattern. Sixteen different patterns are available, Figure.

The pixel primitive draws a single pixel at a given point(x and y coordinates), plus a line weight and line pattern. The pixel primitive is drawn by sending out the "Draw rectangle primitive" opcode(0xDC), followed by the x-coordinate of the point, the y-coordinate of the point, the fill pattern and finally the line weight. The x and y coordinates are 16-bit numbers. The fill pattern and line weight are both 4-bit numbers. The line weight specifies the thickness of the pixel in the x direction, range of 1-15. Using a line weight of 2-15 will result in a horizontal line the length of the line weight, starting from a topleft point specified by the point x,y. The fill pattern specifies the desired fill pattern. Sixteen different patterns are available, Figure 1. When dealing with a single pixel, unexpected results can occur if using a pattern other than black(0) or white(15). If a graphics primitive is sent that does not fit within the bounds of the given LCD (*i.e.,* a delta x of 380 pixels on a 320 x 240 LCD) the Amulet will just ignore the request. It will respond back serially, but the graphic primitive will not be drawn.

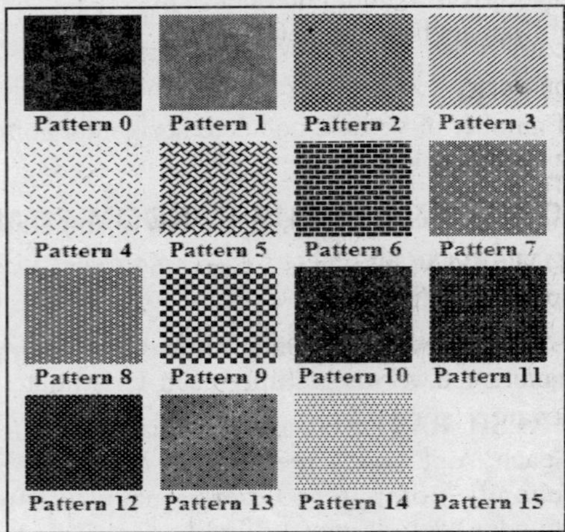

TRANSFORMATIONS

Transformations are what we use to navigate our way around 2 and 3 dimensional space.

Geometrical Transformations

Geometrical transformations are essential to computer graphics. The transformations we will be looking at are (in 2D and 3D):

1. Translation - move an object
2. Scaling - change the size of an object
3. Rotation - rotate an object

Homogenous Coordinates

Homogenous coordinates simplify the way we deal with matrix operations and provide considerable benefits for computer graphics applications.

Combined Transformation Matrices (CTM)

A number of transformations can be combined into a single matrix called a Combined Transformation Matrix or CTM. This drastically reduces the number of calculations a computer graphics application needs to do when rendering a scene.

2D TRANSFORMATIONS

Translation

Translation can be thought of as moving something. In translation a point is moved a distance in a given direction.

For example, when point A(ax, by) is translated d_x units in the x direction and d_y units in the y direction becomes:

A¢($ax + d_x, by + d_y$)

Representing the points as column matrices we have:

$$P = \begin{bmatrix} x \\ y \end{bmatrix}, \quad P' = \begin{bmatrix} x' \\ y' \end{bmatrix}, \quad T = \begin{bmatrix} d_x \\ d_y \end{bmatrix}$$

the translation can be expressed thus: $P' = P + T$

In general we only need to translate the vertices (*i.e.,* corners or endpoints) of an object. Lines or polygons can then be drawn using the transformed vertices.

Scaling

In scaling we stretch or change the size of something. Scaling will make an object bigger or smaller in the x and/or y direction.

To scale a point (x, y) by s_x along the x axis and s_y along the y axis we multiply each coordinate by the relevant scaling factor.

$$x' = x \cdot s_x \quad y' = y \cdot s_y$$

$$\begin{bmatrix} x' \\ y' \end{bmatrix} = \begin{bmatrix} s_x & 0 \\ 0 & s_y \end{bmatrix} \begin{bmatrix} x \\ y \end{bmatrix} \text{ or } P' = S \cdot P$$

Rotation about the origin

In rotation we rotate an object by the angle q around the origin.

$$x = r \cdot \cos\phi, \quad y = r \cdot \sin\phi$$

In the rotation, the new values of x and y are as follows:

$$x' = r \cdot \cos(\theta + \phi) = r \cdot \cos\phi \cdot \cos\theta - r \cdot \sin\phi \cdot \sin\theta$$

$$y' = r \cdot \sin(\theta + \phi) = r \cdot \cos\phi \cdot \sin\theta + r \cdot \sin\phi \cdot \cos\theta$$

The matrix form of rotation (about the origin)is:

$$\begin{bmatrix} x' \\ y' \end{bmatrix} = \begin{bmatrix} \cos\theta & -\sin\theta \\ \sin\theta & \cos\theta \end{bmatrix} \begin{bmatrix} x \\ y \end{bmatrix} \text{ or } P' = R \cdot P$$

Where R is the 2 X 2 rotation matrix.

Rotation about an arbitrary point

The rotation matrix (above) is fine if all we want to do it rotate a point around the origin. But how do we rotate the point (x_p, y_p) around the point $P_1 = (x_1, y_1)$?

The answer is that we must use the following steps:

1. Translate so that P_1 is at the origin. *i.e.,* by $(-x_1, -y_1)$
2. Perform the rotation.
3. Translate so that point at the origin returns to P_1. *i.e.,* by (x_1, y_1)

Homogenous Coordinates

We've seen the following matrix transformations:

Translation: $P' = T + P$

Sacling: $P' = S \cdot P$

Rotation: $P' = R \cdot P$

Translation is achieved through matrix addition while Scaling and Rotation are achieved by matrix multiplication. We can combine any number of translation matrices through addition, and we can combine any number of scaling and rotation matrices through multiplication. But we cannot combine all three into a single CTM. It would be very handy if we could do this.

We achieve our ends by using Homogenous Coordinates. With homogenous coordinates all three transformation matrices are applied using matrix multiplication Thus our transformations using homogenous coordinates become:

Translation: $P_h' = T_h \cdot P_h$

Scaling: $P_h' = S_h \cdot P_h$

Rotation: $P_h' = R_h \cdot P_h$

$$X = \frac{x}{W}$$

In homogenous coordinates a point P(x,y) is represented by the homogenous point P(X,Y,W) where: In computer graphics mostly W = 1.

$$Y = \frac{y}{W}$$

Using homogenous coordinates our transformation matrices become:

Translation: $T(d_x, d_y) = \begin{bmatrix} 1 & 0 & d_x \\ 0 & 1 & d_y \\ 0 & 0 & 1 \end{bmatrix}$

Scaling: $S(s_x, s_y) = \begin{bmatrix} s_x & 0 & 0 \\ 0 & s_y & 0 \\ 0 & 0 & 1 \end{bmatrix}$

Rotation: $R(\theta) = \begin{bmatrix} \cos\theta & -\sin\theta & 0 \\ \sin\theta & \cos\theta & 0 \\ 0 & 0 & 1 \end{bmatrix}$

ORDER OF TRANSFORMATIONS

Matrix multiplication is associative.

$$A \cdot B \cdot C = (A \cdot B) \cdot C = A \cdot (B \cdot C)$$

$$A \cdot B \cdot C = (A \cdot B) \cdot C = A \cdot (B \cdot C)$$

When multiplying matrices the order we carry out the multiplications is irrelevant. Matrix multiplication is not commutative. When multiplying numbers together, the order of the numbers in the expression is irrelevant to the outcome.

COMPUTER SCIENCE

i.e., 2 X 4 X 3 = 24 and
4 X 2 X 3 = 24

In matrix expressions this is not the case!

$$A \cdot B \neq B \cdot A$$

i.e.,

How do we work out the order of our expression when creating our CTM?

If we remember the steps to rotate the point $P(x_p, y_p)$ around the point $P_1 = (x_1, y_1)$?

1. Translate so that P_1 is at the origin. i.e by $(-x_1, -y_1)$
2. Perform the rotation.
3. Translate so that point at the origin returns to P_1. i.e by (x_1, y_1)

It is helpful to think that the transformation closest to the point in the expression is the first transformation to be done.

Another way to remember the order of transformations is as follows.

$$P' = T_1 \,.\, P$$

$$P'' = T_2 \,.\, P'$$

Substituting we get $P'' = T_2 \cdot (T_1 \cdot P) = (T_2 \cdot T_1) \cdot P$

To rotate a shape made up of 5 vertices each transformation would need to be done 5 times.

3 Transformations X 5 Vertices = 15 calculations
This is computationally expensive.

COMBINED TRANSFORMATION MATRIX (CTM)

The answer is to combine the transformations into a single CTM.

3 Transformations X Identity Matrix = 3 calculations

1 Transformation(CTM) X 5 Vertices = 5 calculations

Total calculations = 8

3D TRANSFORMATIONS

The following are the 3D transformations for points represented in homogenous coordinates.

Translation

$$T(d_x, d_y, d_z) = \begin{bmatrix} 1 & 0 & 0 & d_x \\ 0 & 1 & 0 & d_y \\ 0 & 0 & 1 & d_z \\ 0 & 0 & 0 & 1 \end{bmatrix}$$

Scaling

$$S(s_x, s_y, s_z) = \begin{bmatrix} s_x & 0 & 0 & 0 \\ 0 & s_y & 0 & 0 \\ 0 & 0 & s_z & 0 \\ 0 & 0 & 0 & 1 \end{bmatrix}$$

Rotation

3D rotation is a little more complicated than 2D rotation. We in fact have three separate rotation matrices, one each for the z, x and y axes.

Rotation around the z axis is similar to the 2D rotation:

$$R(\theta) = \begin{bmatrix} \cos\theta & -\sin\theta & 0 & 0 \\ \sin\theta & \cos\theta & 0 & 0 \\ 0 & 0 & 1 & 0 \\ 0 & 0 & 0 & 1 \end{bmatrix}$$

Rotation around the x axis:

$$R(\theta) = \begin{bmatrix} 1 & 0 & 0 & 0 \\ 0 & \cos\theta & -\sin\theta & 0 \\ 0 & \sin\theta & \cos\theta & 0 \\ 0 & 0 & 0 & 1 \end{bmatrix}$$

Rotation around the y axis:

$$R(\theta) = \begin{bmatrix} \cos\theta & 0 & \sin\theta & 0 \\ 0 & 1 & 0 & 0 \\ -\sin\theta & 0 & \cos\theta & 0 \\ 0 & 0 & 0 & 1 \end{bmatrix}$$

The rules for the order of transformations and CTMs are the same as for 2D transformations.

MULTIMEDIA

MULTIMEDIA

The wireless Web is an exciting new development, but it is not the only one. For many people, multimedia is the holy grail of networking. When the word is mentioned, both the propeller heads and the suits begin salivating as if on cue. The former see immense technical challenges in providing (interactive) video on demand to every home. The latter see equally immense profits in it. Since multimedia requires high bandwidth, getting it to work over fixed connections is hard enough. Even VHS-quality video over wireless is a few years away, so our treatment will focus on wired systems. Literally, multimedia is just two or more media. If the publisher of this book wanted to join the current hype about multimedia, it could advertise the book as using multimedia technology.. After all, it contains two media: text and graphics (the figures). Nevertheless, when most people refer to multimedia, they generally mean the combination of two or more **continuous media**, that is, media that have to be played during some well-defined time interval, usually with some user interaction. In practice, the two media are normally audio and video, that is, sound plus moving pictures.

1661 (CS)–25-II

DIGITAL AUDIO

An audio (sound) wave is a one-dimensional acoustic (pressure) wave. When an acoustic wave enters the ear, the eardrum vibrates, causing the tiny bones of the inner ear to vibrate along with it, sending nerve pulses to the brain. These pulses are perceived as sound by the listener. In a similar way, when an acoustic wave strikes a microphone, the microphone generates an electrical signal, representing the sound amplitude as a function of time. The representation, processing, storage, and transmission of such audio signals are a major part of the study of multimedia systems. The frequency range of the human ear runs from 20 Hz to 20,000 Hz. Some animals, notably dogs, can hear higher frequencies.

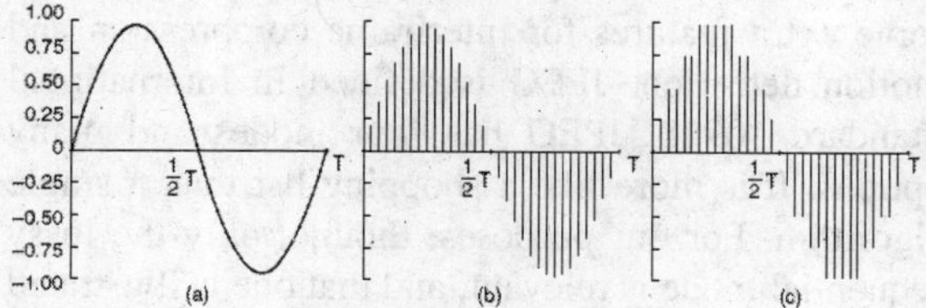

AUDIO COMPRESSION

CD-quality audio requires a transmission bandwidth of 1.411 Mbps, as we just saw. Clearly, substantial compression is needed to make transmission over the Internet practical. For this reason, various audio compression algorithms have been developed. Probably the most popular one is MPEG audio, which has three layers (variants), of which **MP3 (MPEG audio layer 3)** is the most powerful and best known. Large amounts of music in MP3 format are available on the Internet, not all of it legal, which has resulted in numerous lawsuits from the artists and copyright owners. MP3 belongs to the audio portion of the MPEG video compression standard. We will discuss video compression later in this chapter; let us look at audio compression now.

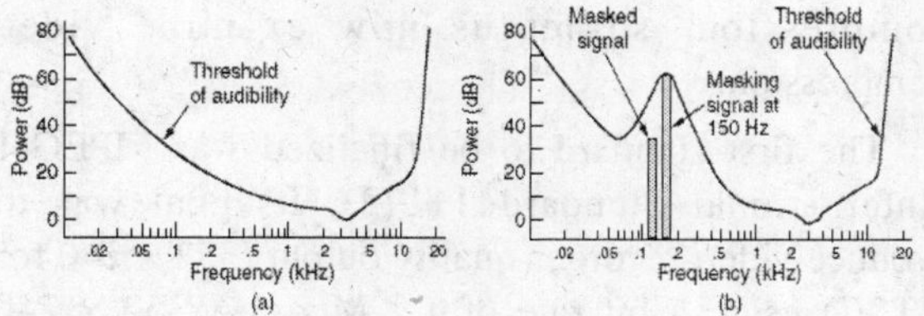

STREAMING AUDIO

The technology of digital audio to three of its network applications. Our first one is streaming audio, that is, listening to sound over the Internet. This is also called music on demand. In the next two, we will look at Internet radio and voice over IP, respectively. The Internet is full of music Web sites, many of which list song titles that users can click on to play the songs. Some of these are free sites (*e.g.*, new bands looking for publicity); others require payment in return for music, although these often offer some free samples as well (*e.g.*, the first 15 seconds of a song). The most straightforward way to make the music play is illustrated in Fig

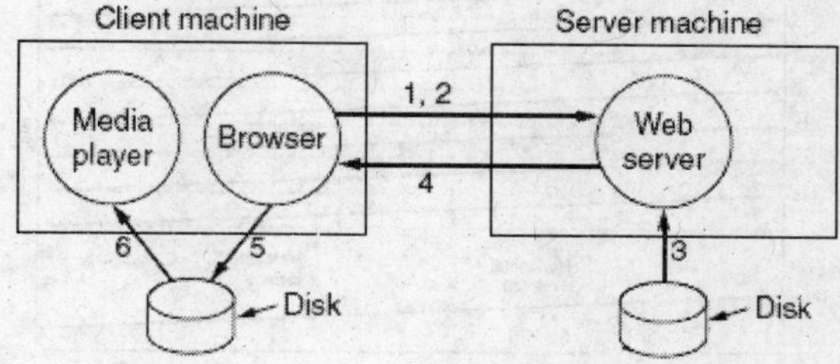

The process starts when the user clicks on a song. Then the browser goes into action. Step 1 is for it to establish a TCP connection to the Web server to which the song is hyperlinked. Step 2 is to send over a *GET* request in HTTP to request the song. Next (steps 3 and 4), the server fetches the song (which is just a file in MP3 or some other format) from the disk and sends it back to the browser. If the file is larger than the server's memory, it may fetch and send the music a block at a time.

INTERNET RADIO

Once it became possible to stream audio over the Internet, commercial radio stations got the idea of broadcasting their content over the Internet as well as over the air. Not so long after that, college radio stations started putting their signal out over the Internet. Then college *students* started their own radio stations. With current technology, virtually anyone can start a radio station. The whole area of Internet radio is very new and in a state of flux, but it is worth saying a little bit about.

INTRODUCTION TO VIDEO

The human eye has the property that when an image appears on the retina, the image is retained for some number of milliseconds before decaying. If a sequence of images is drawn line by line at 50 images/sec, the eye does not notice that it is looking at discrete images. All video (*i.e.*, television) systems exploit this principle to produce moving pictures.

ANALOG SYSTEMS

To understand video, it is best to start with simple, old-fashioned black and white television. To represent the two-dimensional image in front of it as a onedimensional voltage as a function of time, the camera scans an electron beam rapidly across the image and slowly down it, recording the light intensity as it goes. At the end of the scan, called a **frame**, the beam retraces. This intensity as a function of time is broadcast, and receivers repeat the scanning process to reconstruct the image. The scanning pattern used by both the camera and the receiver is shown in Fig. (As an aside, CCD cameras integrate rather than scan, but some cameras and all monitors do scan.)

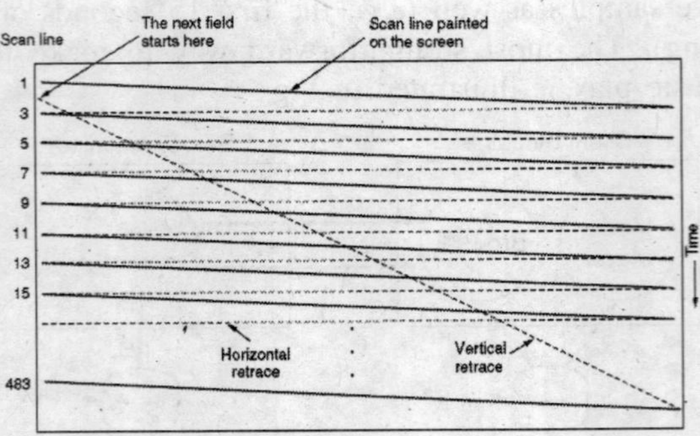

DIGITAL SYSTEMS

The simplest representation of digital video is a sequence of frames, each consisting of a rectangular grid of picture elements, or **pixels**. Each pixel can be a single bit, to represent either black or white. The quality of such a system is similar to what you get by sending a color photograph by fax—awful. (Try it if you can; otherwise photocopy a color photograph on a copying machine that does not rasterize.)

VIDEO COMPRESSION

It should be obvious by now that transmitting uncompressed video is completely out of the question. The only hope is that massive compression is possible.

Fortunately, a large body of research over the past few decades has led to many compression techniques and algorithms that make video transmission feasible. In this section we will study how video compression is accomplished.

All compression systems require two algorithms: one for compressing the data at the source, and another for decompressing it at the destination. In the literature, these algorithms are referred to as the **encoding** and **decoding** algorithms, respectively. We will use this terminology here, too. These algorithms exhibit certain asymmetries that are important to understand. First, for many applications, a multimedia document, say, a movie will only be encoded once (when it is stored on the multimedia server) but will be decoded thousands of times (when it is viewed by customers). This asymmetry means that it is acceptable for the encoding algorithm to be slow and require expensive hardware provided that the decoding algorithm is fast and does not require expensive hardware. After all, the operator of a multimedia server might be quite willing to rent a parallel supercomputer for a few weeks to encode its entire video library, but requiring consumers to rent a supercomputer for 2 hours to view a video is not likely to be a big success. Many practical compression systems go to great lengths to make decoding fast and simple, even at the price of making encoding slow and complicated.

THE JPEG STANDARD

A video is just a sequence of images (plus sound). If we could find a good algorithm for encoding a single image, this algorithm could be applied to each image in succession to achieve video compression. Good still image compression algorithms exist, so let us start our study of video compression there.

The **JPEG (Joint Photographic Experts Group)** standard for compressing continuous-tone still pictures (*e.g.*, photographs) was developed by photographic experts working under the joint auspices of ITU, ISO, and IEC, another standards body. It is important for multimedia because, to a first approximation, the multimedia standard for moving pictures, MPEG, is just the JPEG encoding of each frame separately, plus some extra features for interframe compression and motion detection. JPEG is defined in International Standard 10918. JPEG has four modes and many options. It is more like a shopping list than a single algorithm. For our purposes, though, only the lossy sequential mode is relevant, and that one is illustrated in Fig. Furthermore, we will concentrate on the way JPEG is normally used to encode 24-bit RGB video images and will leave out some of the minor details for the sake of simplicity.

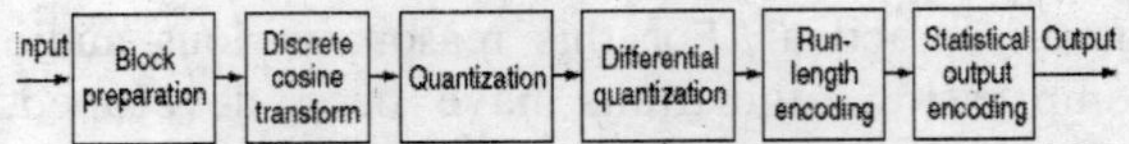

THE MPEG STANDARD

Finally, we come to the heart of the matter: the **MPEG (Motion Picture Experts Group)** standards. These are the main algorithms used to compress videos and have been international standards since 1993. Because movies contain both images and sound, MPEG can compress both audio and video. We have already examined audio compression and still image compression, so let us now examine video compression.

The first standard to be finalized was MPEG-1 (International Standard 11172). Its goal was to produce video-recorder-quality output (352 × 240 for NTSC) using a bit rate of 1.2 Mbps. A 352 × 240 image with 24 bits/pixel and 25 frames/sec requires 50.7 Mbps, so getting it down to 1.2 Mbps is not entirely trivial. A factor of 40 compression is needed. MPEG-1 can be transmitted over twisted pair transmission lines for modest distances. MPEG-1 is also used for storing movies on CD-ROM.

The next standard in the MPEG family was MPEG-2 (International Standard 13818), which was originally designed for compressing broadcast-quality video into 4 to 6 Mbps, so it could fit in a NTSC or PAL broadcast channel. Later, MPEG-2 was expanded to support higher resolutions, including HDTV. It is very common now, as it forms the basis for DVD and digital satellite television. The basic principles of MPEG-1 and MPEG-2 are similar, but the details are different. To a first approximation, MPEG-2 is a superset of MPEG-1, with additional features, frame formats, and encoding options. We will first discuss MPEG-1, then MPEG-2.

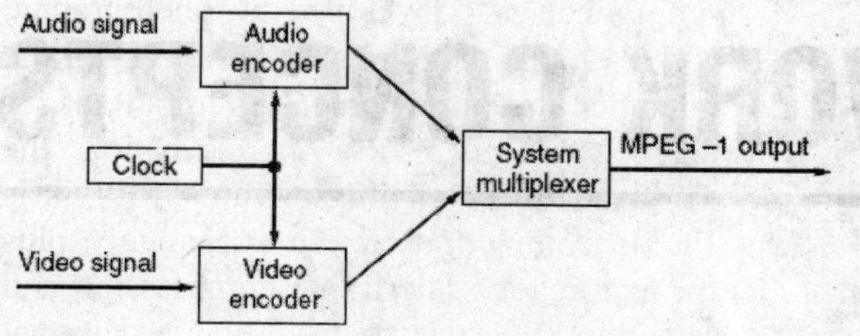

Consider MPEG-1 video compression. Two kinds of redundancies exist in movies: spatial and temporal. MPEG-1 uses both. Spatial redundancy can be utilized by simply coding each frame separately with JPEG. This approach is occasionally used, especially when random access to each frame is needed, as in editing video productions. In this mode, a compressed bandwidth in the 8- to 10-Mbps range is achievable.

Additional compression can be achieved by taking advantage of the fact that consecutive frames are often almost identical. This effect is smaller than it might first appear since many moviemakers cut between scenes every 3 or 4 seconds (time a movie and count the scenes). Nevertheless, even a run of 75 highly similar frames offers the potential of a major reduction over simply encoding each frame separately with JPEG.

11 COMMUNICATION AND NETWORK CONCEPTS

NETWORK FUNDAMENTALS

In the early 19th century, telegraphy systems were first encoded into strings of binary symbols, and were then manually transmitted and received. In the ensuing years developments and implementations of communication systems employing electrical signals became increasingly sophisticated leading, in turn, to the birth of telephone, radio, television, radar, and microwave links. Today, these communication systems have become an integral part of everyday life with circuits spanning the entire world carrying voice, text, pictures, and many other types of information.

Along with the development of faster and higher-capacity transmission systems, the past several decades have witnessed a phenomenal growth in the computer industry. As recent advances in integrated circuit technology have allowed computers to become smaller, less expensive, and widely available, people have become increasingly interested in connecting them together to form networks.

During the first two decades of their existence, computer systems were highly centralised, usually within a single large room. Not infrequently, this room had glass walls, through which visitors could gawk at the great electronic wonder inside. A medium-size company or university might have had one or two computers, while large institutions had at most a few dozen. The idea that within 20 years equally powerful computers smaller than postage stamps would be mass produced by the millions was pure science fiction.

The merging of computers and communications has had a profound influence on the way computer systems are organised. The term network is defined as a set of communication links for interconnecting a collection of terminals, computers, telephones, printers, or other types of data-communicating and data-handling devices. These devices are called *stations.* This interconnection allows these elements to exchange information. The concept of the "computer centre" as a room with a large computer to which users bring their work for processing is now totally obsolete. The old model of a single computer serving all of the organisation's computational needs has been replaced by one in which a large number of separate but interconnected computers do the job. These systems are called computer networks.

Computer network means an interconnected collection of autonomous computers. Two computers are said to be interconnected if they are able to exchange information. The connection need not be via a copper wire; fibre optics, microwaves, and communication satellites can also be used.

The key distinction is that in a distributed system, the existence of multiple autonomous computers is transparent (i.e., not visible) to the user. It can type a command to run a programme, and it runs. It is up to the operating system to select the best processor, find and transport all the input files to that processor, and put the results in the appropriate place. In other words, the user of a distributed system is not aware that there are multiple processors; it looks like a virtual uniprocessor. Allocation of jobs to processors and files to disks, movement of files between where they are stored and where they are needed, and all other system functions must be automatic.

With a network, users must explicitly log on to one machine, explicitly submit jobs remotely, explicitly move files around and generally handle all the network management personally. With a distributed system, nothing has to be done explicitly; it is all automatically done by the system without the users' knowledge.

In effect, a distributed system is a software system built on top of a network. The software gives it a high degree of cohesiveness and transparency. Thus the distinction between a network and a distributed system lies with the software (especially the operating system), rather than with the hardware both distributed systems and computer networks need to move files around. The difference lies in who invokes the movement, the system or the user.

Need for using network now a days by many companys

A company uses network for the following reasons

- **Resources sharing:** To provide programmes equipment, data, information to all the concerned persons of the company irrespected of physical location of the resources and the user.
- **Reliability:** All files could be replicated on two or three machines, so if one of them is unavailable due to a hardware failure, the other copies could be used.
- **To save money:** A company uses client server model which takes the form of a request message from the client to the server taking for some work to be done.

The server then does the work and sends back the reply. Usually, there are many clients uses a small number of servers.

- To increase system performance gradually as the workload grows just by adding more processors.
- To provide a powerful communication medium among widely separated employees.

APPLICATIONS OF COMPUTER NETWORKS

A computer network can provide a powerful communication medium among widely separated employees.

In 1990s, computer networks began to delivering services to private individuals at home. These services and the movitation for using them developes a keen interest among users to use **computer networks provide the following services to the users:**

1. Access to remote information
2. Person-to-person communication
3. Interactive entertainment

Access to remote information will come in many forms. One area in which it is already happening is access to financial institutions. Many people pay their bills, manage their bank accounts, and handle their investments electronically. Home shopping is also becoming popular, with the ability to inspect the on-line catalogues of thousands of companies. Some of these catalogues will soon provide the ability to get an instant video on any product by just clicking on the product's naipe.

Newspapers will go on-line and be personalised. It will be possible to tell the newspaper that you want everything about corrupt politicians, big fires, scandals involving celebrities, sad epidemics, but no football, thank you. At night while you sleep, the newspaper will be downloaded to your computer's disk or printed on your laser printer. On a small scale, this service already exists.

Another application that falls in this category is access to information systems like the current World Wide Web, which contains information about the arts, business, cooking, government, health, history, hobbies, recreation, science, sports, travel, and too many other topics to even mention.

All of the above applications involve interactions between a person and a remote database. The second broad category of network use will be, person-to-person interactions, basically the 21st Century's answer to the 19th Century's telephone. Electronic mail or **email** is already widely used by millions of people and will soon roll like audio and video as well as text. Smell in messages will take a bit longer to perfect.

Real-time email will allow remote users to communicate with no delay, possibly seeing and hearing each other as well. This technology makes it possible to have virtual meetings, called **videoconference,** among far-flung people. It is sometimes said that transport for off and communication are having a race, and whichever wins will make the other obsolete. Virtual meetings could be used for remote school, getting medical opinions from distant specialists, and numerous other applications.

Networking provide entertainment, which is a huge and growing industry. New films may become interactive, where the user is occasionally prompted for the story direction (should Macbeth murder Duncan or just bide his time?) with alternative scenarios provided for all cases. Live television may also become interactive, with the audience participating in quiz shows, choosing among contestants, and so on.

The ability to merge information, communication, and entertainment will surely give rise to a massive new industry based on computer networking. One such network is the worldwide telephone system which is an example of the so-called long-haul network or wide-area network (WAN) that interconnects widely dispersed telecommunication elements.

Elements of Computer Networks and Characteristic of Network Types

A network consists essentially of two kinds of elements:

1. the network nodes which are the actual computing end systems, for example larger

computer systems, personal workstations, terminals etc; and
2. the connections between these along which data transmissions travel.

Network nodes can have a greater or lesser degree of autonomy in local processing power and ability to control the communication process. The connections can be implemented in various media, but in some way serve to switch data flows between these network nodes, to pass information from a source to a destination in the most appropriate way. As a first stage, networks can usefully be categorised by the type of switching which is used.

There are three basic types of switching:

1. circuit switching
2. message switching
3. packet switching

Circuit switching occurs when a physical link is made between the two network nodes for the duration of a session, along which the data can flow under the control of the end systems. The connection must be set up before the information exchange can begin, and released once the session is completed; in the interim, the circuit is only available to the two participants even though the channel may have spare capacity which is unused.

Message switching does not establish a physical connection, but relies on the network to deliver a message successfully once sent. The network is used as an intermediary: the source end system delivers the message to the network and then has no further involvement; the network will carry the message to its destination as a discrete process. The source end system is not aware of the details of this process, and does not work interactively with the destination end system. The network may use a broadcast technique to convey the message; or may route it through a series of intermediate staging posts, each of which receives the message, stores it, and forwards it on to the next step when possible.

Packet switching techniques take a more structured approach, dividing an individual message into separate 'packets', each of which can travel independently through the network. The network is responsible for the safe delivery of these packets, creating them from the message dispatched from the source end system at the point of entry to the network, and re-assembling them into the original message at the point of exit for the destination end system. Since the network is dealing with smaller standard size packets in a predetermined way, a faster transmission rate can be achieved. The network is able to make its own decisions on routing, and can change these dynamically as traffic conditions change, with no apparent difference to the end user.

The advantages of packet switching are the following:

- **Integrated services digital networks**: The development of public data networks for digital communications led to the existence of different networks for different purposes—one for voice, one for data—and requiring organisations using these systems to connect to both. A duplication of networks is undesirable, and also works against the integration of information type, for instance the co-ordination of voice, data, and image, which is increasingly needed to support multimedia information networking.
- there is no need for a direct physical connection between sender and receiver;
- information from different calls can then be interleaved on the network channels to make maximum use of the available bandwidth;
- the user, therefore, pays only for information actually transmitted, rather than for elapsed time regardless of the transfer activity;
- standard use of communication protocols facilitates the inter-connection of equipment from different manufacturers, operating at different data rates. The X.25 protocol set is the standard for public packet switched networks. This is an open standard which is available for end systems as well as internally to the network.

A second characteristic of network types concerns the geographical extent of coverage, and the size in terms of the total number of network nodes which can be feasibly connected. A general classification is to describe networks as either LAN, MAN or WAN.

LOCAL AREA NETWORKS (LAN)

LAN is relatively smaller and privately owned network with the maximum span of 10 km to provide local connectivity within a building or small geographical area. LANs are limited to a single site or building, interconnecting nodes within a single organisation.

The LANs are distinguished from other kinds of networks by three characteristics:-

(*i*) Size,
(*ii*) Transmission technology; and
(*iii*) Topology.

A local area network is a means of linking together a collection of computer-based devices, within a limited geographical area, on a more or less equal basis. This equality makes the local area network (LAN) radically different from a terminal-based network, because each of the computer systems connected is an independent self-governing entity working in a co-operative relationship. Local area networks fall principally into two types:

1. proprietary networks which are used to interconnect a number of computers and their peripherals of the same type, for example a network of IBMPC or Macintosh personal computers;
2. standards-based networks which can interlink computer systems and devices whatever their type and specification, through the use of common network technology

For both types of LAN, every device connected to the network must communicate through a uniform hardware interface and software protocol to achieve compatibility. Standardisation of the communication process is therefore very important to the concept of local area networks. Since no one method of operation would be suitable for all possible needs, a number of alternative standards exist, reflected in the different types of LAN available. A local area network will typically be provided to support:

- resource sharing of expensive hardware resources, for example a colour printer, a high-speed modem, or a CDROM drive accessible to all nodes on the network;
- resource sharing of software and access to specialised facilities;
- *file* transfer and access to support the sharing of information between different users, and to provide wider access to central information while ensuring consistency by maintaining a single copy of the data; and
- messaging and conferencing to enhance organisational communications and co-operative working;

The most commonly found use of proprietary local area networks is to interconnect IBM-PCs within a single site or building. There are broadly two types of PC-based LAN, distinguished by the operating system by which they are managed.

1. In peer-to-peer PC networks all the network nodes interrelate as equals, able to call on the services of other nodes and to offer their own at all times. This is an intuitively natural way of sharing resources, and is cheap and effective to implement for small workgroups.
2. In server-based PC networks, one or more network nodes act as a provider of services for the other client nodes. Clients can only call on the services of a server node, which is dedicated to this purpose; there are three main types of server: a file server dispenses data and programme files across the network, either in whole or in part; a print server drives the printing devices and manages the print queues; and a communications server controls external links, such as facsimile machines, or modems.

According to the size of LAN, there are many standards known as the Institute of Electrical and Electronic Engineers (IEEE) area standards 802.x.International standards development for local area networks has been co-ordinated by Electrical and Electronic Engineers (IEEE) in the United States. This work is intended to develop a framework within which the major types of LAN can be encompassed rather than to specify one single standard for all requirements.

The standards are known by numerical, rather than product names, and cover both Ethernet and Token Ring style networks.

1. The 802.3 standard defines a broadcast bus-based network, which is effectively the same as the Ethernet type.
2. The 802.5 standard defines a token pausing ring network similar to the IBM Token Ring local area network.
3. The 802.4 standard describes a token passing bus network, which combines features of the first two types.
4. The 802.6 standard defines a high-speed broadband network, better known as a metropolitan area network (MAN).

METROPOLITAN AREA NETWORKS (MAN)

Metropolitan Area Network is defined for less than 50 km. and provides regional connectivity typically within a campus or small geographical area. It is designed to extend over an entire city. It may be a single network such as cable television network or it may be a means of connecting a number of LANs into a large network, so that resources may be shared LAN to LAN as well as device to device. For example a company can use a MAN to connect to the LANs in all of its offices throughout a city which exploit the new transmission media such as fibre optic cable, to build city-wide capabilities.

WIDE AREA NETWORKS (WAN)

Wide Area Network provides no limits of distance. In most WAN the subnet consists of two distinct components. Transmission lines also called circuits or channels and routers. Transmission lines are used for moving bits between machines whereas routers are used to connect two or more transmission lines. A WAN provides long distance transmission of data, voice, image and video information over large geographical areas that may comprise a country, a continent or even the whole world.

In the wide area environment, the communi-cations process is seen as a multistage process. Networks are constructed from point-to-point links between different nodes on a store and forward basis. Data transmission are passed from one node to the next, and route with each node making its own routing decision based on matching the information which it holds in a routing table with the destination address on the data packet, and in the context of current network traffic conditions.

Control and management of the network is therefore, distributed throughout, and not located in any single central point. The network can be extended by adding new connections between nodes and making appropriate updates to routing tables. There are likely to be alternative routes between nodes which can be used at different times. The relaying of data between nodes in this way requires the use of protocols to ensure correct delivery and protect against the corruption of transmissions on route.

The protocols normally operate both within the end systems and within the network relay nodes themselves. There are several alternative protocols suites which may be in use; however, all nodes on the network must be running the same protocols to communicate successfully, since this is the glue which binds the disparate systems together.

As an indication, some common wide area protocols are:

- the X.25 protocols which have been developed for public telecommunications, and ensure international compatibility in this area; these have also been adopted in some private networks; the TCP/IP protocol suite, widely used in private networks and in the academic and research world.

  Wide area networks can be usefully seen in two groups, distinguishing public and private systems.

- public telecommunications networks are international in scope, and accessible as a publicly available service;
- private data networks may also be on a national or international scale, but are intended for a distinct user group and not for general public access, although they are likely to make use of services offered by public telecommunications operators.

Each of these network types uses networking technologies which are most appropriate for their purposes.

These may be quite unlike each other, employing different techniques, principles and protocols which are not easily compatible. Stemming from these different technologies, there are consequent differences in maximum data transmission rates, number of possible network connections, response times and overloading factors etc.

Not all WANs are packet switched. A second possibility for a WAN is a satellite system. Each router has an antenna through which it can send and receive. All routers can hear the output from the satellite, and in some cases they can also hear the upward transmissions of their fellow routers to the satellite as well. Sometimes the routers are connected to a substantial point-to-point subnet, with only some of them having a satellite antenna. Satellite networks are inherently broadcast and are most useful when the broadcast property is important.

Network can also be classified as the degree of control which is placed within the network, and the location of this control also arises from these differences in approach. This may be characterised along a continuum, which offers at the extremes:

- a centralised network, with a single main switch to which all nodes are connected, and through which they communicate with each other;
- a decentralised peer-to-peer network, in which each node possesses the same status as any other, and can communicate with any other of its peers on an equal basis.

For large and small-scale networks, there are various compromise points along this continuum where they can be placed; an inter-network can also be constructed using various different topological arrangements which are interconnected at specific gateways — links from one type to the other type.

TERMINAL NETWORKS

Terminal networks are perhaps the simplest form of computer network, consisting of a number of relatively unintelligent terminals, each of which is linked to the central computer system and not directly to other terminals. These two elements work in a master-slave relationship to each other, in that the central system has much more extensive control of the process than the terminal, even though this may in fact be a more powerful machine, such as a personal computer emulating a terminal. In such centralized systems, the connections between terminals and central computer are arranged in a star topology, with communications routed through the central switch; if this should fail the main communication channel is cut off.

Terminal networks are very commonly used in large organisations that wish to pursue a centralised information policy, holding data and information systems at a single main point and providing widespread access to this. There may be a high level of communication requirements for this arrangement, however, where speed of response is important for example, a lending desk terminal in a branch public library may be required to transmit loan information to a central database and check appropriate records in a very few seconds.

PRIVATE DATA NETWORKS

Private data networks can be constructed from a number of different elements, as appropriate to requirements and conditions. They may be national or international in scope, and involve the co-ordination of several different network operators and administrations, using elements from:

- public telecommunications operators, in the form of leased data lines or use of the public data network;
- private network operators, including commercial long-haul network operators and satellite communications suppliers; independent local or wider scale data lines directly owned.

Telecommunications Networks

There are three types of telecommunications network presently available for use for computer-based information networking; each of these represents a phase of the developmental efforts to improve services over several decades, using quite different technology and approaches.

Public Switched Telephone Networks

This is an extensive network of cabling reaching into almost all inhabited parts of developed countries, and providing internationai connections worldwide. This made it attractive as an immediately available option for computer networking in its early stages. The PSTN network is designed for voice communication, and therefore requires the use of an interfacing data communication device, usually a modem, to be used. The network makes use of circuit switching technology for the same reason, and is a rather noisy and unreliable channel, prone to errors and mis-connection. It is poorly suited to fast and reliable data transfer and depends on the end systems alone to maintain quality through the use of suitable protocols. The PSTN makes inefficient use of the available carrying capacity because the circuit is idle when neither end system is transmitting but cannot be used by waiting nodes. Since a switched phone line is charged on a time and distance basis, regardless of the amount of traffic, it is not ideal for inter-computer communication over long distances.

Public Data Networks

The public data networks have been constructed specifically for the transmission of computer information, and cannot be used for voice conversations. They provide fast and reliable data transfer, more flexibility and international communications at a reasonable cost, since they are charged for by the amount of data transferred.

Public data networks are mostly managed on a national basis with international connections between them, and so X.25 forms something approaching a global standard in this area. There are, however, two versions of the X.25 protocol; the 1998 version is not used by all public telecommunications operators. The public data network is essentially a store and forward network which operates at speeds fast enough to give the impression of a direct connection to the end user.

The Leasing Telecommunication Lines

The leasing of dedicated digital data lines is an alternative to use of the public data network. These are private circuits, provided as a carrier by the telecommunications authority, but under the control of the organisation which is renting the line.

Leased lines are point to point connections, permanently linking one site with another, rather than dynamically switchable channels. Since they are leased at a fixed annual rate, the greater the use made of the line the more efficient it becomes.

Multiple rented private circuits are used by large organisations to create private networks, linking remote sites together on a point-to-point basis, or providing a high-speed network backbone for a high volume of traffic between main sites. In the United Kingdom BT provide a range of leased circuits with varying data carrying capacities:

- Kilostream and Kilostream N lines provide bulk data transmission at rates from 64 Kbps up to about 1 Megabit per second (Mbps);
- Megastream lines provide higher speeds of up to 2 Mbps;
- Satstream utilises satellite capacity to offer point-to-multi-point connections over a wide geographical area.The use of leased lines is a more secure and flexible option for the larger organisation, which is able to deploy the systems and protocols which it finds most suitable, rather than having to conform to those used in public systems.

Two development programmes in the telecommunications infrastructure provided the platform for the development of integrated services digital networks:

1. The digitisation of the trunk network lines, the main arteries used by the network operator.
2. The replacement of electro-mechanical local telephone exchanges by digital switches, such as System X and System Y.

The ISDN aims to build a public network providing end-to-end digital connectivity which is capable of supporting a range of digital devices and services, both voice and non-voice, on the same basis. This allows users to send and receive data, text and image from computer systems as well as offering an enhanced telephone service. This is achieved over a single ISDN connection, so that one network may be used for all applications, at the same time as providing higher transmission speeds. The ISDN approach is to enable the existing local telephone circuitry-the local loop-to carry digital signals through the use of specialised equipment and adapters, rather than a wholesale and long-term replacement programme.

This requires the installation of suitable network connections in the customer premises, which act as the interface to the digital network. Despite this fully digital transmission system it is still not possible to connect all computer equipment directly to the network, unless the equipment is designed or adapted to work-with the ISDN system. Access to the ISDN network is available at two different capacity rates, known as basic rate and primary rate.

The access rate refers to the number of logical channels which are available on a single ISDN connection. Each of these channels constitutes a circuit which is independently usable by different information media, and can be switched to different destination points.

The Basic Access Rate provides two bearer channels and one data channel, and for this reason is otherwise known as 213 + D. Each of the bearer channels can simultaneously carry a separate information stream, at a transfer rate of 64 Kbps-for example, one for a voice call and the other for data.

The Primary Access Rate gives a higher number of bearer channels, although the exact number is variable between countries — the United Kingdom, Europe and Australia supply 30 bearer channels to the user in one ISDN connection (known as SOB + D); in the United States, Japan and South East Asia 23 channels are used. SOB + D gives an overall data rate of some 2 Mbps (the equivalent to a BT Megastream leased line) and necessitates the usc of extra equipment at the subscriber premises to manage the multiple channels.

Potential benefits from the use of ISDN are the following:

- all 30 ISDN connections can be switched to different locations;
- clearer calls and more reliable data transfers, with less line noise;
- the ability to send two information streams to the same locations, to support remote co-operative working; for example, two users might discuss over the phone the contents of a computer screen which can be transferred between their terminals;
- enabling domestic services, such as home shopping and banking, online database access, security, and control services for the home;
- feasible desktop video conferencing; and
- providing a better infrastructure for teleworking, for example, by providing a gateway to an office LAN for home-based workers.

Frame Relay Networks

Frame relay networks technologies are in development which may threaten to overwhelm ISDN before its full potential is reached. These involve the use of high-speed packet switching on high bandwidth networks which will offer much greater information transmission capabilities than the present public data networks. Frame relay networks are made possible by use of less noisy transmission media, such as fibre optic cable, in the network infrastructure, exploiting this greater reliability to simplify the protocols necessary and thus speed up the transmission process.

Integrated Broadband Networks

Integrated broadband networks are sometimes referred to as broadband ISDN (B-ISDN) systems and will also exploit the advantages of fibre optic to offer a dramatically enhanced communication facility, far more powerful than exists at present and able to deliver a wider range of services more effectively.

The intention of developing integrated broadband communications systems is to provide a single network for all services, which can be flexibly and dynamically configured according to individual circumstances and priorities. Digital networks allow both data, voice and image to be sent along the same connection, but these information types have different desirable transmission characteristics.

Data and text require a high degree of accuracy, since the quality of the received information is more easily affected by corruption, but are more tolerant of short transmission delays. Voice and the moving image, on the other hand, are more tolerant of errors since these can be interpreted by human interpretation, but are more susceptible to variations in transmission delays.

Broadband networks aim to overcome such problems by using a universal fast packet switching technique for all information streams, and allocating 'bandwidth on demand' rather than relying on fixed bandwidth channels. Two rates have been proposed for B-ISDN: a basic rate service with a digital access rate of 155 Mbps, and a primary rate service at 622 Mbps, although the full specifications for these have yet to be defined.

Wireless Networks

Digital wireless communica-tion is not a new idea. As early as 1901, the Italian physicist Marconi demonstrated a ship-to-shore wireless telegraph, using Morse Code (dots and dashes are binary, after all). Modern digital wireless systems have better performance, but the basic idea is the same.

To a first approximation, wireless networks can be divided into three main categories:

1. System interconnection
2. Wireless LANs
3. Wireless WANs

System interconnection is all about interconnecting the components of a computer using short-range radio. Almost every computer has a monitor, keyboard, mouse, and printer connected to the main unit by cables. So many new users have a hard time plugging all the cables into the right little holes (even though they are usually colour coded) that most computer vendors offer the option of sending a technician to the user's home to do it. Consequently, some companies got together to design a short-range wireless network called *Bluetooth* to connect these components without wires. Bluetooth also allows digital cameras, headsets, scanners, and other devices to connect to a computer by merely being brought within range. No cables, no driver installation, just put them down, turn them on, and they work. For many people, this ease of operation is a big plus.

In the simplest form, system interconnection networks use the master-slave paradigm. The system unit is normally the master, talking to the mouse, keyboard, etc., as slaves. The master tells the slaves what addresses to use, when they can broadcast, how long they can transmit, what frequencies they can use, and so on.

The next step up in wireless networking are the wireless LANs. These are systems in which every computer has a radio modem and antenna with which it can communicate with other systems. Often there is an antenna on the ceiling that the machines talk to. However, if the systems are close enough, they can communicate directly with one another in a peer-to-peer configuration. Wireless LANs are becoming increasingly common in small offices and homes, where installing Ethernet is considered too much trouble, as well as in older office buildings, company cafeterias, conference rooms, and other places! There is a standard for wireless LANs, called **IEEE 802.11,** which most systems implement and which is becoming very widespread.

The third kind of wireless network is used in wide area systems. The radio network used for cellular telephones is an example of a low-bandwidth wireless system. This system has already gone through three generations. The first generation was analogue and for voice only. The second generation was digital and for voice only. The third generation is digital and is for both voice and data. In a certain sense, cellular wireless networks are like wireless LANs, except that the distances involved are much greater and the bit rates much lower. Wireless LAN can operate at rates up to about 50 Mbps over distances of tens of meters. Cellular systems operate below 1 Mbps, but the distance between the base station and the computer or telephone is measured in kilometers rather than in meters. In addition to these low-speed networks, high-bandwidth wide area wireless networks are also being developed. The initial focus is high-speed wireless Internet access from homes and businesses, bypassing the telephone system. This service is often called local multipoint distribution service.

Almost all wireless networks hook up to the wired network at some point to provide access to files, databases, and the Internet. There are many ways these connections can be realised, depending on the circumstances.

Many people believe wireless is the wave of the future (e.g., Bi et al., 200 Leeper, 2001; Varshey and Vetter, 2000) but at least one dissenting voice h<1 been heard. Bob Metcalfe, the inventor of Ethernet, has written: "Mobile wire less computers are like mobile pipe less bathrooms-portables. They will be common on vehicles, and at construction sites, and rock concerts.

Home Networks

Home networking is on the horizon. The fundamental idea is that in the future most homes will be set up for networking. Every device in the home will be capable of communicating with every other device, and all of them will be accessible over the Internet. This is one of those visionary concepts that nobody asked for (like TV remote controls or mobile phones), but once they arrived nobody can imagine how they lived without them. Many devices are capable of being networked. Some of the more obvious Categories (with examples) are as follows:

1. Computers (desktop PC, notebook PC, PDA, shared peripherals).
2. Entertainment (TV, DVD, VCR, camcorder, camera, stereo, MP3).
3. Telecommunications (telephone, mobile telephone, intercom, fax).
4. Appliances (microwave, refrigerator, clock, furnace, airconditioner, light.
5. Telemetry (utility meter, smokel burglar alarm, thermostat, babycam).

Home computer networking is already here in a limited way. Many homes already have a device to connect multiple computers to a fast Internet connection. Networked entertainment is not quite here, but as more and more music and movies can be downloaded from the Internet, there will be a demand to connect stereos and televisions to it. Also, people will want to share their own videos with friends and family, so the connection will need to go both ways. Telecommunications gear is already connected to the outside world, but soon it will be digital and go over the Internet. The average home probably has a dozen clocks (e.g., in appliances), all of which have to be reset twice a year when daylight saving time (summer time) comes and goes. If all the clocks were on the Internet, that resetting could be done automatically. Finally, remote monitoring.of the home and its contents is a likely winner. Probably many parents would be willing to spend some money to monitor their sleeping babies on their PDAs when they are eating out, even with a rented teenager in the house. While one can imagine a separate network for each application area, integrating all of them into a single network is probably a better idea.

Home networking has some fundamentally different properties than other network types. First, the network and devices have to be easy to install. The author has installed numerous pieces of hardware and software on various computers over the years, with mixed results. A series of phone calls to the vendor's help-desk typically resulted in answers like (1) Read the manual, (2) Reboot the computer, (3) Remove all hardware and software except ours and try again, (4) Download the newest driver from our Web site, and if all else fails, (5) Reformat the hard disk and then reinstall Windows from the CD-ROM. Telling the purchaser of an Internet refrigerator to download and install a new version of the refrigerator's operating system is not going to lead to happy customers. Computer users are accustomed to putting up with products that do not work; the car, television, and refrigerator-buying public is far less tolerant. They expect products to work for 100% from the word go.

Second, the network and devices have to be foolproof in operation. Air conditioners used to have one knob with four settings: Off, Low, Medium, and High. Now they have 30-page manuals. This will be beyond the comprehension of virtually all the users.

Third, low price is essential for success. People will not pay a $50 premium for an Internet thermostat because few people regard monitoring their home temperature from work that important. For $5 extra, it might sell, though.

Fourth, the main application is likely to involve multimedia, so the network needs sufficient capacity. There is no market for Internet-connected televisions that show shaky movies at 320 × 240 pixel resolution and 10 frames/sec. Fast Ethernet, the workhorse in most offices, is not good enough for multimedia. Consequently, home networks will need better performance than that of existing, office networks and at lower prices before they become mass market items.

Fifth, it must be possible to start out with one or two devices and expand the reach of the network gradually. This means no format wars. Telling consumers to buy peripherals with IEEE 1394 (FireWire) interfaces and a few years later retracting that and saying USB 2.0 is the interface-of-the-month is going to make consumers *skittish*. The network interface will have to remain stable for many years; the wiring (if any) will have to remain stable for decades.

Sixth, security and reliability will be very important. Losing a few files to an e-mail virus is one thing; having a burglar disarm your security system from his PDA and then plunder your house is something quite different. An interesting question is whether home networks will be wired or wireless. Most homes already have six networks installed: electricity, telephone, cable television, water, gas, and sewer. Adding a seventh one during construction is not difficult, but retrofitting existing houses is expensive. Cost favours wireless networking, but security favours wired networking. The problem with wireless is that the radio waves they use are quite good at going through fences. Not everyone is overjoyed at the thought of having the neighbours piggybacking on their Internet connection and reading their *e-mail* on its way to the printer. In short, home networking offers many opportunities and challenges. Most of them relate to the need to be easy to manage, dependable, and 'secure, especially in the hands of nontechnical users, while at the same time delivering high performance at low cost.

INTERNETWORKS

Many networks exist in the world, often with different hardware and software. People connected to one network often want to communicate with people attached to a different one. The fulfillment of this desire requires that different, and frequently incompatible networks, be connected, sometimes by means of machines called gateways to make the connection and provide the necessary translation, both in terms of hardware and software. A collection of interconnected networks is called an **internetwork or internet**. These terms will be used in a general sense, in contrast to the-worldwide Internet (which is one specific internet), which we will always capitalise. A common form of internet is a collection of LANs connected by a WAN. An internetwork is formed when distinct networks are interconnected. Connecting LANs or WANs or connecting LAN and a WAN forms an internetwork. If different organisations paid to construct different parts of the network and each maintains its part, we have an internetwork rather than a single network. Also if underlying technology is different in different parts (e.g broadcast versus point-to-point), we probably have two networks.

REFERENCE MODELS

Now that we have discussed frame relax networks in the abstract, it is time to look at some examples. In

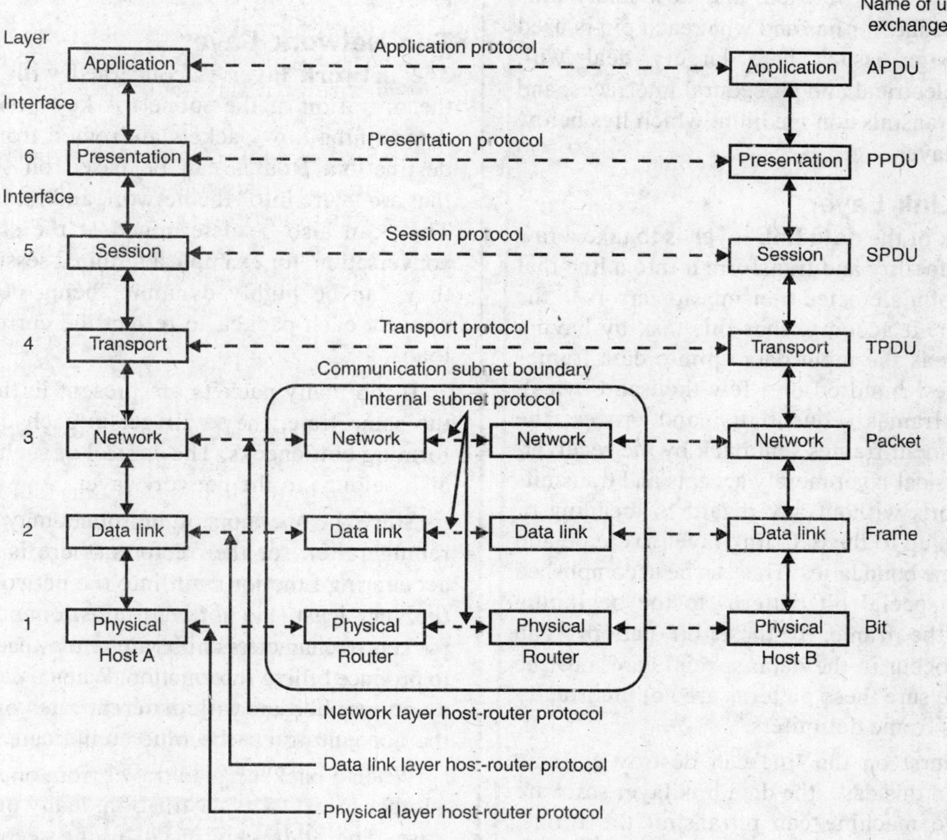

Fig. 11.1: *The OSI reference model.*

the next two sections we will discuss two important network architectures, the OSI reference model and the TCP/IP reference model.

The OSI Reference Model

The **OSI model** is shown in Figure 11.1 (minus the physical medium). This model is based on a proposal developed by the International Standards Organization (ISO) as a first step toward international standardization of the protocols used in the various layers (Day and Zimmermann, 1983). The model is called the ISO OSI (Open Sysem Interconnection) Reference Model because it deals with connecting open systems—that is, systems that are open for communication with other systems. We will usually just call it the OSI model for short.

The OSI model has seven layers. The principles that were applied to arrive at the seven layers are as follows:

1. A layer should be created where a different level of abstraction is needed.
2. Each layer should perform a well defined function.
3. The function of each layer should be chosen with an eye toward defining internationally standardised protocols.
4. The layer boundaries should be chosen to minimise the information flow across the interfaces.
5. The number of layers should be large enough that distinct functions need not be thrown together in the same layer out of necessity, and small enough that the architecture does not become unwieldy.

Below we will discuss each layer of the model in turn, starting at the bottom layer. Note that the OSI model itself is not a network architecture because it does not specify the exact services and protocols to be used in each layer. It just tells what each layer should do. However, ISO has also produced standards for all the layers, although these are not part of the reference model itself. Each one has been published as a separate international standard.

The Physical Layer

The **physical layer** is concerned with transmitting raw bits over a communication channel. The design issues have to do with making sure that when one side sends a 1 bit, it is received by the other side as a 1 bit, not as a 0 bit. Typical questions here are how many volts should be used to represent a 1 and how many for a 0, how many microseconds a bit lasts, whether transmission may proceed simultaneously in both directions, how the initial connection is established and how it is turn down when both sides are finished, and how many pins the network connector has and what each pin is used for. The design issues here largely deal with mechanical, electrical and procedural interfaces, and the physical transmission medium, which lies below the physical layer.

The Data Link Layer

The main task of the **data link layer** is to take a raw transmission facility and transform it into a line that appears free of undetected transmission errors to the network layer. It accomplishes this task by having the sender break the input data up into data frames (typically a few hundred or a few thousand bytes), transmit the frames sequentially, and process the acknowledgement frames sent back by the receiver. Since the physical layer merely accepts and transmits a stream of bits without any regard to meaning or structure, it is up to the data link layer to create and recognise frame boundaries. This can be accomplished by attaching special bit patterns to the beginning and end of the frame. If these bit patterns can accidentally occur in the data, special care must be taken to make sure these patterns are not incorrectly interpreted as frame delimiters.

A noise burst on the line can destroy a frame completely. In this case, the data link layer software on the source machine can retransmit the frame. However, multiple transmissions of the same frame introduce the possibility of duplicate frames. A duplicate frame could be sent if the acknowledgement frame from the receiver back to the sender were lost. It is up to this layer to solve the problems caused by damaged, lost, and duplicate frames. The data link layer may offer several different service classes to the network layer, each of a different quality and with a different price.

Another issue that arises in the data link layer (and most of the higher layers as well) is how to keep a fast transmitter from drowning a slow receiver in data. Some traffic regulation mechanism must be employed to let the transmitter know how much buffer space the receiver has at the moment. Frequently, this flow regulation and the error handling are integrated.

If the line can be used to transmit data in both directions, this introduces a new complication that the data link layer software must deal with. The problem is that the acknowledgement frames for A to B traffic compete for the use of the line with data frames for the B to A traffic. A clever solution (piggybacking) has been devised; we will discuss it in detail later.

Broadcast networks have an additional issue in the data link layer: how to control access to the shared channel. A special sublayer of the data link layer, the medium access sublayer, deals with this problem.

The Network Layer

The **network layer** is concerned with controlling the operation of the subnet. A key design issue is determining how packets are routed from source to destination. Routes can be based on static tables that are "wire into" the network and rarely changed. They can also be determined at the start of each conversation, for example a terminal session. Finally, they can be highly dynamic, being determined a new for each packet, to reflect the current network load.

If too many packets are present in the subnet at the same time, they will get in each other's way, forming bottlenecks. The control of such congestion also belongs to the network layer.

Since the operators of the subnet may well expect remuneration for their efforts, there is often some accounting function built into the network layer. At the very least, the software must count how many packets or characters or bits are sent by each customer, to produce billing information. When a packet crosses a national border, with different rates on each side, the accounting can become complicated.

When a packet has to travel from one network to another to get to its destination, many problems can arise. The addressing used by the second network may be different from the first one. The second one may not accept the packet at all because it is too large. The protocols may differ, and so on. It is up to the network layer to overcome all these problems to allow heterogeneous networks to be interconnected.

In broadcast networks the routing problem is simple, so the network layer is often this or even nonexistent.

The Transport Layer

The basic function of the **transport layer** is to accept data from the session layer, split it up into smaller units if need be, pass these to the network layer, and ensure that the pieces all arrive correctly at the other end. Furthermore, all this must be done efficiently, and in a way that isolates the upper layers from the inevitable changes in the hardware technology.

Under normal conditions, the transport layer creates a distinct network connection for each transport connection required by the session layer. If the transport connection requires a high thoroughput, however, the transport layer might create multiple network connections, dividing the data among the network connections to improve thoroughput. On the other hand, if creating or maintaining a network connection is expensive, the transport layer might multiplex several transport connections onto the same network connection to reduce the cost. In all cases, the transport layer is required to make the multiplexing transparent to the session layer.

The transport layer also determines what type of service to provide the session layer, and ultimately the users of the network. The most popular type of transport connection is an error-free point-to-point channel that delivers messages or bytes in the order in which they were sent. However, other possible kinds of transport service are transport of isolated messages with no guarantee about the order of delivery, and broadcasting of messages to multiple destinations. The type of service is determined when the connection is established.

The transport layer is a true end-to-end layer, from source to destination. In other words, a programme on the source machine carries on a conversation with a similar programme on the destination machine, using the message headers and control messages. In the lower layers the protocols are btween each machine and its immediate neighbours, and not by the ultimate source and destination machines which may be separated by many routers. The difference between layers 1 through 3, which are chained, and layers 4 through 7, which are end-to-end is illustrated in Fig. 6.1.

Many hosts are multiprogrammed, which implies that multiple connections will be entering and leaving each host. There needs to be some way to tell which message belongs to which connection. The transport header is one place this information can be put.

In addition to multiplexing several message streams onto one channel, the transport layer must take care of establishing and deleting connections across the network. This requires some kind of naming mechanism, so that a process on one machine has a way of describing with whom it wishes to converse. There must also be a mechanism to regulate the flow of information, so that a fast host cannot overrun a slow one. Such a mechanism is called *flow control* and plays a key role in the transport layer (also in other layers). Flow control between hosts is distinct from flow control between routers, although we will later see that similar principles apply to both.

The Session Layer

The **session layer** allows users on different machines to establish sessions between them. A session allows ordinary data transport, as does the transport layer, but it also provides enhanced services useful in some applications. A session might be used to allow a user to log into a remote timesharing system or to transfer a file between two machines.

One of the services of the session layer is to manage dialogue control. Sessions can allow traffic to go in both directions at the same time, or in only one direction at a time. If traffic can only go one way at a time (analogous to a single railroad track), the session layer can help keep track of whole turn it is.

A related session service is token management. For some protocols, it is essential that both sides do not attempt the same operation at the same time. To manage these activities, the session layer provides tokens that can be exchanged. Only the side holding the token may perform the critical operation.

Another session service is synchronisation. Consider the problems that might occur when trying to do a 2-hour file transfer between two machines with a 1-hour mean time between crashes. After each transfer was aborted, the whole transfer would have to start over again and would probably fail again the next time as well. To eliminate this problem the session layer provides a way to insert checkpoints into the data stream, so that after a crash, only the data transferred after the last checkpoint have to be repeated.

The Presentation Layer

The **presentation layer** performs certain functions that are requested sufficiently often to warrant finding a general solution for them, rather than letting each user solve the problems. In particular, unlike all the lower layers, which are just interested in moving bits reliably from here to there, the presentation layer is concerned with the syntax and semantics of the information transmitted.

A typical example of a presentation service is encoding data in a standard agreed upon way. Most user programmes do not exchange random binary bit strings. They exchange things such as people's names, dates, amounts of money, and invoices. These items are represented as character strings, integers, floating-point numbers, and data structures composed of several simpler items. Different computers have different codes for representing character strings, (*e.g.*, ASCII and Unicode), integers, (*e.g.*, one's complement and two's complement), and so on. In order to make it possible for computers with different representations to communicate, the data structures to be exchanged can be defined in an abstract way, along with a standard encoding to be used "on the wire." The presentation layer manages these abstract data structures and converts from the representation used inside the computer to the network standard representation and back.

The Application Layer

The **application layer** contains a variety of protocols that are commonly needed. For example, there are hundreds of incompatible terminal types in the world. Consider the plight of a full screen editor that is supposed to work over a network with many different terminal types, each with different screen layouts, escape sequences for inserting and deleting text, moving the cursor etc.

One way to solve this problem is to define an abstract network virtual terminal that editors and other programs can be written to deal with. To handle each terminal type a piece of software must be written to map the functions of the network virtual terminal onto the real terminal. For example, when the editor moves the virtual terminal's cursor to the upper left-hand corner of the screen, this software must issue the proper command sequence to the real terminal to get its cursor there too. All the virtual terminal software is in the application layer.

Another application layer function is file transfer. Different file systems have different file naming conventions, different ways of representing text lines, and so on. Transferring a file between two different systems requires handling these and other incompatibilities. This work, too belongs to the application layer, as do electronic mail, remote job entry, directory lookup, and various other general-purpose and special-purpose facilities.

DATA TRANSMISSION IN THE OSI MODEL

Figure 11.2 shows an example of how data can be transmitted using the OSI model. The sending process has some data it wants to send to the receiving process. It gives the data to the application layer, which then attaches the application header, AH (which may be null), to the front of it and gives the resulting item to the presentation layer.

The presentation layer may transform this item in various ways and possibly add a header to the front, giving the result to the session layer. It is important to realise that the presentation layer is not aware of which portion of the data given to it by the application layer is AH, if any, and which is true user data.

This process is repeated until the data reach the physical layer, where they are actually transmitted to the receiving machine.

IEEE Standard 802.3 and Ethernet

The IEEE 802.3 standard is for a 1-persistent CSMA/CD LAN. To review the idea, when a station wants to transmit, it listens to the cable. If the cable is busy, the station waits until it goes idle; otherwise it transmits immediately. If two or more stations simultaneously begin transmitting on an idle cable, they will collide. All colliding stations then terminate their transmission, wait a random time, and repeat the whole process all over again.

The 802.3 standard has an interesting history. The real beginning was the ALOHA system constructed to allow radio communication between machines scattered over the Hawaiian Islands. Later, carrier

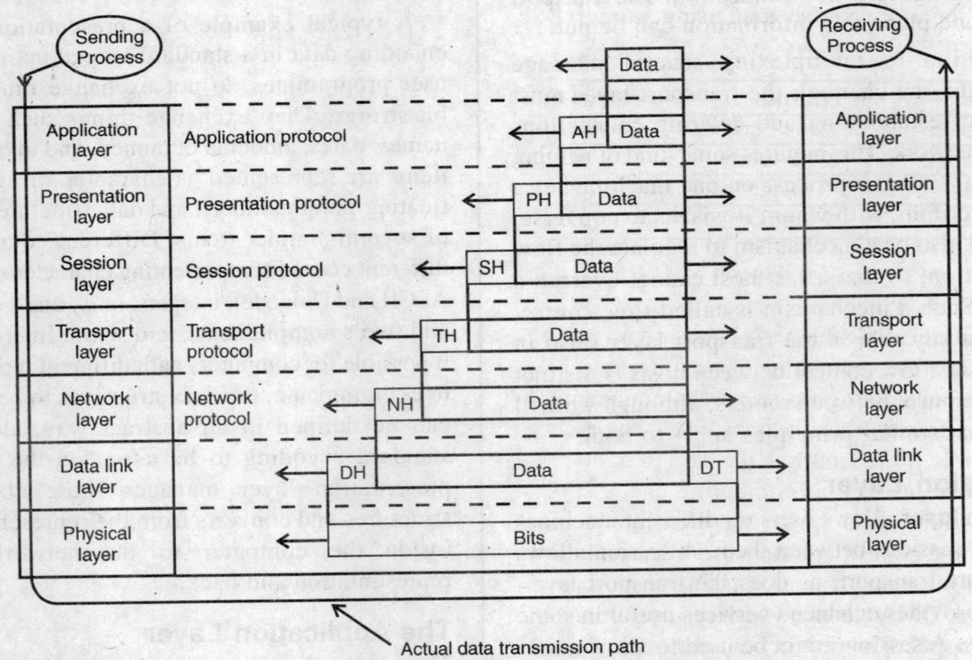

Fig. 11.2: *An example of how the OSI model is used. Some of the headers may be null.*

sensing was added, and Xerox PARC built a 2.94-Mbps CSMA/CD system to connect over 100 personal work-stations on a 1-km cable. This system was called Ethernet after the *luminiferous ether,* through which electromagnetic radiation was once thought to propagate.

The Xerox Ethernet was so successful that Xerox, DEC, and Intel drew up a standard for a 10-Mbps Ethernet. This standard formed the basis for 802.3. The published 802.3 standard differs from the Ethernet specification in that it describes a whole family of 1-persistent CSMA/CD systems, running at speeds from 1 to 10-Mbps on various media. Also, the one-header field differs between the two (the 802.3 length field is used for packet type in Ethernet). The initial standard also gives the parameters for a 10 Mbps base band system using 50-ohm coaxial cable.

Cabling

Since the name "Ethernet" refers to the cable (the ether), let us start our discussion there. Five types of cabling are commonly used, as shown in Figure 6.3. Historically, **10Base5** cabling, popularly called **thick Ethernet,** came first. It resembles a yellow garden hose, with markings every 2.5 meters to show where the taps go. (The 802.3 standard does not actually require the cable to be yellow, but it does suggest it.) Connections to it are generally made using **vampire taps,** in which a pin is carefully forced halfway into the coaxial cable's core. The notation 10Base5 means that it operates at 10 Mbps, uses baseband signaling, and can support segments of up to 500 meters.

Historically, the second cable type was **10Base2** or thin **Ethernet,** which, in contrast to the garden-hose-like thick Ethernet, bends easily. Connections to it are made using industry standard BNC connectors to form T junctions, rather than using vampire taps. These are easier to use and more reliable. Thin Ethernet is much cheaper and easier to install, but it can run for only 200 meters and can handle only 30 machines per cable segment.

The problems associated with finding cable brakes have driven systems toward a different kind of wiring pattern, in which all stations have a cable running to a central hub. Usually, these wires are telephone company twisted pairs, since most office buildings are already wired with way, and there are normally plenty of spare pairs available. This scheme is called **10Base-T.**

These three wiring schemes are illustrated in Figure 6.4. For 10Base5, a tranceiver is clamped securely around the cable so that its tap makes contact with the inner core. The tranceiver contains the electronics that handle carrier detection and collision detection. When a collision is detected, the transceiver also puts a special invalid signal on the cable to ensure that all other transceivers also realise that a collision has occurred.

With 10Base5, a **transceiver cable** connects the transceiver to an interface board in the computer. The transceiver cable may be up to 50 metres long and contains five individually shielded twisted pairs. Two of the pairs are for data in and data out, respectively. Two more are for control signals in and out. The fifth pair, which is not always used, allows the computer to power the transceiver electronics. Some transceivers allow up to eight nearby computers to be attached to them, to reduce the number of transceivers needed.

Name	Cable	Max. segment	Nodes/seg.	Advantages
10 Base5	Thick coax	500 m	100	Gopod for backbones
10 Base2	Thin coax	200 m	30	Cheapest system
10 Base-T	Twisted pair	100 m	1024	Easy maintenance
10 Base-F	Fiber optics	2000 m	1024	Best between buildings

Fig. 11.3: *The most common kinds of baseband 802.3 LANs.*

The transceivers cable terminates on an interface board inside the computer. The interface board contains a controller chip that transmits frames to, and receives frames from, the transceiver. The controller is responsible for assembling the data into the proper frame format, as well as computing check sums on outgoing frames and veryfying them on incoming frames. Some controller chips also manage a pool of buffers for incoming frames, a queue of buffers to be transmitted, DMA transfers with the host computers, and other aspects of network management.

With 10Base2, the connection to the cable is just a passive BNC T-junction connector. The transceiver electronics are on the controller board, and each station always has its own transceiver.

With 10Base-T, there is no cable at all, just the hub (a box full of electronics). Adding or removing a station is simpler in this configuration, and cable breaks can be detected easily. The disadvantage of 10Base-T is that the maximum cable run from the hub is only 100 meters, maybe 150 meters if high-quality (category 5) twisted pairs are used. Also, a large hub costs thousands of dollars. Still, 10Base-T is becoming steadily more popular due to the ease of maintenance that it offers. A faster version of 10Base-T (100Base-T).

A fourth cabling option for 802.3 is **10Base-F,** which uses fibre optics. This alternative is expensive due to the cost of the connectors and terminators, but it has excellent noise immunity and is the method

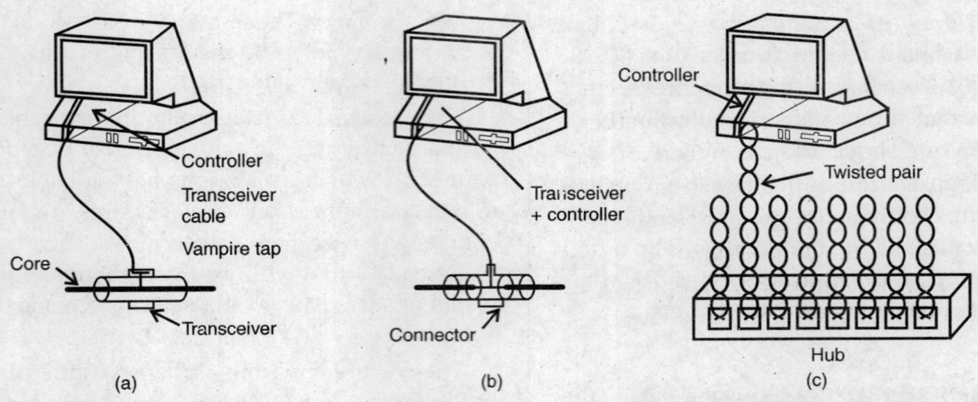

Fig. 11.4: *Three kinds of 802.3 cabling (a) 10Base5(b) 10Base2(c) 10Base-T.*

of choice when running between buildings or widely separated hubs.

Manchester Encoding

None of the version of 802.3 use straight binary encoding (see Figure 6.5(a) with 0 volts for a 0 bit and 5 volts for 1 bit because it leads to ambiguities. If one station sends the bit string 0001000, other might falsely interpret it as 10000000 or 01000000 because they cannot tell the difference between an idle sender (0 volts) and a 0 bit (0 volts).

What is needed is a way for receivers to unambiguously determine the start, end, or middle of each bit without reference to an external clock. Two such approaches are called **Manchester encoding** and **differential Manchester encoding.** With Manchester encoding, each bit period is divided into two equal intervals. A binary 1 bit is sent by having the voltage set high during the first interval and low in the second one. A binary 0 is just the revese; first low and then high. This scheme ensures that every bit period has a transition in the middle, making it easy for the receiver to synchronise with the sender. A disadvantage of Manchester encoding is that it requires twice as much bandwidth as straight binary encoding, because the pulses are half the width. Manchester encoding is shown in Figure 11.5(b).

Differential Manchester encoding, shown in Figure 11.5(c), is a variation of basic Manchester encoding. In it, a 1 bit is indicated by the absence of a transition at the start of the interval. A 0 bit is indicated by the presence of a transition at the start of the interval. In both cases, there is a transition in the middle as well. The differential scheme requires more complex equipment but offers better noise immunity. All 802.3 baseband system use Manchester encoding due to its simplicity. The high signal is +0.85 volts and the low signal is –0.85 volts, giving a DC value of 0 volts.

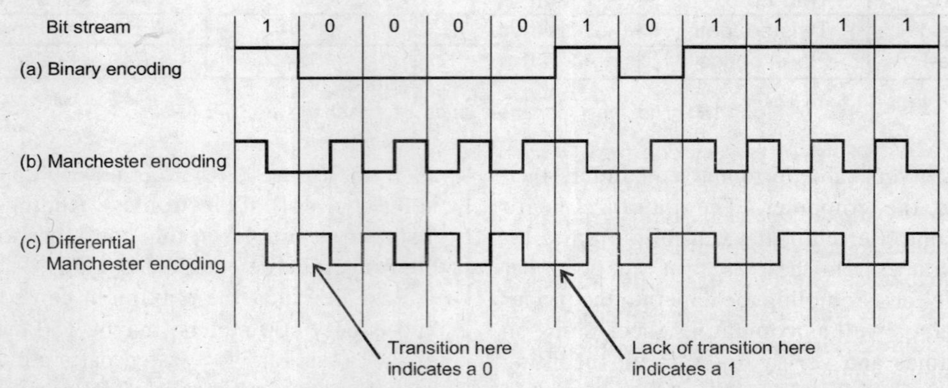

Fig. 11.5: *(a) Binary encoding. (b) Manchester encoding. (c) Differential Manchester encoding.*

The 802.3 MAC Sublayer Protocol

The 802.3 (IEEE, 1985a) frame structure starts with a *Preamble* of 7 bytes, each containing the bit pattern 10101010. The Manchester encoding of this pattern produces a 10-MHz square wave for 5.6 µsec to allow the receiver's clock to synchronise with the sender's. Next comes a *Start of frame* byte containing 10101011 to denote the start of the frame itself.

The frame contains two addresses, one for the destination and one for the source. The standard allows 2-byte and 6-byte addresses, but the parameters defined for the 10-Mbps baseband standard use only the 6-byte addresses. The high-order bit of the destination address is a 0 for ordinary addresses and 1 for group addresses. Group addresses allow multiple stations to listen to a single address. When a frame is sent to a group address, all the stations in the group receive it. Sending to a group of stations is called multicast. The address consisting of all 1 bits is reserved for broadcast. A frame containing all 1s in the destination field is delivered to all stations on the network.

IEEE Standard 802.4 : Token Bus

This standard, 802.4 (Dirvin and Miller, 1986; and IEEE, 1985b), describes a LAN called a token bus. Physically, the token bus is a linear or tree-shaped cable onto which the stations are attached. Logically, the stations are organised into a ring (see Figure 6.6) with each station knowing the address of the station to its "left" and "right". When the logical ring is initialised, the highest numbered station may send the first frame. After it is done, it passes permission to its immediate neighbour by sending the neighbour a special control frame called a token. The token propagates around the logical ring, with only the token holder being permitted to transmit frames. Since only one station at a time holds the token, collisions do not occur.

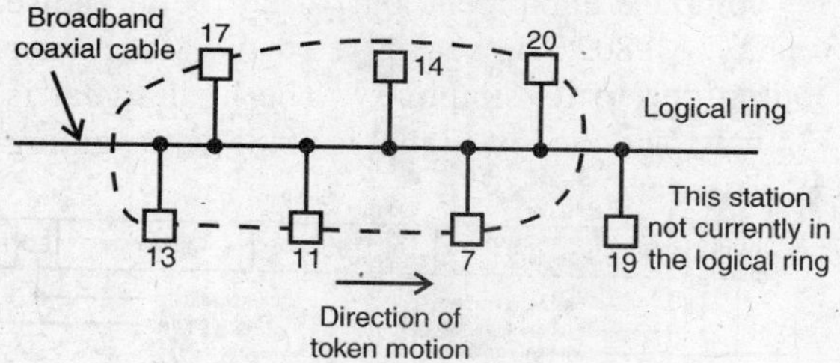

Fig. 11.6: *A token bus.*

The 802.4 MAC protocol is very complex, with each station having to maintain ten different timers and more than two dozen internal state variables. The 802.4 standard is much longer than 802.3 filling more than 200 pages. The two standards are also quite different in style, with 802.3 giving the protocols as Pascal procedures, whereas 802.4 gives them as finite state machines, with the actions written in Ada®.

For the physical layer, the token bus uses the 75-ohm broadband coaxial cable used for cable television. Both single-and dual-cable systems are allowed with or without head-ends. Three different analogue modulation schemes are permitted: phase continuous frequency shift keying, phase coherent frequency shift keying, and multilevel binary amplitude modulated phase shift keying. Speeds of 1, 5, and 10 Mbps are possible.

The Token Bus MAC Sublayer Protocol

When the ring is initialised, stations are inserted into it in order of station address, from highest to lowest. Token passing is also done from high to low addresses. Each time a station acquires the token, it can transmit frames for a certain amount of time; then it must pass the token on. If the frames are short enough, several consecutive frames may be sent. If a station has no data, it passes the token immediately upon receiving it.

The token bus defines four priority classes, 0, 2, 4, and 6 for traffic, with 0 the lowest and 6 the highest. It is easiest to think of each station internally being divided into four substations, one at each priority level. As input comes in to the MAC sublayer from above, the data are checked for priority and routed to one of the four substations. Thus each substation maintains its own queue of frames to be transmitted.

When the token comes into the station over the cable, it is passed internally to the priority 6 substation, which may begin transmitting frames, if it has any.

Token Ring (IEEE Standard 802.5)

Ring networks have been used for both local and wide area networks. Among their many attractive feature is the fact that a ring is not really a broadcast medium but a collection individual point to point links that happen to form a circle. A ring is also fair and has a known upper bound on channel access.

For these reasons, IBM chose the ring as its LAN and IEEE has included, the token ring standard as 802.5.

A major issue in the design and analysis of any ring network is the "physical length" of a bit. If the data rate of the ring is R Mbps, a bit is emitted every $1/R$ μsec. With a typical signal propagation speed of about 200 m/μsec, each bit occupies $200/R$ meters on the ring. This means, for example, that a 1-Mbps ring whose circumference is 1000 meters can contain only 5 bits on it at once. The implications of the number of bits on the ring will become clearer later.

In a token ring a special bit pattern, called the token, circulates around the ring whenever all stations are idle. When a station wants to transmit a frame, it is required to seize the token and remove it from the ring before transmitting. This action is done by inverting a single bit in the 3-byte token, which instantly changes it into the first 3 bytes of a normal data frame. Because there is only one token, only one station can transmit at a given instant, thus solving the channel access problem the same way the token bus solves it.

Ring interfaces have two operating modes, listen and transmit. In listen mode, the input bits are simply copied to output, with a delay of 1 bit time, as shown in Figure 11.7. In transmit mode, which is entered only after the token has been seized, the interface breaks the connection between input and output, entering its own data onto the ring. To be able to switch from listen to transmit mode in 1 bit time, the interface usually needs to buffer one or more frames itself rather than having to fetch them from the station on such short notice.

As bits that have propagated around the ring come back, they are removed from the ring by the sender. The sending station can either save them, to compare with the original data to monitor ring reliability, or discard them. Because the entire frame never appears on the ring at one instant, this ring architecture puts no limit on the size of the frames. After a station has finished transmitting the last bit on its last frame it must regenerate the token. When the last bit of the frame has gone around and come back, it must be removed and the interface must switch back into listen mode immediately, to avoid removing the token that might follow if no other station has removed it.

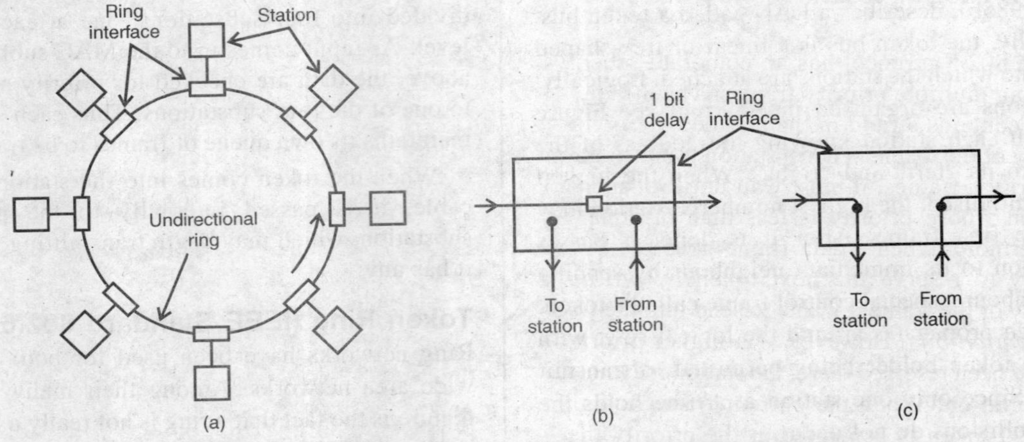

Fig. 11.7: *(a) A ring network. (b) Listen mode. (c) Transmit mode.*

The Token Ring MAC Sublayer Protocol

The basic operation of the MAC protocol is straightforward. When there is no traffic on the ring, a 3-byte token circulates endlessly, waiting for a station to seize it by setting a specific 0 bit to a 1 bit, thus converting the token into the start-of-frame sequence. The station then outputs the rest of a normal data frame, as shown in Figure 11.8.

A station may hold the token for the **token-holding** time, which is 10 msec unless an installation sets a different value. If there is enough time left after the first frame has been transmitted to send more frames, these may be sent as well. After all pending frames have been transmitted or the transmission of another frame would exceed the token-holding time, the station regenerates the 3-byte token frame and puts it out onto the ring.

The *Starting delimiter* and *Ending delimiter* fields of Figure 11.8(b) mark the beginning the ending of the frame. Each contains invalid differential Manchester patterns (HH and LL) to distinguish them from data bytes. The *Access control* byte contains the token bit, and also the *Monitor bit, Priority bits,* and *Reservation bits* (described below). The *Frame control* byte distinguishes data frames from various possible control frames.

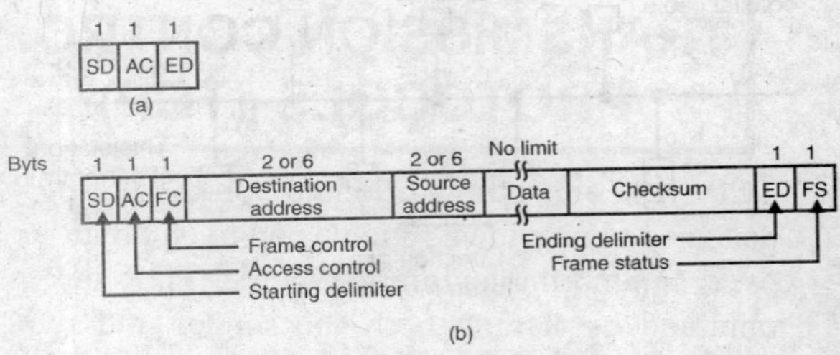

Fig. 11.8: *(a) Token format. (b) Data frame format.*

Next come the *Destination address* and *Source address* fields, which are the same as in 802.3 and 802.4. These are followed by the data, which may be as long as necessary, provided that the frame can still be transmitted within the token-holding time. The *Checksum* field, like the destination and source addresses, is also the same as 802.3 and 802.4

An interesting byte not present in the other two protocols is the *Frame status* byte. It contains the A and C bits. When a frame arrives at the interface of a station with the destination address, the interface turns on the A bit as it passes through. If the interface copies the frame to the station, it also turns on the C bit. A station might fail to copy a frame due to lack of buffer space or other reasons.

When the sending station drains the frame from the ring, it examines the A and C bits. Three combinations are possible:

1. A = 0 and C = 0: destination not present or not powered up.
2. A = 1 and C = 0: destination present but frame not accepted.
3. A = 1 and C = 1: destination present and frame copied.

The A and C bits are present twice in the *Frame status* to increase reliability in as much as they are not covered by the checksum.

The *Ending delimiter* contains an E bit which is set if any interface detects an error (*e.g.,* a non-Manchester pattern where that is not permitted). It also contains a bit that can be used to mark the last frame in a logical sequence, sort of like an end-of-file bit.

The 802.5 protocol has an elaborate scheme for handling multiple priority frames. The 3-byte token frame contains a field in the middle byte giving the priority of the token. When a station wants to transmit a priority *n* frames, it must wait until it can capture a token whose priority is less than or equal to *n*. Furthermore, when a data frame goes by, a station can try to reserve the next token by writing the priority of the frame it wants to send into the frame's *Reservation bits.* However, if a higher priority has already been reserved there, the station may not make a reservation. When the current frame is finished, the next token is generated at the priority that has been reserved.

TRANSMISSION CONTROL PROTOCOLS (TCP)

TCP is connection oriented protocol specially designed to provide a reliable end to end byte stream over an unreliable internet work. TCP service is obtained by having both the sender and receiver create end points called sockets. A TCP connection is byte stream not a message stream. Every byte on a TCP connection has its own 32 bit sequence number. The sending and receiving TCP entitles exchange data in the form of segments. A segment consists of 20 byte header.

The TCP Segment Header

Figure 11.9 shows the layout of a TCP segment. Every segment begins with a fixed-format 20-byte header. The fixed header may be followed by header options. After the options, if any, up to 65,535 – 20 = 65,515 data bytes may follow, where the first 20 refers to the IP header and the second to the TCP header. Segments without any data are legal and are commonly used for acknowledgements and control messages.

Let us dissect the TCP header field by field. The *Source port* and *Destination port* fields identify the local end points of the connection. Each host may decide for itself how to allocate its own ports starting at 256. A port plus its host's IP address forms a 48-bit unique TSAP. The source and destination socket numbers together identify the connection.

The *Sequence number* and *Acknowledgement number* fields perform their usual functions. Note that the latter specifies the next byte expected, not the last byte correctly received. Both are 32 bits long because every byte of data is numbered in a TCP stream.

The *TCP header length* tells how many 32-bit words are contained in the TCP header. This information is needed because the *Option* field is of variable length, so the header is too. Technically, this field really indicates the start of the data within the segment, measured in 32-bit words, but that number is just the header length in words, so the effect is the same.

Next comes a 6-bit field that is not used. The fact that this field has survived intact for over a decade is testimony to how well thought out TCP is. Lesser protocols would have needed it to fix bugs in the original design.

Now come six 1-bit flags. *URG* is set to 1 if the *Urgent pointer* is in use. The *Urgent pointer* is used to indicate a byte offset from the current sequence number at which urgent data are to be found. This facility is in lieu of interrupt messages. As we mentioned above, this facility is a bare bones way of allowing the sender to signal the receiver without getting TCP itself involved in the reason for the interrupt.

The *ACK* bit is set to 1 to indicate that the *Acknowledgement number* is valid. If *ACK* is 0, the segment does not contain an acknowledgement so the *Acknowledgement number* field is ignored.

The *PSH* bit indicates pushed data. The receiver is hereby kindly requested to deliver the data to the application upon arrival and not buffer it until a full buffer has been received (which it might otherwise do for efficiency reasons).

The *RST* bit is used to reset a connection that has become confused due to a host crash or some other reason. It is also used to reject an invalid segment or refuse an attempt to open a connection. In general, if you get a segment with the *RST* bit on, you have a problem on your hands.

The *SYN* bit is used to establish connections. The connection request has *SYN* = 1 and *ACK* = 0 to indicate that the piggyback acknowledgement field is not in use. The connection reply does bear an acknowledgement, so it has *SYN* = 1 and *ACK* = 1. In essence the SYN bit is used to denote Connection Request and Connection Accepted, with the ACK bit used to distinguish between those two possibilities.

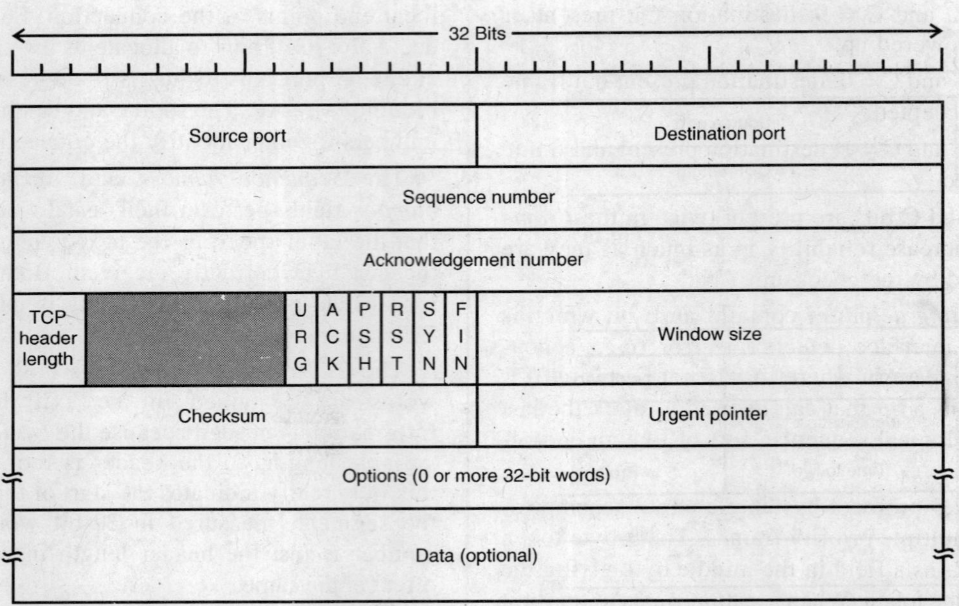

Fig. 11.9: *TCP header.*

The *FIN* bit is used to release a connection. It specifies that the sender has no more data to transmit. However, after closing a connection, a process may continue to receive data indefinitely. Both *SYN* and *FIN* segments have sequence numbers and are thus guaranteed to be processed in the correct order.

Flow control in TCP is handled using a variable-size sliding window. The *Window* field tells how many bytes may be sent starting at the byte acknowledged. A *Window* field of 0 is legal and says that the bytes up to and including *Acknowledgement number* – 1 have been received, but that the receiver is currently badly in need of a rest and would like no more data for the moment. Permission to send can be granted later by sending a segment with the same *Acknowledgement number* and a nonzero *Window* field.

A checksum is also provided for extreme reliability.

User Data Protocol (UDP)

The Internet protocol suite also supports a connectionless transport protocol, **UDP** (User Data Protocol). UDP provides a way for applications to send encapsulated raw IP datagrams and send them without having to establish a connection. Many client-server applications that have one request and one response use UDP rather than go to the trouble of establishing and later releasing a connection. UDP is described in RFC 768.

A UDP segment consists of an 8-byte header followed by the data. The header is shown in Figure 11.10. The two ports serve the same function as they do in TCP: to identify the end points within the source and destination machines. The UDP *length* field includes the 8-byte header and the data. The *UDP checksum* includes the same format pseudoheader, the UDP header, and the UDP data, padded out to an even number of bytes if need be. It is optional and stored as 0 if not computed (a true computed 0 is stored as all 1s, which is the same in 1's complement). Turning it off is foolish unless the quality of the data does not matter (*e.g.,* digitised speech).

THE IP PROTOCOL

An appropriate place to start our study of the network layer in the Internet is the format of the IP datagrams themselves. An IP datagram consists of a header part and a text part. The header has a 20-byte fixed part and a variable length optional part. The header format is shown in Figure 11.11. It is transmitted in big endian order: from left to right, with the high-order bit of the *Version* field going first. (The SPARC is big endian; the Pentium is little endian.) On little endian machines, software conversion is required on both transmission and reception.

The *Version* field keeps track of which version of the protocol the datagram belongs to. By including the version in each datagram, it becomes possible to have the transition between versions take months, or even years, with some machines running the old version and others running the new one.

Since the header length is not constant, a field in the header, *IHL*, is provided to tell how long the header is, in 32-bit words. The minimum value is 5, which applies when no options are present. The maximum value of this 4-bit field is 15, which limits the header to 60 bytes, and thus the options field to

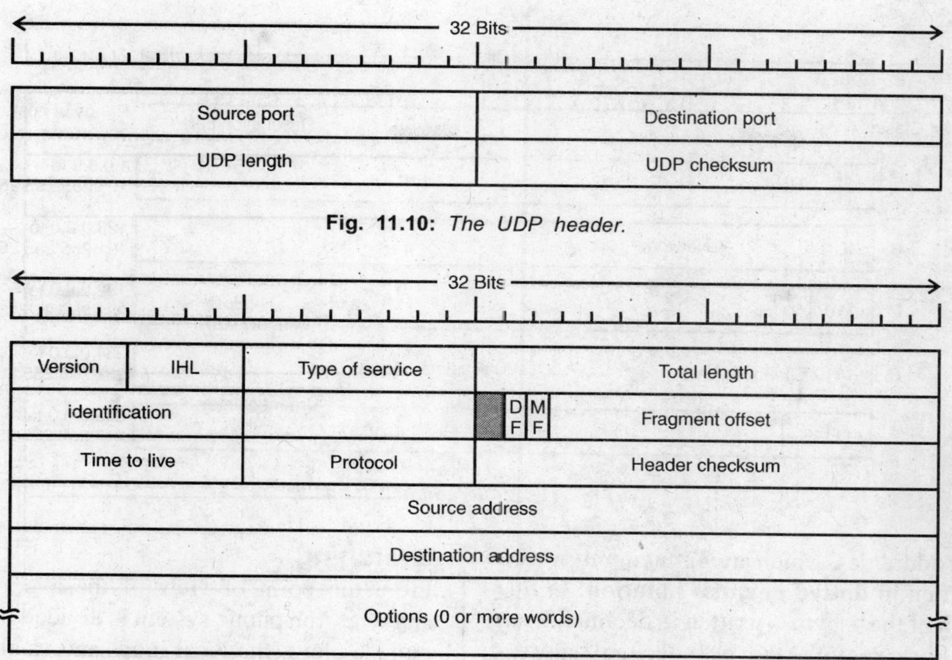

Fig. 11.10: *The UDP header.*

Fig. 11.11: *The IP (Internet Protocol) header.*

40 bytes. For some options, such as one that records the route a packet has taken, 40 bytes is far too small, making the option useless.

The *Type of service* field allows the host to tell the subnet what kind of service it wants. Various combinations of reliability and speed are possible. For digitised voice, fast delivery beats accurate delivery. For file transfer, error-free transmission is more important than fast transmission.

The *Total length* includes everything in the datagram–both header and data. The maximum length is 65,535 bytes. At present, this upper limit is tolerable, but with future gigabit networks larger datagrams will be needed.

The *Identification* field is needed to allow the destination host to determine which datagram a newly arrived fragment belongs to. All the fragments of a datagram contain the same *Identification* value.

Next comes an unused bit and then two 1-bit fields. *DF* stands for Don't Fragment. It is an order to the routers not to fragment the datagram because the destination is incapable of putting the pieces back together again.

MF stands for More Fragments. All fragments except the last one have this bit set. It is needed to know when all fragments of a datagram have arrived.

The *Fragment offset* tells where in the current datagram this fragment belongs. All fragments except the last one in a datagram must be a multiple of 8 bytes, the elementary fragment unit. Since 13 bits are provided, there is a maximum of 8192 fragments per datagram, giving a maximum datagram length of 65,536 bytes, one more than the *Total length* field.

The *Time to live* field is a counter used to limit packet lifetimes. It is supposed to count time in seconds, allowing a maximum lifetime of 255 sec. It must be decremented on each hop and is supposed to be decremented multiple times when queued for a long time in a router.

The header checksum verifies the header only. Such a checksum is useful for detecting errors generated by bad memory words inside a router.

The source address and destination address indicate the network number and host number.

IP Addresses

Every host and router on the Internet has an IP address, which encodes its network number and host number. The combination is unique: no two machines have the same IP address. All IP addresses are 32 bits long and are used in the *Source address* and *Destination address* fields of IP packets. The formats used for IP address are shown in Figure 11.12 on previous page. Those machines connected to multiple networks have a different IP address on each network.

The class A, B, C and D formats allow for up to 126 networks with 16 million hosts each, 16,382 networks with up to 64K hosts, 2 million networks, (e.g., LANs), with up to 254 hosts each, and multicast, in which a datagram is directed to multiple hosts Addresses beginning with 11110 are reserved for future use. Tens of thousands of networks are now connected to the Internet, and the number doubles every year. Network numbers are assigned by the **NIC** (Network Information Centre) to avoid conflicts.

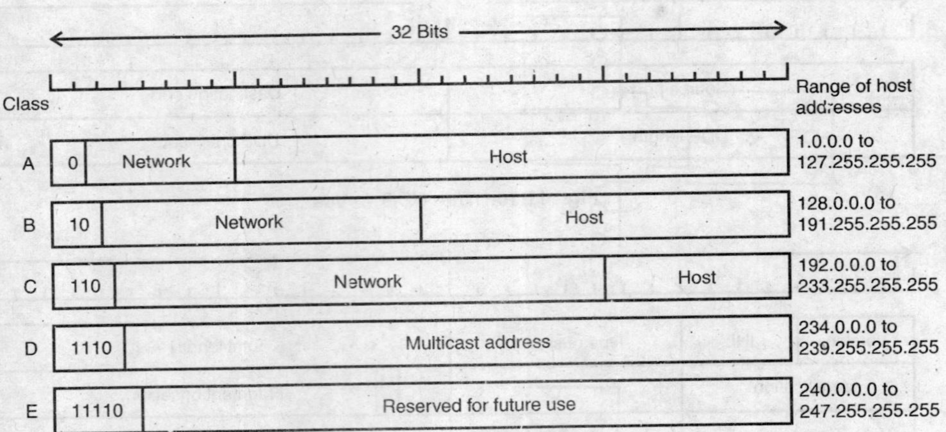

Fig. 11.12: *IP address formats.*

Network addresses, which are 32-bit numbers, are usually written in **dotted decimal notation.** In this format, each of the 4-byte is written in decimal, from 0 to 255. For example, the hexadecimal address C0290614 is written as 192.41.6.20. The lowest IP address is 0.0.0.0 and the highest is 255.255.255.255.

The values 0 and –1 have special meanings as shown in Figure 11.13. The value 0 means this network or this host. The value of –1 is used as a broadcast address to mean all hosts on the indicated network.

The IP address 0.0.0.0 is used by hosts when they are being booted but is not used afterward. IP addresses with 0 as network number refer to the current network. These addresses allow machines to refer to their own network without knowing its number (but they have to know its class to know how many 0s to include). The address consisting of all 1s allows broadcasting on the local network, typically a LAN. The addresses with a proper network number and all 1s in the host field allow machines to send broadcast packets to distant LANs anywhere in the Internet. Finally, all addresses of the form 127.xx.yy.zz are reserved for loopback testing. Packets sent to that address are not put out onto the wire; they are processed locally and treated as incoming packets. This allows packets to be sent to the local network without the sender knowing its number. This feature is also used for debugging network software.

Switching

From the point of view of the average telephone engineer, the phone system is divided into two parts: outside plant (the local loops and trunks, since they are outside the switching offices), and inside plant (the switches). We have just looked at outside plant. Now it is time to examine inside plant.

Two different switching techniques are used inside the telephone system—circuit switching and packet switching.

Circuit Switching

When you or your computer places a telephone call, the switching equipment within the telephone system seeks out a physical "copper" (including fiber and radio) path all the way from your telephone to the receiver's telephone. This technique is called circuit switching and is shown schematically in Figure 11.14(a). Each of the six rectangles represents a carrier switching office (end office, toll office, etc.). In this example, each office has three incoming lines and three outgoing lines. When a call passes through a switching office, a physical connection is (conceptually) established between the line on which the call came in and one of the output lines, as shown by the dotted lines.

The model shown in Fig. 11.14(a) is highly simplified of course, because parts of the "copper"

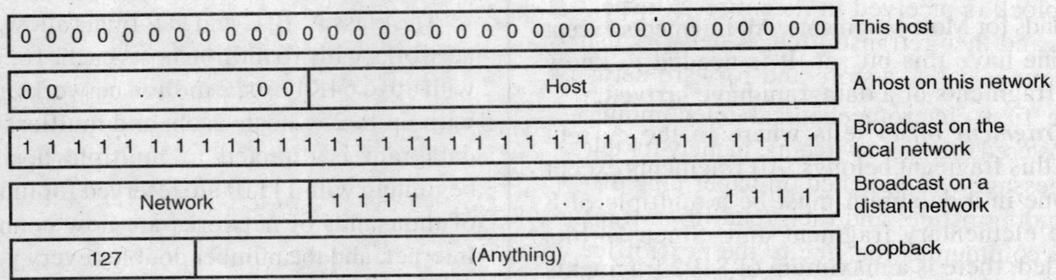

Fig. 11.13: *Special IP addresses.*

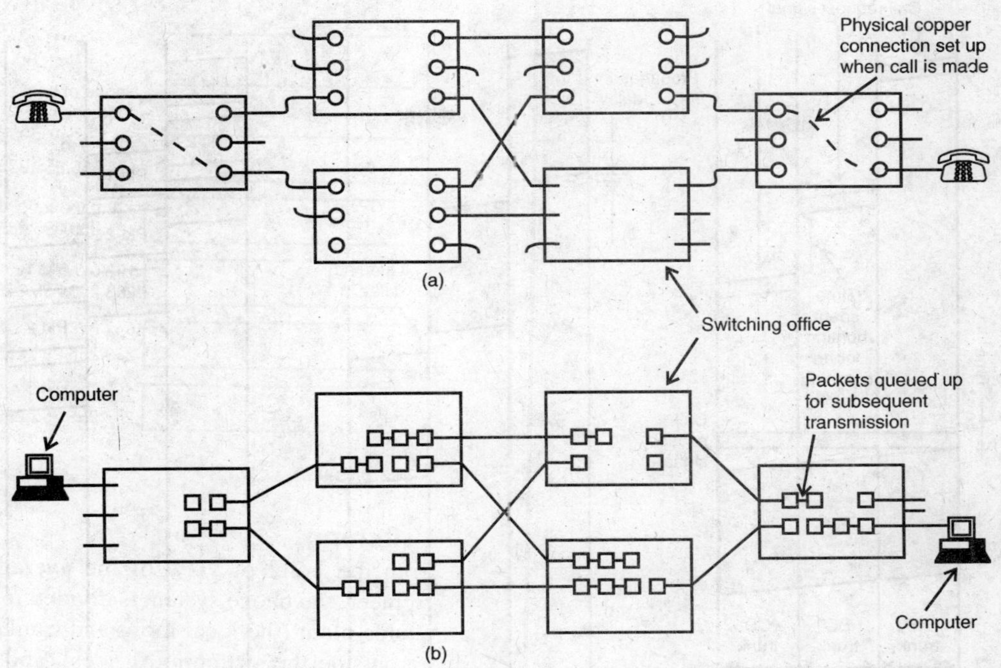

Fig. 11.14: *(a) Circuit switching. (b) Packet switching.*

path between the two telephones may, in fact, be microwave links onto which thousands of calls are multiplexed. Nevertheless, the basic idea is valid: once a call has been set up, a dedicated path between both ends exists and will continue to exist until the call is finished.

An important property of circuit-switching is the need to set up an end-to-end path *before* any data can be sent. The elapsed time between the end of dialing and the start of ringing can easily be 10 sec, more on long-distance or international calls. During this time interval, the telephone system is hunting for a copper path, as shown in Figure 11.15(a).

Message Switching

An alternative switching strategy is message switching, shown in Fig. 6.15(b). When this form of switching is used, no physical copper path is established in advance between sender and receiver. Instead, when the sender has a block of data to be sent, it is stored in the first switching office (i.e., router) and then forwarded later, one hop at a time. Each block is received in its entirety, inspected for errors, and then retransmitted. A network using this technique is called a store-and-forward network.

The first electromechanical telecommunication systems used message switching, namely for telegrams. The message was punched on paper tape off-line at the sending office, and then read in an transmitted over a communication line to the next office along the way, where it was punched out on paper tape. An operator there tore the tape off and read it in on one of the many tape readers, one per out-going trunk. Such a switching office was called a torn tape office.

With message switching, there is no limit on block size, which means that routers (in a modern system) must have disks to buffer long blocks. It also means that a single block may tie up a router-router line for minutes, rendering message switching useless for interactive traffic. To get around these problems, packet switching was invented.

Packet Switching

Packet-switching networks place a tight upper limit on block size, allowing packets to be buffered in router main memory instead of on disk. By making sure that no user can monopolise any transmission line very long (milliseconds), packet-switching networks are well suited to handling interactive traffic. A further advantage of packet switching over message switching is shown in Fig. 11.15(b) and (c) the first packet of a multipacket message can be forwarded before the second one has fully arrived, reducing delay and improving throughput. For these reasons, computer networks are usually packet switched, occasionally circuit switched, but never message switched.

Circuit switching and packet switching differ in many respects. The key difference is that circuit switching statically reserves the required bandwidth in advance, whereas packet switching acquires and releases it as it is needed. With circuit switching, any unused bandwidth on an allocated circuit is just wasted. With packet switching it may be utilised by

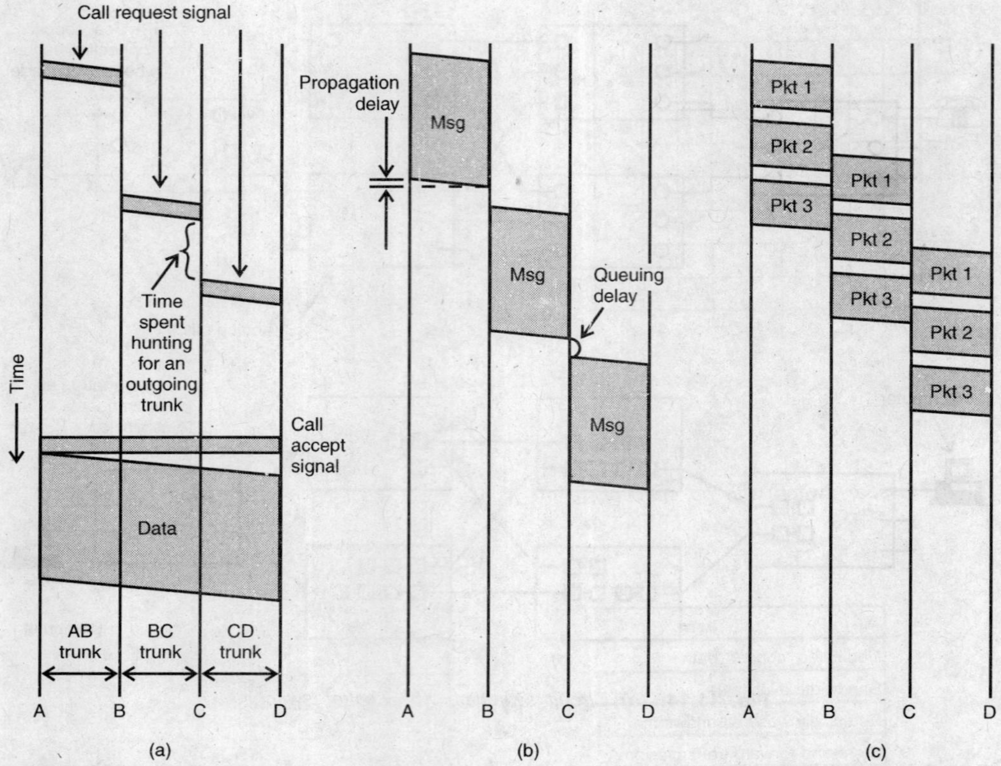

Fig. 11.15: *Timing of events in (a) circuit switching, (b) message switching, (c) packet switching.*

other packets from unrelated sources going to unrelated destinations, because circuits are never dedicated. However, just because no circuits are dedicated, a sudden surge of input traffic may overwhelm a router, exceeding its storage capacity and causing it to lose packets.

In contrast, with circuit switching, when packet switching is used, it is straightforward for the routers to provide speed and code conversion. Also, they can provide error correction to some extent. In some packet-switched networks, however, packets may be delivered in the wrong order to the destination. Reordering of packets can never happen with circuit switching.

Another difference is that circuit switching is completely transparent. The sender and receiver can use any bit rate, format, or framing method they want to. The carrier does not know or care. With packet switching, the carrier determines the basic parameters. A rough analogy is a road versus a railroad. In the former, the user determines the size, speed, and nature of the vehicle; in the latter, the carrier does. It is this transparency that allows voice, data, and fax to coexist within the phone system.

A final difference between circuit and packet switching is the charging algorithm. Packet carriers usually base their charge on both the number of bytes (or packets) carried and the connect time. Furthermore, transmission distance usually does not matter, except perhaps internationally. With circuit switching, the charge is based on the distance and time only, not the traffic. The differences are summarised in Figure 11.16.

Both circuit switching and packet switching are so important, we will come back to them shortly and describe the various technologies used in detail.

Crossbar Switches

Let us now turn from how calls are routed among switches to how individual switches actually work inside. Several kinds of switches are (or were) common within the telephone system. The simplest kind is the **crossbar switch** (also called a **crosspoint switch**), shown in Figure 11.17. In a switch with n input lines and n output lines (*i.e., n* full duplex lines), the crossbar switch has n^2 intersections, called **crosspoints,** where an input and an output line may be connected by a semiconductor switch, as shown in Fig. 11.17(a). In Fig. 11.17(b) we see an example in which line 0 is connected to line 4, line 1 is connected to line 7, and line 2 is connected to line 6. Lines 3 and 5 are not connected. All the bits that arrive at the switch from line 4, for example, are immediately sent out of the switch on line 0. Thus the crossbar switch implement circuit switching by making a direct electrical connection, just like the jumper cables in the first-generation switches, only automatically and within microseconds.

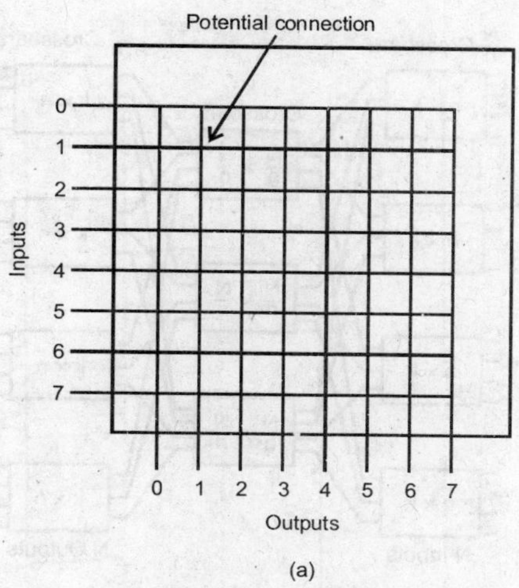

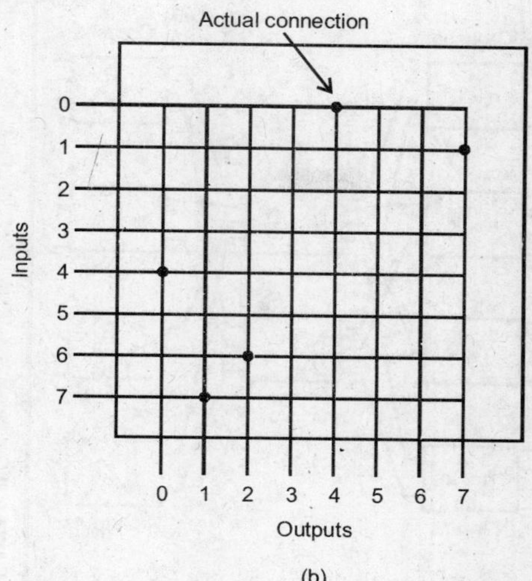

Fig. 11.17: *(a) A crossbar switch with no connections, (b) A crossbar switch with three connections set up: 0 with 4, 1 with 7, and 2 with 6.*

Item	Circuit-switched	Packet-switched
Dedicated "copper" path	Yes	No
Bandwidth available	Fixed	Dynamic
Potentially wasted bandwidth	Yes	No
Store-and-forward transmission	No	Yes
Each packet follows the same route	Yes	No
Call setup	Required	Not needed
When can congestion occur	At setup time	On every packet
Charging	Per minute	Per packet

Fig. 11.16: *A comparison of circuit-switched and packet-switched networks.*

The problem with a crossbar switch is that the number of crossbar grows as the square of the number of lines into the switch. If we assume that all lines are full duplex and that there are no self-connections, only the crosspoints above the diagonal are needed. Still, $n(n-1)/2$ crosspoint are needed. For $n = 1000$, we need 499,500 crosspoints. While building a VLSI chip with this number of transistor switches is possible, having 1000 pins on the chip is not. Thus a single crossbar switch is only useful for relatively small end offices.

Space Division Switches

By splitting the crossbar switch into small chunks and interconnecting them, it is possible to build multistage switches with many fewer crosspoints. These are called **space division switches.** Two configurations are illustrated in Figure 11.18.

To keep our example simple, we will consider only three-stage switches, but switches with more stages are also possible. In these examples, we have a total of N inputs and N outputs. Instead of building a single $N \times N$ crossbar, we build the switch out of smaller rectangular crossbars. In the first stage, each crossbar has n inputs, so we need N/n of them to handle all N incoming lines.

The second stage has k crossbars, each with N/n inputs and N/n outputs. The third stage is a repeat of the first stage, but reversal left to right. Each intermediate crossbar is connected to each input crossbar and each output crossbar. Consequently, it is possible to connect every input to every output using either the first intermediate crossbar in Fig. 11.18 (a) or using the second one. In fact, there are two disjoint paths from each input to each output, depending which intermediate crossbar is chosen. In Fig. 11.18 (b) there are three paths for each input/output pair. With k intermediate stages (k is a design parameter), there are k disjoint paths.

Let us now compute the number of crosspoints needed for a three-stage switch. In the first stage, there are N/n crossbars, each with nk crosspoints, for a total of Nk. In the second stage, there are k crossbars, each with $(N/n)^2$ crosspoints. The third stage is the same as the first. Adding up the three stages, we get.

Number of crosspoints $= 2kN + k(N/n)^2$

For $N = 1000$, $n = 50$ and $k = 10$, we need only 24,000 crosspoints instead of the 499,500 required by a 1000×1000 single-stage crossbar.

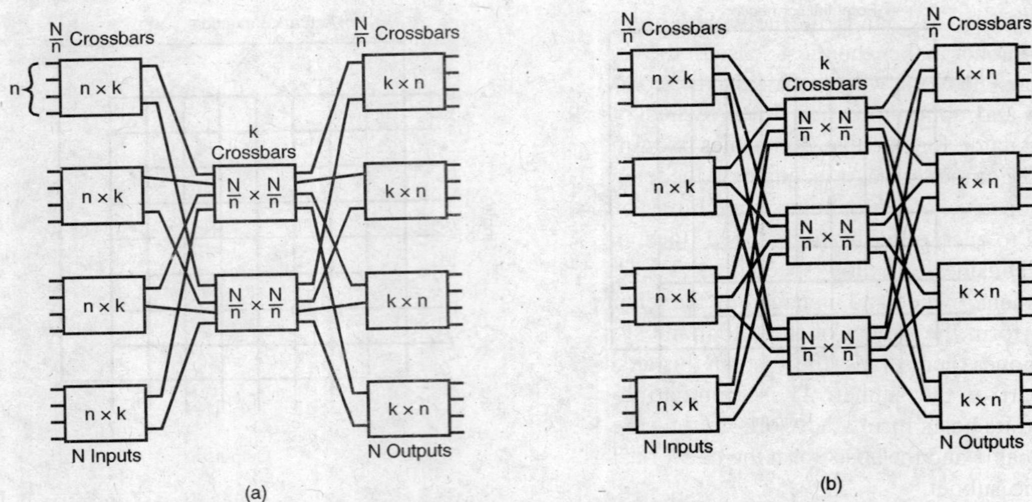

Fig. 11.18: *Two space division switches with different parameters.*

Time Division Switches

A completely different kind of switch is the **time division switch,** shown in Figure 11.19. With time division switching, the *n* input lines are scanned in sequence to build up an input frame with *n* slots. Each slot has *k* bits. For T[1] switches, the slots are 8 bits, with 8000 frames processed per second.

The heart of the time division switch is the time slot interchanger, which accepts input frames and produces out frames in which the time slots have been recorded. In Fig. 11.19, input slot 4 is output first, then slot 7, and so on. Finally, the output frame is demultiplexed, with output slot 0 (input slot 4) going to line, and so on.

Many networks exist in the world, often with different hardware and software. People connected to one network often want to communicate with people attached to a different one. This desire requires connecting together different, and frequently incompatible networks, sometimes by using machines called gateways to make the connection and provide the necessary translation, both in terms of hardware and software. A collection of interconnected networks is called an **internetwork** or just **Internet.**

A common form of Internet is a collection of LANs connected by a WAN. In fact, if we were to replace the label "subnet" by "WAN", nothing also would have to change. The only real distinction between a subnet and a WAN in this case is whether or not hosts are present. If the system within the closed curve contains only routers, it is a subnet. If it contains both routers and hosts with their own users, it is a WAN.

To avoid confusion, please note that the word "Internet" will always be used in this book in a generic sence. In contrast, the **Internet** means a specific worldwide Internet that is widely used to connect universities, government offices, companies, and of late, private individuals.

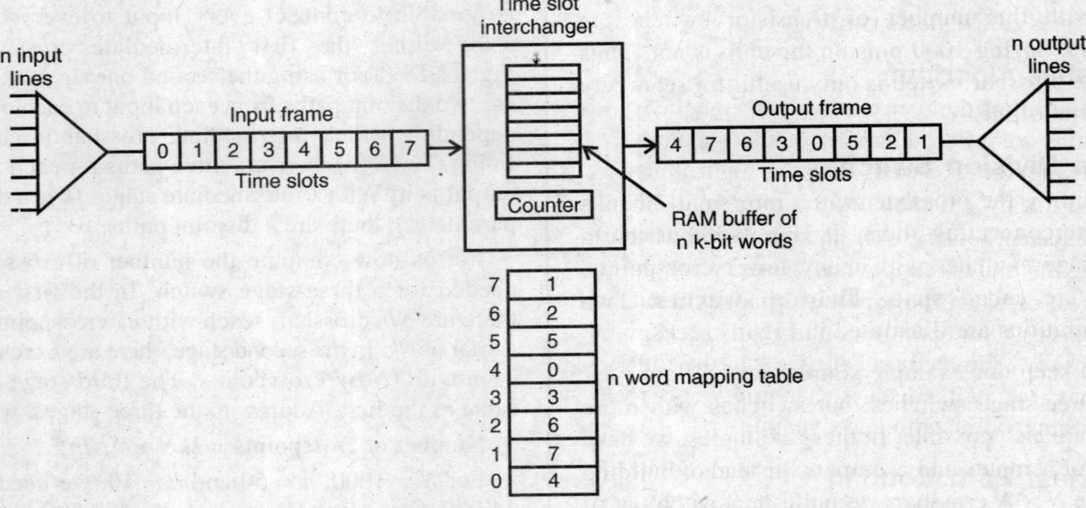

Fig. 11.19: *A time division switch.*

Subnets, network, and internetworks are often confused. Subnet makes the most sense in the context of a wide area network, where it refers to the collection of routers and communication lines owned by the network operator, for example, companies like America Online and CompuServe. As an analogy, the telephone system consists of telephone switching offices connected to each other by high-speed lines, and to houses and businesses by low-speed lines. These lines and equipment, owned and managed by the telephone company, form the subnet of the telephone system. The telephones themselves (the hosts in this analogy) are not part of the subnet. The combination of a subnet and its hosts form a network. In the case of a LAN, the cable and the hosts form the network. There really is no subnet.

An internetwork is formed when distinct networks are connected together. In our view, connecting a LAN and WAN or connecting two LANs forms an internetwork, but there is little agreement in the industry over terminology in this area.

Routers

The main function of the network layer is routing packets from the source machine to destination machine. The routing algorithm is that part of the network layer software responsible for deciding which output line an incoming packet should be transmitted on.

Routing algorithm can be grouped into two major classes non adaptive and adaptive.

Non Adaptive Algorithm

Nonadaptive algorithms do not base their routing decisions on measurements or estimates of the current traffic and topology. Instead, the choice of the route to use to get from I to J (for all I and J) is computed in advance, off-line, and downloaded to the routers when the network is booted. This procedure is sometimes called **static routing.**

Adaptive Algorithm

Adaptive algorithms, in contrast, change the routing decisions to reflect changes in the topology, and usually the traffic as well. Adaptive algorithms differ in where they get their information (e.g., locally, from adjacent routers, or from all routers), when they change the routes (e.g., every ΔT sec, when the load changes, or when the topology changes), and what metrix is used for optimisation (e.g., distance, number of hops, or estimated transit time). In the following sections we will discuss a variety of routing algorithms, both static and dynamic.

Shortest Path Routing

The idea is to build a graph of the subnet, with each node of the graph representing a router and each arc of the graph representing a communication line (often called a link). To choose a route between a given pair of routers, the algorithm just finds the shortest path between them on the graph.

The concept of a shortest path deserves some explanation. One way of measuring path length is the number of hops. Using this metric, the paths ABC and ABE in Figure 11.20 are equally long. Another metric is the geographic distance in kilometers, in which case ABC is clearly much longer than ABE (assuming the figure is drawn to scale).

Flooding

Another static algorithm is flooding, in which every incoming packet is sent out on every outgoing line except the one it arrived on. Flooding obviously generates vast numbers of duplicate packets, in fact, an infinite number unless some measures are taken to damp the process. One such measure is to have a hop counter contained in the header of each packet, which is decremented at each hop with the packet being discarded when the counter reaches zero. Ideally, the hop counter should be initialised to the length of the path from source to destination. If the sender does not know how long the path is, it can initialise the counter to the worst case, namely, the full diameter of the subnet.

A variation of flooding that is slightly more practical is selective flooding. In this algorithm the routers do not send every incoming packet out on every line, only on those lines that are going approximately in the right direction. There is usually little point in sending a westbound packet on an eastbound line unless the topology is extremely peculiar.

Flooding is not practical in most applications, but it does have some uses. For example, in military applications, where large numbers of routers may be blown to bits at any instant, the tremendous robustness of flooding is highly desirable. In distributed database applications, it is sometimes necessary to update all the databases concurrently, in which case flooding can be useful. A third possible use of flooding is as a metrix against which other routing algorithms can be compared. Flooding always chooses the shortest path because it chooses every possible path in parallel.

Distance vector routing: Modern computer networks generally use dynamic routing algorithms rather than the static ones described above. Two dynamic algorithms in particular, distance vector routing and link state routing, are the most popular. In this section, we will look at the former algorithm. In the following one we will study the latter one.

Distance vector routing algorithms operate by having each router maintain a table (i.e., a vector) giving the best known distance to each destination

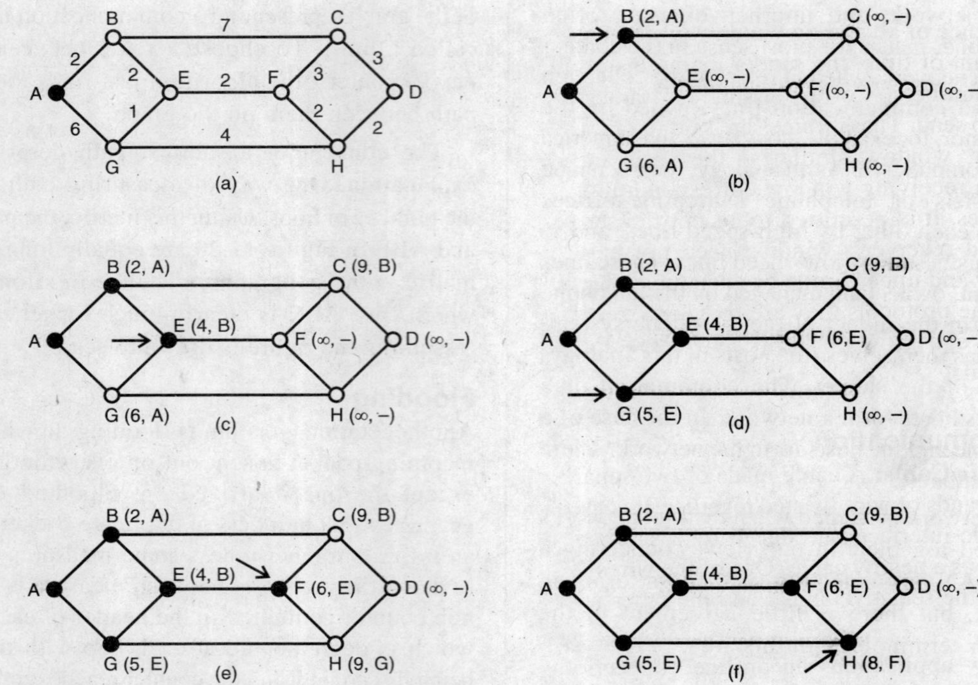

Figure 11.20: *The first five steps used in computing the shortest path from A to D. The arrows indicate the working node.*

and which line to use to get there. These tables are updated by exchanging information with the neighbours.

The distance vector routing algorithm is sometimes called by other names, including the distributed **Bellman-Ford** routing algorithm and the **Ford-Fulkerson** algorithm. AppleTalk and Cisco routers use improved distance vector protocols.

In distance vector routing, each router maintains a routing table indexed by and containing one entry for, each router in the subnet. This entry contains two parts: the preferred outgoing line to use for that destination, and an estimate of the time or distance to that destination.

Sliding Window Protocol

The principle advantage of using piggybacking over having distinct acknowledgement frames is a better use of the available channel bandwidth. The back field in the frame header casts only a few bits, whereas a separate frame would need a header, the acknowledgement and a checksum. In addition fewer frames sent means fewer "Frame arrived" interrupts and perhaps fewer buffer in the receiver, depending on how the receiver's software is organised. In the next protocol to be examined, the piggyback field casts only 1 bit in the frame header. If *r* and *y* costs more than a few bits, the next three protocols are more robust and continue to function even under pathological conditions. All three belong to a class of protocols called sliding window protocols. The three differ among themselves of efficiency, complexity, and buffer requirements.

In all sliding window protocols, each out bound frame contains a sequence number ranging from 0 upto some maximum. The maximum is usually $2^n - 1$. So the sequence number fits nicely in *n* bit field. The stop and wait sliding window protocol uses $n = 1$ restricting the sequence number to 0 and 1, but more sophisticated versions on use arbitrary *n*.

Table 11.1: *Difference between OSI Reference Model and TCP Reference Model*

OSI Reference Model	*TCP Reference Model*
1. It has seven layers.	1. It has 4 layers
2. It distinguishes between service, interface and protocol.	2. It did not distinguishes clearly between service, interface and protocol.
3. First description came and later protocol came.	3. Protocol comes first and description of model later.
4. Both have networks.	4. Transport and Application layer.
5. Supports connection-less and connection oriented communication in network layer and only	5. TCP/IP has only one mode in Network layer (connection less) but supports both modes in Transport layer.
6. Protocols are better hidden and can be replaced relatively easily (No Transparency)	6. Protocols are not hidden and can not be replaced easily.

The essence of all sliding window protocol is that at any instant of time, the sender maintains a set of sequence numbers. Corresponding to frames it is permitted to send. These frames are said to fail within the sending window similarly, the receiver also maintains a receiving window corresponding to the set of frames, it is permitted to accept the sender's window and receiver's window need not have the same lower and upper limits or even have the same size. In some protocols they are fixed in size, but in others they can grow or shrink as frames are sent and received.

Data Communication

Twisted Pair Cable: A cable made of two separated insulated strands of wire twisted together. It is used to reduce single interface introduced by a strong radio source such as a nearby cable. One of the wires in the pair carries the sensitive signal and the other wise is grounded.

For many applications an on-line connection is needed. One of the oldest and still most common transmission media is twisted pair. A twisted pair consists of two insulated copper wires, typically about 1 mm thick. The wires are twisted together in a helical form, just like a DNA molecule. Twisting is done because two parallel wires constitute a fine antenna. When the wires are twisted, the waves from different twists cancel out, so the wire radiates less effectively.

The most common application of the twisted pair is the telephone system. Nearly all telephones are connected to the telephone company (telco) office by a **twisted pair**. Twisted pairs can run several kilometers without amplification, but for longer distances, repeaters are needed. When many twisted pairs run in parallel for a substantial distance, such as all the wires coming from an apartment building to the telephone company office, they are bundled together and encased in a protective sheath. The pairs in these bundles would interfere with one an- other if it were not for the twisting. In parts of the world where telephone lines on poles above ground, it is common to see bundles several centimeters in diameter. Twisted pairs can be used for transmitting either analogue or digital signals. The bandwidth depends on the thickness of the wire and the distance traveled, but their megabits/sec can be achieved for a few kilometers in many cases. Due to adequate performance and low cost, twisted pairs are widely used and are remain for years to come.

Twisted pairs cabling comes in several varieties, two of which are important for computer networks. Category 3 twisted pairs consist of two insulated wires to protect them together. Four such pairs are typically grouped in a plastic sheath to protect the wires and keep them together.

Coaxial Cable: It is an electric cable having two or more conducting paths, one conducting path being surrounded by but insulated from another conducting path, which way in turn be surrounded by and insulated from a third conductor and soon. It provides a continuous path along which electrical signals can be conveyed from one point of another in a system. It has better shielding than twisted pairs, so it can span longer distances at higher speeds. Two kinds of coaxial cable are widely used. One kind, 50-ohm cable, is commonly used when it is intended for digital transmission from the start. The other kind, 75.ohm cable, is commonly used for analogue transmission and cable television but becoming more important with the advent of Internet over cable. This distinction is based on historical, rather than technical, factors (e.g., early dipole antennas had an impedance of 300 ohms, and it was easy to use existing 4 : 1 impedance matching transformers).

A coaxial cable consists of a stiff copper wire as the core, surrounded by insulating material. The insulator is encased by a cylindrical conductor, often as a closely-woven braided mesh. The outer conductor is covered in a protective Plastic sheath. The construction and shielding of the coaxial cable give it a good combination of high bandwidth and excellent noise immunity. The bandwidth possible depends on the cable quality, length, and signal-to-noise ratio of the data signal. Modem cables have a bandwidth of close to 1 GHz. Coaxial cables used to be widely used within the telephone system for long-distance lines but have now largely been replaced by Fibre optics on long-haul routes. Coax is still widely used for cable television and metropolitan area networks, however.

Fibre Optic Cables: It is a form of cable used in networks that transmits signals optically, rather than electrically as do coaxial and twisted pair cable. The light-conducting heart of a fibreoptic cable is a fine glass of plastic fibre called the care. Fibreoptic cable can transmit clean signals at speed as high as 2Gbps because it transmits light, not electricity, it is also immune to evesdropping.

An optical transmission system has three key components: the light source, the transmission medium, and the detector. Conventionally, a pulse of light indiates a 1 bit and the absence of light indicates a 0 bit. The transmission medium is an ultra-thin fibre of glass. The detector generates an electrical pulse when light falls on it. By attaching a light source to one end of an optical fibre and accepts to the other, we have a unidirectional data transmission system that accepts an electrical signal, converts and transmits it by light pulses, and then reconverts the output to an electrical signal at the receiving end.

This transmission system would leak light and be useless in practice except for an interesting principle of physics when a light ray passes from one medium to another.However, if the fibre's diameter is reduced to a few wavelengths of light. The fibre acts like a wave guide, and the light can propagate only in a straight line without bouncing, yielding a single-mode fibre. Single-mode fibers are more expensive but are widely used for longer distances. Currently available single mode fibres can transmit data at 50 Gbps for 100 km without amplification. Higher data rates have been achieved in the laboratory for shorter distances.

Optical fibres are made up of glass. The glass used for modern optical fibres is so transparent that if the oceans were full of it instead of water, the seabed would be as visible from the surface as the ground is from an airplane on a clear day. The attenuation of light through glass depends on the wavelength of the light as well as on some physical properties of the glass. The attenuation in decibels is given by the formula:

Attenuation m decibels = 10 log10 'transmitted power/received power

Fibre optics can be used for LANs as well as for long-haul transmission although tapping into it is more complex than connecting to an Ethernet. Only way around the problem is to realise that a ring network is really just a collection of point-to-point links.

Fibre Cables : Fibre optic cables are similar to coax, except without the braid. At the centre is the glass core through which the light propagates. In multimode fibres, the core is typically 50 microns in diameter, about the thickness of a human hair. In single-mode fibres, the core is 8 to 10 microns.

The core is surrounded by a glass cladding with a lower index of refraction than the core, to keep all the light in the core. Next comes a thin plastic jacket to protect the cladding. Fibres are typically grouped in bundles, protected by an outer sheath.

Terrestrial fibre sheaths are normally laid in the ground within a meter of the surface, where they are occasionally subject to attacks by blackholes or gophers. Near the shore, transoceanic fiber sheaths are buried in branches by a kind of seaplow. In deep water, they just lie on the bottom, where they can be snagged by fishing trawlers or attacked by giant squid.

Fibres can be connected in three different ways. First, they can terminate *1n* connectors and be plugged into fibre sockets. Connectors lose about 10 to 20 per cent of the light, but they make it easy to reconfigure systems.

Second, they can be spliced mechanically. Mechanical splices just lay two carefully-cut ends next to each other in a special sleeve and clamp the W II place. Alignment can be improved by passing light through the junction and then making small adjustments to maximise the signal. Mechanical splices take travelled personnel about 5 minutes and result in a 10 per cent light loss.

Third, two pieces' of fibre can be used (melted) to form a solid connection. A fusion splice is almost as good as a single drawn fibre, but even here, a small amount of attenuation occurs.

For all three kinds of splices, reflections can occur at the point of the splice, and the reflected energy can interfere with the signal.

Two kinds of light sources are typically used to do the signaling, LEOs (Light Emitting Diodes) and semiconductor lasers. They have different properties, as shown in Figure 6.21. They can be tuned in wavelength by inserting Fabry-Perot or Mach-Zehnder interferometers between the source and the fibre. Fabry-Perot interferometers are simple resonant cavities consisting of two parallel mirrors. The light is incident perpendicular to the mirrors. The length of the cavity selects out those wavelengths that fit inside an integral number of times. Mach-Zehnder interferometers separate the light into two beams. The two beams travel slightly different distances. They are recombined at the end and are in phase for only certain wavelengths.

Item	LED	Semiconductor laser
Data rate	Low	High
Fiber type	Multimode	Multimode or single mode
Distance	Short	Long
Lifetime	Long life	Short life
Temperature sensitivity	Minor	Substantial

Fig. 6.21: *Light Emitting Diodes*

WIRELESS TRANSMISSION

Wireless has advantages for even fixed devices in some circumstances. Modern wireless digital communication began in the Hawaiian Islands, where large chunks of Pacific Ocean separated the users and the telephone systems was inadequate.

The Electromagnetic spectrum : When electrons move, they create electromagnetic waves that can propogate through space (even in a vaccum). The amount of information carried by electromagnetic wave can carry is related to its bandwidth. In some cases, a wide band is used with two variations. In frequency hopping spread spectrum, the transmitter hops from frequency to frequency hundreds of times per second. It is popular for military communication because it makes transmissions hard to detect and next to impossible to jam. It also offers good resistance to multipath fading because the direct signal always arrives at the receiver first. Reflected signals follow a longer path and arrive later. By then the receiver may have changed frequency and no longer accepts signals on the previous frequency, thus eliminating interference between the direct and reflected signals. In recent years, this technique has also been applied commercially-both 802.11 and Bluetooth use it, for example. As a curious footnote, the technique was co-invented by the Austrian-born sex goddess Hedy Lamarr, the first woman to appear nude in a motion picture (the 1933 Czech film *Extase*). Her first husband was an armaments manufacturer who told her how easy it was to block the radio signals then used to control torpedos. When she discovered that he was selling weapons to Hitler, she was horrified, disguised herself as a maid to escape him, and fled to Hollywood to continue her career as a movie actress. In her spare time, she invented frequency hopping to help the Allied war effort. Her scheme used 88 frequencies, the number of keys (and frequencies) on the piano. For their invention, she and her friend, the musical composer George Antheil, received U.S. patent 2,292,387. However, they were unable to convince the U.S. Navy that their invention had any practical use and never received any royalties. Only years after the patent expired did it become popular.

The other form of spread spectrum, direct sequence spread spectrum which spreads the signal over a wide frequency band, is also gaining popularity in commercial world. In particular, some second-generation mobile phones use it; and it will become dominant with the third generation

Radio Transmission

Radio waves are easy to generate, can travel long distances, and can penetrate buildings easily, so they are widely used for communication, both indoors and outdoors. Radio waves also are omnidirectional, meaning that they travel in all directions from the source, so the transmitter and receiver do not have to be carefully aligned physically. Sometimes omnidirectional radio is good, but sometimes it is bad. Due to radio's ability to travel long distances, interference between users is a problem. For this reason, all government tightly licence the use of radio transmitters with one exception i.e VLF, LF, MF bands, radio waves follows the ground. MF band has low bandwidth and it is used by AM. In the HF and VHF bands, the ground waves tend to be absorbed by the earth. The military communicates in these bands.

Microwave Transmission

Above 100 MHz, the waves travel in nearly straight lines and can therefore narrowly focused. Concentrating all the energy into a small beam by means of parabolic antenna (like the familiar satellite TV dish) gives a much higher signal to noise ratio, but the transmitting and receiving antennas must be accurate aligned with each other. In addition, this directionality allows multiple transmitters lined up in a row to communicate with multiple receivers in a row without interference, provided some minimum spacing rules are observed. Before fibres optics, for decades these microwaves formed the heart of the long-distance tellephone transmission system. In fact, MCI, one of AT&T's first competitors after it was deregulated, built its entire system with microwave communications going from tower to tower tens of kilometers apart. Even the company's name reflect, this MCI (stood for Microwave Communications, Inc.). MCI has since gone over to fibre and merged with WorldCom.

Since the microwaves travel in a straight line, if the towers are too far apart the earth will get in the way. Consequently, repeaters are needed periodically. The higher the towers are, farther apart they can be. The distance between repeaters goes up very roughly with the square root of the tower height. For 100-meter-high towers, repeaters can be spaced 80 km apart. Unlike radio waves at lower frequencies, microwaves do not pass through buildings well. In addition, even though the beam may be well focused at transmitter, there is still some divergence in space. Some waves may refract off low-lying atmosphere layers and may take slightly longer to arrive than; direct waves. The delayed waves may arrive out of phase with the direct waves and thus cancel the signal. This effect is called multipath fading and is often serious problem. It is weather and frequency dependent. Some operators keep10 per cent of their channels idle as spares to switch on when multipath fading wipes out some frequency band temporarily. The demand for more and more spectrum drives operators to yet higher frequencies. Bands up to 10 GHz are now in routine use, but at about 4 GHz a new problem sets in absorption by water. These waves are only a few centimeters long and are absorbed by rain. This effect would be fine if one were planning to build an huge outdoor microwave oven for roasting passing birds, but for communication, it is a severe problem. The solution is to shut off links that are emerged on an route around ten.

Microwave communication is so widely used for long-distance telephone communication, mobile phones, television distribution, and other uses that a severe shortage of spectrum has developed. It has several significant advantages over fibre.

Microwave is also relatively inexpensive.

They are used for short wave communication. Infrared waves do not pass through solid walls well is also a plus. It means that an infrared system in one room of a building will not interfere with a similar system in adjacent rooms or buildings: you cannot control your neighbour's television with your remote control. Furthermore, security of infrared systems against eavesdropping is better than that of radio systems precisely for this reason. Therefore, no government license is needed to operate an infrared system, in contrast to radio systems, which must be licensed outside the ISM bands. Infrared communication has a limited use on the desktop, for example, connecting notebook computers and printers, but it is not a major player in the communication game.

LIGHTWAVE TRANSMISSION

Laser beams cannot penetrate rain or thick fog but they work well on sunny days.

Communication Satellites

In the 1950s and early 1960s, people tried to set up communication systems bouncing signals off metallised weather balloons. Unfortunately, the received bits were too weak to be of any practical use. Then the U.S. Navy noticed communication satellites have some interesting properties at matter attractive for many applications. In its simplest form, a communication satellite can be thought of as a big microwave repeater in the sky. It contains several transponders; each of which listens to some portion of the spectrum, amplifies the incoming signal, and then rebroadcasts it at another frequency to avoid interference with the incoming signal. The downward beams can be broad, covering a substantial fraction of the earth's surface, or narrow, covering an area only hundreds of kilometers in diameter. This mode of operation is known as a bent pipe.

According to Kepler's law, the orbital period of a satellite varies as the radius of the orbit to the 3/2 power. The higher the satellite, the longer the period. Near the surface of the earth, the period is about 90 minutes. Consequently, low-orbit satellites pass out of view fairly quickly, so many of them are needed to provide continuous coverage. At an altitude of about 35,800 km, the period is 24 hours. At an altitude of 384,000 km, the period is about one month, as anyone who has observed the moon regularly can testify.

A satellite's period is important, but it is not the only issue in determining speed here to place it. Another issue is the presence of the Van Allen belts, layers of highly charged particles trapped by the earth's magnetic field. Any satellite flying within them would be destroyed fairly quickly by the highly-energetic charged particles trapped there by the earth's magnetic field. These factors lead to three regions in which satellites can be placed safely.

Geostationary Satellites

In 1945, the science fiction writer Arthur C. Clarke calculated that a satellite at an altitude of 35,800 km in a circular equatorial orbit would appear to remain motionless in the sky. So it would not need to be tracked (Clarke, 1945). He went to describe a complete communication system' that used these (manned) geostationary satellites, including the orbits, solar panels, radio frequencies, and launch procedures. Unfortunately, he concluded that satellites were impractical due to the impossibility of putting power-hungry, fragile, vacuum tube amplifier into orbit, so he never pursued this idea further, although he wrote some science fiction stories about it.

The invention of the transistor changed all that, and the first artificial communication satellite, **Telstar**, was launched in July 1962. Since then, communication satellites have become a multibillion dollar business and the only aspect of outer space that has become highly profitable. These high-flying satellites are often called GEO (Geostationary Earth Orbit) satellites.

With current technology, it is unwise to have geostationary satellites space much closer than 2 degrees in the 360-degree equatorial plane, to avoid interference. With a spacing of 2 degrees, there can only be 360/2 = 180 of these satellites in the sky at once. However, each transponder can use multiple frequencies and polarisations to increase the available bandwidth.

To prevent total chaos in the sky, orbit slot allocation is done by ITU. This process is highly political, with countries barely out of the stone age demanding in "their" orbit slots (for the purpose of leasing them to the highest bidder). Other countries, however, maintain that national property rights do not extend up to moon and that no country has a legal right to the orbit slots above territory. To add to the fight, commercial telecommunication is not the only application. TV broadcasters, governments, and the military also want a piece of the orbiting pie.

Modem satellites can be quite large, weighing up to 4000 kg and consuming several kilowatts of electric power produced by the solar panels. The effects of solar, lunar, and planetary gravity tend to move them away from their assigned orbit slots and orientations, an effect countered by on-board rocket motors. This fine tuning activity is called station keeping. However, when the fuel for the motor has been exhausted, typically in about 10 years, the satellite drifts and tumbles helplessly, so it has to be turned off. Eventually, the orbit decays and the satellite re-enters the atmosphere and burns up or occasionally crashes to earth.

Orbit slots are not the only bone of contention. Frequencies are, too, because the downlink transmissions interfere with existing microwave users. Conseuently, ITO has allocated certain frequency bands to satellite users. The C band was the first to be designated for commercial satellite traffic. Two frequency ranges are assigned in it, the lower one for downlink traffic (from the satellite) and the upper one for uplink traffic (to the satellite). To allow traffic to go both ways at the same time, two channels are required, one going each way. These bands are already overcrowded because they are also used by the common carriers for terrestrial microwave links. The L and S bands were added by international agreement in 2000. However, they are narrow and crowded. (see Figure 11.22)

Band	*Downlink*	*Uplink*	*Bandwidth*	*Problems*
L	1.5 GHz	1.6 GHz	15 MHz	Low bandwidth; crowded
S	1.9 GHz	2.2 GHz	70 MHz	Low bandwidth; crowded
C	4.0 GHz	6.0 GHz	500 MHz	Terrestrial interference
Ku	11 GHz	14 GHz	500 MHz	Rain
Ka	20 GHz	30 GHz	3500 MHz	Rain, equipment cost

Fig. 11.22: *The principal satellite bads.*

TELEPHONE SYSTEM

The telephone system consists of three major components:

1. Local loops (analogue twisted pairs going into houses and businesses)
2. Trunks (digital fibre optics connecting the switching offices)
3. Switching offices (where calls are moved from one trunk to another)

The local loops provide everyone access to whole system, so they are critical. Unfortunately, they are also the weakest link in the system. For the long-haul trunks, the main issue is how to collect multiple calls together and send them out over the same fibre. This subject is known as multiplexing.

Wireless Local Loops: Since 1996 in the U.S. and a bit later in other countries, companies that to compete with the entrenched local telephone company called an ILEC (Incumbent LEC), are free to do so. The most likely long-distance telephone companies (IXCs). Any IXC wishing to get local phone business in some city must do the following things. First, lease a building for its first end office in that city. Second, it must fill the office with telephone switches and other equipment, Third, it must run a fibre between the end office and its nearest toll office so the new local customers will have access to its national network. Fourth, it must acquire customers, typically by advertising better service or lower prices than those of the ILEc. Fixed wireless (local telephone and Internet service run by CLECs over wireless local loops).

Although WLLs began serious operation in 1998. In 1969 the FCC allocated two television channels (at 6 MHz each) for instructional television at 2.1 GHz. In subsequent years, 31 more channels were added at 2.5 GHz for a total of 198 MHz. Instructional television never took off and in 1998, the FCC took the frequencies back and allocated them to two-way radio. They were *immediately seized* upon for wireless local loops. At these frequencies, the microwaves are 10-12 cm long. They have a range of about 50 km and can penetrate vegetation and rain moderately well. The 198 MHz of new spectrum was immediately put to use for wireless local loops as a service called MMDS (Multichannel Multipoint Distribution Service). MMDS can be regarded as a MAN (Metropolitan Area Network), as can its cousin LMDS. The big advantage of this service is that the technology is well established and equipment is readily available. The disadvantage is that the total bandwidth available is modest and must be shared by many users over a fairly large geographical area. Low bandwidth of MMDS led to interest in millimeter waves as an alternative. Gallium arsenide integrated circuits solved the problem by opening up millimeter bands for radio transmission.

Like ADSL, LMDS uses an asymmetric bandwidth allocation favouring downstream channel. With current technology, each sector can have 36 Gpbs downstream and 1 Mbps upstream, shared among all the users in that sector.If each active user downloads three 5- KB pages per minute, the user is occupying average of 2000 bps of spectrum, which allows a maximum of 18,000 active users per sector. To keep the delay reasonable, no more than 9000 active users should be supported, though. With four sectors, LMDS has a few problems, however. For one thing, millimeter waves propagate in straight lines, so there must be a clear line of sight between the roof top antennas and the tower. For another, leaves absorb these waves well, so the tower must be high enough to avoid having trees in the line of sight. And what may have looked like a clear line of sight in December may not be clear in July when the trees are full of leaves. Rain also absorbs these waves. To some extent, errors introduced by rain can be compensated for with error correcting codes or turning up the power when it is raining. Wireless local loops are not likely to catch on unless there are standards, to encourage equipment vendors to produce products and to ensure that customers can change CLECs without having to buy new equipment. To provide this satellization, IEEE set up a committee called 802.16 to draw up a standard FES. The 802.16 standard was published in April 2002. IEEE calls 802.16 a wireless MAN.

IEEE 802.16 was designed for digital telephony, Internet access, connection of two remote LANs, television and radio broadcasting, and other uses.

Trunks and Multiplexing

Economies of scale play an important role in the telephone system. It costs essentially the same amount of money to install and maintain a high-bandwidth trunk as a low-bandwidth trunk between two switching offices (i.e., the cm come from having to dig the trench and not from the copper wire or optical fibre. Consequently, telephone companies have developed elaborate schemes for multiplexing many conversations over a single physical trunk. These multiplexing schemes can be divided into two basic categories: FDM (Frequency Division Multiplexing) and TDM (Time Division Multiplexing). In FDM, the frequency spectrum is divided into frequency bands, with each user having exclusive position of some band. In TDM, the users take turns (in a round-robin fashion), each one periodically getting the entire bandwidth for a little burst of time.

AM radio broadcasting provides illustrations of both kinds of multiplexing The allocated spectrum is about 1 MHz, roughly 500 to 1500 kHz. Different frequencies are allocated to different logical channels (stations), each operating in a portion of the spectrum, with the interchannel separation great enough to prevent, interference. This system is an example of frequency division multiplexing (in some countries), the individual stations have two logical subchannel music and advertising. These two alternate in time on the same frequency, first a burst of music, then a burst of advertising, then more music, and so on.

Frequency Division Multiplexing

The FDM schemes used around the world are to some degree standardised. Widespread standard is twelve 4000-Hz voice channels multiplexed into the 60 to 108 kHz band. This unit is called a *group*. The 12-kHz to 60-kHz band is sometimes used for another group. Many carriers offer a 48- to 56-kbps leased line service to customers, based on the group. Five groups (60 voice channels) call\ multiplexed to form a supergroup. The next unit is the mastergroup, which is five supergroups (CCITT standard) or ten supergroups (Bell system). Other standards of up to 230,000 voice channels also exist.

Wavelength Division Multiplexing

For fibre optic channels, a variation of frequency division multiplexing is used. It is called WDM (Wavelength Division Multiplexing). WDM technology has been progressing at a rate that puts computer technology to shame. WDM was invented around 1990. The first commercial systems had eight channels of 2.5 Gbps per channel. By 1998, systems with 40 channels of 2.5 Gbps were on the market. By 2001, there were products with 96 channels of 10Gbps, for a total of 960 Gbps. This is an enough bandwidth to transmit 30 full length movies per second (in MPEG-2). Systems with 200 channels are already working in the laboratory. When the number of channels is very large and the wavelength are spaced close together, for example, 0.1 ohm, the system is referred to as DWDM (Dense WDM).

Another new development is all optical amplifiers. Previously, every 100 km it was necessary to split up all the channels and convert each one to an electron signal for amplification separately before reconverting to optical and combine them. Nowadays, all optical amplifiers can regenerate the entire signal on every 1000 km without the need for multiple opto-electrical conversions.

Time Division Multiplexing

WDM technology is wonderful, but there is still a lot of copper wire in all telephone system, so let us turn back to it for a while. Although FDM is still used over copper wires or microwave channels, it requires analogue circuitry and is amenable to being done by a computer. In contrast, TOM can be handled by digital electronics, so it has become far more widespread in recent years. Unfortunately, it can only be used for digital data. Since the local loops produce analogue signals, a conversion is needed from analogue to digital in the end ohm where all the individual local loops come together to be combined onto outgoing trunks.

How multiple analogue voice signals are digitised and combined onto a single outgoing digital trunk?

Computer data sent over a modem also analogue, so the following description also applies to them. The analogue signal are digitised in the end office by a device called a codec (coder-decoder), producing a series of 8-bit numbers. The codec makes 8000 samples per second because the Nyquist theorem says that this is sufficient to capture the information from the 4-kHz telephone channel bandwidth. At a lower sampling rate, information would be lost; at a higher one, no extra information would be gained. This technique is called PCM (Pulse Code Modulation) the heart of the modem telephone system. As a consequence, virtually all time intervals within the telephone system are multiples of 125 msec. When digital transmission began emerging as a feasible technology, CCIT was unable to reach agreement on an international standard for PCM. A variety of incompatible schemes are now in use in different countries around the world.

The method used in North America and Japan is the -'T1 carrier, (Technically speaking, the format is called DS I and the carrier is called Tl, but following widespread industry tradition, we will not make the distinction here). The Tl carrier consists of 24 voice channels multiplexed.

Usually, the analogue signals are sampled on a round-robin basis with the resulting analogue stream being fed to the codec rather than having 24 separate codec and then merging the digital output. Each of the 24 channels, in turn, get to insert 8 bits into the output stream. Seven bits are data and one is for control yielding $7 \times 8000 = 56{,}000$ bps of data, and $1 \times 8000 = 8000$ bps of signaling information per channel.

A frame consists of $24 \times 8 = 192$ bits plus one extra bit for framing, yielding 193 bits every 12511 sec. This gives a gross data rate of 1.544 Mbps. The 193rd bit is used for frame synchronization. It takes on the pattern 01010 10 10 1....

Normally, the receiver keeps checking this bit to make sure that it has not lost synchronisation. If it does get out of sync, the receiver can scan for this pattern to get resynchronised. Analogue customers cannot generate the bit pattern at all because it corresponds to a sine wave at 4000 Hz which would be filtered out.

Digital customers can, of course, generate this pattern, but the odds are against its data present when the frame slips. When a T1 system is being used entirely for data only 23 of the channels are used for data. The 24th one is used for a special synchronised pattern, to allow faster recovery in the event that the frame slips.

ATM

Since ATM networks are connection-oriented, sending data requires first sending a packet to set up the connection. As the setup packet wends its way through the subnet, all the routers on the path make an entry in their internal tables noting the existence of the connection and reserving whatever resources are needed for it. Connections are often called virtual circuits, in analogy with the physical circuits used within the telephone system. Most ATM networks also support permanent virtual circuits, which are permanent connections between two (distant) hosts. They are similar to leased lines in the telephone world. Each connection, temporary or permanent, has a unique connection identifier. Asynchronous transfer mode (ATM) was much more successful than OSI, and it is now widely used deep within the telephone system, often for moving IP packets. Because it is now mostly used by carriers for internal transport, users are often unaware of its existence, but it is definitely alive and well.

ATM Virtual Circuits

Since ATM networks are connection-oriented, sending data requires first sending a packet to set up the connection. As the setup packet wends its way through the subnet, all the routers on the path make an entry in their internal tables noting the existence of the connection and reserving whatever resources are needed for it. Connections are often called virtual circuits, in analogy with the physical circuits used within the telephone system. Most ATM networks also support permanent virtual circuits, which are permanent connections between two (distant) hosts. They are similar to leased lines in the telephone world. Each connection, temporary or permanent, has a unique connection identifier. Once a connection has been established, either side can begin transmitting data. The basic idea behind ATM is to transmit all information in small, fixed size packets called cells. The cells are 53 bytes long, of which 5 bytes are header and 48 bytes are payload, part of the header is the connection identifier, so the sending and receiving hosts and all the intermediate router can tell which cells belong to which connections. This information allows each router to know how to route each incoming cell. Cell routing is done in hardware at high speed. It is easy to build hardware routers to handle short, fixed-length cells. Cable-length IP packets have to be routed by software, which is a slower process. The hardware can be set up to copy one incoming cell to multiple output lines, a property that is required for handlling a television program that is being broadcast to many receivers. Finally, small cells do n<;>t block any line for very long, which makes guaranteeing quality of service easier.

All cells follow the same route to the destination. Cell delivery is not guaranteed, but their order is. If cells 1 and 2 are sent in that order, then if both arrive, they will arrive in that order, never first 2 then 1. But either or both of them can be lost along the way. It is up to higher protocol levels to recover from lost cells. Note that although this guarantee is not perfect, it is better than what the Internet provides. There packets can not only be lost, but delivered out of order as well. ATM, in contrast, guarantees never to deliver cells out of order.

ATM networks are organised like traditional WANs, with lines and switches (routers). The most common speeds for ATM networks are 155 Mbps and 622 Mbps, although higher speeds are also supported. The 155-Mbps speed was chosen because this is about what is needed to transmit high definition television. The exact choice of 155.52 Mbps was made for compatibility with AT&T's SONET transmission system. The 622 Mbps speed was chosen so that four 155-Mbps channels could be sent over it.

The ATM Reference Model

ATM has its own reference model, different from the OSI model and also different from the TCP/IP model. It consists of three layers, the physical, ATM, and ATM adaptation layers, plus whatever users want to put on top of that.The physical layer deals with the physical medium: voltages, bit timing, and various other issues. ATM does not prescribe a particular set of rules but instead says that ATM cells can be sent on a wire or fibre by themselves, but they can also be packaged inside the payload of other carrier systems. In other words, it has been designed to be independent of the transmission medium. The ATM layer deals with cells and cell transport. It defines the layout of a cell and tells what the header fields mean. It also deals with establishment and case of virtual circuits. Congestion control is also located here so because most applications do not want to work directly with cells (although some may), a layer above the ATM layer has been defined to allow users to send packets larger than a cell. The ATM interface segments these packets, transmits the cells individually, and reassembles them at the other end. This layer is the AAL (ATM Adaptation Layer). Unlike the earlier two-dimensional reference models, the ATM model is defined as being three-dimensional. The user plane deals with data transport, flow control, error correction, and other user functions. In contrast, the control plane is concerned with connection management. The layer and plane management functions relate to resource management and interlayer coordination.

The physical and AAL layers are each divided into two sublayers, one at the bottom that does the work and a convergence sublayer on top that provides the proper interface to the layer above it.

The PMD (Physical Medium Dependent) sublayer interfaces to the actual cable. It moves the bits on and off and handles the bit timing. For different carriers and cables, this layer will be different.

The other sublayer of the physical layer is the TC (Transmission Convergence) sublayer. When cells are transmitted, the TC layer sends them as a string of bits to the PMD layer. Doing this is easy. At the other end, the TC sublayer gets a pure incoming bit stream from the PMD sublayer. Its job is to convert this bit stream into a cell stream for the ATM layer. It handles all the issues related to telling where cells begin and end in the bit stream. In the ATM model, this functionality is in the physical layer. In the OSI model and in pretty much all other networks, the job of framing, that is, turning a raw bit stream into a sequence of frames or cells, is the data link layer's task.

The ATM layer manages cells, including their generation and transport. Most of the interesting aspects of ATM are-located here. It is a mixture of the OSI data link and network layers; it is not split into sublayers.

The AAL layer is split into a SAR (Segmentation And Reassembly) sublayer and a CS (Convergence Sublayer). The lower sublayer breaks up packets into cells on the transmission side and puts them back together again at the destination. The upper sublayer makes it possible to have ATM systems offer different kinds of services to different applications (e.g., file transfer and video on demand have different requirements concerning error handling, timing, etc.).

ATM advantages include handling or minimising the severity of

(*a*) Out of sequence packets

(*b*) Delay time between packets of a message

(*c*) Bit errors

The ATM standard features three layers:

1. Application Adaptation Layer(AAL): Accepts transmissions from upper layer services into ATM cells.
2. ATM layer: Provides routing, traffic management, switching, and multiplexing services.
3. Physical layer: Defines transmission medium, bit transmission, encoding and electrical Tl conversion, the ATM has become the new buzzword on the Information Highway today with its attractive implement and inexpensive features.

The Advantages of ATM: Asynchronous Transfer Mode (ATM) is the cell relay protocol that is considered as the highest information superhighway ahead.

ATM enjoys several distinct advantages over conventional data transmission techniques including witching. Some of these advantages are:

1. Optimising use of high data rate transmission media like optical fibre.
2. Less prone to noise degradation.
3. Capable of interfacing with existing systems like LAN without lowering their effectiveness.
4. Implementation is inexpensive.
5. It is connection-oriented. Hence, accurate and predictable delivery is ensured.
6. Some software functions have been moved to hardware. Thus the data rate is increased.
7. Any delay in transmission can be compensated by increasing data rate or changing bandwidth,
8. Provides automatic error correction rather than relying on retransmission.
9. Small cell sizes of ATM offer fewer chances of inroducing errors, as constrasted with large packets in packet switching.
10. There are no complex flow or congestion control mechanisms in ATM.

ATM comunicates by cells and not by transmitting frames. A cell is exactly 5 bytes long specifying the source and destination addresses of the stations communicating, an ATM cell indicates I data will flow through intermediate devices (called switches) , II can maintain a very high data rate.

On an ATM network layer station is always transmitting. However, most of the cell transmitt, cells that can be discarded at the switch. When a cell that is not empty enters the switch, the address determine where the cell will go next. The cell is then sent out in the next available slot and according to cell ATM is a circuit-based network. A virtual circuit is set up between two devices to communicate, network. There are two types of circuits in an ATM network. These are:

1. Permanent Virtual Circuit (PVC): A circuit that is set up in the switches to allow connect between two devices.
2. Switch Virtual Circuit (CVC): A circuit that is temporarily set up just for the duration of a con between two devices.

At each switching node, the ATM header identifies a virtual circuit that will route the cell's no. to destination computer. The cell header enables the switches to forward the cell and data to the next J1 link in the circuit. The virtual circuit is set up through the appropriate ATM switches when two end p communicate. This scheme allows ATM switching to be implemented in hardware that is fast enough transmission rates to 2.488' gigabits per second.

ATM is compatible with current and widely used cable media such as twisted pair, coaxial and as well as LAN, WAN and MAN technology.

INTERNETWORKING

Message Switching: A messaging hub that provides protocol conversion between several messaging systems. Examples of switches include Soft-Switch's, EMX, HP's openmail and Digital's Mailbus. A Messaging Switch differs from messaging gateway in that it supports more than two protocols and connections as well as providing management and directory integration.

Routers: It is a specialised computer. An electronic message is sent to its proper destination by this computer. It selects the most efficient route for sending the messages like a travel agent. Any e-mail message sent through the Internet is passed through a number of routers. A route server provides a more global view of a geographic area than a router, which is only aware of the destinations that it can reach.

Gateways : A network connection device similar to a bridge except that it is visible to the user. It translates data between one type of network and another. Gateway first sold peripheral to owners of Texas Instrument Computers. Gateways are used to connect two dissimilar LANs. The term gateways and routers are used interchangeable, though there is a difference between the two. A router operates at the network layer (layer 3) of the OSI model whereas a gateway operates on, the application Layer (Layer 7) of the OSI model.

E-mail : (Electronic mail) An e-mail system requires a messaging system which provides the store and forward capability and a mail programme that provides the user interface with send and receive functions.

The transmission of memos and messages over a network. Users can send mail to a single recipient or broadcast it to multiple users. With multitasking workstations, mail can be delivered and announced while the user is working in an application.

E-mail Vs fax : Fax documents are scanned images and are thus treated like pictures even if they contain only text. E-mail messages are raw ASCII text, which can be edited immediately in any text editor or word processor that imports ASCII text.

One of the advantages of E-mail is that it gives users the ability to review, respond to a file and discard message quickly. E-mail is becoming an important communication medium and infrastructure for work group applications, that make it easier for people to work together.

EDI: Electronic Data Interchange (EDI) is a set of standards for controlling the transfer of business documents, such as purchase orders and invoices, between computers. The goal of EDI is the elimination of paperwork and increased response time. For EDI to be effective, users must agree on certain standards for formatting and exchanging information, such as the X-400 protocol.

EDI has become a major means of business communications among large companies in the U.S.

The advantage is that it generates the functional acknowledgement whenever an EDI message is received it is electronically transmitted to the sender.

EDI eliminates the paper documents associated with common business transactions. Electronic messages can be duplicated and routed instantly to anyone in an organisation.

Concatenated Virtual Circuits

Two styles of internetworking are possible: a connection-oriented concatenation of virtual-circuit subnets, and a datagram internet style.In the concatenated virtual-circuit model, a connection to a host in a distant network is set up in a way similar to the way connection normally established. The subnet sees that the destination is remote at virtual circuit to the router nearest the destination network. Then it constructs a virtual circuit from that router to an external gateway (multiprotocol gateway) records the existence of the virtual circuit in its tables and proceeds to build another virtual circuit to a router in the next subnet. This process continues until the destination host has been reached.

The essential feature of this approach is that a sequence of virtual circuits is setup from the source through one or more gateways to the destination. Each gateway maintains tables telling which virtual circuits pass through it, where they are to be routed, and what the new virtual-circuit number is.

This scheme works best when all the networks have roughly the same properties. For example, if all of them guarantee reliable delivery of network layer packets, then barring a crash somewhere along the route will also be reliable. Similarly, if none of.them guarantee reliable delivery, then the concatenation of the virtual circuits is not reliable either. On the other hand, if the source machine is on a network that does guarantee reliable delivery but one of the intermediate networks can lose packets, the concatenation fundamentally changed the nature of the service.

Concatenated virtual circuits are also common in the transport layer. In particular, it is possible to build a bit pipe using, say, SNA, which terminates in a way, and have a TCP connection go from the gateway to the next gateway. In this manner, an end-to-end virtual circuit can be built spanning different networks and protocols.

Connectionless Internetworking

An alternative internetwork model is the datagram model. The only service the network layer offers to the transport layer is the ability to inject datagrams-into the subnet and hope for the best. There is none of a virtual circuit at all in the network layer, let alone a concatenation of them. This model does not require all packets belonging to one connection to traverse the same sequence of gateways. A routing decimade separately for each packet, possibly depending on the traffic at the moment the packet is sent. This strategy can use multiple routes and thus achieve bandwidth than the concatenated virtual-circuit model. But there is no guarantee that the packets arrive at the destination in order, assuming that they arrive at all. The model is not quite as simple as it looks. For one thing, if network has its own network layer protocol, it is not possible for a packet from one network to transmit to transit another one. One could imagine the multiprotocol actually trying to translate from one format to another, but unless the two are close relatives with the same information fields, such conversions will be incomplete and often doomed to failure. For this reason, conversion is tempted. Second, and more serious, problem is addressing. Imagine a simple case: a host on the Internet is trying to send an IP packet to a host on an adjoining SNA. The IP and SNA addresses are different. One would need a mapping between IPand SNA addresses in both directions. Furthermore, the concept of what is addressable is different. In IP, hosts (actually, interface cards) dresses. In SNA, entities other than hosts (e.g., hardware devices) can also have addresses. At best, someone would have to maintain a database mapping to the extent possible, but it would constantly be a trouble.

Another idea is to design a universal "internet" packet and have recognise it. This approach is, in fact, what IP is-a packet designed to 1 through many networks. Of course, it may turn out that IPv4 (the current protocol) drives all other formats out of the market, IPv6 (the future Intitocol) does not catch on, and nothing new is ever invented, but history otherwise. Getting everybody to agree to a single format is difficult companies perceive it to their commercial advantage to have a proprietary format they control.

The two ways internetworking can be approached. The concatenated virtual-circuit model has essentially the same advantages as using virtual circuits within a single subnet: buffers can be reserved in advance sequencing can be guaranteed, short headers can be used, and the trouble caused by delayed duplicate packets can be avoided.

It also has the same disadvantages: table space required in the routers for each open connection, no alternate routing to avoid congested areas, and vulnerability to router failures along the path. It also has the disadvantage of being difficult, if not impossible, to implement if one of the networks involved is an unreliable datagram network.

The properties of the datagram approach to internetworking are pretty much the same as those of datagram subnets: more potential for adapting to it, robustness in the face of router failures and longer headers needed. Various adaptive routing algorithms are possible in an internet, just as they are within a single datagram network. A major advantage of the datagram approach to inerrnetworking is that it can be used over subnets that do not use virtual Circuits Inside. Many LANs, mobile networks (e.g. aircraft and naval fleets), and even some WANs fall into this category. Serious problem occurs if internetworking is based on virtual circuits.

Tunnelling

Handling the general case of making two different networks interwork is major difficulty. However, there is common special case manageable. This case is where the source and destination hosts are on the same type of network, but there is a different network in between. As an example, think of an international bank with a TCP/IP-based Ethernet in Paris, a TCP/IP-based Ethernet in London and a non-IP wide area network (e.g., ATM) in between, the solution to this problem is a technique called tunnelling. To send an IP packet to host 2, host 1 constructs the packet containing the IP address of host 2, inserts it into an Ethernet frame addressed to the Paris multiprotocol router, and puts it on the Ethernet. When multi Protocol router gets the frame, it removes the IP packet, inserts it in the payload field of the WAN network layer packet, and addresses the latter to the WAN address of the London multlprotocol router. When it gets there, the London router removes the IP packet and sends it to host 2 inside the Ethernet frame.

The WAN can be seen a big tunnel extending from one mutiprotocol router to the other. The IP packet just travels from one end of the tunnel to the other snug in its nice box. It does not have to worry about dealing with the WAN at all. Neither do the hosts on either Ethernet. Only the multiprotocol router has to understand IP and WAN packets. In effect, the entire distance from the middle of one protocol router to the middle of the other acts like a serial line.

Interworking Routing

One of the differences between internetwork routing and an intranetwork routing is that internetwork routing may require crossing international boundaries. Various law suddenly come into play: such as Sweden's strict privacy laws about exporting personal data about Swedish citizens from Sweden. Another example, Canadian law saying that data traffic originating in Canada and ending in Canada may not leave the country. This law means that traffic from Windsor, Ontario to Vancouver may not be routed via nearby Detroit, even if that route is the fastest and cheapest.

Another difference between interior and exterior routing is the cost. Within a single network, a single charging algorithm normally applies. However, different works may be under different managements, and one route may be less expensive than another. Similarly, the quality of service offered by different networks may be different, and this may be a reason to choose one route over another.

Fragmentation: If the original source packet is too large to be handled by the destination network, then the solution is to allow gateways to breakup packets into fragments, sending each fragment as a separate internet packet. Packet switching networks too have trouble putting the fragments back together again.Two strategies exists for recombining the fragments back into the original packet. The first strategy is to make fragmentation caused by a "small packet" network transparent to any subsequent networks through which the packet must pass on its way to the ultimate destination. In this approach, the small-packet network has gateways e.g specialised routers that interface to other networks. When an oversized packet arrives at a gateway, the gateway breaks it up into fragments. Each fragment is addressed to the same exit gateway, where the pieces are recombined. In this way passage through the small-packet network has been made transparent. Subsequent networks are not even aware that fragmentation has occurred. ATM networks, for example, have special hardware to provide transparent fragmentation of packets into cells and then reassembly of cells into packets. In the ATM world, fragmentation is called segmentation; the concept is the same, but some of the details are different.

Transparent fragmentation is straightforward but has some problems. For one thing, the exit gateway must know when it has received all the pieces, so either a count field or an "end of packet" bit must be provided. For another thing, all packets must exit via the same gateway. By not allowing some fragments to follow one route to the ultimate destination and other fragments a disjoint route, some performance may be lost. A last problem is the overhead required to repeatedly reassemble and then refragment a large packet passing through a series of smallpacket networks. ATM requires transparent fragmentation.

The other fragmentation strategy is to refrain from recombining fragments at any intermediate gateways. Once a packet has been fragmented, each fragment is treated as though it were an original packet. All fragments are passed through the exit gateway (or gateways). Recombination occurs only at the destination host. IP works this way.

Nontransparent fragmentation also has some problems. For example, it requires every host to be able to do reassembly. Yet another problem is that when a large packet is fragmented, the total overhead increases because each fragment must have a header. Whereas in the first method this overhead disappears as soon as the small-packet network is exited, in this method the overhead remains for the rest of the journey. An advantage of nontransparent fragmentation, however, is multiple exit gateways can now be used and higher performance can be achieved. Of course, if the concatenated virtual-circuit model is being used, this advantage is of no use.

When a packet is fragmented, the fragments must be numbered in such a way that the original data stream can be reconstructed. One way of numbering the fragments is to use a tree. If packet 0 must be split up, the pieces are called 0.0, 0.1, 0.2, etc. If these fragments themselves must be fragmented later on, the IDs are numbered 0.0.0, 0.0.1, 0.0.2,..., 0.1.0, 0.1.1, 0.1.2, etc. If enough, IDs have been reserved in the header for the worst case and no duplicates are generated anywhere, this scheme is sufficient to ensure that all the pieces can be correctly reassembled at the destination, no matter what order they arrive in.

However, if even one network loses or discards packets, end-to-end retransmissions are needed, with unfortunate effects for the numbering system. Suppose a 1024-bit packet is initially fragmented into four equal-sized fragments, 0.0, 0.2, and 0.3. Fragment 0.1 is lost, but the other parts arrive at the destination. Eventualy naturally, the source times out and retransmits the original packet again. Only this time Murphy's law strikes and the route taken passes through a network with a 512 bit limit, so two fragments are generated. When the new fragment 0.1 arrives at the destination, the receiver will think that all four pieces are now accounted for and reconstruct the packet incorrectly.

A completeiy different and better numbering system is for the internetwork protocol to define an elementary fragment size small enough that the elementary fragment can pass through every network. When a packet is fragmented, all the pieces are equal to the elementary fragment size except the last one, which may be shorter. An internet packet may contain several fragments, for efficiency reasons. The internet header must provide the original packet number and the number of the (first) elementary fragment contained in the packet. There must be bit indicating that the last elementary fragment contained within the internet packets is the last one of the original packet. This approach requires two sequence fields in the head, the original packet number and the fragment number. Some internet protocols take this method even further and consider the entire transmission on a virtual circuit to be one giant packet, so that each fragment contains the absolute byte number of the first byte within the fragment.

NETWORK SECURITY

Cryptography

Cryptography means secret writing. In this the message to be encrypted known as the *plaintext*, are transformed by a function that is parameterised by a key. The output of the encryption process known as ciphertext, is then transmitted often by messenger or radio. We assume that the enemy, or intruder, hears and accurately copies down the complete cipher text but unable to decrypt the message as he is unaware of the decryption key. Sometimes the intruder cannot only listen to the communication channel(passive intruder) but can also record messages and play them back later, inject his own messages or modify legitimate messages before they get to the receiver(active intruder). The art of breaking ciphers, called cryptanalysis and the art devising them(cryptography) is collectively known as cryptology.

Two fundamental Cryptographic principles are as follows:-

Redundancy-Cryptographic principle 1: *Messages must contain some redundancy'*. In other words, upon decrypting a message, the recipient must be able to tell whether it is valid by simply inspecting it and perhaps performing a simple computation. This redundancy is needed to prevent active intruders from sending garbage and tricking the receiver into decrypting the garbage and acting on the Plaintext. However, this same redundancy makes it much easier for passive intruders to break the system, so there is some tension here. The redundancy should never be in the form of *n* zeros at the start or end of a message. Since running such messages through some cryptographic algorithms gives more predictable results, making the cryptanalysts' job easier. A CRC polynomial is much better than a run of Os. Since the receiver can easily verify it, but it generates more work for the cryptanalyst. Even better is to use a cryptographic hash.

Freshness: The second cryptographic principle is that some measures must be taken to ensure that each message received can be verified as being fresh, that is, said recently. This measure is needed to prevent active intruders from playing back old messages. If no such measures were taken, our ex-employee could tap TCP's phone line and just keep repeating previously sent valid messages. Restating this idea

Cryptographic principle 2: *Some method is needed to foil replay attacks.* One such measure is including in every message a time stamp valid only for say 10 seconds. The receiver can then just keep messages around for 10 seconds to compare newly arrived messages to previous ones to filter out duplicates. Messages older than 10 seconds can be thrown out, since any replays sent more than 10 seconds later will be rejected as too old.

Comparison of Old Cryptography Method versus Modern Method

Symmetric-Key Algorithms: Modern cryptography uses the same basic ideas as traditional cryptography (transposition and substitution) but its emphasis is different. Traditionally, cryptographers have used simple algorithms. Nowadays the reverse is true: the object is to make the encryption algorithm so complex and involuted that even if the crypanalysts acquire vast mounds of enciphered text of his own choosing, he will not be able to make any sense of it at all without the key. Symmetric key algorithm also used the same key for encryption: decrypdtion.

Data Encryption Standard (DES): This method was widely adopted by the industry for in use for security products. Plaintext is encrypted in blocks of 64 bits, yielding 64 bits of ciphertext. The algorithm which is parameterised by a 56 bit key has 19 distinct stages. The algorithm has been designed to allow decryption to be done with the same key as encryption. *DES* and *Rijndael* are the best known symmetric-key, cryptographic algorithms.

DOMAIN NAME SYSTEM (DNS)

The mechanism that implements a machine name hierarch for TCP/IP Internets is called Domain Name Systems(DNS). It has two conceptually independent aspects. The first is abstract; it specifies the name syntax and rules for delegating authority over names. The second is concrete; it specifies the implementation of a distributed computing system that efficiently maps names to addresses. This section. considers the name syntax, and later sections examine the implementation.

The domain name system uses a hierarchical naming scheme as domain names. A domain name consists of a sequence of sub names separated bv a delimitor character, the period in our examples we take that individual sections of the name might represent sites or groups, but the domain system simply calls each section a label. Thus, the domain name *cs.delhi.org*

contains three labels: CS, delhi and ORG. Any suffix of a labels in a domain name is also called a domain. In the above example the lowest level domain is CS. delhi.org (the domain name for the Computer Science Department at IGNOU), the second level domain is ignou.org (the domain name for ignou) and the top level domain is *org*. As the example shows, domain names are written with the local label first and the top domain last. As we will see, writing them in this order makes it possible to compress messages that contain multiple domain **names**.

Table 11.2 ***Domain name System***

Domain Name	Meaning
Com	Commercial Organizations
Edu	Educational Institutes
Gov	Government Institutions
Mil.	Military Groups
Net	Major network support centers
Org	Organisations other than those above
Arpa	Temporary ARPANET domain (obsolete)
INT	International Organisations
Country code	Each country (geographic scheme)

Electronic Mail

This is the most widely used service facilitating users to send and receive messages electronically in a store and forward manner. Different E-mail standards, viz., SMTP, UUCP and X400 Message Handling system are supported on ERNET.

Electronic Mail is a system whereby a computer user can exchange messages with other computer users or group of users via a communications network.

The backbone of an electronic mail system is a communication network that connects remote terminals to a central system or a local area network that interconnects personal computers. Users can send mail to a single recipient or they can broadcast it to any number of selected users on the systems. The method for receiving mail'depends on the sophistication of the system. When multitasking personal computer and workstation are used mail can be delivered to users while they are working on something else. Otherwise, users have to interrogate their mailboxes in a central systems, or file server.

Many users first encounter computer networks when they send or received electronic mail to or from a remote site. E-mail is the most widely used application service. Indeed, many computer users access networks only through electronic mail.

E-mail is popular because it offers a fast, convenient method of transferring information. E-mail can accommodate small notes with a single mechanism.

WWW (World Wide Web)

The World Wide Web is a system for linking up hypertext documents. Each document is a page written in HTML, possible with hyperlinks to other documents. A browser can display a document by establishing a TCP connection to its server, asking for the document, and then closing the connection. When a hyperlink is selected by the user, that document can also be fetched in the same way. This manner, documents all over the world are linked together in a giant web. Some fact about WWW are:

- Fastest growing discovery and retrieval system;
- Presently servers, growing at an astounding rate;
- Retrieve "hypermedia" documents, with text, graphics, audio, video, and links to other hypermedia documents;
- A navigational system based on "hyperlink"; and
- State-less interaction between client and server, conforming to "http" protocol.

12 MULTIPLE CHOICE QUESTIONS

1. A file is downloaded in a home computer using a 56 kbps MODEM connected to an Internet Service Provider. If the download of file completes in 2 minutes, what is the maximum size of data downloaded?
(*a*) 112 Mbits (*b*) 6.72 Mbits
(*c*) 67.20 Mbits (*d*) 672 Mbits

2. In ______ CSMA protocol, after the station finds the line idle, it sends or refrains from sending based on the outcome of a random number generator.
(*a*) Non-persistent (*b*) 0-persistent
(*c*) 1-persistent (*d*) p-persistent

3. Which of the following substitution technique have the relationship between a character in the plaintext and a character in the ciphertext as one-to-many?
(*a*) Monoalphabetic (*b*) Polyalphabetic
(*c*) Transpositional (*d*) None of the above

4. What is the maximum length of CAT-5 UTP cable in Fast Ethernet network?
(*a*) 100 meters (*b*) 200 meters
(*c*) 1000 meters (*d*) 2000 meters

5. The ______ is a set of standards that defines how a dynamic web document should be written, how input data should be supplied to the program, and how the output result should be used.
(*a*) Hyper Text Markup Language
(*b*) File Transfer Protocol
(*c*) Hyper Text Transfer Protocol
(*d*) Common Gateway Interface

6. The count-to-infinity problem is associated with
(*a*) Flooding algorithm
(*b*) Hierarchical routing algorithm
(*c*) Distance vector routing algorithm
(*d*) Link state routing algorithm

7. The IEEE single-precision and double-precision format to represent floating-point numbers, has a length of ______ and ______ respectively.
(*a*) 8 bits and 16 bits
(*b*) 16 bits and 32 bits
(*c*) 32 bits and 64 bits
(*d*) 64 bits and 128 bits

8. Consider an undirected graph G with 100 nodes. The maximum number of edges to be included in G so that the graph is not connected is
(*a*) 2451 (*b*) 4950
(*c*) 4851 (*d*) 9900

9. The amortized time complexity to perform ______ operation(s) in Splay trees is O(Ig n).
(*a*) Search
(*b*) Search and Insert
(*c*) Search and Delete
(*d*) Search, Insert and Delete

10. Suppose that the splits at every level of Quicksort are in proportion $1 - \beta$ to β, where $0 < \beta \leq 0.5$ is a constant. The number of elements in an array is n.
The maximum depth is approximately
(*a*) $0.5\ \beta$ Ig n (*b*) $0.5\ (1 - \beta)$ Ig n
(*c*) $-$(Ig n)/(Ig β) (*d*) $-$(Ig n)/Ig $(1 - \beta)$

11. The minimum number of nodes in a binary tree of depth d (root is at level 0) is
(*a*) $2^d - 1$ (*b*) $2^{d+1} - 1$
(*c*) $d + 1$ (*d*) d

12. The efficient data structure to insert/delete a number in a stored set of numbers is
(*a*) Queue
(*b*) Linked list
(*c*) Doubly linked list
(*d*) Binary tree

13. The number of states in a minimal deterministic finite automaton corresponding to the language $L = \{ a^n \mid n \geq 4 \}$ is

(*a*) 3 (*b*) 4
(*c*) 5 (*d*) 6

14. Regular expression for the language $L = \{w \in \{0, 1\}^* \mid w$ has no pair of consecutive zeros$\}$ is
(*a*) $(1 + 010)^*$
(*b*) $(01 + 10)^*$
(*c*) $(1 + 010)^* (0 + \lambda)$
(*d*) $(1 + 01)^* (0 + \lambda)$

15. Consider the following two languages:
$L_1 = \{a^n b^l a^k \mid n + l + k > 5\}$
$L_2 = \{a^n b^l a^k \mid n > 5, l > 3, k \leq l\}$
Which of the following is true?
(*a*) L_1 is regular language and L_2 is not regular language.
(*b*) Both L_1 and L_2 are regular languages.
(*c*) Both L_1 and L_2 are not regular languages.
(*d*) L_1 is not regular language and L_2 is regular language.

16. LL grammar for the language $L = \{a^n b^m c^{n+m} \mid m \geq 0, n \geq 0\}$ is
(*a*) $S \rightarrow aSc \mid S_1 ; S_1 \rightarrow bS_1c \mid \lambda$
(*b*) $S \rightarrow aSc \mid S_1 \mid \lambda ; S_1 \rightarrow bS_1c$
(*c*) $S \rightarrow aSc \mid S_1 \mid \lambda ; S_1 \rightarrow bS_1c \mid \lambda$
(*d*) $S \rightarrow aSc \mid \lambda ; S_1 \rightarrow bS_1c \mid \lambda$

17. Assume the statements S_1 and S_2 given as :
S_1 : Given a context free grammar G, there exists an algorithm for determining whether L(G) is infinite.
S_2 : There exists an algorithm to determine whether two context free grammars generate the same language.
Which of the following is true?
(*a*) S_1 is correct and S_2 is not correct.
(*b*) Both S_1 and S_2 are correct.
(*c*) Both S_1 and S_2 are not correct.
(*d*) S_1 is not correct and S_2 is correct.

18. The number of eight-bit strings beginning with either 111 or 101 is ______.
(*a*) 64 (*b*) 128
(*c*) 265 (*d*) None of the above

19. Find the number of ways to paint 12 offices so that 3 of them will be green, 2 of them pink, 2 of them yellow and the rest ones white.
(*a*) 55,440 (*b*) 1,66,320
(*c*) 4.790E+08 (*d*) 39,91,680

20. Consider the following statements :
(*i*) A graph in which there is a unique path between every pair of vertices is a tree.
(*ii*) A connected graph with $e = v - 1$ is a tree.
(*iii*) A graph with $e = v - 1$ that has no circuit is a tree.
Which of the above statements is/are true?
(*a*) (*i*) & (*iii*) (*b*) (*ii*) & (*iii*)
(*c*) (*i*) & (*ii*) (*d*) All of the above

21. Consider the In-order and Post-order traversals of a tree as given below :
In-order : j e n k o p b f a c l g m d h i
Post-order : j n o p k e f b c l m g h i d a
The Pre-order traversal of the tree shall be
(*a*) a b f e j k n o p c d g l m h i
(*b*) a b c d e f j k n o p g l m h i
(*c*) a b e j k n o p f c d g l m h i
(*d*) j e n o p k f b c l m g h i d a

22. A simple graph G with n-vertices is connected if the graph has
(*a*) $(n - 1)(n - 2)/2$ edges
(*b*) more than $(n - 1)(n - 2)/2$ edges
(*c*) less than $(n - 1)(n - 2)/2$ edges
(*d*) $\sum_{i=1}^{k} C(n_i, 2)$ edges

23. Which one of the following set of gates is best suited for 'parity' checking and 'parity' generation?
(*a*) AND, OR, NOT (*b*) NAND, NOR
(*c*) EX-OR, EX-NOR (*d*) None of the above

24. The quantification $\exists!x\ P(x)$ denotes the proposition "There exists a unique x such that P(x) is true", express the quantification using universal and existential quantifications and logical operators :
(*a*) $\exists x\ P(x) \vee \forall x \forall y\ ((P(x) \vee P(y)) \rightarrow x = y)$
(*b*) $\forall x\ P(x) \wedge \forall x \forall y\ ((P(x) \vee P(y)) \rightarrow x = y)$
(*c*) $\exists x\ P(x) \wedge \forall x \forall y\ ((P(x) \wedge P(y)) \rightarrow x = y)$
(*d*) $\exists x\ P(x) \wedge \exists x \exists y\ ((P(x) \vee P(y)) \rightarrow x = y)$

25. If F and G are Boolean functions of degree n. Then, which of the following is true?
(*a*) $F \leq F + G$ and $F G \leq F$
(*b*) $G \leq F + G$ and $F G \geq G$
(*c*) $F \geq F + G$ and $F G \leq F$
(*d*) $G \geq F + G$ and $F G \leq F$

26. Match the following identities/laws to their corresponding name :

A.	$x + x = x$ $x \bullet x = x$	(*i*) Dominance
B.	$x + 0 = x$ $x \bullet 1 = x$	(*ii*) Absorption
C.	$x + 1 = 1$ $x \bullet 0 = 0$	(*iii*) Idempotent
D.	$x \bullet (x + y) = x$	(*iv*) Identity

Codes:

	A	B	C	D
(*a*)	(*iii*)	(*iv*)	(*i*)	(*ii*)
(*b*)	(*iv*)	(*iii*)	(*i*)	(*ii*)
(*c*)	(*iv*)	(*iii*)	(*ii*)	(*i*)
(*d*)	(*iii*)	(*iv*)	(*ii*)	(*i*)

27. In which one of the following, continuous process improvement is done?
(*a*) ISO9001

(*b*) RMMM
(*c*) CMM
(*d*) None of the above

28. The ______ of a program or computing system is the structure or structures of the system, which comprise software components, the externally visible properties of these components, and the relationship among them.
(*a*) E-R diagram
(*b*) Data flow diagram
(*c*) Software architecture
(*d*) Software design

29. Working software is not available until late in the process in
(*a*) Waterfall model
(*b*) Prototyping model
(*c*) Incremental model
(*d*) Evolutionary Development model

30. Equivalence partitioning is a ______ testing method that divides the input domain of a program into classes of data from which test cases can be derived.
(*a*) White box
(*b*) Black box
(*c*) Regression
(*d*) Smoke

31. Consider the following characteristics :
(*i*) Correct and unambiguous
(*ii*) Complete and consistent
(*iii*) Ranked for importance and/or stability and verifiable
(*iv*) Modifiable and Traceable

Which of the following is true for a good SRS?
(*a*) (*i*), (*ii*) and (*iii*)
(*b*) (*i*), (*iii*) and (*iv*)
(*c*) (*ii*), (*iii*) and (*iv*)
(*d*) (*i*), (*ii*), (*iii*) and (*iv*)

32. Linked Lists are not suitable for _____.
(*a*) Binary Search
(*b*) Polynomial Manipulation
(*c*) Insertion
(*d*) Radix Sort

33. What is the size of the following Union? Assume that the size of int = 2, size of float = 4, size of char = 1

```
union tag {
int a;
float b;
char c;
};
```

(*a*) 2 (*b*) 4
(*c*) 1 (*d*) 7

34. What is the output of the following program segment?

```
sum(n)
{
  if ( n < 1 ) return n;
  else return (n + sum(n-1));
}
main()
{
  printf("%d", sum(5));
}
```

(*a*) 10 (*b*) 16
(*c*) 15 (*d*) 14

35. Assume that x and y are non-zero positive integers. What does the following program segment perform?

```
while (x!=0)
{
if (x>y)
  x = x-y
  else
  y=y-x;
printf("%d",x);
```

(*a*) Computes LCM of two numbers
(*b*) Computes GCD of two numbers
(*c*) Divides large number with small number
(*d*) Subtracts smaller number from large number

36. Consider the following program segment:

```
d=0;
for(i=1; i<31, ++i)
for(j=1; j<31, ++j)
for(k=1; k<31, ++k)
if ((i+j+k)%3)= = 0);
d = d + 1;
printf("%d", d);
```

The output will be
(*a*) 9000 (*b*) 3000
(*c*) 90 (*d*) None of these

37. Usage of Preemption and Transaction Rollback prevents _____.
(*a*) Unauthorised usage of data file
(*b*) Deadlock situation
(*c*) Data manipulation
(*d*) File preemption

38. The _____ language was originally designed as the Transformation Language for Style Sheet facility.
(*a*) XSTL (*b*) XML
(*c*) XQuery (*d*) XPath

39. Views are useful for ______ unwanted information, and for collecting together information from more than one relation into a single view.
(*a*) Hiding (*b*) Deleting
(*c*) Highlighting (*d*) All of the above

40. The decision tree classifier is a widely used technique for ______.

(*a*) Classification (*b*) Association
(*c*) Partition (*d*) Clustering

41. Cross_tab displays permit users to view ______ of multidimensional data at a time.

(*a*) One dimension (*b*) Two dimensions
(*c*) Three dimensions (*d*) Multidimensions

42. A method to provide secure transmission of email is called ____.

(*a*) TLS (*b*) SA
(*c*) IPSec (*d*) PGP

43. Thoma's-write rule is

(*a*) Two phase locking protocol
(*b*) Timestamp ordering protocol
(*c*) One phase locking protocol
(*d*) Sliding window protocol

44. Match the following :

List-I Process state transition	**List-II** Reason for transition
A. Ready→ Running	(*i*) Request made by the process is satisfied or an event for which it was waiting occurs.
B. Blocked→ Ready	(*ii*) Process wishes to wait for some action by another process.
C. Running→ Blocked	(*iii*) The process is dispatched.
D. Running→ Ready	(*iv*) The process is preempted.

Codes:

	A	B	C	D
(*a*)	(*iii*)	(*i*)	(*ii*)	(*iv*)
(*b*)	(*iv*)	(*i*)	(*iii*)	(*ii*)
(*c*)	(*iv*)	(*iii*)	(*i*)	(*ii*)
(*d*)	(*iii*)	(*iv*)	(*ii*)	(*i*)

45. The hit ratio of a Translation Look Aside Buffer (TLAB) is 80%. It takes 20 nanoseconds (ns) to search TLAB and 100 ns to access main memory. The effective memory access time is ______.

(*a*) 36 ns (*b*) 140 ns
(*c*) 122 ns (*d*) 40 ns

46. Consider the input/output (I/O) requests made at different instants of time directed at a hypothetical disk having 200 tracks as given in the following table:

Serial No.	1	2	3	4	5
Track No.	12	85	40	100	75
Time of arrival	65	80	110	100	175

Assume that :

Current head position is at track no. 65

Direction of last movement is towards higher numbered tracks

Current clock time is 160 milliseconds

Head movement time per track is 1 millisecond.

"look" is a variant of "SCAN" disk-arm scheduling algorithm. In this algorithm, if no more I/O requests are left in current direction, the disk head reverses its direction. The seek times in Shortest Seek First (SSF) and "look" disk-arm scheduling algorithms respectively are:

(*a*) 144 and 123 milliseconds
(*b*) 143 and 123 milliseconds
(*c*) 149 and 124 milliseconds
(*d*) 256 and 186 milliseconds

47. Assume that an implementation of Unix operating system uses i-nodes to keep track of data blocks allocated to a file. It supports 12 direct block addresses, one indirect block address and one double indirect block address. The file system has 256 bytes block size and 2 bytes for disk block address. The maximum possible size of a file in this system is

(*a*) 16 MB (*b*) 16 KB
(*c*) 70 KB (*d*) None of these

48. Which of the following set of Unix commands will always display "WELCOME"?

(*a*) export title = WELCOME; Echo $title
(*b*) title = WELCOME; export $ title ; sh –c "echo $title"
(*c*) title = WELCOME; export title ; sh –c "echo $title"
(*d*) title = WELCOME; echo $title

49. What type of logic circuit is represented by the figure shown below?

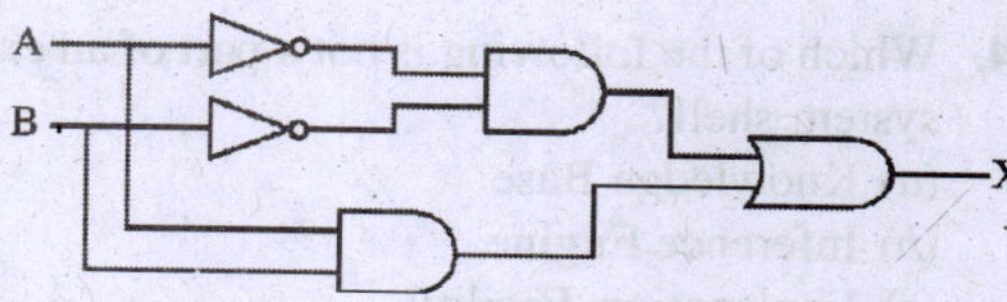

(*a*) XOR (*b*) XNOR
(*c*) XAND (*d*) XNAND

50. The speed up of a pipeline processing over an equivalent non-pipeline processing is defined by the ratio:

(*a*) $S = \dfrac{nt_n}{(k+n-1)t_p}$

(*b*) $S = \dfrac{nt_n}{(k+n+1)t_p}$

(*c*) $S = \dfrac{nt_n}{(k-n+1)t_p}$

(*d*) $S = \dfrac{(k+n-1)t_p}{nt_n}$

COMPUTER SCIENCE

Where $n \rightarrow$ no. of tasks
$t_n \rightarrow$ time of completion of each task
$k \rightarrow$ no. of segments of pipeline
$t_p \rightarrow$ clock cycle time
$S \rightarrow$ speed up ratio

51. Which of the following is a correct predicate logic statement for "Every Natural number has one successor"?
(*a*) $\forall x \exists y$ (succ(x, y) $\wedge$ ($\exists z$ succ(x, z) $\Rightarrow$ equal (y, z)))
(*b*) $\forall x \exists y$ (succ(x, y) $\vee$ ($\exists z$ succ(x, z) $\Rightarrow$ equal (y, z)))
(*c*) $\exists y \forall x$ (succ(x, y) $\wedge$ ($\exists z$ succ(x, z) $\Rightarrow$ equal (y, z)))
(*d*) $\forall x \exists y$ succ (x, y)

52. $\alpha - \beta$ cutoffs are applied to ______
(*a*) Depth first search
(*b*) Best first search
(*c*) Minimax search
(*d*) Breadth first search

53. Assume that each alphabet can have a value between 0 to 9 in a cryptoarithmetic problem

```
  CROSS
 +ROADS
--------
 DANGER
--------
```

Which of the following statement is true?
(*i*) No two alphabets can have the same numeric value.
(*ii*) Any two alphabets may have the same numeric value.
(*iii*) D = 0
(*iv*) D = 1
(*a*) (*i*) and (*iii*) (*b*) (*i*) and (*iv*)
(*c*) (*ii*) and (*iii*) (*d*) (*ii*) and (*iv*)

54. Which of the following is not a part of an expert system shell?
(*a*) Knowledge Base
(*b*) Inference Engine
(*c*) Explanation Facility
(*d*) None of the above

55. The Blocks World Problem in Artificial Intelligence is normally discussed to explain a ______
(*a*) Search technique
(*b*) Planning system
(*c*) Constraint satisfaction system
(*d*) Knowledge base system

56. Means-Ends Analysis process centres around the detection of difference between the current state and the goal state. Once such a difference is found, then to reduce the difference one applies ______
(*a*) a forward search that can reduce the difference.
(*b*) a backward search that can reduce the difference.
(*c*) a bidirectional search that can reduce the difference.
(*d*) an operator that can reduce the difference.

57. Suppose a file of 10,000 characters is to be sent over a line at 2400 bps. Assume that the data is sent in frames. Each frame consists of 1000 characters and an overhead of 48 bits per frame. Using synchronous transmission, the total overhead time is ______.
(*a*) 0.05 second (*b*) 0.1 second
(*c*) 0.2 second (*d*) 2.0 second

58. Which of the following is the size of Network bits and Host bits of Class A of IP address?
(*a*) Network bits 7, Host bits 24
(*b*) Network bits 14, Host bits 16
(*c*) Network bits 15, Host bits 16
(*d*) Network bits 16, Host bits 16

59. Which of the following field of the TCP header tells how many bytes may be sent starting at the byte acknowledged?
(*a*) TCP header length
(*b*) Window size
(*c*) Acknowledgement number
(*d*) Urgent pointer

60. Which of the following is a bit rate of an 8-PSK signal having 2500 Hz bandwidth?
(*a*) 2500 bps (*b*) 5000 bps
(*c*) 7500 bps (*d*) 20000 bps

61. Match the following :

A.	UDP	(*i*)	Message Transfer Protocol
B.	OSPF	(*ii*)	Bit-oriented Protocol
C.	SMTP	(*iii*)	Interior Gateway Routing Protocol
D.	HDLC	(*iv*)	Connectionless Transport Protocol

Codes:

	A	B	C	D
(*a*)	(*iii*)	(*iv*)	(*ii*)	(*i*)
(*b*)	(*iv*)	(*iii*)	(*ii*)	(*i*)
(*c*)	(*iv*)	(*iii*)	(*i*)	(*ii*)
(*d*)	(*iii*)	(*iv*)	(*i*)	(*ii*)

62. Given the IP address 201.14.78.65 and the subnet mask 255.255.255.224. What is the subnet address?
(*a*) 201.14.78.32
(*b*) 201.14.78.64
(*c*) 201.14.78.65
(*d*) 201.14.78.224

63. If an artificial variable is present in the 'basic variable' of optimal simplex table then the solution is ______
(*a*) Alternative solution
(*b*) Infeasible solution

(c) Unbounded solution
(d) Degenerate solution

64. An optimal assignment requires that the minimum number of horizontal and vertical lines that can be drawn to cover all zeros be equal to the number of
(a) rows or columns
(b) rows + columns
(c) rows + columns – 1
(d) rows + columns + 1

65. Which of the following is the minimum cost for an assignment problem given below?

		Jobs			
		A	B	C	D
	I	5	3	2	8
	II	7	9	2	6
Workers	III	6	4	5	7
	IV	5	7	7	8

(a) 13 (b) 16
(c) 17 (d) 18

66. Assume, L is regular language. Let statements S_1 and S_2 be defined as :
S_1 : SQRT(L) = { x| for some y with $|y| = |x|^2$, xy ∈ L}.
S_2 : LOG(L) = { x| for some y with $|y| = 2^{|x|}$, xy ∈ L}.
Which of the following is true?
(a) S_1 is correct and S_2 is not correct.
(b) Both S_1 and S_2 are correct.
(c) Both S_1 and S_2 are not correct.
(d) S_1 is not correct and S_2 is correct.

67. A regular grammar for the language
$L = \{a^n b^m \mid n$ is even and m is even$\}$ is given by
(a) $S \to aSb \mid S_1;\ S_1 \to bS_1a \mid \lambda$
(b) $S \to aaS \mid S_1;\ S_1 \to bSb \mid \lambda$
(c) $S \to aSb \mid S_1;\ S_1 \to S_1ab \mid \lambda$
(d) $S \to aaS \mid S_1;\ S_1 \to bbS_1 \mid \lambda$

68. Given the following productions of a grammar:
$S \to aA \mid aBB;$
$A \to aaA \mid \lambda;$
$B \to bB \mid bbC;$
$C \to B$
Which of the following is true?
(a) The language corresponding to the given grammar is a set of even number of a's.
(b) The language corresponding to the given grammar is a set of odd number of a's.
(c) The language corresponding to the given grammar is a set of even number of a's followed by odd number of b's.
(d) The language corresponding to the given grammar is a set of odd number of a's followed by even number of b's.

69. The language accepted by the non-deterministic pushdown automaton
$M = (\{q_0, q_1, q_2\}, \{a, b\}, \{a, b, z\}, \delta, q_0, z, \{q_2\})$ with transitions
$\delta(q_0\ a, z) = \{(q_1\ a), (q_2\ \lambda)\};$
$\delta(q_1, b, a) = \{(q_1, b)\}$
$\delta(q_1, b, b) = \{(q_1\ b)\},\ \delta(q_1, a, b) = \{(q_2, \lambda)\}$
is
(a) L(abb*a) (b) {a} U L(abb*a)
(c) L(ab*a) (d) {a} U L(ab*a)

70. The language $L = \{a^n b^n a^m b^m \mid n \geq 0, m \geq 0\}$ is
(a) Context free but not linear
(b) Context free and linear
(c) Not Context free and not linear
(d) Not Context free but linear

71. Assume statements S_1 and S_2 defined as:
S_1 : $L_2 - L_1$ is recursive enumerable where L_1 and L_2 are recursive and recursive enumerable respectively.
S_2 : The set of all Turing machines is countable.
Which of the following is true?
(a) S_1 is correct and S_2 is not correct.
(b) Both S_1 and S_2 are correct.
(c) Both S_1 and S_2 are not correct.
(d) S_1 is not correct and S_2 is correct.

72. Non-deterministic pushdown automaton that accepts the language generated by the grammar: $S \to aSS \mid ab$ is
(a) $\delta(q_0, \lambda, z) = \{(q_1, z)\};$
$\delta(q_0, a, S) = \{(q_1, SS)\}, (q_1, B)\}$
$\delta(q_0, b, B) = \{(q_1, \lambda)\},$
$\delta(q_1, \lambda, z) = \{(q_f, \lambda)\}$
(b) $\delta(q_0, \lambda, z) = \{(q_1, Sz)\};$
$\delta(q_0, a, S) = \{(q_1, SS)\}, (q_1, B)\}$
$\delta(q_0, b, B) = \{(q_1, \lambda)\},$
$\delta(q_1, \lambda, z) = \{(q_f, \lambda)\}$
(c) $\delta(q_0, \lambda, z) = \{(q_1, Sz)\};$
$\delta(q_0, a, S) = \{(q_1, S)\}, (q_1, B)\}$
$\delta(q_0, b, \lambda) = \{(q_1, B)\},$
$\delta(q_1, \lambda, z) = \{(q_f, \lambda)\}$
(d) $\delta(q_0, \lambda, z) = \{(q_1, z)\};$
$\delta(q_0, a, S) = \{(q_1, SS)\}, (q_1, B)\}$
$\delta(q_0, b, \lambda) = \{(q_1, B)\},$
$\delta(q_1, \lambda, z) = \{(q_f, \lambda)\}$

73. Match the following :

A. Dangling pointer	(i) Buffer replacement policy
B. Page fault	(ii) Variable-length records

C. List representation (*iii*) Object identifier
D. Toss-immediate (*iv*) Pointer-swizzling

Codes:

	A	B	C	D
(*a*)	(*iii*)	(*iv*)	(*ii*)	(*i*)
(*b*)	(*iv*)	(*iii*)	(*ii*)	(*i*)
(*c*)	(*iv*)	(*iii*)	(*i*)	(*ii*)
(*d*)	(*iii*)	(*iv*)	(*i*)	(*ii*)

74. _______ constraints ensure that a value that appears in one relation for a given set of attributes also appears for a certain set of attributes in another relation.
(*a*) Logical Integrity
(*b*) Referential Integrity
(*c*) Domain Integrity
(*d*) Data Integrity

75. The SQL expression
Select distinct T, branch_name from branch T, branch S
where T.assets>S.assets and S.branch_city="Mumbai" finds the names of
(*a*) All branches that have greater assets than some branch located in Mumbai.
(*b*) All branches that have greater assets than all branches in Mumbai.
(*c*) The branch that has greatest asset in Mumbai.
(*d*) Any branch that has greater assets than any branch in Mumbai.

76. Let A be the set of comfortable houses given as

$$A = \left\{\frac{x_1}{0.8}, \frac{x_2}{0.9}, \frac{x_3}{0.1}, \frac{x_4}{0.7}\right\}$$

and B be the set of affordable houses

$$B = \left\{\frac{x_1}{0.9}, \frac{x_2}{0.8}, \frac{x_3}{0.6}, \frac{x_4}{0.2}\right\}$$

Then the set of comfortable and affordable houses is

(*a*) $\left\{\frac{x_1}{0.8}, \frac{x_2}{0.8}, \frac{x_3}{0.1}, \frac{x_4}{0.2}\right\}$

(*b*) $\left\{\frac{x_1}{0.9}, \frac{x_2}{0.9}, \frac{x_3}{0.6}, \frac{x_4}{0.7}\right\}$

(*c*) $\left\{\frac{x_1}{0.8}, \frac{x_2}{0.8}, \frac{x_3}{0.6}, \frac{x_4}{0.7}\right\}$

(*d*) $\left\{\frac{x_1}{0.7}, \frac{x_2}{0.7}, \frac{x_3}{0.7}, \frac{x_4}{0.9}\right\}$

77. Support of a fuzzy set

$$A = \left\{\frac{x_1}{0.2}, \frac{x_2}{0.15}, \frac{x_3}{0.9}, \frac{x_4}{0.95}, \frac{x_5}{0.15}\right\}$$

within a universal set X is given as

(*a*) $\left\{\frac{x_1}{0.15}, \frac{x_2}{0.15}, \frac{x_3}{0.15}, \frac{x_4}{0.15}, \frac{x_5}{0.15}\right\}$

(*b*) $\left\{\frac{x_1}{0.95}, \frac{x_2}{0.95}, \frac{x_3}{0.95}, \frac{x_4}{0.95}, \frac{x_5}{0.95}\right\}$

(*c*) $\{x_3, x_4\}$
(*d*) $\{x_1, x_2, x_3, x_4, x_5\}$

78. In a single perceptron, the updation rule of weight vector is given by
(*a*) w(n + 1) = w(n) + η[d(n) – y(n)]
(*b*) w(n + 1) = w(n) – η[d(n) – y(n)]
(*c*) w(n + 1) = w(n) + η[d(n) – y(n)]* x (n)
(*d*) w(n + 1) = w(n) – η[d(n) – y(n)]* x (n)

79. _______ refers to the discrepancy among a computed, observed or measured value and the true specified or theoretically correct values.
(*a*) Fault (*b*) Failure
(*c*) Defect (*d*) Error

80. Which logic family dissipates the minimum power?
(*a*) DTL (*b*) TTL
(*c*) ECL (*d*) CMOS

81. Which of the following electronic component is not found in IC's?
(*a*) Diode (*b*) Resistor
(*c*) Transistor (*d*) Inductor

82. A given memory chip has 14 address pins and 8 data pins. It has the following number of locations.
(*a*) 2^8 (*b*) 2^{14}
(*c*) 2^6 (*d*) 2^{12}

83. The instruction: MOV CL, [BX] [DI] + 8 represents the _______ addressing mode.
(*a*) Based Relative
(*b*) Based Indexed
(*c*) Indexed Relative
(*d*) Register Indexed

84. The power dissipation of a flip-flop is 3 mW. The power dissipation of a digital system with 4 flip-flops is given by
(*a*) 3^4 mW (*b*) 4^3 mW
(*c*) 4/3 mW (*d*) 12 mW

85. An astable multivibrator using the 555 timer to generate a square wave of 5 KHz with 70% duty cycle will have
(*a*) R_A = 40.4 KΩ, R_B = 17.25 KΩ, C = 2000 pF
(*b*) R_A = 17.25 KΩ, R_B = 40.4 KΩ, C = 2000 pF
(*c*) R_A = 40.4 KΩ, R_B = 17.25 KΩ, C = 5000 pF
(*d*) None of these

86. A binary ripple counter is required to count up to 16383. How many flipflops are required?

(*a*) 16382 (*b*) 8191
(*c*) 512 (*d*) 14

87. The time complexity of recurrence relation

T(n) = T(n/3) + T(2n/3) + O(n) is

(*a*) O(lg n) (*b*) O(n)
(*c*) O(n lg n) (*d*) $O(n^2)$

88. How many people must there be in a room before there is a 50% chance that two of them were born on the same day of the year?

(*a*) At least 23 (*b*) At least 183
(*c*) At least 366 (*d*) At least 730

89. The number of possible parenthesizations of a sequence of n matrices is

(*a*) O(n) (*b*) θ(n lg n)
(*c*) $\Omega(2^n)$ (*d*) None of the above

90. The time complexity of an efficient algorithm to find the longest monotonically increasing subsequence of n numbers is

(*a*) O(n) (*b*) O(n lg n)
(*c*) $O(n^2)$ (*d*) None of the above

91. Given a binary search trees for a set of n = 5 keys with the following probabilities :

i	0	1	2	3	4	5
pi	–	0.15	0.10	0.05	0.10	0.20
qi	0.05	0.10	0.05	0.05	0.05	0.10

The expected optimal cost of the search is

(*a*) 2.65 (*b*) 2.70
(*c*) 2.75 (*d*) 2.80

92. Given 0-1 knapsack problem and fractional knapsack problem and the following statements :

S_1 : 0-1 knapsack is efficiently solved using Greedy algorithm.

S_2 :Fractional knapsack is efficiently solved using Dynamic programming.

Which of the following is true?

(*a*) S_1 is correct and S_2 is not correct.
(*b*) Both S_1 and S_2 are correct.
(*c*) Both S_1 and S_2 are not correct.
(*d*) S_1 is not correct and S_2 is correct.

93. Equivalence class partitioning approach is used to divide the input domain into a set of equivalence classes, so that if a program works correctly for a value, then it will work correctly for all the other values in that class. This is used _____.

(*a*) to partition the program in the form of classes.
(*b*) to reduce the number of test cases required.
(*c*) for designing test cases in white box testing.
(*d*) all of the above.

94. The failure intensity for a basic model as a function of failures experienced is given as λ(μ) – λ_0[1 – (μ)/(V_0)] where λ_0 is the initial failure intensity at the start of the execution, μ is the average or expected number of failures at a given point in time, the quantity V_0 is the total number of failures that would occur in infinite time.

Assume that a program will experience 100 failures in infinite time, the initial failure intensity was 10 failures/CPU hr. Then the decrement of failures intensity per failure will be

(*a*) 10 per CPU hr.
(*b*) 0.1 per CPU hr.
(*c*) –0.1 per CPU hr.
(*d*) 90 per CPU hr.

95. Improving processing efficiency or performance or restructuring of software to improve changeability is known as

(*a*) Corrective maintenance
(*b*) Perfective maintenance
(*c*) Adaptive maintenance
(*d*) Code maintenance

96. In ______, modules A and B make use of a common data type, but perhaps perform different operations on it.

(*a*) Data coupling (*b*) Stamp coupling
(*c*) Control coupling (*d*) Content coupling

97. Consider the following schemas :

Branch_Schema = (branch_name, assets, city)

Customer_Schema = (cutstomer_name, street, city)

Deposit_Schema = (branch_name, account_number, customer_name, balance)

Borrow_Schema = (branch_name, loan_number, customer_name, amount)

Which of the following tuple relational calculus finds all customers who have loan amount more than ₹12,000?

(*a*) {t(customer_name) | t∈borrow[?] t[amount]>12000}
(*b*) {t|t(customer_name) | t∈borrow[?] t[amount]>12000}
(*c*) {t |[?] ∈ borrow (t(customer_name=s(customer_name))[?] [amount]>12000}
(*d*) {t |[?] ∈ borrow(t(customer_name)[?] s[amount] >12000}

98. Match the following :

A. Create	(*i*) The E-R Model
B. Select	(*ii*) Relationship Model
C. Rectangle	(*iii*) DDL
D. Record	(*iv*) DML

Codes:

	A	B	C	D
(a)	(iii)	(iv)	(i)	(ii)
(b)	(iv)	(iii)	(ii)	(i)
(c)	(iv)	(iii)	(i)	(ii)
(d)	(iii)	(iv)	(ii)	(i)

99. Match the following :

A.	◇R	(i) One to one relationship
B.	—◇R—	(ii) Relationship
C.	—◇R→	(iii) Many to many relationship
D.	←◇R→	(iv) Many to one relationship

Codes:

	A	B	C	D
(a)	(iii)	(iv)	(ii)	(i)
(b)	(iv)	(iii)	(ii)	(i)
(c)	(ii)	(iii)	(iv)	(i)
(d)	(iii)	(iv)	(i)	(ii)

100. Sixty (60) reusable components were available for an application. If only 70% of these components can be used, rest 30% would have to be developed from scratch. If average component is 100 LOC and cost of each LOC is ₹ 14, what will be the risk exposure if risk probability is 80%?

(a) ₹ 25,200 (b) ₹ 20,160
(c) ₹ 25,160 (d) ₹ 20,400

101. Consider the following two function declarations :

(i) int *f( ) (ii) int (*f)( )

Which of the following is true?

(a) Both are identical.
(b) The first is a correct declaration and the second is wrong.
(c) Both are different ways of declaring pointer to a function.
(d) The first declaration is a function returning a pointer to an integer and the second is a pointer to function returning integer.

102. Assume that we have constructor function for both Base and Derived classes. Now consider the declaration :

main ( )
Base *p = new Derived;

In what sequence, the constructor will be executed?

(a) Derived class constructor is followed by Base class constructor.
(b) Base class constructor is followed by Derived class constructor.
(c) Base class constructor is never called.
(d) Derived class constructor is never called.

103. What is the output of the following program?

```
#include<stdio.h>
main( )
{
int a, b = 0;
static int c[10] =
{1, 2, 3, 4, 5, 6, 7, 8, 9, 0};
for (a=0; a<10;++a);
    if ((c[a]%2)= =0) b+=c[a];
printf("%d",b);
}
```

(a) 15 (b) 25
(c) 45 (d) 20

104. A Program contains the following declarations and initial assignments

```
int i = 8, j = 5;
double x = 0.005, y = -0.01;
char c='c', d='d';
```

Determine the value of the following expressions which involve the use of library functions:

`abs(i-2*j); log(exp(x));`
toupper(d)

(a) 2; 0.005; D (b) 1; 0.005; D
(c) 2; 0.005; E (d) 1; 0.005; E

105. MPEG involves both spatial compression and temporal compression. The spatial compression is similar to JPEG and temporal compression removes ______ frames.

(a) Temporal (b) Voice
(c) Spatial (d) Redundant

106. If the data unit is 111111 and the divisor is 1010. In CRC method, what is the dividend at the transmission before division?

(a) 1111110000 (b) 1111111010
(c) 111111000 (d) 111111

107. If user A wants to send an encrypted message to user B. The plain text of A is encrypted with the ______.

(a) Public Key of user A
(b) Public Key of user B
(c) Private Key of user A
(d) Private Key of user B

108. A ______ can forward or block packets based on the information in the network layer and transport layer header.

(a) Proxy firewall
(b) Firewall
(c) Packet filter firewall
(d) Message digest firewall

109. Which of the following graphics devices are known as active graphics devices?

(i) Alphanumeric devices
(ii) Thumb wheels
(iii) Digitizers
(iv) Joystics
(*a*) (*i*) and (*ii*)
(*b*) (*iii*) and (*iv*)
(*c*) (*i*), (*ii*) and (*iii*)
(*d*) (*i*), (*ii*), (*iii*) and (*iv*)

110. A diametric projection is said to be trimetric projection when
(*i*) two of the three foreshortening factors are equal and third is arbitrary.
(*ii*) all of the three foreshortening factors are equal.
(*iii*) all of the three foreshortening factors are arbitrary.
Which of the above is true?
(*a*) (*i*) and (*ii*) (*b*) (*ii*) and (*iii*)
(*c*) (*i*) only (*d*) (*iii*) only

111. Which of the following is/are fundamental method(s) of antialiasing?
(*i*) Increase of sample rate.
(*ii*) Treating a pixel as a finite area rather than as a point.
(*iii*) Decrease of sample rate.
(*a*) (*i*) and (*ii*) (*b*) (*ii*) and (*iii*)
(*c*) (*i*) only (*d*) (*ii*) only

112. The two colour systems—the HSV and HLS are
(*a*) Hue, Saturation, Value and Hue, Lightness, Saturation.
(*b*) High, Standard, Value and High, Lightness, Saturation.
(*c*) Highly, Saturated, Value and Highly, Lightened, Saturation.
(*d*) Highly, Standard, Value and Hue, Lightness, Saturation.

113. The parametric representation of the line segment between the position vectors $P_1(2, 3)$ and $P_2(5, 4)$ is given as
(*a*) $x(t) = 2 + 7t,\ y(t) = 0 \le t \le \propto 3 + 7t$
(*b*) $x(t) = 2 + 10t,\ y(t) = 0 \le t \le 1\ 3 + 12t$
(*c*) $x(t) = 2 + 3t,\ 0 \le t \le 1\ y(t) = 3 + t$
(*d*) $t(x, y) = 14t\ 0 \le t \le 1$

114. Consider the following transformation matrix for rotation (clockwise) :

$$[T] = \begin{bmatrix} \cos\theta & \sin\theta & 0 & 0 \\ -\sin\theta & \cos\theta & 0 & 0 \\ 0 & 0 & 1 & 0 \\ 0 & 0 & 0 & 1 \end{bmatrix}$$

This matrix rotates an object by an angle θ about:
(*a*) X-axis (*b*) Y-axis
(*c*) Z-axis (*d*) All of the above

115. Consider the following sequence of operations:
(*i*) Pointer p_1 is set to point at a new heap-dynamic variable.
(*ii*) Pointer p_2 is assigned p_1's value.
(*iii*) The heap dynamic variable pointed to by p_1 is explicitly de-allocated, but p_2 is not changed by the operation.
This situation leads to which of the following:
(*a*) p_1 becomes a dangling pointer
(*b*) p_2 becomes a dangling pointer
(*c*) Both p_1 and p_2 are now dangling pointers
(*d*) Neither p_1 nor p_2 is now a dangling pointer

116. The programming languages C and C++ are not strongly typed languages because:
(*a*) Both C and C++ allow functions for which parameters are not type checked.
(*b*) Both C and C++ allow functions for which parameters are type checked.
(*c*) Both C and C++ allow functions for which parameters are not type checked and also the union types in these languages are not type checked.
(*d*) Union types in these (C and C++) languages are not type checked.

117. The tracing model in Prolog describes program execution in terms of certain events. These events are
(*a*) call and exit
(*b*) call and fail
(*c*) call, exit and redo
(*d*) call, exit, redo and fail

118. Which of the following statements is not correct with reference to distributed systems?
(*a*) Distributed system represents a global view of the network and considers it as a virtual uniprocessor system by controlling and managing resources across the network on all the sites.
(*b*) Distributed system is built on bare machine, not an add-on to the existing software.
(*c*) In a distributed system, kernel provides smallest possible set of services on which other services are built. This kernel is called microkernel. Open servers provide other services and access to shared resources.
(*d*) In a distributed system, if a user wants to run the program on other nodes or share the resources on remote sites due to their beneficial aspects, user has to log on to that site.

119. A system contains 10 units of resource of same type. The resource requirement and current allocation of these resources for three processes P, Q and R are as follows:

	P	Q	R
Maximum requirement	8	7	5
Current allocation	4	1	3

Now, consider the following resource requests:

(*i*) P makes a request for 2 resource units.

(*ii*) Q makes request for 2 resources units.

(*iii*) R makes a request of 2 resource units.

For a safe state, which of the following options must be satisfied?

(*a*) Only request (*i*)

(*b*) Only request (*ii*)

(*c*) Only request (*iii*)

(*d*) Request (*i*) and (*ii*)

120. Consider the following set of processes with the length of CPU burst time in milliseconds (ms) :

Process	A	B	C	D	E
Burst time	6	1	2	1	5
Priority	3	1	3	4	2

Assume that processes are stored in ready queue in following order :

A – B – C – D – E

Using round robin scheduling with time slice of 1 ms, the average turn around time is

(*a*) 8.4 ms (*b*) 12.4 ms

(*c*) 9.2 ms (*d*) 9.4 ms

121. Consider a main memory with 3 page frames for the following page reference string :

5, 4, 3, 2, 1, 4, 3, 5, 4, 3, 4, 1, 4

Assuming that the execution of process is initiated after loading page 5 in memory, the number of page faults in FIFO and second chance replacement respectively are

(*a*) 8 and 9 (*b*) 10 and 11

(*c*) 7 and 9 (*d*) 9 and 8

122. Which of the following shell scripts will produce the output "my first script"?

(*a*) for i in my first script { echo –i $i}

(*b*) for my first script; do echo –n; done

(*c*) for i in my first script; do echo –i $i; done

(*d*) for n in my first script; do echo –i $i; done

123. The portion of Windows 2000 operating system which is not portable is

(*a*) processor management

(*b*) user interface

(*c*) device management

(*d*) virtual memory management

124. Match the following for Windows Operating System:

A. Hardware abstraction layer — (*i*) Starting all processes, emulation of different operating systems, security functions, transform character based applications to graphical representation.

B. Kernel — (*ii*) Export a virtual memory interface, support for symmetric multiprocessing, administration, details of mapping memory, configuring I/O buses, setting up DMA.

C. Executive — (*iii*) Thread scheduling, interrupt and exception handling, recovery after power failure.

D. Win32 sub-system — (*iv*) Object manager, virtual memory manager, process manager, plug-and-play and power manager.

Codes :

	A	B	C	D
(*a*)	(*i*)	(*iii*)	(*ii*)	(*iv*)
(*b*)	(*iv*)	(*iii*)	(*ii*)	(*i*)
(*c*)	(*ii*)	(*iii*)	(*iv*)	(*i*)
(*d*)	(*iii*)	(*ii*)	(*i*)	(*iv*)

125. Which of the following statements is not true for UNIX Operating System?

(*a*) Major strength of UNIX Operating System is its open standards which enabled large number of organizations ranging from academicia to industries to participate in its development.

(*b*) UNIX kernel uses modules with well specified interfaces and provides advantages like simplified testing and maintenance of kernel. It has better extensibility as the kernel is not monolithic.

(*c*) UNIX is kernel based operating system with two main components viz. process management subsystem and file management subsystem.

(*d*) All devices are represented as files which simplify the management of I/O devices and files. The directories structure used is directed acyclic graph.

126. COCOMO stands for

(*a*) COmposite COst MOdel

(*b*) COnstructive COst MOdel

(*c*) COnstructive COmposite MOdel

(*d*) COmprehensive COnstruction MOdel

127. Match the following :

A. Good quality — (*i*) Program does not fail for a specified time in a given environment

B. Correctness — (*ii*) Meets the functional requirements

C. Predictable — (*iii*) Meets both functional and non-functional requirements

D. Reliable — (*iv*) Process is under statistical control

Codes :

	A	B	C	D
(*a*)	(*iii*)	(*ii*)	(*iv*)	(*i*)
(*b*)	(*ii*)	(*iii*)	(*iv*)	(*i*)
(*c*)	(*i*)	(*ii*)	(*iv*)	(*iii*)
(*d*)	(*i*)	(*ii*)	(*iii*)	(*iv*)

128. While estimating the cost of software, Lines Of Code (LOC) and Function Points (FP) are used to measure which one of the following?
(*a*) Length of code
(*b*) Size of software
(*c*) Functionality of software
(*d*) None of the above

129. A good software design must have
(*a*) High module coupling, High module cohesion
(*b*) High module coupling, Low module cohesion
(*c*) Low module coupling, High module cohesion
(*d*) Low module coupling, Low module cohesion

130. Cyclometric complexity of a flow graph G with n vertices and e edges is
(*a*) V(G) = e+n–2 (*b*) V(G) = e–n+2
(*c*) V(G) = e+n+2 (*d*) V(G) = e–n–2

131. When the following code is executed what will be the value of x and y?

```
int x = 1, y = 0;
y = x++;
```

(*a*) 2,1 (*b*) 2,2
(*c*) 1,1 (*d*) 1,2

132. How many values can be held by an array A(–1,m;1,m)?
(*a*) m (*b*) m^2
(*c*) m(m+1) (*d*) m(m+2)

133. What is the result of the expression (1&2)+(3/4)?
(*a*) 1 (*b*) 2
(*c*) 3 (*d*) 0

134. How many times the word 'print' shall be printed by the following program segment?

```
for (i=1, i<2,i++)
for (j=1,j<2,j++)
for (k=1,k<2,k++)
printf("print/n")
```

(*a*) 1 (*b*) 3
(*c*) 6 (*d*) 8

135. Which of the following is not a type of Database Management System?
(*a*) Hierarchical (*b*) Network
(*c*) Relational (*d*) Sequential

136. Manager's salary details are to be hidden from Employee Table. This Technique is called as
(*a*) Conceptual level Datahiding
(*b*) Physical level Datahiding
(*c*) External level Datahiding
(*d*) Logical level Datahiding

137. A Network Schema
(*a*) restricts to one to many relationship
(*b*) permits many to many relationship
(*c*) stores Data in a Database
(*d*) stores Data in a Relation

138. Which normal form is considered as adequate for usual database design?
(*a*) 2NF (*b*) 3NF
(*c*) 4NF (*d*) 5NF

139. If $D_1, D_2, ...D_n$ are domains in a relational model, then the relation is a table, which is a subset of
(*a*) $D_1 + D_2 + ... + D_n$
(*b*) $D_1 \times D_2 \times ..... \times D_n$
(*c*) $D_1 \cup D_2 \cup ..... \cup D_n$
(*d*) $D_1 - D_2 - .... - D_n$

140. Which of the following addresses is used to deliver a message to the correct application program running on a host?
(*a*) Port (*b*) IP
(*c*) Logical (*d*) Physical

141. In ______ substitution, a character in the plaintext is always changed to the same character in the ciphertext, regardless of its position in the text.
(*a*) polyalphabetic (*b*) monoalphabetic
(*c*) transpositional (*d*) multialphabetic

142. In classful addressing, the IP address 190.255.254.254 belongs to
(*a*) Class A (*b*) Class B
(*c*) Class C (*d*) Class D

143. In hierarchical routing with 4800 routers, what region and cluster sizes should be chosen to minimize the size of the routing table for a three-layer hierarchy?
(*a*) 10 clusters, 24 regions and 20 routers
(*b*) 12 clusters, 20 regions and 20 routers
(*c*) 16 clusters, 12 regions and 25 routers
(*d*) 15 clusters, 16 regions and 20 routers

144. In IPv4 header, the ______ field is needed to allow the destination host to determine which datagram a newly arrived fragments belongs to.
(*a*) identification (*b*) fragment offset
(*c*) time to live (*d*) header checksum

145. Given L_1 = L(a*baa*) and L_2 = L(ab*). The regular expression corresponding to language $L_3 = L_1/L_2$ (right quotient) is given by
(*a*) a*b (*b*) a*baa*
(*c*) a*ba* (*d*) None of the above

146. Given the production rules of a grammar G_1 as
$S_1 \to AB \mid aaB$
$A \to a \mid Aa$

$B \to b$

and the production rules of a grammar G_2 as

$S_2 \to aS_2bS_2 \mid bS_2aS_2 \mid \lambda$

Which of the following is correct statement?

(*a*) G_1 is ambiguous and G_2 is not ambiguous.

(*b*) G_1 is ambiguous and G_2 is ambiguous.

(*c*) G_1 is not ambiguous and G_2 is ambiguous.

(*d*) G_1 is not ambiguous and G_2 is not ambiguous.

147. Given a grammar : $S_1 \to Sc$, $S \to SA \mid A$, $A \to aSb \mid ab$, there is a rightmost derivation $S_1 \Rightarrow Sc \Rightarrow SAC \Rightarrow SaSbc$

Thus, SaSbc is a right sentential form, and its handle is

(*a*) SaS (*b*) bc

(*c*) Sbc (*d*) aSb

148. The equivalent production rules correspon-ding to the production rules

$S \to S\alpha_1 \mid S\alpha_2 \mid \beta_1 \mid \beta_2$ is

(*a*) $S \to \beta_1 \mid \beta_2, A \to \alpha_1 A \mid \alpha_2 A \mid \lambda$

(*b*) $S \to \beta_1 \mid \beta_2 \mid \beta_1 A \mid \beta_2 A, A \to \alpha_1 A \mid \alpha_2 A$

(*c*) $S \to \beta_1 \mid \beta_2, A \to \alpha_1 A \mid \alpha_2 A$

(*d*) $S \to \beta_1 \mid \beta_2 \mid \beta_1 A \mid \beta_2 A, A \to \alpha_1 A \mid \alpha_2 A \mid \lambda$

149. Given a Non-deterministic Finite Automation (NFA) with states p and r as initial and final states respectively and transition table as given below:

	a	b
p	–	q
q	r	s
r	r	s
s	r	s

The minimum number of states required in Deterministic Finite Automation (DFA) equivalent to NFA is

(*a*) 5 (*b*) 4

(*c*) 3 (*d*) 2

150. Which is the correct statement(s) for Non Recursive predictive parser?

S_1 : First(α) = $\{t \mid \alpha \Rightarrow * t\beta$ for some string $\beta\}$ $\Rightarrow *t\beta$

S_2 : Follow(X) = $\{a \mid S \Rightarrow *\alpha Xa\beta$ for some strings α and $\beta\}$

(*a*) Both statements S_1 and S_2 are incorrect.

(*b*) S_1 is incorrect and S_2 is correct.

(*c*) S_1 is correct and S_2 is incorrect.

(*d*) Both statements S_1 and S_2 are correct.

151. Given an open address hash table with load factor $\alpha < 1$, the expected number of probes in a successful search is

(*a*) Atmost $\frac{1}{\alpha}\ln\left(\frac{1-\alpha}{\alpha}\right)$

(*b*) Atmost $\frac{1}{\alpha}\ln\left(\frac{1}{1-\alpha}\right)$

(*c*) Atleast $\frac{1}{\alpha}\ln\left(\frac{1}{1-\alpha}\right)$

(*d*) Atleast $\frac{1}{\alpha}\ln\left(\frac{\alpha}{1-\alpha}\right)$

152. For a B-tree of height h and degree t, the total CPU time used to insert a node is

(*a*) O(h log t) (*b*) O(t log h)

(*c*) $O(t^2h)$ (*d*) O(th)

153. The time complexity to build a heap with a list of n numbers is

(*a*) O(log n) (*b*) O(n)

(*c*) O(n logn) (*d*) $O(n^2)$

154. The value of postfix expression :
8 3 4 + – 3 8 2 / + * 2 $ 3 + is

(*a*) 17 (*b*) 131

(*c*) 64 (*d*) 52

155. Consider the following statements for priority queue :

S_1 : It is a data structure in which the intrinsic ordering of the elements does determine the result of its basic operations.

S_2 : The elements of a priority queue may be complex structures that are ordered on one or several fields.

Which of the following is correct?

(*a*) Both S_1 and S_2 are incorrect.

(*b*) S_1 is correct and S_2 is incorrect.

(*c*) S_1 is incorrect and S_2 is correct.

(*d*) Both S_1 and S_2 are correct.

156. Repository of information gathered from multiple sources, storing under unified scheme at a single site is called as

(*a*) Data mining (*b*) Meta data

(*c*) Data warehousing (*d*) Database

157. The task of correcting and pre processing data is called as

(*a*) Data streaming (*b*) Data cleaning

(*c*) Data mining (*d*) Data storming

158. Using data p=3, q=11, n=pq, d=7 in RSA algorithm find the cipher text of the given plain text SUZANNE

(*a*) BUTAEEZ (*b*) SUZANNE

(*c*) XYZABCD (*d*) ABCDXYZ

159. The relation "divides" on a set of positive integers is ________.

(*a*) Symmetric and transitive

(*b*) Anti symmetric and transitive

(*c*) Symmetric only

(*d*) Transitive only

160. Give as good a big–O estimate as possible for the following functions:
$(n\log n + n^2)(n^3 + 2)$ and $(n! + 2^n)$
$(n^3 + \log(n^2 + 1))$
(*a*) $O(n^5 + 2n^2)$ & $O(n^3 * n!)$
(*b*) $O(n^5)$ & $O(n^3 * 2^n)$
(*c*) $O(n^5)$ & $O(n^3 * n!)$
(*d*) $O(n^5 + 2n^2)$ & $O(n^3 * 2^n)$

161. A test contains 100 true/false questions. How many different ways can a student answer the questions on the test, if the answer may be left blank also.
(*a*) $^{100}P_2$ (*b*) $^{100}C_2$
(*c*) 2^{100} (*d*) 3^{100}

162. Which of the following connected simple graph has exactly one spanning tree?
(*a*) Complete graph
(*b*) Hamiltonian graph
(*c*) Euler graph
(*d*) None of the above

163. How many edges must be removed to produce the spanning forest of a graph with N vertices, M edges and C connected components?
(*a*) M + N – C (*b*) M – N – C
(*c*) M – N + C (*d*) M + N + C

164. Which of the following shall be a compound proposition involving the propositions p, q and r, that is true when exactly two of the p, q and r are true and is false otherwise?
(*a*) $(p \vee q \wedge \neg r) \vee (p \wedge q \wedge r) \wedge (\neg p \wedge q \vee r)$
(*b*) $(p \wedge q \vee r) \wedge (p \wedge q \wedge r) \vee (\neg q \wedge \neg p \wedge \neg r)$
(*c*) $(p \wedge q \wedge \neg r) \vee (p \wedge \neg q \wedge r) \vee (\neg p \wedge q \wedge r)$
(*d*) $(p \vee r \wedge q) \vee (p \wedge q \wedge r) \vee (\neg p \wedge q \wedge r)$

165. The truth value of the statements:
$\exists!xP(x) \rightarrow \exists xP(x)$ and $\exists!x\neg P(x) \rightarrow \neg\forall x P(x)$, (where the notation $\exists!xP(x)$ denotes the proposition "There exists a unique x such that P(x) is true") are:
(*a*) True and False (*b*) False and True
(*c*) False and False (*d*) True and True

166. How many different Boolean functions of degree 4 are there?
(*a*) 2^4 (*b*) 2^8
(*c*) 2^{12} (*d*) 2^{16}

167. A Boolean operator *s* is defined as follows:
$1 \ominus 1 = 1, 1 \ominus 0 = 0, 0 \ominus 1 = 0$ and $0 \ominus 0 = 1$
What will be the truth value of the expression $(x \ominus y) \ominus z = x \ominus (y \ominus z)$?
(*a*) Always false
(*b*) Always true
(*c*) Sometimes true
(*d*) True when x, y, z are all true

168. Which one of the following is decimal value of a signed binary number 1101010, if it is in 2's complement form?
(*a*) – 42 (*b*) – 22
(*c*) – 21 (*d*) – 106

169. A set of processors $P_1, P_2, ..., P_k$ can execute in parallel if Bernstein's conditions are satisfied on a pairwise basis; that is
$P_1 \| P_2 \| P_3 \| ..... \| P_k$ if and only if :
(*a*) $P_i \| P_j$ for all $i \neq j$
(*b*) $P_i \| P_j$ for all $i = j+1$
(*c*) $P_i \| P_j$ for all $i \leq j$
(*d*) $P_i \| P_j$ for all $i \geq j$

170. When a mobile telephone physically moves from one to another cell, the base station transfers ownership to the cell getting strongest signal. This process is known as ________.
(*a*) handoff
(*b*) mobile switching
(*c*) mobile routing
(*d*) cell switching

171. A virtual memory based memory management algorithm partially swaps out a process. This is an example of
(*a*) short term scheduling
(*b*) long term scheduling
(*c*) medium term scheduling
(*d*) mutual exclusion

172. Assuming that the disk head is located initially at 32, find the number of disk moves required with FCFS if the disk queue of I/O block requests are 98, 37, 14, 124, 65, 67 :
(*a*) 310 (*b*) 324
(*c*) 320 (*d*) 321

173. Let the page fault service time be 10 millisecond (ms) in a computer with average memory access time being 20 nanosecond (ns). If one page fault is generated for every 10^6 memory accesses, what is the effective access time for memory?
(*a*) 21 ns (*b*) 23 ns
(*c*) 30 ns (*d*) 35 ns

174. Consider the following UNIX command:
sort <in> temp; head – 30 <temp; rm temp
Which of the following functions shall be performed by this command?
(*a*) Sort, taking the input from "temp", prints 30 lines from temp and delete the file temp
(*b*) Sort the file "temp", removes 30 lines from temp and delete the file temp
(*c*) Sort, taking the input from "in" and writing the output to "temp" then prints 30 lines from temp on terminal. Finally "temp" is removed.
(*d*) Sort, taking the input from "temp" and then prints 30 lines from "temp" on terminal. Finally "temp" is removed.

175. The *mv* command changes
(*a*) the inode

(*b*) the inode-number
(*c*) the directory entry
(*d*) both the directory entry and the inode

176. The Software Maturity Index (SMI) is defined as

$SMI = [M_f - (F_a + F_c + F_d)] / M_f$

Where

M_f = the number of modules in the current release.

F_a = the number of modules in the current release that have been added.

F_c = the number of modules in the current release that have been changed.

F_d = the number of modules in the current release that have been deleted.

The product begins to stabilize when
(*a*) SMI approaches 1
(*b*) SMI approaches 0
(*c*) SMI approaches –1
(*d*) None of the above

177. Match the following:

A. Watson-Felix model	(*i*) Failure intensity
B. Quick-Fix model	(*ii*) Cost estimation
C. Putnam resource allocation model	(*iii*) Project planning
D. Logarithmetic-Poisson Model	(*iv*) Maintenance

Codes:

	A	B	C	D
(*a*)	(*ii*)	(*i*)	(*iv*)	(*iii*)
(*b*)	(*i*)	(*ii*)	(*iv*)	(*iii*)
(*c*)	(*ii*)	(*i*)	(*iii*)	(*iv*)
(*d*)	(*ii*)	(*iv*)	(*iii*)	(*i*)

178. ________ is a process model that removes defects before they can precipitate serious hazards.
(*a*) Incremental model
(*b*) Spiral model
(*c*) Cleanroom software engineering
(*d*) Agile model

179. Equivalence partitioning is a ________ method that divides the input domain of a program into classes of data from which test cases can be derived.
(*a*) White-box testing
(*b*) Black-box testing
(*c*) Orthogonal array testing
(*d*) Stress testing

180. The following three golden rules :
(*i*) Place the user in control
(*ii*) Reduce the user's memory load
(*iii*) Make the interface consistent are for
(*a*) User satisfaction
(*b*) Good interface design
(*c*) Saving system's resources
(*d*) None of these

181. Software safety is a ________ activity that focuses on the identification and assessment of potential hazards that may affect software negatively and cause an entire system to fail.
(*a*) Risk mitigation, monitoring and management
(*b*) Software quality assurance
(*c*) Software cost estimation
(*d*) Defect removal efficiency

182. The "PROJECT" operator of a relational algebra creates a new table that has always
(*a*) More columns than columns in original table
(*b*) More rows than original table
(*c*) Same number of rows as the original table
(*d*) Same number of columns as the original table

183. The employee information of an Organization is stored in the relation:

Employee (name, sex, salary, deptname)

Consider the following SQL query

Select deptname from Employee
Where sex = "M"
group by deptname
having avg (salary) > {select avg (salary) from Employee}

Output of the given query corresponds to
(*a*) Average salary of employee more than average salary of the organization.
(*b*) Average salary less than average salary of the organization.
(*c*) Average salary of employee equal to average salary of the organization.
(*d*) Average salary of male employees in a department is more than average salary of the organization.

184. For a database relation R(a, b, c, d) where the domains of a, b, c, d include only the atomic values. The functional dependency $a \rightarrow c$, $b \rightarrow d$ holds in the following relation
(*a*) In 1NF not in 2NF
(*b*) In 2NF not in 3NF
(*c*) In 3NF
(*d*) In 1NF

185. Match the following :

A. RAID 0	(*i*) Bit interleaved parity
B. RAID 1	(*ii*) Non redundant stripping
C. RAID 2	(*iii*) Mirrored disks
D. RAID 3	(*iv*) Error correcting codes

Codes:

	A	B	C	D
(*a*)	(*iv*)	(*i*)	(*ii*)	(*iii*)
(*b*)	(*iii*)	(*iv*)	(*i*)	(*ii*)
(*c*)	(*iii*)	(*i*)	(*iv*)	(*ii*)
(*d*)	(*iii*)	(*ii*)	(*iv*)	(*i*)

186. The golden ratio φ and its conjugate $\overline{\varphi}$ both satisfy the equation
(*a*) $x^3 - x - 1 = 0$ (*b*) $x^3 + x - 1 = 0$
(*c*) $x^2 - x - 1 = 0$ (*d*) $x^2 + x - 1 = 0$

187. The solution of recurrence relation,
T(n) = 2T(floor $(\sqrt{n})$) + log*n* is
(*a*) O(*n* log log log*n*)
(*b*) O(*n* log log*n*)
(*c*) O(log log*n*)
(*d*) O(log*n* log log*n*)

188. In any *n*-element heap, the number of nodes of height *h* is
(*a*) less than equal to $\left\lceil \frac{n}{2^h} \right\rceil$
(*b*) greater than $\left\lceil \frac{n}{2^h} \right\rceil$
(*c*) greater than $\left\lceil \frac{n}{2^{h+1}} \right\rceil$
(*d*) less than equal to $\left\lceil \frac{n}{2^{h+1}} \right\rceil$

189. A data file of 1,00,000 characters contains only the characters g-l, with the frequencies as indicated in table:

	g	h	i	j	k	l
Frequency in thousand	45	13	12	16	9	5

using the variable-length code by Huffman codes, the file can be encoded with
(*a*) 2,52,000 bits (*b*) 2,64,000 bits
(*c*) 2,46,000 bits (*d*) 2,24,000 bits

190. A vertex cover of an undirected graph G(V, E) is a subset $V_1 \subseteq V$ vertices such that
(*a*) Each pair of vertices in V_1 is connected by an edge
(*b*) If (u, v) ∈ E then u ∈ V_1 and v ∈ V_1
(*c*) If (u, v) ∈ E then u ∈ V_1 or v ∈ V_1
(*d*) All pairs of vertices in V_1 are not connected by an edge

191. In a fully connected mesh network with *n* devices, there are ________ physical channels to link all devices.
(*a*) n(n–1)/2 (*b*) n(n+1)/2
(*c*) 2n (*d*) 2n+1

192. The baud rate of a signal is 600 baud/second. If each signal unit carries 6 bits, then the bit rate of a signal is ________.
(*a*) 3600 (*b*) 100
(*c*) 6/600 (*d*) None of the above

193. Match the following :
A. Data link layer (*i*) Flow control
B. Network layer (*ii*) Node to node delivery
C. Transport layer (*iii*) Mail services
D. Application layer (*iv*) Routing

Codes:

	A	B	C	D
(*a*)	(*ii*)	(*i*)	(*iv*)	(*iii*)
(*b*)	(*ii*)	(*iv*)	(*i*)	(*iii*)
(*c*)	(*ii*)	(*i*)	(*iii*)	(*iv*)
(*d*)	(*ii*)	(*iv*)	(*iii*)	(*i*)

194. An image is 1024 * 800 pixels with 3 bytes/pixel. Assume the image is uncompressed. How long does it take to transmit it over a 10-Mbps Ethernet?
(*a*) 196.6 seconds (*b*) 19.66 seconds
(*c*) 1.966 seconds (*d*) 0.1966 seconds

195. The ________ measures the relative strengths of two signals or a signal at two different points.
(*a*) frequency (*b*) attenuation
(*c*) throughput (*d*) decibel

196. Which one of the following media is multidrop?
(*a*) Shielded Twisted pair cable
(*b*) Unshielded Twisted pair cable
(*c*) Thick Coaxial cable
(*d*) Fiber Optic cable

197. What is the baud rate of the standard 10 Mbps Ethernet?
(*a*) 10 megabaud (*b*) 20 megabaud
(*c*) 30 megabaud (*d*) 40 megabaud

198. At any iteration of simplex method, if Δ_j ($Z_j - C_j$) corresponding to any non-basic variable X_j is obtained as zero, the solution under the test is
(*a*) Degenerate solution
(*b*) Unbounded solution
(*c*) Alternative solution
(*d*) Optimal solution

199. A basic feasible solution to a m-origin, n-destination transportation problem is said to be ________ if the number of positive allocations are less than m + n – 1.
(*a*) degenerate (*b*) non-degenerate
(*c*) unbounded (*d*) unbalanced

200. The total transportation cost in an initial basic feasible solution to the following transportation problem using Vogel's Approximation method is

	W_1	W_2	W_3	W_4	W_5	Supply
F_1	4	2	3	2	6	8
F_2	5	4	5	2	1	12
F_3	6	5	4	7	3	14
Demand	4	4	6	8	8	

(*a*) 76 (*b*) 80
(*c*) 90 (*d*) 96

201. An actor in an animation is a small program invoked ________ per frame to determine the characteristics of some object in the animation.

(*a*) once (*b*) twice
(*c*) 30 times (*d*) 60 times

202. Bresenham line drawing algorithm is attractive because it uses
(*a*) Real arithmetic only
(*b*) Integer arithmetic only
(*c*) Floating point arithmetic
(*d*) Real and integer arithmetic

203. The refresh rate above which a picture stops flickering and fuses into a steady image is called ________.
(*a*) Crucial fusion frequency
(*b*) Current frequency fusion
(*c*) Critical fusion frequency
(*d*) Critically diffused frequency

204. In homogenous coordinate system (x, y, z) the points with $z = 0$ are called
(*a*) Cartesian points
(*b*) Parallel points
(*c*) Origin point
(*d*) Point at infinity

205. If 40 black lines interleaved with 40 white lines can be distinguished across one inch, the resolution is
(*a*) 40 line-pairs per inch
(*b*) 80 line-pairs per inch
(*c*) 1600 lines per inch
(*d*) 40 lines per inch

206. Images tend to be very large collection of data. The size of memory required for a 1024 by 1024 image in which the colour of each pixel is represented by a n-bit number, (in an 8 bit machines) is
(*a*) n × 8 MB
(*b*) n / 8 MB
(*c*) (1024 × 1024) / 8 MB
(*d*) 1024 MB

207. Arrays in C language can have ________ with reference to memory representation.
(*a*) n-subscripts
(*b*) two-subscripts
(*c*) only one subscript
(*d*) three subscripts only

208. Refer the points as listed below :
A. What are the operator precedence rules?
B. What are the operator associativity rules?
C. What is the order of operand evaluation?
D. Are there restrictions on operand evaluation side effects?

Which of the above must be considered as primary design issues for arithmetic expressions?
(*a*) A, B and C (*b*) A, C and D
(*c*) A, B and D (*d*) A, B, C and D

209. Horn clauses are special kinds of propositions which can be described as
(*a*) Single atomic proposition on left side.
(*b*) Single or multiple atomic proposition on left side.
(*c*) A single atomic proposition on left side and a single atomic proposition on right side.
(*d*) A single atomic proposition on left side or an empty left side.

210. Which of the following is/are the fundamental semantic model(s) of parameter passing?
(*a*) in mode (*b*) out mode
(*c*) in-out mode (*d*) all of the above

211. The grammar with production rules $S \rightarrow aSb \mid SS \mid \lambda$ generates language L given by :
(*a*) $L = \{w \in \{a, b\}^* \mid n_a(w) = n_b(w)$ and $n_a(v) \geq n_b(v)$ where v is any prefix of w$\}$
(*b*) $L = \{w \in \{a, b\}^* \mid n_a(w) = n_b(w)$ and $n_a(v) \leq n_b(v)$ where v is any prefix of w$\}$
(*c*) $L = \{w \in \{a, b\}^* \mid n_a(w) \neq n_b(w)$ and $n_a(v) \geq n_b(v)$ where v is any prefix of w$\}$
(*d*) $L = \{w \in \{a, b\}^* \mid n_a(w) \neq n_b(w)$ and $n_a(v) \leq n_b(v)$ where v is any prefix of w$\}$

212. A pushdown automation $M = (Q, \Sigma, \Gamma, \delta, q_0, z, F)$ is set to be deterministic subject to which of the following condition(s), for every
$q \in Q$, $a \in \Sigma \cup \{\lambda\}$ and $b \in \Gamma$
(s_1) $\delta(q, a, b)$ contains at most one element
(s_2) if $\delta(q, \lambda, b)$ is not empty then $\delta(q, c, b)$ must be empty for every $c \in \Sigma$
(*a*) only s_1 (*b*) only s_2
(*c*) both s_1 and s_2 (*d*) neither s_1 nor s_2

213. For every context free grammar (G) there exists an algorithm that passes any $w \in L(G)$ in number of steps proportional to
(*a*) $\ln|w|$ (*b*) $|w|$
(*c*) $|w|^2$ (*d*) $|w|^3$

214. Match the following :

A.	Context sensitive language	(*i*)	Deterministic finite automation
B.	Regular grammar	(*ii*)	Recursive enumerable
C.	Context free grammar	(*iii*)	Recursive language
D.	Unrestricted grammar	(*iv*)	Pushdown automation

Codes:

	A	B	C	D
(*a*)	(*ii*)	(*i*)	(*iv*)	(*iii*)
(*b*)	(*iii*)	(*iv*)	(*i*)	(*ii*)
(*c*)	(*iii*)	(*i*)	(*iv*)	(*ii*)
(*d*)	(*ii*)	(*iv*)	(*i*)	(*iii*)

215. The statements S_1 and S_2 are given as :
S1 : Context sensitive languages are closed under intersection, concatenation, substitution and inverse homomorphism.

S2 : Context free languages are closed under complementation, substitution and homomorphism.

Which of the following is correct statement?
(*a*) Both S_1 and S_2 are correct.
(*b*) S_1 is correct and S_2 is not correct.
(*c*) S_1 is not correct and S_2 is correct.
(*d*) Both S_1 and S_2 are not correct.

216. Which one of the following is not an addressing mode?
(*a*) Register indirect
(*b*) Autoincrement
(*c*) Relative indexed
(*d*) Immediate operand

217. Computers can have instruction formats with
(*a*) only two address and three address instructions
(*b*) only one address and two address instructions
(*c*) only one address, two address and three address instructions
(*d*) zero address, one address, two address and three address instructions

218. Which is not a typical program control instruction?
(*a*) BR (*b*) JMP
(*c*) SHL (*d*) TST

219. Interrupt which arises from illegal or erroneous use of an instruction or data is
(*a*) Software interrupt
(*b*) Internal interrupt
(*c*) External interrupt
(*d*) All of the above

220. The simplified function in product of sums of Boolean function F(W, X, Y, Z) = Σ(0, 1, 2, 5, 8, 9, 10) is
(*a*) (W' + X') (Y' + Z') (X' + Z)
(*b*) (W' + X') (Y' + Z') (X' + Z')
(*c*) (W' + X') (Y' + Z) (X' + Z)
(*d*) (W' + X') (Y + Z') (X' + Z)

221. Match the following :

A.	TTL	(*i*)	High component density
B.	ECL	(*ii*)	Low power consumption
C.	MOS	(*iii*)	Evolution of "diode-transistor-logic"
D.	CMOS	(*iv*)	High speed digital circuits

Codes:

	A	B	C	D
(*a*)	(*iii*)	(*ii*)	(*i*)	(*iv*)
(*b*)	(*i*)	(*iv*)	(*iii*)	(*ii*)
(*c*)	(*iii*)	(*iv*)	(*i*)	(*ii*)
(*d*)	(*i*)	(*ii*)	(*iii*)	(*iv*)

222. Match the following :

A.	Foreign keys	(*i*)	Domain constraint
B.	Private key	(*ii*)	Referential integrity
C.	Event control action model	(*iii*)	Encryption
D.	Data security	(*iv*)	Trigger

Codes:

	A	B	C	D
(*a*)	(*iii*)	(*ii*)	(*i*)	(*iv*)
(*b*)	(*ii*)	(*i*)	(*iv*)	(*iii*)
(*c*)	(*iii*)	(*iv*)	(*i*)	(*ii*)
(*d*)	(*i*)	(*ii*)	(*iii*)	(*iv*)

223. When an array is passed as a parameter to a function which of the following statements is correct?
(*a*) The function can change values in the original array.
(*b*) The function cannot change values in the original array.
(*c*) Results in compilation error.
(*d*) Results in runtime error.

224. Suppose you want to delete the name that occurs before "Vivek" in an alphabetical listing. Which of the following data structures shall be most efficient for this operation?
(*a*) Circular linked list
(*b*) Doubly linked list
(*c*) Linked list
(*d*) Dequeue

225. What will be the output of the following segment of the program?

```
main( )
{
    char *s = "hello world";
    int i = 7;
    printf("%, *s", i, s);
}
```

(*a*) Syntax error (*b*) hello w
(*c*) hello (*d*) None of these

226. Trace the error :

```
void main( )
{
    int *b, &a;
    *b = 20
    printf("%d, %d", a, *b)
}
```

(*a*) No error (*b*) Logical error
(*c*) Syntax error (*d*) Semantic error

227. Match the following :

A.	calloc( )	(*i*)	Frees previously allocated space
B.	free( )	(*ii*)	Modifies previously allocated space
C.	malloc( )	(*iii*)	Allocates space for array
D.	realloc( )	(*iv*)	Allocates requested size of space

Codes:

	A	B	C	D
(a)	(iii)	(i)	(iv)	(ii)
(b)	(iii)	(ii)	(i)	(iv)
(c)	(iii)	(iv)	(i)	(ii)
(d)	(iv)	(ii)	(iii)	(i)

228. Binary symmetric channel uses
(a) Half duplex protocol
(b) Full duplex protocol
(c) Bit oriented protocol
(d) None of the above

229. Hamming distance between 100101000110 and 110111101101 is
(a) 3 (b) 4
(c) 5 (d) 6

230. Given code word 1110001010 is to be transmitted with even parity check bit. The encoded word to be transmitted for this code is
(a) 11100010101 (b) 11100010100
(c) 1110001010 (d) 111000101

231. The number of distinct binary images which can be generated from a given binary image of right $M \times N$ are
(a) $M + N$ (b) $M \times N$
(c) 2^{M+N} (d) 2^{MN}

232. If $f(x, y)$ is a digital image, then x, y and amplitude values of f are
(a) Finite
(b) Infinite
(c) Neither finite nor infinite
(d) None of the above

233. Consider the following processes with time slice of 4 milliseconds (I/O requests are ignored) :

Process	A	B	C	D
Arrival time	0	1	2	3
CPU cycle	8	4	9	5

The average turn around time of these processes will be
(a) 19.25 milliseconds
(b) 18.25 milliseconds
(c) 19.5 milliseconds
(d) 18.5 milliseconds

234. A job has four pages A, B, C, D and the main memory has two page frames only. The job needs to process its pages in following order :
ABACABDBACD
Assuming that a page interrupt occurs when a new page is brought in the main memory, irrespective of whether the page is swapped out or not. The number of page interrupts in FIFO and LRU page replacement algorithms are
(a) 9 and 7 (b) 7 and 6
(c) 9 and 8 (d) 8 and 6

235. Suppose S and Q are two semaphores initialized to 1. P1 and P2 are two processes which are sharing resources.

P1 has statements	**P2 has statements**
wait(S) ;	wait(Q) ;
wait(Q) ;	wait(S) ;
critical-section 1;	critical-section 2;
signal(S) ;	signal(Q) ;
signal(Q) ;	signal(S) ;

Their execution may sometimes lead to an undesirable situation called
(a) Starvation (b) Race condition
(c) Multithreading (d) Deadlock

236. An operating system using banker's algorithm for deadlock avoidance has ten dedicated devices (of same type) and has three processes P1, P2 and P3 with maximum resource requirements of 4, 5 and 8 respectively. There are two states of allocation of devices as follows :

State 1	Processes	P1	P2	P3
	Devices allocated	2	3	4
State 2	Processes	P1	P2	P3
	Devices allocated	0	2	4

Which of the following is correct?
(a) State 1 is unsafe and state 2 is safe.
(b) State 1 is safe and state 2 is unsafe.
(c) Both, state 1 and state 2 are safe.
(d) Both, state 1 and state 2 are unsafe.

237. Let the time taken to switch between user mode and kernel mode of execution be T1 while time taken to switch between two user processes be T2. Which of the following is correct?
(a) T1 < T2
(b) T1 > T2
(c) T1 = T2
(d) Nothing can be said about the relation between T1 and T2.

238. Working set model is used in memory management to implement the concept of
(a) Swapping
(b) Principal of Locality
(c) Segmentation
(d) Thrashing

239. A UNIX file system has 1 KB block size and 4-byte disk addresses. What is the maximum file size if the inode contains ten direct block entries, one single indirect block entry, one double indirect block entry and one triple indirect block entry?
(a) 30 GB (b) 64 GB
(c) 16 GB (d) 1 GB

240. A thread is usually defined as a light weight process because an Operating System (OS) maintains smaller data structure for a thread than for a process. In relation to this, which of the following statement is correct?

(*a*) OS maintains only scheduling and accounting information for each thread.
(*b*) OS maintains only CPU registers for each thread.
(*c*) OS does not maintain a separate stack for each thread.
(*d*) OS does not maintain virtual memory state for each thread.

241. The versions of windows operating system like windows XP and window Vista uses following file system :

(*a*) FAT-16
(*b*) FAT-32
(*c*) NTFS (NT File System)
(*d*) All of the above

242. Which one of the following is a correct implementation of the metapredicate "not" in PROLOG (Here G represents a goal)?

(*a*) not(G):– !, call(G), fail. not(G).
(*b*) not(G):– call(G), !, fail. not(G).
(*c*) not(G):– call(G), fail, !. not(G).
(*d*) not(G):– call(G), fail. not(G):– !.

243. Which one of the following is not an informed search technique?

(*a*) Hill climbing search
(*b*) Best first search
(*c*) A* search
(*d*) Depth first search

244. If we convert

$\exists u\ \forall v\ \forall x\ \exists y\ (P(f(u),v,x,y) \rightarrow Q(u,v,y))$ to

$\forall v\ \forall x\ (P(f(a),v,x,g(v,x)) \rightarrow Q(a,v,g(v,x)))$

This process is known as

(*a*) Simplification (*b*) Unification
(*c*) Skolemization (*d*) Resolution

245. Given two jugs of capacities 5 litres and 3 litres with no measuring markers on them. Assume that there is endless supply of water. Then the minimum number of states to measure 4 litres water will be

(*a*) 3 (*b*) 4
(*c*) 5 (*d*) 7

246. The map colouring problem can be solved using which of the following technique?

(*a*) Means-end analysis
(*b*) Constraint satisfaction
(*c*) AO* search
(*d*) Breadth first search

247. Which of the following is a knowledge representation technique used to represent knowledge about stereotype situation?

(*a*) Semantic network
(*b*) Frames
(*c*) Scripts
(*d*) Conceptual Dependency

248. A fuzzy set A on R is ________ iff

$A(\lambda x_1 + (1 - \lambda)x_2) \geq \min [A(x_1), A(x_2)]$

for all $x_1, x_2 \in R$ and all $\lambda \in [0, 1]$, where min denotes the minimum operator.

(*a*) Support (*b*) α-cut
(*c*) Convex (*d*) Concave

249. If A and B are two fuzzy sets with membership functions

$\mu_A(x) = \{0.6, 0.5, 0.1, 0.7, 0.8\}$

$\mu_B(x) = \{0.9, 0.2, 0.6, 0.8, 0.5\}$

Then the value of $\mu_{\overline{A \cup B}}(x)$ will be

(*a*) {0.9, 0.5, 0.6, 0.8, 0.8}
(*b*) {0.6, 0.2, 0.1, 0.7, 0.5}
(*c*) {0.1, 0.5, 0.4, 0.2, 0.2}
(*d*) {0.1, 0.5, 0.4, 0.2, 0.3}

250. Consider a single perception with weights as given in the following figure:

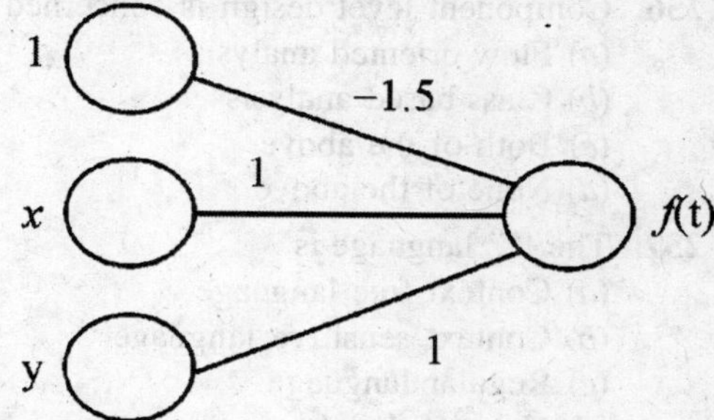

and $f(t)$ defined as

$$f(t) = \begin{cases} 1, & t > 0 \\ 0, & t \leq 0 \end{cases}$$

The above perception can solve

(*a*) OR problem
(*b*) AND problem
(*c*) XOR problem
(*d*) All of the above

251. Consider the circuit shown below. In a certain steady state, Y is at logical '1'. What are possible values of A, B, C?

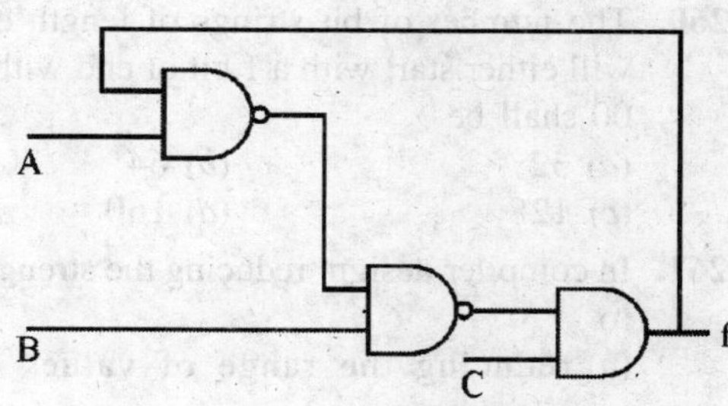

(*a*) A = 0, B = 0, C = 1
(*b*) A = 0, B = C = 1

COMPUTER SCIENCE

(c) A = 1, B = C = 0
(d) A = B = 1, C = 1

252. The worst case time complexity of AVL tree is better in comparison to binary search tree for
(a) Search and Insert Operations
(b) Search and Delete Operations
(c) Insert and Delete Operations
(d) Search, Insert and Delete Operations

253. The GSM network is divided into the following three major systems:
(a) SS, BSS, OSS (b) BSS, BSC, MSC
(c) CELL, BSC, OSS (d) SS, CELL, MSC

254. The power set of the set {ϕ} is
(a) {ϕ} (b) {ϕ, {ϕ}}
(c) {0} (d) {0, ϕ, {ϕ}}

255. If the disk head is located initially at 32, find the number of disk moves required with FCFS if the disk queue of I/O blocks requests are 98, 37, 14, 124, 65, 67.
(a) 239 (b) 310
(c) 321 (d) 325

256. Component level design is concerned with
(a) Flow oriented analysis
(b) Class based analysis
(c) Both of the above
(d) None of the above

257. The 'C' language is
(a) Context free language
(b) Context sensitive language
(c) Regular language
(d) None of the above

258. The Mobile Application Protocol (MAP) typically runs on top of which protocol?
(a) SNMP (Simple Network Management Protocol)
(b) SMTP (Simple Mail Transfer Protocol)
(c) SS7 (Signalling System 7)
(d) HTTP (Hyper Text Transfer Protocol)

259. If a packet arrive with an M-bit value is '1' and a fragmentation offset value '0', then it is ______ fragment.
(a) First (b) Middle
(c) Last (d) All of the above

260. The number of bit strings of length eight that will either start with a 1 bit or end with two bits 00 shall be
(a) 32 (b) 64
(c) 128 (d) 160

261. In compiler design 'reducing the strength' refers to
(a) reducing the range of values of input variables.
(b) code optimization using cheaper machine instructions.
(c) reducing efficiency of program.
(d) None of the above

262. In which addressing mode, the effective address of the operand is generated by adding a constant value to the contents of register?
(a) Absolute (b) Indirect
(c) Immediate (d) Index

263. Which of the following is true?
(a) A relation in BCNF is always in 3NF.
(b) A relation in 3NF is always in BCNF.
(c) BCNF and 3NF are same.
(d) A relation in BCNF is not in 3NF.

264. Given memory partitions of 100 K, 500 K, 200 K, 300 K and 600 K (in order) and processes of 212 K, 417 K, 112 K, and 426 K (in order), using the first-fit algorithm, in which partition would the process requiring 426 K be placed?
(a) 500 K (b) 200 K
(c) 300 K (d) None of these

265. What is the size of the Unicode character in Windows Operating System?
(a) 8-Bits (b) 16-Bits
(c) 32-Bits (d) 64-Bits

266. In which tree, for every node the height of its left subtree and right subtree differ almost by one?
(a) Binary search tree
(b) AVL tree
(c) Threaded Binary Tree
(d) Complete Binary Tree

267. The design issue of Datalink Layer in OSI Reference Model is
(a) Framing
(b) Representation of bits
(c) Synchronization of bits
(d) Connection control

268. Given the following expressions of a grammar
$E \to E * F / F + E / F$
$F \to F - F / id$
Which of the following is true?
(a) * has higher precedence than +
(b) – has higher precedence than *
(c) + and – have same precedence
(d) + has higher precedence than *

269. The maturity levels used to measure a process are
(a) Initial, Repeatable, Defined, Managed, Optimized.
(b) Primary, Secondary, Defined, Managed, Optimized.
(c) Initial, Stating, Defined, Managed, Optimized.
(d) None of the above

270. The problem of indefinite blockage of low-priority jobs in general priority scheduling algorithm can be solved using:

(*a*) Parity bit (*b*) Aging
(*c*) Compaction (*d*) Timer

271. Which API is used to draw a circle?
(*a*) Circle ( ) (*b*) Ellipse ( )
(*c*) Round Rect ( ) (*d*) Pie ( )

272. In DML, RECONNCT command cannot be used with
(*a*) OPTIONAL Set (*b*) FIXED Set
(*c*) MANDATOR Set (*d*) All of the above

273. Coaxial cables are categorized by Radio Government rating are adapted for specialized functions. Category RG-59 with impedance 75 Ω used for
(*a*) Cable TV (*b*) Ethernet
(*c*) Thin Ethernet (*d*) Thick Ethernet

274. RAD stands for ______.
(*a*) Rapid and Design
(*b*) Rapid Aided Development
(*c*) Rapid Application Development
(*d*) Rapid Application Design

275. Suppose that someone starts with a chain letter. Each person who receives the letter is asked to send it on to 4 other people. Some people do this, while some do not send any letter. How many people have seen the letter, including the first person, if no one receives more than one letter and if the chain letter ends after there have been 100 people who read it but did not send it out? Also find how many people sent out the letter?
(*a*) 122 & 22 (*b*) 111 & 11
(*c*) 133 & 33 (*d*) 144 & 44

276. A hash function f defined as f (key) = key mod 13, with linear probing is used to insert keys 55, 58, 68, 91, 27, 145. What will be the location of 79?
(*a*) 1 (*b*) 2
(*c*) 3 (*d*) None of these

277. Which of the following is true while converting CFG to LL(I) grammar?
(*a*) Remove left recursion alone
(*b*) Factoring grammar alone
(*c*) Both of the above
(*d*) None of the above

278. Identify the Risk factors which are associated with Electronic payment system.
(*a*) Fraudulent use of Credit Cards.
(*b*) Sending Credit Card details over internet.
(*c*) Remote storage of Credit Card details.
(*d*) All of the above

279. Which of the following are two special functions that are meant for handling exception, that occur during exception handling itself?
(*a*) Void terminate ( ) and Void unexpected ( )
(*b*) Non void terminate ( ) and void unexpected ( )
(*c*) Void terminate ( ) and non void unexpected ( )
(*d*) Non void terminate ( ) and non void unexpected ( )

280. Which of the following memory allocation scheme suffers from external fragmentation?
(*a*) Segmentation
(*b*) Pure demand paging
(*c*) Swapping
(*d*) Paging

281. Basis path testing falls under
(*a*) system testing (*b*) white box testing
(*c*) black box testing (*d*) unit testing

282. The User Work Area (UWA) is a set of Program variables declared in the host program to communicate the contents of individual records between
(*a*) DBMS & the Host record
(*b*) Host program and Host record
(*c*) Host program and DBMS
(*d*) Host program and Host language

283. Consider the tree given below:

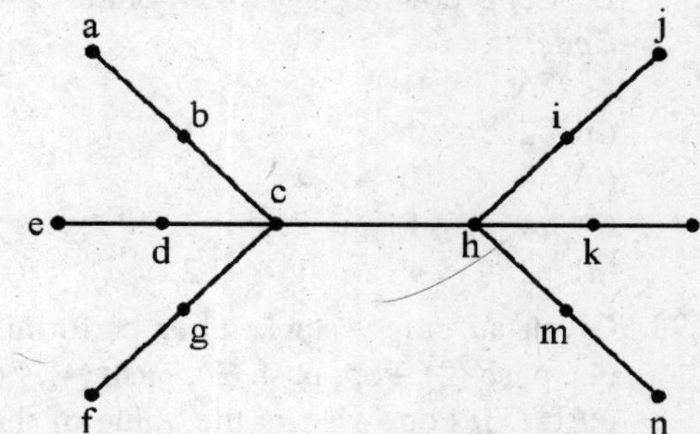

Using the property of eccentricity of a vertex, find every vertex that is the centre of the given tree.
(*a*) d & h (*b*) c & k
(*c*) g, b, c, h, i, m (*d*) c & h

284. The maximum number of keys stored in a B-tree of order *m* and depth *d* is
(*a*) $md + 1 - 1$
(*b*) $\frac{md+1-1}{m-1}$
(*c*) $(m - 1)(md + 1 - 1)$
(*d*) None of these

285. Which of the following is the most powerful parring method?
(*a*) LL(I) (*b*) Canonical LR
(*c*) SLR (*d*) LALR

286. In UNIX, which of the following command is used to set the task priority?
(*a*) init (*b*) nice
(*c*) kill (*d*) PS

287. AES is a round cipher based on the Rijndal Algorithm that uses a 128-bit block of data. AES has three different configurations. ______ rounds with a key size of 128 bits, ______ rounds with a key size of 192 bits and ______ rounds with a key size of 256 bits.

(*a*) 5, 7, 15 (*b*) 10, 12, 14
(*c*) 5, 6, 7 (*d*) 20, 12, 14

288. Match the following IC families with their basic circuits:

A. TTL 1. NAND
B. ECL 2. NOR
C. CMOS 3. Inverter

Code:

	A	B	C
(*a*)	1	2	3
(*b*)	3	2	1
(*c*)	2	3	1
(*d*)	2	1	3

289. Match the following with respect to C++ data types :

A. User defined type 1. Qualifier
B. Built in type 2. Union
C. Derived type 3. Void
D. Long double 4. Pointer

Code:

	A	B	C	D
(*a*)	2	3	4	1
(*b*)	3	1	4	2
(*c*)	4	1	2	3
(*d*)	3	4	1	2

290. Given an empty stack, after performing push (1), push (2), Pop, push (3), push (4), Pop, Pop, push (5), Pop, what is the value of the top of the stack?

(*a*) 4 (*b*) 3
(*c*) 2 (*d*) 1

291. Enumeration is a process of

(*a*) Declaring a set of numbers
(*b*) Sorting a list of strings
(*c*) Assigning a legal values possible for a variable
(*d*) Sequencing a list of operators

292. Which of the following mode declaration is used in C++ to open a file for input?

(*a*) ios : : app (*b*) in : : ios
(*c*) ios : : file (*d*) ios : : in

293. Data Encryption Techniques are particularly used for ______.

(*a*) protecting data in Data Communication System.
(*b*) reduce Storage Space Requirement.
(*c*) enhances Data Integrity.
(*d*) decreases Data Integrity.

294. Let L be a set accepted by a non-deterministic finite automaton. The number of states in non-deterministic finite automaton is |Q|. The maximum number of states in equivalent finite automaton that accepts L is

(*a*) |Q| (*b*) 2|Q|
(*c*) $2^{|Q|} - 1$ (*d*) $2^{|Q|}$

295. What is the result of the following expression?
(1 & 2) + (3 & 4)

(*a*) 1 (*b*) 3
(*c*) 2 (*d*) 0

296. Back propagation is a learning technique that adjusts weights in the neural network by propagating weight changes.

(*a*) Forward from source to sink
(*b*) Backward from sink to source
(*c*) Forward from source to hidden nodes
(*d*) Backward from since to hidden nodes

297. Match the following :

A. TTL (*i*) High fan out
B. ECL (*ii*) Low propagation delay
C. CMOS (*iii*) High power dissipation

Code:

	A	B	C
(*a*)	(*iii*)	(*ii*)	(*i*)
(*b*)	(*i*)	(*ii*)	(*iii*)
(*c*)	(*i*)	(*iii*)	(*ii*)
(*d*)	(*iii*)	(*i*)	(*ii*)

298. ______ is an "umbrella" activity that is applied throughout the software engineering process.

(*a*) Debugging
(*b*) Testing
(*c*) Designing
(*d*) Software quality assurance

299. Identify the operation which is commutative but not associative?

(*a*) OR (*b*) NOR
(*c*) EX-OR (*d*) NAND

300. Given a Relation POSITION (Posting-No, Skill), then query to retrieve all distinct pairs of posting-nos. requiring skill is

(*a*) Select p.posting-No, p.posting-No
from position p
where p.skill = p.skill
and p.posting-No < p.posting-No

(*b*) Select p_1.posting-No, p_2.posting-No
from position p_1, position p_2
where p_1.skill = p_2.skill

(*c*) Select p1.posting-No, p2.posting-No
from position p_1, position p_2
where p_1.skill = p_2.skill
and p_1.posting-No < p_2.posting-No

(*d*) Select p_1.posting-No, p_2.posting-No
from position p_1, position p_2
where p_1.skill = p_2.skill
and p_1.posting-No = p_2.posting-No

301. Eco system is a Frame work for
(*a*) Building a Computer System
(*b*) Building Internet Market
(*c*) Building Offline Market
(*d*) Building Market

302. The efficiency (E) and speed up (sp) for Multiprocessor with p processors satisfies:
(*a*) $E \leq p$ and $s_p \leq p$
(*b*) $E \leq 1$ and $s_p \leq p$
(*c*) $E \leq p$ and $s_p \leq 1$
(*d*) $E \leq 1$ and $s_p \leq 1$

303. Match the following:

List-I	*List-II*
A. Critical region	(*i*) Hoares Monitor
B. Wait/signal	(*ii*) Mutual exclusion
C. Working set	(*iii*) Principal of locality
D. Dead lock	(*iv*) Circular wait

Codes:

	A	B	C	D
(*a*)	(*ii*)	(*i*)	(*iii*)	(*iv*)
(*b*)	(*i*)	(*ii*)	(*iv*)	(*iii*)
(*c*)	(*ii*)	(*iii*)	(*i*)	(*iv*)
(*d*)	(*i*)	(*iii*)	(*ii*)	(*iv*)

304. The technique of temporarily delaying outgoing acknowledgements so that they can be hooked onto the next outgoing data frame is known as
(*a*) Bit stuffing (*b*) Piggy backing
(*c*) Pipelining (*d*) Broadcasting

305. ______ is process of extracting previously non known valid and actionable information from large data to make crucial business and strategic decisions.
(*a*) Data Management (*b*) Data base
(*c*) Data Mining (*d*) Meta Data

306. The aspect ratio of an image is defined as
(*a*) The ratio of width to its height measured in unit length.
(*b*) The ratio of height to width measured in number of pixels.
(*c*) The ratio of depth to width measured in unit length.
(*d*) The ratio of width to depth measured in number of pixels.

307. Which of the following features will characterize an OS as multiprogrammed OS?
A. More than one program may be loaded into main memory at the same time.
B. If a program waits for certain event another program is immediately scheduled.
C. If the execution of a program terminates, another program is immediately scheduled.
(*a*) A only (*b*) A and B only
(*c*) A and C only (*d*) A, B and C only

308. Using RSA algorithm, what is the value of cipher text C, if the plain text M = 5 and p = 3, q = 11 & d = 7?
(*a*) 33 (*b*) 5
(*c*) 25 (*d*) 26

309. You are given an OR problem and a XOR problem to solve. Then, which one of the following statements is true?
(*a*) Both OR and XOR problems can be solved using single layer perception.
(*b*) OR problem can be solved using single layer perception and XOR problem can be solved using self organizing maps.
(*c*) OR problem can be solved using radial basis function and XOR problem can be solved using single layer perception.
(*d*) OR problem can be solved using single layer perception and XOR problem can be solved using radial basis function.

310. Match the following:

List-I	*List-II*
A. Application layer	(*i*) TCP
B. Transport layer	(*ii*) HDLC
C. Network layer	(*iii*) HTTP
D. Data link layer	(*iv*) BGP

Codes:

	A	B	C	D
(*a*)	(*ii*)	(*i*)	(*iv*)	(*iii*)
(*b*)	(*iii*)	(*iv*)	(*i*)	(*ii*)
(*c*)	(*iii*)	(*i*)	(*iv*)	(*ii*)
(*d*)	(*ii*)	(*iv*)	(*i*)	(*iii*)

311. The time complexities of some standard graph algorithms are given. Match each algorithm with its time complexity? (n and m are no. of nodes and edges respectively)

A. Bellman Ford algorithm	(*i*) O (m log n)
B. Kruskals algorithm	(*ii*) $O(n^3)$
C. Floyd Warshall algorithm	(*iii*) O(mn)
D. Topological sorting	(*iv*) O(n + m)

Codes:

	A	B	C	D
(*a*)	(*iii*)	(*i*)	(*ii*)	(*iv*)
(*b*)	(*ii*)	(*iv*)	(*iii*)	(*i*)
(*c*)	(*iii*)	(*iv*)	(*i*)	(*ii*)
(*d*)	(*ii*)	(*i*)	(*iii*)	(*iv*)

312. Let $V_1 = 2I - J + K$ and $V_2 = I + J - K$, then the angle between V_1 & V_2 and a vector perpendicular to both V_1 & V_2 shall be:
(*a*) 90° and (–2I + J – 3K)
(*b*) 60° and (2I + J + 3K)
(*c*) 90° and (2I + J – 3K)
(*d*) None of these

313. Consider a fuzzy set A defined on the interval X = [0, 10] of integers by the membership Junction

COMPUTER SCIENCE

$$\mu_A(x) = \frac{x}{x+2}$$

Then the α cut corresponding to α = 0.5 will be

(*a*) {0, 1, 2, 3, 4, 5, 6, 7, 8, 9, 10}
(*b*) {1, 2, 3, 4, 5, 6, 7, 8, 9, 10}
(*c*) {2, 3, 4, 5, 6, 7, 8, 9, 10}
(*d*) { }

314. Let T(*n*) be the function defined by T(*n*) = 1 and T(*n*) = 2T (*n*/2) + $\sqrt{n}$, which of the following is TRUE?

(*a*) $T(n) = O(\sqrt{n})$ (*b*) $T(n) = O(\log_2 n)$
(*c*) $T(n) = O(n)$ (*d*) $T(n) = O(n^2)$

315. In classful addressing, an IP address 123.23.156.4 belongs to ______ class format.

(*a*) A (*b*) B
(*c*) C (*d*) D

316. The Mandelbrot set used for the construction of beautiful images is based on the following transformation:

$$x_{n+1} = x_n^2 + z$$

Here,

(*a*) Both *x* & *z* are real numbers.
(*b*) Both *x* & *z* are complex numbers.
(*c*) *x* is real & *z* is complex.
(*d*) *x* is complex & *z* is real.

317. Which of the following permutations can be obtained in the output using a stack of size 3 elements assuming that input, sequence is 1, 2, 3, 4, 5?

(*a*) 3, 2, 1, 5, 4 (*b*) 5, 4, 3, 2, 1
(*c*) 3, 4, 5, 2, 1 (*d*) 3, 4, 5, 1, 2

318. In a Linear Programming Problem, suppose there are 3 basic variables and 2 non-basic variables, then the possible number of basic solutions are

(*a*) 6 (*b*) 8
(*c*) 10 (*d*) 12

319. Identify the following activation function:

$$\phi(V) = Z + \frac{1}{1+\exp(-x * V + Y)},$$

Z, X, Y are parameters

(*a*) Step function
(*b*) Ramp function
(*c*) Sigmoid function
(*d*) Gaussian function

320. The no. of ways to distribute *n* distinguishable objects into *k* distinguishable boxes, so that n_i objects are placed into box *i*, *i* = 1, 2, ... *k* equals which of the following?

A. $\dfrac{n!}{n_1! + n_2! + ... + n_k!}$

B. $\dfrac{n_1! + n_2! + ... + n_k!}{n_1!\, n_2!\, n_3! .... n_k!}$

C. $\dfrac{n!}{n_1!\, n_2!\, n_3! .... n_k!}$

D. $\dfrac{n_1!\, n_2! .... n_k!}{n_1! - n_2! - n_3! ..... - n_k!}$

321. How many solutions do the following equation have

$$x_1 + x_2 + x_3 = 11$$

where $x_1 \geq 1$, $x_2 \geq 2$, $x_3 \geq 3$

(*a*) C(7, 11) (*b*) C(11, 3)
(*c*) C(14, 11) (*d*) C(7, 5)

322. Which provides an interface to the TCP/IP suit protocols in Windows95 and Windows NT?

(*a*) FTP Active-X Control
(*b*) TCP/IP Active-X Control
(*c*) Calinsock Active-X Control
(*d*) None of these

323. What are the final values of Q_1 and Q_0 after 4 clock cycles, if initial values are 00 in the sequential circuit shown below:

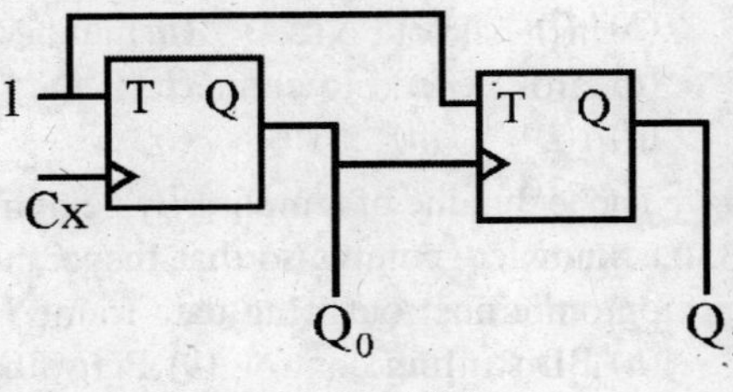

(*a*) 11 (*b*) 10
(*c*) 01 (*d*) 00

324. If dual has an unbounded solution, then its corresponding primal has

(*a*) no feasible solution
(*b*) unbounded solution
(*c*) feasible solution
(*d*) none of these

325. The number of distinct bracelets of five beads made up of red, blue, and green beads (two bracelets are indistinguishable if the rotation of one yield another) is,

(*a*) 243 (*b*) 81
(*c*) 51 (*d*) 47

326. Which are the classifications of data used in Mobile Applications?

(*a*) Private data, User data, Shared data.
(*b*) Public data, User data, Virtual data.
(*c*) Private data, Public data, Shared data.
(*d*) Public data, Virtual data, User data.

327. In an enhancement of a CPU design, the speed of a floating point unit has been increased by 20% and the speed of a fixed point unit has been increased by 10%. What is the overall speed achieved if the ratio of the number of floating point operations to the number of fixed point operations is 2 : 3 and the floating point

operation used to take twice the time taken by the fixed point operation in original design?
(*a*) 1.62 (*b*) 1.55
(*c*) 1.85 (*d*) None of these

328. The initial basic feasible solution to the following transportation problem using Vogel's approximation method is

	D_1	D_2	D_3	D_4	Supply
S_1	1	2	1	4	30
S_2	3	3	2	1	50
S_3	4	2	5	9	20
Demand	20	40	30	10	

(*a*) $x_{11} = 20$, $x_{13} = 10$, $x_{21} = 20$, $x_{23} = 20$, $x_{24} = 10$, $x_{32} = 10$, Total cost = 180
(*b*) $x_{11} = 20$, $x_{12} = 20$, $x_{13} = 10$, $x_{22} = 20$, $x_{23} = 20$, $x_{24} = 10$, Total cost = 180
(*c*) $x_{11} = 20$, $x_{13} = 10$, $x_{22} = 20$, $x_{23} = 20$, $x_{24} = 10$, $x_{32} = 10$, Total cost = 180
(*d*) None of the above

329. 58 lamps are to be connected to a single electric outlet by using an extension board each of which has four outlets. The number of extension boards needed to connect all the light is
(*a*) 29 (*b*) 28
(*c*) 20 (*d*) 19

330. Match the following with respect to the Mobile Computing Architecture.

A.	Downlink control	(*i*)	100 Mbps
B.	Radio communication data rate	(*ii*)	Residency latency (RL)
C.	The average duration of user's stay in cell	(*iii*)	Sending data from a BS to MD
D.	FDDI bandwidth	(*iv*)	2-Mbps

Codes:

	A	B	C	D
(*a*)	(*ii*)	(*i*)	(*iv*)	(*iii*)
(*b*)	(*iii*)	(*iv*)	(*ii*)	(*i*)
(*c*)	(*iv*)	(*iii*)	(*ii*)	(*i*)
(*d*)	(*iv*)	(*iii*)	(*i*)	(*ii*)

331. Which of the following flags are set when 'JMP' instruction is executed?
(*a*) SF and CF (*b*) AF and CF
(*c*) All flags (*d*) No flag is set

332. A thread is a light weight process. In the above statement, weight refers to
(*a*) time
(*b*) number of resources
(*c*) speed
(*d*) All the above

333. The Z-buffer algorithm is used for Hidden surface removal of objects. The maximum number of objects that can be handled by this algorithm shall
(*a*) Depend on the application
(*b*) Be arbitrary no. of objects
(*c*) Depend on the memory availability
(*d*) Depend on the processor

334. The power set of $A \cup B$, where $A = \{2, 3, 5, 7\}$ and $B = \{2, 5, 8, 9\}$ is
(*a*) 256 (*b*) 64
(*c*) 16 (*d*) 4

335. In Win32, which function is used to create Windows Applications?
(*a*) Win APP (*b*) Win API
(*c*) Win Main (*d*) Win Void

336. Suppose a processor does not have any stack pointer registers, which of the following statements is true?
(*a*) It cannot have subroutine call instruction.
(*b*) It cannot have nested subroutine calls.
(*c*) Interrupts are not possible.
(*d*) None of these

337. Everything below the system call interface and above the physical hardware is known as ______.
(*a*) Kernel (*b*) Bus
(*c*) Shell (*d*) Stub

338. Which is not the correct statement?
(*a*) The class of regular sets is closed under homomorphisms.
(*b*) The class of regular sets is not closed under inverse homomorphisms.
(*c*) The class of regular sets is closed under quotient.
(*d*) The class of regular sets is closed under substitution.

339. When a programming Language has the capacity to produce new datatype, it is called as,
(*a*) Overloaded Language
(*b*) Extensible Language
(*c*) Encapsulated Language
(*d*) Abstraction Language

340. Which of the following operating system is better for implementing client-server network?
(*a*) Windows 95 (*b*) Windows 98
(*c*) Windows 2000 (*d*) All of these

341. Consider a system having *m* resources of the same type. These resources are shared by 3 processes A, B and C which have peak demands of 3, 4 and 6 respectively. For what value of m deadlock will not occur?
(*a*) 7 (*b*) 9
(*c*) 10 (*d*) 13

342. The grammar 'G1'
$S \rightarrow OSO| ISI | 0|1| \in$ and the grammar 'G2' is
$S \rightarrow as |asb| X, X \rightarrow Xa | a$.
Which is the correct statement?
(*a*) G1 is ambiguous, G2 is unambiguous
(*b*) G1 is unambiguous, G2 is ambiguous

(c) Both G1 and G2 are ambiguous
(d) Both G1 and G2 are unambiguous

343. Consider n processes sharing the CPU in round robin fashion. Assuming that each process switch takes s seconds. What must be the quantum size q such that the overhead resulting from process switching is minimized but, at the same time each process is guaranteed to get its turn at the CPU at least every t seconds?

(a) $q \le \frac{t-ns}{n-1}$ (b) $q \ge \frac{t-ns}{n-1}$
(c) $q \le \frac{t-ns}{n+1}$ (d) $q \ge \frac{t-ns}{n+1}$

344. The Default Parameter Passing Mechanism is called as
(a) Call by Value (b) Call by Reference
(c) Call by Address (d) Call by Name

345. Which of the following regular expression identities are true?
(a) $(r+s)^* = r^* s^*$ (b) $(r+s)^* = r^* + s^*$
(c) $(r+s)^* = (r^* s^*)^*$ (d) $r^* s^* = r^* + s^*$

346. Two graphs A and B are shown below: Which one of the following statement is true?

A 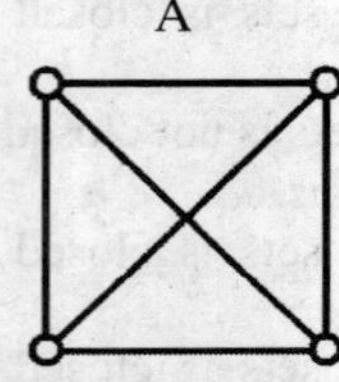 B 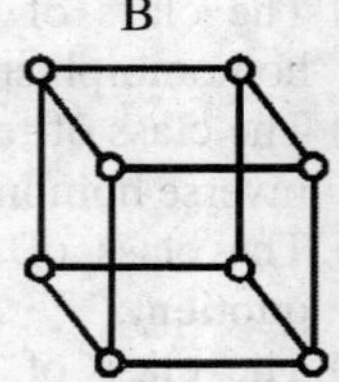

(a) Both A and B are planar.
(b) Neither A nor B is planar.
(c) A is planar and B is not.
(d) B is planar and A is not.

347. The minimum number of states of the non-deterministic finite automation which accepts the language
$\{a\,b\,a\,b^n | n \ge 0\} \cup \{a\,b\,a^n | n \ge 0\}$ is
(a) 3 (b) 4
(c) 5 (d) 6

348. Functions defined with class name are called as
(a) Inline function (b) Friend function
(c) Constructor (d) Static function

349. Let f be the fraction of a computation (in terms of time) that is parallelizable, P the number of processors in the system, and s_p the speed up achievable in comparison with sequential execution – then the s_p can be calculated using the relation:

A. $\frac{1}{1-f-f/P}$ B. $\frac{P}{P-f(P+1)}$
C. $\frac{1}{1-f+f/P}$ D. $\frac{P}{P+f(P-1)}$

350. Which of the following definitions generates the same Language as L, where L = $\{WW^R \mid W \in \{a, b\}^*\}$
(a) S → asb|bsa|∈
(b) S → asa|bsb|∈
(c) S → asb|bsa|asa|bsb|∈
(d) S → asb|bsa|asa|bsb

351. Suppose there are $\log_n$ sorted lists of $n \log_n$ elements each. The time complexity of producing a sorted list of all these elements is (use heap data structure)
(a) O $(n \log \log_n)$ (b) θ $(n \log_n)$
(c) Ω $(n \log_n)$ (d) Ω $(n^{3/2})$

352. Consider the program below in a hypothetical programming language which allows global variables and a choice of static or dynamic scoping

```
int i;
program Main( )
  {
    i = 10;
    call f ( );
  }
  procedure f( )
  {
    int i = 20;
    call g ( );
  }
  procedure g( )
  {
    print i;
  }
```

Let x be the value printed under static scoping and y be the value printed under dynamic scoping. Then x and y are
(a) $x = 10, y = 20$ (b) $x = 20, y = 10$
(c) $x = 20, y = 20$ (d) $x = 10, y = 10$

353. If the parse tree of a word w generated by a Chomsky normal form grammar has no path of length greater than i, then the word w is of length
(a) no greater than 2^{i+1}
(b) no greater than 2^i
(c) no greater than 2^{i-1}
(d) no greater than i

354. The Object Modelling Technique (OMT) uses the following three kinds of model to describe a system
(a) Class Model, Object Model and Analysis Model.
(b) Object Model, Dynamic Model, and Functional Model.
(c) Class Model, Dynamic Model and Functional Model.
(d) Object Model, Analysis Model and Dynamic Model.

355. The factors that determine the quality of a software system are
(*a*) correctness, reliability
(*b*) efficiency, usability, maintainability
(*c*) testability, portability, accuracy, error tolerances, expandability, access control, audit.
(*d*) All of the above

356. If a relation with a Schema R is decomposed into two relations R_1 and R_2 such that $(R_1 \cup R_2) = R_1$ then which one of the following is to be satisfied for a lossless joint decomposition (→ indicates functional dependency)
(*a*) $(R_1 \cap R_2) \to R_1$ or $R_1 \cap R_2 \to R_2$
(*b*) $R_1 \cap R_2 \to R_1$
(*c*) $R_1 \cap R_2 \to R_2$
(*d*) $R_1 \cap R_2 \to R_1$ and $R_1 \cap R_2 \to R_2$

357. Given the following statements:
(*i*) Recursive enumerable sets are closed under complementation.
(*ii*) Recursive sets are closed under complementation.
Which is/are the correct statements?
(*a*) only (*i*) (*b*) only (*ii*)
(*c*) both (*i*) and (*ii*) (*d*) neither (*i*) nor (*ii*)

358. Skolmization is the process of
(*a*) bringing all the quantifiers in the beginning of a formula in FDL.
(*b*) removing all the universal quantifiers.
(*c*) removing all the existential quantifiers.
(*d*) all of the above.

359. Which level of Abstraction describes how data are stored in the data base?
(*a*) Physical level (*b*) View level
(*c*) Abstraction level (*d*) Logical level

360. The transform which possesses the "multi-resolution" property is
(*a*) Fourier transform
(*b*) Short-time-Fourier transform
(*c*) Wavelet transform
(*d*) Karhunen-Loere transform

361. Which one is a collection of templates and rules?
(*a*) XML (*b*) CSS
(*c*) DHTML (*d*) XSL

362. A program P calls two subprograms P_1 and P_2. P_1 can fail 50% times and P_2 40% times. Then P can fail
(*a*) 50% (*b*) 60%
(*c*) 10% (*d*) 70%

363. Third normal form is based on the concept of ______.
(*a*) Closure Dependency
(*b*) Transitive Dependency
(*c*) Normal Dependency
(*d*) Functional Dependency

364. If the Fourier transform of the function $f(x, y)$ is $F(m, n)$, then the Fourier transform of the function $f(2x, 2y)$ is:
A. $\frac{1}{4}F\left(\frac{m}{2}, \frac{n}{2}\right)$ B. $\frac{1}{4}F(2m, 2n)$
C. $\frac{1}{4}F(m, n)$ D. $\frac{1}{4}F\left(\frac{m}{4}, \frac{n}{4}\right)$

365. ______ establishes information about when, why and by whom changes are made in a software.
(*a*) Software Configuration Management.
(*b*) Change Control.
(*c*) Version Control.
(*d*) An Audit Trail.

366. Match the following with respect to HTML tags and usage.

A. CITE	(*i*) Italic representation
B. EM	(*ii*) Represents output from programmes
C. VAR	(*iii*) Represents to other source
d. SAMP	(*iv*) Argument to a programme

Codes:

	A	B	C	D
(*a*)	(*iii*)	(*i*)	(*iv*)	(*ii*)
(*b*)	(*ii*)	(*iii*)	(*i*)	(*iv*)
(*c*)	(*iv*)	(*ii*)	(*iii*)	(*i*)
(*d*)	(*ii*)	(*iii*)	(*iv*)	(*i*)

367. An expert system shell is an expert system without
(*a*) domain knowledge
(*b*) explanation facility
(*c*) reasoning with knowledge
(*d*) all of the above

368. An example of a dictionary-based coding technique is
(*a*) Run-length coding
(*b*) Huffman coding
(*c*) Predictive coding
(*d*) LZW coding

369. Which is the method used to retrieve the current state of a check box?
(*a*) get State ( ) (*b*) put State ( )
(*c*) retrieve State ( ) (*d*) write State ( )

370. Referential integrity is directly related to
(*a*) Relation key (*b*) Foreign key
(*c*) Primary key (*d*) Candidate key

371. You are given four images represented as

$$I_1 = \begin{bmatrix} 0 & 0 \\ 0 & 0 \end{bmatrix}, \quad I_2 = \begin{bmatrix} 0 & 1 \\ 0 & 0 \end{bmatrix},$$

$$I_3 = \begin{bmatrix} 0 & 1 \\ 1 & 0 \end{bmatrix}, \quad I_4 = \begin{bmatrix} 1 & 1 \\ 1 & 0 \end{bmatrix}$$

The value of entropy is maximum for image
(a) I_1 (b) I_2
(c) I_3 (d) I_4

372. A cryptarithmetic problem of the type

SEND
+ MORE
MONEY

Can be solved efficiently using
(a) depth first technique
(b) breadth first technique
(c) constraint satisfaction technique
(d) bidirectional technique

373. Match the following:

A. Supervised learning	(i) The decision system receives rewards for its action at the end of a sequence of steps.
B. Unsupervised learning	(ii) Manual labels of inputs are not used.
C. Reinforcement learning	(iii) Manual labels of inputs are used.
D. Inductive learning	(iv) System learns by example

Codes:

	A	B	C	D
(a)	(i)	(ii)	(iii)	(iv)
(b)	(ii)	(iii)	(i)	(iv)
(c)	(iii)	(ii)	(iv)	(i)
(d)	(iii)	(ii)	(i)	(iv)

374. A* algorithm is guaranteed to find an optimal solution if
(a) h' is always 0.
(b) g is always 1.
(c) h' never overestimates h.
(d) h' never underestimates h.

375. Let $\theta(x, y, z)$ be the statement "$x + y = z$" and let there be two quantifications given as
(i) $\forall x\ \forall y\ \exists Z\ \theta(x, y, z)$
(ii) $\exists Z\ \forall x\ \forall y\ \theta(x, y, z)$
Where x, y, z are real numbers. Then which one of the following is correct?
(a) (i) is true and (ii) is true.
(b) (i) is true and (ii) is false.
(c) (i) is false and (ii) is true.
(d) (i) is false and (ii) is false.

376. The postfix expression AB + CD – * can be evaluated using a
(a) stack (b) tree
(c) queue (d) linked list

377. The post order traversal of a binary tree is DEBFCA. Find out the preorder traversal.
(a) ABFCDE (b) ADBFEC
(c) ABDECF (d) None of the above

378. The branch logic that provides making capabilities in the control unit is known as
(a) Controlled transfer
(b) Conditional transfer
(c) Unconditional transfer
(d) None of the above

379. The number of colours required to properly colour the vertices of every planer graph is
(a) 2 (b) 3
(c) 4 (d) 5

380. Networks that use different technologies can be connected by using
(a) Packets (b) Switches
(c) Bridges (d) Routers

381. Both hosts and routers are TCP/IP protocol software. However, routers do not use protocol from all layers. The layer for which protocol software is not needed by a router is
(a) Layer – 5 (Application)
(b) Layer – 1 (Physical)
(c) Layer – 3 (Internet)
(d) Layer – 2 (Network Interface)

382. In multiuser database if two users wish to update the same record at the same time, they are prevented from doing so by
(a) Jamming (b) Password
(c) Documentation (d) Record lock

383. A binary search tree is a binary tree:
(a) All items in the left subtree are less than root
(b) All items in the right subtree are greater than or equal to the root
(c) Each subtree is itself a binary search tree
(d) All of the above

384. What deletes the entire file except the file structure?
(a) ERASE (b) DELETE
(c) ZAP (d) PACK

385. Which command is the fastest among the following?
(a) COPY TO <NEW FILE>
(b) COPY STRUCTURE TO <NEW FILE>
(c) COPY FILE <FILE 1> <FILE 2>
(d) COPY TO MFILE-DAT DELIMITED

386. B^+ tree are preferred to binary tree in Database because
(a) Disk capacity are greater than memory capacities
(b) Disk access is much slower than memory access
(c) Disk data transfer rates are much less than memory data transfer rate
(d) Disks are more reliable than memory

387. A Transaction Manager is which of the following?

(*a*) Maintains a log of transactions
(*b*) Maintains before and after database images
(*c*) Maintains appropriate concurrency control
(*d*) All of the above

388. Leaves of which of the following trees are at the same level?
(*a*) Binary tree (*b*) B-tree
(*c*) AVL-tree (*d*) Expression tree

389. Which of the following TCP/IP Internet protocol is diskless machine uses to obtain its IP address from a server?
(*a*) RAP (*b*) RIP
(*c*) ARP (*d*) X.25

390. Decryption and encryption of data are the responsibility of which of the following layer?
(*a*) Physical layer (*b*) Data Link layer
(*c*) Presentation layer (*d*) Session layer

391. In which circuit switching, delivery of data is delayed because data must be stored and retrieved from RAM?
(*a*) Space division (*b*) Time division
(*c*) Virtual (*d*) Packet

392. In which Routing Method do all the routers have a common database?
(*a*) Distance vector (*b*) Link state
(*c*) Link vector (*d*) Dijkestra method

393. Page Shift Keying (PSK) Method is used to modulate digital signal at 9600 bps using 16 level. Find the line signals and speed (*i.e.* modulation rate).
(*a*) 2400 bauds (*b*) 1200 bauds
(*c*) 4800 bauds (*d*) 9600 bauds

394. The station to hub distance in which it is 2000 metres.
(*a*) 100 Base-T_x (*b*) 100 Base-F_x
(*c*) 100 Base-T_4 (*d*) 100 Base-T_1

395. Main aim of software engineering is to produce
(*a*) program
(*b*) software
(*c*) within budget
(*d*) software within budget in the given schedule

396. Key process areas of CMM level 4 are also classified by a process which is
(*a*) CMM level 2 (*b*) CMM level 3
(*c*) CMM level 5 (*d*) All of the above

397. Validation means
(*a*) are we building the product right
(*b*) are we building the right product
(*c*) verification of fields
(*d*) None of the above

398. If a process is under statistical control, then it is
(*a*) Maintainable (*b*) Measurable
(*c*) Predictable (*d*) Verifiable

399. In a function oriented design, we
(*a*) minimize cohesion and maximize coupling
(*b*) maximize cohesion and minimize coupling
(*c*) maximize cohesion and maximize coupling
(*d*) minimize cohesion and minimize coupling

400. Which of the following metric does not depend on the programming language used?
(*a*) Line of code
(*b*) Function count
(*c*) Member of token
(*d*) All of the above

401. A/B$^+$ tree index is to be built on the name attribute of the relation STUDENT. Assume that all students names are of length 8 bytes, disk block are of size 512 bytes and index pointers are of size 4 bytes. Given this scenario what would be the best choice of the degree (*i.e.* the number of pointers per node) of the B$^+$ tree?
(*a*) 16 (*b*) 42
(*c*) 43 (*d*) 44

402. The inorder traversal of the tree will yield a sorted listing of elements of tree in
(*a*) Binary tree (*b*) Binary search tree
(*c*) Heaps (*d*) None of the above

403. Mobile IP provides two basic functions.
(*a*) Route discovery and registration
(*b*) Agent discovery and registration
(*c*) IP binding and registration
(*d*) None of the above

404. Pre-emptive scheduling is the strategy of temporarily suspending a gunning process
(*a*) before the CPU time slice expires
(*b*) to allow starving processes to run
(*c*) when it requests I/O
(*d*) to avoid collision

405. In round robin CPU scheduling as time quantum is increased the average turn around time
(*a*) increases (*b*) decreases
(*c*) remains constant (*d*) varies irregularly

406. Resources are allocated to the process on non-sharable basis is
(*a*) mutual exclusion (*b*) hold and wait
(*c*) no pre-emption (*d*) circular wait

407. Cached and interleaved memories are ways of speeding up memory access between CPU's and slower RAM. Which memory models are best suited (i.e. improves the performance most) for which programs?
(*i*) Cached memory is best suited for small loops.
(*ii*) Interleaved memory is best suited for small loops
(*iii*) Interleaved memory is best suited for large sequential code.

(*iv*) Cached memory is best suited for large sequential code.
(*a*) (*i*) and (*ii*) are true.
(*b*) (*i*) and (*iii*) are true.
(*c*) (*iv*) and (*ii*) are true.
(*d*) (*iv*) and (*iii*) are true.

408. Consider the following page trace:
4, 3, 2, 1, 4, 3, 5, 4, 3, 2, 1, 5

Percentage of page fault that would occur if FIFO page replacement algorithm is used with number of frames for the JOB $m = 4$ will be
(*a*) 8 (*b*) 9
(*c*) 10 (*d*) 12

409. Check sum used along with each packet computes the sum of the data, where data is treated as a sequence of
(*a*) Integer (*b*) Character
(*c*) Real numbers (*d*) Bits

410. If an integer needs two bytes of storage, then the maximum value of a signed integer is
(*a*) $2^{16} - 1$ (*b*) $2^{15} - 1$
(*c*) 2^{16} (*d*) 2^{15}

411. Which of the following logic families is well suited for high-speed operations?
(*a*) TTL (*b*) ECL
(*c*) MOS (*d*) CMOS

412. Interrupts which are initiated by an instruction are
(*a*) Internal (*b*) External
(*c*) Hardware (*d*) Software

413. printf("%c", 100);
(*a*) prints 100
(*b*) prints ASCII equivalent of 100
(*c*) prints garbage
(*d*) none of the above

414. For the transmission of the signal, Bluetooth wireless technology uses
(*a*) time division multiplexing
(*b*) frequency division multiplexing
(*c*) time division duplex
(*d*) frequency division duplex

415. Consider the following statements:
I. Recursive languages are closed under complementation.
II. Recursively enumerable languages are closed under union.
III. Recursively enumerable languages are closed under complementation.

Which of the above statements are true?
(*a*) I only (*b*) I and II
(*c*) I and III (*d*) II and III

416. What is the routing algorithm used by RIP and IGRP?
(*a*) OSPF (*b*) Link-state
(*c*) Dynamic (*d*) Dijkestra vector

417. Identify the incorrect statement:
(*a*) The overall strategy drives the E-Commerce data warehousing strategy.
(*b*) Data warehousing in an E-Commerce environment should be done in a classical manner.
(*c*) E-Commerce opens up an entirely new world of web server.
(*d*) E-Commerce security threats can be grouped into three major categories.

418. Reliability of software is directly dependent on
(*a*) quality of the design
(*b*) number of errors present
(*c*) software engineers experience
(*d*) user requirement

419. ______ is not an E-Commerce application.
(*a*) House banking
(*b*) Buying stocks
(*c*) Conducting an auction
(*d*) Evaluating an employee

420. ______ is a satellite based tracking system that enables the determination of person's position.
(*a*) Bluetooth
(*b*) WAP
(*c*) Short Message Service
(*d*) Global Positioning System

421. A complete microcomputer system consists of
(*a*) Microprocessor
(*b*) Memory
(*c*) Peripheral equipment
(*d*) All of the above

422. Where does a computer add and compare data?
(*a*) Hard disk (*b*) Floppy disk
(*c*) CPU chip (*d*) Memory chip

423. Pipelining strategy is called implement
(*a*) instruction execution
(*b*) instruction prefetch
(*c*) instruction decoding
(*d*) instruction manipulation

424. Which of the following data structure is linear type?
(*a*) Strings (*b*) Lists
(*c*) Queues (*d*) All of the above

425. To represent hierarchical relationship between elements, which data structure is suitable?
(*a*) Dequeue (*b*) Priority
(*c*) Tree (*d*) All of the above

426. Consider the following pseudocode segment:

```
K: = 0
   for i1: = 1 to n
      for i2: = 1 to i1
         :
         :
         :
```

```
for i_m : = 1 to i_m - 1
    K: = K+1
```

The value of K after the execution of this code shall be

(*a*) C(n + m – 1, m)
(*b*) C(n – m + 1, m)
(*c*) C(n + m – 1, n)
(*d*) C(n – m + 1, n)

427. In Delta Rule for error minimization

(*a*) weights are adjusted w.r.to change in the output
(*b*) weights are adjusted w.r.to difference between desired output and actual output
(*c*) weights are adjusted w.r.to difference between input and output
(*d*) none of the above

428. The concept of pipelining is most effective in improving performance if the tasks being performed in different stages:

(*a*) require different amount of time
(*b*) require about the same amount of time
(*c*) require different amount of time with time difference between any two tasks being same
(*d*) require different amount with time difference between any two tasks being different

429. What is Granularity?

(*a*) The size of database
(*b*) The size of data item
(*c*) The size of record
(*d*) The size of file

430. Suppose that a given application is run on a 64-processor machine and that 70 per cent of the application can be parallelized. Then the expected performance improvement using Amdahl's law is

(*a*) 4.22 (*b*) 3.22
(*c*) 3.32 (*d*) 3.52

431. If two fuzzy sets A and B are given with membership functions

$\mu_A(x) = \{0.2, 0.4, 0.8, 0.5, 0.1\}$
$\mu_B(x) = \{0.1, 0.3, 0.6, 0.3, 0.2\}$

Then the value of $\overline{A \cap B}$ will be

(*a*) {0.9, 0.7, 0.4, 0.8, 0.9}
(*b*) {0.2, 0.4, 0.8, 0.5, 0.2}
(*c*) {0.1, 0.3, 0.6, 0.3, 0.1}
(*d*) None of these

432. Match the following:

(*i*) OLAP	1. Regression
(*ii*) OLTP	2. Data Warehouse
(*iii*) Decision Tree	3. RDBMS
(*iv*) Neural Network	4. Classification

	(*i*)	(*ii*)	(*iii*)	(*iv*)
(*a*)	2	3	1	4
(*b*)	2	3	4	1
(*c*)	3	2	1	4
(*d*)	3	2	4	1

433. Which level of Abstraction describes what data are stored in the Database?

(*a*) Physical level (*b*) View level
(*c*) Abstraction level (*d*) Logical level

434. The problem that occurs when one transaction updates a database item and then the transaction fails for some reason is ______.

(*a*) Temporary Select Problem
(*b*) Temporary Modify Problem
(*c*) Dirty Read Problem
(*d*) None of these

435. In an image compression system 16384 bits are used to represent 256 × 256 image with 256 gray levels. What is the compression ratio for this system?

(*a*) 1 (*b*) 2
(*c*) 4 (*d*) None of these

436. X.25 is ________ Network.

(*a*) Connection Oriented Network
(*b*) Connection Less Network
(*c*) Either Connection Oriented or Connection Less
(*d*) Neither Connection Oriented nor Connection Less

437. Which of the following can be used for clustering of data?

(*a*) Single layer perception
(*b*) Multilayer perception
(*c*) Self organizing map
(*d*) Radial basis function

438. Which of the following is scheme to deal with deadlock?

(*a*) Time out (*b*) Time in
(*c*) Both (*a*) & (*b*) (*d*) None of the above

439. If the pixels of an image are shuffled then the parameter that may change is

(*a*) Histogram (*b*) Mean
(*c*) Entropy (*d*) Covariance

440. The common property of functional language and logical programming language:

(*a*) Both are declarative
(*b*) Both are based on λ-calculus
(*c*) Both are procedural
(*d*) Both are functional

441. Given the following statements:

(*i*) The power of deterministic finite state machine and non-deterministic finite state machine are same.
(*ii*) The power of deterministic pushdown automaton and nondeterministic pushdown automaton are same.

Which of the above is the correct statement(s)?

(*a*) Both (*i*) and (*ii*) (*b*) Only (*i*)
(*c*) Only (*ii*) (*d*) Neither (*i*) nor (*ii*)

442. Let Q(x, y) denote "$x + y = 0$" and let there be two quantifications given as
(*i*) $\exists y \forall x$ Q(x, y)
(*ii*) $\forall x \exists y$ Q(x, y)
where x & y are real numbers. Then which of the following is valid?
(*a*) (*i*) is true & (*ii*) is false.
(*b*) (*i*) is false & (*ii*) is true.
(*c*) (*i*) is false & (*ii*) is also false.
(*d*) both (*i*) & (*ii*) are true.

443. Consider a schema R(A, B, C, D) and functional dependencies A → B and C → D. Then the decomposition R_1(A, B) and R_2(C, D) is
(*a*) Dependency preserving but not lossless join
(*b*) Dependency preserving and lossless join
(*c*) Lossless join but not dependency preserving
(*d*) Lossless join

444. The quantiser in an image-compression system is a
(*a*) lossy element which exploits the psychovisual redundancy
(*b*) lossless element which exploits the psychovisual redundancy
(*c*) lossy element which exploits the statistical redundancy
(*d*) lossless element which exploits the statistical redundancy

445. Data Warehouse provides
(*a*) Transaction Responsiveness
(*b*) Storage, Functionality Responsiveness to queries
(*c*) Demand and Supply Responsiveness
(*d*) None of the above

446. A* algorithm uses $f' = g + h'$ to estimate the cost of getting from the initial state to the goal state, where g is a measure of the cost of getting from initial state to the current node and the function h' is an estimate of the cost of getting from the current node to the goal state. To find a path involving the fewest number of steps, we should set
(*a*) $g = 1$ (*b*) $g = 0$
(*c*) $h' = 0$ (*d*) $h' = 1$

447. The transform which possesses the highest 'energy compaction' property is
(*a*) Slant transform
(*b*) Cosine transform
(*c*) Fourier transform
(*d*) Karhunen-Loeve transform

448. Which one of the following prolog programs correctly implement "if G succeeds then execute goal P else execute goal θ?"
(*a*) if-else (G, P, θ) :- !, call(G), call(P). if-else (G, P, θ) :- call(θ).
(*b*) if-else (G, P, θ) :- call(G), !, call(P). if-else (G, P, θ) :- call(θ).
(*c*) if-else (G, P, θ) :- call(G), call(P), !. if-else (G, P, θ) :- call(θ).
(*d*) All of the above

449. The ______ memory allocation function modifies the previous allocated space.
(*a*) calloc( ) (*b*) free( )
(*c*) malloc( ) (*d*) realloc( )

450. Which is not the correct statement(s)?
(*i*) Every context sensitive language is recursive.
(*ii*) There is a recursive language that is not context sensitive.
(*a*) (*i*) is true, (*ii*) is false.
(*b*) (*i*) is true and (*ii*) is true.
(*c*) (*i*) is false, (*ii*) is false.
(*d*) (*i*) is false and (*ii*) is true.

451. The mechanism that binds code and data together and keeps them secure from outside world is known as
(*a*) Abstraction (*b*) Inheritance
(*c*) Encapsulation (*d*) Polymorphism

452. Identify the addressing modes of below instructions and match them :

A. ADI	(*i*) Immediate addressing
B. STA	(*ii*) Direct addressing
C. CMA	(*iii*) Implied addressing
D. SUB	(*iv*) Register addressing

	A	B	C	D
(*a*)	(*i*)	(*ii*)	(*iii*)	(*iv*)
(*b*)	(*ii*)	(*i*)	(*iv*)	(*iii*)
(*c*)	(*iii*)	(*ii*)	(*i*)	(*iv*)
(*d*)	(*iv*)	(*iii*)	(*ii*)	(*i*)

453. Which one of the following is not a Greibach Normal form grammar?
(*i*) S → a | bA | aA | bB
A → a
B → b
(*ii*) S → a | aA | AB
A → a
B → b
(*iii*) S → a | A | aA
A → a
(*a*) (*i*) and (*ii*) (*b*) (*i*) and (*iii*)
(*c*) (*ii*) and (*iii*) (*d*) (*i*), (*ii*) and (*iii*)

454. Which of the following IP address class is a multicast address?
(*a*) Class A (*b*) Class B
(*c*) Class C (*d*) Class D

455. While unit testing a module, it is found that for a set of test data, maximum 90% of the code alone were tested with a probability of success 0.9. The reliability of the module is
(*a*) at least greater than 0.9
(*b*) equal to 0.9

(c) atmost 0.81
(d) at least 1/0.81

456. The upper bound of computing time of m colouring decision problem is
(a) $O(nm)$ (b) $O(n^m)$
(c) $O(nm^n)$ (d) $O(n^m m^n)$

457. The equivalent grammar corresponding to the grammar G : $S \rightarrow aA, A \rightarrow BB, B \rightarrow aBb \mid \in$ is
(a) $S \rightarrow aA, A \rightarrow BB, B \rightarrow aBb$
(b) $S \rightarrow a|aA, A \rightarrow BB, B \rightarrow aBb \mid ab$
(c) $S \rightarrow a \mid aA, A \rightarrow BB \mid B, B \rightarrow aBb$
(d) $S \rightarrow a \mid aA, A \rightarrow BB \mid B, B \rightarrow aBb \mid ab$

458. Which one of the following statements is incorrect?
(a) The number of regions corresponds to the cyclomatic complexity.
(b) Cyclometric complexity for a flow graph G is V(G) = N – E + 2, where E is the number of edges and N is the number of nodes in the flow graph.
(c) Cyclometric complexity for a flow graph G is V(G) = E – N + 2, where E is the number of edges & N is the number of nodes in the flow graph.
(d) Cyclometric complexity for a flow graph G is V(G) = P + 1, where P is the number of predicate nodes contained in the flow graph G.

459. Consider a weighted undirected graph with positive edge weights and let (u, v) be an edge in the graph. It is known that the shortest path from source vertex s to u has weight 53 and shortest path from s to v has weight 65. Which statement is always true?
(a) Weight $(u, v) \leq 12$ (b) Weight $(u, v) = 12$
(c) Weight $(u, v) \geq 12$ (d) Weight $(u, v) > 12$

460. Consider the regular expression $(a + b)(a + b) \ldots (a + b)$ (n-times). The minimum number of states in finite automaton that recognizes the language represented by this regular expression contains
(a) n states (b) $n + 1$ states
(c) $n + 2$ states (d) 2^n states

461. Number of binary trees formed with 5 nodes are
(a) 32 (b) 36
(c) 120 (d) 42

462. Are we building the right product? This statement refers to
(a) Verification
(b) Validation
(c) Testing
(d) Software quality assurance

463. The following postfix expression is evaluated using a stack

823^/23* + 51* –

The top two elements of the stack after first * is evaluated
(a) 6, 1 (b) 5, 7
(c) 3, 2 (d) 1, 5

464. The following CFG
$S \rightarrow aB \mid bA, A \rightarrow a \mid as \mid bAA,$
$B \rightarrow b \mid bs \mid aBB$
generates strings of terminals that have
(a) odd number of a's and odd number of b's
(b) even number of a's and even number of b's
(c) equal number of a's and b's
(d) not equal number of a's and b's

465. Consider the following pseudo-code :
If (A > B) and (C > D) then
A = A + 1
B = B + 1
Endif
The cyclomatic complexity of the pseudo-code is
(a) 2 (b) 3
(c) 4 (d) 5

466. Which layer of OSI reference model uses the ICMP (Internet Control Message Protocol)?
(a) Transport layer (b) Data link layer
(c) Network layer (d) Application layer

467. Which one of the following binary search tree is optimal, if probabilities of successful search and unsuccessful search are same?

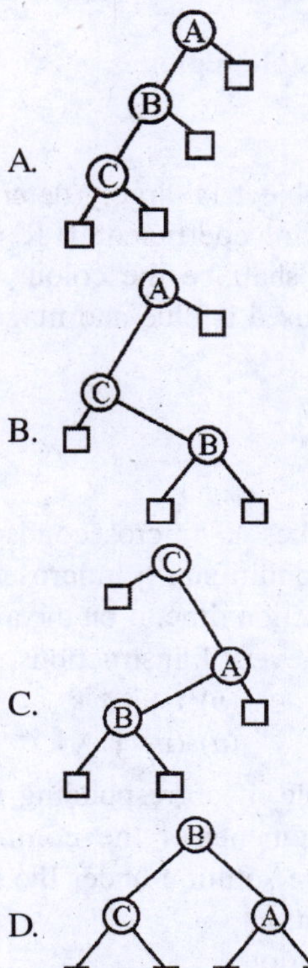

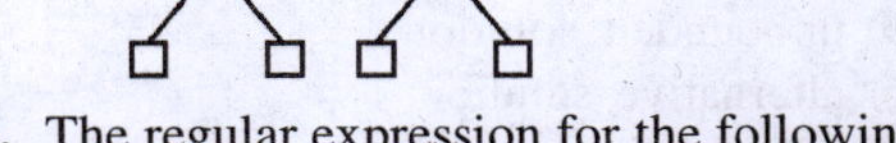

468. The regular expression for the following DFA

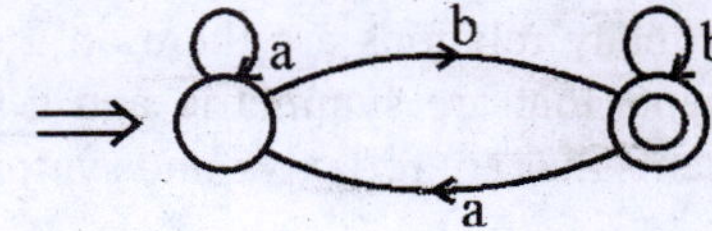

is

(*a*) ab*(b + aa*b)*
(*b*) a*b(b + aa*b)*
(*c*) a*b(b* + aa*b)
(*d*) a*b(b * + aa*b)*

469. Which diagram provides a formal graphic notation for modelling objects, classes and their relationships to one another?
(*a*) Object diagram (*b*) Class diagram
(*c*) Instance diagram (*d*) Analysis diagram

470. A computer system supports 32 bit virtual address as well as 32 bit physical addresses. Since the virtual address space is of same size as that of physical address space, if we want to get rid of virtual memory, which one of the following is true?
(*a*) Efficient implementation of multiuser support is no longer possible.
(*b*) The processor cache can be made more efficient.
(*c*) Hardware support for memory management is not needed.
(*d*) CPU scheduling can be made more efficient.

471. The feasible region represented by the constraints $x_1 - x_2 \leq 1$, $x_1 + x_2 \geq 3$, $x_1 \geq 0$, $x_2 \geq 0$ of the objective function Max $Z = 3x_1 + 2x_2$ is
(*a*) A polygon
(*b*) Unbounded feasible region
(*c*) A point
(*d*) None of these

472. The colour of an object is largely determined by its diffuse reflection coefficient. If $K_d = (0.8, 0.4, 0)$, then what shall be the colour of the object, if the light used is blue and magenta?
(*a*) White and Red
(*b*) Red and Blue
(*c*) Black and White
(*d*) Black and Red

473. If an instruction takes 'i' microseconds and a page fault takes an additional 'j' microseconds. The effective instruction time, if on the average a page fault occurs every k instructions, is
(*a*) i + j/k (*b*) i + j * k
(*c*) (i + j)/k (*d*) (i + j) * k

474. In any simplex table, if corresponding to any negative Δj, all elements of the column are negative or zero, the solution under the test is
(*a*) degenerate solution
(*b*) unbounded solution
(*c*) alternative solution
(*d*) non-existing solution

475. How many relations are there on a set with *n* elements that are symmetric and a set with *n* elements that are reflexive and symmetric?
(*a*) $2^{n(n+1)/2}$ and $2^n.3^{n(n-1)/2}$
(*b*) $3^{n(n-1)/2}$ and $2^{n(n-1)}$
(*c*) $2^{n(n+1)/2}$ and $3^{n(n-1)/2}$
(*d*) $2^{n(n+1)/2}$ and $2^{n(n-1)/2}$

476. The strategy used to reduce the number of tree branches and the number of static evaluations applied in case of a game tree is
(*a*) Minmax strategy
(*b*) Alpha-beta pruning strategy
(*c*) Constraint satisfaction strategy
(*d*) Static max strategy

477. Match the following:

1. Regular Grammar	(*i*) Pushdown automaton
2. Context free Grammar	(*ii*) Linear bounded automaton
3. Unrestricted Grammar	(*iii*) Deterministic finite automaton
4. Context Sensitive Grammar	(*iv*) Turing machine

	1	2	3	4
(*a*)	(*iii*)	(*i*)	(*ii*)	(*iv*)
(*b*)	(*iii*)	(*i*)	(*iv*)	(*ii*)
(*c*)	(*iii*)	(*ii*)	(*i*)	(*iv*)
(*d*)	(*iii*)	(*ii*)	(*iv*)	(*i*)

478. Consider the below circuit and find the output function *f*(*x*, *y*, *z*).

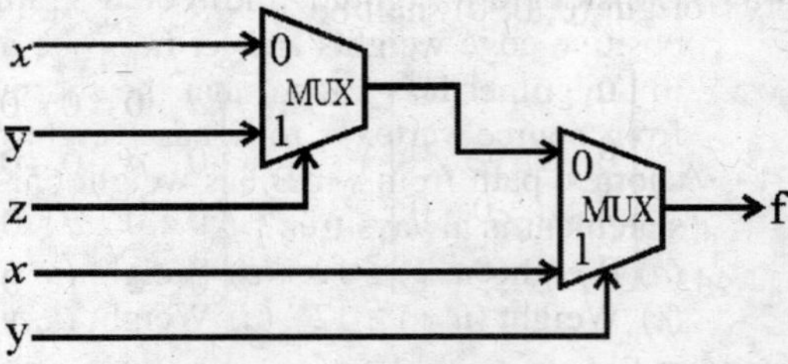

(*a*) $x\bar{z} + xy + \bar{y}z$ (*b*) $x\bar{z} + xy + \bar{y}\,\bar{z}$
(*c*) $xz + xy + \bar{y}\,\bar{z}$ (*d*) $xz + x\bar{y} + \bar{y}z$

479. What is the size (in terms of bits) of Header length field in IPV4 header?
(*a*) 2 (*b*) 4
(*c*) 8 (*d*) 16

480. Match the following with respect to java.util.* class methods:

A. Bit Set	(*i*) Time zone getTimezone( )
B. Calendar	(*ii*) int hashcode( )
C. Time zone	(*iii*) int nextInt( )
D. Random	(*iv*) Void setID(String tzName)

	A	B	C	D
(*a*)	(*ii*)	(*i*)	(*iv*)	(*iii*)
(*b*)	(*iii*)	(*iv*)	(*i*)	(*ii*)
(*c*)	(*iv*)	(*iii*)	(*ii*)	(*i*)
(*d*)	(*ii*)	(*i*)	(*iii*)	(*iv*)

481. _____ is sometimes said to be object oriented, because the only way to manipulate kernel objects is by invoking methods on their handles.
(*a*) Windows NT (*b*) Windows XP
(*c*) Windows VISTA (*d*) Windows 95/98

482. A user level process in Unix traps the signal sent on a Ctrl + C input and has a signal handling routine that saves appropriate files before terminating the process. When a Ctrl + C input is given to this process, what is the mode in which the signal handling routine executes?
(*a*) User mode
(*b*) Kernel mode
(*c*) Superuser mode
(*d*) Privileged mode

483. A CPU generally handles an interrupt by executing an interrupt service routine
(*a*) as soon as an interrupt is raised
(*b*) by checking the interrupt register at the end of fetch cycle
(*c*) by checking the interrupt register after finishing the executing the current instruction
(*d*) by checking the interrupt register at fixed time intervals

484. The perspective projection matrix, on the view plane $z = d$ where the centre of projection is the origin (0, 0, 0) shall be

A. $\begin{bmatrix} 0 & 0 & 0 & d \\ 0 & 0 & d & 0 \\ 0 & d & 0 & 0 \\ d & 0 & 0 & 1 \end{bmatrix}$ B. $\begin{bmatrix} d & 0 & 0 & 0 \\ 0 & d & 0 & 0 \\ 0 & 0 & d & 0 \\ 0 & 0 & 1 & 0 \end{bmatrix}$

C. $\begin{bmatrix} 0 & 0 & 0 & d \\ 0 & 0 & d & 0 \\ 0 & d & 0 & 0 \\ 1 & 0 & 0 & 0 \end{bmatrix}$ D. $\begin{bmatrix} d & 0 & 0 & 0 \\ 0 & d & 0 & 0 \\ 0 & 0 & d & 0 \\ 0 & 0 & 0 & 1 \end{bmatrix}$

485. Radio signals generally propagate according to the following mechanisms:
(*a*) Modulation, Amplification, Scattering
(*b*) Reflection, Diffraction, Scattering
(*c*) Amplification, Diffraction, Modulation
(*d*) Reflection, Amplification, Diffraction

486. Identify the devices given below with their IC numbers:

(*i*) USART	1. 8251		
(*ii*) Micro controller	2. 8051		
(*iii*) Interrupt controller	3. 8259		
(*iv*) DMA controller	4. 8257		

	(*i*)	(*ii*)	(*iii*)	(*iv*)
(*a*)	1	2	3	4
(*b*)	2	1	4	3
(*c*)	3	4	1	2
(*d*)	4	1	2	3

487. The optimal solution of the following assignment problem using Hungarian method is

	I	II	III	IV
A	8	26	17	11
B	13	28	4	26
C	38	19	18	15
D	19	26	24	10

	A	B	C	D
(*a*)	(I)	(II)	(III)	(IV)
(*b*)	(I)	(III)	(II)	(IV)
(*c*)	(I)	(III)	(IV)	(II)
(*d*)	(I)	(IV)	(II)	(III)

488. If *a* and *b* are the end points of a line, then which one of the following is true?
(*a*) If both end points are left, right, above or below the window, the line is invisible.
(*b*) If both end points are left, right, above or below the window, the line is completely visible.
(*c*) If both end points are left, right, above or below the window, the line is trivially visible.
(*d*) If both end points are left, right, above or below the window, the line is trivially invisible.

489. Match the following with link quality measurement and handoff initiation :

A. Networked-Controlled Handoff (NCHO)	(*i*) MS connect to BS
B. Mobile-Assisted Handoff (MAHO)	(*ii*) Process via channel the target BS
C. Forward Handoff	(*iii*) First Generation Analog Cellular System
D. Hard Handoff	(*iv*) Second Generation Digital Cellular System

	A	B	C	D
(*a*)	(*iii*)	(*iv*)	(*ii*)	(*i*)
(*b*)	(*ii*)	(*iii*)	(*i*)	(*iv*)
(*c*)	(*ii*)	(*i*)	(*iv*)	(*iii*)
(*d*)	(*iv*)	(*iii*)	(*i*)	(*ii*)

490. Consider the methods used by processes P_1 and P_2 for accessing their critical sections. The initial values of shared Boolean variables S_1 and S_2 are randomly assigned,

P_1	P_2
while ($S_1 == S_2$);	while ($S_1 == S_2$);
critical section	critical section
$S_1 = S_2$;	$S_1 = S_2$;

COMPUTER SCIENCE

Which one of the following statements describes the properties achieved?
(*a*) Mutual exclusion but not progress
(*b*) Progress but not mutual exclusion
(*c*) Neither mutual exclusion nor progress
(*d*) Both mutual exclusion and progress

491. If the period of a signal is 1000 ms, then what is its frequency in kilohertz?
(*a*) 10^{-3} KHz (*b*) 10^{-2} KHz
(*c*) 10^{-1} KHz (*d*) 1 KHz

492. Let a * H and b * H be two cosets of H.
(*i*) Either a * H and b * H are disjoint
(*ii*) a * H and b * H are identical
Then,
(*a*) only (*i*) is true (*b*) only (*ii*) is true
(*c*) (*i*) or (*ii*) is true (*d*) (*i*) and (*ii*) is false

493. HTML is defined using SGML – an ______ standard, information processing-text and office systems (SGML) for text information processing.
(*a*) ISO – 8878 (*b*) ISO – 8879
(*c*) ISO – 8880 (*d*) ISO – 8881

494. What is the meaning of 'Hibernate' in Windows XP/Windows 7?
(*a*) Restart the computers in safe mode.
(*b*) Restart the computers in normal mode.
(*c*) Shutdown the computer terminating all the running applications.
(*d*) Shutdown the computer without closing the running applications.

495. Assume that we have constructor functions for both base class and derived class. Now consider the declaration in main( ). Base * P = New Derived; in what sequence will the constructor be called?
(*a*) Derived class constructor followed by Base class constructor.
(*b*) Base class constructor followed by derived class constructor.
(*c*) Base class constructor will not be called.
(*d*) Derived class constructor will not be called.

496. Which one of the following options is not a shell in UNIX system?
(*a*) Bourne Shell (*b*) C Shell
(*c*) Net Shell (*d*) Korn Shell

497.

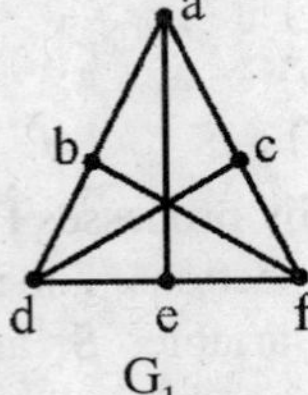

G_1

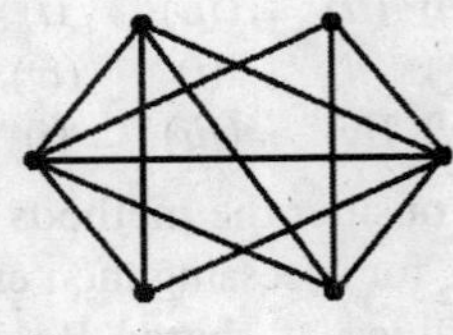
G_2

G_1 and G_2 are two graphs as shown :
(*a*) Both G_1 and G_2 are planar graphs.
(*b*) Both G_1 and G_2 are not planar graphs.
(*c*) G_1 is planar and G_2 is not planar graph.
(*d*) G_1 is not planar and G_2 is planar graph.

498. In which file the compiler manage the various objects, which are used in windows programming?
(*a*) Control File (*b*) Binary File
(*c*) Text File (*d*) Obj File

499. On a disk with 1000 cylinders (0 to 999) find the number of tracks, the disk arm must move to satisfy all the requests in the disk queue. Assume the last request service was at track 345 and the head is moving toward track 0. The queue in FIFO order contains requests for the following tracks :
123, 874, 692, 475, 105, 376
(Assume SCAN algorithm)
(*a*) 2013 (*b*) 1219
(*c*) 1967 (*d*) 1507

500. Halftoning is defined as
(*a*) a technique to obtain increased visual resolution using multiple intensity levels.
(*b*) a technique for using minimum number of intensity levels to obtain increased visual resolution.
(*c*) a technique to obtain increased visual resolution using maximum number of intensity levels.
(*d*) a technique for using appropriate number intensity levels to obtain increased visual resolution.

501. Boolean Algebra is an attempt of representing the
(*a*) True-false logic of humans in mathematical form
(*b*) Zero's in mathematical form
(*c*) One's in mathematical form
(*d*) none of the above

502. George Boole proposed the idea of
(*a*) Algebra (*b*) Boolean Algebra
(*c*) Unitary Method (*d*) none of the above

503. Boolean Algebra is used for designing and analysing
(*a*) digital circuits
(*b*) secondary storage devices
(*c*) CD-ROMs
(*d*) none of the above

504. A variable in Boolean Algebra can take
(*a*) At the most two values
(*b*) More than two values
(*c*) Two values only
(*d*) none of the above

505. There are three basic operations in Boolean Algebra *viz.*
(*a*) AND, OR and NOT
(*b*) IS, AND, OR
(*c*) NOT, TRUE, FALSE
(*d*) none of the above

506. XOR (Exclusive OR), NOR (Not OR), NAND (Not AND)
(*a*) are also Boolean operators
(*b*) are not a Boolean operators
(*c*) are binary operators
(*d*) none of the above

507. The basic logical identities used in Boolean Algebra is
(*a*) Commutative Law, Distributive Law, Identity Law
(*b*) Inverse Law, Associative Law
(*c*) DeMorgan's Theorem
(*d*) All the above

508. A Boolean function can be broken into
(*a*) Relational Model
(*b*) Logic diagram
(*c*) Flowchart and Trees
(*d*) Data Dictionary

509. A Boolean function is defined as an algebraic expression formed with the binary variables
(*a*) the logic operation symbols
(*b*) parenthesis
(*c*) equal to sign
(*d*) All of the above

510. A logic diagram can also be broken into
(*a*) Boolean function (*b*) De-Logic State
(*c*) Identities (*d*) none of the above

511. A logic gate is an electronic circuit, which produces a typical output signal depending on its
(*a*) Output signal (*b*) Input signal
(*c*) I/O signal (*d*) none of the above

512. The output signal of a gate is a simple Boolean operation of its
(*a*) Input signal (*b*) Output signal
(*c*) I/O signal (*d*) none of the above

513. Gates are the basic
(*a*) Logic elements
(*b*) Division method
(*c*) Need to express plus (addition) sums
(*d*) none of the above

514. Any Boolean function can be represented in the form of gates
(*a*) Graphical symbols, Algebraic notation
(*b*) Truth table
(*c*) (*a*) and (*b*)
(*d*) none of the above

515. The truth table of NAND and NOR can be made from
(*a*) NOT (A AND B) and NOT (A OR B) respectively
(*b*) NOT (A OR B) and NOT (A AND B) respectively
(*c*) NOT (A = B) in both cases
(*d*) none of the above

516. Exclusive OR (XOR) is a special gate whose output is one
(*a*) only if two inputs are not equal
(*b*) only if three inputs are not equal
(*c*) only if four inputs are not equal
(*d*) none of the above

517. The inverse of exclusive OR can be a comparator which will produce a one output if two inputs are
(*a*) unequal
(*b*) equal
(*c*) from different sources and are unequal
(*d*) none of the above

518. The digital circuits use only
(*a*) one or two types of gates for simplicity in fabrication purposes
(*b*) three gates or seven gates
(*c*) four gates
(*d*) none of the above

519. A functionally complete set implies
(*a*) a set of gates by which any Boolean function can be implemented
(*b*) a set of gates by which any non Boolean function can be implemented
(*c*) a set of gates by which only true values can be implemented
(*d*) none of the above

520. The functionally complete sets are
(*a*) {AND, NOT}, {NOR}
(*b*) {NAND}
(*c*) {OR, NOT} etc.
(*d*) All the above

521. In two languages (propositional calculus, predicate calculus), a formula may admit several interpretations. It may be true under some, while it may be false under others, the formula are classified as
(*a*) satisfiable (*b*) unsatisfiable
(*c*) (*a*) or (*b*) (*d*) none of the above

522. A satisfiable formula is true under
(*a*) some interpretation
(*b*) no interpretation
(*c*) leading outputs only
(*d*) none of the above

523. An unsatisfiable formula is true under
(*a*) some interpretation
(*b*) no interpretation
(*c*) leading inputs only
(*d*) none of the above

524. The propositional calculus is a
(*a*) weak language (*b*) strong language
(*c*) string language (*d*) none of the abve

525. In propositional calculus, the algorithm for determining satisfiability are

(*a*) hard to design (*b*) not hard to design
(*c*) (*a*) or (*b*) (*d*) none of the above

526. Turing machine was invented
(*a*) as a formalisation of the notion of algorithm, specifically to settle the question of whether satisfiability in the predicate calculus was a solvable problem or not
(*b*) to oppose Pushdown Automata
(*c*) to support Pushdown Automata
(*d*) none of the above

527. The string in propositional calculus is called
(*a*) expressions
(*b*) algebraic expressions
(*c*) formulas
(*d*) none of the above

528. Formulas are constructed by combining
(*a*) atomic formulas with the aid of Logical connectives
(*b*) expressions and multiplication symbol
(*c*) addition and subtraction symbol
(*d*) none of the above

529. The grammar generating the formula of the propositional calculus is
(*a*) simple (*b*) unambiguous
(*c*) temporary (*d*) none of the above

530. A formula is valid if and only if its negation is
(*a*) unsatisfiable
(*b*) unsatisfiables if and only if its negation is valid
(*c*) (*a*) or (*b*)
(*d*) none of the above

531. Two formulas are equivalent if and only if they are assigned the
(*a*) same truth-value by every truth-assignment appropriate to both
(*b*) different truth-value by every truth-assignment to appropriate to both
(*c*) (*a*) or (*b*)
(*d*) none of the above

532. Every formula has at least one conjunctive normal form and at least one disjunctive normal form, and there is an algorithm that transforms any formula F into
(*a*) a conjunctive normal form if desired
(*b*) a disjunctive normal form if desired
(*c*) (*a*) or (*b*)
(*d*) none of the above

533. A Literal is an
(*a*) atomic formula
(*b*) the negation of an atomic formula
(*c*) (*a*) or (*b*)
(*d*) none of the above

534. A set of formulas, finite or infinite is called satisfiable
(*a*) if there is a single truth-assignment that verifies every formula in the set
(*b*) if there is a double truth-assignment that verifies every formula in the set
(*c*) (*a*) or (*b*)
(*d*) none of the above

535. The satisfiability of an infinite set of formulas depends only on the
(*a*) satisfiability of its finite subsets
(*b*) satisfiability of its infinite subsets
(*c*) double sets
(*d*) none of the above

536. In mathematics, any property that can be inferred of an infinite object on the basis of finite "approximations" to that object is called a
(*a*) compactness phenomenon
(*b*) query
(*c*) subsidary equational values
(*d*) none of the above

537. Compactness Theorem for the propositional calculus states that
(*a*) a set of formulas is satisfiable if and only if each of its finite subsets is satisfiable
(*b*) all subset are unsatisfiable
(*c*) only few sets are unsatisfiable
(*d*) none of the above

538. A formula F is valid if every truth-assignment appropriate to F verifies F we say that F is
(*a*) tautology (*b*) binary
(*c*) subformula (*d*) none of the above

539. A clause is called a tautology if it contains
(*a*) both A and ¬A for some atomic formula
(*b*) either A or ¬A for some atomic formula
(*c*) neither A nor ¬A for some atomic formula
(*d*) none of the above

540. In the predicate calculuş, we can make general statements about all objects in affixed set, called
(*a*) the universe (*b*) the relation set
(*c*) the subset (*d*) none of the above

541. In predicate calculus, the atomic formulas are
(*a*) built up from atomic formulas by means of logical connectives.
(*b*) themselves constructed out of names for relations and names for individual objects in the universe.
(*c*) neither (*a*) nor (*b*)
(*d*) (*a*) and (*b*) both

542. In predicate calculus every formula of the predicate calculus is equivalent
(*a*) to at least one rectified formula
(*b*) to at least one formula in prenex form
(*c*) (*a*) and (*b*)
(*d*) none of the above

543. In predicate calculus, every formula without quantifier's is equivalent to

(*a*) at least one formula in conjunctive normal form
(*b*) at least one formula in disjunctive normal form
(*c*) (*a*) and (*b*)
(*d*) none of the above

544. In predicate calculus, every formulas is equivalent to at least
(*a*) one formula in prenex form with matrix in conjunctive normal form
(*b*) at least one formula in prenex form with matrix in disjunctive normal form
(*c*) (*a*) and (*b*)
(*d*) none of the above

545. In predicate calculus, there exists algorithms for
(*a*) transforming a formula into prenex form
(*b*) transforming a formula into conjunctive normal form
(*c*) transforming a formula into disjunctive normal form
(*d*) all of the above

546. There are logic circuits whose present output depends on
(*a*) the past inputs and can store and remember information
(*b*) the present inputs and can store and remember information
(*c*) I/O values and cannot store and remember information
(*d*) none of the above

547. The sequential circuits unlike combinational circuits and time
(*a*) dependent (*b*) independent
(*c*) (*a*) or (*b*) (*d*) none of the above

548. Normally, the current output of a sequential circuit depends on the state of the circuit and on the current
(*a*) input to the circuit
(*b*) output to the circuit
(*c*) I/O to the circuit
(*d*) none of the above

549. Sequential circuits can be of two types
(*a*) Synchronous and Asynchronous
(*b*) Synchronous and edge-triggered
(*c*) Transition and non transition
(*d*) none of the above

550. Synchronous circuits use flip-flops and their status
(*a*) can change only at discrete instants
(*b*) can change only at continous/uncontinous instants
(*c*) can change only at random
(*d*) none of the above

551. The Synchronisation in sequential circuits can be achieved
(*a*) using a anticlock pulse generator
(*b*) using a clock pulse generator
(*c*) logic gates and anticlock pulse generator
(*d*) none of the above

552. The asynchronous sequential circuits may be regarded as
(*a*) combinational circuits with advanced path
(*b*) combinational circuits with narrow path
(*c*) combinational circuits with feedback path
(*d*) none of the above

553. A flip-flop is a
(*a*) binary cell which can store a bit of information
(*b*) dual cell which can store two bits of information
(*c*) tri cell which can store three bits of information
(*d*) none of the above

554. The main feature in R-S flip-flop is the addition of
(*a*) a clock pulse input
(*b*) a clock pulse output
(*c*) a clock pulse I/O
(*d*) none of the above

555. D flip-flop is a special type flip-flop in the sense that it
(*a*) represents the currently applied input as the state of flip-flop
(*b*) represents the currently applied output as the state of flip-flop
(*c*) represents the currently applied I/O as the state of flip-flop
(*d*) none of the above

556. In D flip-flop, the state of flip-flop changes for
(*a*) the applied input/output
(*b*) the applied input
(*c*) the applied output
(*d*) none of the above

557. The basic drawback with R/S flip-flop is, that one set of input condition are not utilised and this
(*a*) cannot be used with a little change in the circuit
(*b*) can be used with a little change in the circuit
(*c*) can be used with a little lot of change in the circuit
(*d*) none of the above

558. In J-K flip-flop, the last combination is used to
(*a*) complement the state of flip-flop
(*b*) condition the state of flip-flop
(*c*) condition the end of flip-flop
(*d*) none of the above

559. A register is a binary function, which holds the
(*a*) binary information in digital form

(b) three bit information
(c) five bit information
(d) none of the above

560. A register consists of a group of binary
(a) storage cells (b) data
(c) digits (d) none of the above

561. A register consists of one and more flip-flops
(a) depending on the number of bits to be stored in a word
(b) depending on the I/O operation
(c) depending on the output operation only
(d) none of the above

562. Register are normally coupled with
(a) combinational gates enabling certain data processing tasks
(b) sequential circuit
(c) (a) and (b) both
(d) none of the above

563. Counter is another useful
(a) sequential circuit
(b) combinational circuit
(c) both (a) and (b)
(d) none of the above

564. A counter in principle is a register whose value is
(a) incremented by one on the occurrence of some event
(b) incremented by two on the occurrence of some event
(c) incremented by three on the occurrence of some event
(d) none of the above

565. The counters are used for
(a) counting the number of times of an event occurs
(b) for generating the timing signal for controlling the sequence of operation in digital computers and generation of counting signals of clock pulse
(c) (a) and (b) both
(d) none of the above

566. Counters are of two types
(a) Joint and Disjoint
(b) Asynchronous and Synchronous
(c) Registered and Unregistered
(d) None of the above

567. In Asynchronous counter
(a) the state of one flip-flop changes at a time
(b) the state of all flip-flop changes at same time
(c) there will be no effect on flip-flop
(d) none of the above

568. In Synchronous counter
(a) the state of one flip-flop changes at a time
(b) the state of all flip-flop changes at same time
(c) there will be no effect in flip-flop
(d) none of the above

569. Asynchronous counter is also termed as
(a) ripple counter
(b) nibble counter
(c) dentle counter
(d) none of the above

570. Asynchronous counter is also called ripple counter because
(a) changes occur to decrement the ripple counter
(b) the changes that occurs in order to increment the counter ripples through the counter from one end to other
(c) changes occur from both end
(d) none of the above

571. Information is represented in a computer in the form of Binary Digit popularly known as
(a) bit (b) radix
(c) base byte (d) none of the above

572. A number system of base r is a system, which have r distinct symbols for r digits
(a) radix (b) byte
(c) decimal (d) none of the above

573. To determine the quantity that the number represents, we multiply the number by an integer power of r depending on the place it is located and then find the sum of
(a) digits (b) weighted digits
(c) decimals (d) none of the above

574. Decimal number system has ten digits represented by
(a) 0 to 9 (b) 1 to 10
(c) A1 to a10 (d) none of the above

575. The base or radix for decimal number system is
(a) 2 (b) 5
(c) 10 (d) none of the above

576. In binary numbers we have
(a) two digits 0 and 1
(b) two digits 1 and 2
(c) two digits A1 and A2
(d) none of the above

577. In binary number system 0 and 1 can be represented
(a) as a weighted digit
(b) as a string of 0's and 1's called bits
(c) as a log
(d) none of the above

578. The base of binary number system is
(a) 2 (b) 3
(c) 4 (d) none of the above

579. An octal system has
(a) 8 digits represented as 0 to7
(b) 8 digits represented as 1 to 8
(c) 8 digits represented as A1 to A2
(d) none of the above

580. For finding equivalent decimal number of an octal number one have to find
(*a*) the quality of the octal number
(*b*) the quantity of the octal number
(*c*) (*a*) and (*b*)
(*d*) none of the above

581. The hexadecimal system has 16 digits which are represented as
(*a*) 0 to 9, A to F (*b*) 1 to 9, A to F
(*c*) 1 to 10, A to F (*d*) none of the above

582. For converting a decimal number to binary number, the integer and fractional part are:
(*a*) handled separately
(*b*) handled together
(*c*) always equal
(*d*) none of the above

583. For converting binary to octal; the binary number is divided into groups of..., which are then combined by place value to generate equivalent octal
(*a*) two
(*b*) three
(*c*) (*a*) and (*b*) depending on the case
(*d*) none of the above

584. Normally the decimal digits are coded in 6-8 bits as alphanumeric characters but for the purpose of arithmetic calculations the decimal digits are treated as
(*a*) four bit binary code
(*b*) six bit binary code
(*c*) 8 bit binary code
(*d*) none of the above

585. ASCII stands for
(*a*) American National Service Code for Inter Transmission Inst
(*b*) American National Standard Code for Information Interchange
(*c*) American National Standard Code for Information Inst
(*d*) none of the above

586. Binary codes can be formulated for any set of
(*a*) sequential series
(*b*) cononical form and elements
(*c*) discrete elements
(*d*) none of the above

587. Basic requirements of the computational date representation in binary form are
(*a*) Representation of sign
(*b*) Representation of magnitude
(*c*) If the number is fractional, then binary or decimal point and exponent
(*d*) All the above

588. The decimal position can be represented by a position
(*a*) between the flip-flop (storage cells in computer)
(*b*) between the flip-flop (storage cells in disk)
(*c*) between the flip-flop (storage cells in UPS)
(*d*) none of the above

589. There are two types of complements for a number of base *r*, these are called *r*'s complement and
(*a*) $(r-1)$'s complement
(*b*) $(r-2)$'s complement
(*c*) $(r-3)$'s complement
(*d*) none of the above

590. The fixed point numbers in binary uses a
(*a*) number division method
(*b*) sign bit
(*c*) exponent and addition symbol
(*d*) none of the above

591. In fixed point representation, the decimal position is
(*a*) assumed either at the beginning or at the end of a number
(*b*) assumed either at the middle or at the end of a number
(*c*) assumed either at the beginning or at the middle of a number
(*d*) none of the above

592. In floating point representation, a second register is used
(*a*) to keep the value of exponent that determines the position of the binary or decimal point in the number
(*b*) to keep the value of complement of a number
(*c*) (*a*) and (*b*) both
(*d*) none of the above

593. Floating-point numbers are often represented in
(*a*) normalised forms (*b*) denormalised forms
(*c*) (*a*) and (*b*) (*d*) none of the above

594. Arithmetic operations involved with floating point numbers are more
(*a*) complex in nature
(*b*) take longer time for execution
(*c*) require complex hardware
(*d*) all the above

595. Floating-point representation is a must as
(*a*) it is useful in mathematics
(*b*) it is useful in scientific calculations
(*c*) it is useful in biology
(*d*) none of the above

596. A parity bit is an extra bit added with
(*a*) binary data such that it makes total number of 1's in data either odd or even
(*b*) binary data such that it makes total number of 0's in data either odd or even
(*c*) Both (*a*) and (*b*)
(*d*) none of the above

597. The parity bit is only an error detection code. The concept of parity bit has been developed and error detection and correction code has been developed using
(*a*) two parity bits only
(*b*) one parity bits only
(*c*) more than one parity bits
(*d*) none of the above

598. Hamming Error-correcting code uses
(*a*) more than one parity bits
(*b*) zero parity bit
(*c*) (*a*) and (*b*) both
(*d*) none of the above

599. Normally, SEC code may be used in semiconductor memories for correction of
(*a*) double bit errors (*b*) single bit errors
(*c*) Both (*a*) and (*b*) (*d*) none of the above

600. Basically, the SEC-DED code guards against the errors of two bits in
(*a*) DEC codes (*b*) DILE codes
(*c*) SEC codes (*d*) none of the above

601. In Symbolic logic, a proposition can be defined as a
(*a*) set of words
(*b*) statement which can be either true or false
(*c*) set of numerical symbols
(*d*) none of the above

602. Formal logic can be regarded as a
(*a*) development of symbolic logic
(*b*) development of numeric logic
(*c*) development of relational logic
(*d*) none of tha above

603. A programming language is one example of
(*a*) formal logic (*b*) ordinary arithmetic
(*c*) both (*a*) and (*b*) (*d*) none of the above

604. In any logical system, certain WFFS (Well Formed Formulae) are taken to be
(*a*) theorems
(*b*) compound propositions
(*c*) both (*a*) and (*b*)
(*d*) none of the above

605. Digital electronics such as that used in computer hardware is based on Switching various points in a circuit
(*a*) between a 'high' voltage and 'low' voltage
(*b*) between a 'high' voltage and 'low' voltage and 1 represent no voltage
(*c*) between a 'high' voltage and 'low' voltage and 1 represent high voltage, represents low voltage
(*d*) none of the above

606. Gates are special circuits that produce
(*a*) input values
(*b*) output values (1 or 0) depending upon the input voltage
(*c*) (*a*) and (*b*) both
(*d*) none of the above

607. A gate acts as a
(*a*) mathematical theorem
(*b*) function which 'calculate' an output values from the input values
(*c*) non mathematical function
(*d*) none of the above

608. In circuit logic, the function can be specified by listing all the possible combinations of input and giving the output in each case. Such a listing is often referred to as
(*a*) a truth table (*b*) gates
(*c*) proposition logic (*d*) none of the above

609. Two propositions *p* and *q* can be combined to form a more complex propositions called a
(*a*) compound proposition
(*b*) true proposition
(*c*) false proposition
(*d*) none of the above

610. Connectives may be used to represent
(*a*) gates (*b*) statement
(*c*) (*a*) and (*b*) (*d*) none of the above

611. The connectives used for negation [NOT], disjunction [OR], conjunction [AND] respectively are
(*a*) $\neg, \vee, \wedge$ (*b*) $\vee, \wedge, \neg$
(*c*) $\wedge, \vee, \neg$ (*d*) none of the above

612. A form such as $(P \wedge \neg q) \Rightarrow P$ whose truth value is always T is called
(*a*) tautology
(*b*) complex equation
(*c*) compound equation
(*d*) none of the above

613. Semantic turnstile $\neq$ is an important
(*a*) metasymbol and used to denote logical implication
(*b*) metasymbol and used to denote illogical implication
(*c*) Both (*a*) and (*b*)
(*d*) none of the above

614. If a propositional form always has the value F irrespective of the values of the logical variable, it is called a
(*a*) diction (*b*) contradiction
(*c*) (*a*) and (*b*) both (*d*) none of the above

615. The order of precedence in the expression $1+2\times5^3$ will be passed as $(1 + (2 \times 5^3))$ and evaluates to
(*a*) 251 (*b*) 120
(*c*) 210 (*d*) none of the above

616. The universal quantifier in predicate logic indicates that

(*a*) all the propositions are false
(*b*) all the propositions are true
(*c*) (*a*) or (*b*) depending on the case
(*d*) none of the above

617. The Existential quantifier $\exists$ indicates that
(*a*) at least one proposition is true
(*b*) at least two propositions are true
(*c*) at least two propositions are true
(*d*) none of the above

618. Evaluate $\Sigma\, x : \in N \mid x < 3 \bullet x^2$, the result will be
(*a*) $0^2+1^2+2^2=5$ (*b*) 4
(*c*) 9 (*d*) none of the above

619. Determine the truth value $\exists Z : \in P\,N \bullet \# Z = S$
(*a*) T (*b*) F
(*c*) T or F (*d*) none of the above

620. Determine the truth value
$\exists Z : \in P\,N \bullet (\forall\, x : \in N \bullet \# Z = x)$
(*a*) F (*b*) T
(*c*) (*a*) or (*b*) (*d*) None of the above

621. Booting a computer means
(*a*) loading the operating system into its memory
(*b*) loading any programme from disk to memory
(*c*) starting the work of processing
(*d*) illuminating the video screen

622. A 3-variable Boolean function (or ternary Boolean operator) *f* (A, B, C) is defined by the given table. The rows with 1 in the output *f* (A, B, C) column are

$100 = a.\bar{b}.\bar{c}$

$110 = a.b.\bar{c}$

$111 = a.b.c$

Boolean expression can be written as
(*a*) $y = a.b.c + a.b.\bar{c} + a.\bar{b}.\bar{c}$
(*b*) $y = a$
(*c*) $y = b$
(*d*) None

623. The symbol .... is used for multiple licats operator in logical multiplication.
(*a*) '.' (*b*) ,
(*c*) : (*d*) None

624. Every Boolean function can be expressed in terms of
(*a*) AND alone (*b*) OF alone
(*c*) NOT alone (*d*) NAND alone

625. A tree is made up
(*a*) multilevel group of elements called nodes
(*b*) single level elements
(*c*) (*a*) or (*b*)
(*d*) none

626. $1101_2 = ?$
(*a*) 25_{10} (*b*) 10_{10}
(*c*) 15 (*d*) None

627. MIPS is an acronym for :
(*a*) Monitoring Input and Peripheral System
(*b*) Million Instructions Per Second
(*c*) Monitor Input Processing System
(*d*) Multiple Instruction Processing System

628. Time sharing operating system have
(*a*) high through put
(*b*) low execution time
(*c*) faster 1/C
(*d*) none of these

629. Robots are now used in industry for process control. A robot is a
(*a*) Mainframe computer
(*b*) Supercomputer
(*c*) Minicomputer
(*d*) Special purpose computer

630. 'Volatile memory' means the memory which
(*a*) can be expanded
(*b*) cannot be expanded
(*c*) retains information even after the power is switched off
(*d*) cannot retain the information if power is cut-off

631. Select the statement which is not correct?
(*a*) RF modulator is a device which can be used with a microcomputer to make an ordinary TV set on output device
(*b*) The three main bases are control bus, data bus and address bus
(*c*) PROM means Programmable Read Only Memory
(*d*) Programme Counter is type of cheek fitted in the CPU

632. An 'assembler' in computer terminology means
(*a*) A person who assembles a computer
(*b*) A high level language
(*c*) A programmer who makes a complete programme by assembling smaller programme segments
(*d*) A programme which converts assembly language programme in machine code.

633. Class of regular sets is closed under
(*a*) union, concatenation, closure
(*b*) union only
(*c*) closure only
(*d*) None of these

634. The set of languages accepted by Pushdown Automata is the set of
(*a*) Regular languages
(*b*) Context-free languages
(*c*) Decursive languages
(*d*) Context sensitive languages

635. For a binary tree T with n vertices, the minimum possible height is
(*a*) $\log_2 (n + 1) - 1$ (*b*) $\log_2$
(*c*) n (*d*) none of these

636. Which of the following statement is true?
(*a*) LAN is an acronym for Local Area Network
(*b*) WAN is an acronym for Wide Area Network
(*c*) ISDN is an acronym for Intergrated System Design Network
(*d*) Both (*a*) and (*b*)

637. Buffer caches are used
(*a*) to handle interrupts
(*b*) to speed up main memory read operation
(*c*) to increase the capacity of the main memory
(*d*) to improve disk performance

638. In an undirected graph, the number of nodes with odd degree must be
(*a*) zero (*b*) even
(*c*) odd (*d*) prime

639. In computer terminology 'bug' means
(*a*) the programmer
(*b*) a defect in the computer
(*c*) an error in the programme
(*d*) a person interested in computers

640. In Boolean Algebra. $\neg(a \wedge B) = \neg a \vee b$ is referred to as
(*a*) DeMorgan's law (*b*) Distributive law
(*c*) Idempotence law (*d*) Absorption law

641. In a rule-based system, procedural domain knowledge is in the form of
(*a*) Meta–rules (*b*) Control rules
(*c*) Production rules (*d*) Rule interpreters

642. The central processing unit of a computer consists of
(*a*) Arithmetic and Logic Unit
(*b*) Primary Storage
(*c*) Control Unit
(*d*) All of these

643. The number of instruction which may possibly be executed by a computer depends upon the size of
(*a*) Opcode
(*b*) Programme counter
(*c*) Memory Address Register
(*d*) A word

644. Programme counter contents indicate
(*a*) the time elapsed since execution began
(*b*) the address where next instruction is stored
(*c*) the count of programme being executed after switching the power ON
(*d*) none of these

645. In Linked Lists as compared to arrays
(*a*) Insertions/deletions are faster, but searching is slower
(*b*) Searching is faster, but insertions/deletions are slower
(*c*) Insertion/deletions are perfomed at comparable speed, but searching is slower
(*d*) Searching is perfomed at comparable speed, but insertion/deletions is slower

646. Which of the following is not a type of databases?
(*a*) Hierarchial (*b*) Network
(*c*) Relational (*d*) Sequential

647. Select the incorrect statement
(*a*) Ferrite core memory is a non-volatile memory
(*b*) Information from auxiliary memory is transferred to ALU via main memory
(*c*) Main memory unit of a computer supervises the working of all other units
(*d*) The computer hardware units are of no use without a programme

648. UNIX is
(*a*) A name of a high-level language
(*b*) A type of computer
(*c*) A peripheral device
(*d*) An operating system

649. The data structure used for staring return addresses in subroutine calls is
(*a*) ARRAY (*b*) STACK
(*c*) LINKED LIST (*d*) HEAP

650. Which one of the following is not a type of flip-flop?
(*a*) RS (*b*) JK
(*c*) GH (*d*) T

651. An AI technique that allows computers to understand association and relationship between objects and events is called
(*a*) Pattern matching
(*b*) Relative symbolism
(*c*) Heuristic processing
(*d*) Cognitive science

652. Consider a hypothetical 4-bit machine. Using 2's complement representation, the range of values that can be stored in the system is
(*a*) –8 to 8 (*b*) –8 to 7
(*c*) –7 to 8 (*d*) –7 to 7

653. The Boolean expression $AB + \overline{ABC}$ is equal to
(*a*) A (*b*) $A \wedge B$
(*c*) B (*d*) none of these

654. The last statement of any BASIC programme is
(*a*) STOP (*b*) FINISH
(*c*) END (*d*) OVER

655. A computer virus is
(*a*) a pirated copy of a licensed software
(*b*) a programme designed to lead to malfunctioning of computer or data corruption

(c) malfunctioning of computer due to overheating
(d) a disease caused by too much use of computer

656. Select the incorrect statement
(a) PASCAL uses':' as separator between statements
(b) PASCAL is an object oriented language
(c) PASCAL is highly suitable for teaching programming concepts
(d) PASCAL allows recursion

657. A 'logical statement' means
(a) a statement which is grammatically correct
(b) a statement which is syntactically correct
(c) a statement which involves only Boolean variables
(d) a statement which is semantically correct

658. A 'queue' is also called a
(a) LIFO list (b) FIFO list
(c) Linked list (d) none of these

659. Which of the following language supports sub–range data types?
(a) PASCAL (b) FORTRAN
(c) BASIC (d) COBOL

660. A programme which converts 'Source programme' into 'Object programme' for some other machine is called
(a) Interpreter (b) Compiler
(c) Cross-compiler (d) Linker

661. Greedy algorithm works for the following graph problems
(a) Minimum Spanning Tree
(b) Shortest Path
(c) Both (a) and (b)
(d) Neither (a) nor (b)

662. Every comparison based sorting algorithm must perform
(a) at least n^2 comparisons
(b) at least O (n $\log_n$) comparisons
(c) at most n comparisons
(d) at most $\log_n$ comparisons

663. 'Garbage Collection' is a technique of
(a) Memory management
(b) Processor management
(c) I/O management
(d) File management

664. What type of system software provides information on processor utilisation?
(a) Utility programme
(b) Communication software
(c) Performance monitoring software
(d) Operating System

665. In DOS the command used for removing a file from the disk is
(a) REM (b) KILL
(c) CLEAR (d) DEL

666. The UNIX command to see the names of all files in a directory is
(a) dir (b) list
(c) ls (d) none of these

667. Which one of the following is not an addressing technique?
(a) Direct addressing
(b) Indirect addressing
(c) Semi-direct addressing
(d) Immediate addressing

668. The Wordstar Commands LM and RM are used for
(a) Adjusting the paragraph heading
(b) Setting number of lines per inch
(c) Setting number of characters in a line
(d) Setting the left and right margins, respectively

669. Select the correct statement
(a) The term software refers to such material as punched cards, paper tapes etc.
(b) The most important characteristics of a high-level is that it is machine based
(c) An error in a computer programme is known as a bug and the process of removing it is called debugging
(d) A pictorial representation of the steps of computation for solving a problem is known as programme

670. Which of the following is true for paper tapes?
(a) It is difficult to delete or add data
(b) They are easily torn or mutilated
(c) They are non-reusable
(d) All of the above

671. Generally, which C statement is placed at the top of the C programme.
(a) Print (b) Control statement
(c) # Define statement (c) none of the above

672. Relational expressions are sometimes called
(a) conditions (b) control
(c) declaration (d) none of the above

673. The scanf() function tends to be of limited usefulness for String input because it terminates input -------
(a) when a blank is encountered
(b) when a blank is not encountered
(c) when a blank and a backslash is encountered
(d) none of the above

674. Whenever an instance of a class is created, the C++ compiler automatically calls the _______ of that class.
(a) Constructor (b) Abs function
(c) Operators (d) none of the above

COMPUTER SCIENCE

675. If the class instance an automatic variable, then C++ compiler calls the ____, when the instance goes out of scope and has to be destroyed.
(*a*) Constructor (*b*) Destructor
(*c*) Operators (*d*) none of the above

676. Object Oriented Programming (OOP) relies on three basic concepts :
(*a*) data abstraction, inheritance and arrays
(*b*) data abstraction, inheritance and polymorphism
(*c*) I/O, inheritance and polymorphism
(*d*) none of the above

677. In C++, genericity is achieved by the use of templates, a template will operate on
(*a*) any data type for which the internal implementation is appropriate.
(*b*) text data type for which the internal implementation is appropriate.
(*c*) numeric data type for which the internal implementation is appropriate.
(*d*) none of the above

678. A *reference* is
(*a*) an alternate name for an object.
(*b*) use it just as you would use the object itself.
(*c*) the address of an item except that unlike a pointer, a reference is not a real variable.
(*d*) all the above

679. A reference is
(*a*) initialised when it is defined, and you cannot modify its value.
(*b*) not initialised when it is defined, and you cannot modify its value;
(*c*) initialised when it is defined, and you can modify its value.
(*d*) none of the above

680. Basic data types such as int and float are simply a ——
(*a*) chunk of memory holds a single value
(*b*) chunk of memory holds a double value
(*c*) chunk of memory holds a cache value
(*d*) none of the above

681. A constructor for a class like String will allocate extra memory for the null terminated string. To release this memory when the string is no longer needed. C++ handles this through
(*a*) destructor, which is a function with the same name as the class but with a tilde (~) as prefix
(*b*) destructor, which is a function with the same name as the class but with a tilde (~) as suffix
(*c*) destructor, which is not a function with the same name as the class but with a tilde (~) as prefix
(*d*) none of the above

682. C++ allows multiple constructors for a single class to be defined, known by the number and types of their arguments called
(*a*) overloading (*b*) destructor
(*c*) struct (*d*) none of the above

683. C++ does not have
(*a*) garbage collector (*b*) constructors
(*c*) struct (*d*) none of the above

684. In C++ heap-based objects must be explicitly deallocated by the
(*a*) delete operator (*b*) Insert operator
(*c*) (*a*) and (*b*) (*d*) none of the above

685. In C++ constructors and destructors simply
(*a*) insert object
(*b*) initialise and clean up objects
(*c*) (*a*) and (*b*)
(*d*) none of the above

686. Memory allocation and deallocation are invoked explicitly
(*a*) by the *new* and *delete* operators
(*b*) implicitly by declaration of level variables
(*c*) (*a*) or (*b*)
(*d*) none of the above

687. C++ allows
(*a*) flexibility in memory allocation
(*b*) a complete control on allocation and creation of objects
(*c*) (*a*) and (*b*)
(*d*) none of the above

688. The *default constructor* is a constructor that takes
(*a*) no arguments (*b*) one argument
(*c*) two arguments (*d*) none of the above

689. For the String class, you can define the default constructor
(*a*) as a function that allocates a single chunk of bytes
(*b*) initialises it to a zero-length string
(*c*) (*a*) and (*b*)
(*d*) none of the above

690. If you define constructors for a class, you
(*a*) should always define a *default constructor* as well
(*b*) should not define a *default constructor* as well
(*c*) (*a*) or (*b*)
(*d*) none of these

691. According to the rules of C++, a const member variable and a reference member variable
(*a*) must be initialised when they are defined
(*b*) must have a constant value as soon as the class instance is created.
(*c*) (*a*) or (*b*)
(*d*) none of these

692. There are two special functions that are meant for handling exceptions that occur during exception handling itself:

(a) void terminate ( ) and void unexpected ()
(b) non void terminate ( ) and void unexpected ()
(c) void terminate ( ) and Non void unexpected ()
(d) none of the above

693. Overloading
(a) means defining several functions with the same name but varying arguments.
(b) permits to redefine the meanings of operators such as + – * / % += -= for any class.
(c) (a) and (b)
(d) none of the above

694. In C++, there is
(a) also a data type called ''void'', which means no data type at all
(b) no data type called ''void''
(c) also a data type called ''void'', which means single data type
(d) none of these

695. Pointers are declared using the
(a) Unary *Operator (b) Alpha Operator.
(c) Beta Operator (d) none of the above

696. C++ was originally developed by
(a) Nicolas Wirth (b) Donald Knuth
(c) Bjarne Stroustrup (d) Ken Thompson

697. The standard C++ comment
(a) / (b) //
(c) /* and */ (d) none of these

698. The preprocessor directive #inlcude is required if
(a) Console output is used
(b) Console input is used
(c) Both console input and output is used
(d) none of these

699. The operator << is called
(a) an insertion operator
(b) put to operator
(c) either (a) or (b)
(d) none of these

700. The operator >> is called
(a) an extraction operator
(b) a get from operator
(c) either (a) or (b)
(d) get to operator

701. When a language has the capability to produce new data type, it is called
(a) Extensible (b) Overloaded
(c) Encapsulated (d) Reprehensible

702. The C++ symbol <<
(a) perform the action of sending the value of expression listed as its right to the outputs strewn as the left
(b) is used to indicate the action from right to left
(c) is adopted to resemble an arrow
(d) All the above

703. C++ name was suggested by
(a) Rrick Mascitti (b) Bjarne Stroustrup
(c) Donald Knuth (d) Ken Thompson

704. What is a reference?
(a) an operator
(b) a reference is an alias for an object
(c) used to rename an object
(d) none of these

705. A constructor is called whenever
(a) an object is declared
(b) an object is used
(c) a class is declared
(d) a class is used

706. State the object oriented languages
(a) C++ (b) Java
(c) Eiffel (d) All of the above

707. Overload function in C++
(a) a group function with the same name
(b) all have the same number and type of arguments
(c) functions with same name and same number and type of arguments
(d) All of the above

708. Operator overloading is
(a) making C++ operator works with objects
(b) giving new meaning to existing C++ operators
(c) making new C++ operator
(d) both (a) and (b) above

709. Which of the following backslash codes used for bell?
(a) \b (b) \a
(c) \r (d) \s
(e) none

710. A class having no name
(a) is not allowed
(b) can't have a constructor
(c) can't have a destructor
(d) can't be passed as an argument

711. The difference between constructors and destructor are
(a) constructors can take arguments but destructor can't
(b) constructors can be overloaded but destructors can't be overloaded
(c) both (a) and (b)
(d) none of these

712. A destructor takes
(a) one argument (b) two arguments
(c) three arguments (d) zero arguments

713. Constructors are used to
(a) initialise the objects

COMPUTER SCIENCE

(*b*) construct the data members
(*c*) both (*a*) and (*b*)
(*d*) none of these

714. In C++ a function contained within a class is called
(*a*) a member function (*b*) an operator
(*c*) a class function (*d*) a method

715. The fields in a class of C++ programme are by default
(*a*) protected (*b*) public
(*c*) private (*d*) none of these

716. The braces that surround the code in 'C' programme
(*a*) Show what code goes in a particular function
(*b*) Delimit a section of code
(*c*) Separate the codes from the constant
(*d*) Separate the source file from the subject file
(*e*) none of the above

717. Every C programme begins with the statement
(*a*) main () (*b*) printf ()
(*c*) # include <stdio.h> (*d*) scanf ()
(*e*) none of the above

718. A single character input from the key board can be obtained by using the function
(*a*) printf () (*b*) getchar ()
(*c*) putchar () (*d*) scanf ()
(*e*) none of the above

719. An identifier in C
(*a*) is a name of a thing such as variable and function
(*b*) is made up of letters, numerals and the underscore
(*c*) can contain both uppercase and lowercase letters
(*d*) all of the above
(*e*) none of the above

720. The function scanf() reads
(*a*) a single character
(*b*) characters and strings
(*c*) any possible variable type
(*d*) any possible number
(*e*) none of the above

721. The library files that come with C are
(*a*) text editors for programme development
(*b*) the compiler and linker
(*c*) programme examples
(*d*) files that contain functions which carry out various operations and calculations
(*e*) none of the above

722. In C, square bracket [] are used in
(*a*) functions (*b*) arrays
(*c*) statements (*d*) all of the above
(*e*) none of the above

723. The single character input/output functions are
(*a*) scanf () and printf ()
(*b*) getchar () and printf ()
(*c*) scanf () and put char ()
(*d*) getchar () and putchar ()
(*e*) none of the above

724. The general form of do-while statement is
(*a*) do expressions while statement
(*b*) do while expressions
(*c*) do statement while (expressions)
(*d*) do statement while statement
(*e*) none of the above

725. The operators << (left shift) and >> (right shift) are
(*a*) assignment operators
(*b*) relational operators
(*c*) logical operators
(*d*) bitwise logical operators
(*e*) none of the above

726. In C, the NULL statement which does nothing is just
(*a*) a., (*b*) ;
(*c*) : (*d*) .
(*e*) none of the above

727. The strong containing certain required formatting information is called
(*a*) argument (*b*) character array
(*c*) character string (*d*) control string
(*e*) none of the above

728. The two statements that can be used to change the flow of control are
(*a*) if and switch
(*b*) if and while
(*c*) switch and do-while
(*d*) break and continue
(*e*) none of the above

729. Precedence determines which operator
(*a*) is evaluated first
(*b*) is most important
(*c*) is fastest
(*d*) operates on the largest number
(*e*) none of the above

730. Any programme in C has access to three standard files
(*a*) standard input file, standard output file, standard error file
(*b*) stdin, stdout, stderr
(*c*) keyboard, screen, screen
(*d*) all of the above
(*e*) none of the above

731. Which of the following is a storage class specification of C?
(*a*) automatic (*b*) external
(*c*) internal (*d*) all of the above
(*e*) none of the above

732. The most common use of one-dimensional array in C is
(*a*) string (*b*) character
(*c*) data (*d*) function
(*e*) none of the above

733. C contains two special pointer operators
(*a*) * and & (*b*) * and &&
(*c*) & and && (*d*) % and &
(*e*) none of the above

734. In C, the address of m's memory location
(*a*) * m (*b*) m &
(*c*) & m (*d*) m *
(*e*) none of the above

735. Main () is an example of
(*a*) library function
(*b*) user-defined function
(*c*) header
(*d*) statement
(*e*) none of the above

736. A variable can be declared static using the keyword
(*a*) extern (*b*) static
(*c*) register (*d*) auto
(*e*) none of the above

737. In C, structure values can be passed as arguments to functions by
(*a*) passing each member of the structure as an actual argument of function code
(*b*) passing a copy of the entire structure to the called function
(*c*) passing the structure as an argument using pointers
(*d*) All of the above
(*e*) none of the above

738. Variables that are both alive and active throughout the entire programme are known as
(*a*) local variables (*b*) private variables
(*c*) automatic variables (*d*) global variables
(*e*) none of the above

739. The header file 'ctype.h' can be used for
(*a*) providing links to assembly language for calls
(*b*) providing diagnostic and debugging assistance
(*c*) providing support for string handling functions
(*d*) providing character type identification (boolean) and translation
(*e*) none of the above

740. The header file 'math.h' can be used for
(*a*) providing links to assembly language for calls
(*b*) providing diagnostic and debugging assistance
(*c*) providing support for string handling functions
(*d*) providing character type
(*e*) none of the above

741. C provides loop constructs for performing loop operations. They are
(*a*) the while statements
(*b*) the do statements
(*c*) the for statements
(*d*) all of the above
(*e*) none of the above

742. C includes two types of modifiers that affect the way variables are accessed by both user's programme and the compiler. These modifiers are
(*a*) extern, static (*b*) auto, register
(*c*) auto, extern (*d*) const, volatile
(*e*) none of the above

743. Arrays that do not have their dimensions explicitly specified are called
(*a*) unsized arrays
(*b*) undimensional arrays
(*c*) initialised arrays
(*d*) no-size arrays
(*e*) none of the above

744. A variable that holds the memory address of another object is called
(*a*) integer (*b*) pointer
(*c*) constant (*d*) memory variable
(*e*) none of the above

745. A computer system having 64K memory will have its last address as
(*a*) 65536 (*b*) 64000
(*c*) 65535 (*d*) 65530
(*e*) none of the above

746. A C function contains
(*a*) function body
(*b*) argument declarations
(*c*) a function header
(*d*) other 'C' functions
(*e*) none of the above

747. A string is like an array because
(*a*) an array is a kind of array
(*b*) they are both character arrays
(*c*) they both access functions in the same way
(*d*) a string is a kind of array
(*e*) none of the above

748. Which of the following expressions will return 1 if both bits have value of 1; otherwise will return a value 0?
(*a*) AND (*b*) OR
(*c*) XOR (*d*) I's complement
(*e*) none of the above

749. A compound statement does not consist of
(*a*) control statements
(*b*) other compound statement
(*c*) a single statement

(*d*) expression statements
(*e*) none of the above

750. A function can
(*a*) perform a task
(*b*) return a value
(*c*) change value of actual arguments in call by reference
(*d*) all of the above
(*e*) none of the above

751. If a painter is arranged value NULL it means
(*a*) the value can not be assigned
(*b*) it points to a memory location 0
(*c*) # define is missing
(*d*) it does not point to any location
(*e*) none of the above

752. Heap
(*a*) is a region from where memory is allocated
(*b*) lies between your programme and the stack
(*c*) is a finite area
(*d*) all of the above
(*e*) none of the above

753. If a static array is net initialised, the elements will be set to
(*a*) an undetermined value
(*b*) zero
(*c*) a floating point number
(*d*) the character constant '\0'
(*e*) none of the above

754. Enumeration is
(*a*) set of numbers
(*b*) a list of strings
(*c*) a set of legal values possible for a variable
(*d*) a list of operators
(*e*) none of the above

755. If an error occurs, while opening a file, the file pointer as assigned a value
(*a*) NULL (*b*) stdout
(*c*) sstderr (*d*) not defined
(*e*) none of the above

756. * ptcount = 2 is
(*a*) a valid statement
(*b*) valid if ptcount is declared pointer 81
(*c*) undefined
(*d*) valid if ptcount is declared a pointer an integer
(*e*) none of the above

757. The array of definition int marks [10] [5] defines an array of
(*a*) 5 tables, 10 rows
(*b*) 10 columns, 5 rows
(*c*) 10 rows, 15 tables
(*d*) 10 rows, 5 columns
(*e*) none of the above

758. A subscript of an array can be
(*a*) any +ve or –ve value
(*b*) a –ve integer
(*c*) an expression giving +ve value
(*d*) zero
(*e*) none of the above

759. A union consists of a members of elements that
(*a*) occupy the same space in memory
(*b*) must be structures
(*c*) are grouped next to each other in memory
(*d*) all have the same type
(*e*) none of the above

760. A C programme contains the following declaration static char *colour[6] = {"red", "green", "blue", "white", "black", "yellow"}; what is the value of * (colour + 2)?
(*a*) yellow (*b*) green
(*c*) red (*d*) blue
(*e*) none of the above

761. Which of the following numerical values is/an invalid constant?
(*a*) 0.7 (*b*) 9.3e12
(*c*) 27.512 (*d*) 12345678
(*e*) none

762. Which of the following is (are) invalid character constants?
(*a*) 'a' (*b*) 'b'
(*c*) '\h' (*d*) '/n'
(*e*) none

763. Which of the following is (are) invalid string constant(s)?
(*a*) '7.15 pm' (*b*) "i like c"
(*c*) "7.3e12" (*d*) "1234e12"
(*e*) none

764. Which of the following is (are) valid identifier(s)?
(*a*) record/ (*b*) /record
(*c*) return (*d*) $tax
(*e*) none

765. A C programme contains the following declaration int i = 8, j = 5
What would be the value of following expression? abs (i – 2*j)
(*a*) 2 (*b*) 4
(*c*) 6 (*d*) 8
(*e*) none

766. A C programme contains the following declarations?
int i, j:
long ix:
What would be the value of the following expression?
ix + j
(*a*) integer (*b*) float
(*c*) long integer (*d*) double precision
(*e*) none

767. In fopen (), the mode that appends to a binary file is
(*a*) ab (*b*) a
(*c*) a^+ (*d*) r^+
(*e*) none of the above

768. In fopen (), the mode, that opens a binary file for reading is
(*a*) r^+ (*b*) r
(*c*) rb (*d*) r + b
(*e*) none of the above

769. Which of the following is not a linked data structure?
(*a*) linear linked list (*b*) circular linked list
(*c*) linked list with multiple pointersd.frees
(*d*) all of the above
(*e*) none of the above

770. The math library is setup for the user by the file
(*a*) float.h (*b*) limits.h
(*c*) math.h (*d*) time.h
(*e*) none of the above

771. Which of the following does not have an unary operator?
(*a*) –7 (*b*) ++i
(*c*) i (*d*) all of the above
(*e*) none of the above

772. The two operators && and || are
(*a*) arithmetic operators
(*b*) equality operators
(*c*) logical operators
(*d*) relational operators
(*e*) none of the above

773. In printf (), the appearance of the output can be affected by
(*a*) field width
(*b*) conversion character
(*c*) flag
(*d*) all of the above
(*e*) none of the above

774. Which of the following operators cannot be applied to a pointer?
(*a*) Increment operator
(*b*) Decrement operator
(*c*) Relational operator
(*d*) All of the above
(*e*) None of the above

775. The link between member of a structure and a variable is established using the member operator
(*a*) ; (*b*) :
(*c*) & (*d*) all of the above
(*e*) none of the above

776. The purpose of a conditional operator is to
(*a*) select one of the two values alternately
(*b*) select the highest of the two values
(*c*) select one of the two values depending on a condition
(*d*) select the more equal of the two values
(*e*) none of the above

777. The meaning of conversion character h for data input is
(*a*) data item is an unsigned decimal integer
(*b*) data item is a short integer
(*c*) data item is a hexadecimal integer
(*d*) data item is a string followed by white space character
(*e*) none of the above

778. The values that can legally appear to the right of assignment operator are called
(*a*) r values (*b*) int values
(*c*) variables (*d*) constants
(*e*) none

779. The conversion, character 's' for data input means that the data item as
(*a*) an unsigned decimal integer
(*b*) a short integer
(*c*) a hexadecimal integer
(*d*) a string followed by a white space character
(*e*) none of the above

780. What will this programme display?
```
# include <stdio.h)>
main ()
{
float = f;
f = 10/3;
print f ("%f", f);
}
```
(*a*) 3.3 (*b*) 3.0
(*c*) 3 (*d*) 3.1
(*e*) none

781. Find out the incorrect statement for strlen () function
(*a*) returns the length of a string incomplete question
(*b*) returns the number of characters
(*c*) returns the string passed as parameter
(*d*) all of the above
(*e*) none of the above

782. Which of the following statements is not true for structure in C?
(*a*) A structure is a method for packing data of different types
(*b*) A structure is a convenient tool for handling a group of logical data items
(*c*) A structure helps to recognise data in a more complex way
(*d*) A structure is a powerful concept and can be used in programme design
(*e*) none of the above

783. The malloc () function
(*a*) returns a pointer to the allocated memory
(*b*) returns a pointer to the first byte of region of memory

(c) changes the size of the allocated memory
(d) deallocates the memory
(e) none of the above

784. If p1 and p2 are properly declared and initialised points then which of the following statements is invalid?
(a) y = *p1 **p2; (b) *p2 = *p2 + 10
(c) a = 6 * _ *p2/*p1; (d) all of the above
(e) none of the above

785. Given the declaration
struct s -type
{int i;
char str [60];
}, s' *p;
The statement that assign to 'p' the address of 's' is
(a) p = &s; (b) p = s.i;
(c) s = &p; (d) p = *s;
(e) none

786. Which of the following I/O functions can be used to write a set of data values to a file?
(a) fscanf (b) fseek
(c) getc (d) fprint f ()
(e) none

787. The function ftell ()
(a) reads a character from a file
(b) reads an integer from a file
(c) gives the current position in the file
(d) sets the position to the beginning of the file
(e) none of the above

788. A programme can be terminated at any time by calling the function
(a) flush( ) (b) error ( )
(c) exit ( ) (d) clearer ( )
(e) none

789. The logical bitwise operator is
(a) bitwise AND (&) (b) bitwise XOR (^)
(c) bitwise OR (|) (d) all of the above
(e) none of the above

790. Which of the following is an incorrect statement regarding array
(a) is a First-In-First-Out (FIFO) structure
(b) is a buffer in which data items are retrieved in reverse order from which they are placed in buffer
(c) can be created as an array
(d) all of the above
(e) none of the above

791. ..... is an important phase in designing a successful database application
(a) E-R modelling
(b) System modelling
(c) Conceptual modelling
(d) none of these

792. The term database application generally refers to a particular
(a) field (b) database
(c) records (d) none of these

793. Traditionally, the design and testing of application programmes has been considered to be more in the realm of the software engineering domain than in the—
(a) database domain (b) data modeling
(c) E-R model (d) none of these

794. There is ..... commonality between database design methodologies and software engineering design methodologies.
(a) some (b) no
(c) (a) or (b) (d) none of these

795. To specify functional requirements in software design, it is common to use
(a) data flow diagrams, sequence diagrams, scenarios and other techniques
(b) DFD only
(c) E-R diagram
(d) none of these

796. The conceptual schema is a concise description of the data requirements of the users and includes detailed descriptions of the entity types, relationship and constraint, so these are expressed using the concepts
(a) Low Level data model
(b) High Level data model
(c) (a) or (b)
(d) (a) and (b)

797. Conceptual schema.....include implementation details
(a) do (b) always
(c) do not (d) none of these

798. Conceptual schema are easier to understand and can be used to communicate with
(a) Technical users
(b) Technical users only
(c) Non technical users
(d) none of these

799. Transformation of conceptual schema from the high level data model into the implementation data model is known as
(a) logical model
(b) data model mapping
(c) (a) and (b)
(d) none of the above

800. The ER model describes data as
(a) entities only
(b) entities, relationships and attributes
(c) attributes only
(d) none of the above

801. The basic object that the ER model represents is an entity, which is a "thing" in the real world with an

(a) dependent existence
(b) unidentified existence
(c) independent existence
(d) none of these

802. An entity may be an object with a
(a) physical existence
(b) physical or conceptual existence
(c) physical and conceptual existence
(d) none of the above

803. Each entity has
(a) attributes (b) records
(c) fields (d) database

804. Attributes are the particular properties that describes the
(a) fields (b) entity
(c) records (d) none of the above

805. In ER-diagrams composite versus simple (atomic subparts, which represent more basic attributes with)
(a) independent meanings
(b) dependent meanings
(c) deep meanings
(d) none of the above

806. The value of a composite attribute is the concatenation of the values of its constituent
(a) Simple attributes (b) Complex
(c) Real (d) None of the above

807. A multivalued attribute may have lower and upper bounds on the number of values allowed for
(a) two entities
(b) three entities
(c) each individual entity
(d) none of these

808. When a particular entity may not have an applicable value for an attribute, then a special value is created which is known as
(a) Null value (b) Empty value
(c) ϕ (phy) value (d) None of the above

809. Composite and multivalued attributes can be.....in an arbitrary way.
(a) nested (b) merged
(c) (a) and (b) (d) none of these

810. The collection of all entities of a particular entity type in the database at any point in time is called
(a) entity set (b) unit
(c) field (d) none of these

811. Composite attributes are attached to their component attributes by
(a) Rectangle (b) Straight Lines
(c) Oval (d) None of these

812. The collection of entities of a particular entity type are grouped into an entity set, which is also called the
(a) extension of the entity type
(b) unit
(c) record
(d) none of these

813. An important constraint on the entities of an entity type is the key or
(a) duplicacy constraint on attributes
(b) uniqueness constraint on attributes
(c) (a) and (b)
(d) none of these

814. Specifying that an attribute is a key of an entity type means that the preceding uniqueness property must hold for
(a) any two entities
(b) any complex entities
(c) every extension of the entity type
(d) none of these

815. An entity which has no value is called
(a) slow entity (b) weak entity
(c) poor entity (d) none of these

816. Value sets (Domains) of Attributes are not displayed in
(a) ER diagrams (b) Flowcharts
(c) Programmes (d) none of the above

817. In ER-diagrams, relationship types are displayed as
(a) rectangular boxed
(b) square boxes
(c) diamond-shaped boxes
(d) none of the above

818. A relationship type of degree two is called
(a) Binary (b) Twice
(c) Ternary (d) none of the above

819. Cardinality ratios for binary relationships are displayed on ER diagrams by displaying
(a) L, M and N on the diamonds
(b) M on the squares
(c) N on the rectangles
(d) none of the above

820. In ER diagrams, total participation is displayed as a double line connecting the participating entity type to the relationship, where as partial participation is represented by a
(a) Three lines (b) Two lines
(c) Single line (d) none of the above

821. .....existence dependency results in a weak entity type.
(a) Every (b) Not every
(c) All (d) none of the above

822. In the worst case, a composite attribute of all the weak entity's attributes will be the partial
(a) key (b) field
(c) record (d) none of the above

COMPUTER SCIENCE

823. The partial key is sometimes called the
(*a*) discriminator (*b*) originator
(*c*) developer (*d*) none of the above

824. In ER diagrams, the partial key attribute is underlined with a
(*a*) straight line
(*b*) double line
(*c*) dashed or dotted line
(*d*) none of the above

825. Weak entity types can sometimes be represented as
(*a*) Simple attributes
(*b*) Complex attributes
(*c*) (*a*) and (*b*)
(*d*) none of these

826. In ER diagram, any overlapping specialisaton would require
(*a*) multiple additional subclasses
(*b*) single additional subclasses
(*c*) (*a*) or (*b*)
(*d*) none of the above

827. A functional dependency (FD) is a property of the relation schema (intension) R and cannot be inferred automatically from a given relation extension *r* but must be defined explicitly by some one who knows the semantics of the
(*a*) attributes of R (*b*) schema
(*c*) relation (*d*) none of the above

828. Normalisation is a process of analysing the given relation schemas based on their FDs and primary keys to achieve the desirable properties of
(*a*) minimising redundancy
(*b*) minimising redundancy and minimising the insertion, deletion and updation anamolies
(*c*) primary key
(*d*) none of the above

829. The database designers need not normalize to the highest possible
(*a*) normal form (*b*) denormal form
(*c*) (*a*) or (*b*) (*d*) none of the above

830. The process of storing the join of higher normal form relations as a base relation which is in a lower normal form is called
(*a*) Normalisation (*b*) Programming
(*c*) Denormalisation (*d*) none of the above

831. 1NF disallows having a set of values, a tuple of values or a combination of both as an attribute value for a
(*a*) Double tuple (*b*) Binary tuple
(*c*) Single tuple (*d*) none of the above

832. Second normal form is based on the concept of
(*a*) full functional dependency
(*b*) half functional dependency
(*c*) semi functional dependency
(*d*) none of the above

833. Third normal form is based on the concept of
(*a*) Transitive dependency
(*b*) Closure dependency
(*c*) Normal dependency
(*d*) none of the above

834. In 1NF, relations should have no non
(*a*) atomic attributes or nested relations
(*b*) only nested relations
(*c*) single relations
(*d*) none of the above

835. According to Codd's original definition, a relation schema R is in 3NF if it satisfies 2NF and no nonprime attribute of R is transitively dependent on
(*a*) secondary key
(*b*) primary and secondary key
(*c*) primary key
(*d*) none of the above

836. In BCNF a relation schema R is in BCNF if whenever a nontrivial functional dependency $X \rightarrow A$ hold in R, then X is a
(*a*) superkey of R
(*b*) primary and secondary key of R
(*c*) binary key of R
(*d*) none of the above

837. SQL is a comprehensive database language and it is both
(*a*) LLL and HLL (*b*) a DLL and a HLL
(*c*) LLL and a DML (*d*) none of the above

838. SQL has one basic statement for retrieving information from a database, that statement is
(*a*) the START statement
(*b*) the SELECT statement
(*c*) the SINGLE statement
(*d*) none of the above

839. The SELECT statement has
(*a*) no relationship to SELECT operation of relational algebra
(*b*) a relationship to SELECT operation of relational algebra
(*c*) sometimes (*a*) or (*b*)
(*d*) none of the above

840. SQL allows a
(*a*) table (relation) to have two or more tuples that are identical in all their attribute values
(*b*) table (relation) to have only one tuple
(*c*) table (relation) to have no tuple
(*d*) none of the above

841. SQL table is
(*a*) not a set of tuples because a set does not allow two identical members
(*b*) a set of tuples because a set does not allows two identical members

(*c*) may or may not set of tuples
(*d*) none of the above

842. Some SQL relations are constrained to be sets because
(*a*) a key constraint has been declared
(*b*) the DISTINCT option has been used with SELECT statement
(*c*) (*a*) or (*b*)
(*d*) none of the above

843. In SQL, the same name can be used for two (or more) attributes as long as the attributes are in
(*a*) different relations (*b*) same relations
(*c*) (*a*) or (*b*) (*d*) none of the above

844. A missing WHERE clause indicates
(*a*) no condition on tuple selection
(*b*) a condition on tuple selection
(*c*) all possible tuple selection
(*d*) none of the above

845. To retrieve all the attribute values of selected tuples, we don't have to list the attribute names explicitly in SQL; we just specify
(*a*) an asterisk (*), which stands for all the attributes
(*b*) a hyphen (-) which stands for all the attributes
(*c*) a slash (/) which stands for all the attributes
(*d*) none of the above

846. SQL usually treats a table not as a set but as a
(*a*) multi set (*b*) mini set
(*c*) mix set (*d*) none of the above

847. A reference to an unqualified attribute refers to the relation, declared (in SQL) in the
(*a*) outermost query
(*b*) innermost nested query
(*c*) only outermost query
(*d*) none of the above

848. In SQL, whenever a condition in the WHERE-clause of a nested quey references some attribute of a relation declared in the outer query, the two queries are said to be
(*a*) inter active (*b*) inter related
(*c*) correcated (*d*) none of the above

849. The exists function is SQL is used to check whether
(*a*) the result of a correlated nested query is empty (no tuples) or not
(*b*) the result of a correlated nested query is based on selected values
(*c*) the result of a inter boundary query is based on selected values
(*d*) none of the above

850. EXISTS and NOT EXISTS are usually used in
(*a*) conjunction with a correlated nested query
(*b*) single query
(*c*) duplicate queries
(*d*) none of the above

851. It is also possible to use an explicit set of values in WHERE clause rather than a
(*a*) single query (*b*) nested query
(*c*) double query (*d*) none of the above

852. A query in SQL can consist of upto
(*a*) Six clauses, but only first two-SELECT and FROM are mandatory
(*b*) Five clauses but only first two-SELECT and FROM are mandatory.
(*c*) Three clauses but only first two-SELECT and FROM are mandatory
(*d*) none of the above

853. The User Work Area (UWA) is a set of programme variables, declared in the host programme to communicate the contents of individual records between
(*a*) DBMS and the host program
(*b*) DBMS and BASIC language
(*c*) DBMS and COBOL language
(*d*) none of the above

854. In the network, DML, retrievals and updates are done by navigating through the database records, hence keeping a trace of the search is
(*a*) easy (*b*) critical
(*c*) elementary (*d*) none of the above

855. ..... are a means of keeping track of the most recently accessed records and set occurrences by the DBMS.
(*a*) currency indicaters
(*b*) RS indicators
(*c*) record indicators
(*d*) none of the above

856. Several status indicators return an indication of successor failure
(*a*) after each DML command is executed
(*b*) before each DML commnad is executed
(*c*) before end of status only
(*d*) none of the above

857. The commands for manipulating a network database are called
(*a*) Data Mini Language (DML)
(*b*) Data Manipulation Language (DML)
(*c*) Data Max Language (DML)
(*d*) None of the above

858. DML commands are embedded in a general-purpose programming language called
(*a*) hand pilot language
(*b*) host programming language
(*c*) hard programming language
(*d*) none of the above

859. The DML commands can be grouped into
(*a*) navigation commands
(*b*) retrieval and update commands
(*c*) (*a*) and (*b*)
(*d*) none of the above

860. In DML update commands can be divided in two subgroups one
(*a*) for updating records and other for updating set occurences
(*b*) no need for second group
(*c*) (*a*) or (*b*)
(*d*) none of the above

861. In DML, RECONECT command can be used with both OPTIONAL and MANDATORY sets but not with
(*a*) FIXED set (*b*) FIRM set
(*c*) Recognise set (*d*) None of the above

862. In many DBMSs where no strict separation of levels is maintained one language called
(*a*) DDL (data definition language) is used by DBA & database designer to define both schemas
(*b*) DML
(*c*) DCL
(*d*) None of the above

863. In DBMS where a clear separation is maintained between conceptual and internal levels the
(*a*) DDL is used to specify conceptual schema only
(*b*) DML is used to specify conceptual schema only
(*c*) DQL is used to specify conceptual schema only
(*d*) None of the above

864. The language SDL (Storage definition language) is used to
(*a*) specify internal schema in DBMS
(*b*) specify external schema in DBMS
(*c*) specify I/O schema in DBMS
(*d*) none of the above

865. A highlevel DML used in a stand-alone interactive manner is called a
(*a*) SQL language (*b*) query language
(*c*) foreign language (*d*) none of the above

866. Data are represented by data values held temporarily
(*a*) within programme's data area
(*b*) recorded permanently on a file
(*c*) (*a*) or (*b*)
(*d*) none of the above

867. The organised collection of data is called a
(*a*) file structure (*b*) record structure
(*c*) data structure (*d*) none of the above

868. The programmes have to follow certain rules to access and
(*a*) process the structured data
(*b*) redefine the structured data
(*c*) redefine the data
(*d*) none of the above

869. Data are represented as:
(*a*) data structure = Organised Data + Allowed operations
(*b*) data structure – set value
(*c*) (*a*) or (*b*)
(*d*) none of the above

870. Simple data types can be used to build
(*a*) new scalar data types
(*b*) new arrays
(*c*) old scalar data types
(*d*) none of the above

871. There are standard data structures which are often used in their own right and can form the basis for
(*a*) simple data structures
(*b*) complex data structures
(*c*) permanent files
(*d*) none of the above

872. .....are basic building block for more complex data structures.
(*a*) Arrays (*b*) files
(*c*) records (*d*) none of the above

873. Classification of data structure can be
(*a*) linear and non linear data structures
(*b*) static and dynamic structures
(*c*) (*a*) and (*b*) both
(*d*) none of the above

874. An array is a homogeneous structure in which all
(*a*) elements are of different type
(*b*) elements are of same type
(*c*) (*a*) or (*b*)
(*d*) none of the above

875. Static structures are ones whose sizes and structures associated memory location are
(*a*) fixed at compile time
(*b*) dynamic at compile time
(*c*) (*a*) or (*b*)
(*d*) none of the above

876. Dynamic structures are ones
(*a*) which expand or shrink as required during the programme execution
(*b*) their associated memory location change
(*c*) (*a*) and (*b*)
(*d*) none of the above

877. .....are a common example of non-homogeneous data structures.
(*a*) files (*b*) records
(*c*) data (*d*) none of the above

878. For finding time and efficiency, two algorithms may compare with each other by a
(*a*) constant factor
(*b*) improvement from one to another does not change as the problem size gets larger.
(*c*) (*a*) or (*b*)
(*d*) none of the above

879. Suppose that we are given two algorithms for finding the largest value in a list of N numbers. It is also given that second algorithm executes twice the number of instructions executed by the first algorithm for each N value.
If the problem size doubles and the algorithm takes one more step, we relate the number of steps to the number of steps to the problem size by
(*a*) O (Log_2 N) (*b*) O (N)
(*c*) O (N Log_2 N) (*d*) none of the above

880. An algorithm chooses an execution path depending
(*a*) on the set of data values (input)
(*b*) on the set of data values (output)
(*c*) (*a*) or (*b*)
(*d*) none of the above

881. The simplest form of an array is a non-dimensional or
(*a*) scalar array (*b*) vector array
(*c*) (*a*) and (*b*) (*d*) none of the above

882. The various elements of an array are distinguished by giving each piece of data separate
(*a*) index (*b*) subscript
(*c*) (*a*) or (*b*) (*d*) none of the above

883. Arrays can be multidimensional *i.e.*
(*a*) An array with vector distribution
(*b*) An array with scalar distribution
(*c*) An array defined to have more than one dimension is considered to be multi dimensional
(*d*) none of the above

884. In general, an array of order M×N (read as M by N)
(*a*) consists of M rows, N columns
(*b*) MN elements
(*c*) (*a*) and (*b*) both
(*d*) none of the above

885. The things need to be specified to declare an array in most of the programming languages are
(*a*) the array name
(*b*) the type of data to be stored in array elements
(*c*) the subscript range
(*d*) none of the above

886. An array declaration tells the computer major pieces of information about an array.
(*a*) the range of subscripts allow the computer to determine how many memory locations must be allocated
(*b*) the array type tells the computer how much space is required to hold each value
(*c*) (*a*) and (*b*) both
(*d*) none of the above

887. The array structure is a
(*a*) homogeneous *i.e.* elements of an arrays are of same type
(*b*) homogeneous *i.e.* the elements of an array are of different type
(*c*) (*a*) and (*b*) both
(*d*) none of the above

888. In 2–dimensional array, we think of data
(*a*) being arranged vertically
(*b*) being arranged in row & column
(*c*) being arranged horizontally
(*d*) none of the above

889. Sparse arrays are of special arrays and it has a relatively
(*a*) number of zero elements
(*b*) number of one's elements
(*c*) number of two's elements
(*d*) none of the above

890. For sparse arrary, to solve only non-zero elements, two representations are used namely
(*a*) vector and linked list representation
(*b*) vector and scalar
(*c*) vector and queues
(*d*) none of the above

891. The set of operation defined for arrays are
(*a*) creating and initialising an array
(*b*) storing retrieving, inserting, deleting an element
(*c*) searching & sorting, printing an array
(*d*) All the above

892. A linear list is an ordered set consisting of
(*a*) a variable number of elements only.....in computer
(*b*) code only
(*c*) variable and code only
(*d*) none of the above

893. The first element of a list is called
(*a*) head of list (*b*) tail of list
(*c*) (*a*) and (*b*) both (*d*) none of the above

894. The last element of a list is called
(*a*) head of LIST (*b*) tail of LIST
(*c*) (*a*) and (*b*) both (*d*) none of the above

895. The next element to the head of the LIST is called its
(*a*) successor (*b*) predecessor
(*c*) headtail (*d*) none of the above

896. The previous element to the tail (if it is not head of the List) of the List is called
(*a*) successor (*b*) predecessor
(*c*) headtail (*d*) none of the above

897. A head.....have a predecessor
(*a*) does (*b*) does not
(*c*) (*a*) or (*b*) (*d*) none of the above

COMPUTER SCIENCE

898. A tail.....have a successor
(*a*) does (*b*) does not
(*c*) (*a*) or (*b*) (*d*) none of the above

899. Any other elements of the List has both one
(*a*) successor & predecessor
(*b*) head and tail
(*c*) top and bottom
(*d*) none of the above

900. The elements in a List are together by their
(*a*) Top-bottom relationship
(*b*) Successor-predecessor relationship
(*c*) Frontend-Backend
(*d*) none of the above

901. A List can be implemented static or dynamically using
(*a*) an array index
(*b*) pointers
(*c*) (*a*) or (*b*) respectively
(*d*) none of the above

902. Lists like arrays are used to store
(*a*) ordered data (*b*) input data
(*c*) current data (*d*) none of the above

903. Static implementation of Lists is the
(*a*) simplest implementation
(*b*) complex implementation
(*c*) (*a*) and (*b*) both
(*d*) none of the above

904. A List can be implemented as an array and
(*a*) its size is fixed and allocated at compilation time
(*b*) its size is dynamic and allocated at compilation time
(*c*) (*a*) or (*b*) depending on the case
(*d*) none of the above

905. Array implementation of a List has certain drawbacks
(*a*) Memory storage space is wasted, very often the list is much shorter than the array size declared.
(*b*) List cannot grow in its size beyond the size of the declared array if reused during programme
(*c*) Operation like insertion and delition at a specified location in List requires a lot of movement of data; thus leading to inefficient and time consuming algorithme.
(*d*) All the above

906. The primary advantage of linked list over arrays is that
(*a*) Items can be rearranged efficiently
(*b*) Linked list can grow and shrink in size during their lifetime and their maximum size need not be known in advance
(*c*) (*a*) and (*b*) both
(*d*) none of the above

907. List of several data structures
(*a*) can share same place
(*b*) cannot share same place
(*c*) do not provide flexibility & sharing of same place
(*d*) none of the above

908. The Linked List is not suited for
(*a*) find the 'Kth' item (find an item given its index),
(*b*) find the item before a given item
(*c*) (*a*) and (*b*) both
(*d*) none of the above

909. In Linked List, we traverse the List in
(*a*) only one direction
(*b*) two direction
(*c*) Sometimes (*a*) or (*b*)
(*d*) none of the above

910. Each element of a doubly Linked List Structure has
(*a*) three field namely data value, a link to its successor, a link to its predecessor
(*b*) four fields namely data, datavalue, structured data, successor
(*c*) a link to its head & tail
(*d*) none of the above

911. The term 'node' is used to designate
(*a*) a unit of storage space
(*b*) data
(*c*) an item
(*d*) none of the above

912. Nodes are allocated to users in response to their
(*a*) requests (*b*) access
(*c*) activity selection (*d*) none of the above

913. The number of nodes and the size of each node are decided keeping the following factors in mind.
(*a*) contiguity of space improves performance, especially for sequential access
(*b*) having a large number of nodes leads to greater storage management effort
(*c*) having fixed size nodes can lead to wastage of space
(*d*) all the above

914. Large nodes provide
(*a*) contiguous space
(*b*) improve performance
(*c*) (*a*) and (*b*) both
(*d*) none of the above

915. Large nodes should
(*a*) not be variable in size
(*b*) be variable in size to prevent excessive wastage of space
(*c*) not prevent excessive wastage of space
(*d*) none of the above

916. Small nodes improve
(*a*) flexibility
(*b*) much space is not wasted but their management is complex
(*c*) (*a*) and (*b*) both
(*d*) none of the above

917. The disadvantages of best fit method is
(*a*) it involves searching all available nodes
(*b*) it tends to increase the number of very small free blocks when D is not equal to 0.2
(*c*) (*a*) and (*b*) both
(*d*) none of the above

918. The advantage of first fit method is
(*a*) smaller search among the available list of nodes
(*b*) major search among the available list of nodes
(*c*) better search among the available list of nodes
(*d*) none of the above

919. The collection of all nodes available is the
(*a*) Storage (*b*) Pool
(*c*) Storage Pool (*d*) none of the above

920. In Linked allocation nodes can be linked together to over the limitations of
(*a*) Bit tables
(*b*) Table of contents
(*c*) Both (*a*) & (*b*)
(*d*) none of the above

921. In Linked allocation when a node is deallocated, it is detached from the allocated List of the file and
(*a*) attached to the free nodes list
(*b*) not need to attach to the free nodes list
(*c*) no need to attach to the free nodes list
(*d*) none of the above

922. Deallocation of nodes can take place in
(*a*) Two Levels (*b*) Three Levels
(*c*) Four Levels (*d*) None of the above

923. The two levels of Deal location of nodes are
(*a*) the application which claimed the node releases it back to the operating system
(*b*) the operating system calls storage management routines to return free nodes to the free space
(*c*) (*a*) and (*b*) both
(*d*) none of the above

924. Garbage collection is usually called
(*a*) when some programme runs out of space
(*b*) when three programme runs out of space
(*c*) when five programme runs out of space
(*d*) none of the above

925. Garbage collection is a
(*a*) slow process
(*b*) process which use should be obviated by efficient programming methods
(*c*) (*a*) and (*b*) both
(*d*) none of the above

926. Framgmentation means
(*a*) splitting (*b*) spotting
(*c*) sampling (*d*) none of the above

927. Relocation and compaction usually form the
(*a*) second phase of Garbage collection
(*b*) first phase of Garbage collection
(*c*) third phase of Garbage collection
(*d*) none of the above

928. Stacks are used in
(*a*) compilers in passing an expression by recussion
(*b*) in memory management in operating system etc.
(*c*) (*a*) and (*b*) both
(*d*) none of the above

929. Queues are used in
(*a*) CPU scheduling, in printer spooling
(*b*) message queuing in computer network etc.
(*c*) (*a*) and (*b*) both
(*d*) none of the above

930. A stack is a linear data structure in which
(*a*) data is inserted at one end (same end)
(*b*) data is stored and retrieved in a LIFO order
(*c*) Both (*a*) and (*b*)
(*d*) none of the above

931. The open end of the stack is called the
(*a*) top of the stack
(*b*) bottom of the stack
(*c*) head of the stack
(*d*) none of the above

932. The store and retrieval operations for a stack are called
(*a*) Push and pop respectively
(*b*) Pop and push respectively
(*c*) Head and tail respectively
(*d*) none of the above

933. The most recently arrived data object is the
(*a*) first one to depart from a stack
(*b*) last one to depart from a stack
(*c*) second one to depart from a stack
(*d*) none of the above

934. Two basic operations are involved in queue
(*a*) one can insert an item into the queue at the beginning and remove an item from the end
(*b*) one can insert an item into the queue at the end and remove an item from the beginning
(*c*) (*a*) or (*b*)
(*d*) none of the above

935. In a stack, something can get burried at the bottom, but a queue everything is processed in the

COMPUTER SCIENCE

(*a*) end (*b*) order received
(*c*) front (*d*) none of the above

936. The simplest way to represent a stack is by using a
(*a*) one-dimensional array
(*b*) two-dimensional array
(*c*) multi-dimensional array
(*d*) none of the above

937. In some application we store a stack element in a
(*a*) structure with a pointer to the next lower element on the stack
(*b*) structure with a pointer to the upper cell on the stack
(*c*) structure without a pointer to the upper cell on the stack
(*d*) none of the above

938. Many machines implement basic stack operations in hardware because they naturally implement
(*a*) procedure method
(*b*) function call mechanism: save the current environment on entry to a procedure by pushing information onto a stack, restore the environment on exit by using information popped from the stack
(*c*) conversion method
(*d*) none of the above

939. Some calculators and some computing languages base their method of calculation on
(*a*) stack operations explicitly
(*b*) queues operations explicitly
(*c*) (*a*) or (*b*)
(*d*) none of the above

940. In computer network, messages need to be buffered until the receiving computer is ready for it. These communication buffers make extensive use of
(*a*) queues by storing messages in a queue
(*b*) stacks
(*c*) stacks & queues
(*d*) none of the above

941. Queues are important in
(*a*) simulation models
(*b*) data models
(*c*) trees
(*d*) none of the above

942. The another approach for implementing queues is by using the
(*a*) dynamic storage allocation through the use of pointers
(*b*) sequential storage allocation through the use of stacks
(*c*) trees
(*d*) none of the above

943. We can define a queue consisting of records where each record contains records that comes
(*a*) before it (*b*) inbetween it
(*c*) after it (*d*) none of the above

944. We must also specify the items at the
(*a*) Front and rear of the queue
(*b*) Top and bottom of the queue
(*c*) Middle of the queue
(*d*) none of the above

945. Many application involving queue priority queues rather than the simple
(*a*) FIFO-strategy (*b*) LIFO-strategy
(*c*) End-strategy (*d*) none of the above

946. Queues are employed in many situations such as
(*a*) Vehicle waiting at a crossing
(*b*) Car waiting at the service station
(*c*) Customers in a check-out line at a departmental store etc.
(*d*) All the above

947. Historically, graph theory originated in
(*a*) Konigsberg bridge problem
(*b*) Mathematical problem
(*c*) Computer problem
(*d*) None of the above

948. We use graphs as models of practical situations involving
(*a*) routes: the vertices represent the cities and edges represent the roads or some other links
(*b*) electric circuits
(*c*) transportation
(*d*) all the above

949. A Graph G consists of
(*a*) a set V of Vertice (nodes)
(*b*) a set E of edge (arcs)
(*c*) both (*a*) and (*b*)
(*d*) none of the above

950. In a Digraph the path is called a
(*a*) directed path
(*b*) a cycle as directed cycle
(*c*) (*a*) and (*b*) both
(*d*) none of the above

951. A digraph is called strongly connected if there is
(*a*) any other vertex (*b*) two vertices
(*c*) one vertex (*d*) none of the above

952. A graph is a tree if it has properties
(*a*) it is connected
(*b*) there are no cycles in the graph
(*c*) (*a*) and (*b*) both
(*d*) none of the above

953. Graph is a mathematical structure and finds its application in many areas of interest in which problems need to be solved using

(*a*) tables (*b*) computers
(*c*) trees only (*d*) none of the above

954. In representing graphs, two most common representation are—
(*a*) Adjacent Matrix and tables
(*b*) Adjacency List representation and tables
(*c*) Adjacent Matrix and Adjacency List representation
(*d*) none of the above

955. In Adjacency List representation, we store a graph as a
(*a*) Cross Linked structure
(*b*) Linked structure
(*c*) (*a*) & (*b*) both
(*d*) None of the above

956. The disadvantages of using Adjacency matrix are :
(*a*) It takes $O(n^2)$ space to represent a graph with *n* vertices even for sparse graph
(*b*) It takes --n^2 time to solve most of the graph problems
(*c*) (*a*) and (*b*) both
(*d*) None of the above

957. The Adjacency List representation is better for
(*a*) sparse graphs: the space required. O (V + E) as contrasted with O (V^2) required by adjacency matrix representation
(*b*) trees
(*c*) matrix
(*d*) none of the above

958. A graph traversal means
(*a*) combining nodes of the graph
(*b*) visiting all the nodes of the graph
(*c*) joining nodes of the graph
(*d*) none of the above

959. Two graph traversals methods which are commonly used methods are
(*a*) Depth first search (DFS) and shortest path problem
(*b*) Breadth first search (BFS) and shortest path problem
(*c*) DFS and BFS
(*d*) none of the above

960. Depth-First search immediately solves some
(*a*) basic graph-processing problems
(*b*) last lines of the programme
(*c*) first-five lines of the programme
(*d*) none of the above

961. A graph has cycle if and only if a
(*a*) node that is not unseen is discovered in visit
(*b*) node that is seen is discovered in visit
(*c*) we encounter an edge pointing to a vertex that we have already visited, then we have a cycle
(*d*) (*a*) or (*c*)

962. A path in a graph is sequence of vertices such that
(*a*) there is an edge that we can follow between each consecutive pair of vertices
(*b*) we visit each edge
(*c*) no need of visiting each edge
(*d*) none of the above

963. No efficient algorithm is known for finding the minimum cost tour that visits each vertex in a weighted graph. This problem called the
(*a*) Translating problem
(*b*) Graphic problem
(*c*) Travelling salesman
(*d*) none of the above

964. An important class of Graphs is called
(*a*) trees (*b*) sectors
(*c*) (*a*) and (*b*) (*d*) none of the above

965. A tree contains
(*a*) no loops (*b*) no cycles
(*c*) (*a*) or (*b*) (*d*) none of the above

966. Trees are useful in computer science such as
(*a*) compiler construction
(*b*) database design windows
(*c*) operating system programmes etc.
(*d*) All the above

967. A tree structure is one in which items of data are related by
(*a*) edges (*b*) branches
(*c*) (*a*) or (*b*) (*d*) none of the above

968. In a tree, leave with no children are called
(*a*) leaves (*b*) terminal nodes
(*c*) (*a*) or (*b*) (*d*) none of the above

969. Nodes with at least
(*a*) one child are sometimes called nonterminal nodes
(*b*) two children are sometimes called nonterminal nodes
(*c*) three children are sometimes called nonterminal nodes
(*d*) none of the above

970. Sometimes nonterminal nodes are referred to as
(*a*) internal nodes (*b*) external nodes
(*c*) (*a*) and (*b*) both (*d*) none of the above

971. Sometimes terminal nodes are referred as
(*a*) internal nodes
(*b*) external nodes
(*c*) internal or external nodes
(*d*) none of the above

972. The length of a path is number of
(*a*) branches on the path
(*b*) trees on the graph
(*c*) nodes on the graph
(*d*) none of the above

973. The depth of any node *n* is the length of the path from

COMPUTER SCIENCE

(a) root to n (b) edge
(c) vertex (d) none of the above

974. A set of tree is called a
(a) graph (b) forest
(c) nodes (d) none of the above

975. A tree in which the root is not identified is called a
(a) free tree (b) undeveloped tree
(c) developed tree (d) none of the above

976. A tree in which the root is identified is called
(a) forest (b) complete tree
(c) rooted tree (d) none of the above

977. A tree with N nodes has
(a) N – 1 edges (b) N – 2 edges
(c) N – 3 edges (d) none of the above

978. A binary tree with N internal nodes has
(a) maximum of N external nodes
(b) maximum of (N + 1) external nodes
(c) maximum of (N + 2) external nodes
(d) none of the above

979. The external path length of any binary tree with N internal nodes is
(a) 2N greater than the internal path length
(b) 3N greater than the internal path length
(c) 4N greater than the internal path length
(d) none of the above

980. The height of a full binary tree with N internal nodes
(a) is about Log_2N (b) is about Log_3N
(c) is about $Log_{2-1}N$ (d) none of the above

981. A special case of binary tree is called a 2-tree or a
(a) ordinary binary tree
(b) strictly binary tree
(c) specially binary tree
(d) none of the above

982. Strictly binary tree is a non empty binary tree in which
(a) either both sub trees are empty
(b) both sub trees are 2-trees
(c) (a) or (b)
(d) none of the above

983. Binary trees appear extensively in computer applications and performance is best when the binary tree are
(a) full (b) nearly full
(c) (a) or (b) (d) none of the above

984. Every binary tree is a tree, not every tree is a
(a) binary tree (b) strictly binary tree
(c) 2-tree (d) none of the above

985. Linked List most commonly represent
(a) levels (b) binary trees
(c) (a) and (b) (d) none of the above

986. A complete binary tree contains the maximum number of nodes possible for its height (K Levels) contains
(a) $K_{1=0}$ 2^1 nodes (b) 2^2 nodes
(c) 2^3 nodes (d) none of the above

987. A binary tree can be used to represent arithmetic expressions if the node value can be either operators or operand values and are such that
(a) each operator node has exactly two branches
(b) each operand node has no branches, such trees are called expression trees
(c) (a) and (b) both
(d) none of the above

988. Preorder traversal is employed in
(a) DFS (b) BFS
(c) AFS (d) None of the above

989. A BST is an ordered binary tree T such that either it is an empty tree or
(a) each data value in its left sub-tree less than the root value
(b) each data value in its right sub-tree greater than the root value
(c) left and right sub-trees are again binary search tree.
(d) all of the above

990. .....allowed in a binary search tree
(a) Duplicate items are not
(b) Duplicate items are
(c) Single items is not allowed
(d) None of the above

991. In order traversal of a BST yields a sorted list in
(a) descending order (b) ascending order
(c) (a) or (b) (d) none of the above

992. In a binary search tree, each nodes holds a single value and has
(a) at most one branch
(b) at most two branches
(c) at most three branches
(d) none of the above

993. A binary search tree is a
(a) two-way tree (b) five-way tree
(c) three-way tree (d) none of the above

994. A binary tree of height h is completely balanced or balanced
(a) if all leaves occur at nodes of level h or h-1
(b) if all nodes at levels lower than h-1 have two children
(c) (a) and (b) both
(d) none of the above

995. A tree's height balanced if
(a) for each node in the tree, the height of the left subtree differs from the height of the right subtree by no more than 1

(*b*) for each node in the tree, the height of the left subtree differs from the height of the right subtree by no more than 2

(*c*) for each node in the tree, the height of the left subtree differs from the height of the right subtree by no more than 3

(*d*) none of the above

996. A B-tree is also known as

(*a*) balanced sort tree

(*b*) balanced unsort tree

(*c*) balanced search tree

(*d*) none of the above

997. A B-tree is used in

(*a*) external sorting (*b*) internal sorting

(*c*) (*a*) and (*b*) both (*d*) none of the above

998. A B-tree is

(*a*) not a binary tree (*b*) a binary tree

(*c*) complex tree (*d*) none of the above

999. To reduce disk accesses, several conditions of the tree must be true

(*a*) the height of the tree must be kept to a minimum

(*b*) there must be no empty sub tree above the leaves of the tree

(*c*) the leaves of tree must all be on same level, all nodes except the leaves must have at some minimum number of children

(*d*) All the above

1000. B-tree of order M has properties

(*a*) Each node has a maximum of M children and minimum of M/2 children or any no. from 2 to the maximum

(*b*) Each node has one fewer keys than children with a maximum of M-1keys

(*c*) Keys are arranged in a defined order within the nodes and all leaves are on the same level

(*d*) All of the above

ANSWERS

1	**2**	**3**	**4**	**5**	**6**	**7**	**8**	**9**	**10**
(*b*)	(*d*)	(*b*)	(*a*)	(*d*)	(*c*)	(*c*)	(*c*)	(*d*)	(*d*)
11	**12**	**13**	**14**	**15**	**16**	**17**	**18**	**19**	**20**
(*c*)	(*c*)	(*c*)	(*d*)	(*a*)	(*c*)	(*a*)	(*a*)	(*b*)	(*d*)
21	**22**	**23**	**24**	**25**	**26**	**27**	**28**	**29**	**30**
(*c*)	(*b*)	(*c*)	(*c*)	(*a*)	(*a*)	(*c*)	(*c*)	(*a*)	(*b*)
31	**32**	**33**	**34**	**35**	**36**	**37**	**38**	**39**	**40**
(*d*)	(*a*)	(*b*)	(*c*)	(*b*)	(*d*)	(*b*)	(*a*)	(*a*)	(*a*)
41	**42**	**43**	**44**	**45**	**46**	**47**	**48**	**49**	**50**
(*b*)	(*d*)	(*b*)	(*a*)	(*b*)	(*b*)	(*d*)	(*c*)	(*b*)	(*a*)
51	**52**	**53**	**54**	**55**	**56**	**57**	**58**	**59**	**60**
(*a*)	(*c*)	(*b*)	(*a*)	(*b*)	(*d*)	(*c*)	(*a*)	(*b*)	(*c*)
61	**62**	**63**	**64**	**65**	**66**	**67**	**68**	**69**	**70**
(*c*)	(*b*)	(*b*)	(*a*)	(*c*)	(*b*)	(*d*)	(*b*)	(*b*)	(*a*)
71	**72**	**73**	**74**	**75**	**76**	**77**	**78**	**79**	**80**
(*b*)	(*b*)	(*a*)	(*b*)	(*a*)	(*a*)	(*d*)	(*c*)	(*d*)	(*d*)
81	**82**	**83**	**84**	**85**	**86**	**87**	**88**	**89**	**90**
(*d*)	(*b*)	(*b*)	(*d*)	(*d*)	(*d*)	(*c*)	(*a*)	(*c*)	(*b*)
91	**92**	**93**	**94**	**95**	**96**	**97**	**98**	**99**	**100**
(*c*)	(*c*)	(*b*)	(*c*)	(*b*)	(*b*)	(*c*)	(*a*)	(*c*)	(*b*)
101	**102**	**103**	**104**	**105**	**106**	**107**	**108**	**109**	**110**
(*d*)	(*b*)	(*d*)	(*a*)	(*d*)	(*c*)	(*b*)	(*a*)	(*d*)	(*c*)
111	**112**	**113**	**114**	**115**	**116**	**117**	**118**	**119**	**120**
(*a*)	(*a*)	(*c*)	(*c*)	(*b*)	(*c*)	(*d*)	(*d*)	(*c*)	(*a*)
121	**122**	**123**	**124**	**125**	**126**	**127**	**128**	**129**	**130**
(*d*)	(*c*)	(*d*)	(*c*)	(*b*)	(*b*)	(*a*)	(*b*)	(*c*)	(*b*)
131	**132**	**133**	**134**	**135**	**136**	**137**	**138**	**139**	**140**
(*a*)	(*d*)	(*d*)	(*d*)	(*d*)	(*c*)	(*b*)	(*b*)	(*b*)	(*a*)
141	**142**	**143**	**144**	**145**	**146**	**147**	**148**	**149**	**150**
(*b*)	(*b*)	(*d*)	(*a*)	(*c*)	(*b*)	(*d*)	(*d*)	(*c*)	(*d*)
151	**152**	**153**	**154**	**155**	**156**	**157**	**158**	**159**	**160**
(*b*)	(*d*)	(*b*)	(*d*)	(*d*)	(*c*)	(*b*)	(*a*)	(*b*)	(*c*)
161	**162**	**163**	**164**	**165**	**166**	**167**	**168**	**169**	**170**
(*d*)	(*d*)	(*c*)	(*c*)	(*d*)	(*d*)	(*b*)	(*b*)	(*a*)	(*a*)

171	172	173	174	175	176	177	178	179	180
(c)	(d)	(c)	(c)	(c)	(a)	(d)	(c)	(b)	(b)
181	182	183	184	185	186	187	188	189	190
(b)	(c)	(d)	(a)	(*)	(c)	(d)	(d)	(d)	(c)
191	192	193	194	195	196	197	198	199	200
(a)	(a)	(b)	(c)	(d)	(c)	(b)	(c)	(a)	(b)
201	202	203	204	205	206	207	208	209	210
(a)	(b)	(c)	(d)	(a)	(b)	(c)	(d)	(d)	(d)
211	212	213	214	215	216	217	218	219	220
(a)	(c)	(d)	(c)	(b)	(c)	(d)	(c)	(b)	(a)
221	222	223	224	225	226	227	228	229	230
(c)	(b)	(a)	(b)	(d)	(c)	(a)	(a)	(d)	(a)
231	232	233	234	235	236	237	238	239	240
(d)	(a)	(b)	(c)	(d)	(a)	(a)	(b)	(c)	(b)
241	242	243	244	245	246	247	248	249	250
(d)	(b)	(d)	(c)	(d)	(b)	(c)	(c)	(c)	(b)
251	252	253	254	255	256	257	258	259	260
(a)	(d)	(a)	(b)	(c)	(c)	(a)	(c)	(a)	(d)
261	262	263	264	265	266	267	268	269	270
(b)	(d)	(a)	(d)	(b)	(b)	(a)	(b)	(a)	(b)
271	272	273	274	275	276	277	278	279	280
(b)	(b)	(a)	(c)	(c)	(d)	(c)	(d)	(a)	(a)
281	282	283	284	285	286	287	288	289	290
(b)	(c)	(d)	(d)	(b)	(b)	(b)	(a)	(a)	(d)
291	292	293	294	295	296	297	298	299	300
(c)	(d)	(a)	(d)	(d)	(b)	(a)	(d)	(d)	(c)
301	302	303	304	305	306	307	308	309	310
(b)	(b)	(a)	(b)	(c)	(a)	(d)	(d)	(d)	(c)
311	312	313	314	315	316	317	318	319	320
(a)	(d)	(c)	(c)	(a)	(b)	(a, c)	(c)	(c)	(c)
321	322	323	324	325	326	327	328	329	330
(d)	(d)	(d)	(a)	(c)	(c)	(d)	(d)	(d)	(b)
331	332	333	334	335	336	337	338	339	340
(d)	(b)	(b)	(b)	(c)	(d)	(a)	(b)	(b)	(c)
341	342	343	344	345	346	347	348	349	350
(d)	(b)	(b)	(a)	(c)	(a)	(c)	(c)	(c)	(b)
351	352	353	354	355	356	357	358	359	360
(a)	(d)	(c)	(b)	(d)	(a)	(b)	(c)	(a)	(c)
361	362	363	364	365	366	367	368	369	370
(d)	(d)	(b)	(a)	(d)	(a)	(a)	(d)	(a)	(b)
371	372	373	374	375	376	377	378	379	380
(c)	(c)	(d)	(c)	(b)	(a)	(c)	(a)	(d)	(d)
381	382	383	384	385	386	387	388	389	390
(a)	(d)	(d)	(c)	(b)	(b)	(d)	(b)	(c)	(c)
391	392	393	394	395	396	397	398	399	400
(b)	(b)	(a)	(b)	(d)	(c)	(b)	(c)	(b)	(b)
401	402	403	404	405	406	407	408	409	410
(a)	(b)	(b)	(a)	(d)	(a)	(b)	(c)	(d)	(b)
411	412	413	414	415	416	417	418	419	420
(b)	(d)	(b)	(c)	(b)	(d)	(d)	(b)	(d)	(d)
421	422	423	424	425	426	427	428	429	430
(d)	(c)	(b)	(d)	(c)	(a)	(b)	(b)	(b)	(b)
431	432	433	434	435	436	437	438	439	440
(d)	(b)	(d)	(c)	(d)	(a)	(c)	(a)	(d)	(a)
441	442	443	444	445	446	447	448	449	450
(b)	(b)	(a)	(a)	(a)	(a)	(d)	(b)	(a)	(b)

451	452	453	454	455	456	457	458	459	460
(c)	(a)	(c)	(d)	(c)	(c)	(d)	(b)	(c)	(b)
461	**462**	**463**	**464**	**465**	**466**	**467**	**468**	**469**	**470**
(d)	(b)	(a)	(c)	(b)	(c)	(d)	(d)	(a)	(c)
471	**472**	**473**	**474**	**475**	**476**	**477**	**478**	**479**	**480**
(b)	(d)	(a)	(b)	(d)	(b)	(b)	(a)	(b)	(a)
481	**482**	**483**	**484**	**485**	**486**	**487**	**488**	**489**	**490**
(a)	(b)	(c)	(b)	(b)	(a)	(b)	(d)	(a)	(c)
491	**492**	**493**	**494**	**495**	**496**	**497**	**498**	**499**	**500**
(a)	(c)	(b)	(d)	(b)	(c)	(d)	(c)	(b)	(b)
501	**502**	**503**	**504**	**505**	**506**	**507**	**508**	**509**	**510**
(a)	(b)	(a)	(c)	(a)	(a)	(d)	(b)	(d)	(a)
511	**512**	**513**	**514**	**515**	**516**	**517**	**518**	**519**	**520**
(b)	(a)	(a)	(c)	(a)	(a)	(b)	(a)	(a)	(d)
521	**522**	**523**	**524**	**525**	**526**	**527**	**528**	**529**	**530**
(c)	(a)	(b)	(a)	(b)	(a)	(c)	(a)	(b)	(c)
531	**532**	**533**	**534**	**535**	**536**	**537**	**538**	**539**	**540**
(a)	(c)	(c)	(a)	(a)	(a)	(a)	(a)	(a)	(a)
541	**542**	**543**	**544**	**545**	**546**	**547**	**548**	**549**	**550**
(d)	(c)	(c)	(c)	(d)	(a)	(a)	(a)	(a)	(a)
551	**552**	**553**	**554**	**555**	**556**	**557**	**558**	**559**	**560**
(b)	(c)	(a)	(a)	(a)	(b)	(b)	(a)	(a)	(a)
561	**562**	**563**	**564**	**565**	**566**	**567**	**568**	**569**	**570**
(a)	(a)	(a)	(a)	(c)	(b)	(a)	(b)	(a)	(b)
571	**572**	**573**	**574**	**575**	**576**	**577**	**578**	**579**	**580**
(a)	(a)	(b)	(a)	(c)	(a)	(b)	(a)	(a)	(b)
581	**582**	**583**	**584**	**585**	**586**	**587**	**588**	**589**	**590**
(a)	(a)	(b)	(a)	(b)	(c)	(d)	(a)	(a)	(b)
591	**592**	**593**	**594**	**595**	**596**	**597**	**598**	**599**	**600**
(a)	(a)	(a)	(c)	(b)	(a)	(c)	(a)	(b)	(c)
601	**602**	**603**	**604**	**605**	**606**	**607**	**608**	**609**	**610**
(b)	(a)	(c)	(a)	(c)	(b)	(b)	(a)	(a)	(a)
611	**612**	**613**	**614**	**615**	**616**	**617**	**618**	**619**	**620**
(a)	(a)	(a)	(b)	(a)	(b)	(a)	(a)	(b)	(a)
621	**622**	**623**	**624**	**625**	**626**	**627**	**628**	**629**	**630**
(a)	(a)	(a)	(d)	(a)	(a)	(b)	(a)	(d)	(d)
631	**632**	**633**	**634**	**635**	**636**	**637**	**638**	**639**	**640**
(d)	(d)	(a)	(b)	(a)	(d)	(b)	(b)	(c)	(a)
641	**642**	**643**	**644**	**645**	**646**	**647**	**648**	**649**	**650**
(b)	(d)	(a)	(b)	(a)	(a)	(c)	(d)	(b)	(c)
651	**652**	**653**	**654**	**655**	**656**	**657**	**658**	**659**	**660**
(a)	(b)	(d)	(b)	(b)	(b)	(c)	(b)	(a)	(c)
661	**662**	**663**	**664**	**665**	**666**	**667**	**668**	**669**	**670**
(c)	(b)	(a)	(d)	(d)	(c)	(c)	(d)	(c)	(d)
671	**672**	**673**	**674**	**675**	**676**	**677**	**678**	**679**	**680**
(c)	(a)	(a)	(a)	(b)	(b)	(a)	(d)	(a)	(a)
681	**682**	**683**	**684**	**685**	**686**	**687**	**688**	**689**	**690**
(a)	(a)	(a)	(a)	(b)	(c)	(c)	(a)	(c)	(a)
691	**692**	**693**	**694**	**695**	**696**	**697**	**698**	**699**	**700**
(c)	(a)	(c)	(a)	(a)	(c)	(b)	(c)	(c)	(c)
701	**702**	**703**	**704**	**705**	**706**	**707**	**708**	**709**	**710**
(a)	(d)	(a)	(b)	(a)	(d)	(a)	(d)	(a)	(c)
711	**712**	**713**	**714**	**715**	**716**	**717**	**718**	**719**	**720**
(c)	(d)	(a)	(a)	(c)	(b)	(c)	(b)	(d)	(c)

721 (*d*)	**722** (*b*)	**723** (*d*)	**724** (*c*)	**725** (*d*)	**726** (*b*)	**727** (*d*)	**728** (*a*)	**729** (*a*)	**730** (*d*)
731 (*d*)	**732** (*a*)	**733** (*a*)	**734** (*c*)	**735** (*b*)	**736** (*b*)	**737** (*d*)	**738** (*d*)	**739** (*d*)	**740** (*e*)
741 (*d*)	**742** (*d*)	**743** (*a*)	**744** (*b*)	**745** (*c*)	**746** (*d*)	**747** (*d*)	**748** (*a*)	**749** (*c*)	**750** (*d*)
751 (*d*)	**752** (*d*)	**753** (*b*)	**754** (*c*)	**755** (*a*)	**756** (*b*)	**757** (*d*)	**758** (*c*)	**759** (*a*)	**760** (*d*)
761 (*c*)	**762** (*d*)	**763** (*a*)	**764** (*a*)	**765** (*a*)	**766** (*c*)	**767** (*a*)	**768** (*c*)	**769** (*e*)	**770** (*c*)
771 (*d*)	**772** (*c*)	**773** (*d*)	**774** (*e*)	**775** (*e*)	**776** (*c*)	**777** (*b*)	**778** (*a*)	**779** (*d*)	**780** (*b*)
781 (*e*)	**782** (*c*)	**783** (*b*)	**784** (*e*)	**785** (*a*)	**786** (*d*)	**787** (*c*)	**788** (*c*)	**789** (*d*)	**790** (*a*)
791 (*c*)	**792** (*b*)	**793** (*a*)	**794** (*a*)	**795** (*a*)	**796** (*b*)	**797** (*c*)	**798** (*c*)	**799** (*c*)	**800** (*b*)
801 (*c*)	**802** (*b*)	**803** (*a*)	**804** (*b*)	**805** (*a*)	**806** (*a*)	**807** (*c*)	**808** (*a*)	**809** (*a*)	**810** (*a*)
811 (*b*)	**812** (*a*)	**813** (*b*)	**814** (*c*)	**815** (*b*)	**816** (*a*)	**817** (*c*)	**818** (*a*)	**819** (*a*)	**820** (*c*)
821 (*b*)	**822** (*a*)	**823** (*a*)	**824** (*c*)	**825** (*b*)	**826** (*a*)	**827** (*a*)	**828** (*b*)	**829** (*a*)	**830** (*c*)
831 (*c*)	**832** (*a*)	**833** (*a*)	**834** (*a*)	**835** (*b*)	**836** (*a*)	**837** (*b*)	**838** (*b*)	**839** (*a*)	**840** (*a*)
841 (*a*)	**842** (*c*)	**843** (*a*)	**844** (*a*)	**845** (*a*)	**846** (*a*)	**847** (*b*)	**848** (*c*)	**849** (*a*)	**850** (*a*)
851 (*b*)	**852** (*a*)	**853** (*a*)	**854** (*b*)	**855** (*a*)	**856** (*a*)	**857** (*b*)	**858** (*b*)	**859** (*c*)	**860** (*a*)
861 (*a*)	**862** (*a*)	**863** (*a*)	**864** (*a*)	**865** (*b*)	**866** (*c*)	**867** (*c*)	**868** (*a*)	**869** (*a*)	**870** (*a*)
871 (*b*)	**872** (*a*)	**873** (*c*)	**874** (*b*)	**875** (*a*)	**876** (*c*)	**877** (*b*)	**878** (*c*)	**879** (*a*)	**880** (*a*)
881 (*b*)	**882** (*c*)	**883** (*c*)	**884** (*c*)	**885** (*d*)	**886** (*c*)	**887** (*a*)	**888** (*b*)	**889** (*a*)	**890** (*a*)
891 (*d*)	**892** (*a*)	**893** (*a*)	**894** (*b*)	**895** (*a*)	**896** (*b*)	**897** (*a*)	**898** (*b*)	**899** (*a*)	**900** (*b*)
901 (*c*)	**902** (*a*)	**903** (*a*)	**904** (*a*)	**905** (*d*)	**906** (*c*)	**907** (*a*)	**908** (*c*)	**909** (*a*)	**910** (*a*)
911 (*a*)	**912** (*a*)	**913** (*d*)	**914** (*c*)	**915** (*b*)	**916** (*c*)	**917** (*c*)	**918** (*a*)	**919** (*c*)	**920** (*c*)
921 (*a*)	**922** (*a*)	**923** (*c*)	**924** (*a*)	**925** (*c*)	**926** (*a*)	**927** (*a*)	**928** (*c*)	**929** (*c*)	**930** (*c*)
931 (*a*)	**932** (*a*)	**933** (*a*)	**934** (*a*)	**935** (*b*)	**936** (*a*)	**937** (*a*)	**938** (*b*)	**939** (*a*)	**940** (*a*)
941 (*a*)	**942** (*a*)	**943** (*c*)	**944** (*a*)	**945** (*a*)	**946** (*d*)	**947** (*a*)	**948** (*d*)	**949** (*c*)	**950** (*a*)
951 (*a*)	**952** (*c*)	**953** (*b*)	**954** (*c*)	**955** (*b*)	**956** (*c*)	**957** (*a*)	**958** (*b*)	**959** (*c*)	**960** (*a*)
961 (*d*)	**962** (*a*)	**963** (*c*)	**964** (*a*)	**965** (*c*)	**966** (*d*)	**967** (*a*)	**968** (*c*)	**969** (*a*)	**970** (*a*)
971 (*b*)	**972** (*a*)	**973** (*a*)	**974** (*b*)	**975** (*a*)	**976** (*c*)	**977** (*a*)	**978** (*b*)	**979** (*a*)	**980** (*a*)
981 (*b*)	**982** (*c*)	**983** (*c*)	**984** (*a*)	**985** (*b*)	**986** (*a*)	**987** (*c*)	**988** (*a*)	**989** (*d*)	**990** (*a*)
991 (*b*)	**992** (*b*)	**993** (*a*)	**994** (*c*)	**995** (*a*)	**996** (*a*)	**997** (*a*)	**998** (*a*)	**999** (*d*)	**1000** (*d*)